The Cambridge Encyclopedia of Historical Performance in Music

Recent decades have seen a major increase of interest in historical performance practice, but until now there has been no comprehensive reference tool available on the subject. This fully up-to-date, illuminating and accessible volume will assist readers in rediscovering and recreating as closely as possible how musical works may originally have sounded. Focusing on performance, this *Encyclopedia* contains entries in categories including issues of style, techniques and practices, the history and development of musical instruments, and the work of performers, scholars, theorists, composers and editors. It features contributions from more than 100 leading experts who provide a geographically varied survey of both theory and practice, as well as evaluation of and opinions on the resolution of problems in period performance. This timely and groundbreaking book will be an essential resource for students, scholars, teachers, performers and audiences.

COLIN LAWSON is Director of the Royal College of Music in London. He is a world-renowned period clarinettist and has played principal in most of Britain's leading period orchestras, with which he has recorded and toured worldwide. He has published extensively and is co-editor, with Robin Stowell, of a series of Cambridge Handbooks to the Historical Performance of Music as well as of *The Cambridge History of Musical Performance* (Cambridge, 2012).

ROBIN STOWELL is Emeritus Professor of Music at Cardiff University. As a violinist he has performed, broadcast and recorded with the Academy of Ancient Music and other period ensembles. He is the author of *Violin Technique and Performance Practice in the Late Eighteenth and Early Nineteenth Centuries* (Cambridge, 1985) and his other major publications include *The Early Violin and Viola* (Cambridge, 2001) and three Cambridge Companions – to the violin (1992), cello (1999) and string quartet (2003).

The Cambridge Encyclopedia of Historical Performance in Music

Edited by
COLIN LAWSON
Royal College of Music, London

ROBIN STOWELL
Cardiff University

CAMBRIDGE
UNIVERSITY PRESS

University Printing House, Cambridge CB2 8BS, United Kingdom

One Liberty Plaza, 20th Floor, New York, NY 10006, USA

477 Williamstown Road, Port Melbourne, VIC 3207, Australia

314-321, 3rd Floor, Plot 3, Splendor Forum, Jasola District Centre, New Delhi - 110025, India

79 Anson Road, #06-04/06, Singapore 079906

Cambridge University Press is part of the University of Cambridge.

It furthers the University's mission by disseminating knowledge in the pursuit of education, learning and research at the highest international levels of excellence.

www.cambridge.org
Information on this title: www.cambridge.org/9781107518476
DOI: 10.1017/9781316257678

© Cambridge University Press 2018

This publication is in copyright. Subject to statutory exception and to the provisions of relevant collective licensing agreements, no reproduction of any part may take place without the written permission of Cambridge University Press.

First published 2018
First paperback edition 2021

A catalogue record for this publication is available from the British Library

Library of Congress Cataloging in Publication data
NAMES: Lawson, Colin (Colin James) | Stowell, Robin.
TITLE: The Cambridge encyclopedia of historical performance in music / edited by Colin Lawson, Robin Stowell.
DESCRIPTION: Cambridge, United Kingdom ; New York : Cambridge University Press, 2019. | Includes bibliographical references and index.
IDENTIFIERS: LCCN 2018034167 | ISBN 9781107108080 (hardback : alk. paper) | ISBN 9781107518476 (pbk. : alk. paper)
SUBJECTS: LCSH: Music–Performance–Encyclopedias.
CLASSIFICATION: LCC ML100 .C28 2018 | DDC 781.4/309–dc23
LC record available at https://lccn.loc.gov/2018034167

ISBN 978-1-107-10808-0 Hardback
ISBN 978-1-107-51847-6 Paperback

Cambridge University Press has no responsibility for the persistence or accuracy of URLs for external or third-party internet websites referred to in this publication, and does not guarantee that any content on such websites is, or will remain, accurate or appropriate.

Contents

List of Illustrations   p. vi

List of Music Examples   p. vii

List of Contributors   p. ix

Editors' Preface   p. xiii

List of Bibliographical Abbreviations   p. xxii

Selected Treatises Commonly Cited in Abbreviated Forms   p. xxiii

A–Z General Entries   *p.* 1

Index   *p.* 701

Illustrations

1 The Greek bagpipe, which is often played along with a small drum (photograph by Cassandre Balosso-Bardin). *p.* 50
2 Examples of John Bulwer's illustrations of gestures for words, deeds, emotions and rhetorical devices. *p.* 57
3 The action of a fretted clavichord, showing two keys sharing one pair of strings (Christopher Nobbs). *p.* 136
4 Plan view of an unfretted clavichord by J. A. Hass, 1763 (by kind permission of the Friends of St Cecilia's Hall, Edinburgh). *p.* 137
5 Section through the action of a typical eighteenth-century double-manual French harpsichord (Christopher Nobbs). *p.* 288
6 Plan view of a double-manual French harpsichord (1769) by Pascal Taskin (by kind permission of the Friends of St Cecilia's Hall, Edinburgh). *p.* 290
7 German tablature from Hans Neusidler's *Der ander Theil des Lauthenbuchs* (Nuremberg, 1536). *p.* 375
8 French tablature from Pierre Attaingnant's *Très brève et familière introduction*... (Paris, 1529). *p.* 375
9 Italian tablature from Giacomo Gorzanis's *Intabolatura di liuto* (Venice, 1561). *p.* 375
10 a and b Lute (c1580) by Sixtus Rauwolf of Augsburg, later converted into an eleven-course Baroque lute (belonging to Jakob Lindberg). *p.* 377
11 Mallorcan pipe and tabor player Tomas Salom (photograph by Cassandre Balosso-Bardin). *p.* 496
12 Francesco Rognoni, *Selva de varii passaggi* (Milan, 1620), pt 1, p. 29. *p.* 551
13 Francesco Rognoni, *Selva de varii passaggi* (Milan, 1620), pt 2, p. 5. *p.* 551
14 a, b and c New German keyboard tablature (in Johann Woltz, *Nova musices organicae tabulatura* (Basle: Johann Jacob Genath, 1617)). *p.* 595
15 Italian lute tablature. *p.* 595
16 French lute tablature. *p.* 595
17 Fourteen-course chitarrone by Magno Dieffopruchar, Venice 1608. String lengths 930 mm and 1703 mm (by kind permission of the Royal College of Music, London). *p.* 616
18 Detail from lid painting by Frederik van Valckenborch or Falckenberg (c1570–1623), *The Four Seasons* (1619). Paul Wismayer Virginal, Germanisches Nationalmuseum, Nürnberg (photograph by Malcolm Rose). *p.* 675

Music Examples

1. Baroque methods and symbols for arpeggiation.   *p. 28*
2. Alberti bass (Domenico Alberti: *Sonate per Cembalo* Op. 1 No. 2 (1748)).   *p. 28*
3. (a) Hans Buchner: 'Quem terra pontus' (*Fundamentum*, 1551); (b) Elias Ammerbach: *Exercises* (1583).   *p. 228*
4. (a) John Bull: *Fantasia* (*GB-Lbl* Add. 36661); (b) Anon. [Bull?]: *Prelude* (*GB-Lcm* MS 2093).   *p. 229*
5. François Couperin: *Premier Prélude* (*L'art de toucher le clavecin*, 1716).   *p. 230*
6. (a–d) Shifting in accordance with the musical punctuation (Leopold Mozart: *Versuch* (1756), 155, 168, 155 and 156).   *p. 233*
7. An example of the kind of bold shift employed by Francesco Geminiani (*The Art of Playing on the Violin* (1751), 14).   *p. 233*
8. Chromatic fingerings: (a) by Francesco Geminiani (*The Art of Playing on the Violin* (1751), 2); (b) by Leopold Mozart (*Versuch* (1756), 66–7).   *p. 234*
9. The finger-replacement shift as illustrated by Charles Baudiot (*Méthode*, Op. 25, 2 vols. [1826, 1828], I, 21).   *p. 237*
10. The 'Italian' appoggiatura (Alexis de Garaudé: *Méthode de chant*, Op. 40).   *p. 258*
11. The so-called 'Geminiani grip'.   *p. 264*
12. (a) Geminiani's sign for vibrato; and (b) his recommendation of when to introduce the effect (*The Art of Playing on the Violin* (1751), 26 and 33).   *p. 265*
13. C. P. E. Bach: *Versuch* (1753–62), trans. W. J. Mitchell (1949), 442–3.   *p. 324*
14. C. P. E. Bach: *Versuch* (1753–62), trans. W. J. Mitchell (1949), 443–5.   *p. 325*
15. Joseph Joachim and Andreas Moser: *Violinschule*, 3 vols. (1905), III, 7.   *p. 340*
16. Six-course lute tuning, showing the positions of octave strings.   *p. 376*
17. Eleven-course D minor lute tuning, showing the positions of octave strings.   *p. 377*
18. Handel: 'Hush ye pretty warbling Quire' (*Acis and Galatea*): (a) London: Walsh, 1734; (b) arr. Mozart (from *Neue Mozart-Ausgabe*).   *p. 418*
19. Francesco Rognoni: *Selva de varii passaggi* (Milan, 1620), facing 2.   *p. 502*
20. Bernardo Mengozzi: *Méthode de chant du Conservatoire de Musique* (1804), 16.   *p. 503*
21. Manuel García I: *Exercices pour la voix* (c1820), 14.   *p. 503*

22 Manuel García II: *Traité complet de l'art du chant* (1840), 64. *p.* 504
23 (a) and (b) Leopold Mozart: *Versuch* (1756), 241 and 178. *p.* 504
24 Haydn: String Quartet in E flat major, Op. 33 No. 2, 2nd movement. *p.* 505
25 Louis Spohr: *Violinschule* (1832), 120. *p.* 505
26 (a) Louis Spohr: Violin Concerto No. 10 in A, Op. 62, 2nd movement; (b) and (c) Pierre Rode: Violin Concerto No. 7, 2nd movement, quoted in Spohr: *Violinschule* (1832), 209. *p.* 505
27 (a) uninterrupted slide on one finger; (b) 'B-portamento'; (c) 'L-portamento'. *p.* 506
28 Louis Couperin: Prélude in C major. *p.* 539
29 François Couperin: Prélude (*L'art de toucher le clavecin*, 2/1717). *p.* 539
30 Henry Purcell: Prelude from Suite No. 4 in A minor (1696). *p.* 540
31 J. S. Bach: Corrente (Partita No. 1 (BWV825)), bars 1–5. *p.* 540
32 J. S. Bach: Organ Sonata No. 4 (BWV528), final movement, bars 14–15. *p.* 541
33 J. S. Bach: Sonata in C minor for violin and harpsichord (BWV1017), 3rd movement, bars 9–12. *p.* 541
34 (a) and (b) J. S. Bach: Overture in the French Style (BWV831), bars 1–3. *p.* 542
35 (a) and (b) Froberger: Gigue, Partita No. 1 in E minor ((a) Libro Quarto 1656 and (b) Bauyn MS). *p.* 543
36 J. S. Bach: Gigue (French Suite No. 1 in D minor (BWV812)). *p.* 543
37 (a) J. S. Bach: Gigue (Partita No. 6 in E minor (BWV830)); (b) J. S. Bach: Gigue (Partita No. 6 in E minor (BWV830)), translated into compound metre. *p.* 544
38 Beethoven: Sonata in E Op. 14 No. 1, Rondo, bars 1–5. *p.* 545
39 Franz Schubert: 'Wasserflut' (*Winterreise* No. 6), bars 1–4. *p.* 546
40 J. F. Schubert: *Neue Singe-Schule* (1804). *p.* 569
41 Chitarrone tuning (the top six courses were often double). *p.* 616
42 English theorbo tuning (the courses seem to have been double throughout). *p.* 616
43 German theorbo tuning (the distribution of double courses is unknown). *p.* 616
44 Girolamo Diruta: *Il Transilvano*, part I (1593), 10. *p.* 628
45 Antonio Cesti: *Il pomo d'oro* (1666), Act IV, scene 4, violin I. *p.* 629
46 Nicola Vaccai: *Metodo pratico* (1832). *p.* 643
47 (a) Leopold Mozart: *Versuch* (1756), 239; (b) Leopold Mozart: *Versuch* (1756), 240, trans. Knocker, 204–5. *p.* 652
48 Pierre Baillot: *L'art du violon* (1835), 138. *p.* 653
49 Louis Spohr: *Violinschule* (1832), 176. *p.* 653
50 Louis Spohr: *Violinschule* (1832), 228. *p.* 654

Contributors

SIMON BAINES
University of Leeds

CASSANDRE BALOSSO-BARDIN
University of Lincoln

JON BANKS
Anglia Ruskin University

PAUL BANKS
London

JEREMY BARLOW
London

DIETRICH BARTEL
Canadian Mennonite University

ROBERT BEALE
Manchester

ALEXANDER EVAN BONUS
Bard College, NY

JOSÉ ANTONIO BOWEN
Goucher College, MD

EDWARD BREEN
City Literary Institute, London

DAVID BREITMAN
Oberlin College and Conservatory, OH

BOJAN BUJIĆ
Magdalen College, University of Oxford

GEOFFREY BURGESS
Eastman School of Music

SCOTT BURNHAM
City University of New York

JOHN BUTT
University of Glasgow

MURRAY CAMPBELL
University of Edinburgh

STEWART CARTER
Wake Forest University, NC

TIM CARTER
University of North Carolina, Chapel Hill, NC

DAVID F. CHAPMAN
Rutgers University, NJ

TERENCE CHARLSTON
Royal College of Music, London

STUART CHENEY
Texas Christian University, TX

NICHOLAS CLAPTON
Oxford

SUZANNE COLE
Melbourne Conservatorium of Music, University of Melbourne

JEFFREY DEAN
Birmingham City University

BRUCE DICKEY
Schola Cantorum Basiliensis

ELIZABETH DOBBIN
Leiden University and The Orpheus Institute, Ghent

ROSS DUFFIN
Case Western Reserve University, OH

CONTRIBUTORS

Cliff Eisen
King's College London

Paul Ellison
San Francisco State University, CA

Don Fader
University of Alabama, AL

David Fallows
University of Manchester

Nicholas Gebhardt
Birmingham City University

Malcolm Gillies
King's College London and
　Australian National University

Geoffrey Govier
Royal College of Music, London

John Haines
University of Toronto

Kenneth Hamilton
Cardiff University

Roger Heaton
Bath Spa University

Trevor Herbert
The Open University and
　Royal College of Music,
　London

Rebecca Herissone
University of Manchester

Claire Holden
University of Oxford

Peter Horton
Royal College of Music, London

Patricia Howard
The Open University

Roy Howat
Royal Academy of Music, London
　and Royal Conservatoire of
　Scotland

John Humphries
Epsom

John Irving
Trinity Laban Conservatoire of Music
　and Dance, London

Paul Israel
Rutgers University, NJ

David Wyn Jones
Cardiff University

Richard D. P. Jones
Abingdon, Oxfordshire

Simon Jones
Royal Welsh College of Music and
　Drama

Lindsay Kemp
London

George Kennaway
University of Huddersfield

Richard Langham Smith
Royal College of Music, London

Andrew Lawrence-King
Guildhall School of Music & Drama,
　London

Colin Lawson
Royal College of Music, London

David Ledbetter
Manchester

Daniel Leech-Wilkinson
King's College London

Erik Levi
Royal Holloway, University of
　London

Robert D. Levin
Harvard University, MA and The
　Juilliard School

Jakob Lindberg
Royal College of Music, London

Peter Linnitt
Royal College of Music, London

Natasha Loges
Royal College of Music, London

TIMOTHY J. MCGEE
University of Toronto

SIMON MCVEIGH
Goldsmiths, University of London

STEFANO MENGOZZI
University of Michigan, MI

JEREMY MONTAGU
Wadham College, University of Oxford

MICHAEL MUSGRAVE
Goldsmiths, University of London;
   Visiting Research Fellow, Royal
   College of Music; Graduate
   Faculty, The Juilliard School

HERBERT MYERS
Stanford University, CA

CORMAC NEWARK
Guildhall School of Music & Drama, London

MICHAEL O'DEA
Université Lumière Lyon 2

MICHAEL OLIVA
Royal College of Music, London

KATE VAN ORDEN
Harvard University, MA

MAX PADDISON
University of Durham

INGRID E. PEARSON
Royal College of Music, London

JULIAN PERKINS
London

DAVID PONSFORD
Cirencester

ANTHONY PRYER
Goldsmiths, University of London

OWEN REES
The Queen's College, University of Oxford

LUCY ROBINSON
Royal Welsh College of Music and Drama

ELEONORA ROCCONI
University of Pavia

STEPHEN ROSE
Royal Holloway, University of London

GABRIELE ROSSI ROGNONI
Royal College of Music, London

ANTONIO ROSTAGNO
Sapienza University of Rome

DAVID ROWLAND
The Open University

JULIAN RUSHTON
University of Leeds

SUSAN RUTHERFORD
University of Manchester

JAMIE SAVAN
Birmingham City University

THOMAS SCHMIDT
University of Huddersfield

GISELHER SCHUBERT
Hameln

BRIAN SIEMERS
Southern State Community College, Hillsboro, OH

NIGEL SIMEONE
Rushden, Northamptonshire

URI SMILANSKY
King's College London

ASHLEY SOLOMON
Royal College of Music, London

ROBIN STOWELL
Cardiff University

JEREMY SUMMERLY
St Peter's College, University of Oxford

MATTHIAS THIEMEL
Freiburg im Breisgau

DAVID TUNLEY
University of Western Australia

xi

CONTRIBUTORS

MELVIN P. UNGER
State University of New York at Fredonia, NY

WOUTER VERSCHUREN
Royal College of Music, London

JONATHAN WAINWRIGHT
University of York

JOHN WALLACE
Royal Conservatoire of Scotland

WILLIAM WEBER
California State University, CA

JAMES WESTBROOK
Wolfson College, University of Cambridge and The Guitar Museum, Brighton

RICHARD WIDDESS
SOAS, University of London

AARON WILLIAMON
Royal College of Music, London

MAGNUS WILLIAMSON
Newcastle University

DAVID K. WILSON
Berkeley, CA

NICK WILSON
King's College London

RICHARD WISTREICH
Royal College of Music, London

IAN WOOD
University of Leeds

ALISON WRAY
Cardiff University

DAVID C. H. WRIGHT
London

STEVEN ZOHN
Temple University, PA

Editors' Preface

The enormous growth of interest in historical performance practice among scholars and executants during the twentieth and twenty-first centuries lies at the core of our vision for *The Cambridge Encyclopedia of Historical Performance in Music*. We have ourselves had the opportunity to combine our own scholarly interests with first-hand practical experience within ensembles under directors whose names are synonymous with period performance, including Mark Elder, Christopher Hogwood, Charles Mackerras, Roger Norrington, Trevor Pinnock, Simon Rattle and Joshua Rifkin, touring and recording a wide range of repertory on historical instruments.

Although there were attempts in the 1880s at using instruments and performance styles contemporary with and appropriate to Baroque and Classical music, the study of performance practice (*Aufführungspraxis*) did not evolve until the early twentieth century, when it began to reflect in print the crucial realisation during the nineteenth century that contemporary performing styles did not necessarily suit music from earlier times; such stylistic awareness was now attempting to view older music in terms of its original period rather than transplanting it to the present. In the later nineteenth century, the establishment of texts from preferred sources in scholarly collected editions was soon to make possible the concepts of faithfulness to the text, performance practice and 'authenticity' itself. A collected edition of Bach's works was soon followed by scholarly editions of Handel, Rameau, Palestrina, Buxtehude, Corelli, Schütz, Purcell, Sweelinck and many other composers. And in the late nineteenth century, Brahms was a composer whose own compositions were deeply affected by his experience of old music.

Important influences in England were Arnold Dolmetsch (*The Interpretation of the Music of the Seventeenth and Eighteenth Centuries Revealed by Contemporary Evidence* (London, 1915)), Thurston Dart (*The Interpretation of Music* (London, 1954)) and Robert Donington (*The Interpretation of Early Music* (London, 1963)) and they were matched by the perspectives of German scholars such as Robert Haas (*Aufführungspraxis* (Potsdam, 1931)) and Arnold Schering (*Aufführungspraxis alter Musik* (Leipzig, 1931)). These writers were among the first to sow the seeds of the so-called 'early music movement' and to establish in print many of the premises and assumptions that have been made regarding how music was performed in earlier times. Their theories and opinions were eagerly absorbed and put into practice by specialist performers.

A large number of small-scale institutions dedicated to historical performance began to develop throughout Europe. For example, there had already been a long tradition of early music at Basle when the viola da gamba player August

Wenzinger co-founded the Schola Cantorum Basiliensis in 1933 as a teaching and research institution for early music from the Middle Ages to Mozart. The revolution in listening habits prompted in the first half of the twentieth century by the advent of recordings also worked well in favour of early music, boosting the reputations of many artists and making ever more forgotten music familiar to a wider public. From the 1920s onwards, broadcasting also played a major part in raising appreciation of early music, especially in Britain, Germany and France, where public service broadcasters promoted a rich mix of live events, recording and talks. In Britain the BBC played a huge part, driving up technical standards and audience expectations. 'Early music' had become a highly marketable commodity.

Period performance after 1945 centred upon Amsterdam, The Hague, London and Vienna. An influential figure was the Dutch harpsichordist Gustav Leonhardt, whose meticulous care for historical accuracy in his texts and instruments avoided the trappings of showmanship. Early post-war milestones were Wenzinger's performance of Monteverdi's *Orfeo* in 1955 and Nikolaus Harnoncourt's Brandenburg Concertos a decade later. In London Thurston Dart symbolised a new coming together of the performer and scholar; in 1954 at the conclusion of his book he wrote: 'The written text must never be regarded as a dead laboratory specimen; it is only sleeping, though both love and time will be needed to awaken it. But love and time will be wasted without a sense of tradition and of historical continuity' (*The Interpretation of Music*, 168). In the 1960s, groups such as London-based Musica Reservata gave Medieval and Renaissance music new energy by integrating sounds and techniques derived from folk music. The Julian Bream Consort introduced many to the world of Elizabethan ensemble music. Above all, the versatile David Munrow won a wide new audience with his Early Music Consort of London (founded in 1967), which brought new life to Medieval and Renaissance repertory and acted as a springboard for its members, such as Christopher Hogwood. All this complementary solo and ensemble practical activity of the time has been usefully summarised by Harry Haskell (*The Early Music Revival: A History* (London: Thames & Hudson, 1988)) and is also surveyed in this volume (see EARLY MUSIC IN EUROPE and EARLY MUSIC IN NORTH AMERICA).

Significantly, there was a belief until about sixty years ago that 'early music' signified Medieval, Renaissance and Baroque music and that there could be no benefit in restoring music written after 1750 to period instruments. As late as 1980 the article 'performing practice' in *The New Grove Dictionary of Music and Musicians* claimed that there had been no severance of contact with post-Baroque music as a whole, nor with the instruments used in performing it. The article at the same time observed how revealing it would be to hear Beethoven symphonies on period instruments, but added that 'the practical difficulties of assembling and equipping such an orchestra would be almost insuperable' (xiv, 389). Musical revelations soon proved much of the arguments in the *NG* article to be false, as period interpretations of Mozart and Beethoven were followed by an exploration of much later repertory. And so the term 'early music', once applied to music of the Baroque and earlier periods, has largely given way to terms such as 'historically informed performance', in recognition that this later repertory also presents some formidable challenges in the restoration of original intent. Indeed, adventurous period ensembles such as the Orchestra of the Age of Enlightenment and Les Siècles have ventured into such territory as Glinka, Borodin, Tchaikovsky, Mahler, Fauré, Stravinsky and Ravel.

Since the last quarter of the twentieth century, historically informed performance (HIP) in theory and practice has truly established itself as part of mainstream musical life, remaining enormously influential. As Nicholas Kenyon expressed it in his Royal Philharmonic Society Lecture of 2001, 'there is no worthwhile, thoughtful and intellectually stimulating and musically adventurous performance going on today that has not been touched by the period instrument movement'. Throughout the world there has developed an unprecedented interest in discovering the original intentions and expectations of composers in terms of sound and musical style and in acquiring appropriate instrumental techniques for their faithful realisation. Furthermore, the explosion in the recording industry in the 1960s and 1970s attracted an ever-increasing number of converts to historical performance and led to a further expansion of scholarly and practical enquiry, as performers extended their repertories from the Baroque in each direction.

Stylistic cross-fertilisation has become a feature of today's musical climate. As Kenyon has observed, more than a generation has passed since the pioneers of the period performance movement began to work with modern orchestras to encourage them to change their sound: Roger Norrington and John Eliot Gardiner with the Vienna Philharmonic, Simon Rattle and William Christie with the Berlin Philharmonic, several period-instrument conductors including Trevor Pinnock and Christopher Hogwood with the American orchestras and opera houses. Partly this has been a question of bringing conductors who have worked with period-instrument orchestras more into the centre of our musical life: Norrington's work with the Stuttgart Radio Symphony Orchestra, pursuing a non-vibrato string sound but on modern instruments, was typically individual. At the same time conductors brought up with conventional instruments began to work in the period field: Ivan Fischer, Vladimir Jurowski and Robin Ticciati. Especially effective have been projects with chamber orchestras, merging traditions: Nikolaus Harnoncourt recording Beethoven symphonies with the Chamber Orchestra of Europe to great acclaim with modern instruments but vigorously individual period insights; Daniel Harding performing Beethoven with the Mahler Chamber Orchestra using natural trumpets but modern horns. It is not an exaggeration to say that these performers and others have transformed public taste.

Almost more remarkable is the change in those who have not used period instruments at all but whose performance style has evolved dramatically as a result of change around them, such as Bernard Haitink in his increasingly sharp-edged, fleet performances with the London Symphony Orchestra and the Chamber Orchestra of Europe. Some thirty-five years ago Paul Henry Lang wrote: 'Success will come when we are able to forgo the restrictive category "old music" and make it an integral part of our musical experience' ('Rigor Antiquarii: The Great "Performance Practice" Muddle', *High Fidelity/Musical America*, 29 (July 1979), 126). It is perhaps no coincidence that early music reached its zenith at a time when the original-state product was also popular in so many areas of activity: stripped wood, organic farming, natural foods and so on.

What is historically informed performance? In the mid-1990s the distinguished palaeoclimate scientist and instrument collector Sir Nicholas Shackleton answered the question by asserting that 'our primary objective in playing historic instruments is to gain a better feeling for what classical music actually sounded like when it was first heard in favourable circumstances' ('The development of the clarinet', in C. Lawson (ed.), *The Cambridge Companion to the Clarinet* (Cambridge University Press, 1995), 17). So, what kind of performance did composers of the past intend? What sounds did they expect? We will never really know, because in terms of sound, the entire history of music has all but disappeared before recording began by about 1890. Even a large library of musical dictionaries, biographies and analytical works cannot do more than hint at how music used to sound or the nature of the musical environment; it would be unrealistic to presume that the present volume can break through such limitations. As Mozart's contemporary Daniel Türk wrote (1789: 337), 'certain subtleties of expression cannot really be described; they must be *heard*'. Words really are inadequate to communicate some aspects of art, especially those tiny differences in emphases and timing that distinguish a great performance from a merely good one. Those aspects of music that are most precious are also the most difficult to put into words. Quantz warned as long ago as 1752 that it was not sufficient merely to read the notes on the page; flair and imagination were essential.

The musical score itself is an imprecise mechanism, which by its very nature offers even the most dutiful performer a rich variety of possibilities. There has always been much detail that a composer did not trouble to notate, knowing that certain conventions would be observed; some of these are no longer current or have undergone significant changes of meaning. For example, musical notation can give little indication of tempo flexibility or the balance of instruments within an ensemble. Those elements of style which a composer found it unnecessary to notate will always have the character of a foreign language, but one within which today's musicians can learn to converse freely. Using the resources and techniques for which a particular repertory was intended may well make more sense of what the composer actually wrote, re-creating something of its initial impact on the listener.

Performers and scholars have increasingly been collaborating to recreate original performance conditions, drawing upon source material including archives, literature, iconography and old instruments. As we remarked some time ago, one might argue that each period performer occupies a distinctive position on the spectrum of historical accuracy (insofar as it can be determined) and practical expediency.

In terms of historical shortcuts, copies of old instruments have a long tradition of wanting not only to revive the past, but also to improve upon it. In 1932 Arnold Dolmetsch's pupil Robert Donington remarked that 'the old harpsichord has certain limitations and produces a jangle, slight in the treble but audible in the bass . . . Dolmetsch's new instruments, which remedy these historical oversights, have proved both purer and more sustained than any previous harpsichord' (see L. Dreyfus, 'Early music defended against its devotees: A theory of historical performance in the twentieth century', *MQ*, 49 (1983), 305–6). Dolmetsch's historical position is interesting, but so is Donington's view of these improvements as sound common sense. And in the 1990s the trumpeter-scholar Robert Barclay drew attention to the finger-holes often placed on copies of the Baroque trumpet, so that 'the so-called out-of-tune harmonics of the natural series ... will not be unpleasant to modern sensitivity'. He was able to claim that the natural trumpet was the one instrument not yet fully revived for use in the performance of Baroque music. Barclay observed that many so-called copies of Baroque trumpets are often equipped with so many anachronistic features that the result is 'a trumpet which resembles its Baroque counterpart only superficially, whose playing technique is quite different, and whose timbre is far removed from that expected for baroque music' ('A new species of instrument: the vented trumpet in context', *HBSJ*, 10 (1998), 1).

Modern musical life has certainly dictated a virtuosity and flexibility that incorporate some decidedly unhistorical elements. Importantly, we are naturally selective in our interpretation of the evidence. There are many clues that testify to unsympathetic performance conditions that were not always what composers might have wished; and it can be convenient to ignore such evidence. For example, Bach was short of singers and players for his weekly church service at Leipzig. Beethoven wrote his symphonies at a time when the situation for orchestras in Vienna was very difficult – culturally, politically and musically.

Other evidence is often absorbed but then discarded for today's purposes. For example, Agricola advised in 1757 that the castrato Farinelli was in the habit of eating one uncooked anchovy before going on stage. Two generations later, when health was still a fragile affair, Joseph Fröhlich (1810–11) recommended for wind players a moderate lifestyle and the avoidance of anything that could damage the chest, such as running, horseback riding and the excessive consumption of hot drinks. One should not practise after a meal, so the afternoon was best avoided; furthermore, one should not drink immediately after practising if the lungs are still warm, since this had been the cause of many early deaths. In the case of dry lips – very bad for the embouchure – the mouth should be rinsed with an alcoholic beverage to give one new strength. Evidence must indeed be read in the spirit of the times.

And times have changed, as illustrated by the sheer responsiveness of Mozart's audience in Paris that testifies to a very different concert environment. He wrote of a tremendous burst of applause during the first movement of the Paris Symphony that he had composed especially for the occasion. In the finale he surprised everyone by starting with just two violin parts and everyone exclaimed 'hush' at the beginning and then, when the whole orchestra came in, they immediately began to clap their hands. Mozart, we may note, was *delighted* by all of this. But would today's audience tolerate such behaviour?

Christopher Hogwood's set of Mozart symphonies from the early 1980s ignited a particular debate about how much of his own personality a conductor should impose on the music. Others pointed out that merely following textbook rules was never going to satisfy an earlier composer's intentions. And around the same time the American scholar Richard Taruskin was already viewing the need to satisfy a composer's intentions as a failure of nerve, if not infantile dependency. He famously argued that historical performance was completely of our own time and that the historical hardware had won its wide acceptance and above all its commercial viability precisely by virtue of its novelty, not its antiquity. The vexed question of an earlier composer's intentions – or even their expectations – could occupy several conferences. When they express intentions as to how their music is to be performed, composers may be unaware of all the possibilities or they may be honestly mistaken, owing to the passage of time or changes of taste. We may want to bear in mind that Brahms relished conducting both the forty-nine-strong orchestra at Meiningen and the one hundred-strong Vienna Philharmonic. Listen to Stravinsky's very different five recordings of *The Rite of Spring* and then decide how he meant it to go.

Significantly, the age of digital technology brings its own challenges. We have become so used to so-called 'perfect' performances on disc that extreme technical accuracy in the concert hall is taken for granted. The danger remains that this element – the craft of musical performance – is achieved at the expense of art – the development of real musical personality. Reproduction instruments are often standardised in all kinds of unhistorical ways. For example, the use of an electronic tuner to impose equal temperament can be misguided. Furthermore, pitch has been unrealistically standardised to $a' = 415$ for Baroque and $a' = 430$ for Classical instruments, no more than a conventional and over-simplified response to the evidence. Ironically, Quantz in 1752 lamented the lack of a uniform pitch throughout Europe, which he thought was detrimental to his work as a flautist and to music in general.

Faced with such historical complexities, those actively pursuing the historical performance of music have thus far lacked a reliable scholarly reference tool to assist the rapid fulfilment of their ideals of rediscovering and recreating as closely as possible how musical works may have sounded at the time of their composition. A similar void exists for listeners to historically informed performance. Since the scholarly territory was traversed by the present editors in 1999 (*The Historical Performance of Music: An Introduction* (Cambridge University Press, 1999)), students have been served primarily by philosophical tracts, notably by Bruce Haynes (*The End of Early Music: A Period Performer's History of Music for the Twenty-First Century* (New York: Oxford University Press, 2007)) and John Butt (*Playing with History: The Historical Approach to Musical Performance* (Cambridge University Press, 2002)), more 'practical' period-defined texts such as Clive Brown's *Classical & Romantic Performing Practice 1750–1900* (Oxford University Press, 1999) or the instrument-focused *Violin Technique and Performance Practice in the Late Eighteenth and Early Nineteenth Centuries* (Cambridge University Press, 1985) by Robin Stowell, *Theory and Practice in Late Nineteenth-century Violin Performance: An Examination of Style in Performance, 1850–1900* (Aldershot: Ashgate, 2003) by David Milsom, *One Hundred Years of Violoncello* (Cambridge University Press, 1998) by Valerie Walden and *Playing the Cello, 1780–1930* (Farnham: Ashgate, 2014) by George Kennaway. It therefore scarcely requires justification to claim that an ambitious, encyclopedic 'one-stop-shop' for accessible, up-to-date and illuminating information about historical performance is necessary and long overdue.

This encyclopedia is intended to serve as a source of vital background information about performance practices, facilitate the understanding and solution of problems encountered in performance and keep historical performers abreast with the literature. It by no means supplants some of the seminal writings that have preceded it; rather, it reviews them in summary form, offers a wide range of information about specific musical personalities, concepts or historical performance practices and provides a valuable summation of the latest thinking behind many of the diverse issues which historical performers may want to assimilate in their interpretations. Inevitably, some of the entries contain discussions that may be familiar to some readers already wise to the world of historical performance, but many represent the latest research in the field and provide valuable new information and ideas. It is hoped that performers, teachers, students, audiences, music-lovers in general and perhaps even scholars will learn from dipping into the book's contents.

Rather than divide the volume into subsections dealing with separate categories of performance issues (tempo, ornamentation, pitch, etc.) *The Cambridge Encyclopedia of Historical Performance in Music* adopts the traditional encyclopedic approach of organising entries alphabetically by article name. In order to be suitably discriminative and to focus more sharply our extensive list of articles, we resolved that subjects for inclusion should fall broadly into the following categories: generic issues of style and performance techniques and practices; organology and the history and development of musical instruments; ensemble directors and performers; theorists; composers; and editors. Broadly, the entries on style and performance techniques/practices are the most extended, establishing the principal focus of the volume and spawning further entries in their wake; those relating to organology embrace largely the instruments of the late nineteenth-century symphony orchestra as well as a selection of significant keyboard and early instruments; those about directors/performers are confined to personalities whose contribution has been innovative or influential and brought significant change in the field; those on theorists are restricted to figures from whose work practical applications can be readily sought; those on composers are confined to musicians who were either actively concerned with music of the past beyond merely promoting/performing it or who made particular contributions to performance practice; and those about editors are limited to scholars/performers whose work has contributed fresh insights in relation to repertoire and style. Certain categories of encyclopedia entry, notably those involving the sociology of musical performance or genres of music composition, which tend not to provide information on specific techniques or interpretative issues of musical execution, are included only where essential.

Many of the world's leading HIP scholars and performers are among the volume's 115 or so contributors, who form a remarkably broad church of evaluation and opinion about theory and practice. Our contributors determined the general shape and focus of their entries within flexible parameters, so there is a fair amount of variety in content and format. All entries are intended to synthesise and present reliable and authoritative information of use to specialists and non-specialists alike more than to present new arguments. In cases where issues may be controversial, contributors have been requested to present all relevant aspects of the debate as well as a current assessment. Their aim is to provide readers with accessible, comprehensive information about the principal practices involved in historical performance. For their part, the editors have tried to make the reading experience a pleasantly informative one, while also preserving the individual style of each author; hence readers will find that some entries are more conversational, some more essayistic, some more formal and academic. Many authors have gone beyond the basics and offer thoughtful reflections on some of the pressing issues.

A detailed index provides the key to the relevance of certain topics to other entries and facilitates finding many more names and terms than could be accommodated as entry headwords; and helpful cross-references to related subject entries (distinguished throughout by the use of small capital letters (or sometimes preceded by *see* or *see also*) and usually marked only on their first appearance in each entry) should also assist readers in navigating their way around the volume. Where a person's birth/death dates are shown in the body of an article, they normally indicate that there is no article specifically about that person.

A select further reading list is provided at the end of each article wherever this has been deemed useful. Each list, presented alphabetically by author (or, for the same author, by title), is intended to provide friendly signposts largely for the uninitiated, allowing readers quickly to assess the sources which might most profitably be looked into further. It normally includes studies on which an author has drawn as well as suggested sources for further investigation. However, these lists are as a rule selective and are not intended to represent comprehensive summaries of the literature on the topic. Inquisitive readers are further encouraged to investigate, in conjunction with the present volume, excellent reference works such as the *New Grove Dictionary of Music and Musicians* and *Die Musik in Geschichte und Gegenwart*, as well as other more specialist HIP volumes.

Abbreviations for commonly cited literature have been used throughout the book (*see* list below). Pitches are identified by the Helmholtz system, where middle C is identified as c′, the c above as c″ and the c above that as c‴ and so on; similarly, the C below middle C is identified as c, the C below that as C, the C below that as C′ and so on. All pitches within any particular ascending octave are similarly identified. All translations are by the contributors unless otherwise stated.

Our guiding principle has been to make this encyclopedia a useful and effective starting point for the diverse readership the volume has the potential to attract. We hope that it will prove an effective tool for those wishing to lay their hands rapidly on essential information for specific purposes. We are all too conscious that compiling and editing it has been an exercise in compromise and we are acutely aware that our principal problem has been what to include and what to omit. Comprehensiveness is impossible within the confines of our publishing brief. Further, a work of this kind is necessarily incomplete, not least because much research in the field still remains to be undertaken. Consequently, the volume may not give the answer to every question readers might have about historical performance, but it will provide the background and basics, as well as some ideas about where to venture for additional reliable information. Even though not everyone or every issue connected with historical performance has a dedicated entry, we have endeavoured to cover what we and our advisers have deemed to be the most important topics somewhere in the volume.

As a final preliminary, some words of acknowledgement are in order for the assistance that we have received from many colleagues during the long process of compiling, organising and editing this volume. Writing a succinct and informative encyclopedia entry is an art form unto itself. We are therefore grateful beyond measure to all our contributors, especially those who submitted their entries on schedule, for their willingness to accept the challenge, their cooperation in discussing details of their material with us and with each other, and for putting up with our repeated bibliographic queries, suggestions for revisions, and other editorial meddling with their texts. Many of them have shown enormous patience in waiting for the final pieces of a complex jigsaw to be put in place. We have also greatly valued the advice and encouragement of the members of our editorial board – the American pianist, musicologist and composer Robert D. Levin (Harvard University and The Juilliard School), Andrew Parrott (Founder and Director, Taverner Choir, Consort and Players), Ashley Solomon (Chair of Historical Performance, RCM and Director of Florilegium) and Richard Wistreich (Director of Research, RCM) – who read some of the drafts and provided us with editorial guidance appropriate to some historical periods in which we questioned our own expertise. Special thanks are due to Natasha Loges, who furnished English translations of German-language submissions and Akos Lustyik, who prepared the music examples for printing. We are also grateful for financial support for the project from our respective institutions, the Royal College of Music and (up to December 2013) Cardiff University, and Cambridge University Press. Finally, thanks are due to Vicky Cooper, our original Senior Commissioning Editor at Cambridge University Press, who showed faith and confidence in inviting us to take on this exciting, draining, occasionally frustrating and ultimately highly rewarding project, and her successor Kate Brett and her production team, especially our eagle-eyed copy editor, Janice Baiton, for their practical guidance in bringing the book into print.

COLIN LAWSON AND ROBIN STOWELL

Bibliographical Abbreviations

AM	*Acta musicologica*
AMZ	*Allgemeine musikalische Zeitung*
BJb	*Bach Jahrbuch*
BJhM	*Basler Jahrbuch für historische Musikpraxis*
EMc	*Early Music*
GSJ	*Galpin Society Journal*
HBSJ	*Historic Brass Society Journal*
JAMS	*Journal of the American Musicological Society*
JM	*Journal of Musicology*
JMR	*Journal of Musicological Research*
JMT	*Journal of Music Theory*
JRMA	*Journal of the Royal Musical Association*
JVdGSA	*Journal of the Viola da Gamba Society of America*
MGG	*Die Musik in Geschichte und Gegenwart*, 2nd edn, 28 vols. (Kassel: Bärenreiter, 1994–2008)
M&L	*Music and Letters*
MQ	*Musical Quarterly*
MT	*The Musical Times*
NG	*New Grove Dictionary of Music and Musicians*, 2nd edn, 29 vols. (London: Macmillan, 2001)
NZfM	*Neue Zeitschrift für Musik*
18CM	*18th-Century Music*
19CM	*19th-Century Music*
PPR	*Performance Practice Review*
PRMA	*Proceedings of the Royal Musical Association*
RIM	*Rivista italiana di musicologia*
RM	*Revue de musicologie*

Selected Treatises Commonly Cited in Abbreviated Forms

Agazzari (1607) — *Del sonare sopra'l basso con tutti li stromenti e dell'uso loro nel conserto* (Siena, 1607); facsim. (Milan, 1933; Bologna, 1969).

Agricola J. F. (1757) — *Anleitung zur Singkunst* (Berlin, 1757).

Agricola M. (1529) — *Musica instrumentalis deudsch* (Wittenberg, 1529; R/ 1545). Trans. and ed. W. Hettrick as *The 'Musica instrumentalis deudsch' of Martin Agricola: A Treatise on Musical Instruments, 1529 and 1545* (Cambridge, 1994).

Bach C. P. E. (1753, 1762) — *Versuch über die wahre Art das Clavier zu spielen*, 2 vols. (Berlin, 1753, 1762). Trans. W. J. Mitchell as *Essay on the True Art of Playing Keyboard Instruments* (New York, 1949).

Baillot (1835) — *L'art du violon, nouvelle méthode* (Paris, 1835). Trans. L. Goldberg as *The Art of the Violin* (Evanston, IL, 1991).

Berlioz (1843) — *Grand traité d'instrumentation et d'orchestration modernes* (Paris, 1843). Trans. M. C. Clarke as *A Treatise on Modern Instrumentation and Orchestration* (London, 1855).

Bermudo (1555) — *El libro llamado declaración de instrumentos musicales* (Osuna, 1555).

Bismantova (1677) — *Compendio musicale* (Ms., 1677).

Couperin F. (1716, 1717) — *L'art de toucher le clavecin* (Paris, 1716, rev. 2/1717). Trans. and ed. M. Halford as *The Art of Playing the Harpsichord* (New York, 1974).

Diruta (1593, 1609) — *Il transilvano dialogo sopra il vero modo di sonar organi, et istromenti da penna*, 2 pts. (Venice, 1593, 1609). Facsim. edn with intro. by M. C. Bradshaw and E. J. Soehnlen (Henryville, PA, 1984).

Fröhlich (1810–11) — *Vollständige theoretisch-praktische Musikschule* (Bonn, 1810–11).

Ganassi (1535) — *Opera intitulata Fontegara* (Venice, 1535). Trans. D. Swainson as *Sylvestro Ganassi: Opera intitulata Fontegara* (Berlin and Lichterfelde, 1956).

SELECTED TREATISES COMMONLY CITED IN ABBREVIATED FORMS

Ganassi (1542)	*Regola rubertina* (Venice, 1542). Trans. in *JVdGSA*, 18 (1981), 13–66.
Ganassi (1543)	*Lettione seconda* (Venice, 1543). Trans. in *JVdGSA*, 19 (1982), 99–163.
Gasparini (1708)	*L'armonico pratico al cimbalo* (Venice, 1708). Trans. F. S. Stillings as *The Practical Harmonist at the Keyboard* (New Haven, CT, 1963).
Hotteterre J. (1707)	*Principes de la flûte traversière, ou flûte d'allemagne, de la flûte à bec, ou flûte douce, et du haut-bois* Op. 1 (Paris, 1707). Trans. and ed. D. Lasocki as *Principles of the Flute, Recorder and Oboe* (London, 1968).
Koch (1802)	*Musikalisches Lexikon, welches die theoretische und praktische Tonkunst, encyclopädisch bearbeitet, alle alten und neuen Kunstwörter erklärt, und die alten und neuen Instrumente beschrieben, enthält* (Frankfurt am Main, 1802, 2/1817).
L'Abbé *le fils* (1761)	*Principes du violon pour apprendre le doigté de cet instrument, et les différens agrémens dont il est susceptible* (Paris, 1761, 2/1772). Facsim. edn with introduction by Aristide Wirsta (Paris, 1961). Facsim. of 1772 edn (Geneva, 1976).
Lanfranco (1533)	*Scintille di musica* (Brescia, 1533). Trans. in B. Lee, 'Giovanni Maria Lanfranco's "Scintille di Musica" and its relation to 16th-century music theory', PhD dissertation, Cornell University (1961).
Mancini (1774)	*Pensieri e riflessioni prattiche sopra il canto figurato* (Vienna, 1774, enlarged 3/1777). Trans. E. Foreman as *Practical Reflections on Figured Singing* (Princeton, NJ, 1967).
Mattheson (1713)	*Das neu-eröffnete Orchestre* (Hamburg, 1713).
Mattheson (1739)	*Der vollkommene Capellmeister* (Hamburg, 1739). Trans. E. C. Harris (Ann Arbor, MI, 1981).
Mersenne (1636–7)	*Harmonie Universelle* (Paris, 1636–7).
Morley (1597)	*A Plaine and Easie Introduction to Practicall Musicke* (London, 1597).
Mozart L. (1756)	*Versuch einer gründlichen Violinschule* (Augsburg, 1756, 2/1769–70). Trans. E. Knocker as *A Treatise on the Fundamental Principles of Violin Playing* (London, 2/1951).
Ortiz (1553)	*Trattado de Glosas sobre Clausulas y otros generos depuntos en la Musica de Violones* (Rome, 1553).
Praetorius (1619)	*Syntagma musicum II–III* (Wolfenbüttel, 1619). Trans. D. Crookes (Oxford, 1986).
Quantz (1752)	*Versuch einer Anweisung die Flöte traversiere zu spielen* (Berlin, 1752). Trans. E. R. Reilly as *On Playing the Flute* (London, 1966).
Rode, Baillot, Kreutzer (1803)	*Méthode de violon* (Paris, 1803). Facsim. (Geneva, 1974).

Santa María (1565)	*Libro llamado el Arte de tañer Fantasia* (Valladolid, 1565).
Spohr (1832)	*Violinschule* (Vienna, 1832). Trans. J. Bishop as *Louis Spohr's Celebrated Violin School* (London, [1843]).
Tosi (1723)	*Opinioni de' cantori antichi e moderni o sieno Osservazioni sopra il canto figurato* (Bologna, 1723). Trans. J. E. Galliard as *Observations on the Florid Song* (London, 1742); ed. with additional notes M. Pilkington (London, 1987).
Tromlitz (1791)	*Ausführlicher und gründlicher Unterricht die Flöte zu spielen* (Leipzig, 1791). Trans. A. Powell as *The Virtuoso Flute-Player by Johann Georg Tromlitz* (Cambridge, 1991).
Türk (1789)	*Klavierschule, oder Anweisung zum Klavierspielen für Lehrer und Lernende mit kritischen Anmerkungen* (Leipzig and Halle, 1789). Trans. R. H. Haggh as *School of Clavier Playing* (Lincoln, NB, 1982).
Virdung (1511)	*Musica getutscht* (Basel, 1511).
Walther (1732)	*Musicalisches Lexikon oder musicalische Bibliothec* (Leipzig, 1732).
Zarlino (1558)	*Le istitutioni harmoniche* (Venice, 1558).

Aaron, Pietro (b. Florence, ?1480; d. after 1545) Italian theorist and composer.
One of the most prolific writers on music of the early sixteenth century, Aaron dealt with issues directly relating to musical performance in the final sections of his *Toscanello in musica* (Venice, 1523). The last chapter of Book 2 provides a practical guide to meantone TEMPERAMENT. It divides the octave into three major thirds, each regarded as the product of four perfect fifths, and recommends that each fifth should be made 'a little short' (*un poco scarsa*) so that the resulting major third is pure (5:4). The next section (the 'Supplement', which closes the treatise) offers a lengthy discussion of the use of accidentals in musical notation. The author argues that the signs of 'b rotondo' (flat) and 'diesis' (sharp) should be notated consistently and precisely, so that singers can perform their parts following the composers' intentions.

FURTHER READING

M. Bent, 'Accidentals, counterpoint, and notation in Aaron's *Aggiunta* to the *Toscanello*', *JM*, 12 (1994), 306–44.
P. Bergquist, 'The theoretical writings of Pietro Aaron', PhD dissertation, Columbia University (1964).
B. J. Blackburn, E. E. Lowsinky and C. Miller (eds.), *A Correspondence of Renaissance Musicians* (Oxford: Clarendon Press, 1991), 74–100, *passim*.

STEFANO MENGOZZI

Abel, Carl Friedrich (b. Cöthen, 22 December 1723; d. London, 20 June 1787) Composer, concert organiser, VIOL player and pupil of J. S. BACH.
His father was a colleague of Bach at Cöthen, and in the 1740s Abel was connected with members of the Bach family in Leipzig and Dresden. The Seven Years' War forced Abel to leave Dresden and during the 1758–9 season he arrived in London (probably visiting Mannheim and Paris en route) where he immediately started arranging concerts. Fresh from Italy, J. C. BACH arrived in London in 1762 and the pair collaborated on their first concert on 29 February 1764. Between January 1765 and May 1781 they ran their famous Bach/Abel series, the first regular subscription concerts in London, which consisted of ten to fifteen concerts annually. Here they performed their latest concertos, symphonies and chamber music and those of other members of the avant-garde; Abel delighted audiences with solos on the viol. In mid-1775 they built a new concert hall, the Hanover Square Rooms, furnished with paintings by their friend Thomas Gainsborough. Competition from the Pantheon concerts from 1774 helped to lead to the series' decline.

FURTHER READING

P. Holman, *Life After Death: The Viola da Gamba in Britain from Purcell to Dolmetsch* (Woodbridge: Boydell Press, 2010).
S. McVeigh, *Concert Life in London from Mozart to Haydn* (Cambridge University Press, 1993).

LUCY ROBINSON

Academy of Ancient Music (Eighteenth Century) London's Academy of Ancient Music, founded in 1726, played a pioneering role in the preservation and performance of earlier music, and thus in the development of the very concept of a historical canon of classical works. The Academy of Vocal Musick (as it was first known) was essentially a private club revolving round the main London choral foundations and dedicated to the enjoyment of 'Grave ancient vocell Musick' from the sixteenth and seventeenth centuries – sacred music and madrigals by Palestrina, Victoria and Marenzio, by Tallis, Byrd and MORLEY. With the change of name in 1731 and the addition of extra instrumentalists, the repertoire expanded to Purcell theatre music and (in 1732) a groundbreaking performance of Handel's *Esther*. Meanwhile the ever-expanding library was formalised and an educational arm formed under the leadership of Johann Christoph Pepusch.

While the term 'ancient' clearly reflected an antiquarian interest in older music, it also came to signify an ideological advocacy of the serious values of dignified contrapuntal music – pointedly reflected in the writings of JOHN HAWKINS, author of an account of the Academy printed in 1770. As a bulwark against the supposed triviality of modern *galant* idioms, the Academy translated a passionate commitment towards older values into both performance and composition. Thus as well as absorbing the music of Handel and his English contemporaries into the repertoire, it encouraged the composition of glees in madrigalian style and larger choral works by Benjamin Cooke and others. Yet gradually the original mission was diluted as the Academy came to resemble a public concert series for the wealthier bourgeoisie, and it entered a period of decline until a final season in 1802. Something of the Academy's spirit, however, lived on in the quite distinct, and decidedly aristocratic, CONCERT OF ANTIENT MUSIC which survived until 1848.

FURTHER READING

C. Hogwood, '"Gropers into Antique Musick" or "A very ancient and respectable Society"? Historical views of the Academy of Ancient Music', in C. Eisen (ed.), *Coll' astuzia, Col giudizio: Essays in Honor of Neal Zaslaw* (Ann Arbor, MI: Steglein, 2009), 127–82.

SIMON McVEIGH

Academy of Ancient Music (Twentieth Century) English ensemble.
The Academy of Ancient Music (AAM) was founded in 1973 by CHRISTOPHER HOGWOOD. Flexible through chamber formations or as a small orchestra, AAM's repertoire ranges from Locke and Purcell through the high Baroque to MOZART and BEETHOVEN. The keyboard player Richard Egarr succeeded Hogwood as music director in September 2006. Guest directors have included Giuliano Carmignola, Stephen Cleobury, Edward Gardiner, Paul Goodwin,

Bernard Labadie, Stephen Layton and MASAAKI SUZUKI. In addition to its regular series of concerts in Cambridge and London, the ensemble tours internationally, and has performed live on every continent except Antarctica. AAM has been an Associate Ensemble at London's Barbican Centre as well as Orchestra-in-Residence at the University of Cambridge.

The ensemble's current discography embraces chamber, symphonic and operatic repertoire and its recordings have enjoyed industry recognition from Gramophone, Edison, Brit and MIDEM awards. AAM enjoyed a particularly fruitful association with Decca's L'Oiseau Lyre label and 'emerged from the studio to become one of the most prolific early music groups on records' (H. Haskell, *The Early Music Revival: A History* (London: Thames & Hudson, 1988), 123). Its first recording, of overtures by Thomas Arne, was released in 1974. Four years later it began its pioneering set of the complete Mozart symphonies, which was completed in 1985. This was followed in 1989 by the Beethoven symphonies. Although incomplete, a project to record all the HAYDN symphonies for Decca under Hogwood's baton stands as a legacy to both Hogwood's development as a conductor as well as AAM's developing fluency. In the opinion of some aficionados, the Decca recordings of eighteen of Mozart's piano concertos with ROBERT LEVIN (released 1994–2001) represent the historical performance movement at its absolute zenith. In 2009 a performance of *Messiah*, from King's College Chapel, Cambridge, was broadcast internationally in real-time to cinemas in over 250 cities. Since 2013 the ensemble has recorded for AAM Records, utilising new technologies in the wider dissemination of its music making.

INGRID E. PEARSON

Accademia Monteverdiana Vocal and instrumental ensemble.

Of variable constitution and wide-ranging early music repertory, the Accademia Monteverdiana (AM) was founded in 1961 by the English musicologist, violinist and conductor Denis Stevens (1922–2004), who was its artistic director and president. Yehudi Menuhin was its vice-president, and NADIA BOULANGER and IGOR STRAVINSKY were among its trustees.

Inspired by recordings by Boulanger's ensemble of some of MONTEVERDI's madrigals, Stevens intended the AM to encompass research, performance and publication and thereby encourage public appreciation and understanding of early music, especially of Monteverdi's *oeuvre*. The AM grew out of the Ambrosian Singers, co-founded in 1951 by Stevens and tenor John McCarthy (1919–2009), because of the perceived need to establish an ensemble of appropriate touring proportions to give concert performances of largely Medieval, Renaissance and Baroque music. Consisting basically of five singers and a harpsichordist, its complement varied according to programming, performance circumstances and locale (in a 1974 BBC Promenade Concert in Westminster Cathedral, for example, the ensemble comprised about 100 performers).

The AM presented its inaugural concert in the City of Bath Festival (1961), featuring violinists Menuhin and Robert Masters, keyboard player Kinloch Anderson and the core vocal quintet, and including spoken introductions by Stevens. Later that year, AM performed Monteverdi's *Vespers of 1610* in

Westminster Abbey, using Stevens's edition. Recordings and radio broadcasts followed, along with concert tours throughout Europe and in the USA and performances (1967) in BBC Promenade Concerts and prestigious festivals such as those in Salzburg and Lucerne. Recordings embraced repertory ranging from Medieval carols, conductus, motets, masses and plainsong to works by Gesualdo, Grandi, Monteverdi, Albicastro, Vivaldi and other composers, including BEETHOVEN.

Although they played an invaluable role in bringing this repertory to public awareness, Stevens and the AM never resorted to experimentation with original instruments or period playing techniques, resisting many of the musicological propositions and organological revivals that burgeoned during the 1970s and 1980s.

FURTHER READING

D. Stevens, *Monteverdi in Venice* (London: Associated University Presses, 2001).

ROBIN STOWELL

Accent According to Cooper (1565) and Thomas (1587), an accent or a tune is 'the rysynge or fallynge of the voice' (G. Strahle, *An Early Music Dictionary* (Cambridge University Press, 1995), 1–3). The accentuation of sixteenth-century vocal music is shaped by its inherent rhythms and language; the mensural system itself seems not to embody notions of accentuation, though that particular issue has proved controversial. In 1706 Kersey-Phillips defined accentuation as follows: '*Accent in Musick* is a Modulation, or warbling of the Voice, to express the Passions, either Naturally or Artificially' (Strahle, 1). Terms used for metrical accentuation in the eighteenth century include *thesis* versus *arsis*, strong versus weak and finally *accented* versus *unaccented*. In H. C. Koch's *Kompositionslehre* (Leipzig, 1787, ii, § 51), an emphasis by means of duration rather than dynamic amounts in aesthetic terms to a stress accent. Such agogic accentuation is essential for interpretation not just on the ORGAN and HARPSICHORD. *Meyers Großes Konversations-Lexikon* (Leipzig and Vienna, 1902–8, art. 'accent') made the following claim:

> In music, one understands by the term accent the emphasis upon individual notes through greater strength of sound and (minimal) elongation of the sound. Regular bearers of accents are the main points of the themes, which are articulated in our notation through the barline as well as (in compound time signatures) through the break in the beaming of the quavers, semiquavers etc. However, the accentuation of these is not achieved abruptly or jerkily, but rather through the culmination of a *crescendo* approaching the upbeat; if, because of a so-called feminine ending, the motive extends beyond the barline, then the *diminuendo* is the obvious solution. These fundamental accentuations arising from the arrangement of the bars are in contrast to the accentuation of individual notes for melodic reasons (melodic climax) or harmonic reasons (dissonances, modulating notes), as well as the individual stronger emphasis of the opening notes of motives.

Meyer's contemporary HUGO RIEMANN declared in general terms: 'Just as with striking melodic intervals, so every striking chord, complex dissonance or far-reaching harmonic step demands accentuation ... a gentle lingering (agogic accent) is generally suitable to illustrate dissonances' (*Handbuch des Klavierspiels* (Berlin: Max Hesses, 1905), 92).

In 1722 MATTHESON labelled strong beats of the bar such as the first and fourth quavers in 6/8 'accents', as distinct from 'emphases'. LEOPOLD MOZART (1756, § 9) similarly defines an 'accent ... an expression, stress or emphasis', which occurs 'mostly ... on the ... *nota buona*', that is, a stress on the strong beats of the bar. Realising the hierarchy of the bar involved due emphasis on the so-called *note buone*, the notes of natural rhythmic stress – particularly the first note of each bar, but also other notes, depending on the TEMPO. This concept, already well developed by the end of the sixteenth century, was restated in many TREATISES of the eighteenth century. J. A. P. Schulz (*Article I. Allgemeine Theorie der schönen Künste* (Leipzig, 1794)) was probably one of the first to stress that those who constantly strongly mark the first beat of the bar destroy the whole piece. Similarly, KOCH (1802, 49–52) warned that the 'grammatical accents' relating to beaming and barring 'in performance, especially ... of passages of similar notes in lively motion, must not be as pronounced as the rhetorical or pathetic accent ... but rather must be so finely nuanced as to be barely perceptible, otherwise a tasteless, limping style of performance results which has the same effect as when one, for example, scans the verse while reading a poem aloud'. He observes that the vivid presentation of a melody within a piece of music depends largely upon the correct rendition of the rhetorical and pathetic accents, while adding that the effect of the stress on these notes is better sensed than described. Generations later, rhetorical, pathetic, melodic, harmonic, rhythmic, thematic, quantitative and extreme accents were distinguished from one another in A. F. Christiani's *Verständnis im Klavierspiel* (Leipzig, 1886). However, this type of terminology has never really become established. Furthermore, it has not always been remembered that meaningful, musical accentuation is applied not only to individual notes, but also to figurations.

Composers have taken a rather less structured approach. In 1923 SCHOENBERG remarked that perfect symmetry is not suited to music, since it impedes any freely flowing, spiritually uplifting phrasing; for instance, through an amateurish over-emphasis on the strong beats. The barline, which should be a regulating 'servant', should not become the 'master'; over-accentuation of strong beats shows poor musicianship, but to bring out the centre of gravity of a phrase is indispensable to its intelligent and intelligible presentation. Musicians such as BUSONI strongly prioritised the melodic line over the metric downbeat; according to him, the barline was just for the eye! One composition student of ALBAN BERG (T. Adorno, *Zu einer Theorie der musikalischen Reproduktion*, ed. H. Lonitz (Frankfurt am Main, Suhrkamp Verlag, 2001), 171f.) believed: 'In traditional music it is insufficient to perform independently of the barline; rather one must *simultaneously* feel the absolute and the bar emphases, in other words, bring out the conflict between the two ... for example in the second theme of the Finale of [Schumann's] Piano Concerto, one must not only emphasise the apparent 3/2 metre, but also always allow the 3/4 to be audible, so as to give some emphasis to the rest in the second bar.'

Explicitly notated accentuation marks are rarely encountered before the Baroque since such nuance was left to the good TASTE of the musician, especially in instrumental music. 'The staccato mark's dual function was never clearly differentiated'; in HAYDN's later works, '(v) was used occasionally as an accent sign' (Brown, 98). *Rinforzando* was sometimes intended to signify more than punctual accentuation or emphasising; it was 'sometimes synonymous with *crescendo*' (Brown, 62). Carl Czerny understood ^, >, *rf, sf, fz* and even *fp* as identical signs.

Erwin Stein (60) claimed that 'there is considerable confusion about the significance of *marcato*, >, ^, *sf, fp*, etc., because the practice of composers varies, even during their lifetime'. A. B. Marx had already ranked *sf* and *ff* as of lesser intensity in early and middle BEETHOVEN than in his late works. In the Septet, Op. 20, the small vertical staccato wedge does indeed indicate an accent. In Schubert, directions such as *fz, sfz, ffz, fp, sfp* and >

> indicate which aspects of the melody, harmony or rhythm are to be emphasized: they clarify the structure of the musical fabric, though often they merely reflect the impetus of the composer. They cannot always be assigned unambiguously to particular instruments [of the full score] or incorporated within the flow of the music ... The accent marks (>), fz (sfz) and fp (sfp) are often used synonymously and interchangeably ... Where ff and fz occur together, the first refers to the dynamic level in general whereas the second calls for a particular accent with respect to a rhythmic figure.
>
> (NEUE SCHUBERT-AUSGABE V. 1, PREFACE)

If the *Moment Musical*, Op. 94 No. 5 has an accent > on the first beat of virtually every bar, then there must surely be a subtle differentiation according to the degree of dissonance and tonal syntax in order to avoid the 'accursed chopping' which Schubert expressly 'could not stand' (Letter 25 July 1824, in O. E. Deutsch (ed.), *Schubert: Die Dokumente seines Lebens* (Kassel: Bärenreiter, 1964), 299), and which occasionally mars the playing of even great pianists. The symbol ^, which usually denotes a lesser intensity than *sf* and *rfz*, was regarded by Riemann as an indication of agogic elongation. Conversely, '*Sforzatos* are often exaggerated, or neglected, by performers ... and composers would do well to accept Stravinsky's method of indicating the dynamic level: *sf* in *pp*, or *marc* in *p*' (Stein, 62).

'Intervals which do not ... belong to the diatonic scale' – the notes through which one modulates – are perceptibly emphasised, to a greater or lesser extent. Intervals which are dissonant to the bass, or which prepare dissonant intervals, as well as 'notes which noticeably stand out because of their length, high or low pitch, etc' should be emphasised (Türk, 1789, 337). Chopin also adhered to this practice, which 'he often repeated to his pupils', according to Jan Kleczynski (*Chopin's Greater Works* (London: Reeves, 1896), 23); 'a long note should be played more strongly, just like a stressed note. Equally, a dissonance should be more pronounced', as well as syncopations. Conversely, the end of a phrase, before a comma or a full stop, is always weak. When a melody ascends, one should *crescendo*; when it descends, *decrescendo*. Decisions must be made according to the context and aesthetic function. Chopin was called the Ariel of the PIANO in the nineteenth century on account of the lightness, tenderness, cleanness, elegance and grace of his playing (see M. Tomaszewski, *Chopin* (Poznań: Podsiedlik-Raniowski i Spólka, c1998), 53).

FURTHER READING

C. Brown, *Classical and Romantic Performing Practice 1750–1900* (Oxford University Press, 1999).
E. Stein, *Form and Performance* (London: Faber, 1962).

MATTHIAS THIEMEL (TRANS. NATASHA LOGES)

Accentuation *see* ACCENT

Adam, (Jean-) Louis (Johann Ludwig) (b. Muttersholtz, 3 December 1758; d. Paris, 8 April 1848) French composer, music teacher and piano virtuoso.

Louis Adam composed primarily for the piano but also for the orchestra and the voice. He arrived in Paris in the mid-1770s and taught at the PARIS CONSERVATOIRE from 1797. With Ludwig-Wenzel Lachnith he published the *Méthode ou principe général du doigté* (Paris: Sieber, 1798, R/2001), but of greater significance was his official *Méthode de piano du Conservatoire* (Paris: Conservatoire de Musique, 1804). Adam's tutor stresses a quiet, finger-based technique and a legato approach; super-legato (in which the notes are held for longer than indicated) is also described. With one exception, he advocates upper-note trills and all his ornament explanations start on the beat. He describes a rubato in which the beat of the melody line is displaced from the accompaniment. Adam's tutor also contains an extensive and robust defence of PEDALLING. He describes the lute, moderator, sustaining and lid-swell (squares only) and *una corda* (grands only) of French pianos. Examples are included for all the pedals except the lid-swell, but he reserves his longest discussion for the sustaining pedal, his approach to which is the most modern of the period.

FURTHER READING

J.-M. Fauquet, *Dictionnaire de la musique en France au XIXe siècle* (Paris: Fayard, 2003).
M. van Epenhuysen Rose, '*L'art de bien chanter*: French pianos and their music before 1820', PhD dissertation, New York University (2006).

DAVID ROWLAND

Adam of Fulda *see* FULDA, ADAM OF

Adler, Guido (b. Eibenschütz [now Ivančice], Moravia, 1 November 1855; d. Vienna, 15 February 1941) Austrian musicologist.

Adler established himself as one of the pioneers of modern musicology with his article 'Umfang, Methode und Ziel der Musikwissenschaft', printed in the first issue (1885) of the *Vierteljahrsschrift für Musikwissenschaft*, which he founded with Spitta and Chrysander. As professor for musicology at the University of Vienna, he founded and acted as general editor (1894–1938) of the *Denkmäler der Tonkunst in Österreich*.

FURTHER READING

C. Rosenthal, 'Reminiscences of Guido Adler (1855–1941)', *Musica Judaica*, 8 (1985–6), 13–22.

DAVID FALLOWS

Adlung, Jakob (b. Bindersleben, nr Erfurt, 14 January 1699; d. Erfurt, 5 July 1762) German organist and scholar.

After university studies at Jena, Adlung returned to his home town of Erfurt to succeed Buttstedt as organist of the Prediger Church. His two extant books, *Anleitung zur musikalischen Gelahrtheit* (Erfurt, 1758) and *Musica mechanica organoedi* (Berlin, 1768) are major sources about music in the German Baroque. *Anleitung* contains his knowledge of music history, tuning, ORGAN history, construction and registration as well as SINGING, thoroughbass, IMPROVISATION, Italian TABLATURE and composition. In *Musica mechanica* he recorded unique data concerning early eighteenth-century organs in middle Germany. It serves as an encyclopedia, with details of organ-builders, organ construction and tonal characteristics, cases, wind chambers, pipes and registers, tuning and TEMPERAMENT, methods of testing new instruments as well as giving detailed descriptions of more than eighty German organs. The editorial notes made by J. L. Albrecht and J. F. AGRICOLA reveal J. S. BACH's opinions on organ building and design.

FURTHER READING

J. Adlung, *Musica mechanica organoedi* (1726) 2 vols. (Berlin, 1768); ed. C. Marenholz (Kassel, 1931); Trans. Q. Faulkner as *Musical Mechanics for the Organist* (Lincoln, NE: Zea E-Books, 2011).

P. Williams, *The European Organ 1450–1850* (London: B. T. Batsford, 1966).

DAVID PONSFORD

Adorno, Theodor W. (b. Frankfurt, 11 September 1903; d. Brig, Switzerland, 6 August 1969) German philosopher and sociologist.

Adorno studied at Frankfurt University (1921–4), and became professor of philosophy there in 1949, after fifteen years of exile in the 1930s and 1940s in Britain and the USA. His most important philosophical works are *Negative Dialectics* (1966) and *Aesthetic Theory* (1970), and his most infamous book on music is *Philosophy of New Music* (1949). He was also a musician and music critic, and had studied the piano and composition at the Hoch Conservatory in Frankfurt with Bernhard Sekles, later studying composition in Vienna in the mid-1920s with ALBAN BERG and piano with Eduard Steuermann.

Adorno wrote extensively on music, publishing many books and essays on a wide range of musical subjects, including the Second Viennese School, STRAVINSKY, BACH, BEETHOVEN, JAZZ and mass culture. His approach is always to understand the music as mediated by its historical and political context, an example of which is his critique of 'AUTHENTICITY' and the historical performance movement in his article 'Bach defended against his devotees' (1951, in *Prisms*, trans. S. and S. Weber (London: Spearman, 1967), 133–46). He worked sporadically over a period of forty years on a 'theory of musical reproduction', orientated towards the aesthetics of performance rather than directly towards musical practice. He began the project in the mid-1920s, and pursued it in the 1930s and 1940s initially as a proposed collaboration with the violinist RUDOLF KOLISCH, finally returning to it in the 1950s and 1960s. It was never completed, and remained at his death in fragmentary form as notes, drafts and outlines. These fragments were finally published in German

(*Zu einer Theorie der musikalischen Reproduktion*, ed. H. Lonitz (Frankfurt am Main: Suhrkamp Verlag, 2001)) and in an English translation (as *Towards a Theory of Musical Reproduction*, ed. H. Lonitz, trans. W. Hoban (Cambridge: Polity Press, 2006)).

The fundamental idea underlying the 'theory of reproduction' is that performance as interpretation is a form of critique, a critical practice. An important focus is the relationship of performer to score. Adorno conceives the musical score as having three elements: 1) the *mensural* (i.e. the score as rationalised 'sign-system' indicating duration, pitch, barlines and so on); 2) the *neumic* (i.e. the gestural/mimetic aspects of the score, including phrasing, directions for EXPRESSION and DYNAMICS); and 3) the *idiomatic* (i.e. directions suggesting the 'language-like' aspects of the music – although this is the least developed of his three basic concepts). He says that 'the theme of the study is really the dialectic between these elements'. The question of what it means to play a piece 'correctly', and the conviction that a theory of musical reproduction would concern the idea of a 'true interpretation' (*die Idee der wahren Interpretation*) is inseparable for Adorno from what might seem to be its opposite – the idea that interpretation changes historically, as he argues do musical works and our reception of them. He sees performance both as a process of interpretation and as an autonomous form in its own right, just as he sees composition as a process and the musical work as an autonomous form. Only one short essay from the project was published during Adorno's lifetime: 'Zum Problem der Reproduktion' (1925. In *Pult und Taktstock* 2, vol. 4. Republished in Adorno, *Gesammelte Schriften*, vol. 19, ed. R. Tiedemann (Frankfurt am Main: Suhrkamp Verlag, 1984), 440–4).

FURTHER READING

H. Danuser, '"Zur Haut zurückkehren". Zu Theodor W. Adornos Theorie der musikalischen Reproduktion', *Musik & Ästhetik*, 7/25 (January 2003), 5–22.
M. Paddison, *Adorno's Aesthetics of Music* (Cambridge University Press, 1993).
  'Riddle-character, interpretation, and dialectical image: Adorno's philosophy and the case of musical performance', *New German Critique* (special edition: *Adorno and Music: Critical Variations*), 43/3(129) (November 2016), 139–54.

MAX PADDISON

Aesthetics

Aesthetics and the Performing Arts

The word 'aesthetics' derives from the Greek 'aisthesis' meaning 'perception'. It is now commonly used in two broad senses to indicate: 1) any theoretical or experiential engagement with the arts in relation to their 'art-ness'; or 2) any focus on those attributes and qualities – such as design, colour, gesture, appearance or manner of execution – that appeal to the senses and are valued for their own sake wherever they are found (e.g. in nature, ordinary objects).

The relationship between art and aesthetic perception is problematic, as is the notion of beauty that is assumed by many to be perceived through those activities. In Plato and Aristotle art is discussed in relation to craftsmanship and the imitation of nature, but almost never in conjunction with beauty (a brief exception can be found in Plato's *De Re Publica*, Book III), and the notion of perception is analysed (notably in Aristotle's *De Anima*) but never in relation to art. These disjunctions open up a number of intriguing questions. Do all things done with skill and artistry necessarily lead to the creation of artworks? Is the possession of aesthetic attributes on its own sufficient to designate something as art? And is musical performance an art or a craft?

An early attempt to designate performance as a distinct type of art can be found in Quintilian's *Institutio Oratoria* (Book II, xviii, 1), dating from c60AD, where he separately discusses the arts of theory (e.g. mathematics), practice (e.g. dance or music) and production (e.g. painting). However, he leaves open the question of whether the second category is able to create an artistic product purely in its own right, or whether it merely reveals an artwork conceived under the third, 'productive', category. From at least the eighteenth century music was categorised as one of the 'fine arts', which also included painting, sculpture, architecture, poetry, theatre and dance. This system separated the fine arts from the so-called 'applied arts' (decorative crafts, etc.). In doing that it contrasted the full imaginative control that originating artists had over form and content in the former, with the routinised and repetitive skills found in the latter, no matter how expertly and sensitively executed. It is a legacy of this system that the level of creativity required by musical performers, actors and dancers is sometimes called into question.

It was Alexander Baumgarten in his *Aesthetica* (1750) who established aesthetics as a distinct discipline. He argued that knowledge derived from the senses is of a special kind that can stand alongside conceptual knowledge and logical truth. His engagement with the aesthetic was transformed in Immanuel Kant's *Kritik der Urteilskraft* (1790) into a sophisticated theory of how we perceive the aesthetically beautiful through judgements of TASTE. This theory has much relevance for our experiences of art, but in Kant's writings the connection between the two is not altogether transparent. This is because his categories of art are based on a system that emphasises the senses and skills involved rather than the art objects themselves, and because his notion of aesthetic experience is not primarily concerned with art. A sunset, for example, may be aesthetically beautiful without our being able to speak of it in terms normally applied to art – it cannot in itself be well crafted, ironic, a profound commentary on the human condition, or a transformation of a genre.

Aesthetics is often associated with a rather simplistic notion of 'the beautiful', sometimes meaning little more in popular usage than the 'pleasing' or the 'pretty'. Kant himself was at pains to make a distinction between the beautiful and the awe-inspiring sublime, and later developments in art, such as Realism and Brutalism, and the gradual displacement of 'beauty' by 'truth' as an artistic paradigm meant that aesthetic properties expanded to include the disturbing, the shocking and – more recently – the camp, the cute and much else besides.

Issues of Identity and Definition

How we define something partly determines how we value it and how we ready ourselves for the types of experience we think we are likely to get from it. For the musical performer the most pressing issues come not from questions about how we might define music itself, but how we might construct a viable notion of the identity of a musical work (and the 'mode of its existence' – its 'ontology') given the variety of its performances. This question underpins debates concerned with what used to be called 'authentic' performance, the status of URTEXT editions, the notion of 'the music itself', the transient nature of improvisations, the status of fakes and forgeries (can musical performances be forged?), and with our attempts to distinguish 'acceptable' novel or interesting performance interpretations from 'unacceptable' bizarre ones.

Several theories attempt to accommodate the special problem of identity v. performance variety in the performing arts, though most get further in their descriptions of the paradox than in offering clear solutions as to how identity is maintained in the face of variety. For example, Richard Wollheim (*Art and Its Objects* (Cambridge University Press, 1980)) distinguishes between non-performance 'Individuals' (e.g. Mona Lisa) and performance 'Types-and-their-Tokens' (e.g. the idea of Beethoven's Ninth Symphony, which is its 'type' and its many performance instantiations, which are the type's 'tokens'). Related systems have been developed by Nelson Goodman (*Languages of Art* (Indianapolis: Hackett, 1976)), Roman Ingarden (*The Work of Music and the Problem of Its Identity*, trans. A. Czerniawski, ed. J. G. Harrell (Basingstoke: Macmillan Press, 1986)) and others.

The difficulty with many of these systems rests on the question of whether we should consider the 'identity' of a work to include only the material notes and performance instructions (the 'exhibited' features), or also indirect ('non-exhibited') features such as irony or composer intentions, or culturally understood and intentionally implied performance conventions and appropriate styles – in other words, the 'reading cultures' that surround the works. These arguments are not entirely resolved by the claim (argued by Ben Caplan, Carl Matheson and others) that the identity of a work arises from the sum of its performances. After all, how can we know which of the many performances in the world are relevant to the construction of a particular work unless we already have a shadowy notion of the work's identity – the very thing the theory is supposed to supplant? And what could any of those 'relevant' performances possibly be interpretations of, if the work does not exist until they are over?

Musical Meanings

Two general theories of meaning lie behind many traditional attempts to explain how artworks and performances can seem 'meaningful': the correspondence theory and the coherence theory.

Correspondence theories claim that artworks accrue meanings because they refer to ('correspond to') things in the world such as human emotions, social functions, or programmatic and narrative ideas. Coherence theories claim that artworks can be meaningful in virtue of being integrated, balanced, or having well-formed processes or structures. 'Coherence' approaches generally lead to formalist theories, though sometimes with the additional claim that the forms themselves have a transcendental import, or a metaphysical content. Modern notions of the metaphysical import of artworks are derived in part from Hegel who linked the insights of art to the gradual revelation through history of our true nature and the fulfilment of its promise.

In recent times the more tangible attributes of expression, representation, language and narrative have received sophisticated theoretical examination from

Peter Kivy, Stephen Davies, Jerrold Levinson and others. Discussions have tended to focus on how our vague sensations in the presence of sounds become defined into emotional experiences. The mechanisms explored include the clarifications given by our knowledge of composer intentions, the additional impact of our subjective associations with music, the kinetic and physiological mechanisms of sonic 'arousal', and our 'reading' of the contours of music as metaphorical gestures. Such approaches have generally had less to say about the specific contribution of performers to our 'expression experiences'. Performers as human agents not only reveal sounds appropriate to (say) sadness or joy or narration, but also respond to them with (say) pity or elation or expectation, and persuade us to hear sonic events symbolically and as appropriate to distinct feelings.

Theories of musical narration and language (by Deryck Cooke, Leonard Bernstein, Anthony Newcomb and others) have different problems. Unlike language, music on its own is 'non-propositional' – it cannot make clear assertions, it has no past or future tense and it cannot distinguish between subjects and predicates (e.g. an angry man and anger). Moreover, although a composer may write music in response to thoughts, texts or events, some (e.g. Carl Dahlhaus) have argued that, at best, such ideas can only become the 'subject' of music, not its 'content'. Equally problematic is the notion that music forms a 'communication' system. It may be that we could share with others a sense of absorption, mood and involvement at a musical event (this would be an experience of 'communion') but this is not equivalent to sharing exact and particular meanings (which would constitute a 'communication').

Much of philosophy has been concerned with what goes on in the mind, but in recent years attention has turned towards the apparently 'unproblematic' body – including the bodily presence of the performer. The claim is that performance does not just reveal or communicate the meaning(s) of the work, but also, through the very act of performing and the physical attributes and mannerisms of the performer, further meanings are created and projected. These additional meanings are 'performative' meanings and encompass variously: 1) those meanings that can only arise through an action in a particular context (e.g. the 'aura' of a prize-winning performance in a competition); 2) the body's distinctive physiological effects on the specific sounds produced in performance (see R. Barthes, 'The Grain of the Voice', in his *Image-Music-Text*, trans. S. Heath (London: Fontana, 1977), 179–89); or 3) aspects of the gendered or sexualised bodily presence of the performer (as explored by Lawrence Kramer, Susan McClary and others).

Coherence theories of meaning give rise to different kinds of problem. Do all works with the same form have the same meaning and value? What exactly is a well-formed structure? How can the materials of a 'non-propositional' abstract art like music have 'logical' consequences, where 'statement x' necessarily and always entails 'statement y'? (SCHOENBERG, for example, claimed that his song *Vorgefühl*, Op. 22 No. 4 followed 'musical logic', even though some of its instigating material turns up again in his *Die Jakobsleiter* with very different musical consequences.) For performers, there is also the question of whether to take integration, coherence and closure as the 'natural' aim of performance, or to leave audiences with questions about works – to reveal their 'riddle characters' as ADORNO might say.

The relation of musical form to expression is often neglected. However, much that is felt in music emerges cumulatively through time in conjunction with formal development and intellectual understanding (as with emotions such as fascination, or states of mind, or reflective moods). The performer needs to be aware of the graduated manner of musical expression; 'art' emotions, unlike 'human' emotions, are always controlled formally to some extent (see R. Scruton, *The Aesthetics of Music* (Oxford: Clarendon Press, 1997), 155 ff.).

Interpretation and Value
In philosophical terms 'interpretation' normally implies the 'critical negotiation' or 'sophisticated adjudication' of meaning. It differs subtly from 'hermeneutics' in that the latter is more centrally concerned with the analysis of human understanding as such, rather than with what exactly is understood. For musical performers the difficulties begin with the fact that in the realm of musical performance the term 'interpretation' is employed promiscuously and opaquely.

At its most basic, it indicates the routine reading and realisation of the notation, or the conventional articulation of aspects of the musical material, or the unplanned emergence of patterns of intensity in performance (as effects without interpretative causes). None of these implies a 'critical negotiation' or 'sophisticated adjudication' of meaning, and therefore it is hard to regard such performances as having interpretations at all in the technical sense: they are 'displays' rather than 'interpretations'.

Genuine acts of interpretation in performance include elucidations (the effective resolution of formal and other kinds of ambiguity in the music), elaborations (through ornaments, cadenzas, or improvisations upon models), and characterisations (whether of mood, narrative, or stylistic or emotive 'colouring') – all of which require the performance interpretation to be underpinned, whether consciously or unconsciously, by some kind of critical understanding.

Many have argued that, none the less, we should not see a simple equivalence between genuine performance interpretations and critical interpretations (see, for example, J. Levinson, 'Performative versus critical interpretation in music', in M. Krausz (ed.), *The Interpretation of Music: Philosophical Essays* (Oxford: Clarendon Press, 1993), 33–60). Critical interpretations tend to focus only on those elements that support the 'explanation', whereas performers need to play every note in a meaningful way. Also, the purpose of criticism is to reveal meaning, whereas performance through time may, for the sake of impact or narrative, be required temporarily to conceal the wider meaning or connections of a passage. And, of course, analyses and criticisms need have no allegiance to aesthetic effect in the manner of their presentations.

The term 'evaluate' has two distinct meanings – 'to come to understand' and 'to reach a verdict'. In practice the two are related. For example, a performance might sound bizarre (e.g. GLENN GOULD's recording of the first movement of MOZART's A major Piano Sonata, K331) but, once the rationale is known, it can attain a significance and interest not immediately apparent. Moreover, performances have their own communal and personal qualities, values and meanings that lie beyond a narrow focus on a competent display of the work. That being so we can make an evaluative distinction between 'the perfect performance of music' and 'the perfect musical performance' (L. Goehr, *The Quest for Voice: Music, Politics and the Limits of Philosophy* (Oxford: Clarendon Press, 1998), 134).

Some have seen the value systems we employ as being merely reflective of transient social contexts and forces. Instead of 'value' they prefer the notion of 'value-relation', a term established by the sociologist Max Weber, which asserts a causal link between the needs and interests of a particular society and its value systems. Those who largely place their faith in this relativistic approach (e.g. the French sociologist Pierre Bourdieu) tend to have a reductionist approach to attributes of art, largely denying that there can be inherent values or permanent qualities to a work. This merging of social functions and aesthetic purposes is problematic because it eradicates the 'specificity' of particular works of art. After all, all fanfares have similar social functions, but some are arresting and majestic while others are merely 'calls to attention', and some are ingenious and intriguing (BRITTEN, *Fanfare for St Edmundsbury*, 1959) while others are triadic and conventional.

A different approach is found from those who believe in qualities such as profundity or beauty. The difficulty is that these notions are resistant to explanation. Is beauty a 'logically primitive' quality that can be sensed but not defined, or a combination of more specific aesthetic qualities (grace, elegance, etc.), or does it proceed from non-aesthetic properties (proportion, symmetry), or does it emerge via a special kind of judgement (as claimed by Kant)? In short, is beauty 'real' (existing independently of any particular way of perceiving it) or 'non-real' (a mind-dependent concept, a way of experiencing something that arises out of certain attitudes)? Similar difficulties arise with the notion of 'musical profundity' (for a penetrating analysis of which, see A. Neill and A. Ridley, 'Musical profundity', in their *Arguing About Art* (New York: McGraw-Hill, 1995), 241–71).

Ultimately, we tend to value art works and musical performances if they represent unusual achievements in the realm of human endeavour – that is, if they display imagination, creativity and originality. But the force of those values depends on our being able to distinguish creativity from mere self-expression, paradigm-changing originality from mere novelty, and imaginative insight from indulgent fantasy. Not all imaginings are imaginative and not all creations are creatively done.

FURTHER READING

S. Davies, *Musical Meaning and Expression* (Ithaca: Cornell University Press, 1994).
S. Davies, K. M. Higgins, R. Hopkins, R. Stecker and D. Cooper (eds.), *A Companion to Aesthetics* (Chichester: Wiley-Blackwell, 1992/R 2009).
S. Godlovitch, *Musical Performance: A Philosophical Study* (London: Routledge, 1998).
T. Gracyk and A. Kania (eds.), *The Routledge Companion to Philosophy and Music* (Abingdon: Routledge, 2011).
P. Kivy, *Introduction to a Philosophy of Music* (Oxford: Clarendon Press, 2002).

ANTHONY PRYER

Affections (*Affektenlehre*) The theory of the affections is rooted in Greek and Roman writings on rhetoric, and focuses on instructing the orator in how to control and direct the emotional state or affections of the audience. With the growing importance of the linguistic disciplines in the Renaissance and the accompanying rise of humanistic musical thought, a new emphasis on text expression rooted in rhetoric began to replace the Medieval supremacy of speculative music theory. Increasingly music theorists pointed to the importance of expressing and moving the affections through music, parallel to how rhetoricians had talked about oratory since antiquity. Both disciplines sought to present and evoke the intended affections, thereby persuading and edifying the listener. Wolfgang Caspar Printz's statement that 'the ultimate and final purpose of music is the moving of the human affections' (*Historische Beschreibung der edelen Sing und Kling Kunst* (Dresden, 1690), 173) or JOHANN MATTHESON's proclamation: 'In summary, everything that occurs without affections means nothing, does nothing, and is worth nothing' (1739, 146) express a commonly held understanding of music by Baroque musicians and composers.

While the centrality of presenting and moving the affections through music can be found in all European Baroque traditions, it was particularly in German circles that this teaching was vigorously explored, parallel to a similar embrace of a musical rhetoric, including the teaching of the musical-rhetorical figures. However, a common theory or doctrine was never established. Indeed, during this period the term *Affektenlehre* is only used by Mattheson, and even then only rarely. It is a verbal construct parallel to *Naturlehre*, through which he refers to Descartes's teachings on the temperaments and bodily humours, the physiological explanation of how the affections are aroused in the human body. While Mattheson refers the reader to *Leidenschaften* under the entry *Affekten* in the *Capellmeister*'s index, the term *Affektenlehre* warrants no entry whatsoever.

At the very heart of the Baroque concept of the affections lay a quasi-Newtonian premise of law and order, action and reaction mutually accepted by musician and audience. The Cartesian pathology used to explain the process adopted the ancient teaching of the four humours and their related body organs, in conjunction with the teaching of the four temperaments. The melody, rhythm and harmony of music would impact these complexities in a predictable way. Based on such rational explanations, the Baroque composer counted on a calculated emotional response from the listener, the desired affection being presented and aroused through the appropriate mode or key, time signature and tempo, cadence and progression of intervals, along with the entire arsenal of rhetorical methods and devices, particularly the musical-rhetorical figures. Differences in individuals' responses were explained by the differences in their temperaments.

In listing the affections, authors frequently identified two general categories: joyful or agreeable affections, and sorrowful or unpleasant ones, at times including a third intermediary affection with all other affections flowing out of these. However, there was limited consensus regarding the number of specific affections. One of the more exhaustive lists is found in FRIEDRICH MARPURG's *Kritische Briefe zur Tonkunst* (1762, 273ff.), beginning with the three fundamental affections: sorrow, joy, contentment (including patience and solace), remorse, hope, fear (including anxiety and despair), longing, doubt, timidity, love, hate, envy, sympathy, jealousy, anger, pride, shame, courage, cowardice, vainglory, humility, geniality, revenge, apathy, innocence, impatience, and gloating. Marpurg also includes short directives to composers regarding the expression of the various affections. For example, in expressing sorrow the composer is to use a slow tempo with a languishing melody interrupted by many sighs (*Seufzer*) and using smaller intervals and dissonant harmonies. HEINRICH KOCH (1802) suggests that when expressing the great variety of affections composers ought to consider TEMPO, metre, tessitura, stepwise or leaping melodic structure, the use of more or less consonant or dissonant intervals, the use of accented metres and syncopations, the variety of notes, natural or strange chord progressions and more or less dissonant or consonant harmonies.

Some writers ascribed certain affective qualities to the various modes or keys, although there was little agreement on specific details, and a number felt that any affection could be portrayed in any given mode. One of the better-known lists of affective attributes of keys is found in Mattheson (1713), where he discusses the affections for seventeen of the most commonly used keys. Noteworthy is his caveat following these descriptions, where he clearly allows for alternate KEY CHARACTERISATIONS, acknowledging that individuals of varying temperament will be affected very differently by the same key. Similarly Johann Kuhnau 'is surprised, that many musicians and especially those who are familiar with the fundamentals of their art ... adhere to the preconceptions of the past and continue to repeat in simple blind faith that each mode has a certain precise effect' (*Musicalische Vorstellung einiger biblischer Historien* (Leipzig: Immanuel Tietzen, 1700), xii), a sentiment echoed by his student JOHANN DAVID HEINICHEN.

Virtually every theorist admonished the composer to examine the text which was to be set to music for affective words or implied affections. Indeed, many of the individual affections can only be identified through the associated text, with instrumental music being limited to more general affections. Theorists frequently included lists of words closely resembling lists of affections which were to receive particular attention in the composition, such as the list Johannes Nucius presents in his *Musices poeticae* (1613): rejoicing, weeping, fearing, lamenting, bewailing, mourning, raging, laughing and pitying. Beginning with Kircher the musical expression of the affections became more closely linked to rhetorical structures and devices. He equated the musical figures with their rhetorical counterparts, both being used to express diverse affections. In so doing, Kircher established the pattern of tying the musical expression of the affections to the musical-rhetorical figures, being the first of many following theorists to emphasise consistently the expression of both the affections and the text in figure definitions, frequently including examples of a suitable affection as well as appropriate affective words for a figure. While the various *FIGURENLEHRE* or interpretations of the musical-rhetorical figures varied significantly from one theorist to the next throughout the German Baroque, a common theme after Kircher is the assumption that it is through the musical-rhetorical figures that the affections are most convincingly and forcefully expressed, leading JOHANN SCHEIBE to declare: 'For the figures themselves are a language of the affections' (*Der critische Musicus*, rev. edn (Leipzig: Breitkopf, 1745), 683).

Enlightenment thought fundamentally altered the orientation of the prevailing concept of music towards an empirical, natural aesthetic. Towards the end of the Baroque era, the mechanistic explanations of the affections were found increasingly unnatural and artificial. Enlightenment composers rejected such a rationally determined explanation of music's emotional content in favour of a personal, subjective expressiveness and a pervading presence of the emotional utterance of the individual, ushering in an era with a radically altered understanding of music.

FURTHER READING

D. Bartel, 'The concept of the affections in German Baroque music', in *Musica Poetica: Musical-Rhetorical Figures in German Baroque Music* (Lincoln: University of Nebraska Press, 1997), 29–56.

G. J. Buelow, 'Johann Mattheson and the invention of the *Affektenlehre*', in G. J. Buelow and H. J. Marx (eds.), *New Mattheson Studies* (Cambridge University Press, 1983), 293–407.

R. Damann, *Der Musikbegriff im deutschen Barock*, 2nd edn (Regensburg: Laaber-Verlag, 1984).

U. Thieme, *Die Affektenlehre im philosophischen und musikalischen Denken des Barock: Vorgeschichte, Ästhetik, Physiologie* (Celle: Moeck Verlag, 1984).

DIETRICH BARTEL

Agazzari, Agostino (b. Siena, 2 December 1578; d. Siena, ?10 April 1640) Italian composer, organist and theorist.

After an early career in Rome, Agazzari returned in 1607 to Siena, his home town, where he was organist and subsequently *Maestro di cappella* until his death. He was one of the first to adopt FIGURED BASS, and in 1607 published instructions concerning figured bass realisation in *Del sonare sopra'l basso*. This is a fundamental reference for early Baroque performance practice and an indispensable guide to continuo players, particularly concerning unfigured basses. Discussions include the use of various instruments (foundational and ornamental) and the essential prerequisites for continuo players: a good musical ear, an excellent playing technique, knowledge of counterpoint, rules of harmonic progression, consonance and dissonance, cadences, proportions, clefs, TABLATURE, divisions, score-reading and TRANSPOSITION. The treatise was quoted by MICHAEL PRAETORIUS (1619). In the prefaces to his various collections of music (1603, 1609, 1611, 1613), Agazzari discussed ORNAMENTATION and TEMPO as well as musical style.

FURTHER READING

A. Agazzari, 'Del sonare sopra'l basso', trans. O. Strunk, in *Source Readings in Music History* (New York: W. W. Norton, 1950).

C. Reardon, *Agostino Agazzari and Music at Siena Cathedral, 1597–1641* (Oxford: Clarendon Press, 1993).

DAVID PONSFORD

Agricola, Johann Friedrich (b. Dobitschen, Saxe-Altenburg, 4 January 1720; d. Berlin, 2 December 1774) German music historian, composer, singing teacher and music director.

Although Agricola was a distinguished opera composer and court music director, he is best known today for his *Anleitung zur Singkunst* (1757), a translation of PIER FRANCESCO TOSI's seminal *Opinioni de' cantori antichi e moderni* (1723) that Agricola undertook in order to help reform German singing by disseminating the Italian *bel canto* style. Justly recognised within his own lifetime as an important treatise in its own right, Agricola's translation contains substantial additional commentary and updating of the original work, making considerable interventions in Tosi's lengthy chapters on the appoggiatura, *passaggi* (divisions), trills, recitative and CADENZAS respectively. Agricola applies the latest knowledge of vocal anatomy and physiology to the pedagogy of SINGING, and his is 'the first German vocal research to have examined the connection between breathing and laryngeal function' (Baird, 9). Indeed, Agricola was really the first to discuss breathing in a vocal treatise, stipulating for example, that singers should not breathe in the middle of a word, and nor should they break a cadenza.

One of Agricola's most important insights into vocal production relates to the key question of 'joining the registers', so critical to *bel canto* technique. Rather than simply learning to make as imperceptible a transition between the chest and falsetto registers as possible, the main concern of Tosi, whose treatise was primarily aimed at training castratos like himself, Agricola recognised that singers in fact need to develop a 'middle' register or head voice, a blending of chest and falsetto over most of the range. Although he revered Italian vocal singing in general, and Tosi's teaching in particular, Agricola did not agree with the degree of liberty in ORNAMENTATION that was not only allowed but also strongly encouraged by the Italian pedagogues of the previous generation. For example, Tosi castigates composers for notating appoggiaturas, insisting that singers need to learn how to apply them spontaneously in performance; but in line with a general tendency towards a rigorous systematisation of ornamentation, Agricola wishes to see all appoggiaturas written out. Likewise, Tosi stressed the importance of *messa di voce* ('placing the voice'), achieved by gradually swelling a tone from the softest to the loudest sound and then diminishing back to the softest, as important for learning to control the voice, but that in performance it should be 'used sparingly and only on bright vowels', whereas Agricola maintained that it must be applied to any note of substantial length (Baird, 11).

FURTHER READING

M. Elliott, *Singing in Style: A Guide to Vocal Performance Practices* (New Haven, CT and London: Yale University Press, 2006).

Introduction to the Art of Singing by Johann Friedrich Agricola, trans. and ed. J. C. Baird (Cambridge University Press, 1995).

F. Neumann, *Ornamentation in Baroque and Post-Baroque Music* (Princeton University Press, 1978).

RICHARD WISTREICH

Agricola, Martin (b. Schwiebus, Silesia, c1486; d. Magdeburg, Saxony, 10 June 1556) German music teacher, composer and theorist.

Originally known as Martin Sore, he adopted the Latin name Agricola (meaning 'farmer'), reflecting both his educated status and his humble origins, in typical Lutheran fashion. Agricola was active as a teacher in Magdeburg by 1520, and later became cantor at the Protestant school and director of music at the church of St Ulrich. He is best known today for his TREATISES on the fundamentals of music, written in German (rather than Latin) as textbooks for the emerging Lutheran school curriculum, and printed by Georg Rhau in Wittenberg. Foremost among these were *Ein kurtz deudsche Musica* (1528), later reissued as *Musica choralis deudsch* (1533), which focuses on unison singing, unmeasured chant notation and solmisation; and *Musica figuralis deudsch* (1532), which deals with part-singing, mensural notation and rhythmic PROPORTIONS. Perhaps the most important of his writings for the study of performance practice is *Musica instrumentalis deudsch* (1529; significantly revised and enlarged, 1545). The 1529 edition is substantially modelled on SEBASTIAN VIRDUNG's *Musica getutscht* (Basel, 1511), copying many of the latter's woodcut illustrations of musical instruments – although Agricola extends the nascent CONSORT principle by including transverse FLUTES, VIOLS and rebecs in groups of three or four different sizes, in addition to the RECORDERS and CRUMHORNS that had previously been so depicted by Virdung. The revised 1545 edition goes much further in explaining details of instrumental performance, including instructions for paired TONGUING (di-ri di-ri) on wind instruments, and descriptions of VIBRATO on the Swiss flute and Polish fiddle. Agricola's FINGERING charts for wind instruments provide important evidence for TRANSPOSITION practice, with the implication that SHAWMS (and other loud winds) sounded a fifth higher than written. On the subject of ORNAMENTATION, he recommends that instrumentalists follow the method of contemporary organists in playing graces and fast passagework.

FURTHER READING

H. Funck, *Martin Agricola: ein frühprotestantischer Schulmusiker* (Wolfenbüttel: Georg Kallmeyer Verlag, 1933).
W. E. Hettrick, *The 'Musica instrumentalis deudsch' of Martin Agricola: A Treatise on Musical Instruments, 1529 and 1545* (Cambridge University Press, 1994).
D. Howlett, 'A translation of three treatises by Martin Agricola: *Musica choralis deudsch, Musica figuralis deudsch* and *Von den Proporcionibus*', PhD dissertation, Ohio State University (1979).

JAMIE SAVAN

Alard, (Jean-)Delphin (b. Bayonne, 8 March 1815; d. Paris, 22 February 1888) French violinist, composer and pedagogue.

A violin pupil of HABENECK (1827–30) and a composition student of FÉTIS (1831–3) at the PARIS CONSERVATOIRE, Alard was praised by PAGANINI for his debut at the Société des Concerts du Conservatoire in 1831 and was eventually appointed to the royal orchestra (1840–8), succeeding BAILLOT as solo violinist in 1842; he later assumed a similar post in Napoleon's imperial orchestra (1853). He was also renowned as a chamber musician, establishing in 1835 a string quartet, which played a prominent role in Parisian musical life and beyond.

Alard also succeeded Baillot as violin professor at the Paris Conservatoire (1843–75), disseminating the Italian-French principles of Viotti to his students, among whom were Jules Garcin, Jean Becker, Adolf Pollitzer and Pablo Sarasate. His significance as a pedagogue is amplified by his *École du violon: méthode complète et progressive* (Paris: Schonenberger, 1844), which synthesised the treatises of Baillot and Habeneck, was translated widely, and incorporated numerous progressive studies, including many as duos. Also noteworthy are his independent study collections (especially his six *Études dédiées à Paganini*, Op. 2, ten *Études Artistiques*, Op. 19, and twenty-four *Études*, Op. 41) and his editions, particularly his *Maîtres classiques du violon*, which was among the first significant collections of 'historical' pieces by a variety of Baroque and Classical composers. Published in fifty-six parts (1862–83), each with a preface, composer biography and 'general observations' on performance issues, this faithfully edited collection resurrected works (principally sonatas, but also some concertos and other genres) by composers as diverse as Ferrari, CORELLI, J. S. BACH, TARTINI, Locatelli, Leclair, Stamitz, Viotti, KREUTZER, MOZART, BEETHOVEN and Paganini. It may have inspired FERDINAND DAVID's comparable and even more influential *Die hohe Schule des Violinspiels* (1867–72). Alard's original violin works include two concertos (Opp. 15, 34), three *symphonies concertantes* (Opp. 31, 33, 34b), a *grand duo concertant* (Op. 25), virtuoso variation sets, opera fantasias and salon pieces.

FURTHER READING

E. van der Straeten, *The History of the Violin*, 2 vols. (London: Cassell & Co., 1933).

J.-M. Fauquet, *Les sociétés de musique de chambre à Paris de la Restauration à 1870* (Paris: Aux Amateurs de Livres, 1986).

ROBIN STOWELL

Albert, Eugène d' (b. Glasgow, 10 April 1864; d. Riga, 3 March 1932) German composer and pianist.

D'Albert was, as both pianist and composer, one of the most notable students of Liszt. He was also remarkable for the radical reshaping of his own public image from that of a Glasgow-born, London-trained musician of English, French and Italian descent to that of a naturalised German, who affected to speak his native language with a foreign accent, and loudly condemned the musical education he had undergone in England. His celebrity was yet further increased by a colourful personal life that included (successively) six wives. D'Albert was an astonishingly prolific composer who produced twenty-one operas and a host of instrumental music, but only *Tiefland* has remained in the repertory – and that chiefly in Germany. He was, however, renowned as one of the greatest pianists of his day, famed as much for his cavalier heedlessness of wrong notes as for the overwhelming verve and sweep of his playing. Although his studies with Liszt were of relatively short duration, some of his editions give a valuable insight into his master's teaching of his own compositions. D'Albert's recorded legacy is relatively small, but does vividly illustrate the energetic spontaneity of his playing that so impressed contemporaries.

FURTHER READING

C. Pangels, *Eugen d'Albert: Wunderpianist und Komponist. Eine Biographie* (Zürich and Freiburg: Atlantis, 1981).

KENNETH HAMILTON

Albrechtsberger, Johann Georg (b. Klosterneuburg, 3 February 1736; d. Vienna, 7 March 1809) Austrian organist, composer and theorist.

Albrechtsberger was a renowned organist and composer but had special influence through his teachings and writings. His *Gründliche Anweisung zur*

Composition (Leipzig, 1790) and *Kurzgefasste Methode den Generalbass zu erlernen* (Vienna, c1792) achieved wide circulation; his intensive study of polyphonic writing (largely borrowed from Fux and MARPURG) was influential in the formulation of the classical style. His treatise on composition also provides a variety of evidence relevant to historical performance practice. For example, he attributes the provision of the BASSET HORN's chromatic extension to the STADLER brothers, valuable information since virtually all surviving instruments have only a diatonic extension, including examples by Anton Stadler's maker, Theodor Lotz. Furthermore, in addition to the basset horns in F and G used by MOZART, Albrechtsberger provides evidence of instruments pitched in E, E♭ and D.

FURTHER READING

E. Paul, *Johann Georg Albrechtsberger: Ein Klosterneuburger Meister der Musik und seine Schule* (Klosterneuburg: Jasomirgott Verlag, 1976).

COLIN LAWSON

Altenburg, Johann Ernst (b. Weissenfels, 15 June 1734; d. Bitterfeld, 14 May 1801) German trumpeter, organist and composer.

Brought up immersed in the European natural TRUMPET traditions of the seventeenth and eighteenth centuries, Altenburg served a long apprenticeship from the age of two to seventeen with his father, the notable trumpet player Johann Caspar Altenburg (1689–1761). Altenburg junior became a field trumpeter in the French Army during the Seven Years War (1756–63). He lived through a period where the changing social order saw the decline of both the status and the number of trumpeters employed by courts for all functional reasons. Changing tastes and styles in art music also saw a decline in the melodic use of the natural trumpet in the upper, *clarino* register. As a consequence, Altenburg failed to obtain a position as a court trumpeter and spent most of his working life in relative obscurity as the organist of Bitterfeld in Saxony.

Altenburg is known chiefly for his treatise, *Versuch einer Anleitung zur heroisch-musikalischen Trompeter- und Pauker-Kunst* (Halle, 1795), which had existed substantially in manuscript form, available through subscription, from 1770. The treatise covers the technique and practice of the trumpet and TIMPANI throughout the Baroque and early Classical periods, including style, phrasing, ARTICULATION and ORNAMENTATION, as well as advice on 'lipping', tuning, mouthpieces, crooking and muting. It lays particular importance on the Imperial Privileges which resided with trumpeters of the courts within the Holy Roman Empire from 1623. The high status of these individuals may have resulted from the other important ambassadorial duties for which trumpeters were responsible, to which Altenburg alludes, such as carrying despatches to the enemy. His treatise also contains a musical appendix containing an important Concerto for seven trumpets and timpani, attributed to him.

FURTHER READING

J. E. Altenburg, *Versuch einer Anleitung zur heroisch-musikalischen Trompeter- und Pauker-Kunst* (Halle, 1795), trans. E. H. Tarr as *The Art of the Trumpeter and Kettledrummer* (Nashville, TN: Brass Press, 1974).

JOHN WALLACE

Altès, Joseph Henry (b. Rouen, 18 January 1826; d. Paris, 24 July 1895) French flautist.

Altès entered the PARIS CONSERVATOIRE in 1840 to study with Jean-Louis Tulou. He was an outstanding flautist and in 1848 was appointed first flute at the Paris Opéra, a position he held for twenty-four years. In 1869 he became the first professor at the Paris Conservatoire to teach the new BOEHM flute. He composed numerous works for his instrument, including twenty-six études; his *Méthode complète de flûte* dates from 1880. Focusing on intonation, he described the semitone as the smallest interval appreciable to the ear. Significantly, he discussed the importance of alternative FINGERINGS to help achieve perfect intonation, giving numerous exercises in duet form to help achieve precision. Discussion of other aspects of technique such as breathing and embouchure is much more general and comments on TASTE rather vague. He retired from the Conservatoire due to ill health in 1893, when Paul Taffanel succeeded him.

FURTHER READING

A. Powell, *The Flute* (New Haven, CT and London: Yale University Press, 2002).

ASHLEY SOLOMON

Ammerbach, Elias Nikolaus (b. Naumburg c1530; d. Leipzig, bur. 29 January 1597) German organist.

Ammerbach was organist of the Thomaskirche, Leipzig (1561–95). His *Orgel oder Instrument Tabulatur*, published in 1571 and expanded in 1583, was the first printed organ music in Germany, and the first printed in new German organ TABLATURE, with letter names and rhythmic symbols in open score. The introduction contains extensive examples of FINGERINGS based on sequential figures, in which RH and LH second and fourth fingers are 'good', as well as the RH third finger to begin some four-note sequences. There are also two ornaments: 'mordents' in ascending and descending contexts, signifying that ornaments begin on the main note; ornaments occupied half of the written value of the principal note, and the choice of auxiliary was determined by context. The book, of which J. S. BACH owned copies, contains German religious songs, with sometimes crude voice-leading and harmonies, followed by dances. Finally, there is a series of four- and five-part vocal INTABULATIONS, with lavish diminutions. In 1575, Ammerbach published *Ein new künstlich Tabulaturbuch*, containing forty vocal intabulations and one praeambulum.

FURTHER READING

Anthology of Early Keyboard Methods, trans. and ed. B. Sachs and B. Ife (Cambridge: Gamut Publications, 1981), 57–9.

W. Apel, *The History of Keyboard Music to 1700*, trans. and rev. H. Tischler (Bloomington, IN and London: Indiana University Press, 1972).

J. Butt, 'Germany and the Netherlands', in A. Silbiger (ed.), *Keyboard Music before 1700* (New York and London: Routledge, 2004), 147–234.

DAVID PONSFORD

Anglebert, Jean Henry d' *see* D'ANGLEBERT, JEAN HENRY

Applause Applause as a way of showing acclamation or approval is described several times in the Old Testament, and was used as a formal sign of appreciation in theatres of ancient Rome. It became something that musicians both encouraged and craved. In the Preface to his Eighth Book of Madrigals (Venice, 1638), MONTEVERDI wrote that the *Combattimento di Tancredi e Clorinda* was 'received by the best citizens of the noble city of Venice with much applause and praise'. A century later, the London press measured Handel's success in terms of applause-related superlatives: *The London Magazine* (April 1732) noted that *Esther* was greeted 'with vast applause' and a year later *The Bee* (14 July 1733) reported that *Athalia* was 'performed with the utmost applause'.

MOZART was well aware how an audience might react – during the music as well as after it. He wrote to his father in 1778 about the first performance of the 'Paris' Symphony K297/300a: 'Just in the middle of the first Allegro there was a passage that I felt sure must please. The entire audience was quite carried away – and there was a tremendous burst of applause ... I introduced the passage again near the close – and off they went again.' Applause was contentious at the first performance of BEETHOVEN's 'Eroica' Symphony, as reported in *Der Freymüthige* (4 August 1806): the public found Beethoven 'discourteous because he did not nod his head in recognition of the applause which came from a portion of the audience. On the contrary, Beethoven found that the applause was not strong enough.'

At his London debut in 1829, MENDELSSOHN reported that his First Symphony provoked a reaction 'beyond anything that I could ever have dreamed. I was received with immense applause ... The Scherzo was so vigorously encored that I felt obliged to repeat it' (W. S. Rockstro, *Mendelssohn* (London: Sampson Low, 1884), 39). Later, Mendelssohn came to dislike applause between movements, and it is probable that he linked the movements of the Violin Concerto in order to prevent interruptions.

MAHLER was sensitive about applause in his own works: a footnote in the score of *Kindertotenlieder* states that the songs were conceived as a whole and 'must not be interrupted, e.g. by applause'. Mahler's own performances were customarily punctuated by applause between movements and when Fred Gaisberg recorded Mahler's Ninth Symphony with the Vienna Philharmonic under Bruno Walter in 1938, he noted that the applause after each movement had to be edited out. Such audience reaction was common before WWII. At the first concert performance of Fauré's Requiem on 12 July 1900, the 'Pie Jesu' was encored on the spot. Hans Richter usually discouraged applause between movements, but at the premiere of ELGAR's First Symphony with the Hallé in Manchester, *The Times* (4 December 1908) reported that: 'the outburst at the end of the *Adagio* represented a heartfelt response ... The composer was called to the platform before the finale in order to acknowledge the applause.'

Concert etiquette from Richter onwards tended towards withholding applause between movements, but opera performances have remained a different matter. Even the best-behaved opera audience might applaud a singer after an aria while the orchestra is still playing. WAGNER, and particularly his *Parsifal*, became an exception: at the first performance, the composer asked the audience neither to clap for prolonged curtain calls between acts nor to applaud during the music. This was misinterpreted by zealous Wagnerites, who hissed anyone daring to applaud, including Wagner himself when he shouted an enthusiastic 'Bravo' to the Flowermaidens in Act II (during the eighth Bayreuth performance). The myth persisted, and in 1951 the programme for a revival at Covent Garden contained the startling claim that 'In accordance with the composer's wish there will be no curtain calls and the audience is requested to refrain from applause.' In his review, Winton Dean protested that this was 'complete humbug' (*Opera*, August 1951, 485).

The opera house claque – audience members paid by the administration or individual singers to provide enthusiastic applause – has origins as old as opera itself, but reached its dubious zenith in Paris during the 1830s, led by Auguste Levasseur. In a letter probably from just before the premiere of Meyerbeer's *Les Huguenots*, Levasseur wrote to the administration of the Paris Opéra: 'It will be possible to guarantee all the arias and almost all the duos ... I expect to have the trio in the fifth act cheered. I await the orders of the administration as to what must be done on behalf of the performers and the authors' (quoted in G. Hauger, 'Auguste and the Opéra claque', *Opera* (March 1980), 243). Later in the nineteenth century, the claque became active at La Scala and at the Vienna Court Opera. Both Toscanini and Mahler attempted to suppress its activities, but neither was entirely successful. In 1929, there was an active claque in Vienna when Toscanini took La Scala there in 1929, with the young Herbert von Karajan as one of its ringleaders.

In orchestral concerts, Furtwängler and Koussevitzky both discouraged applause except at the end of a work, but in an article in the *New York Times* (21 August 1938), Olin Downes deplored the 'ridiculous banning and absence of applause between the movements of symphonies', describing it as 'snobbism *in excelsis* '. Other conductors agreed: in 1959 Pierre Monteux said, 'I have one big complaint about audiences in all countries, and that is their artificial restraint from applause between movements of a concerto or symphony', a view echoed by Erich Leinsdorf, who described this practice as 'utter nonsense. The notion, once entertained by questionable historians, was that an entity must not be interrupted by the mundane frivolity of hand clapping. The great composers were elated by applause, wherever it burst out' (Monteux and Leinsdorf, both quoted in Ross, 3). ROGER NORRINGTON is among current HIP practitioners who have encouraged applause between movements. In a blog post from 2008, the pianist Emanuel Ax published a plea for common sense rather than convention:

> I really hope we can go back to the feeling that applause should be an emotional response to the music, rather than a regulated social duty. I am always a little taken aback when I hear the first movement of a concerto which is supposed to be full of excitement, passion, and virtuoso display (like the BRAHMS or BEETHOVEN concertos), and then hear a rustling of clothing, punctuated by a few coughs; the sheer force of the music calls for a wild audience reaction ... Most composers trust their listeners to respond at the right time, and if we feel like expressing approval, we should be allowed to, anytime!

FURTHER READING

E. Ax, 'When to applaud'. https://emanuelax.wordpress.com/2008/11/14/when-to-applaud/
H. Rosenthal, 'Applause for *Parsifal*?', *Opera* (Feburary 1966), 88.

A. Ross, 'Hold your applause: Inventing and reinventing the classical concert', Royal Philharmonic Society Lecture, Wigmore Hall, 8 March 2010. http://royalphilharmonicsociety.org.uk/images/uploads/RPS_Lecture_2010_Ross.pdf.

NIGEL SIMEONE

Arban, (Joseph) Jean-Baptiste (Laurent) (b. Lyons, 28 February 1825; d. Paris, 9 April 1889) French cornet player, composer and conductor.

Arban spent his working life in Paris, travelling widely in Europe as soloist and conductor. He entered the trumpet class of Dauverné at the PARIS CONSERVATOIRE aged sixteen at a pivotal moment in the advancement of brass instruments. The development of valve mechanisms was transforming the technical capabilities of brass instruments, and the cornet had only recently been invented (c1835). Arban was to become the pre-eminent champion of the cornet. His influence from the mid-nineteenth century remains evident in current brass didactic practice.

Arban's *Grande méthode complète pour cornet à pistons et de saxhorn* (Paris, 1864) has remained a core text for both cornet and TRUMPET players. As a composer, Arban's melodic gift and his ability to imbue technical exercises with balletic grace ensured his prominence over contemporary cornet virtuoso composer/performers. During his lifetime, it seemed possible that the cornet would replace the trumpet. He lobbied Auber, director of the Paris Conservatoire, for recognition of the cornet. After initial resistance, Auber compromised, putting the cornet and trumpet on equal footing. From 1868 students were obliged to study both instruments there. The consequence was that the trumpet and cornet converged rather than developing distinct orchestral idioms, with the eventual eclipse of the cornet in the orchestra. The lyrical cornet idiom continued to flourish in brass bands.

Arban played an important role in the cornet's technical development. In 1883 he patented a fully compensating cornet in C, which attracted praise but never gained commercial success. His greatest triumphs were achieved in 1870s Russia, where his influence was considerable. With his own full-sized *Orchestre Arban* in St Petersburg, he played cornet solos and conducted his own dance music and popular operatic excerpts.

FURTHER READING

J.-B. Arban, *Grande méthode complète pour cornet à pistons et de saxhorn* (Paris: Léon Escudier, 1864).
J.-P. Mathez, *Joseph Jean-Baptiste Laurent Arban 1825–1889* (Moudon: Editions BIM, 1977).

JOHN WALLACE

Arbeau, Thoinot (b. Dijon, 17 March 1520; d. Langres, 23 July 1595) French cleric and author whose actual name was Jehan Tabourot.

Thoinot's most celebrated work is his *Orchésographie* (1588, rev. 1596), a dance treatise written in the form of a dialogue. Choreographies and melodies include branles, galliards and its variant the volta, the coranto, the alman, as well as the only examples for the sword-wielding bouffons. Arbeau also offers insights into Western dance culture, commenting on social etiquette, physical comportment and the differing customs of peoples and classes.

Orchésographie notates drumming rhythms for DANCE, vocal and military accompaniment, presenting the first published PERCUSSION music in Western history. Arbeau also addresses wind performance through player illustrations and suggestions for ensemble instrumentation. Using a novel printing method, Arbeau's verbal step instructions correspond directly to notes on a vertically placed musical staff, thereby documenting the parallels between physical movements and dance melodies with unmatched clarity. The combination of verbal explanations, musical excerpts and step illustrations makes *Orchésographie* the most detailed social-dancing account in the fifteenth and sixteenth centuries.

FURTHER READING

T. Arbeau, *Orchésographie: traité en forme de dialogue par lequel toutes les personnes peuvent facilement apprendre & pratiquer l'honnête exercice des danses* (Langres, 1588; repr. Langres: Dominique Guéniot, 1988).

Y. Kendall, 'Early Renaissance Dance, 1450–1520', in J. Kite-Powell (ed.), *A Performer's Guide to Renaissance Music* (Bloomington, IN: Indiana University Press, 2007), 377–98.

The Music of Arbeau's Orchésographie (Hillsdale, NY: Pendragon Press, 2013).

ALEXANDER EVAN BONUS

Archlute (*arciliuto*) *see* LUTE

Arezzo, Guido d' (b. 990s; d. after 1033) Benedictine monk and music educationalist from Northern Italy.

When Guido was in his mid-30s, he compiled a manual entitled *Micrologus* ('Short Treatise'), which became the most widely transmitted musical pedagogical text of the Medieval era. *Micrologus* presented a method whereby young people could accurately learn plainchant melodies using a monochord. Later, Guido described staff NOTATION (in a Prologue to a now lost antiphoner). And in his *Epistola* ('Letter') to Brother Michael in Pomposa, near Ferrara, Guido explained how to derive solmisation syllables (*ut, re, mi, fa, sol, la*) from the plainchant hymn '*Ut queant laxis*'. Guido recommended that musical notation should not use a staircase staff (where successive lines represent diatonic steps), but a ladder staff instead (where lines represent pitches a third apart). Guido also pioneered the use of clefs and coloured lines (yellow for c', red for f) as an elegant way of indicating where semitones occur within the stave.

Guido was opinionated and outspoken, and consequently he was ostracised by the other monks at the monastery in Pomposa. What irked Guido's colleagues was that by providing a method whereby even young people could teach themselves how to sight-sing plainchant melodies, educational control was wrested from the monks. Guido's unpopularity prompted his move to Arezzo, where the Bishop arranged for Guido to train the cathedral's singers. *Micrologus* followed in 1025 or 1026. Although the celebrated Guidonian Hand was an elaboration of Guido's innovations, the fully fledged hexachordal system was not Guido's own. But Guido's pioneering use of staff notation, his belief in the benefit of developing pitch memory, and his promotion of a direct correspondence between graphic notation and vocalised sound, make him a founding father of Western classical music's sight-reading culture and its reliance on the musical score.

FURTHER READING

W. Babb and C. Palisca (eds.), *Hucbald, Guido, and John on Music: Three Medieval Treatises*. Music Theory Translation Series 3 (New Haven, CT and London: Yale University Press, 1978).
S. Mengozzi, *The Renaissance Reform of Medieval Music Theory: Guido of Arezzo between Myth and History* (Cambridge University Press, 2010).
D. Pesce (trans. and ed.), Guido d'Arezzo's *Regule Rithmice, Prologus in Antiphonarium*, and *Epistola ad Michahelem: A Critical Text and Translation with an Introduction, Annotations, Indices, and New Manuscript Inventories* (Ottawa: Institute of Mediaeval Music, 1999).

JEREMY SUMMERLY

Arnulf of St Ghislain (*fl. c*1400) Writer about music, perhaps a member of the Benedictine community at St Ghislain in Hainaut.

Arnulf's treatise, *Tractatulus de differentiis et gradibus cantorum*, divides musicians into four categories: those who are ignorant of music and do not perform correctly; unschooled but talented laymen who perform well by imitating those who are trained; well-schooled teachers with inadequate voices who produce fine students; schooled and talented musicians who know to sing according to the rule in mode, measure, number and colour. In the last category he praises both women and men with fine voices who not only sing correctly but who are able to embellish (colour) the music by employing throat ARTICULATION to subdivide tones into semitones and semitones into microtones.

FURTHER READING

T. McGee, *The Sound of Medieval Song: Ornamentation and Vocal Style according to the Treatises* (Oxford: Clarendon Press, 1998), 8–10, 18–20, 24–5, 88–9, 115, 163–4.
C. Page, 'A treatise on musicians from ?c1400: The *Tractatulus de differentiis et gradibus cantorum* by Arnulf de St Ghislain', *JRMA*, 117 (1992), 1–21.

TIMOTHY J. MCGEE

Aron, Pietro *see* AARON, PIETRO

Arpeggiando Literally, to play like a harp; an instruction to arpeggiate.

In string playing, the sounding of each note of a broken chord on a different string, sometimes using a bouncing bow stroke, also called *batterie*. The effect can be achieved with arpeggios, Alberti bass figurations, or bariolage, depending on the context. *See* ARPEGGIO.

TERENCE CHARLSTON

Arpeggio The performance of a chord 'spread' from bottom to top or top to bottom, or the displacement of its notes in successive order, often with a regular rhythm (e.g. a broken chord).

A feature of stringed and keyboard music from at least the seventeenth century onwards (*see* ARPEGGIANDO), it is also an integral technique of *bel canto* singing. The manner of arpeggiation was often left to the discretion of the player. In the Baroque period, chordal passages could be marked 'arpeggio' and rudimentary symbols to indicate upward or downward arpeggiation and broken chords were introduced as in Example 1.

Example 1: Baroque methods and symbols for arpeggiation.

Example 2: Alberti bass (Domenico Alberti: *Sonate per Cembalo* Op. 1 No. 2 (1748)).

The Alberti bass (Example 2), a left-hand keyboard accompaniment pattern consisting of a triad broken into four notes – bottom, top, middle, top – is named after the keyboard composer who first frequently used it.

Subtle gradations of arpeggio were universally employed by harpsichordists (e.g. RAMEAU, 1722) and arpeggio-based passagework became ubiquitous for pianists and later virtuoso instrumentalists.

TERENCE CHARLSTON

Articulation The attack, release, sustaining and decay of individual notes and the ways in which these connect and divide musical constituents.

Together with phrasing, articulation is one of the defining characteristics of musical EXPRESSION, shaped by circumstances and events often at a regional rather than a national level. Choice and enactment of articulation is guided by performers' musical education and TASTE, as well as their familiarity with stylistic and idiomatic characteristics of the repertory. An awareness of the interrelationship between notated and non-notated features is crucial, as elements including TEMPO and genre also condition a performer's articulatory choices. Such decisions also reflect differing expectations across solo, chamber, choral, orchestral and operatic repertory as well as those pertaining to sacred and secular music.

An array of documentary materials can corroborate or supplement articulatory information provided by NOTATION. From the sixteenth century, as the impact of the printing press spread across Europe, an increase in the number of published TREATISES helped to codify, preserve and spread practices, as well as either enhancing or substituting for individual musical instruction. In seeking to recreate past articulation practices, we have yet comprehensively to take account of the many extant performance VENUES, including churches, rooms in private houses and palaces, theatres and concert halls. Aural evidence recorded by musicians born in the nineteenth century, as well as the growing corpus of historically informed approaches, offer a variety of idiosyncratic accounts of articulation in practice. An increasing number of REPLICAS complements evidence from original organological specimens and associated paraphernalia, allowing a more tactile understanding of articulation. In comparison with their modern counterparts, many instruments made before the early nineteenth century facilitate a more expressive and articulate approach in performance by virtue of their relatively small dynamic range.

Whilst articulation on stringed instruments is intimately connected with matters of BOWING and FINGERING, pizzicato became another important articulatory device from the early seventeenth century. Mentioned in most sources from GANASSI's *Regola rubertina* (Venice, 1542) through French treatises of the seventeenth century to SPOHR's *Violinschule* (Vienna, 1832), the rule of the down-bow remained a remarkably consistent feature of string articulation. Historical performers have long recognised the wider range of detached articulatory nuances facilitated by the various pre-Tourte bows which are appropriate for string repertory pre c1790. In music composed before c1830, before the prevalence of an almost ubiquitous legato style, the relationship between bowing and fingering and between phrasing and articulation was more interdependent. BAILLOT's *L'art du violon* (Paris, 1835) conveys contemporary performers' increasingly prescriptive expectations of notation amidst a large palette of articulatory nuances, facilitated by a variety of bow strokes. As the nineteenth century progressed, a seamless legato masking necessary changes of bow stroke became a desirable element of string technique. The influence of virtuosos such as PAGANINI and the emerging French (later Franco-Belgian) and Germanic schools of violin playing saw a further extension of the palette of bowed strokes.

Keyboard articulation is closely associated with fingering, which helped to cultivate a musical hierarchy in which unevenness was initially a virtue. Other related parameters include touch, PEDALLING and phrasing. ORNAMENTATION also provides articulatory colour, particularly in repertory for the HARPSICHORD and the ORGAN. The nature of each instrument, particularly its action, affects both sound quality and resonance, thus exerting a significant impact on a player's choice of articulation. DIRUTA's *Il transilvano* (Venice, 1593) provides early evidence of the distinction between a legato touch, ensuring a continuity of sound more conducive to the organ, and a more detached style for quilled instruments such as the harpsichord. Single-manual harpsichords produce a clarity which fosters a more detached style of performance particularly suited to the contrapuntal styles of the seventeenth and eighteenth centuries. With the rise of the BASSO CONTINUO both the speed of arpeggiation and the texture chosen by the player had implications for articulation practices. This was a time of transition from a style seeking primarily to articulate so-called 'good' and 'bad' notes to one of finger evenness, as seen in the works of JOHANN SEBASTIAN BACH. Despite the CLAVICHORD's small dynamic range, the close connection between the tangent, the strings and the player's fingers makes available a range of expressive nuances. This was praised by C. P. E. BACH in his *Versuch* (1753) in contrast to the touch of the recently invented PIANOFORTE. From Bartolomeo Cristofori's innovations of the 1720s to the exhibition in Vienna of the so-called 'Steinway system' in 1873, the development of hammer-struck keyboard instruments, capable of dynamic gradations and sustaining power, had a momentous impact on the development of articulatory nuances. Milestones include the emergence of two main traditions of piano manufacture towards the end of the eighteenth century. MALCOLM BILSON and ROBERT D. LEVIN, amongst others, recognise a resultant difference of articulation between the music of HAYDN and MOZART and repertory by London-based musicians such as Dussek and

CLEMENTI. By the mid-nineteenth century the characteristics of English-style pianos enabled a growing number of players to cultivate a more virtuoso style of performance. The *sostenuto* pedal, first exhibited in 1844, encouraged an increasingly prevalent legato style and subsequently exerted a profound effect on piano sound and technique.

Singers create arguably the most sensitive and nuanced articulation through the attack and decay of consonants and vowels, usually within the context of the delivery of a text. PORTAMENTO and the judicious use of the breath also create articulatory colour. During the Renaissance, vocal articulation was produced by the throat, the tongue and the chest, although references to the latter indicate the area of support for the sound rather than an actual register. In virtuoso music the use of throat articulation or *gorgie* was essential for performing divisions and *passaggi*. During the sixteenth and seventeenth centuries this technique reached considerable refinement amongst Italian singers. They were able to match the considerable facility of instrumentalists in achieving a style characterised by speed and clarity of articulation, as reported in Ganassi's *Opera intitulata Fontegara* (Venice, 1535) and ZACCONI's *Prattica di Musica* (Venice, 1596). Until well into the eighteenth century, vocal passaggi were rendered in the prevailing detached style, as TOSI's *Opinioni* (1723) testifies. Amongst an increasing number of vocal treatises published from the mid-eighteenth century, JOHANN FRIEDRICH AGRICOLA's translation (1757) helped disseminate Tosi's practices whilst also addressing a lacuna in comprehensive German-language singing manuals. A detached style of performing divisions was preferable and Agricola chides contemporary singers in Italy who 'tend to slur almost all, even the liveliest divisions'. MARPURG (1755–61) and JOHANN HILLER (1774) document a preference for a more sustained vocal line which had begun to emerge during the second half of the eighteenth century. By the second quarter of the nineteenth century the impact of the so-called 'Rossinian' revolution was reflected in the practice of SINGING a smooth *portamento di voce* and introducing various ornamental devices. The *cantabile* style favoured the *cavatina* (also the *Andante* or *Largo*) and provided the main focus for decorative nuance, contrasting with the *staccato* style employed in faster tempos. In GARCÍA II's *Traité complet* (Paris, 1840, rev. 1847) slurring is still chiefly an ornamental device to obtain melodic colour, with detached nuances used for light and graceful sentiments. García reports that one of the singer's hidden resources is the ability to modify notated articulation in order more faithfully to portray the character of a given piece. Evidence of nineteenth-century practice, can also be found amongst arias annotated by or associated with prominent singers, including GARCÍA I, Angelica Catalani, Giovanni Velluti, LAURE CINTI-DAMOREAU, Jenny Lind and Pauline Viardot.

Wind articulation is primarily concerned with single, double and triple tonguing, for which the breath, the chest and the throat were employed until the nineteenth century. It is conditioned by a wide range of embouchures from those of the RECORDER and CORNETT to instruments of the orchestral wind and brass families, many of whose design changed dramatically during the nineteenth century. Despite scant documentary evidence concerning tongued articulation before the sixteenth century, onomatopoeic imitations of 'trompeurs', 'cornemuses' and drums in the texts of two anonymous chansons preserved in the *Ivrea Codex* suggest that double and triple tonguing had been in use since at least the first third of the fourteenth century. MARTIN AGRICOLA's *Musica instrumentalis deudsch* (1529, R/1545), which includes an early description of flutter tonguing, shows the interrelationship of articulation and rhythm manifest in the use of different syllables for notes of contrasting durations, a practice which continued until well into the eighteenth century. A player's native language affects the use of syllabically based articulation. For example, the syllables 't' and 'd' in combination with vowels produce contrastingly hard and soft sounds. Renaissance theorists distinguish between single tonguing for long and slow notes and compound tonguings for faster virtuoso passages. This inequality helped to distinguish between 'good' and 'bad' notes, creating an effect similar to the up- and down-bows of stringed instruments and paired fingerings of keyboard players. North Italian sources from Ganassi to BISMANTOVA's *Compendio Musicale* (ms, 1677) confirm that articulation was a highly cultivated and refined characteristic of wind performance in which instrumentalists sought to imitate the best singers. During the late seventeenth and early eighteenth centuries, the choice and execution of tongued articulation was a hallmark of a highly skilled performance style, often reflected in the didactic works for individual wind instruments published in France, particularly those for the FLUTE. A mid-eighteenth-century performer's repertoire of articulatory effects included intricate patterns of tonguing and those which facilitated velocity, as well as combinations of slurred and detached strokes, providing markedly contrasting approaches. Wind players increasingly utilised the slur as an expressive device rather than for technical reasons.

By the late eighteenth century, more sophisticated and dexterous modes of single tonguing heralded a decline in the use of double tonguing. Adding to the work of QUANTZ, TROMLITZ's *Ausführlicher und gründlicher Unterricht...* (1791) offers a particularly comprehensive and systematic account of wind articulation. A high level of agility and dexterity as well as a gradual standardisation of articulatory practice is reflected in early nineteenth-century methods published by the PARIS CONSERVATOIRE. Tutors for CLARINET by LEFÈVRE (1802), for HORN by Frédéric Nicolas Duvernoy (1802), for BASSOON by OZI (1803) and for flute by Antoine Hugot and Jean-Georges Wunderlich (1804) regard the tongue as the most satisfactory means of articulation, although other nuances were still practised. In reconciling the often contradictory theoretical evidence with inconsistent notational practices, we observe a gradual shift from a detached style towards a legato mode of delivery. A symbiosis between articulation and tempo is a particular feature of tonality, and until well into the nineteenth century the characteristics of Allegro, Andante and Adagio movements existed in contrast to each other, necessitating the use of different articulatory mechanisms. The Adagio was performed in a manner more sustained than the Andante or Allegro. Seventeenth- and eighteenth-century sources testify that performers were expected to distinguish between 'good' and 'bad' notes, reconciling the music's metrical hierarchy, and singers' decisions concerning emphases were dictated by the syntax of the text.

Notes seemingly left unmarked may be the most ambiguous in terms of articulatory choice; indeed, articulation marks are relatively rare in music before the seventeenth century. Whilst a distinct and separated manner of performance for unmarked notes was more common before 1750, over the next century their interpretation favoured an increasingly less articulated style with notes held for their full notated length. Whilst a type of legato was almost certainly used for notes bound by ligatures in music before 1600, a nuanced and detached style of articulation was the most prevalent, certainly in secular repertoire. Sixteenth- and seventeenth-century keyboard repertory contains specific markings, with early seventeenth-century VIRGINAL repertory revealing much about contemporary English fingering practices. Mid-eighteenth-century sources, including those by Quantz and C. P. E. Bach, recognise three broad categories of articulation: *legato* or a slurring, a semi-detached style in the middle and then *staccato*. The subsequent broadening of notated articulation signs is likely to have grown from this accord. An increasing amount of notated detail in late eighteenth-century repertory coincides with the emerging market for published music. From the early nineteenth century, a performer's choice of articulation began to be determined by individual musical ideas or characteristics within a single piece, a trend which heralded the use of more prescriptive notation. Whilst certain elements of standardisation began to appear by the mid-nineteenth century, composers often also added supplementary symbolic and/or written instructions. Their music displays an increasing use of terms such as *leggiero* and *staccatissimo*. Today's performers must reconcile ambiguities in the notation of detached strokes such as the dot and wedge, which were used inconsistently. There was often no clear distinction between intermediate detached strokes such as mezzo- and semi-staccato.

Late seventeenth- and early eighteenth-century French practices attest to the intimate connection between ornamentation and articulation, manifest in the small-scale slurring associated with the *port de voix* and documented in RAISON (*Livre d'orgue* (Paris: l'auteur, 1688), SAINT LAMBERT (*Les principles du clavecin* (Paris: Christophe Ballard, 1702) and JEAN-PHILIPPE RAMEAU (*Pièces de clavecin avec une méthode* (Paris: l'auteur, [1724]). Repertory from 1670 to 1750 suggests that slurs were usually confined to small intervals, whilst larger slurs (e.g. over sixths and sevenths) had more expressive qualities. In proposing that slurs were best employed only for small intervals and that marked divisions were more frequent than gliding ones, Tosi codifies practices from c1690 to 1710, eschewing a style more contemporary with the era in which his treatise was published. At that time a discreet amount of slurring was usually reserved for slower arias and pieces in a *cantabile* style, with a more distinct mode of articulation for faster tempi. The slurs in FRANÇOIS COUPERIN's *Pièces de clavecin* (Paris, 1713-30) suggest that he was an early proponent of a legato style which did not come into its own for another hundred years. A discernible increase in the frequency of slurred passagework in HOTTETERRE's *L'art de préluder sur la flûte traversière* (1719) probably reflects the influence of Italian violin performance practices. MATTHESON's *Der vollkommene Capellmeister* (1739) acknowledges the importance of knowing when to slur and when a more detached mode is more appropriate. LEOPOLD MOZART (1756) advises the performer to adhere to notated slurs but to exercise taste in determining articulation choices where notation is less fulsome.

The so-called legato style began to gain converts from the middle of the eighteenth century as reflected in Marpurg's *Anleitung zum Clavierspielen* (Berlin: A. Haude & J. C. Spener, 1755–61) and TÜRK's *Klavierschule* (1789). Slurred bowings were increasingly utilised for their capacity to imitate the human voice. Even when a legato style became more prevalent, performers still calibrated other elements such as character and tempo in deciding the degree of separation to use. By the second quarter of the nineteenth century the slur indicated phrasing rather than implying small-scale articulatory nuances with implications for tonguing and bowing. As the nineteenth century progressed, a seamless legato style found favour although subtle articulatory nuances within slurred passages were undoubtedly retained in performance.

The delineation between the roles of composer and performer did not occur until well into the nineteenth century; thus for the music of earlier periods the process of determining articulation calls for a more explicit acknowledgement of the extent to which the act of performance also embodied elements of composition and improvisation. For example, despite 'problems of consistency and completeness' (Butt, 210), J. S. Bach's articulatory palette appears to have been wider and more comprehensive than that of many of his contemporaries. JOHN BUTT's study of autograph MANUSCRIPTS, copies and engravings confirms the need to differentiate between 'interpretative' and 'instructive' markings, often added at different stages in a work's genesis. Many of Bach's initial slurrings accentuate the harmonic rhythm and thus might be considered primarily compositional in nature, whilst those added subsequently saw Bach function 'primarily as a performer and elaborator'. In acknowledging the notational fluidity of a musical work, historical performers would do well to recognise the more transient temporal quality of the articulation marks with which they are presented.

Indeed, much progress has already been made in restoring the articulatory variety and colours of the past, suggesting a larger palette of nuances than previously explored. As RICHARD TARUSKIN has observed, 'there can be no denying either the beauty or the communicative power of the new rhetorical approach, which is based not on the long legato lines of romantic music but on short, pointed phrases in exact alliance with the metrical scheme and in continual dialogue with one another' (*Text and Act: Essays on Music and Performance* (Oxford University Press, 1995), 278–9).

FURTHER READING

C. Brown, *Classical and Romantic Performing Practice, 1750–1900* (Oxford University Press, 1999).
J. Butt, *Bach Interpretation: Articulation Marks in Primary Sources of J. S. Bach* (Cambridge University Press, 1990).
B. Dickey and E. Tarr, *Articulation in Early Wind Music* (Winterthur: Amadeus Verlag, 2007).
S. P. Rosenblum, 'Concerning articulation on keyboard instruments: Aspects from the Renaissance to the present', *PPR*, 10/1 (2007), http://scholarship.claremont.edu/ppr/vol10/iss1/4/

INGRID E. PEARSON

Artusi, Giovanni Maria (b. c1540; d. Bologna, 18 August 1613) Italian theorist and composer.

A canon regular in the Congregation of S. Salvatore at Bologna who studied under GIOSEFFO ZARLINO in Venice, he is best known for having initiated in

1600 the Artusi–MONTEVERDI controversy over the irregular dissonances and other solecisms espoused by modern composers. However, he also issued attacks in print and in manuscript on the Florentine VINCENZO GALILEI and, with particular animosity, on his fellow Bolognese, Ercole Bottrigari.

Artusi's treatises from 1586 to 1608 – the last a final assault on Monteverdi written under the pseudonym Antonio Braccino da Todi – clearly draw on Zarlino's teachings presented in more digestible form. Monteverdi deflected his criticisms by distinguishing between the *prima* and *seconda pratica*. Bottrigari had a harder time in their dispute over tuning systems, wherein Artusi took the somewhat progressive stance of favouring a form of equal temperament as the only viable option for modern ensembles mixing voices and instruments.

FURTHER READING

T. Carter, 'Artusi, Monteverdi, and the poetics of modern music', in N. K. Baker and B. R. Hanning (eds.), *Musical Humanism and Its Legacy: Essays in Honor of C.V. Palisca*, (Stuyvesant, NY: Pendragon, 1992), 171–94.

TIM CARTER

Audiences Until the late eighteenth century, patronage of musicians came almost entirely from the aristocracy. As a consequence, the audience for music – both concerts and opera – was generally made up of the ruling classes, and by other professional musicians. There were some early exceptions. The emerging middle class – a term first coined in English in 1745 – developed an enthusiasm for music through concerts held in London taverns as early as the 1650s, and later through events such as the series of concerts run from 1678 onwards by the coal merchant Thomas Britton in Clerkenwell. In several German cities, similar concerts started to be given in coffee houses, the most famous being those at the Café Zimmermann in Leipzig, where TELEMANN and J. S. BACH performed. One of the earliest series of public concerts to attract audiences from a slightly broader social spectrum in France was the *Concert Spirituel*, inaugurated in Paris in 1725, and attended by merchants as well as aristocrats. In London, the New Spring Gardens (later known as the Vauxhall Gardens) was a large public space at which concerts of vocal music were introduced in 1745. In 1749 a public rehearsal of Handel's *Fireworks Music* was exceptionally well attended. *The Gentleman's Magazine* (April 1749, 185) reported:

> Friday 21 [April]: Was performed at Vauxhall Gardens the rehearsal of the music for the fireworks, by a band of 100 musicians, to an audience of above 12,000 persons (tickets 2s. 6d.). So great a resort occasioned such a stoppage on London Bridge, that no carriage could pass for 3 hours.

Though the details of this report have been challenged (*see* Hunter, 75–89), the substantial crowd attending the event suggests that Handel's appeal went well beyond the social elite that customarily attended his operas and oratorios in the theatre. This was certainly the exception rather than the rule at the time, and remained so until the nineteenth century.

Opera audiences in seventeenth-century Italy were predominantly aristocratic (many of the theatres were owned by the nobility), though in some cities there was also an enthusiastic following for opera by members of the professional and merchant classes. By 1800, those attending opera were from a broader public, but this was partly because aristocrats brought a retinue of servants to performances, and were allocated tickets for them in cheaper parts of the theatre. The claim by the government of Lombardy-Venetia in 1820 that La Scala was the only meeting place of all the classes (Rosselli, 39–40) is somewhat idealistic, though significant change had come in Milan during the years of French rule (1796–1814). According to a pamphlet from the time, the rear stalls of La Scala by 1821 were attended by 'well-bred men and women who did not dress elegantly, had no carriage, and might arrive dusty or muddy from the Milan streets' (Rosselli, 44) – tradesmen, civil servants and other professionals. These members of the audience were there to enjoy the performance, while the aristocrats in the boxes 'did little besides talk, eat, drink, gamble, and visit each other' (Rosselli, 10). Things were little better at the other end of the social hierarchy: the gallery at La Scala during a performance of the ballet *Il Prometeo* in 1813 was the subject of a poem in Milanese dialect by Carlo Porta (*Olter desgrazzi de Giovannin Bongee*). The riotous behaviour described involved a fireman, soldiers, a lamplighter and a tailor (Rosselli, 45).

By the middle of the nineteenth century, regular concert series were established in most cultural centres, attracting a wider audience. William Weber has written that 'by 1848 a commercial concert world had emerged in each city, over which the middle class exerted powerful, if not dominant, control' (Weber, 7). August Manns and George Grove began their Saturday afternoon concerts at the Crystal Palace in 1855, a series that ran until 1901, and which quickly became the most important source of classical music at affordable prices. The programmes were extremely enterprising, with the British premieres of Schubert's 'Great' C major Symphony and Schumann's Fourth Symphony both given in the first season. Later Manns introduced works by BRAHMS, Dvořák, Liszt and RICHARD STRAUSS, as well as promoting British composers including Sullivan, ELGAR, Parry and Stanford. The Promenade Concerts were established by Robert Newman in 1895, with Henry Wood as the conductor. Newman's aim was to educate a large audience at cheap prices. He wrote to Wood: 'I am going to run nightly concerts and train the public by easy stages. Popular at first, gradually raising the standard until I have created a public for classical and modern music' (quoted in Wood, 92). The atmosphere for the promenaders was informal (smoking, eating and drinking were all permitted in the early seasons), and has remained so, with standing tickets for more than 1,000 people available on the day for £6.00 each in 2016. The BBC took over the running of the concerts in 1927.

Programming of new music has provoked some celebrated cases of audience disruption. The most notorious (though by no means the first) is the 'riot' at the first night of STRAVINSKY's *Sacre du printemps* in the Théâtre des Champs-Elysées on 29 May 1913. There is disagreement among those who were present about whether it was the choreography or the music that sparked the demonstrations. In the era of radio, it is possible to hear the results of rowdy audience behaviour. The premiere of Varèse's *Déserts* at the Théâtre des Champs-Elysées on 2 December 1954 was broadcast, and the increasingly disruptive behaviour of enraged audience members can be heard all too clearly throughout the performance.

Opera has often provoked extreme reactions. When Patrice Chéreau's production of WAGNER's *Ring* was first given at Bayreuth in 1976, conducted by PIERRE BOULEZ, the first few minutes of Act III of *Götterdämmerung* as broadcast on Bavarian Radio were rendered inaudible by boos, howls and shouts from the audience. A few months later at La Scala, Milan, Zeffirelli's new production of Verdi's *Otello* conducted by Carlos Kleiber (7 December 1976) was disrupted for different reasons: demonstrators 'had gathered outside the theatre in order to protest the costs and subsidies of opera in the face of other social needs. Some of them had purchased tickets and were in the house' (Barber, 90). When Kleiber started Act III, the protestors erupted with shouting over the music – witnessed by twenty-four million viewers of the live television relay broadcast around the world – while an imperturbable Kleiber kept conducting.

Over a century earlier, the audience at Auber's opera *La Muette de Portici* on 25 August 1830 played a part in the start of the Belgian Revolution:

> When Lafeuillade and Cassel began singing the celebrated duet 'Amour sacré de la patrie', enthusiasm exploded irresistibly and it was necessary to start again in the middle of the cheering. Finally, when Masaniello (Lafeuillade) launched into the invocation 'Aux Armes!', the public could no longer be restrained. They acclaimed aria and singer, they booed the fifth act in order to stop the performance, and the delirious crowd rushed out of the theatre – into history ... It joined in the demonstrations that launched the revolution of 1830.
>
> (RENIEU, 744–5)

Concerts are less often disrupted by audiences inflamed for political reasons. There was, however, a disturbance on 21 August 1968 when Rostropovich, Svetlanov and the USSR State Symphony Orchestra appeared in London at the Proms on the very the day Soviet tanks rolled into Prague. The bitter irony of Soviet artists playing Dvořák's Cello Concerto was not lost on the audience, and the start of Shostakovich's Tenth Symphony was interrupted by loud protests around the hall (some shouting 'Go home!'). The broadcast of the performance (released on CD by ICA Classics) demonstrates the audience's violent change of mood from open hostility at the start to wild enthusiasm at the end of the symphony.

FURTHER READING

C. Barber, *Corresponding with Carlos: A Biography of Carlos Kleiber* (Lanham, MD: Scarecrow Press, 2011).
D. Hunter, *The Lives of George Frideric Handel* (Woodbridge: Boydell Press, 2015).
M. Musgrave, *The Musical Life of the Crystal Palace* (Cambridge University Press, 1995).
L. Renieu, *L'histoire des théâtres de Bruxelles: depuis leur origine jusqu'à ce jour* (Brussels: Duchartre and Van Buggenhoudt, 1928).
J. Rosselli, *The Italian Opera Industry from Cimarosa to Verdi* (Cambridge University Press, 1984).
W. Weber, *Music and the Middle Class: The Social Structure of Concert Life in London, Paris and Vienna between 1830 and 1848* (New York: Holmes and Meier, 1975).
H. Wood, *My Life of Music* (London: Gollancz, 1938).

NIGEL SIMEONE

Auer, Leopold (von) (b. Veszprém, 7 June 1845; d. Loschwitz, nr Dresden, 15 July 1930) Hungarian violinist and teacher.

Auer completed his violin studies with JOSEPH JOACHIM in Hanover (1863–4), following instruction from Ridley Kohne and Jakob Dont (1857–8). After brief appointments as concertmaster in Düsseldorf and Hamburg, he settled in St Petersburg, where he succeeded Wieniawski as professor at the conservatoire (1868–1917). Auer led the string quartet of the Imperial Music Society (1868–1906) and conducted that society's orchestra (1883, 1887–92). He also made summer teaching visits to London (1906–11) and Dresden (1912–14). Like Joachim, he was renowned as a 'finishing teacher', guiding technically proficient students in matters of TASTE, style, interpretation and professional discipline. Foremost among his pupils were Mischa Elman, Efrem Zimbalist, Jascha Heifetz, Nathan Milstein, Cäcilia Hansen, Kathleen Parlow, May Harrison and Oscar Shumsky. Many of his students followed him to New York, where he settled in 1918. He gave masterclasses at the Juilliard School and taught at Philadelphia's Curtis Institute.

Auer's *Graded Course of Violin Playing* (8 vols., New York: Carl Fischer, c1926), 'arranged' by Gustav Saenger, embraces violin study from the earliest stages. It aims to establish good posture, early BOWING proficiency and tonal appreciation before even introducing the left hand. Volume three develops tonal sonority and left-hand agility and includes duets; technical demands increase rapidly thereafter, with double-stopping, whole-tone and diatonic scales as particular foci; the final volume considers CADENZAS.

Catering for advanced students and teachers, Auer's *Violin Playing as I Teach it* (New York: Frederick A. Stokes, c1921) acknowledges the increasing contemporary emphasis on physiological considerations, stressing also the importance of mental and psychological factors and a keen aural and rhythmic sense. Significant recommendations include: rejecting a shoulder pad; using a special chin rest adapted to the individual's neck; cultivating free left-hand movement by raising the violin as high as feasible; and adopting a forward thumb position with the 'Geminiani grip'; applying wrist (as opposed to arm) pressure on the strings; and making the violin 'sing'. For him, VIBRATO is an expressive embellishment that should never be continuous nor employed to conceal poor intonation. Similarly, he advocates tasteful employment of PORTAMENTO, in moderation, stressing its vocal basis in lending 'animation and expression' to a melody. Further chapters focus on the execution of various bow strokes, left-hand technique, and scales. Auer favours 'rhythmic' FINGERING (shifts on the beats of the bar) and inaudible shifting but considers fingering choices primarily a matter for the individual. In the concluding chapters, he discusses ORNAMENTATION, pizzicato, HARMONICS, phrasing, DYNAMICS, timbre, TEMPO and rhythm, along with matters of style, stage fright and the violin repertory.

Auer's *Violin Masterworks and their Interpretation* (New York: C. Fischer, [1925]) offers a detailed interpretative approach to selected violin works of various genres from the Baroque to the late nineteenth century. A final chapter addresses transcriptions and MEMORY performance. His own TRANSCRIPTIONS and arrangements are tasteful and his careful, practical editions of works from the standard repertory still have currency, even if some, notably of PAGANINI's Caprice No. 24 and Tchaikovsky's Violin Concerto, present the parent work in a very different light – and not just in terms of fingerings and BOWINGS. His autobiographical *My Long Life in Music* (1923) offers interesting insights into his interaction with contemporary performers, composers and many aspects of musical performance of his times.

FURTHER READING

L. Auer, *My Long Life in Music* (New York: Frederick A. Stokes Co., 1923).
G. Kosloski, 'The teaching and influence of Leopold Auer', PhD dissertation, Indiana University (1977).
B. Schwarz, *Great Masters of the Violin* (New York: Simon & Schuster, 1983).

ROBIN STOWELL

Aurelian of Réôme (*fl.* ?840–50) Frankish writer.

Generally regarded as the earliest surviving Medieval musical treatise, Aurelian's *Musica disciplina* (from the 840s) is an attempt to integrate the Boethian tradition of *musica mathematica* with ninth-century plainsong practice. The penultimate chapter of the treatise offers a wealth of information on PLAINCHANT performance. The author painstakingly prescribes the intonation of introits, responses and antiphons in each of the eight church modes, specifying the particular accents and durations that singers should choose for each syllable of the text, while criticising faulty practices that do not adhere to his rules. In this and earlier chapters, Aurelian occasionally resorts to neumatic NOTATION to illustrate the melodic contour of verses and melodic formulae (*nonannoeane*, *noeagis*, etc.), showing that such a system was already in use by the mid-ninth century. Finally, *Musica disciplina* cites over one hundred chant melodies that were presumably in common use at the time.

FURTHER READING

L. A. Gushee, 'Questions of genre in Medieval treatises on music', in W. Arlt, E. Lichtenhahn and H. Oesch (eds.), *Gattungen der Musik in Einzeldarstellungen: Gedenkschrift Leo Schrade* (Bern and Munich: Francke, 1973), 365–433.
A. Morelli, Il *'Musica disciplina' di Aureliano di Réôme: Fondamenti teorico-disciplinari dell'ars musica nel IX secolo* (Udine: Forum, 2007).

STEFANO MENGOZZI

Authenticity Few would disagree that the concept of authenticity has been central to the historical performance of music. Fewer still, it would seem, agree over precisely what authenticity in musical performance actually entails. The early music movement has been characterised almost as much by the heated debate over 'authentic' performance as by its distinctive musical offerings. Over the years, a very broad selection of international performers, musicologists, cultural theorists and philosophers has written extensively on the topic.

The Greek ancestry of the word authentic, *authenteo*, means 'to have full power', that is, being 'the master of his or her domain'. The *Oxford English Dictionary* refers to 'possessing original or inherent authority', or 'acting of itself, self-originated'. The authentic is that 'which is sufficient unto itself, which commends, sustains, proves itself, and hath credit and authority from itself' (Kenyon, 24–5). With respect to art in general, we can usefully distinguish *nominal authenticity* – the correct identification of the origins, authorship or provenance of an object – from *expressive authenticity* – having to do with an object's character as a true expression of an individual's or society's values and beliefs (D. Dutton, 'Authenticity in Art', in J. Levinson (ed.), *The Oxford Handbook of Aesthetics* (Oxford University Press, 2003), 258–74).

In the context of musical performance, Stephen Davies makes a persuasive case for authenticity being an ontological requirement not an interpretative option on account of its being essentially implicated in a work's performance (S. Davies, *Musical Works & Performances* (Oxford University Press, 2001)). A performance has to be minimally (nominally) authentic in order to be the work being performed. The central challenge for the historical performance of music, however, concerns expressive authenticity and stems from the fact that original 'authors' (i.e. composers) are no longer able to assert their authority and power through telling us how their music should sound.

Peter Kivy argues that all performances are essentially the emergent outcome of competing demands or 'authenticities' – of *intention, sound, practice* and also *personal* authenticity, with this latter category overlapping with a broad sweep of scholarship devoted to identity and authenticity of the self (P. Kivy, *Authenticities* (New York: Cornell University Press, 1995)). More recently, Nick Wilson offers a justification of authentic performance in terms of 'historical (dispositional) authenticity': for the performer this means asking questions about what must have been *possible* to perform the musical work at the time and place, rather than what were the *actual* conditions of any first performance, what the piece sounded like, or what the composer's intentions actually were (N. Wilson, *The Art of Re-enchantment: Making Early Music in the Modern Age* (Oxford University Press, 2014)).

The original early music view was that 'music sounds best when played as the composer expected it would be played' (Sherman, 10); this is often discussed in terms of being 'faithful to the work' (see WERKTREUE). HOWARD MAYER BROWN lays this 'cult of authenticity' at the feet of ARNOLD DOLMETSCH, who 'more than anyone else ... was committed to the idea that performers should try to play music in the way its composers intended' (Kenyon, 39). Dolmetsch also led the way for makers of authentic instruments, who, following an 'ideology of replication' (Haynes, 140–1), sought to replicate the original instruments they were copying. Unfortunately, leaving aside the issue of whether authenticity was a legitimate aim, the standard of many early authentic performances, especially when period instruments were yet to be mastered, left much to be desired. As Nicholas Kenyon (ix) wrote, 'There was on the one hand such wide acceptance of the evident (and indeed moral) rightness of an approach to performance which "respected the composer's original intentions", and on the other hand such a violent dismissal of the end results by many thinking and articulate musicians that it was time for a reappraisal of the situation.'

Kenyon's book on the movement's 'ominous theory' and 'arrogant claim' comprised a collection of essays, some of which had been published earlier in the decade. In February 1984 a group of articles appeared in the journal *Early Music* under the title 'The limits of authenticity'. The most critical voice amongst them belonged to RICHARD TARUSKIN. Motivated by what he regarded as the conceptual constraints that prevented historical performance from being 'truly historical', Taruskin cast doubt on the whole 'authenticity' project. Performers were not really being authentic in their practices, since it was impossible to know what the composer's intentions were. Furthermore, as CHRISTOPHER HOGWOOD acknowledged, 'There just wasn't enough evidence for all the things we were doing ... It was just one invention on top of another all the time' (Kenyon, 3-4). For Taruskin, early music performance was really about how modern performers *wanted* it to sound. Taruskin was also critical of musicology, which he described as a 'Johnny-come-lately to the authentic performance movement', adding 'musicology has been responsible for more of what has gone wrong with "authentic" performance than what has gone right with it' (R. Taruskin, *Text & Act* (Oxford University Press, 1995), 96-7). By the end of the 1990s, 'authenticity' had become 'virtually taboo among historicists' (Sherman, 8). The new term of choice – HISTORICALLY INFORMED PERFORMANCE (HIP) (see J. Butt, *Playing with History* (Cambridge University Press)) – conveyed an altogether more modest agenda.

With the benefit of hindsight, it is hard not to agree with Bruce Haynes's observation that 'More than anything else, authenticity seems to be a statement of intent' (Haynes, 10). Haynes acknowledges that totally accurate historical performance is probably impossible to achieve, but adds that it is 'the *attempt* to be historically accurate, that is, authentic'. For many, it has been by 'taking the indefensible ideal of authenticity seriously that our knowledge has been increased and our musical life enriched' (C. Rosen, *Critical Entertainments: Music Old and New* (Cambridge, MA: Harvard University Press, 2000), 221). Judging by a recent tongue-in-cheek press release from one prominent historical performance ensemble, 'period ensemble to perform *Clapping Music* using Steve Reich's original hands', it remains to be seen just how 'seriously' musicians will take authenticity in the future.

FURTHER READING

B. Haynes, *The End of Early Music* (Oxford University Press, 2007).
N. Kenyon (ed.), *Authenticity and Early Music* (Oxford University Press, 1988).
B. D. Sherman, *Inside Early Music* (Oxford University Press, 1997).

NICK WILSON

Avison, Charles (b. Newcastle upon Tyne, ?early February (bap. 16 February) 1709; d. 9 or 10 May 1770) English composer, conductor, organist and writer on music.

Based in Newcastle upon Tyne for much of his life, Avison had early connections to London, where he took lessons with GEMINIANI and gave concerts in Hickford's Rooms (beginning in March 1734). Two years later he moved to Newcastle following his appointment as organist at St Nicholas's, the principal church in that city. He organised subscription concerts there, as well as in Durham, and brought together a gifted group of musicians including William Herschel, William Shield and Felice Giardini. He wrote over sixty concerti grossi, and, beginning with his Op. 5 (1756), the earliest chamber sonatas for keyboard to be composed in England.

Avison's important treatise, *An Essay on Musical Expression* (London: C. Davis, 1752; rev. 3rd edn, London; Lockyer Davis, 1775), is in three parts. The first deals with musical EXPRESSION in general and pursues a long analogy with painting. The second treats expression in relation to composition, where a balance of interest between melody and harmony is advised if expressive music is to be produced. The third section, on expression in relation to performance, is the most insightful and practical. It distinguishes expression from mere execution and has many remarks on textural balance, ARTICULATION, the use of DYNAMICS, and ORNAMENTATION (which, in ensemble works, must not disrupt the time or obscure the harmony). More originally Avison emphasises the need for the performer to be aware of the design of the work as a whole, and he devises a special sign (a florid 'V') to indicate the leading subjects and ideas. He therefore recommends performing from full scores, and in 1758 published twenty-six of his concerti (Opp. 3, 4 and 6) in that format. BURNEY (7) described Avison as 'the first, and almost the only writer' who attempted musical criticism in his day in England.

FURTHER READING

C. Burney, 'Essay on Musical Criticism', in *A General History of Music from the Earliest Ages to the Present Period (1789)*, ed. F. Mercer, 2 vols. (London: Foulis, 1935; repr. New York: Dover, 1957), II, 7–11.

P. le Huray and J. Day (eds.), *Music and Aesthetics in the Eighteenth and Early-Nineteenth Centuries* (Cambridge University Press, 1987).

A. Longo, 'Charles Avison estetico della Musica', *RIM*, 27 (1992), 183–204.

ANTHONY PRYER

B

'Bach' Bow A specially curved violin BOW developed in the first half of the twentieth century as the result of a misconception that the multiple stopping in J. S. BACH's Sonatas and Partitas for unaccompanied violin, BWV1001–1006, should be realised literally, and without arpeggiation. Its highly arched, convex stick enabled the player to sound all four strings simultaneously; many believed that the resultant organ-like polyphony was how Bach intended his works to be heard.

The misconception originated in two 1904 articles by Arnold Schering (1877–1941), supported by Albert Schweitzer (1875–1965). Although Schering modified his position in 1920, Schweitzer persisted in his belief in the 'Bach' bow, of which there have been several prototypes, ranging from Hermann Berkowskis's 'Polyphon-Bogen' to models developed respectively by Hans Baumgart, Günther Hellwig, Georges Frey and Rolph Schroeder. The Hungarian violinist Emil Telmányi (1892–1988) also championed the cause, commissioning the 'Vega Bach bow' from the Dane Knud Vestergaard (Vega is an abbreviation of VEsterGAard) in 1954. The Vega's bowstick is convex, of high arch (about 10–12 cms/4–5 inches separating the hair and stick at the highest point) and has a thumb-operated mechanical lever to loosen or tighten the hair immediately while playing. When the hair is loose, the player can execute and sustain full chords, wrapping the bow hair around the curve of the bridge; when the hair is tightened, he can play freely on individual strings, as with a regular modern bow.

The case against the 'Bach' bow's existence has been particularly well made by DAVID BOYDEN, who points to: the complete lack of surviving Baroque-era bows of its design or any relevant evidence; the fact that bow hair could not be loosened or tightened mechanically at that time; the lack of evidence for the use of a relaxed right thumb; and the suitability of the old French bow hold required for simple dance music, but not for the execution of sustained chords. Sonically, sustaining the notes as notated does not serve the music's purpose as may clear differentiation of parts through timbre, ARTICULATION and bowing. Use of a 'Bach' bow results in a noticeable loss of brilliance, especially on single strings; chords tend to sound louder than individual notes because the overtones are reinforced by the sustained notes; the melodic and harmonic functions of the texture are less clearly differentiated; and the violin sounds rather more like a synthesiser or even an accordion.

Nevertheless, violinist Tossy Spivakovsky endorsed the 'Bach' bow as late as 1967 and some performers still promote its use. Violinist Rudolf Gähler not only recorded solo Bach using such a bow as recently as 1996 but also published a book about the bow's merits. German cellist Michael Bach (Bachtischa), encouraged by Mstislav Rostropovich, also championed the 'Bach' bow concept in the 1990s, performing solo Bach and newly commissioned works from composers such as Walter Zimmermann and JOHN CAGE. However, the 'Bach' bow succeeds in realising Bach's polyphonic string music only in the image of its twentieth-century inventors, not as Bach intended or heard it.

FURTHER READING

D. D. Boyden, *A History of Violin Playing from its Origins to 1761* (London: Oxford University Press, 1965).

R. Gähler, *Der Rundbogen für die Violine – ein Phantom?* (Regensburg: ConBrio Verlagsgesellschaft, 1997).

A. Schering, 'Verschwundene Traditionen des Bach-Zeitalters', *NZfM*, 80 (1904), 675–8 and *BJb*, 1 (1904), 104–15.

ROBIN STOWELL

Bach, Carl Philipp Emanuel (b. Weimar, 8 March 1714; d. Hamburg, 14 December 1788) Composer and church musician, second surviving son of JOHANN SEBASTIAN BACH and his first wife, Maria Barbara.

Emanuel Bach was, like his younger half-brother, Johann Christian, a tremendously successful composer, performer and catalyst for music culture in the years after Sebastian's death. Indeed, to many in the later eighteenth century he was far more significant and relevant than his father. Whether through his own attitude or with his father's encouragement, he showed more independence from his father's methods and attitudes than his elder brother, WILHELM FRIEDEMANN. He constitutes one of the most significant sources of performance practice from the middle of the century, showing vestiges of his early education and providing much of the basis for later pedagogy.

As the writer of the *Versuch* (1753/1762), Emanuel reflects a new trend within eighteenth-century performance, namely the development of a systematic pedagogical method in line with Enlightenment thought, one that reflected and influenced professional practice, but which also provided a significant basis for a newly energised amateur culture of music making (hence his employment of the term 'für Kenner und Liebhaber' in some of his keyboard music). On the other hand, the growing culture of individual style and originality could be taken to suggest that his methodology is really only applicable to his own highly individual musical style (one that is steadily becoming recognised as highly significant in its own right, rather than merely transitional between the supposedly stable Baroque and Classical styles). While this limitation is true in a literal sense, Emanuel's pedagogy is also excellent evidence that performance practices were (as they probably always had been) in flux and that they provide a snapshot of a practice far more varied and dynamic than many looking for certain answers might assume. Furthermore, such was Emanuel's influence that his methodology was all but ubiquitous for composers and performers of the classical era (including BEETHOVEN), and his FIGURED BASS method was an essential source well into the next century. In other words, Emanuel's rich pedagogy points to traces of practice that were in some ways relevant to the entire eighteenth century even if we are inevitably unable to abstract from it the precise performance practice for any particular decade, composer, piece or even performance.

Emanuel's advice on performance (and much can be substantiated from other sources, such as CHARLES BURNEY) covers many categories of practice, primarily, but not exclusively, relating to keyboard performance. At the most basic level is his advice on FINGERING, which shows both the growing importance and the diversity of fingering discipline. He provides some examples of the old paired style that he states was common in his father's youth (when the use of the thumb was restricted), but he also reflects the burgeoning tonal system, which he must have first encountered through *The Well-Tempered Clavier* and which demanded a much more flexible method. Through his many examples we can almost see the basis of modern, thumb-under fingering emerging, a sort of methodology that has become typical of the professionalisation of the modern age. Less obvious from a modern viewpoint, though, is Emanuel's strong advocacy of the CLAVICHORD as the basis of the technique on all keyboard instruments, something that cultivates the firm and engaged employment of each individual finger. Coupled with this is a style of ARTICULATION that is undoubtedly more separated than the essential legato touch that began to develop from around 1800. Again, this suggests the cultivation of clarity and speech as an essential element of performance style.

The *Versuch* is also one of the most important sources of ornamental practice, essentially showing an updated version of French symbol ORNAMENTATION and establishing rules of thumb that are largely relevant for the remainder of the century in Austro-German culture. These include rules on long appoggiaturas and trills largely beginning on the upper note. As with all aspects of any pedagogical method, it is clear that these elements are to be taken as starting points rather than absolutely rigid instructions.

Perhaps most interesting, and indeed challenging, from the point of view of historical performance practice, are Emanuel's comments on performance and his emphasis on IMPROVISATION. While many early pioneers of historically informed performance practice understandably tried to distance seventeenth- and eighteenth-century performance from the so-called 'romantic' accretions of the nineteenth, there is no doubt that Emanuel reflects an extraordinarily intense engagement with the experience of music, its performance and audition. Far from advocating a rational, objective or speech-like (in the sense of prosaic) approach, his own performance seems to have been intensely passionate and even 'possessed'. It may be that many modern views on the 'doctrine of AFFECTIONS' have seen affects in eighteenth-century music as representations of a pre-established catalogue, each mood conforming to some assumed scale of correctness. What the evidence from Emanuel Bach suggests, however, is a sense of moods actually taking over the performer and thence affecting the listener in turn. This is therefore a very real and embodied sense of emotion, every bit as 'romantic' as that assumed for later generations. In a sense, then, the implications of Emanuel's embodied approach to music – although undoubtedly individual, and perhaps extreme in some respects – open up a broader range of possibilities for performance practice than may have traditionally been assumed in modern historical performance.

Emanuel's approach to embodied emotion, fully integrated with the playing technique and attitudes to the act of performance, ties in directly with his famed art as an improviser. The *Versuch* contains much information on ornamenting pre-existing music, particularly in his emphasis on CADENZAS and 'varied repeats' ('Veränderungen'). This advice, together with much of Emanuel's own notated music, also points towards a freely improvised practice embodied in the fantasia. The 'fantastic' style sits behind, rather than necessarily apart from, the standard forms of the eighteenth century. The unexpected and whimsical progress of such music presupposes a deep understanding of harmonic procedures and tonal trajectories, and in turn may lie behind the ways even seemingly fixed NOTATION was devised. Therefore, even if we choose not to alter one note, knowledge of the dynamic relationship between improvisation and notated composition has the potential to inflect our performance of eighteenth-century music.

FURTHER READING

C. P. E. Bach, *Essay on the True Art of Playing Keyboard Instruments*, trans. W. J. Mitchell (London: Eulenburg Books, 1974).
S. Rampe, *Carl Philipp Emanuel Bach und seine Zeit* (Laaber Verlag, 2014).
D. Schulenberg, *The Music of Carl Philipp Emanuel Bach* (University of Rochester Press, 2014).

JOHN BUTT

Bach, Johann Sebastian (b. Eisenach, 21 March 1685; d. Leipzig, 28 July 1750) German composer and organist.

While Bach's biography and compositional output hardly require reiteration, his contribution to performance and the development of various types of performance practice is also very significant. Most obviously, he was the ORGAN virtuoso of his age, rivalled only by Handel (although the two were never directly heard together) and, in most of the posts he held, he was the director of musical ensembles. He stands at an interesting juncture in the history of performance, since he was brought up in the performance traditions of his family and the Lutheran culture of Thuringia, yet in many ways he heralded the more modern approach to performance as a targeted, specialist art. Coming from a family of musicians stretching right back to the turn of the seventeenth century, his musical culture would have been along the lines of a family trade, in which the skills were passed from one musician to another. Many in his family had been church organists or worked as court or town musicians ('Kunstgeiger' and 'Stadtpfeiffer'). Within the guild culture of these various established groups, musicians learned as apprentices, mastering what could be an extraordinarily wide range of skills. These might include proficiency on instruments from several families, the fundamentals of composition and arrangement, together with skill in the design, construction or maintenance of instruments (including, in Bach's case, the organ). Performance practice was thus marked by its versatility and the ability to switch from one performance medium to another. It was craft-like in the sense that musicians would have had knowledge of a wide range of the stages in the production of music, even if they were not consistently involved in every element simultaneously.

Bach acquired his more 'modern' attitude to performance partly through the intense focus of his own keyboard virtuosity but also through frequent exposure to some of the most skilled musicians of the age, in the various court appointments he held (particularly that at Cöthen). In 1730 he expressed his envy of the musicians in Dresden, who were only required to specialise in one instrument, thus engendering an overall higher standard of performance. This notion of specialisation would, by the end of the eighteenth century, become the standard ideal of the music conservatoire, in which musicians become responsible for only one element in the process of musical production. Orchestras and other ensembles could therefore benefit from the 'division of labour' even if they lost something of the craft-like versatility of the older cultures of performance.

Bach never lost his own sense of versatility, though. He was concerned with every element of music, from the construction of instruments, through composition to performance; and each stage in this process was mutually influential. The close link between composition and performance seems to have been particularly important, bridged by the art of IMPROVISATION (a central element of the organist's art), in which Bach excelled. This intense concern for the broad culture of music may well have had religious and vocational motivations, but it meant that Bach never ceased to be interested in every style of music that he encountered. Most obviously he, like other composers in his environment (such as TELEMANN), was concerned with assimilating the performance practices of France and Italy, both separately and together, which in turn informed his development of the indigenous German styles. And even within the latter, he seemed keen to master every stylistic level, from the most contrapuntally severe *stile antico* to the much more popular *galant* style, which became an essential aspect of musical fashion from the 1720s onwards. Anecdotes concerning his own manner of performance abound, with his organ playing characterised by its relaxed and effortless technique, resulting in a performance that sounded like a lively conversation. Particularly interesting is the description by the school rector J. M. Gesner of his lively direction of music in ensembles, directing from the keyboard, with every limb embodying the pulse, and correcting players both with his own playing and with his voice.

Bach's imperative to assimilate styles, techniques and idioms seems to have gone hand in hand with his work as a teacher. Here again, we see him as one of the earliest teachers of finished compositional inventions (discrete pieces of music as opposed to the more traditional exercises in counterpoint). This was coupled with performance as a contiguous learning process (at least for those students who were capable of both performance and composition). Sources of Bach's music and his specifically pedagogical productions (such as the music book for WILHELM FRIEDEMANN BACH and the published four-part collection of the *Clavier Übung*) all suggest an increasing specificity of performance practice as his career progressed. Casual indications of ORNAMENTATION and ad lib playing out of chordal patterns are replaced by an increasingly didactic presentation of notes, together with a French system of ornament symbols (*agréments*) and greater specificity of ARTICULATION patterns. In many ways, Bach was part of a general movement, as the century progressed, towards providing more notational detail; but the notion that he was exceptional in the level of detail he provided is suggested by the dispute of 1737, when the musician and journalist J. A. SCHEIBE inveighed against Bach's style and notation, leaving nothing to singers' discretion and providing every little note and nuance. He also observed that Bach assumed that all singers and players could do what the composer could do with his own fingers as a keyboard player.

It may be that we are quite fortunate that Bach worked with such a diverse range of performers, since if he had always had consistently excellent collaborators, he might not have developed so much detail in his notation, nor provided the pedagogic background for the seminal work on performance practice written by his son C. P. E. BACH (1753/62). In fact, his many pupils and grandpupils dominated the pedagogic landscape of northern Europe throughout the remainder of the century, so it is probably fair to say that Bach influenced both the composition and the performance of music in the decades after his death far more than might first appear.

FURTHER READING

J. Butt, *Bach Interpretation: Articulation Marks in Primary Sources of J. S. Bach* (Cambridge University Press, 1990).

L. Dreyfus, *Bach and the Patterns of Invention* (Cambridge, MA: Harvard University Press, 2004).

JOHN BUTT

Bach, Wilhelm Friedemann (b. Weimar, 22 November 1710; d. Berlin, 1 July, 1784) German composer and organist, eldest son of J. S. BACH.

Wilhelm Friedemann seems to have benefitted in the strongest measure from his father's pedagogic methods. The single most significant element surviving from this early education is the *Klavierbüchlein* (1720), which shows the beginnings of a graduated method that embraces both keyboard performance and compositional methodology. We can learn much about aspects of performance practice that were current in Germany during the early decades of the eighteenth century, at least as a starting point for incipient performers. This includes the wholesale appropriation of the French symbol style of ORNAMENTATION and also some of the most detailed information on keyboard FINGERING of the period (and by far the most significant examples by J. S. Bach). This shows the old-style, paired form of fingering as the basis of technique, but clearly adapted to account for the increase in accidentals that came with the development of the full tonal system. Some of the fingerings also show the shape of the hand accommodating the shape of the figuration in each bar, as if to suggest a development of a local form of phrasing and shaping.

The father's traditional advice on fingering takes on added resonance given that W. F. Bach was singled out later in the century by TÜRK as being particularly conservative in his use of paired fingering. This implies both that it was possible to retain traditional methods of the high Baroque era and that newer styles of fingering (making active use of the thumb) were becoming ubiquitous.

Virtually all J. S. Bach's keyboard pieces of the 1720s may have been written with Friedemann's education in mind (and these include the demanding trio sonatas for organ). It is clear that the son kept much of his father's attitude towards performance alive when he held his own appointments in Dresden and Halle. Although the sources are patchy, his apportionment of instrumental and vocal parts in his own cantatas conforms to earlier practice, particularly in the production of only one copy of each vocal part in surviving sets.

FURTHER READING

D. Schulenberg, *The Music of Wilhelm Friedemann Bach* (University of Rochester Press, 2010).

JOHN BUTT

Bacilly, Bertrand 'Bénigne' de (b. ?Normandy, ?c1625; d. Paris, 27 September 1690) French composer, singing teacher and theorist active in Paris.

Bacilly's enduring legacy is his treatise, *Remarques curieuses sur l'art de bien chanter et particulièrement pour ce qui concerne le chant françois par le sieur B.D.B.* (Paris: R. Ballard, 1668), which is considered fundamental to the development of the French style of writing and interpretation. The treatise contains detailed rules of PRONUNCIATION and syllabic quantity in relation to singing in French, rules as to seventeenth-century ornamentation and guidance on correct breathing. For Bacilly, the ability to determine syllable length (categorised as long, short or in between the two) was critical to the art of SINGING and composing vocal music in French; long syllables should be sung with greater force, energy and weight than short or medium ones and syllabic length should also determine the addition of ornaments and their length. This carefully balanced, syllabic approach creates a lilting sense of refinement and inflection in the music.

FURTHER READING

C. Gordon-Seifert, *Music and the Language of Love: Seventeenth-Century French Airs* (Bloomington, IN and Indianapolis: Indiana University Press, 2011).

A.-M. Goulet, *Poésie, musique et sociabilité au XVIIe siècle: Les livres d'airs de différents auteurs publiés chez Ballard de 1658 à 1694* (Paris: Honoré Champion Éditeur, 2004).

H. Prunières, 'Un maître de chant au XVIIe siècle: Bénigne de Bacilly', *RM*, 4/8 (November 1923), 156–60.

ELIZABETH DOBBIN

Backofen, Johann Georg Heinrich (b. Durlach, 6 July 1768; d. Darmstadt 10 July 1839) German clarinettist, composer and painter.

Backofen studied composition and the CLARINET in Nuremberg and later took up the FLUTE. He was also a celebrated harpist and basset horn player. After a period as court chamber musician at Gotha (where he worked with SPOHR), he was appointed to the Darmstadt court, where he manufactured clarinets. Backofen wrote a HARP method (*Antleitung zum Harfenspiel* (Leipzig: Breitkopf, 1801), and compositions for harp, clarinet, basset horn and wind band. He is now best remembered for his *Anweisung zur Klarinette, nebst einer kurzen Abhandlung über das Bassett-Horn* (Leipzig: Breitkopf, 1803; completely revised 1824 to take account of the new mechanism devised by MÜLLER). This tutor is significant as the first German source for playing the clarinet since EISEL (*Musicus Autodidaktos* (Erfurt: Finke, 1738)).

Backofen's work is full of practical advice. He remarked that he had never encountered a clarinet with absolutely pure intonation and could not decide whether this was inherent in the instrument or the fault of makers. He recommends wax for adjusting individual tone-holes, while remarking that embouchure has an important part to play, together with liberal use of alternative FINGERINGS. Suspicious of additional mechanism, Backofen observes that broken springs were all too common. He counsels that all clarinettists should prepare their own reeds, recognising individual preferences for hard or soft strengths. He stresses the importance of obtaining hard cane, which is brownish-gold in appearance and has an ivory colour when cut across. Among his reed tools are a sharp knife, a large wide file and a small piece of glass or a piece of horsetail dipped in water. Significantly, he noted in 1803 that reed-above and reed-below embouchure were equally popular.

Backofen recommends a relaxed posture, instructing players to place their feet as if they were about to make a large leap. With the head held too far back the clarinettist appears cheeky and shameless, but when held too far forward, the posture of the head gives a shy and unpromising appearance.

FURTHER READING

C. Lawson, *The Early Clarinet: A Practical Guide* (Cambridge University Press, 2000).
P. Weston, *More Clarinet Virtuosi of the Past* (London: The Author, 1977).

COLIN LAWSON

Badura-Skoda, Eva (née Halfar) (b. Munich, 15 January 1929) German/Austrian musicologist.

Badura-Skoda, Paul (b. Vienna, 6 October 1927) Austrian pianist.
Distinguished husband-and-wife team (now separated) making significant contributions as scholar (she) and performer (he) to our understanding of eighteenth- and early nineteenth-century music.

After studies in viola d'amore, piano and theory at the Vienna Conservatory (now the University of Music and Performing Arts), Eva pursued musicology, philosophy and art history at the universities of Heidelberg, Regensburg, Vienna and Innsbruck, receiving a PhD (Vienna, 1953) for the thesis 'Studien zur Geschichte des Musikunterrichtes in Österreich im 16., 17. und 18. Jahrhundert'. Paul Badura-Skoda won first prize in the Austrian Music Competition in 1947 and subsequently appeared with many of the world's most illustrious conductors, including Wilhelm Furtwängler, Herbert von Karajan and George Szell. Although primarily known for his MOZART, BEETHOVEN and Schubert performances, his repertoire has a broad range. His playing shows deep stylistic understanding and cultivation. He has made over 200 recordings. For many years he formed a piano duo with Jörg Demus.

Eva and Paul met in 1950 and married in 1951. His acute understanding of the details of musical style and her erudition inspired fruitful collaboration. His powerful intuition has clarified errors in standard works and questions of authenticity. Together they amassed a collection of historic keyboard instruments; he made one of the very first recordings of Mozart on a period piano from the Kunsthistorisches Museum, Vienna. They collaborated on an authoritative treatise, *Mozart-Interpretation* (Vienna, 1957), trans. L. Black as *Interpreting Mozart on the Keyboard* (New York, 1962); 2nd edn as *Interpreting Mozart: The Performance of His Piano Pieces and Other Compositions* (New York and London: Routledge, 2008), followed by Paul's *Bach-Interpretation* (Laaber bei Regensburg, 1990), trans. A. Clayton as *Interpreting Bach at the Keyboard*

(Oxford: Clarendon Press, 1993; 2nd edn, 2014), and the fifth volume of the Mozart piano concertos (containing the concertos K453, 456 and 459) for the *Neue Mozart-Ausgabe*. The scholarly initiative was hers; the musical breadth and practical application of the scholarship largely his. Both have contributed numerous articles to reference works and periodicals; she has edited works of DITTERSDORF, HAYDN, Mozart, and Schubert, and co-edited *Schubert Studies: Problems of Style and Chronology* (Cambridge University Press, 1982) with Peter Branscombe. She also edited the report of the international Haydn congress held in Vienna in 1982 (Munich, 1986) and was an editor of a volume on Schubert and his friends (Cologne and Vienna, 1999). She has taught at the Salzburg Mozarteum (1962, 1963), the University of Wisconsin (1966–74), Boston University (1976), Queen's University at Kingston, Ontario (1979), McGill University (1981–2) and the University of Göttingen (1982–3). Both have contributed numerous articles to reference works and periodicals. Both have received numerous honorary doctorates and other distinctions and awards.

ROBERT D. LEVIN

Bagpipes Mouth or bellows-blown instrument featuring a bag that distributes the air into one or several single- or double-reed pipes.

Bagpipes can feature one or two melodic pipes and up to six drones. They can be classified into three categories: single-reed bagpipes, hybrid bagpipes and double-reed bagpipes (Van Hees, 42). Single-reed bagpipes have single reeds in all the pipes and are found from India to Spain with predominance in northern, eastern and Mediterranean countries such as Sweden (*säckpipa*), Bulgaria (*gaida*) or Greece (*tsampouna, askomandoura*; Figure 1).

Hybrid bagpipes feature double reeds in the melodic pipe and single reeds in the drones; they are mainly found in France (*cornemuse, chabrette, biniou,* etc.), Spain (*gaita, xeremies,* etc.), and the British Isles (Great Highland bagpipes, *uilleann* pipes, smallpipes, etc.). Finally, double-reed bagpipes that feature one or two melodic pipes and from two to six double-reed drones are found in Italy (*zampogna a chiave*...) and historically in France (*musette, grande cornemuse à miroirs,* etc.) and England (shuttle pipe, Cornish double pipe). Vernacular bagpipes can be found as far as India (*mashak*), Western Russia (*shuvyr*) and

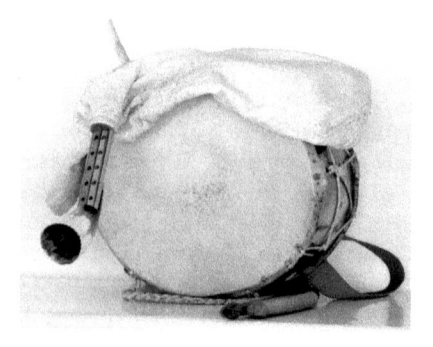

Figure 1: The Greek bagpipe, which is often played along with a small drum. (photograph by Cassandre Balosso-Bardin)

Northern Africa (*mezwed*). About 150 different models have been documented (Van Hees, 45), many of which are still played today. In some regions, however, local bagpipes disappeared over time or were replaced by more dominant instruments such as the Scottish Highland bagpipes or the accordion.

The origins of bagpipes are unclear. The earliest documentation of bagpipes is in *De vita Caesarum* by Gaius Suetonius Tranquillus (c70–c140) and in *Orationes LXXI* by Dio Chrysostom (c40–112), who mention that Emperor Nero played an *aulos* with a bag and that he hoped to become an *utricularius* (player of a small skin reservoir). Although bagpipes occasionally emerge in the literature around the ninth and eleventh centuries, bagpipe ICONOGRAPHY explodes in the thirteenth century, appearing all over Europe. Droneless until the twelfth or thirteenth century, bagpipes were loud instruments, associated with official functions and outdoor activities. Documents show that pipers were often hired by the town or the court, playing for festivities and religious ceremonies. Rich ICONOGRAPHY can be found on religious buildings or illuminated documents such as the *Cantigas de Santa Maria* (1258).

During the Renaissance, bagpipes were played in both rural and aristocratic environments. It was also an era of many inventions, one of which was the ancestor of the French baroque *musette*. It appeared around the 1550s and was later further developed by Martin HOTTETERRE (c1635–1712), who added a second melodic chanter to extend its range. This expensive instrument was used in art music for over two hundred years until c1760; it featured in compositions by Boismortier, Campra, CORRETTE, Hotteterre, LULLY and RAMEAU amongst others. The organology of the Baroque *musette* later inspired the creation of the Northumbrian and *uilleann* pipes. Other instruments featuring in art music at the time include Polish, Italian and Czech bagpipes (see Van Hees, 139–43). In Scotland, the *piobaireachd* art form performed on the *piob mhor*, the Highland bagpipes, flourished between the sixteenth and eighteenth centuries.

Bagpipe performance practice varies widely. Bagpipes can be played solo or in duo, trio, quartet and larger formations such as pipe-bands. They are often traditionally coupled with another PERCUSSION or melody instrument such as SHAWMS, FLUTES, VIOLINS, HURDY-GURDIES or small drums (France, Greece, Italy, Mallorca, Malta, Poland, etc.). Scottish pipe and drum bands began to emerge in military regiments around the mid-nineteenth century (West, 657). This formation was later emulated in other countries, both with Scottish bagpipes (many Commonwealth countries, USA and more recently Central America and South East Asia) and vernacular pipes (Brittany, Bulgaria, Galicia, etc.). Since the last quarter of the twentieth century, many piping cultures have produced large bagpipe ensembles although rarely with the military or competition aspects found in Scotland.

Bagpipes provided music for entertainment and dancing but were also functional instruments played at specific moments of the year including rituals and ceremonies such as weddings, funerals, patron saint days and official events. In Italy and Malta, for example, the sound of bagpipes is still closely associated with Christmas. Repertoire was generally transmitted orally and only very few bagpipe traditions boast early TRANSCRIPTIONS or MANUSCRIPTS. The earliest known collection of bagpipe tunes in Britain is the

William Dixon manuscript for border bagpipes, written between 1733 and 1738. EARLY RECORDINGS and personal sound archives have become essential as the ORAL TRADITION led to great loss of repertoire with the decline of the instrument in the nineteenth and twentieth century. Thanks to a widespread renaissance in the second half of the twentieth century, many bagpipes were revived or even reinvented along with their repertoire. Today, bagpipes from both unbroken and re-established traditions are played regularly all over the world.

FURTHER READING

H. Cheape, *Bagpipes: A National Collection of a National Treasure*, 2nd rev. edn (Edinburgh: NMSE Publishing, 2011).
J. Dixon (ed.), *The Highland Bagpipe: Music, History, Tradition* (Farnham: Ashgate, 2009).
J.-P. Van Hees, *Cornemuses: un infini sonore* (Kerangwenn: Coop Breizh, 2014).
G. West, 'Scottish military music', in E. M. Spiers, J. A. Crang and M. J. Strickland (eds.), *A Military History of Scotland* (Edinburgh University Press, 2012), 648–68.

CASSANDRE BALOSSO-BARDIN

Baillot, Pierre (Marie François de Sales) (b. Passy, nr Paris, 1 October 1771; d. Paris, 15 September 1842) French violinist, composer and pedagogue.

Taught initially by Polidori and Sainte-Marie, Baillot later studied with Nardini-pupil Pollani. He settled in Paris (1791–5) as a violinist in the Théâtre Feydeau orchestra, but later worked in the ministry of finance before undertaking military service. He was appointed violin professor at the PARIS CONSERVATOIRE in 1795, first temporarily and later permanently (1799–1842), including Mazas, Sauzay, Charles and Léopold DANCLA, the HABENECKS, Auguste Kreutzer, Lalo, Urhan, BÉRIOT and Maurer among his pupils. He joined Napoleon's private orchestra (1802), toured Russia successfully (1805–8) and became an esteemed chamber music performer (with Quatuor Baillot), leading a concert series in Paris (from 1814) and disseminating hitherto little-known repertory. Further touring followed, along with leadership of the Paris Opéra Orchestra (1821–31) and the Chapelle Royale (from 1825).

Baillot composed nine violin concertos, variation sets, studies and chamber music. He prepared some editions (notably of BEETHOVEN's Violin Concerto), 'resurrected' music by various Baroque composers and, along with RODE and RODOLPHE KREUTZER, codified Viotti's principles in the Conservatoire's first official violin treatise (1803).

Baillot also edited a cello treatise co-edited by JEAN HENRI LEVASSEUR, Charles-Simon Catel and Charles-Nicolas Baudiot (*Méthode de violoncelle et de basse accompagnement* (Paris: Janet et Cotelle, n.d. [1804]). DUPORT's principles are evident in their consideration of some technical issues, notably the FINGERING of HARMONICS and chromatic scales, but they are progressive in their recommended cello hold, associating the fourth finger with thumb position fingerings, exploiting varied BOWINGS and dynamic levels suited to the Tourte-model bow and urging taste and restraint in implementing expressive devices such as PORTAMENTO and ORNAMENTATION. They also include a detailed account of bass accompaniment, including recitative accompaniment, even though that art was dying out by that time.

Describing the collaborative 1803 violin method as 'an experiment', Baillot resolved to remedy its omissions in his *L'art du violon* (1835). One of the most comprehensive and significant nineteenth-century violin treatises, *L'art* was translated into German twice within a year of its Paris publication and soon appeared in a second French edition and Spanish translation. It comprises two parts. Section two is a reprint, with a brief introduction, of the earlier *Méthode*'s text about EXPRESSION. Part one integrates technical, musical and artistic elements in unprecedented detail, using a three-step pedagogical approach: explanation of the technique; exercises for its practice; and examples of its application. Baillot's violin hold approximates modern methods and even allows a shoulder pad for comfortable support of the instrument. The 'Geminiani grip' retains its currency, but with a more advanced thumb position for greater mobility and facility with extensions. Baillot's mix of thumb, index-finger and wrist-joint pressure on the bow relates to the Tourte model and approximates current practice.

Baillot divides bow strokes into two categories according to speed (slow or fast), stressing the importance of bow division for optimum effect, but includes a 'composite' stroke, which adopts elements of slow and fast strokes simultaneously. His fundamental fast strokes are different types of *détaché*, which may be 'muted' (*mats*) – on-the-string strokes articulated by wrist and forearm (*grand détaché, martelé*, staccato); 'elastic' (*élastiques*) – mostly off-string strokes (*détaché léger, perlé, sautillé, staccato à ricochet*, 'flying staccato'); or 'dragged' (*traînés*) – composite on-the-string strokes (*détaché plus ou moins appuyé, détaché flûté*). He thoroughly surveys specific and extempore ORNAMENTATION, including some elaborate endings in his fermata embellishments, and distinguishes three VIBRATO types: a wavering effect caused by variation of bow-stick pressure; normal left-hand vibrato; and a combination of the two. He advocates its sparing employment, using only narrow finger movement and allowing notes to be begun and terminated without vibrato for intonation purposes. He illustrates Viotti's vibrato usage, linking it with the *messa di voce*.

Baillot distinguishes three kinds of fingering: the most secure; the easiest (for small hands); and the expressive. He contrasts Viotti's string-crossing and general avoidance of shifts, Kreutzer's frequent shifts and Rode's more uniform timbral goals incorporating portamento. He approves of tasteful portamentos, especially in slow movements and sustained melodies. His consideration of extensions introduces for the first time the fingered-octave technique.

Baillot makes the traditional connection between music and speech in his consideration of phrasing, equating musical rests with punctuation marks and introducing unannotated 'light separations'. Musical character, ACCENT and various effects (notably unisons and octaves, harmonics, muted sounds, pizzicato, difference-tones, quadruple stopping, SCORDATURA and rhythm) come under close scrutiny, but Baillot's advice extends beyond violin study to PRELUDING, career guidance, programme planning, PLAYING FROM MEMORY and platform manner; he even lobbies for the introduction of a standard PITCH.

Many of Baillot's other writings are significant for their critical insights into Parisian musical life during the period from the Revolution to the July Monarchy.

FURTHER READING

P. M. F. Baillot, *The Art of the Violin*, ed. and trans. L. Goldberg (Evanston, IL: Northwestern University Press, 1991).

B. François-Sappey, 'Pierre Marie François de Sales Baillot (1771–1842) par lui-même: étude de sociologie musicale', *RMFC*, 18 (1978), 126–211.

A. Penesco, 'Pierre Baillot et l'école franco-belge de violon', in A.-M. Bongrain and A. Poirier (eds.), *Le Conservatoire de Paris: deux cents ans de pédagogie, 1795–1995* (Paris: Buchet-Chastel, 1999), 91–9.

ROBIN STOWELL

Baines, Anthony (Cuthbert) (b. London, 6 October 1912; d. Farnham, 2 February 1997) Organologist, bassoonist and conductor.

Anthony Baines was a leading authority on wind instruments. His books *Woodwind Instruments and their History* (London: Faber, 1957), *Bagpipes* (Oxford University Press, 1960) and *Brass Instruments, their History and Development* (London: Faber, 1976) have all proved highly influential. His broader organological interests are represented in his comprehensive study *European and American Musical Instruments* (London: Batsford, 1966) and *The Oxford Companion to Musical Instruments* (Oxford University Press, 1992), notable for its breadth and succinct but eminently readable style. In 1968 he catalogued the non-keyboard instruments of the Victoria and Albert Museum collection (now disbanded).

In 1946 Baines was a founder member (with ten others) of the Galpin Society. The inaugural meeting in May the following year comprised music by C. P. E. BACH, Dowland, Falconieri, LULLY, HANDEL, MORLEY, Neruda, PHILIDOR *l'aîné* and Carl Stamitz. In 1948 he published an article on the wind instruments of the TALBOT MANUSCRIPT in the library of Christ Church, Oxford. This appeared in the first volume of the *Galpin Society Journal*, of which he was editor from 1956 to 1963 and again from 1970 to 1983. In the 1950s he provided material for the new English Consort which was run by Marilyn Wailes, producing specifications for a thirteenth–fourteenth-century psaltery, which was then recreated. He published performing editions of *Music for Sagbutts* and the *Water Music* and also provided a number of articles on instruments for *Grove* V. He edited *Musical Instruments throughout the Ages*, published by Penguin for the Galpin Society in 1961. Apart from the preface, his own contribution was on 'Ancient and folk backgrounds', a topic which had not previously been encapsulated for a general readership.

Baines's organological expertise was founded on practical experience. Having read chemistry at Oxford, he changed direction with an open scholarship to the ROYAL COLLEGE OF MUSIC, before joining the London Philharmonic Orchestra, where he played BASSOON and CONTRABASSOON from 1935 until the outbreak of war. He continued his musical activities as a prisoner of war and then returned to the LPO. After a period as associate conductor with the International Ballet, he joined the music staff of Uppingham School and later moved to Dean Close School. At this time he travelled extensively in Europe, studying both folk and art instruments and taking part in international conferences. After Philip Bate presented his remarkable collection of woodwind instruments to Oxford University, Baines was a natural choice as its first curator from 1970 to 1980. During that decade, the collection expanded rapidly, initially through his own generosity. The Bate Collection of Historical Woodwind Instruments soon attracted other loans and gifts, widening its scope with brass instruments and specimens from other cultures. Among significant donors were Reginald Morley-Pegge and Edgar Hunt. Baines's curatorship was highly influential, because in accordance with Bate's wishes he ran the collection not merely as a museum but also as a centre for the study of musical instruments of all periods. He was thus an important influence on many younger players of historical instruments. The American Musical Instrument Society presented the CURT SACHS Award to him in 1985 for his contribution to 'a fuller understanding of the parallels and interactions between folk and art traditions'. His writings are informed by a rare combination of enthusiasm, wit and authority, which reflect Baines's exuberant personality.

FURTHER READING

J. Montagu, 'Anthony Baines, 1912–97', *EMc*, 25 (1997), 345–6.
J. Rimmer, 'Anthony Cuthbert Baines (1912–1997): A biographical memoir', *GSJ*, 52 (1999), 11–26.

COLIN LAWSON

Banchieri, Adriano (b. Bologna, 3 September 1568; d. Bologna, 1634) Italian organist, composer and theorist.

As a Benedictine monk, Banchieri was organist at a number of monasteries in Lucca, Siena and Bologna, as well as churches in Venice and Verona. In 1604 he met GIROLAMO DIRUTA at the monastery of San Pietro, Gubbio, and described the important Fiammingo organ in *Conclusioni nel suono dell'organo* (Bologna, 1608). In *L'Organo suonarino* (Venice, 1605) and its various revisions and editions (1611, 1622, 1638), Banchieri describes the realisation of bass figures and gives instructions for the accompaniment of liturgical chant. In the *Dialogo musicale ... sopra un basso continuo* (1611), instruction is given to organists on registration and continuo playing, including such advice as not to spoil with runs and ornaments the ornamental passages notated in singers' parts. An early direction to play *arpeggiato* is found in the 1638 edition, and in *Cartella musicale* (1614), his counterpoint treatise, a table of vocal ornaments was included. Banchieri was one of the first composers to notate dynamic markings.

FURTHER READING

Anthology of Early Keyboard Methods, ed. and trans. B. Sachs and B. Ife (Cambridge: Gamut Publications, 1981).
A. Silbiger (ed.), *Keyboard Music before 1700* (New York and London: Routledge, 2004).
C. Zotti, *Le sourire du moine: Adriano Banchieri da Bologna: musicien, homme de lettres, pédagogue, équilibriste sur le fil des querelles du Seicento* (Nice: Serre Editeur, 2008).

DAVID PONSFORD

Baroque Gesture The art of gesture, founded on principles of Greek and Roman oratory, was practised until the mid-nineteenth century as an indispensable element of rhetorical delivery. Performance was studied as *pronuntiatio* (vocal delivery) and *actio* or gesture, the 'action and position of all the parts of the body' (G. Austin, *Chironomia* (London: printed for T. Cadell and W. Davies by W. Bulmer, 1806), 133). Austin's notational system specifies positions and movements of hands and feet within an imaginary sphere extending outwards from the performer. John Bulwer retells Cicero's and Quintilian's story of Demosthenes being asked to list the three principal points of eloquence: the answers were 'Action!', 'Action!', 'Action!' (*Chirologia & Chironomia* (London, 1644), pt 2, 22). Quintilian advised a gesture every three or four words, though Shakespeare's Hamlet warned, 'do not saw the air too much with your hand' (Act III, scene ii). Within the philosophical framework of AFFECTIONS and the four humours, gesture unites heart and hand to give 'shape, figure and winning glory unto eloquence' (Bulwer, 5).

In current usage, opera 'with Baroque gesture' can imply historically informed stage production, extending to scenery, lighting, actors' positions and movements. Nevertheless, gesture is not limited to theatrical performance, but – with due allowance for propriety in varied situations – was employed whenever words were pronounced. The 'speaking action' of John Donne's sermons, his 'carriage' and 'gesture' were 'such as could divide the heart' (Bulwer, 20). Historical action refined natural gestures according to artistic principles, social etiquette and rhetorical teachings. Giovanni Bonifacio's *L'arte de' cenni* (Vicenza, 1616) catalogues gestures of the entire body from head to toe, commenting on their dignity, delightfulness and efficacy: 'sincerity of the spirit is better revealed by gestures than by words' (ch. 2). Baroque performers' bodies were conditioned by walking, horse riding, dancing and swordfighting. The default stance was the *contrapposto* familiar from period art: diagonally on to the spectators, weight on one leg, the right hand presented, the fingers progressively more curved from index to little finger, and the middle two fingers close together.

Bulwer's illustrations (Figure 2) show gestures for words (immensity, worthlessness), deeds (begging, threatening), emotions (sadness, triumph, awe, anger) and rhetorical devices (irony, distinguishing contraries, arguing, numbering points). He emphasises the dominance of the right hand, with the left hand alone used only for negative gestures of rejection or abhorrence. The hands normally remain above the waist and below the eyes. Sung texts offer many opportunities for contrasting gestures. When Orfeo bids 'farewell to earth, farewell to heaven and sun!', MONTEVERDI's low and high phrases would have been accompanied with low and high gestures (Act II). Such frequently encountered pointing-words as 'here', 'now' and 'I' encourage gestures that reinforce the sense of immediacy. Monteverdi remarked that one should: 'Make steps and gestures according to the text ... so that the three actions [text, music, movement] meet in a unified representation' (*Combattimento* in *Madrigali Libro Ottavo* (Venice, 1638), BASSO CONTINUO partbook, 19). This reflects Cavalieri's earlier view that 'Words should be accompanied with gestures and movements, both hands and feet, which are very effective means to move the passions' (*Rappresentatione di Anima et di Corpo* (Rome, 1600), preface).

In spite of the historical importance of gesture and the increasing prevalence nowadays of historically informed productions of early opera, most current conservatoire training does not equip young singers with the rhetorical skill set

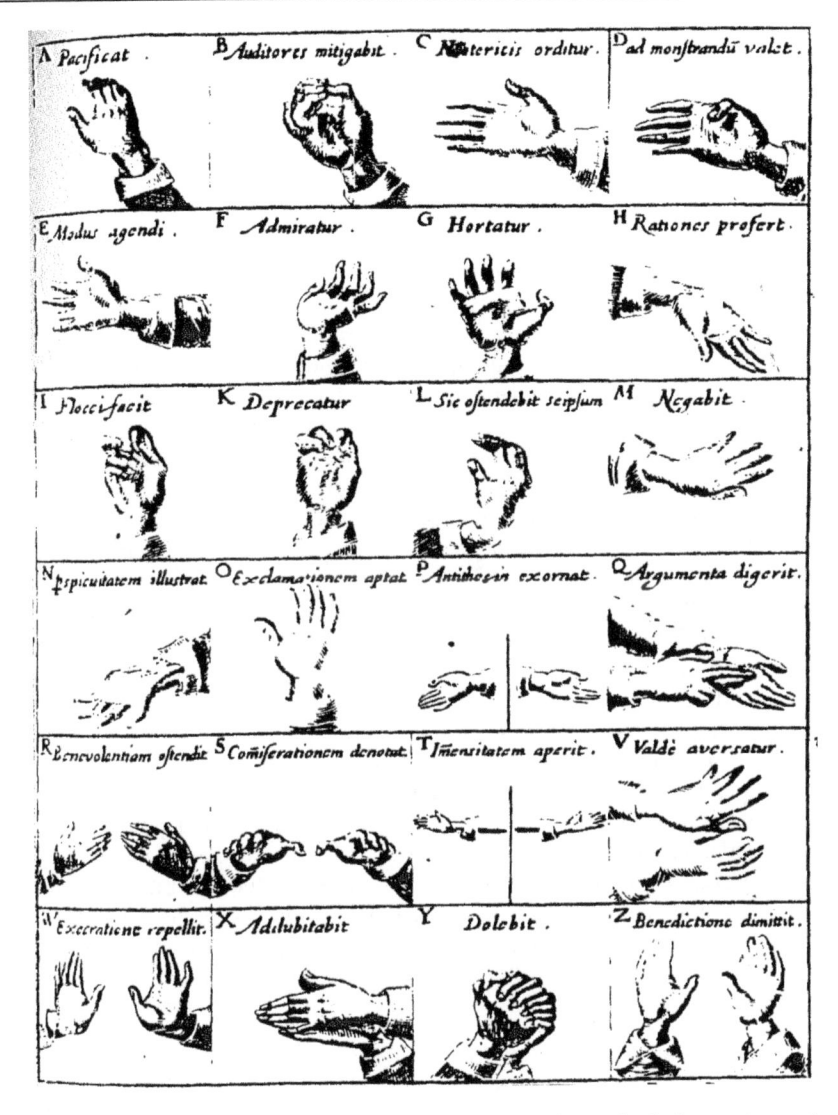

Figure 2: Examples of John Bulwer's illustrations of gestures for words, deeds, emotions and rhetorical devices.

of their Baroque predecessors. Until action is trained as a fundamental skill alongside foreign languages and period ORNAMENTATION, gesture risks being seen as 'bolted on', when it should be 'built in'.

FURTHER READING

D. Barnett, *The Art of Gesture: The Practices and Principles of Eighteenth-century Acting* (Heidelberg: C. Winter, 1987).

G. Bonifacio, *L'arte de' cenni* (Vicenza: F. Grossi, 1616), trans. in A. Lawrence-King, *The Art of Gesture* (Moscow: Opera Omnia, 2018).

P. Fabbri and A. Pompilio, *Il Corago o vero alcune osservazioni per metter bene in scena le composizioni drammatiche* (Florence, 1983), partial trans. in R. Savage and M. Sansone. '"Il Corago" and the staging of early opera: four chapters from an anonymous treatise circa 1630', *EMc*, 17/4 (1989), 495–511.

D. Harrán, 'Toward a rhetorical code of early music performance', *JM*, 15/1 (1997), 19–42.

ANDREW LAWRENCE-KING

Barrel Organ A mechanical instrument, the notes of which are defined by pins hammered into a horizontal, normally wooden cylinder.

When the cylinder is set in motion, usually through a hand-operated crank, the pins lift pivoted levers, or keys, which in turn open the valve of the corresponding pipe or reed-pipe arranged in one to four stops. The crank also operates a bellow which pumps air through the pipes.

Mentions of instruments of this kind survive from as early as the ninth century in Byzantine sources and recur often in European treatises of the sixteenth and seventeenth centuries, including Salomon de Caus, Robert Fludd, Athanasius Kircher and later Filippo Bonanni. However, it is between the second half of the eighteenth and the first of the nineteenth centuries that the popularity of the barrel organ reached its peak, with over 130 makers active in the UK alone: sizes varied from the single-stop *serinette*, used to train birds to sing, to the large church and chamber instruments which were used as replacement for church bands and home entertainment. Each instrument would typically be sold with a selection of barrels, to offer a choice of hymns, dance and opera repertoire, each including several tunes that could be selected by sliding the barrel sideways.

The use of barrels as sources for the study of TEMPO, ORNAMENTATION and performance practice is tantalising and has been discussed on several occasions, without yet reaching a convincing conclusion regarding its actual potential and reliability: texts of the time refer to the capability of the best makers to obtain effects equal to the fingers of the first-rate performers and the study of surviving barrels sometimes shows irregularities which might in fact reflect musical intention. An increasing number of digital scanning projects is currently being undertaken and might soon shed further light on the issue.

FURTHER READING

A. W. J. G. Ord Hume, *Barrel Organ: The Story of the Mechanical Organ and How to Restore it* (London: George Allen & Unwin, 1978).

M. Di Sandro, *Macchine musicali al tempo di Händel* (Firenze: Leo S. Olschki, 2012).

GABRIELE ROSSI ROGNONI

Bartók, Béla (b. Nagyszentmiklós, Hungary (now Sânnicolau Mare, Romania), 25 March 1881; d. New York, 26 September 1945) Hungarian composer, pianist, ethnomusicologist and teacher.

Although a leader of the first generation of modernist composers, Bartók performed in a largely late Romantic style, inherited from his piano teacher István Thomán, a pupil of Liszt. In his earlier years Bartók edited several Hungarian-themed works for the first Liszt Critical Edition, including the Hungarian Rhapsodies; he also produced highly prescriptive editions of core piano repertory by J. S. BACH, BEETHOVEN, HAYDN, MOZART, Chopin,

COUPERIN, Scarlatti, Schubert and Schumann. From the mid-1920s, his creative ideal shifted from Beethoven towards Bach, influencing his compositional techniques, choice of performing repertory and performance style. This shift led him, for instance, to perform his own concert arrangements of works by Bach, Purcell and a series of Baroque Italian masters in the later 1920s.

The scores of Bartók's compositions disclose his distinctive performing interests, such as with timings – through TEMPO, METRONOME and durational annotations – and ARTICULATIONS – through wedge, staccato, PORTA(MEN)TO, half-staccato, tenuto, slur signs and their various combinations, reflecting his wide array of percussive and non-percussive touch-types. His mature practice is perhaps most comprehensively codified in his six volumes of *Mikrokosmos* piano pieces and associated exercises (1926–39).

Unlike STRAVINSKY, Bartók neither aspired to an 'objective music' nor to minimising the intervention of the performer. In his essay 'Mechanical Music' (1937), he asserted the primary importance of live performance, considering any recording was, at best, 'a surrogate'. But he recognised the pedagogic and scientific importance of recordings: to communicate 'those infinite, minute nuances which cannot be expressed notationally, yet can be immortalized in their totality on gramophone records'. The recording was invaluable through preserving a composer's 'works according to his own idea at a given moment', although it always involved 'the variability of live music' because 'perpetual variability is a trait of a living creature's character'. Bartók, none the less, did claim some of his own later recordings as 'authentic', and his publisher acknowledged these recordings as such in the relevant scores.

László Somfai (1996) described the six-hour heritage of Bartók's recordings of his own music (*Bartók at the Piano*, 1994) as 'extremely large, many-sided and important', leading to detailed studies of Bartók's use of RUBATO (from four extant recordings of his 'Evening in Transylvania') and of his substantial variability in tempos, DYNAMICS, touch, and even in adding or deleting sections (from *Allegro Barbaro* recordings). Somfai also tracked how the various elements of Bartók's interpretation changed, both over time and between genres. These recordings have influenced not just performance of Bartók's piano works but also his works for strings and for voice. High-quality HMV recordings of 1928, of *Eight Hungarian Folksongs* (1917/27) and *Five Hungarian Folk Tunes* (1928), with Bartók accompanying three leading Hungarian singers, are authoritative guides to such issues as portamento, rubato, intonation, ORNAMENTATION and rhythmic adaptation to linguistic features, as well as tempo and timing issues.

Hungaroton's *Bartók New Series* of recordings of his compositions, issued since 2008 under Zoltán Kocsis's direction, explicitly perpetuates a Hungarian performance tradition rooted in the playing of Bartók and his associates. The six string quartets, for instance, in this series played by the Mikrokosmos Quartet led by Gábor Takács-Nagy, lie in an interpretative tradition stretching back to the Waldbauer-Kerpely and KOLISCH Quartets, which premiered most of these works under Bartók's original guidance. Nowhere is this legacy seen more strongly than in the very consistency in rendition of Bartók's most distinctive string techniques, including *sul tasto, sul ponticello*, glissando,

HARMONICS, multiple-stopping, strumming, *martellato*, and the signature 'Bartók pizzicato'.

The complete critical edition of Bartók's works, launched by G. Henle Verlag and Editio Musica Budapest in 2015, with László Vikárius as editor-in-chief, recognises Bartók's recordings, along with his sketch-to-score materials, correspondence and editions of other composers' works, as essential sources to imaginative, informed, yet twenty-first-century interpretations of his *oeuvre*.

FURTHER READING

B. Bartók, 'Mechanical music', in B. Suchoff (ed.), *Béla Bartók Essays* (London: Faber & Faber, 1976), 289–98.
Z. Kocsis (ed.), *Bartók New Series* (Budapest: Hungaroton, 2008–).
L. Somfai, 'On Bartók's notation and performing style', in *Béla Bartók: Composition, Concepts, and Autograph Sources* (Berkeley, CA: University of California Press, 1996).
L. Somfai and Z. Kocsis (eds.), *Bartók at the Piano, 1920–1945* (Budapest: Hungaroton, 1994), HCD 12326–31.

MALCOLM GILLIES

Baryton (bariton, barydon, paradon, paridon, pariton, viola di bardone, viola di bordone) A bass stringed instrument that can be simultaneously bowed from above and plucked from behind.

The baryton probably originated in the early seventeenth century in England as an amalgamation of features of the bass viol (gut strings and fretted fingerboard), lyra viol and bandora (wire 'sympathetic' strings, strung below the fingerboard) into one hybrid instrument. The earliest extant example, by Magnus Feldlen (Vienna, 1647) is preserved in the ROYAL COLLEGE OF MUSIC, London. In its original state, it had the standard six-string bowed manual and nine wire, sympathetic strings of the Baroque instrument; it would have been played 'lyra-way' as a solo instrument from TABLATURE, the bowed strings defining the melody line to an accompaniment plucked by the left thumb.

The Classical form of the instrument involved modification of the Baroque set-up, the lower manual strings being tuned to the same pitch range as the upper four strings of the bowed manual (c–d′). A seventh string was also added to the bowed manual, and the number of lower manual strings, differently attached, was increased, sometimes to fifteen or more; a third manual, with gut strings, was also added by some makers. HAYDN and his Esterházy colleagues (Luigi Tomasini, Joseph Purksteiner and Anton Neumann) composed the most significant corpus of music for the Classical baryton at the behest of Prince Nicolas, who was a keen barytonist. The prince's instrument, by Johann Joseph Stadlmann (Vienna, 1750), had seven bowed strings (tuned A′, D, G, c, e, a, d′) and ten sympathetic strings (tuned A, d, e, f♯, g, a, b, c♯, d′, e′). Haydn himself composed *c*200 works involving the instrument between *c*1765 and *c*1775, including duets, trios, quintets, divertimentos and concertos. He notated them in the treble clef, sounding an octave below; the plucked notes were indicated by numbers below the treble staff, the strings numbered from lowest to highest (opposite to earlier practice). This system of tuning and NOTATION has become standard in the instrument's modern revival.

FURTHER READING

C. Gartrell, *A History of the Baryton and its Music: King of Instruments, Instrument of Kings* (Lanham, MD: Scarecrow Press, 2009).
T. M. Pamplin, 'The Baroque baryton: The origin and development in the 17th century of a solo, self-accompanying, bowed and plucked instrument played from tablature', PhD dissertation, Kingston University (2000).

ROBIN STOWELL

Bassano, Giovanni (b. ?Venice, *c*1560/61; d. Venice, 16 August 1617) Venetian cornett virtuoso and composer.

At the age of fifteen or sixteen Bassano was named cornettist in the Doge's wind band and later in the musical chapel of St Mark's. From 1601 he was leader of the instrumental ensemble there. He also taught singing, solfeggio and counterpoint at the ducal seminary from 1583. He was a skilful composer of polychoral motets and canzonettas, but is best known for his two volumes dedicated to the art of improvised divisions. One contains solo ricercars, probably intended as models for IMPROVISATION, and patterns for ornamenting intervals and cadences. The other (destroyed in WWII but surviving in a manuscript of Friedrich Chrysander) consists of complete sets of divisions on motets, chansons and madrigals from the second half of the century. These divisions are carefully and elegantly constructed and show different styles for instrumental and vocal improvisation, with the former displaying quicker note values, greater rhythmic variety and larger intervals.

FURTHER READING

G. M. Ongaro, 'New documents on the Bassano family', *EMc*, 20/3 (August, 1992), 409–13.
E. Selfridge-Field, 'Bassano and the orchestra of St Mark's', *EMc*, 4/2 (April, 1976) 152–8.

BRUCE DICKEY

Bass Clarinet *see* CLARINET

Basset Clarinet *see* CLARINET

Basset Horn *see* CLARINET

Basso Continuo The term 'basso continuo' was first coined by Lodovico Viadana in his *Cento concerto ecclesiastici ... con il basso continuo* (Venice, 1602). It refers to the pan-European practice, fundamental to seventeenth- and eighteenth-century ensemble music, in which keyboards and string instruments (plucked and bowed) 'realised' the harmonies implied by instrumental and vocal bass lines, the individual notes of which were sometimes figured (either above or below) by numerals and accidentals. The figures indicated the musical intervals to be played above the written bass to produce the correct harmonies within the given key, irrespective of the octave. Within this practice there were various conventions involving figures (and their omission), the application of accidentals and procedures relating to standard chord progressions. Essentially, the practice was that of directed IMPROVISATION, but the system became an important tool in the teaching of harmony.

Throughout the period, the system contained ambiguities and lacked precision, but among the issues for consideration by performers are the choice of instruments, the manner of realisation (complexity *versus* simplicity), types of arpeggiation, treatment of contrapuntal parts, the doubling of upper parts, the addition of dissonances, the elaboration or simplification of the written bass, the placing of cadences (in recitatives) and the choice of chords for unfigured basses. Information relating to such topics is dependent on chronology, geographic region, musical genre, instrumental idiom and individual compositional style.

During the late sixteenth century, the development of the practice of organists accompanying from full scores to playing from a single bass line appears to have emerged for reasons of convenience. However, it was with the development of the self-consciously expressive, harmonically orientated *seconda pratica* around 1600 that basso continuo became a fundamental component of musical style in both composition and performance. The practice lasted until c1800 when more sophisticated harmony led to ever more complex figures. The last examples of the practice occurred in both theatre and church, and both MOZART and BEETHOVEN included figures in their piano concertos.

In the late sixteenth century, unfigured basses were often used in large-scale, vertically conceived polychoral works, such as Striggio's forty-part motet *Ecce beatam lucem* (extant parts 1587), in which the continuous bass line is a compilation of several vocal bass parts. Whilst the earliest sources teaching the improvisation of a chordal texture date back to Hans Buchner's *Fundamentum* (c1525), the first scores with FIGURED BASS were Peri's opera *Euridice* (1600), Cavalieri's *Rappresentatione di anima, et di corpo* (1600) and CACCINI's *Nuove musiche* (1602). However, in the introduction to his *Concerti ecclesiastici* (1610), Piccioni deliberately omitted accidentals and numerals on the grounds that it would confuse unskilled organists, and skilled players would not need them. Nevertheless, unfigured basses do pose problems for modern editors and players, leading to ambiguities over harmony (even the choice between major and minor chords), particularly so within a period that spanned the decline of the modal system and witnessed the emergence of the major–minor key system. Such harmonic ambiguities can only be informed, together with guides to realisation of unfigured basses, with reference to seventeenth-century rules of consonance and dissonance, counterpoint, interval regulation and voice-leading, found in treatises by Bermudo (1555), SANTA MARÍA (1557), ZARLINO (1558), DIRUTA (1593, 1609), MORLEY (1597) up to GASPARINI (1708). Furthermore, analysis of these topics in contemporaneous compositions is crucial to an understanding of stylistic continuo playing in seventeenth-century music. For example, many theorists recommended points of imitation to be doubled, a practice that was retained in fugal textures into the eighteenth century. However, the doubling of a solo part was contentious. It was recommended by Diruta (1609), Penna (*Li primi albori musicali*, Bologna, 1672) and BISMANTOVA (1677), but discouraged by AGAZZARI (1607), Da Gagliano (1608) and Gasparini (1708).

In England, playing from unfigured or figured basses developed later than in Italy, probably as a result of the predominantly polyphonic compositional styles of early seventeenth-century church and consort music. The earliest extant example of an English 'thorough basse' is probably that for Tallis's forty-part *Spem in alium*, written possibly in 1571. Instructive examples of written-out organ parts occur in consort music by Coperario (c1575–1626), Jenkins (1592–1678) and William Lawes (1602–45).

During the first decades of the seventeenth century, many German composers (under Italian influence) prefaced their compositions with instructions on how to realise figured basses, although in 1648 Schütz only presented a continuo part for his *Geistliche Chormusik* at the request of his publisher. Written-out accompaniments survive from the mid-sixteenth century, including realised accompaniments to songs by Peri, CACCINI, Dowland, MORLEY, Le Roy, Moulinié, Kapsberger and Castaldi. These are instructive for their lute and keyboard textures, overt parallel fifths and octaves, the melodic relationship between accompaniment and vocal line, treatment of dissonance, choice of chords and treatment of passing notes in the bass.

Numerals indicating musical intervals were used in counterpoint treatises from the sixteenth century, so it was logical that they came to be used to indicate chords above a bass. Initially, sharps and flats were added (signifying major or minor chords), followed (sparingly) by digits such as '6' and '4' to clarify ambiguous passages. MONTEVERDI and Cavalieri specified 3–4–4–3 progressions, although figures are mostly absent from their scores. Such pieces as Monteverdi's *Orfeo* (1609) and *Vespro della Beata Vergine* (1610) are full of ambiguities as to what chords were intended, and whether the chords should agree harmonically with the soloist or consciously disagree to create expressive false relations. Theory books often prescribed that certain bass progressions (such as C♯ to D) would imply a $^6_3$ chord, and players would learn standard rules such as the 'Rule of the Octave'. Furthermore, Italian typefaces did not always clearly differentiate between flats ('♭') and '6', and sometimes accidentals on their own above a note would indicate a sharp or flat '6' in addition to a sharp or flat '3'. Compound figures (those above '9', so that '10' would indicate an octave and a third) were used to indicate an actual pitch, not only its harmonic position. Caccini used figures up to '14', and Cavalieri up to '18'.

Fundamental to the manner of realising figured basses on the HARPSICHORD are the differences between national schools of harpsichord building. The immediate attack, tone colour and limited sustaining power of the Italian harpsichord contrast markedly with the sonorous tenor and bass, and long sustaining quality, of a French instrument. The realisation given in J. H. D'ANGLEBERT's *Principes de l'accompagnement* (*Pièces de clavecin*, 1689) exploits the French qualities with seven-part chords in the tenor–bass register, incorporating arpeggio, *acciaccature* and *coulés*.

Reports of J. S. BACH's continuo playing suggest a vivid accompanist who elaborated continuo parts into obbligato pieces, converted trios into quartets and constantly produced unexpected counter-subjects. However, the rules at the end of Anna Magdalena's book support C. P. E. BACH's claim that his father taught strict four-part thoroughbass. Pieces such as the *Largo e dolce* from J. S. Bach's Sonata in B minor (BWV1030) for flute and harpsichord provide us with an ideal continuo realisation of a slow movement. Accompaniment of German recitative on the ORGAN also calls for comment. The custom, established by around 1750, was to accompany recitative with short chords, no matter how long the bass notes were notated. This practice is described in TÜRK's *Von den wichtigsten Pflichten eines Organisten* (Halle, 1787, 162–4) as 'one of the organist's most important rules', and is exemplified by the short notes in the continuo parts of Bach's *St Matthew Passion*, even though the autograph full score contains conventional long notes with ties.

Instruments

Although the organ was understood to be the principal continuo instrument for church music, with parts from 1600 to 1800 labelled '*organo*' or '*basso per l'organo*', harpsichords were used when the organ was, in some countries, banned in Lent or just in Holy Week. Many Italian organs were provided with a harpsichord manual for this purpose, and larger German churches such as the Thomaskirche, Leipzig, retained a harpsichord. For his *Historia der Auferstehung* (1623), Schütz suggested that the evangelist be accompanied by 'a large or small organ, or also a harpsichord, lute or pandora, according to choice'. In the English Chapel Royal, two THEORBOS were sometimes used with the organ for accompanimental purposes. In Spain, from the 1550s throughout the period, the HARP was used in larger churches and was expected to play elaborate accompaniments, with the organ joining in tutti sections.

Organ registrations changed throughout the period and from country to country. Antegnati (*L'arte organica*, 1608) and MONTEVERDI (*Vespers*, 1610) recommend Principals 8' up to 8', 4' and 2' and so on to *organo pleno* on the single manual Italian organ. The more varied German organ allowed greater variety, with PRAETORIUS (1619) recommending two keyboards of differing DYNAMICS, loud and soft. Schütz (1623) advised accompanying recitative on a quiet 8' flute.

From its first use in the Florentine *intermedii* in 1589, the chitarrone became the prime instrument for accompanying monodic song. Other instruments mentioned in publications were the harpsichord, LUTE, GUITAR and double harp. For monodic songs, a single instrument was considered sufficient, but melodic bass instruments were used in stage works. Monteverdi's *Combattimento* (1624) uses a *contrabasso da gamba* with harpsichord throughout, although the combination of harpsichord and the (later) CELLO was not common in Italy before the last decade of the seventeenth century. Even so, many publications into the eighteenth century specified harpsichord as an alternative to the violone/cello, suggesting that the cello played a partially chordal accompaniment. CORELLI's *Sonate da chiesa* Opp. 1 and 3 specify violone or ARCHLUTE together with the organ. Multiple plucked stringed instruments played continuo in large concerto orchestras at the end of the century. GEORG MUFFAT (*Auserlesene Instrumentalmusik*, 1701) suggested an accompaniment of harpsichords, theorbos, harps and 'similar instruments' depending on resources, although the *concertino* should be played only by either an organist or a theorbo player. 'Violone' in Italy usually signified an 8' pitch, with the 16' CONTRABASSO appearing in larger orchestras in the later part of the seventeenth century. After 1700, opera orchestras supported a continuo group of two harpsichords, sometimes with theorbo, or one harpsichord with cello and DOUBLE BASS.

In early eighteenth-century Germany, the largest centres had the most elaborate instrumental resources. The Dresden court chapel employed a continuo group of two or more cellos, BASSOONS, VIOLONES and theorbos. The harpsichord was used in Lamentations, oratorios and passions in Holy Week, when the organ was silent. In Leipzig, J. S. Bach used one or two cellos and sometimes a violone to reinforce the continuo. His use of the harpsichord is evident, either singly or in combination with the organ, and Bach himself directed the funeral music for the Queen and Electress Christiane Eberhardine from the harpsichord in 1727. The earliest example of a double bassoon occurred in Georg Österreich's *Actus funebris* (1702), giving strength to the *bassono grosso* in Bach's *St John Passion* (1749 version) being a double bassoon at 16' pitch.

In England, the harpsichord was rarely mentioned as an accompanying instrument for songs before 1660, the theorbo being most important right through to c1700 when it became overshadowed by the archlute. Some books of songs include accompaniments for bass VIOL, either chordal in TABLATURES or just a single line. Later publications such as PLAYFORD's *Select Musical Ayres* (1652) specify theorbo, lute and bass viol as alternatives. Theatrical works after the Restoration were influenced by French practices, particularly those of LULLY, but after 1700 fashion swung in favour of Italian opera, with a standard continuo section of two harpsichords, continuous cello and (probably) double bass.

France was later than Italy in adopting the continuo. The first published work to contain a '*bassus continuus*' was Henri Du Mont's *Cantica sacra* (1652), a collection of motets and instrumental pieces in three or four parts. The organ was most important, but Charpentier called also for harpsichord and theorbo. The theorbo came into fashion c1660 and its first recorded use was in Lully's *Ballet d'Alcidiane* (1558).

In 1701 Dieupart's *Six suites pour le clavecin* contained parts for *basse de viole* and archlute in the chamber music version. Some cantata arias, such as Clérambault's, are completely Italian in style, but require a virtuoso French seven-string bass viol. After 1720, the wave of enthusiasm for Italian sonatas and cantatas that began in the 1690s had reached its height, and Italian influence predominated. J.-J.-B. Anet and J. P. Guignon's sonatas include the standard combination of VIOLIN and cello (as an alternative to harpsichord).

In the Classical period, sources indicate that basso continuo remained standard practice. Forty-eight of HAYDN's symphonies were arranged by J. P. Salomon as quintets with keyboard continuo. The first performances of these took place in London (where they were published) with Haydn playing the FORTEPIANO. For his oratorio *The Creation*, sources are ambiguous. The most complete score, the 'Engraver's' score with a set of parts, has figures from the beginning of the work to the middle of No. 7, whereas the 'Estate' score from Haydn's library has figures throughout Parts 1 and 2 plus the final chorus. In the first edition, figures only occur in No. 7, but chords for the fortepiano are essential in the *secco* recitatives.

The figures in the tutti passages in MOZART's piano concertos imply continuo throughout, and the autograph additions to the keyboard part of K246 may suggest help to an amateur player who needed to realise the continuo. Several points can be gleaned from this: 1) the soloist played continuo when the double basses played; 2) when playing continuo, the piano played continuously in the middle register; 3) the piano's allegiance was to the strings, not to the wind; 4) the string bass line was adapted to be idiomatic for the keyboard.

Before BEETHOVEN wrote his *Materialien zum Generalbass* (1809), he evidently left continuo realisation to the performer, but afterwards he stated explicitly how the figured bass should be realised, using 't. s.' to signify when the pianist was to abstain from realising the harmony. The marking '*Col basso continuo*' occurs as late as the *Missa Solemnis*, Op. 123, in whose original edition the basso continuo was realised, and it is clear that the soloist was expected to realise to some extent the figured bass in the piano concertos, right through to the 'Emperor' Concerto, Op. 73.

FURTHER READING

F. T. Arnold, *The Art of Accompaniment from a Thorough-Bass as Practised in the 17th and 18th Centuries* (London: Holland Press, 1931/1961).

T. Borgir, *The Performance of the Basso Continuo in Italian Baroque Music* (Ann Arbor, MI: UMI Research Press, 1987).

J. B. Christensen, *Die Grundlagen des Generalbass-spiels im 18. Jahrhundert* (Kassel: Bärenreiter, 1997).

L. Dreyfus, *Bach's Continuo Group* (Cambridge, MA, and London: Harvard University Press, 1987).

T. M. Klinkhamer, 'Del sonari sopra 'l basso: The theory and practice of basso continuo accompaniment in the seventeenth century', PhD dissertation, University of Leeds (2014).

N. North, *Continuo Playing on the Lute, Archlute and Theorbo: A Comprehensive Guide for Performers* (London and Boston: Faber, 1987).

P. Williams, *Figured Bass Accompaniment*, 2 vols. (Edinburgh University Press, 1970).

DAVID PONSFORD

Bassoon (Fr. *Basson*; Ger. *Fagott*; It. *Fagotto*; Sp. *Fagot* or *Bajon*) Double-reed wind instrument made out of wood, with a conical, folded bore.

The bassoon has appeared in a variety of designs and sizes ever since its development in the early sixteenth century. The one-piece CURTAL developed via a three-piece transitional instrument into the final four-piece bassoon known today. The reed is placed on a bocal, which is fitted into the small end of the bore and traditionally made of metal, such as brass or silver.

The curtal (Engl. also *Dulcian*; Ger. *Dulzian* or *Chorist Fagott*; It. *Fagotto*; Sp. *Bajon*) is a conical, high pitched (*Chorton*), double-reed instrument, usually made of maple. It was originally built as a bass instrument with an open, often flared bell; later in the seventeenth century, it was also made with a covered bell (*gedackt*). In the sixteenth century the curtal was built as a consort, ranging from soprano to octave bass. In the seventeenth century, the smaller curtals went out of vogue, except for Spain, where the smaller instruments (*bajoncillos*) remained popular. Most curtals have two covered keys, one on the front, and one on the back of the instrument. The compass of the bass curtal is, according to the few fingering charts and tables still extant, such as those by MICHAEL PRAETORIUS (1619), Daniel Speer (1697) and Verschuere Reynvaan (1795), C′ to f′ or g′. There is reason to believe that the curtal originates from the first quarter of the sixteenth century in the proximity of Venice, and can be linked to the BASSANO family. Later in the century, the instrument spread through the rest of Europe and was brought to Latin America by the missionaries. In this period, the main use of the curtal was reinforcing or replacing singers in vocal repertoire. With the development of instrumental music in Venice in the first half of the seventeenth century, the role of the *fagotto* drastically changed, instigated by virtuosi on the curtal, such as Bartolomé de Selma y Salaverde (*fl.* 1638), Giovanni Antonio Bertoli (1598–after 1645) and Philip Friedrich Böddecker (1607–83), into a highly virtuosic solo instrument. In the last quarter of the seventeenth century, with the development of the new French-style instruments in low pitch (*Tief-Kammerton*), the curtal, together with other wind instruments such as the cornetto and the sackbut, slowly receded into the background, though in Spain the curtal, with several added keys, remained in use in church until the twentieth century.

During the reign of Louis XIV, Nicolas HOTTETERRE and other members of the family developed the Baroque bassoon. The function of the *basson* was the accompaniment of the Baroque oboe (as JOHANN MATTHESON later describes in 1713) and to reinforce the bass group in the orchestra. Among the first composers to write music for this new instrument were LULLY and CHARPENTIER. Compared with the curtal, its bell was prolonged to produce a low B♭, the lowest string of the *basse de violon*. The Baroque bassoon was made out of four joints. The earliest specimens were fitted with three keys; later the fourth key for g♯ was added. A fifth key for low E♭ appears only in the third quarter of the eighteenth century. The French, low-pitched bassoon was soon emulated by various instrument makers through Europe, such as Jakob Denner in Nürnberg and Richard Haka in Amsterdam. In the first half of the eighteenth century, Leipzig became an important centre of bassoon making, with leading makers such as JOHANN HEINRICH EICHENTOPF, Johann Poerschmann and G. H. Scherer. It is likely that these makers provided instruments for the performances of cantatas by J. S. BACH in Leipzig. Thomas Stanesby junior was an important English contemporary. In the seventeenth and eighteenth century, there were great differences in pitch across different geographical areas. In the Baroque period the role of the bassoon was a supporting rather than solo one. However, the instrument was also used in an obbligato capacity in cantatas and in chamber music repertoire by composers such as J. S. Bach and Telemann. Composers such as Johann Friedrich Fasch, Capel Bond and, most importantly, Antonio Vivaldi, with thirty-nine works for bassoon and strings, composed concertos which are often demanding.

During the second half of the eighteenth century the bassoon underwent major changes. The instrument developed from 'the proud bassoon' described by Mattheson, to a much more refined and elegant instrument. Its function changed from a fundamental bass instrument to a lyrical tenor instrument. This transformation is likely to have been instigated by the famous Besozzi family of double-reed players, whose members spread through Europe during the middle of the eighteenth century, introducing the northern Italian oboes and bassoons made by makers such Palanca and Anciuti to the countries north of the Alps. These instruments had narrower bores than the traditional instruments in northern Europe, and inspired Dresden makers such as August and HEINRICH GRENSER and Jakob Grundmann to develop a new style classical instrument with an easier high register, which formed the foundation for the development of the German school of bassoon making in the nineteenth century. In France, the forerunners of bassoon making in the second half of the century were, among others, Prudent Thiériot and Dominique Antony Porthaux. The instruments of these fine makers can be seen as the foundation of the French-system bassoon developed in the nineteenth century. In addition to the change in the bore, in the Classical era, three to five keys were added for low E♭, F♯, B♭, high a' and high c''. The most important keys were the latter ones on the wing-joint, which enlarged the range in the high register, facilitated the tenor register and improved slurring over octaves. Select examples of classical bassoon concertos are that of Mozart (KV191), those of FRANÇOIS DEVIENNE and the two by Johann Christian Bach.

The early nineteenth century was a period of technical experimentation. Among composers of notable concertos for bassoon were JOHANN NEPOMUK HUMMEL and Carl Maria von Weber. A need for greater volume, a more even sound and a higher range instigated major changes in the construction of the bassoon, which lead to a fundamental division between the German- and French-system bassoon incited by two contrasting virtuosi. Carl Almenräder (1786–1846), self-taught bassoonist and inventor, was dissatisfied with the tuning and evenness in sound of the traditional *Dresden* bassoon made by Grenser. While serving as first bassoonist in the Mainz Theatre, Almenräder met composer and theorist GOTTFRIED WEBER. The latter's writings on acoustics and improvements on musical instruments inspired Almenräder to experiment with the design of the bassoon. In 1817 he was employed at the factory of B. Schott Söhne in Mainz, where he was able to apply his improvements. In 1831, Almenräder started a firm with Johann Adam Heckel called 'Almenräder und Heckel' which lasted until 1838. After their separation, J. A. Heckel started his own company. It is likely that he started using the Heckel/Biebrich stamp by 1845. In 1877 Wilhelm Heckel took over the firm after his father's death.

In France, Jean Nicolas Savary (also called Savary *jeune*) and Frédérique Guillaume Adler were the most influential bassoon makers of their time. Savary's instruments show more continuity with the past than those of Almenräder. Savary seemed less concerned with increasing the volume of the bassoon, changing the bore, moving tone-holes or evenness in sound. His inventions mainly deal with the improvement of keywork and adjustability of pitch. His main inventions are the rollers on the F and A♭ keys, the key on the crook hole to facilitate the high register and the ingenious systems to extend the bore in various places on the instrument in order to lower the pitch evenly through the entire range of the instrument. In 1844 Jean-Louis Buffet added his wife's name to the name of his firm, establishing the name Buffet Crampon. In cooperation with the bassoon virtuoso Louis-Marie-Eugène Jancourt, Buffet Crampon became one of the leading makers of French bassoons in the second half of the nineteenth century. French-system bassoons became popular in England, Belgium, Italy and Spain and were in use until the 1970s. Compositions by French composers, such as SAINT-SAËNS, Ravel, STRAVINSKY (e.g. *Le Sacre du Printemps*) and Poulenc, as well as works by Italian and English composers, such as Puccini, Verdi, VAUGHAN WILLIAMS and Holst, were probably intended to be played on a French-system bassoon. It slowly lost popularity in favour of the Heckel model; and eventually, in 1969, the Orchestre de Paris switched to Heckel-system instruments.

The practice of doubling the bass part an octave lower on wind instruments stems from the early seventeenth century, and is already described by Praetorius (1619). Three kinds of dulcians descend lower than eight-foot: the quart, the quint and the octave dulcian. The latter is pitched exactly an octave lower than the bass-size dulcian. The quart bass descends only to GG and the quint bass to FF. Praetorius describes how the quint bass is preferred for playing in flat keys, whereas the quart bass functions better in sharp keys, because of the FINGERINGS for sharps and flats on the instrument. On the octave bass, one can play all the notes in 16 foot range.

The first mention of octave doubling on bassoons was at the Chapelle Royale of the court of Louis XIV. JACQUES DANICAN PHILIDOR is recorded to have played a 'gros basson à la quarte et à l'octave'. Earliest surviving CONTRABASSOONS include a three-key instrument by Andreas Eichentopf dated 1714 and a remarkable instrument of 1732 by Maria Anciuti Mediolani with a bell designed as a dragon's head; Thomas Stanesby junior announced in 1739 that he was manufacturing two contrabassoons. Austria gradually became the centre of classical contrabassoon making. The traditional model was replaced by a more tractable design and the gigantic Baroque bocal was shortened. Later in the nineteenth century, contrabassoon makers focused on developing a more compact and convenient design by introducing new technologies such as rod-axle keys. The modern contrabassoon is based on the 1879 Heckel model.

FURTHER READING

W. Jansen, *The Bassoon, Its History, Construction, Makers, Players and Music* (Buren: Frits Knuf, 1978).
M. Kilbey, *Curtal, Dulcian, Bajón: A History of the Precursor to the Bassoon* (St Albans: the Author, 2002).
J. B. Kopp, *The Bassoon* (New Haven, CT and London: Yale University Press, 2012).
L. G. Langwill, *The Bassoon and Contrabassoon* (London: Benn, 1965).

WOUTER VERSCHUREN

Baumgartner, Johann Baptist (b. Augsburg, 1723; d. Eichstätt, 18 May 1782) German cellist.

Baumgartner was the son of an Augsburg court flautist, and worked both there and at an Augsburg seminary. From 1768 he toured extensively in England (with the patronage of J. C. Bach), Holland, Sweden, Denmark and Germany, and for some years lived in Amsterdam. In 1776 he was elected to the Swedish Academy of Music. He continued to tour widely, in Hamburg, Augsburg, Salzburg and Vienna. In 1778 he joined the Eichstätt Hofkapelle. His *Instructions de musique, théorique et pratique, à l'usage du violoncelle* (The Hague: possibly 1766, or c1774) discusses music theory, left-hand and BOWING techniques, the chordal accompaniment of *secco* recitative (unnecessary in *accompagnato*), and the occasional addition of chords in orchestral playing. His scale FINGERINGS show an attempt to avoid excessive stretches between the third and fourth fingers, but he still adopts a fundamentally tetrachordal approach to scales. Some of his compositions (including a set of six solos with thirty-five CADENZAS in all keys) have survived in manuscript; his posthumously published *Fuga* for solo cello (Vienna, 1797) was included in GRÜTZMACHER's *Höhe Schule* (Leipzig, 1891).

FURTHER READING

G. Kennaway, *Playing the Cello, 1780–1930* (Farnham: Ashgate, 2014).
V. Walden, *One Hundred Years of Violoncello* (Cambridge University Press, 1998).

GEORGE KENNAWAY

Beethoven, Ludwig van (b. Bonn, bap. 17 December 1770; d. Vienna, 26 March 1827) German pianist, conductor and composer.

Beethoven has consistently been at the centre of debates about historical performance. His works challenge performers with confounding and conflicting interpretative choices. These tensions pit individual expressivity against the composer's written intention, and place improvisatory delivery in opposition to an objective, literal rendering. Other interpretative conflicts arise with regard to Beethoven's instrumentation and TEMPO indications.

Beethoven's own pianism raises issues about performance technique, expressivity, good TASTE and insightful interpretation. His reputation as an excellent sight-reader and improviser was sustained throughout his career, and he was noted at various times for rapid-fire execution, a beautiful legato touch and sustained lyricism. Yet critics commonly described a rough-hewn, inconsistent approach – impetuous and energetic as it may have been. Affected by deafness, by 1814 Beethoven's unwieldy, loud style was straining the limits of PIANO construction, while his soft passages were occasionally inaudible. Beethoven's playing abilities by most accounts then deteriorated further. The character of Streicher, Graf, Broadwood and Érard instruments – with which Beethoven became familiar over his lifetime – varied in terms of touch, timbre, dynamic contrast and sustaining potential. No single instrument ever seemed to match his ideal. Writing in 1810, Beethoven offers one definitive insight regarding the appropriate instrument: 'My motto is either to play on a good instrument or not at all' (Newman, 55).

Beethoven's CONDUCTING ability was occasionally seen as wanting in accuracy and clarity. SPOHR described a jumping and crouching technique, seemingly uncoordinated with the orchestra's DYNAMICS and tempo, or the music NOTATION itself (Thayer, II, 257). With imprecision, ambiguity and impetuosity being hallmarks of Beethoven's directing style – traits attributed to deafness – it is no small irony that his METRONOME markings have been attended to so faithfully by many twentieth-century trained conductors and scholars who desire to recreate his precise performance intentions. Seldom considered is the possibility that Beethoven's inability fully to hear a piano or an orchestra by 1813 had also made metronome clicks somewhat if not totally inaudible to him by 1818, the year he had publicly endorsed the device for pedagogical and compositional purposes.

The posthumous history of Beethoven's works provides constant evidence of changing performance practices. Liszt's piano TRANSCRIPTIONS of the nine symphonies offer solo performers showcases for their technical and interpretative prowess. VON BÜLOW, RIEMANN and BARTÓK modernised Beethoven's piano publications for their respective ages, re-editing ARTICULATIONS, adding metronomic data and even recomposing cadential passages with an eye towards greater rhythmic precision. MAHLER revised Beethoven's Symphony No. 9 to reflect expanded, late nineteenth-century orchestration techniques. In his article on PERFORMANCE PRACTICE in *The New Grove Dictionary* of 1980, HOWARD MAYER BROWN noted that it would be revealing to hear Beethoven's symphonies on period instruments, but the practical difficulties of assembling such an orchestra would be almost insuperable. But revelatory accounts by BRÜGGEN, NORRINGTON and others in the 1980s and beyond attempted to recreate the sonic world inhabited by Beethoven, though the subjectivities and idiosyncrasies surrounding his creativity have proved to be elusive.

FURTHER READING

C. Czerny, *Theoretical and Practical Piano Forte School*, Op. 500, trans. J. A. Hamilton, 3 vols. (London: R. Cocks, 1846).
W. S. Newman, *Beethoven on Beethoven: Playing His Piano Music His Way* (New York: Norton, 1988).
A. Schindler, *The Life of Beethoven*, ed. I. Moscheles (London: Henry Colburn, 1841).
A. W. Thayer, *The Life of Ludwig van Beethoven*, ed. H. Deiters and H. Riemann, trans. H. Krehbiel, 3 vols. (New York: Beethoven Association, [1921]).

ALEXANDER EVAN BONUS

Benda, Franz (František) (b. Staré Benátky, Bohemia, bap. 22 November 1709; d. Nowawes, nr Potsdam, 7 March 1786) Bohemian violinist and composer.

Trained in Prague and Dresden, Benda became one of northern Germany's most influential violinists. As a soloist, chamber musician, teacher and member of Frederick the Great of Prussia's court for more than half a century, he was especially renowned for his skills in melodic embellishment. MANUSCRIPTS of his concertos and sonatas commonly include much specific ORNAMENTATION (trills, mordents, etc.), indicated by signs; but White (1992) refers to two concerto manuscripts (in Vienna and Melk) which include written-out elaborated versions of slow movements, and Lee (1976) discusses manuscripts (in Berlin), probably not in Benda's hand, of thirty-two three-movement violin sonatas; all but two of their movements include at least one written-out embellished version placed below the original melodic line. These elaborations, preserved in various archives, are potentially significant records of mid-eighteenth-century performance practice; however, they may have been prepared only for pedagogical purposes and copied by Benda's pupils to facilitate their emulation of his playing style. Short CADENZAS appear in twenty-two of the Adagios and in one concluding Allegro. Among Benda's pupils who disseminated his influence were Friedrich Rust and Johann Peter Salomon.

FURTHER READING

S. Gerlach, 'Gedanken zu den "veränderten" Violinstimmen der Solosonaten von Franz Benda in der Staatsbibliothek Preussischer Kulturbesitz, Berlin', in M. Bente (ed.), *Musik–Edition–Interpretation* (Munich: Henle, 1980), 199–212.

D. A. Lee, 'Some embellished versions of sonatas by Franz Benda', *MQ*, 62/1 (January, 1976), 58–71.

E. C. White, *From Viotti to Vivaldi: A History of the Early Classical Violin Concerto* (Philadelphia: Gordon and Breach, 1992).

ROBIN STOWELL

Bérard, Jean-Antoine (b. Lunel, ?1710; d. Paris ?1772) French music teacher, composer and singer of small roles at the Paris Opéra and Théâtre-Italien.

Bérard's treatise, *L'art du chant* (1755), the authorship of which is mooted, was dedicated to Madame de Pompadour. It was one of the first works to take a scientific approach in discussing the mechanics of voice production and the effect of physiology on tone, diction and ORNAMENTATION. The treatise is arranged in three parts which address, respectively, the function of the anatomical structure (lungs, trachea, larynx, glottis and vocal cords) in SINGING, ARTICULATION and PRONUNCIATION, and ornamentation (function, execution and NOTATION). Although some of Bérard's theories are considered flawed today, his discussion of syllabic quantity and his analysis as to how each letter of the French alphabet is produced by the voice reflect the French preoccupation with text declamation and provide a practical performance guide for the modern singer.

FURTHER READING

B. Jerold, 'Mystery in Paris, the German connection and more: the Bérard-Blanchet controversy revisited', *18CM*, 2/1 (2005), 91–112.

K. Kenaston-French, 'The teachings of Jean-Antoine Bérard: content, context and legacy', *Journal of Singing*, 66/2 (November/December, 2009), 149–55.

ELIZABETH DOBBIN

Berg, Alban (b. Vienna, 9 February 1885; d. Vienna, 24 December 1935) Austrian composer.

Unlike the other members of the Second Viennese School, Berg had somewhat limited experience as a performing musician. Nevertheless, as a proactive member of the Society for Private Music Performance in Vienna, he laid down some clear guidelines regarding the interpretation of new orchestral music performed with drastically reduced instrumental forces. Pianists, for example, were exhorted to apply an instinctive feeling for tonal colour that should exceed the conventional expressive possibilities of their instrument.

Berg's densely textured scores are littered with detailed instructions relating to the characterisation, ARTICULATION and expressive intent of individual melodic lines. Following Schoenberg's example, many works, including the *Drei Orchesterstücke*, Op. 6 and *Lyrische Suite*, designate a clear delineation between *Hauptstimme* (main voice) and *Nebenstimme* (subsidiary voice).

Berg left very extensive instructions regarding the most desirable performance practice with regard to his opera *Wozzeck*. He called for a measured and somewhat leisurely approach to the overall TEMPO. Furthermore, the principal dynamic level of the opera should be *piano*, not merely to allow the text to be easily heard, but also to make the explosive passages in each scene sound all the more powerful. With regard to the execution of *Sprechstimme* in the vocal parts, he clarified the necessity for all pitches in the score to be presented exactly as indicated by the notes in the score. These had to be projected with the tone quality of the speaking voice which in itself could and, in some cases, should involve the use of head tones.

Berg expanded the range of vocal possibilities in his opera *Lulu*. In the brief Prologue, for example, different types of NOTATION are employed in quick succession to make an explicit distinction between the spoken word, *Sprechstimme*, *halb gesungen*, *parlando gesungen*, *parlando* and *cantabile*.

FURTHER READING

A. Berg, 'The preparation and staging of *Wozzeck*', *MT*, 109 (June, 1968), 518–21.
B. R. Simms (ed.), *Pro Mundo – Pro Domo: The Writings of Alban Berg* (New York: Oxford University Press, 2014).

ERIK LEVI

Bériot, Charles-Auguste de (b. Leuven, 20 February 1802; d. Brussels, 8 April 1870) Belgian violinist, composer and teacher.

Bériot studied the violin with Jean-François Tiby, Viotti's pupil André Robberechts and briefly in BAILLOT'S PARIS CONSERVATOIRE class. He was solo violinist to King William I of the Netherlands (1826–30) and toured in Europe with mezzo-soprano Maria Malibran (1830–6). They married in 1836, but Maria died later that year. Bériot resumed concert touring in 1838, performing with Maria's younger sister, the singer Pauline García. He developed the violin playing traditions of Viotti, Baillot, RODE and KREUTZER, combining them with PAGANINI's virtuoso vocabulary and Maria's *bel canto* style, as demonstrated in his ten violin concertos, *Scène de ballet*, opera fantasias, variation sets and other bravura pieces.

Bériot declined a violin professorship at the Paris Conservatoire (1842) in favour of one in Brussels (1843–52), where he established a Franco-Belgian 'school' of violin playing, counting Henri Vieuxtemps among his most celebrated pupils. He published various pedagogical works, including violin studies and duos of varying technical difficulty, a *Méthode de violon*, Op. 102 (1858) and two 'annexes', the concert studies in *L'école transcendante du violon*, Op. 123 (1867) and *L'art du prélude*. Bériot's *Méthode* unsurprisingly focuses on 'imitating the accents of the human voice'. Its first two parts cover technique and mirror much of Baillot's instruction; part 3 concentrates on style. Bériot illustrates his instruction with duet arrangements of opera arias, complete with texts; he consistently provides analogies with vocal performance, in terms of capturing the ARTICULATION, EXPRESSION, phrasing and ACCENTUATION appropriate to the prevailing sentiment or character. Viewing the bow as the violinist's equivalent of the singer's breath, he observes the hierarchy of the bar by taking long syllables in a down-bow and short ones in an up-bow. He recommends the introduction of VIBRATO and PORTAMENTO in moderation, considering portamento an important facilitator for *cantabile* performance. His numerous musical examples are notated with FINGERINGS, BOWINGS and symbols indicating vibrato and portamento usage.

FURTHER READING

N. de Carteret Hammill, 'The ten violin concertos of Charles-Auguste de Bériot: a pedagogical study', DMA dissertation, Louisiana State University (1994).

E. Heron-Allen, *A Contribution Towards an Accurate Biography of Charles Auguste de Bériot and Maria Felicita Malibran-Garcia* (London: Heron-Allen, 1894).

ROBIN STOWELL

Berlioz, (Louis-)Hector (b. La Côte-Saint-André, Isère, 11 December 1803; d. Paris, 8 March 1869) French composer and conductor.

Berlioz conducted his own music in France, Belgium, Germany, Russia, and England, necessarily accommodating himself to the musicians available. His comments on performance under other conductors such as HABENECK suggest that his own rehearsals (including sectionals) concentrated on accuracy, rather than combating stylistic habits with respect to VIBRATO or PORTAMENTO. A prime concern was TEMPO; Berlioz almost always supplied METRONOME marks, and meant them. His tempi may have seemed fast to the players and, in his interpretation of BEETHOVEN, to WAGNER, who criticised what he considered insufficient flexibility – marking a difference of approach that has been compared to that between Toscanini and Furtwängler.

Berlioz's *Grand traité d'instrumentation et d'orchestration modernes* (1843) discusses the techniques of standard instruments, and some experimental ones, as well as solo and choral voices; he also considers instrumental combinations. The work is profusely illustrated with music he admired, by Gluck, Beethoven, Weber and Meyerbeer, as well as his own. He added an important essay on CONDUCTING to the revised second edition (1855).

Always conscious of technical developments, mainly affecting brass, Berlioz revised the instrumentation of some of his scores, removing the SERPENT from *Symphonie fantastique*. Ever practical, he sometimes adopted the formula 'OPHICLEIDE or TUBA'. He introduced *Cornets à piston* into several works, alongside natural TRUMPETS. For most of his career he could expect only natural HORNS, at least in France, and to increase chromatic coverage he required four in different keys (e.g. *Roméo et Juliette*), and used horns in unusual keys such as D♭ (*La Damnation de Faust*: 'Invocation'). In the *Traité* he defines precisely the quality of stopped notes, and deplores the decline of hand stopping when, by means of pistons or valves, notes were played 'open' that composers expected (and wanted, for expressive reasons rather than necessity) to be stopped. Always interested in new possibilities, in *La Damnation* (1846) he specifies in one section a fourth horn 'à pistons', and in the *Marche hongroise* he reinforced the climax with a valve TROMBONE. He also wrote on, and composed for, Alexandre's 'orgue-mélodium'.

More generally, horns and trombones had narrower bores than today. The reedy timbre of French BASSOONS makes a marked difference in the grotesque movements IV and V of *Symphonie fantastique* – IV has a unison counterpoint by four bassoons (the standard complement), and in V the diminished seventh (bar 3, bassoons *divisi à* 4) has a sharp attack lost on the widely used 'German' bassoon.

The *Traité*, and other evidence, clarifies Berlioz's preferred ORCHESTRAL PLACEMENT. The violin sections are to the left and right of the conductor; principal CELLO and DOUBLE BASS are to be near the conductor, the other lower strings arrayed centrally (if possible on risers). Chorus and soloists should be in front of the orchestra, some even between conductor and audience, requiring a sub-conductor; off-stage forces could be controlled by the so-called 'electric metronome'. Proper proportions were essential to him, in chamber orchestras (e.g. *Les Nuits d'été*) or the vast forces he imagined, and was occasionally able to assemble.

FURTHER READING

H. Berlioz, *Grand traité d'instrumentation et d'orchestration modernes* (Paris: Schonenberger, 1843; 2nd rev. edn, 1855).
P. Bloom (ed.), *New Berlioz Edition*, vol. 24 (Kassel: Bärenreiter, 2003; trans. H. Macdonald as *Berlioz's Orchestration Treatise* (Cambridge University Press, 2002)).

JULIAN RUSHTON

Bernhard, Christoph (b. Kolberg, Pomerania, 1 January 1628; d. Dresden, 14 November 1692) German music theorist, composer and singer.

Bernhard's *Von der Singe-Kunste, oder Maniera* (manuscript, c1650) is a systematic theoretical treatment of advanced vocal style summarising contemporary Italian regional practices of embellishment: *Cantar sodo* (Rome), *cantar d'affetto* (Naples) and *cantar passagiato* (Lombardy). Roman style is the most conservative, singers sticking closely to the written notes save for application of the *trillo* ('the most difficult, but also most attractive ornament; difficult to describe in words, it is best learned by ear') (1926/1999, 32). Other Roman-style ornaments are *Accento* (a tiny ARTICULATION at the end of a note); *anticipatione della Syllaba* (like the French *port-de-voix*); *cerca della nota* (intonation from below); and *ardire* (a TREMOLO on a cadential final). The Neapolitan style focuses on the precise PRONUNCIATION and EXPRESSION of text. The ornamental style of Lombardy is characterised by diminution, or *Coloraturen*, which should be used sparingly. Bernhard concludes with standard admonitions to singers to avoid facial grimaces (which should be reserved for 'singenden Comoedie') (1926/1999, 37), singing through the nose or teeth, lisping, or opening the mouth too wide.

FURTHER READING

J. Müller-Blattau, *Die Kompositionslehre Heinrich Schützens in der Fassung seines Schülers Christoph Bernhard* (Kassel: Bärenreiter, 1926/1999); trans. in W. Hilse, 'The treatises of Christoph Bernhard', *Music Forum* 3 (1973), 1–196.

RICHARD WISTREICH

Berr, Frédéric (b. Mannheim, 17 April 1794; d. Paris, 24 September 1838) Clarinettist, bassoonist, bandmaster, administrator, composer and pedagogue.

An itinerant military musician from his mid-teens, Berr settled in Paris around 1818. This greatly enhanced his further musical development, particularly as a CLARINET player. Berr abandoned military employment in the early 1820s to work as an orchestral player. Between 1831 and 1838 he taught at the PARIS CONSERVATOIRE and in 1836 founded the *Gymnase de Musique Militaire*. Berr's two clarinet tutors, the *Traité complet de la clarinette à 14 clefs* and the *Méthode complete de clarinette*, published in 1836, were particularly influential not least because of their advocacy of the reed-below embouchure. The *Traité* sets out Berr's credo of clarinet performance practices, providing much informative detail, whilst the *Méthode* addresses both the art and the craft of clarinet playing. Celebrated by FRANÇOIS-JOSEPH FÉTIS as the founder of the

French clarinet school, Berr's legacy was perpetuated by his most celebrated pupil HYACINTHE KLOSÉ.

FURTHER READING

D. Charlton, 'The Berr clarinet tutors', *GSJ*, 40 (1987), 48–52.
F.-J. Fétis, 'Berr (Frédéric)', *Biographie universelle des musiciens et bibliographie générale de la musique* (Brussels: Meline, Cans et Compagnie, 1837), ii, 164.

INGRID E. PEARSON

Bilson, Malcolm (b. Los Angeles, 24 October 1935) American pianist and scholar.

Bilson began an active performing and recording career on Philip Belt FORTEPIANOS in the early 1970s. His set of MOZART concertos with JOHN ELIOT GARDINER was the first on historic instruments; other recordings include the solo sonatas of Mozart, BEETHOVEN and Schubert. Bilson has influenced generations of keyboard players, through the doctoral programme in historical performance practice he founded at Cornell University in the 1980s, worldwide lectures and masterclasses, and educational videos (www.knowingthescore.com).

DAVID BREITMAN

Binkley, Thomas (Eden) (b. Cleveland, OH, 26 December 1931; d. Bloomington, IN, 28 April 1995) American musicologist, lutenist and player of early wind instruments.

Binkley founded the STUDIO DER FRÜHEN MUSIK at Munich in 1959, together with ANDREA VON RAMM, Sterling Jones and Nigel Rogers, internationally known as the EARLY MUSIC QUARTET. In later years Rogers was replaced by Willard Cobb and then Richard Levitt. Together the group made over forty recordings. Binkley later directed the Early Music Institute at the University of Indiana (1979–95).

FURTHER READING

D. Lasocki, 'The several lives of Tom Binkley: a tribute', *Early Music America*, I/i (1995), 16–24.

DAVID FALLOWS

Birnbaum, Johann Abraham (b. Leipzig, 30 September 1702; d. Leipzig, 8 August 1748) Legal theoretician and Leipzig orator.

Birnbaum famously defended J. S. BACH against SCHEIBE's criticisms first published from 1737 onwards. His writings reveal Bach's aesthetic views and appreciation of older styles of music, alongside anecdotes such as the cancelled competition with Louis Marchand.

FURTHER READING

M. Boyd, *Bach* (Oxford University Press, 2000), 174–5, 284–5.
J. Butt, 'Bach's metaphysics of music', in J. Butt (ed.), *The Cambridge Companion to Bach* (Cambridge University Press, 1997), 46–59.
C. Wolff, *Johann Sebastian Bach: The Learned Musician* (Oxford University Press, 2000).

TERENCE CHARLSTON

Bismantova, Bartolomeo (b. Reggio Emilia, ?; d. ?Ferrara, after 1694) Italian cornettist, composer and writer.

According to the title page of his *Compendio musicale*, Bismantova was a musician at the cathedral and cornettist at the *Accademia dello Spirito Santo* in Ferrara in 1677. The *Compendio*, extant in manuscript only, was probably a copy prepared for the printer, but a note on the back of the title page apparently in the same hand but dated 1694 states that it was not submitted for print because of the death of Bismantova's patron. It also specifies that at this time instructions for the *violoncello da spalla*, the CONTRABASSO and the OBOE were added. Those for oboe are missing from the manuscript but appeared in 1688–9 as a supplement to the author's *66 Duetti a due trombe da camera*, written for two trumpets or cornetts. An additional manuscript containing a brief *Preludio* for cornett solo has recently come to light.

The *Compendio* deals with mensural SINGING, plainsong, counterpoint, BASSO CONTINUO and tuning of keyboard instruments, but it is decidedly most interesting for its discussion of instruments, both wind (RECORDER, flageolet and CORNETT), and string (VIOLIN and *violoncello da spalla*, a small CELLO played on the shoulder).

Bismantova's instructions for BOWING, using dots above and below the notes, demonstrate a strict application of bowing patterns (e.g. 'good' notes are played with a down-bow, 'bad' notes up; dotted notes must be down), though he briefly describes 'modern' patterns which contradict these principles. There is no shifting of the left-hand position.

Bismantova uses the term *flauto italiano* for a three-piece Baroque-style recorder in G. This is an early appearance of a Baroque-type instrument in Italy and indeed seems to be the oldest existing method-book for this type of instrument. Bismantova gives FINGERINGS, including trills, which he says should be done on all notes, as far as permitted by their length. He also speaks extensively about ARTICULATION. Also mentioned is a recorder a fourth lower, corresponding to what was later known as the voice flute. His comments on the flageolet, which he calls the *fasoletto* or *flautino francese*, are without much detail.

Playing the recorder is, according to the author, a prerequisite for learning the cornett. Of particular importance is his illustration and description of joints to be added to the cornett at the top and bottom in order to tune to ORGANS at different pitches. He also gives fingerings for very high notes (up to d''') and for *tremoli* and *trilli*; the difference between the two is not addressed, but fingerings suggest that the TREMOLO has smaller intervals than the *trillo*.

Of greatest interest are Bismantova's comments on TONGUING for the recorder and cornett. In general he employs softer syllables on the recorder (*de*) than on the cornett (*te*). Also of interest is the observation that notes under a slur are not to be played altogether without tonguing, but rather in pairs with such syllables as *de, a*. He appears to misconstrue the *lingua roversa*, that is, the tonguing (*lere lere*) deemed most important in division playing by earlier writers, a confusion probably explained by the fact that divisions were nearly a lost art in Italy by 1677.

FURTHER READING

M. Castellani, 'The *Regola per suonare il Flauto Italiano* by Bartolomeo Bismantova (1677)', *GSJ*, 30 (1977), 76–85.

B. Dickey, P. Leonards and E. H. Tarr, 'The discussion of wind instruments in Bartolomeo Bismantova's *Compendio musicale* (1677)', *BJhM*, 2 (1978), 143–87.

BRUCE DICKEY

Blasius, (Mathieu-) Frédéric (b. Lauterbourg, Bas-Rhin, 24 April 1758; d. Versailles, 1829) French clarinettist, violinist, conductor and composer.

Frédéric Blasius was born in the far north-eastern corner of France on the Rhineland border of Alsace. His birthplace, the frontier town of Lauterbourg, had a large military presence, including many musicians. From 1780 to 1782 Blasius worked for the Bishop of Strasbourg and encountered the composer and leading theoretician Franz Xavier Richter, who was the cathedral *Kapellmeister* and municipal music director. In 1784 Blasius went to Paris and performed one of his own violin concertos at a *Concert Spirituel*. He joined the orchestra of the Opéra-Comique and became concertmaster two years later. In 1795 he was appointed professor of VIOLIN at the newly founded PARIS CONSERVATOIRE. During the succeeding years he became very active as a conductor and as a composer of stage and other works. At the Théâtre de la Gaîté in 1801 he conducted the first Parisian performance in German of MOZART's *Die Entführung aus dem Serail*.

In addition to the violin, Blasius also played the CLARINET and BASSOON, for which he wrote methods, and the FLUTE. He held appointments as director of the National Guard Band, the bands of the Garde Consulaire and the Grenadiers de la Garde de Napoléon. Blasius wrote a *Méthode de clarinette* (c1795), which is presumed lost; his *Méthode de basson* dates from 1800. He is now especially remembered for his *Nouvelle méthode de clarinette et raisonnement des instruments, principes et théorie de musique dédiés aux élèves du Conservatoire* (Paris, 1796). This includes a FINGERING chart for a five-keyed instrument, notably incorporating some enharmonic fingerings. Blasius advocated a double-lip embouchure to avoid either lips or teeth touching the reed. He noted that it was necessary to support the mouthpiece on the lower lip and to cover the reed with the upper lip, without the teeth touching any of it.

FURTHER READING

E. T. Hoeprich, *The Clarinet* (New Haven, CT and London: Yale University Press, 2008).
C. Pierre, *Le Conservatoire national de musique et de declamation: documents historiques et administratifs* (Paris: Imprimerie nationale, 1900).
A. R. Rice, *The Clarinet in the Classical Period* (Oxford University Press, 2003).

COLIN LAWSON

Boethius, Anicius Manlius Torquatus Severinus (b. Rome, c480; d. Pavia, c524–6) Italian writer and statesman.

A member of a patrician family educated in Greek philosophy and the liberal arts, Boethius was *magister officiorum* at the court of Theodoric the Ostrogoth in Ravenna, the former capital of the Western Roman Empire. He authored several didactic, theological and philosophical works, but he is best known in musical circles for his *De institutione musica* in five books, the last of which survives incomplete. This treatise summarising ancient Greek ideas about music profoundly influenced the development of Western musical thinking and established the canon of Medieval culture – the term *quadrivium*, denoting the four mathematical disciplines of antiquity (arithmetic, music, geometry and astronomy), was first introduced by Boethius.

De institutione is based on a neo-Pythagorean and neo-Platonic approach (as are its main sources, Nicomachus and Ptolemy), according to which music was a preparatory tool for philosophy. Boethius classified music into three categories: *musica mundana* (i.e. of the universe), the highest kind of music; *musica humana*, the unifying principle for the human being; *musica instrumentalis*, produced by musical instruments. The true *musicus* is neither the performer nor the composer, but the man 'who has the faculty to judge' music through a rational approach. Hence, in order to become a real *scientia*, music theory had to translate sounds and intervals into mathematically measurable quantities and ratios.

Boethius's mathematical calculations of Greek musical scales influenced considerably the development of European music. On the one hand, the detachment of theory from practice (begun in theoretical TREATISES long before Boethius) reinforced the rational approach to musical knowledge which prevailed until the late Renaissance; on the other, the application – from the ninth century onwards – of Boethian tonal system to modal classification of Gregorian melodies (based on his short explanation of the theory of 'modes', as he called them, literally translating the Greek term *tonoi/tropoi* with the Latin word *modi*) provoked a deep and long-lasting misunderstanding of the ancient theory.

FURTHER READING

M. Bernhard, 'Il *De institutione musica* di Boezio nell'alto Medioevo', in M. Cristiani, C. Panti and G. Perillo (eds.), *Harmonia mundi. Musica mondana e musica celeste fra Antichità e Medioevo* (Firenze: Sismel–Edizioni del Galluzzo, 2007), 77–93.

C. M. Bower, 'The role of the *De Institutione Musica* in the speculative tradition of Western musical thought', in M. Masi (ed.), *Boethius and the Liberal Arts: a Collection of Essays* (Berne and Las Vegas: Peter Lang, 1981), 157–74.

C. M. Bower (trans. and ed.), *Anicius Manlius Severinus Boethius, Fundamentals of Music* (New Haven, CT and London: Yale University Press, 1989).

ELEONORA ROCCONI

Boracchi, Carlo Antonio (*fl.* early nineteenth century) Italian timpanist of the Royal Opera Orchestra (La Scala), Milan.

Boracchi's *Manuale del timpanista* (Milan: Luigi di Giacomo Picola, 1842) was one of the first specialist TIMPANI tutors, following the brief relevant chapter in JOHANN ALTENBURG's *Versuch* (1795). Along with confirming a preference for goatskin heads and perpetuating the practice (no longer implemented in French opera) of improvising rhythmic embellishments to the printed timpani parts, it describes Boracchi's invention to facilitate more rapid tuning. This development comprised a lever at the drum's base, which, when moved to the right or left, turned a central screw, raising or lowering the entire base plate and assembly of eight vertical struts underneath the instrument, thereby altering the tension of the head and the instrument's tuning. The invention's various shortcomings resulted in its limited adoption; however, Verdi may have been familiar with it through its probable use by his favoured timpanist, Pietro Pieranzovini (1814–85), Boracchi's successor at La Scala and also the author of a respected timpani TREATISE (*Método teórico prático per timpani* (Milan: Ricordi, 1860)).

FURTHER READING

J. Beck, *Encyclopedia of Percussion* (New York: Routledge, 1995).

ROBIN STOWELL

Bordes, Charles (b. La Roche Courbon-Vouvray, 12 May 1863; d. Toulon, 8 October 1909) Choral conductor, musicologist, educationist and composer.

Bordes was of considerable importance in the early music revival in France at the turn of the twentieth century. His first major venture in the revival of Renaissance polyphony was his founding of a choir devoted to the repertoire at St Gervais in Paris, a select chamber choir of twenty-four singers who went on to revive BACH cantatas and the music of Carissimi, Schütz and CHARPENTIER among others. In 1890 this venture developed into the Schola Cantorum, founded by Bordes but put under the charge of D'INDY and Guilmant. He paved the way for such composers as Canteloube for whom the regional folk music of France was central, both as a collector and as a composer. Bordes was particularly interested in the music of the Basque country. For his editions he founded his own publishing house and also inaugurated similarly motivated choirs and tirelessly organised lecture-recitals across the whole of France. Although he was deeply involved in the revival of RAMEAU, both in the complete edition and in staged productions, it is widely thought that his legacy of compositions would have been more substantial had he not been such a committed proselytiser for unedited early music and folksong.

FURTHER READING

C. Bordes (ed.), *Anthologie des maîtres religieux primitifs des quinzième, seizième et dix-septième siècles: édition populaire à l'usage des maîtrises et des amateurs, en notation moderne avec clefs usuelles, nuances et indications d'exécution et réduction des voix au clavier*, 6 vols. (Paris: Bureau d'Édition de la Schola Cantorum, [1893–5]; repr. New York: Da Capo, 1981).

RICHARD LANGHAM SMITH

Bottesini, Giovanni (b. Crema, 22 December 1821; d. Parma, 7 July 1889) Italian DOUBLE BASS player, conductor and composer.

Bottesini's earliest training in music was with his father, who was a clarinettist and conductor. He sang in choirs, played TIMPANI and studied VIOLIN with Carlo Cogliati. In 1835, he applied to enter the Milan Conservatory. After passing his audition, Bottesini studied double bass with Luigi Rossi, completing his studies by 1839. He was awarded the sum of 300 francs as a soloist, and applied this sum towards a 1716 Carlo Giuseppe Testore bass, an instrument he played throughout his career.

After leaving the Conservatory, Bottesini was highly successful as a virtuoso soloist, playing many concerts in Italy and Vienna. He was principal double bassist at the Teatro San Benedetto, where he first met Verdi. Bottesini joined the Tacon Theatre in Havana in 1846, touring with the opera company in both the USA and Mexico while continuing to perform as a soloist. Well known throughout Europe as a conductor, he directed the first performance of Verdi's

Aida on 27 December 1871. He often performed as a double bass soloist in intermissions of his opera performances. In recognition of his virtuosity, he was known as the 'Paganini of the double bass'.

Bottesini was a prolific composer for his instrument. His *Metodo di Contrabbasso* (Milan, 1865) defined the standards of double bass playing at the time. It instructs the student in orchestral playing and includes scale, interval, and melodic exercises and tuition regarding embellishments and pizzicato technique. It also discusses correct playing positions, as well as differences between the 'Dragonetti bow' and the French bow, sometimes called the 'Bottesini bow' because he was the first player to use it. In the second section Bottesini discusses the role of the double bass as a solo instrument. He notates the range of the solo bass from A to g'''. His exercises are written for the extended range of the instrument beyond the fingerboard and frequently use harmonics. The placement of the harmonics is shown through graphic representation and the method concludes with a collection of melodic exercises with piano accompaniment.

Bottesini also wrote three concerti for double bass, as well as numerous chamber pieces involving the instrument. His works use the extended techniques described in his method and require a high level of expertise.

FURTHER READING

T. Martin, 'In search of Bottesini', *Journal of the International Society of Bassists*, 10/1 (1983), 6–12, 10/2 (1984) 6–12, 11/2 (1985) 25–39.

B. Siemers, 'The history and development of the double bass', DMA dissertation, University of Cincinnati, College-Conservatory of Music (2001), 125–35.

BRIAN SIEMERS

Boulanger, (Juliette) Nadia (b. Paris, 16 September 1887; d. Paris, 22 October 1979) French composer, conductor, pianist, organist and pedagogue.

Nadia Boulanger is remembered chiefly as one of the twentieth century's foremost teachers of composition, but her principal contribution to historical performance emerged from her role as a conductor. She was a significant advocate of unfamiliar music of the past, directing highly regarded performances of several of J. S. BACH's cantatas and works by Schütz (*Historia der Auferstehung*), Purcell (*The Fairy Queen*), CHARPENTIER (*Pestis Mediolensis*; *Médée*) and Carissimi (*Jephte*).

In 1936 she formed a diverse ensemble of professional and keen amateur singers and performed repertoire ranging from sixteenth-century French music to works by contemporary composers. Building on the groundwork of VINCENT D'INDY, Henri Prunières and Gian Francesco Malipiero, her ensemble's interpretations of CLAUDIO MONTEVERDI's secular chamber music, particularly madrigals from books 7 and 8, generated worldwide acclaim through performances, broadcasts and recordings. Especially significant are their five seminal 78 rpm records of Monteverdi's works for HMV (1937), featuring madrigals, various works for two tenors and extracts for solo voices and strings from *Il Ballo delle ingrate*. These recordings, in which Boulanger accompanies some works at the PIANO (she showed little regard for historical performance practice per se), garnered remarkable interest in Monteverdi worldwide, set a high benchmark for the interpretation of his music and influenced, among many others, Denis Stevens (ACCADEMIA MONTEVERDIANA) and JOHN ELIOT GARDINER.

FURTHER READING

J. Brooks, *The Musical Work of Nadia Boulanger: Performing Past and Future between the Wars* (Cambridge University Press, 2013).
'Nadia Boulanger and the Salon of the Princesse de Polignac', *JAMS*, 46/3 (Autumn, 1993), 415-68.
L. Rosenstiel, *Nadia Boulanger: A Life in Music* (New York and London: Norton, 1982).

ROBIN STOWELL

Boulez, Pierre (b. Montbrison, 26 March 1925; d. Baden-Baden, 5 January 2016) French composer and conductor.

Boulez was central to the evolution of contemporary music during the twentieth century as an influential composer (particularly during the early years 1950–70), as a conductor and as a political force and polemicist for the promotion of modernist music. His skill as a conductor mirrored his application and determination as a musician generally, in terms of the analytical approach he pursued and his clarity of purpose and vision. His early masterpieces, particularly *Le marteau sans maître* (1953–5) and a group of works composed between 1957 and 1962, including *Pli selon pli* and the Third Piano Sonata, reveal his development of integral serialism from WEBERN rather than SCHOENBERG, and later CAGE's influence in terms of indeterminacy and formal procedures of choice or chance. These are works with a sense of energy and urgency that was also part of his mission as a proselytiser for modernism, whereas the later works are more conventionally structured and concerned with colour and elaboration.

As a conductor he is in a line of composer/conductors from BERLIOZ, WAGNER, MAHLER and Schoenberg to his more recent colleague Bruno Maderna with whom he worked closely at the Darmstadt Summer Courses during the 1950s and 1960s: the composer as conductor is central to the evolution of CONDUCTING. In the early years immediately after WWII, however, Boulez's first opportunities to conduct arose largely by chance. In Paris he directed the *Domaines Musicales* concerts and group because of the lack of an alternative conductor and in the early 1950s was working in Paris and Germany often as a result of the illness and unavailability of musicians such as Roger Désormière, Hans Rosbaud and others. Almost from the start Boulez worked with major orchestras such as the West Deutscher Rundfunk in almost exclusively contemporary repertoire, although it was not unknown for him to have to include something from the past, such as a HAYDN symphony or Baroque repertoire including MONTEVERDI and RAMEAU, when taking over concerts from Rosbaud or Ernest Bour, both of whom Boulez acknowledged as influences on his own technique. He stated that his conducting came about because of the poorly prepared and performed concerts of recent music, particularly of works by the Second Viennese School. During 1958–9 he, at first reluctantly, conducted a number of concerts with the SWF orchestra including Webern's Six Pieces Op. 6, three extracts from BERG's *Wozzeck* and BARTÓK's *Miraculous Mandarin*. His repertoire of music from the late nineteenth century onwards was extensive, as is his discography. As early as 1966 he conducted

Wagner's *Parsifal* at Bayreuth, which led to the extraordinary *Ring* in Patrice Chereau's production 1976–80, together with Debussy's *Pelléas et Mélisande* in the early 1960s. He recorded all the music of the Second Viennese School, including two complete Webern recordings, Debussy, Ravel and STRAVINSKY with the orchestras he was most associated with in Cleveland and New York, as well as the BBC Symphony in London. After working abroad from 1959 onwards, he returned to Paris in 1963 to conduct significant performances of Stravinsky's *Le Sacre du Printemps* and Berg's *Wozzeck*; however, his influence on the artistic élite in France was less successful and his ideas about the Opéra and French musical life were rejected by the then minister of cultural affairs, André Malraux. Boulez had considerable success later in the 1970s in Paris because of the similar ambitions of President Georges Pompidou with his research institute IRCAM, which has been particularly influential in electronic developments and the use of computer digital technology. His Ensemble Intercontemporain, founded in 1976, is still one of the world's leading ensembles.

FURTHER READING

P. Boulez, *Boulez on Music Today* (1963), trans. S. Bradshaw and R. R. Bennett (London: Faber & Faber, 1971).
Boulez on Conducting, Conversations with Cécile Gilly (London: Faber & Faber, 2003).
W. G. Harbinson, 'Performer indeterminacy and Boulez's Third Sonata', *Tempo*, 169 (1989), 16–20.

ROGER HEATON

Bovicelli, Giovanni Battista (b. Assisi, mid-sixteenth century; d. after 1627) Italian virtuoso singer.

Bovicelli is best known for his diminution treatise, *Regole, passaggi di musica* (Venice, 1594), published during his tenure as a singer at Milan Cathedral. In his preface, Bovicelli stresses the importance of text setting, and especially the relationship between ORNAMENTATION and the AFFEKT of the words, which he illustrates through sacred *contrafacta* of well-known madrigals. He makes a particular distinction between *passaggi* and *accenti*; his worked examples of the latter, which are more appropriate for sad and serious texts, frequently create dissonances that transgress the boundaries of contemporary contrapuntal theory. In this way his approach clearly anticipates the *seconda pratica*. His TREATISE also contains examples of embellished *falsobordone*, and is an important document of this IMPROVISATION practice.

GIULIO CACCINI's preface to *Le nuove musiche* (1601/2) contains a critique of some of the techniques exemplified by Bovicelli, which he seemingly thought too extravagant for the new monodic style.

FURTHER READING

G. B. Bovicelli, *Regole, passaggi di musica* (Venice, 1594); preface trans. J. Rosenberg, *HBSJ*, 4 (1992), 27–44.
H. M. Brown, *Embellishing Sixteenth-Century Music* (Oxford University Press, 1976).
B. Dickey, '*L'accento*: in search of a forgotten ornament', *HBSJ*, 3 (1991), 98–121.

JAMIE SAVAN

Bow, bowing It has long been acknowledged that choice of bow is one of the most significant considerations in the quest to realise the characteristics of 'period' style in stringed instrument performance. L'ABBÉ LE FILS's description of the bow as 'the soul of the instrument' (1761, 1) is one among many from celebrated violinists to highlight the bow's critical importance. There is little disagreement that the use of pre-Tourte style bows for the performance of Baroque and Classical repertoire affords considerable advantages to performers seeking to reproduce the readily identifiable features of 'period' style such as crisp ARTICULATION, shortened execution of notated rhythmic values, non-uniform note shapes, hierarchy within the bar, and deliberate inequality between consecutive notes.

Although the development of the bow was a gradual evolution, scholars have generally adopted four bow classification categories: short 'Early Baroque'; longer 'High Baroque'; Transitional/Classical; and Tourte model. The distinctions between these categories are often interpreted as being more clear-cut than in fact they are, and many 'period' string players subscribe to a partly apocryphal received history of the bow that has become oversimplified as a result of attempts to delineate the scope of use for different bow types within a modern HIP context.

Since DAVID BOYDEN's seminal *The History of Violin Playing* (1965), research has highlighted the lack of standardisation in pre-Tourte bow design and the overlap in the use and manufacture of different bow types irrespective of dates and national boundaries that were previously considered to be definitive. Robert Seletsky pulls no punches in evaluating the situation thus: 'The late twentieth-century period-instrument movement has codified its perceptions about various bow types into an extremely under-informed methodology that now determines the appropriate bows for given musical repertories' (286). Nevertheless, such categories provide a useful framework within which to consider aspects of historical bows and bowing.

Short 'Early Baroque' Bows

Pre-seventeenth-century bows for stringed instruments were fairly rudimentary, the hair usually being attached at the point through a hole, knotted and often covered with an ornamental cap. 'Pike-head' bows were developed c1625 in response to rapid technical advances in performance. These were more complex in construction and afforded better balance, clearer articulation and superior tone production.

While the short bow (sometimes referred to as the 'Corelli bow' because of illustrations provided in the treatises of WOLDEMAR and FÉTIS) is often considered to be a seventeenth-century bow and/or a bow for French music, Seletsky argues that the use of short bows persisted well into the eighteenth century and that the 'long-lived devotion to the short bow among Italian virtuosos and the simultaneous interest shown in the long bow by French players invalidates an old superstition, often accepted uncritically even now, that the French invariably preferred the short bow because of their interest in dance music' (294–5).

Like most pre-Tourte models, these short bows were manufactured from a variety of different woods. Bows made from cheaper, local wood were generally less durable and not as highly prized as those fashioned from exotic hardwoods; consequently, few have survived. Many of the best-quality sticks were made from snakewood, which was particularly strong and elastic. The profile of the stick (particularly that of Italian bows) was often convex. ROBIN STOWELL gives the lengths of seventeenth-century VIOLIN bows as ranging from c36 cm at the start of the century to at least 61 cm by the end (38). The 61 cm (or two-feet long) bow is frequently referenced in contemporary literature. The weight range associated with violin bows of this length is given by Seletsky as between 36 and 44 g (290).

At the tip of the bow the hair was knotted and curled inside a mortise in the head. At the other end, the hair went into another mortise in the frog, which functioned to separate the stick from the hair. Almost all short bows (and, indeed, longer bows, as well as some transitional models) had clip-in frogs; this hair tension could only be altered by placing pieces of leather (or an equivalent) between the frog and the hair. Clip-in frogs remained in use until beyond 1750 (far later than often assumed), because screw technology was neither reliable nor affordable until the mid-eighteenth century. The much remarked upon dentated *crémaillère*, where a metal loop was hooked over one of various 'teeth' on the bow stick, moving the frog into different positions, is indicative of a desire among performers to 'fine-tune' hair tension before the advent of screw technology.

Despite the qualifications of date and nationality already discussed, there was a gradual move towards longer violin and VIOLA bows by the early 1700s. The development of bows for bass instruments, however, did not follow this trend. It is generally accepted that for much of the seventeenth century there was a loose correlation between instrument size and bow length (larger instruments having longer bows), but this concept became increasingly obsolete as longer bows gained currency; CELLO and VIOLA DA GAMBA bows in fact became shorter than violin bows.

In the early seventeenth century, bows were usually held with the thumb placed on the underside of the hair. This is often referred to as the 'French bow grip'. Italian players introduced a bow hold with the thumb on the stick during the early 1600s, but the practice of holding the bow with the 'thumb-on-hair' persisted into the eighteenth century in France, where it was well suited to playing heavily accented dance music; its decline was linked to the growing popularity of violin sonatas and concertos in France in the early to mid-eighteenth century.

The basic stroke of the short bow was well articulated, non-legato and produced using only the wrist and forearm. Sources pre-dating LEOPOLD MOZART (1756) do not refer to the relationship between bow speed and dynamic level, and so the implication is that the weight from the hand and forearm and the placement of the bow in relation to the bridge and the fingerboard were the methods used to control volume. Despite the clear articulation of these bows (or maybe because of it), there are many references to the desirability of long, smooth bow strokes from very early in the relevant literature; Boyden references PRAETORIUS, MONTEVERDI, Cerreto and Schütz on this point.

Using the bow direction that was naturally more weighted (down-bow on the violin, up-bow on the viol) to provide stress to important beats was an important aspect of phrasing with the short bow. This 'rule of the down-bow' is discussed in a multitude of sources from GANASSI in the mid-sixteenth century, to SPOHR (who describes it as an ancient rule that is now frequently ignored) in the early nineteenth century. Of particular note are the examples given in GEORG MUFFAT's *Florilegium Secundum* (1698).

Longer 'High Baroque' Bows

Although the use of short bows continued well into the 1700s, violin bows of 66–72 cm, weighing 45–55 g, came into common usage in the first quarter of the century. Sticks became straighter, leading to developments in the design of the head. In order to create some space between the tip and the hair, the stick of pike-headed bows was raised towards the point, as a result of either carving, or possibly heating the stick. The 'swan bill' elevated head design was introduced as an alternative. Seletsky points out that 'swan bill' bows appear in iconography from 1685 and that their development predates that of the long bow (290).

Long bows have traditionally been associated with Italian sonata playing and their design allowed greater equality between up- and down-strokes. As the century progressed there was an increasing aesthetic focus on legato and *cantabile* that encouraged performers to sustain more and effect smooth bow changes. The fluting often seen on the top two-thirds of long bows influences their balance and lightens the stick, while preserving its strength. Adoption of these bows resulted in the upper arm being brought into use for longer strokes, explaining in part why playing posture (particularly that of the right elbow and wrist) changed during the course of the eighteenth century.

Transitional/Classical Bows

The transitional bow was created when the shape of the head developed beyond the Baroque 'pike' or 'swan' varieties. It comprises a miscellany of assorted bow designs devised in response to aesthetic transformation, new compositional approaches, and changes in the working conditions and practices of performers and bow makers. It emerged c1760–70 and is often associated with Mannheim, not least because Wilhelm Cramer (1746–99), whose name became attached to the most famous of the various transitional models, began his career there. There is also some suggestion that Mannheim string players later became early advocates of Tourte bows; for example, in 1803 Louis Spohr's Mannheim-trained teacher Franz Eck insisted that Spohr purchase a Tourte bow.

The advent of transitional bows reflected the demand for a bow capable of sustaining *cantabile* melody and projecting in larger performance spaces. Seletsky suggests that lifted bow strokes in the music of the Mannheim school and Viennese classical composers also provided a catalyst for change (416). These strokes were not akin to modern *spiccato* – they were not thrown strokes, but began from the string before being lifted off. Whether or not the desire to play short, 'springing' strokes in the middle of the bow was a factor in the development of the transitional bow, such strokes were certainly executed with bows of this period by Cramer and other contemporary string players, including the cellists DUPORT and ROMBERG. CLIVE BROWN (276) claims that a relatively small number of players employed lifted strokes, and that there is no evidence that lifted strokes were introduced in orchestral playing. By the turn of the nineteenth century, lifted strokes were regarded as old-fashioned and were particularly disliked by Spohr among others.

Examples of transitional bows survive in various woods, but there was an increasing preference for pernambuco. Many transitional models are shorter than the 'long' bows, and although they tend to be thicker, they are usually lighter, because pernambuco is less dense than snakewood. The sticks are either straight, or more usually concave, allowing a weightier sound to be produced at the frog. Transitional 'battle axe'- or 'hatchet'-shaped bow heads were developed to allow legato melodies to be sustained at the tip, the 'battle axe' being cut away on both sides of the head and the 'hatchet' having a solid interior face. The frogs of transitional bows were often ornamentally carved and invariably open channelled. Bows by the Duchaine family, Meauchand and Louis Simon Pajeot in France, and Edward Dodd in England provided some of the most significant examples of transitional bow development.

Early Nineteenth-Century Bows
The early nineteenth century has often been represented as the period during which the history of the bow finally achieved reassuring perspicuity and standardisation as bow design reached its acme in the form of the Tourte model. That François Tourte's (1748–1835) work led to the transformation of future bow-making practices is beyond doubt, but his design was conceived, made and used within a broader context that has not always been fully acknowledged. The development of the Tourte model is generally accepted to have started in the 1780s, arriving at its definitive form by c1810. Many of its identifiable components had been developed by others before Tourte synthesised them so effectively, standardising and refining the dimensions, materials, final design and construction of the bow as developed by his predecessors.

Nicolas Pierre Tourte (*père*) (c1700–64) was already using a fully developed hatchet head and producing concave sticks (as were other French makers and John Dodd in London). Most bow historians draw attention to François Tourte's method of heating a straight stick to produce the camber (as opposed to carving it into the desired shape); but it was the scale and efficacy of Tourte's use of heat to create the camber, rather than the technique of heating the wood per se, that was groundbreaking. Seletsky suggests that (although on a much smaller scale than Tourte's deliberate creation of a mathematically implied inward curve) heating the stick in small amounts to correct anomalies was not uncommon in earlier bow making (290). Snakewood, being strong and elastic, had not required the addition of camber to increase resistance and strength, but as bows became longer and sticks became thicker, the use of pernambuco allowed bows to remain responsive and manageable in weight; and the addition of camber, through heating, preserved elasticity. Stowell (19) states that Tourte determined the ideal violin bow length to be 73.66–74.93 cm and optimum weight to be 56 g and Seletsky (422) gives 74.5 cm as the standard length of a Tourte violin bow with a corresponding weight range of 57–60 g. John Dilworth provides measurements for the Tourte standardised cello bow of length '72–3 cm, with a playing length of hair of 60–2 cm and a balance-point 17.5–18 cm above the frog' (237).

Tourte *père* is generally credited with invention of the ferrule (a 'D' shaped band of metal that encircles the hair where it meets the frog), although other makers in France were also experimenting similarly; but it was François Tourte who brought it into general use. Bow makers had long been interested in increasing the width of hair in their bows, but until the invention of the ferrule, wider ribbons of hair tended to bunch unsatisfactorily. The invention of the tin (later silver) ferrule meant that bow hair could be spread flat, pressed between the metal band and a wooden wedge. Between the mid-eighteenth and early nineteenth centuries, the number of hairs in a bow increased from as few as eighty to as many as 200, although many comprised an amount somewhere within these limits.

Kai Köpp has reassessed the supposed primacy of Tourte model bows in German-speaking territories (where geopolitical sensitivities influenced attitudes against a distinctively French product) and has demonstrated that numerous, more conservative designs of bow were available for purchase well into the nineteenth century (K. Köpp, 'German bows: from "Cramer bow" to "Biedermeier bow"', in J. Akoka (ed.), *L'Archet Révolutionnaire* (Paris: Pietrossel'Arte, 2015), ii, 9–12). Such bows were neither designed for, nor capable of, playing thrown ('off-the-string') strokes with ease, but they were remarkably stable 'on-the-string' in the upper third, a part of the bow exploited by many German bow strokes of the period. Some locally made bows conformed to the Tourte style (i.e. with a hatchet head, closed frog with slide and ferrule), although it is likely that the camber was carved rather than produced by heating.

It is not surprising that German makers were offering a variety of bow types. In Britain, and even in France, traditional open frog bows continued to be made as well as Tourte models because they were cheaper and more affordable. In England, John Dodd (1752–1839), who like François Tourte had a background in metalwork (an expertise evident in his use of screw mechanisms), was making models similar to contemporary French bows, although he mostly carved his sticks into the desired shape. Dodd bows are generally slightly shorter than Tourte bows, and many retain an open frog.

The oft-reiterated precept that the Tourte model heralded the arrival of the 'modern' bow has misled many specialist 'period' instrumentalists into believing that any 'modern' bow they use for nineteenth-century HIP will have playing characteristics similar to those used by nineteenth-century performers. This is not necessarily the case. Even owning a bow made in the early nineteenth century offers no guarantee, since many bows have subsequently been re-cambered to enable them to play thrown strokes more effectively. As the century progressed, the bow continued to develop to suit emergent playing styles; in general terms, there was a move towards the adoption of heavier, more resistant bows that were suited to articulating *spiccato* with great precision and to producing incisive *pesante* accents.

The history of the bow comprises a constant organological evolution in synergy with trends in performance style. This is as true for the development of reproduction bows throughout the early music movement to date, as in earlier centuries. From the revivalist bows of DOLMETSCH, through those made to satisfy the demands of the HIP recording boom in the 1980s and 1990s, to new 'period' bows made today, the requirements of players, and fashions in the stylistic characteristics demanded by professional life have subtly changed and will doubtless continue to do so.

Original Baroque and transitional bows were designed for an age when string playing was highly individualistic. There was far less artistic conformity in the seventeenth and eighteenth centuries than is commonly demonstrated by modern 'period' instrumentalists. As the master/apprentice pedagogical model gave way to conservatoire education at the start of the nineteenth century, and approaches to technique, bow-stroke selection and tone production became formalised and regulated, the institutional aspiration for uniformity and the consequent desire for a standardised bow coincided perfectly with the development of the Tourte model.

Information about the historical bow can be found with relative ease, as can evidence related to historical bow technique and strokes; how to coalesce these constituent components within the exigencies of professional expectations continues to remain more philosophically and practically challenging than might be expected, given the maturity and success of the HIP industry in the twenty-first century.

FURTHER READING

D. D. Boyden, *The History of Violin Playing from its Origins to 1761: and its Relationship to the Violin and Violin Music* (Oxford University Press, 1965).
C. Brown, *Classical and Romantic Performing Practice 1750–1900* (Oxford University Press, 1999).
J. Dilworth, 'The bow: its history and development', in R. Stowell (ed.), *The Cambridge Companion to the Cello* (Cambridge University Press, 1999).
R. E. Seletsky, 'New light on the old bow: 1', *EMc*, 32/2 (2004), 286–302; 'New light on the old bow: 2', *EMc*, 32/3 (2004), 415–26.
R. Stowell, *Violin Technique and Performance Practice in the Late Eighteenth and Early Nineteenth Centuries* (Cambridge University Press, 1985).

CLAIRE HOLDEN

Bowman, James (b. Oxford, 6 November 1941) English countertenor.

Bowman's career spans a crucial half-century in the development of the countertenor voice. Predominantly employed from mediaeval times as a chorus member in sacred music, the countertenor emerged in the second half of the twentieth century as a soloist, capable of undertaking roles in opera and oratorio. Bowman's experience mirrors this progression. After early training as a boy chorister (Ely Cathedral), and later as a choral scholar (New College, Oxford), he made the transition to the operatic stage in a number of contemporary works: in 1967 he sang Oberon in BRITTEN's *A Midsummer Night's Dream*, a role created for ALFRED DELLER. Other roles followed, created to exploit his expressive voice and commanding stage presence, including the Priest in Peter Maxwell Davies's *Taverner* (1972), Apollo in Britten's *Death in Venice* (1973) and Astron in TIPPETT's *The Ice Break* (1977). At the same period, his interest in early music was sparked by his association with DAVID MUNROW and the EARLY MUSIC CONSORT OF LONDON, with whom he recorded a wide repertory, from Gregorian chant, through Machaut and Dufay to music of the early seventeenth century. Later in his career he formed an equally productive relationship with Robert King and The King's Consort, with whom he recorded the complete Purcell odes, anthems and services.

Bowman played a major role in establishing the viability of the countertenor to tackle CASTRATO roles in Baroque opera, overcoming the initial reluctance of directors to cast a voice which was perceived to be quieter and technically more limited than a 'full' voice. In 1970 Bowman made history by becoming the first countertenor soloist at Glyndebourne, as Endymione in Cavalli's *Calisto*. He later became something of a HANDEL specialist, with more than a dozen roles in his repertory, notably Polinesso (*Ariodante*), Giulio Cesare and Orlando.

FURTHER READING

P. Giles, *The History and Technique of the Counter-Tenor: A Study of the Male High Voice Family* (Aldershot: Scolar Press, Ashgate, 1994).

PATRICIA HOWARD

Boyden, David Dodge (b. Westport, CT, 10 December 1910; d. Berkeley, 18 September 1986) American musicologist and violinist.

Boyden studied at Columbia University, Hartt School of Music and Harvard, and taught at the University of California, Berkeley 1938–75, becoming full professor (1955) and chairman of the music department (1955–61). His pioneering research into the history of stringed instruments and string playing, disseminated largely in his *A History of Violin Playing from its Origins to 1761* (1965), considers the violin, its music, technique and performance chronologically from the sixteenth through to the mid-eighteenth century in the light of practical experience and a wide range of evidence. It also challenges established notions, notably of Gasparo da Salò as the violin's inventor and of the authenticity of the 'BACH' BOW. Boyden contributed two other textbooks, significant chapters/articles on organological issues, GEMINIANI, TARTINI, CORELLI and ORNAMENTATION and DYNAMICS, as well as an important facsimile edition of Geminiani's treatise on violin playing and an annotated catalogue of the Hill instrument collection in Oxford's Ashmolean Museum (1969).

ROBIN STOWELL

Brahms, Johannes (b. Hamburg, 7 May 1833; d. Vienna, 3 April 1897) German composer, pianist and conductor.

As the son of a working musician in Hamburg, Brahms gained early practical experience of performance, learning the HORN, VIOLIN and CELLO with Johann Jacob Brahms, as well as the PIANO with Otto Cossel and Eduard Marxsen, and publishing piano arrangements of popular items anonymously for the Hamburg publisher Cranz. He made his solo debut aged fifteen. His concertising was later greatly expanded by collaboration with JOACHIM and others in the chamber repertory, and with the baritone Julius Stockhausen, who promoted Schubert and Schumann in his recitals. At his first appearances in Vienna in 1862, Brahms presented himself both as pianist in his own new Piano Quartets, Opp. 25 and 26, and as soloist in his *Variations and Fugue on a Theme of Handel*, Op. 24. His recital repertory until that point had featured MOZART and BEETHOVEN piano concertos, Beethoven sonatas and variations, Schumann's Piano Concerto and Fantasia in C, and J. S. BACH's *Chromatic*

Fantasia and Fugue. He later confined his performances increasingly to his own works, premiering most of his chamber music with piano, and the Second Piano Concerto (1881 in Budapest), as he had also presented the First Concerto with Joachim and the Hanover Court Orchestra in 1859.

Brahms was a masterly player and composer for the piano, whose execution was described early on by Schumann as essentially orchestral in effect; his *51 Übungen* and *Paganini Variations*, Op. 35 also show the level of his youthful technical virtuosity. But less poetic observers found him to have a somewhat detached playing and platform manner (as is apparent in von Beckerath's posthumous – though reputedly very faithful – sketches). Hanslick found his playing too reticent at his Vienna premiere, and Eugenie Schumann felt him ill at ease with the instrument, as though impatient for orchestral expression. In later years when he did not practise, his performances were very inaccurate, as Stanford observed of his rendering of the Second Piano Concerto. However, Stanford also noted a velvety quality in the slow movement; in his teaching of Florence May and Eugenie Schumann, Brahms certainly stressed variety of touch and tone and distinctive phrasing. In chamber music he was noted as playing in a tight, classical style; and with singers as an equal partner, providing strong basses in the piano part.

Brahms gained his first professional experience as a choral conductor during his engagement at the court of Detmold in the winter seasons of 1857-9 and in his second year in Vienna, 1863-4 with the *Wiener Singakademie*. In Detmold he showed a pioneering spirit in the performance of much little or unknown Baroque and Renaissance music; he even copied out Palestrina's *Missa Papae Marcelli*, though it was never apparently performed. With the *Wiener Singakademie* he presented BACH cantatas (most only becoming available in modern editions through the Leipzig *Bach Gesellschaft* from 1851), and even Schütz's 'Saul, Saul, was verfolgst du mich' from the *Symphoniarum sacrarum*, part 3, copied from Carl von Winterfeld's *Johannes Gabrieli und sein Zeitalter* (1834), music completely unknown to audiences. As director of the Gesellschaft der Musikfreunde in Vienna 1872-5, he added major works of Bach and HANDEL, though he continued his educational bent with comparative performances of settings of the choral 'Es ist genug' by Bach and J. R. Ahle. All this reflected his intimate interest in the work of modern editors of 'early music' and concern for accurate EDITIONS. Among his own editorial work he produced single editions of concertos and sonatas by C. P. E. BACH and W. F. BACH, the *Pièces de Clavecin* of FRANÇOIS COUPERIN for Friedrich Chrysander's series *Denkmäler der Tonkunst* in 1871, and chamber duets for Chrysander's *Händels Werke*, for which he realised the continuo part.

All Brahms's studies ultimately served to stimulate his own composition: he had founded his own Frauenchor in Hamburg in 1859 to bring early music and his own music together in study and performance, and the steady stream of choral works which led to *Ein deutsches Requiem* revived and reinterpreted historical repertory. The theme of his orchestral variations on the 'St Anthony Chorale' was given to Brahms in a manuscript copy by the HAYDN scholar C. F. Pohl and thus first published in this work; Brahms apparently knew the theme of his 'Handel Variations' through the original 1733 print when he published it in 1862 (and some variations simulate Baroque models); the theme of the variation finale of the Fourth Symphony is an adaptation of the bass from a movement from Bach's Cantata 150, hardly known to audiences in its original form, nor evidently to the conductor HANS VON BÜLOW.

Brahms's attitude to performance itself was always practical. To the baritone Georg Henschel, suffering from a cold in Brahms's own *Triumphlied*, he commented that a thinking sensible singer may change a note which for some reason or other was out of his compass into one which he could reach with comfort, provided always that the declamation remained correct and the accentuation did not suffer. As regards style, he always favoured elasticity of tempi, even eventually deleting the METRONOME marks he had provided for the first issues of the full score of *Ein deutsches Requiem* in 1894 following his belief that his musical feeling and a mechanical instrument simply did not go together; but he was also sensitive to dragging, revising the marking 'poco sostenuto' to 'meno allegro' at the end of the first movement of the First Symphony since conductors were taking it too slowly. Opinions differed regarding his CONDUCTING ability. He seems to have been technically adequate if not polished, but, due doubtless to his careful preparation, able to communicate the expressive meaning. Though Brahms could be physically vigorous, Ferdinand Schumann stresses rather his concise, calm gestures and amiable directions to the different instrumental groups, and this is well illustrated in sketches by von Beckerath. His direction of the premiere of *Ein deutsches Requiem* appears to have been very effective, as was the first exposure of his Fourth Symphony under his baton in MEININGEN in 1885.

FURTHER READING

G. Henschel, *Recollections of Brahms* (Boston: R. G. Badger, 1907), 18–19.
F. Schumann, 'Brahms and Clara Schumann', trans. J. Mayer, *MQ*, 2 (1916), 514–15.

MICHAEL MUSGRAVE

Bream, Julian (b. London, 15 July 1933) English guitarist and lutenist.

Bream encouraged many fine composers to write for the GUITAR, introducing new techniques, and he undoubtedly helped to secure the instrument's place in twentieth-century musical culture. His career has been well documented on film and includes BBC programmes featuring The Julian Bream Consort, *Guitarra!* a series for Channel 4 television and the 2003 DVD video profile *Julian Bream: My Life in Music* containing three hours of interviews and performances.

It was Bream's exploration of early guitar TRANSCRIPTIONS which inspired his love of the LUTE. However, to preserve his guitar technique, especially his use of the fingernails, he commissioned his lutes to have a slightly raised ebony fingerboard, with fixed metal frets and a bridge with bone saddle, thus raising the height of the strings over the soundboard. As a result, he adapted the lute to his technique rather than adapting his technique to the lute (he played with thumb out and without resting the little finger on the soundboard, for example). Bream did much to bring early music to the general public, sometimes playing in concert halls rather the more usual chamber settings. He revived the interest in Elizabethan lute-songs with tenor Peter Pears and his period-instrument ensemble The Julian Bream Consort, giving highly expressive performances of John Dowland, William Byrd and THOMAS MORLEY.

FURTHER READING

T. Palmer, *Julian Bream: A Life on the Road* (London: Macdonald, 1982).
G. Wade, *The Art of Julian Bream* (Blaydon on Tyne: Ashley Mark, 2008).

JAMES WESTBROOK

Bremner, Robert (b. ?Edinburgh, c1713; d. London, 12 May 1789) British publisher and music dealer.

In 1754 Bremner opened a music shop in Edinburgh. Its success encouraged him to move to London in 1762 where he established a complementary business in The Strand, with the identical brand name of *Harp and Hautboy*. Over the following twenty years Bremner established himself as the principal music publisher in London, printing music that reflected and promoted the rich musical life of the city.

Bremner had studied the VIOLIN with GEMINIANI and his wider interest in performance is reflected in his publishing activities, including TREATISES on the rudiments of music, THOROUGHBASS, GUITAR and HARPSICHORD playing. A projected treatise on violin playing, written by Bremner himself and aimed at amateur and professional players, was only partially realised. The first part, *Some Thoughts on the Performance of Concert Music*, appeared in 1777 as part of an edition of six quartets by Johann Schetky; the promised one or more further instalments never appeared, denying the public a treatise of major significance. The printed portion, however, achieved wider distribution through its publication in German in the newly founded *Magazin der Musik* of 1783, when the editor Carl Friedrich Cramer provided some dissenting remarks on Bremner's views on VIBRATO. The treatise also contains some informative asides on ORGAN playing and choral singing.

FURTHER READING

J. Preston, *An Additional Catalogue of Instrumental Music and Vocal Music Printed and Sold by Preston and Son ... Late the Property of That Eminent Dealer Mr. Robert Bremner* (London, 1790).
N. Zaslaw, 'The compleat orchestral musician. Text and commentary on Robert Bremner's "Some Thoughts on the Performance of Concert Music" (1777)', *EMc*, 79 (1979), 46–57; 80 (1980), 71–2.

DAVID WYN JONES

Bréval, Jean-Baptiste Sébastien (b. Paris, 6 November 1753; d. Colligis, Aisne, 18 March 1823) Cellist and composer.

Bréval studied with Jean-Baptiste Cupis, and possibly with Martin Berteau. He was a member of the *Concert Spirituel*, the Théâtre Feydeau orchestra, and the Paris Opéra, retiring in 1814. He may have taught at the PARIS CONSERVATOIRE between 1796 and 1802; some of his compositions were used as teaching and examination material. Bréval composed string chamber music, particularly string duos and quartets of the *quatuor concertant dialogué* type, seven CELLO concertos and many sonatas, one of which is still used for teaching purposes. His music is graceful, charming, technically straightforward and popular with amateurs, to whom his 'facile et agréable' Op. 28 set of solos was dedicated. Several sets of duos were published in both Paris and London. His more demanding works require scales and arpeggio passagework in thumb position, bariolage in high registers and occasional extended up-bow staccato. Some of his easier cello duos were re-published in the later nineteenth century, and some sonatas were edited by Alfred Moffat, Carl Schroeder, Diran Alexanian and Gaspar Cassadó. His own performances were said to have had fine style but lacked energy.

His *Traité du violoncelle*, Op. 42 (Paris: Janet et Cotelle, 1804) was his last published work. This large treatise (over 200 pages, with hundreds of music examples) was written for provincial players unable to find a teacher. It covers a very wide range of topics, including extremely complex arpeggio BOWING, HARMONICS, thumb position on the upper strings (illustrated by twelve of Bréval's sonatas and six duos), double stops (with an exercise very similar to one by DUPORT) and virtuosic material including passages in broken tenths. For some scales Bréval gives several different FINGERINGS in addition to that given by GUNN and Duport. He does not, however, deal with any aspect of ORNAMENTATION, and his verbal explanations are few. A free English adaptation was prepared by John Peile – *Bréval's New Instructions for the Violoncello* (London: C. Wheatstone & Co., [1810]). This amplifies some sections such as the shape of the left hand (opposing the 'violinistic' shape), while over-simplifying others such as posture (not clarifying the importance of holding the cello by the edges). While his compositions had some longevity, Bréval's *Traité* had only limited success and was perceived as old-fashioned even at the time.

FURTHER READING

G. Kennaway, *Playing the Cello, 1780–1930* (Farnham: Ashgate, 2014).
S. Milliot, *Le violoncelle en France au XVIIIe siècle* (Paris and Geneva: Champion-Slatkine, 1985).
V. Walden, *One Hundred Years of Violoncello* (Cambridge University Press, 1998).

GEORGE KENNAWAY

Britten, (Edward) Benjamin (b. Lowestoft, 22 November 1913; d. Aldeburgh, 4 December 1976) English composer, conductor and pianist.

Britten had a significant impact on musical life as composer, pianist and conductor, although on a psychological level he had a complex relationship with his role as a performer: private music making was a source of pleasure and enjoyment, but performing in public often entailed off-stage symptoms of intense nervousness. The establishment of the English Opera Group (1946) and the Aldeburgh Festival (1948) as the focus of Britten's work as an interpreter can be seen as an attempt to establish an ensemble and a local, semi-private environment in which he could work most effectively.

It was as accompanist for his partner, the tenor Peter Pears, that Britten attracted attention as a performer from the early 1940s, initially for his acutely characterised PIANO playing and later his increasingly accomplished CONDUCTING. In the latter role Britten's approach was a reaction against what he felt to be the sentimental expressivity of earlier conductors (e.g. Bruno Walter): no string PORTAMENTI or fussy dynamic inflections, a strong rhythmic pulse (though with subtle RUBATO) and responsiveness to dramatic and structural features. His performances of earlier repertoires (Purcell, BACH and MOZART), in part reflected contemporary attitudes towards appropriate orchestra size and string VIBRATO, but the imaginative continuo realisations, textural lucidity, crisp rhythms, sprightly TEMPI and often detached string ARTICULATION can be heard as anticipations of later approaches, and in the mid-1950s he borrowed a Stein FORTEPIANO for performances of Mozart. By this time, thanks to the imaginative programming of Imogen Holst (artistic director with Britten and Pears), the Aldeburgh Festival's programmes had expanded in historical range from organum to the avant-garde, and it has since hosted several generations of specialist HIP ensembles. The whole gamut of Britten's own activity as a performer was exceptionally well documented through recordings and broadcasts.

FURTHER READING

P. Kildea (ed.), *Britten on Music* (Oxford University Press, 2003).
C. Grogan (ed.), *Imogen Holst: A Life in Music* (Woodbridge: Boydell Press, 2007).
D. Mitchell, P. Reed and M. Cooke (eds.), *Letters from a Life: The Selected Letters of Benjamin Britten* vols. 1–3 (London: Faber & Faber, 1991, 2004); vols. 4–6 (Woodbridge: Boydell Press, 2008, 2010, 2012).

PAUL BANKS

Broadcasting Radio played a crucial role in fostering HISTORICALLY INFORMED PERFORMANCE, particularly in Europe. The situation in Great Britain provides a good example. The British Broadcasting Company (founded in 1922) became the British Broadcasting Corporation (BBC) in 1927. From the start, it introduced unfamiliar repertoire and unusual instruments. VIOLET GORDON WOODHOUSE and Anne E. Farnell-Watson broadcast HARPSICHORD recitals in 1924, and the CHAPLIN Trio (sisters Nellie, Kate and Mabel Chaplin) played the harpsichord, viola d'amore and viola da gamba. A pair of 1934 programmes from the Primitive Methodist Chapel, Upper Ettingshall included 'the playing of an ophicleide ... Black Country melodists of the last century loved to write parts for it ... Joseph Kirkland, who is to play it, is self-taught, there being no teachers left.'

At a time when recordings of BACH's cantatas scarcely existed, the BBC broadcast one cantata a week over a four-year period (1928–31). Rarely seen opera flourished: HANDEL's *Rodelinda* and MONTEVERDI's *Il ritorno d'Ulisse in patria* were both broadcast in 1928, and BBC staff undertook musicological projects. For the Handel anniversary in 1935, Julian Herbage prepared a new edition of *Messiah* conducted by Adrian Boult, which aimed to present, according to the *Radio Times*, 'a version as true to the original score as it is possible to make it'. Boult and Herbage returned to *Messiah* in 1942 but Herbage's material had been destroyed in the Blitz, so the work had to be done all over again (and was subsequently used for Boult's Decca recording in 1954).

The post-war period saw projects on the BBC Third Programme (established in 1946) such as the *History in Sound of European Music* devised by Gerald Abraham. The first of seventy episodes ('The oldest surviving secular music') was broadcast on 3 January 1948; episode 40 was devoted to 'Baroque ornamentation in vocal and instrumental music'. Programmes which raised questions about how old music should be performed were a feature of the time. In

1950, Arnold Goldsbrough conducted Handel's *Acis and Galatea* in a new edition made with Basil Lam. According to the *Radio Times*, the editors aimed to restore 'the spirit of Handel's own performances. A small orchestra and chorus will be used. Ornaments have been added in the arias, especially in the repeats.' Programmes specifically about vocal style included two on 'Ornamentation in Mozart's vocal music' presented by CHARLES MACKERRAS and Fritz Spiegl in 1957, the same year in which the phrase 'authentic performance' first appeared in the *Radio Times* to describe a concert by the Philomusica of London directed by THURSTON DART. Dart made his BBC debut as a boy chorister singing lute songs on *Children's Hour* in 1936. From 1948 onwards, he gave numerous broadcasts as a harpsichordist and devised programmes of music ranging from Josquin to C. P. E. BACH.

Repertoire that was then uncommon in the concert hall flourished on the radio. Between 1947 and 1959, the BBC broadcast six performances of Monteverdi's *Vespers*; the 1959 account from Brompton Oratory used 'a chamber orchestra including recorders, cornetts, and sackbuts'. Early pianos featured regularly, and in 1959 MOZART's Piano Quartet K493 was broadcast with Joyce Rathbone using a FORTEPIANO. The violinist Alan Loveday gave a Bach recital in 1961 on 'an unaltered instrument dating from Bach's time'. The size of performing forces was another preoccupation, and in 1970 James Loughran conducted a specially recorded BEETHOVEN symphony cycle 'with an orchestra of the size Beethoven knew'.

Radio stations all over Europe followed a similar pattern, but German radio did most to encourage the diffusion of early music. On Easter Sunday 1931, *Mitteldeutscher Rundfunk AG* (MIRAG) broadcast Bach's cantata *Christ lag in Todesbanden* from Leipzig, performed by the Thomanenchor and Gewandhaus Orchestra under Karl Straube, the first of a series that ran until 1937, broadcast to many countries in mainland Europe. A Leipzig newspaper claimed that the Bach cantata series was 'Europe's biggest shared radio event' at the time. After the war, German radio stations supported early music energetically, and in 1954 *Nordwestdeutscher Rundfunk* (later WDR) in Cologne even established its own ensemble, the Cappella Coloniensis. This was an initiative of the station's musicologist, Eduard Gröninger, who amassed the old instruments (or replicas), and recruited players from all over Europe. Its first director was AUGUST WENZINGER and early projects included Monteverdi's *Orfeo* with period instruments (at the 1955 Hitzacker Festival, subsequently recorded). This pioneering ensemble applied research into historical performance practice and radio was the ideal medium to demonstrate the results, including Handel's *Alcina* in 1959, conducted by Ferdinand Leitner. In 1966 Archiv issued a recording of Mozart's Serenade K203 under Leitner – one of the earliest discs of Mozart's orchestral music on period instruments – and the advertisement in *The Gramophone* described the ensemble as 'the Barock orchestra of the WDR'.

Austrian Radio in Vienna broadcast Monteverdi's *Orfeo* in 1954, presenting the reconstruction edited and conducted by PAUL HINDEMITH, using mostly old instruments, and an edition that attempted to get back to Monteverdi's original. The small orchestra included NIKOLAUS HARNONCOURT, who later described the occasion as 'like being struck by lightning'.

In France, the *Société de Musique d'Autrefois* broadcast Baroque repertoire on period instruments from the late 1920s onwards, conducted by Jean Huré and then by Roger Désormière (more usually associated with new music). NADIA BOULANGER also made frequent appearances on French radio during the 1930s, often performing unfamiliar repertoire.

Though television has been less dominant in presenting historical performance, there have been notable moments: NOAH GREENBERG'S NEW YORK PRO MUSICA appeared on the CBS *Omnibus* series in 1955, *The Play of Daniel* was televised from the Cloisters in 1958, and for Canadian television, Greenberg and his players made 'The Renaissance Band' in 1965. In Britain, DAVID MUNROW'S EARLY MUSIC CONSORT OF LONDON reached a large television audience with music for *The Six Wives of Henry VIII* (1970) and *Elizabeth R* (1971). The early years of BBC Two (which opened in 1964) produced several enterprising music programmes, including a rare venture into televised musicology. In 1965 the *Workshop* series devoted a programme to Beethoven's 'Eroica' Symphony presented by Bernard Keeffe and including Keeffe's orchestrations of sketches to demonstrate the compositional process.

Recording companies increasingly led the way in fostering historical performance from the 1970s onwards, but radio and television have continued to play an important part. One of the most imaginative initiatives in the twenty-first century was the French television series *Presto!* (2007–9) in which Pierre Charvet introduced music from LULLY to Shostakovich with LES SIÈCLES and François-Xavier Roth performing all the works on instruments appropriate to the time and place.

FURTHER READING

H. Haskell, *The Early Music Revival: A History* (London: Thames & Hudson, 1988).
C. Lawson (ed.), *The Cambridge Companion to the Orchestra* (Cambridge University Press, 2003).
D. Stevens, 'Performance practice issues on the BBC Third Programme', *PPR*, 2/1 (1989), 3–81.
'BBC Genome Project', http://genome.ch.bbc.co.uk

NIGEL SIMEONE

Brossard, Sébastien de (b. Dompierre, bap. 12 September 1655; d. Meaux, 10 August 1730) French lexicographer, collector, theorist, historian and self-taught composer.

Brossard occupies a unique place in the history of French music. His tenure as *Maître de chapelle* at the cathedral of Strasbourg brought him into contact with a wide range of musical and theoretical traditions from Germany, France and Italy, on which he drew to assemble his enormous collection of scores and writings, and as inspiration for his own work. The main source of his pronouncements on performance is his *Dictionnaire de musique* (Paris: Christophe Ballard, 1701, with several later editions), whose encyclopedic breadth defies generalisation. Other sources include the autograph catalogue of his collection, along with a number of manuscript writings and the prefaces to his published music. Brossard's works shed considerable light on musical theory, on choral practices in provincial churches, on the SINGING of Gregorian chant and *chant sur le livre* (improvised polyphony), as well as the arrangement of others' works, among further topics.

FURTHER READING

C. Cessac, 'The presentation of Lully's *Alceste* at the Strasbourg Académie de Musique', in J. Hajdu-Heyer (ed.), *Lully Studies* (New York: Cambridge University Press, 2000), 199–215.

J. Duron, *L'oeuvre de Sébastien de Brossard (1655–1730): Catalogue thématique* (Versailles: Éditions du Centre de Musique Baroque de Versailles, 1995).

J. Duron (ed.), *Sébastien de Brossard, musicien* (Paris: Klincksieck, 1998).

DON FADER

Brown, Clive (b. Bolton, 7 May 1947) English musicologist and emeritus professor, University of Leeds.

Brown read history and then music at the University of Cambridge. After a period of teaching music and performing as a violinist, he gained a DPhil at the University of Oxford (1980), with a thesis on LOUIS SPOHR. He remained at Oxford as a lecturer, but later moved to Bretton Hall College and eventually the University of Leeds. His seminal *Classical & Romantic Performing Practice 1750–1900* (Oxford University Press, 1999), a wide-ranging work with an emphasis on the German school of string playing (SPOHR, DAVID, JOACHIM), but with considerable material on matters of style in general, inspired a generation of researchers in nineteenth-century performance practice. At Leeds he directed the CHASE research project (http://chase.leeds.ac.uk), which assembled a database of nineteenth-century annotated EDITIONS of string music now widely used in universities and conservatoires. He has published extensively on eighteenth- and nineteenth-century topics, and remains active as a violinist specialising in historically informed performance. He has directed workshops and lectured at many institutions in Europe, the USA and Australia.

GEORGE KENNAWAY

Brown, Howard Mayer (b. Los Angeles, 13 April 1930; d. Venice, 20 February 1993) American musicologist.

Brown's groundbreaking approach to performance practice paired close study of repertoire with the information that could be gleaned from contemporaneous depictions and written accounts of music making. Concentrating largely on instruments and instrumentation, the research Brown conducted for his landmark *Musical Iconography* (Cambridge, MA: Harvard University Press, 1972) led to detailed considerations of the Trecento fiddle, SHAWM, HARP and gittern; his expertise in theatrical music resulted in studies of instrumentation in French chansons and Florentine *intermedii* (*Sixteenth-Century Instrumentation: Music for the Florentine Intermedii*. Musicological Studies and Documents 30 (Middleton, WI: American Institute of Musicology, 1973)); and he literally wrote the book on *Embellishing Sixteenth-Century Music* (London: Oxford University Press, 1976). In 1980 he drew much of this research together in a richly illustrated article 'Performing Practice' in *NG* (1980, 14: 370–93), which treated Western music up to the era of sound recordings. His discussion of notational styles and their musical rendering reminded readers that all textual interpretation must be paired with social history, ICONOGRAPHY, organology and 'le bon goût'. He also acknowledged the unique sound of the hand-stopped HORN and early nineteenth-century PIANO in performances of sonatas such as BEETHOVEN's Op. 17, but felt that 'almost insuperable' obstacles prevented early music ensembles from assembling the gut-strung string instruments, early woodwinds, and valveless brass required to perform Beethoven's symphonies.

With STANLEY SADIE, Brown edited *Performance Practice* (2 vols., London: Macmillan Press, 1989), an invaluable guide to 'the study of past performance', dealing with performance contexts, sources, theory, instruments and their techniques and other relevant topics such as NOTATION, PITCH, TEMPO, tuning and ORNAMENTATION. Brown was a fine flautist and conductor and a determined gambist. He recorded the first volume of the *Historical Anthology of Music* edited by Davison and Apel (10 LPs, Pleiades Recordings, 1973–6) and mounted the first American performance of Jacopo Peri's *Euridice* in January 1967 with the Collegium Musicum of the University of Chicago. His edition of *Euridice* appeared in 1980.

FURTHER READING

R. Jackson, 'Pathfinder in performance practice: Howard Mayer Brown, 1930–1993', *PPR*, 6 (1993), 107–12.

KATE VAN ORDEN

Brüggen, Franciscus Jozef (b. Amsterdam, 30 October 1934; d. Amsterdam, 13 August 2014) Dutch pioneer of the early music movement, recorder player, flautist and co-founder of the Orchestra of the Eighteenth Century.

Brüggen studied FLUTE and RECORDER at the Amsterdam Conservatory and at the age of 21 was appointed professor of Baroque music at the ROYAL CONSERVATORY OF THE HAGUE. Initially a solo recorder player and chamber musician, he often worked in partnership with GUSTAV LEONHARDT and ANNER BYLSMA. In 1972 he founded the avant-garde recorder trio Sour Cream with Kees Boeke and Walter van Hauwe and elevated the profile of the instrument with his expressive, flexible approach. With the ORCHESTRA OF THE EIGHTEENTH CENTURY, Brüggen explored repertoire ranging from J. S. BACH and RAMEAU to Schubert and MENDELSSOHN.

From 1988 he became closely associated with the ORCHESTRA OF THE AGE OF ENLIGHTENMENT, being appointed emeritus conductor in 2007. He was particularly noted for unstinting exploration of subtle and varying colours in the wind section.

ASHLEY SOLOMON

Brunelli, Antonio (b. San Croce sull'Arno, Tuscany, 20 December 1577; d. Pisa, before 19 November 1630) Italian composer, organist, teacher and writer on music.

Brunelli was active in Florence and collaborated with the singer-composer architects of the new monodic style, such as GIULIO CACCINI and Jacopo Peri. He published two short TREATISES: *Regole utilissime* (1606) 'for scholars who wish to learn to sing', a primer covering rudiments and simple counterpoint; and *Varii esercitii* (1614), a book of more advanced exercises. It begins with simple diminutions in plain (*ordinario*) equal note values, each followed by dotted versions of the same (labelled *meglio* or *migliore*); these are followed by duets designed for the teacher to sing with his pupil in order to teach first simple and then florid counterpoint. Exercise 6 consists of imitative diminutions highly reminiscent of the instrumental interludes in the aria 'Possente spirto' in MONTEVERDI's *Orfeo* (1607). Brunelli's volume is, indeed, addressed not just to singers but also 'for practising on cornetts, flutes, recorders, viols, violins and similar instruments'.

FURTHER READING

A. Brunelli, *Varii esercitii 1614*, ed. R. Erig (Zurich: Musik Hug, 1977).

RICHARD WISTREICH

Brunold, Paul (b. Paris, 14 October 1875; d. Paris, 14 September 1948) French harpsichordist, organist and musicologist.

Brunold studied at the PARIS CONSERVATOIRE under the direction of Lavignac, Leroux and Marmontel, and later Paderewski. His possession from 1910 onwards of an eighteenth-century harpsichord began a lifelong study of its repertoire. He published the pioneering series *Les maîtres français du clavecin* (Paris, 1914–25), an influential performance textbook, *Traité des signes* (Lyons, 1925) and the first critical editions of the harpsichord music of CHAMBONNIÈRES, Clérambault and Dieupart, and (also including their organ music) of LOUIS COUPERIN and FRANÇOIS COUPERIN. In 1915 he was appointed organist of Saint-Gervais in Paris and in 1934 published a monograph on its historic organ. From 1946 he was curator of the instrument collection at the Paris Conservatoire, where he supervised the restoration of many instruments to playing condition and promoted them in a series of concerts.

FURTHER READING

Nécrologie, 'Paul Brunold (1875–1948)', *RM*, 30, 85/88 (1948), 137.
Obituary, 'Paul Brunold', *MT*, 89/1269 (November, 1948), 350.

TERENCE CHARLSTON

Buchner, Hans (Johannes) (b. Ravensburg, 26 October 1483; d. ?Konstanz, 1538) German organist and composer.

A pupil of Paul Hofhaimer, Buchner (also known as Hans von Constanz) was organist in Konstanz from 1506 to 1526. Highly esteemed by his contemporaries as an organist, ORGAN builder and teacher, his most important work was his *Fundamentum*, written about 1520. This was divided into three sections: keyboard performance, arranging vocal pieces for the keyboard and techniques for contrapuntal development of a cantus firmus. *Fundamentum* contains the earliest known keyboard FINGERINGS and the earliest extant collection of liturgical organ music.

Buchner affirms that his fingerings are only a guide, to be modified with further experience, but his principles suggest a non-legato technique with paired fingerings that imply a variety of ARTICULATIONS. Metrically 'good' notes in both hands are played with the second and fourth fingers. The third finger is sometimes 'bad', sometimes 'good'. Consecutive fifth fingers are used when playing two parts with one hand, as is (rarely) the thumb.

FURTHER READING

Anthology of Early Keyboard Methods, trans. and ed. B. Sachs and B. Ife (Cambridge: Gamut Publications, 1981), 63–5.

W. Apel, *The History of Keyboard Music to 1700*, trans. and rev. H. Tischler (Bloomington, IN: Indiana University Press, 1972).

J. Butt, 'Germany and the Netherlands', in A. Silbiger (ed.), *Keyboard Music before 1700* (New York and London: Routledge, 2004), 147–234.

DAVID PONSFORD

Bülow, Hans von (b. Dresden, 8 January 1830; d. Cairo, 12 February 1894) German conductor and pianist.

Hans von Bülow studied with Friedrich Wieck, Louis Plaidy and Franz Liszt. He transformed the process of orchestral preparation through his rigorous approach to sectional REHEARSAL and his demand that his musicians memorise their parts. His orchestral innovations (some of which were short-lived) included the use of the five-stringed DOUBLE BASS, the 'Ritter' VIOLA and pedal TIMPANI.

He conducted legendary performances of WAGNER's *Tristan und Isolde* and *Die Meistersinger von Nürnberg* in the 1860s in Munich, as well as the premiere of BRAHMS's Symphony No. 4 in 1885 in Meiningen. Other radical performance practices included CONDUCTING Brahms's First Piano Concerto from the keyboard, and performing BEETHOVEN's *Grosse Fuge* with a full string section. An outstanding pianist, von Bülow was the first to perform all of Beethoven's piano sonatas as a cycle, a practice which has gained in popularity.

NATASHA LOGES

Burney, Charles (b. Shrewsbury, 7 April 1726; d. Chelsea, London, 12 April 1814) English musician, composer and music historian.

Son of a dancer, violinist and portrait painter originally named Macburney, Charles Burney was educated in Chester and Shrewsbury, benefiting from the many musicians travelling between London and Dublin. After moving to London in 1744, he apprenticed successively to Thomas Arne and gentleman Fulke Greville while playing ORGAN at St Dionis Backchurch and VIOLIN in concerts at the Swan Tavern. Ill health forced Burney to move to King's Lynn in 1751 for nine years; working as an organist, he developed high-level social and professional contacts, most notably with David Garrick for producing pieces by William Shakespeare and J.-J. ROUSSEAU.

As Roger Lonsdale suggested, '[Burney's] chief ambition and achievement was to be accepted as a "man of letters" rather than as a "mere musician"' (viii). In 1770 and 1772 Burney published books on the state of musical life in European countries, depicting what Vanessa Agnew interprets as 'orphic powers' parallel to what Captain James Cook saw in music of the Pacific islands at that time. The *General History of Music*, published in three volumes in 1776, 1782 and 1789, established a public for music history among 'polite' amateurs. Indeed, his supporters waged a bitter war in the press against the competing music history written by JOHN HAWKINS, which also appeared in 1776. Even though Burney's opinions on Renaissance music and English music have often been criticised, he has been respected for intelligently depicting the evolution of music in the eighteenth century, showing where the all-Italian repertory of the King's Theatre had come from. Burney devoted the last fifteen years of his life to writing articles on music for Abraham Rees's *Cyclopaedia* and setting forth a detailed memoir. His collections of music and contemporary newspapers proved to be invaluable for scholars from many fields.

FURTHER READING

V. Agnew, *Enlightenment Orpheus: The Power of Music in Other Worlds* (New York: Oxford University Press, 2008).
J. Hemlow et al. (eds.), *The Journals and Letters of Fanny Burney (Madame D'Arblay)* 12 vols. (Oxford University Press, 1972–84).
R. Lonsdale, *Dr. Charles Burney: A Literary Biography* (Oxford: Clarendon Press, 1965).

WILLIAM WEBER

Busoni, Ferruccio (b. Empoli, 1 April 1866; d. Berlin, 27 July 1924) Italian composer and pianist.

Busoni was probably the most influential pianist of the generation after Anton Rubinstein. His contemporary Ignacy Paderewski toured more widely and left a more extensive legacy of recordings, but Busoni's outstanding intellectual engagement with the AESTHETICS and practicalities of performance – its outcome enshrined in a series of visionary compositions, uniquely characteristic TRANSCRIPTIONS, polemical essays and thought-provoking EDITIONS – ensured that even today his ideas remain discussed, debated and frequently applied. His quasi-Platonic conception of the 'musical essence' of a composition, the score of which is already a realisation and therefore a type of transcription (with subsequent performances effectively also transcriptions) gave both a philosophical licence for freedom in performance and a validation of the sometimes despised art of transcription itself. Busoni's aesthetic approach, which stemmed originally from his intense admiration of J. S. BACH and Liszt, was most trenchantly expounded in his editions of the first book of Bach's *48 Preludes and Fugues* and of Liszt's *Reminiscences de Don Juan*, his *Entwurf einer neuen Ästhetik der Tonkunst* and his *Clavierübung*.

FURTHER READING

K. Hamilton, *After the Golden Age: Romantic Pianism and Modern Performance* (New York: Oxford University Press, 2008).
G. Kogan, *Busoni as Pianist*, trans. S. Belsky (University of Rochester Press, 2010).

KENNETH HAMILTON

Butt, John (b. Solihull, England, 17 November 1960) British musicologist, organist, harpsichordist and conductor.

An organ scholar at King's College, Cambridge (1979–82), Butt then undertook doctoral research published as *Bach Interpretation: Articulation Marks in Primary Sources of J. S. Bach* (Cambridge University Press, 1990). He has taught at the universities of Aberdeen, Berkeley (CA), Cambridge and (since 2001) Glasgow. His prolific scholarship includes monographs published by Cambridge University Press on Bach's B minor Mass (1991) and St Matthew and St John Passions (*Bach's Dialogue with Modernity: Perspectives on the Passions*, 2010), *Music Education and the Art of Performance in the German Baroque* (1994) and *Playing with History: The Historical Approach to Musical Performance* (2002).

His many recordings cover a wide range of Baroque keyboard music and, as musical director of the Dunedin Consort, historical reconstructions of works by Bach, HANDEL and MOZART. Honours include the Royal Musical

Association's Dent Medal (2003), fellowships of the Royal Society of Edinburgh (2003) and the British Academy (2006), and an OBE (2013) for services to music in Scotland.

TIM CARTER

Bylsma, Anner (b. The Hague, 17 February 1934) Dutch cellist and pioneer of historical performance.

Bylsma studied with Carel van Leeuwen Boomkamp at the ROYAL CONSERVATORY OF THE HAGUE (1950–5) and shares his teacher's preference for gut strings and the sound of early CELLOS. In 1959 Bylsma won the Casals Competition in Mexico, and between 1962 and 1968 he was principal cellist of the Amsterdam Concertgebouw Orchestra. He is legendary for his versatility across the whole repertory for his instrument. In the early 1960s Bylsma began his long association with GUSTAV LEONHARDT and FRANS BRÜGGEN, and describes Leonhardt as one of his major influences. He played regularly with the Leonhardt Consort and LA PETITE BANDE. Bylsma's 1979 recording of J. S. BACH's Cello Suites (BWV 1007–12) – on his Goffriller Baroque cello and five-string violoncello piccolo for the sixth – took the musical world by storm and people flocked to hear his live performances. In marked contrast to contemporary legato renditions, his lively articulated BOWING and rhetorical silences threw new light on these masterpieces. In 1992 he made a second recording on the 'Servais' Stradivari. In 1998, Bylsma published *Bach, the Fencing Master* with the primary goal of bringing players new ideas, notably using the bow to express the musical intent.

FURTHER READING

A. Bylsma, *Bach, the Fencing Master: Reading Aloud from the First Three Cello Suites* (Basel: Bylsma Fencing Mail, 1998).
P. Laird, *The Baroque Cello Revival: An Oral History* (Lanham, MD: Scarecrow Press, 2004), 63–87.

LUCY ROBINSON

C

Cabezón, Antonio de (b. Castrillo de Matajudíos, c1510; d. Madrid, 26 March 1566) Spanish composer and organist.

Cabezón was a renowned blind keyboard player who served as a chamber musician and chapel organist to the Spanish Habsburgs, including Emperor Charles V, the Empress Isabella and Charles's heir Philip II. His surviving output is transmitted largely in two printed collections, compiled by Luis Venegas de Henestrosa (*Libro de cifra nueva*, 1557) and by Cabezón's son HERNANDO (*Obras de música*, 1578). These present the music using the same system of number TABLATURE, the numbers showing the 'white notes' of the keyboard, with accidentals placed after or beneath the relevant numbers (or presented as a B♭ signature) to indicate inflections, although these indications are far from comprehensive, presenting modern editors and performers with many choices. While both compilers claim that their collections are suitable for performance on keyboard instruments, HARP and VIHUELA (and the preface to the *Obras* also mentions ensemble performance), the suitability of Cabezón's published music to the vihuela or harp seems in practice to be limited. Each collection provides guidance to keyboard players, including on FINGERING and ORNAMENTATION, while more extensive coverage of relevant performance practices is found in TOMÁS DE SANTA MARÍA's *Arte de tañer fantasia* (1565), which was inspected and approved by Cabezón. Many of Cabezón's works are suited to liturgical performance, alongside their didactic purposes. These works, incorporating chant, reflect the fact that the principal role of the organist during the celebration of the Divine Office (principally Vespers) and Mass was to provide versets in alternation with the singers performing chant or polyphony. Cabezón's output of items for such *alternatim* performance includes psalm and hymn *versos*, settings of the canticle *Magnificat*, and Kyrie *versos*. The sets of variations and the numerous decorated transcriptions (*glosados*) of polyphonic vocal works in Cabezón's *oeuvre* demonstrate his inventive approach to the art of embellishment.

FURTHER READING

G. Doderer and M. B. Ripoll (eds.), *A. de Cabezón: Ausgewählte Werke für Tasteninstrumente* (Basel: Bärenreiter, 2010), Introduction.

OWEN REES

Cabezón, Hernando de (b. Madrid, 5 September 1541; d. Valladolid, 1 October 1602) Spanish keyboard player and composer.

Youngest of the five children of ANTONIO DE CABEZÓN (c1510–66), Hernando served as a keyboard player in the households of Kings Philip II and Philip III of Spain. He compiled, transcribed into TABLATURE, and published an anthology of his father Antonio's instrumental works, entitled *Obras de musica para tecla arpa y vihuela* (Madrid: Francisco Sánchez, 1578). The collection – issued twelve years after Antonio's death – presents music which Antonio used in his teaching, and its organisation likewise reflects a pedagogical intent, opening with two-part pieces for beginners and proceeding to more difficult and complex works, including *tientos*, *glosas* of vocal works and sets of variations. Although it is much the largest source of Antonio's music, it represents only a fraction of the works known to Hernando, who stated in his will that two further volumes were ready for publication. The numerical system of tablature used in the *Obras* – indicating the notes within an octave starting from F by the numerals 1 to 7 – had previously appeared in Luis Venegas de Henestrosa's *Libro de cifra nueva* (1557), which includes many works by 'Antonio'. Hernando employs barlines marking units a semibreve in length. His instructions to keyboard players in the prefatory matter include FINGERING patterns: Hernando treats the right and left hands in contrasting ways, advocating paired fingering in the right hand but more extensive use of the thumb and first three fingers in succession for scalic figures in the left hand. The editions in the *Obras* provide an abundance of written-out ornamental figuration, providing models for keyboardists, vihuelists and *ministriles* playing in instrumental ensembles, but in his preface Hernando mentions only one specific type of ornament, the *quiebro*, which is to be played as quickly as possible and kept short.

OWEN REES

Caccini, Giulio (b. Rome, 8 October 1555; d. Florence, bur. 10 December 1618) Italian singer, teacher and composer.

Caccini is best known today for his two volumes of 'New Songs' (*Le nuove musiche*, 1602 and 1614), a compendium of relatively conservative settings of madrigal poetry, scored for self-accompanied solo voice. By 1602, he had for thirty-seven years been a leading singer and composer at the Medici court in Florence, and also Italy's most celebrated singing teacher. *Le nuove musiche* (1602) opens with a Preface addressed 'to the reader' that sets out not only the theoretical principles, but also the practical technicalities of turning a song into a convincingly expressive performance. The theory is based on ideals he had developed during his participation in the 'Camerata', a humanistically inspired academy active in Florence during the 1570s. Dedicated to recreating what they believed was a lost Classical style of monodic SINGING that prioritised text, as opposed to the prevailing contemporary predilection for excessive virtuoso vocal display, the Camerata's experiments undoubtedly contributed to the creation of new musical forms, including 'singing recitation' (*recitar cantando*) that led to the invention of opera. Based on both his practical experience as a singer educated in the Neapolitan technique of vocal agility and refined chamber music style (*see* MAFFEI, GIOVANNI CAMILLO), and his subsequent training of many successful singers (including members of his own family), Caccini claims that he alone was responsible for eschewing singing that 'offered no pleasure beyond that which pleasant sounds give' in favour of music in which 'one could almost speak in tones' (*quasi che in armonia favellare*), employing in it 'a certain noble negligence in singing' (*una certa nobile sprezzatura di canto*). He goes on to describe a range of performance interventions that singers should make, including expressive swelling and diminishing of the voice, ACCENTS and PORTAMENTI, and various types of throat-articulated ORNAMENTATION (*cantar di gorga*), including the seminal *trillo* (Wistreich, 2000, 187–8; Wistreich, 2013). Caccini stresses the importance of only applying melismatic divisions (*passaggi*) sparingly and with discretion to enhance expression of specific words – a thinly veiled criticism of 'the vocal incontinence that has overtaken his contemporaries' (Potter and Sorrell, 78–9). The Preface to *Le nuove musiche* was already internationally circulated within a few years of its publication, and continues to be cited as *the* authority on early Baroque singing. Ironically, as with many other treatises, it is in fact essentially reactionary: a somewhat idealistic rearguard action by one of the last great Renaissance singers.

FURTHER READING

G. Caccini, *Le nuove musiche* (Florence: Marescotti, 1602 and 1614), ed. and trans. H. Wiley Hitchcock (Madison, WI: A-R Editions, 1970 and 1978).
J. Potter and N. Sorrell, *A History of Singing* (Cambridge University Press, 2012).
R. Wistreich, 'Re-constructing pre-Romantic singing technique', in J. Potter (ed.), *The Cambridge Companion to Singing* (Cambridge University Press, 2000), 178–91.
'"Nach der jetzig Newen Italienischen Manier zur guten Art im singen sich gewehnen": The trillo and the migration of Italian noble singing', in S. Ehrmann-Herfort and S. Leopold (eds.), *Migration und Identität: Wanderbewegungen und Kulturkontakte in der Musikgeschichte: Analecta musicologica 49* (Kassel: Bärenreiter, 2013), 137–49.

RICHARD WISTREICH

Cadenza A passage normally near the end of a movement or piece (principally a concerto movement or aria but occasionally a movement for solo keyboard or chamber ensemble), in which the soloist decorates a cadence, usually indicated by a fermata (or 'solo', 'tenuto', 'ad arbitrio', 'a piacimento', or even by a rest, however short), and may introduce some virtuosity. A cadenza is usually unaccompanied and most commonly for one player or singer; it may be either improvised or composed. 'Concerted cadenzas' for two or more soloists were of necessity written out, as in HAYDN's *Sinfonia concertante* H.I:105 and MOZART's Quintet K452.

The cadenza's origins are clouded by terminological inconsistencies in describing a passage of extempore decoration at or around a cadence, especially at the end of a movement or piece. The passage often included the bravura content of a rudimentary cadenza, even if this diverted attention momentarily from the core substance of the movement/piece. Florid cadences ('copula') appear in Franco of Cologne's *Ars cantus mensurabilis* (1260–80), and examples of embellished cadences were provided by Renaissance theorists such as SYLVESTRO DI GANASSI (*Opera intitulata Fontegara*, 1535; *Regola rubertina*, 1542), GIROLAMO DALLA CASA (*Il vero modo di diminuir*, 1584) and Pietro Cerone (*El melopeo y maestro*, 1613). The first to use the term 'cadenza' for these decorated cadences was probably PIETRO AARON (*Toscanello de la musica*, 1523).

Other non-Italian writers on diminution and ORNAMENTATION, such as Juan Bermudo (1555), TOMÁS DE SANTA MARIÁ and DIEGO ORTIZ, discussed similar ornamented cadences, but used different terminology. GIOVANNI BASSANO demonstrated how to devise ornamented cadences (*cadenza fiorita*) in his *Ricercate, passaggi et cadentie* (1585), but some composers, among them GIULIO CACCINI, wrote out such ornamentations. In French sources, the increasing interchangeability of the terms 'tremblements' and 'cadences' in the seventeenth and eighteenth centuries caused considerable confusion, but QUANTZ (1752) confirms that the French style's prescribed nature essentially restricted the introduction of cadenzas only into works written in the Italian idiom.

Quantz ascribes the origins of the cadenza proper, characterised by its placement within a structural cadence, to early eighteenth-century Italy and describes it as an extempore embellishment intended to 'surprise' and 'leave behind a special impression' (1752, 180), such as LEOPOLD MOZART (1756) achieved with his accelerating trill or trill in sixths. Quantz considered the inclusion of more than one cadenza in a movement wearying. For him, cadenzas 'must stem from the principal sentiment of the piece' and make reference to some of its ideas. He favours extempore cadenzas which are short and sound spontaneous, and warns against introducing too many ideas, repeating motives too often or straying from related keys into tonal areas that are too remote. A short cadenza should not modulate; longer ones may modulate to the subdominant, and still longer ones to the subdominant and dominant (but not without exception); changes in mode should be brief and regular metre should not be observed. Vocal cadenzas or cadenzas for a wind instrument should be performed in one breath (1752, 181–5), a guideline endorsed by TROMLITZ (1791, 298) but one clearly not without exception through history.

The growing popularity of vocal virtuosity in the late seventeenth and early eighteenth centuries, particularly in opera, began increasingly to place the spotlight on an aria's final cadenza. The nature and content of cadenzas was left to individual singers, who, drawing on the rich tradition of diminution and *fioritura*, tended to mould them to their own technical strengths. Some singers used cadenzas to excess, TOSI (1723, §2) indicating the possibility of introducing three in each aria (one at the end of each of its sections, with the most elaborate coming last), but recommending only one. J. F. AGRICOLA (1757) claims that this limitation was often ignored. A surviving written-out cadenza example attributed to FARINELLI is extraordinarily long and clearly intended to showcase his virtuosity. Extant TRANSCRIPTIONS of eighteenth-century vocal cadenzas demonstrate little by way of thematic correlation with the parent aria. MANCINI (1774) was one of few vocal theorists to recommend such motivic interconnection and Quantz suggests resorting to it only if one is short of new ideas.

Instrumental cadenzas appear to have originated in the early concertos composed in Italy c1700 by Torelli and others; they comprised repetitive passagework over a sustained bass pedal note (Torelli termed them 'perfidia'). Vivaldi introduced free-standing and entirely unaccompanied cadenzas in several sections. A few of these cadenzas survive in notated form; some bear the additional comment 'Qui si ferma a piacimento poi segue' ('here one pauses ad. lib. [for the solo cadenza] and then resumes'). Primarily cadential, their effect might be enhanced by tonal change, heightening the suspense before the arrival of a new key or a return to the tonic key, normally for the concluding ritornello. Such were the models for the 'capriccios' of Pietro Locatelli, who positioned them in the outer (fast) movements of each of his twelve concertos Op. 3, just before the final tutti section; in many cases he added an improvised embellishment of the final cadence, using the term 'cadenza', and completed the movement with a reprise of the ritornello. J. S. BACH included brief, decorative *ad libitum* passages in some of his concerto movements (notably before the reprise in the first movement of his Violin Concerto in E major (BWV1042)), but his extended (sixty-five bars), written-out passage for solo harpsichord in the first movement of his Fifth Brandenburg Concerto (BWV1050) anticipated the later desire (c1750 onwards) for cadenzas to incorporate motivic relevance to its parent movement alongside virtuoso flights of fancy.

The practice of including cadenzas within instrumental concertos was not universal. Cadenzas were omitted from most Parisian 'Classical' concertos and *symphonies concertantes*, but most German concertante works included them. TARTINI's guidelines for cadenza construction (*Traité des agréments*, 1771, but written before 1756) resemble in principle those addressed to singers and seem to have been widely followed: cadenzas may start with a swelled note (*messa di voce*), *passaggi* or a trill, succeeded by metrically free notes of smaller value and then a high note that may match or be followed by the highest note in the piece; this melodic peak usually led swiftly to the concluding trill.

Surviving examples by W. A. MOZART and the description given by TÜRK (1789) offer the best guides to the 'Classical' instrumental cadenza. Mozart's cadential formula begins with harmonic tension created by the orchestral pause on an inconclusive chord (normally the tonic $^6_4$). The soloist's cadenza carries the tension through to the final trill on a played/implied dominant seventh chord, which resolves on the tonic and the orchestral re-entry. It thus differs fundamentally from the EINGANG (lead-in), which emanates typically from a fermata on the dominant (usually dominant seventh) and comprises a short improvised link typically to the reprise of the principal theme, particularly in rondo structures. Some Classical concertos indicate a cadenza in each movement, though the trend in the later eighteenth century was towards one or at most two cadenzas per work.

ROBERT LEVIN has calculated that Mozart's extant keyboard cadenzas are about 10 per cent of the length of their respective parent movements (in Brown and Sadie, 282–3; see also Badura-Skoda and Badura-Skoda, 216–34). He subdivides the typical Mozart cadenza into four sections: brief introductory passagework (optional); first section, often derived from the primary group of themes with harmonic stability removed from quoted material. Following an arrival either on V^7 or I^6_4 (often underscored by a fermata) and an optional bridge of passagework, the second main section is often derived from the secondary group of ideas. The stability of root position tonic is again normally avoided, and non-modulating sequences are sometimes made chromatic (or more chromatic). This section culminates in a clear arrival, this time on I^6_4, elaborated by passagework and with a fermata. The final section comprises a flourish or running scale passage, which prepares for the concluding trill. Significantly, an idiomatic cadenza does not depend entirely upon the systematic quotation of themes; apart from an initial motivic citation, Mozart's cadenza for the first movement of his Piano Concerto K488 is virtually a free fantasia. Withheld harmonic stability from the initial fermata to the final trill, rather than thematic reference, seems to be the more important integrating ingredient.

TÜRK (1789, 298–301) provides the most detailed late eighteenth-century guidelines for cadenza creation. His text largely aligns with Mozart's extant cadenzas. He states that a cadenza should: contain material pertinent to and in character with the relevant piece; not present difficulties for difficulties' sake; be rich in ideas from the movement and not overlong (especially in melancholy movements); not modulate widely or beyond the tonal range of the piece; achieve unity, but include some musical variety for interest. Frequent repetition of any idea should be avoided. The same tempo and metre should not be maintained throughout and a fantasia-like impression of 'ordered disorder' should be given, the performance sounding as if extemporised. Interestingly, CZERNY's cadenza instruction (*Systematische Anleitung zum Fantasieren auf dem Pianoforte*, Op. 200, Vienna, 1829) includes some examples which are considerably more extended than surviving eighteenth-century models.

Existing sketches/drafts for some early cadenza attempts by BEETHOVEN demonstrate that he, like Mozart, favoured quoting an important idea (usually the principal second-group theme) at the cadenza's heart. Contrary to Mozart's practice, however, he included this theme on a scale-step harmonically remote from the tonic (e.g. the flattened third, sixth or seventh). Many of Beethoven's mature cadenza examples (c1809) expand upon Mozartian models in terms of length, thematic concentration, register and technical demand. His written-out cadenza for the first movement of the Violin Concerto, Op. 61, as arranged for piano and orchestra (Op. 61a), broke new ground in incorporating a substantial part for the TIMPANI (as does the cadenza for the finale of his Fifth Piano Concerto towards its close). Beethoven's written-out cadenzas for Mozart's D minor Piano Concerto K466, although stylistically inappropriate, are amongst his best examples of the genre; written-out examples also appear in his solo and chamber works such as the first movements of his Piano Sonata, Op. 2 No. 3 and Cello Sonata, Op. 5 No.1.

Following Beethoven's lead, spontaneous, improvisatory creation of the cadenza was gradually overtaken in the nineteenth century by composers' preference either to write their own cadenzas or dispense with a cadenza altogether. It may be inferred from HUMMEL's piano treatise (1828) that he considered the improvised cadenza *passé*; and composers such as BRAHMS, Liszt, Schumann and MENDELSSOHN (whose first-movement cadenza for his Violin Concerto, Op. 64 has a structural function, appearing immediately prior to the reprise) preferred in most cases to write their own. After c1880, most composers have written out cadenzas for their concertos (the violin concertos of Brahms, Szymanowski and Khachaturian are among the exceptions); some have considered accompanied cadenzas more appropriate to their works

(Elgar, Violin Concerto), while others have allotted them the status of, effectively, an extra movement in their concerto scheme (e.g. Shostakovich, Violin Concerto No. 1; Walton, Cello Concerto).

This general trend of composers keeping cadenza practices in check also filtered into most vocal arenas. The vocal cadenza became a more formal affair. While many Italian composers of the first half of the nineteenth century still persisted with fermatas to signal the introduction of an improvised cadenza (e.g. Bellini), similar practices in Germany and France became increasingly rare. In Meyerbeer's operas, places for cadenzas are found mainly in those arias written in an Italian style. In Italy, Rossini eventually wrote out his fermata embellishments in full. Having indicated fermatas for improvised cadenzas in many of his earlier operas, Verdi decided to write out the cadenzas for his mature operas. The art of improvising cadenzas thus gradually died out around the nineteenth century's end, although remnants of the practice survive in various EARLY RECORDINGS.

Readers seeking modern idiomatic cadenzas for some of Mozart's concertos are referred to those of PAUL BADURA-SKODA, Marius Flothius and Robert Levin. Other composers' cadenzas for works of their predecessors (e.g. Clara Schumann's for Mozart's D minor Piano Concerto K466; BUSONI's and Reinecke's for numerous Classical works), though important documents of their times, are stylistically inappropriate for historical performers either to adopt or emulate. Brahms's Violin Concerto (1876) was one of the last theoretically to indicate an improvised cadenza; more than twenty violinist-composers have provided examples, but the cadenza composed by his close friend JOSEPH JOACHIM has become almost inseparable from the work, providing an ideal match of style and mind.

FURTHER READING

E. Badura-Skoda and P. Badura-Skoda, *Mozart-Interpretation* (Vienna: Edward Vancura Verlag, 1957; trans. L. Black as *Interpreting Mozart on the Keyboard* (New York: St Martin's Press, 1962)).

H. M. Brown and S. Sadie (eds.), *Performance Practice: Music after 1600* (London: Macmillan, 1989) [especially R. Levin: 'Instrumental ornamentation, improvisation and cadenzas', 267–91; W. Crutchfield: 'Voices', 292–319, 424–58].

M. Edin, 'Cadenza improvisation in nineteenth-century solo piano music according to Czerny, Liszt and their contemporaries', in R. Rasch (ed.), *Beyond Notes: Improvisation in Western Music of the Eighteenth and Nineteenth Centuries* (Turnhout: Brepols, 2011), 168–74.

D. Lasocki and B. B. Mather, *The Classical Woodwind Cadenza: A Workbook* (New York: McGinnis & Marx, 1978).

F. Neumann, *Ornamentation and Improvisation in Mozart* (Princeton University Press, 1986).

P. Whitmore, *Unpremeditated Art: the Cadenza in the Classical Keyboard Concerto* (Oxford University Press, 1991).

ROBIN STOWELL

Cage, John (Milton, Jr) (b. Los Angeles, 5 September 1912; d. New York, 12 August 1992) American composer.

John Cage is arguably the most influential figure in twentieth-century music, far beyond the narrow world of contemporary art music, through compositional explorations, artistic innovation, writings, lectures, performances and collaborations with other artists. Cage met SCHOENBERG in 1934 and was struck by his remarkable passion for music: Cage's early works show an influence but even here his characteristically questioning aesthetic led him to manipulate and alter Schoenberg's serial technique. More important was his encounter with dance and particularly Merce Cunningham in 1937, which led to music that embraced noise, writing for PERCUSSION groups including non-percussion instruments and those from other cultures. At this time he was also pioneering the use of electronic possibilities. His work with percussion and dance resulted in the 'invention' of the prepared piano in 1938. Influenced by the earlier works of Henry Cowell, Cage discovered a percussion ensemble sound world by inserting different objects between the strings of the piano. It is the works of the mid-1940s – for example, *The Perilous Night* (1944) – that expanded the technique in more extended pieces. At this time he studied Indian philosophy, particularly the writings of Coomaraswamy, which influenced the composition of his most important work for prepared piano, *Sonatas and Interludes* (1946–8). He travelled to Europe in 1949 and met BOULEZ (there is significant correspondence between them in the period 1949–54) returning to New York where he met Feldman, Christian Wolff and the virtuoso pianist David Tudor together with a number of abstract Expressionist painters. It is also at this time he began to develop ideas about silence influenced by Hinduism and Zen Buddhism. Silence is central to both his way of life and his art as is the idea of indeterminacy after encountering the *I Ching* in the early 1950s when he developed techniques of deriving material, ordering and coordinating, by chance operations. *Music of Changes* for solo piano (1951) is the first important example of these techniques and 1952 sees his most infamous conception *4' 33"*.

FURTHER READING

J. Lockhead, 'Performance practice in the indeterminate works of John Cage', *PPR*, 7/2 (1994), 233–41.
D. Nicholls (ed.), *The Cambridge Companion to John Cage* (Cambridge University Press, 2002).
D. Nicholls, *John Cage* (Urbana and Chicago: University of Illinois Press, 2007).

ROGER HEATON

Cambini, Giuseppe Maria (Gioacchino) (b. Livorno, ?13 February 1746; d. ?Netherlands, c1818) Italian composer and violinist.

Details of Cambini's early career are unreliable and shrouded in mystery, but he is known to have settled in Paris in the early 1770s, performing one of his *symphonies concertantes* at the *Concert Spirituel* on 20 May 1773. However, it was largely as a prolific composer that he made his living, contributing to a wide range of instrumental and vocal repertory, including fourteen operas, several concertos and *symphonies concertantes*, string quartets and much other chamber music. He also held positions at the Théâtre des Beaujolais (1788–94) and later at the Théâtre Louvois and he seems to have thrived during the Revolution, composing several popular revolutionary hymns and odes. After 1794 he led private concerts for the munitions maker Armand Seguin, for whom he wrote several string quintets.

Cambini's popularity as a composer waned somewhat after c1795. He resorted instead to writing about musical performance, publishing his *Nouvelle méthode théorique et pratique pour le violon* in 1795. This tripartite VIOLIN tutor deals respectively with principles of left- and right-hand technique and general matters of expressive execution. Remarkable amongst its largely elementary instruction is its recommended method of holding the violin – horizontally at about shoulder height, with chin, shoulder and additional wrist and (at the neck–body joint of the instrument) heel-of-the-hand support and the chin positioned on the G-string side of the tailpiece. This instruction anticipates that of BAILLOT and SPOHR in the early 1830s. Cambini also stresses the importance of the left-hand thumb in leading the movement of the hand in shifts and advocates large hand-shifts in fast movements and small ones in slow movements. He treats the BOW as an expressive tool and emphasises the importance of both the right wrist for regulating bow pressure and the fingers as 'springs which set the bow in motion' (3). He invokes operatic tableaux to illustrate expressive performance and annotates his examples (particularly the last three of the six graduated sonatas which conclude the treatise) with appropriate FINGERINGS (some involving PORTAMENTO implications), ARTICULATIONS, ornaments and DYNAMICS.

Cambini's elementary *Méthode pour la flûte traversière* (1799) includes surprisingly little textual instruction and consists largely of melodic passages in various keys, twenty airs for two flutes, including many of the same pieces found in FRANÇOIS DEVIENNE's earlier *Nouvelle méthode théorique et pratique pour la flûte* (Paris: Naderman, n.d. [1794]), and six duets. Among Cambini's other writings of significance is an article about string quartet performance for the *Allgemeine musikalische Zeitung* ('Ausführung der Instrumentalquartetten', AMZ 47 (22 August 1804), cols. 781–3), in which he severely criticises the contemporary practice of performing string quartets at sight and argues passionately for ensembles to adopt a new regime of studying thoroughly and rehearsing intensely their concert repertory in order effectively to move their audiences. He also collaborated with ALEXIS DE GARAUDÉ briefly as the anonymous editor of *Tablettes de Polymnie* and gained some notoriety for his alleged role in Legros's cancellation of the performance of MOZART's *Symphonie concertante* for winds at the *Concert Spirituel*. Little is known about his work after c1810. FÉTIS's record of his death (Paris, 1825) is of doubtful accuracy.

FURTHER READING

E. Borrel, 'Un cours d'interprétation de la musique de violon au 18e siècle par Cambini', *RdM*, 10/30 (1929), 120–4.
G. M. Cambini, 'Ausführung der Instrumentalquartetten', *AMZ*, 6 (1803–4), 781–3.

ROBIN STOWELL

Campagnoli, Bartolomeo (b. Cento, nr Bologna, 10 September 1751; d. Neustrelitz, 7 November 1827) Italian violinist, composer and pedagogue.

Campagnoli studied the VIOLIN with TARTINI's pupils Paolo Guastarobba, Paolo Alberghi and Pietro Nardini. Following a brief orchestral appointment in Rome (1775), he entered the service of the Bishop of

Freysingen. He toured widely from 1778, combining travel with the post of music director at the Duke of Courland's court in Dresden (1779–97), and later served as leader of Leipzig's Gewandhaus Orchestra (1797–1818), resigning to assist his daughters in furthering their operatic careers in Hanover (1820) and later Neustrelitz (1826).

Campagnoli is most important for his Preludes, Op. 12, Fugues, Op. 9, Polonaises, Op. 13 and Divertissements, Op. 18 for solo violin and his pedagogical works, notably his forty-one Caprices for VIOLA, Op. 22, *L'art d'inventer à l'improviste des fantaisies et cadences pour le violon*, Op. 17, *Receuil de 101 pièces faciles et progressives*, Op. 20, and especially his systematically organised *Nouvelle méthode de la mécanique progressive du jeu de violon*, Op. 21 (1824). The existence of an original Italian version of this method (1797?) has never been proved, but the treatise was later disseminated in various other editions as well as Italian (undated) and English (1856) translations. Subdivided into five parts, its introduction discusses general technical matters and comprises a mixture of progressive (notably on tuning) and outdated (notably regarding the bow hold) principles. The first four sections instruct students in applying the 250 progressive exercises (including 132 duets) in part five. Campagnoli cites LEOPOLD MOZART's description of the four divisions of the BOW almost *verbatim*, but he omits mention of any 'small softness' at the stroke's beginning and end, suggesting his employment of a bow similar to Tourte's model in design, attack and musical effect. He links VIBRATO usage explicitly to the bow's DYNAMICS, especially to the *messa di voce*, and he was one of the first writers to advocate the Pythagorean tuning system.

FURTHER READING

D. Hays, 'The "messa di voce" as an ornament in the string playing of the seventeenth, eighteenth and nineteenth centuries', PhD dissertation, Northwestern University (2000).
U. Montanari, *Bartolomeo Campagnoli violinista compositore* (Cento: Bagnoli, 1969).
Z. Szabo, 'The violin method of Bartolomeo Campagnoli: An analysis and evaluation', PhD dissertation, Indiana University, Calgary (1978).

ROBIN STOWELL

Cartier, Jean Baptiste (b. Avignon, 28 May 1765; d. Paris, ?, 1841) French violinist, composer and pedagogue.

Cartier studied the VIOLIN with *L'Abbé* Walraef and Viotti; he served Queen Marie Antoinette, was assistant leader of the Paris Opéra Orchestra (1791–1821) and played in the court orchestra (1804–30) of both Napoleon and the Bourbon regime. He taught many students privately and supported his teaching with an important treatise, *L'art du violon* (Paris: Decombe, 1798), dedicated to the PARIS CONSERVATOIRE.

The third and most valuable part of *L'art* comprises an anthology of pieces by French, German and Italian composers of the seventeenth and eighteenth centuries. It embraces a variety of compositions and styles, ranging from music for unaccompanied violin (including works by Stamitz, Nardini, Spadina, Locatelli, Moria and the first ever printed example of unaccompanied BACH – the fugue of the C major Sonata, BWV1005 – courtesy of a copy owned by Gaviniès), to the first publication of TARTINI's 'Devil's Trill' sonata (courtesy of a manuscript owned by BAILLOT), seven sonatas by Nardini with written-out ornamentation of the Adagios (after an edition of 1760, now lost), the first complete republication of Tartini's *L'arte del arco*, a collection of *chasses* and, as an appendix to the second and later editions, an Adagio by Tartini with eighteen different embellishments of its melody. In collecting and publishing these works (and rescuing some from oblivion), Cartier secured an important place in the history of violin literature. He sparked an interest in the revival of pre-1750 music which flourished in the nineteenth century not only in performances (notably with MENDELSSOHN's centenary revival of Bach's *St Matthew Passion* in Berlin (1829) and the 'Concerts historiques' promoted in Paris by ALEXANDRE CHORON and FRANÇOIS-JOSEPH FÉTIS) but also through collections of earlier music, notably by EDOUARD DELDEVEZ (twenty-six *Pièces diverses* (1857–8)), DELPHIN ALARD (*Maîtres classiques du violon* (1862–83)) and FERDINAND DAVID (*Hohe Schule des Violinspiels* (1867) and his somewhat simpler, preparatory *Vorstudien zur Hohen Schule des Violinspiels* (1872–3)).

The first two parts of Cartier's treatise are disappointing by comparison. The text of the first section, a brief survey of the main principles of violin playing, comprising the violin and bow holds, bow division and management, ornaments, EXPRESSION and other technical and interpretative matters, is especially retrospective. Cartier admits in his preface that this material simply amalgamates extracts from the treatises of GEMINIANI, LEOPOLD MOZART, Tarade and L'ABBÉ LE FILS. Nevertheless, this hotch-potch of ideas from different national schools confirms the advent of a more uniform, international approach to violin playing. The second part, intended primarily to acquaint students with the geography of the fingerboard, includes nine scales (illustrating the positions) and discusses in turn the FINGERING of fifths (of all kinds), Italian terms, HARMONICS, double stopping and ornaments. Three duos by Cartier himself are included for the perfection of slurred bowings (No. 1) and elementary position-work (Nos. 2 and 3) together with a survey of various ARPEGGIANDO bowings.

Cartier's other works comprise duos, potpourris, *airs variés* and sonatas, including a two-violin sonata 'in the style of Lolli', Op. 7, for which the first violin part adopts a SCORDATURA tuning.

FURTHER READING

K. M. Stolba, 'J. B. Cartier's *L'art du violon* and its significance in the history of violin literature', *Pro Musica Magazine*, 2/1 (1977), 6–15.

R. Stowell, *Violin Technique and Performance Practice in the Late Eighteenth and Early Nineteenth Centuries* (Cambridge University Press, 1985).

ROBIN STOWELL

Casadesus, Henri (b. Paris, 30 September 1879; d. Paris, 31 May 1947) French composer, VIOLA and viola d'amore player and one of an extensive family of musicians.

With his brother, Francis (1870–1954), Henri Casadesus founded the *Société des instruments Casadesus* (1901) in collaboration with SAINT-SAËNS, and this ensemble gave concerts until the outbreak of WWII. A viola player originally, he mastered the virtually extinct viola d'amore and throughout his life was interested in the revival of forgotten and obscure instruments and their repertoire. His reputation has been somewhat tarnished by his hoodwinking the musical public by publishing pieces – mainly concertos – under the names of celebrated composers of the eighteenth century, including MOZART, HANDEL and both J. C. BACH and C. P E. BACH. These pieces were in fact composed by himself and his brothers. His collection of rare instruments survives in the collection of the Boston Symphony Orchestra and his 'forgeries' enjoyed more success than his other compositions, which include ballets, chamber music and film music.

RICHARD LANGHAM SMITH

Casals, Pau (Pablo) (b. Vendrell, Catalonia, 29 December 1876; d. Puerto Rico, 22 October 1973) Catalonian cellist and teacher.

Casals started studying the CELLO with José Garcia at Barcelona's Escuela Municipal de Música in 1887. After further studies in Madrid and a period working in Paris, he returned to Barcelona as García's successor in 1896. His international career began with performances in London and Paris in 1899, and he continued to perform and record as a cellist (and conductor) until the 1960s. Casals recorded extensively in every genre, including shorter light pieces, sonatas, chamber music, concertos and J. S. BACH's Solo Suites. He was not the first to play Bach's Suites complete in public (GRÜTZMACHER and Piatti had already done this on occasions), nor did he 'discover' them (several EDITIONS had been published by the late nineteenth century), but his advocacy of these works made them central to the cello canon. Concertos were written for him by Móor, SCHOENBERG and Tovey, but, unlike Rostropovich, Casals had little influence on new repertoire for the cello.

Casals was one of the most influential cello teachers of the twentieth century – his many students included Feuermann, Tortelier and Rostropovich – but he never published a method nor any studies. Nevertheless, his preface to his pupil Diran Alexanian's *Traité théorique et pratique du violoncelle* (Paris: Mathot, 1922, but written 1910–14) unreservedly endorses this work. Alexanian includes an explanation of 'expressive intonation', a technique strongly associated with Casals, where notes are adjusted according to their harmonic direction. Casals taught a subtler and more resilient left-hand action than the conventional 'hammered' approach. While he used PORTAMENTO, he evolved an elastic shifting technique that minimised inadvertent sliding. Although credited with a new approach to the use of the BOWING arm (compared with García's conservative teaching), other cellists were exploring a higher elbow position at that time. Casals eschewed facile virtuosity, but brought a fresh analytical approach both to repertoire and to technique. His performances of Baroque repertoire often highlighted (or even created) motivic aspects, such as his bowing for Valentini's Sonata in D, Bach's Suites, or his CONDUCTING of Bach's Brandenburg Concertos. The edition of Bach's Suites by Madeleine Foley, completed by David Soyer with assistance from Casals's widow Marta (Ann Arbor: Continental, 1986), attempts to notate some details of his teaching and performance, but in spite of demand, Casals did not publish his own edition, objecting to editions that were full of personal elements.

FURTHER READING:

R. Baldock, *Pablo Casals* (London: Gollancz, 1994).
D. Blum, *Casals and the Art of Interpretation* (Berkeley and Los Angeles: University of California Press, 1980).
G. Kennaway, *Playing the Cello, 1780–1930* (Farnham: Ashgate, 2014).

GEORGE KENNAWAY

Castil-Blaze, François Henri Joseph (Blaze, François-Henri-Joseph) (b. Cavaillon, Vaucluse, 1 December 1784; d. Paris, 11 December 1857) French critic, translator, librettist, composer, arranger and author of historical surveys.

Castil-Blaze is remembered mainly for his music criticism, which during the 1820s in Paris marked a turn away from the dilettantism of men of letters towards the technical competence and philosophical seriousness of composers and other trained professionals. His efforts to bring before the French public music by foreign composers, in particular through his own arrangements, raised questions of fidelity to the text versus intelligibility to audiences in the here and now, questions that embraced performance practice not only as it pertained to the EDITING of musical texts, but also to the institutional frameworks (in the case of opera especially strict) then governing the production and reception of music.

FURTHER READING

K. Ellis, *Music Criticism in Nineteenth-Century Paris: 'La Revue et Gazette Musicale de Paris', 1834–80* (Cambridge University Press, 1995).

CORMAC NEWARK

Castrato The centrality of the castrato voice to eighteenth-century opera, oratorio and chamber music makes it impossible to ignore the problems it raises for performance in the twenty-first century. Although the practice of castrating boys for religious, medical or punitive purposes can be traced back to prehistoric times, and continued in rare and special circumstances into the twentieth century, the professional castrato singer only emerged in the late sixteenth century, flourishing until the end of the eighteenth century. The engagement of castratos in church and theatre was the direct result of restrictions placed on the employment of women singers. A ban on women in church choirs in Spain and Italy created a gap only partly filled by male altos (falsettists), whose voices were thought to be inferior to those of boy trebles, who, in their turn, were considered expensive to train for the short duration of their voices, and troublesome to control. Another church ruling, prohibiting the appearance of women on stage in the Papal States, created opportunities for castratos in opera in that region and encouraged their acceptance in theatres across Europe (with the exception of France). There is evidence that many were exceptionally skilled. Their training, which began in childhood, was longer, broader and more intensive than that of any other class of singer. By the mid-eighteenth century the finest were among the most highly paid soloists in Europe.

Recreating early opera in modern times causes problems that were not formerly perceived as such. By the early eighteenth century it had become the norm for opera to be performed predominantly by high voices – female sopranos or castratos – whether the characters they represented were male or female. While in Rome all female roles were necessarily undertaken by castratos, in London HANDEL created such overtly masculine roles as lovers (Medoro in *Orlando*) or villains (Polinesso in *Ariodante*) for contraltos. There was moreover a continuous process of replacement casting, driven by the availability of singers. The scale of substitutions and transference of voice types is indicated by the various alterations Handel made to the role of David in his oratorio *Saul*: having originally written the role for a countertenor, he subsequently adapted it for soprano, soprano-register castrato, mezzo-soprano, alto-register castrato, tenor and bass. This apparent disregard for gender by classical composers (see Burrows, 1988; Leopold, 2000) suggested an obvious solution for later directors: from the beginning of the nineteenth century until well after WWII it became the norm to assign castrato roles to female singers. The only argument against this choice is the scarcely disguised feminine appearance of some singers: Pauline Viardot García made minimal concessions to masculinity in costume or gesture when portraying Orphée in Berlioz's version of Gluck's *Orphée et Eurydice*.

In the last fifty years, the use of a countertenor has become increasingly common (*see* BOWMAN, JAMES). Its timbre was initially considered inadequate in the theatre because of the voice's inherently small volume, but this problem has disappeared with improved technique. Modern countertenors such as David Daniels and Iestyn Davies have demonstrated that volume is no longer an issue, and the voice has the advantage of retaining the other-worldly resonance that the castrato seems to have held for eighteenth-century listeners, who called them 'angels'.

Transferring castrato roles to tenor or bass has clear disadvantages. It involves TRANSPOSITIONS that inevitably upset textures and orchestration, and occasionally destroy key schemes. There is also the loss of the expressive tension created in duets between equal voices (e.g. in 'Pur ti miro', the final duet in *L'incoronazione di Poppea*). However, there are ample historical precedents in the adaptations composers made to their own scores, especially those that recast the castrato role for tenor. Handel, for example, adapted the castrato role of Silvio (*Il pastor fido*) for the tenor John Beard, and Gluck reworked Guadagni's alto-register castrato title role in *Orfeo ed Euridice* for the *haute-contre* Le Gros. The transposition of castrato roles for the bass voice has been less well received. In the 1920s Oskar Hagen attracted much opprobrium when he prepared a series of editions for the Göttingen Handel Festival with octave transpositions (among other gratuitous modifications). The practice, however, remained popular in Germany: in the 1960s, both Walter Berry and Dietrich Fischer-Dieskau undertook the title role in *Giulio Cesare*.

In eighteenth-century usage, the term 'castrato' always contained a hint of disparagement or mockery – in England they were often called 'capons'. 'Evirato' was a common and accurate alternative term, while 'musico' was preferred within the singers' own professional ambit.

FURTHER READING

D. Burrows, 'Die Kastratenrollen in Händels Londoner Opern: Probleme und Lösungsvorschläge', in H. J. Marz (ed.), *Händel auf dem Theater: Bericht über die Symposien 1986 und 1987, Internationalen Händel-Akademie, Karlsruhe* (Laaber-Verlag, 1988), 85–93.

P. Howard, 'The castrato', in B. Gustafsen (ed.), *Oxford Bibliographies in Music* (New York: Oxford University Press, 2014).

S. Leopold, 'Not sex but pitch: Kastraten als Liebhaber – einmal über der Gürtellinie betrachtet', in H. M. Linde and R. Rapp (eds.), *Provokation und Tradition. Erfahrungen mit der alten Musik* (Stuttgart: Metzler, 2000), 219–40.

PATRICIA HOWARD

Cavaillé-Coll, Aristide (b. Montpellier, 4 February 1811; d. Paris, 13 October 1899) French ORGAN builder.

Cavaillé-Coll can justly be credited with the creation of the French Romantic organ, which inspired compositions from Franck to Messiaen. In contrast to the French Classical organ, Cavaillé-Coll developed the concept of each department (*Grand Orgue, Positif, Récit*) having its own *grand choeur*, complete with flue and reed ranks, so that *crescendo*s and *diminuendo*s from the loudest to the quietest DYNAMICS were obtainable, whilst retaining the same basic timbres at every dynamic level. His first success was winning a competition for the design of the organ at the abbey of St Denis. Henceforth, he built about 500 organs in France, Western Europe and South America. His largest organs, including *Grand Orgue* (the lowest manual), *Positif, Récit, Bombarde* and *Grand Choeur* divisions, were those in St Sulpice (1862; five manuals/one hundred stops) and Notre-Dame Cathedral (1868; five manuals/eighty-six stops).

When rebuilding Classical organs, Cavaillé-Coll retained the traditional *Positif* and *Grand Orgue* cases, but his newly constructed organs placed all divisions within one case. He was faithful to mechanical action, but employed Barker levers to lighten the touch on larger instruments, and he developed the detached and reversed console. Wind pressures of 90–110 mm were not significantly different from Classical organs, to which he introduced and perfected overblowing flutes, expression boxes for *Récit* and *Positif* (after 1865), chamade trumpets on large organs and German-inspired string stops. *Récit* departments were initially relatively small but were later developed into symphonic dimensions, and often the *Pédale* was relatively sparse. He conducted scientific experiments in pipe construction and scaling diameters, which can be accessed through his writings. Amongst the orchestral sounds that he added to the organ were the *Basson* and *Cor anglais* 16', the *Voix humaine, Hautbois* and *Clarinette* 8', as well as the *Voix celeste* and *Unda maris*.

FURTHER READING

A. Cavaillé-Coll, *Complete Theoretical Works*, facsim. edn G. Huybens (Buren: F. Knuf, 1978).

DAVID PONSFORD

Cello (violoncello,'cello) Bass instrument of the VIOLIN family (although its name means literally 'small violone', incorrectly implying an association with the VIOL family).

The cello's immediate antecedent was the seventeenth-century bass violin. There are, however, earlier representations of cello-type instruments, such as the three-stringed cello described by AGRICOLA (1529) and depicted by Gaudenzio Ferrari in the cupola fresco of Saronno Cathedral (1535). The bass violin was a larger instrument than the modern cello and played at a lower pitch (the lowest string tuned to B♭). It used gut strings, and the lower strings of the instrument were therefore particularly thick. The development of wire-wound strings, which seems to have begun in Bologna, meant that string thicknesses could be reduced and thus the overall size of the instrument – many bass violins were later reduced in size. Bologna became a centre of cello playing due to the presence of three cellists who all played at the church of San Petronio: Petronio Franceschini (c1650–80), Domenico Gabrielli (1651–90) and Giuseppe Maria Jacchini (c1663–1727). The seven *Ricercari* by Gabrielli are among the earliest works for solo cello.

Terminology in this field is diverse; in the seventeenth century in particular terms such as 'violone', 'violonzino', 'bassetto', 'bassetto di viola', 'basso da brazzo', 'basso viola da brazzo', or even 'viola' – among many other Italian, French and German terms – all referred to a bass string instrument deeper in pitch than a modern VIOLA. However, 'violoncello' appears to have originated in northern Italy, first used in print there in 1665.

The size and overall dimensions of the cello became largely standardised (e.g. a back length of c75 cm) by the beginning of the nineteenth century, with most instruments corresponding to one of a relatively small number of variants. However, in the seventeenth and eighteenth centuries there was considerable variety in these respects. The earliest surviving instrument is one made by Andrea Amati in 1572. Early Cremonese instruments were larger than Brescian instruments of the same period, and the co-existence of two fundamental sizes of cello appears to have continued into the eighteenth century. QUANTZ (1752) advised players to have one of each, the smaller being used for solos and the larger for orchestral playing. Stradivarius (1644–1737) and Rugeri (c1630–98) both made instruments of the size familiar today, and Stradivarius's second version of the pattern based on this size, the so-called 'B' pattern, is the most commonly used. An example of a longer Stradivarius model from c1701, known as the 'Servais', is held in the Smithsonian Museum. Many eighteenth-century cellos made to a larger pattern were later modified to match the Stradivarius model B dimensions. However, earlier eighteenth-century instruments varied significantly in size, even those from the same region or town. Surviving early eighteenth-century cellos show a higher fingerboard angle (with a proportionally higher bridge) than violins of the same period.

Towards the end of the eighteenth century, most instruments underwent modification, all designed to increase tonal power and projection: the neck angle was increased, bass bars became thicker and fingerboards themselves became longer to enable use of a wider tessitura. Unmodified eighteenth-century instruments are therefore relatively rare. The modern cello is in essence a nineteenth-century instrument, with few developments. In the 1950s Carleen Hutchins developed a range of violin family instruments in collaboration with players including the cellist Sterling Hunkins, many of which were played in the manner of the cello rather than the violin. In this new system the cello was redefined as a baritone violin.

Although cellos with four strings predominated in Italy by the end of the seventeenth century, five-string cellos (with an upper E string) were used into the middle of the eighteenth century, as many paintings of the period show. J. S. BACH in particular wrote for this instrument; in addition to the Sixth Solo Suite BWV1012, there are several instances of its use in his cantatas. Other five-string cellos included the *viola [violoncello] da spalla*, or 'shoulder viola' (Walther, 1732), which was a smaller instrument tuned as a five-string cello but held from the shoulder by a strap. There has been renewed interest in this instrument in modern times.

The standard tuning for the cello from the early eighteenth century onwards is (ascending) C–G–d–a. The tuning C–G–d–g occurs in the later seventeenth century and is specified by Bach for the Fifth Solo Suite BWV1011. SCORDATURA tunings for special effects or sonorities occur occasionally in the nineteenth and twentieth centuries. Schumann's Piano Quartet, Op. 47 (1842) requires a temporary re-tuning of the C string to B; Kodály's Solo Sonata, Op. 8 (1921) requires the tuning B'–$F\sharp$–D–A; and George Crumb's *Vox Balaenae* uses an electric cello tuned B'–$F\sharp$–$d\sharp$–a.

Like the instrument, the BOW also varied considerably in size at first; eighteenth-century cello bows could vary in length by as much as 7 cms and weigh from 65 to 86 grams. QUANTZ suggests that a heavier bow with coarser black hair be used for orchestral playing, and a lighter bow with white hair for solo playing. Bow design also varied widely, with older Baroque bows using a convex stick, and later models having a stick more or less parallel to the hair. Some repertoire requiring particular staccato effects suggests that a concave stick may have been in use before the model developed by François Tourte. Tourte's design rapidly became the preferred type of bow. DUPORT endorsed it (*Essai*, c1806) and ROMBERG owned two Tourte bows, which are still extant. Later modifications of Tourte's design were aimed at increasing strength or ease of use.

Although there is pictorial evidence of players using various forms of support (cushions or boxes) for the instrument, these are predominantly used by amateurs. Until late in the nineteenth century, many cellists were still holding the instrument without an endpin, cradling it between the legs. No cello method recommends the use of a support of any kind except as a makeshift arrangement (CORRETTE, Crome) until this period (however, the 'bass-Geig di bracio' shown in PRAETORIUS (1619) clearly has a wooden support). The first important player/teacher to use the endpin was the Belgian Adrien Servais (1807–66). Photographs show that the traditional explanation – that he used an endpin because of his obesity – is untenable. The use of the endpin spread gradually and enabled a greater number of female cellists to succeed as soloists, several of whom were Servais's pupils. However, a number of leading players did not adopt it, including Haussmann, Piatti and Popper. Even in the early twentieth century, CARL FUCHS insisted on pupils mastering the traditional posture first, claiming that the use of the endpin could encourage histrionic body movement. Changes to the endpin's materials and design have been driven not by comfort but by a search for improved tone. The first were of wood, but these were soon replaced by metal; carbon fibre is now frequently used. Paul Tortelier introduced a bent endpin in order to raise the cello so that the fingerboard was more nearly horizontal, and variations on this design are now widespread.

The left-hand technique of the cello, unlike that of the violin, is based on the fingers being a semitone apart, extending this to a tone between the first and second fingers when required. Thus, in the neck positions, the maximum normal span is a major third, although a span of a fourth is possible (the twentieth-century cellist Joachim Stutchewsky was one of few offering a systematic training in a larger extension, the *'grosse Spannung'*). The thumb can be placed on the string in higher positions, where the fourth finger was frequently used until the mid-nineteenth century; nowadays it is used much less often. Thumb technique originated in the eighteenth century; at first the thumb was used as a movable nut (the Italian term for this technique is *capotasto* – it occurs in the sonatas by Stephen Paxton c1780), but it became a fully independent digit in the later nineteenth century. The fingers can drop perpendicularly to the string or can be slightly slanted back; some cellists used a very slanted left hand analogous to violin technique, but this was never widespread. The modern bow is held with all fingers, including the fourth, over the stick, rather than with the fourth finger touching the stick as in the case of the violin or viola, and with the thumb at the edge of the frog, roughly opposite the second finger. Baroque and Classical bows were held further down the stick with the second finger touching the hair. In the earlier eighteenth century an underhand grip (as with the viol) was sometimes used.

Several accessories are used for either musical or technological reasons. MUTES made of wood that clip on to the bridge dampen the resonance of the instrument. These are rarely required in earlier music. Indeed, in the orchestra the violins are often expected to play with the mute but the lower strings do not – this practice lasted until at least the time of BEETHOVEN. An extreme example of muted playing occurs in the opening bars of Shostakovich's Second Piano Trio, where the cello begins unaccompanied, muted, playing in artificial HARMONICS. Devices to eradicate 'wolf notes' – jarring vibrations set up by particular pitches, usually around E or F – are also used, such as rubber-filled tubes attached to the string below the bridge, or more sophisticated devices attached inside the instrument. Some cellists have experimented with metal bridges or systems of mechanical amplification but these have not found favour.

The earliest surviving cello method of any substance is that by MICHEL CORRETTE (Paris, 1741); the earliest English and German methods are from 1765 (Robert Crome, London) and 1788 (Ferdinand Kauer, Vienna) respectively. Eighteenth-century cello methods frequently adopted fingering systems that appear cumbersome today – neither Corrette nor Crome used the third finger in low positions. The more logical and ergonomic fingerings used by GUNN and DUPORT became standard in the nineteenth century. Later eighteenth-century and early nineteenth-century tutors were notable for their elaborate bowing techniques in arpeggios. Duport in particular explored sophisticated bowing in his studies. ROMBERG's tutor is a much more encyclopedic work which prioritises more legato bowing and more flexible left-hand techniques. The most widely used nineteenth-century cello TREATISES were those by Duport (Paris, c1806), BAILLOT et al. (Paris, 1805), DOTZAUER (Mainz, c1825) and Kummer (Leipzig, 1839) – the last-named work was successively re-edited by Alfredo Piatti (1877) and Hugo Becker (1909). Dotzauer and Kummer extend Romberg's work – all three demonstrate PORTAMENTO by example, and on the whole avoid elaborate spiccato. The twentieth century saw fewer discursive cello methods, as opposed to those consisting of graded exercises, and the most influential performers and teachers, such as Popper, CASALS or Rostropovich, did not write down their teaching principles. Casals's teaching was codified by Alexanian (*Traité théorique et pratique du violoncelle*, Paris: Mathot, 1922) and was an important part of the teaching of one of his later pupils, Christopher Bunting (*Essay on the Craft of Cello Playing*, 2 vols., Cambridge University Press, 1982). Other significant twentieth-century cello treatises include those by Maurice Eisenberg (*Cello Playing of Today*, London: The Strad, 1957), Gerhard Mantel (*Cello Technique: Principles and Forms of Movement*, Bloomington, IN: Indiana University Press, 1975), and Paul Tortelier (*How I Play*, London: Chester Music, 1975). William Pleeth also set down some of his ideas in *The Cello* (London: Macdonald, 1982).

In chamber ensembles and orchestral playing, the cello had a primarily accompanying role until the nineteenth century, although it was never restricted to such a role. As a continuo instrument, it gradually replaced the bass VIOL (although the latter instrument never entirely disappeared, and continued longer in France than elsewhere). Many continuo parts are technically challenging, especially those of HANDEL and CORELLI. In addition to the notated continuo part, cellists would also elaborate these with chordal harmony, sometimes in the absence of a keyboard continuo instrument in the case of instrumental sonatas, and sometimes in operatic recitative (notated examples of the latter are given well into the nineteenth century after the practice had become obsolete).

There is a very large repertoire of sonatas for cello in the eighteenth century, and an equally large nineteenth-century repertoire, although much of the latter consists of ephemeral works such as operatic TRANSCRIPTIONS, variation sets, fantasias and other virtuoso showpieces written by cellists. The modern canonic repertoire consists of the Bach Solo Suites, the sonatas by BEETHOVEN and BRAHMS, the sonatas, concertos and other works by MENDELSSOHN, Schumann, Tchaikovsky, Debussy, Prokofiev and Shostakovich, and the concertos of HAYDN, Schumann, Dvořák and ELGAR. There is a very considerable mainstream twentieth-century cello repertoire partly inspired by cellists such as Casals and Rostropovich. However, in common with other instruments, many composers have extended the range of sonorities and playing techniques, using microtones, left-hand percussion, playing with two bows at once, playing under instead of over the strings, electronic amplification and distortion, and using pre-recorded tracks. Lachenmann's *Pression* (1969) contains no conventionally produced pitched sounds, and Xenakis's *Nomos Alpha* has passages which are equally extreme.

FURTHER READING

L. Ginsburg, trans. T. Tchistyakova, ed. H. R. Axelrod, *History of the Violoncello* (Neptune City, NJ: Paganiniana Publications, 1983).
G. Kennaway, *Playing the Cello, 1780–1930* (Farnham: Ashgate, 2014).
D. Markevitch, trans. F. Seder, *Cello Story* (Princeton, NJ: Summy-Birchard Music, 1984).
R. Stowell (ed.), *The Cambridge Companion to the Cello* (Cambridge University Press, 1999).
V. Walden, *One Hundred Years of Violoncello: A History of Technique and Performance Practice, 1740–1840* (Cambridge University Press, 1998).

GEORGE KENNAWAY

Chalumeau see CLARINET

Chambonnières, Jacques Champion, Sieur de (b. 1601/2; d. Paris, before 4 May 1672) French composer and harpsichordist.

Chambonnières established a new and distinctive style of HARPSICHORD playing and was widely influential both within and outside France. Born into a distinguished family of musicians (his father, Jacques Champion, was harpsichordist to Louis XIII), Chambonnières was granted reversion of his father's post in 1611. Declared the 'ultimate master' of the harpsichord by MERSENNE in 1636, he was finally appointed *joueur d'espinette ordinaire de la Chambre du Roy* after his father's death in 1642 but subsequently fell from favour at court. In 1657 he was passed over in the selection of the royal harpsichord teacher and he retired in 1662, selling his position to JEAN HENRY D'ANGLEBERT. Amongst his distinguished pupils were LOUIS COUPERIN, whom he discovered and brought to Paris, and Jacques Hardel.

Performance in Chambonnières's time was essentially an improvised art and the printed and manuscript sources of his music (dating from the end of the seventeenth century) give only a limited impression of his documented reputation. His playing was characterised by a 'beauty of rhythm, fine touch or lightness and speed of hand' (MERSENNE, 1636) and a flair for 'natural, tender, well-turned melodies' (*Lettre de Mr Le Gallois à Mademoiselle Regnault de Solier touchant la musique* (Paris: Estienne Michallet, 1680)). He used LUTE-inspired ORNAMENTATION to exploit the resonance of the harpsichord, although his basic keyboard texture is polyphonic, often in four voices, suggesting ORGAN or CONSORT origins, rather than the lute. Le Gallois (1680) described his playing as 'flowing' (*coulant*) as opposed to the brilliance of others, notably Louis Couperin.

There are 153 pieces surviving with attributions to Chambonnières. All are dance movements, some with additional character titles; unlike the works of Louis Couperin and D'Anglebert, there are no preludes. Chambonnières published two books (both 1670) which contain sixty pieces arranged into suites by tonality.

FURTHER READING

B. Gustafson, *Chambonnières: A Thematic Catalogue*, JSCM Instrumenta 1, http://sscm-jscm.org/instrumenta/instrumenta-volumes/instrumenta-volume-1.

TERENCE CHARLSTON

Chant see PLAINCHANT

Chaplin sisters Nellie (Eleanor Mary) (b. London, 11 February 1857; d. London, 16 April 1930); Kate (b. London, 3 July 1865; d. London, 9 December 1948); Mabel (b. London, 19 October 1870; d. London, 6 November 1960). Nellie (piano), Kate (violin) and Mabel (cello) trained at the London College of Music. They achieved early recognition and in 1893 Kate and Nellie played before Queen Victoria. In 1903 Nellie began investigating early DANCE and on 6 July 1904 presented a programme of French and English dances from the seventeenth and eighteenth centuries in the Royal Albert Hall. That summer Nellie also played a J. S. BACH double concerto on the HARPSICHORD with

Kathleen Salmon in a DOLMETSCH concert, and probably at around the same time Kate took up the viola d'amore and Mabel the VIOLA DA GAMBA. Their concerts of early dance and music proved popular until Nellie's death in 1930. Nellie wrote several instruction books for early dances.

In 1920 the sisters lent period flavour to the eight-piece female ensemble that accompanied a hugely successful revival of *The Beggar's Opera* at the Lyric Theatre, Hammersmith, London.

FURTHER READING

F. Hoffman, 'Chaplin, Schwestern', *Europäische Instrumentalistinnen des 18. und 19. Jahrhunderts*. www.sophie-drinker-institut.de/cms/index.php/chaplin-schwestern (1912).

M. Macdonald, 'Nellie Chaplin and her sisters: Forgotten pioneers of early music & dance with authentic instruments. Part 1'. www.semibrevity.com/2015/05/nellie-chaplin-and-her-sisters-forgotten-pioneers-of-early-music-dance-with-authentic-instruments-part-1/.

JEREMY BARLOW

Charpentier, Marc-Antoine (b. in or nr Paris, 1643; d. Paris, 24 February 1704) French composer.

A product of Roman training and a French career, Charpentier's music presents a particularly complex set of performance practice issues, reflecting both the wide range of genres he composed for nearly every setting or institution in the Île-de-France and his unique mixing of contemporary and antiquarian styles. Fortunately, most of Charpentier's pieces are preserved in his autograph collection (the *Mélanges*), which provides many clues to performance.

Charpentier's directions in the *Mélanges* make possible some generalisations about his practices: some common to French music, others unique to him. For example, Charpentier combines French *agréments* with his own specifications. He notates ornaments both on and before the beat, usually indicated in his vocal music by text syllable placement. Among the signs unique to Charpentier are dots before or after a trill, which indicate that it begins on the main note. He also uses a dot above a note to indicate that no ornament should be added. Another important issue of NOTATION is Charpentier's use of 'croches blanches' (flagged white notes in 3/2 time) and coloration (unflagged black note-heads), found in the works of earlier seventeenth-century Italian composers. While the former seem to be markers of Italian style rather than TEMPO, the latter are often used to indicate hemiolas.

Scoring is another major issue because Charpentier utilises virtually every combination of voices and instruments, from solo soprano to polychoral motet. He rarely indicates at the beginning of scores whether a piece, a movement, or an individual voice should be performed one or more per part, but this sometimes becomes evident via later annotations. Other instances can only be inferred from practice in similar works. This problem is especially evident in continuo parts, often labelled simply 'accompagnement'. Even some parts labelled 'orgue' refer later to doubling instruments, including VIOLA DA GAMBA, THEORBO and basse de violon; a few sacred pieces are labelled 'clavecin'. Some of Charpentier's works can be traced to particular institutions whose performing forces are known. For example, the composer uses six-part vocal writing for his first employer, Mlle de Guise.

Charpentier's writings are aimed primarily at teaching the 'Règles de composition', as the title of his primary treatise suggests. Only the very brief list of principles in the 'Abrégé des règles d'accompagnement' (Summary of the rules of accompaniment) and the 'Énergie des modes' – the composer's list of the affective associations of various keys in the 'Règles' – address performance.

FURTHER READING

M.-A. Charpentier, 'Règles de composition' (and other writings), in C. Cessac, *Marc-Antoine Charpentier*, 2nd edn (Paris: Fayard, 2004), 461–96; see also www.chmtl.indiana.edu/tfm/17th/CHAREG_MPBN6355.html.
S. Thompson, 'The autograph manuscripts of Marc-Antoine Charpentier: Clues to performance', PhD dissertation, University of Hull (1997). http://ethos.bl.uk/, thesis ID 389291.
S. Thompson (ed.), *New Perspectives on Marc-Antoine Charpentier* (Farnham: Ashgate, 2010).

DON FADER

Choir Choir derives from the Greek *choros*. Chorus lines in Ancient Greek drama, the Judaic Psalms of David, Delphic hymns and early Christian chant were all vehicles for monophonic or heterophonic choral singing. When voices are deployed chorally (i.e. with several singers per voice part), words are sung simultaneously or proximately (or occasionally in opposition), depending on the textural sophistication of the medium. The wordless chorus did not feature in Western music until the nineteenth century (e.g. HECTOR BERLIOZ, Funeral March for the final scene of *Hamlet*, Op. 18 No. 3), although the untexted voice parts of Medieval motets have been taken by some to imply wordless performance, most usually to the vowels 'ah' or 'ü'.

The earliest improvised Christian polyphony – simple (parallel) *organum* – lent itself to choral performance. But as vocal IMPROVISATION above a preexistent melody became more sophisticated (e.g. the florid *organa* of twelfth-century Aquitaine and Paris), solo renditions of the organal voice became the norm. In the late Medieval period, choral foundations proliferated, and vocal music was composed to be sung in the refectory or at the fireside, as well as to enhance the liturgy. Polyphony was the province of the small ensemble while choral performance was reserved for monophonic chant. This view was challenged by some early twentieth-century interpretations of Medieval polyphony, some of which involved very large groups of singers, both with and without instruments – Carl Orff's *Carmina Burana* was a homage to such a sound-world, now regarded as anathema in the performance of Medieval music.

Late Medieval and early Renaissance *Contratenor* parts lie very low in places for modern altos, and *Tenor* parts lie rather high in places for modern tenors. One solution is to combine voices of different ranges in order to create a seamless timbral spectrum. Sometimes instruments are used to paper over the vocal cracks. Sometimes TRANSPOSITIONS are enacted so that anomalies of tessitura are moved to a part of the gamut where the problem is dissipated. And sometimes singers toggle between head voice, chest voice and falsetto as practicable. All these solutions are aided by choral rather than solo performance, and the size of early Renaissance choirbooks indicates that between a dozen and twenty people could have surrounded one of the larger books. Experiments in the contrast between high and low textures within a choir were a feature of the early Renaissance, and by the mid-sixteenth century, enjoyment of such sonorities created a demand for music where whole choirs were pitted against one another. Ultimately this gave way to the split choirs (*cori spezzati*) of the late Renaissance.

While Renaissance choirs rarely comprised more than thirty people, certain establishments boasted more (e.g. the *Hofkapelle* in Munich, where Lassus had musical responsibility for over sixty singers, all of whom sang together on special occasions). Large choirbooks on music stands were replaced by handheld partbooks and the use of instruments to accompany choirs also became commonplace. In some cases instruments doubled the voices; in other cases instruments supplied notes that the singers themselves could not provide with enough power or with requisite timbre; in yet other cases instruments deputised for missing voices. Alongside the use of (primarily brass) instruments within choirs, from the very opening of the fifteenth century the ORGAN emerged as an accepted component of the sacred choral sound.

Antiphonal singing of polyphonic music came to the fore in the mid-sixteenth century. On the continent it initially appeared in the work of lesser-known northern Italian composers, but achieved excellence in Adrian Willaert's collection of vespers psalms (composed in collaboration with Jacquet of Mantua) published in Venice in 1550. At the same time in England, post-Reformation composers of the Chapel Royal used Latin terms to distinguish between the *Decani* (Dean's) and *Cantoris* (Cantor's) sides of the choir. Meanwhile, amateur music making saw small choirs gathering in the homes of the emerging middle classes, where collections of madrigals were billed as 'apt for the viols and voices'.

The advent of virtuosic vocal writing in the Baroque era ushered in a two-tier system of part-singing – one was demonstrably choral and the other soloistic. The debate surrounding Baroque vocal forces has tended to centre on the music of J. S. BACH, where it is argued that the default disposition (irrespective of financial considerations) was solo voices, and that choral bolstering was a special effect used in certain pieces or within certain movements of large-scale works. In England, however, HANDEL's music for the coronation of King George II in 1727 was performed by a choir of forty-seven singers, while the 1784 Handel Commemoration used a choir of 274.

In America in the mid-eighteenth century, the choral guru William Billings believed that a balanced choir should have as many basses as all the other parts put together. A century later, the Belgian conductor and pedagogue FRANÇOIS-JOSEPH FÉTIS opted for a nearly equal disposition of voices: fourteen each of sopranos and basses with twelve altos and ten tenors. It was during Fétis's career that the term *a cappella* began to be used to describe unaccompanied choral singing. Indeed, the early nineteenth century had witnessed an explosion of interest in choral singing, of which BEETHOVEN's Symphony No. 9 in D minor, Op. 125 ('Choral') from 1822–4 and MENDELSSOHN's celebrated 1829 Berlin performance of J. S. Bach's *St Matthew Passion* BWV244 were obvious manifestations. And late eighteenth-century French experiments in the use of large forces led to works such as Jean-François Le Sueur's *Chant de 1er vendémiaire an IX* ('Song of 23 September 1800'), a Napoleonic choral ode for four choirs and four orchestras. This had its noblest influence in the work of Le Sueur's pupil BERLIOZ, most notably in his *Grande messe des morts*, Op. 5 ('Requiem'), which was first performed in 1838 with a choir of 210 (eighty sopranos, sixty tenors, seventy basses) and an orchestra of 190 (including four brass bands), although Berlioz ultimately envisioned a choir numbering between 700 and 800 singers. In nineteenth-century Germany, choral singing became a nationalistic pastime, and in England, the use of women's voices in church choirs (which had begun around northern Europe in a small way in the late eighteenth century) burgeoned. Rallies of hundreds, or even thousands, of singers became features of nineteenth-century America and Europe. The 1857 Handel Festival at London's Crystal Palace used a choir of over 2,000, whereas the Anniversary Festival of Charity Children at St Paul's Cathedral in 1851 had – according to Berlioz's report – hosted a choir of 6,500.

In the twentieth century, choral performance practice was affected by sound recording techniques and the advent of playback. Western choir training began to focus on balance, clarity and control. Within mixed choruses, countertenors were replaced by mezzo-sopranos and contraltos. Single-sex choirs also flourished, in particular the robed men-and-boys choirs of the English cathedral tradition. These choirs still act as indispensable training grounds for young musicians and, since a pioneering move at Salisbury Cathedral in 1991, have broadened their catchment to include girls' choirs to run alongside, or in combination with, the existing choir. Ironically for a medium with its roots in DANCE – such as the *paean* of Ancient Greece or *carole* of Medieval France – Western choral performance is mainly a stylised static offering.

Later in the twentieth century, much was made of differences between training methods within the choral world, and vocal and presentational techniques were borrowed from, and shared between, countries and genres. Latterly, choirs have become definers of orientation – political, religious, cultural and sexual. Choirs have also become iconic in branding and profiling institutions, since choral singing is perceived to foster group discipline and goal-sharing. Add to that the required skills of time management and non-verbal communication, and choral singers are deemed to be especially employable in many non-musical roles.

FURTHER READING

C. Alwes, *A History of Western Choral Music*, 2 vols. (Oxford University Press, 2015, 2016).
R. Minor, *Choral Fantasies: Music, Festivity, and Nationhood in Nineteenth-Century Germany* (Cambridge University Press, 2012).
A. Parrott, *Composers' Intentions? Lost Traditions of Musical Performance* (Woodbridge: Boydell & Brewer, 2015).

JEREMY SUMMERLY

Choron, Alexandre(-Étienne) (b. Caen, 21 October 1771; d. Paris, 29 June 1834) French writer on music, publisher and composer.

Choron was largely self-taught and his interest in contrapuntal technique developed through study of such theoreticians as ZARLINO, Martini, Fux and ALBRECHTSBERGER. This led him to publish his own *Principes* of accompaniment and composition of the Italian School, in 1804 and 1808 respectively.

This was followed by a two-volume dictionary, largely concerned with musicians of preceding centuries. From 1812 he became director of *Fêtes publiques* and he was also responsible for the reform of church music in French cathedrals and their choir-schools (*maîtrises*), particularly during the reign of Louis-Philippe. His overriding interest for *ars perfecta* church music led him to found his own institution for its study, the École royale et spéciale du chant, which became particularly important later in the century when it was revived as the École Niedermeyer. It was through his initiatives in the unearthing of the music of the past that lay his greatest contribution to historical performance, training musicians to appreciate and perform the music of the Renaissance masters, especially Palestrina but also French composers. This interest expanded into larger-scale Baroque works with orchestra and also the symphonies of HAYDN.

In his concerts of largely unknown earlier music he achieved considerable success, partly through his choir, which performed at the Sorbonne every Sunday, always matching the repertoire to the church calendar. Among those who attended his concerts in the *École* were Bourbon royalty as well as musicians as celebrated as Cherubini and Rossini. He continued to publish various pedagogical *cours* and *méthodes* right up to his death; their whole approach to education was entirely different from that of the Conservatoire. Although he also published his own compositions, it was through his many EDITIONS of old music that he exerted his most important influence; along with his entourage of students he catalysed the interest in early music in France in the second half of the century, laying the foundations for Cecilianism, a French adaptation of the principles of the Saint-Cecilia Academy in Rome.

FURTHER READING

K. Ellis, *Interpreting the Musical Past: Early Music in Nineteenth-Century France* (London: Oxford University Press, 2005).

RICHARD LANGHAM SMITH

Christiani, Adolph Friedrich (b. Kassel, 1836; d. New Jersey, 1885) German piano pedagogue.

Christiani's *Principles of Expression of the Pianoforte* (1885) concerns practical and aesthetic aspects of piano performance, though his instructions and insights are applicable to the majority of instrumental and vocal repertoire from the nineteenth century. Detailing nuanced approaches to performance, his discussions of TEMPO, rhythm, metre and TACTUS offer fundamentals for interpreting most music from the so-called Romantic tradition.

Christiani also considers the nature of musicianship and expressivity using hierarchical frameworks, not entirely dissimilar to biological classification systems. He divides musical ability into four criteria: talent, emotion, intelligence and technique. Those who possessed all qualities in equal measure were performing artists of the first order; he labels those who claimed technique alone 'virtuosos of the music-box kind' (Christiani, 16). Christiani finds that vocalists, violinists and cellists exhibit the most expressive potential, because they possess the greatest abilities to vary tone, timbre and ARTICULATION.

Pianists, he believes, are 'the last and least qualified' to be expressive agents due to their instrument's limitations in modifying sound (Christiani, 20).

Christiani's pedagogy mainly concerns various types of ACCENTUATION. Not simply a quantifiable articulation, an ACCENT is a 'tone-pressing, emphasising [which] is the chief means and the basis of musical expression' (Christiani, 20). He counts four distinct accent varieties: rhythmical, metrical, melodic and harmonic. Each accent includes subtypes, all of which are not typically notated, but rather sensed or intuited by the performer, given the musical context. Through examples drawn from nineteenth-century repertoire and treatises by CZERNY, LUSSY, KULLAK and Köhler, Christiani argues that expressive techniques are not consigned to good TASTE alone, nor are they mystically derived moments of genius. Since 'intelligence, not feeling, is the chief requirement of expression' (Christiani, 5), excellent musicality is teachable through a pedagogy that, beyond stressing shallow physical-technical achievement, aims towards the deeper goal of musical eloquence and artistry.

FURTHER READING

A. F. Christiani, *The Principles of Expression in Pianoforte Playing* (New York: Harper & Brothers, 1885).

ALEXANDER EVAN BONUS

Christie, William (b. Buffalo, 19 December 1944) American harpsichordist and conductor, best known as founder-director of the French Baroque ensemble LES ARTS FLORISSANTS.

Christie studied art history at Harvard University and musicology at Yale, where he was taught HARPSICHORD by RALPH KIRKPATRICK. In 1971 he moved to France to work as a keyboard player, performing in RENÉ JACOBS's ensemble Concerto Vocale among others, and in 1979 he founded his own mixed ensemble of voices and instruments Les Arts Florissants, taking the name from a work by MARC-ANTOINE CHARPENTIER, who was the focus of much of their early activity.

Success came quickly for the group, and since the early 1980s many recordings of seventeenth- and eighteenth-century sacred, secular and dramatic music with voices have followed for Harmonia Mundi, then Erato, and latterly the Les Arts Florissants label. Although they performed numerous works by English and Italian composers, it was in the French repertoire that they won particular recognition. Christie's insistence on attention to the meaning of text and the inflections of speech gave his performances a natural means of communication, while his grip of dramatic pacing and tonal beauty helped revive much forgotten repertoire from the Baroque era, including works by Charpentier (his opera *Médée*), RAMEAU and LULLY. A staged production of Lully's *Atys* in New York in 1987 made an especially strong impact.

Christie later widened his operatic repertoire to include HANDEL and MOZART, and, following an admired 1996 production of Handel's *Theodora* (with director Peter Sellars) at Glyndebourne, has returned there for *Rodelinda*, *Giulio Cesare*, Purcell's *The Fairy Queen* and Rameau's *Hippolyte et Aricie*. He has also been influential as a teacher: from 1982 to 1995 he taught at the PARIS CONSERVATOIRE, and in 2002 he founded *Le Jardin des Voix*, an 'academy' ensemble for younger singers. He has made a small number of recordings as a solo harpsichordist.

LINDSAY KEMP

Cimbasso see TUBA AND OPHICLEIDE

Cinti-Damoreau, Laure (Laure-Cinthie Montalant) (b. Paris, 6 February 1801; d. Paris, 25 February 1863) French soprano admired for her impeccable technique, stylistic nuance and inventive ORNAMENTATION.

Refused entry to the vocal class at the PARIS CONSERVATOIRE (where she studied PIANO, HARP and composition), Cinti-Damoreau trained privately with Charles-Henri Plantade and then gained much from her early years at the Théâtre-Italien following her debut with Angelica Catalani's company in January 1816. She subsequently became the 'French spearhead of Rossini's Italian invasion' (Caswell, 462), creating a number of principal roles in the composer's operas for Paris (1825–31). Cinti-Damoreau sang at the Opéra-Comique (1835–40) in premieres of works by Auber, Puget and Adam, but subsequently devoted herself solely to concert performance (1841–5), touring with, for example, the soprano Cornélie Falcon (1841) and the violinist Alexandre Artôt. She taught at the Paris Conservatoire (1833–56). As well as two SINGING manuals and some songs, she left a series of notebooks that provide valuable evidence about melodic embellishment during the period. Her combination of Italianate vocal technique with French adherence to textual subtlety made an important contribution to the development of singing in France.

FURTHER READING

A. Caswell, 'Mme Cinti-Damoreau and the embellishment of Italian opera in Paris 1820–1845', *JAMS*, 28/3 (Autumn 1975), 459–92.
A. Caswell (ed.), *Embellished Opera Arias. Recent Researches in the Music of the Nineteenth and Early Twentieth Centuries*, vols. VII–VIII (Madison, WI: A-R Editions, 1989).
L. Cinti-Damoreau, *Méthode de chant composée pour ses classes du Conservatoire* (Paris: au Ménestrel, 1849).
Nouvelle méthode de chant à l'usage des jeunes personnes, introduction à sa méthode d'artiste (Paris: Heugel et Cie, 1855).

SUSAN RUTHERFORD

Clarinet A woodwind instrument with predominantly cylindrical bore, played with a single reed.

The clarinet developed around 1700; since then it has been subject to a large number of changes in design. The Boehm-system instrument in common use today was patented in 1844 and has gradually found universal favour outside Germany and Austria, where clarinets have remained more closely related to earlier models. From the 1970s and 1980s, as historical performance began to embrace music of the Classical and Romantic periods, the distinctive tone-quality of clarinets from different eras has become more widely appreciated. However, in the copying of old clarinets, historical accuracy has sometimes been overtaken by practical expediency, 'normalised' pitches and modernised mouthpieces having become regular concessions to market forces.

An immediate predecessor of the clarinet was the CHALUMEAU, which evolved in the late seventeenth century, probably from attempts to increase the volume of sound produced by the RECORDER; the retention of the latter's foot-joint and manufacture of four sizes is evidence of the close physical relationship between the two instruments. Two diametrically opposed keys were soon added above the seven finger-holes and the thumb-hole, in order to bridge the gap between the highest fundamental note and lowest note of the (scarcely available) upper register. The relatively large dimensions of the vibrating reed and the mouthpiece to which it was tied, however, were principally designed to produce the fundamental register. Of the half dozen or so chalumeaux still in existence, one (in Munich) is the work of J. C. Denner, widely acknowledged as the inventor of the clarinet. Recent research has uncovered a substantial chalumeau repertory from 1700 to 1770 and beyond. In Viennese opera the instrument was favoured by Ariosti, the brothers Bononcini, Caldara, Conti, Fux and Emperor Joseph I; later it was revived by Gluck in *Orfeo* (1762) and *Alceste* (1767), with an even later appearance in Gassmann's *I rovinati* (1772). Instrumental pieces include a concerto by Hoffmeister, divertimenti by DITTERSDORF, Gassmann and Pichl, and ballet music by Asplmayr and Starzer. A *Musica da camera* by Starzer was formerly attributed to MOZART as part of K187/159c. In Germany one of the most prolific composers for the chalumeau was TELEMANN, who played it early in his career and wrote a double concerto for the middle two sizes. In Darmstadt, Christoph Graupner variously employed the four sizes in as many as eighty cantatas and eighteen instrumental works. For other German composers the chalumeau was an occasional colour, including J. L. Bach, Harrer, Hasse, Keiser, König, Molter, Schürmann, Steffani and von Wilderer. Although the overall delicacy of the chalumeau repertory is not reflected in contemporary criticism of the instrument, Daniel Schubart in 1784–5 paid tribute to its individual and infinitely pleasant character, belatedly adding that the whole world of music would suffer a grievous loss if the instrument ever fell into disuse.

The two-keyed clarinet came into being when the thumb-hole was repositioned, the mouthpiece was reduced in size to facilitate overblowing and the foot-joint was replaced by a bell to improve the projection of sound. The chalumeau was able for a time to retain its separate identity partly because the clarinet functioned rather unsatisfactorily in its lowest register. Like other woodwinds of the time, it was normally constructed of boxwood. The clarinet finds an early mention in Nuremberg records from 1710, its early trumpet-like character reflected in its name (clarinetto = small clarino). Clarinets in C and D were used orchestrally by Telemann and Caldara in the 1720s, in concertos by Vivaldi and in Handel's Overture HWV 424 for two clarinets and horn. The clarinet gradually began to find a place in the orchestra in the works of Rameau, Arne and the Mannheim School. During the second half of the century the five-keyed classical instrument enabled the clarinet to emulate the human voice across its entire range and all but three (C, B♭, A) of the seven pitches listed in Roeser's *Essai d'instruction à l'usage de ceux qui composent pour la clarinette et le cor* (Paris, 1764) fell from favour. The articulated style known to Mozart is somewhat in contrast to the smooth, seamless approach adopted by many modern clarinettists – and has been found to be well worth recapturing. The practice of playing with reed against the top lip was abandoned at the PARIS CONSERVATOIRE only in 1831 and was also slow to be abandoned in England and Italy; Mozart's clarinettist ANTON STADLER is believed to have played reed-below and this has provided sufficient reason for modern players to take insufficient interest in the earlier practice.

Mozart's early and occasional encounters with the clarinet were outside his home in Salzburg; for example, in London, Milan, Mannheim and Paris. It was shortly after Mozart met Stadler at the beginning of the 1780s that an enormous leap in Mozart's appreciation of the clarinet took place, both in opera and in the wind serenades K375 and K388. But it was the serenade for thirteen instruments, the *Gran Partita* K361, in which Mozart's range of idiomatic writing for clarinets and basset horns radically advanced, as his exploration of the possibilities in the chalumeau register entered a new phase. In addition to Mozart's Clarinet Trio K498, the mid-1780s witnessed important clarinet parts in three piano concertos, K482, 488 and 491; then in *Don Giovanni* (1787) the clarinets in the opera orchestra finally began to threaten the dominance of the oboes as the principal woodwind colouring. There is some justification for the assertion that at the end of the eighteenth century the relatively new clarinet came to symbolise power and new ideals, whereas the OBOE retained an association with the aristocracy and the monarchy. The development of Stadler's BASSET CLARINET (with a downward extension by four chromatic semitones) inspired the dramatic contours of Mozart's Quintet K581 and Concerto K622. In the 1780s the BASSET HORN, a type of tenor clarinet, was shaped in two straight joints angled at a knee, whereas today it resembles a bass clarinet, with curved crook and upturned bell. The basset horn's sombre tone quality (arising from its relatively narrow bore) made it especially suitable for the ceremonial and religious contexts of *Die Zauberflöte* and the Requiem.

In the nineteenth century the clarinet acquired more mechanism, which contributed to greater evenness of tone and a more resonant sound, as well as making tractable the highly chromatic style of writing that was then evolving. For tonal reasons the B♭ clarinet was by then established as the main solo instrument and in 1812 IWAN MÜLLER presented at the Paris Conservatoire his *omnitonique* thirteen-keyed instrument, which he claimed made A and C clarinets redundant. Although rejected on the grounds that the special tone colour of each size would be sorely missed, his model was highly influential and remained the basis for the German clarinet. Between 1839 and 1843 KLOSÉ and Buffet *jeune* developed a clarinet system similar to that of BOEHM's for the flute and known initially as the 'clarinet with moving rings'. Composers took different views of the relationship of A and B♭ clarinets; for Dvořák the choice appears to have rested entirely on technical considerations, whereas STRAVINSKY's Three Pieces for Clarinet (1919) requires a change from A to B♭ for the last piece. The C clarinet deserves wider revival (and is technically essential on period instruments) for orchestral contexts such as BEETHOVEN, BERLIOZ, Liszt and BRAHMS (Symphony No. 4, Scherzo). RICHARD STRAUSS made a keen distinction between all the different clarinets and was a particular advocate of the C clarinet.

Throughout the nineteenth century the clarinet was (with the HORN) the orchestral romantic tone colour par excellence. Weber and SPOHR were inspired respectively by the playing of Heinrich Baermann and Simon Hermstedt, writing concertos and chamber music for the clarinet. Larger ensembles of mixed wind and strings involving clarinet became popular in the wake of Beethoven's Septet, Op. 20, which was a palpable influence upon Schubert's Octet, D803. Notwithstanding Schumann's *Fantasiestücke*, Op. 73, the clarinet gradually fell from favour as a solo instrument until Richard Mühlfeld inspired BRAHMS to abandon his retirement to compose the highly influential Trio, Op. 114, Quintet, Op. 115 and the two sonatas, Op. 120. It is notable that Mühlfeld continued to play an instrument manufactured in boxwood (rather than the already popular blackwoods) until his death in 1907; at a time when orchestras were expanding, the MEININGEN ORCHESTRA to which he belonged consisted of a mere fifty players, just half the size of the Vienna Philharmonic. Grenadilla became the usual material for clarinets, both because it enabled greater projection of sound and offered more stable support for the mechanism.

In the twentieth century, the versatility of the clarinet was able to match the plethora of compositional styles, which brought ever increasing technical demands on the player. Many composers of significance, from BERG, Debussy and Nielsen through to Berio, Carter, BOULEZ and Reich, made important contributions to the solo repertory. The cultivation of multiphonics is charted in Bartolozzi's *New Sounds for Woodwinds* (Oxford, 1967), while Roger Heaton (1995) has provided an important survey of other contemporary techniques, including use of microtones. The profile of the clarinet as a JAZZ instrument was perhaps strongest before 1945, though its advocates continued to expand its range of vocalised expression through use of a wide VIBRATO, glissandi and PORTAMENTI. The clarinet's emulation of the human voice also forms part of the rich tradition of Klezmer. Sidney Bechet and Benny Goodman were among those jazz clarinettists whose work was greatly appreciated by classical musicians.

The BASS CLARINET was already in existence by the 1790s and acquired its modern form in 1830s at the hands of ADOLPHE SAX and Buffet *jeune*. Meyerbeer included a bass clarinet obbligato in *Les Huguenots* (1836) and WAGNER's integration of it into the orchestra was followed by MAHLER, Stravinsky, SCHOENBERG and a host of others. Since the 1950s a substantial solo repertory has been created, while in its search for original colours the period movement has sought to revive the bass clarinet in A, which was explicitly required by Wagner for performances of *Tristan und Isolde*.

FURTHER READING

R. Heaton, 'The contemporary clarinet', in C. Lawson (ed.), *The Cambridge Companion to the Clarinet* (Cambridge University Press, 1995), 163–83.
E. Hoeprich, *The Clarinet* (New Haven, CT and London: Yale University Press, 2008).
C. Lawson (ed.), *The Cambridge Companion to the Clarinet* (Cambridge University Press, 1995).

COLIN LAWSON

Classification of instruments Various approaches to the grouping and systematisation of musical instruments have appeared at least since the second century BC in Greece, the Arab world and India. Since then, most societies have developed their own classifications, often taking into account elements relevant to their specific culture, sets of values and musical traditions.

The division of instruments into 'strings', 'wind' and 'percussion', still the most widely used among Western musicians, was introduced by Porphyry (242–c305 AD) and later reorganised by BOETHIUS. Through its history it underwent several revisions and developments usually inspired by the specific characteristics of the instruments typical of each period: SEBASTIAN VIRDUNG (1511) replaces the category of percussion with 'instruments made of metal or other resonant substances', notably ignoring drums, which he hails as an invention of the devil; MICHAEL PRAETORIUS (1619) undertakes a first theoretical discussion of the rationale of classification, stating that instruments can only be divided based on their pitch and sound, 'examining how and with what kind of motion of the instrument and of the human limbs their sound is generated' and 'by measuring their range in pitch'. He then distinguishes the classes of wind (further divided into piped or blown, with holes on the front, front and back, front back and sides, with or without bags), percussion (struck by beaters or in the shape of clappers or metal globes), stringed instruments (with gut or metal strings, plucked or bowed, with keyboard) and a class for 'hybrids'. The same system remained popular in treatises as well as in common usage until the mid-nineteenth century, when BERLIOZ further rationalised and adopted it in his instrumentation treatise (1843), restoring the Boethian order of strings (further divided into bowed, plucked and with keyboard), wind (with or without reed, with keyboard, brass with mouthpiece, woodwind with mouthpiece, voices) and percussion (fixed, audible pitch and indeterminate pitch).

Since the growth in number and breadth of musical instrument collections in Europe in the last quarter of the nineteenth century, new systems were developed with the aim of giving order and comparing instruments from a wider variety of periods, places and cultures. The most influential attempt was developed by VICTOR-CHARLES MAHILLON in Brussels in the late 1870s, and was based on traditional systems that had been used in India for centuries. Based on the primary source of vibration, it divided instruments into autophones (where the sound is generated by the elasticity of the instrument's body itself), *instruments à membranes* (sound generated by a tensioned membrane), *instruments à vent* (sound produced by the oscillatory movement of air) and *instruments à cordes* (based on the vibration of strings under tension). Following examples from the natural sciences, each class was then subdivided into branches, sections, *sous*-sections. This system became rapidly popular after its application to the 3,000+ instruments catalogued by Mahillon over the following years and was soon translated into several languages. In contrast with the systems previously described, it had the advantage of being culturally neutral, and therefore applicable to any known or unknown instrument of any provenance and time. It also facilitated the identification of common features between otherwise unrelated instruments, highlighting lines of 'development' from simpler to more complex models and, in accordance with the ideas of the time, facilitating an understanding of the history of musical instruments.

In 1914 CURT SACHS and Eric von Hornbostel undertook a major revision of Mahillon's method, strengthening its coherence and introducing a numerical system based on the decimal classification devised by Melvil Dewey in 1876. Instruments were divided into 1) idiophones, 2) membranophones, 3) cordophones and 4) aerophones, each class having up to eight further divisions. Each numerical identifier is followed by one or more suffixes, preceded by a dash, to indicate further accessories or physical characteristics. In 1937 Canon FRANCIS GALPIN introduced the fifth category of 'electrophonic instruments', further reorganised by Sachs in 1940 under the name 'electrophones'.

Notwithstanding frequent criticism of its ontology, coherence and appropriateness to current research goals, the Hornbostel-Sachs classification remains the most popular system in museums and organological research, particularly thanks to its flexibility – the number of instruments that it cannot include is limited to a few examples – and ease of use with computers and automated systems. A recent revision was undertaken by an international group and is available through the website of the International Committee of Museums of Instruments and Music of the International Council of Museums. Among other updates, it includes the most articulate attempt to systematise electric and electronic instruments.

Two alternative streams of research have emerged particularly since the 1970s: one concerns the development of more complex and content-driven methods and the other the cultural study of traditional classification systems. Several of the new proposals reflect an emancipation from the study of the musical instrument as an object, to its understanding as a medium between cultural, musical and technical dimensions in relation to the requirements of the human body. Examples are Hans Heinz Dräger's principles and Mantle Hood's organograms – both taking into account elements related to musical function, decoration and performance practice – and Hans Peter Reinecke's correlation of instrument families and emotions. In the same period Herbert Heyde developed a classification based on eleven elements that aimed to correlate instruments with the historical and technical context that generated them. All these methods have proved superior to Hornbostel-Sachs in their capacity to lead to a fuller understanding of the anthropological and cultural value of the instruments classified, but have had limited circulation due to the wealth of information and preliminary understanding required in order to adopt them, and the complexity in the interpretation of results.

Traditional classification systems began to be studied in the 1970s. In 1990 Margaret Kartomi published an influential overview of classification systems, particularly focusing on the value of their comparative study in developing an understanding of elements of the musical cultures that produced them. It led to a new and unprecedented interest in this area of organology that might eventually lead to the development of a long overdue alternative to the Hornbostel-Sachs classification combining cultural richness and simple application.

FURTHER READING

N. A. Jairazbhoy, 'An explication of the Hornbostel-Sachs instrument classification system', in S. C. de Vale (ed.), *Selected Reports in Ethnomusicology*, vol. VIII: *Issues in Organology* (Los Angeles: University of California, 1990), 81–104.

M. J. Kartomi, *On Concepts and Classifications on Musical Instruments* (University of Chicago Press, 1990).

Revision of the Hornbostel-Sachs Classification of Musical Instruments by the MIMO Consortium, M. Birley et al. (eds.). www.cimcim.icom.museum.

GABRIELE ROSSI ROGNONI

Clavichord (Fr. *clavicorde, manicorde, manicordion*; Ger. *Clavichord, Klavichord*; It. *clavicordio, clavicordo, manicordo, monacordo, monocordo, sordino*; Lat. *clavicordium*; Port. *clavicórdio*; Sp. *clavicordio, manicordio, manucordio, monacordio*) The earliest, simplest, quietest and arguably the most expressive of all stringed keyboard instruments.

The sound of the clavichord is produced by depressing a pivoted key-lever which raises a narrow metal blade (the tangent) attached to its distal end. The tip of the tangent strikes a pair (or course) of strings dividing them into two halves, the right side of which is free to vibrate, the left being damped by a piece of cloth (the listing). The sounding length (and therefore the pitch) is defined by the contact point of the tangent on the course and the strings continue to sound only while the key is depressed and the tangent remains in contact with them. The player can control the initial dynamic of each note by varying the force and speed of the touch, and alter the sounding string after its initiation by changing the pressure on the key and even raise the pitch. The clavichord is the only keyboard instrument which allows this degree of touch sensitivity (*see* Figure 3).

The clavichord is related to the monochord, a single-string scientific instrument, said to have been invented by Pythagoras. The earliest reference to the 'clavichord' (*clavichordium*) is from the early fifteenth century and the oldest datable representation, the carved altarpiece in Minden, Germany, is dated 1425. Early clavichords were fretted (*gebunden*); one course provided more than one pitch. The earliest technical information on fretting comes from the manuscript treatise (c1440) by HENRI ARNAUT DE ZWOLLE: a small, multiple-fretted clavichord with up to four notes sharing each course and a compass of three chromatic octaves (thirty-seven notes), B to b". The tangents are positioned to give a Pythagorean TEMPERAMENT. Mid-fifteenth-century

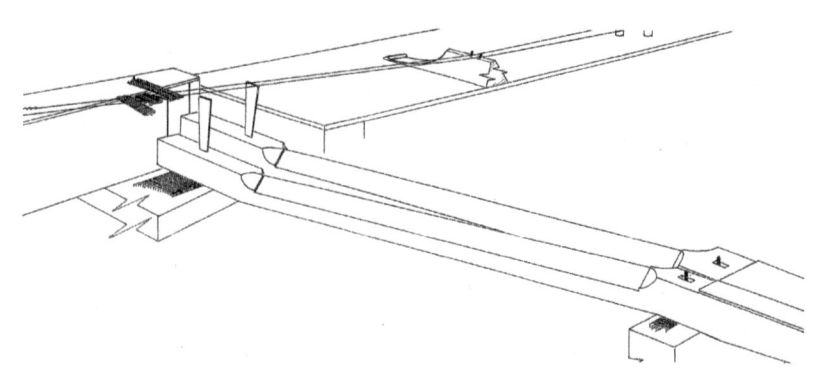

Figure 3: The action of a fretted clavichord, showing two keys sharing one pair of strings. (Christopher Nobbs)

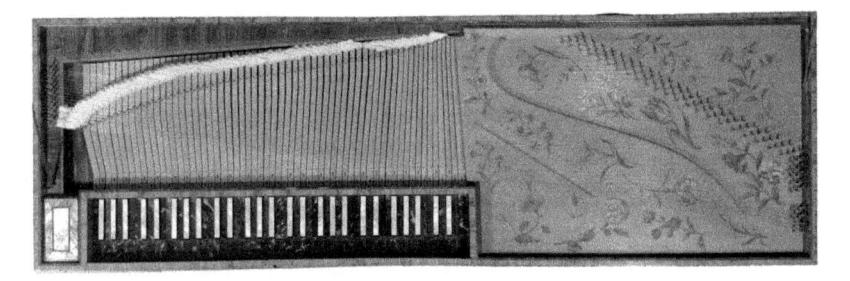

Figure 4: Plan view of an unfretted clavichord by J. A. Hass, 1763.
(by kind permission of the Friends of St Cecilia's Hall, Edinburgh)

clavichords had a soundboard located near the bottom of the instrument, extending underneath the keys. Clavichords were common all over Europe by the sixteenth century. The earliest surviving signed and dated clavichord (Domenico da Pesaro, 1543) is one of only five remaining from before 1600. Sixteenth-century clavichords were polygonal or rectangular in shape (*see* VIRGINAL) with the soundboard to the right and the keyboard off-centre to the left. The keyboard had a bass short octave and protruded from the longest side. Four courses were provided for each upper octave.

From the seventeenth century onwards Germany, Spain, Portugal and Scandinavia became the main centres of clavichord playing and making. Multiple fretting gave way to diatonic fretting (where each course provides either one or two notes) and the keyboard became incorporated within a larger case. Unfretted (*bundfrei*) clavichords (with one course per note) first appeared towards the end of the sixteenth century. JOHANNES SPETH stipulates an unfretted instrument for clavichord performance of his *Ars magna consoni et dissoni* (Augsburg, 1693): the oldest surviving unfretted clavichord, however, dates from a little later (Johann Michael Heinitz, 1716). Large instruments with a compass of five octaves or even more were made from the 1730s. The Hass family in Hamburg built many such large, unfretted models. They included 4' strings to re-enforce the bass, a feature which C. P. E. BACH detested, preferring the work of the Saxon maker, Christian Ernst Friederici (*see* Figure 4).

The Saxon GOTTFRIED SILBERMANN invented the *cembal d'amour*, a clavichord with strings of double length, struck exactly in their middle. JAKOB ADLUNG (1758) describes movable keyboards, leather-covered tangents and the pantalon stop, an ingenious sustaining device (of which examples survive), which raised a set of extra fixed tangents turning the clavichord into an undamped keyed dulcimer. The lost Harmonic Clavichord (Mazlowski, 1800) may have included sympathetic strings. Large, strong-toned clavichords continued to be made in Sweden in competition with the piano until 1832.

SANTA MARÍA published his treatise, largely devoted to clavichord playing, in 1565 and the clavichord was used for teaching and practice (especially by organists) for at least 300 years. Attaingnant (1531), Speth (1693) and J. C. F. Fischer (1698) allowed for clavichord performance of their keyboard music and MATTHESON (1713) admired its potential for *cantabile* playing. J. S. BACH regarded the clavichord as the best instrument for study (Forkel, *Ueber Johann Sebastian Bachs Leben, Kunst und Kunstwerke*, 1802) and many of his keyboard works were probably played on it. C. P. E. Bach was the first among many German composers to conceive music specifically for the clavichord. His pieces epitomise *Sturm und Drang* and *Empfindsamkeit* sensibilities and use VIBRATO (*Bebung*), tone swelling (*Tragen der Töne*) and extreme dynamic contrasts. Primarily a solo instrument for private recreation, the clavichord was also used to accompany solo SINGING and occasionally solo instruments. HAYDN and W. A. MOZART owned and played the clavichord, and BEETHOVEN knew it through his teacher, Neefe.

ARNOLD DOLMETSCH began the revival of clavichord making in 1894, starting with copies of original instruments, before creating his own 'improved' designs. No new music was written for the instrument until Herbert Howells's *Lambert's Clavichord*, published in 1928. Since then a steady flow of works has appeared but, unlike the HARPSICHORD, its contemporary repertoire remains meagre.

FURTHER READING

B. Brauchli, *The Clavichord* (Cambridge University Press, 1998).

TERENCE CHARLSTON

Clavicytherium *see* HARPSICHORD

Clementi, Muzio (bap. Rome, 24 January 1752; d. Evesham, Worcs., 10 March 1832) Naturalised English composer, keyboard player and teacher, music publisher and piano manufacturer of Italian birth.

Following a brief career as an organist in Italy, Clementi moved to Dorset in c1766. From c1775 he earned a living as a harpsichordist/pianist, composer and teacher in London. From 1798 he was a partner in one of Europe's largest music publishing and instrument-making businesses.

Clementi's concerts during the 1770s were performed on the HARPSICHORD, but his Op. 2 Sonatas (1779) were 'for Piano Forte or Harpsichord' and changing performing styles appropriate to the piano are seen in the revised editions he published up to 1819. In the 1779 edition slurs are usually over two or three notes and never over a barline, trends which disappear in later editions in favour of long slurs and the more legato approach articulated in Clementi's influential treatise: 'N.B. When the composer leaves the LEGATO and STACCATO to the performer's taste; the best rule is, to adhere chiefly to the LEGATO' (*Introduction to the Art of Playing on the Piano Forte*, 1801, 9). This transition is also described in the accounts of Clementi's pianistic 1781 duel with MOZART. Clementi described to Ludwig Berger how in those days he had 'taken particular delight in brilliant feats of technical proficiency', only later adopting 'a more melodic and noble style of performance' (*Caecilia*, 10 (1829), 239). Mozart's letters corroborate Clementi's version. The 1779 version of Op. 2 contains a few *piano* and *forte* indications, but by 1819 there is a full dynamic range from pp to ff with many *crescendo* and *diminuendo* indications. There is also PEDALLING, a feature that Clementi adopted only cautiously from 1798, and which was not mentioned in his *Introduction* until the fifth edition (1810/

11). Like other contemporary 'updated' scores, the later editions of Op. 2 extend the compass beyond the five octaves of earlier pianos, and they are also more highly ornamented. Second repeats in sonata movements disappear in later editions, a further feature already cautiously described in the *Introduction* (8): 'the second part of a piece, if VERY LONG, is seldom repeated, notwithstanding the DOTS'. Also evident in the *Introduction* is a modern approach to ORNAMENTATION, including instruction for short trills to begin on the main note, long appoggiaturas, and the clarification that turns usually encompass a minor third.

Clementi's EDITIONS of earlier music demonstrate a changing approach to the repertoire. In his 1791 edition of Scarlatti's sonatas a liberal approach is evident, especially to DYNAMICS, which are freely added to the score. In the four volumes of his *Clementi's Selection of Practical Harmony* (4 vols. (London: Clementi, Banger, Hyde Collard and Davis, 1801–c15)), which contain works by over twenty Baroque composers, and in his *Introduction*, which includes 31 works by Baroque composers, a more restrained approach is seen, Clementi keeping mainly to the original notation. There are few performance indications and no added notes, unlike the editions by Czerny, for example, with their copious dynamic markings and octave TRANSPOSITIONS and doublings (although Clementi transposes some works of RAMEAU and FRANÇOIS COUPERIN). But there is no evidence that Clementi's pursuit of authenticity went as far as that of his friend and neighbour, IGNAZ MOSCHELES, who played some of this repertoire on the HARPSICHORD.

FURTHER READING

M. Clementi, *Introduction to the Art of Playing on the Piano Forte* (London: Clementi, Banger, Hyde, Collard and Davis, 1801/R).
B. Harrison, 'The revision of Clementi's Op. 2 and the transformation of piano performance style', in R. Illiano, L. Sala and M. Sala (eds.), *Muzio Clementi: Studies and Prospects* (Bologna: Ut Orpheus Edizioni, 2002), 303–21.
D. Rowland, 'From harpsichordist to "Father of the Pianoforte": changes in performance styles in the lifetime of Muzio Clementi', in B. E. H. Schmul (ed.), *Zur Aufführungspraxis von Musik der Klassik* (Augsburg: Wißner-Verlag, 2011), 273–86.

DAVID ROWLAND

Codex The term 'codex' can describe any collection of manuscript leaves that survives as a bound book with protective outer covers. As such it is routinely applied to a huge variety of historical music sources, dating from the ninth century, when chant books containing neumatic NOTATION first appear, until the sixteenth, when print became the dominant medium. In many of these sources the binding is contemporary with the copying of the music contained in the codex and in such cases the structure of a codex can be suggestive about the way that it might have been used by performers. Details such as the size, paper quality, legibility, repertory, organisation and reliability of attributions vary widely from one codex to another; each is conditioned by the unique set circumstances of the institution for which it was copied and the individuals responsible for its production.

Establishing the relationship between any of these codices and the act of performance is problematic, since evidence for such things in this early period remains scant. Certainly the notion of sight-reading, which is so fundamental to modern performance, would have been alien to an era when repertories were smaller and the skill of PERFORMING FROM MEMORY was so much more extensively cultivated. However there is little doubt that codices would have been used in the performance of liturgical plainsong, if only to guide the singers through the complex and ever changing sequences of ritual chants. Many sources, especially from the later Medieval period, are large, well-ordered and conspicuously legible; and some pictorial representations of liturgical performance do include a book on a stand.

The situation with codices of liturgical polyphony is somewhat different and most commentators now agree that surprisingly few can be stated with any certainty to have been used in the course of a performance. The most likely candidates date from the end of the fifteenth and beginning of the sixteenth centuries, such as the GAFFURIUS Codices that were prepared for the choir of Milan Cathedral. These are much bigger than most polyphonic sources; the folios in the first two each measure 64 × 45 cm and the notation is proportionally enlarged such that it can be read from a distance. The resulting books are physically awkward and must have been expensive but they make sense in the context of a large choir, such as Milan had, reading from a single copy. It is of note that the earliest survivals of another type of source clearly used by performers, the set of part-books, are from the same period.

In other cases, the relationship between codex and performer is more ambiguous. Books, especially beautifully illustrated ones, were expensive items and were collected in their own right. A number of those containing music have been identified as wedding gifts for aristocratic patrons or presentation copies for institutions and though they may well faithfully preserve a favoured repertory are unlikely to have been used by the musicians themselves. This is particularly true of the more elaborately illuminated productions, which show few, if any, signs of daily use. One such is the Mellon Chansonnier, whose first song bears a cryptic dedication to Beatrice of Aragon; this subtle positioning was for her benefit and would have been wasted on singers. At the other end of the scale, there are small untidy books that would be hard to read by more than one person at a time; these are clearly unsuited to ensemble performance *in situ*, but may well have been used by actual musicians, for reference and even in REHEARSAL.

Codices containing solo instrumental TABLATURE might be assumed to have been used for performance but this has been increasingly called into question. The keyboard music in the Robertsbridge Codex (c1360), for example, contains a unique combination of tablature and staff notation and it has been suggested that in performance this complex music would have been memorised. Similarly the tablature of the Faenza Codex (c1420) is now considered to have been for private study and it is assumed that any performance of its music would have been from memory, the book itself serving as a repository of material for reference. The situation with lute tablature is rather different; it seems eminently suited to performance but this is a later invention and exclusive sources of it are rarely referred to as codices.

Nevertheless, even with the caveat that a codex may well not have been physically in front of the musicians as they performed its music, the way that it presents its repertory can still be suggestive about its relationship to performance. There are a number of late fifteenth-century Italian MANUSCRIPTS that preserve French chansons with either no text, or occasionally fragments of texts that are so corrupt as to be unusable. The practice is too consistent to be accidental and suggests that these sources, though ostensibly full of songs, served a vigorous instrumental tradition. The way that pieces seem occasionally to be grouped together on grounds of range or genre can also suggest a practical use, as, for example, in the Segovia Codex.

There are a few performance contexts where contemporary accounts imply that a codex might have been used directly in performance. There is evidence that stringed instruments were kept and played in some Renaissance Italian libraries and such a situation might explain some of the features of certain codices. For example, the chansonnier Florence 229, of about 1490, was owned by a Florentine nobleman, which accounts for its lavish decoration, but at the same time certain features of its repertory suggest practical use by lutenists, as does a quotation about playing music among friends that is inscribed at the beginning. In this intimate context, players and audience alike could share in the beauty of the codex simultaneously with the sounds that it recorded, allowing it to be shown off as a multimedia artefact.

FURTHER READING

J. Banks, *The Instrumental Consort Repertory of the Late Fifteenth Century* (Aldershot: Ashgate Press, 2006).

JON BANKS

Collegium Aureum German period-instrument ensemble.

Collegium Aureum was founded in Cologne in 1962 by the recording company Deutsche Harmonia Mundi and within a year made its first commercial recordings of works by Carl Stamitz and HAYDN. The violinist Franzjosef Maier (1925–2014) was named as the orchestra's concertmaster in 1964, and over the next two-and-a-half decades led its performances on a *primus inter pares* basis. Although the Collegium undertook several concert tours, it was primarily as a studio orchestra covering a wide range of repertoire that it made its name; while it recorded much Baroque music (including some of the earliest sets of BACH's Brandenburg Concertos and HANDEL's Op. 6 Concerti grossi), it was perhaps the first period ensemble to devote significant time to Classical-period works by Haydn, MOZART and other, lesser-known figures such as Durante and J. C. Bach. The recordings of BEETHOVEN's Fourth Piano Concerto and Triple Concerto (both 1974) and Third and Seventh Symphonies (1981) are thought to be the first on period instruments. The Collegium Aureum also functioned as a chamber ensemble, recording Mozart's wind serenades, Beethoven's Septet and Schubert's Octet and 'Trout' Quintet among other repertoire.

Although it was always a period ensemble which paid attention to historical techniques, the Collegium Aureum's sound was noticeably different, indeed more 'modern-sounding', from those of the newer ensembles that began to appear from the mid-1970s onwards, a factor that may explain why it gradually ceased to operate during the 1990s. Yet its list of members and collaborators includes important and influential period-performance names such as GUSTAV LEONHARDT, PAUL BADURA-SKODA, ANNER BYLSMA, Hans-Martin Linde and the KUIJKEN brothers, while its willingness to break new ground in later repertoire was not only pioneering, but also did much to acquaint the larger public with the concept of period performance.

LINDSAY KEMP

Concentus Musicus Wien Pioneering period-instrument ensemble founded in 1953 by NIKOLAUS HARNONCOURT, who was its only director until his retirement in 2015.

One of the first ensembles of its kind, Concentus Musicus undertook four years of preparation before giving its first concert, and made its first recording, of Purcell viol fantasies, in 1962. It was as a Baroque orchestra, however, that it built a reputation through the 1960s, with revelatory recordings of J. S. BACH's major orchestral and choral works, MONTEVERDI operas and works by Austrian composers such as Biber, Schmelzer and Fux, all characterised by radical interpretative rethinking based on extensive historical research. Harnoncourt directed many of the earlier performances from the CELLO, but later turned more to CONDUCTING. His wife, Alice, was for many years the ensemble's leader and VIOLIN soloist, including in a vividly revisionist 1977 recording of Vivaldi's *Le quattro stagioni*. In 1971 Harnoncourt and the ensemble began a complete recorded cycle of Bach's church cantatas, sharing it with GUSTAV LEONHARDT and the Leonhardt Consort. This influential project, completed in 1990, was the first to use all-male voices as a historically informed principle. From the late 1990s onwards, Harnoncourt took the group increasingly into Classical repertoire, producing acclaimed recordings of HAYDN and MOZART symphonies and choral works. The Concentus Musicus's performances are generally characterised by high standards of preparation and execution, and a cleaner but more opaque sound than most modern period orchestras. In 1985 four of its players – Erich Höbarth, Andrea Bischof, Anita Mitterer and Christophe Coin – were foundermembers of the QUATUOR MOSAÏQUES, one of the world's most successful period string quartets.

LINDSAY KEMP

Concerts of Antient Music Founded in 1776, the Concerts of Antient Music, like the ACADEMY OF ANCIENT MUSIC, promoted the performance of earlier music, explicitly works more than twenty years old. Unlike the Academy, it was an aristocratic society which saw the appreciation of earlier music as elevating audiences and promoting traditional social values, features seen as wanting in modern music. Its Register of Performances (Royal College of Music MS 1159) lists the collection and records when individual works were performed up to the mid-1790s. This shows that the society collected and played music from across Europe – but HANDEL's work increasingly dominated its programmes. The directors were involved in promoting the 1784 Handel Commemoration in London. From 1785, George III and the court became prominent supporters. The society continued to promote concerts until 1848, but its repertoire did not develop, so it was increasingly seen as a relic of an earlier age.

FURTHER READING

J. Brewer, *The Pleasures of the Imagination. English Culture in the Eighteenth Century* (London: Harper Collins, 1997).
S. Wollenberg and S. McVeigh, *Concert Life in Eighteenth-Century Britain* (Aldershot: Ashgate, 2004).
B. Zon (ed.), *Music and Performance Culture in Nineteenth-Century Britain, Essays in Honour of Nicholas Temperley* (Farnham: Ashgate, 2012).

PETER LINNITT

Conducting and Direction Musical direction developed gradually to deal with larger groups and more complex music. By the first half of the nineteenth century, new forms of conducting emerged and often competed within a variety of genres, VENUES and national traditions: audible time beating, different forms of divided leadership and violin-bow direction all persisted into the second half of the century, as modern baton conducting gradually became the norm. Known as cheironomy (from the Greek *cheir* for 'hand'), conducting began with hand signals that could indicate PITCH or melodic shape as well as TEMPO. Medieval choir directors held a staff in the left hand as a symbol of office, but led the CHOIR with the right hand. In the eighteenth century, a rolled-up paper was used to beat time for large choral groups. This was replaced by the baton for the large choral festivals of the nineteenth century, but conducting with the hands has remained standard for *a cappella* choirs.

With the rise of polyphonic choral music, many sixteenth-century TREATISES gave instructions for how to mark the TACTUS with a visible pulse. Some authors complained about audible time beating and generally prescribed a simple up and down motion of the hand to control the music. KOCH (1802) stated that the strong beat is called a 'down-beat' because the hand moved down on this beat and up on the weaker beats. ROUSSEAU (*Dictionnaire de musique* (Paris: Chez la veuve Duchesne, 1768) claimed that the Italians also beat time up and down, but that the French also moved the hand to the left and right. Lexicographer Thomas Janowka (*Clavis ad thesaurum magnae artis musicae*, Prague, 1701) described tactus for an ordinary bar as a right-hand movement of down, left, right, up: the pattern that became the standard. Until the early nineteenth century, either silent or audible time-beating (*tactieren*) with batons, rolled-up papers or the hands remained largely a church choir activity, while directing (*dirigieren*) with an instrument (i.e. leading by example with a keyboard or the VIOLIN) was the standard procedure for opera or instrumental music. This was not only a reflection of the differing musical styles and conventions, but also of practical logistics; the more scattered the forces for a large choral work, the more likely there was to be a time-beater.

As the BASSO CONTINUO became the rhythmic engine of seventeenth-century music, it became easy for the keyboard player to lead. The keyboard player was often the *Kapellmeister*, who organised, rehearsed and usually composed the music, and the keyboard was always part of the ensemble. C. P. E. BACH was an advocate for keyboard leadership, as the left hand could fortify the bass line while the right hand could add notes or be raised to signal an entrance. If things began to fall apart, both hands could quickly pound out a rhythm, returning the conductor from a signal giver to an audible time-keeper.

Playing the melody and standing in front, the violinist was also in a good position to lead by example. As musical style changed during the eighteenth century and the keyboard bass was gradually eliminated, the leader (in England), *Konzertmeister* (in Germany), *premier violon* (in France) or *capo d'orchestra* (in Italy) could direct the orchestra by beating time with the neck of the violin, making other movements or simply playing louder (again leading by sound rather than by sight). QUANTZ and LEOPOLD MOZART lobbied in favour of violin leadership, arguing that melodic nuances were more important than the rhythmic and harmonic control possible at the keyboard.

As the keyboard disappeared from orchestral music at the close of the eighteenth century, it appeared that the violinist/leaders such as FRANÇOIS-ANTOINE HABENECK would predominate, as indeed they did in France. In England, Italy and Germany, however, opera and concert music in the eighteenth and early nineteenth centuries were most often led by some form of divided or alternating leadership, although these arrangements varied greatly. Composers such as J. C. BACH, HAYDN and MOZART could lead from either position depending on the situation. In German and Italian opera houses, the violinist was responsible for the orchestra and led the instrumental music, while the keyboard player focused on the singers. Leipzig's Gewandhaus Orchestra (est. 1781) was the first orchestra devoted exclusively to symphonic music rather than opera, and retained this model of alternating leadership. The Gewandhaus had four keyboard conductors until MENDELSSOHN became its first baton conductor in 1835. These early leaders mostly sat at the keyboard and only 'conducted' the numbers with singers. BEETHOVEN's Ninth Symphony created new challenges; the first three movements were led by the concertmaster, but since the final movement involved the chorus, it was 'conducted' from the keyboard. Eventually, neither a violin nor a keyboard conductor proved to be adequate.

This German practice of alternating leadership between the keyboard and the first violin became an established system of divided leadership in England. When Haydn came to London in 1791 and 1792, he sat at the keyboard while Johann Peter Salomon, the impresario who had arranged the concerts, led from the violin. From the middle of the eighteenth until the middle of the nineteenth century, English concert notices were distinctive in listing two directors for most performances, the violinist leader to direct the ensemble and the keyboard player to correct mistakes. Divided leadership forced the Philharmonic to limit its repertoire to older and easier works and the press began to complain.

The baton or staff, long a symbol of power, was also used for directing others musically. One of the earliest reports of a huge ensemble (800 performers in 709 BC) also mentions a staff, waving 'up and down in equal movements so that all might keep together' (Galkin, 245). In 1594, the nuns at St Vito sat at a long table to be led silently in their music making by a wand-bearing Maestra. A large visible staff (grasped in the middle) was used from the seventeenth century for leading marching bands. LULLY, the *maître de musique* for Louis XIV, also used *une canne*, a very large stick which he banged on the floor as required. Audible time-keeping continued in French opera until the nineteenth century. Early baton use was also recorded by Haydn at the first performance of *The Creation* in 1798. Further instances include JOHANN REICHARDT, who removed the piano from the court opera in Berlin in 1776 and directed from a separate desk, and Ignaz Franz Mosel in Vienna (from 1812); HALLÉ reported that in 1810 TÜRK was using a baton with motions so exuberant that he occasionally hit the chandelier over his head and showered himself with glass. SPOHR claimed to have introduced the baton to the Philharmonic Society on 10 April 1820, but in 1832 the leader still objected to Mendelssohn's desire to use a baton. Both a leader and a conductor continued to appear until 1846, when Sir Michael Costa (1806–84) was appointed the first permanent conductor, on the understanding that he would have full responsibility for the performance.

Carl Maria von Weber conducted by beating a roll of paper silently, but not continuously, and experimented with re-organised seating, administration and REHEARSALS. Weber was also the first to articulate for the conductor a role beyond keeping the band together; he outlined a relationship between TEMPO and inner feeling that would become the core of WAGNER's theories a generation later. Weber saw the conductor initially as a referee between the singers who bring 'a certain undulation to the metre' and the instrumentalists who divide time 'into sharp grooves like the swing of a pendulum'. Weber wanted to encourage individuality, which was required for the 'emotional expression' of music, while 'preventing the singer from letting himself go too much' (Bamberger, 20). Gaspare Spontini brought discipline and sectional rehearsals to the Berlin Opera from 1820 to 1842. He held a thick ebony staff in the middle and emphasised the use of the eyes, which required that he face the orchestra, in defiance of eighteenth- and early nineteenth-century concert etiquette.

Like the opera conductors Weber and Spontini, Mendelssohn was also interested in raising standards of ensemble. He also used a baton, largely faced the band while conducting (standing sideways in his early days), and took rehearsal seriously, even stopping the orchestra in rehearsal to correct mistakes. BERLIOZ, too, thought the conductor needed to 'criticise the errors and defects ... economy of time should be reckoned among the most imperative requisites of the orchestral conductor' (246). After ten years (1848–58) as a resident conductor, Liszt continued to conduct and teach into the 1880s and many of the conductors in the next generation (including VON BÜLOW, Damrosch, Mottl, Arthur Nikisch and Weingartner) were deeply influenced by his introduction of a vocabulary of gesture. Like Schopenhauer, Hegel and later Wagner, Liszt thought that music expressed ideal 'passions and feelings', but translating this from the piano to an orchestra proved difficult, as he avoided beating time and instead crouched low for soft passages and jumped and flailed his arms when he wanted more expression. Liszt's contemporaries found these gestures original and strange, but they became the physical vocabulary of modern conducting.

While the word *interprétation* is largely absent from Berlioz's treatise and other mid-century writing, it is at the heart of Wagner's *Über das Dirigieren*. Berlioz wrote about rehearsals and beating time, but for Wagner these were only the means to an end. For him, interpretation was the art of discovering the 'poetic object' and tempo and its subtle modifications were the way a conductor brings the inner character of the music to life. Wagner's theory and practice remained at the heart of central European conducting until the middle of the twentieth century, and can be heard in the slow and flexible tempos of Nikisch, Furtwängler and Knappertsbusch. Wagner's prioritisation of expression of the inner spirit of music led some (notably MAHLER) to take further liberties with the surface details, most commonly instrumentation. Conductors quite routinely, for example, substituted (by now valved) HORNS for Beethoven's notated BASSOONS in the recapitulation of the first movement of his Fifth Symphony.

Arturo Toscanini eventually led a counter movement that was more loyal to the NOTATION in the score. For him, *come scrito* meant a rejection of tempo and instrumentation modifications (although he compromised with one bassoon and one horn in the recapitulation of Beethoven's Fifth). This new loyalty to the score would eventually be merged with the twentieth-century early music revival to create a movement for HISTORICALLY INFORMED PERFORMANCE. While ARNOLD DOLMETSCH was initially interested in reproducing early instruments (VIOLS, RECORDERS, LUTES and early keyboard instruments), the historical performance movement eventually also rejected Wagner's romantic ideology of interpretation and his tempo variations, and history would seem to confirm that, as conducting emerged, tempos were indeed more steady (in orchestral music) as a technical limitation. This new ideology and style had a profound effect on the performance of both early and contemporary music in the twentieth century. Directors of early music, however, were reluctant to revert to earlier leadership practices such as divided leadership, audible time beating or no leadership at all.

Conductors have remained at the heart of debates about the goals of performance, not least the vexed issue of a composer's expectations. EARLY RECORDINGS have complicated this discourse; Willem Mengelberg's close working relationship with Mahler, for example, might suggest that the deliberate use of PORTAMENTO, varying degrees of VIBRATO, TEMPO fluctuation and even lack of alignment between melody and accompaniment in his recordings constitute further unnotated performance instructions for Mahler's music. Mengelberg's recordings of other composers' music (and Nikisch's Beethoven recordings), however, contain many of the same traits; they contain work-specific traditions but are deeply enmeshed with the performance conventions of the day. Some conductors (e.g. ROGER NORRINGTON) have attempted to recreate historical performance attributes with modern instruments. In the twentieth century, therefore, conducting largely changed from an aesthetic practice, where musical TASTE and intuition were used to bring stable poetic objects to musical life (largely as articulated by Wagner) to a more confined space where scholarship and historical evidence were expected to inform musical judgement. Where the nineteenth century was focused on internal qualities, the twentieth century became more concerned with external ones, as jet travel and recordings further eliminated listeners' tolerance for technical inaccuracies, while homogenising national styles and raising standards of ensemble uniformity.

FURTHER READING

C. Bamberger (ed.), *The Conductor's Art* (New York: McGraw-Hill, 1965).
H. Berlioz, *Grand traité d'instrumentation et d'orchestration modernes: nouvelle édition augmentée de l'art du chef d'orchestre* (Paris: Schonenberger, 1855).

E. W. Galkin, *A History of Orchestral Conducting: In Theory and Practice* (New York: Pendragon Press, 1988).

R. Wagner, *Über das Dirigieren* (Leipzig: Breitkopf & Härtel, 1869).

JOSÉ ANTONIO BOWEN

Conforti, Giovanni Luca (b. Mileto, Calabria, c1560; d. Rome, 11 May 1608) Italian soprano and composer.

Conforti was a virtuoso singer in Rome in the latter decades of the sixteenth century, celebrated for his highly ornamented singing as a 'falsettist, great singer of *gorge* and *passaggi*, who could sing as high as the stars' (Pietro delle Valle, *Discorso sulla musica dell'eta nostra* (Rome, 1640/1763), 255), although in the Papal chapel he sang contralto in his chest voice (*voce piena*), 'perhaps to avoid joining his falsetto to the natural voices of the castrati' (Sherr, 43). His *Breve et facile maniera d'essercitarsi* (Rome: s.n., 1593) is one of the earliest compendia of ORNAMENTATION, written 'in compact form, such that all those who sing and play can acquire good and pleasing *dispositione* in less than two months' (33–4). It includes the earliest representations of the iconic *trillo* (single pitch) and *groppo* (TREMOLO on adjacent pitches), as well as exercises in dividing different intervals into *passaggi* of increasing elaboration. The application of such improvisatory techniques in professional liturgical singing is demonstrated in *Salmi passaggiati* (1601–3), containing examples of how a solo singer can embellish *falsobordoni* psalm verses.

FURTHER READING

M. C. Bradshaw (ed.), *Giovanni Luca Conforti 'Salmi passaggiati' (1601–1603)* (Neuhausen-Stuttgart: American Institute of Musicology, 1985).

R. Sherr, 'Guglielmo Gonzaga and the castrati', *Renaissance Quarterly*, 33 (1980), 33–56.

RICHARD WISTREICH

Consort/consort music A small instrumental group for playing music written before about 1700.

The term 'consort' encompasses vocal ensembles and ensembles mixing voices and instruments and is also used for the music itself. Its meaning has changed since its early usage; for example, there is little evidence that a 'broken' consort signified a consort of mixed instruments. It probably indicated a consort that 'breaks' long notes into small ones and thus played divisions.

'Consort' was the English translation of the early sixteenth-century Italian word 'concerto', meaning an ensemble of voices or instruments. Its earliest use in Britain around 1575 seems to have indicated a mixed ensemble of instruments from different families. The anonymous chronicler of *The Honourable Entertainment... at Elvetham* (London, 1591) describes how the Queen was entertained by 'a song of six partes, with the musicke of an exquisite consorte, wherein was the Lute, Bandora, Base-violl, Citterne, Treble-violl, and Flute' (17). MORLEY's *Consort Lessons* (1599, 2/1611) and Rosseter's *Lessons for Consort* (1609) were also written for this combination. But by the early seventeenth century this usage was giving way to a more general one as stated in Bullokar's *English Expositor* (London, 1616/R): 'a company of Musitions together'. The French 'concert' had the same meaning and Cotgrave's *Dictionarie of the*

French and English Tongues (London, 1611/R) equates 'concert de musique' with 'a consort of musicke'.

The function of a consort commonly determined its instrumentation. Thus in the English Jesuit College at St Omer during the seventeenth century, young musicians were taught the VIOL, mixed consort music was performed for the reception of guests of distinction, whilst OBOES and RECORDERS were reserved for persons of high standing. In the theatre, the choice of instruments was governed by symbolic connotation; strings (viols or VIOLINS) signified harmony, oboes were linked to magic, and recorders and FLUTES often symbolised death. The social position of the players was also significant; professional musicians tended to play violins and wind instruments whereas amateurs played the viol. Whilst SIMPSON in his *Compendium* (London, 1667) discusses 'Fancies of 6, 5, 4 or 3' under 'Of Music design'd for Instruments', he adds that they are 'intended commonly for Viols' (115).

MACE describes the ideal viol consort: 'Your *Best Provision* ... will be, a *Good Chest of Viols; Six*, in *Number*; viz. 2 *Basses*, 2 *Tenors*, and 2 *Trebles*' (245). He emphasises the importance of the relative size of the instruments within the consort to give a good balance to the individual parts and advocates that the basses 'be *Large*'. Then the trebles should have half their string length 'because they stand 8 *Notes Higher*', the tenors need a string length from the fifth fret to the bridge of the bass 'because they stand a *4th. Higher*' (246). Mace explains the different distances to bow from the bridge: on 'a *Large Consort-Viol*' about '2 *Inches* and a *Half*' and about 'an *Inch* and a *Half*' for the treble, and 'so upon all *Others*, according to *This Suitable Proportion*' (248). For '*Consort Use*', he continues, 'Play nearer the *Bridge*, than you would Play *Alone*; which although It be not so *Sweet*, yet it is more *Lusty*, and that little *Ruffness* is *Lost* in the *Crowd*' (249).

Mace outlines the forms of music commonly played by a viol consort and how their performance was underpinned by RHETORIC: 'We had for our *Grave Musick, Fancies* of 3, 4, 5, and 6 *Parts* to the *Organ*; Interpos'd (now and then) with some *Pavins, Allmaines, Solemn, and Sweet Delightful Ayres*; all of which were (as it were) so many *Pathetical Stories, Rhetorical, and Sublime Discourses*' (234).

Viol consorts were also found in Italy, Spain, France, Germany and the Low Countries. Jacques Maudit (1557–1627) brought the viol consort into fashion with Parisian society by introducing it to the musical gatherings of the *Académie de Poésie et de Musique*. MERSENNE writes in praise of the beautiful melodies and variety of invention found in Le Jeune's *fantaisies*, explaining: 'it is why' Le Jeune's music 'is widely favoured in viol consorts' (1636, II, vii, 61). In Germany, Schütz employed a consort of four bass viols to accompany the Evangelist in his *Historia der Auferstehung Jesu Christi*, SWV 50 (Dresden, 1623); he requests that 'the gambas must follow the Evangelist's words so that he can recite his part with as much flexibility as if he were speaking', adding that one of the gambas can break up the chords 'in arpeggios as is customary and of good effect' (Preface). In 1680, Buxtehude uses a consort of five bass viols in *Ad cor: Vulnerasti cor meum*, BuxWV 75, to address Christ's heart, and uses deeply expressive TREMOLO quavers in the final movement.

FURTHER READING

W. A. Edwards, 'The performance of ensemble music in Elizabethan England', *PRMA*, 97 (1970–1), 113–23.
T. Mace, *Musick's Monument or, a Remembrancer of the Best Practical Musick* (London, 1676), 231–50.

LUCY ROBINSON

Contrabasso *see* DOUBLE BASS

Contrabassoon *see* BASSOON

Copies of Instruments The practice of making modern copies of early musical instruments began at least as far back as the 1870s and served a variety of purposes; makers such as ARNOLD DOLMETSCH made more or less accurate reproductions of surviving historical instruments to be used in the performance of early music, whilst museum curators and collectors such as VICTOR-CHARLES MAHILLON and FRANCIS GALPIN commissioned copies that, although often unplayable, filled gaps in their collections for educational purposes. However, since the 1970s a new type of replica began to be developed, mainly by museums and public institutions, with the aim of empirically exploring the making techniques of the past, rarely documented by other sources, through the accurate study and reproduction of historical instruments using exclusively tools and techniques known at the time of the original.

The idea of what a copy should achieve has also greatly changed over time: when Dolmetsch produced a copy of a Pui Bressan recorder in the 1920s, providing the model for thousands of further copies worldwide, he proceeded from memory, trial and error, since the original had been lost. The playability of replicas also now represents a key factor in the making of copies, even as historical accuracy has developed alongside further understanding of performance practice. Sometimes makers deviate from originals in order to fill gaps in knowledge or reflect the expectations of modern listeners or larger concert halls, as happened with the introduction of vent-holes in Baroque brass instruments in mid-twentieth-century copies to facilitate the intonation of some of the upper HARMONICS. Further exploration of historical sound and ARTICULATION soon demonstrated the importance of copying appropriate accessories, such as BOWS and mouthpieces. Variations in the mechanical and acoustical behaviour of materials – particularly wood – also require the makers to adapt and find a balance between faithfully reproducing the original and reaching an outcome acceptable to modern audiences.

A long-lasting debate exists about the validity of copies as alternatives to restored originals; while the advantages of copies are obvious in terms of conservation, availability and sometimes cost, objections are usually raised about whether an accurate reproduction of the original sound can be obtained, particularly because this sound changes throughout the life of both the original and the copy, and not necessarily in the same way. The fact that a high degree of consistency is often found at least among groups of instruments by the same maker has also led to the development of the idea of copies 'after a maker or School' instead of 'after a specific instrument', which allows the maker greater flexibility in the combination of historical accuracy and musical efficiency.

The hard sciences (chemistry, physics and acoustics) are now providing an increasing number of investigatory techniques that allow very accurate documentation in relation to the reproduction of original materials, dimensions and craftsmanship, allowing copying to be undertaken with greater accuracy. At the same time, new materials and the possibilities offered by 3D printing and reverse engineering (the regression of the dimensional effects of aging such as warping and shrinking) are opening new pathways for very accurate and affordable copies, particularly of wind instruments.

FURTHER READING

R. Barclay, *The Preservation and Use of Historic Musical Instruments* (London: Earthscan, 2004).
M. Campbell, *Dolmetsch: The Man and his Work* (London: Hamilton, 1975).
Copies of Historic Musical Instruments, CIMCIM Publications, 3 (1994).

GABRIELE ROSSI ROGNONI

Cor Anglais *see* OBOE

Corelli, Arcangelo (b. Fusignano, 17 February 1653; d. Rome, 8 January 1713) Italian violinist and composer.

Corelli's *oeuvre*, comprising largely instrumental works (solo sonatas, trio sonatas and concerti grossi), is modest; yet through his compositions, performances and teaching, he exerted a profound influence on the development of VIOLIN playing.

Confusion surrounds the detail of Corelli's early violin instruction, but his musical stature developed quickly after he settled in Rome (c1675); he engaged and led/directed most of Rome's large ensembles between c1680 and 1712, having clearly absorbed LULLY's influence as both composer and concertmaster. That he adapted French orchestral discipline to Italian music and insisted on unanimity of bow strokes and direction is confirmed not only by GEMINIANI (Burney, *A General History of Music from the Earliest Ages to the Present Period* (London, 1776–89, 1957), II, 443) but also by the first movement of his concerto, Op. 6 No. 3, which, though not so designated, is a French overture viewed through his Italian eyes.

Payrolls and other archival documents preserved in the Vatican library relating to his (from 1690) patron Cardinal Pietro Ottoboni's household indicate that Corelli's orchestra often exceeded forty players; for oratorios it sometimes increased to seventy plus (H. J. Marx, *Analecta musicologica* 5 (1968), 104–77 and *Studi musicali*, 12 (1983), 121–87). Although orchestral sizes between 1690 and the early 1720s varied from event to event, instrumental balance and proportions remained consistent. The number of violins tended to equal approximately the sum of the other stringed instruments, regardless of the overall total of players; the introduction of wind instruments sometimes resulted in a corresponding increase in the number of violins (S. Hansell, 'Orchestral practice at the court of Cardinal Pietro Ottoboni', *JAMS* 19 (1966), 398–403). SCIPIONE MAFFEI remarked not only about the skill of Corelli's orchestra at playing *forte* and *piano* in alternation, but also on its 'artful way of letting the sound grow softer little by little and then all of a sudden resuming clamorously' with the full ensemble (*Giornale dei letterati* (Venice, 1711), v.144, in R. Harding, *Origins of Musical Time and Expression* (London: Oxford University Press, 1938), 94).

Corelli's twelve *Sonate a Violino e Violone o Cimbalo*, Op. 5 have courted controversy as to their intended execution due to the ambiguity of their title. Historical performers have generally opted for accompaniment by either harpsichord or cello, the latter filling out the harmonic background in the manner discussed by David Watkin ('Corelli's Op. 5 Sonatas: "Violino e violone o cembalo"?', *EMc*, 24 (1996), 645–63). A similar ambiguity regarding the ensemble's constitution applies to Corelli's trio sonatas. While Corelli evidently used four partbooks for his church sonatas (Opp. 1 and 3) – two for the violins, one for *violone o arcileuto* (cello or archlute) and one for *basso per l'organo* (organ continuo) – he employed only three for the chamber sonatas Opp. 2 and 4, two for the violins and one for the *violone o cembalo* (cello or harpsichord). The implied continuo options for these *opera* open up a variety of potential interpretations (*see* S. Mangsen, 'The trio sonata in pre-Corellian prints: When does 3 = 4?', *PPR*, 3 (1990), 138–64).

Corelli's Op. 5 sonatas are also renowned for the numerous extant eighteenth-century sources which incorporate lavish embellishment of his original text, some allegedly (and probably genuinely) by the composer himself (for the slow movements of Nos. 1–6) and others by violinists such as GEMINIANI, Dubourg and TARTINI (see Boyden (1972), Marx (1975) and various articles in *EMc*, 24 (1996) 95–115, 119–30, 133–42, 623–33).

FURTHER READING

P. Allsop, *Arcangelo Corelli: 'New Orpheus of Our Times'* (Oxford and New York: Oxford University Press, 1999).
D. D. Boyden, 'Corelli's solo violin sonatas "grac'd" by Dubourg', in N. Schiørring, H. Glahn and C. E. Hatting (eds.), *Festskrift Jens Peter Larsen* (Copenhagen: Hansen, 1972), 113–26
'The Corelli "Solo" Sonatas and their ornamental additions by Corelli, Geminiani, Dubourg, Tartini, and the "Walsh Anonymous"', *Musica antiqua III* (1972), 591–606.
H. J. Marx, 'Some unknown embellishments of Corelli's violin sonatas', *MQ*, 61 (1975), 65–76.

ROBIN STOWELL

Cornett (German: *Zink*) Made primarily of wood, bound in leather or parchment and sounded by the player's lips vibrating in a mouthpiece; as such, the cornett belongs to the same family as brass instruments.

It flourished throughout Europe from the late fifteenth to the end of the seventeenth century as a solo and ensemble instrument in both sacred and secular contexts. The two main treble forms of the instrument share the same pitch and range but differ in shape and timbre; the most common had a curved shape while the straight form was called 'mute cornett' because of its soft and subtle timbre. The former was played with a detachable mouthpiece while the mouthpiece of the latter is integrated into the body of the instrument. Both were pitched from g to a'' but some seventeenth-century parts have the upper register extended by up to a fifth. The tenor size was pitched a fifth below the treble instrument, and the cornettino was a fifth or fourth higher and used mainly in Austria in the later seventeenth century. Both these instruments were used less frequently than the treble instrument.

In the preface to his division manual *Il vero modo di diminuir* (Venice: Angelo Gardano, 1584), the Venetian cornettist GIROLAMO DALLA CASA provides advice on playing technique and especially the ARTICULATION of syllables. The first source that explains FINGERINGS specifically for the cornett is Aurelio Virgiliano's unpublished *Il dolcimelo* (c1590), which also shows TRANSPOSITIONS of the decorative patterns that were so important in cornett playing. Instruction books for the RECORDER and other instruments can often be taken as relevant to the cornett as far as fingering is concerned; this is suggested, for example, by GANASSI's *Opera intitulata la Fontegara* of 1535, which, though written for the recorder, shows two cornetts on its title page.

The American cornett player BRUCE DICKEY has been the seminal influence in the rediscovery of the idiom of the instrument in modern times. He and other players have revealed the astonishing virtuosity exhibited by performers in the centuries when it was regarded as the most important of all wind instruments. Few timbres in Western music have flourished so intensely for such a relatively short period before descending so quickly into obscurity. Many florid lines in seventeenth-century Italian music are marked '*per violino overo cornetto*' (for violin or cornett), but by the end of the century new musical TASTES and fashions were favoured. Its use lasted longer in northern than southern Europe, but only by a few decades.

The instrument was prized because of the range of its expressive qualities and the ability of its players to improvise. It was often matched with TROMBONES, which could also be played with a wide range of articulations, and was prominent in civic ensembles such as *piffari*, *Stadpfeifer* and waits, as well as sacred institutions. Dickey and Edward H. Tarr have compiled a wide-ranging anthology of Renaissance and Baroque sources concerning articulations on wind instruments which is relevant to performance technique on cornetts, and Dickey and Michael Collver have assembled a near-comprehensive catalogue of works for which there are labelled cornett parts.

FURTHER READING

M. Collver and B. Dickey, *A Catalog of Music for the Cornett* (Bloomington, IN: Indiana University Press, 1996).

T. Herbert and J. Wallace (eds.), *The Cambridge Companion to Brass Instruments* (Cambridge University Press, 1997).

E. H. Tarr and B. Dickey, *Bläserartikulation in der Alten Musik / Articulation in Early Wind Music* (Winterthur: Amadeus, 2007).

TREVOR HERBERT

Corrette, Michel (b. Rouen, 10 April 1707; d. Paris, 21 January 1795) French organist, composer and pedagogue.

One of the first French composers to write concertos in the Italian manner (e.g. his twenty-five *Concertos Comiques*, Op. 8, 1733), Corrette was a dedicated teacher and published several TREATISES covering a wide range of instrumental/vocal techniques (VIOLIN, VIOLA, CELLO, DOUBLE BASS, FLUTE, RECORDER, BASSOON, HARPSICHORD, HARP, GUITAR, mandolin and voice).

Corrette's violin method, *L'école d'Orphée*, Op. 18 (1738), includes music in the French and Italian styles, recommends the Italian manner of holding the instrument under the chin and contrasts the Italian and French BOW holds and attitudes towards position-work and shifting, encouraging players to secure the instrument with the chin in order to liberate the left hand. It is also prescriptive about the introduction of rhythmic inequality relative to the note values and time signatures. Its sequel, *L'art de se perfectionner sur le violon* (1782), has more Italian bias and is technically more advanced, notably in its bowing requirements, emphasis on tone quality and EXPRESSION, use of positions up to the eleventh, CADENZAS and preludes and graduated exercises in double stopping. Textually sparse, its main substance comprises several compositions, mostly of Italian origins, by such composers as Alberti, Albinoni, CORELLI, Dall'Abaco, Locatelli, GEMINIANI, HANDEL, Vivaldi and Corrette himself, with recommended FINGERING.

Corrette's *Méthode théorique et pratique*, Op. 24 (1741) for cello signals the increasing popularity of that instrument over the VIOLA DA GAMBA in professional and amateur circles. It is particularly interesting for its espousal of the overhand bow grip, its cultivation of the 'reprise d'archet' in realising the rule of down-bow and its instructions on fingering. Corrette's cello fingerings correspond with violin or gamba fingering patterns, although he substitutes the fourth for the third finger in the cello's lower positions. He also divides the fingerboard into the customary four positions, addresses basic concepts in shifting and specifies where and how the thumb position should be included in fingering patterns.

Corrette's other treatises offer enlightening insights into the performing practices of his time, particularly regarding ORNAMENTATION and NOTES INÉGALES. His flute method (1735/1740) incorporates informative instruction on specific and extempore ornamentation and TRANSPOSITION; his *Le parfait maître à chanter* (1758) describes French ornamentation practices from a vocal perspective; his *Les dons d'Apollon* (1762) considers guitar playing from both music NOTATION and TABLATURE; his viola da gamba method (1781) embraces the five- and six-string instrument and includes lessons in one and two parts; and his multi-instrument treatise (*Méthode pour apprendre à jouer de la contre-basse à 3, à 4, et à 5 cordes, de la quinte ou alto et de la viole d'Orphée* (Paris: adresses ordinaires, 1773)) includes practical instruction for proficient violinists to play the viola and cellists to switch to the three-, four-, or five-string double bass, with guidance regarding bass-line simplification practices. Corrette also attempts a revival of the bass viol as the *viole d'Orphée* by tuning it in fifths, adopting overhand bowing, removing frets and using brass strings. Further, his *Le maître de clavecin pour l'accompagnement* (Paris: l'auteur, Bayard, Leclerc, 1753), a companion to his *Les amusemens du Parnasse* (Paris: l'auteur, 1749), includes information about harpsichord string gauges and lengths and their association with 'the diapason of the instrument'; and his *Premier livre de pièces de clavecin* (1734) includes fingerings and a table of ornaments typical of French publications of the time.

FURTHER READING

D. D. Boyden, *The History of Violin Playing from its Origins to 1761* (London: Oxford University Press, 1965).

Y. Jaffrès, 'Michel Corrette (1707–1795), sa vie, son oeuvre', PhD dissertation, University of Lyon II (1989).

P. Lescat, *Méthodes et traités musicaux en France de 1660 à 1800* (Paris: Institut de pédagogie musicale et chorégraphique-La Villette, 1991).

ROBIN STOWELL

Corri, Domenico (b. Rome, 4 October 1746; d. London, 22 May 1825). Italian singer, singing teacher, publisher and composer.

Corri had a varied career after leaving Italy, first as a singing teacher in Edinburgh for eighteen years, and later running Vauxhall Gardens in London and a music publishing business in Soho; he also composed successful operas. *A Select Collection of the Most Admired Songs, Duetts* (3 vols., c1779) was designed for transmitting the artistry of the greatest *bel canto* performers to non-professional singers, and includes fully worked-out ornamented aria repeats and realisations of the BASSO CONTINUO. In the Introduction, Corri explains that 'the principal refinements in song; such as cadences, divisions, and all those intervening ornaments, the proper use of which alone can give to song its highest degree of grace and elegance ... have never yet been written down' (Corri, I, 4), and he seeks to remedy this with annotations to a wide range of popular opera arias.

In 1810, he published *The Singer's Praeceptor* (2 vols. (London: Longman, Hurst, Rees and Orme, 1810)), a systematic method for amateurs, closely modelled on the pedagogy of TOSI (1723), published almost ninety years earlier, and that of his own teacher, Nicola Porpora (who also taught FARINELLI); Corri, in turn, passed it on to a younger generation of singing pedagogues, notably Isaac Nathan (1790–1864). Corri emphasises key traditional aspects of perfecting vocal technique, including *messa di voce*, 'soul of music', which should be used 'on every note of any duration' (i, 14, 15); *portamento di voce*, 'the perfection of vocal music; it consists of the swelling and dying of the voice, the sliding and blending one note into another with delicacy and expression' (i, 3). He prioritises the proper accentuation and rhetorical delivery of texts ('Words the origin of music'; i, 2), often referring to speech as an analogy for SINGING. For example, he advocates the audible breaking of the voice in a word such as 'sigh – (suspiration) – ing' (i, 65), and writes longer note values in his 'performing versions' of well-known recitatives to indicate accentuated words (Toft, 30–6). The book concludes with a collection of arias, recitatives and songs, annotated to indicate the additions that singers need to make to the basic text.

FURTHER READING

D. Corri, *Singers' Praeceptor* (London: Silvester, 1810), facsim. edn R. Maunder as *Domenico Corri's Treatise on Singing* (New York: Garland, 1995).
J. Potter and N. Sorrell, *A History of Singing* (Cambridge University Press, 2012), esp. ch. 4.
R. Toft, *Bel Canto: A Performer's Guide* (Oxford University Press, 2013).

RICHARD WISTREICH

Cossmann, Bernhard (b. Dessau, 17 May 1822; d. Frankfurt, 7 May 1910) German cellist and teacher.

Cossmann studied the CELLO first with Espenhahn and then DOTZAUER's pupil Karl Drechsler in Dessau. He continued his studies with Theodore Müller in Brunswick (1837–40) and Friedrich Kummer (another of Dotzauer's pupils) in Dresden. In 1848 he was appointed principal cellist of the Leipzig Gewandhaus Orchestra (succeeding Kummer) but moved at Liszt's invitation to Weimar (1850), where he remained for sixteen years. Appointments followed as professor of cello at the Moscow Conservatoire (1866–70) and, after a spell in Baden-Baden (1870–8), as the first professor of cello at Frankfurt's Hoch Konservatorium (1878).

According to CARL FUCHS, Cossmann's teaching owed much to the so-called 'Dresden School' and was based on the concertos of ROMBERG and Schumann. Praised for his sonorous tone and phrasing, Cossmann was considered conservative in his approach to expression. He composed several works for the cello and edited MENDELSSOHN's cello sonatas and the cello parts of Mendelssohn's piano trios, but he is remembered principally for his collections of studies and exercises. His *Fünf Concert Etuden*, Op. 10 (Leipzig, 1876) concentrate on left-hand technique and complex passagework, incorporating extensive passages of double stopping and arpeggiation, but require little in the way of complex BOWINGS such as up- and down-bow staccato, explored at length by contemporaries such as Alfredo Piatti (*Capricen*, Berlin, 1874). This reflects the more conservative attitudes of the 'Dresden' cellists towards right-hand technique; although ROMBERG, Dotzauer, Kummer, and GRÜTZMACHER included exercises for cultivating slurred staccato, such strokes were not as important in their bowing vocabulary as they were for Servais, Piatti, or Popper, for example. Cossmann's *Etudes ... pour développer l'agilité et la force des doigts et la pûreté de l'intonation* (Mainz, [1876]) also focus on the left hand and are still used nowadays. These are repetitive exercises for double trills, arpeggios, scales (including scales in thirds), and drills for the use of the fourth finger in thumb position, a technique that was becoming old fashioned by the later nineteenth century.

FURTHER READING

G. Kennaway, *Playing the Cello, 1780–1930* (Farnham: Ashgate, 2014).

GEORGE KENNAWAY

Couperin, François (*le grand*) (b. Paris, 10 November 1668; d. Paris, 11 September 1733) French composer, harpsichordist and organist.

Couperin's thoughts on how to perform his music are all contained in the Prefaces to his works and in his guide to performance: *L'Art de toucher le clavecin*. Very much a man of his time, his views are also useful in the wider context of French and Italian styles, which in some of his pieces he sought to unite.

Couperin is known especially through his 234 HARPSICHORD pieces, mostly published in four suites which he called *Ordres* (perhaps to indicate that they were more than mere collections of dance movements), which represent the quintessence of French Baroque music with their fanciful titles and links to social life, and in particular through their rich ORNAMENTATION. Whereas most composers of the time left it to performers to improvise their ornamentation, Couperin was adamant that those who played his harpsichord pieces must follow to the letter all that he had indicated on the score (Preface, *Pièces de clavecin*, Bk. 3, 1722), pointing to his harpsichord method of 1716 (rev. 1717). His list of ornaments and their execution in his first *Ordre*, omitted in the L'Oiseau Lyre collected edition of 1932, is restored in the revised edition by Kenneth Gilbert (*Oiseau Lyre*, ed M. Cauchie, rev. K. Gilbert, *Oeuvres complètes de François Couperin* (Monaco, 1980, ii–iii)).

Couperin's concern for correctness when playing his harpsichord music stands in striking contrast to what appears to be an almost cavalier approach to other aspects of Baroque performance practice – and a salutary lesson to modern performers who seek historical authenticity in the recreation of early music. In his choice of instruments, for example, Couperin is no purist. For his orchestral suite *L'Apothéose de Lully* he suggests possible performance on two harpsichords, and some of the harpsichord duets in his *Ordres* can be played as solos by leaving out the middle line. Many of the harpsichord solo pieces can be played by FLUTE, VIOLIN or other treble instruments (*L'Apothéose de Lully*, 'Avis'). His *Leçons de ténèbres* can be sung by all voice-types, especially as he says 'most accompanists nowadays know how to transpose' (*Leçons de ténèbres*) (For matters concerning ways to transpose, see MICHEL CORRETTE's *Méthode pour apprendre aisément à jouer de la flûte traversière* (Paris: Boivin [et[Le Clerc, 1735)).

In the vehement debates on the merits of French and Italian styles that arose during his career, Couperin professed his admiration of both schools and his deep love of the music of both LULLY and CORELLI, believing that, by uniting the seemingly opposed styles, music will be led to a state of perfection. It was through this embrace that the so-called 'Classical' style of French music moved into its 'Baroque' phase. In a much-quoted dictum Couperin pointed out that 'We [the French] notate our music differently from how we play it ... On the other hand the Italians write their music with the correct note–values' (F. Couperin, *L'art de toucher le clavecin* (Paris: Chés l'auteur, le Sieur Foucat, 1716), 39). In particular, this refers to the French practice of notating a smooth flow of melody that in performance is played or sung in a dotted rhythm (NOTES INÉGALES), the style moulded by the expressive intent. Thus, in the harpsichord piece *Allemande La Laborieuse* Couperin recommends that the semiquavers be 'ever so slightly dotted' ('les double croches tant-soit peu pointées'). Where stepwise phrases are to be played as written, Couperin writes 'notes égales'. Unlike as in Italian scores where words indicating TEMPO (allegro, andante, etc.) are widely employed, Couperin (1716) explains their absence in French music, 'We try to remedy this by marking the beginning of our pieces with words such as *tendrement* [tenderly], *vivement* [brightly] as close as we can to what we would like to be heard' (*L'art de toucher le clavecin*, 40–1).

The picturesque titles of his harpsichord pieces have intrigued performers and listeners for generations, and they spring from various sources: personalities, the social scene, literature, mythology and gossip. The meaning behind many of the titles is still often obscure, but Clark and Connon have been closest to demystifying them. Couperin expressed strong views on teaching harpsichord to children. In *L'art de toucher le clavecin* he maintained that they must only be shown NOTATION after they have committed a number of pieces to MEMORY, so that they can give full attention to hand-shape and note-correctness.

FURTHER READING

J. Clark and D. Connon, *The Mirror of Human Life – Reflections on François Couperin's Pièces de Clavecin*, 2nd edn (London: Keyword Press, 2011).
P. le Huray, 'Couperin's *Huitième Ordre*', in *Authenticity in Performance* (Cambridge University Press, 1990), 45–69.
W. Mellers, *François Couperin and the French Classical Tradition*, 2nd edn (London: Faber, 1987).
D. Tunley, *François Couperin and 'The Perfection of Music'* (Aldershot: Ashgate, 2004).

DAVID TUNLEY

Couperin, Louis (b. Chaumes, c1626; d. Paris, 29 August 1661) French composer, harpsichordist, organist and viol player.

Like so many of the Couperin dynasty, Louis Couperin was an accomplished and versatile musician highly regarded in his day as a composer, violist, organist and harpsichordist. Uncle to FRANÇOIS COUPERIN *le grand*, as a child Louis came to the attention of CHAMBONNIÈRES, founder of the French harpsichord school. During his short life, Louis composed some 200 works mostly for HARPSICHORD, but he left no TREATISE nor instructions on how to play these idiosyncratic works, especially the so-called 'unmeasured preludes' of which he was the pioneer in France (see Moroney, 1985).

In Couperin's NOTATION the long strands of semibreves weaving around and through the treble and bass staves can be considered as a guide to IMPROVISATION, the notes fixed but the rhythms free. In a real sense this is 'wordless recitative', or, as Louis's famous young nephew (who left the form alone) was to put it, a kind of 'prose', in contrast to 'poetry' as in the traditional 'measured' preludes. Yet, the younger composer, obviously influenced by his uncle, was to declare that his own preludes written in traditional notation should also be played freely without too much attention to the note values (unless marked *mesuré*). Whether measured or not, Louis Couperin's harpsichord pieces are filled with phrases which are unexpectedly extended, often in hemiola rhythm, and touching unusual harmonic progressions, all of which seem to suggest a free fantasy style. As he left no performance instructions, it is reasonable to assume that his model was Chambonnières, whose influence on his student was profound.

FURTHER READING

D. Moroney (ed.), *Pièces de clavecin de Louis Couperin* (Monaco: Editions de l'Oiseau-Lyre, 1985).

DAVID TUNLEY

Criticism of Music As an intellectual discipline, criticism is the process of explaining and elucidating the artistic and social significance of works of art, either as uniquely individual objects or larger groups and genres. In music, 'criticism' in its most commonly encountered usage refers to the journalistic activity of commenting on and assessing the degree of success with which performers have achieved their goal of making a written object – the musical score – come to life in an act of performance. This, however, leads one to ask 'What is the object a critic describes?' Most readers of eighteenth-century music journals, the first widely disseminated sources of critical writings, needed to be educated in the skill of being able to judge a particular manner of composing and performing, such as 'French' or 'Italian', where the terms did not refer to national identities in the modern sense but to stylistic features governing both composition and performance. Such a unified concept of style rendered the distinction between the score and its performance redundant and the act of performance was judged as a logical completion of the score. This judgement presupposed a continuity of action between the composer and the performer, often embodied in the same person.

Abandoning the unified concept of style, Romantic critics stressed the role of a work as a vehicle for individual expression and looked for originality above all else. With the rise of the public concert, especially in the decades between the 1830s and 1860s, critical accounts of performance as a vehicle for the expression of a performer's personality led to the cult of the virtuoso, and stress was placed on reports of concerts as social events. A reaction to this type of criticism arose in conjunction with the impact that nineteenth-century philosophical thought had on criticism in general and the study of music history. German critics reflected Kantian formalism and Hegelian philosophy of history, whereas the French and English ones were influenced by the positivist search for origins and an 'orderly' evolution. Without renouncing its earlier function of reporting on musical events, music criticism expanded to include discussions of historical development of repertories and modes of reception. A new category of scholar-critics was thus established and, inevitable exceptions aside, the division among the critics into the two groups, motivated respectively by critical theory and journalistic service to readers, persists to the present day.

In the nineteenth century, the dominance of German critics and the study of music history in German-language universities resulted in a strong preference being given to the German symphonic and instrumental tradition – a canon of works since c1750 – relegating older music to a category of interesting works allegedly flawed by a lack of 'depth'. Some German critics, such as Philipp Spitta and A. W. Ambros, reacted against this limited view and turned their attention to older music, while in England, Italy and France, the Germanocentric view was countered by efforts to bring to life forgotten national musical treasures, most of these significantly pre-dating the Germanic canon. In this way, by the early twentieth century a significant body of early music was brought to performers' and listeners' awareness and a long battle for its proper understanding ensued. From an initial belief that early music had to conform to modern sonorities and performing styles, artistic and critical attitudes swung in the direction of a positivist-inspired desire to recreate allegedly accurate past practices. Such a purist attitude failed to recognise the inevitable changes in human sensibility and modes of reception, and a more balanced approach, usually referred to as HISTORICALLY INFORMED PERFORMANCE, gained in importance. Scholar-critics played an important part in this development while the journalistic critics were made to realise that they could not fulfil their duties without being significantly better informed about the historical aspects of performance than was the case with some of their predecessors.

Early music is still not an equal partner in the commercially dictated canon as perceived by concert promoters, while listeners' awareness of early music has been significantly aided by the wealth of recordings. Only a minority of these reproduce live concert performances, becoming instead art-works shaped jointly by the performers and electroacoustical experts. This in turn raises the old question of what a musical work is: a composer's idealised internal sound-representation, its transformation through the intervention of the performers, or a manufactured, marketable object? Such dilemmas, rather than endangering the role of criticism, make it even more challenging and give an added significance to the role of a critic.

FURTHER READING

L. Goehr, *The Imaginary Museum of Musical Works: an Essay in the Philosophy of Music* (Oxford: Clarendon Press, 1992; rev. edn Oxford University Press, 2007).
M. Graf, *Composer and Critic: Two Hundred Years of Musical Criticism* (London: Chapman & Hall, 1947).
R. Taruskin, *Text and Act: Essays on Music and Performance* (New York: Oxford University Press, 1995).
L. Treitler, *Music and the Historical Imagination* (Cambridge, MA and London: Harvard University Press, 1989).

BOJAN BUJIĆ

Crumhorn (Ger. *Krummhorn* – 'curved horn'; It. *storta, cornamuta*) Capped double-reed wind instrument with narrow cylindrical bore.

The crumhorn is defined by the J-shaped profile of its body; this is surmounted by a 'windcap' (or 'wind capsule'), which surrounds the reed and prevents direct contact with the lips. The result is a 'buzzy' timbre, dynamically inflexible but quite effective in making polyphony clear. The crumhorn does not overblow, so its range is limited to the number of finger-holes plus one – that is, generally to a ninth. Some of the larger members of the family possess lower – but not upper – extension keys; the upper extension keys often fitted to modern reproductions are unhistorical.

Arising during the closing years of the fifteenth century, the crumhorn was one of the first winds to be developed into a family (it was not identical to the Medieval *douçaine*, as was at one time believed, despite some similarities). The instrument remained in vogue through the first few decades of the seventeenth century, declining with the advent of more expressive musical styles. Even in its heyday it was rarely found outside Germany, the Netherlands and northern Italy.

FURTHER READING

B. Boydell, *The Crumhorn and Other Renaissance Windcap Instruments* (Buren: Frits Knuf, 1982).

HERBERT MYERS

Curtal *see* BASSOON

Cyr, Mary (b. Fargo, N. Dakota, 20 August 1946) Naturalised Canadian gambist, teacher and musicologist.

Cyr studied musicology at the University of California, Berkeley (1965–75), Baroque CELLO in Amsterdam with ANNER BYLSMA and VIOLA DA GAMBA in Brussels with WIELAND KUIJKEN. She then pursued a concert career as cellist and gambist with various US and Canadian ensembles, while maintaining her musicological interests, and made some notable recordings of French and English VIOL music. A Rockefeller scholar, she was also co-recipient of the American Musicological Society's NOAH GREENBERG prize for early music performance (1983).

Following fifteen years' teaching at McGill University, Montreal, she was appointed chair of music (1992), and later director of the School of Fine Art, at the University of Guelph, Ontario, where she worked until her retirement in 2005. She has lectured and performed extensively as a gambist and Baroque cellist in Europe, North America, Australia and New Zealand and she has published widely, including contributions to *NG*, focusing on gamba technique and repertoire, the music of RAMEAU, and early music performance. Her *Performing Baroque Music* (Aldershot: Scolar Press, 1992) is a practical guide to Baroque music interpretation, exploring through score study matters of TEMPO, DYNAMICS, PITCH and TEMPERAMENT, BASSO CONTINUO, ARTICULATION, rhythm and NOTATION, ORNAMENTATION, continuo playing and SINGING, with a bias towards French music. Her subsequent *Style and Performance for Bowed String Instruments in French Baroque Music* (Farnham: Ashgate, 2012) confirms this specialism, dealing with the interpretation of French Baroque music for VIOLIN, CELLO, viol and contrebasse in their various roles as solo and ensemble instruments c1680–1760, with case studies focusing on works by MARIN MARAIS, Jean-Baptiste Barrière, Elisabeth-Claude Jacquet de la Guerre and the Forqueray family. Her critical editions of the music of Jacquet de la Guerre and the Forquerays have also received acclaim.

ROBIN STOWELL

Czerny, Carl (b. Vienna, 21 February 1791; d. Vienna, 15 July 1857) Austrian pianist, teacher, composer, theorist and historian.

Czerny was a prolific composer of studies and other piano works who spent almost all his life in Vienna. He was a pupil of BEETHOVEN, who encouraged him to study C. P. E. BACH's treatise, and whose nephew he taught using CLEMENTI's tutor. Among Czerny's high-profile students were KULLAK, LESCHETIZKY and Liszt.

Most of what is known about Czerny's performance preferences comes from his various didactic works, especially his *Systematische Anleitung zum Fantasieren auf dem Pianoforte*, Op. 200 (Vienna: Diabelli & Cappi, 1829; trans., 1983) and *Vollständige theoretisch-praktische Pianoforte-Schule*, Op. 500 (3 vols., Vienna: Diabelli & Cappi, 1839; trans., 1839); *Supplement* (Vienna: Diabelli, 1846; trans., 1846; R/1970 (chs. 2, 3)). From these publications we learn that Czerny, like his teacher, favoured a quiet hand position, with little use of the wrist or arm. Staccato was generally achieved without wrist movement; instead, the fingers were drawn back into the palm of the hand, although for energetic octaves the wrist was also required. Czerny stressed the need for a legato approach, following his teacher's style, and advocating an extreme form of legato (e.g. in chordal passages) not achieved with the sustaining pedal, but with an over-legato touch of the fingers alone. He generally played in strict time, varying the TEMPO only occasionally, and like Beethoven, HUMMEL and MOSCHELES his METRONOME markings have been thought excessively fast by some modern commentators. He observed that the capabilities of 'Viennese' pianos in the 1820s offered performers the ability to vary the tone of their performances and encouraged pianists to exploit the full possibilities of the instrument.

A striking aspect of Czerny's performance was his ability to play from MEMORY – a much less usual feature then than now – and in his Op. 500 he offers advice on how to do so. A further unusual feature of his didactic literature was his teaching on IMPROVISATION; although pianists of his time were expected to improvise in several contexts, there is little or no literature as comprehensive as Czerny's that offers advice on how to achieve this. As well as including many sample preludes, Czerny's Op. 200 explains how to improvise them in their various forms. He also provides tuition on CADENZAS, with some very long examples compared with eighteenth-century models. More generally, he explains that improvised material should only be introduced into works of a lighter character, acknowledging that his contemporaries were more inclined than their predecessors to include all the notes necessary to the performer. Czerny also offers advice on improvising fantasias, potpourris and fugues.

Czerny's relationship with earlier music is difficult to characterise. His approach to MOZART was conservative, advising against the use of the pedal. Especially in the Op. 500 *Supplement* he provided valuable insights into the way Beethoven played his own works. He draws a distinction between earlier performance practices and those relevant to the pianos of the 1830s. Czerny observes that it would be inappropriate for the sustaining pedal to be depressed throughout the theme of the slow movement of Beethoven's Third Concerto, a technique evidently favoured by the composer. His approach to BACH was to update the scores (e.g. of the 48 Preludes and Fugues) with DYNAMICS, tempo fluctuation marks and phrasing, and occasional added octaves.

FURTHER READING

M. Edin, 'Cadenza improvisation in nineteenth-century solo piano music according to Czerny, Liszt and their contemporaries', in R. Rasch (ed.), *Beyond Notes: Improvisation in Western Music of the Eighteenth and Nineteenth Centuries* (Turnhout: Brepols, 2011), 168–74.

S. P. Rosenblum, *Performance Practices in Classic Piano Music* (Bloomington, IN and Indianapolis: Indiana University Press, 1988).

M. Noorduin, 'Czerny's "impossible" metronome marks', *MT*, 154/1925 (Winter 2013), 19–46.

DAVID ROWLAND

D

Dalla Casa, Girolamo (b. ?Udine, ?; d. Venice, 1601) Virtuoso of the CORNETT and author of a two-volume division manual with instructions on playing the instrument.

In 1568 Dalla Casa was hired as a wind player in the first fixed instrumental ensemble at St Mark's. In the 1580s he was named *maestro de' concerti*. He was thus, together with GIOVANNI BASSANO, the principal cornettist during the tenure at St Mark's of GIOVANNI GABRIELI.

Dalla Casa is most important for his two-volume instruction book *Il vero modo di diminuir*, published in 1584. This treatise is of particular interest for its detailed explanation of TONGUING patterns for use in playing divisions. Echoing GANASSI's remarks of almost fifty years earlier, he sets forth three tonguing patterns with differing degrees of smoothness. His divisions on pre-existing pieces include extremely fast passages with sometimes six and eight divisions to the semiminim (crotchet), as well as specific ornaments which he calls the *groppo battuto* (measured [?] *groppo*) and the *tremolo groppizato* (TREMOLO with termination). His complete divisions include a rare and instructive example of a madrigal with divisions in all the parts.

FURTHER READING

T. A. Collins, '"Reactions against the Virtuoso." Instrumental ornamentation practice and the Stile Moderno', *International Review of the Aesthetics and Sociology of Music*, 32/2 (December 2001), 137–52.

B. Dickey, 'Ornamentation in sixteenth-century music', in J. Kite-Powell (ed.), *A Performer's Guide to Renaissance Music*, 2nd edn (Bloomington, IN and Indianapolis: Indiana University Press, 2007), 300–24.

BRUCE DICKEY

Dance

Sources

The re-creation of Renaissance and Baroque dance relies primarily on instructions in dance manuals from the mid-fifteenth century onwards. Supplementary information may come from judicious interpretation of ICONOGRAPHY and further documentary evidence. The earliest manual, *De arte saltandi et choreas ducendi* by the Italian dancing master Domenico da Piacenza (c1455), gives instructions for individual *balli* and *bassedanze*; an introductory section promotes the benefits of dance and analyses the qualities needed of a dancer. Understanding of the steps, tempi, metre and form of the dances is necessary to co-ordinate the instructions with the melodies provided. The first manual to synchronise music and steps clearly on the page is the French treatise *Orchésographie* (1588), written by Jehan Tabourot under the pseudonym THOINOT ARBEAU (see Hutchinson Guest, 47).

In the late seventeenth century, increasingly complex dances in the Baroque style – known as *la belle danse* or *la danse noble* – at the court of Louis XIV led to the development of the Beauchamp Feuillet NOTATION system, which indicates, in relation to the music, the steps, other physical movements and floor pattern of the dance. (See, e.g., facsimiles of treatises by Feuillet, Rameau (Pierre) and Tomlinson in Aldrich (n.d.); for a comprehensive list of works with dance instructions from c1450 to 1750, see Nevile, 313–19.)

Music

The melodies in dance manuals acted as an *aide mémoire*; instrumentation for a ball depended on the period, region, scale of the occasion, acoustic environment and the social rank of those dancing. Iconography may help to identify the constitution of dance bands within these categories. For example, a pair of prints by Théodore de Bry (c1550) contrasts courtly with rustic dancers; a band of two VIOLINS, bass VIOL and LUTE accompanies courtly dancers indoors, while SHAWM and BAGPIPES play for rustics dancing outside. Over the next two centuries ballroom scenes from England, France and the Low Countries typically show two fiddles and a bass stringed instrument as the basic line-up; some images add or substitute OBOE and BASSOON in large halls. Musicians seldom play from music in illustrations and little functional dance music survives for the combination.

Although instrumental music with dance titles abounds from the Renaissance onwards, much of it is music *from* dance, not *for* dance. Not even the highly danceable arrangements produced by Attaingnant, Susato and PRAETORIUS necessarily replicate performance at a ball. The extent to which a piece embodies the spirit of the dance depends on its complexity and technical demands, the composer's knowledge and treatment of dance forms and the date of the piece in relation to the era of the dance: allemandes in J. S. BACH's keyboard suites are far removed from their seventeenth-century dance origins, whereas his minuets often prove suitable for dancing (the minuet was the chief couple dance in the ballroom at the time).

Scores for stage dance survive with increasing abundance from the late sixteenth century. The published account of *Le balet comique de la royne* (1581) – sometimes taken as a starting point in histories of ballet because it was the first work with 'ballet' in the title to have an overall story – includes the earliest set of parts for the five-part string orchestra later employed by LULLY at the court of Louis XIV. Similar scores survive for dances in seventeenth-century English court masques (see also Nevile, 26–33).

Re-Creation

Interest in re-creating Renaissance and Baroque dances gathered momentum during the years around 1900 and thus coincided with the start of the early music revival. In the early 1890s, influential dance teacher and stage choreographer Robert Crompton formed the Renaissance Dancers (a troupe of eight young women) and also worked in London with stage director William

Poel – as did ARNOLD DOLMETSCH – on dances for historically informed Shakespeare productions (Buckland, 37, 46). Writers on dance in France during the 1880s and 1890s noted a growth of interest in early dances, while instructions and recommendations for the minuet occur in two German dance manuals of the 1880s.

The minuet, increasingly obsolete in the ballroom after 1800, survived through the nineteenth century as an instructional dance for inculcating grace, decorum and bearing in upper-class children. Crompton taught the pavan and gavotte as well as the minuet to society dance teacher Elizabeth Garratt for her youthful pupils. In 1892 the Children's Salon, a charitable organisation, arranged performances by the genteel young in aid of the poor; the first entertainment included the minuet, gavotte and morris dances, as well as 'old English village games'. The same year, musical antiquary FRANCIS GALPIN published *Ye Olde Englysshe Pastymes. Old English Dances and Rustic Sports*; in England, a nostalgia for times past fed into the early dance revival (Buckland, 48).

Historic dances at that time were seen as 'fancy dances', even if performers and audiences believed in their authenticity (Buckland, 37). Illustrations of re-created Renaissance and Baroque dances commissioned for dance history books published between the 1890s and 1920s reveal a style that commonly features high-raised arms and toe pointing, quite at variance with dance illustrations from the original period (only the late eighteenth-century allemande involved raising the arms high); see Lilly Grove's *Dancing* (1895), Gaston Vuillier's *A History of Dancing from the Earliest Ages to Our Own Time* (trans. from *La Danse*, 1898) and Ardern Holt's *How to Dance the Revived Ancient Dances* (1907). Holt dedicated her book to the CHAPLIN SISTERS; Nellie Chaplin promoted a similar style in photographs for her own instruction books.

Prominent English dance historians of the next generation included Mabel Dolmetsch (1874–1963), Arnold's third wife, and Melusine Wood (1889–1971). Both derived their instructions directly from the early dance manuals. In America the pianist and composer Louis Horst (1884–1964) utilised early dances as a teaching tool in his work with modern dancers and choreographers; he encouraged students to use the structure of the music and its relationship to the steps of the dance as a starting point for their own dance compositions.

As in the early music revival, succeeding generations of dance historians and performers have challenged the notions of authenticity promulgated by their predecessors. Specialised research, improved performance technique in particular genres, fresh historical perspectives (see Carter, 10–19) and shifting audience expectations continue to refashion interpretations of source material.

FURTHER READING

E. Aldrich (ed.), *An American Ballroom Companion: Dance Instruction Manuals c1490–1920*. www.loc.gov/collections/dance-instruction-manuals-from-1490-to-1920.

T. J. Buckland, 'Dance and cultural memory: interpreting *fin de siècle* performances of "Olde England"', *Dance Research*, 31/1 (2013), 29–66.

A. Carter (ed.), *Rethinking Dance History: A Reader* (London and New York: Routledge, 2004).

A. Hutchinson Guest, *Dance Notation: The Process of Recording Movement on Paper* (London: Dance Books, 1984).
J. Nevile (ed.), *Dance, Spectacle, and the Body Politick, 1250–1750* (Bloomington, IN and Indianapolis: Indiana University Press, 2008).

JEREMY BARLOW

Dancla, (Jean Baptiste) Charles (b. Bagnères de Bigorre, 19 December 1817; d. Tunis, 10 November 1907) French violinist, composer and pedagogue.

Dancla studied the VIOLIN initially with Dussert, impressed RODE with his playing and attended the PARIS CONSERVATOIRE to study with Paul Guérin and PIERRE BAILLOT. He gained a *premier prix* in 1833, but continued there as a student of counterpoint and composition and played the violin in Parisian theatre orchestras, succeeding Javault as leader at the Opéra-Comique. He also participated in HABENECK's *Société des Concerts du Conservatoire* from 1834 and was its foremost violinist from 1841 to 1863, modelling his playing style after Henri Vieuxtemps.

Inspired by Baillot's quartet performances, the Dancla family established a chamber ensemble (*c*1839), giving regular concerts at the home of the pianomaker Hesselbein. However, circumstances in Paris were such that Charles left the capital in 1848 to become a postmaster in Cholet. He later returned as a postal administrator and was eventually offered employment at the Conservatoire in 1855, being appointed violin professor from 1860 until his enforced retirement (1892). Among his celebrated pupils was Maud Powell, who considered him her most inspiring teacher.

Dancla never toured as a concert artist; his reputation outside Paris was therefore based largely on his teaching, compositions and didactic works. A prolific composer, he wrote four symphonies, six violin concertos, numerous *symphonies concertantes*, *airs variés*, fantasias, souvenirs, romances and salon pieces, fourteen string quartets and much other chamber music. Among his pedagogical works are several sets of violin études catering for various different technical levels from beginners (*36 études mélodiques et très faciles*, Op. 84) through to advanced players (*20 études brillantes et caractéristiques*, Op. 73).

Dancla's instruction books cover a similarly wide range. He perpetuated Baillot's principles in his substantial *L'école de violon: méthode complète et progressive* (1844) and *Méthode élémentaire et progressive pour violon*, Op. 52 (1855). The latter discusses fundamental musical and technical principles in its first part, providing scales, duos, studies and exercises for specific aspects of left- and right-hand technique and dealing, as in Dancla's *L'école des cinq positions*, Op. 193 (incorporating the three books of études, Opp. 90, 122, 128), with the first five hand positions. Part 2 is technically more advanced and deals more with artistic factors such as VIBRATO, PORTAMENTO, ORNAMENTATION and even HARMONICS, supported throughout by exercises and study material. Some of Dancla's 'schools' address specific technical or pedagogical issues. His *L'école de l'archet*, Op. 110 aims at improving proficiency in BOWING, his *L'école de mécanisme*, Op. 74 comprises fifty daily exercises written expressly for the development of digital independence in the violinist's left hand, his *Petite école de la mélodie*, Op. 123 consists of three graded suites of melodious pieces for violin and piano, designed to improve tone and *cantabile* playing, and his *Le Semainier du jeune violoniste*, Opp. 144 and 150 guides students through a week's regular daily practice regime of exercises and violin duos.

Dancla is also important for his EDITIONS of works by, for example, Viotti, Rode, BEETHOVEN, BÉRIOT and Vieuxtemps, and his *Notes et Souvenirs* (1893), memoirs which include letters from colleagues, insightful reminiscences of famous musicians, advice on performance and interpretation and other issues.

FURTHER READING

J. B. C. Dancla, *Notes et souvenirs* (Paris: Delamotte, 1893).
J.-M. Fauquet, *Les sociétés de musique de chambre à Paris de la Restauration à 1870* (Paris: Aux Amateurs de livres, 1986).
E. van der Straeten, *The History of the Violin*, 2 vols. (London: Cassell and Co., 1933).

ROBIN STOWELL

D'Anglebert, Jean Henry (bap. Bar-le-Duc, 1 April 1629; d. Paris, 23 April 1691) French composer, harpsichordist and organist.

As Louis XIV's harpsichordist and through the publication of his *Pièces de clavecin* (1689), D'Anglebert represents the highest development of harpsichord music of the *ancien régime*. His manner of notating *préludes non mesurés*, with black quavers as well as white semibreves, suggests a more intelligible performance manner than LOUIS COUPERIN's blanket white NOTATION. D'Anglebert's ornament table is the most elaborate and precise in the harpsichord repertoire, and J. S. BACH's copy made in 1709/12 no doubt influenced the *Explicatio* for W. F. BACH. D'Anglebert's HARPSICHORD TRANSCRIPTIONS are models of their kind. They include fifteen transcriptions of LUTE pieces and twenty transcriptions from LULLY (overtures, airs and ballets). D'Anglebert's five ORGAN fugues, composed c1660, were profusely ornamented perhaps for their publication in 1689. His *Principes de l'accompagnement* contains ornamented full-voiced accompaniments similar to the GUITAR accompaniments written out by Francesco Corbetta, guitar teacher to the young Louis XIV.

FURTHER READING

C. D. Harries (ed.), *Jean Henry D'Anglebert: The Collected Works* (New York: The Broude Trust, 2009).
B. Scheibert, *Jean-Henry D'Anglebert and the Seventeenth-Century French Clavecin School* (Bloomington, IN: Indiana University Press, 1986).

DAVID PONSFORD

Dart, (Robert) Thurston (b. Kingston, 3 September 1921; d. London, 6 March 1971) English musicologist and performer.

As a choirboy at the Chapel Royal, Hampton Court, Thurston Dart was encouraged by the early English choral music scholar EDMUND H. FELLOWES. He later studied the harpsichord with Arnold Goldsborough at the ROYAL COLLEGE OF MUSIC before reading mathematics at Exeter University. After war-time service he studied with the Flemish musicologist Charles van den Boren before becoming assistant to the music lecturer Henry Moule at Cambridge University in 1946. He became assistant lecturer when awarded a

Cambridge MA in 1948, and was appointed professor in 1962. In 1964 he was appointed the first full-time professor of music of the University of London. He founded the Faculty of Music at King's College and rewrote the London syllabus.

Dart's book *The Interpretation of Music* (1954) is largely concerned with EDITING and performance. It promoted the principles of distinguishing editorial interventions from original text and the pursuit of historically informed instrumental sonorities and acoustic conditions for performances. During the 1950s, Dart performed widely, appearing regularly on the BBC Third Programme, forming (with Neville Marriner) the Jacobean Consort and performing in the Boyd Neel Orchestra. In 1955 Neel moved to Canada and Dart became artistic director. His remodelled ensemble – the Philomusica of London – specialised in Baroque repertoire and performed from his own editions, aiming to pay the utmost attention to authenticity and sonority. He directed from the harpsichord and commissioned 'Corelli bows' to recreate a period string tone. He resigned in 1959, citing exhaustion.

Dart's editorial activities can be traced through his positions as secretary of *Musica Britannica*, an active board member of music publishers Stainer & Bell, editor of the *Galpin Society Journal* and contributions to *Grove's Dictionary of Music and Musicians*. Dart's work with Éditions de l'Oiseau-Lyre led to a close friendship with its founder, Louise Dyer, with whose patronage he recorded early keyboard music and several orchestral discs. Dart's later research continually questioned established performance norms – and particularly concerning J. S. BACH's Brandenburg Concertos BWV1046–51, which he was recording with Marriner (1971) when admitted to hospital with stomach cancer. His editions (re)assigned the flauti d'echo parts to RECORDERS and were performed by DAVID MUNROW and John Turner.

FURTHER READING

E. Breen, *Thurston Dart and the New Faculty of Music at King's College, London* (London: King's College London, 2014). www.kcl.ac.uk/artshums/depts/music/newsrecords/2015/50th-anniversary-biography-of-the-department.aspx.

T. Dart, *The Interpretation of Music* (London and New York: Hutchinson's University Library, 1954).

EDWARD BREEN

Dauprat, Louis François (b. Paris, 24 May 1781; d. Paris, 16 July 1868) French HORN player, teacher and composer.

Although Dauprat was renowned for his beautiful tone and elegant and pure manner of phrasing, he felt increasingly uncomfortable performing in public and his most important legacies are his pupils at the PARIS CONSERVATOIRE and his magnificent, three-volume *Méthode de cor alto et cor basse* (1824).

His *Méthode* is an extraordinarily comprehensive work with detailed advice on both performance and style. It consists of forty-seven 'articles', thirty 'lessons', twelve 'studies' and 700 'exercises'. The articles go into detail on the technique of playing the hand horn to an advanced level, including playing different crooks, and the so-called 'factitious tones' (low register notes bent downwards to obtain otherwise impossible pitches) as well as on matters such as TONGUING, legato playing, breathing, learning to lip trill and tone production. There is advice on crooks, mouthpieces and instruments as well as suggestions on style and interpretation, including the performance of ORNAMENTATION and a host of suggestions of ideas for incorporation into CADENZAS, while the final part contains advice for composers on writing for the horn. Dauprat expressed distaste for the new *cor mixte* style, in which performers concentrated just on a narrow range, preferring to divide players into *cor alto* or *cor basse* performers, and the *Méthode* provides separate exercises for each class of player. While he favoured the hand horn, he acknowledged MEIFRED's work in promoting the valve horn. The most celebrated of his compositions for the horn, the Sextet, Op. 10 is scored for six natural horns crooked in different keys and is a compendium of the potential of the instrument.

FURTHER READING

B. Coar, *A Critical Study of the Nineteenth-Century Horn Virtuosi in France* (De Kalb, IL: B. Coar, 1952).
L.-F. Dauprat, *Méthode de cor alto et cor basse* (Paris: Zetter, 1824); trans. V. Roth (Bloomington, IN: Birdalone Music, 1994).
R. Morley-Pegge, *The French Horn. Some Notes on the Evolution of the Instrument and of its Technique* (London: Benn, 1960, 2/1973).

JOHN HUMPHRIES

David, Ferdinand (b. Hamburg, 19 June 1810; d. Klosters, Switzerland, 18 July 1873) German violinist, composer and teacher.

A VIOLIN pupil (1823–5) of SPOHR, Ferdinand David undertook concert tours to Copenhagen, Leipzig, Dresden and Berlin with his pianist sister before being appointed as a violinist in Berlin's Königstadt Theatre (1826–9), where he befriended MENDELSSOHN. After a period as a chamber musician for Karl von Liphart in Dorpat (now Tartu, Estonia; 1829–35), he moved to Leipzig to lead both the Gewandhaus Orchestra (under Mendelssohn) and the Stadttheater Orchestra, taking responsibility also for Leipzig's church music. He quickly established himself as a violinist, composer, teacher and conductor, making only occasional concert trips abroad. He was appointed violin professor at the newly established Leipzig Conservatoire in 1843, including among his pupils JOSEPH JOACHIM, August Wilhelmj, Friedrich Hermann, Arno Hilf and Wilhelm von Wasielewski. In 1845 he premiered Mendelssohn's Violin Concerto, Op. 64, having advised the composer on technical matters.

David's best-known composition, his Concertino, Op. 34, is a staple of the TROMBONE repertory; his violin works include five concertos, variation sets, an unaccompanied Suite, Op. 43, study materials and a corpus of chamber music, salon pieces and other miniatures. His *Violinschule* (Leipzig: Breitkopf & Härtel, 1863) perpetuated and broadened Spohr's pedagogical principles; subdivided into two parts, the first section is designed for beginners and the second for advanced students. It includes exercises and duets for master and pupil, along with some significant textual instruction and illustrations, notably of the typical German right-arm position with the elbow low and close to the body. The BOW is held at the first joint of the first three fingers, which remain stiff, requiring the wrist to be extremely supple. Particularly significant is David's focus on scales in various forms, his recommendation of the 'Geminiani grip', his appreciation of the inter-relationship between bow pressure, bow speed and contact point, and his adoption of various springing bowings previously rejected by Spohr. David extends Spohr's four VIBRATO types to thirteen, all relating to dynamic EXPRESSION, and he admits virtuoso techniques such as single and double artificial HARMONICS, left-hand pizzicato, and simultaneous bowing and pizzicato. Some of David's principles influenced other nineteenth-century Austro-German writers, among them his pupils Henry Schradieck and Karl Courvoisier and Boehm-pupil Jakob Dont; some were even reproduced verbatim, notably by Joachim and Moser in their *Violinschule* (1905).

David later supplemented his *Violinschule* with a two-volume companion work, *Zur Violinschule* Opp. 44 and 45 (1873), which develops further its technical principles in violin duet format. Op. 44 comprises twenty-four studies for beginners, graded into two groups of twelve and limited to first position. Op. 45 consists of eighteen studies using the higher positions; the concluding eight are the most challenging.

David's contribution as an editor and arranger (e.g. he arranged BEETHOVEN's cello sonatas for violin and piano) to the dissemination of the string repertoire is particularly significant. A few years after his pioneering 1843 EDITION of J. S. BACH's solo sonatas and partitas he began editing in earnest core Baroque and Viennese Classical repertory, annotating his editions with his own bowings, FINGERINGS (some suggesting PORTAMENTO), expressive and other markings and, in the case of one concerto by RODE, additional ORNAMENTATION, while remaining substantially faithful to the sources available to him. A catalogue of published editions in his *Violinschule* demonstrates his productiveness by the early 1860s; it includes editions of studies by KREUTZER, Fiorillo and Rode, TARTINI (*L'art de l'archet*), PAGANINI (caprices), J. S. Bach (solo sonatas and partitas) and his own Opp. 8, 20 and 39, as well as concertos by Viotti, Rode and Kreutzer (four by each published as *Conzert-Studien*), Maurer, Spohr, Molique, Lipinski, Vieuxtemps, Joachim, BÉRIOT, Ernst, Paganini, Mendelssohn and Beethoven. His *Violinkonzerte neuere Meister* (1865) made available in one-volume editions the violin concertos of Beethoven, Mendelssohn, Lipinski (Op. 21) and Ernst (Op. 23) and the enthusiastic reception of his *Die hohe Schule des Violinspiels* (1867-72), a three-volume set of twenty works – mostly Baroque sonatas for violin and continuo arranged for violin and piano – resulted in several reissues of the collection under one cover. David also edited a technically easier collection of thirteen sonatas and suites, *Vorstudien zur hohen Schule des Violinspiels* (1872-3), including CORELLI's Sonatas, Op. 5 Nos. 7-11 and works by Leclair and Aubert. His editions of the core Classical chamber music repertoire (including Beethoven's string trios, piano trios by HAYDN, MOZART, Beethoven and Schubert, string quartets by Haydn, Mozart, Beethoven, Mendelssohn and Schubert, string quintets by Mendelssohn and Schubert and violin sonatas/sonatinas by Mozart, Beethoven, Raff and Schubert) offer invaluable insights into the technical, expressive and interpretative practices of one of the nineteenth century's most influential performers and pedagogues.

FURTHER READING

C. Brown, *Classical & Romantic Performing Practice 1750–1900* (Oxford University Press, 1999).
D. Milsom, *Theory and Practice in Late Nineteenth-Century Violin Performance: an Examination of Style in Performance, 1850–1900* (Aldershot: Ashgate, 2003).
R. Stowell, 'Mozart's "Viennese" sonatas for keyboard and violin according to Ferdinand David: a survey of editorial and violin performance practices', in M. Harlow (ed.), *Mozart's Chamber Music with Keyboard* (Cambridge University Press, 2012), 69–103.

ROBIN STOWELL

Davies, Fanny (b. Guernsey, 27 June 1861; d. London, 1 September 1934) English pianist.

Fanny Davies was raised in Birmingham. As a teenager, she had lessons with CHARLES HALLÉ in London. She went to Leipzig in 1882 and studied with Clara Schumann in Frankfurt in 1883. Following her debut in 1885 at the Crystal Palace, she established a steady concert career. She gave several English premieres of chamber and solo works by BRAHMS, particularly the late solo piano miniatures, Opp. 116 and 117. Although she was chiefly associated with the core German repertoire, she also played Debussy and Scriabin, and was an early pioneer of English virginal music.

Davies's concert career reflected the values of her celebrated teacher Clara Schumann, namely integrity and absence of extrovert display onstage. As a member of the Schumann/Brahms circle, Davies performed with soloists including the violinist JOSEPH JOACHIM, the clarinettist Richard Mühlfeld and the cellist Robert Hausmann. She also heard Brahms play his own works, and wrote a detailed account of his piano playing. In particular, she noted in her score the details of his performance of the Piano Trio, Op. 101. Her copies of the Piano Trio, Op. 8 and the Clarinet Trio, Op. 114 also contain annotations and METRONOME marks, which probably reflect the practices of Brahms's musical circle. These scores, as well as her clean copies of numerous other chamber works, are held by the ROYAL COLLEGE OF MUSIC, London.

Davies made several rolls for the Welte-Mignon reproducing piano in 1909. She recorded (1928–30) piano works by Schumann, including his Piano Concerto, Op. 54 with the Royal Philharmonic Orchestra under Ernest Ansermet. These recordings capture her sweet tone, characteristic chord arpeggiation and dislocation between the left and right hand. They are a valuable document of early twentieth-century pianism.

FURTHER READING

F. Davies, 'Some personal recollections of Brahms as pianist and interpreter', in W. W. Cobbett (ed.), *Cobbett's Cyclopedic Survey of Chamber Music*, 2nd edn, 3 vols. (London: Oxford University Press, 1963), I, 182–4.
D. Mayer, 'Fanny Davies', *Recorded Sound*, 70–1 (1978), 776–9.

NATASHA LOGES

Deldevez, Edmé (Edouard) Marie Ernest (b. Paris, 31 May 1817; d. Paris, 6 November 1897) French violinist, conductor, composer and teacher.

A VIOLIN pupil of François Sudre (1823–5) and later FRANÇOIS-ANTOINE HABENECK at the PARIS CONSERVATOIRE, Deldevez joined the Paris Opéra

Orchestra (1833) and the orchestra of the *Société des Concerts du Conservatoire* (1839), but later turned to a CONDUCTING career. He was appointed assistant conductor at L'Opéra (1847–70), its principal conductor (1872–77), conductor of the Conservatoire Concerts (1873–85) and became the Paris Conservatoire's first professor of conducting (1873–85). He published a detailed treatise (*L'art du chef d'orchestre*, 1878), which comprises much significant technical detail but perpetuates the (by then old-fashioned) French tradition of conducting with the violin BOW, more than twenty years after BERLIOZ had issued his treatise on baton conducting.

Deldevez's sacred, dramatic, orchestral, chamber and solo works were strongly influenced by his composition teachers REICHA, Halévy and Berton and achieved some popularity; but he is most remembered for his theoretical works on various musical topics (NOTATION, harmony, ensemble performance), his historical reminiscences and especially his collection of seventeenth- and eighteenth-century violin music (*Pièces diverses*, Op. 19, 1857) 'with concertante parts added to the original text and arranged for piano and violin'. This collection of twenty-six pieces follows JEAN-BAPTISTE CARTIER's in the third part of his *L'art du violon* (1798) and anticipates similar anthologies by DELPHIN ALARD, FERDINAND DAVID and others; it comprises complete sonatas and separate movements by Italian, French and German composers from CORELLI to Viotti. Adopted by the Paris Conservatoire for its didactic intentions, it introduces performers to various interpretative issues, including the execution of the notated ornaments, and provides bowings and FINGERINGS and PIANOFORTE accompaniments realised from the FIGURED BASS. Although it includes eighteen pieces that had already appeared in Cartier's anthology, Deldevez's publication is no duplicate, for he frequently takes liberties with the music, whether with the order of movements or with the content of some of his 'creative' accompaniments.

FURTHER READING

E. Deldevez, *Mes mémoires* (Paris: Le Pluy, 1890).
D. K. Holoman: *The Société des Concerts du Conservatoire, 1828–1967* (Berkeley, CA: University of California Press, 2004).
G. Streletski, 'Les chefs d'orchestre-violonistes dans la France du XIXe siècle', in A. Penesco (ed.), *Du baroque à l'époque contemporaine: aspects des instruments à archet* (Paris: Champion, 1993), 87–106.

ROBIN STOWELL

Deller, Alfred George (b. Margate, 31 May 1912; d. Bologna, 16 July 1979) English countertenor and conductor, and one of the most important singers to emerge in the post-war period as a performer of early repertoire.

Completely self-taught as a singer and from a socially modest background, Deller was brought to public notice after MICHAEL TIPPETT heard him sing in Canterbury in 1944, by which date Deller was a lay clerk at the cathedral. On 29 September 1946, in the opening broadcast of the new BBC Third Programme (now Radio 3), he was a soloist in Purcell's Ode on St Cecilia's Day 'Come ye Sons of Art'. In 1947 he became a vicar choral at St Paul's Cathedral and in 1948 founded the DELLER CONSORT, an important British vocal ensemble that popularised a wide range of vocal chamber music from the thirteenth to the eighteenth centuries. In 1962 he established the Stour Festival in Kent, one of the first in Britain to specialise in 'early music'. He performed worldwide and made many recordings, being particularly well known for his emotionally vivid performances of LUTE songs (frequently in partnership with Desmond Dupré) and the works of Purcell, as well as premiering many new works, most famously BRITTEN's *A Midsummer Night's Dream* (Oberon). His range was approximately g to e″, with little use of chest voice; whenever possible, he sang the upper few semitones very lightly (one element in what some regarded as a mannered performing style). He preferred an essentially instinctive approach to music making, disliking REHEARSALS, and with trenchant views about such matters as AUTHENTICITY, which he feared could become an end in itself. This did not prevent GUSTAV LEONHARDT from citing him as his greatest influence.

FURTHER READING

J. Drillon, *Sur Leonhardt* (Paris: Gallimard/L'Infini, 2009).
M. Hardwick and M. Hardwick, *Alfred Deller: A Singularity of Voice* (London: Proteus, 1980).

NICHOLAS CLAPTON

Deller Consort English vocal ensemble.

Founded by Alfred Deller in 1950, the Consort's original members were sopranos April Cantelo and Eileen McLoughlin, Deller himself, tenors Harry Barnes (from Westminster Abbey Choir) and Eric Barnes, and baritone Maurice Bevan (the last two colleagues of Deller at St Paul's Cathedral). Lutenist Desmond Dupré (and, from 1974, Robert Spencer) frequently accompanied them. The personnel varied over the years, with Bevan and soprano Honor Sheppard (from 1961) being especially long-serving.

Immediately successful, the group toured internationally from 1955 and built up an extensive discography, especially for the labels Vanguard (USA) and Harmonia Mundi (France). A celebratory compilation, *50 Years of the Deller Consort*, appeared in 2000 (Vanguard Classics). Its core repertoire was from the English secular and sacred Renaissance, but it ranged from Pérotin to HANDEL, including large-scale works, such as the latter's *Acis and Galatea*, and works by Purcell, as well as occasional commissions. They often performed with other notable musicians of the early music movement, including NIKOLAUS HARNONCOURT, CONCENTUS MUSICUS and COLLEGIUM AUREUM. Deller's son, Mark, joined the group in 1963, and continued to direct it after his father's death in 1979. Its final appearance was at the Stour Music Festival on 30 June 2012.

In founding the Consort, Deller aimed to achieve inspired, almost improvisatory live performance. Contemporary reviews of concerts abound in phrases like 'wonderfully polished' and 'thus angels in heaven may sing', though the sparing, general use of VIBRATO marks this ensemble out from the straight-toned voice production favoured by many groups now active in similar repertoire.

NICHOLAS CLAPTON

Delusse, Charles (b. Paris, 1720; d. Paris, after 1774) French flautist, composer and writer.

Charles Delusse was active at the Opéra-Comique in the 1760s. He published a number of works between 1751 and 1757, including six sonatas for FLUTE and BASSO CONTINUO (Op. 1) and six sonatas for two unaccompanied flutes (Op. 2). These three-movement sonatas contain complex rhythms, specific DYNAMICS and numerous ARTICULATION markings. Delusse also composed music for the one-act comic opera *L'amant statue* (1759), as well as various songs and romances. His modest treatise *L'art de la flûte traversière*, published in 1760, describes a more advanced level of flute playing than most previous tutors, especially regarding different styles of ORNAMENTATION and the use of HARMONICS and VIBRATO. It also contains preludes in twenty different keys and twelve long and difficult caprices or CADENZAS, which display an exceptional level of fantasy and virtuosity. These are the earliest independent cadenzas in French flute literature. In the 1770s he contributed articles to the *Encyclopédie* of Diderot and d'Alembert.

FURTHER READING

N. Toff, *The Flute Book* (Oxford University Press, 1996).

ASHLEY SOLOMON

Denis, Jean (b. Paris?, 1600; d. Paris?, January 1672) French HARPSICHORD maker and organist.

Although Denis described himself as a 'simple artisan', his family were renowned instrument makers and he was organist of Saint Barthélemy in Paris. His patrons included musical aristocrats and he was acquainted with leading theorists and musicians, including MERSENNE and his contemporary, CHAMBONNIÈRES. His short TREATISE on keyboard tuning (*Traité de l'accord de l'espinette* (Paris: Ballard and Jean Denis, 1643)) is a rare but important document written at the time when the harpsichord was rapidly gaining ascendancy over the LUTE. The first edition of 1643 contains his instructions for tuning meantone TEMPERAMENT and includes a short prelude to prove its efficacy once tuned. The second edition of 1650 gives additional advice on liturgical ORGAN playing, TRANSPOSITION, IMPROVISATION, ORNAMENTATION and keyboard technique. The unusual combination of practical and theoretical insight in the *Traité* is given extra significance by Denis's status as both craftsman and musician.

FURTHER READING

D. H. Boalch, *Makers of the Harpsichord and Clavichord 1440–1840* (Oxford University Press, 1956; 3/1995, ed. C. Mould), 45–6.

J. Denis, *Treatise on Harpsichord Tuning by Jean Denis*, trans. and ed. V. J. Panetta (Cambridge University Press, 1987).

E. Kottick, *A History of the Harpsichord* (Bloomington, IN: Indiana University Press, 2003), 165–8.

TERENCE CHARLSTON

Devienne, François (b. Joinville, Haute-Marne, 31 January 1759; d. Paris, 5 September 1803) French flautist, bassoonist, composer and teacher.

Devienne occupied a number of orchestral positions in Paris from 1779 as bassoonist and flautist and increasingly made appearances as soloist. In addition to concertos and *symphonies concertantes* featuring wind instruments, he wrote a number of *operas comiques*, of which the most successful was *Les visitandines* (1792), which achieved over 200 performances in Paris between 1792 and 1797. His concertos and chamber music were highly influential in raising the musical level of French works written for wind instruments at the time. His music for FLUTE was championed by Jean-Pierre Rampal in the 1960s and has become popular among players of the instrument; two of his CLARINET sonatas have gained a toehold in the repertory, though largely in EDITIONS which replace Devienne's simple bass line with over-elaborate keyboard realisations, tending to distort his musical ideas.

Devienne's influential *Nouvelle méthode théorique et pratique pour la flûte* (Paris, 1794) is an important method for the one-keyed flute, containing information on flute techniques and performing practice, especially in relation to late eighteenth-century ARTICULATION. Although Devienne acknowledged the use of more mechanism, he never employed it himself. Some ten years later the four-keyed flute was adopted at the PARIS CONSERVATOIRE, when Hugot and Wunderlich's *Méthode de flûte* (Paris, 1804) fully embraced the use of four keys and gave systematic exercises for acquiring fluency. Both methods favoured mellow tone colours, denouncing hard sounds, and both rejected double TONGUING. Devienne's views on articulation include a rejection of *tu-ru*, which was such an integral part of eighteenth-century flute playing and is still retained today for dotted rhythms. He described it as 'a disagreeable roll, which gives no clarity in execution, preventing those who use it from either shaping passagework or giving any expression'. He calls it *brouillage* ('stuttering') and remarks that it was never used on clarinet, BASSOON, OBOE or HORN.

FURTHER READING

J. Bowers, *François Devienne's 'Nouvelle méthode théorique et pratique pour la flûte'* (Aldershot: Ashgate, 1999).
W. Montgomery, 'The life and works of François Devienne, 1759–1803', PhD dissertation, Catholic University of America (1975).

COLIN LAWSON

Dickey, Bruce (Howard) (b. South Bend, IN, 3 March, 1949) American CORNETT player, teacher and musicologist.

Dickey read music at Indiana University before proceeding to the SCHOLA CANTORUM, Basel to study RECORDER. He has lived in Europe since 1974. In 1987, with the trombonist Charles Toet, he formed the cornett/TROMBONE group Concerto Palatino. He has worked with most of the major historical performance groups in the world and has taught generations of cornetto players.

Dickey was not the first modern player to have taken up the cornett, but he was the first to explore the idiom of the instrument in its entirety through painstaking research and virtuoso performance. He has been widely influential in unveiling the character of an instrument that was of the greatest importance in the sixteenth and seventeenth centuries, but had subsequently become obscure and often misunderstood.

FURTHER READING

M. Collver and B. Dickey, *A Catalogue of Music for the Cornett* (Bloomington, IN: Indiana University Press, 1996).
B. Dickey, 'The cornett', in T. Herbert and J. Wallace (eds.), *The Cambridge Companion to Brass Instruments* (Cambridge University Press, 1997), 51–67.
E. H. Tarr and B. Dickey, *Bläserartikulation in der alten Musik /Articulation in Early Wind Music* (Winterthur: Amadeus, 2007).

TREVOR HERBERT

Diémer, Louis-Joseph (b. Paris, 14 February 1843; d. Paris, 21 December 1919) French pianist, composer and harpsichordist.

Diémer studied the PIANO with Antoine Marmontel and works dedicated to him include Franck's *Symphonic Variations* (1885). In the 1860s, Diémer began to introduce the HARPSICHORD into his solo recitals, and he later owned the magnificent 1769 Taskin now in the Russell Collection. At the 1889 Paris Exposition he played the harpsichord (including newly constructed instruments by Pleyel and Érard) in concerts with Jules Delsart (VIOLA DA GAMBA) and others with whom he founded the pioneering *Société des Instruments Anciens*.

FURTHER READING

I. Kipnis (ed.), *The Harpsichord and Clavichord: An Encyclopedia* (New York: Routledge, 2007, 2/2014).

NIGEL SIMEONE

Dietrich, Albert (b. Forsthaus Golk, nr Meissen, 28 August 1829; d. Berlin 20 November 1908) German composer and conductor

Dietrich was *Kapellmeister* at Oldenburg between 1861 and 1890. Closely connected with BRAHMS (with whom and with Schumann he contributed to the composite 'FAE Sonata' for JOSEPH JOACHIM in October 1853), his *Erinnerungen an Johannes Brahms* is especially valuable concerning the origins and first performance of *Ein deutsches Requiem*.

FURTHER READING

A. Dietrich, *Erinnerungen an Johannes Brahms in Briefen besonders aus seiner Jugendzeit* (Leipzig: Otto Wigand, 1898).

MICHAEL MUSGRAVE

Diruta, Girolamo (b. ?Deruta nr Perugia, c1554; d. ?Choggia after 1612) Italian organist and theorist.

Having studied with ANDREA GABRIELI, ZARLINO, Merulo and Porta, Diruta thoroughly absorbed the practical and theoretical traditions of Venetian keyboard music. His two-part treatise *Il transilvano* (Venice, 1593 and 1609) was the first work to distinguish between ORGAN and HARPSICHORD playing. Published at the instigation of Merulo, whose teaching it probably encapsulated, it was written in dialogue form. Diruta discussed the following topics: playing position; FINGERING ('good' and 'bad' fingers corresponding to 'good' and 'bad', i.e. metrically strong or weak, notes); diminutions; ORNAMENTATION; rules of counterpoint; church modes and organ registrations; TRANSPOSITION; methods for intabulating vocal music; accompanying; intoning and responding to the choir. He also included toccatas by Merulo, A. and G. GABRIELI amongst others, and (in the second part) ricercars by Luzzaschi and BANCHIERI. Unlike the toccatas of A. Gabrieli and Merulo, who alternated chordal and imitative sections with passagework, Diruta's toccatas consist entirely of passagework accompanied by chords.

FURTHER READING

Anthology of Early Keyboard Methods, trans. and ed. B. Sachs and B. Ife (Cambridge: Gamut Publications, 1981).

A. Silbiger (ed.), *Keyboard Music before 1700* (New York and London: Routledge, 2004).

DAVID PONSFORD

Dittersdorf, Carl Ditters von (Ditters, Carl) (b. Vienna, 2 November 1739; d. Neuhof, Pilgram, Bohemia, 24 October 1799) Austrian violinist and composer.

Raised in Vienna, Dittersdorf began his musical career as a jobbing violinist when he was a young boy, gradually established himself as a leading virtuoso, turned to composition in the mid-1750s and worked as *Kapellmeister* at three different courts in the Austrian territories. He composed in a wide variety of genres, sonatas, concertos and symphonies, masses, oratorios and opera, and enjoyed the friendship of Gluck, HAYDN, MOZART, CLEMENTI, REICHARDT and others.

Towards the end of his life he dictated his autobiography to his son; the work was first published by Breitkopf & Härtel in 1801. Rich in entertaining anecdotes, it also reveals many details about the training of young violinists, REHEARSAL practices and the sizes of orchestras (in northern Italy and Berlin, as well as in the Austrian territories).

FURTHER READING

The Autobiography of Karl von Dittersdorf, trans. A. D. Coleridge (London: Bentley, 1896; repr. New York: Da Capo Press, 1970).

DAVID WYN JONES

Dolmetsch, Arnold (and family) (b. Le Mans, 24 February 1858; d. Haslemere, 28 February 1940) French-born instrument maker, performer, musicologist and teacher.

Of mixed Swiss and French ancestry, Dolmetsch was apprenticed at fourteen to his parents' ORGAN factory and music shop in Le Mans. As a VIOLIN student at Brussels Conservatoire (1879–83) he bought and restored a square PIANO; after moving to London (1883) he had, by 1890, restored a viola d'amore, LUTE and several early keyboard instruments. The first instrument he made was a lute (1893); then, with encouragement from William Morris, a batch of four CLAVICHORDS (1894) and a HARPSICHORD (1896), followed by the first of three BEETHOVEN PIANOFORTES (1898). As well as building instruments in his own workshop, Dolmetsch made HARPSICHORDS, CLAVICHORDS, VIOLS and lutes in association with piano manufacturer Chickering (USA, 1906–11), and harpsichords and clavichords with Gaveau (Paris, 1911–14).

Dolmetsch's important discovery in the late 1880s of the English viol CONSORT repertoire led to extensive performances in the following decade and growing recognition. Praise was not universal, but George Bernard Shaw among others gave him enthusiastic reviews and personal support. Over the years Dolmetsch's consort incorporated several family members: his daughter Hélène (1878–1924) by his first marriage (an outstanding viol player, according to Shaw), his second wife, harpsichordist Élodie, and third wife, Mabel (1874–1963), also a viol player who developed an interest in historical DANCE, writing two treatises on the subject. In due course Mabel's children Cécile (1904–97), Nathalie (1905–89), Rudolph (1906–42) and Carl (1911–97) joined the consort. Nathalie later wrote about the viola da gamba and lyra viol; she, too, was a dancer and in 1970 founded the Dolmetsch Historical Dance Society. Rudolph's promising career as a harpsichordist ended prematurely with his death at sea during WWII. Carl became the leading RECORDER player of his generation and supervised Dolmetsch recorder production from 1926, seven years after his father had made the first instrument, a treble. From 1978 a new firm marketed redesigned recorders under the name J & M Dolmetsch, after Carl's twin daughters Jeanne and Marguerite. The workshop closed in 2010.

Throughout his career Arnold Dolmetsch produced numerous EDITIONS of music from the sixteenth to eighteenth centuries and wrote many articles, but his greatest musicological contribution was *The Interpretation of the Music of the Seventeenth and Eighteenth Centuries Revealed by Contemporary Evidence* (London: Novello & Co., 1915), a successor to Edward Dannreuther's *Musical Ornamentation* (1893/5) (*see* DONINGTON, ROBERT). The family settled at Jesses, near Haslemere, Surrey (1917). Recordings made by Columbia in 1921, 1929, 1932/3 and 1938 attest to the power and individuality of his musicianship. He founded the Haslemere Festival, the first early music festival (1925–2001 in its original format); the Dolmetsch Foundation (est. 1928) continues to promote his work. That year Dolmetsch made his first violin and completed a 'New Action' harpsichord. It incorporated a jack action which eliminated the sound of the plectrum touching the string on its return, a *Bebung* device and a sustaining pedal. He was awarded the Croix de Chevalier de la Légion d'Honneur (1938). For almost half a century he had dominated period-instrument performance and overshadowed other pioneers (DIÉMER, FÉTIS, GALPIN, HIPKINS, FULLER-MAITLAND), laying sound foundations for the twentieth-century 'early music revival'.

FURTHER READING

M. Campbell, *Dolmetsch: The Man and His Work* (London: Hamish Hamilton, 1975).
M. Dolmetsch, *Personal Recollections of Arnold Dolmetsch* (London: Routledge and Kegan Paul, 1957).
R. Donington, *The Work and Ideas of Arnold Dolmetsch* (Haslemere: The Dolmetsch Foundation, 1932).

JEREMY BARLOW

Donington, Robert (b. Leeds, 4 May 1907; d. Firle, Sussex, 20 January 1990) English musicologist, violist and violinist.

Donington's contribution to historical performance practice lies chiefly in *The Interpretation of Early Music* and *A Performer's Guide to Baroque Music*; in the former book he acknowledges a debt to ARNOLD DOLMETSCH's *The Interpretation of the Music of the Seventeenth and Eighteenth Centuries*

Revealed by Contemporary Evidence (London: Novello & Co., 1915). Although Donington advised caution in inferring fixed rules of performance practice from his copious musical and textual examples, FREDERICK NEUMANN considered him to be too prescriptive over practices such as double dotting and starting trills on the beat with the upper note. In later editions of *The Interpretation of Early Music*, Donington responded to the criticisms and, when he felt Neumann was justified, modified his views. Donington has also been criticised over his support for Dolmetsch's 'improvements' to the HARPSICHORD in *The Work and Ideas of Arnold Dolmetsch* (Haslemere: Dolmetsch Foundation, 1932) and for his use of a mix of VIOLINS in modern set-up (played by Yehudi Menuhin) with a Baroque BOW, a modern Goble harpsichord (played by George Malcolm), and a Baroque gamba and bow in the recording that accompanies his *String Playing in Baroque Music* (London: Faber & Faber, 1977).

Donington's interest in early music arose from hearing the Dolmetsch family and colleagues give a concert of English VIOL music at a Haslemere Festival in the mid-1920s. He took lessons on the viol from Arnold Dolmetsch, and together with his sister Margaret – also a viol player – performed with the family in ensuing years. Between 1935 and 1961 he played in the English Consort of Viols, the London Consort and the Donington Consort, which he directed from 1956 to 1961. Involvement as a founder member of the Galpin Society in 1946 led to publication of *The Instruments of Music* three years later. From 1961 Donington spent much time in America, performing and lecturing extensively; the University of Iowa appointed him visiting professor of music in 1964 and professor of music from 1968 to 1974. He returned to England for the last part of his life and continued to write and to revise earlier publications. His several works on opera include *The Rise of Opera* (1981) and *Opera and its Symbols: The Unity of Words, Music, and Staging* (1990).

FURTHER READING

R. Donington, *The Instruments of Music* (London: Methuen & Co Ltd, 1949; rev. 1970).
The Interpretation of Early Music (London: Faber & Faber, 1963; rev. 1974; repr. with corrections 1975; rev. edn New York: W. W. Norton, 1992).
A Performer's Guide to Baroque Music (London: Faber & Faber, 1973; repr. with corrections, 1975).

JEREMY BARLOW

Dotzauer, Justus Johann Friedrich (b. Häselrieth, nr Hildburghausen, Thüringen, 20 January 1763; d. Dresden, 6 March 1860) German cellist, teacher, and composer.

Dotzauer learnt the CELLO initially from the Hildburghausen court trumpeter but furthered his studies in Meiningen (from 1799) with J. J. Kriegck, a pupil of the elder Duport, and played in the Meiningen Hofkapelle (1801–5). After six months in Berlin in 1806, where his playing was strongly influenced by ROMBERG, he moved to a position in the Leipzig Gewandhaus Orchestra. In Leipzig, his string quartet gave some of the first public quartet concerts in Europe. In 1811 he joined the Dresden royal orchestra, becoming principal in 1821 and remaining there until his retirement (1850). SPOHR spoke highly of his intonation and technical refinement in chamber music. Evidence that he was at one time connected with the Naples conservatoire has not been corroborated; however, an Italian translation of his *Violonzellschule* (*Metodo per il Violoncello*, Milan, 1838) was adopted by the Milan Conservatoire.

In his *Violonzellschule* (Mainz: Schott, [1825]), Dotzauer stresses the importance of cultivating a fine tone and melodiousness in cello playing. He rejects excessive decoration and technical display, quoting ROUSSEAU on the value of simplicity. Like Duport, he considers PORTAMENTO more as a technical aid for shifting than as an expressive device, providing only a few examples and eschewing detailed explanation. He gives VIBRATO even less attention, providing only a short verbal description of left-hand vibrato and 'bow-vibrato' (one of very few cello teachers to describe this latter). His remark that vibrato was more popular with Italians was not included in the Italian text of the Milan edition, nor the German text of the first edition. Dotzauer was also interested in HARMONICS and published a tutor on the subject (*Violoncello Flageolett-Schule*, Op. 147), comprising largely scales and duets involving harmonic effects and even incorporating left-hand pizzicato. He describes other acoustic phenomena in his *Violonzellschule*, especially the 'Pochen', an effect achieved by touching a lower sympathetically vibrating string to create a sensation of a beating tone quality. Dotzauer also endorses Romberg's fingerboard groove below the C string (Spohr advocated a similar modification on the violin) but this did not become widespread.

Dotzauer's EDITION of J. S. BACH's Cello Suites (Leipzig: 1826) was the first with a named editor, and also the first to appear without egregious errors. It has few FINGERINGS, directional BOWINGS or additional dynamic markings, but includes many slurs, some staccato indications, and TEMPO markings for almost every movement. Dotzauer sometimes indicates ascending portamentos on the D string, to a register he called '*moelleux*' ('mellow'), an effect which Romberg and Kummer also favoured. Dotzauer's edition was reissued throughout the nineteenth century and was referred to by Hugo Becker in his own edition (Leipzig, c1907).

His compositions fell from favour, but his teaching material, still in use, was edited by several cellists, including GRÜTZMACHER's pupils Klingenberg and Becker. Piatti included several of Dotzauer's studies in his cello method. Dotzauer's scale fingerings (he offers more than one option for several scales) are mainly in the GUNN/DUPORT system (increasingly widespread by the mid-1820s), but his use of the thumb is more flexible than Duport's and owes more to Romberg's approach. Dotzauer's pupils included Friedrich Kummer, Karl Schuberth and Karl Drechsler, who themselves taught Grützmacher, Carl Schröder and Robert Hausmann.

FURTHER READING

G. Kennaway, *Playing the Cello, 1780–1930* (Farnham: Ashgate, 2014).
   'Bach Solo Cello Suites – an overview of editions', University of Leeds, 2013. http://chase.leeds.ac.uk/article/bach-solo-cello-suites-an-overview-of-editions-george-kennaway/.
V. Walden, *One Hundred Years of Violoncello* (Cambridge University Press, 1998).

GEORGE KENNAWAY

Double Bass The largest and lowest-pitched stringed instrument in the symphony orchestra.

The double bass is unique among bowed string instruments for its ability to reach the contra octave. An early use of the term 'double bass' was by the seventeenth-century English composer Orlando Gibbons who wrote a set of VIOL fantasias, two of them including a 'great dooble bass'. However, 'double bass' generally refers to the practice in some symphonic repertoire of doubling the cello line an octave lower. This was not always the instrument's function; and although the double bass sometimes doubles the CELLO line in repertoire after BEETHOVEN, its contribution eventually evolved into a separate voice.

The earliest record of large viols with a range reaching into the contrabass octave may be found in the late fifteenth century. In 1493 an Italian chancellor, Bernadino Prospero, described a consort of Spanish viols including 'viole grandi come me' ('large viols as big as myself'). Iconic evidence of early upright basses may be found in a set of woodcuts from *Das Schempartbuch* (1518), preserved in the German National Museum in Nuremburg. Of the three musicians pictured, one is playing a large bowed string instrument similar in size to the double bass.

Because of the early influence of the VIOLA DA GAMBA on the double bass, elements of its construction are different from other instruments of the VIOLIN family. These include a tuning in fourths, or thirds and fourths, low sloping shoulders, a flat back and the traditional gamba shape without outward turning 'violin corners'. As the violin family became predominant, elements of its design were incorporated into the double bass, resulting in a hybrid instrument.

The immediate predecessor of the double bass, however, was the VIOLONE. Literally, the Italian term 'violone' describes a large viol and was applied to a variety of instruments. It emerged as early as the beginning of the fifteenth century, was cited by Lanfranco (1533), GANASSI (1542) and ORTIZ (1553) and was used by composers to describe a variety of stringed instruments in the contrabass register. Seventeenth-century Italian composer Giovanni Colonna used the terms *violoncello* and *violone* to describe bass instruments, but described stringed instruments reaching the 16′ octave as CONTRABASSO. In his First Brandenburg Concerto, J. S. BACH uses not only the term *continuo è violono grosso* but also *violone*. There is still debate among scholars and practitioners as to the exact nature of instruments described as violones in original scores.

Violones normally had six strings tuned in thirds and fourths. Although there was a wide variety of tunings, the two most commonly cited were D′-G′-C-E-A-d and G′-C-F-A-d-g. Violones were fitted with gut frets, for the first seven semitones. As with the viola da gamba, these frets could be moved to accommodate different tuning systems. Early double basses, such as those by Gasparo da Salò and Giovanni Paolo Maggini, were originally built as six-string violones but have since been modified to take a more modern, four-string tuning. Period players prefer the original set-up of these historic instruments, which is often carefully copied by modern luthiers.

The hybrid nature of the double bass is also reflected in the two types of BOW employed through its history. The German bow, also known as the Butler bow or Simandl bow (after Viennese bassist Franz Simandl), is the oldest bow-type used in the modern orchestra; it is employed primarily in Germany and Austria as well as in the USA. Its underhand grip developed from the viola da gamba bow. There are both concave and convex variations of the underhand bow, including the so-called 'Dragonetti bow', which was in use in England until the early twentieth century. The French bow requires an overhand grip similar to that used by modern violinists. It was not used widely until it was adopted and popularised by the nineteenth-century Italian virtuoso, GIOVANNI BOTTESINI.

In eighteenth-century Austria, a school of double bass playing emerged that put an emphasis on technical virtuosity and the solo possibilities of the double bass. The bass of the Viennese Classic School was a five-string fretted violone tuned $F'-A'-D-F\sharp-A$. The D major chord formed by the open strings made solo works with arpeggiated chordal passages easier to execute. The leading double bassist of that School was Johann Matthias Sperger, who was also a prolific composer and wrote some eighteen concertos for the instrument. Other composers who wrote for the Viennese Classical double bass included Capuzzi, DITTERSDORF and Vanhal. The tradition of the double bass virtuoso was also in the ascendancy in Italy, first with Dragonetti, who began his career in the orchestra of San Marco in Venice, and emigrated (1794) to England where he performed in London's King's Theatre, and later with Bottesini. The latter, known as 'the Paganini of the double bass', further developed the instrument's virtuoso solo potential, exploiting techniques such as HARMONICS to striking effect and performing in the high range of the instrument.

From the middle of the eighteenth century, many double bassists played three-stringed instruments. Different tunings were used for these instruments. In Italy, England and Spain the most common tuning for the three-stringed double bass was $A'-D-G$. Dragonetti and Bottesini played such instruments. In France, a tuning of $G'-D-A$ was employed, while in Germany a four-stringed bass was used with the tuning $E'-A'-D-G$. This tuning is the most widely used tuning in modern orchestras and was cited by QUANTZ (1752), Nicolai ('Das Spiel auf dem Contrabass', *AMZ*, 16 (1816), cols. 257–66) and Wettengel (*Vollständiges Lehrbuch der Geigen- und Bogenmacherkunst* (Ilmenau: Bernh. Fr. Voigt, 1828)). A fifth string, tuned to either C' or B'', was added to some double basses to accommodate the increased range of music in the Romantic era.

The Prague Double Bass School was founded in the early nineteenth century at the Prague Conservatory by Wenzel Hause. Various left-hand FINGERING systems were in use at this time, including 1–2–3–4, 1–2–4 and 1–3–4 (with each number representing a successive semitone). In his *KontrabaßSchule*, he established a system based on the 1–2–4 fingering system that was widely adopted and standardised left-hand technique for double bassists. His students Josef Hrabě and Emanuel Storch established a school in Leipzig based on Hause's methods. One of Hrabě's students, Franz Simandl, developed a school in Vienna using this system; his *Nouvelle Méthode* for double bass established it as a standard and is still widely used in conservatoires today.

By the twentieth century, the double bass had retained a relative level of equality with other members of the string section. In the symphony orchestra it had fully realised an independent role, and was no longer restricted to doubling the bass line an octave lower. A tuning in fourths was standardised, although a small number of double bassists, such as Canadian Joel Quarrington, advocate tuning the instrument in fifths. One of the most significant double bassists of the twentieth century was the Russian virtuoso Serge Koussevitzky, whose Concerto, Op. 3 is now standard repertory. Koussevitzky was also an important conductor, leading the Boston Symphony Orchestra from 1924 to 1949. Twentieth-century composers Lars Erik-Larsson, Gunther Schuller and Frank Proto have also written notable concertos. The American composer Paul Ramsier has devoted much of his career to writing for the double bass and has attempted through his work to give audiences a greater understanding of the musical potential of the modern bass. Other notable players and composers of the twentieth and twenty-first centuries include Gary Kerr, Bertram Turetzky and Edgar Meyer. Turetzky's *The Contemporary Contrabass* (1974) considers various contemporary techniques and expressive devices and how to realise them.

The double bass has also played a highly significant role in the development of JAZZ AND POPULAR MUSIC in the twentieth and twenty-first centuries. Both it and the TUBA were used in early New Orleans jazz. Bassists such as Pops Foster played the roots of chords, or the root and fifth, on beats one and three. As the instrument had the lowest volume in early jazz ensembles, bassists developed a slap technique, which allowed them to be heard more easily above other instruments. Walter Page was one of the first jazz bassists to walk a bass line or play scalar passages over chord changes on all four beats. Other significant jazz bassists include Oscar Pettiford, Jimmie Blanton, Charles Mingus and Paul Chambers.

Although the double bass is still a popular instrument for jazz, it has been replaced for the most part in rock and pop music by the electric bass. As early as 1924, Lloyd Loar developed a prototype of an electric upright bass. It was not mass-produced, but by the 1930s Rickenbacker, Gibson and Vega were all developing electric instruments, including basses. During the 1930s Paul Tutmarc Jr invented what is often considered to be the first electric bass, a fretted instrument made to be played horizontally. The first electric bass to be mass-produced was developed by Leo Fender in 1951. Electric basses were easier to transport and less prone to feedback than their acoustic counterparts. By the mid-1960s the electric bass had, for the most part, replaced the double bass in rock and popular music.

FURTHER READING

P. Brun, *A New History of the Double Bass* (Villeneuve d'Ascq: Paul Brun Productions, 2000).
R. Elgar, *Introduction to the Double Bass* (Princeton, NJ: Basso Continuum, 1960).
A. Planyavsky, *Die Geschichte des Kontrabasses* (Tutzing: Hans Schneider, 1984).

BRIAN SIEMERS

Dreyfus, Laurence (b. Boston, 28 July 1952) American viol player, cellist and musicologist, specialising in Bach and Wagner.

Dreyfus studied the CELLO with Leonard Rose at the Juilliard School and the VIOL with WIELAND KUIJKEN at the Brussels Conservatoire, and received his PhD (supervised by Christoph Wolff) at Columbia University. In 1992, he took up a chair in performance studies at King's College, London University in association with the ROYAL ACADEMY OF MUSIC. Two years later he founded the viol CONSORT Phantasm, whose activity relates to his practice-based research. The consort received a Gramophone Award for its debut CD of the Purcell fantasias and since then has travelled the world and made around twenty CDs of sixteenth- and seventeenth-century English music, including *William Byrd: Complete Consort Music* (2011) and *Lawes: Royal Consort* (2015). In 2005 Dreyfus joined Magdalen College, Oxford and Phantasm became consort-in-residence in 2010, collaborating and recording with the college choir on CDs such as *Ward: Fantasies and Verse Anthems* (2014) and *Tomkins Anthems and Canticles* (2016). In 1987, Dreyfus's meticulous study of surviving parts to J. S. BACH's vocal works bore fruit in his first book, *Bach's Continuo Group*. Here he examines the function of the ORGAN and HARPSICHORD, the accompaniment of recitatives, the role of the BASSOON, the CELLO, the challenging identity of the VIOLONE, the bass VIOL and the LUTE. In *Bach and the Patterns of Invention* (1996), Dreyfus explores J. S. Bach's compositional process and demonstrates in detail how he uses 'invention', which is then disposed, elaborated and decorated. He speculates about the order in which the inventions of a work are created and argues that through a thorough exploration of this process we as performers can use it to play a part in our interpretation of Bach's music. He gives an enlightening and thought-provoking analysis of the G minor Viol Sonata (BWV1029).

FURTHER READING

L. Dreyfus, *Bach's Continuo Group: Players and Practices in his Vocal Works* (Cambridge, MA: Harvard University Press, 1987).
Bach and the Patterns of Invention (Cambridge, MA: Harvard University Press, 1996).

LUCY ROBINSON

Duport, Jean-Louis (the younger) (b. Paris, 4 October 1749; d. Paris, 7 September 1819) French cellist and composer.

Jean-Louis Duport studied the CELLO with his older brother Jean-Pierre. He performed as a soloist and chamber musician in Paris, and was a friend of Viotti from 1782. The Revolution forced him to move to Berlin in 1790, where he played in the court orchestra with ROMBERG. Duport returned to France after the dissolution of the Berlin court in 1806, but could only find a post in Marseilles, and did not re-settle in Paris until 1812 when he joined the Imperial Chapel with Baudiot. He became professor at the CONSERVATOIRE in 1814, retiring when the institution was restructured in 1816. He wrote much for the cello including six concertos (passages from which were used by GUNN) and some twenty-four sonatas, but his most influential work was his *Essai sur le doigté du violoncelle et sur la conduite de l'archet* (Paris: Imbault, [c1806]), and its concluding collection of twenty-one studies. The *Essai* is quoted in later tutors as late as the mid-nineteenth century and was reprinted and translated into several languages – August Lindner even prepared a trilingual edition (Offenbach: André, [1864]). The studies, which are still in use, were edited by GRÜTZMACHER (Leipzig, c1895), Robert Hausmann (Leipzig, c1900), Hugo Becker (Hamburg: Simrock, c1921), Paul Bazelaire (Paris: Leduc, c1924) and others.

Duport's diatonic and chromatic scale FINGERING systems (the former anticipated by Gunn) eventually became standard. However, Duport considered his diatonic system, based on fingering a scale in successive groups of three notes, challenging for less advanced players, as the lack of open strings could lead to insecure intonation. His scales in thumb position remain on the upper two strings of the cello. Like DOTZAUER, he discusses HARMONICS and sympathetic vibration. Duport acknowledges that same-finger PORTAMENTO can help when playing difficult passages at sight, but only recommends it cautiously on musical grounds. However, he is almost unique in the nineteenth century in discussing different speeds of sliding between notes. Like Gunn, Duport deprecated the 'violinistic' left-hand shape used by Romberg. He apparently originally only wished to discuss fingering, but the section on BOWING ('quickly thrown down') was included after many requests. Duport recommended the Tourte bow, saying that everyone regarded it as a natural first choice. He gives many exercises with complex bowings including up- and down-bow staccato and describes a lifted bow-stroke ('*petit détaché*') in the upper part of the bow, rarely mentioned by other cellists.

FURTHER READING

S. Milliot, *Le violoncelle en France au XVIIIe siècle* (Paris and Geneva: Champion-Slatkine, 1985).
G. Kennaway, *Playing the Cello, 1780–1930* (Farnham: Ashgate, 2014).
V. Walden, *One Hundred Years of Violoncello* (Cambridge University Press, 1998).

GEORGE KENNAWAY

Dynamics *see* EXPRESSION

E

Early Music (Concepts of) Early music is a catch-all term. Most centrally, it applies to a particular repertoire of musical works, and a movement dedicated to the authentic and historical performance of this music. Broadly speaking, early music repertoire refers to any classical music where there is either an interrupted or lost interpretative tradition. The term 'early muisc' has to some extent fallen out of fashion, reflecting changes in approaches to the music involved and the role of the movement today. However, it remains associated with a range of key concepts and rhetorics relevant to historical performance, including early music repertoire, movement, industry, ensembles, training and festivals.

For most of the twentieth century, the German term *Alte Musik* held greater currency than its Anglicised form. *Alte Musik* denoted a rejection of the 'overheated emotionalism of the age of romanticism and the increasing secularism of the age' (Brown, in Kenyon, 36). Writing in 1954, NIKOLAUS HARNONCOURT summarised early music's developing agenda as ignoring the entire Romantic tradition of performance. He called for musicians to 'hear and perform [music] as if [it] had never been interpreted before, as though [it] had never been formed nor distorted' (in Kenyon, 4). As THURSTON DART pointed out in relation to BEETHOVEN's Ninth Symphony, the only instruments whose sounds had not changed since the symphony was first performed in 1824 were the kettle drum, the triangle and the trombone (T. Dart, *The Interpretation of Music* (London: Harper Collins, 1954), 34).

The RHETORIC surrounding early music has been lively and diverse, ranging from the movement's 'revolutionary' credentials, where those involved are seen as breaking away from the status quo; the 'commercial', in which early music is portrayed as little more than a promotional exercise to sell more records; the 'amateur', referring to the perspective held by some commentators and musicians that the standard of performance of early music was generally not as high as across the wider classical music profession; to the 'modernist' rhetoric, in which the movement's advocates are charged with making up a justification for the sounds they wanted to make.

Detailed discussion of early music is impossible without understanding more about the movement that bears its name. Accounting for when, where and how exactly the movement emerged is itself problematic. For Friedrich Blume, the movement stemmed from the BACH revival, sparked off by MENDELSSOHN's 1829 performance of the *St Matthew Passion* (F. Blume, *Two Centuries of Bach* (Oxford University Press, 1950)). ROBERT DONINGTON held that 'it all pretty much began, as such movements must, in a single man's visionary initiative' (in M. Campbell, *Dolmetsch: The Man and his Work* (London: Hamish Hamilton, 1975), ix–x); that man was ARNOLD DOLMETSCH (1858–1940). Elizabeth Roche takes Harry Haskell's history of *The Early Music Revival* (London: Thames & Hudson, 1988) to task for being 'too simplistic' in suggesting that 'everything that has happened in this field within the last 150-years plus can be seen as part of a definable "early music movement"' (Roche, 382).

Early music gained a particular momentum with the launch in 1967 of DAVID MUNROW'S EARLY MUSIC CONSORT OF LONDON. Munrow's influence as a performer and passionate advocate for early music was pervasive. Over and above his dazzling musicianship, he even had a hand in the launch of the Early Music Shop (which promotes the Early Music Festival and Exhibition in Greenwich). Founder Richard Wood recalls: 'we even sat down and talked about a name – because "early music" was not a generic term at that stage – and I can well remember the conversation we had. "Shall we call it *Old Music* or *Olde Music*?" We actually invented the name, and people like the *Early Music* magazine and even the *Early Music Centre* had to write to us for permission to use it' (Wilson, 100).

As a comparative term, *early* music has been used to refer to a widely different set of historical periods. During the 1950s and 1960s, early music denoted music primarily of the Medieval and Renaissance periods, no later than 1640. Performances by the likes of the Early Music Consort of London and Musica Reservata drew huge audiences, often comprising a string of short dance pieces (as many as sixty-five in some concerts). By the 1970s it referred to music composed in the Baroque era or earlier. During the 1970s there was an exponential rise in the number of instrument makers working in the field. The *Register of Early Music* listed sixty-two instrument makers in 1971, ninety-five by 1973, and a staggering 597 by 1976, many of whom were 'DIY enthusiasts'. By the 1980s, early music performances of MOZART, HAYDN, BEETHOVEN and other Classical or early Romantic composers were increasingly frequent. A decisive point for the movement was reached in 1986 with the launch of the ORCHESTRA OF THE AGE OF ENLIGHTENMENT (OAE). This group was distinctive for being player-led, rather than under the control and direction of a permanent artistic director. The OAE's association with conductor SIMON RATTLE, particularly performing Mozart operas at Glyndebourne, signalled the early music movement's 'coming of age' within the mainstream musical establishment in Britain. In practice, though 'HISTORICALLY INFORMED PERFORMANCE' (HIP) has become the preferred term, 'early music' now can take in almost any music where a historically appropriate style of performance is reconstructed on the basis of surviving instruments, treatises and other evidence. However, in doing so, it arguably 'painted itself into an ideological corner' on account of its practices being increasingly at odds with the drive to 'wipe the distortions of Romanticism from the face of the pre-Romantic repertory' (M. Dulak, 'The quiet metamorphosis of "Early Music"', *Repercussions*, 2/2 (1993), 45).

The list of prominent figures associated with early music in the formative years of the twentieth century (practitioners, musicologists, instrument makers, record company representatives, promoters) is far too extensive to include here (entries in this encyclopedia provide bibliographic background to some of them). From the point of view of the historical performance of instrumental music, it is not unreasonable to suggest that it was largely the Austrians and the Dutch who were the real pioneers of the modern revival, with English period instrument specialists following their lead some ten to twenty years later. Peter Phillips (The Tallis Scholars) argues that the early music 'revolution' had a rather different trajectory with regard to VOCAL PERFORMANCE: 'One of the reasons why the revolution in choral sound of the last thirty years has been so much slower to be accepted and appreciated for what it is, is just that it didn't have such a good story-line to sell it. We were obviously making it up. We couldn't fall back on historical evidence to boost our credentials' (P. Phillips, 'Hip replacements', *MT*, 155/1928 (2014), 99). Phillips also claims that the 'sound' associated with small professional mixed choirs had its origins in Britain, and has been successfully exported.

The extent to which early music represented a *coordinated* attempt to upset the status quo of musical performance as a unified movement is a matter of contention. Intriguingly, the first reference to a 'movement' of any kind in the journal *Early Music*, launched in 1973 by Oxford University Press, was not until 1975. The first mention of the 'early music movement' was not until 1977, in a piece devoted to the York Early Music Week. It is striking then to note that in RICHARD TARUSKIN's influential article on 'The limits of authenticity' in 1984 (R. Taruskin, 'The limits of authenticity', *EMc*, 12/1 (1984), 3–12), he uses the word 'movement' no fewer than thirteen times (though his term of choice is the 'authenticity movement').

One of the targets of Taruskin's critique was what might be thought of as the early music 'industry'. By the mid-1980s 'a huge industry connected to the revival of early music and HIP was blossoming' (J. Butt, *Playing with History* (Cambridge University Press, 2002), ix–x). To a significant extent, early music's successes were contingent on strong relationships between musicians, musicologists and representatives of record companies and BROADCASTING (especially the BBC). There was a very strong tie-up between many of the leading Oxbridge educated pioneers of historical performance musicology and those working for the BBC Music Department, who produced programmes for the Third Programme (later Radio Three) and the Proms.

With the benefit of hindsight it is not unfair to suggest that music colleges and conservatories in the twentieth century were initially slow to catch up with the developing wave of early music in professional performance. Today, however, nearly all have specialist departments, but have dropped 'early music' in favour of 'historical performance'. The label lives on in the market for early music instruments, and many early music festivals throughout the world. These range from very well-established and dedicated festivals (e.g. in Boston, Indianapolis, Innsbruck, Utrecht and York), to newer events in countries where interest in early music is still emerging.

FURTHER READING

H. Haskell, *The Early Music Revival: A History* (London: Thames & Hudson, 1988).
B. Haynes, *The End of Early Music* (Oxford University Press, 2007).
N. Kenyon, *Authenticity and Early Music* (Oxford University Press, 1988).

E. Roche, 'Early music: its revival and interpretation', M&L, 70/3 (1989), 382–4.

N. Wilson, *The Art of Re-enchantment. Making Early Music in the Modern Age* (Oxford University Press, 2014).

NICK WILSON

Early Music Consort of London British early music ensemble.

Founded in 1967 by DAVID MUNROW, the Early Music Consort of London gave its first concert in Leuven that year and made its London debut in 1968. Early members included Munrow on wind instruments, countertenor JAMES BOWMAN, viol player Oliver Brookes, keyboard-player CHRISTOPHER HOGWOOD and, from 1969, lutenist James Tyler. The group performed across the range of Medieval and Renaissance music using appropriate performing styles and a wide variety of instruments, and quickly gained success thanks to high levels of technical and musical polish and the charismatic energy of Munrow's leadership.

Munrow was sometimes criticised for his colourful instrumental scorings and showmanlike interpretations, but their attraction to non-specialist listeners made the group's performances both popular and influential in bringing new audiences to early music. The Consort made numerous recordings, many with appealing and intelligently realised themes such as 'Music of the Crusades', 'Two Renaissance Dance Bands', 'The Art of Courtly Love' and 'Instruments of the Middle Ages and Renaissance'. Soundtrack recordings for the high-profile BBC television series *The Six Wives of Henry VIII* (1970) and *Elizabeth R* (1971) also brought them to greater notice, and several new works were written specially for them, including Peter Dickinson's *Translations*, Elisabeth Lutyens's *The Tears of Night* and a role for stage band in Peter Maxwell Davies's opera *Taverner*. They also made forays into Baroque music with recordings of MONTEVERDI's contemporaries and two Purcell birthday odes. Although the group's performances tended at first to draw on the excitement of exotic instrumental colour, they later shifted their emphasis more towards voices, as in the acclaimed recordings of Dufay's Missa 'Se la face ay pale' and the collection 'The Art of the Netherlands', one of their last releases. The group ceased to function following Munrow's suicide in 1976.

FURTHER READING

D. Munrow, *Instruments of the Middle Ages and Renaissance* (London: Oxford University Press, 1976).

LINDSAY KEMP

Early Music in Europe

To 1880

Early music in Europe began, as it were, within itself. Among the first stirrings of special interest in the first quarter of the eighteenth century was the founding in London of the ACADEMY OF ANCIENT MUSIC, and other organisations to follow in its footsteps were the Madrigal Society and the CONCERTS OF ANTIENT MUSIC. The HANDEL centenary celebrations in Westminster Abbey in 1784 did much to fix a place in the repertoire for the composer's oratorios, which also found favour around the same time in Vienna, where

Gottfried van Swieten organised performances, some directed by W. A. MOZART. Van Swieten's promotion of the music of J. S. BACH – then a relatively forgotten figure – also exercised a powerful effect on Mozart. Bach's music was also championed from 1808 onwards in London concerts by Samuel Wesley, while influential semi-private events devoted to Renaissance and Baroque music were promoted in Vienna from 1816 by R. G. Kiesewetter and in Heidelberg by A. F. J. Thibaut; in Paris in 1816 CHORON founded the Institution Royal de Musique Classique et Réligieuse to promote fortnightly recitals of pre-Classical choral works. The groundbreaking performances of J. S. Bach's *St Matthew Passion* conducted by MENDELSSOHN at the Berlin Singakademie in 1829 did much to propel Bach's music for the first time into the domain of public and professional music making, not only spawning further presentations of the work in Germany and beyond, but also contributing to a significant surge of interest in the composer.

Before about 1830 few practitioners of earlier music had worried much about what would now be called 'HISTORICALLY INFORMED PERFORMANCE'. Mozart and Mendelssohn both adapted scores without compunction for the performing forces of their time, while interpretative styles in Renaissance polyphony were often dictated more by subjective notions of appropriate religious sentiment than by anything its composers could be shown to have been familiar with. The issue was addressed to a certain extent by figures such as FÉTIS – who in 1832 instigated at the PARIS CONSERVATOIRE a series of themed 'historical concerts' making use of original instruments such as LUTES, VIOLS and HARPSICHORDS – and the pianist MOSCHELES, who around the same time in London was playing Scarlatti and Bach on the harpsichord in public. And while BRAHMS edited freely for the many performances of pre-Classical choral music he conducted, his friend JOACHIM surprised the audience at a performance of Bach's B minor Mass at Eisenach in 1884 by using a modern replica of an oboe d'amore and a 'Bach trumpet'.

In general, however, the nineteenth-century early music revival was one of rediscovery and re-evaluation (assisted by a boom in published *intégrales* and anthologies and a growth in amateur choral singing that brought wider awareness of the Renaissance masters of the madrigal and sacred polyphony) rather than one that concerned itself with issues of performance practice.

1880–1945

The impetus for historical performance in Europe appears to have arisen out of a growing curiosity during the last decades of the nineteenth century for early instruments. International exhibitions in London in 1885 and Paris in 1889 both included displays and demonstration-performances on original and reconstructed examples. DIÉMER played the harpsichord at the Paris event, and subsequently formed a Baroque chamber ensemble, the *Société des Instruments Anciens*; and it was a concert involving original instruments from Fétis's private collection in Brussels in 1879 that fired the interest of the young DOLMETSCH.

Meanwhile early vocal music was beginning to flourish in England. Performances of Renaissance masters by Daniël de Lange's Amsterdam A Cappella

Choir at the London exhibition made a big impression, but in the early decades of the twentieth century the works of English Tudor composers in particular were advanced by scholars such as EDMUND FELLOWES, conductors such as Richard Terry (choir director at Westminster Cathedral from 1901) and choirs such as the English Singers and the Fleet Street Choir. Meanwhile Purcell's *Dido and Aeneas* had begun its rehabilitation in 1895 with the first modern staging (with 'additional accompaniments' by Charles Wood) by students from the ROYAL COLLEGE OF MUSIC under Stanford.

In France, developments focused at first on vocal music. In 1892 CHARLES BORDES, choirmaster at St Gervais in Paris, formed the Chanteurs de St Gervais, who enjoyed considerable success with concerts of Renaissance vocal music, as well as an annual Bach cantata series. In 1894, together with D'INDY and the organist Alexandre Guilmant, Bordes founded the Schola Cantorum, a teaching establishment that focused on the study of pre-Classical church music, but which also mounted performances of operas by MONTEVERDI, LULLY and RAMEAU, culminating in a staging of Rameau's *Castor et Pollux* in Montpellier in 1908; subsequently an opera society, La Petite Scène, was established to further this work.

Other ensembles to play on Baroque instruments included the Versailles-based chamber orchestra La Couperin (convened by instrument collector Eugène de Bricqueville) and the *Société des Instruments Anciens*, founded in 1901 by the violist HENRI CASADESUS (who, however, presented a repertoire largely consisting of forgeries). In 1903, WANDA LANDOWSKA began her career as the most influential harpsichordist of the first half of the twentieth century with her first public performance on the instrument in Paris. Important presences in Paris after WWI included Geneviève Thibault and her all-female Société de Musique d'Autrefois and, in the field of pre-Baroque vocal music, Jacques Chailley's Psalette de Notre Dame and de Van's Paraphonistes de St Jean-des-Matines.

The early 1900s also saw the creation of German Baroque instrumental ensembles such as the Deutsche Vereinigung für alte Musik (founded by gambist Christian Döbereiner), but after WWI early music activity in Germany tended to centre on scholarship and academic institutions. Following the lead of HUGO RIEMANN, who in 1908 started an informal Collegium Musicum at Leipzig University to perform Baroque music, similar groups were founded in other German universities; the one founded in Freiburg in 1922 by Wilibald Gurlitt included in its concerts not only Baroque but also chant and Medieval music, thought to have been among the first performances of this repertoire in Germany in modern times. Other contributors to the expansion of German early music making included the growth of interest in historic organs (whose influence spread widely throughout Europe), the rise of the RECORDER as an instrument for popular amateur use, the energetic revival of the music of Schütz, and the participation of choirs such as Karl Straube's Leipzig Thomanerchor, responsible for regular performances of Bach's church cantatas. The long road back to visibility for stagings of Handel's operas, too, began in earnest with the first (heavily edited) revival for nearly 200 years of *Rodelinda* at the inaugural Göttingen Festival in 1920.

Elsewhere in Europe the growth of early music between the wars was more haphazard, though there were performing organisations in Holland, Denmark, Finland, Czechoslovakia, Hungary, Poland and Spain. A notable figure was the American Safford Cape, whose Pro Musica Antiqua, formed in Brussels in 1933, gave admired performances of Medieval and Renaissance repertoire. Italy rediscovered Monteverdi with a concert performance of *Orfeo* in Milan in 1909, and Vivaldi in a 'Settimana Vivaldi' at the Accademia Musicale Chigiana in Siena in 1939. In Switzerland musicians such as gambist AUGUST WENZINGER and harpsichordist Fritz Neumeyer had made headway, but in 1933 one of the most significant events in the advancement of early music performing standards in Europe occurred with the founding in Basel by Wenzinger and Paul Sacher of a teaching institute 'to establish a lively interaction between musicology and performance': the SCHOLA CANTORUM BASILIENSIS.

The revolution in listening habits prompted in the first half of the twentieth century by the advent of recordings also worked well in the favour of early music, boosting the international reputations of many artists and making ever more 'forgotten' music familiar to a wider public. Several companies launched substantial historical anthologies, including Columbia's *History of Music by Ear and Eye*, Parlophone's *Two Thousand Years of Music* and *L'Anthologie Sonore*. From the 1920s onwards, BROADCASTING also played a major part in raising appreciation of early music, especially in Britain, Germany and France, where public service broadcasters served a richly educative mix of live events, recording and talks.

Post-1945

While formerly 'obsolete' instruments such as the harpsichord, lute and viol had played a part in early music performance almost from the beginnings of historically informed practice, most orchestras and ensembles still used those instruments which had not gone out of continuous use, such as the violin family and standard orchestral woodwind, in their modern developed form. This applied even to leading chamber orchestras, who in the decades around WWII were created largely to play Baroque- and Classical-period music, including Sacher's Basler Kammerorchester, the Boyd Neel Orchestra (later, under THURSTON DART, renamed the Philomusica of London), Renato Fasano's I Virtuosi di Roma, Karl Münchinger's Stuttgarter Kammerorchester, the Goldsbrough Orchestra (later English Chamber Orchestra), I Musici, MILAN MUNCLINGER's Ars Rediviva, the Jean-François Paillard Chamber Orchestra, Neville Marriner's Academy of St Martin in the Fields and Claudio Scimone's I Solisti Veneti, as well as in otherwise historically aware performances in the 1950s and 1960s conducted by the likes of ANTHONY LEWIS, CHARLES MACKERRAS, RAYMOND LEPPARD, Karl Richter, Karl Münchinger and Denis Stevens.

The move towards more thorough use of period instruments began in the 1950s, most influentially with the founding of CONCENTUS MUSICUS WIEN and the Leonhardt Consort. Even so, the modest number of available players and instruments meant that most period performances in the 1950s and 1960s tended to be for small to medium-sized ensembles rather than full Baroque or

Classical orchestras. Among these period pioneers were the Alarius Ensemble, EDUARD MELKUS's Capella Academica Wien and the quartet of GUSTAV LEONHARDT, FRANS BRÜGGEN, ANNER BYLSMA and JAAP SCHRÖDER.

It was perhaps rather in the performance of pre-Classical music – instrumental music in particular – that developments ran fastest in the 1950s and 1960s. Dutch recorder-player Kees Otten formed Muziekkring Obrecht in 1952 and Syntagma Musicum twelve years later and Konrad Ruhland founded Cappella Antiqua München in 1956. Medieval and Renaissance music was further enlivened in the 1960s by the importation of sounds and techniques derived from European and non-European folk music by THOMAS BINKLEY's STUDIO DER FRÜHEN MUSIK and by London-based MUSICA RESERVATA. The JULIAN BREAM Consort introduced many to the world of Elizabethan ensemble music, and DAVID MUNROW won a wide new audience for the pre-Classical repertoire with his EARLY MUSIC CONSORT OF LONDON, founded in 1967. Munrow was also influential in Britain in the later creation of THE CONSORT OF MUSICKE and Philip Pickett's New London Consort among others. Renaissance *a cappella* music had meanwhile been well served by, among others, the DELLER CONSORT, Grayston Burgess's Purcell Consort of Voices, David Wulstan's Clerkes of Oxenford (who carried out important experiments with pitch) and Pro Cantione Antiqua.

Holland and Belgium had become the main centre of gravity for period performance by the time SIGISWALD KUIJKEN founded LA PETITE BANDE as an orchestra in 1972, but it was perhaps something of Munrow's influence that led to Britain taking up the cause soon afterwards, with the formation in 1973 of its two first period orchestras, the ACADEMY OF ANCIENT MUSIC and THE ENGLISH CONCERT. Recording companies and broadcasters again played a large part in these developments: La Petite Bande was convened at the request of Harmonia Mundi, while the Academy of Ancient Music gained much of its early reputation from its recordings for Decca's specialist label L'Oiseau-Lyre.

Other larger period ensembles were formed as the 1970s progressed, including ANDREW PARROTT's Taverner Consort and Players, TON KOOPMAN's Amsterdam Baroque Orchestra and ROGER NORRINGTON's London Classical Players, while smaller groups emerged such as London Baroque, RENÉ JACOBS's Concerto Vocale and REINHARD GOEBEL's MUSICA ANTIQUA KÖLN. In 1979 JOHN ELIOT GARDINER switched his Monteverdi Orchestra to period instruments and renamed them the ENGLISH BAROQUE SOLOISTS. It was in the 1980s, however, that most of these grew to prominence along with newer arrivals such as THE KING'S CONSORT, the ORCHESTRA OF THE EIGHTEENTH CENTURY, the ORCHESTRA OF THE AGE OF ENLIGHTENMENT and Paul McCreesh's Gabrieli Consort & Players. Prominent smaller ensembles meanwhile included PETER HOLMAN's The Parley of Instruments, the Purcell Quartet, Trio Sonnerie and Fretwork.

France began to rediscover its interest in historical performance at this time too. Although a vocal/instrumental model had been around since the 1960s in Jean-Claude Malgoire's La Grand Écurie et la Chambre du Roy, the most influential ensemble of this kind was LES ARTS FLORISSANTS, a group founded by WILLIAM CHRISTIE in 1979 and particularly expert in French

Baroque music that would later inspire followers such as Marc Minkowski's Les Musiciens du Louvre, Hervé Niquet's Le Concert Spirituel, Christophe Rousset's Les Talens Lyriques and Emanuelle Haïm's Le Concert d'Astrée.

For choral music with orchestra all-male choirs of men and boys prevailed at first in Britain and Germany, where cathedral and collegiate traditions were strong, but from the mid-1980s onwards professional mixed-voice choirs became the customary choice even for Baroque and Classical music. Elsewhere, professional choral groups had been more common both with and without orchestra, but the founding of ensembles such as PHILIPPE HERREWEGHE's Collegium Vocale Gent and Harry Christophers's The Sixteen firmly established the precedent for such groups. Vocal consorts also flourished, notably Paul Van Nevel's Huelgas Ensemble, the HILLIARD ENSEMBLE, Peter Phillips's The Tallis Scholars, Dominique Visse's Ensemble Clément Janequin, Konrad Junghänel's Cantus Cölln, Andrew Carwood's The Cardinall's Musick and Robert Hollingworth's I Fagiolini. Medieval music, meanwhile, took a commercial boost from the success of Gothic Voices' hugely successful Hildegard of Bingen debut recording *Feather on the Breath of God* (1985); other leading European Medieval ensembles from this time included Ensemble Organum, SEQUENTIA, Ensemble Micrologus and the Dufay Collective.

The application of period principles to Classical and Romantic music developed significantly in the 1970s: Alan Hacker's MUSIC PARTY investigated the wind repertoire, Hausmusik followed in the 1980s, while early string quartets included the Esterhazy Quartet, and later the Salomon Quartet and QUATUOR MOSAÏQUES. The COLLEGIUM AUREUM was responsible for many period orchestra 'firsts' in the 1970s, and cycles such as the MOZART symphonies (CHRISTOPHER HOGWOOD), BEETHOVEN symphonies (Norrington) and Mozart piano concertos (Gardiner with fortepianist MALCOLM BILSON) were important milestones of the 1980s and early 1990s. Norrington, Gardiner, Jos Van Immerseel's Musica Aeterna, the Orchestra of the Age of Enlightenment and others have since extended period performance well into the nineteenth-century repertoire and beyond.

The 1990s saw the start of a wide geographical expansion beyond the heartlands of Britain, Germany, France and the Low Countries. Perhaps the most significant newcomers were the Italian Baroque orchestras; groups such as Sonatori de la Gioiosa Marca, Accademia Bizantina, Rinaldo Alessandrini's Concerto Italiano (which also functioned as a madrigal ensemble) and Giovanni Antonini's Il Giardino Armonico were all founded in the 1980s, but emerged more fully in the following decade, to be joined by Fabio Biondi's Europa Galante and Andrea Marcón's Venice Baroque Orchestra in doing much to revitalise their own musical heritage. By the turn of the century, period performance had reached most corners of Europe. In Spain JORDI SAVALL's versatile Hespèrion XX (later Hespèrion XXI) had been a distinguished presence since 1974, but new groups such as Eduardo López Banzo's Al Ayre Español and José Miguel Moreno's Ensemble La Romanesca now added to the mix; Cappella Savaria had been pioneers in Hungary since 1981, but elsewhere in Eastern Europe the fall of the Berlin Wall in 1989 allowed groups such as the Akademie für Alte Musik Berlin, the Polish orchestra Arte dei Suonatori and Collegium 1704 from the Czech Republic to emerge and flourish.

Prominent ensembles to appear in Scandinavia include the Drottningholm Court Baroque Ensemble and Concerto Copenhagen.

Other important developments in recent decades include increasing sophistication and freedom in continuo playing, in terms of both the number and variety of instruments used and the inventiveness of their players; among the results has been the creation of continuo-based ensembles such as Tragicomedia, The Harp Consort and L'Arpeggiata. The sounds and techniques of world music have also continued to play a part in performances of Medieval music by Hespèrion XXI, Ensemble Sarband, Oni Wytars and Joglaresa among others. And, led by the resurgence of interest in Handel starting in the early 1990s, Baroque opera productions reflecting historical practice (musically if not always dramaturgically) have increasingly made their way into the repertoires of the mainstream opera houses.

Among the most interesting developments in the early twenty-first century has been the growing contribution of 'modern orchestras' which have adapted to historical performance, whether symphony orchestras restoring Baroque music to their normal programming, or specially formed ensembles such as Combattimento, Claudio Abbado's Ensemble Mozart and the Berliner Barock Solisten.

FURTHER READING

H. Haskell, *The Early Music Revival: A History* (London: Thames & Hudson, 1988).

LINDSAY KEMP

Early Music in North America The first North American inklings of interest in earlier repertoire appeared with the HANDEL AND HAYDN SOCIETY (H+H), which was established in 1815 as a choral organisation to perform the oratorios of those masters. HAYDN had died only six years earlier, but the society's agenda still represented a conscious preservation of earlier music, as the ACADEMY OF ANCIENT MUSIC had attempted in London almost a century before. J. S. BACH was more slowly rediscovered, but there were various performances of the B Minor Mass in the late nineteenth century, culminating in the foundation of the Bach Choir of Bethlehem (PA) in 1898, which inspired the Baldwin Wallace Bach Festival, founded by Albert Riemenschneider in Cleveland in 1932, and the Carmel (California) Bach Festival, founded by Dene Denny and Hazel Watrous in 1935.

Interest in historical performance came later, spurred by the establishment of societies for the various instruments over the ensuing decades: the American Recorder Society was first established in 1939 with Suzanne Bloch, a DOLMETSCH disciple and daughter of Ernest Bloch, as the first president. The Viola da Gamba Society of America was founded in 1962 by George Glenn, and holds an annual conclave. The Lute Society of America came shortly afterwards, in 1966, and hosts annual summer seminars on alternating coasts (usually Vancouver and Cleveland). A national service organisation, Early Music America, was established in 1985 by Ben Peck and continues to promote earlier repertoires and historical performance across the continent. In 1988, the Historic Brass Society was founded by Jeffrey Nussbaum. Most of these societies produce publications, offer scholarships and/or promote competitions, and sponsor summer programmes.

By 1971, interest in historical instruments encouraged James Caldwell and Catharina Meints to establish the Oberlin Baroque Performance Institute (BPI), a summer teaching festival which originally built on regular conservatory faculty interest in historical instruments. Summer festivals then became a focus for introducing young musicians to early instruments, as well as providing ensemble opportunities for amateurs and professionals alike. In 1972 harpsichordist Albert Fuller established the Aston Magna Foundation at Bard College, devoted to researching and performing Baroque and Classical music on period instruments. The Amherst Early Music Festival, one of the largest summer teaching festivals, began at Hampshire College in Massachusetts in 1979, before moving to Amherst College and then elsewhere in New England. Early Music Vancouver (EMV, originally the Vancouver Society for Early Music), led from 1979 to 2013 by José Verstappen, has similarly offered summer teaching programmes. Some summer teaching festivals, such as EMV, have incorporated concerts with professional series that have extended into the regular concert season. Summer festivals that were established primarily to promote concerts include harpsichordist Frank Cooper's Festival Music Society (now Indianapolis Early Music) from 1966, Boston Early Music Festival and Exhibition (BEMF&E), founded in 1980 and the Berkeley Early Music Festival, initiated by Robert Cole and Joseph Spencer in 1990. Around that time in San Francisco, tenor and conductor Jeffrey Thomas helped to found the American Bach Soloists, a performing ensemble which established a summer academy in 2010.

There are early music societies throughout the continent, from Victoria (BC) to Phoenix to Miami, from Hilo (Hawaii) to Calgary to Milwaukee and Houston. Some prominent presenters include the pioneering Cambridge (MA) Society for Early Music, founded by Erwin Bodky in 1943. The success of that organisation helped establish Boston as a leading centre for early music, and led to BEMF&E becoming a significant operation. Pittsburgh's Renaissance and Baroque Society, founded by Colin Sterne, has presented artists in Synod Hall since 1969. The concert series Music Before 1800 was established at Corpus Christi Church in New York by Louise Basbas in 1975 and the Early Music Guild of Seattle (EMG) began in 1977. Also central to the field was Cleveland's Chapel, Court & Countryside concert series, established by Ross Duffin and Beverly Simmons, which ran at Case Western Reserve University from 1986 to 2011.

North America has a long tradition of leaders in the construction of early instruments. ARNOLD DOLMETSCH was a pioneer in this, dating to his time with the Chickering Piano Company in 1905–10, when he made some seventy-five early keyboard and stringed instruments. That was an isolated forerunner, but Dolmetsch was the teacher of John Challis, who returned from Haslemere in 1931 to set up his own harpischord-building shop in Ipsilanti, Michigan. Challis was interested in 'modernising' the HARPSICHORD, but his student William Dowd later became a leader in making historically based harpsichords, along with his colleague Frank Hubbard, who also studied at Haslemere. They later went their separate ways but both were extremely influential in harpsichord building according to historical principles. Other early keyboard building pioneers include Charles Fisk, who established the first historically oriented tracker ORGAN building firm in Massachusetts in 1961, and his apprentice John Brombaugh, who began his own firm in Ohio in 1968. Brombaugh's partners included George Taylor and John Boody, whose own firm was established in 1979, and his former apprentices include Paul Fritts and Bruce Fowkes (of Richards & Fowkes), all of whom are leaders in historical organ manufacture.

Other instrument-making pioneers include Friedrich von Huene, whose workshop was founded in 1960 and who designed historically based RECORDERS, including many production models for larger firms, as well as his own handmade instruments. Among his apprentices was Bob Marvin, a recluse in the Eastern Townships of Québec, and universally respected as a maker of Renaissance recorders. From 1978 Cathy Folkers and Ardal Powell made historical FLUTES, sparked by Powell's research into the history of the instrument. Ray Nurse, a mainstay of the early music making in Vancouver, is widely esteemed as a LUTE builder, having apprenticed with Ian Harwood, and Nurse's former apprentice, Grant Tomlinson, is an important lute builder in his own right.

North American instrument builders have had access to specimens for examination in many excellent collections. The instrument collection at the Metropolitan Museum in New York was established with donations from the Drexel and Brown families in 1889. It was curated for decades by Emanuel Winternitz and then Laurence Libin. Yale University's superb collection of historical keyboards began with the acquisition of Morris Steinert's collection in 1900 and the Boston Museum of Fine Arts began its collection with the purchase of Canon Francis Galpin's instruments in 1916. In Washington DC the Library of Congress has a collection of Stradivari instruments inaugurated by Gertrude Clarke Whittall in 1935, as well as an extraordinary collection of some 1,600 historical flutes, bequeathed by Dayton C. Miller in 1941. The Smithsonian Institution in Washington also boasts an important collection of early stringed instruments, including several Stradivari that were donated in 1998 by Herbert and Evelyn Axelrod and curated by Kenneth Slowik (also the director of Oberlin's BPI since 1993). A more recent (1973) impressive collection of 15,000 items is preserved at the National Music Museum (formerly the Shrine to Music) in Vermillion, South Dakota.

Early music ensembles in North America have included NOAH GREENBERG's pioneering NEW YORK PRO MUSICA (originally, the Pro Musica Antiqua), established in 1952-3 in emulation of the Pro Musica Antiqua of Brussels, founded in 1933 by Denver-native Safford Cape. The success of the Pro Musica inspired other ensembles such as the Waverly Consort, founded in 1963 by Michael and Kay Jaffee, and Early Music New York (formerly the New York Ensemble for Early Music), founded by former Pro Musica keyboardist Frederick Renz in 1974. Meanwhile the Boston Camerata began in the 1960s at the Museum of Fine Arts under HOWARD MAYER BROWN and others from Harvard, but from 1968 to 2008 was under the direction of Joel Cohen. It is now led by French singer Anne Azéma. THOMAS BINKLEY founded the STUDIO DER FRÜHEN MUSIK (Early Music Quartet) in Munich in 1960, including expatriate Americans Sterling Jones and later tenor Willard Cobb, then countertenor Richard Levitt, along with Estonian mezzo ANDREA VON RAMM. They opened up repertoires of Medieval music not previously explored in performance. During their residence at the SCHOLA CANTORUM in Basel, they also taught many future leaders of the early music movement, including Benjamin Bagby and Barbara Thornton, who founded the Medieval ensemble SEQUENTIA in 1977. Other expatriates who established early music ensembles in Europe include WILLIAM CHRISTIE, who founded LES ARTS FLORISSANTS in 1979; BRUCE DICKEY, who founded Concerto Castello c1980, and Concerto Palatino in 1987; Eric Hoeprich, a leading early CLARINET player who was a founding member of the ORCHESTRA OF THE EIGHTEENTH CENTURY and many other groups; and David Skinner, co-founder of The Cardinall's Musick in 1989 and founder of Alamire vocal consort in 2005.

North American ensembles breaking ground in special repertoires include the short-lived Musicans of Swanne Alley, led by PAUL O'DETTE and Lyle Nordstrom, and important for opening up the so-called broken consort repertoire, a tradition continued by the Baltimore Consort. A veteran of Swanne Alley, violinist David Douglass, later founded The King's Noyse, a pioneering Renaissance VIOLIN band. The Toronto Consort, founded in 1972 by David Klausner and Timothy McGee, and led since 1990 by David Fallis, performs a wide range of Medieval and Renaissance music for voices and instruments. VIOL consorts include the New England Consort of Viols, founded by Grace Feldman in 1973; Les Filles de Sainte Colombe, a 1980s consort featuring Wendy Gillespie, Sarah Cunningham and Mary Springfels; Les Voix Humaines, a Montreal duo founded in 1985 by gambists Susie Napper and Margaret Little; and Parthenia, founded in New York in 2002. Renaissance wind bands include Piffaro (originally the Philadelphia Renaissance Wind Band), founded by Robert Wiemken and Joan Kimball in Philadelphia in 1980, and Ciaramella, established in 2003 by Adam and Rotem Gilbert in Los Angeles. A wind band crossing over into the seventeenth century is Dark Horse Consort, led by trombonist Greg Ingles. Instrumental chamber ensembles performing later music include the seventeenth-century focused Quicksilver, led by violinists Robert Mealy and Julie Andrijeski, and Les Délices, founded by early reed player Debra Nagy to perform French music of the late Baroque and early Classical periods. These groups continue to unearth previously unexplored repertoire and perform it at an extraordinarily high level.

The earliest dedicated Baroque orchestra was the Clarion Concerts Orchestra, founded by Newell Jenkins in New York in 1958 and refounded as a period band in 2006 by Steven Fox. Other orchestras include Boston Baroque (originally Banchetto Musicale), founded in 1973–4 and led by Martin Pearlman, Toronto's TAFELMUSIK (1979), still the only full-time Baroque ensemble in North America, led for many years by American violinist Jeanne Lamon and famous in recent years for its memorised programmes designed by violone player Alison Mackay. Other pioneering orchestras include San Francisco's Philharmonia Baroque, founded by Laurette Goldberg in 1981 and directed since 1985 by NICHOLAS MCGEGAN, Smithsonian Chamber Players, established in 1981 by James Weaver and led since 1989 by Kenneth Slowik, and Apollo's Fire, founded by Jeannette Sorrell in Cleveland in 1992.

Baroque opera companies include the Boston Early Music Festival, led by Paul O'Dette and Stephen Stubbs; Toronto's Opera Atelier, created by Marshall Pynkosky and Jeannette Zingg in 1983, with music direction by David Fallis; and Opera Lafayette, in Washington DC, founded in 1995 by Ryan Brown.

Vocal ensembles include Pomerium, established in 1972 by Alexander Blachly, and focusing on choral music of the late Middle Ages and Renaissance; Studio de Musique Ancienne de Montréal, founded in 1974 by Christopher Jackson; Anonymous 4 (1992–2016), famous for close-harmony performances of a wide range of music (but especially Medieval); the Rose Ensemble, founded in St Paul, Minnesota in 1996 by Jordan Sramek, performing a wide range of music but with specialties in early Slavic and Hawaiian music; and Boston-based Blue Heron, established in 1999 by Scott Metcalfe, and specialising in sixteenth-century vocal polyphony.

Historical DANCE was represented from 1969 by the work of Ingrid Brainard and her Cambridge Court Dancers, pursuing her specialisation in courtly dance of the fifteenth century. Baroque dance specialist and historian Wendy Hilton taught at Juilliard from 1972 and during summers at Stanford University, training a generation of dance specialists such as Linda Tomko, Susan Bindig and Julie Andrijeski. Catherine Turocy studied under Shirley Wynne and formed the New York Court Dance Company in 1976, presenting historical dance performances, often in collaboration with the ensemble Concert Royal, led by James Richman.

North American soloists known for their performances of early music were inspired originally by the work of Arnold Dolmetsch in the first decades of the twentieth century, then later WANDA LANDOWSKA, beginning with her tour of 1923, and then after she emigrated from Nazi-held France in 1941. Landowska taught famous harpsichord scholar and player RALPH KIRKPATRICK and Canadian Kenneth Gilbert, who made his career in Europe. Also based in Europe is Mitzi Meyerson, who assumed the professorship in harpsichord at the Hochschule in Berlin in 1989. In that post she followed another Canadian, Bradford Tracy.

American lutenists include: Paul O'Dette, who trained at the Schola Cantorum, returning to teach at Eastman from 1976; Hopkinson Smith, who attended the Schola in 1973 and remained there as a teacher; and Robert Barto, former rock guitarist who established a career in Europe as a leading interpreter of late Baroque lute music, especially by Weiss and Hagen.

Vocal soloists of note include Judith Nelson, who was one of the early soprano soloists in the English Baroque revival of the 1970s and 1980s; Julianne Baird, whose scholarship on eighteenth-century vocal treatises has been complemented by her career as a soprano soloist; and Ellen Hargis, whose recitals with Paul O'Dette and collaboration with the Newberry Consort, among other groups, have been significant. Others include countertenor, David Daniels, a Handel specialist who debuted with the Metropolitan Opera in 1999; and Daniel Taylor, a widely recorded Canadian countertenor, who is now head of early music at the University of Toronto.

North American schools have also been important. PAUL HINDEMITH's pioneering Collegium Musicum at Yale University drew the attention of a wide musical public to earlier repertoires. His students included George Hunter, who ran a famous Collegium at the University of Illinois, as well as Albert Fuller, founder of Aston Magna, who was the only early music faculty member at Juilliard for decades. HOWARD BROWN led the Cambridge Society and other groups while a graduate student at Harvard, then went on to direct the

Collegium at the University of Chicago. Putnam Aldrich studied with Landowska, then established the early music performance practice programme at Stanford University, for many years the leading school in that field. Early music programmes were established at McGill University by Kenneth Gilbert in 1960, at Oberlin in connection with the Baroque Performance Institute in 1971, at Case Western Reserve in Cleveland in 1972, at Peabody Conservatory in Baltimore around 1980, at the University of Southern California in 1986 by lutenist James Tyler, and at Juilliard in 2009, led by violinist Robert Mealy. Some believe that the Juilliard programme has begun to 'legitimise' early music programmes in traditional music conservatories across North America.

Finally, radio has served to advance public understanding and appreciation of early music. Among pioneering programmes was *Chapel, Court & Countryside*, hosted by Joseph Spencer, first in Los Angeles and then in Berkeley; *Millennium of Music*, hosted by Robert Aubrey Davis, begun in 1975 and syndicated in 1990; *Micrologus: Exploring the World of Early Music*, the first nationally syndicated programme devoted to early music (in 1981); and *Harmonia*, hosted by Angela Mariani, begun in 1991 and nationally syndicated in 1995.

FURTHER READING

H. Haskell, *The Early Music Revival* (London: Thames & Hudson, 1988).
T. F. Kelly, *Early Music: A Very Short Introduction* (New York: Oxford University Press, 2011).

ROSS DUFFIN

Early music in the digital age In recent decades the music business has been reshaped by the rise of digital media (here defined as machine readable data that can be transmitted online). The recording industry, which in the 1970s and 1980s supported the boom in historical performance, has now been partly supplanted by online audio streaming. Yet performers of early music have benefited from digitisation unlocking access to many of the musical sources that inspire and inform their work. Such expanding digital horizons open new opportunities, yet can also undermine the role of scholarly authority in historical performance.

Digitisation

Since the late 1990s large-scale projects have collected and archived digital images of sources from many locations. The Digital Image Archive of Medieval Music (www.diamm.ac.uk) contains high-quality scans of polyphonic manuscripts to c1550. Music also features in digitisation projects of broader scope: Early English Books Online (http://eebo.chadwyck.com) includes scans from microfilm of most English printed music before 1700.

Digitisation is increasingly led by research libraries aiming to make their collections more accessible. Notable are the digital archives developed by the Bibliothèque Nationale, Paris (http://gallica.bnf.fr, documenting France's cultural heritage); the Bayerische Staatsbibliothek, Munich (www.bsb-muenchen.de, rich in printed music from the sixteenth century onwards); the Sächsische

Landesbibliothek, Dresden (http://digital.slub-dresden.de, including seventeenth-century Lutheran music and the Schrank II collection of eighteenth-century instrumental repertory); and the Museo internazionale e biblioteca della musica in Bologna (www.bibliotecamusica.it) with notable holdings of Italian printed music of the sixteenth to seventeenth centuries.

Some sites present digitised sources for a specific composer's output, often including lists of works and concordances, as with BACH Digital for members of the Bach family (www.bach-digital.de). The Online Chopin Variorum Edition contains facsimiles of nineteenth-century printed and manuscript sources, with variants displayed when the user clicks on any individual bar of music (www.chopinonline.ac.uk).

These online repositories democratise access to many of the primary sources of pre-1900 music. Digital surrogates can be consulted by multiple readers worldwide, with no conservation restrictions. They allow users to magnify details too small for the naked eye, and may permit the digital enhancement of damaged or illegible sources. Yet digitisation can diminish awareness of the aura and material format of the original; it may also lead musicians to overlook non-digitised sources, which now seem less accessible.

The full value of digitised sources can be realised only when they are accompanied by high-quality metadata (catalogue descriptions). A few digitisation projects have included upgrades of metadata. The British Library's Early Music Online not only digitised sixteenth-century anthologies but also provided inventories, allowing compositions within these books to be easily located (www.earlymusiconline.org). The Düben Collection Database Catalogue combined re-cataloguing and digitisation of this manuscript collection at Uppsala University Library (www.musik.uu.se/duben/Duben.php). Currently no union catalogue exists of digitised early music. Recently RISM (Répertoire internationale des sources musicales) released online many of its catalogues of printed and manuscript music (http://opac.rism.info), but these records only sometimes link to digitised sources. Moreover, the RISM databases for the United Kingdom and Switzerland remain on separate systems. Whereas much digitisation is led by local or national initiatives using customised platforms or databases, many users would prefer digital content to be consolidated in a single location for ease of access.

Editions

The authority of scholarly editing has recently been challenged by a proliferation of online editions. Pioneers in this field included music-loving computer scientists such as Werner Icking (1943–2001), who shared music-processing files online. By the early 2010s such TRANSCRIPTIONS became consolidated in two main sites, the Choral Public Domain Library (www.cpdl.org) and the International Music Score Library Project (www.imslp.org). Both are run on a wiki basis, inviting all users to contribute: consequently, the quality is uneven, including non-scholarly transcriptions by enthusiasts alongside scans of nineteenth-century complete EDITIONS (such as the Bach-Gesellschaft edition or Friedrich Chrysander's Handel edition). Because of copyright restrictions, modern scholarly editions are rarely available on such sites, and this has reduced their visibility among performers. Musicians should thus approach online editions with caution and discrimination. In response, some specialist sites are making refereed critical editions available online, as with the Web Library of Seventeenth-Century Music (www.sscm-wlscm.org).

Music publishers have found their profitability threatened by the free availability of online editions, but can also learn from these new models for dissemination. A future ideal might be editions in dual format: a scholarly copy for the library shelf, and an electronic performing version. Indeed, Stainer & Bell sells electronic offprints for individual compositions from the series Early English Church Music.

A truly digital edition is not a static document, but uses digital tools or formats such as presenting the musical text in XML (eXtensible Markup Language) following the rules of the Music Encoding Initiative (http://music-encoding.org). Such texts can be dynamic, capable of being customised for users or updated to reflect new discoveries; they can be linked to other data such as facsimile images or critical reports; and they can be searched to locate melodic or harmonic features. Digital editions were pioneered by the Computerized Mensural Music Editing Project (www.cmme.org), where the user can choose the degree of notational modernisation in editions of Renaissance polyphony. The Lost Voices project (http://digitalduchemin.org/) uses MEI to compare reconstructions of missing voice parts of sixteenth-century chansons. Aruspix (www.aruspix.net), developed by Laurent Pugin, is a system of optical music recognition for typeset music of the sixteenth century; it can convert an image into an XML music file, and can carry out collation (to show the typographical differences between individual copies). The Electronic Corpus of Lute Music (www.ecolm.org) has applied optical character recognition to printed TABLATURES, and has crowd-sourced members of the UK's Lute Society to check its encodings. A challenge for these digital editions is to show how they can be sustained beyond their academic sponsors, and to secure their durability in a fast-changing technological world.

Other digital transformations

The November 2014 and November 2015 issues of *Early Music* showcased a range of digital projects that are transforming the field: computer tomography and 3D printing to analyse and copy antique instruments; signal processing techniques to analyse keyboard temperaments; computer-aided analysis of compositional or notational features; and Big Data analysis of the bibliographical records for early repertories. Although such initiatives may require specialist computing skills, they also offer new ways for historically informed performers to link past traditions with present-day concerns.

FURTHER READING

T. Dumitrescu, K. Kügle and M. van Berchum (eds.), *Early Music Editing: Principles, Historiography, Future Directions* (Turnhout: Brepols, 2013).
  'Early Music and Modern Technology', special issue of *EMc*, 42/4 (2014).
  'Early Music and Modern Technology II', special issue of *EMc*, 43/4 (2015).

STEPHEN ROSE

Early Music Quartet *see* STUDIO DER FRÜHEN MUSIK

Early recordings The record industry has been influential in promoting historical performance since the 1920s. As well as promoting new styles, recordings (especially up to the 1920s) preserve many older styles now superseded.

THOMAS EDISON invented the first device able to record and replay sound in 1877. His PHONOGRAPH focused sound pressure onto a needle, which cut a groove in a rotating cylinder. The groove stored an analogue representation of the sound wave. Rotating the cylinder with the needle tracking the groove reproduced the sounds, albeit with much reduced quality. A similar process applied to a wax disc introduced the gramophone to the public in 1895. Few recordings of classical music survive from before 1897, though an important exception is a poor-quality recording of BRAHMS playing the piano in 1889.

It is important to understand what early recordings could and could not reproduce. At first recording was restricted to loud sounds in the frequency band between around 100 Hz and 4000 Hz. This enabled recording of the fundamentals of musical pitches but of only the lowest of their partials. Recording horns (which focused sound onto a diaphragm to drive the needle) tended, individually, to strengthen and weaken specific frequency bands. Thus voices and instruments on early recordings sound different in tone from their modern equivalents; some (though not all) of this is due in varying degrees to the recording process. Because the earliest machines required performances to be as loud as possible, little subtlety was available to the performer in terms of DYNAMICS. All these limitations were eased gradually up to 1925, when the introduction of new technology (the microphone and electrical amplification) offered immediate and significant improvement. From here it became possible to record all orchestral instruments, many of which had previously been replaced by more penetrating substitutes.

During the acoustic era (pre-1925) the 78 rpm shellac disc became the standard recording medium. The speed 78 rpm was a notional one: many discs were recorded faster or slower, and the recording speed cannot normally be known today. Thus speed and therefore pitch may sometimes be misrepresented in modern transfers. At first discs generated much surface noise but this reduced somewhat up to the end of the shellac era, allowing greater subtlety in performance nuance to become audible. Discs were limited in duration until the introduction of the long-playing vinyl disc in 1948. Before then typical durations were three minutes for 10-inch discs and four and a half minutes for 12-inch discs. Examples survive of performances that were obviously speeded up to fit onto one side of a disc, but normal practice was to split longer performances across two or more sides, often with newly composed cadences or *ritardandos* at the end of each side (the ritardandi tend to survive in modern digital transfers and need to be allowed for in commenting on performance style). These problems largely disappear with the introduction of the long-playing, 33⅓ rpm disc.

An advantage of early recording technology for students of performance practice is that editing performances was impossible until the introduction of magnetic tape after 1945. An exception was the piano roll (see Peres da Costa, 2012). Recordings up to that date preserve a performance made in one unedited take. Serious mistakes would lead to a further take being recorded, but the prevalence of mistakes by performers suggests that performers and listeners were less concerned than we are by slips. Once editing became possible, however, it became commonly employed and is believed by many to have been the driver behind the focus on accuracy that has occupied musicians since c1950.

Early recordings show indisputably that performance style changes greatly over time, to the extent that what is considered musical in the early twenty-first century is in many respects opposite to what were considered musical ideals c1900. A consequence is that recorded evidence from the past can seem somewhat unpalatable, notably recordings of musicians whose training dates back to the 1840s to 1870s – Carl Reinecke (1824–1910) recorded in 1905 on Welte-Mignon reproducing piano rolls, or violinist JOSEPH JOACHIM, recorded on disc in 1903. Although these musicians were elderly when recorded, there are stylistic consistencies among recorded musicians born before c1870 evidencing a mid- to later nineteenth-century performance style in which musicians speeded up between phrases, varied the extent of synchronisation between parts, spread chords, varied TEMPO from note to note (RUBATO), and used extensive PORTAMENTO (but only to a small extent VIBRATO) as essential tools in expressive or nuanced performance. The amount of recorded evidence is such that we must conclude that these practices, though unacceptable today, were considered ideal by performers, expected by composers and illustrated by composer-performers such as Grieg and Debussy.

With performers born in and after the 1870s, non-synchronisation, rubato, RHYTHMIC ALTERATION and portamento began to decline, albeit slowly; and in their place vibrato becomes gradually wider, slower and continuous, and a regular relationship between tempo and loudness became established, in which phrases tend simultaneously to get faster and louder or slower and quieter, together. This new alliance is used to define structural phrases in compositions (Cook, 2013). Volume thus appears to become a more important ingredient in performance nuance. However, at the same time recording was becoming more sensitive to differences in DYNAMICS, and thus there may have been more subtle use among older musicians than is audible to us. The increasing interest in making composition structure audible may have developed in the first half of the twentieth century alongside an increasing concern with music analysis.

Significant and widespread stylistic changes happened after WWII, as a new generation focused attention on vibrato and dynamics as the main carriers of performance expressivity. It was this sound world to which 'historically informed performance' reacted in the 1970s and thereafter, regarding it as overly 'romantic', although in fact it had little historically to do with Romanticism. Regularity, precision and consistency, features of Modernism, became (and currently remain) overriding virtues in professional performance.

As well as period changes, there were also national differences audible 100 years ago. At least four national styles of FLUTE playing have been identified among early recordings (Dolan, 2010). German, English, French, Russian and Italian approaches to vocal production were substantially different. Elements of this distinctiveness remain in singing, but in instrumental playing only facets of Russian pianism show signs of being recognisably distant from a homogeneous international style at the moment. Furthermore, performers were notably individual a hundred or more years ago: generalisations about period style must take into account the greater differences between personal styles to which the earliest recordings bear witness.

It follows that early recordings have implications for modern reflection on historical performance and its practice. Recorded sound preserves performance styles at a level of detail that textual description cannot equal. This helps to explain the wide discrepancies between modern 'historically informed performance' of nineteenth-century scores and the recorded evidence, features of which could not have been anticipated from the written documentation. These discrepancies demand attention, with performers heeding the evidence of non-synchronisation, frequent rubato and frequent portamento, techniques that may also have been in use long before recording began (Reinecke's performances of MOZART are provocative in this respect).

Equally significant are the implications for today's interpreters of a composer's scores. Despite their greater rubato and portamento, early recorded performances are often lighter than we would expect: faster, less regular, less serious than is acceptable today. BRAHMS is an interesting example, a composer whose music we approach with reverence and imagine as weighty, sonorous and profound. Yet in the hands of musicians he chose to represent him in the 1880s and 1890s he sounds light-hearted and fantastical, thanks to fast speeds, constantly varying tempi and non-synchronised parts. Modern performers can thus seem quite mistaken in their beliefs about his intentions and about the nature of his music. Such a case severely tests beliefs about obligations to composers and our ability to discern what belongs to their music.

Recent projects emulating performances from early recordings (Slåttebrekk and Harrison, 2010, on Grieg; Scott, 2014, on Brahms) reveal many historical principles for modern performers who wish to play historically, while allowing, with the safety net of historical correctness, alternative approaches to nuance. Yet the wide differences between past and present styles, and among performers a hundred years ago, all documented in recordings, show that scores still have the dangerous potential to be performed in ways yet to be imagined and attempted.

FURTHER READING

N. Cook, *Beyond the Score* (New York: Oxford University Press, 2013).
A. Dolan, 'Landmarks in flute performance style in 78 rpm recordings 1900–1950', PhD dissertation, King's College London (2010).
N. Peres da Costa, *Off the Record: Performing Practices in Romantic Piano Playing* (New York: Oxford University Press, 2012).
A. Scott, 'Romanticizing Brahms: Early recordings and the reconstruction of Brahmsian identity', PhD dissertation, University of Leiden (2014).
S. Slåttebrekk and T. Harrison, *Chasing the Butterfly: Recreating Grieg's 1903 Recordings and Beyond*. www.chasingthebutterfly.no/ (2010).

DANIEL LEECH-WILKINSON

Edison, Thomas Alva (b. Milan, OH, 11 February 1847; d. West Orange, NJ, 18 October 1931) American inventor.

Edison was a major figure in the development of recorded sound. He invented the PHONOGRAPH (1877), the first device to record and reproduce sound. The first phonographs proved inadequate for commercial use and were never more than exhibition devices. Spurred on by the work of other inventors, Edison resumed work on the phonograph in 1887. By 1889, he and his West Orange laboratory staff produced an improved machine that recorded on wax cylinders.

Edison's and other early phonographs were primarily marketed for dictation rather than for recording music. None the less, Edison envisioned a market for music recordings. His laboratory staff experimented extensively to improve the technology for music and developed wax cylinders designed especially for this purpose. Most importantly, Edison worked on a method for moulding and duplicating records in anticipation of becoming a record manufacturer. His laboratory also became the first recording studio, making hundreds of music recordings between 1888 and 1891, including many for the Exposition Universelle in Paris (1889).

Although recordings of music became more popular in the 1890s with the development of nickel-in-slot amusement phonographs, Edison remained primarily a manufacturer of phonographs until the late 1890s. As improvements in phonograph technology drove down the price of machines and created a growing market for recorded sound, Edison resumed his efforts to develop a commercial record duplication process, finally succeeding in 1901. During the first few years of the twentieth century, Edison was the industry leader, but by the end of the decade was falling behind competitors, especially the Victor Talking Machine Company and its disc gramophone and records. In response, Edison developed his own disc phonograph and records but he focused on creating the highest fidelity sound. To secure recognition for his new technology, he selected artists based on their recording abilities rather than their musical reputations and he also played a major role in the selection of repertoire. As a consequence, Edison became known for recording less popular artists and music; by 1929, facing new competition from radio, he left the music business.

FURTHER READING

L. DeGraaf, 'Confronting the mass market: Thomas Edison and the entertainment phonograph', *Business and Economic History*, 24/1 (1995), 88–96.
P. Israel, *Edison: A Life of Invention* (New York: John Wiley & Sons, 1998).
E. Thompson, 'Machines, music, and the quest for fidelity: marketing the Edison phonograph in America, 1877–1925', *MQ*, 79/1 (Spring 1995), 131–71.

PAUL ISRAEL

Editing/editions Musical editing, as traditionally conceived, is a process of mediation between existing written witnesses of a musical 'text' or 'work' and a printed (or, in recent years, digital) publication. The term is sometimes used as an analogy for the remediation or documentation of audiovisual sources. Any editing is the result of a critical process: it necessitates a whole series of decisions on the part of the editor(s) regarding the selection, organisation and reproduction of its material base.

The initial impetus for editing music of earlier periods – as opposed to the publication of contemporary repertoire – is found in the historicism of the nineteenth century, where an interest in the rediscovery of music of bygone periods emerged. Virtually from the beginning, different kinds of editions evolved which reflect the different attitudes by editors to the historical record and its function. These are in principle the types still encountered today. Some editions were intended as antiquarian monuments, to record canonical repertoire to be venerated and preserved for posterity (usually in large representative multi-volume editions often ill-suited to actual practice); some were pedagogical or instructive, explicitly adapting and annotating the musical text to facilitate the rediscovery of repertoire through musical performance. Starting with the *Bach Gesellschaft* in 1851, methods of source-critical philology found their way into musical editing; and from the late nineteenth century, so-called URTEXT editions sought to combine critical authority with accessibility for performers. In contrast, diplomatic editions aimed to reproduce every aspect of a single source perceived as authoritative.

The emerging and lasting consensus that historically aware performers as well as scholars should use 'authoritative' editions has resulted in a standard of critical editions based on the oldest and best sources. As in editions of verbal text, the critical approach underlying music editions can follow the 'best text' method, after the French medievalist Henri Bédier (1864–1938), or the 'stemmatic' method established by German classicists and biblical scholars in the early nineteenth century. Where clearly accredited sources exist – such as autographs or authorised first editions – the best-text approach is often the most appropriate, whereas the stemmatic process (the reconstruction of a hypothetical archetype through recension and collation, and evaluation of all extant witnesses by way of identifying and classifying separative and conjunctive errors) is used where directly authorised sources no longer exist, or never existed. This applies mostly to music of earlier periods: pioneering use of the stemmatic method has been made in CHANT scholarship and the *New Josquin Edition*.

Regardless of the degree of philological ambition, editions of notated music have always differed from most editions of verbal texts insofar as their implied readership has included practitioners, as opposed to (or in addition to) silent readers or scholars. This requires a greater degree of adaptation or 'translation' (Bent, 1994) of the original notation to facilitate legibility by modern recipients. The resulting notational gap to be bridged is the greater the earlier the repertoire, but also affects eighteenth- and, up to a point, nineteenth-century compositions. This implies processes of normalisation (converting parts or TABLATURE into score, arrangement of voices, barring, cleffing, proportional reduction of note values, converting mensural into rhythmic notation, etc.) as well as completion or adaptation (complementing and aligning ARTICULATION and DYNAMICS, specifying the TEXT UNDERLAY, realising the FIGURED BASS).

In recent years this process of translation has come under increased scrutiny, with a concurrent tendency to produce editions that reproduce as closely as possible the graphic choices of the original. This tendency is driven by performers and scholars who argue that in order to read the music with true understanding and empathy, one has to engage with the visual and textual manifestation of the original; some indeed have rejected translation-through-editing altogether and perform directly from original NOTATION, whether fifteenth-century manuscripts or eighteenth-century engraved parts. Simulating the 'original' reading experience has its rewards: the performers themselves become the editors, as it were, translating the written text into sound without the intervening mediation of a printed modern score. But it comes at the cost of being able to engage with one witness only, and its success is much dependent on the expertise of the musicians; it can be 'informed', but not 'critical' in a philological sense.

Another issue affecting the edition of music regards the status one accords its witnesses. The concept of editing, especially critical editing, has traditionally assumed an attitude towards textuality, authoriality and the work that allows the distinction between right and wrong, or at least between more or less credible variants when comparing the written testimonies; stemmatics in particular is based on the concept of error. However, the greater fluidity of attitudes towards authorship and textual fixity that we now tend to ascribe to earlier periods of music history in particular – and which are inextricably linked to the performative implications of the notation – lends itself less easily to such apodictic judgements. The acknowledged existence of genuinely equivalent readings or entire versions, of 'background variation' in the notational detail, of mnemonic rather than fully prescriptive types of notation more generally, cast doubt on the idea of privileging one reading by including it in the main text while relegating the others to the critical notes. Musical editing is still searching for rigorous and at the same time pragmatic ways of presenting the musical text that do justice to its specific nature. Digital editions which can present very effectively alternative readings (and indeed alternative ways of visual representation) may offer solutions here, but issues of editorial control avoiding the arbitrary conflation of incompatible readings have not yet been satisfactorily resolved.

FURTHER READING

M. Bent, 'Editing early music: the dilemma of translation', *EMc*, 22 (1994), 373–92.
J. Caldwell, *Editing Early Music* (Oxford University Press, 1995).
M. Caraci Vela, *Musical Philology. Institutions, History, and Critical Approaches*, I: *Historical and Methodological Fundaments of Musical Philology* (Pisa: ETS, 2015).
G. Feder, *Music Philology. An Introduction to Music Textual Criticism, Hermeneutics, and Editorial Technique*, trans. B. C. McIntyre (Hillsdale: Pendragon Press, 2011).
J. Grier, *The Critical Editing of Music: History, Method, and Practice* (Cambridge University Press, 1996).

THOMAS SCHMIDT

Eichentopf, Johann Heinrich (b. Stollberg, *c*1678; d. Leipzig, 30 March 1769) German maker of woodwind and brass instruments.

Eichentopf's name appears for the first time in the Leipzig city archives in 1707 as 'demobilised soldier' (*abgedankter Soldat*). He married in the Thomaskirche in 1710, when he was described as 'flute maker' (*Instrumentalischer*

Pfeiffenmacher), and retired in 1749. Some of the godparents of his eight children and grandchildren were celebrated instrument makers, such as the luthier Johann Christian Hoffmann, who was also a dear friend of JOHANN SEBASTIAN BACH, and the brass instrument maker Christoph Stephan Scheinhardt.

Eichentopf was active as an instrument maker between 1710 and 1749. He made OBOES, OBOES D'AMORE and OBOES DA CACCIA, BASSOONS (among them an octave and a quart bassoon), FLUTES, RECORDERS, TRUMPETS, TROMBONES and natural HORNS; he may have made stringed instruments as well. In an inventory of the *Köthener Hofkapelle* (1773), five instruments by J. H. Eichentopf are listed, among them a VIOLA dated 1726. These instruments are lost and no other stringed instruments by Eichentopf are known to have survived.

Legend has it that J. S. Bach, during his employment as *Kapellmeister* at the Thomaskirche, suggested that Eichentopf should make an oboe da caccia, the instrument of which Bach would make frequent use. However, Johann Kaspar Gleditsch, Bach's principal oboist, had been playing oboe da caccia at least one year before Bach arrived in Leipzig (1723). Two oboes da caccia by Eichentopf have been preserved, both stamped 1724, which are distinctive because of their brass bell, imitating the corno da caccia, an instrument that he also manufactured. Eichentopf is also reputed to have invented a special kind of tuning device, built into the cork of an ivory flute.

Eichentopf is classified as one of the most important Leipzig wind instrument makers. His instruments are of high quality and fine craftsmanship.

FURTHER READING

W. Jansen. *The Bassoon, its History, Construction, Makers, Players and Music* (Buren: Frits Knuf, 1978), 364–5.

P. Rubardt, 'Johann Heinrich und Andreas Eichentopf', in *Wissenschaftliche Zeitschrift der Humboldt-Universität zu Berlin, Gesellschafts- und sprachwissenschaftliche Reihe*, 15 (1966), 411–13.

W. Waterhouse, *The New Langwill Index: A Dictionary of Musical Wind-Instrument Makers and Inventors* (London: Bingham, 1993), 103–4.

WOUTER VERSCHUREN

Eigeldinger, Jean-Jacques (b. Neuchâtel, Switzerland, 9 March 1940) Professor emeritus of musicology, University of Geneva.

Besides a critical edition of JEAN-JACQUES ROUSSEAU's *Dictionnaire de musique* (Paris: Chez la veuve Duchesne, 1768) and several publications devoted to Stephen Heller, Eigeldinger's large bibliography is mainly centred on mid-nineteenth-century France and Chopin. His primary impact on performance practice comes from *Chopin vu par ses élèves* (*Chopin, Pianist and Teacher*), a detailed and annotated compilation of Chopin's teaching and playing as recounted by Chopin's students and associates; this offers radical revisions to twentieth-century Chopin performing habits, notably as regards Chopin's insistence on simplicity and clarity of musical line and diction, ease and fluidity in performance and retention of early Classical (or *bel canto*) usages in ORNAMENTATION, with trills normally starting on the dissonant note and grace-note figurations on the beat. Several augmented re-editions have appeared in French, as well as in English, Polish, Italian, Chinese and Japanese translations.

Related books are Eigeldinger's annotated first complete edition of Chopin's project for a teaching method (French, Polish), studies of Chopin in relation to Parisian salons and to his PIANO maker Pleyel, plus two general surveys (*L'Univers musical de Chopin* and *Frédéric Chopin*, both translated into several languages). A pioneer in the study of composers' annotated scores, Eigeldinger has published numerous facsimile volumes, including newly discovered Chopin manuscripts, Jane Stirling's integral collection of Chopin scores showing Chopin's performing indications, and Chopin's own annotated score of BACH's '48'. A chapter of *L'Univers musical de Chopin* links Chopin's practices to the various European HARPSICHORD schools; other studies consider Liszt and Schumann relative to Bach. Eigeldinger's 2016 publication *Chopin and Baroness Nathaniel de Rothschild* (Polish, French, English) clarifies long-standing mysteries about a nocturne and waltz apparently from Chopin's last years, revealing them to be Chopin's elaboration of pieces by his pupil Charlotte de Rothschild; it also presents a hitherto unknown version of Chopin's own Mazurka, Op. posth. 67 No. 4.

Eigeldinger is a founding editor of the Peters Edition *Complete Chopin: A New Critical Edition*, for which he edited all the Preludes. While never aspiring to a concert career, he is a fine pianist who can give revealing performances at lecture presentations, and has given memorable masterclasses.

FURTHER READING

J.-J. Eigeldinger, *Chopin vu par ses élèves* (Neuchâtel: La Baconnière, 1970; rev. edns. 1979, 1986, 2006); trans. N. Shohet, K. Osostowicz and R. Howat as *Chopin, Pianist and Teacher* (Cambridge University Press, 1986).

(ed.), *Stephen Heller, lettres d'un musicien romantique à Paris* (Paris: Flammarion, 1981).

(ed.), *Interpréter Chopin. Actes du colloque des 25 et 26 mai 2005* (Paris: Cité de la Musique, 2006).

ROY HOWAT

Eingang A short improvised link in a concerto movement or aria, most commonly before the return of the principal theme, especially in rondos.

The term *Eingang* (lead-in) is used particularly by MOZART. It differs from a CADENZA not only in its shorter length but also in its linguistic function. Whereas a cadenza begins upon the orchestra's arrival on the tonic $^6_4$ and ends with a trill by the soloist that resolves into the re-entry of the orchestra, an *Eingang* is signalled typically by a fermata on the dominant (usually V^7) – thus one step closer to the tonic resolution – and connects to the soloist's reiteration of the main theme. Although the V^7–I progression is the most common, Mozart's VIOLIN concertos also call for *Eingänge* upon arrivals on the dominant above a sounded or implied dominant seventh chord, or on the tonic or dominant of related keys – most commonly, the relative minor. A census of *Eingänge* in the rondos of Mozart's violin concertos makes this clear:

Concerto in D, K211: lead-ins at bb. 39 (V of D), 89 (i of B minor = vi), 141 (V of D)

Concerto in G, K216: lead-ins at bb. 121–4 (V of G, written out), 217 (V of e = vi) (the fermatas at bb. 252 and 290 do not call for *Eingänge*), 377 (V of G)

Concerto in D, K218 (no *Eingänge* at bb. 14, 84, 184, 216): lead-ins at bb. 70 (V of D), possibly 126 (V of G = IV), 178 (V of D), 209–10 (V of D)
Concerto in A, K219: bb. 58 (V of A), 109 (V of f sharp = vi) (no *Eingang* at b. 131), 262 (V of a/A)
Concert Rondo in B♭, K269 (261a) (replacement finale for K207): bb. 74 (V of B♭), 147 (V of g = vi)

There is a third type of improvisation in arias and concertos: the *fermata*, which calls for an elaboration on the tonic common chord (triad), most commonly at the soloist's first entry – for example, in the first movement of the Piano Concerto in B♭, K450, and in numerous arias.

Mozart composed numerous *Eingänge* for others, such as his sister. Portions, or their entirety, can be non-metrical.

ROBERT D. LEVIN

Eisel, Johann Philipp (b. Erfurt, 1698; d. 1763) German composer, theorist, cellist and lawyer.

Eisel composed a number of motets and cantatas, as well as divertimenti and sonatas for the FLUTE and a concerto for BASSOON. He is now remembered for his *Musicus Autodidaktos, oder der sich selbst informirende Musicus...* (Erfurt: J. M. Funcken, 1738), a primer for instrumentalists and singers that is an important source for performance practice and pedagogy across a wide range of instruments. Butt (67) observes that by the beginning of the eighteenth century TREATISES were destined for the growing amateur market in addition to their traditional school usage. Yet Eisel points to the lofty God-given status of music, one that was being greatly enhanced by the growth in musical expertise among royal amateurs, from whom the rising bourgeoisie took their lead. His work shares a great deal of material with MAJER's *Museum musicum* (Schwäbisch Hall, G. M. Majer, 1732) and he belongs to a period in which 'writers seem positively to be proud to have drawn their material from important authors; evidently adherence to tradition was often more desirable than originality' (Butt, 52). But Eisel offers important additional material, apparently drawn from first-hand experience; for example, he is one of very few authors to make an important distinction between the CLARINET and CHALUMEAU. He further notes that clarinet virtuosi could reach a fifth or sixth higher than the normal upper limit of c''', a significant remark in the light of the high tessitura of the concertos by his contemporary Johann Melchior Molter. In recent times Eisel has been cited by organologists and practitioners across topics ranging from DOUBLE BASS tunings to advice for timpanists. On the latter subject he recommends that TIMPANI heads be made by a parchment or harness maker and that the knobs on the wooden sticks be covered with woollen or leather cloth, both comments reflecting his contemporaries' need to be more responsive to expressive musical requirements.

FURTHER READING

J. Butt, *Music Education and the Art of Performance in the German Baroque* (Cambridge University Press, 2006).

COLIN LAWSON

Electronic instruments Electronic instruments fall into two broad categories: those which produce sounds themselves (synthesisers) by generating electrical oscillations that are converted to sound by means of amplifiers and loudspeakers; and those which can be used to modify recordings or other live sound sources such as instruments (samplers and effects units).

Synthesisers have a venerable history dating back to the 1920s with the development of instruments such as the ondes martenot (much used by Messiaen), the theremin and the trautonium. Later significant instruments include the Hammond organ, Moog synthesiser and the Yamaha DX7.

A characteristic of early synthesisers in particular was a desire to create control inputs that expand an organ/keyboard model to enable more expressive playing. In the ondes martenot PITCH can be controlled by both a standard keyboard or a sliding metal ring which lines up in front of the keys, allowing for smooth continuous glissando or VIBRATO effects. The theremin dispenses with the keyboard altogether, pitch and volume being controlled by the position of the performer's hands relative to two metal antennae. This tradition continues to the present day with the development of a host of interfaces based on computer touch screens, breath sensors, or even EEG brain wave activity. Naturally this requires the development of a unique playing technique for many synthesisers.

Samplers use recordings (samples) loaded into the instrument, which are then played back by means of a keyboard or other interface. Early examples such as the Mellotron (developed in the early 1960s) were electro-mechanical, but the development of digital sound technology in the late 1970s led to the creation of much more practical and highly influential instruments such as the Fairlight CMI. It should be emphasised that even if the same sample is used, it is easy to distinguish the sound quality of, say, a Fairlight from an instrument by another manufacturer.

Effects units are used to alter an incoming audio signal – for example, from a microphone. Originally these were often test equipment used in the radio or telecommunications industry, repurposed by composers as instruments – for instance, STOCKHAUSEN's use of the Maihak W49 filter in works from *Mikrophonie I* onwards. Nowadays there are literally thousands of software effects units, each with its own timbral characteristics.

The extremely rapid development of electronic technology has created significant challenges for the modern interpreter, most frequently because the particular hardware or software specified in the score is obsolete. Even if vintage instruments can be found, the surprisingly rapid degradation of electronic components such as capacitors or integrated circuit boards may mean that the instrument no longer behaves as it did originally. Even if the machine does work well, having that instrument is not equivalent to having the sounds it is supposed to play. In a piece such as Jonathan Harvey's *From Silence*, the Yamaha DX7 synthesiser will require settings (sometimes provided by the publisher and stored on an obsolete medium such as floppy disc) which define the timbres it is required to produce.

The modern solution to many of these problems is generally to create a software emulation of the original hardware in a computer program such as Max (although of course this software itself needs regular updating). For the more successful historical instruments such as the Hammond organ and DX7, commercially produced simulations may be available.

All this may involve a certain amount of research and interpretation. Even well-presented published scores are often lacking in detail when it comes to electronic elements, and in some cases written information can be woefully inadequate – this applies both to equipment and to method of performance, given that composers will often have invented new types of NOTATION for electronic instruments. But former performers (building an ORAL TRADITION of performance) and recordings can be consulted. Often these software versions are a considerable improvement on the original in terms of sound quality and ease of operation.

An extreme example of obsolescence concerns works from the 1940s onwards, which use shortwave radios as sound sources. Examples include important works by composers such as Stockhausen and CAGE. Due to the replacement of morse code broadcasts (so beloved of many composers) with more modern means of communication, and ultimately the 'analogue switch-off', which will lead to a total lack of any shortwave broadcasts, we may have to accept that these works will never be performed again.

FURTHER READING

S. Emmerson, *Living Electronic Music* (Hampshire and Burlington: Ashgate, 2007).
F. Weium and T. Boon (eds.), *Material Culture and Electronic Sound* (Washington DC: Smithsonian Institution Scholarly Press, 2013).

MICHAEL OLIVA

Elgar, Edward (b. Broadheath, Worcester, 2 June 1857; d. Worcester, 23 February 1934) English composer and conductor.

Elgar formed a close relationship with the Gramophone Company that resulted in an unprecedented legacy of EARLY RECORDINGS, bridging the acoustic and electrical eras. Besides five PIANO 'improvisations', he conducted recordings of nearly all his orchestral music; even on his deathbed, he monitored recordings by telephone. Photographs show what might be inferred from the musical evidence: Elgar retained the standard seating position, with first and second violins respectively on the left and right of the conductor.

Elgar's scores are replete with DYNAMIC and ACCENTUATION markings, METRONOME indications, and directions to broaden or accelerate the TEMPO. His own performances do not adhere strictly to these markings, perhaps intended more as guidelines than rigid prescription. For example, 'Nimrod', from the *Variations for Orchestra* ('Enigma'), recorded in 1926, is markedly slower in Elgar's recording than his printed metronome mark, starting at crotchet = 40 rather than the score's 52 – a liberty which too many conductors take as an excuse to go even slower; there follows an unmarked *accelerando*.

Aspects of Elgar's performance style exhibit freedoms now considered normal for the time, in flexible tempi and (in piano IMPROVISATION) arpeggiating chords. It is a pity that despite his considerable keyboard fluency, Elgar (whose first instrument was the VIOLIN) declined an invitation to make what could have been a revealing recording of his Piano Quintet. In his orchestral recordings, it is clear that his players made sensitive use of string PORTAMENTO: there are five audible slides in the first four bars of 'Nimrod'.

Elgar's attitude to vibrato is less clear. ROGER NORRINGTON has divided opinion by performances of the First Symphony, on modern instruments but with minimal string vibrato. Elgar studied the violin with Adolphe Pollitzer, whose own teacher was also JOACHIM's; Elgar was briefly acquainted with the latter near the end of his life. Joachim's selective use of vibrato contrasts with Fritz Kreisler's, who is credited with the growing acceptance of near-continuous vibrato, and for whom Elgar wrote his Violin Concerto. If attitudes to vibrato changed during his lifetime, Elgar seems to have accepted this development – witness his 1932 recording of the Violin Concerto with Menuhin, who still offers a fair amount of portamento. Elgar would not have expected wind instruments to use vibrato, or not prominently, although late in life he admired Léon Goossens; low clarinets in No. 5 of his *Sea Pictures* are directed 'vibrato' in the printed score (the MS has 'reedy').

Elgar was friendly with many solo singers (Edward Lloyd, Andrew Black, Clara Butt, Muriel Foster) and composed with their capabilities in mind. Contemporary sources suggest that the standard of preparation for choral performance was variable; Elgar's markedly original choral writing caused problems, more evidence that in his day he was considered an advanced, even modernist composer. The freedom of his recorded performances, in details such as over-dotting (e.g. *In the South*) and emphatic *tenuto* (e.g. 'Dorabella' in the *Variations*), as well as their rhythmic flexibility and vitality, makes them all the more an indispensable benchmark for stylistically informed performance.

FURTHER READING

R. Philip, 'The recordings of Edward Elgar (1857-1934): authenticity and performance practice', *EMc*, 12 (1984), 481–9.

JULIAN RUSHTON

Enescu (Enesco), George (Georges) (b. Liveni Vîrnav, Romania, 19 August 1881; d. Paris, 4 May 1955) Romanian composer, conductor, violinist, pianist and teacher.

Hailed by his friend and colleague PABLO CASALS for the depth and range of his gifts as undoubtedly the 'greatest musical phenomenon since Mozart' (in Malcolm, 263), Enescu excelled as both a practical and a creative musician. A prodigy violinist who became a pupil of Josef Hellmesberger Jr in Vienna in 1887, he was a pioneer in incorporating the microtonal inflections of Romanian folk music into his own compositions for the instrument (Sonata for Violin and Piano No. 3 *dans le caractère populaire roumain* (1926) and *Impressions d'enfance* (1938)). In the USA, he was widely recognised as an inspirational conductor, praised in particular for his masterly sense of TEMPO, instinctive understanding of the ebb and flow of the musical argument and a profound awareness of form and line. Such principles guided him as a performer and pedagogue.

Enescu left a small number of commercial recordings. As a violinist, he can be heard at his best in a charismatic and pure-toned account of Chausson's *Poème* recorded in 1928. Towards the end of his life he set down memorable, if occasionally flawed, performances of the sonatas and partitas for unaccompanied VIOLIN by J. S. BACH, the composer with whom he felt the closest affinity. In contrast to many of his contemporaries, Enescu eschewed the exaggerated use of RUBATO and fluctuating changes of TEMPO favoured by Romantic virtuosi, adopting a more objective approach which he imparted to his pupils – Yehudi Menuhin, Arthur Grumiaux and Christian Ferras. In essence, he argued that the rhythmic pulse in Bach has to be unshakeable because it 'corresponds to the beating of the heart' (C. Chailley-Richez, 'Une visite parmi les dernières à Georges Enesco', *Musique et Radio*, 529 (June 1955), 370, quoted in Malcolm, 242).

The French violinist Serge Blanc, who studied with Enescu after WWII, has published an insightful EDITION of Bach's unaccompanied violin works which contains valuable annotations of his teacher's interpretative approach to the music, including extensive details on matters of tempo, DYNAMICS, ARTICULATION, FINGERING and BOWING.

FURTHER READING

J. S. Bach, *6 Sonatas & Partitas for Violin Solo*, BWV 1001–1006. Educational edition with technical indications and comments by Georges Enescu. Collected and edited by S. Blanc. www.sergeblanc.com/files/bach-sonatas-partitas-en.pdf.

N. Malcolm, *George Enescu: His Life and Music* (London: Toccata Press, 1990) [with list of recordings by Enescu, pp. 278–90].

ERIK LEVI

Engel, Carl (b. Thiedewiese, Hanover, 6 July 1818; d. London, 17 November 1882) German collector, organologist, musicologist.

Engel studied composition with Carl Loewe and Johann Christian Lobe and PIANO with JOHANN NEPOMUK HUMMEL. In 1845 he moved to Manchester and then to London, where he was mostly active as a scholar and music consultant for the South Kensington Museum.

His work was fundamental in developing a new approach to the use of ICONOGRAPHY in relation to musical instruments, particularly from ancient and extra-European sources, in the reappraisal of the history of Western music. His *Essay on the History of Musical Instruments*, first published as an introduction to the *Descriptive Catalogue of Musical Instruments in the South Kensington Museum* (London: South Kensington, 1874), is the first systematic attempt to present a comprehensive history of musical instruments from pre- to early modern history, strictly based on first-hand sources. Since the 1870s he also played an active role in reviving interest in the CLAVICHORD in Britain.

FURTHER READING

C. Engel, 'Some letters to a namesake', *MQ*, 28/3 (July, 1942), 337–79.
A. J. Hipkins, 'Engel, Carl', in G. Grove (ed.), *A Dictionary of Music and Musicians*, 4 vols. (London: Macmillan and Co., 1879–90), iv (supplement), 627–8.
B. Zon, *Representing Non-Western Music in Nineteenth-Century Britain* (University of Rochester Press, 2007).

GABRIELE ROSSI ROGNONI

English Baroque Soloists The debut of the English Baroque Soloists (EBS) took place in 1977 at the Innsbruck Festival of Early Music with a concert performance of HANDEL's *Acis and Galatea*. Founded by JOHN ELIOT GARDINER to succeed his Monteverdi Orchestra, and as a companion ensemble for the Monteverdi Choir, EBS performs worldwide. London based, the orchestra traverses chamber, symphonic and operatic repertoire, complementing its sister ensemble, the ORCHESTRE RÉVOLUTIONNAIRE ET ROMANTIQUE.

Following two discs of music by Handel released in 1981, EBS's subsequent association with major recording labels established an international following. Recordings for DGArchiv from the 1980s include music by J. S. BACH, Buxtehude, Handel, MONTEVERDI, Schütz and the first set of MOZART piano concertos on period instruments with soloist MALCOLM BILSON. During the following decade, they recorded seven Mozart operas for DG and the late symphonies for Philips, as well as maintaining an association with the Erato label.

EBS often presents canonic works to mark significant dates, including a live broadcast of Mozart's *Requiem* K626 in December 1991 from Barcelona's Palau de la Música Catalana, and in 1995, for the Purcell tercentenary, concerts and the soundtrack recording of *England, My England*, Tony Palmer's film portrait of the composer. Its most ambitious and celebrated project took place over twelve months from Christmas Day 1999. With the Monteverdi Choir, EBS performed Bach's 198 extant sacred cantatas on appropriate liturgical feast days, described by founding VIOLA player Annette Isserlis in the liner notes as 'an exceptionally intense and illuminating immersion in the music's context'. More than forty of fifty-nine concerts were recorded and their release on CD, between 2005 and 2010, heralded the establishment of Soli Deo Gloria, Gardiner's in-house label. This development has allowed EBS to revisit works recorded during its formative years. Drawing upon vocal soloists from the larger *ripieno*, the 2015 recording of Bach's B minor Mass continues to ignore JOSHUA RIFKIN's research but is an obvious interpretative successor to the cantata project. Gardiner himself has acknowledged a change in perspective in recalibrating the relationships between movements and the Mass's overall shape.

FURTHER READING

L. Kemp, 'Sir John Eliot Gardiner returns to Bach's B minor Mass', *Gramophone*, 93/1121 (2015), 10–15.

INGRID E. PEARSON

The English Concert *see* PINNOCK, TREVOR

Engramelle, Marie Dominique Joseph (b. Nédonchel, Artois, 24 March 1727; d. Paris, 9 February 1805) French monk and maker of MECHANICAL INSTRUMENTS.

Engramelle experimented with the craft of barrel pinning, mentioned in texts as early as the ninth century, and developed the principles by which keyboard performances could be preserved through 'translation' to pins and staples on a barrel and repeated at will. He describes the process in *La tonotechnie ou l'art de noter des cylindres ... dans les instruments de concerts méchaniques* (Paris: Delaguette/Basan & Poignant, 1775; facsimile éditions Hermann, 1993), which also includes charts for pinning twelve pieces of music. These charts afford valuable insights into eighteenth-century performance practices, most notably regarding RHYTHMIC ALTERATION, ORNAMENTATION, TEMPO and ARTICULATION. They reveal that tempos were markedly fluid; endings were strikingly retarded; the variable inequality of NOTES INÉGALES ranged in proportion from 3:1 to 9:7; staccato (variously graded but normally very short) took precedence over legato (also variously shaded); grace notes were short and sounded on the beat; and trill repercussions were never of uniform speed throughout. The French organ builder François Bédos de Celles subsequently revised and expanded Engramelle's work in his *L'art du facteur d'orgues* (Paris, 1766–78).

FURTHER READING

D. Fuller, *Mechanical Musical Instruments as a Source for the Study of Notes Inégales* (Cleveland Heights, OH: Divisions, c1979).
A. W. J. G. Ord-Hume, *The Mechanics of Mechanical Music* (London: The Author, 1973).
'Ornamentation in mechanical music', *EMc*, 11 (1983), 185–93.

ROBIN STOWELL

Europa Galante Italian period-instrument ensemble founded by the violinist Fabio Biondi in 1990.

Alhough Europa Galante was not among the first wave of Baroque orchestras to be formed in Italy – period performance had been slow to take hold there in comparison with the Netherlands, Germany and Great Britain – this ensemble's arrival helped power a surge of interest among Italian musicians through the 1990s. Since then the orchestra has toured and recorded extensively, performing repertoire largely focused on Italian composers, encompassing string ensemble music from the early seventeenth century, the concerto grosso and solo concerto repertory (especially Vivaldi, including two recordings of *Le quattro stagioni* in 1991 and 2003 respectively) and Boccherini string quintets, as well as oratorios and operas by, for example, Alessandro Scarlatti, Caldara, Handel and Vivaldi (the latter including Biondi's own completions of the operas *Bajazet*, *Ercole sul Termodonte* and *L'oracolo in Messenia* with eminent singers such as David Daniels, Joyce DiDonato, Philippe Jaroussky and Rolando Villazón). The ensemble has also performed and recorded concertos by J. S. BACH and MOZART and in 2016 produced the first period recording of Bellini's *I Capuleti e i Montecchi*. Early recordings were with the French specialist label Opus 111, but towards the end of the 1990s a move was made to the more mainstream Virgin Classics and more recently the Spanish label Glossa.

Europa Galante's playing centres on a boldly projected and virile string sound, firmly driven from Biondi's VIOLIN with strong, often sudden dynamic contrasts and a quick-witted and imaginative approach to phrasing and ARTICULATION which, while risking accusations of exaggeration, can be vividly exciting, especially in live performance.

LINDSAY KEMP

Expression The term stems from Roman RHETORIC, as defined by writers such as Cicero and Tertullian. In musical theory it was associated with the stirring of emotion in late Antiquity; for example, by such writers as Horace, Seneca and Pliny.

Until the middle of the eighteenth century, music was not bound up with individual personality or interpretation. So-called expressivity – for instance, in Heinrich Schütz's *Cantiones sacrae* – primarily signifies representation. Furthermore, throughout history each composer has operated within different styles and expressive parameters: Gesualdo differs from CACCINI, BUSONI from Reger or Scriabin. 'The more distinctive the emotional and expressive content of a piece of music, the greater its demands in terms of expression in musical performance' (H. Eggebrecht and G. Kwiatkowski (eds.), *Meyers Taschenlexikon der Musik*, 3 vols. (Berlin: Bibliographisches Institut, 1984), I, 68). The term 'expression' embraces subtleties which can scarcely be adequately understood, including nuances of colour, the shaping of groups of notes into actual phrases and finally, the formulation of coherent, linked formal sections. Therefore, alongside all the emotional implications, tonal expression implies the clear manifestation of musical thought, the tangible ARTICULATION of motives and themes and the transparency of the entire design of the piece (H. Riemann, *Der Ausdruck in der Musik*, in P. Graf Waldersee (ed.), *Sammlung Musikalischer Vorträge* (Leipzig: Breitkopf & Härtel, 1884), v, 43).

Performance indications or directions such as 'espressivo' or 'with expression' are suggestive of a metaphorical gateway; to pass through this, musicians must be actively creative on each occasion, in that they must ultimately balance spontaneously tested tensions and releases in the acoustic of the space, within strict performance parameters. Friedrich Gutmann's 'Thoughts on musical performance and expression' (*AMZ* (1804–5), 345) have the effect of a geological watershed; they may be read as a backward projection onto previous generations, or alternatively a cautionary looking forward: 'No matter how much this differs from what very many musicians say, I would assert: true expression must lie in the phrase itself... it must be felt and developed; one cannot apply expression from the outside; then it is just an affectation, in that it wavers here and there, produces all sorts of twists and turns, exclamations and exaltations, which one instantly identifies as merely artificial, rather than the essence of true expression.'

It appears from pedagogical sources over many generations that the conditions of expression in successful performance can be described, but that there are no comprehensive recipes for it. TÜRK (1789) elevates 'expression of the respective dominating character' to the 'highest goal of musical art' and insists: 'nevertheless, everything mechanical... can be learnt through much practice'. But it is fruitless to try to determine expression through rules, 'because in expression, so much depends on that which no rules can teach, namely upon one's own feelings'. The relationship of performing musicians to an ideally realised expression reflects that of Socrates to ethics and wisdom.

Directions such as *espressivo* did not exist in the Baroque era; after all, expression was more or less written into the music of that time. For example, J. S. BACH regularly used 'out-of-tune' seventh, eleventh and thirteenth partials on the natural TRUMPET to represent terror, death and evil. He used the very flat seventh partial of the trumpet in the cantata *Gott fähret auf mit Jauchzen* BWV 43 at the word 'Qual' ('torment'). In the aria 'Zerfließe, mein Herze' in the *St John Passion*, the FLUTE part is in F minor, a very weak, 'tragic'-sounding key using frequent cross-FINGERINGS, corresponding to the desperate, suffocating emotion of the aria. Bach's preferred keyboard instrument was the gentle CLAVICHORD, capable of a short *Bebung* (VIBRATO), and not the HARPSICHORD. Terraced DYNAMICS were the exception rather than the rule.

The evolution of the explicit direction *espressivo* began after the principal TREATISES of the 1750s (by QUANTZ, LEOPOLD MOZART and C. P. E. BACH) had already appeared. Around 1770 expression was regarded as the 'soul of music: without it, music is just a pleasant diversion ... Happiness is conveyed in full sonorities without exaggerated tempo, and measured inflection of the stronger and weaker, the higher and lower notes. Sadness expresses itself in slow delivery, from deep in the heart, and fewer vivid sounds' (J. G. Sulzer, *Allgemeine Theorie der schönen Künste* (Leipzig: M. G. Weidemanns Erben und Reich, 1771–4), I, 101 ff.). A letter of MOZART (November 1777) to his father reveals that expression was by then a common concept. In preparing to teach Mademoiselle Rose a sonata, he observes that the Andante will cause the most work, for it is full of expression and must be played accurately with TASTE and the dynamics as indicated. J. A. P. Schulz, SULZER and subsequent authors make it clear that any description of expression is difficult for those who do not have experience and sensibility.

Nevertheless, for Mozart, expression is more redolent of the court and more impersonal than for the next generation. Expression coalesces and expands with BEETHOVEN. Ries declared: 'when I mistakenly played something wrong in a passage, or if there was figuration that he wanted to stand out more, he rarely said anything; but, when I missed something in the expression, in crescendi etc., or in the character of the work, he became upset because, he said, the former was accident, but the latter was lack of knowledge, of feeling, or of attentiveness. The former happened to him quite frequently, even when he played in public' (in A. W. Thayer, *Ludwig van Beethovens Leben*, 2nd edn, 3 vols. (Leipzig: Breitkopf & Härtel, 1910), II, 293).

Franz Schubert could not bear the 'cursed chopping' of many, even exceptional pianists, as he stressed in a letter to his parents on 25 July 1824 (in O. E. Deutsch (ed.), *Schubert: Die Dokumente seines Lebens* (Kassel: Bärenreiter, 1964), 299), whose sentiments bring us fundamentally closer to the expression of the music of his century. For KALKBRENNER (1831) musical expression consisted entirely of nuance. In common with many other nineteenth-century authors he recommended that rising passages must be played *crescendo*, descending *diminuendo*, giving the music a certain wave-like motion that greatly intensified its expression. CZERNY states that where a composer wants the opposite, he must stipulate it. Similarly, conscientious twentieth-century pianists taught that *crescendo* should be avoided in descending passages – unless clearly indicated by the composer (see L. Kozubek, *Arturo Benedetti Michelangeli as I Knew Him*, Frankfurt/Main: Peter Lang, 2011). In the *Damen-Conversations-Lexikon* (C. Herlosssohn (ed.), 10 vols. (Adorf: Verlags-Bureau, 1834), I, 379)), Schumann defined expression in music as follows:

> To play with expression commonly means nothing more than with feeling.
> In a wider sense, it is the specific emphasising of thoughts, feelings, passions through sounds, whether this lies in a composition's rhythm, melody or harmony, in the presentation of the performer, in the particular timbre of the instruments, or in a combination of all of these ... Only when everything – composer, virtuoso and instrument – work together in beautiful harmony, for example, when Szymanowska performed the Hummel B minor Concerto on a Stein grand piano, does the informed listener recognise the ideal of musical expression.

As a result of conflict, European performance practice has suffered ruptures of tradition and amputations of style, and has been affected by diverse later ideologies, in particular the 'new purism' post-1945. Even in this postmodern age, tensions between schools of virtuoso instrumentalists and singers (as well as idiosyncrasies and prejudices) militate against any stylistic consistency. On the other hand, the past and the idealised past cannot really be reproduced; for example, we know practically nothing about how Bach's music sounded in the nineteenth century. Moreover, we know far less about whether Bach's music in his day was in any sense faithful to the score.

Research and analysis and musical expression are effectively two sides of the same coin. For example, in VIOLIN playing before 1750, it is widely agreed that the left hand contributed less, the BOW hand more to expressive playing. In contrast, it can be argued that modern violin playing has gained a robustness of tone, in some respects also of scale and expression, whilst sacrificing sweetness, nuance and natural ARTICULATION. According to Thomas Kabisch's exposition of nineteenth-century performance pedagogy, 'musical expression and individuality of performance do not emerge according to a model in which musical expressivity and inspiration is added to a finished performance and which can always be "adjusted"' (in D. Torkewitz, *Im Schatten des Kunstwerks II. Theorie und Interpretation des musikalischen Kunstwerks im 19. Jahrhundert* (Vienna: Praesens, 2014), 47–106). R. S. Hatten (*Interpreting Musical Gestures, Topics and Tropes. Mozart, Beethoven, Schubert* (Bloomington IN: Indiana University Press, 2004), 9) advocates the notion that expression is a *translation* of structure (or structural relationships) at all levels. Hatten presents an analogy to biological DNA, RNA, aminosaurs and proteins: 'Structure is the generative code for which expression is the structured result.' This 'investigation into the qualitative aspects of musical gesture . . . with phenomenological character (287) . . . helps bridge the gap in the irrelevant opposition "musical structure *or* expression"' (10); 'theorists can learn to appreciate the structural role of performers' expressive nuances, and performers can learn to recognise the expressive significance of the structures analysed by theorists' (3).

Furthermore, it is clear from the performances of, for example, BARTÓK, Rachmaninov, Medtner or Messiaen that music speaks to us from a level that cannot be deduced from the mere NOTATION. The vocal quality of Rachmaninov's and Bartók's piano playing also has characteristics that could not be deduced from the scores, and that are unlike modern performances. RICHARD STRAUSS declared in 1924: 'The excessively large opera houses and unfortunately, the tastelessness of the general public, which . . . prefers a strong voice to a beautiful one, have turned beautiful piano and mezza voce singing into rarities' (R. Strauss, *Betrachtungen und Erinnerungen*, ed. W. Schuh (Zurich: Atlantis-Verlag, 1949/1989), 138). In 1928, after the end of expressionism, SCHOENBERG recalled MAHLER saying that he could not understand why WAGNER singers on the stage screamed so much.

Closely connected with expression and *cantabile* is PORTAMENTO, still maligned in the post-modern era, but nevertheless characteristic of the nineteenth and early twentieth centuries. FINGERINGS by violinists such as BAILLOT and JOACHIM show this in detail, as do such later players as Ysaÿe and Kreisler; string quartets in the 1930s still utilised portamento. Sliding shifts were also occasionally abused, as already pointed out by SPOHR. But it is clear that the expressive slide through shifts was a recognised expressive device for generations. As David Epstein argued (*Beyond Orpheus. Studies in Musical Structure* (Cambridge MA and London: MIT Press, 1979), 202): 'It is widespread experience that much of the power of musical communication lies within the domain of the ineffable and nonverbal – call it affect, expression, gesture, or whatever ... Structure ... is not all ... Certainly a return to the subjectivities of the past is not the answer.'

Some new music demands 'an expression of expressionlessness, of calm, of indifference and apathy to be realised in a way that is impossible for traditional music' – 'ever since Satie, Stravinsky and Hindemith' (T. Adorno, *Gesammelte Schriften*, 20 vols. (Frankfurt: Suhrkamp Verlag, 1970–86), xv, 45). For example, the mature Debussy composed neither 'sound as speech' in the eighteenth-century sense, nor expression in the nineteenth-century sense; the prélude *Voiles*, for example, can hardly be understood as an intention to express, but rather an *impression*. Unsynchronised lengthening of time-values can also be seen in Debussy's and Mary Garden's 1904 recording of *Ariettes oubliées* (see J. Briscoe (ed.), *Debussy in Performance* (New Haven and London: Yale University Press, 1999), 137). Debussy (at the piano) adheres to the pulse while Garden holds back or rushes ahead; for instance, in the ariette 'Il pleure' (bars 23–7) the expressive RUBATO creates the effect of softly falling rain.

Tempo rubato and portamento were less viable after the end of WWII. BOULEZ observed: 'My generation took Webern first and foremost as the renewer of musical language ... we neglected expressivity. With ... distance, I now see that this was too one-sided ... pure structure is uninteresting, academic. Just intuition is not enough ... The most important thing in music [is] a balance between structure and intuition.' But ultimately, why an outcome is musically 'really convincing, one cannot say' ('Interview: Pierre Boulez', *Fono Forum* (March 1995), 28 f.).

Ludwig Wittgenstein went one step further in 1949: 'Soulful expression in music cannot be described as degrees of strength and tempo, any more than the soulful expression on a person's face through spatial measurements. Indeed, it cannot be explained through a paradigm either, because the same piece can be played with genuine expression in countless ways' (in G. H. von Wright (ed.), *Vermischte Bemerkungen* (Frankfurt am Main: Suhrkamp Verlag, 1977)). Ultimately, 'expression is to be inferred from the form, and not to be poured into it ... To play music correctly means ... to speak its language correctly. This attracts imitation of itself, not decoding' (J. Uhde and R. Wieland, *Denken und Spielen* (Kassel: Bärenreiter, 1988), 291).

FURTHER READING

D. Torkewitz, *Im Schatten des Kunstwerks II. Theorie und Interpretation des musikalischen Kunstwerks im 19. Jahrhundert* (Vienna: Praesens, 2014), 47–106.

D. G. Türk, *Klavierschule*, trans. R. Haggh as *School of Clavier Playing* (Lincoln: University of Nebraska Press, 1982).

MATTHIAS THIEMEL (TRANS. NATASHA LOGES)

F

Facsimile (from the Latin *fac simile*, 'make alike') In music, a reproduction of a composer's autograph manuscript, manuscript copy, or printed edition with the aim of maximum accuracy.

The clarity and precision of facsimile EDITIONS have improved with the evolution of the supporting technologies. Their earlier evolution reflects that of print-making as a whole. Earlier facsimiles were lithographs, whose basic procedure creates prints made by drawing on limestone with wax crayons, applying ink onto the stone and printing the image onto paper. Lithographic facsimiles of music were created by placing a sheet of tracing paper on the autograph or other source and copying the pen strokes or printed music as closely as possible. The completed tracing paper was turned over, placed on a prepared, blank lithographic plate and traced with sufficient pressure that the markings were transferred to the lithographic plate as a mirror image. The plate was inspected to make sure that all the lines were visible, and any lines that were broken or too faint to reproduce properly were fixed freehand. The plate was then inked and used to print copies. In short, such a lithographic facsimile is a printing of a tracing of a tracing, and (as Neal Zaslaw has shown) all stages – the tracing, the mirror-image transfer and the free-hand corrections – are subject to imprecision and error. A later stage, photolithography, printed a lithograph from a stone or metal plate upon which a picture or design was formed by photography, thus measurably improving the accuracy of the result.

With improvement in photographic reproduction techniques came the photostat – the earliest form of photographic copying. George C. Beidler (Oklahoma City, OK) founded the Rectigraph Company in 1906 or 1907, which produced the first such photographic copying machines. In 1909 Beidler moved the company to Rochester, NY in order to obtain locally supplied photographic paper and chemicals, then produced by the Haloid Company, which acquired Rectigraph in 1935 and later purchased the rights to Chester Carlson's xerographic equipment; in 1958 the firm became Haloid Xerox and in 1961 was renamed the Xerox Corporation. Thus photostats are direct ancestors of the photocopying machines of today. They were used primarily to create single copies of sources, however; printed facsimiles continued to use photolithography and photographic reproductions into the twentieth century. In addition, autographs, MANUSCRIPTS and prints could be duplicated on 35 mm microfilm, viewed in a reader and, later, photocopied.

In recent decades improvements in photographic and scanning techniques have made colour facsimiles more common, though facsimile editions remain very expensive and therefore have limited press runs.

ROBERT D. LEVIN

Fantini, Girolamo (b. Spoleto, bap. 11 February 1600; d. Florence, after 6 May 1675) Italian trumpeter and writer.

Fantini wrote the first known published TRUMPET method: *Modo per imperare a sonare di tromba tanto di guerra quanto musicalmente in organo* (*Method for Learning to Play the Trumpet Both in War and Musically with Organ*), published in Florence in 1638. The first part contains military signals and the second the earliest known solo sonatas for trumpet and continuo.

Fantini was active as a player from the 1620s. Employed by Cardinal Borghese in Rome from 1626 to 1630, he subsequently entered the musical household in Florence of Ferdinand II of Tuscany, to whom he dedicated his trumpet method. During this period, Fantini's reputation grew and in 1634 he revisited Rome to give a solo performance, accompanied by GIROLAMO FRESCOBALDI on Cardinal Borghese's chamber organ, one of the earliest documented instances of a trumpet being played in recital. A contemporaneous letter from French physician Pierre Bourdelot to MARIN MERSENNE (*Harmonicorum libri* (Paris: Lutetiae Parisorum, 1635–6), II, 109) refers to Fantini's playing ability, to 'so regulate the breath so as to emit all the individual tones from the third or fifth ascending' – that is, to 'lip' notes that do not exist in the harmonic series. In the solo sonatas of his TREATISE, Fantini also increases the upper range used by earlier trumpeters such as Cesare Bendinelli by a fourth, going up to the eighteenth natural note (d''') on the C trumpet.

Fantini is an important figure in the development of the trumpet in the early Baroque period. In his treatise, he sets out many of the underlying principles of ARTICULATION, breathing and phrasing which underpinned trumpet technique and practice in art music in the seventeenth and eighteenth centuries.

FURTHER READING

I. Conforzi, 'Girolamo Fantini, "Monarch of the Trumpet": recent additions to his biography', *HBSJ*, 5 (1993), 159–73.
'Girolamo Fantini, "Monarch of the Trumpet": new light on his works', *HBSJ*, 6 (1994), 32–59.

JOHN WALLACE

Farina, Carlo (b. Mantua, c1604; d. end July?, Vienna, 1639) Italian violinist and composer.

Details of Farina's musical education are uncertain. He was appointed *Konzertmeister* at the Dresden court (1625–8) under Heinrich Schütz and was later variously employed for short spells in Parma, Lucca, Danzig and Vienna. His compositions, largely for instruments of the VIOLIN family, comprise five printed volumes mostly of three- and four-part dance pieces, along with some two- and three-part sonatas, canzonas and sinfonias and the notorious *Capriccio stravagante* (1627). They are significant in their cultivation of a distinct violin idiom, particularly the violin/continuo sonatas, with their rapid passagework, double stopping and exploitation of the G string (e.g. *La franzosina* and *La desperata*). The four-part, virtuoso *Capriccio stravagante*, the descriptive pieces ('curious inventions') of which imitate the sounds of instruments and animals, capitalise innovatively on the violin's expressive and technical potential by introducing effects such as glissando, pizzicato (including plucking guitar-style), TREMOLO, double stopping, *col legno* and *sul ponticello*. The execution of some effects is explained with verbal instruction. Farina's impact on German violinist-composers such as David Cramer, the elder Johann Schop, Johann Vierdanck and others was far-reaching and long-lasting.

FURTHER READING

W. Apel, *Italian Violin Music of the Seventeenth Century*, ed. T. Binkley (Bloomington, IN: Indiana University Press, 1990).

D. D. Boyden, *The History of Violin Playing from its Origins to 1761* (London: Oxford University Press, 1965).

ROBIN STOWELL

Farinelli (Carlo Broschi) (b. Andria, Apulia, 24 January 1705; d. Bologna, ?17 September 1782). Italian singer and composer.

The most famous of all the CASTRATOS, Farinelli was celebrated in his own lifetime with popular adulation and acclamation from the most judicious critics of his age. Descriptions of his SINGING are unusually precise. At the heart of his technique was a rare degree of breath control that enabled him to sustain both single notes and whole phrases with no discernible taking of breath. BURNEY famously described an aria with obbligato TRUMPET in which his ability to sustain a note, ornament it, and go on to execute rapid passagework far excelled that of the trumpeter (*The Present State of Music in France and Italy*, 2nd edn (London, 1773), 213–14); Burney also praised Farinelli's *messa di voce* which astonished listeners suspected was sustained by 'the latent help of some instrument by which the tone was continued while he renewed his powers by respiration' (1776–89, II, 790).

In common with most castrato singers, Farinelli impressed with his agility in ORNAMENTATION, examples of which, including florid CADENZAS, are preserved in a volume of arias presented to the Hapsburg Emperor Francis I in 1753 (http://data.onb.ac.at/rec/AL00543417). On the evidence of his repertory, his range was a remarkable c–d′′′, which he exploited in passagework across tenor, alto and soprano registers and displayed in large leaps of up to two octaves (Clapton, 326). He also made frequent use of the *trillo* (rapid repeated notes), an ornament more typical of the early seventeenth century (Clapton, 333).

Farinelli composed a number of arias, most of them settings of Metastasian texts. In these he sometimes showed a simpler, more expressive style, though how far this was embellished in performance cannot be known.

FURTHER READING

S. Cappelletti, *La voce perduta: vita di Farinelli evirato cantore* (Turin: EDT, 1995).

N. Clapton, 'Carlo Broschi Farinelli: aspects of his technique and performance', *British Journal for Eighteenth-Century Studies*, 28 (2005), 323–38.

D. Heartz, 'Farinelli revisited', *EMc*, 18/3 (1990), 430–43.

PATRICIA HOWARD

Fellowes, Edmund H(orace) (b. London, 11 November 1870; d. Windsor, 21 December 1951) English editor, scholar and clergyman.

Fellowes was educated at Winchester College and at Oriel College, Oxford, where he read theology. He was ordained in 1894 and took the Oxford BMus in 1896. He spent the majority of his career as a minor canon at St George's Chapel, Windsor (1900–51), where from 1924 to 1927 he took charge of the choir during an interregnum between Masters of Music. Fellowes's numerous critical writings and editions, being solidly source based, provided the bedrock for modern scholarly editorial practice of English music from c1545 to c1645. Of particular significance is the fact that, excepting his contribution to the library edition of Tudor Church Music (10 vols., 1922–9), his EDITIONS were designed to be practical and all were issued in a format for use in performance. His editions of cathedral repertoire have proved particularly enduring but his work also included madrigals and lute songs.

Fellowes's collected editions are as follows: *The English Madrigal School* (36 vols., 1913–24); *The English School of Lutenist Song Writers* (32 vols., 1920–32); *The Collected Works of William Byrd* (20 vols., 1937–50).

FURTHER READING

E. H. Fellowes, *Memoirs of an Amateur Musician* (London: Methuen, 1946).
W. Shaw, 'Edmund H. Fellowes, 1870–1951', *MT*, 111 (1970), 1104–5.

JONATHAN WAINWRIGHT

Fenkner, Johann August (fl. c1770–c1810) German violinist and teacher.

Little is known about Fenkner's training or career. His *Anweisung zum Violinspielen* (1803) incorporates information about VIOLIN maintenance, rosin, general musical issues, markings and terminology, TEMPO, FINGERING, BOWING, EXPRESSION and fundamental technique. It concludes with guidance on style and phrasing, recitative accompaniment and issues of musical form. Intended for amateur violinists, much of Fenkner's elementary instruction was already out of date.

FURTHER READING

J. Pulver, 'Violin methods old and new', *PRMA*, 50 (1923–4), 101–27.
E. van der Straeten, *The Romance of the Fiddle* (London: Rebman Ltd., 1911), 262–8.

ROBIN STOWELL

Fétis, François-Joseph (b. Mons, 25 March 1784; d. Brussels, 26 March 1871). Belgian musicologist, critic, teacher and composer.

Fétis moved to Paris to study at the CONSERVATOIRE aged sixteen; though he returned to his native Belgium following independence to take up the posts of director of the Brussels Conservatory and *maître de chapelle* to Léopold I, he continued to exercise considerable intellectual influence throughout France and beyond. His activities ranged widely from organist to librarian, probably attracting most general public attention during the period when he was working to complete Meyerbeer's *L'Africaine* following the composer's death in 1864. In the realm of historical performance, however, they were concentrated around his musicological and historiographical research; his collection of early instruments and c10,000 volumes, acquired by the Belgian state on his

death and still a central part of national institutional holdings, includes TREA-
TISES and studies from every era in many languages. Fétis disseminated this
learning in the form of philosophical writings, journalistic criticism (he
founded, and for seven years published, the *Revue Musicale*, arguably the first
significant publication of its kind) and educational concerts. This series of
Concerts Historiques, instituted in 1832, was not by any means the first such
initiative even in Paris, but it was influential. The concerts comprised a careful
thematic selection of repertoire (occasionally presented using original instruments) introduced by lectures which were then printed in the *Revue Musicale*.
Performances were not always wholly satisfactory, but more significant in
retrospect is the fact that among them was included at least one fake, the aria
'Pietà, signore' supposedly by Stradella. The Stradella myth – that, following an
amorous escapade which incurred the wrath of a powerful nobleman, this aria
persuaded the assassins sent after him not to carry out their task – ranks with a
number of similar examples of the mystique of 'old' music used as a marketing
ploy for sheet music on the one hand and scholarship on the other. What
makes it remarkable is that Fétis himself may have been the author. If so, such
apparently unscholarly behaviour may merely be further evidence that Fétis,
despite his antiquarianism, did not consider most of the items in the *Concerts
Historiques* as potentially part of the living repertory, but rather as test-cases for
a theory of music history. Essentially his thinking appears to have vacillated
between ideas of historical progress (indebted to the philosophy of Auguste
Comte) and of universal truths clothed in idioms that change with musical
fashion (derived from Victor Cousin), eventually settling on a fittingly *juste
milieu* compromise, one that became common in the revival of early music in
nineteenth-century France and Belgium.

FURTHER READING

P. Bloom, 'François-Joseph Fétis and the "Revue Musicale" (1827–1835)', PhD dissertation, University of Pennsylvania (1972).
K. Ellis, *Music Criticism in Nineteenth-Century Paris: 'La Revue et Gazette Musicale de Paris'*, *1834–80* (Cambridge University Press, 1995).
Interpreting the Musical Past: Early Music in Nineteenth-Century France (New York: Oxford University Press, 2005).

CORMAC NEWARK

Figured bass *see* BASSO CONTINUO

Figurenlehre Musical-rhetorical figures.

The term *Figurenlehre* was coined by German musicologists to identify a widespread practice found in German Baroque TREATISES of defining and explaining expressive devices identified as *Figuren* with terminology borrowed from RHETORIC. Names for musical figures were either adopted from rhetoric or newly coined to emulate a rhetorical term, reflecting the growing influence of rhetorical concepts on musical thought during this time. The hundred or so musical figures identified with such terminology in the treatises can be generally organised into the following categories: melodic repetition, harmonic repetition and fugal figures, representation and depiction, dissonance and displacement, interruption and silence, melodic and harmonic ornamentation,

as well as some miscellaneous figures. Although the musical and linguistic figures use contrasting methods of expression unique to their respective disciplines and media, many of them are constructed in a similar or related manner, and they share a common affective goal. In the same way that orators were to ornament and heighten their speech through rhetorical figures to lend greater persuasive effect, so too could the musician portray and arouse the AFFECTIONS through comparable musical figures.

In designing the curriculum for the German *Lateinschulen*, Luther's humanistically oriented associate Philipp Melanchthon ensured that rhetoric received a prominent place in students' education. It was in these schools that the vast majority of the authors who wrote the treatises containing the various *Figurenlehren* received their training and taught not only music but also Latin and rhetoric. Rhetorical figures of speech were dealt with in the third step of rhetorical structuring, *decoratio*, where, after identifying the argument (*inventio*) and organising it (*dispositio*), figures of speech and thought would be added. It is above all these figures of speech, used to embellish, amplify and vividly portray the ideas and arguments, which were considered the most useful rhetorical devices in presenting and arousing the affections. Throughout the sixteenth century, German music treatises increasingly referred to rhetorical methods and techniques, culminating in Joachim Burmeister's treatises which enshrined rhetorical terminology and methodology in German compositional theory at the beginning of the seventeenth century. His novel systematic discussion of musical-rhetorical figures profoundly influenced German compositional theory throughout the Baroque era. The desire to identify pre-existing musical phenomena with familiar but newly defined rhetorical terminology was explicitly affirmed by Burmeister, thereby opening up a new world of analytical and compositional possibilities.

Both rhetoric and music are disciplines which involve performance, identified as *actio* in rhetoric, and as such embrace both the process of composition and the act of performance. Many authors blurred the distinction between figures which concern the composition of a piece and the figures which pertain to its delivery, in music the latter referred to as ORNAMENTATION. Indeed, the classical rhetorical process called *ornatus*, the third step within *decoratio/elocutio*, is the step involving the application of the rhetorical figures. Virtually all the authors of the various treatises were practising musicians, equally concerned with teaching, writing and performing. Knowledge of the musical figures was as important to the composer as it was to the performer.

The concept of the musical-rhetorical figures developed from an early Baroque understanding of figures as aberrations from the simple or traditional compositional norms, primarily for the sake of variety, interest and colour, to a late Baroque understanding in which they were defined as the primary agents for presenting and arousing the affections. The large number of German treatises which are in one way or another indebted to Burmeister's *Figurenlehre* attests to the wide support and general acceptance of this rhetorical approach to music. Upon closer examination of the many different treatises, however, it becomes apparent that the development of the musical-rhetorical figures was anything but uniform, with substantial differences even between authors of the same generation. While some writers viewed the figures primarily as legitimising dissonance or unusual musical syntax, others regarded their main function as the expression of the text and the affections. In spite of the substantial differences between the various concepts of the musical-rhetorical figures, certain fundamental elements are common to all *Figurenlehren*: a musical-rhetorical figure was generally regarded as an artful and expressive musical device which digressed from either the simple, unadorned musical idiom or the established rules of counterpoint.

Early seventeenth-century references to the figures, including the writings of Burmeister, Nucius and THURINGUS, focused on text expression and musical embellishment, developed by musicians who thought, wrote and composed in the style and context of sixteenth-century imitative counterpoint. While the early *Figurenlehren* referred only periodically or indirectly to the figures' powers to evoke the affections, this function became increasingly important throughout the century. Athanasius Kircher highlighted the figures' role in text and affection expression in all his figure definitions. CHRISTOPH BERNHARD's discussion of *Figurenlehre* concerned itself with explaining *seconda pratica* dissonances in the context of *stylus gravis* rules of counterpoint. Johann Georg Ahle explained the figures in a purely rhetorical context, focusing on the literary figures found in a composition's text. JOHANN MATTHESON also regarded the musical figures as virtually identical to their rhetorical counterparts. Furthermore, he introduced a subjective and empirical element into his concept of the musical-rhetorical figures, which corresponded to parallel developments in contemporary German rhetoric. JOHANN ADOLF SCHEIBE related his *Figurenlehre* more closely to a rhetorical concept of the figures than any previous author had done, modelling his discussion of the musical-rhetorical figures directly on Johann Christoph Gottsched's literary publications, likewise insisting that the figures were the very language of the affections. The source of the musical figure became the affection which lies at the heart of the text, rather than the text itself. This facilitated a natural transfer of the musical-rhetorical figures to instrumental music, away from a primary focus on text-expressive vocal music. Johann Nikolaus Forkel's discussion of the figures brought the discourse about musical-rhetorical figures to its conclusion. Although he had high praise for a musical rhetoric, his terminology betrays a concept of music which was foreign to the Baroque period. Individualisation, subjectivity and feeling replaced an authoritative, objective and affection-driven Baroque concept of music. Not insignificantly, Forkel's discussion of the figures no longer takes place in the context of a compositional treatise or music dictionary but in the foreword to a history of music.

FURTHER READING

D. Bartel, *Musica Poetica: Musical-Rhetorical Figures in German Baroque Music* (Lincoln, NE: University of Nebraska Press, 1997).

J. Cameron, 'Rhetoric and music: the influence of a linguistic art', in J. Williamson (ed.), *Words and Music* (Liverpool University Press, 2005).

DIETRICH BARTEL

Fingering This summary of fingering principles for keyboard, bowed string and wind instruments through history follows modern practice in the numbering of fingers: for keyboard instruments, 1 = thumb, 2 = index finger, 3 = middle finger, 4 = annular, 5 = little finger; for bowed string instruments, 0 = open (i.e. unstopped) string, 1 = index finger, 2 = middle finger, 3 = annular, 4 = little finger. Specific fingering is not normally prescribed in music for wind instruments.

1 Keyboard Instruments

Historical keyboard fingering can be studied from surviving instructions and fingered pieces. Although relatively scarce in earlier times, information from the mid-eighteenth century onwards is more plentiful. Keyboard fingerings show which digit is required for a particular note and commentators have inferred from these indications a number of principles by which the fingers must therefore move over the keys. The extent to which these movements affect the sound of the music in performance depends ultimately upon the executant, and since no two players will produce the same results using the same fingering, keyboard fingerings are open to considerable interpretative latitude. Nevertheless, fingering is inseparable from keyboard technique, hand shape and the fundamentals of touch, ARTICULATION and sound production.

The earliest fingerings come from HANS BUCHNER's *Fundamentum*, a tutor dated 1551 but probably written in the 1520s. His rules show that conjunct notes were taken by alternate neighbouring fingers from the middle of the hand (paired fingering) and that the two hands used the same patterns in mirror image. The thumb and little finger are seldom used, although consecutive thirds and sixths are fingered '2' and '4' and '2' and '5' respectively. Most importantly, Buchner initiates the rhythmic principle of consistently allocating fingers '2' and '4' (the 'good' fingers) to play on strong ('good') beats (Example 3(a)). His system was widely adopted in Germany but gradually gave way to '3' being the 'good' finger, especially in the right hand, during the later seventeenth century. ELIAS AMMERBACH's two sets of fingered exercises (1571, 1583) show the left hand developing different patterns from the right hand and a preference for scale groups of fours (4321) (Example 3(b)).

GIROLAMO DIRUTA published the first comprehensive TREATISE on ORGAN playing, *Il transilvano*, in Venice in 1593. In Italy, the 'good' fingers '2' and '4' generally led the hand on strong beats and Diruta disapproved of the newer method of leading with '3' as in ADRIANO BANCHIERI's writings. He also expressed concern at the resulting stiffness in the hands of some of his colleagues. A follower of the virtuoso Claudio Merulo, Diruta discussed

Example 3: (a) Hans Buchner: 'Quem terra pontus' (*Fundamentum*, 1551); (b) Elias Ammerbach: *Exercises* (1583).

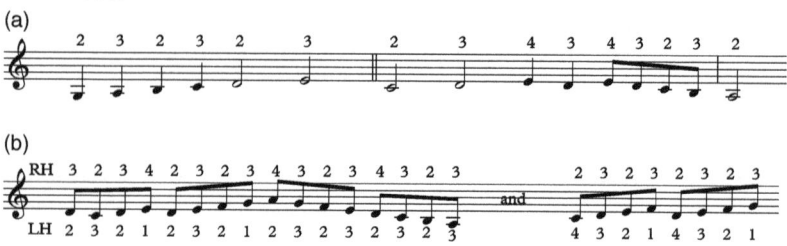

Example 4: (a) John Bull: *Fantasia* (*GB-Lbl* Add. 36661); (b) Anon. [Bull?]: *Prelude* (*GB-Lcm* MS 2093).

fingering in the context of technique and articulation. He advises a 'quiet' (i.e. still) hand with a slightly high wrist and the fingers somewhat curved or arched ('alquanto inarcate'), and recommends that passagework must be played cleanly with a short, clear but close articulation between the notes, the fingers moving up and down at the same time.

No sixteenth-century Spanish music survives with fingerings but rules are given in four treatises and prefaces: Bermudo (1555), Venegas de Henestrosa (*Libro de cifra nueva*, 1557), SANTA MARÍA (1565) and Hernando de Cabezón (*Obras de música para tecla, arpa y vihuela*, 1578). These represent a variety of approaches, of which Santa María's are the most elaborate, and can be summed up in the advice of Correa de Arauxo (*Libro ... intitulado Facultad organica*, 1626). Correa stipulates that for runs on diatonic notes, the right hand should go up 34–34 and down 32–32, and the left hand, up 21–21 and down 34–34, but these pairings often extend to groups of threes (234–234) or fours (1234). In England, hundreds of fingerings survive from the virginalist era but no tutors. From these a consensus emerges broadly in line with the Spanish rules with similar scale patterns, including paired fingerings, and Santa María's repetition of the same finger on different pitches (probably a CLAVICHORD technique). The 'good' finger is now '3' (Example 4(a)). Newly emerging techniques include changing finger on repeated notes and greater use of finger '5'; for example, at the end of right-hand runs (Example 4(b)). Fingerings often occur in close proximity to ornament symbols informing both the choice of fingers and the note pattern required.

Towards the end of the seventeenth century as touch and articulation became more nuanced, fingering is increasingly indicative of the execution of subtleties. In addition to detached playing, NIVERS (*Livre d'orgue* (Paris: l'auteur & R. Ballard, 1665)) advises organists to slur some notes as a singer would, and RAISON (*Livre d'orgue* (Paris: l'auteur, 1688)) goes further, requiring legato notes to be overlapped. FRANÇOIS COUPERIN considered fingering essential to the correct realisation of his pieces. His *L'art de toucher le clavecin* (1716), the most influential treatise of the period, includes eight preludes to demonstrate his method. He recommends finger substitution (depressing a key with one finger then continuing to hold it down with another) and joined fingering to achieve the required overlapped legato, and reassigns the old manner of paired fingerings and limited use of the thumb to achieve a new and often complex micro-phrasing (Example 5). He requires perfect execution of ornaments and, like RAMEAU (*Pièces de clavecin avec une méthode* (Paris:

Example 5: François Couperin: *Premier Prélude* (*L'art de toucher le clavecin*, 1716).

Chez Charles-Etienne Hochereau; Boivin: l'auteur, n.d. [1724])), includes progressive exercises for developing evenness of touch.

In Germany, fingering and touch were in transition between old and new practices. Several pieces by J. S. BACH are fingered – the earlier instructional ones use old-style paired fingering while the later pieces, copied by one of his pupils, confirm the use of the thumb in chords and for frequent hand shifts. C. P. E. BACH states that for his father the thumb was the 'chief finger' and advocates using the thumb to orientate hand position shifts and to act as an additional finger (*Versuch*, 1753). He also lists modern scale fingerings although he does not always recommend their use. Some later eighteenth-century treatises are less conservative and much of their advice (e.g. TÜRK, 1789) has remained valid for over two hundred years.

Old scale fingerings and techniques persisted in Germany, perhaps a reflection of the delicate actions of the clavichord and Viennese FORTEPIANO. J. H. Knecht (*Vollständige Orgelschule*, 1795) complained that many players failed to use the thumb and little finger. Modern fingerings were widely adopted elsewhere, however. In England, Niccolò Pasquali advocated proper use of the thumb in the 1760s, while more than twenty years later Robert Broderip instructed that the long fingers should 'never be turned over or under each other' (*Plain and Easy Instructions for Young Performers on the Piano-forte or Harpsichord*, c1788). Modern scale fingerings were fully accepted by the nineteenth century in both theory and practice (e.g. CLEMENTI, *Introduction to the Art of Playing on the Piano Forte*, 1801 and CZERNY, *Complete Theoretical and Practical Pianoforte School*, Op. 500, 1839).

The final stages in the development of modern keyboard fingering reflect the general adoption of legato phrasing and touch. Czerny, for example, praised BEETHOVEN's legato tone over W. A. MOZART's detached style of playing, which he called 'clipped'. César Franck taught organists an absolute legato achieved by tying common pitches together (even when notated otherwise) and through continuous finger substitution. Nevertheless, the playing of great artists often rejected the accepted norms. Beethoven frequently included unusual fingerings in his piano sonatas to explain the proper execution of his more obscure NOTATION and CHOPIN's exceptional style required specific fingering for every passage. Like Buchner in the sixteenth century, Chopin admitted the uniqueness of each hand and the possibility to adapt fingerings when required.

FURTHER READING

J.-J. Eigeldinger, *Chopin vu par ses élèves* (Neuchâtel: Editions de la Baconniére, 1970), trans. as *Chopin, Pianist and Teacher: As Seen by His Pupils* (Cambridge University Press, 1986).

M. Lindley and M. Boxall (eds.), *Early Keyboard Fingerings* (London: Schott, 1992).

D. Rowland, *Early Keyboard Instruments: A Practical Guide* (Cambridge University Press, 2001), 58–67.

B. Sachs and B. Ife (eds.), *Anthology of Early Keyboard Methods* (Cambridge: Gamut Publications, 1981).

J. Swinkin, 'Keyboard fingering and interpretation: a comparison of historical and modern approaches', *PPR*, 12/1 (2007). http://scholarship.claremont.edu/cgi/viewcontent.cgi?article=1210&context=ppr.

2 Bowed Stringed Instruments

Fingering on bowed string instruments has rather more interpretative implications than on keyboards; in addition to articulation issues, it may have associations with intonation, timbre or EXPRESSION. Its conventions have evolved through history in line with developments in instrumental techniques, accessories and construction, and musical TASTE.

Viol

Early VIOL fingerings were based on LUTE fingerings, as demonstrated by GANASSI (*Regola Rubertina* (Venice: Author, 1542)), who presents some advanced examples in Italian lute TABLATURE, with fingering indicated by dots in four different positions around the fret number. In keeping with the principle of *tenüe* ('hold') practised by French players, SIMPSON (*The Division Viol* (London: W. Godbid, 1659)) advises keeping the fingers on the string as long as possible to gain the optimum *cantabile*, sonority and resonance. French violists such as ROUSSEAU (*Traité de viole* (Paris: Christophe Ballard, 1687)), Sainte-Colombe, MARAIS (*Pièces de violes*) and Forqueray annotated their works copiously, including fingerings (*see* Hsu, 1981). As Danoville (*L'art de toucher le dessus et le basse de violle* (Paris: Christophe Ballard, 1687)) and CORRETTE (*Méthode pour apprendre facilement à jouer du par-dessus de viole à 5 et à 6 cordes* (Paris: l'auteur, 1748)) verify in their methods, bass viol fingering systems generally require one finger for each semitone, with occasional extensions of a tone, almost always between 1 and 2; however, the smaller, treble viol is sometimes played with one finger for each tone.

Among other related indications is *le doigt couché*, which, derived from *barré* in lute playing, involved placing the first (or occasionally fourth) finger across two or more strings, freeing up the other three fingers to stop other notes, especially in chordal or ARPEGGIANDO passages. Marais also prescribed the string to be played by adding an equivalent number of dots around the fingering annotation. Bol (1973) summarised the fundamentals of Baroque viol fingering as follows: the outer notes of broken chords should be sustained as long as possible for optimum sonority and resonance; if possible, the same finger should not be used for two different notes on the same fret (except in *le doigt couché*); shifting should only be executed during a single bow stroke via an open string, extension or *'le système-reptiles'* ('creeping', involving finger substitution); in stepwise shifts, the finger employed last in the position being left should be used first, if possible, in the new position; if two or more fingers stop the same fret, the lowest numbered finger normally plays on the lowest string.

FURTHER READING

H. Bol, *La basse de viole du temps de Marin Marais et d'Antoine Forqueray* (Bilthoven: A. B. Creyghton, 1973).
J. Hsu, *A Handbook of French Baroque Viol Technique* (New York: Broude Bros., 1981).
I. Woodfield, *The Early History of the Viol* (Cambridge University Press, 1984).

Violin and Viola
To c1800

VIOLIN and VIOLA fingering was closely related to the set-up of the instrument, the manner of holding it, and the player's hand conformation. MERSENNE (1636–7) offers the earliest instruction, which is elementary and confined to first position, although he describes the instrument's range as g–d'''. Not until the mid-eighteenth-century treatises of GEMINIANI, LEOPOLD MOZART, HERRANDO and L'ABBÉ LE FILS are there more advanced surveys of fingering techniques; even then, fingering principles were unstandardised.

Broadly, unnecessary finger activity was avoided; much of the Baroque repertory required only the first three positions and the most common annotated fingering in early violin music is the fourth finger to indicate open-string avoidance. Although open strings were sometimes necessarily employed in the execution of shifts, bariolage, double and multiple stopping, and SCORDATURA, they were generally avoided (at least from the early eighteenth century onwards) when stopped notes were viable. This was particularly the case in descending (especially slurred) scale passages involving more than one string, trills, appoggiaturas and most melodic or expressive contexts.

Leopold Mozart (1756), in his progressive survey of the various left-hand positions, claims that 'necessity, convenience, and elegance' justify the use of positions other than the first, elegance being aligned with timbral consistency and *cantabile* delivery. Modern half and second positions assumed greater importance from c1750 onwards, when most advanced TREATISES embraced at least the first seven positions; some even extended to eleventh position and beyond in supplementary study material. However, excessively high position-work with the short fingerboard was comparatively rare (Locatelli's Op. 3 was exceptional), because clarity of stopping was difficult to achieve; later fingerboard modifications (*see* VIOLIN) enabled exploitation of a wider range.

Shifts generally conformed to the music's punctuation: on the beat or on repeated notes (Example 6a), by the phrase in sequences (Example 6b), after an open string (Example 6c), on a rest or pause between staccato notes or after a dotted figure played with a lifted bowstroke (Example 6d). L'Abbé *le fils* (1761) indicates them with the letter D (*démancher*). The unbraced methods of holding the instrument placed the onus more on the fingers than the arm to effect shifts; if possible, one position was chosen to accommodate an entire phrase, and extensions and contractions were often used (but HARMONICS rarely so in the eighteenth century, despite Mondonville's advocacy (*Les sons harmoniques*)) to avert shifting. The adoption of the chin-braced hold liberated the hand's shifting potential. Emphasis was placed rather more on the odd-numbered positions, and cultivation of semitone shifts facilitated achievement of the prevalent legato ideal.

Example 6: (a–d) Shifting in accordance with the musical punctuation (Leopold Mozart: *Versuch* (1756), 155, 168, 155 and 156).

Example 7: An example of the kind of bold shift employed by Francesco Geminiani (*The Art of Playing on the Violin* (1751), 14).

The mechanics of shifting are sparsely documented, but inevitably depended on whether or not the instrument was stabilised by the chin. The thumb's independent role in following the fingers (as opposed to the modern ideal of the hand moving as a unit) was paramount (Geminiani, 1751). Upward shifts increased the instrument's stability against the player's neck. Most eighteenth-century writers advocated small upward shifts, using adjacent fingers (23–23; 12–12), but some, notably Geminiani, Tessarini and CORRETTE, prescribed bold leaps (Example 7). Downward shifts, particularly when playing 'chin-off', were less easily realised; but, GALEAZZI (*Elementi teorico-pratici di musica*, 2 vols. (Rome: Nella Stamperia Pilucchi Cracas, 1791–6)) excepted, large leaps (4321–4321) were generally favoured. Some eighteenth-century writers reject outright PORTAMENTO in shifting, but evidence suggests that it was introduced by some players, especially in solo contexts, either as part of the shift mechanism or as an expressive device.

Some composers prescribed fourth-finger extensions to avert shifts. ZANETTI (1645) and, for example, Castrucci indicate them with the figure 5, while others (e.g. L'Abbé *le fils*) place the letter *e* above the prescribed fingering. Leopold Mozart (1756) illustrates how a first-finger contraction can sustain a suspension satisfactorily. Some fingerings were prescribed to ensure the faithful realisation of cross-string effects such as bariolage or *ondeggiamento*, voice-leading in polyphony or timbral considerations. Diminished fifth/augmented

Example 8: Chromatic fingerings: (a) by Francesco Geminiani (*The Art of Playing on the Violin* (1751), 2); (b) by Leopold Mozart (*Versuch* (1756), 66–7).

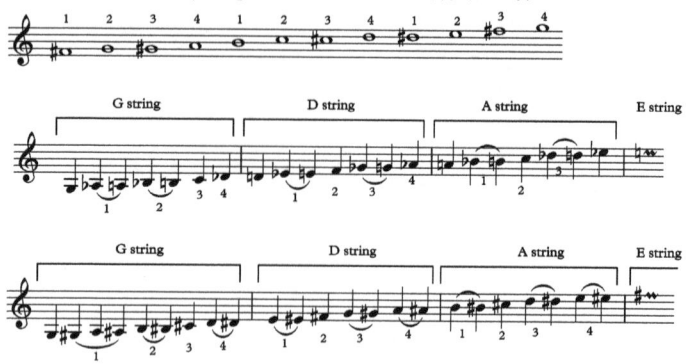

fourth fingerings (L'Abbé's *croisé* (crossed) or Leopold Mozart's *Überlegung* (overlapping)) were often specified; Francoeur and Leclair sometimes involved the left thumb in certain chord fingerings.

Considerations of timbral uniformity played little part in seventeenth-century fingering principles, but Leopold Mozart (1756) encourages the execution of entire passages on one string and sequences with matching fingerings, bowing articulations and string changes. The two principal chromatic scale fingerings were Geminiani's (1751) one-finger-per-note method and Leopold Mozart's 'slide-fingering' (Examples 8a and 8b), adopted by most of his immediate successors, which involves different fingerings for chromatic scales written in sharps from those in flats; it highlights the contemporary concept of unequal semitones and intonation systems in which flats were considered higher than their 'enharmonic' sharps.

Post-c1800
Modified instrument necks (*see* VIOLIN) facilitated shifting and playing in the higher positions. The chin-braced grip on the G-string side of the tailpiece, confirmed by RODE, BAILLOT and KREUTZER (1803), liberated the left hand for increasingly adventurous passagework in high positions on all strings. The chin rest provided additional security. The higher positions were exploited more frequently for expressive and timbral reasons, and the increased use of extensions and semitone shifts facilitated achievement of the prevalent legato ideal. *Una corda* playing was especially encouraged, reaching its zenith with the sul-G extravaganzas of PAGANINI and his successors.

Baillot (1835) distinguishes between the most secure fingering, the easiest fingering for small hands and expressive fingering, contrasting Viotti's string-crossing and general avoidance of shifts, Kreutzer's frequent shifts on all strings for brilliant effect and Rode's more uniform timbral goals, incorporating portamento. Paganini opened up unlimited possibilities for the left hand, many of his fingerings (*see* GUHR, 1829) demonstrating scant regard for the traditional concept of positions disseminated in contemporary treatises by SPOHR (1832), BAILLOT (1835) and HABENECK (c1840), and later by BÉRIOT (1858),

DAVID (1864), and JOACHIM and Moser (1905). As harmonic language and musical styles evolved in the twentieth century, the left hand's liberation extended beyond any diatonic fingering ideology, thanks to increased chromaticism, whole-tone, microtone and other scale patterns, and unusual non-consonant double and multiple stopping. Players were encouraged to adapt fingering to their own style and technique and make it an integral part of musical interpretation and creative individual expression (Yampolsky, *Osnovi Skripichnoy Applikaturi* (Moscow, 1933); trans. A. Lumsden as *The Principles of Violin Fingering* (Oxford University Press, 1971); Flesch, *Alta scuola di diteggiatura violonistica* (Milan, 1960); trans. B. Schwarz as *Violin Fingering, Its Theory and Practice* (London: Barrie & Rockliffe, 1966)).

As shifting became more of an expressive resource during the nineteenth century, the introduction of portamento increased. In Baillot's (1835) discussion of *ports de voix* and expressive fingering, anticipatory notes (unsounded, like Spohr's, 1832) indicate his approach to shifting. Nevertheless, fingerings indicate that tasteful introduction of slides was permitted, especially in slow movements and sustained melodies when a passage ascends or descends by step, accompanied respectively by a *crescendo* or *diminuendo*. Spohr (1832), among others, admitted the use of natural harmonics in shifting, especially to make one note in a passage stand out. Exploitation of slides to articulate melodic shape and emphasise structurally important notes became so prevalent in the late nineteenth century that succeeding generations reacted strongly against it (e.g. Flesch, *see* PORTAMENTO).

AUER (1926) favours 'rhythmic' (on-beat) over 'antirhythmic' (off-beat shifting) fingering, but acknowledges that fingering is primarily an individual matter dependent on the conformation of hand and fingers. Influenced by twentieth-century musical developments, Babitz (*Principles of Extensions in Violin Fingering* (Los Angeles: Delka, 1947)), Flesch (1960), Galamian (*Principles of Violin Playing and Teaching* (Englewood Cliffs, NJ: Prentice-Hall, 1962)) and others aim to achieve a 'cleaner' style of playing. Galamian distinguishes between the 'complete shift', in which both hand and thumb assume a new position, and the 'half shift', using the thumb as a pivot to allow the fingers to straddle positions. Concurrent with this 'cleaner' approach came a renaissance of Geminiani's chromatic fingering principles, championed by Flesch for its greater evenness, articulation and clarity, and the increased popularity of the fingered-octave technique, first discussed by Baillot (1835), for its clarity, accuracy, and less frequent hand displacements.

FURTHER READING

D. D. Boyden, *The History of Violin Playing from its Origins to 1761* (London: Oxford University Press, 1965).

R. Stowell, *Violin Technique and Performance Practice in the Late Eighteenth and Early Nineteenth Centuries* (Cambridge University Press, 1985).

P. Walls, 'Violin fingering in the 18th century', *EMc*, 12 (1984), 300–15.

Violoncello

To c1800

Early cello fingering was influenced by violin and viol technique, as is evident in BISMANTOVA (1694) and Corrette's (*Méthode pour apprendre le violoncelle*

(Paris: s.n., 1741)) treatises. Corrette's fingerings for consecutive note patterns suggest his use of an oblique left-hand position, employing the first, second or fourth fingers in first and second positions but limiting fourth finger usage above third position. He considers the chromatic system of fingering old-fashioned, preferring instead a system based on violin fingering (intervals of both semitones and whole tones being executed with the same finger). Many followed his lead, introducing diatonic extensions without shifts and fingerings based on semitone finger-spacing; the use of extensions between the first and second fingers only in lower positions became more common as the eighteenth century progressed. However, BAUMGARTNER (1774) introduced variations, using an extension between the second and third fingers, and employing the third finger (as opposed to the fourth) from the third position upwards.

The French school's adoption of a more perpendicular left-hand position in relation to the neck facilitated the use of chromatic fingering, in which each semitone was stopped with a separate finger throughout the first four positions, with no compression of third and fourth positions. Extensions were limited largely to the second finger, and notes above fourth position were stopped by the first, second and third fingers. This more idiomatic system, emanating from Berteau and his pupils, was eventually codified by DUPORT (c1806).

Thumb position, with the thumb placed horizontally across the strings and acting as a movable nut, was first introduced in the 1730s sonatas of Lanzetti. It was instrumental in expanding considerably the cello's range and bravura capability and was especially nurtured by Mannheim cellists Danzi and Filtz. Their virtuoso use of blocked hand positions across two or more strings in thumb position was perpetuated in works such as HAYDN's C major Concerto. These cellists used the fourth finger over the entire compass of positions, including extensions between the third and fourth fingers.

GUNN (1789), the first theorist to attempt to systematise cello fingering principles, rejected the slanted left-hand position and recommended fingerings based on the principle that all scales can be played in groups of three fingered notes, irrespective of key-signature. He anticipated Duport's detailed treatment (c1806), which provided the true basis for modern left-hand technique.

Post c1800

Like Gunn, Duport recommended a left-hand position perpendicular to the neck. His fingering system involved successive semitone spacings between each finger, with extensions possible between the first and second, and between the second and third (but only above fourth position), and only very rarely between the third and fourth. He disapproved of sliding with the same finger when shifting, unless executed for expressive reasons or technical exigency, and discouraged shifting within slurs.

Duport's system was disseminated through the *Méthode* [1804] edited by his pupil Levasseur with Catel, Baudiot and Baillot and adopted by the PARIS CONSERVATOIRE. Most French and English cellists of the first half of the nineteenth century subscribed to it, along with DOTZAUER (1825); but some (e.g. Alexander, 1802; Bideau, 1802; ROMBERG, 1840), and particularly those with German associations, considered same-finger shifting more reliable for intonation accuracy. Romberg advocated an oblique left-hand position and

Example 9: The finger-replacement shift as illustrated by Charles Baudiot (*Méthode*, Op. 25, 2 vols. [1826, 1828], I, 21).

became renowned for his mastery of thumb position, extending its boundaries by using blocked hand positions and exploiting the upper registers of the G and C strings. His use of the fourth finger in thumb position set him apart from most French players. The finger-replacement shift was a common expressive ploy for use with articulated same-note slurs (Example 9) and portamento became increasingly employed to express emotion.

Developing technical requirements and ever-changing expressive and timbral ideals led to the cultivation of a completely mobile hand untrammelled by fixed positions based on the thumb. Instrumental in this transformation were Rabaud (*Méthode complète de violoncelle* (Paris: Leduc, n.d. [1878])) and especially Davidov (*Violoncello-Schule* (Leipzig: C. F. Peters, [1888])), whose methods, inspired by observing violinists, involved shifting with either the finger in play or the finger about to be used, the hand guided (if necessary) by anticipatory notes. But German fingering systems prevailed with GRÜTZMACHER (*Daily Exercises for the Cello* (New York: Schirmer, 1891)) and Popper (*Hohe Schule des Violoncellspiels* (Leipzig: F. Hofmeister, 1901–5)), the latter expanding the range of thumb position, using logical fixed positions, to its maximum potential.

Casals's individual approach to fingering, perpetuated by his pupils Alexanian (*Traité théoretique et pratique du violoncelle* (Paris: A. Z. Mathot, 1922)) and Eisenberg (*Cello Playing of Today* (London: Novello, 1957)), provided the foundations from which flexible twentieth-century fingering approaches developed. It acknowledged a need to favour the innately stronger fingers when musical values required but emphasised the importance of maximum finger-independence for facility in stretching and shifting and diversity of vibrato colouring. Casals rejected conventional fingerings unsuited to musical phrasing, used semitone shifts generously and often permitted same-finger re-use in the upper register whenever finger spacing was limited. Like his mentor Stutschewsky, his optimum fingering minimised shifts using extensions, achieving greater clarity and eliminating inappropriate slides. He often chose 1 23 for tone-semitone rather than 1 34, and even extended 1 4 for the interval of the fourth. He also pioneered percussive fingering, stopping the strings decisively and making note-beginnings clear, 'expressive intonation', and fingering techniques for double and multiple stopping.

Double Bass
The very size of and the stringing differences between the various double bass models have spawned such a variety of fingering systems through history that standardisation has only partially been achieved. Two principal systems developed: 'extended fingering', formed from viol or cello technique, and

'Simandl', based on nineteenth-century Austro-German methods. The first involves positioning the hand so that semitones lie between each of the fingers in all positions; thus, the fingers are 'extended' and the need for shifting reduced. With the 'Simandl' system the hand is positioned so that a semitone lies between 1 and 2 and another between 2 and 4. The third finger is used only as a support for 4 until the higher positions are reached, when it is used instead of 4. BOTTESINI (c1865?), however, fingered semitones 1-3-4 (sometimes 1-4 in the lower positions) and some of his successors adopted his methods.

FURTHER READING

G. Kennaway, *Playing the Cello, 1780–1930* (Farnham: Ashgate, 2014).
R. Stowell (ed.), *The Cambridge Companion to the Cello* (Cambridge University Press, 1999).
V. Walden, *One Hundred Years of Violoncello* (Cambridge University Press, 1998).

3 Wind Instruments

Fingering on woodwind instruments concerns the opening and closing of tone holes so as to produce the required sequence of pitches. Woodwinds developed on the principle of six finger-holes (for the first three fingers of each hand) plus left-hand thumb. A seventh hole for the right-hand little finger increased the lower range and on larger instruments this was replaced by a key, as on recorders. Around the middle of the seventeenth century, the natural scale began to be standardised to conform to the diatonic scale. After c1800 the positioning of left above right hand was established, coinciding with addition of a further key for the right-hand little finger and gradually more complex mechanisms. Half-holing lowers a fingered note by a semitone by half-closing the next lowest hole; to ensure greater accuracy, such holes were often doubled, as on the hautboy. Cross (or fork) fingerings lower a simple fingering by closing one or more holes below the first open hole. Such 'resistant' fingerings were largely eliminated by the provision of complex mechanisms in the nineteenth century, which (as HEINRICH GRENSER noted) somewhat altered the instrument's character. Most woodwinds access the upper register via an octave hole or speaker key operated by the left-hand thumb; reed instruments with cylindrical bore (such as the clarinet) have registers a twelfth (rather than an octave) apart, with additional keys near the top of the instrument to bridge the gap.

Notwithstanding such general principles, it is significant that JOSEPH FRÖHLICH observes (1810–11, 15):

> Owing to the different construction and various manners of blowing wind instruments, there are no generally applicable rules of fingering. All one can do is give the usual fingerings and a critique for each note, and, at the same time, to inform the student of the various manners in which the same note can be fingered, in order to make the dark notes brighter and more sonorous, and to improve the bad ones. Consequently, one must really see to it that each player evolves the fingering for himself.

Some sixty years earlier, QUANTZ advised that notes indicated with flats were to be played a little sharper than those with sharps, insisting that a player must have a good understanding of the proportion of intervals in the scale. Fingering charts became an essential part of tutors and instruction books from c1700 and show

how finger technique developed alongside the acoustic qualities of each instrument. They are a valuable source for the use of different TEMPERAMENTS and approaches to tone quality and interval placement. Sometimes, they offer further valuable historical information; for example VANDERHAGEN's chart in his *Nouvelle méthode pour la clarinette* (Paris, 1819) shows the mechanism for the clarinet on which Heinrich Baermann played Weber's solo works. The application of radical keywork and acoustic design to the flute by THEOBALD BOEHM in the first half of the nineteenth century led to radical new fingerings that enabled greater sound projection and equality of tone. These ideals have been challenged more recently by the cultivation of micro-intervals and multiphonics.

FURTHER READING

A. Baines, *Woodwind Instruments and Their History* (London: Faber, 1957).
B. Bartolozzi, *New Sounds for Woodwinds* (Oxford University Press, 1967).
J. L. Voorhees, *The Development of Woodwind Fingering Systems in the Nineteenth and Twentieth Centuries* (Hammond LA: Voorhees Publishing Co., 2003).
T. E. Warner, *An Annotated Bibliography of Woodwind Instruction Books, 1600–1830* (Detroit: Information Coordinators, 1967).

1. TERENCE CHARLSTON; 2. ROBIN STOWELL; 3. COLIN LAWSON

Florilegium British ensemble specialising in historical performance.

Florilegium focuses on seventeenth- and eighteenth-century music, taking its name from MUFFAT's 1695 *Suavioris harmoniae instrumentalis hyporchematicae florilegium primum*. The ensemble is based around a nucleus of principal players, comprising FLUTE/RECORDER, VIOLIN, VIOLA DA GAMBA, CELLO and HARPSICHORD/ORGAN. As co-founder and artistic director Ashley Solomon has observed, Florilegium's flexibility of personnel enables it to perform variously scored repertoire. The ensemble usually performs without a conductor, a feature which enhances the intimacy and spontaneity of the music making.

Florilegium made its London debut in 1991, at a time when HISTORICALLY INFORMED PERFORMANCE in the UK appeared to be flourishing. However, the independent orchestras formed during the 1970s and 1980s had largely drawn upon the same pool of established musicians, and a younger generation sought to create their own opportunities. In 1992 Florilegium won the prestigious International Van Wassenaer Competition in Utrecht and made its first commercial recording. Released in 1993, this CD of chamber music by TELEMANN was awarded a Diapason d'Or and Choc de monde de la musique, marking the beginning of a fruitful collaboration with the Dutch label Channel Classics. Florilegium's reputation as 'one of the most flamboyant of the younger generation of British Baroque ensembles' (*The Times*, 15 August 1996) was further enhanced by its residency at London's Wigmore Hall between 1998 and 2000. Since its foundation Florilegium has presented more than 1,000 performances, throughout the UK and internationally, receiving widespread recognition.

A close association with music from Bolivian Chiquitos and Moxos archives at Jesuit missions during the era of Spanish colonialism has further advanced the ensemble's profile. Three highly acclaimed CDs of Bolivian Baroque music (released in 2005, 2006 and 2009) include performances by the Arakaendar Bolivia Choir, co-founded with Polish musicologist Piotr Nawrot and Bolivia's Asociación pro Arte y Cultura.

A commitment to future generations of musicians underpins the ensemble's educational work; Florilegium has developed a special association with the ROYAL COLLEGE OF MUSIC, London.

FURTHER READING

A. Solomon, 'A look back at Bolivian Baroque'. www.gramophone.co.uk/blog/gramophone-guest-blog/a-look-back-at-bolivian-baroque.

INGRID E. PEARSON

Flute A term used to denote various instruments of many different cultures worldwide with a hollow body containing an air column which is activated by a stream of air striking the edge of an opening. Thus, flutes are classed acoustically as 'edge-tone instruments'.

In Europe prior to the late eighteenth century, the term *flauto* and its variants normally referred to the RECORDER, reflecting that instrument's prevalence. To denote the flute, the adjective *transverse, traverse,* or *allemande* (referring to its early popularity in Germany and its military use by German mercenaries) was added to the simple term *flauto* or *flûte*. As the flute became more popular, the need for a classifying adjective waned, and the instrument eventually superseded the recorder as the default *flauto*.

Flutes of various kinds have long been played worldwide, with Plato referring to them (*The Republic, c*375 BC) as the original instrument of wide range imitated by all others, but it is likely that transverse flutes appeared much later than their end-blown relatives. They probably came to Europe from India, where the flute has long been associated with Krishna, by way of Byzantium. The Veroli Casket, housed in London's Victoria and Albert Museum (no. 216–1865), is a carved ivory box dating from the second half of the tenth century and fashioned in what is now Istanbul, Turkey. Probably made for a member of the Umayyad house, this casket bears one of the earliest certain depictions of the transverse flute in Europe, being played by a centaur to the accompaniment of a lyre (*see* http://collections.vam.ac.uk/item/O70463/veroli-casket-casket-unknown/).

Music of the tenth to fourteenth centuries was predominantly vocal; although instruments were used either in place of or alongside voices, they were not specified. Only a handful of bone flutes from that period have survived (it is of course likely that more perishable materials were generally used) and references to the flute in contemporary literature and TREATISES are rare, although some visual depictions are informative. A manuscript of the *Cantigas de Santa Maria* (E-E, *c*1270–90) is one of the first sources to link the transverse flute with an existing repertory, the collection of songs associated with the court of Alfonso, King of Castile and León. Here an image of two seated flautists suggests that flutes may have been used in the performance of these vocal works.

One of the earliest sources to discuss the distinction between transverse flutes and recorders is Guillaume de Machaut's epic narrative poem *La Prise d'Alexandrie* (*c*1367). In an extended passage describing musical instruments (ll. 1152–68) he mentions both 'flaustes traverseinnes' (transverse flutes), followed by 'flaustes dont droit joues quant tu flaustes' – 'those which you play straight as you make music with the flute' – indicating the recorder or some sort of tabor PIPE.

Throughout the fifteenth century the flute was often described as a military-band instrument coupled with the field drum, but the inconsistency of iconographical sources depicting military scenes makes it difficult to distinguish between the flute and the fife, a much smaller instrument with a very narrow bore in relation to its length, resulting in a high-pitched, shrill sound.

Court inventories offer ample evidence of a surge in flute ownership in the sixteenth century; Henry VIII of England possessed seventy-four flutes in 1547, Maria of Hungary had more than fifty in 1555 and, most impressively, the Stuttgart court had 220 flutes in 1589, compared with only forty-eight recorders. Throughout the century flutes were typically made as CONSORT instruments, appearing in many different sets that displayed a variety of tunings, which enabled them to play in a wide range of modes. These Renaissance flutes were simple, one-piece cylindrical tubes, generally made from maple, plum or boxwood, with six finger-holes and a somewhat limited range. Like most wind instruments of the time, they followed a Guidonian scheme, resulting in three instruments of different sizes pitched a fifth apart. The bass had G (gamma ut) as its lowest written note, the tenor and contra-tenor D (sol re), and the descant A (la mi re). The four-part transverse flute consort appeared in France, Germany and England, and is also reported in Italy as early as 1529, when a quartet of flutes played at a dinner given by Ercole d'Este for his father Alfonso I, Duke of Ferrara.

MARTIN AGRICOLA (1529) offers an insight into the flute's place in sixteenth-century German musical culture. In the first edition of his TREATISE, after presenting a woodcut of a flute consort, Agricola describes how best to play this simple six-holed flute:

> Blow the lowest eight notes very moderately; let the next seven be somewhat faster; the next four require a faster breath; and the highest three go very quickly. Also if you want to master the fundamentals and basics, then learn to play with quivering breath, for it graces the music very much on all wind instruments that one plays.
>
> (TRANS. W. E. HETTRICK, 12)

The notion that this flute had a three-octave range is quite extraordinary, but Agricola's revised version of the treatise contains sets of scales that limited the range more predictably to just over two octaves. Agricola also advocates the use of VIBRATO or 'quivering breath' ('mit zitterndem Winde'), and other sixteenth-century sources affirm that both breath and finger vibrato were seen as essential elements in expressive woodwind playing.

In sixteenth-century France, the Roman city of Lyon claimed significance as the cultural capital, particularly before the French Wars of Religion (1562–98). Records of 'Grand Spectacles' and theatrical performances there reveal an Italian influence, including for their prominent use of transverse flutes in these events. At least two of the eight flute makers listed in Lyon archives were members of the Rafi family, from whom four recorders and seven transverse flutes survive today, and on whose instruments many modern reproductions of historical flutes are based. François Rabelais has Gargantua learn the *flûte allemande* in his *Gargantua et Pantagruel* (Lyon, 1535) and the Burgundian musician PHILIBERT JAMBE DE FER gives the transverse flute much attention in his *Epitome musical* (Lyon, 1556).

GIOVANNI BASSANO's *Ricerate, passaggi et cadentie* (1585) is the earliest surviving collection of solo pieces to mention the transverse flute, closely followed by Aurelio Virgiliano's *Il Dolcimelo* (c1600). MARIN MERSENNE's *Harmonie Universelle* (1636–7) later heralded some significant changes in the construction of the D flute, proposing fingerings similar to those presented by HOTTETERRE seventy years later. Mersenne's flutes were made in one piece (occasionally two pieces) and probably had a conical rather than cylindrical bore, but still had no key.

The change from the one-piece cylindrical flute to a one-keyed conical instrument in three parts transformed not only the musical but also the cultural role of the flute throughout the seventeenth century. Despite a tendency today to ascribe a narrative of chronological development from 'simple' to 'complex', changes were in no way uniform or standardised, with an enormous range of variation in flute pitches, bore diameters and tapers, timbres, ranges, intonations and tones. The common early Baroque flute had a cylindrical head, a conical body (narrowing from the head towards the foot) with six finger-holes and a foot joint with a single key which, when opened, raised the lowest note d' to $d\sharp'$; other chromatic notes were obtained by cross-fingering (closing holes under the lowest open hole, thereby flattening the pitch). Most instruments were made of boxwood, ebony or ivory. In France developments in flute design coincided with changes in the character of the music composed for the instrument. Formerly associated with war, the flute began to be affiliated with gentler, softer music, especially that expressing love. Flautist Philbert Rebillé (1639–1717) attracted attention in the French court to the qualities of this new instrument. MARIN MARAIS published the first French trios in 1692, illustrating the title page with flutes in the new style, and in 1702 Michel de La Barre published the first book of solo pieces for transverse flute to appear in print in any country.

Five years later, Jacques-Martin Hotteterre (1707) made clear his intentions to establish a dedicated pedagogy, performing practice and repertory for the transverse flute. His treatise offers a fascinating insight into flute playing at this time, notably mentioning different fingerings for 'enharmonic equivalents', providing instructions on the uses of *tu* and *ru* in woodwind ARTICULATION, and explaining the execution of the French graces, including *flattements*, *ports-de-voix*, *accents* and *battements*. Translations of Hotteterre's treatise appeared in Dutch (1729) and English (1730), and the book was also closely imitated by Pablo Minguet y Yrol in his *Reglas, y advertencias generales* (Madrid, 1754), the only known eighteenth-century Spanish flute treatise.

As the transverse flute in D was becoming standardised, references to other sizes of flute as instruments in their own right also appeared. MICHEL CORRETTE mentioned the piccolo flute, pitched an octave higher, in his *Méthode* (1740), while RAMEAU and Gluck scored for it. The *flûte d'amour*, pitched a third lower, was written for by Molter and Graupner, but there is very little repertoire compared with the number of surviving instruments; it is possible that these flutes were used as transposing instruments.

JOSEPH JOACHIM QUANTZ contributed significantly both to the flute's development and to our knowledge of the eighteenth-century flute and performance practices. In addition to instruction on flute playing, his *Versuch* (1752) contains the only contemporary account of the modifications made to the instrument in the late seventeenth century, referring to Quantz's own innovations in flute construction: the second key (1726) enabling a different note for $d\sharp'$ and $e\flat'$, and the division of the head joint into two sections to create a tuning slide. By this time the body of the flute had been divided into two, ensuring greater ease and accuracy in reaming the bore (using shorter tools) but also allowing the flautist to play at different pitches by using interchangeable joints of slightly differing lengths. However, variations in PITCH were such that the slide advocated by Quantz was helpful in ensuring true intonation.

The addition of keys and chromatic holes provided with closed keys continued throughout the eighteenth century, though there is conflicting information concerning the provenance of these developments, many of which were short-lived. FRANÇOIS DEVIENNE criticised several new fashions in flute playing in his *Nouvelle méthode* (1794) whilst JOHANN GEORG TROMLITZ strongly advocated the keyed flute and the stronger sound it produced. By 1780 keys for f', $g\sharp'$ and $b\flat'$ were in use and the range was extended with further keys for c', $c\sharp'$ and later c''; eight-key flutes like this were available into the twentieth century.

By 1800, the flute was probably enjoying its most successful phase as a solo instrument. As its capabilities were explored and exploited by composers and performers, corresponding experiments in construction were undertaken by instrument makers, leaving a colourful legacy of innovation. As early as 1803, Dr Pottgieser, a medical doctor, set out plans to revise the flute's construction. Although he was unable to bring his ideas to fruition, he proposed equalised holes for every finger and thumb, with the right thumb operating the only key he then declared necessary, and a more pronounced taper and therefore a shorter tube, which would allow the finger-holes to be closer together. In 1808, Charles Townley patented his invention of two levers operated by the left thumb to control the tuning slide during performance (a device seldom, if ever, used) and, more importantly, Rev. Frederick Nolan proposed what is thought to be the first contrivance for using the same finger to close both an open key and a normal hole, in the form of open-standing keys with rings as their touch-pieces.

The most important figure in the development of the modern flute was THEOBALD BOEHM. In 1831 he heard the renowned flautist CHARLES NICHOLSON play and was inspired to remodel his instruments. Nicholson, appointed joint professor of flute at London's ROYAL ACADEMY OF MUSIC on its foundation in 1822, was credited with producing a sonorous tone. This resulted not only from his personal playing style but also from his unusual instrument, which had the standard eight keys but a huge embouchure hole and very large finger-holes.

In the same year, Boehm met the amateur flautist Captain Gordon, an officer in Charles X's Swiss Guards. Gordon had decided to eschew his military career for that of a flute designer, and by 1831 had already had some instruments made for him by a Swiss watchmaker and in London by Rudall and Rose and Cornelius Ward. At their meeting, Gordon and Boehm are said to have compared flutes, the former sporting a completely open-keyed mechanism and the latter his first improved model, which was not fully open-keyed. It is not clear what impact Gordon's flute had on Boehm, although it may well have influenced his later reforms. Gordon continued to work on this design, but with little further success. His case was taken up by several rivals of Boehm in the following years, who claimed that Gordon was the true inventor of the new flute. The ensuing public dispute had the invaluable consequence of encouraging Boehm to write his essay on flute construction, in which he presented his detailed knowledge of the design to prove his inventor's role.

Boehm had an extraordinary understanding of the standard flute's deficiencies and spent his whole life working on developments, first by improving the old system flute, and then by inventing a whole new system, which brought a dramatic change to the world of flute playing. His studies of the principles of acoustics in 1846 with the scientist Carl Emil von Schafhäutl (1803–90) helped him discover that the sound was improved when the bore of the instrument was cylindrical, and that a silver flute had the most sonorous tone. The instrument finally established in his Munich workshop in 1847 with a metal cylindrical body, a head joint that narrows parabolically towards its top and a cylindrical foot joint is still the basis of the flute played almost universally today. The sophisticated mechanism, open-standing keys and large holes in acoustically correct positions overtook the design principles of the old flute, effectively giving birth to a new kind of instrument, a flute that has hardly changed in the last 160 years. Naturally there was considerable resistance to this new instrument and many felt that these innovations meant that the essence, charm and character of the old flute was lost forever.

Indeed, it looked likely that confusion and disagreement over the benefits of the new design would lead to the flute's irrelevance; James Browne observed in 1910 that though between 1821 and 1846 twenty-one flute solos had been performed at Philharmonic concerts, since 1846 there were records of only one, and there was a noticeable decline in repertoire across Europe. However, Paul Taffanel, a professor of flute at the PARIS CONSERVATOIRE, founded the *Société d'Instruments à Vent* in 1879, insisting on high standards of performance and composition, and thus inspired a new generation of flautists as well as works from many respected contemporary composers, including Widor, SAINT-SAËNS and later Debussy. A thriving French school of flute playing soon developed, becoming globally recognised and admired, especially after Georges Barrère emigrated to the USA in 1905. One of the most striking differences (aside from increased use of vibrato) was a preference for silver flutes, whilst the English and German schools still used wooden flutes well into the twentieth century.

Avant-garde composers often turned to the flute to facilitate special acoustic effects in their music, including the use of harmonics and pitch manipulation both with the fingers and the breath to produce microtones and glissandos.

William Kincaid pioneered the production of whistle or whisper tones (high, clear sounds created by blowing extremely gently across the embouchure hole), initially as a warm-up exercise before they gained popularity with composers. Early examples of the technique of flutter-tonguing are found in works by RICHARD STRAUSS and MAHLER, with notable use in Ravel's *La Valse* and SCHOENBERG's *Pierrot Lunaire*; it soon began to appear in conjunction with other effects, including whisper tones and multiphonics. Percussive sounds were also being developed, the most common being the key slap; in fact it had long been known that slapping the keys down at the same instant as the tongue attack facilitated clarity in the lower register, but now it began to be used as a sound in its own right. Bruno Bartolozzi gives details of many of these new techniques in his *New Sounds for Woodwind* (trans. R. Smith Brindle, London and New York: Oxford University Press, 1967).

Although the Boehm flute is considered sufficient for most extended techniques, the Dutch maker Eva Kingma has developed new system quarter-tone flutes in various sizes, as well as an open-holed alto flute (in G) and later a bass version (in C). These innovative instruments have inspired contemporary composers in their constant search for fresh sounds.

FURTHER READING

P. Bate, *The Flute: A Study of its History, Development and Construction* (London: Benn, 1969).
R. Bigio, *Readings in the History of the Flute* (Cambridge University Press, 2006).
J. Haar (ed.), *European Music, 1520–1640* (Woodbridge: Boydell Press, 2006).
A. Powell, *The Flute* (New Haven, CT and London: Yale University Press, 2002).
N. Toff, *The Development of the Modern Flute* (New York: Taplinger, 1979).

ASHLEY SOLOMON

Fortepiano The term 'fortepiano' differentiates pianos of the eighteenth and early nineteenth centuries from their modern descendant. Strictly speaking, however, it could be said to represent all forms of the PIANO from its origin up to those at the beginning of the twentieth century, when the modern form of the piano became fairly standardised (indeed the term for the standard instrument in Russian remains 'fortepiano'). It is most likely that it derives from the first known description of a piano by SCIPIONE MAFFEI, who in 1711 referred enthusiastically to an instrument made by BARTOLOMEO CRISTOFORI, who was keeper of instruments at the Medici Court in Florence, as a '*gravecembalo [gravicembalo] col piano, e forte*', literally 'harpsichord with soft and loud'. The fundamental challenge in constructing a piano was to create a mechanism that would cause a hammer to strike a string and then fall away so that it did not immediately dampen the sound that it had initiated. The tangents of CLAVICHORDS remain in contact with the string but given that they are constructed of metal they do not dampen the sound when the key is depressed, and indeed allow the production of VIBRATO – an effect valued by C. P. E. BACH, among others. Cristofori's instruments were very sophisticated mechanically and it is therefore surprising that the piano took so long to become adopted as a standard keyboard instrument. It seems that the ability to play loudly and softly and to *crescendo* and *diminuendo* between these levels needed to be reflected by composers before the advantages of the instrument became apparent. Once music of the second half of the eighteenth century demanded these musical effects, the instrument quickly started to be preferred – and the HARPSICHORD, in a desperate attempt to compete, started to acquire machine stops, swell pedals and other such devices in order to match this newly required dynamic versatility. The ability of the clavichord to produce varied, though very subtle, levels of sonority, as required by C. P. E. Bach's fantasies, some of which date from the 1760s, also deserves to be part of this discussion. There is little doubt that by the mid-1770s leading keyboard composers such as HAYDN and MOZART were writing for the piano.

By the late eighteenth and early nineteenth centuries pianos could be broadly classified as either Viennese or English. Most of the Viennese builders originated from Swabia, including the Stein family, Walter and Graf. The instruments of the Viennese school dominated the German-speaking world and had an extremely light and responsive action that was directly mounted on the key. The notes were damped all the way to the top and clarity and ARTICULATION were the primary means of EXPRESSION, due to the construction that created high hammer velocity (*Prellmechanik*). These instruments were able to articulate discreetly without disturbing the natural flow of the music. By contrast the articulation of English instruments, used also in France and much of Scandinavia, was less clear. The top strings were left free to vibrate, as on the modern piano, so as to create a more resonant sound quality, the lyrical singing line being heavily prioritised over clarity. These instruments were also more robustly constructed, generally louder and therefore able to project more easily in larger halls. The instruments were wooden-framed; their strings were much thinner and their hammers consequently much smaller than those of the modern piano. Damping on English pianos was created by superimposing layers of felt laid loosely over the keys as opposed to the V-shaped Viennese dampers for bi-chordal stringing and flat felt dampers for tri-chordal stringing, which gave the Viennese instruments clearer damping.

At the end of the eighteenth century, a typical Viennese piano would have a five-octave range (F'–f''') and composers exploited the full range of the instrument in virtually all compositions. The English instruments had a slightly wider range of about five and a half octaves (F'–c''''). Haydn used this wider range in his 'English' Sonata in C major, Hob XVI/50 (in fact only up to a''', a pitch BEETHOVEN does not employ until his 'Waldstein' Sonata, Op. 53) and Dussek, Beethoven and others published music with optional ranges according to the instrument in use. As the piano range expanded, the demand for new instruments was made particularly acute because new repertoire was unplayable on shorter keyboards.

The physical development of the piano was one of gradually increasing power and resonance. At all stages en route to the modern piano, however, there were some distinctive instruments; the Pleyel of Chopin's day is as revolutionary, in terms of revealing differing conceptual possibilities, as are the Walters of Mozart's. To an extent these pianos represent native speakers of the composer's language and therefore can instruct players more directly than other instruments.

From the 1970s onwards, a number of pioneering pianists and pedagogues have demonstrated that early pianos have the capacity radically to influence a musician's responses. Rhetorical gestures, rhythmic flexibility and much more attention to articulation have been prioritised over more traditional lyrical elements. There have also been significant advancements in the construction of COPIES OF INSTRUMENTS, the best of which show subtlety and finesse. The agility of articulation that is an essential part of the character and vitality of the music of earlier times is nowadays all too readily sacrificed in favour of greater projection within large concert halls.

FURTHER READING

M. N. Clinkscale, *Makers of the Piano*, 2 vols. (Oxford University Press, 1993 and 1999).
R. Harding, *The Piano-Forte: Its History Traced to the Great Exhibition of 1851* (Cambridge University Press, 1933).
S. Pollens, *The Early Pianoforte* (Cambridge University Press, 1995).

GEOFFREY GOVIER

Freiburger Barockorchester German period orchestra formed in 1985 by students at the Freiburg Musikhochschule.

The Freiburger Barockorchester ensemble gave its inaugural public concert (of music by Purcell, LULLY, CORELLI, MUFFAT and Wassenaer) in Lahr in November 1987, made its first appearance abroad in Amsterdam in 1989 and undertook its first visit to the USA in 1995. By that time it had already secured a reputation as one of the world's premier Baroque groups, consistently capable of delivering performances combining high technical standards, precise ensemble and refined but vital tonal blend with evident group spirit and controlled interpretative energy.

The orchestra functions as a collective, and has never had a formal music director. In the first decade many of its concerts were either conducted or led by violinist Thomas Hengelbrock, but over the years the majority have been led from within by one or other of its two concertmasters, Gottfried von der Goltz and Petra Müllejans. In this form it has recorded much late Baroque repertory, including J. S. BACH's orchestral suites and concertos for VIOLIN and HARPSICHORD, Vivaldi's *Le quattro stagioni* and TELEMANN's complete *Musique de table*. It has also recorded a number of Classical and pre-Classical works including symphonies and concertos by C. P. E. BACH, HAYDN and MOZART.

The orchestra has worked with guest conductors on larger-scale projects, including NICHOLAS MCGEGAN in HANDEL operas at the Göttingen Handel Festival and RENÉ JACOBS on projects including Haydn's *Die Schöpfung* and *Die Jahreszeiten* and several Mozart operas. More recently it has recorded symphonies by Schubert and Schumann with Pablo Heras-Casado.

A parallel ensemble, the Freiburg BarockConsort, exists to explore repertoire for smaller instrumental groupings; its recordings include Telemann's 'Paris' Quartets and works by Biber, Schmelzer, Bertali and Muffat.

LINDSAY KEMP

Freillon-Poncein, Jean-Pierre (b. France, c1655; d. France, c1720) French composer and writer on music.

Freillon-Poncein is believed to have lived in the Dauphiné province from 1700 until 1708. Little else is known about his life, although according to FÉTIS he was 'prévost (deputy) des hautbois' of the 'grande écurie' at the French court.

Strangely, however, he does not appear in any known court records. Freillon-Poncein's treatise *La véritable manière d'apprendre à jouer en perfection du haut-bois, de la flûte et du flageolet, avec les principes de la musique pour la voix et pour toutes sortes d'instrumens* (Paris: Collombat, 1700) is significant for being the first published French tutor for the OBOE, RECORDER and flageolet. The book sets out to teach the rudiments of music and offers guidance for composing dance movements, before providing FINGERING charts, trill fingerings and instructions for ORNAMENTS and ARTICULATIONS. Interestingly, Freillon-Poncein uses the tonguing syllables *tu* and *ru* (like LOULIÉ and JACQUES HOTTETERRE) and assumes equal temperament for wind instruments, while acknowledging the existence of major and minor semitones. The treatise ends with four short pieces: *L'Embarras de Paris* in six parts, a Trio for recorders, *Bruits de guerre* in three parts, and a *Passacaille* and two minuets for recorder.

FURTHER READING

D. Lasocki, 'Freillon Poncein, Hotteterre and the recorder', *American Recorder*, 10/2 (Spring, 1969), 40–3.

L. Pottier, *Les 3 méthodes de flûte à bec en France à l'époque baroque – Loulié, Freillon-Poncein, Hotteterre* (Bourg la Reine: Zurfluh, 1996).

ASHLEY SOLOMON

Frescobaldi, Girolamo Alessandro (b. Ferrara, bap. mid-September 1583; d. Rome, 1 March 1643) Italian composer and keyboard player.

Frescobaldi was one of the first composers to devote his energies to instrumental composition. Although he journeyed outside Italy only once, his keyboard music was known all over Europe. He taught many players, including his most famous pupil J.J. Froberger. He published seven keyboard books (many of which were reprinted several times) and instrumental music, motets and secular songs. He became organist to the Capella Giulia of San Pietro, Rome in 1608. His keyboard music consists of more than 150 printed pieces plus many attributed to him only in manuscripts. In addition to liturgical ORGAN music, the printed keyboard music consists of two books of toccatas, contrapuntal pieces (ricercare, canzona and capriccio) and variation sets based on dances and songs. His use of chromaticism and the wide range of modulation of the later pieces stretched meantone TEMPERAMENT to its limits.

Frescobaldi recognised the interpretative challenge set by his keyboard pieces and he included performance instructions in the prefaces to *Il primo libro di toccate* (1615), *Il primo libro di capricci* (1624) and *Fiori Musicali* (1635). His guidelines concern the freedoms of TASTE which cannot be conveyed by the musical NOTATION but which he considered necessary for stylish interpretation. These include the selection of appropriate tempi and a flexible pulse for expressive reasons (as in the contemporary madrigal), the ARTICULATION of the overall musical structure, the execution and shaping of trills, unwritten rhythmic inequality, options to omit sections at will, and techniques to combat the short decay of harpsichord sound – arpeggiation and the restriking of dissonances and suspensions. He recommends that a toccata or capriccio should begin slowly to contrast with the following faster sections and he requires a relaxation of the tempo at cadences to signal the end of a section and to lend clarity in fast or harmonically complex passages.

FURTHER READING

Frescobaldi Thematic Catalogue Online (FTCO). http://frescobaldi.music.duke.edu.
F. Hammond, *Girolamo Frescobaldi* (Cambridge, MA: Harvard University Press, 1983).
R. Judd, 'Italy', in A. Silbiger (ed.), *Keyboard Music before 1700* (New York: Schirmer Books 1995), 235–311.

TERENCE CHARLSTON

Fröhlich, (Franz) Joseph (b. Würzburg, 28 May 1780; d. Würzburg, 5 January 1862) German teacher, administrator, critic, theorist, conductor and composer.

Joseph Fröhlich was a prolific composer, but is now remembered for his influential theoretical, didactic and critical writings. He was keen to link theory and practice, as is especially evident from his *Vollständige theoretisch-praktische Musikschule* (Bonn, 1810–11), which includes instructions for playing the full range of musical instruments. Some of Fröhlich's advice to wind players reflects an era when health was an altogether more fragile affair. He recommended a moderate lifestyle and the avoidance of anything that could damage the chest, such as running, horseback riding and the excessive consumption of hot drinks. One should not practise after a meal, so the afternoon was best avoided; furthermore, one should not drink immediately after practising if the lungs are still warm, since this had been the cause of many an early death. In the case of dry lips – very bad for the embouchure – the mouth should be rinsed with an alcoholic beverage to give the lips new strength.

Fröhlich was a contributor to one of the most ambitious (yet incomplete) encyclopedia projects ever attempted, the *Allgemeine Encyclopädie der Wissenschaften und Künste* published by Johann Samuel Ersch and Johann Gottfried Gruber from 1818. His critical work also includes perceptive contributions to the journal *Caecilia*. John Warrack has observed that in his final years Fröhlich was engaged in writing a history of early music.

Fröhlich made an influential contribution to the development of holistic musical education. His work as a teacher and administrator encompassed several disciplines, notably AESTHETICS. In his youth he was a student of law and philosophy as well as music, founding the Akademische Bande, a student choral and orchestral group, which in 1804 became part of the university. This first German state music school established a singing school in 1820, for which Fröhlich wrote his *Systematischer Unterricht zum Erlernen und Behandeln der Singkunst überhaupt* (Würzburg, 1822–9).

FURTHER READING

H. Unverricht, 'Franz Joseph Fröhlich als Musikhistoriker und Musikschriftsteller', *Musik in Bayern*, 22 (1981), 151–62.

COLIN LAWSON

Fuchs, Carl (b. Offenbach am Main, 3 June 1865; d. Manchester, 9 June 1951) German cellist and teacher.

Fuchs was a pupil of BERNHARD COSSMANN in Frankfurt and Carl Davidov in St Petersburg. He was co-principal cello in the Scottish Orchestra for the winter season 1887–8, and on Clara Schumann's recommendation succeeded Ernest Vieuxtemps as principal cellist of the Hallé Orchestra 1887–1914. He played chamber music with SIR CHARLES and Lady (Wilma Neruda) HALLÉ, played quartets with Ernest Schiever (a JOACHIM pupil), and was a member of the Brodsky Quartet (1895–1926). He was professor of cello at the Royal Manchester College of Music (1893–1914 and 1921–42), and also taught regularly in Newcastle upon Tyne from 1918. His *Violoncello-Schule* (3 vols., London, 1906; 2/1909) was notable for recommending retention of the older posture, without tailpin. His teaching was strongly influenced by Davidov, especially as regards BOWING technique. Fuchs gave the English premiere of BRAHMS's C minor Piano Trio, and was the soloist in the Hallé Orchestra's first performances of the Lalo and Dvořák concertos, STRAUSS's *Don Quixote,* and Tchaikovsky's *Variations on a Rococo Theme.* He was associated with John Ireland, with whom he performed Ireland's Cello Sonata (1923). Fuchs only made one (private) recording (1930), that of Tricklir's *Adagio and Rondo* (in *The Recorded Cello Volume II,* Pearl, GEMM 9984–6).

FURTHER READING

C. Fuchs, *Erinnerungen eines Offenbacher Cellisten* (Bethel bei Bielefeld: Buchdruckerei der Anstalt Bethel, 1932), trans. H. Fuchs as *Musical and Other Recollections of Carl Fuchs, Cellist* (Manchester: Sherrat & Hughes, 1937).

GEORGE KENNAWAY

Fuhrmann, Martin Heinrich (b. Templin, Uckermark, bap. 29 December 1669; d. Berlin, bur. 25 June 1745) German cantor, organist and writer on music.

Of Fuhrmann's many publications, most important for performers are *Musicalischer Trichter* (Frankfurt a. d. Spree, 1706) and its concise version, *Musica vocalis in nuce* (Berlin, [1715]). The *Trichter* (a 'funnel' for pouring musical knowledge into a pupil) is concerned with the training of all-male church choirs. The musical style envisaged is similar to the rather chaste version of concertato style exemplified by Johann Schelle, Leipzig Thomascantor from 1676 to 1701, with whom Fuhrmann studied counterpoint. Fuhrmann explains a relatively small number of *Manieren*, more in order that singers may recognise them as ornaments than that they should add them. He considers virtuoso ORNAMENTATION unsuitable for church music where it interferes with the comprehensibility of the words, and it should not be used where voices and instruments are doubled. For this he cites Buxtehude in Lübeck, who used up to thirty and more VIOLINS with Lullian discipline, allowing them to play only what was written. Fuhrmann also considers the lighter French dance types (bourrée, passepied etc.) unsuitable. For the performance of motets without instruments, such as those published by Andreas Hammerschmidt, he prefers those in four parts and recommends a cohort of two trebles and one each of alto, tenor and bass. For the more elaborate style with instruments (*Concerto*), he envisages a quartet of *Concertisten* with the option of an additional quartet (*Cappella*), located separately, to reinforce tuttis. In large churches he recommends the addition of a 16′ VIOLONE.

For basic training, he stresses the absolute necessity of the pupil possessing a CLAVICHORD of four octaves (C–c‴) in order to learn pitches and

TRANSPOSITION. In spite of the limitations of the clavichord fretted in quarter-comma meantone the singer must learn to distinguish the diesis (differentiate d♯ from e♭ etc.). Fuhrmann is advanced in using modern German nomenclature: *dur* and *moll* for major and minor; and *ces, des* etc. for flattened notes, so that note names can replace Guidonian syllables in sight singing. He also uses modern key signatures (although for only sixteen keys). He has much to offer in relation to trills, VIBRATO and other essential ornaments. The *Trichter* ends with a crash course over a three-month period for teaching a private pupil to sing in this style.

FURTHER READING

J. Butt, *Music Education and the Art of Performance in the German Baroque* (Cambridge University Press, 1994).

DAVID LEDBETTER

Fulda, Adam of (b. Fulda, c1450; d. Wittenberg, 1505?) German composer, singer, theorist and historiographer.

According to Adam, his *De Musica* was completed at the Benedictine monastery of Wormbach on 5 November 1490, where the author had retired from nearby Passau. Adam spent the rest of his life in the service of Ferdinand the Wise of Saxony at Torgau, becoming *Kapellmeister* in 1498. Most of his surviving compositions are sacred, but his best-known work was (and remains) the secular song 'Ach hülf mich leid', which enjoyed numerous reworkings, retextings and reprintings. His TREATISE is important as a snapshot of purely northern theoretical preoccupations and solutions, as it shows no knowledge of contemporaneous Italian thought. Noteworthy are the aesthetic judgements integrated into his composition rules, the early discussion of the notion of TACTUS, and his elaborations of the *musicus and cantor* trope into polemics against bad musicians and musicianship in his immediate surroundings.

FURTHER READING

P. J. Slemon, 'Adam von Fulda on *musica plana* and *compositio: De musica*, book II: a translation and commentary', PhD dissertation, University of British Columbia (1994). https://open.library.ubc.ca/circle/collections/ubctheses/831/items/1.0088909).

URI SMILANSKY

Fuller-Maitland, John Alexander (b. London, 7 April 1856; d. Carnforth, 30 March, 1936) English critic, editor and scholar.

After studying at Trinity College, Cambridge, where he came under the influence of Stanford, Fuller-Maitland took piano lessons with Edward Dannreuther and W. S. Rockstro. Rockstro introduced him to the HARPSICHORD and together they organised a concert of ancient music at the 1885 Music and Inventions Exhibition. At this time he also came under the influence of A. J. HIPKINS and acquired a harpsichord by Kirkman with which he gave many performances in the years before WWI. Alongside his journalistic career, which began at the *Pall Mall Gazette* (1882–4), followed by *The Guardian* (1884–9) and *The Times* (1889–1911), he pursued antiquarian research which resulted in editions of Purcell's *Twelve Sonatas of Three Parts* (1893), *Ode on St Cecilia's Day* (1895) and *Catches, Rounds, Two-Part and Three-Part Songs*

(1922). The last was a collaboration with William Barclay Squire, with whom he had already worked on his best-known publication, an edition of *The Fitzwilliam Virginal Book* (1894–9). His interest in early keyboard music was further reflected in EDITIONS of music by Benjamin Cosyn and William Byrd (both 1923) and by short monographs on the music of J. S. BACH – *The Suites of Bach* (1924), *The '48': Bach's Wohltemperirtes Clavier* (1925), *The Keyboard Suites of J. S. Bach* (1925) and *Bach's Brandenburg Concertos* (1929). In collaboration with Mrs Clara Bell, he translated Spitta's *Life of Bach* (1894–5), served as editor for the second edition of *Grove's Dictionary of Music and Musicians* (1904–10) and wrote *The Age of Bach and Handel*, the fourth volume of the *Oxford History of Music* (1904). As an editor, Fuller-Maitland produced reliable editions that conformed to the scholarly norms of his time; only the continuo realisations show their age. Following his retirement from *The Times*, he moved to Carnforth, Lancashire, where he published a volume of memoirs (1929).

FURTHER READING

H. C. Colles, 'J. A. Fuller-Maitland: Vale', *MT*, 77 (1936), 419–21.
J. A. Fuller-Maitland, *A Door-Keeper of Music* (London: John Murray, 1929).

PETER HORTON

G

Gabrieli, Andrea (b. Venice, 1532 or 1533; d. Venice, 30 August 1585) Italian composer and organist.

Andrea Gabrieli's teachers may have included Adriano Willaert and Vincenzo Ruffo. From 1555 to 1557 he was organist at San Geremia, Venice; in 1562 he was associated with Orlande de Lassus in the service of Albrecht V, Duke of Bavaria; by 1566 he was organist at St Mark's, Venice, alongside Claudio Merulo, influencing the growth of instrumental forces there until his death. His students included Gregor Aichinger, Hans Leo Hassler and LODOVICO ZACCONI.

The large-scale works for two or more choirs in the posthumous *Concerti* (1587) met sacred and civic ceremonial needs in Venice. However, Gabrieli also wrote smaller-scale motets (1565, 1576), Masses (1572) and psalm settings (1583), as well as books of madrigals (1556–89), settings of the choruses for Sophocles's *Oedipus tyrannus* at the Teatro Olimpico, Vicenza (1585), and many keyboard ricercars, toccatas and canzonas published only after his death.

FURTHER READING

F. Degrada (ed.), *Andrea Gabrieli e il suo tempo: atti del convegno internazionale (Venezia 16–18 settembre 1985)* (Florence: Olschki, 1987).

TIM CARTER

Gabrieli, Giovanni (b. ?Venice, c1554–7; d. Venice, August 1612) Italian composer and organist, nephew of ANDREA GABRIELI.

Giovanni Gabrieli was trained by his uncle Andrea and served under Lassus at the court of Albrecht V, Duke of Bavaria, c1575–9. In 1585 he succeeded Claudio Merulo as organist at St Mark's, Venice. His large-scale works in the 1587 *Concerti* (alongside pieces by Andrea) and in two books of 'sacred symphonies' (1597, 1612) typify Venetian ceremonial music in the early Baroque period, whether for St Mark's or for other rich institutions such as the Scuola di San Rocco. However, they remain fraught with performance problems in terms of their scoring for voices and instruments.

Gabrieli's output also included madrigals, keyboard *intonationi* (1593), and canzonas and sonatas for instrumental ensemble. Among his students were the Italians Francesco Stivori and Taddeo del Guasto (who edited the posthumous *Canzoni e sonate* of 1615), as well as northerners such as Melchior Borchgrevinck, Mogens Pedersøn and Heinrich Schütz.

FURTHER READING

D. Arnold, *Giovanni Gabrieli and the Music of the Venetian High Renaissance* (London: Oxford University Press, 1979).

TIM CARTER

Gaffurius, Franchinus (b. Lodi, 14 January 1451; d. Milan, 25 June 1522) Italian theorist, composer and choirmaster.

Arguably the most accomplished and influential music theorist around 1500, Gaffurius gives valuable information about aspects of musical performance of his time, particularly in his widely influential *Practica musicae* of 1496. In Book 1 he offers a rare account of the Ambrosian psalm tones, illustrated through musical examples, and observes that the TEMPO of a plainsong melody should be somewhat slower on solemn feasts than on normal ones. In Book 3, Gaffurius deals with the issue of tempo in polyphonic music, pointing out that one TACTUS (i.e. the unit of time marked by the up-and-down motion of the hand, now commonly called 'beat' or 'pulse') was equivalent to the pulse of a man breathing normally (the meaning of this observation, however, is ambiguous). Gaffurius also discusses at length the topic of the proportional relationships between different time signatures. By advocating (with TINCTORIS) that minims retain their value across different metres, he departed from the standard 'equal breve' (or 'equal semibreve') position (Busse Berger, 212–32).

FURTHER READING

A. M. Busse Berger, *Mensuration and Proportion Signs: Origins and Evolution* (Oxford: Clarendon Press, 1993), *passim*.

C. A. Miller, 'Gaffurius's *Practica musicae*: origin and contents', *MD*, 22 (1968), 105–28.

E. Segerman, 'A re-examination of the evidence on absolute tempo before 1700 – I', *EMc*, 24/2 (1996), 227–48.

STEFANO MENGOZZI

Galeazzi, Francesco (b. Turin, 1758; d. Rome, January 1819) Italian theorist, violinist and composer.

Trained in Turin, Galeazzi settled in Rome, where he was a VIOLIN teacher, composer and music director of the Teatro Valle for fifteen years. By c1780 he was in Ascoli Piceno, where he married and spent his later years. Few of his compositions have survived.

Galeazzi's *Elementi teorico-pratici di musica* (2 vols., Rome, 1791, 1796) is the most comprehensive eighteenth-century Italian TREATISE and an important source of information about Classical style. Each volume is divided into two parts. The first part of volume one is an elementary musical grammar, and the second provides a methodical survey of violin technique and general performance practice, with a hypothetical three-year study plan for beginners. It includes chapters on INTONATION, tonal uniformity, BOWING, multiple stopping, HARMONICS, ORNAMENTS, diminution, IMPROVISATION and other issues such as TEMPO and the expressive associations of keys and modulation. Galeazzi describes ornaments as 'improvisatory' and considers EXPRESSION and the tasteful improvisation of 'diminutions' as the two principal ingredients of style. He is reserved about VIBRATO usage, claiming that its vacillations in pitch can be in poor TASTE. Notable also are his more user-friendly focus on the G major (as opposed to the traditional C major) scale and his chapters on the duties of the orchestral leader, the proportion of instruments in ORCHESTRAS of various sizes and the distribution of orchestras in church, chamber and theatre, including seating plans of the Turin and Dresden orchestras.

The second volume comprises a brief history of music, with emphasis on theory and a study of harmony, counterpoint, melody, structure, instrumentation and other aspects of composition. A supplement to the first volume describes Galeazzi's METRONOME invention and the second edition of this volume adds four tables of bowings, some brief studies and two examples of ornamentation of a slow movement by CORELLI.

FURTHER READING

A. Frascarelli, '*Elementi teorico-pratici di musica* by Francesco Galeazzi: an annotated English translation and study of volume 1', DMA dissertation, University of Rochester (1968).
J. E. Smiles, 'Directions for improvised ornamentation in Italian method books of the late eighteenth century', *JAMS*, 31 (1978), 495–509.
M. Sutter, 'Francesco Galeazzi on the duties of the leader or concertmaster', *The Consort*, 32 (1976), 185–92.

ROBIN STOWELL

Galilei, Vincenzo (b. S Maria a Monte, Tuscany, ?1520; d. Florence, bur. 2 July 1591) Italian lutenist, teacher, composer and theorist.

Galilei was a pivotal figure within Giovanni Bardi's Florentine Camerata, where he found a fertile context for intellectual discussions on poetry, music and musical theory. He wrote and published two EDITIONS of the *Fronimo* (1568 and 1584), a didactic dialogue on playing, composing and intabulating music for the LUTE, and many other works (some unpublished) on theoretical matters and musical composition; especially significant is his *Dialogo della musica antica et della moderna* (1581), in which he presented the first known examples of ancient Greek songs, four hymns later ascribed to the second-century AD citharode Mesomedes.

In 1572 Galilei started an extensive correspondence with the humanist Girolamo Mei, whose influence led him to claim the inferiority of modern polyphonic music, the intricacies of which tended to obscure the poetic text (although in his two manuscript treatises on counterpoint he showed a deep knowledge of contemporary polyphony) and programmatically to adhere to Mei's appreciation of monody inspired by the ancient Greek ideal of song, the only genre that could realise music's true aim – the EXPRESSION of the AFFECTIONS.

Thanks to Mei, Galilei had access to the work of Aristoxenus, the Peripatetic philosopher who, through an empirical tuning system that avoided giving a mathematical quantification of intervals, had admitted the possibility of dividing the tone (9:8, mathematically indivisible in equal parts) into two semitones. This rediscovery supported contemporary musicians' need to adopt a system of tuning that could solve the problems inherent in Pythagorean INTONATION (based on 'pure' consonances), especially during modulation. Realising that mathematical theory and musical practice do not always coincide and taking Aristoxenus as a model of empiricism, Galilei engaged in a polemic against his former teacher ZARLINO; and he carried out acoustical experiments with lute strings of various materials, influencing his son Galileo to develop similar experimental interests.

FURTHER READING

C. V. Palisca, *Girolamo Mei (1519–1594): Letters on Ancient and Modern Music to Vincenzo Galilei and Giovanni Bardi. A Study with Annotated Text* (Rome: American Institute of Musicology, 1977).
Humanism in Italian Renaissance Musical Thought (New Haven, CT and London: Yale University Press, 1985).
The Florentine Camerata: Documentary Studies and Translations (New Haven, CT and London: Yale University Press, 1989).

ELEONORA ROCCONI

Gallay, Jacques François (b. Perpignan, 8 December 1795; d. Paris, 18 October 1864) French HORN player, teacher and composer.

Gallay was the last great natural horn specialist in France, renowned for his quality of tone in both open and stopped notes, his certainty of attack and clarity in rapid passages. Compared to his teacher DAUPRAT's tutor, his *Méthode pour le cor* is limited to basic technical issues. There are paragraphs on holding the instrument, the position of the mouthpiece on the lips, TONGUING and others including emptying water from the instrument. He recommends that players should maximise the variety of tone colour while avoiding uneven volume, by blowing less hard on open notes and harder on stopped ones. The *Méthode* also includes a chart showing the different hand positions required to produce all the notes through the range of the instrument and detailed descriptions of his preferred mouthpieces: his 'model no. 1' for high horn players had an internal diameter of 16½ mm, his 'model no. 2' for low players 18½ mm. He recommended a rim width of 2½ mm, a total length of 72 mm and a diameter at the 'tail' of the mouthpiece of 7 mm.

Gallay was a *cor alto* (high horn player), though he preferred to use only the middle register for solo performances. His preference for horns with a relatively small bell throat influenced French design long after his death. His compositions include caprices and studies for solo horn, numerous fantasies for horn and piano, duets, trios and a Grand Quartet, Op. 26 for four horns, each crooked in a different key. Although the fantasies use the era's characteristic theme and variation form, they are musically more significant than most and the *Préludes mesurés et non mesurés* retain their value both musically and as study material.

FURTHER READING

B. Coar, *A Critical Study of the Nineteenth-Century Horn Virtuosi in France* (De Kalb, IL: Coar, 1952).
J.-F. Gallay, *Méthode pour le cor*, Op. 54 (Paris: Colombier, c1845).
R. Morley-Pegge, *The French Horn. Some Notes on the Evolution of the Instrument and of its Technique* (London: Benn, 1960, 2/1973).

JOHN HUMPHRIES

Galpin, Francis William (b. Dorchester, 25 December 1858; d. Richmond, Surrey, 30 December 1945) English organologist and collector of musical instruments.

Galpin developed an interest in music from an early age and in the early 1880s played clarinet under Charles Villiers Stanford in the orchestra of the Cambridge University Musical Society. During this period he started a collection that grew to include over 300 European musical instruments, focusing on the seventeenth, eighteenth and early nineteenth centuries, also including copies of early models for practical use.

Galpin's musical interests were equally divided between the history, description and classification of instruments, with particular attention towards the English ones, and actual performance on them. His *Old English Instruments of Music* (London: Methuen & Co., 1910) and *A Textbook of European Musical Instruments* (London: Williams & Norgate, 1937) are among the most extensive organological discourses of his time, and he is one of the major contributors of entries on musical instruments in the third and fourth editions of *Grove's Dictionary*. Between 1900 and 1903 he consulted extensively for the International Exhibition at the Crystal Palace in London, for which he developed an extension of VICTOR-CHARLES MAHILLON's classification system, and for the Metropolitan Museum of Art in New York and the Musikhistoriska Museet in Stockholm.

The records of his activity during his years as a vicar in Essex (1891–1933) give an example of the broadness of his interests as a performer: in a series of annual concerts he played on the SERPENT, BARYTON, marimba, nyastaranga (an Indian instrument introduced into Europe by Rajah Sourindro Mohun Tagore during this period) and a variety of HORNS. He also oversaw local musical programmes, which included some of the earliest practical revivals of English Medieval country songs and dances, the establishment of a stable RECORDER quartet – among the earliest within the early music revival – and performances on LUTES, VIRGINALS, and SHAWMS. His musical activity drastically declined when in 1916 he transferred his collection to the Museum of Fine Arts in Boston, where it is still preserved.

FURTHER READING

N. Bessaraboff, *Ancient European Musical Instruments* (Cambridge, MA: Harvard University Press, 1941).

S. Godman, 'Francis William Galpin: music maker', *GSJ*, 12 (1959), 8–16.

A. Myers, 'Galpin, Francis William', in *Oxford Dictionary of National Biography*, 60 vols. (Oxford University Press, 2004), xxi, 334–6.

GABRIELE ROSSI ROGNONI

Ganassi dal Fontego, Sylvestro di (b. Fontego, nr Venice, 1492; d. c1550) Italian instrumentalist and writer.

Ganassi was employed as an instrumentalist in Venice from 1535, supplying court music for the Doge of Venice and sacred instrumental music for St Mark's. He was an excellent player of both the RECORDER and VIOLA DA GAMBA and also owned a small printing press. This enabled him to publish his own works, including two TREATISES, one for the recorder and the other for wind instruments, *Opera intitulata Fontegara* (1535), and one (in two volumes) for the VIOLA DA GAMBA, *Regola rubertina* (1542) and *Lettione seconda* (1543). Both treatises are more than simple instruction manuals; they include in-depth discussion of technique, with the main focus on subtleties of EXPRESSION, how to produce a good sound, rules to execute ORNAMENTATION successfully and numerous examples for ARTICULATION (BOWING, TONGUING and FINGERING). Ganassi always refers to the human voice as a model for expression and tonal variety.

FURTHER READING

H.-M. Linde, *The Recorder Player's Handbook* (Mainz: Schott, 1962).
J. M. Thomson, *The Cambridge Companion to the Recorder* (Cambridge University Press, 1995).

ASHLEY SOLOMON

Garaudé, Alexis de (b. Nancy, 21 March 1779; d. Paris, 23 March 1852) French singer, teacher and composer.

Garaudé was one of the most important French voice teachers of the early nineteenth century. At the age of twenty he enrolled at the PARIS CONSERVATOIRE, where he studied composition with REICHA and CAMBINI and SINGING with Crescentini and Garat, and where, from 1816 to 1841, he was professor of singing. During most of his tenure, the Conservatoire was directed by Cherubini, who promoted the Italian vocal style, based on didactic material prepared by Bernardo Mengozzi. Garaudé's *Méthode de chant*, first published in 1809, aimed to complete Mengozzi's work, and made constant comparison between French and Italian techniques.

Garaudé revived the eighteenth-century debate on the suitability of the French language for singing, and having illustrated the Italian accentual patterns of *troncho*, *piano* and *sdrucciolo*, he argued the case for long and short syllables in the French language, while deploring the lack of resonant vowel sounds in French. He advocated singing 'r' in the Italian manner (à la Piaf) rather than the guttural consonant in spoken French. He followed Mengozzi in differentiating between simple legato (PORTAMENTO) and *porte de voix*, which should always contain an audible slide and involve an anticipation of the final note. A large part of his *Méthode* is devoted to the performance of recitative, where he encouraged French singers to adopt the 'Italian' appoggiatura (Example 10).

The exercises incorporated in the *Méthode* are in the form of wordless vocalises, each of which isolates a particular mood or style; for example, *cantabile, bravura, agitato*. He repeatedly praised Gluck, Piccini and Sacchini for their effective setting of the French language and their understanding of extremes of emotion. His theories were further developed in the composition of more than 200 songs, chiefly romances.

Example 10: The 'Italian' appoggiatura (Alexis de Garaudé: *Méthode de chant*, Op. 40).

FURTHER READING

A. de Garaudé, *Méthode de chant*, Op. 40 (Paris: l'auteur, 1809, rev. 1811, 1830, 1854).
H. Gougelot, *La Romance française sous la Révolution et l'Empire* (Mehun: Legrand et fils, 1937).
D. Kauffman, 'Portamento in Romantic opera', *PPR*, 5 (1992), 139–58.

PATRICIA HOWARD

García, Manuel (I) (b. Seville, 21 January 1775; d. Paris, 10 June 1832) Spanish composer, singer and SINGING teacher.

García was active in a number of musical fields, and influential in all of them. The early years of his career were spent in Spain, where he made his mark as a composer and performer in a variety of dramatic forms. He subsequently composed over thirty dramatic works, rarely performed today, including *tonadillas*, *opere serie*, comic opera in both French and Italian traditions and one *tragédie lyrique*. Singing dominated García's middle years. From 1808 he travelled extensively in Spain, France and Italy. As Rossini's favourite tenor, he created the role of Norfolk in *Elisabetta regina d'Inghilterra* in Naples in 1815, and Almaviva in *Il barbiere di Siviglia* in Rome in 1816 (he had already sung the Count in MOZART's *Le nozze di Figaro* in Naples in 1812). In 1818 he spent a season in London where his Rossini roles included Lindoro in *L'italiana in Algeri*, and Otello.

García later returned to London where in 1824 he founded two singing academies, one offering a general musical education that included acting besides solo and ensemble singing, another for advanced professional training. García himself was self-taught; the only singing lessons he is known to have taken were at the age of thirty-seven with the tenor Giovanni Ansani. García's method, based on traditional Italian pedagogy, was set down in *Exercises and Method for Singing*, devised for his own students. Beginning with practice on *messe di voce*, his exercises progress to rapid scales and finally to PORTAMENTO. He gives exact instructions for the proper execution of the trill, 'beginning piano and adagio ... gradually increasing its force and accelerating the movement to a prestissimo'. The most useful content for twenty-first-century singers is the portfolio of CADENZAS of increasing elaboration.

In 1825 he travelled to New York where he sang and directed two seasons of Italian opera, the first performances of opera in Italian in the USA; besides a selection of his own operas and those of Rossini, he also sang the title role in Mozart's *Don Giovanni* (1826). His next venue was Mexico City, where he translated some of his own operas and Rossini's into Spanish. He returned to Paris in 1829 to devote his energies to teaching.

García's voice illustrates several aspects of early nineteenth-century performance practice. Always described as a tenor, the fact that he sang Mozart's Count Almaviva and Don Giovanni suggests he could adequately tackle baritone roles. As was customary at the time, he probably made extensive use of falsetto to perform the top range of his tenor roles, though he is also known to have transposed some of them down by as much as a third. His enduring reputation is as a singing teacher, a vocation he adopted almost accidentally but with spectacular success. Among his most distinguished pupils were the tenor

Adolphe Nourrit and two of his own children, Pauline Viardot and Maria Malibran. His pedagogical methods were further developed by his son MANUEL GARCÍA (II).

FURTHER READING

M. García, *Exercices pour la voix avec un discours préliminaire en français et italien* (Paris: Petit, c1820).
Exercises and Method for Singing with an Accompaniment for the Piano Forte (London: T. Boosey, 1824).
J. Radomski, *Manuel García (1775–1832): Chronicle of the Life of a 'bel canto' Tenor at the Dawn of Romanticism* (Oxford University Press, 2000).

PATRICIA HOWARD

García, Manuel (II) (b. Madrid, 17 March 1805; d. London, 1 July 1906) Spanish SINGING teacher.

Manuel García II's career as a singer was short and undistinguished, and in 1829 he abandoned the professional stage and dedicated his life to teaching. He had studied singing with his father MANUEL GARCÍA (I) and was thoroughly grounded in the older García's traditional method before developing his own more innovative approach. He is widely credited with undertaking the first scientifically based investigation into the art of singing. His study of physiology came about almost by accident: service in the French army in Algeria in 1830 led to his employment in military hospitals, which provided the opportunity for him to pursue his anatomical interests. His research was immediately recognised as groundbreaking. While teaching at the PARIS CONSERVATOIRE in 1830 to 1848, he attracted widespread interest with his paper 'Mémoire sur la voix humaine' presented to the *Académie des sciences* in 1841 and his *Traité complet de l'art du chant*, published in 1840, revised and expanded in 1847. In 1848 he moved to London to teach at the ROYAL ACADEMY OF MUSIC (1848–95). It was here that he invented the laryngoscope, an instrument which, with the use of mirrors, allowed the movement of the larynx during singing to be studied. García reported his studies in 'Observations on the human voice' presented to the Royal Society in 1855 and incorporated them in a further revision of his *Traité complet* in 1872.

From his father, García absorbed the traditional teaching of the great CASTRATO pedagogues, including TOSI and MANCINI, based on flexibility, evenness of tone and control of volume, especially in the highly valued technique of *messa di voce*. Their methods sought to inculcate a perfect legato and the smooth transition from one register to another. The younger García did not reject this approach, and many of his exercises have the same aim; for example, to pass smoothly from one register to another by alternating notes of the same pitch in head and chest registers. Where he broke new ground was in teaching a different understanding of cause and effect, based on his physiological research. García's method required the singer to transfer his attention from how he heard his voice to the sensations he felt during the process of singing. He was also influenced by changing musical styles and the demands of nineteenth-century opera for greater volume and a more dramatic manner of delivery.

Some of his recommendations are obscured by the ambiguous vocabulary endemic in writing about voice production. His insistence on beginning each note with a *coup de glotte* has been widely misunderstood (García later described it as a mental preparation rather than a physical one); his use of 'falsetto' to describe the register between chest voice and head voice is misleading, and his explanation of 'dark' and 'light' timbres is far from precise. He was, nevertheless, the most celebrated singing teacher of the nineteenth century. His pupils included Jenny Lind, Mathilde Marchesi and Charles Santley.

FURTHER READING

M. García, 'Observations on the human voice', *Proceedings of the Royal Society of London*, 7 (1854–5), 399–410.
Traité complet de l'art du chant (Mainz: Schott, 1840, 1847).

PATRICIA HOWARD

Gardiner, John Eliot (b. Fontmell Magna, England, 20 April 1943) English conductor and musical entrepreneur.

Gardiner's childhood encounters with the music of MONTEVERDI at Dartington directed by NADIA BOULANGER and Walter Goehr's 1957 performance of the *Vespro della Beata Vergine* at York Minster proved to be catalytic. Gardiner began CONDUCTING during his teens. In March 1964, whilst an undergraduate at Cambridge, he mounted a seminal performance of Monteverdi's *Vespro* in the chapel of King's College Cambridge, a work with which he has since enjoyed a long and fruitful relationship, having almost singlehandedly reinvented it for the age of commercial recordings. After Cambridge he studied with THURSTON DART and the conductor George Hurst, and in Paris with Boulanger between 1966 and 1968. Gardiner made his London conducting debut in 1966; his first Proms appearance was in 1968, the year before his operatic debut.

Gardiner's repertoire ranges from the Venetian Baroque to the early twentieth century. He has conducted orchestras worldwide, in Amsterdam, Berlin, Boston, Cleveland, Hamburg, Leipzig, London, Munich, Paris, Vancouver, Vienna and Zurich. He enjoys an ongoing relationship with the London Symphony Orchestra, in concerts and in the studio. He began his association with the Royal Opera House Covent Garden in 1973, since when he has also appeared at the Glyndebourne Festival and in houses throughout Europe.

Gardiner is best known, however, as a pioneering figure in HISTORICALLY INFORMED PERFORMANCE, a reputation enhanced by having founded three ensembles now based in London: the Monteverdi Choir, the ENGLISH BAROQUE SOLOISTS and the ORCHESTRE RÉVOLUTIONNAIRE ET ROMANTIQUE. Whilst much of the repertoire of these groups was not conducted in its time, Gardiner's role as their artistic director allows him to assert his strong personality, both on and off stage, and in rehearsal. With his Monteverdi Ensembles, Gardiner has disseminated his music making via the recording studio and BROADCAST media as well as making judicious use of new technologies.

The recipient of more Gramophone awards than any other living artist, Gardiner has made over 250 recordings, encompassing international labels such as Deutsche Grammophon, Decca, Erato and Philips, as well as his own Soli Deo Gloria. These recordings have been awarded most of the industry's leading honours, including the Diapason d'Or and two Grammys.

Gardiner's monograph *Music in the Castle of Heaven* (London: Allen Lane, 2013) draws upon his experiences of the texted works, the passions, masses and cantatas of J. S. BACH. Rather than a biographical account, the book presents a succession of fourteen contextualising approaches to Bach through his music.

Gardiner's achievements have been widely recognised. He became the inaugural president of the Bach-Archiv Leipzig in 2014, and in 2016 was awarded the Concertgebouw Prize. Gardiner maintains 500 acres in Dorset, England, organically farming sheep, cattle and cereals.

FURTHER READING

C. da Fonseca-Wollheim, 'Crops and music, each in its season', *The New York Times*, 5 April 2013.

INGRID E. PEARSON

Gasparini An Italian family of musicians, remembered for three brothers: Francesco (b. Camaiore, nr Lucca, 19 March 1661; d. Rome, 22 March 1727), a celebrated composer and teacher; Paolo Lorenzo (b. Camaiore, nr Lucca, 10 August 1668; d. ?Rome, after 1725) who worked in Rome as a violinist and violist; Michelangelo (b. Lucca, ?1670; d. Venice, ?1732), a singer in Venice who composed opera and taught SINGING, most famously to Faustina Bordoni.

Francesco Gasparini probably studied with CORELLI and Bernardo Pasquini in Rome in the early 1680s and became a member of the Accademia Filarmonica, Bologna in 1684. He returned to Rome in 1687, where he established his reputation as a composer of opera and occupied prominent church posts. He moved to Venice between 1701 and 1713 as *maestro di coro* at the Ospedale della Pietà, where he employed Vivaldi. He was a prolific composer of theatre and church music and a much sought-after teacher. His many pupils included the prominent Baroque composers Benedetto Marcello and Domenico Scarlatti and influential doyens of the *galant* style, including Galuppi, Platti and QUANTZ.

His BASSO CONTINUO tutor, *L'armonico pratico al cimbalo*, is an important witness to the full-voiced HARPSICHORD accompaniment style prevalent in Italy and explored in greater detail by the German theorist HEINICHEN. It was first published in Venice in 1708 and reissued many times in the eighteenth century, with the sixth and last edition appearing in 1802. Practical advice is given concerning the realisation of unfigured basses, the correct recognition of basic progressions and cadences, and the addition of dissonant notes, which Gasparini calls acciaccatura and *mordente*, to enrich the harmony of recitative. Read alongside its French equivalent, SAINT LAMBERT's *Nouveau traité de l'accompagnement* (Paris: Christophe Ballard, 1707), these accounts have been used to reconstruct continuo playing in modern times.

FURTHER READING

F. T. Arnold, *The Art of Accompaniment from a Thorough-Bass* (London: Oxford University Press, 1931; New York: Dover Publications, 1965), 250–5.

M. R. Butler, 'Italian opera in the eighteenth century', in S. P. Keefe (ed.), *The Cambridge History of Eighteenth-Century Music* (Cambridge University Press, 2009), 201–71.

F. Gasparini, *L'armonico pratico al cimbalo* (Venice, 1708), trans. F. S. Stillings and ed. D. L. Burrows as *The Practical Harmonist at the Keyboard* (New Haven, CT: Yale School of Music, 1963).

TERENCE CHARLSTON

Geminiani, Francesco (Saverio) (Xaviero) (b. Lucca, bap. 5 December 1687; d. Dublin, 17 September 1762) Italian composer, violinist and theorist.

Geminiani studied VIOLIN in Milan and later (evidently) in Rome with CORELLI. He held orchestral appointments in Rome (April 1704–December 1706), Naples (1706–7, 1711–14 as leader) and Lucca (1707–10) before moving to London (1714). He spent periods in Dublin (1733–40, 1759–62) and Paris (1749–55) and worked as a violinist, teacher, composer, music theorist, impresario and art dealer, performing mostly in aristocratic circles. His pupils included Matthew Dubourg, CHARLES AVISON, Michael Festing, Joseph Kelway and ROBERT BREMNER.

Like Corelli, Geminiani focused on instrumental composition, particularly the sonata and concerto grosso. Initially following Corelli's structural models, he developed an individual style, introducing French and other influences, increasing technical demands and adding a VIOLA to the customary concerto grosso *concertino* group. His adaptations of Corelli's Op. 5 sonatas as two sets of concerti grossi (1726; 1729) are also notable, along with his transcriptions derived largely from Corelli's Trio Sonatas, Op. 3 (1735). Some elaborate embellished versions of Corelli's Op. 5 sonatas have also been ascribed to him.

Geminiani's theoretical writings focus on practical matters, musical content outweighing textual instruction. His *Rules for Playing in a True Taste* (1748) and *A Treatise of Good Taste in the Art of Musick* (1749) discuss tasteful, expressive performance of ORNAMENTS and DYNAMICS, the later work describing the affective meaning of individual ornaments and providing a table 'of the elements of playing and singing in a good Taste'. Especially interesting are Geminiani's views about VIBRATO (summarised below). It is no coincidence that he significantly increased his annotation of phrasing, nuance and ARTICULATION in his later works; the application of *messe di voce*, previously sparingly used on long notes in slow movements, was especially extended.

Intended to broaden a composer's range of harmonic and tonal thought, Geminiani's *Guida Armonica* (c1752) comprises brief phrases of FIGURED BASS alongside annotations regarding their potential combination into longer sentences. His *The Art of Accompaniment* (c1756) demonstrates a range of keyboard realisations achievable from sample series of figured-bass patterns. *The Art of Playing the Guitar or Cittra* (1760) caters for the six-course 'English GUITAR', 'lesser guitar', or pandora and comprises a short introduction and eleven sonatas (in TABLATURE and staff notation) for that instrument (or violin).

Geminiani's most significant theoretical publication is his *The Art of Playing on the Violin* (1751), which appeared in several editions and in French, Dutch and German translations; subsequent TREATISES were based on its principles, and plagiarised versions were published well into the nineteenth century. Intended largely for advanced players, its textual content is relatively sparse.

Example 11: The so-called 'Geminiani grip'.

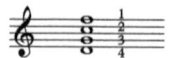

Although Geminiani recommends an old-fashioned violin hold with the instrument 'rested just below the collar-bone' without chin support, his so-called 'Geminiani grip' (Example 11) for acquiring the optimum hand placement in first position was adopted by LEOPOLD MOZART in the second edition of his *Versuch* (1769–70) and perpetuated well into the nineteenth century.

The Art... demands facility in seven positions ('orders') on all four strings. As Geminiani's violin-hold requires the thumb to shift *after* the movement of the hand, he favours bold leaps (such as 123–123, or 1234–1234) for upward shifts, often using adjacent fingers (23–23 or 12–12), and large hand movements (e.g. 4321–4321) for downward shifts. He acknowledges the importance of scales for cultivating intonation accuracy, finger independence, strength and agility, tone-quality, BOW division, and DYNAMICS. His guiding principle to raise the left-hand fingers only when necessary was mirrored in most eighteenth-century methods. His various exercises cultivate finger flexibility to facilitate extensions and contractions and reduce the need for shifts. His innovative one-finger-per-note FINGERING for chromatic scales, eventually championed in the twentieth century, offers greater evenness, articulation and clarity than the traditional 'slide' fingering (see Example 8, p. 234).

Geminiani encourages practice of his first six exercises in the various positions without the bow. He describes the typical early eighteenth-century Italian bow hold a short distance from the nut. His instruction about bow management, including the largely non-participatory role of the upper arm and shoulder, the need for flexibility of the wrist in order to cultivate a straight bow-stroke and the control of bow pressure – and hence, tonal quality and volume – by the index finger rather than the weight of the hand, underpins that of many treatises. He illustrates a wide range of bow strokes but rejects the long-standing rule of down-bow, whereby the 'good notes' of each bar are played with the stronger down-bow, in favour of a more flexible regime. He specifically warns against 'marking the Time' with the bow and encourages greater equality of ACCENTUATION between up and down strokes.

Geminiani consistently emphasises the performer's responsibility to convey the composer's intentions with accuracy, EXPRESSION and TASTE. His model is the human voice and he encourages an expressive performing style through imaginative, yet controlled employment of ORNAMENTATION, dynamics, varied and nuanced bowings, vibrato and other such means. He reproduces his table of ornaments and supporting text from his 1749 treatise on taste and relates how some ornaments can change their character or AFFECT according to their manner of execution. He considers vibrato ('close shake') an ornament, associating it with affective performance that may express majesty and dignity as well as affliction and fear. His recommendation to use vibrato 'as often as possible' to make sounds 'more agreeable', contrary to the sparing use advocated by his contemporaries, has been interpreted as *carte blanche* for the

Example 12: (a) Geminiani's sign for vibrato; and (b) his recommendation of when to introduce the effect (*The Art of Playing on the Violin* (1751), 26 and 33).

(a)

Tremolo

(b)

adoption of a 'modern' continuous vibrato; however, such an interpretation is highly controversial. Geminiani admits elsewhere that 'the Melody would be too much diversified' if the 'pure note' is not heard occasionally and annotates vibrato usage only once in a 13-bar Adagio (Example 12). Robert Bremner's re-issue (1777) of *The Art...* omits Geminiani's vibrato references entirely, thereby complementing the conservative views expressed in his *Some Thoughts on the Performance of Concert Music* (1777).

Geminiani's *The Art...* was the predominant treatise in England for over seventy-five years, eventually being superseded by SPOHR's *Violinschule* (1832). It was to re-emerge into the spotlight through DAVID BOYDEN'S FACSIMILE reproduction in the early 1950s and was eagerly adopted by the 'early music movement' as a seminal eighteenth-century text.

FURTHER READING

D. D. Boyden, 'Prelleur, Geminiani, and just intonation', *JAMS*, 4 (1951), 202–19.
  'The Corelli "solo" sonatas and their ornamental additions by Corelli, Geminiani, Dubourg, Tartini, and the "Walsh Anonymous"', *Musica antiqua III* (Bydgoszcz, 1972), 591–606.
  The History of Violin Playing from its Origins to 1761 (London: Oxford University Press, 1965).
P. Walls, '"Ill-compliments and arbitrary taste"? Geminiani's directions for performers', *EMc*, 14/2 (1986), 221–35.
N. Zaslaw, 'Ornaments for Corelli's Violin Sonatas, Op. 5', *EMc*, 24/1 (1996), 95–118.

ROBIN STOWELL

Gerle, Hans (b. Nuremberg, *c*1500; d. Nuremberg, 1570) German instrumentalist, LUTE maker and music arranger/compiler.

As performer, instrument builder and arranger, Gerle was well integrated into the musical powerhouse that was Nuremberg in the fifteenth and sixteenth centuries, where it is likely he spent his entire life. Unlike earlier virtuoso instrumentalists such as Conrad Paumann, who left the city to perform, teach and find wider circulation for his materials and playing style, Gerle's contribution consisted of the importation and popularisation in print of works from elsewhere, allowing them to resonate also within the German-speaking world. His *Tabulatur auff die Laudten* (Nuremburg: Hieronymus Formschneider,

1533) presents INTABULATIONS for lute of works mostly by Franco-Flemish composers of his as well as the earlier generation, while his *Eyn newes sehr künstlichs Lautenbuch* (1552) presents fantasias and dances transcribed into German TABLATURE from earlier Italian lutebooks. His first publication, *Musica teutsch, auf die Instrument der grossen unnd kleinen Geygen, auch Lautten* (1532), concentrates mostly on German composers, and presents versions for bowed-strings ensembles, as well as for solo lute. The importance of this publication for modern practitioners, though, is in the introductory essays it contains. These offer step-by-step instruction in the setting up, use and NOTATION relevant to the lute as well as the VIOL and VIOLIN families. For the bowed strings, they offer the first surviving instance of such detailed instruction, and enable the reconstruction of the tuning system and technique. The presentation makes it clear that the target audience need not have any prior musical knowledge, and was imagined as bourgeois amateurs interested in teaching themselves music for personal consumption at home, perhaps having just bought a set of instruments from the publication's author. This opens a window on the otherwise rather elusive world of non-aristocratic and non-professional music making.

FURTHER READING

J. Pierce, 'Hans Gerle: sixteenth-century lutenist and pedagogue', PhD dissertation, University of North Carolina (1973).
A. Silbiger, 'The first viol tutor: Hans Gerle's *Musica Teutsch*', *JVdGSA*, 6 (1969), 34–48.

URI SMILANSKY

Gesture ('Historical Action') *see* BAROQUE GESTURE

Giorgetti, Ferdinando (b. Florence, 25 June 1796; d. Florence, 22 March 1867) Italian violinist, composer and teacher.

Giorgetti studied with Nardini's pupil Francesco Giuliani and served as court chamber musician to Elisa Bonaparte in Lucca. After a sojourn in Paris (1812–14) he returned to Florence, renouncing his performing career due to paralysis in his legs. He turned to composition (studying with Ugolini) and teaching and became one of the first of a Florence-based movement (Orchestra Filarmonica) to encourage wider appreciation in Italy of the works of the German Classical composers, especially BEETHOVEN. In 1840, he founded (with Luigi Picchianti) the first Italian music journal, *Rivista Musicale Fiorentina*, and ten years later established, with his pupil Giovacchino Giovacchini, an important series of instrumental concerts in Florence, paving the way for the Società del Quartetto, founded (1861) by Abramo Basevi.

Giorgetti composed much chamber music and various sacred works. He taught the VIOLIN and VIOLA at Florence's Istituto Musicale from 1839, counting among his pupils Federico Consolo, Guido Papini, Federico Sarti, Carlo Verardi and cellist Jefte Sbolci. He left four major didactic works: *Piccolo Metodo* (unpublished; ms I-Fc) preparatory to BARTOLOMEO CAMPAGNOLI's *Metodo*; *Studi per violino che comprendono l'esercizio delle sette prime posizioni [...]* (completed by Giovacchini); *6 Studi*, Op. 28 preparatory to PAGANINI's *Capricci*; and *Metodo per Esercitarsi a ben suonare l'alto-viola* (Milan: Ricordi, 1854). The latter addresses the dearth of specialist violists by encouraging talented violinists to make the transition to the viola. Nevertheless, he was convinced that violists required a different training regime from violinists, and his pedagogical methods did much to progress the technical standards demanded by the studies of Alessandro Rolla and Eugenio Cavallini. That said, the technical instruction in Part 1 is conservative; more important are the six character studies in duet format included in Part 2, and particularly the challenging *Gran Solo in forma di Scena drammatica* in Part 3, which involves the violist taking an opera singer's role in music that combines recitatives, passages of arioso and coloratura-like virtuoso figuration. For both violin and viola playing, Giorgetti advocated: as few left-hand movements as possible; sparing VIBRATO usage, and only where indicated (by a dotted line); and, like Campagnoli, right elbow placement close to the body. And he emphasised the viola's potential as an accompanying instrument, devoting the second part of his method to double and triple stopping.

FURTHER READING

M. Fabbri, *Ignoti momenti rossiniani.* [...] *Le segrete confessioni a Ferdinando Giorgetti* [...], *Chigiana*, 25/5 (1968), 265–85.
C. Paradiso (ed.), *Il cavalier Ferdinando Giorgetti musicista romantico a Firenze* (Rome: Società Editrice di Musicologia, 2015).
L. Picchianti, 'La scuola fiorentina di violino', *Gazzetta Musicale di Milano*, 6/10 (7 March, 1847), 74–5.

ROBIN STOWELL

Goebel, Reinhard (b. Siegen, Westphalia, 31 July 1952) German Baroque violinist and conductor.

Goebel studied the VIOLIN with Franz-Josef Maier, Saschko Gawriloff and Marie Leonhardt. In 1973 he and fellow students from the Cologne Conservatoire founded MUSICA ANTIQUA KÖLN, with which he has appeared both as soloist and as director, toured extensively and recorded prolifically. As a result of a career-threatening focal dystonia of his left hand in the early 1990s, Goebel re-learnt the violin, BOWING left handed and scaling down his solo playing. He later reverted to a conventional playing technique and undertook further solo roles, but his dystonia returned in 2006, forcing him to abandon violin playing completely and concentrate on CONDUCTING.

Goebel's discography is extensive, ranging from Biber's 'Mystery' sonatas through concertos, orchestral suites and chamber music by J. S. BACH and TELEMANN, and vocal music of the Bach family to works by Dresden court composers, notably HEINICHEN, Pisendel and Hasse. He has written about Bach and Heinichen performance and is admired for his respect for the composer's annotations, insightful interpretations and slick, clearly articulated performances.

FURTHER READING

M. Elste, 'Alte Musik als ästhetische Gegenwart. Reinhard Goebel im Gespräch', *Fonoforum*, 40/10 (October, 1995), 36–42.
S. Schwarzer, 'Goebel, Reinhard', in S. Drees (ed.), *Lexikon der Violine* (Laaber Verlag, 2004), 264–5.

ROBIN STOWELL

Gordon Woodhouse (née Gwynne), Violet (b. London, 23 April 1871; d. Thrupp, nr Stroud, 9 January 1948) British keyboard player.

Gordon Woodhouse's first-known encounter with early keyboard instruments was in 1896, when she heard a performance by ARNOLD DOLMETSCH. She subsequently studied with him and in 1899 acquired her first HARPSICHORD, a Longman and Broderip with an additional second manual by Dolmetsch. In 1920 she became the first to record on the harpsichord, having been awarded a three-year contract with HMV. She combined her advocacy both for the CLAVICHORD and for Domenico Scarlatti's keyboard sonatas through her performances, and inspired Thomas Goff to make clavichords.

Gordon Woodhouse's social circle included Lawrence of Arabia, Beecham, Diaghilev, Picasso, Walton, Siegfried Sassoon, George Bernard Shaw, Ethel Smyth and the Sitwells. She performed with BUSONI, CASALS, Sarasate, Segovia and Tertis, and her homes were artistic meccas. Her passion for English folksong inspired Warlock and resulted in an unlikely folksong arrangement for harpsichord and FLUTE by VAUGHAN WILLIAMS (Delius also wrote a delightfully unidiomatic harpsichord piece for her). Her broad repertoire ranged from the English virginalists to Albéniz and Granados on the clavichord. One of her two pupils was Valda Aveling.

FURTHER READING

V. J. Douglas-Home, *The Life and Loves of Violet Gordon Woodhouse* (London: Harvill Press, 1996).

JULIAN PERKINS

Gould, Glenn (Herbert) (b. Toronto, 25 September 1932; d. Toronto, 4 October 1982) Canadian pianist, writer and composer.

Gould must be counted as one of the major BACH interpreters of the twentieth century; his recordings of the *Goldberg Variations*, the *48* and *The Art of Fugue*, among others, are legendary. It could be said that he had not the slightest regard for historical performance. His trills were exactly as we know they were not done; his TEMPI were extreme and totally without respect for all that is known about Baroque DANCE. He did what he liked with scores, sometimes to 'correct' the composers whom he believed to have made wrong choices: bringing out melodies, altering accidentals in sequences, adding extra harmonic support and giving thought-out form to improvisatory passages – for example, in Handel's *Suites*. He did a rare recording on the HARPSICHORD but used an instrument that he liked because it resembled a piano (a Wittmayer) but admitted that he never touched this instrument before he entered the recording studio, rehearsing only on the PIANO.

His ideas about music were more deeply rooted in Romantic views than is generally admitted; he subscribed to the hyper-Romantic view that music existed in a purer form before it was interpreted. Thus he practised silently, getting to know pieces not through the keyboard but in his mind; on several occasions he observed that fingers give rise to bad ideas and that music is played with the mind. It has to be remembered that his attitude towards historical performance was based on a 1950s view which prescribed total respect for the written score but was still in its infancy about instruments, EXPRESSION, genre and

ARTICULATION. However, on reading his opinions – which are very coherent and clear – it might be concluded that even if he had known more about historical performance, he would not have altered the way he played one jot.

FURTHER READING

K. Bazzana, *Glenn Gould: The Performer in the Work* (Oxford University Press, 1997).

RICHARD LANGHAM SMITH

Greenberg, Noah (b. New York, 9 April 1919; d. New York, 9 January 1966) American conductor and musicologist.

Greenberg was born to Polish immigrant parents in the Bronx, NY. His career in early music began in the 1950s, when he assembled a group of talented, interested musicians, including Bernard Krainis, LaNoue Davenport, Sheila Schonbrun and Russell Oberlin. These formed the core of the NEW YORK PRO MUSICA Antiqua, founded in 1952–3. Audacious programming and polished, energetic performances established the group as a musical phenomenon. In January 1958 at the Cloisters, Greenberg led a reconstruction of the thirteenth-century *Play of Daniel*, which became a signature production. His hallmark was a combination of scholarship, musicianship and passion for unexplored early repertoires. By the time of his premature death in 1966, he was regarded as the father of the early music revival in the USA; the American Musicological Society makes an annual award in his memory for work of benefit to both scholars and performers.

FURTHER READING

J. Gollin, *Pied Piper: The Many Lives of Noah Greenberg* (Hillsdale, NY: Pendragon, 2001).

ROSS DUFFIN

Gregory of Tours (b. Clermont Ferrand, ?538; d. Rome, 12 March 604). Frankish historian and Bishop of Tours (573–94).

Gregory provides considerable, although imprecise, information on religious music in his historical and hagiographical works. Apart from one reference to non-Christian SINGING, all his information concerns ecclesiastical music, although many of the references concern processions: the major liturgical processions of the Rogations (particularly those from Clermont to Brioude) involved the singing of psalms, but so too did the public movement of bishops. In addition, Gregory comments on the singing of psalms within churches, both episcopal and monastic. Where possible psalms were sung antiphonally, with one part taken by the *cantor*. This is attested in both cathedrals and in monasteries, most notably the monastery of St Maurice d'Agaune in the Valais, where the liturgy of the *laus perennis* (perpetual chant) was performed by CHOIRS which included child oblates with unbroken voices. The scale of psalm-singing is set out in a short work, *De cursu stellarum*, which includes a discussion of the heavens as a guide to the liturgical year and lists the numbers of psalms to be sung daily during the different months. It is sometimes said that this provides a guide to the monastic liturgy, but Gregory refers to the work as being concerned with ecclesiastical offices, and he would seem to be talking about the liturgy in all major ecclesiastical establishments. In addition,

Gregory mentions the singing of hymns, in the context of both the regular performance of the liturgy and such occasions as the death of a ruler. He notes that one ruler, Chilperic I, was responsible for the composition of hymns.

FURTHER READING

Gregory of Tours, *Opera, 1: Libri Historiarum X*, ed. B. Krusch and W. Levison, Monumenta Germaniae Historica I, 1 (Hannover: Hahn, 1951).
Opera, 2: Miracula et opera minora, ed. B. Krusch and M. Bonnet, Monumenta Germaniae Historia, I, 2 (Hannover: Hahn, 1969).
Y. Hen, *The Royal Patronage of Liturgy in Frankish Gaul to the Death of Charles the Bald (877)*, Henry Bradshaw Society Subsidia 3 (Woodbridge and Rochester, NY: Boydell & Brewer, for the Henry Bradshaw Society, 2001).

IAN WOOD

Grenser family The Grenser family of instrument makers comprises (Carl) August (in) I (b. Wiehe, Thuringia, 11 November 1720; d. Dresden, 4 May 1807); (Johann) Heinrich (Wilhelm) (b. Lipprechtsroda, Thuringia, 5 March 1764; d. Dresden, 12 December 1813); Carl Augustin II (b. Dresden 2 May 1757: d. Dresden, 8 January 1814). A family tree appears on page 145 of *The New Langwill Index*.

August Grenser I moved to Dresden in 1744 and in 1753 was appointed *Kurfürstliche-Sächsischer Hofinstrumentenmacher*. LEOPOLD MOZART ordered from him in 1772 three sets of OBOES and BASSOONS for Salzburg. In 1789 he supplied the Duke of Ludwigslust with three bassoons (each with two crooks), two angled BASSET HORNS and a four-keyed FLUTE in ebony and ivory. Waterhouse notes that a 'Clarinett-Bass' by him dated 1795 is a virtual copy of the model whose invention is attributed to Heinrich Grenser in 1793. He specialised in flutes and bassoons, which were highly regarded for their superb workmanship, intonation and tone-quality; he also made oboes, CLARINETS and basset horns.

Heinrich was the nephew and son-in-law of Augustin I, to whom he was apprenticed during 1779–86 and whom he succeeded in 1796. In 1808 he built a special alto clarinet for IWAN MÜLLER, of which he was presumably the inventor; he made an eleven-keyed clarinet for the Swedish virtuoso Bernhard Crusell. Heyde has noted the extent of his workshop inventory (itemised in *Langwill*, 145). On Heinrich's death in 1813 he was succeeded by Samuel Gottfried Wiesner, who had become his journeyman two years earlier and married his widow in 1817. Wiesner used Heinrich Grenser's name at least as late as 1818. In 1978 Phillip Young tracked as many as 127 surviving instruments, most of them flutes and bassoons, but also including basset horns, clarinets, oboes, fagottini and one each of BASS CLARINET, COR ANGLAIS, OBOE D'AMORE, bass HORN, CONTRABASSOON, hunting horn and RECORDER. Heinrich Grenser wrote several articles for the *Allgemeine musikalische Zeitung*; in defending his work against TROMLITZ in 1800, he wrote: 'To add a key for the improvement of this or that tone is not difficult nor skilful. Keys are also nothing new... However, since the greatest art is to make flutes without [extra] keys, it is necessary to correct notes with particular weakness in a way that would be comparable to the addition of keys' ('Bemerkungen über eine neue Erfindung zur Vervollkommung der Flöte', *AMZ*, 13 (1811) 775–8). He also wrote, 'Not in the number of keys, but in the greater simplicity of the flute, without sacrificing its elegance, must we find true perfection of this beautiful instrument' (*Intelligentzblatt zur AMZ*, XI, 44). This philosophy played an important part in organological discourse throughout the nineteenth century. In recent times Heinrich Grenser's instruments have been widely copied; for example, for HISTORICALLY INFORMED PERFORMANCE of Weber's clarinet works.

Carl Augustin II was apprenticed to his father Carl Augustin I and subsequently had his own workshop; he was less known than August I and Heinrich Grenser and according to the flautist and composer Anton Bernhard Fürstenau his career as a maker was unremarkable.

FURTHER READING

H. Heyde, *Musikinstrumentenbau: 15.–19. Jahrhundert, Kunst, Handwerk, Entwurf* (Leipzig: Breitkopf & Härtel, 1986).
W. Waterhouse, *The New Langwill Index* (London: Tony Bingham, 1993).
P. T. Young, 'Inventory of instruments: J. H. Eichentopf, Poerschmann, Sattler, A. and H. Grenser, Grundmann', *GSJ*, 31 (May, 1978), 100–34.

COLIN LAWSON

Grocheio, Johannes de (*fl.* c1300) A music theorist writing around 1300.

Grocheio's *Ars musice* is the only literary work to deal extensively with musical practice of the Middle Ages. Grocheio divides the music performed in Paris at the end of the thirteenth century into three categories following their general sound and place in society. The first, *musica vulgalis* (not *vulgaris*), consists of secular monophonic songs performed in Paris; Grocheio names a few pieces found elsewhere, such as Thibaut de Champagne's 'Ausi com l'unicorne sui', an example of what Grocheio calls a *cantus coronatus*. The second, *musica mensurata*, denotes the different types of polyphony. The third, *musica ecclesiastica*, is the most important category to Grocheio for he lavishes more words on it than the other three, reviewing all the main chants for mass and office according to their sound and role in the liturgy. He often compares these to secular songs; the Kyrie, for example, is like the *cantus coronatus*.

FURTHER READING

J. de Grocheio, *Ars musice*, ed. C. Mews et al. (Kalamazoo, MI: Medieval Institute Publications, 2011).

JOHN HAINES

Grützmacher, Friedrich Wilhelm Ludwig (b. Dessau, 1 March 1832; d. Dresden, 23 February 1903) German cellist and editor.

Grützmacher studied first with his father, then with Karl Drechsler, both of whom played in the Dessau court ORCHESTRA. In 1848 he joined the Leipzig Gewandhaus and Euterpe (choral society) orchestras. From 1850 to 1860 he was principal CELLO in the Leipzig Gewandhaus and professor at the Leipzig Conservatory. He then moved to Dresden as principal cello in the Hofkapelle (1860–77), and was professor at the Dresden Conservatoire from 1866 until 1903. During this period he was also 'Kammermusikus' in Meiningen c1870–2.

Grützmacher was a prolific editor, arranger and composer (these functions often overlapped), publishing approximately 200 works in all (mostly for cello, but also some songs and piano pieces), of which just over a quarter were original compositions. His EDITIONS are notable for their unusually high level of detail, including FINGERINGS, BOWING marks, additional DYNAMICS, but also unusually frequent PORTAMENTO indications (he appears only to have indicated VIBRATO once in print).

Grützmacher was the first documented cellist to play BACH's solo suites complete in concerts, in Dresden and Mannheim (1865 and 1867), and he published two editions of these works: one, 'for public performance', extensively recomposed and with added chords, counterpoint and dynamics, the other with a more conservative text. Grützmacher was also among the first cellists to play the Schumann concerto frequently, and he published a performing edition of that work less than a decade after its 1860 premiere. His other performing editions include all MENDELSSOHN's and BEETHOVEN's works for cello, ROMBERG's concertos and smaller works, DUPORT's *Études* and one concerto, works by Servais and Chopin, and much Classical and Baroque repertoire including works by Boccherini, C. P. E. BACH, J. C. Bach and TARTINI and a concerto attributed at that time to HAYDN. He is now notorious for his version of Boccherini's B♭ major Concerto G482, constructed from several authentic Boccherini concerti and with additional newly composed material (particularly evident in the third movement); even his arrangement of Schumann's *Träumerei* contains five newly composed bars. He also arranged much VIOLIN music for the cello, including the complete violin sonatas of Beethoven, Haydn and MOZART, Beethoven's Romances, Schumann's Violin Sonata, Op. 121, piano works by Chopin and Schumann, and songs by Schubert and Schumann. His technical studies (two books, Op. 38, and collections of smaller exercises) are still in use today. His *Hohe Schule* for the cello, like FERDINAND DAVID's collection of the same name for violin, comprises works by eighteenth- and early nineteenth-century composers; however, unlike David, Grützmacher focused on concertos rather than sonatas.

He was praised for his technique (especially that of the left hand) and for his strong playing, but his tone quality was found lacking by comparison with his Dresden predecessor Kummer. A regular chamber music partner with Clara Schumann, he occasionally played in JOACHIM's quartet; he also played quartets with David, LEOPOLD AUER and August Wilhelmj, and chamber music with Carl Reinecke. His pupils included his younger brother Leopold Grützmacher, Emil Hegar, Wilhelm Fitzenhagen, Josef Werner, Johannes Klingenberg, Oskar Brückner and Dinan Alexanian. He is sometimes confused with his nephew Friedrich, Leopold Grützmacher's son, who gave the premiere of STRAUSS's *Don Quixote* in 1898.

Performing editions and articles about Grützmacher are available at http://chase.leeds.ac.uk.

FURTHER READING

G. Kennaway, 'Friedrich Grützmacher: an overview'. http://chase.leeds.ac.uk/article/friedrich-grützmacher-an-overview-george-kennaway/

GEORGE KENNAWAY

Guhr, Carl (Wilhelm Ferdinand) (b. Militsch [now Milicz], 30 October 1787; d. Frankfurt am Main, 22 July 1848) German conductor, violinist and composer.

Guhr studied in Breslau with Schnabel and Janitschek, and held CONDUCTING appointments in Nuremberg, Wiesbaden, Kassel and Frankfurt (1821–48), raising orchestral standards and earning the praise of, among others, Spontini, WAGNER and BERLIOZ. An accomplished violinist whose playing was influenced initially by RODE, his first-hand experience of PAGANINI's Frankfurt performances inspired him to make a study of the Italian's idiosyncratic style, which he published as *Über Paganinis Kunst die Violine zu spielen* (Mainz: Schott, 1829).

Guhr's TREATISE was intended not as a comprehensive VIOLIN method but 'merely as an appendix to such as already exist' (Preface, 2). It is an informative account of Paganini's performing style from personal observation, with attention paid to his physique, technique and equipment. Without this study, knowledge of Paganini's technical facility, manner of performance and, indeed, some of his compositions would be slighter, since Paganini guarded his works and executive skills with the utmost secrecy. Guhr isolates the main differences between Paganini's imaginative approach and the style of his contemporaries, and focuses in particular on his posture, use of SCORDATURA, BOW strokes, combination of left-hand pizzicato with bowing, use of HARMONICS in single- and double-stopping, *una corda* playing and the extraordinary tours de force for which he was renowned. He provides numerous examples of unorthodox FINGERING employed by Paganini for *una corda* passages, double stops and chords, promoting a debate about the ramifications of the virtuoso's Ehlers-Danlos syndrome and his consequent advanced placement of the thumb in relation to the palm of the left hand; and he includes a reconstruction (from memory) of a set of variations for solo violin on an aria from Paisiello's opera *La molinara*, for which Paganini's original is lost.

Guhr's compositions also include a Violin Concerto in E minor ('Souvenir de Paganini'), operas, a mass, a symphony, quartets, further concertos and violin pieces.

FURTHER READING

P. Borer, 'Paganini and the "philosophy of the violin": aspects of a musical language', *Quaderni dell'Istituto di studi paganiniani*, 8 (1996), 40–8, 9 (1997), 47–58, 10 (1998), 42–6.
R. Stowell, 'The *diabolus in musica* and *Paganini redivivus* phenomena with some thoughts on their relevance to the "German Paganini [August Wilhelmj (1845–1908)]"', in A. Barizza and F. Morabito (eds.), *Nicolò Paganini: Diabolus in Musica* (Turnhout: Brepols, 2010), 3–21.
Violin Technique and Performance Practice in the Late Eighteenth and Early Nineteenth Centuries (Cambridge University Press, 1985).

ROBIN STOWELL

Guitar (Fr *guitare*; Ger *Gitarre*; It *chitarra*; Sp *Guitarre*) A plucked, fretted figure-of-eight-shaped chordophone.

The guitar's direct ancestor (c1500) was a waisted and fretted instrument that might be either strummed, plucked or bowed to produce chords; it was therefore closely related to (and in some respects indistinguishable from) the proto-VIOL with a flat bridge. The *viola da braccio* belongs in the same tradition. Perhaps the earliest textual witness to such chordal playing was Juan Bermudo who, in his

El libro llamado declaración de instrumentos musicales (1555), mentioned *musica golpeada* (struck or strummed music) in relation to the *guitarras* of his day. These *guitarras* were predominantly strung with four courses, the standard disposition during the later sixteenth century throughout Europe. However, the surviving music in printed TABLATURE for such guitars, in French and Spanish sources dating from the 1550s, calls for a plucked technique which is clearly based on the manner of the LUTE and VIHUELA; the role of strumming in this very literate and rather exacting music is not clear. By c1600, however, publications in Italy began to feature instrumental pieces for strumming, or strummed accompaniments to songs, with the chords indicated by letters, supplemented with a few other symbols. This is now called *alfabeto* NOTATION. The guitar in question had by then developed into a five-course instrument, which Italians called the *chitarra spagnuola*, and had become associated with music and performing styles of the Spanish kingdoms and dependencies from Cadiz across to Naples.

The seventeenth-century guitar was commonly employed in the accompaniment of song and DANCE; in this it excelled, using the *rasgueado* (also called *rageo* (*rajeo*), *rasgueo* or *rasgeo*) technique, associated with strumming in flamenco music. Although the term 'flamenco guitar' is a fairly recent one, elements of this emerging genre are witnessed in the eighteenth century, particularly in the works of Santiago de Murcia (1673–1739), who, in addition to including popular regional dances and recognisable flamenco form, exploited the *golpe* (Sp. to strike) technique, where one uses the fingers to tap on the soundboard of the guitar. However, it was not until the early 1900s that some luthiers initiated a distinction between *guitarra de concierto* (concert guitar) and *guitarra de tablao* (flamenco guitar).

Five-course instruments, strung throughout in gut, were tuned in various ways (for details, see Hall, 2003). Some players employed a re-entrant tuning (a–d′–g–b–e′) in which the fourth and fifth courses were both an octave higher than a modern guitarist would expect; others combined this with a lower octave on both courses or only on the fourth (producing the so-called 'French' tuning). The top string might be either single or double. Many guitarist composers used their tunings to achieve a ringing-on effect in scale passages, called *campanellas* (little bells). Gaspar Sanz (Francisco Bartolomé Sanz Celma (bap. 1640–1710)) utilises this effect in his *Pavanas por la D* from his *Libro segundo, de cifras sobre la guitarra española* (Zaragoza, 1675). It is often impossible to reproduce this effect on a modern classical guitar.

In the late 1630s, guitarists such as Giovanni Paolo Foscarini (*fl.* 1600–47) developed a mixed style where the player could sweep some or all of the strings with the nails of the right hand, or upwards with the flesh, while the fingertips could be used for plucking lute-like contrapuntal textures between the chords. This idiom was taken to its highest level by Francesco Corbetta (c1615–81) of Pavia, who served the English court at Whitehall for some twenty years after 1660, especially in his two published collections entitled *La Guitarre Royalle* (Paris, 1671 and 1674). By the 1720s, however, there are signs throughout Europe that the guitar, played in any manner, had begun to lose its attraction at a time when plucked and fretted instruments in general, including the LUTE, were passing out of favour. Yet although the history of the guitar in the eighteenth century is in many respects little understood as yet, it is clear that the instrument did not vanish altogether and that the second half of the century witnessed changes that prepared the way for a remarkable trans-European revival between approximately 1795 and 1845. Re-entrant tunings were abandoned in favour of *bourdons* (bass strings) on both the fourth and the fifth courses, a development exploiting overspun strings with a silk or gut core that had been available since the 1650s but do not seem to have been systematically used until the later eighteenth century. By the 1770s the arrangement with double courses was losing favour, and after a brief spell in which a five-single-string guitar was fashionable, the common form known today was settled upon: the six-string guitar.

Until the late eighteenth century, frets were not fixed but tied round the neck as gut ligatures (few players use double frets today). The player could therefore move the frets to make subtle changes according to key, TEMPERAMENT or intonation, the position of the frets ultimately being a personal and pragmatic choice that was much influenced by the angle of the neck and the string action.

The sounding string-length of guitars in the Baroque period settled at around 69–71 cm, some Stradivarius instruments being larger. Today most players opt for between 63 and 70 cm. The average in the nineteenth century was 63 cm, finally standardised to 65 cm, although there can be no suggestion that one guitar fits all nineteenth-century repertoire. The music of Giulio Regondi (1823–72), for example, requires eight strings; many of Luigi Legnani's (1790–1877) compositions regularly go beyond the then normal compass of a''', thus necessitating guitars with up to five extra frets; Mauro Giuliani's (1781–1829) style of writing benefited from bass stopping, using the left-hand thumb, requiring a guitar with a narrower neck.

The four-course guitars of the Renaissance appear to have been quite small – perhaps no larger than a baritone ukulele – and could be played in a standing position. During the Baroque era, it was usual to support the guitar with a ribbon so that the musician could play it either seated or standing. By the nineteenth century, the use of a ribbon had become vital for free movement of the left hand, but in the most common position the player sat with a leg (either the right or the left) raised on a footstool, and the ribbon was allowed to hang redundantly as a mere ornament (Fernando Sor (bap. 1778–1839) recommended resting the upper bout of the instrument against a table in such a way as made the twelfth fret equidistant between the two hands and facilitated amplification of the sound). In the twentieth century the use of a footstool became well nigh universal, with the guitar's waist resting upon the left thigh. However, players are increasingly re-evaluating this unnatural posture in the light of the strain it exerts upon the body, and are seeking alternative postures. More demanding techniques and larger guitars, with higher string action, have compelled them to reconsider their practices in order to avoid strain injuries.

From the seventeenth century onwards, the use of the nails of the right hand can be tracked among lutenists and guitarists such as Alessandro Piccinini (*Intavolatura di liuto, et di chitarrone, libro primo* (Bologna: Gio Paolo Moscatelli, 1623), 'Prefazione') and Domenico Pellegrini, although it remains unknown how widely that technique (rarely native to the lute) was used. Many of today's period players have come to the early guitar via the lute and are 'flesh players' as a result. An important technical factor is that nail playing is much impeded by the low string action over the soundboard on any guitar with flush fingerboard made before c1820. The reason (or one might say excuse) for using nails nowadays lies with the execution of rapid passages. Perhaps Fernando Sor hints at this with respect to his duo *Les deux amis*, Op. 41, written for the composer and the nail player Dionisio Aguado (1784–1849): Sor comments, 'The Part [music] of Mr. Aguado only has a very rapid variation' (A. Merrick (trans.), *Method for the Spanish Guitar by Ferdinand Sor* (London: Cocks, 1832), 47). One more important distinction between the two performers was that Sor (a 'flesh player') preferred to use slurs during fast passages, while Aguado would articulate each note separately. As with the lute, if loudness is needed – for example, in ensemble playing – the extra volume produced by nails is most welcome, although the technique is very damaging to gut strings. Nails were much in use among members of the 'Tárrega School', but during the late 1940s the introduction of robust synthetic treble strings made nail playing virtually universal. The technique of resting the little finger on the soundboard, inherited from the lute, was abolished and increasing use was made of the ring finger (abbreviated 'a' for *digitus annularis*) of the plucking hand.

Francisco Tárrega (1852–1909) is regarded as having laid the foundations for both the twentieth century's widespread acceptance of the guitar as a concert/recital instrument and the development of modern guitar technique. However, it should be acknowledged that the cornerstone was laid by Aguado; further, in the absence of any direct pedagogical material by Tárrega, Julián Arcas (1832–82), Tárrega's mentor, should not be ignored. Many of Arcas's and Tárrega's compositions are concordant in style, and some of Arcas's works were even published as compositions by Tárrega, among them the *Fantasia sobre los motivos de La Traviata*. Tárrega is also known for a special effect utilised in his *Recuerdos de la Alhambra*, achieved through the creation of a quasi-mandolin 'sustaining' of the upper part by alternating the ring, middle and index fingers (*a, m, i*) against an arpeggiation played by the thumb.

Examples of some 'modern' guitar techniques employed in avant-garde compositions of the second half of the twentieth century had been foreshadowed in various earlier works; thus, the use of harmonics was pre-empted by François Campion (1686–1747) and the imitation of the snare drum by Arcas; and the German-born guitar virtuoso Madame Sidney Pratten (Catharina Josepha Pratten, née Pelzer (1824–95)) composed many bravura compositions which provided the catalyst for technical developments in the twentieth century. Flamenco effects have been introduced in the guitar works of Turina and Falla, and Petrassi has explored string slapping against the frets in his *Suoni notturni* (1959).

FURTHER READING

D. Aguado, *Aguado, New Guitar Method*, 1843, ed. B. Jeffery (London: Tecla, 1981).
M. Hall, *Baroque Guitar Stringing: A Survey of the Evidence* (London: The Lute Society, 2003).
S. F. Josel and M. Tsao, *The Techniques of Guitar Playing* (Kassel: Bärenreiter, 2014).
R. Savino, 'Essential issues in performance practices of the classical guitar, 1770–1850', in V. Coelho (ed.), *Performance on Lute, Guitar, and Vihuela: Historical Practice and Modern Interpretation* (Cambridge University Press, 1997), 195–219.
J. Tyler and P. Sparks, *The Guitar and Its Music: From the Renaissance to the Classical Era* (Oxford University Press, 2002).

JAMES WESTBROOK

Gunn, John (b. Golspie, Caithness [?], 1766; d. Camberwell, Surrey, 1824) British cellist, flautist and scholar.

John Gunn left Scotland at an early age, spent some time in Paris in the later 1770s, and then worked in Cambridge and London. He studied with Hugh Reinagle in the early 1780s. He moved to Edinburgh by 1802, where he married the music teacher Anne Young (c1759–1826). Sometime after 1812 he returned to London.

Gunn was an unusual combination of instrumental teacher and historian – he played in orchestras in Cambridge and London, but there is no other record of him as a performer. He published methods for the CELLO and the FLUTE, a history of the HARP in the Scottish Highlands, a translation of Antonio Borghese's *L'art musical* (not, *pace* the title page, translated from the Italian) and a TREATISE on THOROUGHBASS. He refers in his writings to further historical and musical publications that did not materialise.

As guides to performance, Gunn's books for the cello and the flute are his most important works. *The Theory and Practice of Fingering the Violoncello* (London: The Author, 1/1789; 2/1800–3) was the most ambitious cello treatise to appear in any language. It began with a history of stringed instruments drawing on a range of sources quoted in classical and modern languages, which Gunn may have written while living at Cambridge (he was not, however, a matriculated student there). He was chiefly concerned to establish a rational basis for cello FINGERING, which had been unsystematic. Gunn's fingering system for scales was in effect the modern one, involving playing three notes in one position and then shifting, an approach taken by JEAN-LOUIS DUPORT in his *Essai* (Paris: [c1806]) and often attributed to him. His explanation of basic posture was considerably more detailed than any earlier one, and he strongly deprecated the 'violinistic' (backwards sloped) shape of the left hand. Like Duport's *Essai*, Gunn also deals with aspects of BOWING technique. The second edition of this treatise was more sympathetically directed at the needs of the learner, and may have been influenced by his wife, who herself wrote pedagogical material for the young. Both editions include many musical examples taken from a wide variety of sources from CORELLI to Pleyel, fingered in detail throughout. Gunn's arrangement of forty Scottish airs, published as an appendix to the first edition of *The Theory and Practice*, is likewise fully fingered, and is marked with large asterisks indicating longer musical phrases, similar to those used by CORRI. Gunn's *The Art of Playing the German-Flute* (London: The Author, c1793?) is the most comprehensive work in English on the topic up to that time. Gunn gives fingering information for both the older one-keyed flute and for the more recent six-keyed model. He strikes a balance between the then differing views on the topics of tone colour (the older, softer and varied tone, versus the more modern and consistent tone). His flute method is also notable for rejecting VIBRATO ('sweetening') as an old-fashioned ornament.

FURTHER READING

R. Brown, *The Early Flute: A Practical Guide* (Cambridge University Press, 2002).
G. Kennaway, *Playing the Cello, 1780–1930* (Farnham: Ashgate, 2014).
V. Walden, *One Hundred Years of Violoncello* (Cambridge University Press, 1998).

GEORGE KENNAWAY

H

Habeneck, François-Antoine (b. Mézières, 22 January 1781; d. Paris, 8 February 1849) French violinist, conductor and composer.

Habeneck studied the VIOLIN under BAILLOT at the PARIS CONSERVATOIRE and started his performing career in opera, first briefly at the Opéra-Comique and then at L'Opéra, succeeding KREUTZER as principal violinist in 1817. He later became L'Opéra's director (1821–4) and conductor (1824–46; principal conductor from 1831), overseeing many significant premieres and raising the standards of orchestral playing to critical acclaim.

Habeneck is especially important for introducing BEETHOVEN's music to French audiences and promoting it as director of the Conservatoire students' orchestra (1806–15), the annual Holy Week concerts at L'Opéra (from 1818 onwards) and the *Société des concerts du Conservatoire* (1828–48), of which he was a founder. His initiative prompted the establishment of other important concert societies in Paris at that time, among them Chelard's *L'Athénée Musical* (1829–44) and FÉTIS and CHORON's short-lived, yet significant, *Concerts Historiques* (1827). Habeneck also conducted the premieres of BERLIOZ's *Symphonie fantastique* (preliminary version, 1830), *Requiem* (1837) and *Benvenuto Cellini* (1838). He generally conducted with a violin BOW, reading from a first violin part. WAGNER admired his expertise and authority in this role, but Berlioz criticised him for not using a baton; nevertheless, critical reception confirms that the orchestra was 'a machine ... in perfect order, and under the guidance of experience and intellect' (Henry Chorley, *Music and Manners in France and Germany*, 3 vols. (London: Longman, Brown, Green and Longmans, 1844, I, 20)) and that its performing standards were high.

Habeneck served as assistant violin professor at the Paris Conservatoire (1808–16) and took special violin classes there (1825–48). He recorded his technical and musical principles in his *Méthode théorique et pratique de violon* (Paris, c1840); greatly influenced by the teaching of Baillot, this treatise is of special significance not only for Habeneck's own violin instruction but also for his inclusion of facsimiles of extracts from Viotti's unfinished elementary method, presented to Habeneck for publication by Mrs Chinnery, to whom it had been bequeathed. Habeneck's *Méthode* is divided into three main sections. The first is devoted to fundamental musical rudiments; part two is concerned with violin technique, incorporating information about the violin and bow, extracts from Viotti's treatise and advice about practice, posture, violin and bow holds, bow management, scales (including another extract from Viotti's method), varied BOWINGS, position-work and shifting. Although the final part chiefly concerns EXPRESSION and includes practical advice about bow division (and its relationship to bow speed and the desired effect), DYNAMICS, phrasing, nuances, ornaments, PORTAMENTO and ACCENT, Habeneck makes no mention of VIBRATO and reverts to technical considerations quite unconnected with expression, making special studies of double- and triple-stopping, ARPEGGIOS, HARMONICS, chromatic scales and extempore ORNAMENTATION, including PRELUDES and CADENZAS. He concludes with interesting observations on the performing styles of some contemporary violinists, illustrated by extracts from the compositions of Ernst, Vieuxtemps and PAGANINI.

Among Habeneck's principal pupils were DELPHIN ALARD, Jean-Baptiste de Cuvillon, Hubert Léonard, François-Hubert Prume and Prosper Sainton. His compositions for violin and orchestra include two violin concertos, an *Air varié* and a *Grande polonaise*; he also composed three *duos concertants* for two violins, three caprices for solo violin and a *Grande fantaisie* for violin and piano.

FURTHER READING

F. Bronner, *François-Antoine Habeneck (1781–1849)* (Paris: Hermann, 2014).
J. Cooper, *The Rise of Instrumental Music and Concert Series in Paris 1828–1871* (Ann Arbor, MI: UMI Research Press, 1983).
D. K. Holoman, 'The emergence of the orchestral conductor in Paris in the 1830s', in P. Bloom (ed.), *Music in Paris in the Eighteen-Thirties* (Stuyvesant, NY: Pendragon, 1987), 374–430.

ROBIN STOWELL

Halle, Adam de la (c1245–c88) Considered the last of the *trouvères*.

Adam de la Halle composed primarily monophonic chansons. Like some famous *trouvères* before him, Adam supervised the compilation of his complete works. His musical output is representative of the late thirteenth-century shift away from aristocratic, courtly songs and towards urban, book-centred ones. Unlike most *trouvères*, but like GUILLAUME DE MACHAUT after him, Adam's achievements were both literary and musical, and his musical works were both monophonic and polyphonic. In the latter category are over a dozen *rondeaux* and a handful of motets, all for three voices. Of Adam's *oeuvre* the musical drama *Le Jeu de Robin et de Marion*, first performed in Sicily in the 1280s and revived in the nineteenth century, has received the most attention from performers seeking historical integrity. For example, it was arranged for orchestra first by Julien Tiersot in 1896 and later by Jean Beck for the 1928 Canadian Folk Song and Handicraft Festival.

FURTHER READING

J. Haines, 'Paraphrases musico-théâtrales du *Jeu de Robin et Marion*, 1870–1930', *Revue d'Histoire du Théâtre*, 216/4 (2002), 281–94.
D. H. Nelson and H. van der Werf (eds.), *The Lyrics and Melodies of Adam de La Halle* (New York: Garland, 1985).
J. Saltzstein (ed.), *Musical Culture in the World of Adam de la Halle* (Leiden: Brill, forthcoming)
N. Wilkins (ed.), *The Lyric Works of Adam de la Hale* ([Dallas]: American Institute of Musicology, 1967).

JOHN HAINES

Hallé, Sir Charles [Carl Halle] (b. Hagen, Westphalia, 11 April 1819; d. Manchester, 25 October 1895) German-born PIANO virtuoso, chamber musician and conductor.

Hallé helped establish 'Classical' repertory as the norm of concert giving. As pianist and teacher in Paris (1840–8), he gave performances of BEETHOVEN's sonatas and pioneered chamber music concerts without vocalists. His first known Beethoven sonata cycle took place in London in 1876. In Manchester, from 1848, he gave chamber music concerts and was engaged as 'conductor' of the Gentlemen's Concerts Society over the head of its 'leader'. He made the Society fully professional and (as had Costa in London before him) reformed its ORCHESTRAL PLACEMENT.

As a performer, Hallé's style was likened to that of MOSCHELES, with its even touch and free rhythm. In his mid-career, it was considered apposite, unlike the 'expression' of players such as Anton Rubinstein. His RUBATO was thought excessive by the late 1880s, and a tendency to play chords ARPEGGIANDO was also criticised.

Hallé's editions of standard piano works (including Beethoven's sonatas, 1856 and 1870) paralleled those of Ernst Pauer, Lindsay Sloper and Sterndale Bennett. His added METRONOME counts, phrasing, DYNAMIC markings and FINGERINGS were designed to aid performance (more fully in his pedagogic 'School' editions).

As entrepreneur-conductor, Hallé's formation of an independent Classical concert orchestra in Manchester in 1857 was unique in Britain. Its repertoire initially mixed piano solos and operatic fantasias with major symphonies, and his concerts, up to his death, always included a vocal component (solo or choral). In its heyday he engaged a complement of sixty to seventy string players (and a massed choir) for Manchester and some other performances, though he would conduct elsewhere with a total orchestra of fewer than sixty, even for WAGNER. His readings of Baroque and Classical works were considered 'faithful' to the score, with freedom of interpretation perceived in works of Romantic aesthetics only.

FURTHER READING

R. Beale, *Charles Hallé: A Musical Life* (Aldershot: Ashgate, 2007).
C. E. and M. Hallé (eds.), *The Life and Letters of Sir Charles Hallé* (London: Smith Elder & Co., 1896).
A. Kersting, *Carl Halle – Sir Charles Hallé: Ein europäischer Musiker* (Hagen: Kommissionsverlag von der Linnepe, 1986).

ROBERT BEALE

Hampel, Anton Joseph (b. Prague, c1710; d. Dresden, 30 March 1771) German HORN player, teacher and composer.

Heinrich Domnich (1807) wrote that Hampel was the first horn player to make consistent use of hand stopping to obtain notes lying outside the natural HARMONIC series. This technique first emerged in Dresden, where composers had been writing notes which needed hand stopping from about 1719 and where Hampel played second horn in the Royal Orchestra from 1737. This experience is said to have given him the opportunity to develop the *cor basse* (low horn) technique, the large leaps and rapid arpeggios of which made it distinct from the more melodic *cor alto* (high horn) style.

Hampel's interest in hand stopping is demonstrated by the inclusion of a limited range of stopped notes in some of his trios. However, his tutor is a disappointment. It survives in an edition by his pupil Punto, and opens with some perfunctory thoughts on TONGUING. It also includes a chromatic scale, probably added by Punto, showing the pitches available to the horn, some thoughts on crooks and a warning to composers to avoid writing f″ and a″ together (the out-of-tune eleventh and thirteenth harmonics) as this will lead to a 'terrible dissonance'. There is no other text. All the method's exercises are written as duets and most are variations on the same theme. The opening pages make some suggestions for ARTICULATION, but hand stopping is not mentioned and only rarely features in the exercises; its main appearance is in a minor-key example probably added by Punto.

FURTHER READING

A. J. Hampel, *Seule et vraie méthode pour apprendre facilement des élémens des premier et second cors*, ed. G. Punto (Paris: J. H. Naderman, n.d. [c1794]).

JOHN HUMPHRIES

Harmonics Any note produced by an instrument is accompanied by several other notes (harmonics) at fixed intervals above it. These harmonics are heard as constituents of the single note, but can be produced separately. The lowest tone of the harmonic series (the fundamental) is the first harmonic, the next lowest the second harmonic and so on. Other tones are the 'upper partials' or 'overtones', at fixed intervals above the fundamental (octave, perfect fifth, etc.).

With woodwind instruments, the player is required to modify the tone generator (e.g. by changing the lip pressure on a reed) or sometimes to open a register key to modify the air column, in order to move from one resonance to another. With the long, narrow tubes of 'natural' (i.e. slideless, keyless and valveless) TRUMPETS and HORNS, players are able to produce numerous harmonics by tightening the lips when blowing; these harmonics are the only available notes on those 'natural' instruments. In trumpet playing some harmonics (e.g. the seventh, eleventh, thirteenth and fourteenth) require 'lipping' up or down, as appropriate, for accuracy of tuning; in horn playing, the technique of hand stopping (inserting the hand, cupped, into the bell, thereby reducing the PITCH of a note by a semitone or more), combined with a crook appropriate for the key of the music being performed, increases the number of available notes. J. S. BACH regularly wrote for a trumpet range between the third and eighteenth (and occasionally twentieth) harmonics. MOZART's horn writing covered a range from the second to the twenty-fourth harmonic. The invention and adoption of valves in the early nineteenth century transformed brass playing, having the effect of a simple and rapid crook change and enabling melodies to be executed evenly and with greater facility.

In string playing, 'natural' harmonics are produced from light finger placement on 'open' strings at various points ('nodes'), producing notes of a flute-like quality. 'Artificial' harmonics sound when one finger stops the string firmly and another (usually the fourth) is placed lightly above it. Harmonics have been exploited largely as a contrasting timbre to normal playing (and occasionally, with instruments of the VIOLIN family, as an aid to shifting). Their unanimous acceptance through history was slow owing to their 'dissimilarity of tone' (LEOPOLD MOZART, 1756, ch. 5 sec.13). SPOHR (1832) was similarly reserved about their use, though he introduced natural harmonics into some shifts. Virtuosos such as Jakob Scheller and NICOLÒ PAGANINI aroused public interest in artificial harmonics. Paganini's introduction of artificial harmonics in double stopping was innovatory, as was his exploitation of chromatic slides, single trills, trills in double stopping and double trills, all in harmonics.

'Second harmonics', sounding one octave above, are the most common in HARP playing; they are obtained by plucking the upper half of the string with the side of the thumb and lightly touching the mid-point of the string with the ball of the thumb. Guitarists play natural and 'fretted' (including artificial and 'pinched') harmonics. The timbral effects of harmonics have also long been used in ORGAN building and more recently in synthesising various instrumental timbres on ELECTRONIC keyboard INSTRUMENTS.

FURTHER READING

M. Campbell and C. Greated, *The Musician's Guide to Acoustics* (London: Oxford University Press, 1987).

T. Herbert and J. Wallace (eds.), *The Cambridge Companion to Brass Instruments* (Cambridge University Press, 1997).

R. Stowell, *Violin Technique and Performance Practice in the Late Eighteenth and Early Nineteenth Centuries* (Cambridge University Press, 1985).

ROBIN STOWELL

Harnoncourt, Nikolaus (b. Berlin, 6 December 1929; d. Vienna, 5 March 2016) Austrian conductor, cellist and VIOL player, best known as founder-director of the pioneering period orchestra CONCENTUS MUSICUS WIEN (CMW).

Raised in Graz, Harnoncourt studied at the Vienna Music Academy before joining the Vienna Symphony Orchestra as a cellist. Curiosity about Baroque music led him in 1953 to found his own period-instrument ensemble Concentus Musicus Wien, one of the first of its kind. The group gave its debut concert in 1957 and made its first recording, of Purcell's viol fantasies, in 1962. Acclaimed and revelatory recordings followed throughout the 1960s of J. S. BACH's major orchestral and choral works (all for Telefunken), and in 1965 Harnoncourt made the first recording of Bach's six Cello Suites to use a CELLO in a Baroque set-up. In 1971 CMW (together with GUSTAV LEONHARDT and the Leonhardt Consort) embarked on recording all Bach's church cantatas, a project which was completed in 1990. Other influential projects of the 1970s included MONTEVERDI's operas on stage in Zurich and Edinburgh and on record.

Harnoncourt's programmes with CMW later widened to encompass works of the Classical period, but he also conducted Classical and Romantic repertoire with orchestras of 'modern' instruments such as the Concertgebouw, the Chamber Orchestra of Europe (with whom he recorded the BEETHOVEN symphonies), the Vienna Philharmonic (for whom he twice conducted the New Year's Day concert) and the Berlin Philharmonic. He remained active with both period and modern ORCHESTRAS until his retirement in December 2015, but he never diluted his approach to performance, founded on wide-reaching historical research, radical rethinking and a willingness to make bold interpretative decisions. His influence has also been disseminated through his teaching at Salzburg University and the Salzburg Mozarteum (from 1972), and his thoughts are recorded in numerous articles, essays and liner notes (some of which were republished in English in a book, *Baroque Music Today* (1988)). The depth, uncompromising nature and longevity of his activities, as well as the robustly communicative personality of his performances, qualify him as one of the most important figures of the early music movement.

FURTHER READING

W. Gratzer (ed.), *Ereignis Klangrede. Nikolaus Harnoncourt als Dirigent und Musikdenker* (Freiburg i. Br., Berlin and Vienna: Rombach Verlag, 2009).

N. Harnoncourt, *Baroque Music Today: Music as Speech, Ways to a New Understanding of Music*, trans. M. O'Neill (Portland, OR: Amadeus, 1988).

LINDSAY KEMP

Harp Generic term for chordophones in which the plane of the strings is perpendicular to the soundboard (Hornbostel and Sachs).

The harp is an ancient instrument with a great variety of historical forms and usages. Even in Medieval and early modern Europe, triangular frame-and-pillar harps and related instruments show considerable chronological and regional differences. Certain types have become accepted amongst historical performers; others have yet to be re-established. The revival of early harps has lagged behind other instruments and there are still significant gaps in scholarly knowledge as well as noticeable differences between historical evidence and today's practice. The instrument's traditional identity as a national symbol in Wales, Ireland and some South American countries has added heat, rather than light, to harpists' discussions.

Before 1300 there are difficulties with nomenclature. Early Medieval Germanic and Scandinavian names cognate with *harpa* refer to four-sided lyres, as do Old Irish *cruit* and *crott*, whereas European *rota* signifies a triangular harp-psaltery with two sets of strings either side of a central sound-box. Latin *cithara* and *lira* often (but not exclusively) refer to pillar-harps, but *psalterium* mostly suggests the single-sided trapezoidal psaltery. Harps and psalteries continue to be closely associated until the eighteenth century.

Illustrations in later Medieval *romances* and psalm commentaries connect French *harpe* and Latin *(h)arpa* to the pillar-harp. In late twelfth-century Ireland, it is not certain if Gerald of Wales's *cithara* was a harp, nor if it was strung with metal. Gut-strung harps were played in Ireland until the early sixteenth century, whereas the Irish name *cláirseach* for a strongly constructed harp with thick brass strings first appeared in 1385. In Scotland the first mention of *klerschach* (1434) refers to a player of this type of harp, which may have originated in Scandinavia. European pillar-harps had gut strings (horse-hair strings are documented in Wales) as did triangular harp-psalteries; trapezoidal psalteries had strings of brass or precious metals.

In the French liturgical drama *Ludus Danielis* (c1200), harpists (*cythariste*) march in front of the invading soldiers, who kill Belshazzar. This dramatisation parallels the chronicle of William the Conqueror's harpist Taillesfer striking the first blow at the Battle of Hastings, and Irish legends of battle-harps. Harper-knights from Celtic mythology became the heroes of Medieval French *romances*. Each player had an individual way of tuning the harp and tuning preludes included fragments of melody as well as chords and alterations of PITCH. In literature, scripture and courtly life harps were high-status instruments associated with David the Psalmist and other royalty.

Medieval lap-harps, approximately equilateral, with a handful or up to two octaves of strings, were well suited to monophonic tunes and early polyphony. But during the fourteenth century tall, slender harps with about twenty-four strings emanated from France. MACHAUT's mid-century *Le dit de la harpe* compares each string of the harp to the twenty-five graces of his lady – the poem links the instrument to fundamentals of music theory and artistic philosophy. The subtle NOTATION of Senleches' *La harpe de melodie* (c1395) within an image of a harp, two voices entabulated on strings and a third encoded into a poetic *rondeau* wrapped around the harp-pillar, presents the instrument as a symbol of artistic sophistication.

In Italy, ICONOGRAPHY from 1450 to 1550 shows the most typical duo as harp and LUTE; in many sources, harp and ORGAN are depicted together. The low-tension strings of these 'Gothic' harps were attached at the soundboard by 'bray pins', L-shaped wooden pegs against which the vibrating string rattles, amplifying and transforming the sound. This *angenehm schnarrende* (pleasantly buzzing) effect, similar to a HURDY-GURDY or tromba marina, remained the typical sound of PRAETORIUS's *gemeine Harfe* (ordinary harp) in 1619.

In 1555, the Spanish theorist BERMUDO described three solutions to the challenge of chromaticism on the essentially diatonic harp. According to the mode, one might tune the E strings, for example, to E♭ in one octave, E♮ in another. Alternatively, one might tune more than seven notes to the octave, dedicating colour-coded strings to both B♭ *and* B♮, E♭ *and* E♮. The third solution was to have a complete second row of strings, supplying all the chromatic notes: the second row crosses over the first, in the way in which clasped fingers interlace. Spanish harps of this period stand shoulder-high with a four-octave range; the sound-box is narrow and shallow in the treble, broad and deep in the bass, producing a contrast in timbre between the two hands, emphasised by the playing position with the left hand around the middle of each string, the right hand at the top.

In the last decades of the sixteenth century, Italian harps (still 'Gothic' in shape) with two parallel rows of strings extended northwards from Naples. Harps and psaltery played in the 1589 Florentine *Intermedi*. By the *seicento*, the Italian *arpa doppia* was wider, very large (above head height), with a staved back and three rows of strings – diatonic, chromatic, diatonic – allowing chromaticism throughout the compass, but with easy access for both hands to the diatonic strings. A low sitting position facilitated strong bass-playing *près de la table* for the longest bass strings, corresponding to a THEORBO's diapasons and the lowest notes of a *gravicembalo*. AGAZZARI's TREATISE on continuo, *Del sonare sopra'l basso* (1607), draws attention to the harp's multi-functionality, with its wide range, polyphonic capability and dual roles of fundamental accompaniment in small ensembles and decorative ORNAMENTATION in larger CONSORTS. His description of 'ripostes between the two hands and trills' perfectly characterises the harp solo in MONTEVERDI's *Orfeo* (also 1607).

Alongside the old-style repertory of polyphonic fantasias, transcriptions of vocal music and DANCES, chromatic harps were particularly associated with *seconda pratica* toccatas, opera and oratorio, and continuo playing. Throughout the Baroque period, harps evoked David, Orpheus, Apollo and Arion; pleasure, love and visions of heaven. In early seventeenth-century English masques, large ensembles were centred on a single Irish harp and Jean le Flelle's Italian harp appeared on stage. The scholarly consensus is that William Lawes's *Harp Consorts* were intended for the brass-strung Irish harp (paired with theorbo to accompany VIOLIN and VIOL), though many of today's practitioners prefer gut-strung Italian harps.

The first Spanish operas (1660) were composed by harpist Juan Hidalgo, and harp continuo is specified for the earliest surviving Spanish oratorios (from 1704). Ribayaz's *Luz y norte* (Madrid: Lucas Ruiz de Ribayaz, 1677) links harp technique and repertory to the strumming patterns and dance-music variations of the Spanish Baroque GUITAR. A cantata by Zachow includes a harp solo: the writing keeps the player's hands well separated, suiting the two-row German *Davidsharfe*.

Whilst multi-row harps were favoured by the most famous seventeenth-century virtuosi and have become the accepted standard in Baroque performances nowadays, single-row instruments (sometimes fitted with semitone hooks) were far more common. There are tantalising hints of chromatic Irish harps, but all the surviving instruments are single-row. In London after the Restoration, Italianate triple harps were being built and played by Welshmen. By the 1730s the 'high-head' shape – high at the pillar, low at the top of the soundbox – facilitated the style of virtuoso playing in the high treble register heard in Handel's Concerto in B♭, Op. 4 No. 6 HWV294 (1736). Even higher-headed shapes characterised the triple harp celebrated as the Welsh national instrument later in the century.

Eighteenth-century German dictionaries define *Harfe* variously as: the gut-strung *Davidsharfe*; the Irish harp with its thick brass strings; and the *Spitzharfe* or *Tischharfe*, an upright, double-sided chromatic psaltery with thin brass and steel strings, known in Italy as *arpanetta*. These 'peaked' or 'table' harps were very common as domestic instruments, outnumbering the multi-row pillar-harps that are nowadays regarded as typically Baroque.

The ubiquity of harps in financial records, biographical information, literary sources and iconography begs the question of why so little harp music survives from before 1750. A more fruitful line of enquiry considers what harpists played, revealing a substantial but often unwritten repertory of abstract fantasias, transcriptions of vocal music, DANCES and accompaniment, all having much in common with lute, guitar and keyboard music.

In the second half of the eighteenth century, harps became increasingly fashionable amongst French amateur noblewomen. The single action of pedal harps allows a semitone alteration of any of the seven diatonic notes, simultaneously in every octave. Compared to contemporary Italian triple harps, this *harpe organisée* was small, delicate and lightly strung at low pitch, the epitome of French TASTE. MOZART's Concerto in C K299 (1778) was written for such an instrument, whereas scholars still debate whether C. P. E. BACH's Sonata (1762) was intended for French pedal harp, Italian triple, or even both (one playing continuo for the other).

Petrini's first book of harp sonatas (with optional violin) and Eichner's concerto (for harp or harpsichord) were both published in 1769. Krumpholz's performance in Vienna in 1773 led to his employment at the Esterházy court as HAYDN's pupil; between his Op. 1 sonatas (*c*1775) and first published concertos (*c*1777), he collaborated with harp-maker Steckler to improve harp design; in 1785 he commissioned a harp from Naderman with a bass octave of wire strings and an eighth pedal, which operated shutters in the back of the harp, swelling the sound. The harp represents Orpheus's lyre in Gluck's *Orfeo e Euridice* (1762) and Haydn's *L'anima del filosofo* (1791).

The few surviving seventeenth-century treatises on harp technique emphasise systematic FINGERING according to the principle of 'good' and 'bad' notes (imitating the accented and unaccented syllables of sung texts). Beginning with Meyer's *Essai sur la vraie manière de jouer de la harpe* (Paris: M. de la Chevardière, 1763), many instructional methods survive for *harpe organisée*; these are consistent with C. P. E. Bach's *Versuch* (1753 and 1762, for keyboards) in prioritising fingering systems (i.e. short-term ARTICULATION), ornamentation and accompaniment in which improvised arpeggiation gradually replaced continuo realisation. Bunting's short description (1840) of Irish harp techniques preserved from the previous century is similarly organised, but in that repertory harpists improvised a bass accompaniment according to harmonies implied by the ornamented melody. In spite of repeated attempts at revival, the continuity of Scottish and Irish harp traditions was decisively broken in the nineteenth century.

French harpist, writer and pedagogue the Comtesse de Genlis claimed to be the first to introduce HARMONICS; in her *Nouvelle méthode* (1802 and 1811) she disapproves of excessive use of rallentando, RUBATO and *broderies* (divisions), advising careful attention to 'good' and 'bad' notes. Her virtuosic five-finger technique, although carried forward by her son Casimir and in treatises by Désargus (*Nouvelle méthode de harpe* (Paris: Naderman, 1809)) and Prumier (*Méthode de harpe*, Op. 76 (Paris: Brandus, [1865])), was not generally adopted. Pollet's *Méthode* (*c*1780) includes harmonics for both hands simultaneously, alongside variations on *Les Folies d'Espagne* and advice on ornaments and fingerings for Krumpholz's compositions.

During the Revolution, French harpists sought refuge particularly in London, Germany and St Petersburg. In the years that followed, harp design changed quickly, with increases in pitch, string tension and the angle between strings and soundboard; the decorative styling of the Empire model imitated classical antiquity. Many of SPOHR's compositions for violin and harp notate the harp part in the convenient key of E♭, whilst the violin (tuned a semitone higher) plays in its preferred key of D. Sébastien Érard's double-action harp (1810) allowed each string to be raised one or two semitones, facilitating chromatic complexity and enabling the special effects of *bisbigliando* (rapid 'whispering' between pairs of unisons) and chordal glissandi. In Britain, single- and double-action harps co-existed alongside the Welsh triple-harp, but Pierre-Orphée Erard's 'Gothic' design (1836), a larger and heavier double-action instrument, was the most widely used nineteenth-century harp.

Elias Parish Alvars's transcriptions of works by such composers as Field, Rossini and Donizetti brought him favourable attention from Liszt (1842) and

BERLIOZ, who had included two harps in his *Symphonie fantastique* (1830). In 1894 Lyon's chromatic harp revived the concept of Spanish Baroque X-strung double-harps: his Pleyel company commissioned Debussy's *Danse sacrée et danse profane* (1904), which exploits the instrument's unique capabilities. The Érard company responded by commissioning Ravel's *Introduction and Allegro* (1905) for double-action harp and the work was premiered in the USA by Carlos Salzedo, whose *Modern Study of the Harp* (1921) championed new techniques of percussive effects and unconventional sounds. The rigours of the North American climate encouraged luthiers to improve the robustness of the instrument and its mechanism, and around 1910 the extended soundboard facilitated extra notes and increased resonance in the bass.

During the eighteenth and nineteenth centuries, there was a flourishing tradition of itinerant harpists and harp ensembles from the Austro-Hungarian Empire and Germany, centred on the music-dominated town of Pressnitz. The harp tradition in the Tyrol was admired by Haydn; in the late nineteenth century a local variant of single-action mechanism was revived. Naples and Rome also cultivated strong harp traditions, and the distinctive Norwegian *krogharpe* (first mentioned in 1623) might share a common ancestor with medieval clarsachs. John Eagan's Dital Harp (c1819) sought to evoke ancient Irish instruments but was actually a simplified version of a contemporary pedal harp. The Clark blade harp (1913) and 'Troubadour' lever harp (1962) similarly applied hand-operated semitone systems to small instruments, leading the way for today's Celtic harps. Levers have also been applied to Latin American folk harps (descendants of Spanish Baroque instruments) first brought to wider attention by Paraguayan virtuoso Félix Pérez Cardozo in the 1930s.

Grandjany, professor of harp at Juilliard from 1938, made arrangements of Baroque works in the style of his own times. Zabaleta's mid-century publications offered sensitively edited TRANSCRIPTIONS of music from Spanish Renaissance to French Classical. The modern revival of early harps began in the 1980s with conferences in the USA and Basle and the establishment of the International Historical Harp Society. Further progress would be aided by closer contact between young harpists and historically aware performers and earlier exposure to the challenges of polyphonic music, improvisation and continuo realisation; it is not sufficient simply to exchange one harp-type for another. New historical information is always welcome, but meanwhile there is still much to be done in applying well-established period principles to harpists' performing practices.

FURTHER READING

M. Morrow, 'The Renaissance harp: recreating a lost performing tradition', *EMc*, 7 (1979), 499–510.
R. Rensch, *The Harp: Its History, Technique and Repertoire* (London and New York: Duckworth, 1969).
Harps and Harpists (Bloomington, IN: Indiana University Press, 1989, 2/2007).
C. Salzedo, *Modern Study of the Harp* (NewYork: Schirmer, 1921).

ANDREW LAWRENCE-KING

Harpsichord (Dutch *klavecimbel*; Fr. *clavecin*; Ger. *Cembalo, Clavicimbal, Flügel, Kielflügel*; It. *cembalo, clavicembalo*; Lat. *clavicembalum*; Port. *cravo*; Sp. *clave*,

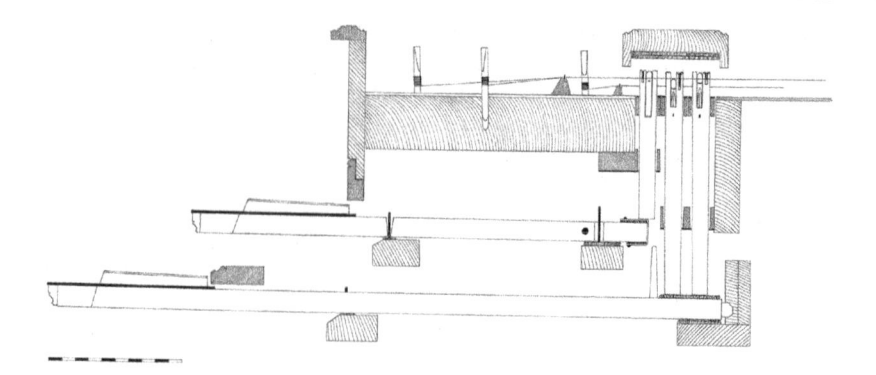

Figure 5: Section through the action of a typical eighteenth-century double-manual French harpsichord (Christopher Nobbs).

clavicordio) A stringed keyboard instrument with an elongated wing shape and plucked strings, which run directly away from the player.

'Harpsichord' is also a generic term for all plucked keyboard instruments including SPINETS and VIRGINALS. It flourished in a variety of different forms from the late fifteenth century until the end of the eighteenth century, when it was completely superseded by the FORTEPIANO. It was widely used as a solo and BASSO CONTINUO instrument and idiomatic performance techniques were gradually developed in tandem with its large and varied repertoire.

The popularity of the harpsichord over four centuries must in part be a reflection of its simple and highly effective action. Each string is plucked by a plectrum made of bird's quill (or a modern nylon alternative). This is fixed in a slip of wood (the tongue), which is mounted in such a way that it can rotate in a slot at the top end of a larger rectangular slip (the jack). The jack stands on the far end of a key and moves vertically upwards when the key is depressed, causing the plectrum to pluck the string. When the key is released, the jack falls and the plectrum briefly makes contact with the string, causing the tongue to rotate and the plectrum to slide back past the string without sounding it again. A light spring of metal or bristle returns the tongue to its starting position and the string is damped by a piece of cloth in a slot at the top of the jack. One row of jacks constitutes a register; large harpsichords have at least two or three registers, each of which produces different sounds and pitches. The registers can be brought in or out of use, like ORGAN stops, by a small sideways movement of the jack rail, so that the jacks engage (or just miss) the strings on their upward motion (Figure 5).

Although early harpsichords were made with just one register at unison pitch (8′), a second 8′ or 4′ (sounding one octave higher) was generally employed, and three choirs of strings (2 × 8′, 1 × 4′) were normal in a two-keyboard instrument. The position of the register relative to the keyboard end sets the plucking point on the string and thus the quality of the sound. Later French instruments placed the 4′ between the two 8′ rows to maximise the difference between the unison sounds, while the English tradition preferred the 4′ jacks to be placed furthest from the player. Various effects could be achieved with additional devices. The buff (or harp) stop brings into play a small piece of buff leather or cloth, which touches the strings lightly, producing a pizzicato quality. The so-called LUTE stop is an additional row of jacks which pluck one of the 8′ choirs very close to the ends of the strings, producing a penetrating 'nasal' sound.

The earliest known reference to the instrument is to the 'clavicembalum' of Hermann Poll mentioned in a letter of 1397, and the carved altarpiece (1425) in Minden Cathedral in Germany depicts a small harpsichord. The earliest detailed description of a harpsichord, however, is the 'clavisimbalum' in the manuscript of HENRI ARNAUT DE ZWOLLE (c1440, Paris: Bibliothèque Nationale, MS. latin 7295), which includes a plan with three plucked mechanisms and a hammer action (called 'dulce melos').

The harpsichord was also constructed in an upright configuration known as the CLAVICYTHERIUM, with a vertical soundboard and the strings running upwards from the keyboard. The manuscript of Paulus Paulirinus (Kraków: Biblioteka Jagiellónska, Ms. 257, c1460) describes such an instrument. That the earliest surviving stringed keyboard instrument is an upright rather than a horizontal harpsichord confirms the importance of such designs between the fifteenth and eighteenth centuries. This clavicytherium (housed in the ROYAL COLLEGE OF MUSIC, London) was made probably in Southern Germany c1480 and exhibits many of the characteristics of sixteenth-century Italian harpsichords, suggesting a common ancestry.

More than forty Italian harpsichords survive from the sixteenth century; the earliest are by Vincentius (1515) and Jerome of Bologna (1521). Early Italian harpsichords are all single-manual instruments within thin cases, which were protected by separate outer cases. They normally had only the one 8′ register, although a second 4′ register could be added. Seventeenth-century Italian instruments tended to have thicker cases (when made to resemble an instrument housed within an outer case this is called 'false inner-outer' construction) with two 8′ registers rather than the earlier 1 × 8′ and 1 × 4′; sometimes they were built with a third 8′ register. As on the ORGAN, split keys were often used to accommodate enharmonic notes in meantone TEMPERAMENT (e.g. A♭ and G♯). Harpsichord making in Italy continued along the same lines into the eighteenth century and apart from an increase in bass compass showed little sign of the developments occurring elsewhere in Europe.

Only a small number of surviving sixteenth-century stringed keyboard instruments originate from northern Europe; notable among them are the German Müller (1537), the Flemish Moermans (1584) and the English-built Theewes (1579) harpsichords. While the Müller and the virginal by Joes Karest (Antwerp, 1548) share many characteristics of earlier Italian instruments, the Moermans and, to a lesser extent, the Theewes exemplify features of the mature Flemish tradition such as long, iron-string scaling and deeper and more substantial casework. The Antwerp-based Ruckers family dominated this tradition for about a century from 1579, building single-manual harpsichords with an 8′ and a 4′ register (eventually adding a second 8′ c1650), and a two-manual harpsichord with its keyboards a fourth apart (the 'transposing double'). From the 1680s onwards the keyboards were rebuilt, aligned to the same PITCH and fitted with a coupling device so that they could be used simultaneously or in contrast. This 'expressive double' with three registers (2 × 8′ and 1 × 4′) became the favoured design and has been frequently copied in the modern revival of the instrument. In the eighteenth century the Dulcken family continued to build harpsichords in Antwerp, often adding a fourth register – the lute stop.

Few harpsichords from France, England or Germany survive from before the eighteenth century. As with the keyboard repertoire, harpsichords in France survive only from the second half of the seventeenth century. These early French instruments stand somewhere between the Flemish and the Italian traditions. Two keyboards were common, some with the 4′ register alone on the upper manual but without a coupler, which was introduced later. Eighteenth-century makers extensively rebuilt (and even faked) valuable Flemish harpsichords in a process known as *ravalement*, whereby the compass and case were widened to accommodate later musical requirements. The rich sonority of the typical two-manual, five-octave French harpsichord of the eighteenth century was rooted in the Flemish tradition of soundboard design. These models were often equipped with registration devices to enable changes of dynamic and colour which composers exploited with specific techniques such as crossing the hands in *pièces croisées* and with registration instructions as in Dandrieu's *Premier Livre* (1724). Pascal Taskin (1723–93) claimed the invention (1768) of the *peau de buffle*, a register of jacks with plectra made from buff leather which affords some possibility of variable DYNAMICS by touch, and knee-levers (*genouillères*) to engage the registers (*see* Figure 6).

The earliest surviving English harpsichord (Theewes, 1579) is a claviorgan, a harpsichord and chamber organ combined within the same case, but few seventeenth-century English harpsichords are extant. Eighteenth-century English harpsichord makers, however, were prolific and over 200 of their instruments survive. Many were emigrants, notably Hermann Tabel (Flanders), Burkat Shudi (Switzerland) and Jacob Kirkman (Alsace), and English instruments were highly sought after across Europe. Later instruments were equipped with *crescendo* pedals either on the organ swell principle ('Venetian swell' and 'lid swell' or

Figure 6: Plan view of a double-manual French harpsichord (1769) by Pascal Taskin. (by kind permission of the Friends of St Cecilia's Hall, Edinburgh)

'nag's head swell') or 'machine stops', fitted by Shudi from at least as early as 1740, which changed registration and allowed a sudden *forte/piano* contrast.

German and Austrian harpsichords display greater tonal and design variation than English instruments, reflecting the geographical spread of the principal German-speaking centres of harpsichord making. The Hass and Fleischer families in Hamburg made large, lavishly decorated harpsichords, incorporating elements from organ building. The Hass family's instruments had 16′ and 2′ registers and an H. A. Hass of 1740 had three manuals. The instruments of Gräbner, Horn and Silbermann in Saxony and Mietke in Berlin are more lightly constructed than those of the Hamburg school; they have been closely studied and copied as models appropriate for performances of works by J. S. BACH and his circle. A few extant harpsichords of Viennese manufacture employ a complicated short-octave arrangement and resemble early fortepianos in their appearance and construction.

The wide variation in national and regional schools of building is reflected, more than with any other keyboard instrument, in the harpsichord's richly diverse repertoire. Keyboard players adapted their musical ideas, often improvised, to the instruments available. DIRUTA (1593) distinguishes between the harpsichord touch required for dances and the sustained approach necessary for the realisation of counterpoint in organ playing; he advocates TREMOLOS and *accenti* to give the illusion of sustained harmony on the harpsichord. FRESCOBALDI (1615) goes further, recommending restriking suspensions or dissonances to counteract the instrument's lack of sustaining power. The main genres of repertory before the eighteenth century include INTABULATIONS or TRANSCRIPTIONS of non-keyboard music, variation sets (often based on song melodies), imitative counterpoint (including fugues, fantasias, canzonas and ricerare), dances, toccatas (most notably by Frescobaldi), sonatas, tombeaux (or memorial pieces) and un-measured preludes (*see* 'PRELUDING').

In the seventeenth century, the availability of more sonorous harpsichords and the emergence of a playing style inspired by lute technique led to a new school of harpsichord performance. Largely driven by the French *clavecinistes*, CHAMBONNIÈRES, D'ANGLEBERT and LOUIS COUPERIN, but also the German Froberger, this style deployed subtle rhythmic nuance and touch sensitivity to create a wider dynamic and expressive range. It reached its compositional apotheosis in the eighteenth century in the published suites of FRANÇOIS COUPERIN and JEAN-PHILIPPE RAMEAU, both of whom wrote technical and interpretative instructions for performers and refined the dedicatory and programmatic character piece.

Harpsichord music was central to the development of eighteenth-century musical forms, particularly the suite, sonata and the prelude and fugue pairing inherited from the seventeenth century and new genres such as the concerto and chamber music with obbligato keyboard parts. All composers were trained as keyboard players and the major figures such as HANDEL, Scarlatti and especially J. S. Bach added significantly to the repertoire. An ideal vehicle for experimentation and instruction, harpsichord music fulfilled a didactic function, both leading and reflecting new aesthetic ideas (*see* AFFECT and RHETORIC), musical TASTE (e.g. through the integration of different

NATIONAL IDIOMS) and compositional principles (especially binary sonata forms). The harpsichord remained the primary keyboard instrument of the Rococo and early Classical periods until the 1770s, embracing the early careers of HAYDN and MOZART. The last surviving harpsichord from its first era of existence dates from 1800.

Harpsichords were occasionally heard in concerts in the nineteenth century, played by, for example, IGNAZ MOSCHELES (1837), Ernst Pauer (1861–7), LOUIS DIÉMER (1860s) and ALFRED HIPKINS (1886); but the revival of harpsichord making dates from the end of the century with the Pleyel piano firm in Paris (1882) and ARNOLD DOLMETSCH in London (1896). An iron-framed harpsichord by Pleyel entered production in the 1920s and was championed by the Polish virtuoso WANDA LANDOWSKA, and the four-register 'Bach harpsichord' with pedals for rapid registral changes became standard in Germany for much of the twentieth century. Other specialist performers on non-historical harpsichords included VIOLET GORDON WOODHOUSE, Eta Harich-Schneider and Rudolph Dolmetsch. Regular production of harpsichords modelled on original instruments did not start until the 1950s (by makers such as Hugh Gough, Frank Hubbard and William Dowd, Rainer Schütze and Martin Skowroneck); with these REPLICAS a new generation of historically aware performers emerged, including RALPH KIRKPATRICK, George Malcolm, THURSTON DART, GUSTAV LEONHARDT and Kenneth Gilbert. The harpsichord revival brought with it a renewed interest from composers, including Falla, Poulenc, Ligeti, Elliott Carter, Górecki and Schnittke, and a place for its timbre in film and popular music.

FURTHER READING

F. Hubbard, *Three Centuries of Harpsichord Making* (Cambridge, MA: Harvard University Press, 1967).
E. L. Kottick, *A History of the Harpsichord* (Bloomington, IN and Indianapolis: Indiana University Press, 2003).
G. O'Brien, *Ruckers: A Harpsichord and Virginal Building Tradition* (Cambridge University Press, 2008).
D. Rowland, *Early Keyboard Instruments: A Practical Guide* (Cambridge University Press, 2001).
R. Russell, *The Harpsichord and Clavichord: An Introductory Study*, 2nd edn, rev. H. Schott (London: Faber & Faber, 1973).

TERENCE CHARLSTON

Hauptmann, Moritz (b. Dresden, 13 October 1792; d. Leipzig, 3 January 1868) German violinist, composer, educator and theorist.

Hauptmann authored *Die Natur der Harmonie und der Metrik* (1853) and helped to found the *Bach Gesellschaft*. After performing and teaching in Dresden, Vienna and Kassel, he became the Kantor of the Thomasschule in Leipzig in 1842.

Beyond connections to Hegelian dialectic philosophy, Hauptmann's theories reveal his early education in mathematics and architecture. They stress principles of balance, symmetry and unity, using abstract, draft-like illustrations of metre, ACCENTUATION and pulse. Hauptmann's depictions of 'rhythmopoeia' enrich the understanding of a practical concept, addressed only partially in contemporaneous method books. Although he claimed that *Harmonie und*

Metrik was not a practical instruction method, Hauptmann's varied schemas of musical-metrical construction may be applied to the interpretation and performance of late eighteenth- and nineteenth-century compositions.

Hauptmann's letters offer keen observations about the state of German musical life in the mid-nineteenth century. Considered are the merits of particular ORCHESTRAS and ensembles; vocalists and SINGING technique; works by Schumann, SPOHR, BERLIOZ and MENDELSSOHN; issues regarding acoustics, INTONATION and TEMPERAMENT; and contemporary performances of Baroque music. Although Hauptmann admitted to being an average orchestral violinist and a lacklustre keyboard player, he garnered adulation in Leipzig and elsewhere as an influential conservatoire professor and intellectual force.

FURTHER READING

M. Hauptmann, *The Letters of a Leipzig Cantor*, ed. A. Schöne and F. Hiller, trans. A. D. Coleridge, 2 vols. (London: Novello, Ewer and Co. and Richard Bentley and Son, 1892).

Die Natur der Harmonie und der Metrik (Leipzig: Breitkopf & Härtel, 1853), trans. W. E. Heathcote as *The Nature of Harmony and Metre* (London: Swan Sonnenschein & Co., 1888).

O. Paul and A. Felchner, *Moritz Hauptmann: eine Denkschrift zur Feier seines siebenzigjährigen Geburtstages am 13. October 1862* (Leipzig: Dörffel, 1862).

ALEXANDER EVAN BONUS

Hawkins, Sir John (b. London, 29 March 1719; d. London, 21 May 1789) English music historian.

John Hawkins grew up in a moderately well off London family, his father styling himself as 'citizen and haberdasher'. Hawkins became articled to an attorney, established a successful business as a solicitor in 1751 and was sworn Justice of the Peace for Middlesex ten years later. The substantial inheritance his wife received that year led them to move to Twickenham, near his friends Horace Walpole and David Garrick. Hawkins belonged to the famous club that surrounded Samuel Johnson; his 1787 *Life of Samuel Johnson* is still well regarded among scholars. He was knighted in 1772 due to his growing prominence in literary and political affairs.

In his youth, Hawkins learnt the VIOLIN and the CELLO and became a *habitué* of music clubs. He played in a prominent series of private concerts in a tavern on Gracechurch Street, joined the musically educated amateurs in the Madrigal Society and supported the ACADEMY OF ANCIENT MUSIC, publishing an account of its activities in 1770. His *A General History of the Science and Practice of Music* (5 vols. (London: T. Payne, 1776)) drew a vicious set of pamphlets from supporters of CHARLES BURNEY, the first volume of whose music history had also appeared that year. In contrast, Dr Johnson opined that it should be put 'in all great libraries', and Hawkins is credited as the main pioneer in establishing scholarly treatment of music history. He abandoned the traditional assumption of the 'progress' of music through the ages and treated works of the sixteenth and seventeenth centuries with special respect. A man of quite unpleasant temperament, Hawkins was honoured by few at his death – Sir Joshua Reynolds, for example, described him as 'mean and groveling [*sic*]' (Grant, xii).

FURTHER READING

K. S. Grant, *Dr Charles Burney as Critic and Historian of Music* (Ann Arbor, MI: UMI Research Press, 1983).
P. A. Scholes, *The Life and Activities of Sir John Hawkins* (London: Oxford University Press, 1953/R).
W. Weber, 'Intellectual foundations of musical canon in eighteenth-century England', *JAMS*, 47 (1994), 488–520.

WILLIAM WEBER

Haydn, Franz Joseph (b. Rohrau, Lower Austria, 31 March 1732; d. Vienna, 31 May 1809) Austrian composer.

Commenting on his abilities as a performer, Joseph Haydn told an early biographer that he 'was a wizard at no instrument, but knew the strength and working of them all' (G. A. Griesinger, *Biographische Notizen über Joseph Haydn* (Leipzig: Breitkopf & Härtel, 1810), 119). While this may be taken as an admission of a weakness, especially in comparison with the celebrated capabilities of two contemporaries, MOZART and BEETHOVEN, it was also a signal strength born out of a way of life that was gradually disappearing at the end of the eighteenth century, the life of a working *Kapellmeister*. From his mid-twenties to his death in 1809, Haydn was employed as a *Kapellmeister*, first for the Morzin family in Bohemia and then, from 1761, for the Esterházy family based mainly in Eisenstadt and the summer palace of Eszterháza in Hungary. His popularity with his employers, as well as with his musicians, gave rise to the nickname of 'Papa' Haydn. Unfortunately, posterity was to emphasise the genial side of this nickname, ignoring the authority, efficiency and experience that went with it. The practicalities of performance were as much part of the required capabilities of a *Kapellmeister* as composition, and Haydn was one of the great exponents of these two complementary activities in the eighteenth century, rivalled only by J. S. BACH. When from the 1780s onwards Haydn began composing more and more music for individuals and institutions beyond the Esterházy court, such as quartets for publishers in Vienna, symphonies for Paris and London and oratorios for van Swieten in Vienna, he applied this same innate professionalism plus an ever-present curiosity about any new and different performing circumstances that he encountered.

If Haydn had been able to document this wide experience, he would almost certainly have talked about practicalities rather than lofty aesthetic ideals and would have provided a late eighteenth-century equivalent to MATTHESON's *Der vollkommene Kapellmeister*, a volume which Haydn himself admired. The absence of such a volume is compensated by a considerable corpus of material from contemporary sources relating to Haydn's personal experience of performance, symphonies for the Esterházy court and for London, opera for Eszterháza, oratorio for Vienna and so on, plus what can be gleaned from the scores themselves. Glancing references in the early biographies by Griesinger and Dies provide some tantalising glimpses of some of his priorities, notably the importance of a SINGING style in performance as well as in composition, and the cautionary comment that minuet movements should not be performed too quickly.

The most substantial set of written comments relating to performance dates from early in Haydn's career, in the so-called 'Applausus' letter of March 1768.

Haydn had been asked to write a cantata for a celebratory occasion in the abbey of Zwettl in Lower Austria. It was an unusual experience for him: he did not know the performers and his duties at the Esterházy court did not allow him to travel to Zwettl to direct the performance. In those circumstances he wrote a letter detailing issues that particularly concerned him, ten numbered points, fastidious products of Haydn the *Kapellmeister*. Strict TEMPI and brisk allegros are a must; real and graded differences between *piano, pianissimo, forte* and *fortissimo* are to be observed, likewise the expressive nature of *crescendo* and *sforzando*; appoggiaturas are to be realised in a particular way; for clarity the bass line should include a BASSOON as well as CELLO and DOUBLE BASS; and delayed rather than simultaneous cadences should be the norm in recitatives.

FURTHER READING

T. Beghin, 'A composer, his dedicatee, her instrument, and I: thoughts on performing Haydn's keyboard sonatas', in C. Clark (ed.), *The Cambridge Companion to Haydn* (Cambridge University Press, 2005), 203–25.

A. P. Brown, B. Harrison, D. W. Jones, R. Rabin and R. Stowell, 'Performance practice', in D. W. Jones (ed.), *Oxford Composer Companions. Haydn* (Oxford University Press, 2002), 271–86.

M. Hunter, 'Haydn's string quartet fingerings: communications to performer and audience', in M. Hunter and R. Will (eds.), *Engaging Haydn: Culture, Context, and Criticism* (Cambridge University Press, 2012), 281–301.

DAVID WYN JONES

Haynes, Bruce (b. Louisville, KY, 14 April 1942; d. Montreal, 17 May 2011) American-Canadian oboist and scholar.

Growing up in California, Haynes played the OBOE and RECORDER. From 1965 to 1967 he studied with FRANS BRÜGGEN and GUSTAV LEONHARDT and then apprenticed with the woodwind instrument builder Friedrich von Huene in Boston. Haynes was a vigorous advocate of historical PITCH standards and for a short time made early oboes (hautboys) after Jakob Denner in a workshop in California. In 1972 he was invited to replace Brüggen as recorder teacher at the ROYAL CONSERVATORY OF THE HAGUE for the year. He established an 'hautboy' class and remained in Holland for the following decade. In addition to teaching some of the most noted players of the next generation and collecting data for his numerous research projects, he played with numerous Dutch early music ensembles, made recordings of oboe concertos and chamber music and participated with the Leonhardt Consort in recording all of J. S. BACH's cantatas for Telefunken. His most significant contributions in the field of performance practice research relate to PITCH standards and TEMPERAMENT, and early oboe technique. Based on exacting historical research, his groundbreaking work was often polemical. *The End of Early Music* is a provocative re-examination of the early music movement's motivations and goals. *The Pathetick Musician*, which remained in draft at his death and was completed by Geoffrey Burgess, considers the rhetorical-based interpretation of Baroque music, and particularly the vocal music of J. S. Bach.

FURTHER READING

B. Haynes, *The Eloquent Oboe: A History of the Hautboy 1640 to 1760* (New York: Oxford University Press, 2001).

A History of Performing Pitch: The Story of 'A' (Lanham, MD: Scarecrow Press, 2002).
The End of Early Music: A Period Performer's History of Music for the 21st Century (New York: Oxford University Press, 2007).
B. Haynes and G. Burgess, *The Pathetick Musician: Moving an Audience in the Age of Eloquence* (New York: Oxford University Press, 2016).

GEOFFREY BURGESS

Heinichen, Johann David (b. Krössuln, nr Weissenfels, 17 April 1683; d. Dresden, 16 July 1729) German composer and theorist.

After formative studies in Leipzig and six years in Italy, Heinichen became *Kapellmeister* at the court of Dresden. His importance for performers derives primarily from his *Neu erfundene und gründliche Anweisung ... zu vollkommener Erlernung des General-Basses...* (Hamburg, 1711, but evidently written before most, if not all, of his Italian travels), and a considerably enlarged version, *Der General-Bass in der Composition...* (Dresden, 1728). The latter's title reflects an expanded purpose: to show how the THOROUGHBASS can provide principles for composition. It also includes more music examples and extensive footnotes, which provide valuable insights into matters of style.

Although Heinichen had addressed the theatrical style in his first volume, he covers it more thoroughly in his revision, having immersed himself in Venetian operatic style during the intervening years. Comparing its bold harmonies and free treatment of dissonance to the learned German church style, he despises the pedantic complexity of German counterpoint, favouring a mixed style combining French and Italian elements. In accordance with contemporary *galant* trends, he observes that 'modern' music allows the ear to dominate reason in determining aesthetic value, a view shared by JOHANN MATTHESON. Above all, musicians must possess good TASTE (*goût*), acquired through talent, scholarship and experience. For Heinichen *goût* embodies a pervading *cantabile*, beneficial and touching accompaniments, harmonic changes recommended by the ear and other qualities suggested by experience.

Heinichen's principal distinction between the theatrical and the traditional church style is the treatment of dissonance - an essential element of the theatrical style's harmonic palette, especially in recitatives. Dissonances in the theatrical style can generally be approached or resolved in unconventional ways (or even left unresolved), if the result does not offend the ear - an idea reminiscent of MONTEVERDI's concept of *seconda pratica*. Related to this more liberal approach is Heinichen's advocacy of full-voiced HARPSICHORD accompaniment (*Vollstimmigkeit*), in which notes are doubled as much as practicable. Evidently, the resulting increase in volume was needed in the larger ORCHESTRAS of his times. Heinichen also advocates using the keyboard's entire compass, with the left hand sometimes playing bass notes an octave lower than written and the right hand sustaining and filling out the sound through chord re-positioning or creating melodies, variations and embellishments. On the ORGAN, however, filling out chords in the left hand is to be avoided, lest the sound become muddy.

Heinichen discusses TEMPO and metre in the context of realising bass lines that contain quick, non-harmonic tones, observing that traditional metrical symbols no longer provide reliable indications of tempo. Heinichen's own sacred works sometimes include time durations, from which likely tempi can be inferred.

Heinichen refers the reader to Mattheson's *Exemplarische Organisten-Probe* (Hamburg: im Schille- und Kißnerischen Buch-Laden, 1719) regarding embellishment. His own treatment of ORNAMENTS (except the acciaccatura, which may emphasise dissonances in recitatives) is cursory. Overly embellished accompaniments should be avoided when accompanying singers, lest the accompaniment detract from the vocal part; any independent melodies should be similarly unobtrusive, and song-like.

In his lengthy introduction to *Der General-Bass* (Dresden: the author, 1728), Heinichen discusses the importance of musical RHETORIC for expressing the AFFECTIONS. Although mostly applicable to composers, his instructions spur the performer to expressive performance, for the aim of making music is 'to stir the affections and delight the ear' (in Buelow, 1992, 278). While discounting a strict connection between keys and particular affects, Heinichen provides valuable insights into the relationship between music and rhetoric as it was understood at the time.

FURTHER READING

G. J. Buelow, 'The Italian influence in Heinichen's *Der General-Bass in der Composition* (1728)', *BJhM*, 18 (1994), 47–65.

Thorough-Bass Accompaniment According to Johann David Heinichen, rev. edn (Lincoln, NE: University of Nebraska Press, 1992).

W. Horn, 'Takt, Tempo, Aufführungsdauer in Heinichens Kirchenmusik', *Musiktheorie*, 9/2 (1994), 147–68.

MELVIN P. UNGER

Herrando, José (b. Valencia, late 1720/early 1721; d. Madrid, 4 February 1763) Spanish violinist and composer.

Many scholars refute Herrando's claim that he was a pupil of CORELLI (*Arte y puntual explicación del modo de tocar el violín con perfección y facilidad*, preface); however, he may have received musical training from Giacomo Facco. Herrando entered the service of the Real Convento de la Encarnación in Madrid, probably in the 1740s, and became principal violinist in 1756. He forged professional affiliations with the GEMINIANI family and the Dukes of Alba and Arcos, and records associate him with numerous performances given by FARINELLI. He composed some of his works at Farinelli's request, notably his six sonatinas for a five-stringed VIOLIN (tuned $c-g-d'-a'-e''$). Another unusual sonata, *El Jardín de Aranjuez*, demands the reproduction of birdsong and other natural sounds on the violin.

Herrando's *Arte y puntual explicación*... was the first published violin TREATISE by a Spaniard. Engraved in Paris in 1756 and published in Madrid in 1757, it comprises a thorough compendium of Italian violin techniques and performing practices, particularly with regard to holding the instrument and BOW. He recommends that the chin should secure the violin over the tailpiece, with the face turned somewhat towards the right hand. In advocating the Italian bow hold, he is precise about the optimum elbow position and stresses the importance of wrist and lower arm movement. His twenty-eight exercises include one study in each of the major and minor keys; these studies become more expansive and technically more challenging as the treatise progresses. Geminiani used Carmona's engraving from the front of Herrando's treatise (in which Herrando is pictured playing the violin) in the French translation (1752) of his own violin method, substituting his own head for that of Herrando. The Spaniard also compiled a significant pedagogical work for VIOLA, *Libro de diferentes lecciones para la viola*.

FURTHER READING

D. D. Boyden, *The History of Violin Playing from its Origins to 1761* (London: Oxford University Press, 1965).
M. Jasinski, 'A translation and commentary on José Herrando's "Arte y puntual Explicación del modo de tocar el violin (1756)"', MA dissertation, Brigham Young University (1974).
E. Moreno, 'Aspectos técnicos del tratado de violín de José Herrando (1756): el violín español en el contexto europeo de mediados del siglo XVIII', *Revista de Musicología*, 11/3 (1988), 555–655.

ROBIN STOWELL

Herreweghe, Philippe (b. Ghent, 2 May 1947) Belgian conductor.
Herreweghe studied in Ghent at both the university (medicine and psychiatry) and the music conservatory (piano). During that time he founded the Collegium Vocale (1970) and was invited by GUSTAV LEONHARDT and NIKOLAUS HARNONCOURT to take part in their recordings of all J. S. BACH's cantatas. In 1977 he founded the ensemble La Chapelle Royale in Paris to perform music of the French Golden Age. From 1982 to 2002 he was artistic director of the Académies Musicales de Saintes, creating the Ensemble Vocal Europeén to specialise in Renaissance polyphony, and the Orchestre des Champs Élysées to play Romantic and pre-Romantic repertoire on original instruments. Building on an already extensive discography, Herreweghe founded his own label, PHI, in 2010 in order to achieve greater artistic freedom. Flagship recordings include Schubert's symphonies (2012) and his remarkable reading of Bach's Mass in B minor (1998). His beautiful balancing of the choir and orchestra make this rendition distinctive, combined with soloists who clearly take the text as paramount. Indeed, Herreweghe's choral awareness always allows the text to shine through and inspire instrumental colours and phrasing. Furthermore, there is a fine attention to detail within a flowing sense of continuity that admirably conveys the grand architecture of the work.

Herreweghe's original, energetic, authentic and rhetorical approach to all genres of music has won many plaudits. He has embraced hundreds of years of repertoire with an extraordinary enthusiasm for discovering the specific styles and approaches needed for each period, always creating specialist ensembles to continue his legacy. He is widely regarded as one of the greatest champions of culture, exploring different repertoire with a genuine curiosity, which is infectious.

ASHLEY SOLOMON

Hey, Julius (b. Irmelshausen, 29 April 1832; d. Munich, 22 April 1909) German SINGING teacher, writer and composer.
Hey studied singing with Friedrich Schmitt (1812–84), whose vocal principles had captured RICHARD WAGNER's attention in Magdeburg (1834–6) and were

published in his *Große Gesangsschule für Deutschland* (Munich: Beim Verfasser, 1854). Wagner and King Ludwig II brought Schmitt to Munich in 1864 as part of their plans not only to establish a Königliche Musikschule there but also to develop singers for performances of Wagner's music dramas. Dissatisfied with singers' limited understanding of drama in German opera, inadequate acting and imperfect realisation of the sonic possibilities of the German language's various combinations of consonants, particularly 'the special quality of semi-vowels as a convenient binding agent for legato text-phrasing' (Hey, 135), Wagner believed that Schmitt's pedagogical focus on his native language, underpinned by knowledge of Italian vocal principles, was the optimum way forward (Hey, 85). However, Schmitt was summarily dismissed in 1867 and Hey was appointed as the Königliche Musikschule's first voice teacher.

Hey systematised Wagner's views in his *Deutscher Gesangsunterricht* (2 vols. (Mainz: Schott, 1885)). He devoted the first volume to spoken discourse, discussing each vowel, semi-vowel, diphthong and, above all, each consonant in minute detail and providing several examples in poetry (not music). Contrary to Italian tutors, which took the vowel 'a' as the foundation of vocal technique, he considered all vowels, diphthongs and consonants equally significant for enhancing the words' 'expressive plasticity' (*Deutscher Gesangsunterricht*, vol. 2, 'Gesanglicher Theil', 3f.). He aimed to develop Wagnerian singers who could 'combine vivid emphasis on the meaning of a word with the melodic accentuation of a vocal phrase in a natural unit, with the aim of creating a "German bel canto", that is: a singing of simplest truth clothed in a declamation of perfect style, the melodic rules of which emanate exclusively from the life-giving rhythm' of the German language (*Deutscher Gesangsunterricht*, vol. 2, 'Gesanglicher Theil', 83). A condensed edition of his TREATISE (by Fritz Volbach and Hans Hey) was later published as *Der kleine Hey* (Mainz and Leipzig: Schott, 1912) and has remained a standard German singing text.

Hey coached many of the singers involved in the first complete *Ring* cycle in Bayreuth (1876), insisting on clear enunciation of the text as a springboard for expressive singing. Among those who came under his influence were Georg Unger, Felix von Kraus, Friedrich Brodersen, Julius von Raatz-Brockman and Ernestine Schumann-Heink. The latter's recordings (c1930) as Erda and Waltraute (*Der Ring*) provide particularly good examples of Hey's approach to textual delivery.

FURTHER READING

R. Fricke, *1875–1876. The Diaries of Richard Fricke*, trans. G. R. Fricke and ed. J. Deaville, with E. Baker (Stuyvesant, NY: Pendragon Press, 1998).
H. Hey (ed.), *Richard Wagner als Vortragsmeister: Erinnerungen von Julius Hey* (Leipzig: Breitkopf & Härtel, 1911).
E. Newman, *The Life of Richard Wagner*, 4 vols. (London: Cassell, 1933–47).

ROBIN STOWELL

Hiller, Ferdinand (von) (b. Frankfurt, 24 October 1811; d. Cologne, 11 May 1885) German conductor, pianist, organist, composer, entrepreneur and musicologist.

A piano pupil of Alois Schmitt (Frankfurt) and JOHANN NEPOMUK HUMMEL (Weimar), Hiller gave the first performance in Paris (1833) of

BEETHOVEN's Fifth Piano Concerto and gained high praise in the French capital over nearly seven years (from 1828) for his performances, compositions and ORGAN teaching. In Frankfurt (1836) he deputised for Johann Schelble as conductor of the *Cäcilienverein*, conducted later in Milan and Leipzig and eventually replaced his then good friend MENDELSSOHN as conductor of the Gewandhaus Orchestra (1843–4).

Hiller was a tireless organiser of concert series. He initiated the orchestral *Abonnement-Konzerte* in Dresden 1845–7 and a series at the *Musikverein* in Düsseldorf (1847–50), where he raised musical standards considerably. He later served as *Kapellmeister* in Cologne (1850–84), reorganised the city's music school on the Leipzig model and directed the annual series of Gürzenich concerts there. He also became one of the directors (with Robert Schumann and Julius Tausch) of Cologne's *Niederrheinische Musikfest* in 1853 (and sole director in eleven subsequent festivals up to 1883) and he conducted most of Schumann's major compositions under the festival's auspices. Liszt described Hiller's CONDUCTING as 'like his whole personality: obliging, rounded, correct, even distinguished, but with no tension, no energy and therefore with no authority and communicative electricity. He could be reproached for having no flaws, and thus with giving criticism no foothold' (La Mara [Ida Marie Lipsius] (ed.), *Franz Liszts Briefe*, 8 vols. (Leipzig: Breitkopf & Härtel, 1893–1905), iv, 217). Hiller's scholarly contributions include a study of early Italian polyphony and his role (from 1854) as Karl Mikuli's adviser for the complete edition of Chopin's music. Although he had conservative musical TASTES, his influence was wide-ranging, as his correspondence with contemporary composers, performers and publishers amply confirms.

FURTHER READING

E. Hanslick, *Sämtliche Schriften. Historisch-kritische Ausgabe*, vol. I (Aufsätze und Rezensionen 1855–1856), ed. D. Strauß (Vienna, Cologne and Weimar: Böhlau, 1995), 76–83 et passim.

F. Hiller, *Erinnerungsblätter* (Cologne: DuMont-Schauenburg, 1884).

R. Sietz (ed.), *Aus Ferdinand Hillers Briefwechsel: Beiträge zu einer Biographie Ferdinand Hillers* (Cologne: Arno Volk Verlag, 1958–70).

ROBIN STOWELL

Hiller, Johann Adam (b. Wendisch-Ossig, 25 December 1728; d. Leipzig, 16 June 1804) German composer, Kantor, writer on music, singing pedagogue.

Hiller was a moderniser, particularly through his tireless advocacy for improving the standard of vocal pedagogy and professional practice, as well as his championing the emancipation of women in music, including their participation in church music. His most important and lasting contributions to performance practice are his two TREATISES on SINGING. His *Anweisung zum musikalisch-richtigen Gesange* (Leipzig, 1774) is a primer 'concerned with the basics – elementary skills of musicianship, theory, harmony and technique' (Butt, 166) based on practical exercises. Hiller explains his motivation for writing it as the lamentable state of German singing compared with Italy in particular, which he attributes to outmoded school music pedagogy, based on his own experience of it as a child as so much dry theory, whereas 'of the good use of the voice, of the comfortable drawing of breath, of a pure and clear pronunciation, however essential these elements of singing were, little or nothing was mentioned' (Butt, 166).

Six years later he published a more advanced treatise on art singing, the *Anweisung zum musikalischen-zierlichen Gesange* (Leipzig: J. F. Junius, 1780). Hiller felt that German professional operatic singing lagged far behind Italy, which he put down partly to the fact that the German language could never be a successful vehicle for the brilliance of Italian declamation. For this reason, he was a strong supporter of the development of the German *Singspiel*, which, rather like English ballad opera, interspersed spoken dialogue with strophic arias, reaching its apogee in MOZART's *Die Zauberflöte* (1791). In order to emulate Italian pedagogical methods as closely as possible, Hiller built on the tradition of the treatises of PIER FRANCESCO TOSI and his successors, including JOHANN AGRICOLA's translation and expansion (1757) of Tosi, FRIEDRICH WILHELM MARPURG and JOHANN MATTHESON. Hiller, like Agricola, strongly supports the idea that while the composer must take responsibility for the proper ACCENTUATION of the text, it is the singer's responsibility to 'go further than the composer in expressing, through swellings and mutings of the voice, that which the composer cannot indicate' (Hiller, ed. Beicken, 21). Another feature of the volume is the section dealing with ORNAMENTATION and other arbitrary variations. While Hiller is a champion of the importance of singers' 'co-compositional' role in the creation of arias in particular, he rejects the complete freedom to improvise ornamentation advocated by Tosi and MANCINI, and argues that it should be written out, not to curtail singers' capriciousness so much as to demonstrate the importance of the link between ornamentation and declamation: 'all musical ornaments are essentially accents, and should be used to emphasise certain notes and syllables' (Hiller (1780), 34). To support this he provides examples in the form of two whole arias, one Italian the other German, with fully written-out ornamentation for the repeats. When it comes to CADENZAS, Hiller is far less restrictive than Tosi, defending singers' right to show their inventiveness. Nevertheless, he imposes certain limits, including the rule that the cadenza must be sung in one breath; he also suggests that singers unable to extemporise should simply sing a few notes that are in the harmony and end with a trill, while he recommends writing out double and triple cadenzas in full.

FURTHER READING

S. J. Beicken (ed. and trans.), *Treatise on Vocal Performance and Ornamentation by Johann Adam Hiller* (Cambridge University Press, 2001).
J. Butt, *Music Education and the Art of Performance in the German Baroque* (Cambridge University Press, 1994).

RICHARD WISTREICH

Hilliard Ensemble British all-male vocal CONSORT, founded in 1973.

Directed until the late 1980s by bass Paul Hillier, the Hilliard Ensemble later crystallised into a directorless quartet (ATTB) to which other voices could be added. The group dissolved in 2014, having gained a worldwide reputation and made over forty recordings. Countertenor David James was a member of the ensemble from beginning to end, while other long-time members include tenors Paul Elliott, Rogers Covey-Crump, John Potter and Steven Harrold, and baritone Gordon Jones. The Ensemble divided its activity between Medieval/Renaissance repertoire and contemporary music, much of the latter written for them by leading composers; and when the two periods were merged in *Officium*, an album project with jazz saxophonist Jan Garbarek, it brought the group its greatest commercial success. *Morimur*, a practical exploration of Helga Thoene's theories that J. S. BACH's *ciaccona* (solo violin Partita No. 2 in D minor BWV1004) represents a memorial to his wife Maria Barbara and that the whole Partita includes references to death by way of quotations from his chorales, was another project to find a wide audience. Violinist Christoph Poppen performed the Partita and the Hilliards sang the chorale quotations, illustrating how they align with the solo VIOLIN part.

The group's performances consistently showed high levels of ensemble expertise and a distinctive and affecting sound that derived much of its colour from its individual voices, in particular James's upper-part countertenor contribution.

LINDSAY KEMP

Hindemith, Paul (b. Hanau, nr Frankfurt, 16 November 1895; d. Frankfurt, 28 December 1963) German composer, theorist, teacher, violist and conductor.

Hindemith's approach towards historical performance practice reveals itself in all his activities. He was a versatile musician, competent on most orchestral instruments, and his concert activities included performances on historical instruments, particularly the viola d'amore. He conceived of early music always as an expression of the here and now, which he gleaned through his engagement with historical performing practices.

Hindemith was first exposed to early music during his studies at Hoch's Conservatory in Frankfurt am Main, where the works of Biber, CORELLI, TARTINI, Vitali, Handel and BACH were integral to the didactic literature. In 1922 his interest in the viola d'amore arose simultaneously from its distinctive sound, from preparations for the staging of Hans Pfitzner's opera *Palestrina* that included a short appearance of the instrument, and from sheer historical curiosity. He composed for the instrument as early as 1922 and proceeded to devote much time to exploring and editing for performance its historical repertoire by Ariosti, Biber, Erlebach, Ganswindt, Rust, Carl Stamitz, Petzold and Vivaldi.

As professor of composition in Berlin from 1927, Hindemith required his students to take lessons on early instruments, which he borrowed from the *Staatliche Instrumentensammlung* that was under the direction of CURT SACHS. In preparing his own theoretical method, *Unterweisung im Tonsatz* (3 pts. (Mainz: Schott, 1937, 1939 and 1970)), he studied historical TREATISES, which gave him much insight into performing practices; crucially, he insisted that performances of early music in which he was to be involved should abandon the customary modern substitute instrumentation and pay heed to historical forces, TEMPERAMENTS and performing practices. After his emigration to the USA in 1940, Tanglewood and Yale University offered further opportunities for him to intensify these activities and broaden their historical basis. Even though he was employed to teach composition, he organised a series of concerts at Tanglewood in 1941 as part of the Boston Symphony Orchestra Summer Academy, during which nearly 200 pieces dating from the twelfth to the sixteenth centuries were performed in his own arrangements. At Yale he turned such concerts into part of the curriculum by attaching a Collegium Musicum to his composition and theory lectures. With this group he followed a systematic chronological path through works from Pérotin to Gesualdo and Bach, interpreting these in as historically accurate a manner as possible at that time in a series of performances that took place between 1945 and 1953. The concerts were hugely successful and have had a lasting influence on historical performance practice in the US.

In his 1952 monograph, *A Composer's World*, Hindemith postulated that any modern performance of early music distorts the music's sound and musical sense, both of which could only be represented adequately through historical performing practices. Towards the end of his life he was still planning an edited series of early music, for which he prepared selections from GIOVANNI GABRIELI's *Symphoniae Sacrae* with extensive performance instructions. Crucially, he sought to publish these supplemented by the FACSIMILES of the original prints to allow performers to control the decision-making. 'Early music' for Hindemith was by no means a musical culture separate from contemporary musical life; instead, he understood this repertoire as an indispensable part of contemporary music culture which ought to be cultivated according to its own historical context just as contemporary music was understood within its own context.

FURTHER READING

P. Hindemith, *A Composer's World* (Cambridge, MA: Harvard University Press, 1952).
I. Kemp, *Hindemith* (London: Oxford University Press, 1970).

GISELHER SCHUBERT

Hipkins, Alfred James (b. London, 17 June 1826; d. London, 3 June 1903) Writer on musical instruments, collector and performer on early keyboards.

In 1840 Hipkins was apprenticed at Broadwood as a PIANO tuner and worked for that firm for the rest of his life. From this position he met and corresponded with key musical figures in Europe, such as Fryderyck Chopin and Clara Schumann, as well as Alexander J. Ellis, with whom he collaborated in the study of equal TEMPERAMENT and PITCH.

Hipkins's studies led to the publication of the first comprehensive monograph in English on the history of musical instruments (*Musical Instruments: Historic, Rare, Unique* (Edinburgh: A & C Black, 1888)) and the first English history of the piano and early keyboard instruments (*A Description and History of the Pianoforte* ... (London: Novello, Ewer & Co., 1896)). Self-taught, he performed in 1886 J. S. BACH's *Chromatic fantasia and fugue* BWV903 on the CLAVICHORD and part of the *Goldberg Variations* BWV1087 on the HARPSICHORD. His work on extra-European music was influenced by CARL ENGEL, with whom he was a close friend.

FURTHER READING

A. Pimlott Baker, 'Hipkins, Alfred James', in *Oxford Dictionary of National Biography*, 60 vols. (Oxford University Press, 2004), xxii, 304.
'Alfred James Hipkins', *MT*, 39/667 (1898), 581–6.
'Alfred James Hipkins', *MT*, 44/725 (1903), 459–60.

GABRIELE ROSSI ROGNONI

Historical concerts The boundary between concerts of a canonic and a historical nature, though often vague, derives from their contrasting relationships with the musical past. While both kinds of events focus on old repertories, the historical concert involves a distancing from the past which was often viewed through an academic perspective. By contrast, canonic valuation of a composer's work has usually stressed continuity with the past, placing it in a tradition alongside figures given more or less equivalent respect. The repertories of string quartets, symphonies and solo sonatas termed 'Classical music' in the nineteenth century were not usually defined in historicist terms. Distancing from the past often involved links with academic study, and the main signal for such a posture can be seen when dates were given for pieces or the birth and death of composers.

The ACADEMY OF ANCIENT MUSIC, founded in London in 1726, was defined explicitly as a historicist institution, since little precedent existed for self-conscious performance of old pieces. Led by the principal singers of the royal chapels and educated amateurs, the Academy intended to revive 'grave Ancient vocell musick', as its minutes of 7 January 1725/26 noted. Tim Eggington's recent history of the Academy shows how the group aimed to develop 'a studious enthusiasm, unusual in its day, for music's august theoretical traditions' (2014, 1). The Academy's meetings offered performance of pieces by Giovanni Palestrina, William Byrd and Luca Marenzio, as well as contemporaries such as Handel and Domenico Scarlatti. Known only among a small specialised public, the Academy shifted to a canonic rather than a historicist repertoire in the 1780s similar to that of the CONCERT OF ANTIENT MUSIC, begun in 1776.

A remarkably systematic programme of historical concerts came about in Vienna under the leadership of Raphael Kiesewetter between 1816 and 1842. Interestingly enough, Kiesewetter acknowledged London's Academy of Ancient Music as a model for his enterprise. An official of the war office from the lesser nobility, he sang in public concerts and devoted himself to music history, publishing *Geschichte der europäisch-abendländischen oder unsrer heutigen Musik* (Leipzig, 1834), a set of lectures on seventeen periods chiefly of sacred music since the tenth century. The concerts, held in his own home, offered a journey through music from the sixteenth century, featuring pieces variously from those of Giovanni Palestrina to J. S. BACH and JOSEPH HAYDN.

Historicist programming emerged with an ideological slant in the *Concerts Historiques* given by FRANÇOIS-JOSEPH FÉTIS in April 1832. Fétis drew on the long-standing battle over Italian versus French music in presenting little-known opera selections at the first of the three concerts, including selections from CLAUDIO MONTEVERDI, Francesco Cavalli, JEAN-BAPTISTE LULLY, Reinhard Keiser, and JEAN-PHILIPPE RAMEAU. As Katharine Ellis put it, his lecture-recitals gave 'a crash course' in separating musical wheat (Italian or

German) from chaff (French) of any era. The series stimulated other musicians to put on comparable concerts; the orchestral concerts of the *Société du Conservatoire* likewise included pieces from operas by Lully, Rameau and André-Modeste Grétry. Programmes focused on old opera similar to Fétis's model had done were occasionally attempted elsewhere in Europe. In 1847 the Subscription Concerts of the Gewandhaus in Leipzig offered a programme of 'works by the Great Masters of the last 100 Years' that included selections from Handel's *Jephtha*, Pergolesi's *Stabat Mater* and Grétry's *Richard Coeur de Lion*.

By the turn of the twentieth century, many organisations and individual musicians were presenting historically informed concerts throughout Europe and the Americas. In 1905 a New York newspaper dubbed British musician ARNOLD DOLMETSCH an 'apostle of retrogression'. The repertory of such events brought along many little-known composers. In 1910, for example, the *Société des instruments anciens*, founded by HENRI CASADESUS, put on a concert for VIOLS in the Salle Pleyel that included pieces by André Cardinal Destouches, J.-A. Hasse, Bonifacio Asioli and Antonio Bruni. It was conventional for a singer or an instrumentalist to open a concert with music composed before 1800, often with the composers' dates supplied. In 1910 Bechstein (later Wigmore) Hall, London, offered a concert by violinist Joseph Debroux that began with sonatas by Diogenio Bigaglia and J.-F. d'Andrieu and continued with pieces by J. S. Bach, Max Bruch, and an adaptation of music of WAGNER by August Wilhelmj. Harry Haskell (194) has pointed out that by the end of the twentieth century the 'omnivorous eclecticism' of such concerts was succeeded by a deeper historical sensibility, which Christopher Hogwood termed a 'healthy didacticism'.

FURTHER READING

T. Eggington, *The Advancement of Music in Enlightenment England: Benjamin Cooke and the Academy of Ancient Music* (Woodbridge: Boydell & Brewer, 2014).
K. Ellis, *Interpreting the Past: Early Music in Nineteenth-Century France* (Oxford University Press, 2005).
H. Haskell, *The Early Music Revival: a History* (London: Thames & Hudson, 1988).
H. Kier, *Raphael Georg Kiesewetter (1773–1850): Wegbereiter des musikalischen Historismus* (Regensburg: Bosse, 1968).

WILLIAM WEBER

Historically informed performance In recent times the intentions and expectations of composers in terms of sound and musical style have become a subject for lively discourse. Performers and scholars have worked together to recreate original practices, drawing upon archival, literary, iconographical, analytical and purely philological studies. The musical score itself is an imprecise mechanism, which by its very nature offers even the most dutiful performer a rich variety of possibilities. There has always been much detail that a composer did not trouble to notate, knowing that certain conventions would be observed; some of these are no longer current or have undergone significant changes of meaning. Those elements of style which a composer found it unnecessary to notate will always have the character of a foreign language, but one within which today's musicians can learn to converse freely. Using the resources for which a particular repertory was intended may well make more sense of what the composer actually wrote, re-creating something of its initial impact on the listener.

Significantly, there was a belief until relatively recently that there was no benefit in restoring music written after 1750 to period instruments. As late as 1980 the article 'performing practice' in *The New Grove Dictionary* claimed that there had been no severance of contact with post-Baroque music as a whole, nor with the instruments used in performing it. Subsequent musical revelations have proved this argument untenable, as period interpretations of MOZART and BEETHOVEN have been followed by a traversal of repertory extending to STRAVINSKY, Ravel and beyond. Thus the term 'early music', once applied to music of the Baroque and earlier periods, has largely given way to terms such as 'historically informed performance', in recognition that this later repertory also presents formidable challenges in relation to the balance of historical accuracy and practical expediency.

Performances of 'early music' have been a feature of Western culture at various times and places – and it seems probable that the extent to which musicians before 1900 performed and studied only the music of their own time has been somewhat exaggerated. In Renaissance England, for example, sacred vocal music often stayed in the repertories of church and cathedral CHOIRS for more than a hundred years. Then in the late eighteenth and early nineteenth centuries, organisations such as the ACADEMY OF ANCIENT MUSIC and the CONCERTS OF ANTIENT MUSIC in London regularly presented early English church music as well as works by Purcell, HANDEL and CORELLI. England was the first country where old works were performed regularly and reverentially and where the idea of musical classics first arose. The crucial realisation gradually developed during the nineteenth century that contemporary performing styles did not necessarily suit music from earlier times. Prominent among advocates of such a viewpoint was FÉTIS, whose historical concerts began at the PARIS CONSERVATOIRE as early as 1832. This stylistic awareness attempted to view older music in terms of its original period rather than transplanting it to the present. The widespread acceptance of so-called faithfulness to the original is much more recent and has been widely seen as symptomatic of the loss of a truly living contemporary music. In the later nineteenth century, the establishment of texts from preferred sources in Collected Editions was soon to make possible the concepts of WERKTREUE (faithfulness to the text), performance practice and AUTHENTICITY itself. Discussion as to whether musical instruments had improved or merely changed was rife during the great technological developments of the nineteenth century. For example, WAGNER was in no doubt that in Beethoven's symphonies valved TRUMPETS and HORNS should be used rather than their natural precursors. On the other hand, BERLIOZ (1843) described the use of valves for stopped notes in Beethoven as a dangerous abuse.

Unsurprisingly, the beginnings of the historical performance movement were modest indeed, though from a European perspective it is significant that in the year 1915 (the year of publication of ARNOLD DOLMETSCH's seminal book *The Interpretation of the Music of the Seventeenth and Eighteenth Centuries Revealed by Contemporary Evidence* (London: Novello & Co.)), SAINT-SAËNS surveyed the principal issues of style, technique and equipment in a lecture in San Francisco. A huge number of fledgling institutions began to develop throughout Europe. There had already been a long tradition of early music at Basle when the gambist AUGUST WENZINGER co-founded the SCHOLA CANTORUM BASILIENSIS in 1933 as a teaching and research institution for early music from the Middle Ages to Mozart. Dolmetsch's special status in the history of period performance is justified as much by the wisdom of his book as the eccentricities of his career. Yet his great gift was to have the imagination and the musicianship to take a work which had become a museum piece and make it speak to the people of his own time. He treated recordings and concerts as works in progress rather than finished articles and was fortunate in having had the opportunity to implement his pioneering work at a time before the pressures of the recording industry were to place such a high premium on technical accuracy at all costs. The art of making music has remained much more difficult to quantify than the craft. This point is well illustrated in TÜRK's *Klavierschule* of 1789, which lays out various stylistic precepts, but finally admits that some aspects of musicianship cannot be taught and that all one can do is simply to listen to the best singers.

Period performance after 1945 centred upon Amsterdam, The Hague, London and Vienna. In London THURSTON DART symbolised a new coming together of the performer and musicologist, who in 1954 at the conclusion of his book wrote (165): 'The written text must never be regarded as a dead laboratory specimen; it is only sleeping, though both love and time will be needed to awaken it. But love and time will be wasted without a sense of tradition and of historical continuity.' A later important practical impetus was the versatile DAVID MUNROW (1942–76), who with THE EARLY MUSIC CONSORT OF LONDON brought new life to Medieval and Renaissance repertory and acted as a springboard for distinguished alumni such as CHRISTOPHER HOGWOOD. A quite different personality and another seminal figure was the Dutch harpsichordist GUSTAV LEONHARDT, whose meticulous care for historical accuracy in his texts and instruments eschewed the trappings of showmanship. Early postwar milestones were Wenzinger's performance of MONTEVERDI's *Orfeo* (1955), and HARNONCOURT's Brandenburg Concertos a decade later. In the early 1970s, English ensembles were formed by JOHN ELIOT GARDINER, Hogwood, ROGER NORRINGTON and TREVOR PINNOCK. At this time enterprising individuals and chamber groups were venturing into the Classical and even early Romantic periods. But this repertory was given particular impetus by Hogwood's complete Mozart symphony cycle in the early 1980s, which ignited further debate about the role of interpretation, to which Hogwood was fundamentally opposed. Like many of his contemporaries, he was decidedly unhistorical in directing with a baton. Soon, Beethoven symphonies played with historical awareness were to prove revelatory, notably at the hands of Roger Norrington, whose recordings aimed to make the music sound new and to recapture much of the exhilaration and sheer disturbance that it certainly generated in his day. Beethoven cycles continued apace, whilst Berlioz, MENDELSSOHN, Schumann, BRAHMS, WAGNER and Verdi were soon to prove ripe for treatment. Thus historical awareness eventually reached the era of early recordings, bringing a further perspective on its aspirations and limitations.

The ethos (rather than the practicalities) of historical performance has continued to attract substantial attention. As long ago as 1983 LAURENCE DREYFUS queried how adherence to textbook rules for 'scientific method' could be magically transformed into a composer's intentions. RICHARD TARU-SKIN (*Text and Act* (Oxford, 1995)) famously argued that historical performance was completely of our own time and that the historical hardware had won its wide acceptance and above all its commercial viability precisely by virtue of its novelty, not its antiquity. Since that time the principles of historical performance have been increasingly absorbed into the mainstream of concert life, not just at the hands of pioneers such as Norrington (who has argued against the use of orchestral VIBRATO in repertory from before the 1930s), but much more generally. While this phenomenon has been widely reported, NICHOLAS KENYON's 2001 Royal Philharmonic Society Lecture, 'Tradition isn't what it used to be' remains its most articulate account.

FURTHER READING

R. T. Dart, *The Interpretation of Music* (London: Hutchinson, 1954).
H. Haskell, *The Early Music Revival: A History* (London: Thames & Hudson, 1988).
N. Kenyon, 'Tradition isn't what it used to be', Royal Philharmonic Society Lecture, 2001.
C. Lawson and R. Stowell, *The Historical Performance of Music: an Introduction* (Cambridge University Press, 1999).
C. Lawson and R. Stowell (eds.), *The Cambridge History of Musical Performance* (Cambridge University Press, 2012).

COLIN LAWSON

Hogwood, Christopher (Jarvis Haley) (b. Nottingham, 10 September 1941; d. Cambridge, 24 September 2014) English conductor, harpsichordist, musicologist and educator.

Christopher Hogwood was one of the most influential of period conductors from the 1970s onwards, an authority on HISTORICALLY INFORMED PERFORMANCE and a persuasive advocate across practice and theory. Taught by RAYMOND LEPPARD, Mary Potts, THURSTON DART, Rafael Puyana, GUSTAV LEONHARDT and Zuzana Růžičková, he co-founded the EARLY MUSIC CONSORT OF LONDON with DAVID MUNROW in 1967. His own ACADEMY OF ANCIENT MUSIC (AAM) was founded in 1973, initially to play Baroque music on period instruments. His 200+ recordings with AAM proved highly influential way beyond the confines of historical performance. His revelatory *Messiah* in 1980 was hailed for the scholarly thoroughness of its conception and its sheer brilliance of execution. By the following year he was CONDUCTING the Los Angeles Philharmonic, which acclaimed him as 'the most stimulating force in years'. By this time he had completed his hugely influential recordings of the MOZART symphonies, the first set on period instruments. Hogwood consistently defended his non-interventionist approach, suggesting that the figure of the grand maestro imposing a highly subjective interpretation was itself a creation of a more recent era. Some critics remained unconvinced; famously a review in the journal *Early Music* controversially suggested that the AAM Mozart symphonies were not merely 'underinterpreted' but 'uninterpreted'. The AAM repertory soon moved into the nineteenth century and Hogwood directed other period orchestras (notably revolutionising the HANDEL AND HAYDN SOCIETY in Boston) and applied period principles on modern instruments across repertory from CORELLI to TIPPETT with diverse ORCHESTRAS from Minnesota, Prague, Basel and Poznań. He conducted opera at Covent Garden, La Scala, the Paris Opéra, the Deutsche Oper and the Sydney Opera House. Hogwood commanded respect for his virtuosity as a keyboard player, demonstrated by such landmark recordings as the *Fitzwilliam Virginal Book, My Ladye Nevells Booke* and J. S. BACH's *French Suites*, as well as discs of Arne, C. P. E. BACH, LOUIS COUPERIN, FRESCOBALDI, Gibbons and others. He had a particular affinity with the CLAVICHORD, which he held up as proof of former generations' greater esteem for domestic and amateur music making; his recordings on that instrument include music by Bach, Handel and Mozart. His scholarly activity was formidable, with essays on Dowland, Purcell, Handel, HAYDN, Mozart, MENDELSSOHN and many others. His classic book on Handel from 1984 was translated into Czech, German, Italian, Japanese, Polish and Spanish. It is a fine illustration of his elegant, articulate and discriminating prose, while commanding a cultural agenda way beyond music. Hogwood's many editions of major chamber and orchestral works encompassed Purcell, Vivaldi, Mendelssohn, BRAHMS and ELGAR. Contemporaneous chamber arrangements of Haydn and Mozart became a speciality. He was a board member of the C. P. E. Bach Complete Edition and general editor of the GEMINIANI *Opera Omnia*. Hogwood had a wide-ranging, intelligent cultural perspective, engaging at various times with period cookery, flower arranging, architecture and fashion. On the occasion of the award of an HonDMus at the ROYAL COLLEGE OF MUSIC in 2013, he was delighted to reveal that he was writing a history of the picnic, a project left incomplete at the time of his death.

FURTHER READING

T. Donahue (ed.), *Essays in Honor of Christopher Hogwood: The Maestro's Direction* (Lanham MD: Scarecrow Press, 2010).

COLIN LAWSON

Holman, Peter (b. London, 19 October 1946). English keyboard player, conductor and musicologist, specialising in English Renaissance and Baroque music.

Holman studied at King's College, London with THURSTON DART, has taught at many conservatoires and universities and is professor emeritus at Leeds University. In 1979 Holman founded (with Roy Goodman) The Parley of Instruments, taking its name from the early public concerts that the violinist John Banister presented in London in 1676. The group specialises in early VIOLIN repertoire and in 1985 pioneered the revival of a Renaissance violin band using copies of late sixteenth-century instruments, the light internal construction, gut strings and short BOWS of which make an attractive, blended sound akin to a VIOL CONSORT. Holman works closely with Judy Tarling (violin) and Mark Caudle (bass violin, bass viol and CELLO); together they have made over seventy recordings with the group. He also became a co-director of Opera Restor'd (1985), which presented productions of lesser-known small-scale operas, many of which were recorded by Hyperion. In 1993, Holman's first book, *Four and Twenty Fiddlers*, mapped the court string ensemble from Henry VIII to Purcell, offering captivating insights into the contemporary music profession; it won a British Academy prize. The following year his *Henry Purcell* was published, setting the historical context for the various genres in which Purcell composed and examining the institutions within which he worked. Holman's essay 'The British Isles: private and public music' (in J. Sadie ed., *Companion to Baroque Music* (London: Dent, 1990), 261-9) gives a focused and pithy account of music of Stuart and Georgian Britain. More recently, *Life after Death* (2010) traces the thread of the viol's survival in Britain from Henry Purcell to ARNOLD DOLMETSCH. Centre stage is ABEL, who Holman believes performed in over 400 concerts after his arrival in Britain; in the course of his research Holman discovered a 'cult of exotic instruments' (135) into which the largely abandoned viol fitted neatly.

FURTHER READING

P. Holman, *Four and Twenty Fiddlers: The Violin at the English Court 1540-1690* (Oxford University Press, 1993).
Henry Purcell (Oxford University Press, 1994).
Life after Death: The Viola da Gamba in Britain from Purcell to Dolmetsch (Woodbridge: Boydell Press, 2010).

LUCY ROBINSON

Horn Lip-vibrated brass instrument with a mainly conical bore; one of the family of trumpets in the Hornbostel-Sachs classification system.

The Baroque and Early Classical Eras

The seventeenth-century European horn existed in two forms. One, with a loosely wound hoop, fitted over the player's shoulder while he was hunting and survives as the French *trompe de chasse*. Circumstantial evidence suggests that the other, a tightly coiled instrument, may have been used on stage in Cavalli's *Le Nozze di Teti e di Peleo* (1639); generally, however, the horn did not appear in ORCHESTRAS until after c1680, when, after hearing the instrument at Versailles, the Bohemian Count Anton von Sporck arranged for two of his servants to learn to play it. The horn also began to appear in operatic scores written in Vienna and Hamburg, and TELEMANN, Zelenka, QUANTZ, Hasse and Vivaldi composed particularly for the players who were based in Dresden. Elsewhere in Europe, J. S. BACH (Cöthen and Leipzig) and HANDEL (London) both used the instrument on a regular basis.

A serious disadvantage of the early horn was that, because it was made from a fixed length of tubing, it could only play in one key. Progress was made in 1703 when the Viennese maker Michael Leichnamschneider made it possible to insert additional circles of cylindrical tubing between the mouthpiece and the horn to lower its PITCH. In the eighteenth century these could come either in the form of a master crook, to which a choice of couplers could be added, or as a series of 'terminal crooks', one for each of the common keys. 'Terminal crooks' had the advantage of keeping the body of the horn at the same distance from the player's lips regardless of the length of tubing involved.

The earliest horn tutors are English, essentially for hunting horn, and say little about Baroque horn technique that cannot be worked out empirically. Although the instrument was limited to playing the notes of the harmonic series, its narrow, tapered tubing meant that it could play up to at least the sixteenth degree of the series, where the close proximity of the notes made it possible – if taxing – to play melodically. Some pictorial evidence suggests that the horn was originally held with the bell in the air, but this seems unlikely as the condensation created in playing would have drained back into the player's mouth, quickly making the instrument unplayable. Other illustrations of horn players show them holding their horses' reins in one hand and their instruments in the other. Following the horn's adoption in the orchestra, it was not long before it was held by both hands, making it possible to occlude the bell with one and thereby create notes outside the harmonic series. Players in Dresden were experimenting with this idea by the 1720s and ANTON HAMPEL is credited both with developing the technique systematically and with teaching it to others, who developed it further. He also helped to design the *Inventionshorn*, an instrument with a fixed mouthpipe and interchangeable central sections of tubing in F, E, E♭ and D, the keys in which the tonal character of the horn was at its finest and in which hand stopping worked best. The non-transposing mute which Hampel developed did not become a regular part of the horn player's equipment until WAGNER recognised its potential, but the addition of the tuning slide by Haltenhof in 1776 had a more immediate impact.

The Late Classical and Early Romantic Eras
One of Hampel's pupils, Giovanni Punto (1746–1803), toured Europe extensively, popularising both hand stopping and the *Inventionshorn* and inspiring BEETHOVEN to write his Sonata, Op. 17. His preferred instrument was made by Lucien-Joseph Raoux, whose horns were also played by Türrschmidt and Palsa from the court at Oettingen-Wallerstein, DAUPRAT (professor at the PARIS CONSERVATOIRE) and Giovanni Puzzi (the leading horn player in England c1817). The elegant bell-shape of Raoux's instruments dictated horn design in France and England throughout the nineteenth century and its influence only faded with the arrival of the German-style double horn after WWII.

Although the finest solo works for horn from the Classical era – HAYDN's Concerto in D major Hob.VIId:3, MOZART's concertos and his Quintet K407 – were composed for Joseph Leutgeb (1732–1811), others were far more virtuosic. Players were increasingly capable of extraordinary technical feats, immense tonal variety and delicacy of style, but by the early nineteenth century they were being pushed to the limit by composers' increasingly chromatic scores. Ways of changing crooks automatically became essential. Friedrich Blühmel and Heinrich Stölzel each invented valves independently, but they took out a joint patent for them in 1818.

The Romantic Era
By 1828 the valve horn was being played by PIERRE-JOSEPH MEIFRED in France and the brothers Joseph and Eduard Lewy in Austria and Germany. In France and England, however, the instrument's consistent tone seemed monotonous by comparison with the wide tonal palette of the hand horn. Dauprat's view (*Méthode de cor alto et cor basse* (Paris: Zetter, 1824) 13) was that far from gaining from the removal of stopped tones, 'the horn would lose a great deal' from the introduction of valves; he and his pupil GALLAY played and

taught the hand horn until their deaths. In contrast, BERLIOZ welcomed the valve horn as a completely new instrument.

Charles Pace built valve horns in England from 1830 but the majority of British players favoured the hand horn until the 1870s. Joseph Lewy used the valve horn in England in 1835 but performances by the German immigrants Adolphe Koenig and Hermann Steglich led to complaints about the loss of the hand horn's veiled stopped notes and 'pure and legitimate tone'. However, when Charles Harper played BEETHOVEN's Quintet, Op. 16 on hand horn in 1870, a reviewer commented that a valve horn 'which avoided all stopped tones ... would be decidedly preferable'.

AUDIENCES in Germany, Austria and Italy were quicker to accept the valve horn but many players continued to play with a mixture of valve and hand technique. Schubert wrote mainly for the hand horn in *Auf dem Strom* D943 but the bass clef passages were clearly designed to show off Joseph Lewy's command of the valves. BRAHMS's horn parts could in theory be played on the hand horn but there is evidence that most players performed them on valve horns. In contrast, progressive composers such as Schumann and Wagner quickly saw the value of the horn as a fully chromatic valved instrument; Schumann's *Konzertstück*, Op. 86, one of the early peaks of valve horn writing, was premiered in Leipzig in 1850 and performed in New York in 1852. Valves were quickly and widely adopted in Italy. Composers as late as Verdi continued to pay lip service to hand horn technique in their musical lines but the players must have had valves in order to be able to cope with other features of the writing. In Russia, Tchaikovsky wrote exclusively for the valve horn.

Stölzel's valves were superseded by other valve-types. Piston valves became popular in France and England; first designed in 1838 by François Périnet, they were often made as a '*sauterelle*' which could be removed so that the instrument could be played as a hand horn. The rotary valve was invented independently by both Josef Kail of Prague and Nathan Adams of Boston and it was used in Germany on horns with a slightly wider bore than was usual in France and England. A third, slightly cumbersome double piston valve designed by the Leipzig trumpeter C. F. Sattler was adopted by Viennese players and continues to influence playing in the city today.

Double Horns

Valve horns in F had a reputation for being treacherous to play because their HARMONICS from around written c' upward are very close together, making accuracy difficult. One solution – the use of a shorter crook (A was often used in England, B♭ in Germany) – increased accuracy but also compromised tone quality. The double horn developed by Kruspe c1897 was more satisfactory as it gave players access to two sets of tubing, one in F and another in B♭, and enabled them to switch between the sets with a fourth valve, usually operated by the thumb.

Although Kruspe's horn was traditionally described as a 'compensating' instrument in which double rotors gave access to the additional lengths of tubing which were needed to convert the B♭ instrument to F, recent research has shown that it was actually a full double horn with completely separate valve slides. The classic Alexander 103, which is still popular today, was designed in 1908.

Double horns soon dominated the market in much of Europe and the USA but single horns hung on tenaciously in the UK and France until WWII; and French players have continued to prefer instruments with a third valve which raises the PITCH by a tone rather than lowering it by three semitones, as is the norm.

Period Instruments
Horns were slower than other instruments to make their mark in HISTORICALLY INFORMED PERFORMANCE. Hermann Baumann was an early pioneer of modern hand horn playing and was followed by Lowell Greer (USA), Michel Garcin-Marrou (France) and Anthony Halstead (UK); the current generation of scholarly performers includes Anneke Scott (UK).

FURTHER READING

T. Hiebert, 'The horn in the Baroque and Classical periods', in T. Herbert and J. Wallace (eds.), *The Cambridge Companion to Brass Instruments* (Cambridge University Press, 1997), 103–14.
J. Humphries, *The Early Horn: A Practical Guide* (Cambridge University Press, 2000).
R. Morley-Pegge, *The French Horn: Some Notes on the Evolution of the Instrument and of its Technique* (London: Benn, 1960, 2/1973).

JOHN HUMPHRIES

Hotteterre family French family of woodwind instrument makers, instrumentalists at the French court, and composers. The Hotteterres are credited with initiating important changes that took place in the construction of woodwind instruments during the second half of the seventeenth century.

Two of the sons of wood turner Loys de Haulteterre (d. before 1628) were Jean *père* (b. La Couture, c1610; d. Paris?, 1692) and Nicolas *père* (b. La Couture, c1615; d. Versailles, 15 May 1693). In about 1660 Nicolas established a workshop on the Rue des Arcis in Paris, where he worked with his sons Nicolas *l'aîné* (b. La Couture, c1637; d. Versailles, 1694), Louis *frère* (b. La Couture, 1647; d. Ivry, 1716), and Nicolas Colin Hotteterre *le jeune* (b. La Couture, 19 February 1653; d. Paris, 14 December 1727). A declaration made by his wife (in connection with a dispute over his estate) states that three of her sons worked with their father making instruments, teaching, and playing at L'Opéra. She adds that the sons were much more skilled in tuning instruments than their father. By c1635 Jean had established a workshop in the Rue Neuve Saint-Louis. According to Borjon de Scellery (*Traité de la musette* (Lyon: Jean Girin & Barthelemy Riviere, 1672)), Jean was unique in constructing all kinds of instruments of wood, ivory and ebony, such as musettes, 'flûtes', flageolets, *hautbois* and *cromornes*; and even for the perfect tuning of these instruments. Jean Hotteterre *père* had two sons, Jean *fils aîné* I (b. Paris? c1630; d. Paris, 1668) and Martin (b. Paris, c1640; d. Paris, 15 November 1712). In Borjon de Scellery's opinion, Jean's sons Jean and Martin were in no way inferior to their father in the art of instrument making, of which they had a complete understanding and they showed a more admirable mastery of musette playing in particular. Martin took over his brother's post as 'hautbois et violon du roi' after the latter's murder in 1668 and also succeeded to his father's workshop and mark. Later that year the workshop was moved to the parish of St Berthélemy. A 1711 inventory of Martin's workshop refers to him as a master maker of instruments and lists, among some seventy instruments, transverse FLUTES, flageolets, RECORDERS, OBOES, BASSOONS and musettes. Martin had two sons, Jacques-Martin 'le Romain', and Jean *fils* II.

Jacques-Martin 'le Romain' (b. Paris, 29 September 1674; d. Paris, 16 July 1763) is now and was even then the most celebrated member of the family, renowned as a performer, teacher and composer. He held the posts of 'grand hautbois du roy' and 'flutte de la chambre de roy', and was ranked one of the most important musicians of France by Titon du Tillet (*Orchestre de Parnasse*, 1743). In Jacques's marriage contract is included an inventory of his music library, in which both French and Italian vocal and instrumental music are represented. In writing his well-known *Principes* (Paris, 1707), Jacques made clear his intentions to establish a dedicated pedagogy, performing practice and repertory for the transverse flute. The book also includes sections on playing the oboe and recorder, and covers posture, embouchure, FINGERING, tonguing and ORNAMENTATION. The description of the principal ornaments and embellishments of the period make it a useful companion to FRANÇOIS COUPERIN's *L'art de toucher le clavecin* (1716). It is also significant as the only known treatise for that particular combination of instruments. As a composer for the transverse flute, Jacques was also active, publishing two books of *Pièces*, the second of which marked the first appearance of multi-movement works for flute and bass designated as sonatas (1715), and *L'art de préluder sur la flûte traversière* (1719), an unusual work and the first to detail the practice of 'PRELUDING'.

Jacques's brother, Jean *fils* II (d. 20 February 1720) took over the workshop from his father in 1712, having served also in the *hautbois et musettes de Poitou*. He also composed a collection of *Pièces pour la muzette*, published by his brother Jacques in 1722. The last known woodwind instrument maker of the Hotteterre family was Louis *fils* (1717–1801), who was born and died in La Couture. In 1748 he married Marie-Anne Lot, a member of a prominent family of woodwind instrument makers also from La Couture. There is an oboe (c1750) marked 'L/Hotteterre' in a music school collection in Tokyo, which was probably made by him.

FURTHER READING

P. Bate, *The Flute: A Study of its History, Development and Construction* (London: Benn, 1969).
R. W. Griscom and D. Lasocki, *The Recorder: A Research & Information Guide* (London: Taylor & Francis, 2003).
W. Waterhouse, *New Langwill Index: Dictionary of Musical Wind-instrument Makers and Inventors* (London: Bingham, 1993).

ASHLEY SOLOMON

Hummel, Johann Nepomuk (b. Pressburg [now Bratislava], 14 November 1778; d. Weimar, 17 October 1837) Austrian composer and virtuoso pianist.

One of the best-known pianists of his era, Hummel studied with MOZART for two years and possibly with CLEMENTI. He was known throughout Europe for his concert tours and for his precise and clean virtuoso performance style. His skills as an improviser were particularly admired.

Hummel was one of the most important teachers of early nineteenth-century pianists. He favoured 'Viennese' pianos and among his pupils were Henselt and

FERDINAND HILLER. His most influential teaching, however, was through his PIANO TREATISE, the most comprehensive of its kind at the time, which sold prolifically after it was published in Germany in 1828 and in translation in England and France in the following year.

Hummel's treatise is in three sections; the first, like many contemporary tutors, addresses the basics of piano playing, including technique, scales and music NOTATION. Unlike a few of his contemporaries such as Dussek, and others of the following generation, most notably Liszt, Hummel advocated a very 'quiet' finger technique. The pianist should sit in the centre of the keyboard and the elbows should be held close to the body with the arms, wrists and hands kept in a horizontal plane. His predominant touch was legato, achieved mainly through the fingers, and on occasions he advocated a superlegato in which the fingers rest on the notes for longer than the notation indicates.

Part two deals with ORNAMENTATION, advocating main-note trills while acknowledging the early nineteenth century to be a period of transition and uncertainty on the issue. He endorses the practice of long appoggiaturas while expressing frustration at their inconsistent notation. The third part deals with many general matters of performance. Hummel emphasises his own approach to metronomic regularity (a frequently remarked upon feature of his own playing), while acknowledging that a certain degree of TEMPO flexibility may be adopted in melodic passages. Examples are supplied. He stresses the benefits of the METRONOME for practice and for indicating the proper tempo, although his own metronome markings for works by Mozart and BEETHOVEN have been seriously questioned as unrealistically fast. He sets himself against the excessive use of ornamentation. Like many German writers before him, Hummel stresses the importance of RHETORIC in performance. His comments on PEDALLING are very conservative; he advocates pedal usage only where necessary, preferring finger-legato in many instances. He dismisses the use of 'special effect' pedals such as the bassoon, although it is indicated occasionally in his own works. He comments at length on the differences between English and 'Viennese' pianos of the period and advocates tuning in equal TEMPERAMENT. Finally, he offers advice on IMPROVISATION, an art that he had practised assiduously and one that was expected by audiences of the day. In sum, Hummel's treatise offers the most complete guide to playing the piano of his time, albeit from a conservative standpoint that was rapidly going out of fashion.

FURTHER READING

J. N. Hummel, *Ausführliche theoretisch-practische Anweisung zum Piano-forte-Spiel* (Vienna: Haslinger, 1828, R/1838).

M. Kroll, '"La Belle Exécution": Johann Nepomuk Hummel's treatise and the art of playing the pianoforte', in S. A. Crist and R. M. Marvin (eds.), *Historical Musicology: Sources, Methods, Interpretations* (University of Rochester Press, 2004), 234–55.

Johann Nepomuk Hummel (Lanham, MD, Toronto and Plymouth UK: Scarecrow Press, 2007).

DAVID ROWLAND

Hurdy-Gurdy A stringed instrument whose strings are bowed by a wooden wheel operated through a crank. It typically includes a set of drones and one of melody strings, whose vibrating length is shortened by tangents to obtain the different notes. A special way of turning the wheel allows clear rhythmic ARTICULATION.

The earliest sources on the instrument appear between the twelfth and thirteenth century in northern Spain and France. At this time the instrument existed in a larger model (the *organistrum*), which required two musicians to operate the crank and the tangents respectively, and a smaller one (the *symphonia*), which became increasingly popular amongst minstrels and pilgrims in sacred and secular music.

In the 1720s the French maker Henri Bâton introduced major innovations in the shape and construction of the instrument, leading to a widespread technical and aesthetical standardisation. The new model had a soundbox in guitar- or vessel-shape, a string length of c360 mm, two melody strings producing a chromatic range g–f♯″ and four drones, one of which rests on a loose bridge that is free to rattle against the soundboard, and gives the instrument a characteristic reedy sound. Decorations often included mahogany, mother-of-pearl and pegboxes in the shape of carved heads.

Written repertoire for the hurdy-gurdy had begun to appear since the 1660s, when LULLY introduced it to the French court. The instrument enjoyed an increasing success in that country, with composers such as Boismortier, Naudot, MICHEL CORRETTE and Jean-Baptiste Dupuits. By the second half of the 1760s it began its decline, but it was still occasionally used by composers, including WOLFGANG AMADEUS and LEOPOLD MOZART, Himmel and Donizetti. Between 1786 and 1792 JOSEPH HAYDN composed a substantial number of pieces for the *lira organizzata* – a variant model with reed pipes instead of strings.

A modern revival of the instrument began in the mid-1970s and several festivals are organised in France every year, the largest being the one in Château d'Ars, attracting over 130 makers.

FURTHER READING

R. A. Green, *The Hurdy-gurdy in Eighteenth-Century France* (Bloomington, IN: Indiana University Press, 1995, 2/2016).
S. Palmer, *The Hurdy-gurdy* (London: David & Charles, 1980).

GABRIELE ROSSI ROGNONI

I

Iconography The field of enquiry which seeks to study, understand and interpret visualisations (paintings, prints, photographs, etc.) and their significance.

Iconography continues to be valued by a wide range of musicians, its relevance reflected in the breadth of approaches. Employing a variety of musicological methodologies as means to an end rather than as ends in themselves, historical performers are adept at utilising a range of sources and approaches to enhance and inform their music making. However, for musicians seeking to reconstruct past performing practices, the judicious and enlightened application of iconography often presents particular challenges. Visual representations in non-didactic works function primarily on extra-musical and symbolic levels. Similarly, representations of musical instruments, whilst amongst the most tantalising of iconographical sources for the historical performer, often manifest little or no intent for contextual and technical accuracy. As Robert Kendrick reminds us, musical instruments as subjects of iconographical representation and iconological dissemination were a cornerstone of the growth of historical performance during the twentieth century. None the less, we must reconcile the availability of such depictions with the growing awareness that much Western art music before 1600 is predominantly vocal, and much of that enacted *a cappella*.

During the 1920s and 1930s, two landmark texts helped establish the field of musical iconography, Georg Kinsky's *Geschichte der Musik in Bildern* (Leipzig: Breitkopf & Härtel, 1929) and Erwin Panofsky's *Studies in Iconology* (New York: Oxford University Press, 1939). Whilst Panofsky's suggestion that visual objects have a meaning which can be interpreted has been influential, casting his thesis as a nuance of our overtly literate society with its omnipresence of text challenges us to recalibrate our *post hoc* interpretations. Panofsky's fellow émigré Emanuel Winternitz joined the staff at New York's Metropolitan Museum of Art in 1941 and by 1949 was the inaugural curator of musical instruments. His recognition of the value of that museum's collection of iconographical images served as a major catalyst to the foundation of the Répertoire International d'Iconographie Musicale (RIdIM). RIdIM's mission is to catalogue visual sources pertaining to music and other performing arts and to lead in the interpretation of these sources and the dissemination of related knowledge. One might argue that the field of iconography had finally arrived in 1980 with the inclusion of RIdIM pioneer HOWARD MAYER BROWN's entry on the subject for *The New Grove Dictionary*. By the early 1990s, following William Mitchell's declaration of the so-called 'pictorial turn', visual objects began to be treated as entities existing on their own terms, capable of a multiplicity of interpretations through time. In the twenty-first century our experience of images is frequently mediated through technology, particularly as digital photography facilitates their manipulation and dissemination. It could be argued that the subsequent distance from reality of many of these images parallels iconographical sources of earlier eras.

Despite our ability to preserve an image for as long as the medium lasts, iconography reminds us of the fallacy of seeking common practice in the light of a plurality of idiosyncratic approaches. Iconographical interpreters who have grown up alongside analogue photography must resist what Alan Trachtenberg terms the 'idea of photo camera', whereby we read an image in its entirety at face value, as if we had experienced it ourselves in real time. Tilman Seebass's comprehensive entry for the second edition of *NG* categorises seven locations of iconographical sources: illustrations in books and manuscripts, theoretical or narrative; pictorial works eschewing text such as frescoes, tapestries and friezes; stand-alone illustrations including photographs, paintings and sculpture; musical instruments themselves; illustrative and/or decorative material on album covers and in theatrical works; performance sites and other contextual locations; and finally, products of artistic synergy across music and visual art. These sources are often underpinned by intricate themes, sacred, profane and/ or metaphorical, as well as those concerning portraiture and synæsthesia. Seebass notes that representations of musical instruments, of musical notation and also of the act and location of performance have proven particularly helpful in the absence of texted, organological and/or aural sources.

Iconographical methodology involves identification, description and analysis of the object of visual representation and its thematic content or subject, followed by a process of interpretation, application and dissemination. This latter stage is sometimes termed 'iconology', often bringing with it 'intellectual penetration on a hermeneutical level' (Seebass, *NG*, xii, 54). The term 'iconography', however, is now used inclusively. By enacting iconographical findings on the stage or in the studio, historical performers create a practical iconology, surely worthy of the status accorded texted outputs.

Twenty-first-century performers now have a sizeable corpus of iconographical/iconological work upon which to reflect, including instances where visual sources have helped as well as hindered the process of realising a musical text through the act of performance. Supplementing the activities of RIdIM are three key journals: *Imago Musicæ: The International Yearbook of Music Iconography* (founded in 1984 under the auspices of RIdIM), *Music in Art* (published since 1984 in conjunction with the *Research Center* [sic] *for Music Iconography* at the City University of New York) and *Musique-Images-Instruments* (publishing organological and iconographical research since 1995 under the auspices of the *Institut de Recherche en Musicologie* in Paris).

The interaction of iconographical, documentary and organological sources has been particularly revealing of performance practices associated with the CLARINET during the eighteenth and nineteenth centuries. Despite the existence of two possible reed positions during the instrument's formative years, the 'reed-above' embouchure has been studiously ignored by most historical performers in favour of the now-universal 'reed-below' embouchure. Iconographical sources confirm that reed-above was still employed in southern Germany in the late eighteenth century, thus enabling a more representative account in the light of a paucity of contemporary German-language documentary sources. Furthermore, evidence from French and Italian didactic sources attests to the use of reed-above until well into the nineteenth century, an impression corroborated by surviving instruments.

In a similar manner, the corroboration of organological and iconographical sources is challenging historical brass players to rethink anachronistic compromises made during the twentieth century in the interests of technical accuracy and the recording industry. Regarding the TRUMPET, this paradigm shift has seen a move away from instruments with vent holes and a small mouthpiece, characteristic of the standardised so-called Baroque instrument, as well as the adoption of an approach to performance which facilitates a wider and more stylistically appropriate dynamic spectrum.

In at least two instances, the same iconographical sources have been invoked to refute and to substantiate JOSHUA RIFKIN's still much-debated thesis concerning the constitution of J. S. BACH's chorus. Whilst JOHANN GOTTFRIED WALTHER's *Musikalisches Lexicon*, published in 1732, remains a landmark source for our understanding of early to mid-eighteenth-century music, its reception may have benefited from the familial connection between Walther and Bach. Its frontispiece, the book's only illustration, contains a wealth of detail and appears to capture the act of performance. However, it cannot be interpreted in validation of claims for either point of view. Similarly, although reproduced in at least two twentieth-century secondary sources devoted to iconography of Bach's life, Ludwig Richter's nineteenth-century drawing of boys from the Thomasschule singing outdoors cannot shed light on earlier choral performance practices, let alone those pertaining to that composer.

The greatest merit of iconographical sources and their interaction with other materials is surely the way in which they make us question what degree of historical practice actually informs our music making if we are too willing to jettison uncomfortable evidence from the past. As Kendrick writes: 'In the world of early modern culture, iconography, conceived broadly, still has much to reveal, sonically and visually' (49), and historical performers are certainly well placed to lead such revelations.

FURTHER READING

A. Buckley, 'Music iconography and the semiotics of visual interpretation', *Music in Art*, 23/1–2 (1998), 5–10.
R. L. Kendrick, 'Iconography', in T. Shephard and A. Leonard (eds.), *The Routledge Companion to Music and Visual Culture* (New York and Abingdon: Routledge, 2014), 43–9.

INGRID E. PEARSON

Improvisation and unwritten performance practices Musical improvisation is central to cultures throughout the world. In Western art music the pendulum swung back and forth between eras of complexity of NOTATION (e.g. at the end of the fourteenth century, exemplified by Baude Cordier (*c*1380–before 1440), a master of *ars subtilior*) and periods of greater freedom in performance (e.g. the unmeasured preludes of LOUIS COUPERIN), but by the nineteenth century progressively less liberty remained for performers as composers' notation grew increasingly explicit. None the less, improvisation was actively perpetuated in performance, particularly by pianists, well into the twentieth century and influenced numerous genres (among them caprice, fantasy and prelude) throughout the Romantic era. In the twentieth century, some composers turned to aleatoric options to introduce elements of creativity that had all but disappeared save by organists, whose practical duties included bridging possible gaps in church services as well as the ability, particularly in France, to improvise fantasies and symphonies.

A prerequisite for the cultivation of improvisation as a primary expressive vehicle was the existence of broad stylistic congruence for composers and performers alike – whereby it is crucial to observe that until the twentieth century virtually all composers were performers and most performers composed. Only within a *lingua franca* can a performer be able to add a large measure of creativity to a written text by working within broadly acknowledged stylistic parameters. It is worth observing the progressive compression in length of style periods throughout much of Western music history: the International style prevailed for some 200 years, 1400–1600; the Baroque era for 150 (1600–1750); the Classical era, following a twenty-year interregnum, for about sixty (1770–1830). The Romantic period that followed lasted in some hands beyond the turn of the twentieth century, but WAGNER's *Tristan und Isolde* and the progressive works of Liszt (1811–86), among others, presaged by the mid-nineteenth century the ultimate disintegration of the tonal system, whose grammar and syntax allowed an able improviser to balance the whims of the moment with structural aspirations. It may be possible to improvise in an atonal idiom, but even a cultivated listener will have some difficulty anticipating the larger arc of such a performance; and it is essentially impossible to improvise beyond a rudimentary level in serial music (and even more decisively so in the total serialism of the Darmstadt orthodoxy).

At the advent of the Baroque era, ornamented and improvised versions of chansons and madrigals had long been cultivated by keyboard players, as were improvised variations (grounds), preludes, toccatas and fantasies. The rise of tonal harmony – whose displacement of the modal system overlapped the latter over centuries – provided a more visceral sense of tension and repose, albeit at the cost of the modal system's greater subtlety. Notwithstanding the superlative achievements of J. S. BACH, Handel, FRANÇOIS COUPERIN and RAMEAU, among others, one could characterise the emergence of tonality, spearheaded by Italian music at the advent of the eighteenth century, as an act of *haute vulgarisation*, employing an harmonic system devolving from a small number of basic syntactic patterns. To be sure, these were animated by master composers with an extraordinary vocabulary of colour and inflection, deriving to a significant degree from the long-established hierarchy and treatment of dissonance within a consonant frame. One could argue, therefore, that the simplified archetypes of the Baroque tonal language make the accomplishment of Baroque and subsequent masters that much more impressive – a fact perhaps less evident to those familiar only with music of the common practice period.

Harmony was distilled into the four basic functions of tonic, dominant, predominant (whether IV or II) and plagal (IV), together with circle of fifth progressions knitting the seven scale degrees together by tolerating the diminished fifth in the root progression IV–VII in major and between VI and II in minor. At the same time the seamless flow of the international style yielded to the use of catchy rhythmic motives, anticipated by the *vers mesuré* of the French *chanson* and already evident in MONTEVERDI's *Orfeo* and the works of his contemporaries. By the time of CORELLI the overtness of simple tonal harmonic formulae with the motoric vitality of recurring rhythmic motives provided an ideal basis for improvisers. Both the melodic surface and the underlying syntax were readily communicable, in a manner that JAZZ would revive in the twentieth century in a new dialect in which the practice of improvisation is quite similar to that of the eighteenth.

Professional vocal soloists and instrumentalists were trained (and expected) to improvise in performance, though there is ample documentation of improvisation in orchestral performances in the eighteenth and early nineteenth centuries (see J. Spitzer and N. Zaslaw, 'Improvised ornamentation in eighteenth-century orchestras', *JAMS*, 39/3 (1986), 524–77). An experience of orchestral improvisation in Rome on 18 December 1816 is recounted by SPOHR in his autobiography the following day (*see Louis Spohr's Autobiography. Translated from the German* 2 vols. (London: Longman, Green, Longman, Roberts, & Green, 1865, I, 309)): 'I certainly forbade several times every note which did not stand in the score; but ornamentation has become so much a second nature to them, that they cannot desist from it.'

The basis of expert improvisation is an ability to animate the melodic line with idiomatic flexibility, taking account of the underlying harmonies; keyboard improvisation may affect a single line – itself varying from stepwise motion to different types of passagework to arpeggiation of the underlying chord progressions – within a texture encompassing rigorous counterpoint or chords, derived once again from the supporting harmonies. Improvisation is mandated by the BASSO CONTINUO, for which keyboard players, lutenists and other continuo instruments improvise an accompaniment from the bass line, whether provided with figures or not. The art of continuo playing was an essential component of musical training into the nineteenth century and has been revived from the mid-twentieth century within the resurgence of interest in early music performance. It was perpetuated in keyboard concertos of the Classical and early Romantic periods, in which the soloist is directed to improvise an accompaniment in all tutti passages not provided with rests, doubling the contrabass line (not the CELLO when the DOUBLE BASSES are silent, nor the BASSOON in wind passages). MOZART designates continuo in his keyboard concertos with the direction *Col Baßo*; his early concertos contain figures for the left hand, mostly supplied by his father, doubling the contrabass. It is revealing that BEETHOVEN does not provide complete continuo notations in his first four piano concertos, which he performed himself; but when it became clear to him that his increasing deafness would impede him from performing the fifth, he provided it with a completely figured continuo part, including *tasto solo, all'ottava, Telemann-Bögen* and strengthening the bass line with added lower octave to provide more emphatic accompaniment in certain tutti passages.

The act of improvisation ranges from the spontaneous decoration of an existing text to the creation of an original, autonomous piece. The former requires a thorough familiarity with the principles of ORNAMENTATION and embellishment within the stylistic era of the piece and the ability to create out of individual decorations a consistent artistic result that enhances the basic character of the piece. Contemporary TREATISES discuss ornamentation in this light; C. P. E. BACH (1714–88), in his *Versuch* (1753, 1762) distinguishes between two basic types – the essential (*wesentliche Manieren*) and the voluntary (*willkürliche Manieren*). Essential ornamentation is signalled by standard symbols, whose execution is universally recognised. Voluntary ornamentation consists of free decoration supplied by the performer, who should respect the language of the work.

The distinction between prepared and improvised contributions to a work was all the more fluid throughout the many centuries during which there was no concept of repertoire and, apart from operatic performances, few works were played publicly more than once. Critics did, however, attend more than one performance of a given opera and at times commented on the imagination (or lack thereof) displayed by the singers in ornamenting their arias. In the seventeenth and early eighteenth centuries schematic NOTATION that was to be fleshed out in performance was common, particularly for slow movements. Perhaps the most familiar case is that of the violin sonatas of Corelli, which were immediately subject to numerous ornamented versions (see inter alia D. Boyden, 'Corelli's solo violin sonatas "grac'd" by Dubourg', in N. Schiørring and H. Glahn (eds.), *Festskrift Jens Peter Larsen* (Copenhagen: Wilhelm Housen Musik-Forlag, 1972), 113–25; ibid., 'The Corelli "solo" sonatas and their ornamental additions by Corelli, Geminiani, Dubourg, and the "Walsh Anonymous"', *Musica antiqua europæ orientalis*, iii (Bydgoszcz, 1972), 591–607). Corelli's practice was taken up by Handel, and the sonatas of both composers enjoyed longevity in circulation and in the practice of embellishment. The distinction between professional musicians and talented amateurs (*Kenner und Liebhaber*, as represented in six important sets of keyboard sonatas by C. P. E. Bach, Wq55–59, 61) is central in this regard; well-schooled professionals would improvise, whereas amateurs required prepared solutions. The first set of C. P. E. Bach's *Sonaten mit veränderten Reprisen* Wq50 (1758–9, published 1760), described in detail below, addresses the need for variation of repeats by writing them out with substantial recomposition.

We are fortunate that pedagogy was such a central aspect of J. S. Bach's personality and activity. The teaching of ornamentation and embellishment is documented throughout his career, from the *Klavierbüchlein* for his son WILHELM FRIEDEMANN BACH through the four-part *Clavier-Übung* (1731–41). Among his numerous prescriptives are the table of ornaments and their execution in the former (including all the essential ornaments employed by Bach himself save for the *Schleifer*) together with the *Applicatio* BWV994, an eight-bar keyboard piece not composed by Bach (*See* P. Wollny, *Händel-Jahrbuch* 61 (2015), 385–6), but taken over by him and supplied with ornaments from the table – both of these from the W. F. Bach *Klavierbüchlein*; the decorations of the sarabandes from the English Suites No. 2 in A minor BWV807 – in which only the upper voice is decorated – and No. 3 in G minor BWV808 – in which the entire texture is subject to ornamentation; highly decorated versions of the Fugue in D minor from the first book of *The Well-Tempered Clavier* BWV851, and of the E♭ major Sinfonia BWV791; and decorations transmitted through handwritten entries into printed copies of the harpsichord partitas, some of which are in Bach's hand and others from those of his immediate circle, as well as MANUSCRIPT copies. In addition, the various autographs and authentic copies of Bach's keyboard works contain numerous essential ornaments and frequent voluntary decoration of originally simpler lines (see R. D. P. Jones's *Kritischer Bericht* (Kassel: Bärenreiter, 1978)) for his edition of the partitas within the *Neue Bach-Ausgabe* (*NBA*)(V/1) and the *Nachtrag* (1997) that re-evaluates individual sources for the partitas in the light of their presumptive authenticity. Jones refers in the *Nachtrag* to a similar source situation involving extravagant decoration of the French Suites in the hand of copyist Anonymous 5 (Heinrich Nikolaus Gerber), discussed in the foreword to the *NBA* by editor Alfred Dürr. In particular, the transcriptions into keyboard concertos of original versions for strings and wind provide ample testimony to Bach's ceaseless elaboration of his works.

In general the seventeenth- and early eighteenth-century performer was expected to provide ornamentation at repeats and da capos, from the outset in slow movements, and elaborations at fermatas, of which there were three basic types: 1) the initial entrance of a soloist, especially a singer in an aria, consisting of melodic decoration of the tonic harmony, called *Fermaten* in German treatises; 2) elaboration of a pause on the dominant or at an arrival at a key other than the tonic, commonly before the reprise of the principal music (called EINGANG by Mozart); and 3) CADENZAS, signalled by an arrival on the tonic $^6_4$ chord. All three were signalled by fermatas. Vocal treatises emphasised that all of these were to be confined to a single breath – a stricture that was not always applied to instrumentalists. Improvisation was thus central to the performance of arias and concertos. Mozart and Beethoven composed cadenzas for their concertos, but these were designed for the use of others – primarily students, and, in Mozart's case, his sister Maria Anna ('Nannerl') (for an example of the latter, see the second set of lead-ins for the third movement of the Piano Concerto in E♭ major, K271 (*Jenamy*) (K624/K³ 626a, No. 5a – K⁶ 626a/I/21 and 22)), sent by Mozart to Nannerl together with cadenzas for the 1782 revision of the Concerto in D, K175 (with the Rondo K382 as finale) in a letter dated 15 February 1783.

The autographs of Mozart's piano concertos contain numerous passages in shorthand, some of which remain undetected in any EDITION. These delineate passages in which scales and arpeggios are to be fleshed out in performance, broken octaves and thirds supplied to apparent two-voiced passages and melodies notated only schematically; for example, the piano recitatives in the concertos K451, 466, 467, 537 and 595, the first of which comes down to us in an authentic embellishment in the hand of Mozart's sister ('Nannerl').

From the Baroque era to the twentieth century, keyboard instruments provided the central impetus to free improvisation, as they permitted complete control of all aspects of musical texture. Stringed instruments can provide harmonic support through multiple stops, but even in the most masterly polyphonic writing of Bach's sonatas and partitas for solo violin and the solo cello suites, absolute polyphony and continuous explicit harmonic progression are not possible to the extent found in his keyboard works. Undoubtedly only virtuoso players whose intellect matched their technical abilities were capable of improvising fugues; but preludes, capriccios, fantasies and toccatas were well within the capabilities of well-trained keyboard players. The final chapter of C. P. E. Bach's *Versuch* teaches improvisation as the invention of a flexible texture (of which Bach gives numerous examples) above a bass line capable of supporting cogent harmonic progressions that can be rendered by figuration. The final two examples of the treatise present such a bass line and a brilliant fantasy derived from it. The numbers in the examples correlate the use of these textures in the foregoing explanation, the figured bass and the realised fantasy (see Examples 13 and 14).

Example 13: C. P. E. Bach: *Versuch* (1753–62), trans. W. J. Mitchell (1949), 442–3.

There were both practical and aesthetic bases for improvisation. Mozart makes a distinction between a PRELUDE designed to allow the performer to try out a keyboard instrument before embarking on a performance of a work and one designed to modulate from one key to another in order to avoid an unpleasant succession of keys. The former consists not only of gaining acquaintance with the tone and sustaining qualities of the instrument and technical matters such as key dip and speed and resistance of the action. Rather, the need to try out a keyboard with an improvised prelude implies that someone other than the performer will have tuned it (else the player already would have knowledge of the instrument), and a crucial element of how the instrument will sound devolves from the TEMPERAMENT employed by the tuning. Equal temperament did not become standard until well into the nineteenth century, and the character of individual tonalities – the result of variant interval size (especially important were thirds and fifths, as they comprise the triads that form the basic material of tonal harmony) – is protocolled in the AFFEKTENLEHRE (doctrine of emotions) with which all musicians working within the tonal system were familiar. Improvised preludes trying out keyboards would normally begin and end in the same key. They could include modulations but often remained in the tonic key throughout, as exemplified in the preludes of HUMMEL and MOSCHELES and Chopin's Prelude, Op. 28 No. 1.

Example 14: C. P. E. Bach: *Versuch* (1753–62), trans. W. J. Mitchell (1949), 443–5.

Mozart's modulating preludes, clearly derived from the precepts of C. P. E. Bach, were composed to satisfy the needs of his sister. Their existence is the result of LEOPOLD MOZART's having tutored Nannerl to perform but not to improvise or compose – a gender-based prejudice that long held sway. One of the preludes modulates first from F major to E minor and continues, after a cadence, to C major. The two sections became physically separated; the first is presently in Budapest, the second in Kraków. On the reverse of both portions are figured bass exercises in Nannerl's hand, reflecting Mozart's tutelage; their blurred syntax reveals her lack of training in composition. A later set of four preludes K284a (formerly known as the Capriccio K395) was sent by Mozart to his sister in response to a request for a brief Praeambulum, but this time modulating from C to B♭. The aesthetic tenet generating such preludes has long disappeared from our concert life, in which performers have few qualms about the AESTHETICS of programming works whose keys are a step or even a half-step apart – a procedure that would have offended musicians of an earlier time. The practice of improvising such preludes survived well into the twentieth century; pianists such as Josef Hofmann were able practitioners of what has become a lost art.

In the eighteenth century the primary vehicles for improvisation, besides preludes, were variations on a popular aria of the moment and free fantasias. These practices extended into the nineteenth century. Beethoven's Fantasy, Op. 77 may well protocol the one he improvised in the famous *Akademie* of 22 December 1808, in which the Fifth and Sixth Symphonies, the Fourth Piano Concerto, three movements from the Mass in C and the Choral Fantasia received their public premieres. Legend has it that when MENDELSSOHN performed his First Piano Concerto before the Prussian king Friedrich Wilhelm III, he was asked by the sovereign to improvise variations on Mozart's 'Non più andrai' (*Le nozze di Figaro*) as an encore. It is assumed that Chopin's ballades are written out versions of improvisations, and Liszt and his many virtuoso contemporaries improvised free fantasies as an essential component of their concerts. In France improvisation reached its heyday with its ORGAN culture; the organ symphonies of Charles-Marie Widor and Louis Vierne reflect that culture, which derived from the influence of César Franck and was exemplified by improvised symphonies, fugues and individual movements.

Practical considerations limited improvisation to genres that were throughcomposed or based on a single idea (such as a fugue). Sonata form in its various incarnations (sonata allegro, second-movement sonata minus development, minuet/scherzo, sonata rondo) would require prodigious feats of memory in order to reproduce substantial portions of the movement verbatim or virtually so and were hence not cultivated even by master improvisers. That improvisation none the less played a central role in the performance of sonatas – in which performers freely embellished and altered the text, even the first time around, and in particular at REPEATS – has received less attention than it deserves. There is certainly intrinsic evidence: sonatas whose expositions and developments plus recapitulations are to be repeated often contain embellished versions at the recapitulation. Literal repeats of both sections undermine the character of spontaneity that led the composer to decorate the theme; indeed, there is no expressive sense to performing an undecorated version twice followed by two iterations of a specific decorated one (though alas this is often done).

The most precious evidence of the idiomatic performance of repeated sections in sonatas is provided by C. P. E. Bach's *Sonaten mit veränderten Reprisen* Wq50 (1759). At the outset of his extensive foreword, Bach remarks, 'At present the variation of repeats is indispensable. It is expected of every performer.' He warns against inappropriate decoration that undermines the writing, the affect and the relationship among the musical thoughts, and continues, 'Is the principal intention in varying this: that the performer brings honour to himself and at the same time to the piece? Must he not consequently present thoughts at least as good the second time [as the first]? Despite these difficulties and their misuse, good variations retain at all times their value. Incidentally, I refer to that which I have presented in the first part of my *Essay*.' Bach states that in composing these sonatas he was thinking of beginners and amateurs who lack the patience and time to practise, thereby providing them an easy way to experience with pleasure a comfortable manner of allowing themselves to be heard with variations without their needing to invent them or having to follow the counsels of others, and having laboriously to memorise them. Bach concludes by claiming to be the first to have produced works that actively demonstrate the usefulness and pleasure of variation. And indeed these sonatas are without parallel in what they reveal of the practice of the time. Rather than supplying the standard repeat signs, Bach writes out the repeats and not only provides richly imaginative embellishment, both essential and voluntary but recomposes the music by altering both harmonies and the texture, not merely the melodic lines. Given the evident influence he exerted on HAYDN, Mozart and Beethoven, one might be justified in concluding that virtually all today's performances of their keyboard music, consisting as they do either of literal execution of the repeats or a few discreet decorations, are very distant indeed from what they expected.

As indicated above, numerous twentieth-century composers sought to reintroduce improvisational elements. These included, but were not limited to: 1) providing a harmonic skeleton upon which the performer could decorate within a metrical frame or at will; 2) notating a group of pitches and/or clusters to be played as specified in instructions; 3) co-ordinating improvisations from instrument to instrument in a chamber or orchestral work; 4) notating a precise pattern prolonged by permutation within boundaries defined by the composer; or 5) calling for free improvisation by the performer without defining any parameters whatsoever. An example of the latter is Edison Denisov's *Ode* (1968) for CLARINET, PERCUSSION and piano; its initial version followed pages of highly complex notation with a group of coloured geometric figures that the performers were to transform into the continuation of the work. A later version continued the complex notation, but abandoned the aleatoric content.

FURTHER READING

R. Levin, 'Mozart's non-metrical keyboard preludes', in C. Hogwood (ed.), *The Keyboard in Baroque Europe* (Cambridge University Press, 2003), 198–216.

ROBERT D. LEVIN

Indy, (Paul-Marie-Théodore-) Vincent d' (b. Paris, 27 March 1851; d. Paris, 2 December 1931) French composer, teacher, conductor and editor.

Indy was important in the early music revival in France. He believed that knowledge of the music of the past was the key to all aspects of its practice and especially of its composition, on which he published a TREATISE concerned largely with the detailed study of music from the Mediaeval period onwards. With CHARLES BORDES he founded in 1894 the Schola Cantorum, a modest rival to the PARIS CONSERVATOIRE, at first concentrating on the revival of Gregorian CHANT but later offering a wider education and fortnightly concerts. These concerts involved some period instruments and programmed much Renaissance and Baroque music which he himself had edited, particularly of J. S. BACH and the music of the *Grand siècle*. He was involved in SAINT-SAËNS'S RAMEAU edition and prepared the material for the first revival (1908) at the Paris Opéra of *Hippolyte et Aricie*, which he also conducted.

FURTHER READING

A. Thomson, *Vincent d'Indy and his World* (Oxford University Press, 1996).

RICHARD LANGHAM SMITH

Instrument collections (historical) Collections of musical instruments are documented from as early as the fourteenth century BC. They became more widespread from the Renaissance onwards, particularly in Europe, as courts began to compete in size and splendour and were emulated throughout all levels of society. On the evidence of surviving inventories, they appear to have been driven either by the practical requirements of music making or, less frequently, by an encyclopedic approach to contemporary instruments (as in, for example, the collection of Lorenzo de' Medici, documented in 1492, which is the earliest example of its kind). The occasional inclusion of older instruments is usually accounted for by their survival in playing condition, sometimes over a period of more than a century and often with major modifications; such instruments may have a particular connection with a celebrated maker.

Specific interest in collecting historical instruments emerged at the end of the eighteenth century as a consequence of the increasing examination of musical history; it continued to develop in the following decades. In 1796 the PARIS CONSERVATOIRE opened a museum of 'antique or foreign instruments and those that could serve as models because of their perfection'. A substantial portion of the 316 instruments which formed its original nucleus – later mostly destroyed – dated from over a century earlier. These comprised keyboards, VIOLINS and GUITARS, some of which were unlikely to have had a role in practical music making and appear mostly to have had a historical value.

A more systematic interest in historical instruments began to appear during the second half of the nineteenth century, when the number of collections steadily increased throughout Europe and later the USA. A central role was played by the new conservatoires and music schools and later by some of the large museums; substantial collections were acquired and displayed by the University of Edinburgh (1859), conservatoires in Florence (1864) and Brussels (1870), the *Königliche Hochschule für Musik* in Berlin (1888) and the ROYAL COLLEGE OF MUSIC in London (1894). The early catalogues of most of these collections represent systematic attempts to combine surviving early instruments with those from so-called 'primitive' societies, conflating distance in time and space into a single evolutionary path to explain the history of Western music. It is no coincidence that the earliest comprehensive 'history of musical instruments' was published by CARL ENGEL (1874) as an introduction to the catalogue of the collection of the Victoria and Albert Museum.

With the burgeoning interest in the performance of early music throughout the twentieth century, museums focused even more on antique instruments, which became a separate acquisitions stream. Although a study of the role of museums in the early music revival is still largely to be written, several such institutions supported musical performances and often had resident *Collegia Musica*, particularly between the 1880s and the mid-twentieth century (e.g. in Paris, Leipzig, Berlin and New York). After the 1960s, when increasing global travel highlighted concerns about the use and restoration of old instruments, conservation became a priority, greatly reducing their usage in order to preserve them as models for the construction of copies and for theoretical and material studies.

The number of public and private collections dramatically increased during the second half of the twentieth century. Full lists are available for only a few countries: the UK alone includes almost 400 musical instrument collections, a similar number is recorded in Italy and over 800 are known in France. Among the most representative institutions currently active are those in Paris, Brussels, Amsterdam and The Hague, Nuremberg, Berlin, Vienna, Basel, Barcelona, Edinburgh, New York and Vermillion (SD). Many of these combine collections of several thousand instruments with a strong involvement in research. An increasing number of music museums is opening in the Far East, some including relevant collections of European historical instruments (e.g. the Chimei Museum in Taiwan). Since the 1960s most of these have been members of the International Committee of Music Museums (CIMCIM) of the International Council of Museums, which maintains a list of music collections and promotes networking and partnership worldwide. While no unified catalogue of historical instruments yet exists, the MIMO project, initiated with a European grant by a consortium of museums led by Edinburgh University in 2009, offers a single access point to almost 80,000 instruments in public collections in Europe, and is expanding to include the USA and China.

FURTHER READING

F. Gétreau, *Aux origins du musée de la musique* (Paris: Clincksieck, 1996).

GABRIELE ROSSI ROGNONI

Intabulations (Ger. *Intabulierung*; It. *Intavolatura*) An arrangement of a vocal or ensemble piece for keyboard, LUTE, or other plucked string instrument, written in TABLATURE.

Keyboard tablatures were in use as early as the fourteenth century, and the earliest surviving examples of lute tablatures date from the latter part of the fifteenth century. Before this time lutenists almost exclusively plucked strings with a quill or plectrum, and would play a single line of music reading from staff NOTATION. Towards the end of the fifteenth century they started to pluck strings with the thumb and fingers, which enabled them to sustain two, three or even four voices at a time. Music for the GUITAR in the sixteenth and seventeenth centuries was also written in various tablatures. The earliest surviving keyboard source to date, the Robertsbridge Codex (*c*1320), contains intabulations of two motets from the *Roman de Fauvel*. These are written in a combination of staff notation and letters, showing the shape of things to come.

An intabulation may be literal, that is, note for note the same as its model in staff notation. Such are the intabulations of Italian madrigals by Gabriel Fallamero, Vincenzo Galilei and others in the latter part of the sixteenth century, where the original polyphony sounds more like a succession of chords. The surviving lute books of Edward Paston contain hundreds of literal intabulations, but they omit the highest voice part, which would have been sung to the lute. Some of the intabulations of Hans Newsidler omit voices just to make the music easier to play. It seems that these incomplete intabulations were intended to be played as solos rather than to accompany a voice or other instrument supplying the missing notes. In the sixteenth century lutenists such as Francesco da Milano (1497–1543) and Valentin Bálint Bakfark (1507–76) would intabulate well-known songs by other composers and superimpose their own elaborate divisions and decorations, creating an entirely new composition. Apart from enhancing the original composition, these ornamented passages compensate for the lute's lack of sustain and enable the player to shape phrases, rather as Italian mandolinists do with the fast repeated notes of their TREMOLO.

The word 'intabulation' was also commonly used in the sixteenth century for any piece of music notated in tablature. For example, the first printed book of lute music is Francesco Spinacino's *Intabulatura de Lauto Libro primo* (Venice: Petrucci, 1507), which includes DANCE music, intabulations of songs, and prelude-like *recercari*. Adrian Le Roy (*c*1520–98) in *Les Instructions pour le Luth* (1574) explains in some detail how to make lute intabulations from *chansons*. After the 1600s the Italians embraced this and re-interpreted it with a system known as *alfabeto* to represent I–IV–V chords at the very beginning of the alphabet.

Musicians incorporated as much of the vocal model they were intabulating as the techniques and constraints of their instruments would allow. Keyboard and lute players commonly played four-part harmonies verbatim. Compositions with greater parts, however, required them to simplify the arrangement. Guitarists and cittern players, on the other hand, did not have the luxury to be so literal; in some instances, they could only give the merest impression of the original composition.

Virtually all sixteenth-century intabulators added ornamentation to their arrangements of vocal music, although this may have been obligatory for players of plucked stringed instruments, since the increased body of notes helped to sustain the fragile sounds of their otherwise restrained instruments. Francesco da Milano, for example, used the original music for a virtuoso display of variation technique. Vihuelist Miguel de Fuenllana was a rare exception to this trend.

Intabulations of sixteenth-century vocal music provide instruction in the techniques of embellishment used by a variety of musicians in performance, and are helpful in indicating the difference between the way music appears on the page and how it must have sounded in the Renaissance. Tablatures, especially those for plucked stringed instruments, are also useful in elucidating how sixteenth-century musicians added accidentals to music, according to the rules of MUSICA FICTA, since tablature indicates precisely where performers were to put their fingers on the strings, and hence is more apt to include the particular chromatic inflections heard in performance than music written in staff notation.

FURTHER READING

H. M. Brown, 'Embellishment in early sixteenth-century Italian intabulations', PRMA, 100/1 (1973), 49–83.

A. Le Roy, *Les instructions pour le luth* (1574). Corpus des luthistes français, 2 vols. (Paris: Editions de centre national de la recherche scientifique, 1977).

JAMES WESTBROOK

Intonation systems Throughout the Middle Ages, theorists acknowledged the authority of Greek theorist Pythagoras, prioritising the perfection of octaves, fifths and fourths with the acoustical ratios of 2:1, 3:2 and 4:3 respectively. The repertoire of Gregorian chant was undoubtedly sung under such a system, with resultant wide whole tones (9:8), wide major thirds (or ditones, consisting of two wide whole tones = 81:64) and narrow leading tones (256:243). Most Medieval polyphony throughout the fourteenth century also works well in such a system, though two apparently English theorists, Anonymous IV and Walter Odington, spoke for the purity of major thirds (5:4) in the late thirteenth and early fourteenth centuries. This may have been because English music seems to have favoured triadic sonorities earlier than continental repertoires. By the late fourteenth century, however, even some continental pieces use triadic harmonies as points of apparent repose rather than as sonorities requiring resolution (Machaut's Mass, for example), and this happens with increasing regularity into the fifteenth century.

The prevailing parallel first inversion sonorities of the Dufay generation – the so-called *contenance angloise* – is inconceivable with Pythagorean ditones, so there must have been a migration towards just intonation, even though theorists did not discuss it systematically until the sixteenth century. There is some evidence that the later stages of Pythagorean tuning included the use of schismatic major thirds (in reality, Pythagorean diminished fourths, e.g. D–G♭) as a way of achieving more euphony in the penultimate sonority at cadences. Eventually, no such rationalisation was needed: such thirds are extremely close to the 5:4 pure major thirds of just intonation. Just intonation further extends the use of intervals with simple acoustical ratios to minor thirds (6:5), major sixths (5:3), minor sixths (8:5), diatonic semitones (16:15) and even tritones (45:32) and diminished fifths (64:45). However, there are complications in practice with just intonation such as the necessity for a second size of whole tone (10:9), possible microtonal migration up or down depending on the succession of intervals and the incompatibility of simple ratios with more complex harmonies. But the sound of triadic just intonation is extremely satisfying and Renaissance theorists are unanimous that it was the constant goal, even if there were complications in practice.

Instruments of fixed PITCH, like keyboards and fretted instruments, were unable to achieve just intonation because they did not offer sufficient flexibility of pitch depending on context, so meantone emerged as a compromise that creates pure major thirds at the expense of noticeably narrow fifths. Each fifth is actually narrowed by one-quarter of the syntonic comma (81:80), the discrepancy between the Pythagorean ditone and the pure major third (four consecutive fifths in a circle create a major third). Meantone is well suited for instruments because it has a single size of whole tone, exactly half (i.e. the mean) of the major third. Its limitation on keyboards of twelve notes per octave is that, while the system contains eight pure major thirds, it also has four excruciatingly wide ones, almost two syntonic commas wider than pure. Some instrument makers mitigated this problem by making keyboards with more than twelve notes per octave (split keys), and in the sixteenth and seventeenth centuries, various schemes appeared with nineteen, thirty-one, thirty-six, forty-two, fifty-two, or even sixty keys per octave. However, these schemes normally had no more than thirty-one different pitches, the number of notes needed to extend quarter-comma meantone fully to create pure major thirds between any two notes. More split-keys make more difficulty for the player, however, and such enharmonic keyboards eventually fell out of use.

Other regular meantone schemes were used as well; each has its advantages. Third-comma meantone possesses pure minor thirds, though its fifths are very narrow. Fifth-comma meantone has good (though not perfect) major thirds, fifths better than those in quarter-comma, and fifths and major thirds that beat at about the same rate, creating a slight VIBRATO effect. Sixth-comma meantone, still quite euphonious, took a further step on the path towards full utility which ends with equal TEMPERAMENT (eleventh-comma meantone) and has the further virtue of having pure tritones and diminished fifths, important constituents of complex tonal harmonies. All regular meantone systems can be achieved in extended form (i.e. with all necessary enharmonics) by non-keyboard instruments and voices. The inability of keyboards to access enharmonic alternatives necessitated other strategies, which involved tempering the fifths by different amounts.

Irregular systems use varying sizes of fifths, with the unwavering condition that the total tempering must always narrow the circle of fifths by one Pythagorean comma (129.75:128), the discrepancy between twelve pure fifths and seven pure octaves. The temperament KIRNBERGER III, for example, has four quarter-comma narrow fifths in a row, then eight pure fifths around the rest of the circle. Four or more consecutive pure fifths make triads with ditones for major thirds, however, so the challenge was to distribute the tempered fifths around the circle to create schemes that sounded good but were useful in a wide variety of keys. ORGANS had less demand for utility since the keys of congregational singing were not so diverse, but J. S. BACH's *Wohltemperirte Clavier* called for a 'well temperament' or 'circulating temperament' that was acceptable in all keys. Inevitably in such schemes, some keys (usually the most commonly used ones) sound better than others, but at least all keys are usable. This is also the period when KEY CHARACTERISTICS proliferated; certainly, keys sound much more distinctive in unequal systems than in equal temperament.

Evidence suggests that although keyboards used the expedient of irregular systems, especially from the late seventeenth to the early twentieth century, non-keyboard instruments and voices maintained a system of extended meantone (originally quarter- then, later, sixth-comma) from the Renaissance through most of the tonal period. That practice is gradually being recovered by today's musicians. The advent of twelve-tone and atonal compositional styles promoted the use of equal temperament, and it became the standard for most music throughout the twentieth century. Composers such as Harry Partch pioneered new music for unequal systems, however, and interest in unequal historical systems intensified from the 1970s.

FURTHER READING

P. Barbieri, *Enharmonic Instruments and Music, 1470–1900* (Latina: Il Levante, 2008).
D. Dolata, *Meantone Temperaments on Lutes and Viols* (Bloomington, IN: Indiana University Press, 2016).
R. W. Duffin, *How Equal Temperament Ruined Harmony (and Why You Should Care)* (New York: W. W. Norton, 2007).

ROSS DUFFIN

J

Jacobs, René (b. Ghent, 30 October 1946) Belgian countertenor and conductor, one of the first modern countertenors from the European continent to achieve prominence.

Jacobs's range is approximately f–f″, with a happy use of 'chest' voice alongside a tangy head register (he disdains those who call him a falsettist). From the 1970s he worked with many important continental early music ensembles and conductors, founding his own group, Concerto Vocale, in 1977. Also active as a conductor since 1983, recordings such as that of MOZART's *Le nozze di Figaro* (2004) have received many awards, but criticism from textual literalists. He was director of opera at the Innsbruck *Festwochen der alte Musik* 1991–2009, and is a professor at the SCHOLA CANTORUM BASILIENSIS. He is thoughtfully unaverse to courting controversy: 'unlike instruments the voice does not evolve. The only thing of which we can be sure is that voices today are identical with those of the past' (Wistreich, 2002).

FURTHER READING

R. Jacobs, *La Controverse sur le timbre de contre-ténor* (Arles/Paris: Actes Sud, 1985).
R. Wistreich, 'Practising and teaching historically informed singing – who cares?', *BJhM*, 26 (2002), 17–30.

NICHOLAS CLAPTON

Jambe de Fer, Philibert (b. Champlitte, ?1515; d. ?Lyons, ?1566) French Huguenot theorist and composer.

Jambe de Fer wrote one of the earliest French TREATISES on music: *Epitome Musical des Tons, Son et Accordz, es Voix Humaines, Fleustes d'Alleman, Fleustes à neufs trous, Violes & Violons* (Lyons, 1556). The first part deals with the rudiments of music; the second – which describes ranges, tunings, FINGERINGS and playing techniques for CONSORTS of transverse FLUTES, RECORDERS, VIOLS and VIOLINS – proffers unique and valuable information.

Jambe de Fer explains that a four-part consort of flutes requires two sizes – three tenors in D for the upper parts and a bass in G; in contrast, the recorder consort needs an additional soprano instrument to play the highest part. He describes how the 'transverse flute has 15 to 16 notes which sound good and natural without much strain or force', adding that it can reach up to nineteen notes but 'they are very crude and rough due to the force of air needed' (47–8) and that for this reason they are rarely used. He also addresses flute embouchure.

Jambe de Fer records that the French 'tune their viols in diverse ways' but always using five strings tuned in fourths, whereas Italian viols have six strings 'tuned exactly like the lute ... The violin is very different to the viol. First it has only four strings, which are tuned in fifths ... It has a much smaller body, flatter and a much more harsh sound. It does not have frets because it is fingered in tones ... Both the French and the Italians play the violin in the same way' (58, 61, 62).

Answering the question: 'Why do you call one viols and the other violins?' Jambe de Fer explains: 'We call viols those with which gentlemen, merchants and other people of virtue pass their time. The Italians call them *viole de gambe* because they are held downwards, some between their legs and others on a seat or stool' (62). The violin 'is used in communal dancing with good reason, because it is much easier to tune, because the fifth is easier to hear than the fourth. It is also more portable, which is very important when transporting it to weddings and mummeries ... Few people play it, save those who earn their living by it' (63).

FURTHER READING

F. Lesure, '*L'Epitome musical* de Philibert Jambe de Fer (1556)', AnnM, 6 (1958–63), 341–86.

LUCY ROBINSON

Jazz and Popular Music From the early decades of the twentieth century, debates about jazz and popular music have focused on origins and AUTHENTICITY with regard to style and genre. These debates reflected immense changes in cultural production, especially the global circulation of jazz and popular music through the media of recording, radio, cinema, television, advertising and the internet. Various historical performance practices were developed in response to the dramatically shifting boundaries of musical cultures, as previous traditions dissolved and newer ones came into being. These included the rediscovery of what were perceived to be original vocal or instrumental techniques associated with specific genres, the exhaustive documentation of past performances, the return to older values and ideas, and the replication of former performance venues and institutions.

Jazz

The historical recreation of jazz performances primarily consists of revival movements which focus on particular styles and ensembles that attempt to reproduce historically faithful renditions of standard repertoire (DeVeaux, 1998). As with many musicians active in early music, there are two ways in which jazz performers generally approach the past. The first is based on the oral transmission of concepts and techniques to recreate note-for-note the earliest performance practices of a specific style such as was exemplified by the Dixieland revival in the 1940s. At that time musicians primarily learned tunes from each other by ear, as well as copying their individual sound and solos from the first recordings of the music. Critics who were sympathetic to the movement emphasised musical risk and experimentation. They disparaged swing musicians for performing in a mechanical, slick, unfeeling manner and relying on scores, and argued instead for the honest, emotional

EXPRESSION they associated with the original New Orleans performance style (Gendron, 44).

The second is based on carefully notated TRANSCRIPTIONS of classic recordings. Historians Gunther Schuller and David Baker were influential practitioners of this approach with the Smithsonian Jazz Masterworks Orchestra, an ensemble created by the United States Congress in 1990 in recognition of the importance of jazz in American culture and currently based within the National Museum of American History in Washington DC. In 1995 the trumpeter Wynton Marsalis initiated a similar project on Duke Ellington's music at the Lincoln Center in New York City. The programme 'Essentially Ellington' distributes free copies of more than one hundred big-band transcriptions to American high schools, with new transcriptions coming out at the rate of about six per year. The publications include transcripts of brass and reed parts, as would appear in most standard big band libraries, as well as detailing improvised solos, bass lines and the piano voicing and 'fills' used by Ellington band members in performance. While at first this repertory was dedicated only to the compositions of Ellington, in 2008 Jazz at Lincoln Center began including non-Ellington repertory in its school programme, such as Mary Lou Williams, Count Basie, Dizzy Gillespie and Charles Mingus. The larger ambition in both these cases is to reconnect performers and audiences to the original creative processes that gave rise to the music and to offer a blueprint for authentic performances of its masterpieces.

In 2014, the band Mostly Other People Do The Killing released its album *Blue*, which set out to perform note-for-note trumpeter Miles Davis's 1959 recording *Kind of Blue*. The project involved meticulous reproduction of the original, including the TRANSCRIPTION of Paul Chambers's bass lines, Jimmy Cobb's drum patterns and pianist Bill Evans's modal harmonisation, along with the solos by Davis and saxophonists Cannonball Adderley and John Coltrane. Even Coltrane's off-microphone entrance on 'Freddie the Freeloader' was carefully duplicated on *Blue* by the group's tenor saxophonist Jon Irabagon. To achieve greater fidelity to the original, the band also decided to record each of the rhythm tracks and the HORN parts separately, rather than performing them together as a single take (which happened at Davis's recording session). In taking this approach, *Blue* highlights some of the key issues surrounding historical performance practice in jazz, especially as they relate to questions of technique, concepts of artistic value and the sources of creativity among performers. As the band's bassist and leader Moppa Elliot claimed in an interview soon after the release of the album, the project was 'a commentary on the relationship between playing jazz now and jazz's own history' (*Time Out*, 4 November 2014, www.timeout.com). Because there is such a high premium placed on IMPROVISATION and spontaneity in jazz, however, these kinds of historical reconstructions can often appear contrary to the music's core principles.

Popular Music

As in the world of jazz, historical performance in popular music is engaged with similar issues of authenticity and originality. In particular, cover bands and tribute acts are an essential part of popular music culture, along with the frequent revival of earlier genres to which these groups often refer. These kinds of historical practices show us the ways in which musicians use their relationship to the music of the past to reflect on the creative possibilities available to them in the present. At the same time, they demonstrate how the strict adherence to past practices can also considerably limit those possibilities.

In his 1949 guide to the vocabulary of the popular music industry, Arnold Shaw explained that when a song had become a hit on one label, other companies then 'covered' themselves against a loss by recording it also. By the early 1950s, covers had become so common within popular music culture that there were often more than ten competing versions of the same song circulating at any given time. Understanding the different approaches that performers take to cover songs opens up a rich and useful discussion of historical practice in popular music. According to Albin Zak (602), Jimi Hendrix's 1968 recording of Bob Dylan's 'All Along the Watchtower' incorporates 'a set of interactions among genres and musical activities – including ballad, blues, rock, rhythm and blues, urban folk, improvisation, composition, performance, and recording – that was characteristic of late 1960s rock'. By engaging with the multiple sources of Dylan's original to produce his cover, Hendrix not only revealed the complex history embedded in the song, but invested it with new meaning. Furthermore, when we return to Dylan's song, we understand its mood and lyricism differently.

Tribute acts or bands now cover the spectrum of post-WWII popular music, from the Beatles, the Rolling Stones, the Doors, Genesis, Pink Floyd, Abba, ACDC and the Eagles, to more recent acts such as Madonna and Nirvana. There is also a growing trend towards solo acts, both for contemporary popular music artists, such as Elvis Presley, Rod Stewart and Neil Diamond, and those from earlier periods, such as Frank Sinatra and Dean Martin. Some of the most prominent are the Presley solo tribute acts, of which there are thousands in the USA alone. These performers focus on recreating a specific phase in the singer's career by reproducing particular performances as faithfully as possible. Annual conventions and festivals in many different countries reinforce their attention to recreating Presley's unique vocal technique, physical gestures, emotional intensity and theatrical presence in great detail.

Historical performance also extends to different musical movements in which the participants collectively perform an authentic musical and cultural identity within a specific scene. British Northern Soul is a good example of this practice. The Northern Soul dance music scene originated in the English North and Midlands in the early 1970s and became identified with venues such as The Twisted Wheel in Manchester and the Wigan Casino. Although generally associated with the African-American dance music produced in the USA by the Tamla Motown label, Northern Soul DJs generally avoided songs that were commercially successful, preferring to focus on performing 'rare grooves'. The most valued recordings in the scene were usually by lesser-known artists, released only in limited numbers, and often by small regional American labels. The contemporary revival of Northern Soul in British cities in the last decade, along with other countries such as Spain and Australia, focuses on recreating the contours of the original scene as accurately as possible, whether through developing an inventory of classic tracks, induction into highly specialised dance steps, or claims about the type of clothing participants should wear. The search for an authentic encounter with the Northern Soul scene in this instance opens up a space in which participants imaginatively reflect on the past in terms of its relevance to their current experiences of music.

Within jazz and popular music studies, the performance practice movement has focused primarily on recreating authentic performance practices with an aim towards recovering and reconstructing the reality of the original performance. Musicians have mobilised a range of historical sources, instrumental and vocal techniques, sound recordings and critical commentary to achieve this. More broadly, their attempts to reconstruct these performances underline the many problems involved in understanding and evaluating musical experiences of the past, as well as the challenges of sustaining them in the future.

FURTHER READING

S. DeVeaux, 'Constructing the jazz tradition', in R. O'Meally (ed.), *The Jazz Cadence in American Culture* (New York: Columbia University Press, 1998), 483–512.
B. Gendron, '"Mouldy figs" and modernists', in K. Gabbard (ed.), *Jazz Among the Discourses* (Durham: Duke University Press, 1995), 31–56.
A. Shaw, 'The vocabulary of Tin-Pan Alley explained', *Notes*, 7/1 (1949), 33–53.
T. Wall, 'Out on the floor: the politics of dancing on the Northern Soul scene', *Popular Music*, 25/3 (2006), 431–45.
A. J. Zak, 'Bob Dylan and Jimi Hendrix: juxtaposition and transformation "all along the watchtower"', *JAMS*, 57/3 (2005), 599–644.

NICHOLAS GEBHARDT

Jerome of Moravia [Hieronymus de Moravia] (*fl.* 1272–1304) A Dominican monk, perhaps from Moravia or from the region of Moray (Scotland), and active in Paris.

Jerome's *Tractatus de musica*, compiled around 1290, possibly in connection with the recent Dominican chant reform, is preserved in only one Parisian manuscript, used as a textbook in the College of Navarre at the Sorbonne. In the chapter on plainsong performance, he recommends that singers use the same type of voice (head, throat, or chest) and keep the same beat, following a leader chosen from among them; PLAINCHANT melodies should be performed in a comfortable range. These rules also apply to the performance of organum. In the last chapter Jerome provides rare information on the different tunings and ranges of two bowed instruments, the *rubeba* (pitched lower than the rebec) and the *viella*, giving basic directions on FINGERING and manner of performance.

FURTHER READING

Hieronymi de Moravia Tractatus de Musica, ed. C. Meyer and G. Lobrichon, Corpus Christianorum 250 (Turnhout: Brepols, 2012).
C. Page, 'Jerome of Moravia on the rubeba and viella', *GSJ*, 32 (1979), 77–98.

STEFANO MENGOZZI

Joachim, Joseph (b. Kitsee, nr Pressburg [now Bratislava, Slovakia], 28 June 1831; d. Berlin, 15 August 1907) Austro-Hungarian violinist, composer, conductor and teacher.

A VIOLIN pupil of Stanislaus Serwaczyński, Georg Hellmesberger (i), Joseph Boehm and eventually FERDINAND DAVID, Joachim became a protégé of FELIX MENDELSSOHN. He followed his successful Leipzig debut (1843) with an acclaimed account in London (1844) of BEETHOVEN's Violin Concerto, which he established in the repertory. Appointed Liszt's concertmaster at Weimar (1850), he resigned (1852) to become royal music director at Hanover, where he renewed friendship with Schumann and established a long association with BRAHMS (temporarily ruptured (1881) by disagreements about Joachim's divorce). Joachim settled in Berlin (1868) as founding director/violin professor at the Königliche Akademie der Künste (later Königliche Hochschule für Musik); he contributed profoundly to that city's cultural development and was a popular and influential visitor to Britain.

The Joachim Quartet, formed in 1869 with colleagues from the Akademie (although personnel changed throughout the ensemble's existence), gave a pioneering annual series of recitals at Berlin's Singakademie and toured Europe to great acclaim. Joachim's concert career included engagements as a conductor, particularly of Brahms's symphonic music, and he freely advised various composers (notably Schumann, Dvořák, Bruch, Gade and Brahms) about matters of string writing. A composition pupil of MORITZ HAUPTMANN, he wrote three violin concertos, five overtures, various songs and salon pieces and some masterly concerto CADENZAS. Among his most celebrated students were LEOPOLD AUER, Bronislav Hubermann, Karl Klingler, Marie Soldat and his eventual assistant/collaborator/biographer Andreas Moser.

Joachim and Moser's comprehensive *Violinschule* (3 vols. (Berlin: N. Simrock, 1905)), though compiled mostly by Moser, incorporates intriguing insights into Joachim's technical and artistic aims. It emphasises the importance of scales in developing fundamental left- and right-hand technique, values economy of shifting in the pursuit of true intonation and generally rejects the customary prioritising of the third over the second position and of the 'uneven' positions. The thumb's contribution towards dexterous shifting in emulation of the human voice is particularly stressed, while PORTAMENTO is endorsed as a means of EXPRESSION and preserving timbral uniformity, provided that it is introduced discerningly, when the starting finger undertakes the slide and the intermediate notes are imperceptible. Sliding with the second of the two fingers is considered faulty, except to a harmonic.

Joachim and Moser advocate free movement of the upper right arm at the shoulder joint. They broaden SPOHR's vocabulary to include spiccato and springing bow strokes and criticise him for rejecting selective use of artificial HARMONICS and left-hand pizzicato. They oppose BÉRIOT's method of chord arpeggiation, opting for the simultaneous execution of the notes of three-note chords wherever possible. However, they cite Spohr on VIBRATO usage, recommending its selective introduction only where the expression demands it and recognising 'the steady tone as the ruling one' (II, 96a). SINGING again provides the model, the addition of words to the opening bars of Joachim's *Romance*, Op. 2 clarifying the ACCENTUATION, character and vibrato usage, which should be 'only, like a delicate breath, on the notes under which the syllables "früh" and "wie" are placed' (III, 7) (*see* Example 15). The few extant

Example 15: Joseph Joachim and Andreas Moser: *Violinschule*, 3 vols. (1905), III, 7.

Hol - der Früh - ling, komm doch wie - der!

recordings of Joachim's playing (1903) confirm his pure steady sound, sparing use of vibrato, long-arched phrasing and subtle RUBATO.

Volume three comprises ten short essays by Moser on 'style and artistic performance' and editions of the solo violin part, with FINGERINGS, BOWINGS, cadenzas (as appropriate) and prefatory remarks by Joachim, of sixteen 'masterworks', including concertos by BACH, Viotti, KREUTZER, RODE, MOZART, Beethoven, Spohr, Mendelssohn and Brahms. Some of Moser's essays relate to issues already considered (vibrato, portamento, accentuation, phrasing and timbre and ORNAMENTATION); others focus on the importance of composer-fidelity regarding expression, style and delivery (a particular Joachim concern), the merits of uniform orchestral bowing, the relationship between violin and continuo, TEMPO modification, rubato and prolongation, and the appreciation of personal artistic idiosyncrasies and NATIONAL IDIOMS.

Joachim also published many independent editions of music. At first he was not especially prescriptive editorially, as evidenced by his 'clean' edition of some of CORELLI's trio sonatas (1869) and his sparing additional indications in his performing editions of Mendelssohn's piano trios, string quintets and quartets and even his first version of Mendelssohn's Violin Concerto (annotated more copiously in the *Violinschule*). Performance directions are more prevalent in his first edition of Brahms's Violin Concerto and in his editorial work generally from the late 1890s, possibly due to Moser's influence as collaborator, his own pedagogical leanings, or his desire to record his interpretative decisions for posterity. These later editions include concertos by Bach, Mozart and Beethoven, Beethoven's string quartets and violin sonatas, and Bach's solo sonatas and partitas (completed by Moser but reflecting Joachim's practice).

Joachim's correspondence, especially that with Brahms which extended over forty-four years and embraced the evolution of Brahms's Violin Concerto, reveals important insights into his character, relationships with other musicians, creative activity and artistic credo.

FURTHER READING

B. Borchard, *Stimme und Geige: Amalie und Joseph Joachim – Frau und Mann. Biographie und Interpretationsgeschichte* (Vienna: Böhlau Verlag, 2005).
C. Brown, 'Joachim's violin playing and the performance of Brahms's string music', in M. Musgrave and B. D. Sherman (eds.), *Performing Brahms: Early Evidence of Performance Style* (Cambridge University Press, 2003), 48–98.
B. Schwarz: 'Joseph Joachim and the genesis of Brahms's Violin Concerto', *MQ*, 69/4 (1983), 503–26.

ROBIN STOWELL

Journals *see* PERIODICALS

Jousse, Jean (b. Orléans, 1760; d. London, 19 January 1837) French theorist and composer.

A refugee of the French Revolution, Jean Jousse settled in London and published several didactic texts, many based on others' work. He translated and expanded 'musical grammars' (notably by Asioli), revised various EDITIONS of Dibdin's *Music Epitomized*, expanded Hudl's work on modulation, translated and edited THOROUGHBASS methods by ALBRECHTSBERGER and Pasquali, penned his *A Catechism of Thoroughbass and Harmony* and published *Lectures* (c1818) and 'dialogues' on that subject. He also compiled a *Guida Armonica* (1808) and *A Catechism of Music* [183_?], as well as dictionaries explaining musical rudiments and terminology in various languages.

Jousse's *The Piano forte, made easy to every capacity* (c1810) reached its twelfth edition by 1830. He also published *Instructions for the Piano forte* and a *Fashionable Preceptor for the Piano-forte*, and some of his piano writings were revised and edited by Henry West [1858], W. Forde [1868] and Henri Hemy [1876]. He wrote piano pieces and *An Essay on Temperament* [1832] to assist students in piano tuning.

Jousse's *The Vocal Primer* (1834) and *A Catechism of Singing* [1835?] place in context his *Introduction to the Art of Sol-Fa-ing & Singing* [1815?]. His *The Modern Violin Preceptor* (1805) is an elementary work with technical instruction assimilated from the treatises of GEMINIANI (1751), PRELLEUR (1731) and Philpot (1766). More advanced is his *The Theory and Practice of the Violin* (1811), which takes inspiration from the TREATISES of Geminiani, LEOPOLD MOZART, Philpot, L'ABBÉ LE FILS and RODE, BAILLOT and KREUTZER and is both progressive (regarding posture, the VIOLIN hold, FINGERING and shifting) and conservative (regarding the bow hold and VIBRATO) in technical content. It devotes seven pages to ORNAMENTATION, includes works by CORELLI, TARTINI's *L'arte del'arco*, some studies by Kreutzer and exercises in duet format, exploiting up to ninth position as well as double stopping in octaves and tenths.

FURTHER READING

D. J. Golby, *Instrumental Teaching in Nineteenth-Century Britain* (Aldershot: Ashgate, 2004).
R. Stowell, 'The contribution of Geminiani's "The Art of Playing on the Violin" to "the improved state of the violin in England"', in C. Hogwood (ed.), *Geminiani Studies* (Bologna: Ut Orpheus Edizioni, 2013), 257–300.
Violin Technique and Performance Practice in the Late Eighteenth and Early Nineteenth Centuries (Cambridge University Press, 1985).

ROBIN STOWELL

Junker, Carl Ludwig (b. Kirchberg an der Jagst, 3 August 1748; d. Ruppertshofen, 30 May 1797) German writer and composer.

Junker became interested in music and art at the court of Hohenlohe-Kirchberg, before he studied theology at the University of Göttingen (from 1769). He settled briefly in Switzerland (1774–7) but returned to Kirchberg as deacon and, in 1779, court chaplain. He held subsequent appointments as pastor in Dettingen (1789), Lendsiedel (1792) and Ruppertshofen (1795). He played the FLUTE, CELLO and keyboards and his compositions comprise symphonies, concertos, a melodrama, songs and keyboard pieces.

Junker wrote extensively about art and music, often comparing drawing, colouring and EXPRESSION in art with melody, harmony and expression in music. Many of his writings about music focus on style issues, using 'sentimentality' (*Empfindsamkeit*) as his benchmark. They embrace a wide range of topics, including description of the music at leading courts, the affective properties and gendering of instruments, sketches of prominent contemporary composers and arguments for music as an 'expressive' rather than 'imitative' art. His *Zwanzig Componisten* (Bern: Typographische Gesellschaft, 1776), for example, includes severe criticism of HAYDN's 'modern' musical style and the view that rondo form was over-used and too 'popular'; a 1783 essay specifies the instruments most appropriate for respectable bourgeois women to play (the PIANO, HARP, LUTE, zither and GUITAR) and bans them from performing on 'male' instruments, thereby fuelling the contemporary division of male and female performing roles respectively in terms of public and domestic settings.

Most significant for historical performers is Junker's *Einige der vornehmsten Pflichten eines Kapellmeisters oder Musikdirectors* (Winterthur: Steiner, 1782), which includes discussions of TEMPO issues and the role of tempo modification for the expression of feelings, the *Kapellmeister*'s role as a 'time-beater', CONDUCTING techniques, the location, distribution and seating of performing forces in specific kinds of VENUES (particularly the problems posed by orchestral performances in churches), REHEARSAL practices and the role of keyboard players, including tuning the ORCHESTRA and filling in missing or errant parts from the score.

FURTHER READING

D. J. Koury, *Orchestral Performance Practices in the Nineteenth Century: Size, Proportions and Seating* (Ann Arbor, MI: UMI Research Press, 1986).

R. Stowell, '"Good execution and other necessary skills": the role of the concertmaster in the late eighteenth century', *EMc*, 16/1 (February, 1988), 21–33.

R. E. Wates, *Karl Ludwig Junker (1748–1797): Sentimental Music Critic* (New Haven, CT: Yale University Press, 1965).

ROBIN STOWELL

K

Kalkbrenner, Frédéric (Friedrich) (b. early November 1785; d. Enghien-les-Bains, 10 June 1849) French pianist, teacher and composer of German extraction.

Kalkbrenner was a prolific composer and pianist of significant if transient influence during the early nineteenth century. Although German by birth, he studied the PIANO with LOUIS ADAM at the PARIS CONSERVATOIRE before continuing his compositional studies in Vienna with Salieri and ALBRECHTSBERGER. After several moderately successful tours in German-speaking lands, he settled in England (1814–23), where he became closely acquainted with the English school of piano manufacturing and was introduced to Johann Bernhard Logier, inventor of the so-called *chiroplast*, a mechanical device attached to the piano, designed to hold the wrist steady while isolating and developing finger action. Kalkbrenner collaborated with Logier in further developing and widely promoting the *chiroplast*, later marketed in France as the *guide-mains* and in Germany as the *Handleiter*. It featured significantly in Kalkbrenner's popular *Méthode pour apprendre le piano-forte à l'aide du guide-mains* (*Method for Learning the Piano With the Help of the Chiroplast* (Paris: Chez Ign. Pleyel & cie, 1831)). This and the finish and elegance of Kalkbrenner's own playing made him one of the most famous pianists in Europe after his return to Paris in 1825, his financial security yet further enhanced by prudent investment in Pleyel's piano manufacturing company and by increasing fame as a teacher. Upon his own arrival in Paris in 1831, the young Fryderyk Chopin was indelibly impressed by Kalkbrenner's exquisitely refined playing. Nevertheless, Kalkbrenner's influence began to decline markedly in the late 1830s, with the impact of the almost infinitely more imaginative compositions of Chopin, the increasing action-weight of pianos that rendered the *chiroplast* both useless and potentially harmful, and the development of a powerfully iconoclastic piano performance style by Liszt that made Kalkbrenner's smooth brilliance seem shallow and outmoded. Aspects of Kalkbrenner's style did, however, survive in the later nineteenth-century French piano school, especially in the music of SAINT-SAËNS, a pupil of Kalkbrenner's pupil Camille Stamaty.

FURTHER READING

A. Marmontel, *Les pianistes célèbres* (Paris: Heugel, 1878).

KENNETH HAMILTON

Kastner, Jean-Georges [Johann Georg] (b. Strasbourg, 9 March 1810; d. Paris, 19 December 1867) French composer and writer about music.

Kastner spent most of his working life in Paris. He was a composer of operas and other large-scale works that gained little success, but a marriage to one of his wealthy students allowed him to pursue whatever caught his interest. His significance rests on his writings about MILITARY MUSIC and wind and brass instruments, principally his *Traité général d'instrumentation* (Paris, 1837, enlarged 2/1844), *Tableaux analytiques et résumé général des principes élémentaires de musique* (Paris, 1838), *Cours d'instrumentation* (Paris, 1839, suppl. 1844), *Mémoire sur l'état de la musique en Allemagne* (Paris, 1843) and *Manuel général de musique militaire* (Paris, 1848). These publications all hold information for students of performance practice because of what they convey about the state of knowledge and the performance conventions at the time of their writing.

Kastner was a scholarly and well-organised writer who, in his 1837 work, identified a disconnection between the richness of contemporary composers' ideas and their general knowledge of musical instruments. He was able to describe instruments such as the CORNETT that were either obsolete or slipping into obscurity, but he also had a keen understanding of the most modern instruments, such as those designed by ADOLPHE SAX, whom he knew well and regarded highly. He is believed to have written the first published works for Sax's most enduring inventions, the saxophone and saxhorn. Kastner's writings provide evidence, both witting and unwitting, of practices and attitudes in Paris at a critical period of musical transformation, especially in respect of brass and woodwind instruments. BERLIOZ was a close friend, and it has been suggested that many of the ideas put forward in the composer's *Grand traité d'instrumentation...* (Paris, 1843) are indebted to Kastner's work, which elevated the importance of instrumentation as a discrete branch of study.

FURTHER READING

S. Carter, 'Georges Kastner on brass instruments: the influence of technology on the theory of orchestration', in S. Carter (ed.), *Perspectives in Brass Scholarship: Proceedings of the International Historic Brass Symposium, Amherst 1995* (Stuyvesant, NY: Pendragon Press, 1997), 171–93.

TREVOR HERBERT

Kenyon, Sir Nicholas Roger (b. Altrincham, 23 February 1951) English editor, administrator and writer on music.

Kenyon was music critic for *The New Yorker* (1979–82) and subsequently worked for *The Times, The Listener* and *The Observer*. He was editor of the journal *Early Music* (1983–92), commissioning a series of articles in 1984 which became the highly influential volume *Authenticity and Early Music* (Oxford, 1988). In 1992 he was appointed Controller of BBC Radio 3 and in 1996 director of the BBC Promenade Concerts. In 1998 he relinquished his position at Radio 3 to concentrate on the Proms and other activities. His Royal Philharmonic Society Lecture (2001), 'Tradition isn't what it used to be', was an influential and astute appraisal of the integration of period principles into the mainstream. Kenyon has been managing director of the Barbican Centre since 2007 and has published books on BACH, MOZART, SIMON RATTLE, the BBC Symphony Orchestra and the City of London. He contributed the opening chapter 'Performance today' to the *Cambridge History of Musical Performance*, edited by COLIN LAWSON and ROBIN STOWELL (Cambridge University Press, 2012).

COLIN LAWSON

Key character A term used from the late seventeenth century onwards to describe the theory that affective meanings are conveyed by the use of individual keys.

Although key character had its roots in affective modality, the transference of these meanings to tonal music is not completely clear. Italian theorist GIOSEFFO ZARLINO differentiated the meaning of the modes in ancient times from those of the contemporaneous Church modes in his influential treatise *Le istitutione harmoniche* (1558). JOHANNES MATTHESON later drew similar conclusions in *Das neu-eröffnete Orchestre* (1713). A crucial element in this transference was the contrasted affective potentiality of thirds. Zarlino identified the premise of associating the major mode with happiness and the minor with sadness. This idea became widely understood, aided by the extensive dissemination of Zarlino's treatise and by the work of various theorists, including Salomon de Caus (*Les raisons des forces mouvantes* (Frankfurt: Jan Norton, 1615)) and Seth Calvisius (*Melopoeia sive melodiae condendae ratio* (Erfurt: Georg Baumann, 1592)).

Tonal rather than modal definitions first began to emerge in France towards the end of the seventeenth century. The earliest known list of key characteristics was published by JEAN ROUSSEAU in his *Méthode claire* (Paris: C. Ballard, 1691), followed immediately by MARC-ANTOINE CHARPENTIER in 'Règles de composition' (Paris, c1692), Charles Masson in *Nouveau traité* (Paris: J. Collombat et chez l'auteur, 1697), and finally JEAN-PHILIPPE RAMEAU, who in his *Traité de l'harmonie* (Paris: J.-B.-C. Ballard, 1722) again affirmed Zarlino's affective characterisation of thirds. While these early French lists may appear subjective, the descriptions of keys found in them focused on instrumental function and capability, and reflected genres of music composed for particular themes or occasions. In the descriptions that follow, definitions for C major are followed by those for G major (representing the sharp side), and F major (representing the flat side).

C major	Rousseau: gay things, grandeur
	Charpentier: gay and militant
	Masson: not mentioned
	Rameau: songs of glee and rejoicing
G major	Rousseau: tenderness
	Charpentier: sweetly joyful
	Masson: gay and brilliant
	Rameau: tender and gay songs
F major	Rousseau: devotional pieces, church songs
	Charpentier: furious and hot-tempered
	Masson: naturally gay mixed with gravity
	Rameau: tempests, furies and other subjects of that nature

In German-speaking lands, similar observations were made. Andreas Werckmeister (*Musicae Mathematicae* (Frankfurt & Leipzig: Theodor

P. Calvisius, 1686)) echoed Zarlino's theory concerning the quality of thirds. However, the sole known contributor of key definitions at this time is Johannes Mattheson (1713 and 1739). Even though Mattheson acknowledged that his opinions were subjective, his definitions proved to be influential. His treatise received wide circulation and his characterisations of the keys were reflective of contemporaneous musical genres.

C Major   rude, impudent ... suited to rejoicing ... where joy is in
            full scope...
            a clever composer ... charming, tender (1713)
            tender and touching (1739)
G Major: insinuating and persuasive ... brilliant, suited to serious and
            cheerful things (1713)
F major: generosity, steadfastness, love ... beautiful sentiments (1713)

Mattheson's descriptions recount his subjective views and also illustrate the beginnings of what Rita Steblin terms the 'sharp/flat principle' (Steblin, 10). They also chronicle and establish contrasted affective traditions in certain individual keys. For instance, his description of C major – triumph, strength, rejoicing versus charming, tender, pure – showed the two parallel traditions of using this key. By the end of the century, two or more contrasted traditions had developed in many keys.

In these early French and German lists, the beginnings of the 'sharp/flat principle' can be seen. C major serves as an affective starting point – a *tabula rasa* – something also supported by tuning. Keys became ever more bright or harsh as sharps were added, since these keys used more open strings. In contrast, keys on the flat side became more melancholy, heavy and dark since they used more stopped strings. Two of the most widely known lists of key characteristics by Christian Friedrich Daniel Schubart (published in 1806) and Georg Joseph Vogler (1779) both reflect this principle. PITCH was not a significant issue, despite the presence of many different pitch levels, since the sharp/flat principle continued to operate regardless.

Tonal symbolism appealed strongly to the Romantic imagination. Writers of the next generation such as E. T. A. Hoffmann were greatly influenced by Schubart's definitions, to the extent of adopting his actual language. Even BEETHOVEN was moved to comment, albeit very sparingly. Schumann and BERLIOZ both wrote extensively about key character and theorists continued to define it throughout the nineteenth century.

Tuning was an important factor that was often used to support the existence of key characteristics. The lengthy progression from meantone via well tempered to equal tempered tuning had profound implications for the meaning of the keys. Meantone tuning, widely used until the early eighteenth century (and rather later in some places), was based on a hierarchy with C major at its centre, preserving the tuning of natural thirds. This meant that keys up to three accidentals could be used successfully. Moving further afield – to F minor for instance – would mean that the minor third of the tonic triad would not be 'in tune'. This explained, for instance, why F minor, a remote, 'out of tune key', came to be universally known for projecting extreme grief or despair. With the advent of well TEMPERAMENTS in the late seventeenth century, it became possible to play in all the keys. Owen Jorgensen defines a well temperament as 'an unrestrictive, irregular, circulating temperament containing key-colour contrasts that supports the characters of the keys' (Jorgensen, 10). He also concludes that equal tempered tuning was not employed on early nineteenth-century pianos, and was only adopted widely at the end of the nineteenth century.

Over the years, many writers have sought simplistic solutions for the meaning of individual keys, yet this is clearly not a historically appropriate stance since many keys actually depicted multiple affective states. However, despite the fact that there was not always agreement as to exactly what each tonality meant, the concept of key character was a critical component of affective theory.

FURTHER READING

W. Auhagen, *Studien zur Tonartencharakteristik in theoretischen Schriften und Kompositionen vom späten 17. bis zum Beginn des 20. Jahrhunderts* (Frankfurt a. M.: Lang, 1983).
P. Ellison, *The Key to Beethoven: Connecting Tonality and Meaning in His Music* (Hillsdale, NY: Pendragon Press, 2014).
O. Jorgensen, *Tuning* (East Lansing, MI: Michigan State University Press, 1991).
R. Steblin, *A History of Key Characteristics in the Eighteenth and Early Nineteenth Centuries* (University of Rochester Press, 2002).
J. Wilson, 'Topos and tonality in the age of Beethoven', PhD dissertation, University of Vienna (2012).

PAUL ELLISON

Kirkby, Dame Emma (b. Camberley, 26 February 1949) English soprano.

Dame Emma Kirkby studied classics at Oxford, devoting her time there to languages, literature and SINGING with the Schola Cantorum and other ad hoc groups. Here she first encountered historical instruments in chamber music ranging from Medieval to Baroque.

Having trained as a teacher, she soon gravitated towards professional performance with pioneering groups. In 1971 she joined the Taverner Choir, which had an important influence on her distinctive style. Two years later she began a long association with lutenist Antony Rooley and THE CONSORT OF MUSICKE. They soon became leading advocates of early music, particularly Renaissance LUTE songs. Kirkby embarked upon nearly two decades of immersion in madrigal repertoire with a stable group of six colleagues, galvanised by Rooley into a full range of responses, from still, contemplative performance to adventurous staging. Performing extensively in Germany, they also collaborated with Co-op Piccionaia of Vicenza in *Commedia dell'Arte* shows across Europe.

Kirkby took part in early Decca Florilegium recordings with The Consort of Musicke and the ACADEMY OF ANCIENT MUSIC at a time when most college-trained sopranos had not developed an appropriate vocal sound for early music. She has since made over 100 recordings, of music by J. S. BACH, MONTEVERDI, Vivaldi, COUPERIN, Dowland, Purcell and Arne, but also of lesser known masters, including John Danyel, the Lawes brothers, Luca Marenzio, Giaches de Wert, Sigismondo D'India and the young Heinrich Schütz. However, she is probably best known for her recordings of Handel.

Kirkby takes the sound of historical instruments as inspiration, reacting to and engaging with the colours and timbres around her in a way that immediately singles her out. She has been praised for singing with a grace, lightness and sparkle that are immediately appealing, always bringing EXPRESSION to the fore. Her clear, agile voice allows her to shade notes carefully, shape melodies subtly and articulate flourishes incisively, maintaining a palpable sense of sheer enjoyment. This infectious delight in music making has given her international recognition; her widespread popularity early in her career gave a significant boost to the early music movement.

Kirkby has taught for many years throughout Europe, the USA and Japan. Whilst stressing that singers learn from historical instruments, she also advises that historical instrumentalists have much to learn from singers, especially in light of efforts to emulate the human voice in music making throughout the centuries. She therefore does not advocate a strict, straight-tone approach (since the voice vibrates naturally), instead suggesting a clean attack, followed by VIBRATO as needed as an enrichment of the note. Above all, vocal sound is hung on words, and in SINGING she insists on the importance of consonants, particularly remarking on the way in which clear consonants can enhance volume.

ASHLEY SOLOMON

Kirkpatrick, Ralph (Leonard) (b. Leominster, MA, 10 June 1911; d. Guilford, CT, 13 April 1984) American harpsichordist, clavichordist, pianist and scholar.

Kirkpatrick was a performer and scholar best known today for his pioneering work on Domenico Scarlatti: the chronological catalogue of Scarlatti sonatas in which he assigned each sonata a 'K.' number, his book *Domenico Scarlatti* (Princeton and London, 1953) and his critical edition of *Sixty Sonatas* (Schirmer, 1953). A pupil of NADIA BOULANGER and WANDA LANDOWSKA in Paris, as well as ARNOLD DOLMETSCH in England, Kirkpatrick's most significant recordings were of Scarlatti and J. S. BACH, but he also recorded eighteenth-century French music and some English VIRGINAL music. Kirkpatrick's complete Bach recordings during the 1960s were made on HARPSICHORDS with metal frames and heavy construction by J.C. Neupert of Bamberg, although his later Bach recordings were made on reproductions of eighteenth-century French harpsichords by Hubbard & Dowd. His recording of *The Well-Tempered Clavier* involved both harpsichord and CLAVICHORD, and he was a significant figure as an interpreter of MOZART'S PIANO music, which he played on the FORTEPIANO.

Kirkpatrick taught at the Salzburg Mozarteum 1933–4, and was subsequently professor of music at both Yale and the University of California (Berkeley). This academic background reaped rewards in the scholarly prefaces to his EDITIONS of all Scarlatti's sonatas in FACSIMILE, Bach's *Goldberg Variations* 'for harpsichord or piano' (Schirmer, 1938), and Scarlatti's *Sixty Sonatas*. These were some of the first critical editions of eighteenth-century keyboard music, a reaction to the subjective 'performing' editions characteristic of the period. In the preface to his edition of the *Goldberg Variations* and in his *Interpreting Bach's Well-Tempered Clavier: A Performer's Discourse* (New Haven, CT, and London, 1984), Kirkpatrick wrote extensively on issues relating to performance practice, thus stimulating an important discipline that continues today. Kirkpatrick also corresponded with important musicians from a variety of disciplines: harpsichord makers, performers and composers.

FURTHER READING

M. Kirkpatrick (ed.), *Ralph Kirkpatrick: Letters of the American Harpsichordist and Scholar* (University of Rochester Press, 2014).
R. Kirkpatrick, 'Fifty years of harpsichord playing', *EMc*, 11 (1983), 31–41.
H. Schott, 'Obituary of Ralph Kirkpatrick', *EMc*, 12 (1984), 585.

DAVID PONSFORD

Kirnberger, Johann Philipp (b. Saalfeld, bap. 24 April 1721; d. Berlin, 26 or 27 July 1783) German composer and theorist.

Kirnberger studied with J. S. BACH in Leipzig (1739–41) and then worked for members of the Polish nobility (1741–51) before returning to Germany as violinist in the Berlin Hofkapelle (1751–4). His last post (1758–83) was as court musician to Princess Anna Amalia of Prussia (sister of Frederick the Great), Berlin. He acted as her musical consultant and composition teacher and helped to compile her music library, the Amalienbibliothek.

One of the most prominent Berlin theorists of his day, Kirnberger promoted J. S. Bach's methods of teaching and composition in his *Die Kunst des reinen Satzes in der Musik* (1771–9; trans. as *The Art of Strict Musical Composition* (New Haven, CT, 1982)) and *Die wahren Grundsätze zum Gebrauch der Harmonie* (Berlin and Königsberg, 1773)). He also co-edited, with C. P. E. BACH, an early edition of J. S. Bach's four-part chorales (Leipzig, 1784–7).

Kirnberger's compositions are in some cases modelled on J. S. Bach's, in others on the *galant* style of Bach's sons. In his *Recueil d'airs de danses caractéristiques* (Berlin: J. J. Hummel, c1777), which mixes traditional French dance style with a more forward-looking pre-Classical style, he advocated the study of keyboard DANCES to help students develop a good sense of time and rhythm. He also published instruction manuals combining theory and practice: on THOROUGHBASS (*Grundsätze des Generalbasses als erste Linien zur Composition* (Berlin, 1781)) and on vocal composition (*Anleitung zur Singekomposition* (Berlin and Leipzig, 1782)). In addition, he contributed to the debate on keyboard TEMPERAMENT (*Clavierübungen*, Part IV, 1766, and *Die Kunst des reinen Satzes*). He criticised equal temperament for its ironing out of individual KEY CHARACTERISTICS and devised three systems of unequal temperament, Kirnberger I, II and III, of which the third is still much used by harpsichordists today.

FURTHER READING

E. R. Blechschmidt, *Die Amalien-Bibliothek. Musikbibliothek der Prinzessin Anna Amalia von Preußen (1723–1787). Historische Einordnung und Katalog mit Hinweisen auf die Schreiber und Handschriften* (Berlin: Merseburger, 1965).
J. Lester, *Compositional Theory in the Eighteenth Century* (Cambridge, MA: Harvard University Press, 1992), 231–57.

RICHARD D. P. JONES

Kit (kytte, treble violin) (Flem. *creytertjes*; Fr. *poche, pochette, pochette d'amour, sourdine*; Ger. *Posch, Tanzmeistergeige, Taschengeige, Trögl-geige*; It. *canino*, *pochetto, sordina, sordino*; Lat. *linterculus*) A small bowed, unfretted VIOLIN (c42 cm long; 24.5 cm string length), generally with four strings but sometimes only three, used from the sixteenth to the nineteenth century.

Although kits were variously shaped, two basic models prevailed: one was rebec-like, either pear-shaped or resembling a narrow boat (*Linterculus*), with a vaulted back; the other resembled a miniature VIOL, violin, *mandore* or GUITAR, with a slightly arched back and long neck. The term 'kit' dates from John Rastell's *Interlude of the Four Elements* (c1517).

Four-stringed kits were generally tuned in fifths, sometimes at violin pitch; but three-stringed models were normally tuned a fourth, fifth, and occasionally even an octave higher than the violin's lowest three strings ($c'-g'-d''$ was most common). Fingerboards were long relative to the instrument in order to maximise its melodic range. The kit's soft, muted sound (hence, *sordino, sourdine*), sufficient for private settings, was due largely to its small size; but some models lacked a soundpost and/or bass-bar.

A kit was commonly employed by travelling minstrels, street musicians and especially dancing masters who taught at courts throughout Europe in the seventeenth and eighteenth centuries (hence *Tanzmeistergeige*). It fitted either in a leather case (*poche*) or in the tail-pocket (*pochette, Taschengeige*) and was withdrawn by the dancing master whenever he needed to play a melody or rhythm while teaching DANCE steps. It was played at the chest, using mainly one left-hand position, and was bowed as a violin. The instrument's repertory comprised dances, marches, popular tunes and some violin pieces. The decline of court dance in Europe in the late eighteenth century led to the instrument's gradual demise.

Surviving kits range from simple rustic instruments to those by Antonio Stradivari, who left working patterns for different types of kit, and Joachim Tielke. Some, particularly boat-shaped models, were elaborately carved or inlaid with ivory, tortoiseshell, ebony, precious stones, silver or gold.

FURTHER READING

D. D. Boyden, *The History of Violin Playing from its Origins to 1761* (London: Oxford University Press, 1965).
D. Fryklund, *Studien über die Pochette* (Sundsvall: Sahlin, 1917).
W. Salmen, *Der Tanzmeister* (Hildesheim: Olms, 1997).

ROBIN STOWELL

Klosé, Hyacinthe-Eléonore (b. Corfu, 11 October 1808; d. Paris, 29 August 1880) French clarinet player and teacher.

Klosé collaborated with Buffet *jeune* to produce a CLARINET that incorporated the ring-mechanism earlier applied by Boehm to the FLUTE. His design was exhibited in Paris in 1839, patented by Buffet in 1843 and first named 'Boehm clarinet' in the 1860s. It enables a perfect scale to be played simply by removing the fingers one by one, without the need for cross-FINGERINGS. As Hoeprich (2008) remarks, an absolute evenness of scale, perfect intonation and a lack of technical difficulties were the qualities sought after by instrument makers and clarinettists by the 1840s. The popularity of the Boehm system after well over a century and a half testifies to the logic and convenience of the new model. Today's players (outside Germany and Austria) take the instrument for granted, without necessarily recognising the design's radical nature, which lies outside the organological history of the clarinet from two-keyed to German system, with their attendant cross-fingerings.

Klosé's *Méthode pour servir à l'enseignement de la clarinette à anneaux mobiles* (Paris: Meissonnier, 1843) proved highly influential and has been reprinted, translated into several languages and revised on many occasions. Significantly, Klosé still found it necessary to advocate playing with reed against the bottom lip. He noted that this method of playing produced a more beautiful sound, allowed greater facility of ARTICULATION and was more graceful and less tiring. Hoeprich (2008) details some of Klosé's more detailed technical and musical advice, while suggesting that 'given the growing number of conservatories in Europe, clarinettists no longer needed detailed instructional material, relying instead on their teachers'. Klosé's text benefits from his experience as player and teacher. BERLIOZ heard him play in 1835 and wrote in *Le Rénovateur* that the human voice, to his taste, does not even have the softness and melancholy of the sound of his clarinet.

FURTHER READING

E. T. Hoeprich, *The Clarinet* (New Haven, CT and London: Yale University Press, 2008).
W. Waterhouse, *The New Langwill Index* (London: Tony Bingham, 1993).

COLIN LAWSON

Koch, Heinrich Christoph (b. Rudolstadt, 10 October 1749; d. Rudolstadt, 19 March 1816) German music theorist.

Although Koch is best known as a music theorist, his musical studies and subsequent career in the Hofkapelle at Rudolstadt were of a firmly practical cast, centred on the VIOLIN as well as composition. At Rudolstadt (where he had first served in 1772), Koch eventually rose to the position of *Kapellmeister* (1792), though he returned to the ranks as a violinist the following year, thereafter concentrating on his theoretical writings, which had widespread influence. Besides examples in his most famous theoretical textbook, the *Versuch einer Anleitung zur Composition* (3 vols. (Leipzig: Böhme, 1782, 1787, 1793)), none of his own compositions survive.

Koch's *Versuch* is perhaps the most comprehensive treatment of musical composition from late eighteenth-century Germany and displays wide knowledge of current repertory. Focusing extensively on both the theory and the AESTHETICS of music, his highlighting of the dynamic interdependency of melody and harmony within a musical texture arguably reflects his experience as a practitioner, and accords well with the real-time experience of a listener to a performance of music.

Koch's aesthetic framework for musical composition (heavily influenced by SULZER) proposes three stages: the initial plan (*Anlage*); its realisation (*Ausführung*); and subsequent elaboration (*Ausarbeitung*). While their sequential presentation on paper suggests artificiality, the teleology shares common ground with contemporary rhetorical understandings suggestive of a performance approach in which the score is regarded as a script whose realisation (by the player, or singer, in real time) proceeds as a creative narrative guided by the art of elaboration.

FURTHER READING

N. K. Baker, 'From "Teil" to "Tonstück": the significance of the "Versuch einer Anleitung zur Composition" by Heinrich Christoph Koch', PhD dissertation, Yale University (1975).
N. K. Baker and T. Christensen (trans. and ed.), *Aesthetics and the Art of Musical Composition in the German Enlightenment: Selected Writings of Johann G. Sulzer and Heinrich C. Koch* (Cambridge University Press, 1995).

JOHN IRVING

Kolisch, Rudolf (b. Klamm am Semmering, 20 July 1896; d. Watertown, MA, 1 August 1978) Austrian violinist, conductor and musical performance theorist.

Kolisch studied at the Vienna Musikakademie and the University of Vienna. In 1919 he began private composition studies with ARNOLD SCHOENBERG, with whom he worked closely in running the Society for Private Music Performances. In 1924 he founded the Neue Wiener Streichquartett, which by 1927 became the Kolisch Quartet, and with which he gave many first performances of new music by Schoenberg, BERG, WEBERN, BARTÓK and other important composers of the period.

As well as his many performances and recordings (which include a definitive recording of all the Schoenberg string quartets), Kolisch made an important contribution to musical performance theory through his teaching and writing. His work with the Kolisch Quartet involved close analysis of the score in REHEARSAL, and he introduced the practice of quartet playing from MEMORY. In the 1920s and 1930s he had considerable influence on the thinking of T. W. ADORNO through their long-standing discussions and correspondence on the development of a theory of musical performance. He also did research into TEMPO in BEETHOVEN's music, on which he published an influential article ('Tempo and character in Beethoven's music', *MQ*, 29/22 (1943), 169–87; 29/3 (1943), 291–312).

In 1941 he went to the USA, where he stayed for the rest of his life. He was invited to lecture at the New School in New York, returning to Europe from time to time in the late 1940s and 1950s to lead classes in the performance of contemporary music at the Darmstadt Summer School. In 1944 he became professor of music at the University of Wisconsin-Madison, and leader of the Pro Arte Quartet. Following his retirement in 1966, he taught at the New England Conservatory, Boston. The extensive papers of Rudolf Kolisch, including writings, correspondence and scores, are held in the Houghton Library at Harvard University.

FURTHER READING

T. W. Adorno, 'Kolisch und die neue Interpretation', *Musikalische Schriften VI. Gesammelte Schriften* Band 19, R. Tiedemann (ed.) (Frankfurt am Main: Suhrkamp Verlag, 1984), 460–2.
R. Kolisch, *Zur Theorie der Aufführung: Ein Gespräch mit Berthold Turcke* (Munich: Edition Text + Kritik, 1983).
A. Shreffler and D. Trippett (eds.), *Rudolf Kolisch in Amerika: Aufsätze und Dokumente*. Special edition of *Zeitschrift zur Musikwissenschaft*, 24/3 (2009).

MAX PADDISON

Koopman, Ton (b. Zwolle, 2 October 1944) Dutch solo harpsichordist, organist, conductor and founder of the Amsterdam Baroque Orchestra.

Koopman studied musicology at Amsterdam University and ORGAN with Simon Jansen and HARPSICHORD with GUSTAV LEONHARDT at the city's Sweelinck Conservatory. By the end of his studies in 1970 he had already founded a small ensemble (Musica da Camera) and a Baroque orchestra (Music Antiqua Amsterdam). He was professor of harpsichord at the Sweelinck Conservatory from 1978 to 1988, following that with ten years in the same post at the ROYAL CONSERVATORY OF THE HAGUE. He now teaches at the University of Leiden and at the ROYAL ACADEMY OF MUSIC in London.

In 1979 he formed the Amsterdam Baroque Orchestra, initially a mix of mainly English string players and Dutch and Belgian winds. With the orchestra he made recordings of Baroque and early Classical orchestral works, at first for Philips and then for the French label Erato. In 1992 he founded the Amsterdam Baroque Choir and expanded into choral repertory, recording among other things the BACH Passions (including his own realisation of the lost *St Mark Passion*), and the world premiere recording of Biber's A major Requiem. In 1994 he began a complete cycle of the Bach cantatas for Erato, completing it on his own newly founded label Challenge Classics in 2005. His career as a leading keyboard soloist has run concurrently with his CONDUCTING, and includes recordings of Bach's major harpsichord works and (for Teldec) complete organ music. All three roles came together between 2005 and 2014 in a project to record the complete works of Buxtehude, also for Challenge.

Koopman's performances as conductor and soloist are carefully shaped and lively in TEMPO and rhythmic ARTICULATION. His solo and continuo playing alike are characterised by a spontaneous and flamboyant approach to ORNAMENTATION.

LINDSAY KEMP

Kreutzer, Rodolphe (b. Versailles, 16 November 1766; d. Geneva, 6 January 1831) Violinist, composer and pedagogue.

Rodolphe Kreutzer received his early musical education from his father and Anton Stamitz (from 1778). He made an acclaimed debut at the *Concert Spirituel* in Paris (1780), performing one of Stamitz's concertos. Influenced by Viotti's style of composition and performance, Kreutzer premiered his own First Violin Concerto at the *Concert Spirituel* in 1784 and was later 'adopted' by Marie Antoinette and the Count of Artois, who probably arranged his acceptance into the King's Music (1785), eventually moving from Versailles to Paris (1789). In the capital he became associated with the *Institut National de Musique* and eventually the CONSERVATOIRE (1795), teaching there until 1826 and serving as a member of its council (1825–30). He continued touring (Italy, 1796), playing his own concertos, and made numerous appearances at Paris's Théâtre Feydeau and L'Opéra, some jointly with PIERRE RODE. He succeeded Rode as solo violinist at L'Opéra and joined Napoleon's chapel ORCHESTRA (1802) and private orchestra (1806). Kreutzer was also a partner (1802–11) in *Le Magasin de Musique*, a publishing and retail concern formed with Cherubini, Méhul, Rode, Isouard and Boieldieu. A broken arm terminated his solo career (1810), but he continued his ensemble playing and started a CONDUCTING career, directing mostly at L'Opéra.

Together with BAILLOT and Rode, Kreutzer formed the founding trinity of the French VIOLIN 'school', based on the Italian traditions disseminated by Viotti and centred at the Paris Conservatoire. Together they published the Conservatoire's first official violin treatise, *Méthode de violon* (1803), which was widely read, translated and imitated (notably by Fauré and Mazas). In two parts, details of the violin's origins and history, artistic matters and taste precede more practical considerations – violin and BOW holds, finger action, posture, bow management, specific and extempore ORNAMENTATION, bowing principles and DYNAMICS. Interestingly, no mention is made of VIBRATO, HARMONICS, or left-hand pizzicato. The second part deals exclusively with EXPRESSION and style, discussed under the headings of tone, TEMPO, style, TASTE, *aplomb* and genius of execution. Exercises and musical examples are freely incorporated, including scales in all keys (with accompaniments for a second violin by Cherubini), scales by intervals, illustrations of position-work, chromatic scales, double stopping and general finger exercises.

As a composer, Kreutzer achieved some success with his operas, ballets and chamber music, but he is remembered mostly for his nineteen violin concertos and especially his *42 études ou caprices* for violin (originally forty; the additional two, nos. 13 and 25, were added by an anonymous French reviser c1850), which appeared initially in 1796, published by the Conservatoire. His *Grande Sonate* for violin and piano probably served as a model for BEETHOVEN's 'Kreutzer' Sonata, Op. 47, which Beethoven dedicated to him without his knowledge. Kreutzer is thought never to have performed the sonata in public.

Kreutzer's numerous pupils included his brother Auguste, Charles Lafont and Joseph Lambert Massart. His letters reveal his significant role in obtaining some of the Paris Conservatoire library's early acquisitions from Italy (1796–1802) and list details not only of the works desired but also the cost of purchases and losses.

FURTHER READING

R. Macnutt, 'Early acquisitions for the Paris Conservatoire Library: Rodolphe Kreutzer's role in obtaining materials from Italy', in D. Hunter (ed.), *Music Publishing and Collecting: Essays in Honor of Donald W. Krummel* (Urbana, IL: Graduate School of Library and Information Science, University of Illinois at Urbana-Champaign, 1994), 167–88.

R. Stowell, *Violin Technique and Performance Practice in the Late Eighteenth and Early Nineteenth Centuries* (Cambridge University Press, 1985).

M. R. Williams, 'The violin concertos of Rodolphe Kreutzer', PhD dissertation, Indiana University (1973).

ROBIN STOWELL

Kuijken brothers

Wieland (b. Dilbeek, nr Brussels, 31 August 1938) VIOL player and cellist.

Sigiswald (b. Dilbeek, nr Brussels, 16 February 1944) Violinist, viol player, *violoncello da spalla* player and conductor.

Barthold (b. Dilbeek, nr Brussels, 8 March 1949) Flautist and RECORDER player. Influential pioneers of historical performance.

The Kuijken brothers are all self-taught, which underpins their open-minded musical approach: one of curiosity, imagination, self-examination and deeply felt EXPRESSION. Barthold explains: 'You learn from your mistakes in a totally different way than when your teacher tells you: "better do it this way because that way doesn't work". So I can recommend it to everyone' (D. Brüggen, *Early Music Icons: Barthold, Sigiswald and Wieland Kuijken*, MusicFrame Films, 2014). Wieland and Sigiswald started by playing 'little fiddles' together and stress the importance of this experience in their musical development. At fifteen Wieland studied CELLO and PIANO full time at the Bruges Conservatoire; he then studied at the Brussels Conservatoire (1957–62). In 1956 he discovered and taught himself the viol. Sigiswald studied the VIOLIN at the Bruges Conservatoire from the age of eight and then at the Brussels Conservatoire (1960–4). He taught himself the Baroque violin, realising that it required a completely new hold to make seventeenth-century music come to life. Both brothers played with the groundbreaking Alarius Ensemble of Brussels – Sigiswald performing on viol as well as the violin – with Janine Rubinlicht and Robert Kohnen, giving them a busy concert and recording schedule until 1972. In 1965 the two brothers played to GUSTAV LEONHARDT. Sigiswald describes it as: 'a kind of "holy moment". He [Leonhardt] was dumbfounded: two unknown boys playing Marais' (Brüggen, 2014). This led to concerts with Leonhardt, and BRÜGGEN asked them to join a RECORDER and viol CONSORT. Wieland and Sigiswald both recorded BACH sonatas with Leonhardt and the three of them made a landmark recording of MARAIS and Forqueray, 'Musique à Versailles', as well as RAMEAU's *Pièces de clavecin en concerts* (rec. 1971) with Brüggen. Barthold studied at the conservatories of Bruges, Brussels and The Hague, including the recorder with Brüggen; but he is self-taught on the Baroque FLUTE. When he found an eighteenth-century instrument it made 'total sense' of the music (Brüggen, 2014). The three brothers with either Leonhardt or Kohnen toured the world together to great acclaim.

In 1972, Sigiswald founded the Baroque orchestra LA PETITE BANDE, which includes Barthold and Wieland. In 2004 he began to re-introduce the *violoncello da spalla*. He strongly debates whether J. S. BACH's Cello Suites (BWV1007–12) were intended for the instrument that today we call the Baroque CELLO, played da gamba. He has persuasive local evidence in Bach's cousin, J. G. WALTHER: 'The Violoncello is an Italian bass instrument ... which is played almost like a violin, namely it is partly held and played with the left hand and partly, because of its weight, hung from a button on the jacket, and bowed with the right hand' (*Praecepta* (Weimar, 1708), 161). MATTHESON commends the da spalla for its excellent ability to play rapidly. Sigiswald finds that 'the use of three violoncelli *da spalla* in Brandenburg No. 3, along with the 8′ violone, is particularly refreshing' (S. Kuijken, 269). In 2006/7 he recorded Bach's Cello Suites on the *violoncello da spalla*, using copies of an instrument by a contemporary of Bach, Johann Christian Hoffmann of Leipzig.

FURTHER READING

B. Kuijken, *The Notation is Not the Music: Reflections on Early Music Practices and Performance* (Bloomington, IN: Indiana University Press, 2013).
S. Kuijken, 'A Bach odyssey', *EMc*, 38/2 (2012), 263–72.
    'Wieland Kuijken and Christopher Hogwood on the viol' (trans., ed. and annotated L. Robinson), *EMc*, 6/1 (1978), 4–11.

LUCY ROBINSON

Kullak, Adolph (b. Meseritz, 23 February 1823; d. Berlin, 25 December 1862) German pianist and writer.

Kullak's elder brother Theodor gained greater renown as a pianist, composer and pedagogue. Adolph's most significant work – indeed the only one of influence – is *Die Ästhetik des Klavierspiels* (*The Aesthetics of Piano Playing* (Berlin: Guttentag, 1860)), although *Das Musikalisch-Schöne, ein Beitrag zur Ästhetik der Tonkunst* (*The Beautiful in Music, A Contribution to the Aesthetics of Composition*) is occasionally cited in discussions of nineteenth-century musical philosophy. The *Aesthetics of Piano Playing* enjoyed considerable popularity in the late nineteenth and early twentieth centuries, going through no fewer than eight EDITIONS, all of them heavily revised by subsequent editors. Owing to Adolph Kullak's early death, the first major expansion of his work was undertaken in 1876 by Theodor Kullak's pupil Hans Bischoff, with a further revision by Bischoff in 1889. The last of these formed the basis of an English translation by Theodore Baker in 1893. Yet more extensive revision and updating of the German edition were undertaken by Walter Niemann in 1906, 1916 and 1920. The result is that what is often regarded today as Kullak's *Aesthetics* is almost as much the work of Bischoff and Niemann as it is of the initial author, but the partially groundbreaking nature of the original edition lay in the attempt to produce a comprehensive PIANO TREATISE growing from aesthetic principles grounded in the history of piano music, rather than starting with foundational technique and exercises. It was this strategy that necessitated regular updating as the piano repertoire changed. It could be argued that both CZERNY's *Grand Piano-School*, Op. 500 and MOSCHELES and FÉTIS's *Method of Methods* (Paris: Schlesinger, 1840) had already adopted elements of this approach, but there is no doubt that the Kullak *Aesthetics* achieved wider resonance, at least in German-speaking lands.

KENNETH HAMILTON

Kürzinger, Ignaz Franz Xaver (b. Rosenheim, Upper Bavaria, 30 January 1724; d. Würzburg, 12 August 1797) Trumpeter, violinist, *Kapellmeister* and composer.

Little of Kürzinger's *oeuvre* has survived, but his vocal/VIOLIN TREATISE, *Getreuer Unterricht zum Singen mit Manieren, und die Violin zu spielen* (Augsburg, 1763), has been preserved. A fundamental question/answer musical instruction manual, it appeared in numerous editions (fifth edition, 1821); its violin instruction is elementary, but its examples of vocal ORNAMENTATION are informative.

FURTHER READING

O. Kaul, *Geschichte der Würzburger Hofmusik im 18. Jahrhundert* (Würzburg: Becker, 1924).

ROBIN STOWELL

L

L'Abbé le fils [Joseph-Barnabé Saint-Sevin] (b. Agen, 11 June 1727; d. Paris, 25 July 1803) French violinist and composer.

A pupil of Leclair (1740–2), L'Abbé worked in the Paris Opéra Orchestra for twenty years; he made his debut at the *Concert Spirituel* in 1741, performing a VIOLIN duo with Pierre Gaviniès. Several further solo performances at the *Concert Spirituel* until 1754 established him as one of the finest violinists of the mid-eighteenth century. His Violin Sonatas Opp. 1 and 8 are modelled on Leclair's sonatas; two movements of the Op. 8 sonatas are notable for their fully written-out CADENZAS. His symphonies were among the earliest to appear in Paris, and his collections of 'Airs' illustrate changing Parisian tastes after the *Querelle des Bouffons*.

L'Abbé's most celebrated publication was his *Principes du violon* (1761). This significant violin method amalgamates the Italian sonata tradition, as represented by its numerous lessons 'in the manner of sonatas', with the French dance tradition, as manifested in its various *Menuets, Airs* and *Rondeaux* and in the two suites of opera airs, which also include dances, in the form of advanced duets for two violins. Music predominates over text in its eighty-one pages such that L'Abbé's violin instruction is scarcely comprehensive and comprises a somewhat ad hoc mixture of ideas lacking in systematic order; but it is progressive on many counts.

L'Abbé was the first to recommend what is essentially the modern method of holding the violin, placing the chin on the left (G string) side of the tailpiece and lowering slightly the E string side of the instrument. He annotates many of his short exercises and pieces with FINGERINGS and often indicates where shifts are to be executed, marking a downward shift with the letter 'D' (an abbreviation for 'descendre la main') under the note and either the word 'monter' or an obvious fingering for an upward shift. He was also the first writer to categorise the use of half position, his abbreviation 'R' indicating that the player should 'move the hand back close to the nut' and use 'borrowed fingers... to stop notes other than those they normally stop'; and he was the first French writer to discuss fully the technique of double stopping, appreciating the roles of both left and right hands in its execution and outstripping LEOPOLD MOZART's 1756 survey. His TREATISE also includes useful advice regarding left-hand extensions and ORNAMENTATION; and, building on Mondonville's prefatory essay to *Les sons harmoniques* (1738), he incorporates natural and artificial HARMONICS, trills in harmonics and harmonics in double stopping in his instruction; he even includes a *Menuet* to be played entirely in harmonics.

L'Abbé calls the BOW 'the soul of the instrument it touches, as it is used to give expression to the sounds, sustain them, swell and diminish them' and he recommends a bow-hold which foreshadows modern concepts, placing the hand at the frog and not slightly above it as GEMINIANI and Leopold Mozart had advised. His advice for bow management is also advanced, requiring pronation of the wrist, instinctive 'imperceptible movements' of the fingers and a slight inclination of the bow towards the fingerboard, a ploy previously discouraged by Leopold Mozart.

FURTHER READING

D. D. Boyden, *The History of Violin Playing from its Origins to 1761* (London: Oxford University Press, 1965).
L'Abbé le fils: Principes du violon (Paris: Centre de Documentation Universitaire, 1961) [facsim. repr. ed. A. Wirsta, with preface by J. Chailley, avant-propos by E. Borrel, and introduction by A. Wirsta].
R. Stowell, *Violin Technique and Performance Practice in the Late Eighteenth and Early Nineteenth Centuries* (Cambridge University Press, 1985).

ROBIN STOWELL

La Borde (or Laborde), Jean Benjamin de (b. Paris, 5 September 1734; d. Paris, 22 July 1794) French composer and writer on music.

La Borde, a First Valet serving Louis XV, was a writer, musician, lover of the dancer Mlle Guimard, later a tax farmer and husband of Adélaïde de Vismes, sister of Jacques de Vismes, director of the Paris Opéra (1778–80). Laborde's many operatic works in various genres were performed at Court and in Paris with modest success.

His anonymous *Essai sur la musique ancienne et moderne* (4 vols. (Paris: Onfroy, 1780)) is an ambitious, intelligent mixture of compilation and original writing, much more an encyclopedia than an essay, handsomely illustrated, with six books devoted respectively to music in different cultures, musical instruments, composition (with engraved examples), a dictionary of lyric poets and song writers, numerous separate dictionaries (composers, poets, musicians, theorists, in Greece, Rome, Italy, France), and diverse matters. Admiration for RAMEAU and Piccinni is evident, Gluck's presence is minimal and ROUSSEAU's views on music are persistently criticised.

The *Essai* has significant historical and documentary value. Book II gives detailed descriptions of orchestral and other instruments, with engravings generally showing instruments in the hands of musicians. The *Essai* also includes thirty pages of scores by Claude Le Jeune, Orlande de Lassus and Charles d'Helfer (Book III), thirty pages of twelfth-century songs by Le Châtelain de Coucy (Book IV (but with few scores)), and 170 pages of four-part settings of old and new French songs, Parisian and rustic. Its dictionaries include entries for MONTEVERDI and Cavalli, who were evidently unknown to Rousseau. The whole reflects a substantial expansion of historical knowledge and musical curiosity (ancient, rustic, exotic music and instruments).

FURTHER READING

M. Couty, *Jean-Benjamin de Laborde, ou le bonheur d'être fermier-général* (Paris: Michel de Maule, 2001).

P. Vendrix, *A l'origine d'une discipline historique. La musique et son histoire en France aux XVIIe et XVIIIe siècles*. Bibliothèque de la Faculté de Philosophie et Lettres de l'Université de Liège No. 260 (Geneva: Droz, 1993).

MICHAEL O'DEA

L'Affilard, Michel (b. c1656; d. Versailles, ?April 1708) French composer, singer and writer.

L'Affilard's *Principes très-faciles pour bien apprendre la musique* was revised five times between 1694 and 1705. The final EDITION was reprinted until 1747. Beyond elementary pedagogical concerns, the TREATISE contains complete airs and dances intended for advanced instrumental and vocal performance. Although each edition offers instrumentalists useful exemplars of French ORNAMENTATION and stylistic conventions, L'Affilard weighted his final edition more towards vocal repertoire with BASSO CONTINUO.

The fifth edition prints numerical indications intended for LOULIÉ's simple tempo-pendulum, the *chronomètre*. Although twentieth-century scholarship has tended to treat this rarified data with an authority usually reserved for composers' modern METRONOME markings, perhaps more illuminating to historical performance practices are L'Affilard's indications about rhythmo-poetic delivery, metric emphasis and time-beating techniques. His instructions suggest a varied range of movements, GESTURES and expressive characteristics for French airs and dances that individual *chronomètre* indications fail to impart.

FURTHER READING

M. L'Affilard, *Principes très-faciles pour bien apprendre la musique* (Paris: Ballard, 1694; 5th edn, 1705).

E. Loulié, *Eléments ou principes de musique* (Paris: Ballard, 1696; Amsterdam: Roger, 1698).

J. Sauveur, *Principes d'acoustique et de musique ou système général des intervalles des sons* (Paris: Académie Royal des Sciences, 1701).

ALEXANDER EVAN BONUS

Lalandi, Lina (b. Athens, 13 July 1920; d. ?London, 8 June 2012) Greek harpsichordist and singer, and founding director of the English Bach Festival.

After initial studies in Athens, Lalandi took HARPSICHORD and voice lessons in London and made her debut at the Royal Festival Hall in 1954. She appeared as a soloist in Paris, Geneva and Athens as a particular advocate of J. S. BACH and FRANÇOIS COUPERIN. In 1963 she founded the English Bach Festival, based first in Oxford and then in London. She was director and chief administrator, and also responsible for research and programme planning. Initially conceived to promote HISTORICALLY INFORMED PERFORMANCES of the Bach family, the Festival was visited by specialists such as Rilling and Karl Richter and (after the full emergence of period orchestras) LEONHARDT and HARNONCOURT, as well as GARDINER, HERREWEGHE, KOOPMAN, NORRINGTON and PINNOCK. In the late 1970s and 1980s, Lalandi formed her own ensembles to promote the fruits of her researches into Baroque opera and DANCE, resulting in extravagant productions such as rarely staged RAMEAU at the Royal Opera House, which then transferred to other European capitals. Earlier, in the 1960s, she had persuaded STRAVINSKY, Bernstein, Xenakis, Messiaen, STOCKHAUSEN and other eminent musicians to come to Britain, many for the first time. In *The Guardian* obituary (8 July 2012), NICHOLAS KENYON remarked, 'For all the chaos, working with her was immense fun; for all the complications, it was artistically wholly worth it; and for all that she was infuriatingly volatile and unpredictable, we all owe her a massively inspiring musical education. She opened our ears.'

COLIN LAWSON

Landowska, Wanda (b. Warsaw, 5 July 1879; d. Lakeville, CT, 16 August, 1959) Polish harpsichordist, pedagogue and writer.

Landowska was a hugely influential pioneer in the revival of early music, and especially of the HARPSICHORD. She performed on the harpsichord in public from 1903 (initially as an aside to the PIANO) after marrying and moving to Paris, but it was only in 1912 that she first acquired a large double-manual Pleyel harpsichord. Although this example was inspired by original instruments, Landowska demanded a 16′ register as a counterpart to the 4′ register. She was encouraged to champion the harpsichord by Fauré, Dukas and Schweitzer and she toured extensively. She moved to Berlin in 1913, returning to Paris as a widow after WWI. A collection of original instruments was assembled at her home at Saint-Leu-La-Forêt, a few miles north of Paris. She was forced to abandon the place in WWII and moved to America (1941), eventually settling in Lakeville, Connecticut in 1947.

Widely read, Landowska compiled numerous documents to write a book and was an early evangelist for HISTORICALLY INFORMED PERFORMANCE. She adopted a combative stance at the outset of her writing career, in which she railed against the then common assumption that the history of music was a continuous Darwinian development. She emphasised the importance of TASTE over 'the vain pride of progress' (Restout, 41), stating that 'Innovation in itself is of little interest' (Restout, 59). In 1909 her much-awaited book *Musique Ancienne* (Paris: Senart, 1909) created a sensation. Thereafter her writings developed specific issues on interpretation such as the French influence on the music of J. S. BACH and his compatriots.

Her many recordings include J. S. Bach's *Goldberg Variations* (1933) and *The Well-Tempered Clavier* (1954). Although her Pleyel harpsichords now sound inappropriate in Baroque repertory and her use of RUBATO somewhat extreme, her performances consistently demonstrate a compelling personal conviction. Landowska also championed the harpsichord in contemporary music, proving an inspiration to composers such as de Falla and Poulenc.

FURTHER READING

D. Restout (ed. and trans.) with R. Hawkins, *Landowska on Music* (New York: Stein and Day, 1969).

JULIAN PERKINS

La Petite Bande An orchestra of internationally renowned specialists in historical performance founded by SIGISWALD KUIJKEN in 1972.

La Petite Bande takes its name from the élite group of string players brought to fame by LULLY at the court of Louis XIV in the late 1650s. It was formed at the request of Harmonia Mundi (Germany) specifically to record Lully's *Le bourgeois gentilhomme* directed by GUSTAV LEONHARDT. Released in 1973, this recording was followed by one of Campra's *L'Europe galante* and, under the direction of Kuijken, music by MUFFAT and CORELLI's Op. 6 concerti grossi. RAMEAU's *Zais* was released in 1978. The ensemble's successful recordings led to concert tours throughout the world. In 2013 the Flemish government withdrew its support for the orchestra but the group has been sustained through private donations and benefit concerts. In 2014 the eighteen-CD series of 'Cantatas of J. S. Bach' was completed, using a vocal quartet and light instrumental scoring. With the ensemble's future in mind, Kuijken has intentionally cultivated a blend of youth and experience in its personnel and appointed the French harpsichordist and organist Benjamin Alard (b. 1985) to assist in its direction.

LUCY ROBINSON

Lawson, Colin (b. Saltburn-by-the-Sea, N. Yorkshire, 24 July 1949) English player of early and modern clarinets, academic, broadcaster, administrator and pedagogue.

Lawson learned both CLARINET and PIANO as a child, and played with the National Youth Orchestra of Great Britain during his teenage years. After reading music at Keble College, Oxford, he was awarded an MA from the University of Birmingham in 1972 for a study of the clarinet in eighteenth-century repertoire. Lawson's doctoral research into the chalumeau was completed in 1976 concurrently with his first academic position at the University of Aberdeen. After twenty years at the University of Sheffield, Lawson became chair of performance studies at Goldsmiths College, University of London in 1998. From 2001 to 2005 he was pro-vice chancellor and dean of the then London College of Music & Media at Thames Valley University (now the University of West London). In July 2005 Lawson became the tenth director of London's ROYAL COLLEGE OF MUSIC, where he holds a personal chair in historical performance.

As one of the foremost post-war exponents of historical woodwind performance and also a leading commentator on the historical performance movement, Lawson has established an international reputation through the symbiosis of his activities across both practice and theory. Maintaining an active performing career alongside academic positions has enabled him to exert a truly profound influence on historical performance. A principal player with leading UK ensembles, including THE ENGLISH CONCERT, THE HANOVER BAND, London Classical Players and ORCHESTRA OF THE AGE OF ENLIGHTENMENT, as well as making regular chamber music appearances, Lawson's concert and recording activities began during the historical performance movement's heyday in the 1980s and 1990s. Benchmark solo recordings include the concertos of WOLFGANG AMADEUS MOZART (1990), Fasch (1996) as well as LOUIS SPOHR and Weber (1998), and amongst chamber repertoire Lawson's CDs of music for BASSET HORNS by Mozart and ANTON STADLER are acclaimed.

Hallmarks of Lawson's research are an understanding of the necessity to prioritise context, together with an approach combining the scholar's insatiable curiosity with the pragmatism and expediency of a skilled practitioner mindful of the evanescence of sound. Early publications concern the CHALUMEAU and performance practices associated with the clarinet's formative years, and

Lawson's first monograph *The Chalumeau in Eighteenth-Century Music* (Ann Arbor, MI: UMI, 1981) remains the most extensive study of that instrument and its repertoire. The work has proven a particularly fertile resource for Lawson himself and subsequent generations to utilise the evidence of history and bring this little-known instrument to life. Other publications include studies of Mozart's Clarinet Concerto (1996) and Brahms's Clarinet Quintet (1998) for Cambridge University Press, combining Lawson's intimate experience of this repertoire across modern and historical instruments with his detailed knowledge of primary and secondary sources. His academic partnership with ROBIN STOWELL began in the 1990s, since when Lawson and Stowell have significantly influenced the discourse around historical performance, particularly through their series of Cambridge Handbooks to the Historical Performance of Music.

INGRID E. PEARSON

Le Blanc (Leblanc), Hubert (d. ?1728) French doctor of law, abbé and amateur VIOL player.

Leblanc's *Défense de la basse de viole contre les entreprises du violon et les prétentions du violoncel* (sic) (Amsterdam, 1740) is significant for his descriptions of early eighteenth-century Parisian musical TASTE and performing practices. It compares French *pièces* and Italian sonatas, favours the delicacy and chordal playing potential of the viol over the VIOLIN, which is more suited to large halls and higher PITCH, and advises about viol tuning, FINGERING and shifting. It also describes MARAIS's six different BOW strokes and 'imperceptible' bow changes, and makes observations about GEMINIANI, Guignon and other violinists.

FURTHER READING

B. G. Jackson, 'Hubert Le Blanc's *Défense de la viole*', *JVdGSA*, 10 (1973), 11–28, 69–80; 11 (1974), 17–58; 12 (1975), 14–36 [Trans. and commentary].

ROBIN STOWELL

Leech-Wilkinson, Daniel (b. Bath, England, 21 October 1954) British musicologist.

Leech-Wilkinson was educated at the ROYAL COLLEGE OF MUSIC, where he studied composition, HARPSICHORD and ORGAN, King's College London and Cambridge University. He then held several academic appointments, primarily at Southampton University and King's College London, where he was appointed professor of music in 2004.

He has made many important contributions to the understanding of performing practice and has been a leading figure in research into Medieval music. Much of this research has been focused on the works of MACHAUT, but he has also demonstrated a broader scope of interest in the period, notably in his *The Modern Invention of Medieval Music* (Cambridge, 2002), which won a prestigious Royal Philharmonic Society award. This book contains a detailed assessment of how Medieval music has been studied and performed and the TASTES and ideologies that such work has stimulated. It has been central to debates about how modern attitudes to this music have been formed.

Leech-Wilkinson's interest in musical performance has also been directed at later historical periods through innovative research into recorded music and the processes performers use to give music shape. He was a prominent member of the group of scholars engaged in the CHARM (Centre for the History and Analysis of Recorded Music) project, and subsequently in the Centre for Musical Performance as Creative Practice (CMPCP). His work has led to insightful and often definitive publications on performance practice topics such as PORTAMENTO (*JRM*, 25/3–4 (2006), 233–61) and several important contributions on the evidence about performance that emerges from early recordings of Schubert's songs.

Leech-Wilkinson's published work is consistently well regarded by performers as well as scholars and is characterised by rigorous primary source research and carefully applied methodologies.

TREVOR HERBERT

Lefèvre, Jean Xavier (b. Lausanne, 6 March 1763; d. Paris, 9. November 1829) Swiss-born French clarinettist and teacher.

Lefèvre studied the CLARINET with Michael Yost in Paris. He played in L'Opéra Orchestra from 1791 to 1817 and was principal clarinet at the Imperial Chapel from 1807. He taught at the PARIS CONSERVATOIRE from its foundation in 1795 until 1824. A highly successful player and teacher, many of his pupils (who included Boufil and Crusell) won first prizes. A prolific composer of concertos and chamber music for his own instrument, Lefèvre is now best remembered for his *Méthode de clarinette* (Paris: Imprimerie du Conservatoire de Musique, 1802), which was reprinted and translated well into the twentieth century. Lefèvre's text dilutes an old-style philosophical approach with sound practical advice. His illustrations and FINGERING charts show that the clarinet was played with the reed against the top lip, a technique officially abandoned at the Conservatoire only in 1831. He includes instruction on posture, holding the clarinet and finger placement. Lefèvre found good cane for reeds difficult to acquire, remarking that cane tended to be cut too green or dry. His detailed list of out-of-tune notes on the clarinet, which needed correcting by means of the embouchure, is important evidence in today's ongoing debate about the INTONATION of Classical wind players. He seems all too realistic about the clarinet's shortcomings and perhaps over-optimistic about the manner in which they might be overcome. Significantly, he stated that performance becomes monotonous without attention to nuance and ARTICULATION, emphasising the importance of sound musical TASTE and a good knowledge of harmony. Recommending players to listen to the best singers, he prioritised musical character, noting that it was not sufficient merely to read the music and play the notes. The coldness and monotony often ascribed to the clarinet was in fact the responsibility of the performer.

FURTHER READING

C. Lawson, 'Lefèvre's *Méthode de clarinette* (1802): the Paris Conservatoire at work', in M. E. Cross and D. Williams (eds.), *The French Experience from Republic to Monarchy, 1792–1824: New Dawns in Politics, Knowledge and Culture* (Basingstoke: Palgrave, 2000), 140–54.

COLIN LAWSON

Lenton, John (? bap. London, 4 March 1657; d. London, ? May 1719) English violinist, singer and composer.

Lenton became a member of Charles II's Twenty-Four Violins in 1681 and of the Chapel Royal in 1685. He remained a member of the royal band at least until 1718 but spent much of his time in theatrical circles from c1688. His compositions include several suites for the court or the theatre.

Lenton's *The Gentleman's Diversion* (1693) is believed to be the earliest extant VIOLIN TREATISE and the model for later tutors such as *Nolens volens* (Anon. (London: T. Cross, 1695)), from which many instruction books were derived. Known from a single, incomplete copy, it was intended for amateurs and beginners and deals only with the fundamentals of music NOTATION, ORNAMENTS and violin technique. Lenton opts largely for French over Italian techniques, proposing positioning the violin 'something higher than your Breast' and using a thumb-under-hair bow hold. He prescribes no general BOWING principles, claiming that these vary considerably amongst teachers, but he subscribes to the rule of the down-bow, illustrating its application in several examples, some of which were imitated in *Nolens volens*.

Instead of concluding with the normal selection of popular tunes, Lenton's treatise terminates with twenty-eight 'Easie Lessons', pieces by Lenton himself and fourteen of his contemporaries, most of whom were colleagues in his circle. Presented in table-book format and thus performable by two players facing each other, twenty-three of these 'lessons' are for violin and bass (probably bass VIOL or CELLO) and five (Nos. 23–7) are for two violins. Most are in binary form, but No. 18 is a ground and No. 26 is a canon at the unison. Nos. 1 and 2, composed by 'M^r. P', have attracted interest for their possible attribution to Henry Purcell, with whom Lenton was doubtless well acquainted; however, their style barely supports such an attribution. The concluding 'lesson', by the Italian violinist NICOLA MATTEIS, is the most advanced and idiomatic for the instrument.

FURTHER READING

M. Boyd and J. Rayson, '*The Gentleman's Diversion*: John Lenton and the first violin tutor', *EMc*, 10/3 (1982), 329–32.

P. Holman, *Four and Twenty Fiddlers: The Violin at the English Court 1540–1690* (Oxford University Press, 1993).

C. Sharpe, 'A re-evaluation of English violin tutors published in the late 17th and early 18th centuries', MMus dissertation, University of Birmingham (1991).

ROBIN STOWELL

Leonhardt, Gustav (b. 's-Graveland, 30 May 1928; d. Amsterdam, 16 January 2012) Dutch solo harpsichordist, organist and conductor.

Leonhardt studied at the SCHOLA CANTORUM BASILIENSIS and in Vienna, before making his debut as a solo harpsichordist in 1950. His first recording (1954) was of English Tudor and Jacobean music with ALFRED DELLER, Desmond Dupré (lute) and a quartet of VIOLS that included himself and NIKOLAUS HARNONCOURT; in 1955 he founded the Leonhardt Consort, a Baroque ensemble of period instruments that was among the first of its kind.

Leonhardt's career as a recitalist was both extensive and long-lasting, extending to within a few weeks of his death. He was recognised as a major interpreter of J. S. BACH, recording all that composer's major HARPSICHORD works, but his repertoire ranged widely across the Baroque period, and performances of important but then lesser-known seventeenth-century keyboard composers such as FRESCOBALDI, Froberger and LOUIS COUPERIN were also influential. Almost from the start he was one of the first to take an interest in the sound of original harpsichords, or faithful copies of them, rather than those of hybrid 'modern' design. Although his manner could seem reserved, his playing carried great authority, while its musicality came from a considered but subtle approach to touch, ARTICULATION, RUBATO and graceful ORNAMENTATION.

Leonhardt collaborated with many of the pioneers of the early music movement, including FRANS BRÜGGEN, ANNER BYLSMA, JAAP SCHRÖDER and the KUIJKEN brothers, and with the Leonhardt Consort (led by his violinist wife Marie) he made one-to-a-part recordings of the Bach harpsichord concertos. In 1971 the Consort joined Telefunken's nineteen-year project to record the complete church cantatas of Bach, sharing it with Nikolaus Harnoncourt's CONCENTUS MUSICUS WIEN. As a conductor he worked with LA PETITE BANDE (recording the Bach Passions with them in the late 1980s) and the ORCHESTRA OF THE AGE OF ENLIGHTENMENT, among others.

A much sought-after teacher, principally at the Amsterdam Conservatory from 1954 to 1988, Leonhardt can be counted not only as a major figure in the early music movement but also as the most influential harpsichordist of the second half of the twentieth century.

LINDSAY KEMP

Leppard, Raymond (b. London, 11 August 1927) British conductor.

After studying music at Cambridge, Leppard made his debut as a conductor in London in 1952, and, while not setting out to be a specialist, quickly established a reputation as a stylish interpreter of Baroque orchestral repertoire and a free-spirited continuo harpsichordist. In the 1950s he worked frequently with the Goldsbrough Orchestra in both roles, continuing the association when that ensemble became the English Chamber Orchestra in 1960. In opera, too, he gravitated towards the Baroque, making his debuts at Covent Garden in 1959 in Handel's *Samson*, Glyndebourne in 1962 in MONTEVERDI's *L'incoronazione di Poppea*, and Sadler's Wells in 1965 in *L'Orfeo*. He himself had edited *Poppea* for the Glyndebourne production, thus instigating a series of revivals through the 1960s of seventeenth-century operas based on his own editions, both at Glyndebourne and elsewhere. These revivals included all the Monteverdi operas as well as works by Cavalli (notably *L'Ormindo* and *La Calisto*) which did much to re-establish that composer in the repertory. Some of these EDITIONS were published and used by Leppard elsewhere and by other conductors, but they had largely fallen out of favour by the 1980s, when attitudes had hardened towards his liberal approach to the texts (he often made substantial cuts, additions and transpositions). For his part, Leppard has been critical of the whole idea of 'AUTHENTICITY', articulating his thoughts in his first book *Authenticity in Music* in 1988, and never embraced the use of period instruments. His later busy CONDUCTING career – which has included posts with the BBC Northern Symphony Orchestra and the Indianapolis Symphony Orchestra – has largely been in later repertory, yet his recorded Baroque legacy remains substantial, extending from Monteverdi to BACH, Handel and RAMEAU and revealing a conductor with a keen sense of beauty, colour and rhythmic definition as well as a strong appreciation of the power of music drama.

FURTHER READING

R. Leppard, *Authenticity in Music* (London: Faber & Faber, 1988).
T. P. Lewis (ed.), *Raymond Leppard on Music: An Anthology of Critical and Personal Writings* (New York: Pro/Am Music Resources Inc., 1993).

LINDSAY KEMP

Les Arts Florissants Influential French ensemble of voices and instruments, founded in 1979 by WILLIAM CHRISTIE.

Although this ensemble has performed Baroque sacred and secular works from England and France, it is most closely associated with French music, especially by RAMEAU, LULLY and CHARPENTIER, from one of whose works it takes its name. Its performances are characterised by a sensitive approach to language, strong dramatic input and an overall beauty of sound. It has taken part in a number of staged operas, including an admired production of Lully's *Atys* in New York in 1987. Singers to have been members include Agnès Mellon, Jill Feldman, Guillemette Laurens, Dominique Visse, Véronique Gens, Sandrine Piau, Patricia Petibon, Sophie Daneman, Mark Padmore, Jean-Paul Fouchécourt and Lorraine Hunt Lieberson, whilst instrumentalists who have gone on to form their own ensembles include the harpsichordists Christophe Rousset and Emmanuelle Haïm. Tenor Paul Agnew became the group's associate director in 2013.

LINDSAY KEMP

Leschetizky, Theodor (b. Łańcut, 22 June 1830; d. Dresden, 14 November 1915) Polish pianist, teacher and composer.

Leschetizky was undoubtedly the most celebrated PIANO pedagogue of the generation after Liszt. Himself a pupil of BEETHOVEN's student CARL CZERNY in Vienna, Leschetizky first performed as a child prodigy and thereafter enjoyed for some years a respectable, if hardly stellar, career as a concert pianist and teacher. Although he was an expressive player, his refined technique lacked the demonic intensity of pianists such as Anton Rubinstein, who – according to Moriz Rosenthal – almost completely drowned Leschetizky out when playing piano duets. Nevertheless, Rubinstein admired Leschetizky's pedagogical gifts enough to invite him to Russia in 1852, initially as a court piano teacher, but from 1862 to 1877 as head of the piano department at the newly founded St Petersburg Conservatory.

On returning to Vienna in 1878, Leschetizky set up a private piano studio, which gained international renown in the wake of the developing fame of Ignacy Paderewski (1860–1941), who studied with him from 1884, and who subsequently gave his teacher generous credit for his success. Paderewski was the most famous of a host of remarkable students, including Artur Schnabel, Elly Ney, Mark Hambourg, Ossip Gabrilovitsch and Benno Moiseiwitsch. In later years, Leschetizky confined his own teaching to advanced students, employing assistants to nurture the more elementary players. Of a notoriously caustic, choleric and impatient disposition, Leschetizky himself never wrote a TREATISE, but authorised two by his assistants. The most comprehensive of these is Malwine Brée's *Die Grundlage der Methode Leschetizky* (*The Groundwork of the Leschetizky Method* (Mainz: Schott, 1902)). This, and even more the twelve piano rolls Leschetizky recorded in 1906, show how closely Paderewski modelled elements of his style on that of his teacher, including copious arpeggiation, dislocation between the hands, and a liberal use of RUBATO. These aspects were common currency in nineteenth-century performance practice, as was Leschetizky's insistence on the primacy of a 'singing' tone at the keyboard.

FURTHER READING

E. Newcomb, *Leschetizky as I Knew Him* (New York: Appleton, 1921).
I. J. Paderewski, *The Paderewski Memoirs* (New York: Scribners, 1938).

KENNETH HAMILTON

Les Siècles French period-instrument orchestra.

Since its foundation in 2003 by the conductor François-Xavier Roth (b. 1971), Les Siècles has specialised in performances of music from the eighteenth to the twentieth centuries, using the instruments appropriate to each work. Its work has included a number of imaginative projects: SAINT-SAËNS's 'Organ' Symphony (No. 3) was recorded in Saint-Sulpice (with Daniel Roth, François-Xavier's father, as the organ soloist), Offenbach's *Les brigands* was filmed at the Opéra-Comique using not only period instruments but also ORCHESTRAL PLACEMENT from the composer's time (familiar from some of Degas's paintings of opera house interiors), with the VIOLINS at the back of the pit, the wind and brass at the front, playing towards the stage, and the conductor in the middle.

To mark the centenary of STRAVINSKY's *Firebird* in 2010, Roth and Les Siècles performed the work on instruments of the period – including narrow-bore French TRUMPETS and TROMBONES – and gave it alongside *Les orientales*, the collection of dances included in the programme of the first performance. Subsequently Roth and his players released a scrupulously researched and musically exciting coupling of Stravinsky's *Petrushka* and *The Rite of Spring*. Other projects have included Debussy's *La mer* and the first performance of the newly discovered *Première suite d'orchestre*, Dukas's *L'apprenti sorcier* (coupled with his Prix de Rome cantata *Velléda* and the overture *Polyeucte*), works by French composers inspired by Spain (including Debussy's *Ibéria*, Chabrier's *España*, Ravel's *Alborada del gracioso*), music by Liszt and Théodore Dubois, and BERLIOZ's *Symphonie fantastique*. These have been released on disc by Actes Sud in performances recorded live, a process Roth prefers.

Roth and Les Siècles devised *Presto!*, a television series that ran for three seasons on France 2, starting in 2007, featuring HISTORICALLY INFORMED PERFORMANCES of a large repertory ranging from BACH to Bernstein. It attracted weekly AUDIENCES of more than three million viewers.

NIGEL SIMEONE

Levasseur, Jean Henri (b. Paris, 1763; d. Paris, 1823) French cellist, composer, and teacher.

Levasseur (sometimes called *le jeune* to distinguish him from the unrelated older cellist Pierre François Levasseur) was a pupil of DUPORT and Cupis. He joined the Paris Opéra in 1789 and was its principal cellist until 1823. He was a professor at the PARIS CONSERVATOIRE from its inception in 1795 and taught there for thirty-eight years. Levasseur's pupils included Lamare, Baudiot and Norblin. He composed several solo and duo sonatas and a set of exercises, but his chief importance is as one of the co-authors (with Catel and Baudiot) of the *Méthode de violoncelle et de basse accompagnement* edited by BAILLOT and adopted for teaching by the Paris Conservatoire (Paris: Janet et Cotelle, 1804). Baillot, a violinist, had some influence on cellists – Olive-Charlier Vaslin (1794–1889) found his classes more useful than those given by cellists. Widely adopted, the *Méthode* was translated into English by Merrick (London: Cocks & Co., c1830). There are exercises in all the keys, exercises in higher registers without the thumb (using operatic themes), exercises with the thumb, chromatic scales, double stop exercises, ORNAMENTATION including double trills (more elaborate embellishments are offered, but with the caveat that the character of the instrument should dictate that fewer should be used), and many BOWING techniques, both technical and expressive. HARMONICS are treated summarily, but there is an exposition of chordal BASSO CONTINUO accompaniment. A substantial quantity of excerpts from the chamber and orchestral works of HAYDN and Boccherini is included, along with three sonatas by Stefano Galeotti (also used by GUNN and BRÉVAL). This *Méthode* is of roughly similar size to that of Bréval, but is much larger in scope and reaches advanced techniques more quickly. It also goes beyond questions of technique by describing at some length the essential character of the CELLO and the importance of the visual appearance of the performer.

FURTHER READING

G. Kennaway, *Playing the Cello, 1780–1930* (Farnham: Ashgate, 2014).
S. Milliot, *Le violoncelle en France au XVIIIe siècle* (Paris and Geneva: Champion-Slatkine, 1985).
V. Walden, *One Hundred Years of Violoncello* (Cambridge University Press, 1998).

GEORGE KENNAWAY

Levin, Robert (David) (b. Brooklyn, NY, 13 October 1947) American pianist and musicologist.

Robert Levin is especially well known for his restoration of the Classical period performance practice of improvised embellishments and CADENZAS. In particular, his MOZART and BEETHOVEN recordings have been widely acclaimed for their active mastery of the Classical musical language. He has performed and recorded with many period groups, including the ACADEMY OF ANCIENT MUSIC, La Chambre Philharmonique, ENGLISH BAROQUE SOLOISTS, HANDEL & HAYDN SOCIETY, London Classical Players, ORCHESTRA OF THE AGE OF ENLIGHTENMENT, ORCHESTRE RÉVOLUTIONNAIRE ET ROMANTIQUE and Philharmonia Baroque. In addition to his concerto cycles with CHRISTOPHER HOGWOOD and JOHN ELIOT GARDINER, he has recorded all the BACH concertos with Helmuth Rilling, together with the English suites and *The Well-Tempered Clavier* (on five keyboard instruments). He has worked with many of the world's great symphony ORCHESTRAS, proving a powerful advocate of period style on modern instruments. His repertory is extensive; in addition to recording the complete PIANO music of Dutilleux, he has commissioned and premiered a large number of new works.

Robert Levin has an international profile as theorist and Mozart scholar. He has written extensively on Mozart performance practice and has completed a number of unfinished works, notably the Mass in C minor K427, the Clarinet Quintet fragment K516c and the Requiem K626. His completion of the Rondo in A K581a for Clarinet Quintet was recorded for the first time by COLIN LAWSON in 2012. Among other such projects was his reworking of Mozart's *Sinfonia Concertante* K297b, which he made the subject of an ingenious but controversial monograph in 1988. He has published cadenzas to Mozart's FLUTE, flute and HARP, OBOE, HORN and BASSOON concertos and to the Beethoven Violin Concerto. Among his recent influential writings is his preface to the Bärenreiter FACSIMILE of Mozart's Piano Concerto K491, whose autograph is held at the ROYAL COLLEGE OF MUSIC in London. He has held teaching positions at the Curtis Institute, Conservatoire Américain Fontainebleau, State University of NY (Purchase), Staatliche Hochschule für Musik Freiburg and Harvard University (1993–2014).

FURTHER READING

B. D. Sherman, 'Speaking Mozart's lingo: Robert Levin on Mozart and improvisation', in *Inside Early Music* (Oxford University Press, 1997), 315–38.

COLIN LAWSON

Lewis, Sir Anthony Carey (b. Bermuda, 2 March 1915: d. Haselmere, 5 June 1983) English conductor, composer and editor with a particular interest in the performance of early music, especially by Purcell and Handel.

Lewis attended Salisbury Cathedral choir school, and later St George's Chapel, Windsor under EDMUND FELLOWES and Sir Walford Davies. He studied at the ROYAL ACADEMY OF MUSIC before taking up an ORGAN scholarship at Peterhouse, Cambridge from 1932 and receiving a studentship for further studies in Paris with NADIA BOULANGER in 1934. In 1935 he won the Barclay Squire prize for musical palaeography.

In 1935, Lewis joined the music staff of the BBC as music planner for the Third Programme, which first broadcast in 1946. There, he revived many pre-Classical works and produced the series 'Foundations of Music'. In this way he balanced the classics with lesser-known works and brought much early music to public attention. In 1947 he was elected Peyton and Barber professor of music at Birmingham University, succeeding JACK WESTRUP, and conducted many early works including revivals of Handel's operas and also the first English recordings of MONTEVERDI's *Vespro della Beata Vergine* and Purcell's *The Fairy Queen*. At the Barber Institute he hosted DAVID MUNROW's debut concert with the EARLY MUSIC CONSORT in 1967. The following year he was appointed principal of the Royal Academy of Music, where he continued to ensure that scholarly research informed musical performance.

Whilst at Birmingham he founded *Musica Britannica*, an influential collection of early British music. The editorial committee included Lewis as general editor and THURSTON DART as secretary. The first three volumes were published in 1951 as part of the Festival of Britain celebrations. Lewis also produced several important editions of operas by Handel and Purcell, and was honorary secretary of the Purcell Society.

FURTHER READING

N. Fortune, 'Sir Anthony Lewis', *MT*, 124/1686 (1993), 503.
M. Pope, 'Lewis, Sir Anthony Carey (1915–1983)', *Oxford Dictionary of National Biography* rev. edn (Oxford University Press, 2004). www.oxforddnb.com.proxy3.library.mcgill.ca/view/article/31358.

EDWARD BREEN

Löhlein (Lelei), Georg Simon (b. Neustadt an der Heide, nr Coburg, bap. 16 July 1725; d. Danzig (now Gdańsk), 16 December 1781) German pedagogue, composer, pianist and violinist.

Löhlein's early musical training from his father was interrupted by a lengthy term of conscription in the Prussian army. He attended the University of Jena (1760) and continued his studies of philosophy, ethics and poetry in Leipzig from 1763, seeking musical instruction from JOHANN ADAM HILLER. He was appointed musical director of the *Grosses Konzert* there, but earned his living largely from private music tuition, supplementing it with theoretical writings about keyboard and VIOLIN playing and composing a variety of works, most notably chamber and keyboard music. Shortly before his death he became *Kapellmeister* of Danzig's *Marienkirche*.

Löhlein's most significant publication was his *Clavier-Schule* (2 vols., Leipzig and Züllichau, 1765 and 1781), which appeared in Dutch and Russian translations and was published in numerous EDITIONS and revisions well into the nineteenth century. Inspired by C. P. E. BACH's *Versuch*, its first volume is directed more towards beginners and amateurs and presents basic musical rudiments and technical principles in a considered, graded order. It includes helpful information on ARTICULATION and RHYTHMIC INTERPRETATION and its simple rules for FINGERING combine new concepts with some paired fingerings of former times. His application of these rules is illustrated in a fully annotated collection of progressively more difficult minuets, gigues, allegros, polonaises and divertimenti, and focuses on musical shaping and expressive realisation of the melodic line. Two further editions of the first volume (1773, 1779) were published before the second volume appeared in print. Based on principles expounded in Sorge's *Compendium harmonicum* (Lobenstein: im Verlag des Verfassers, 1760), this volume provides sound instruction on unfigured bass accompaniment, demonstrating its application in six sonatas with violin accompaniment and a supplementary section on accompanying recitative. Johann Georg Witthauer's edition (1791) combined both volumes, as did those of August Müller (1804), CARL CZERNY (1825) and Julius Knorr (1848), each of whom revised, enlarged and updated Löhlein's instruction for his own times.

Like most German violin methods of the period other than LEOPOLD MOZART's, Löhlein's *Anweisung zum Violinspielen* (Leipzig and Züllichau, 1774) is of an elementary technical level and was designed for amateurs or orchestral violinists (*Ripienisten*). Löhlein discusses fourteen qualities essential to a violinist, notably the importance of good equipment, posture, BOWING facility, position-work, ORNAMENTATION and knowledge of rudiments. Each of the fourteen requirements forms a subdivision in his method; but the method's 136 pages comprise a mixture of both sound and questionable guidance. Especially useful are Löhlein's observations on posture and the position of the feet in relation to the face, the violin hold with the chin on the left (G string) side of the table, VIBRATO (warning against using it too liberally, but providing some examples of its introduction), bowing (even though recommending a bow hold some distance from the frog) and matters of articulation, and metrical and agogic ACCENTUATION, as well as his twenty-four annotated violin duets. He emphasises the importance of scales and deals with positions up to fourth position. His method was published in at least seven editions, the later editions revised and edited by JOHANN FRIEDRICH REICHARDT (1797) and August Müller.

FURTHER READING

C. Brown, *Classical and Romantic Performing Practice 1750–1900* (Oxford University Press, 1999).
F. von Glasenapp, *Georg Simon Löhlein (1725–1781): sein Leben und seine Werke* (Halle: Halle Akademie Verlag, 1937).
D. J. Wilson, 'Georg Simon Löhlein's "Klavierschule": translation and commentary', PhD dissertation, University of Southern California (1979).

ROBIN STOWELL

Loulié, Etienne (b. Paris, 1654; d. Paris, 1702) French performer, composer and theorist.

Loulié is known as the inventor of the *chronomètre*, considered the first practical machine for dictating musical pulse. In his *Éléments ou principes de musique* (Paris, 1696), he considers musical time, ORNAMENTATION, vocal training, monochord use and TRANSPOSITION. His rhythmical realisations demystify certain ambiguities in treating dots of addition and alteration. Special attention is given to time-beating patterns in various simple and compound metres. For Loulié musical temporality originated in the vital, not mechanical, movement of beating time.

Éléments introduces his TEMPO machine, a simple pendulum with a scale marked in seventy-two 'pouces'. As a proxy for composer-directors, it provided the initial pulse 'in their absence as if they were beating the measure themselves' (Loulié, title page). QUANTZ and ROUSSEAU knew the purposes behind Loulié's invention, but both discounted it as an insufficient replacement for musician-derived pulse dictation.

FURTHER READING

P. Ranum, 'A sweet servitude: a musician's life at the court of Mlle de Guise', *EMc*, 15/3 (1987), 346–60.
R. Semmens, 'Étienne Loulié and the new harmonic counterpoint', *JMT*, 28/1 (1984), 73–88.

ALEXANDER EVAN BONUS

Luca, Sergiu (b. Bucharest, 5 April 1943; d. Houston, TX, 7 December 2010) Naturalised American violinist, conductor and pedagogue.

Luca studied at the Bucharest Conservatory, in London with Max Rostal, at the Berne Conservatory (1958–61) and with Ivan Galamian at the Curtis

Institute (1961–3), and made his American debut with the Philadelphia Orchestra in 1965. He served as professor of music at the University of Illinois (1980–3) and VIOLIN professor at Rice University Houston (1983–2010), founded/directed the Chamber Music Northwest Festival (Portland, OR; 1971–80) and the Cascade Head Festival (Lincoln City, OR; 1985–2006), was music director of the Texas Chamber Orchestra (1983–6) and director of the Houston arts organisation Da Camera (1986–93).

Luca's diverse repertory embraced a special affinity with Baroque music. He experimented with period instruments in the mid-1970s and was the first to record J. S. BACH's unaccompanied violin works using a period instrument and BOW (1977). Other recordings, including sonatas by W. A. MOZART (with MALCOLM BILSON), TARTINI, Nardini and Chabran, music by Prince Louis Ferdinand of Prussia and Bach's Brandenburg Concertos (with PABLO CASALS), and his performances and masterclasses inspired a generation of young performers to pursue the study of early music. In 1996, he co-founded Context, a chamber ensemble which performed, as appropriate, on either modern or period instruments.

ROBIN STOWELL

Lully, Jean-Baptiste (b. Florence, 29 November 1632 (as Giovanni Battista Lulli); d. Paris, 22 March 1687) French composer, dancer and instrumentalist of Italian birth.

In his youth Lully was taken by the aristocratic Guise family to Paris, where he quickly shook off Italian traits, embracing those of France to such a degree that his style as composer, dancer and violinist became the cachet of seventeenth-century French Classical music. His arrival in France fortuitously coincided with the young Louis XIV's ambition to create a distinctive French school to rival the Italians in all the arts and crafts. In the young and prodigiously gifted (and ambitious) Lully he found the ideal proponent.

Lully had already mastered his adopted language and its complex rules of prosody when applied to Classical French poetry set down by Malherbe and others in the early years of the century, so that when he set it to music it was universally recognised as the perfect matching of word and note, reflecting both the sentiment and structure of the poetry. It goes without saying that an understanding of the text and clarity of diction is an essential element in recreating the style (*see* Bénigne de Bacilly's *Remarques curieuses sur l'art de bien chanter* (1668), trans. A. B. Caswell as *A Commentary on the Art of Proper Singing* (New York: Institute of Medieval Music, 1968)). BACILLY describes the principles of long and short syllables, ORNAMENTS, diction and other elements of the style. As Lully provided few signs for ornaments, this aspect of performance becomes the responsibility of the singer. Unfortunately, Bacilly's instructions on ornamentation are directed towards the performance of solo songs with LUTE accompaniment in which delicacy and lightness and a fondness for *doubles* (through which the repeat of simple melodies is dissolved into a rapid flow of notes). This did not suit Lully's operatic style, which was far more direct and dramatic and hovered between lyricism and declamation. The NOTATION in his scores includes many changes of metre, largely because of his observing the short and long syllables. However, because 2/4 was rarely (if ever) used in seventeenth-century French music, Lully's solution was to notate the passage using the traditional signs for either 2 or alla breve and to double the speed of the notes.

Lully's orchestral innovations, including uniform BOWING and crisp rhythms, are described by his German student GEORG MUFFAT in the prefaces to his *Florilegia* (1695 and 1698) and concertos (1701). Muffat also describes the various possible combinations of orchestral instruments in Lully's day. Modern musicological research has shown that Lully's music (in both his operas and his sacred music) was usually accompanied by quite large orchestras, the continuo section often including two HARPSICHORDS, six bass VIOLS, THEORBOS and LUTES as well as a *basse de violon*. With lavish costumes and sets and much dancing by both professionals and skilled courtiers, the operas of Lully were spectacular entertainments such as only a court could provide.

FURTHER READING

J. H. Heyer, *Jean-Baptiste Lully and the Music of the French Baroque – Essays in Honor of James R. Anthony* (Cambridge University Press, 1989).

DAVID TUNLEY

Lussy, Mathis (b. Stans, 8 April 1828; d. Montreux, 21 January 1910) Swiss theorist and pianist.

Lussy worked in Paris, mostly as a PIANO teacher. He also wrote five books and several articles about the history of musical NOTATION, the cultivation of musical feeling, and the theory of rhythm and EXPRESSION, and he was dubbed *Chevalier de la légion d'honneur* (1908) in recognition of his contributions to music theory and AESTHETICS.

Lussy undertook the first empirical investigations into expressiveness in performance. He made comparative analyses of performances by some of the most significant pianists of his time, notably HANS VON BÜLOW, Anton Rubinstein and Karl Klindworth (*L'anacrouse dans la musique moderne* (Paris: Heugel, 1903)), copiously annotating details of timing, DYNAMICS and phrasing. These analyses revealed to him that expression in performance originates from the structures and features of the music rather than solely from the performer's inspiration. He thus codified a system of expression that involved identifying 'the notes and passages which most excite and impress the performer', classified them 'to discover the *cause* and the nature of their action upon the sentiment' (*Traité de l'expression musicale* (Paris: Heugel, 1874); 8 editions until 1904; Trans. M. E. Von Glehn as *Musical Expression* (London: Novello, 1885), 4) and devised rules that correspond to specific performative actions. Through his *Traité...*, *Le rythme musical* (Paris: Heugel et Cie, 1883, 4 editions until 1911; abridged E. Dutoit, trans. E. Fowles as *A Short Treatise on Musical Rhythm* (London: Vincent Music Co., 1908)) and *L'anacrouse*, he endeavoured to establish a 'grammar of execution' for his system. For example, he articulated classifications of anacruses and ACCENTS (a three-part categorisation, identifying metric, rhythmic and pathetic accentuation as counterparts respectively to instinct, intelligence and emotion); he also systematised an underlying phrase structure of music and described the relationship between specific rhythmic-tonal structures and the expression that they generate in performance in terms of TEMPO and dynamic fluctuations.

Basing his theories upon the principle of action–repose or tension–relaxation first formulated by Momigny, he concluded that: the source of expressive sentiments lies in unexpected events that disrupt the regularity and symmetry of tonality, metre and rhythm (e.g. syncopations, note repetitions, dissonances and chromatic harmonies); and the more sensitive performers are to those disruptions, the more expressive is their playing. Lussy's theories had their detractors, notably HUGO RIEMANN, but undoubtedly influenced the ideas of, among others, Émile Jaques-Dalcroze.

FURTHER READING

M. Doğantan-Dack, *Mathis Lussy: A Pioneer in Studies of Expressive Performance* (Bern: Peter Lang, 2002).
M. D. Green, 'Mathis Lussy's *Traité de l'expression musicale* as a window into performance practice', *Music Theory Spectrum*, 16/2 (1994), 196–216.

ROBIN STOWELL

Lute (Fr. *luth*; Ger. *Laute*; It. *liuto* or *leuto*; Sp. *laud*) A plucked stringed instrument which flourished in Europe for over five hundred years, from the Middle Ages until its demise towards the end of the eighteenth century.

It derives its name from the Arab lute, *al' ud*, which was probably brought to Europe with the Muslim penetrations into Spain and Sicily. Its rounded back is built up from thin strips of wood to create its characteristic shape. The strings (generally in pairs) run from a bridge, glued to the soundboard, along the neck to the tuning-pegs. These are inserted sideways into a pegbox, which is attached to the neck pointing backwards almost at right angles. The lute became a very important instrument in mainland Italy, as evidenced by numerous fourteenth-century illustrations. It also reached north of the Alps and, by the fifteenth century, the number of strings increased to five pairs and the intervals between the courses were (from bass to treble): fourth, third, fourth, fourth. This is the type of instrument for which the first lute TABLATURE was developed, reputedly invented by the blind musician Konrad Pauman of Nuremberg (c1410–73). Although German lute tablature appears to be the oldest, the three principal systems (German, French and Italian) were developed at roughly the same time during the second half of the fifteenth century (*see* Figures 7, 8 and 9).

JOHANNES TINCTORIS (c1435–1511) observed that the lute could be plucked either with a plectrum or with the fingers, but the latter technique prevailed, enabling execution of more complex polyphony. Coinciding with this development, a sixth course was added towards the end of the fifteenth century. It was tuned a fourth below the fifth course and in order to brighten the sound of the low gut bass strings, the three bottom ones were paired with thinner strings tuned at the upper octave (Example 16).

During the sixteenth century, lute making flourished both north and south of the Alps, and makers such as Laux Maler (d. 1552) and Hans Frei (d. before 1576) were in great demand. Music printing and the invention of tablature meant that lute pieces could be widely disseminated, and an enormous corpus of solo lute music has survived in manuscripts and in print. The six-course lute remained the most common type and some distinguished performers emerged,

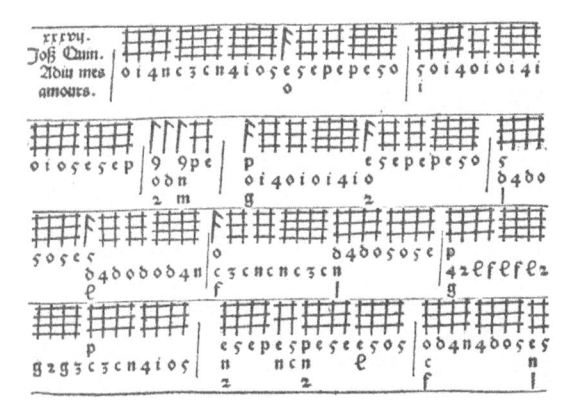

Figure 7: German tablature from Hans Neusidler's *Der ander Theil des Lauthenbuchs* (Nuremberg, 1536).

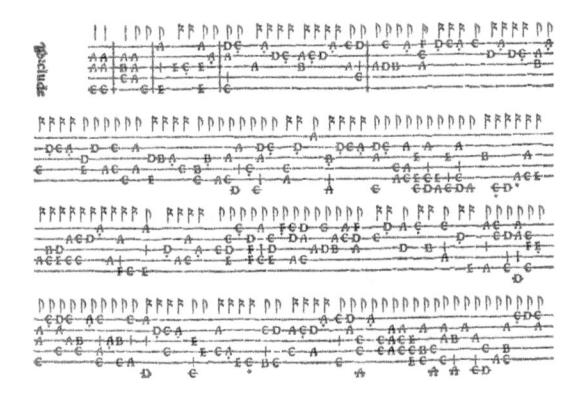

Figure 8: French tablature from Pierre Attaingnant's *Très brève et familière introduction...* (Paris, 1529).

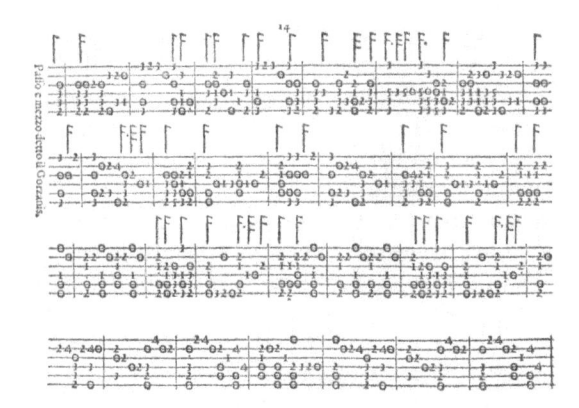

Figure 9: Italian tablature from Giacomo Gorzanis's *Intabolatura di liuto* (Venice, 1561).

Example 16: Six-course lute tuning, showing the positions of octave strings.

such as Francesco da Milano (1497–1543) and Albert de Rippe (c1500–51). Lavish royal patronage was bestowed on lutenists across Europe at this time and the instrument was held in high esteem, not least because it was played by many royals and members of the nobility.

During the latter part of the sixteenth century, a new style of lute making evolved, lute backs being built up with a greater number of ribs. By using a greater number of thin strips of yew, cut in such a way that both the light sapwood and the red heartwood were visible on each rib, makers such as Wendelio Venere (*fl.* 1560–90) and Magno Tieffenbrucker (*fl.* 1589–1621) created some visually stunning instruments. Also around this time the range of the lute was extended in the bass and the number of courses gradually increased to ten soon after 1600. The music by John Dowland (1563–1626) reflects this development. Dowland was one of several prolific English lutenists at that time and famous throughout Europe for his lute compositions.

The seventeenth century was a period of great creativity and experimentation in terms of lute construction, tuning and compositional styles. At the very end of the sixteenth century, Giovanni Antonio Terzi (c1580–1620) and Simone Molinaro (c1565–1615) published books with fantasias, dances and INTABULATIONS, often using technically demanding thick textures. However, a new and more transparent style began to emerge in Italy with composers such as Giovanni Girolamo Kapsperger (c1580–1651) and Alessandro Piccinini (1566-c1638), who exploited more daring harmonies, particularly in their improvisatory toccatas. To meet players' demands, Italian lute makers experimented with increasing the instrument's range, abandoning the bent-back pegbox and instead extending the neck and creating two pegboxes, one for seven 'stopped' courses and one for seven long bass courses. The larger 'arciliuto' or arch lute seems to have evolved a little later, retaining the double fingerboard-courses of the ordinary lute, here usually six in number, and with eight single bass strings tuned to a diatonic scale. These were nearly double the length of the 'stopped' ones and thus the arch lute shared something of the strong bass of the THEORBO and the agility of the treble of the ordinary lute. These became widely used for thoroughbass during the second half of the seventeenth century, continuing to flourish during the following century.

By contrast, lutenists in France and northern Europe were exploiting the natural resonances of the lute by using a number of different tunings on a ten-course instrument. One of these tunings, the so-called D minor tuning, gradually became standard (Example 17) and an eleven-course instrument (Figures 10a and 10b) became the classic French lute during the second half of the seventeenth century. A huge repertoire can be found in a large number of prints and MANUSCRIPTS for this type of lute well into the eighteenth century. The last important French lutenist was Charles Mouton

Example 17: Eleven-course D minor lute tuning, showing the positions of octave strings.

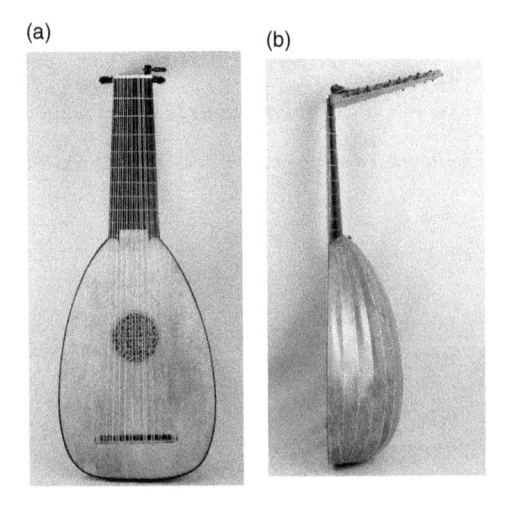

Figure 10a and b: Lute (c1580) by Sixtus Rauwolf of Augsburg, later converted into an eleven-course Baroque lute (belonging to Jakob Lindberg).

(c1626–1710), whose two surviving printed books contain some of the finest examples of the lutenist's art from this period.

Towards the end of the seventeenth century there was a decline in the popularity of the lute in France and England. However, it continued to have strong appeal in German-speaking countries. Esaias Reusner (1636–79) studied with a well-known French lutenist, possibly Dufaut, and published some exceptional music for lute. In Austria, where the French court of Louis XIV was the cultural model, lute playing was something to aspire to and members of aristocratic families would learn to play the instrument. In this fertile climate a number of professional lutenists flourished, notably Graf Johann Losy von Losinthal (c1650–1721), Wolff Jacob Lauffensteiner (1676–1754) and Johann Georg Weichenberger (1677–1740). The emerging musical style shows a fusion of French elements with Italian opera, as in the works of Silvius Leopold Weiss (1687–1750). He was born near Breslau into a family of lutenists and subsequently became celebrated throughout Europe as the finest lutenist of his time and more than 600 of his compositions for the lute survive. Weiss was involved with the last development in the history of the lute: the swan-necked instrument with thirteen courses. This was an ideal instrument for the emerging *stile galante*, which had Italian *bel canto* as an ideal. Weiss's pupil Adam Falckenhagen (1697–1754) adopted this new musical fashion more fully than his teacher. He was employed as lutenist at Bayreuth and published a number of attractive solo sonatas. Other exponents were Bernard Hagen (1720–87) and

Karl Kohaut (1726–84), who wrote solo music as well as fine chamber music with lute obbligato parts and together these virtuosi represent the final flowering of the lute in Europe.

FURTHER READING

V. A. Coelho, *The Manuscript Sources of Seventeenth-Century Italian Lute Music* (New York: Garland Press, 1994).

D. Poulton, *John Dowland: His Life and Work* (London: Faber & Faber, 1972).

D. A. Smith, *A History of the Lute from Antiquity to the Renaissance* (New York: Lute Society of America Inc., 2002).

R. Spencer, *The Burwell Lute Tutor with an Introductory Study by Robert Spencer* (Leeds: Boethius Press, 1974).

M. Spring, *The Lute in Britain: A Historical Survey of the Instrument and its Music* (Oxford University Press, 2001).

JAKOB LINDBERG

M

Mace, Thomas (b. ?Cambridge or York, 1612/13; d. ?Cambridge, ?1706) English singer, lutenist, viol player, composer and theorist.

In 1676, Mace published his *Musick's Monument or, a Remembrancer of the Best Practical Musick* in London. This substantial volume (272 pages plus extensive prefatory material) is an important, albeit conservative, source for English music of the second and third quarters of the seventeenth century. It is in three parts. The first is concerned with church music, particularly how the decline in SINGING might be reversed. He also includes a graphic description of the 'Hellish disturbance' (20) of a service in York Minster during the siege of York in 1644.

By far the largest section (199 pages) is the second, devoted to Mace's favourite instrument, the LUTE, entitled 'The Lute made Easie'. Mace addresses how to obtain a lute, stringing, fretting, 'how to take off the Belly' (56) and 'How to mend a Crack' (57). He then gives a detailed and systematic method for 'a *Very New* Beginner' to learn to play the instrument, including tuning and how to read TABLATURE. Mace adds carefully planned 'setts' (suites) observing that the movements 'ought to be *something a Kin* ... in their *Conceits, Natures or Humours*' (120). In concerts he recommends improvising a smooth modulation between differing tonalities of consecutive pieces and gives examples.

The third part concerns 'The Viol and Musick in General'. Mace discusses the importance of having a music room fit for performance; his '*Touch-stone*' (242) is an ORGAN in the middle of the room and after that 'a *Good Chest of Viols*' (245) for CONSORT playing. He continues: '*The Viol* is an *Instrument* so very much in use' with 'so many *Profess'd Teachers* upon It' (247) and endorses SIMPSON's tutor. He asks the student to pay particular attention to two common faults: first, when playing a chord at the end of a phrase '*be sure to give the Lowest String a Good Full Share of your Bow* (*Singly, by Itself, before you slide It upon the Rest*) ... This will make your Play very *Lovely*' (249). The second rule is to hold the left-hand fingers down '*according to the Propriety, and Necessity of the Composition*' (250).

FURTHER READING

T. Mace, *Musick's Monument or, a Remembrancer of the Best Practical Musick* (London: Ratcliffe & Thompson, 1676).

M. Spring, 'Solo music for tablature instruments', in I. Spink (ed.), *Music in Britain: The Seventeenth Century* (Oxford: Blackwell, 1992), 367–405.

LUCY ROBINSON

Machaut, Guillaume de (b. Reims or Machault, Champagne, c1300; d. Reims, April 1377) French composer and poet.

Machaut is considered today – as he was in his day – a towering figure in the music, poetry and literature of fourteenth-century France. Musically, his position is perhaps overstated today due to the dearth of surviving French MANUSCRIPTS of secular polyphony from this era. While never employed as a musician and leaving no evidence of involvement in performance, he remains an invaluable point of call for performers. His habit of collecting his *oeuvre* in dedicated manuscripts at various points during the last few decades of his life (six such collections are extant) enables the assignation of groups of works to specific decades. Furthermore, his poetry contains references to musical practices. Thus, his *Prologue* and *Remède de Fortune* contain thoughts on the requirements for and process of becoming a poet-musician. The latter work and his *Prise d'Alexandrie* contain lists of instruments within their narrative, and the semi-autobiographical *Voir dit* hints at his personal attitudes to musical consumption. The *Voir dit* is a complex and influential work in which the relationship of a student and teacher that has become amorous is presented through the incorporation of exchanged letters, poetry and music into the narrative. In one such letter he implores his student-beloved to hear and learn a new song of his exactly as written without adding or subtracting anything, and goes on to suggest a general TEMPO and some instruments which will suit its character. In another letter he describes how he is loath to release any new song into circulation without first having heard it performed. Together, they hint at the centrality of performance to his art and the respect he expected performers to show to his written instructions.

FURTHER READING

L. Earp, *Guillaume de Machaut: A Guide to Research* (New York: Garland, 1995).
E. E. Leach, *Guillaume de Machaut: Secretary, Poet, Musician* (Ithaca: Cornell University Press, 2011).
D. Leech-Wilkinson (ed.) and R. B. Palmer (trans.), *Le livre dou voir dit (The Book of the True Poem)* (New York: Garland, 1998).

URI SMILANSKY

Mackerras, Sir (Alan) Charles (Maclaurin) (b. Schenectady, NY, 17 November 1925; d. London, 14 July 2010) Australian conductor and musicologist.

An internationally renowned 'mainstream' conductor, Charles Mackerras had a significant impact on the HISTORICALLY INFORMED PERFORMANCE of music from the eighteenth to the twentieth century, notably Handel, MOZART, BEETHOVEN, BRAHMS and Janáček. He was music director at English National Opera (1970–7) and Welsh National Opera (1987–92), and a regular guest at the Royal Opera House and the Metropolitan Opera. He held positions with ORCHESTRAS, notably the Philharmonia, and worked closely with the Goldsborough Orchestra, English Chamber Orchestra, Orchestra of St Luke's, Scottish Chamber Orchestra and ORCHESTRA OF THE AGE OF ENLIGHTENMENT (OAE).

Mackerras studied the OBOE at the Sydney Conservatorium before travelling to England in 1947, where he made his permanent home. In 1947–8 he studied CONDUCTING with Václav Talich in Prague. At Sadler's Wells he conducted the British premiere of *Kát'a Kabanová* in 1951, the start of a lifelong devotion to Janáček that included the preparation of several important editions of the operas as well as a definitive series of recordings which restored Janáček's original orchestration and removed spurious revisions.

In the mid-1950s, Mackerras combed European libraries for contemporary evidence of performance practice in Mozart's operas. A tenacious self-taught scholar, he quickly applied the fruits of his research. Two BBC broadcasts on 'ornamentation in Mozart's vocal works' (1957) were followed in 1965 by *Le nozze di Figaro* at Sadler's Wells, one of the first productions in modern times to attempt idiomatic SINGING of appoggiaturas as well as using contemporary embellishments. On Mackerras's use of appoggiaturas, Arthur Jacobs commented (*Opera*, June 1965): 'If we dislike them, we dislike Mozart's ideas of Mozart.' While Mackerras used fewer embellishments in later years, his insistence on the proper execution of appoggiaturas influenced generations of singers. He conducted Mozart operas with period instruments (*Die Zauberflöte* and *Così fan tutte* with the OAE at Glyndebourne) and introduced historically informed practice to Mozart at ENO, the Royal Opera House, Welsh National Opera and the Edinburgh Festival.

In 1959 Mackerras recorded the *Music for the Royal Fireworks* in Handel's original scoring for large wind band (including twenty-six oboes), using double dotting and some ORNAMENTATION (in a letter to his mother, he described the result as 'one of the most marvellous noises I have ever heard'). He conducted Basil Lam's edition of *Messiah* for the BBC in 1965 and recorded it a year later. This was advertised as 'performed in a manner approximating as nearly as possible to that of Handel's own time'. Along with variants such as the 12/8 version of 'Rejoice greatly', this recording included vocal embellishments and CADENZAS, and used a relatively small choir and orchestra. Mackerras subsequently conducted productions of Handel's operas in his own editions, including *Semele*, *Julius Caesar* and *Xerxes*.

Mackerras applied historically informed practice to nineteenth-century repertory, including Donizetti's *Lucia di Lammermoor* (experimenting with the original orchestral layout, stripping away later accretions, and recording it with period instruments), and Brahms's symphonies (drawing on accounts of FRITZ STEINBACH's performances). In 1987, he was among the first to record major nineteenth-century orchestral works on period instruments with the OAE, starting with Schubert's 'Great' C major Symphony and MENDELSSOHN's 'Italian'.

Always a pragmatist, Mackerras brought elements of period practice into modern-instrument performances. With the Scottish Chamber Orchestra in Mozart and Beethoven, he used natural TRUMPETS and HORNS, and TIMPANI with calfskin heads, alongside modern strings playing with sparing use of VIBRATO. In the Beethoven cycle recorded at the Edinburgh Festival in 2006 (Hyperion) and his last Mozart recordings (Linn), the results were revelatory, thanks to Mackerras's combination of rhythmic energy and stylistic understanding.

FURTHER READING

N. Phelan, with appendices by C. Mackerras, *Charles Mackerras: A Musician's Musician* (London: Gollancz, 1987).

N. Simeone and J. Tyrrell (eds.), *Charles Mackerras* (Woodbridge: Boydell, 2015).

NIGEL SIMEONE

Maffei, Giovanni Camillo (b. Solofra, nr Salerno, early sixteenth century; *fl.* 1562–73) Italian physician, singer and courtier.

Maffei's *Discourse on the Voice* (1562) is a highly practical TREATISE about the art of refined SINGING. It opens with a discussion of the anatomy, physiognomy and physiology of the voice (closely modelled on Aristotle and Galen). Explaining that the voice is 'nothing more than a sound changed by the minute and ordered repercussions of the air in the throat' (16), Maffei proceeds to teach his courtier pupil, the Count of Alta Villa, the principles of *cantar di gorga* ('singing in the throat'); how to ornament the basic line by breaking up longer note values (*passaggi*); 'how to apply the *passaggi* to madrigals or other things he sings' (20) using worked examples – Layolle's 'Lasciar il velo o per sol' o per ombra' for four voices and an anonymous setting of Petrarch's 'Vago augelletto che cantando vai' arranged for solo voice. The *Discourse* concludes with recipes for treating various vocal disorders.

FURTHER READING

H. M. Brown, 'The geography of Florentine monody: Caccini at home and abroad', *EMc*, 9 (1981), 147–68.

G. C. Maffei, 'Discourse on the voice and the method of learning to sing ornamentation', trans. in E. V. Foreman, *Late Renaissance Singing* (Minneapolis, MN: Pro Musica Press, 2001).

RICHARD WISTREICH

Maffei, Scipione (b. Verona, 1 June 1675; d. Verona, 12 February 1755) Veronese marquis, soldier and academician.

Maffei wrote on many learned topics, composed poetry and collected antiquities. With Apostolo Zeno he published the bi-monthly *Giornale de' letterati d'Italia*, which in 1711 included an extensive article with action diagram of Cristofori's newly invented PIANO, of which Cristofori had already made three. The account was republished by Maffei in 1719 and translated in MATTHESON's *Critica Musica* (1725). The article elaborates upon very brief manuscript notes written by Maffei on a visit to Cristofori, although much of it may have been based on information sent to Maffei by the maker. Maffei states that the action was difficult to understand, but his diagram nevertheless appears workable. His description differs from the four surviving actions of Cristofori dated 1720, 1722, c1725 and 1726, suggesting that the maker was continually experimenting and improving his pianos. Maffei relates how the sound of Cristofori's pianos was considered to be too soft and dull by some, while also making the point that a different approach from conventional HARPSICHORD technique was required to bring out their best qualities. He comments that when played with a new kind of technique, Cristofori's pianos were capable of effective dynamic contrast and a full sound, reproducing the effects he had heard at grand concerts in Rome. He also advocates choosing appropriately delicate repertoire in which the melodic line can be fully brought out, adding that solo and other chamber music was most effective, rather than works for the church, or large ORCHESTRA. Maffei's article additionally describes a five-manual harpsichord in the possession of Signor Casini of Florence and very briefly discusses the consequences of having to tune unequal fifths on keyboard instruments.

FURTHER READING

S. Maffei, 'Nuova invenzione d'un gravecembalo col piano e forte; aggiunte alcune considerazioni sopra gli strumenti musicali', *Giornale de' letterati d'Italia*, 5 (Venice, 1711), 144–59.
S. Pollens, *The Early Pianoforte* (Cambridge University Press, 1995).
D. Wraight, 'Recent approaches in understanding Cristofori's fortepiano', *EMc*, 34/4 (2006), 635–44.

DAVID ROWLAND

Mahaut, Antoine (bap. Namur, 4 May 1719; d. *c*1785) Franco-Flemish flautist, composer and editor.

Mahaut remains a shadowy figure, yet his importance as a musician should not be underestimated. His numerous works for FLUTE include a valuable TREATISE and many concerti, influenced by his French musical education. He embraced a synthesis of French and Italian styles, combining Italian concerto structure and instrumental figuration with French rhythmical practices and ORNAMENTATION. He spent his early career in Amsterdam and Mannheim, before moving to France. In 1735 Mahaut travelled to London where he met the publisher John Walsh, who subsequently published his Six Duets for German Flutes or Violins.

Probably a native of Namur, Mahaut lived in Amsterdam from 1738 to 1745, during which period he published some solo sonatas and duets for flute, edited several collections of Italianate songs in Dutch and composed numerous symphonies and concertos. In 1745 he left Amsterdam for Mannheim to work with Johann Stamitz, whose influence on his own symphonic style is very apparent. He also spent a short period working in Dresden before returning to Amsterdam to publish his flute method entitled *Nouvelle méthode pour apprendre en peu de temps à jouer la flûte traversière* (Paris: de Lachevardiere, 1759). This appeared simultaneously in French and Dutch and mainly focused on technical and musical aspects of playing the flute, adding material to QUANTZ's publication from seven years earlier. Mahaut gives much attention to INTONATION, in particular giving detailed recommendations for different FINGERINGS and varied embouchure on specific notes which are often difficult to tune. It remains significant for its representation of mid-eighteenth-century performance practices in France and the Netherlands. The sheer number of Mahaut's works, together with their wide dissemination throughout Europe, is evidence of the extent of his considerable popularity. He spent his last years in a French monastery.

FURTHER READING

C. Backers, *Dutch Composers from 1400 to Today* ('s-Gravenhage: Beroemde musici, 1942).
H. M. Brown and S. Sadie, *Performance Practice: Music after 1600* (London: Macmillan, 1990).
F.-J. Fétis, *Biographie universelle des musiciens* (Brussels: Meline, Cans et Compagnie, 1835–44).

ASHLEY SOLOMON

Mahillon, Victor-Charles (b. Brussels, 10 March 1841; d. St Jean-Cap Ferrat, 17 June 1924) Belgian organologist, writer and maker of woodwind instruments.

After gaining practice in woodwind instrument making with his father, Mahillon became the first curator of the musical instrument collection of the

Conservatoire Royal de Musique in Brussels in 1877, which he expanded from fewer than 200 to over 3,000 instruments, each described – often with diagrams and scales – in his five-volume catalogue (1893–1922). Since 1869 he published *L'Echo Musicale*, to which he contributed several articles on musical instruments and acoustics.

By 1878 Mahillon had developed an open classification system, influenced by traditional Indian models, which introduced a scientific division into classes and subclasses based on acoustical elements, and was therefore applicable to both European and non-European instruments. It reflected and promoted the interest in comparative studies and the search for a universal history of musical instruments. His classification served as the basis for the one developed by Eric von Hornbostel and CURT SACHS in 1914, which is still largely adopted.

He also remained active in the family business, developing various patents and was involved – as participant, or member of the jury – in several international exhibitions. He made REPLICAS of early brass and woodwind instruments spanning from Roman times to the late Renaissance. Some of these were functional, while some had exclusively aesthetic purposes, aiming to enrich the collections of several European museums to which they were donated.

FURTHER READING

N. A. Jairazbhoy, 'The beginning of organology and ethnomusicology in the West: V. Mahillon, A. Ellis and S. M. Tagore', in S. C. de Vale (ed.), *Selected Reports in Ethnomusicology*, vol. viii: *Issues in Organology* (Los Angeles: University of California, 1990), 67–80.

P. Mahillon, 'Notice biographique', in V.-C. Mahillon, *Catalogue descriptif et analytique du Musée instrumental du Conservatoire royal de musique de Bruxelles* (Gand: Hoste, 1893; repr. Bruxelles: Les Amis de la Musique, 1978).

V.-C. Mahillon, 'Essai de classification méthodique de tous les instruments anciens et modernes', in *Catalogue descriptif et analytique du Musée instrumental du Conservatoire royal de musique de Bruxelles* (Gand: Hoste, 1880), 1–89.

GABRIELE ROSSI ROGNONI

Mahler, Gustav (b. Kalischt, nr Iglau, 7 July 1860; d. Vienna, 18 May 1911) Austrian composer and conductor.

Mahler's early training was in the Czech lands and continued in Vienna (1875–8), where he developed a deep admiration for WAGNER, and had the opportunity to attend opera and orchestral concerts, particularly those of the Vienna Philharmonic (conducted by Hans Richter), the ORCHESTRA that remained his lifelong ideal. He was profoundly influenced by Wagner's readiness to modernise BEETHOVEN's instrumentation and his practice of TEMPO modification; the conductor he admired most was HANS VON BÜLOW.

Mahler's extensive operatic repertoire did not include any pre-Classical works, and from the later eighteenth-century repertoire he only conducted works by Gluck and MOZART. In his championship of the latter he, together with his colleagues Arthur Nikisch (1855–1922), Hermann Levi (1839–1900), Ernst von Schuh (1846–1914) and RICHARD STRAUSS, encouraged a 'rediscovery' of Mozart's stage works, and some aspects of his musical direction reflected a degree of historical awareness, such as the use of small orchestras (with reduced string complement) and, in the Da Ponte operas, the replacement of spoken dialogue (which had become the norm in central Europe) with the original *secco* recitative. From 1887 onwards Mahler accompanied the singers from a keyboard, and as director of the Court Opera in Vienna ordered a Pleyel HARPSICHORD for this purpose in 1905.

With the exception of BACH and Handel, Mahler performed little Baroque music in his concerts, but in 1909 he prepared a compilation from Bach's Second and Third Suites, with a continuo realisation that included parts for 'clavicembalo' – Mahler used a modified Steinway grand PIANO – and (in the first movement only) an ORGAN. The text of the orchestral parts was derived directly from the *Bach-Gesellschaft Ausgabe*, and Mahler's editorial additions are generally limited to ARTICULATION (detached) and DYNAMICS: the latter frequently embody a terraced approach, alternating loud and soft, except for the subtle gradations in the Air from the Third Suite and some other passages. Following Wagner's example, Mahler rescored Beethoven, who he considered had been forced into compromises by the limitations of the available instruments, and did the same for later composers, notably Schumann. But Mahler could also intervene on a structural level, the extreme example being his version of Bruckner's Fourth Symphony (1910), in which the last three movements were all shortened and restructured.

Mahler's own CONDUCTING scores, contemporary reports and photographs and musicians' recollections suggest that when conducting his own music he did not expect continuous VIBRATO in either the strings or woodwind, but rather its use as a modification of the basic sound, and that he normally divided the violins left and right. Although he indicated some string PORTAMENTO, Mahler probably expected additional slides to be supplied. On the other hand, there is evidence that in his own music Mahler did not adopt the more uniformly legato style that was becoming common around 1900 (and went to some pains to use NOTATION to encourage detached articulation when necessary) while his handling of DYNAMICS was unusually detailed and variegated. On a local level, Mahler often indicates subtle RUBATO, and on a larger scale carefully notates both the TEMPO contrasts and the gradual tempo changes that constitute essential structural and expressive elements of his music.

FURTHER READING

R. Kubik (ed.), *Musikinstrumente und Musizierpraxis zur Zeit Gustav Mahler* (Vienna, Cologne and Weimar: Böhlau Verlag, 2007).
H.-L. de La Grange, *Gustav Mahler*, 4 vols. (I: London: Gollancz, 1974; II–IV: Oxford University Press, 1995, 1999, 2008).
K. Martner, *Mahler's Concerts* (New York: Kaplan Foundation/Overlook Press, 2010).

PAUL BANKS

Majer, Joseph Friedrich Bernhard Caspar (b. Schwäbisch Hall, 16 October 1679; d. Schwäbisch Hall, 22 May 1768) German organist and music theorist.

Majer started ORGAN lessons at the age of nine, before completing the curriculum of the local Gymnasium, and acting as municipal clerk in neighbouring towns. In 1724 he became Kantor and Organist of the Church of St Katharina in Schwäbisch Hall. He wrote two musical instruction manuals, of which the *Hodegus musicus* (1718) is now lost.

Majer's own annotated copy of the *Museum musicum theoretico practicum* (Schwäbisch Hall: Georg M. Majer, 1732) is preserved in the Württembergische Landesbibliothek in Stuttgart. It was intended to offer students elementary instruction in music NOTATION and the techniques of playing the RECORDER, CHALUMEAU, FLUTE, OBOE, BASSOON, CORNETT, flageolet, CLARINET, clarino, HORN, TROMBONE, various keyboard instruments (including a section on thoroughbass), LUTE, HARP, TIMPANI, VIOLIN and VIOLS. The book concludes with a dictionary of 260 musical terms. Majer seems to have been well acquainted with earlier and current TREATISES, and mentions his indebtedness to various composers and theorists including TELEMANN, MATTHESON, Baron and WALTHER. The book starts with odes to theorists and composers, before presenting some prose on practical and theoretical music, and finally describing the basics of musical literacy and including FINGERING charts and woodcuts for most of the instruments mentioned. He revised the text in 1741.

Although Majer's work may not have been entirely original, it is valuable as a glimpse into the sorts of texts on music that were circulating, and is also significant for at least one important illustration of a flute with a C-foot, which (in conjunction with a mention by QUANTZ) corroborates a contemporary reference to such an instrument, which the maker Charles Schuchart claims to have seen in Germany. There is one remaining instrument from this period with a low C by the maker Jakob Denner currently held in the Germanisches Nationalmuseum in Nuremberg.

FURTHER READING

J. Lester, *Between Modes and Keys: German Theory 1592–1802* (New York: Pendragon Press, 1989).
A. Powell, *The Flute* (New Haven, CT and London: Yale University Press, 2002).

ASHLEY SOLOMON

Mancini, Giovanni Battista (b. Ascoli, Piacenza, 1 January 1714; d. Vienna, 4 January 1800) Italian CASTRATO and SINGING teacher.

Mancini had a classic eighteenth-century singer's training followed by a modest career in Italy and Germany. He settled in Vienna, becoming a fashionable teacher, and at the age of sixty published *Pensieri, e riflessioni pratiche sopra il canto figurato* (1774, rev. 1777). It is very much in the mould of TOSI's *Opinioni de' cantori antichi e moderni* (1723), testifying to the enduring principles of *bel canto* that would persist until well into the nineteenth century. Like Tosi's treatise, Mancini's is conservative and primarily addressed to the teaching of castrati, but emphasises the perennial elements of fine singing. Pupils spent years in perfecting technical skills (starting as young as eight years old), commencing with balanced vocal emission and joining the chest and falsetto registers; 'placing the voice' (*messa di voce*); and PORTAMENTO (passing between pitches without breaking the line). Embellishments arise organically out of the fundamentals of voice production: thus, the precise ARTICULATION of the trill ('Sustenance, decoration, and life of singing!') is introduced early on, in order 'to facilitate [the pupil's] eventual success' (Foreman, 40–1). From the trill proceed runs, divisions and CADENZAS, which, in turn, necessitate a thorough understanding of harmony and IMPROVISATION. Mancini advocates allowing even the young singer to try making cadenzas ('which, however, should at first be made up of but a few notes'), because 'the cadenza is necessary to every appropriate finale and if [one is] not made by the singer, the whole remains imperfect and languid' (Foreman, 46–7).

Mancini's curriculum is painstakingly incremental, based on the singing of *solfeggi* designed to build strength, agility and musical understanding, in order to prepare for the time – maybe years into the future – when the singer will present himself on stage, fully equipped to operate as the autonomous creator of his performance on any particular occasion. As Mancini explains, from the composer's blueprint 'we find only the concept of a simple cantilena ... enough to let the great singer have full liberty in embellishing the composition in accord with his talent' (Foreman, 12).

FURTHER READING

E. V. Foreman, *A bel canto Method: or How to sing Italian Baroque Music Correctly, Based on the Primary Sources* (Minneapolis, MN: Pro Musica Press, 2006).
G. Mancini, *Practical Reflections on Figured Singing*, trans. and ed. E. V. Foreman (Minneapolis, MN: Pro Musica Press, 1967/1996).
J. Potter and N. Sorrell, *A History of Singing* (Cambridge University Press, 2012), esp. ch. 4.

RICHARD WISTREICH

Mannheim Orchestra The Mannheim Orchestra – largely the creation of the Elector Palatine Carl Theodor (from 1743) – was the most highly regarded orchestra in Europe during the period 1750–80. In 1756 it numbered about fifty-six players including two organs, eleven first violins, nine second violins, four violas, four violoncellos, two DOUBLE BASSES, two FLUTES, two OBOES, three BASSOONS, four HORNS, TRUMPETS (possibly as many as thirteen) and TIMPANI; CLARINETS and additional winds were added in the 1760s. MOZART's *Idomeneo* (1780–1) was written for the Mannheim orchestra, which had relocated to Munich in 1778 when Carl Theodor became Elector of Bavaria.

Praise for the orchestra, as well as a recognition of its historical importance, was unanimous during the eighteenth century. CHARLES BURNEY wrote in his *The Present State of Music in Germany, the Netherlands and United Provinces* (3 vols. (London, 1773), I, 94) that: 'it was here that the *Crescendo* and *Diminuendo* had birth; and the *Piano*, which was before chiefly used as an echo, with which it was generally synonymous, as well as the *Forte*, were found to be musical *colours* which had their *shades*, as much as red or blue in painting'. Similarly, if more poetically, Christian Daniel Friedrich Schubart noted that 'No orchestra in the world has ever excelled the Mannheim. Its *forte* is a thunderclap, its *crescendo* a cataract, its *diminuendo* a crystal stream babbling away into the distance, its *piano* a breath of spring. The wind instruments are everything that they should be: they raise and carry or fill and inspire the storm of the strings' (*Ideen zur Aesthetik der Tonkunst*, Vienna, 1806, 130).

It was not just orchestral effects that made the Mannheimers famous; as Burney noted, orchestral discipline was essential to producing them: 'power will naturally arise from a great number of hands', he wrote, 'but the judicious use of this power, in all occasions, must be the consequence of good discipline; indeed there are more solo players and good composers in this, than perhaps in any other orchestra in Europe; it is an army of generals, equally fit to plan a battle, as to fight it' (Burney, I, 93). The Mannheim orchestra represented a standard to which other orchestras could aspire both musically and socially; when LEOPOLD MOZART and his family visited Mannheim in 1763, he wrote to his Salzburg landlord Lorenz Hagenauer, 'The orchestra is undeniably the best in Germany. It consists altogether of people who are young and of good character, not drunkards, gamblers or dissolute fellows' (letter of 19 July 1763). Mozart himself later remarked, 'one of my chief reasons for detesting Salzburg [is the] coarse, slovenly, dissolute court musicians ... [The Mannheim musicians] certainly behave quite differently from ours. They have good manners, are well dressed and do not go to public houses and swill' (letter of 9 July 1778).

FURTHER READING

L. Finscher (ed.), *Die Mannheimer Hofkapelle im Zeitalter Carl Theodors* (Mannheim: Palatium Verlag im J. & J. Verlag, 1992).
J. Spitzer and N. Zaslaw, *The Birth of the Orchestra: History of an Institution, 1650–1815* (Oxford University Press, 2004), 256–62.
E. K. Wolf, 'The Mannheim court', in N. Zaslaw (ed.), *Man and his Music: The Classical Era: From the 1740s to the End of the 18th Century* (Englewood Cliffs, NJ: Prentice-Hall, 1989), 213–39.

CLIFF EISEN

Manuscripts Manuscripts cover a large range of sources (and not just music), which can illuminate historic performance practice. Manuscript music can comprise autograph scores, copyist scores and parts, while non-music sources include letters and diaries. When looking at any manuscript score, we must be mindful of the circumstances in which the work was composed. Two issues illustrate this: first, all composers work within a performing tradition and what was obvious to the composer and contemporary performers may not be obvious to a modern performer. Second, the system of NOTATION has always developed as composers expanded the musical language and needed to express greater subtlety in their scores.

Autograph Scores

Autograph scores are those written in the composer's hand. Where they are available, they are seen as the primary source for a work, often recording the composer's original version. As such they serve as an important juncture in a work's genesis but they may only be the first step in fully understanding that work. An example of this is HAYDN's String Quartet in C major, Op. 64 No. 1 (RCM MS 283). The first London edition matches the musical text of the autograph score, but Haydn revised it prior to its publication in Vienna.

The scores of composers who were expected to write music on demand can leave many details to the performer's discretion and TASTE. This is especially true where composers were writing works for themselves to perform – for example, MOZART's works for the piano. The manuscripts of his concertos reveal that he completed the piano part once the rest of the score had been finished, often having to squeeze that part into a very small space. More interesting still is a comparison of the autograph score with the first edition of Mozart's Piano Sonata in F major, K332. Many modern editions publish both versions of the middle movement in parallel so that it is clearly evident that the autograph score has relatively few ornaments compared to the published edition, thereby giving an insight into how Mozart expected performers to approach his works.

Copyist Scores

The largest proportion of manuscript scores comprises copyists' scores, that is, scores not in the composer's own hand. This was the principal way in which music was disseminated for many centuries, as the market for music was relatively small and the cost of printing high. In many cases it was cheaper to produce hand-copied scores on demand and some music publishers employed groups of copyists for such work.

Freelance copyists worked for all kinds of music establishments across Europe. CHARLES BURNEY recorded using their services when he was collecting scores in preparation for his history of music. Copyists were also employed by composers. Mozart's correspondence with his father refers to copyists coming to his home so that he could oversee their work. Some composers are known to have had a long-term relationship with a copyist, notably Handel with John Christopher Smith senior. This relationship lasted for many decades; Smith's copies are well documented and often offer alternative musical texts to the autograph sources.

The main issues involving copyists' scores include identifying both the source that was copied and any copyist's errors made during the process. Where a copyist's score can be traced back to the composer, it may show examples of that composer's own self-editing and give invaluable insights into his working methods; notable in this respect is the copy of BEETHOVEN's Symphony No. 9 in D minor, Op. 125 ('Choral'), prepared for the Philharmonic Society in London and preserved in the British Library (shelfmark: RPS MS 5 f.71), which includes amendments in Beethoven's hand.

Where an autograph score is lost, a copyist's score can be the earliest source for a work. A copyist's score can also transmit a version of a work which incorporates alternative readings reflecting performing traditions. The sources for Allegri's *Miserere* offer an interesting example, as the original is much plainer than the work we have come to know. Performance traditions have established the ornamented version that we are used to hearing. When Leopold I, the Holy Roman Emperor, requested a copy from the Vatican for his chapel at the end of the sixteenth century, he famously complained to the Pope that he had been sent an inferior work as it was unadorned and did not represent the work he had heard in the Sistine Chapel. Later sources include various ornamented versions of the work and have been used to create modern editions.

Manuscript Parts

Manuscript performance parts are relatively rare but can be an invaluable source, especially for performance markings. In exceptional cases these can include sets of parts which were used at early performances under the composer's direction. They can give insights into the discussions which took place during the REHEARSAL stages. They can include changes to the music, which are recorded in the parts but not in either the conducting or the autograph score, and to the way of performing the music.

Other Manuscript Sources
Composers' letters can often reveal information about the way in which they wanted their works to be performed. One illustration of this is Haydn's 'Applausus' Cantata, Hob. XXIVa:6. This work was commissioned by an Abbey in Lower Austria. Haydn knew that he would not be able to prepare the performance so he sent a letter detailing his expectations. Although this letter primarily concerns the cantata's performance, it also offers glimpses of Haydn's working practices and performance style.

From an earlier generation, we know that singers were expected to show off their vocal and embellishing talents and musical TASTE in the da capo section of an aria but surviving examples of this ornamentation are not common. However, one interesting example relates to the performance of the aria 'Scherza infida' from Handel's *Ariodante*. A contemporary manuscript source preserved at the ROYAL ACADEMY OF MUSIC, London (RAM MS 139) includes the ornaments with which Carestini, for whom the aria was written, is reputed to have embellished it.

FURTHER READING

T. Best (ed.), *Handel Collections and their History* (Oxford: Clarendon Press, 1993).
M. Elliott, *Singing in Style: A Guide to Vocal Performance Practices* (New Haven, CT and London: Yale University Press, 2006).

PETER LINNITT

Marais, Marin (b. Paris, bap. 31 May 1656; d. Paris, 15 August 1728) French composer and VIOL player, who is an outstanding figure of the French Baroque era.

Marais was a pupil of Sainte-Colombe and LULLY. Between 1693 and 1709 he published four operas (*tragédies en musique*) in which he expands the dramatic role of the French ORCHESTRA using a high degree of virtuosity. Marais's five books of *pièces de viole*, consisting of 596 pieces published between 1686 and 1725, are a remarkable source on the niceties of French Baroque string playing in the *goût français*.

Marais marked up his pieces with all the necessary BOWING, FINGERING and ORNAMENTATION to play the viol with *délicatesse* (good TASTE). Stressing the importance of a flexible wrist for an excellent bow stroke, Marais marks his bowings with 'p' (*poussé*, pushed) and 't' (*tiré*, pulled). In addition, Marais clarifies the type of bowing such as *sec* (dry), *petits coups d'archets* (short bow strokes) and an 'e' to indicate *enfler* (to swell). Chords are played in three manners: normally, arpeggiated marked '/' and *en plein* (all strings together). Marais emphasises the need for a good left-hand position with the thumb opposite the middle finger for ease of playing chords. Fingerings 1, 2, 3 and 4 are used to indicate shifts, and dots are added above the numbers to show the string in ambiguous cases. Marais also uses a dot either side of the number to indicate laying a finger across two or more strings. Recommended ornamentation includes VIBRATO with one and two fingers marked by a vertical or horizontal wavy line respectively, and the highly expressive sliding of one finger up a semitone. In his later books Marais embraces the *goût étranger* (foreign style) and the *goût exotique* (exotic style). HUBERT LE BLANC (83) describes Marais's sonorous sound as like 'the great bell of Saint-Germain' and 'playing on air' by letting the string vibrate after the bow stroke.

FURTHER READING

H. Le Blanc, *Défense de la basse de viole contre les entreprises du violon et les prétentions du violoncelle* (Amsterdam: P. Mortier, 1740).
M. Marais, 'Avertissements' To Five Books of *pièces de viole* (Paris, 1686/9, 1701, 1711, 1717, 1725).
D. A. Teplow, *Performance Practice and Technique in Marin Marais' Pièces de Viole* (Ann Arbor, MI: UMI Research Press, 1986).

LUCY ROBINSON

Marchesi, Luigi (b. Milan, 8 August 1755; d. Milan, ?18 December 1829) Italian singer and composer.

One of the foremost CASTRATOS of the last quarter of the eighteenth century, Marchesi was celebrated for his enormous compass, spanning alto and soprano registers (g–d'''). Pietro Verri (27) judged his voice 'very beautiful, sonorous and equal throughout his range' and 'sufficiently powerful to fill the largest theatre'. For Benedetto Frizzi he was the 'non plus ultra' of singers, equally accomplished in coloratura and expressive SINGING (in Rice, 372–3). BURNEY described his singing as 'refined ... grand and full of dignity'; he also praised his dramatic interpretation of recitatives and 'the grace and propriety of his gestures', adding, 'we expected a great singer, but that does not always include a fine actor' (*A General History of Music from the Earliest Ages to the Present Period* (London, 1776–89, 1957), II, 901–2).

Marchesi was universally commended for his exact intonation, but it was his ORNAMENTATION that attracted the most detailed scrutiny, both for its variety and originality – 'new, elegant, and of his own invention' (Burney, II, 902). Verri (27) described his formidable trill, 'on each of six or seven consecutive notes ... as firm and clear as if played on a violin'. A transcription of Marchesi's ornaments applied to an aria by Zingarelli, in *Pirro, Re di Epiro* (Milan, 1791), is reproduced in Derr (10).

Marchesi sang in all the major opera houses in Italy, with particular successes in Naples, Venice, Florence and Milan. He was also engaged in Munich, Vienna, Warsaw, St Petersburg and London. He was Sarti's favourite leading man, and created roles for Bianchi, Jommelli, Mayr and Mysliveček among others. Reputedly one of the highest earning castratos of his age, he was noted for his charitable works, including the sponsorship of regular benefit concerts for the widows and orphans of musicians in Milan. He composed regularly throughout his life, and left a number of published arias and duets besides several MANUSCRIPT collections.

FURTHER READING

E. Derr, 'Zur Zierpraxis im späten 18. Jahrhundert', *Österreichische Musikzeitschrift*, 32 (1977), 9–10.
J. Rice, 'Benedetto Frizzi on singers', *Studi musicali*, 23 (1994), 372–3.
P. Verri and A. Verri, *Carteggio di Pietro e Alessandro Verri*, ed. G. Seregni (Milan: Giuffre, 1940), 27.

PATRICIA HOWARD

Mariani, Angelo (b. Ravenna, 11 October 1821; d. Genoa, 13 June 1873) Italian conductor and composer.

As a young first violinist-conductor Mariani worked principally in Milan, Copenhagen and Constantinople. He was conductor of Genoa's Teatro Carlo Felice (1853–73) and also undertook important work at Bologna's Teatro Comunale (from 1860), where he directed all Meyerbeer's grand operas and the first Italian performances of WAGNER's *Lohengrin* (1871) and *Tannhaüser* (1872). He also conducted Classical symphonies, directing the first complete performance in Italy of BEETHOVEN's Third Symphony (Genoa, 1853).

Mariani's autobiography (Bologna: Archiginnasio, 1866) and various letters (mostly unpublished) record that he introduced four elements of opera CONDUCTING into modern Italian practice: uniting the roles of vocal rehearser and performance director; using the baton rather than the VIOLIN BOW; introducing independent ORCHESTRA REHEARSALS and sectional rehearsals; and, principally, taking complete control over both music and staging. He realised Verdi and Wagner's wish for *unità* or *Gesamtheit*, pre-empting the practices of Toscanini and Karajan.

FURTHER READING

I. Cavallini, *Il direttore d'orchestra. Genesi e storia di un'arte* (Venice: Marsilio, 1998), 217–39.
A. Rostagno, 'Verdi e Mariani', in R. Iovino and S. Verdino (eds.), *Giuseppe Verdi genovese* (Lucca: Libreria musicale italiana, 2000), 33–60.
'La Scala verso la moderna orchestra. Gli eventi e i motivi delle riforme da Merelli ad "Aida"', *Studi verdiani*, 16 (2002), 157–216.

ANTONIO ROSTAGNO

Marpurg, Friedrich Wilhelm (b. Seehof, nr Wendemark, Brandenburg, 21 November 1718; d. Berlin, 22 May 1795) German composer and writer on music.

In the early 1740s Marpurg resided in Paris, where he was employed as private secretary to a Prussian general who played the FLUTE, Friedrich Rudolph Graf von Rothenburg. The music he must have encountered there clearly made a lasting impression on him, for he became a passionate devotee of the French style. From 1749 to 1763 he made a precarious living in Berlin, devoting himself mainly to music criticism and theoretical writing, though he also composed Lieder and keyboard works. His financial situation improved when, thanks to KIRNBERGER's recommendation, he was offered a post in the Prussian State Lottery in 1763. Three years later, in 1766, he was appointed director of the lottery, a post he held until the end of his life.

On the strength of his writings from 1749 onwards, Marpurg established himself as an important figure in the early Berlin Enlightenment. He was responsible for the EDITING and most of the contents of three periodicals: *Der critische Musicus an der Spree* (Berlin, 1749–50), *Historisch-Kritische Beyträge zur Aufnahme der Musik* (Berlin, 1754–62, 1778) and *Kritische Briefe über die Tonkunst* (Berlin, 1760–4). In *Der critische Musicus* he discussed, among other things, the theory of AFFECTS, the chief NATIONAL IDIOMS of the day – the French, Italian and German styles – and the manner of performance associated with them.

Marpurg's manuals on keyboard playing, *Die Kunst das Clavier zu spielen* (Berlin, 1750 and 1761) and *Anleitung zum Clavierspielen* (Berlin, 1755), contain helpful advice and information on ORNAMENTATION, ARTICULATION, dotted and triplet rhythms, and accompaniment. The second-named manual owes much to FRANÇOIS COUPERIN's *L'Art de toucher le clavecin* (Paris, 1716). Marpurg was also much influenced by RAMEAU, disseminating the Frenchman's harmonic theories in his *Systematische Einleitung in die musikalische Setzkunst, nach den Lehrsätzen des Herrn Rameau* (Leipzig, 1757), a German translation of D'Alembert's *Elémens de musique* (Paris, 1752). Shortly after J. S. BACH's death, Marpurg wrote a substantial preface to the second edition of his *Die Kunst der Fuge* (Leipzig: Breitkopf, 1752), warmly commending its study to students of fugue and identifying it as the inspiration of his TREATISE on the subject, *Abhandlung von der Fuge nach den Grundsätzen der besten deutschen und ausländischen Meister* (2 vols. (Berlin, 1753–4; repr., Hildesheim, 1970)), a major, systematic study of fugal writing in the late Baroque period.

Marpurg's other writings include a manual on thoroughbass, *Handbuch bey dem Generalbasse* (Berlin, 1755–8), which is still useful today for its advice on FIGURED BASS realisation, and manuals on the art of SINGING and composing for the voice: *Anleitung zur Singcomposition* (Berlin, 1758) – a tacit rebuttal of Agricola's *Anleitung zur Singkunst* – and *Anleitung zur Musik überhaupt und zur Singkunst besonders* (Berlin, 1763). He also contributed to the eighteenth-century German debate on keyboard TEMPERAMENT in his *Anfangsgründe der theoretischen Musik* (Leipzig, 1757) and *Versuch über die musikalische Temperatur* (Breslau, 1776). While strongly supporting equal temperament, he believed that a form of *modified* equal temperament was the most useful system of all.

FURTHER READING

A. Mann, *The Study of Fugue* (New Brunswick, NJ: Rutgers University Press, 1958, repr. 1987).
H. Serwer, 'Friedrich Wilhelm Marpurg (1718–95): Music critic in a galant age', PhD dissertation, Yale University (1969).

RICHARD D. P. JONES

Marsh, John (b. Dorking, 31 May 1752; d. Chichester, 31 October 1828) English composer and writer.

John Marsh left behind a thirty-seven-volume *History of My Private Life* that depicts how far an English amateur might go in devoting himself to musical activities. Marsh redrafted an early personal diary and notes on the history of his family, and from 1800 made current entries, all of which has been published in two volumes by Brian Robins (the revised edition of vol. 1 has a longer index). Having grown up as the son of a sea captain, Marsh worked as a solicitor in Romsey and Salisbury and, after coming into his inheritance, moved to Canterbury and then to Chichester. Trained on the VIOLIN and the ORGAN, Marsh helped manage the concert society in each city. He composed organ music and several symphonies and wrote essays on the theory of harmony, but his most impressive publication was a 'comparison between the Ancient and Modern' (*Monthly Magazine*, 1796–7). The *History of My Private Life* provides a vivid picture of the rich musical culture that flourished well outside London, leading one through domestic parties, dances in assembly rooms, public and private concerts, election rituals, lunches with town mayors and dinners of reading societies. The scope of Marsh's musical career led him, as John Brewer suggested, to self-deprecation, indeed to a 'desire to escape censure as a social oddity who considered music more important than anything else' (544).

FURTHER READING

J. Brewer, *The Pleasure of the Imagination: English Culture in the Eighteenth Century* (London: HarperCollins, 1997), 531–72.
J. Marsh, *John Marsh Journals*, vol. 1, rev. edn, ed. B. Robins (Stuyvesant, NY: Pendragon Press, 2011).
John Marsh Journals, vol. 2, ed. B. Robins (Stuyvesant, NY: Pendragon Press, 2013).
W. Weber, 'The fabric of daily life and the autobiography of John Marsh', *Huntington Library Quarterly*, 59 (1996), 145–69.

WILLIAM WEBER

Martinn, Jacob-Joseph-Balthasar (b. Antwerp, 1 May 1775; d. Paris, 10 October 1836) Flemish violinist, composer and pedagogue.

Little is known about Martinn's VIOLIN training. He worked for most of his career in Paris, playing in the Théâtre du Vaudeville orchestra and then at the Opéra Italien. After the foundation of the Imperial schools he taught the violin at the Lycée Charlemagne. His compositions include two *symphonies concertantes*, six string quartets and other chamber pieces; he also published two violin methods and three VIOLA TREATISES, appropriate for students of differing levels of technical proficiency.

Martinn's *Méthode élémentaire de violon* (Paris: Frey, c1815) combines basic technical principles with scales and tunes in the various keys, six *Airs Variés* and six violin duets. His later *Méthode de violon* (Paris: Jouve, [1825]) is only slightly more advanced in its instruction and musical content, which comprises exercises, scales, simple tunes as 'leçons' and twelve *divertissements*.

The most substantial and advanced of Martinn's viola treatises, *Méthode pour l'alto contenant les principes de cet instrument* (Paris: chez Richault, 1823), featured in pedagogical circles well into the twentieth century. Textual content is relatively sparse. Martinn makes some parallels with violin left-hand position-work, but remarks little about bowing. Musical content includes scales and études, three two-movement sonatas for two violas, twelve progressive viola duos and twenty-four challenging études, some clearly influenced by KREUTZER's *Quarante Etudes*. His *Nouvelle méthode d'alto* (Paris: Joly, c1826) takes direct inspiration from BAILLOT, RODE and Kreutzer's violin method (1803), especially regarding holding the instrument. Again, there is little instruction re bowing. The work includes some scales, exercises in all keys, twelve lessons as duos and three easy duo sonatas. Intended as a self-instructor, Martinn's *Nouvelle méthode d'alto, pour apprendre sans maître* (Paris: Joly, c1835) is of more modest content and demand. It embraces general musical as well as some fundamental technical principles, reprints the *leçons* of his treatise of c1826 and includes twenty new airs, six short duos and an *Air varié*.

ROBIN STOWELL

Marx, Adolf Bernard (b. Halle, 15 May 1795; d. Berlin, 17 May 1866) German music theorist, critic and composer.

Marx spent most of his life in Berlin, a city with strong traditions in performance theory (exemplified by the didactic works of C. P. E. BACH, J. J. QUANTZ and F. W. MARPURG) and the technical analysis of music (E. T. A. Hoffmann died there in 1822). He published his own detailed analyses of BEETHOVEN's piano sonatas in an appendix to his biography of the composer (1859), and his rigorously formalist approach implied that performers had a duty to understand the structures of the music. He also established the term 'sonata form' (*Die Lehre von der musikalischen Komposition* (4 vols. (Leipzig: Breitkopf & Härtel, 1837–47), III, 200ff.), characterising its first and second themes as 'masculine' and 'feminine' respectively – a move which has influenced the manner in which they have been performed ever since, and one which has attracted the attention of modern gender theorists.

Marx's famous music journal, the *Berliner allgemeine musikalische Zeitung* (1824–30), contains many comments on performance, as does his *Allgemeine Musiklehre* (Leipzig: Breitkopf & Härtel, 1839), which is a general survey, divided into seven parts, of music theory and practice. The first five deal with rudimentary matters such as NOTATION, keys, rhythm, and instruments and voice types, etc. Part 2, for example, provides a comprehensive discussion of musical ACCENTUATION (122ff.) with a survey of symbols (dots, lines, boxes, etc.) used to indicate the types available. Part 6 of the book attempts a rare analysis of 'artistic performance' (282ff.). It distinguishes between 'correct performance' (which represents the notation accurately), 'intelligent performance' (which attends to the construction of the work and connections between its sections), 'graceful performance' (which by its pleasing manner and interesting accentuation increases the beauty and effectiveness of the music), and 'feeling performance' (which opens us to the spiritual dimension, and 'cannot be taught but only fostered or heightened'). Students are warned (295) against superficial advice on interpretation by 'pseudo-poetical aestheticians', and against misleading, short-cut, characterisations such as 'the clarinet is the instrument of love'. Above all, 'the idea of the whole work should be our guide and rule in interpretation' (316, fn.). The seventh (final) part of the book is concerned with the cultivation and teaching of music.

Marx's contributions to music dictionaries (such as Gustav Schilling's *Encyclopädie*, 1835) are also important, though revised versions of many of his entries are incorporated into his *Allgemeine Musiklehre*. His criticisms of Carl Zelter's Singakademie in Berlin led him to establish, together with THEODOR KULLAK and Julius Stern, the Berliner Musikschule in 1850 (which later became the Stern Conservatoire).

FURTHER READING

C. Brown, *Classical and Romantic Performing Practice 1750–1900* (Oxford University Press, 1999).
T. Christensen (ed.), *The Cambridge History of Music Theory* (Cambridge University Press, 2002).
A. Marx, *Allgemeine Musiklehre* (Leipzig: Breitkopf & Härtel, 1839).
   Musical Form in the Age of Beethoven, ed. and trans. S. Burnham (Cambridge University Press, 1997).

ANTHONY PRYER

Matteis, Nicola (b. Naples?; *fl.* c1670–c1690). Italian violinist, guitarist and composer.

Matteis reputedly walked to London in the 1660s from his native southern Italy, yet through the agencies of wealthy amateur players he attained pivotal influence over the adoption of the Italian style in England. Celebrated for his virtuosity, expressive adagios and holding the VIOLIN almost at his waist, Matteis's main legacy rests in his five sets of *Ayres* for the violin. Ornate copperplate engraving reveals both nuanced, expressive ORNAMENTATION and a significant level of technical difficulty. Optional second and third parts allowed for simple CONSORT performance. Matteis's son (also Nicola) and grandson (John-Nichola) shared his profession, leading to inevitable confusion. His son died in Vienna in 1737, and his grandson (who returned to the UK and taught CHARLES BURNEY the violin) in 1760. North tells us that poor Matteis senior 'dyed miserable' (J. Wilson (ed.), *Roger North on Music* (London: Novello, 1959), 308), in obscurity, as a result of overindulgence brought on by his sudden wealth.

FURTHER READING

M. Cyr, 'Violin playing in late seventeenth-century England: Baltzar, Matteis, and Purcell', *PPR*, 8/1, article 5.

S. Jones, 'The legacy of the "stupendious" Nicola Matteis', *EMc*, 29/4 (November 2001), 553–68.

SIMON JONES

Mattheson, Johann (b. Hamburg, 28 September 1681; d. Hamburg, 17 April 1764) German composer and writer.

A musical child prodigy, Mattheson performed on the ORGAN and sang at Hamburg's churches and at the Opera. After studies with Joachim Gerstenbüttel at the Johanneum, he was briefly a page at the Hamburg court of Count von Güldenlöw, then took on solo roles at the Opera until 1705. Together with his friend Handel, he was invited in 1703 to succeed Buxtehude as organist at the Marienkirche in Lübeck, but both musicians declined the offer. In 1706 he began his long service as secretary to Sir John Wich, the English ambassador to Hamburg. From 1715 he was vicar and from 1718 music director at Hamburg Cathedral, resigning in 1728 over a conflict with his oratorio singers. By this time he had begun to lose his hearing, and eventually went completely deaf. The Duke of Holstein appointed him *Kapellmeister* in 1719, legation secretary in 1741 and 'Legations-Rat' in 1744.

Among Mattheson's many writings on music, the earliest to address performance issues is the *Exemplarische Organisten-Probe* (Hamburg, 1719), extensively revised and expanded as the *Grosse General-Baß-Schule* (Hamburg, 1731). In both books, Mattheson instructs organists on how to improvise solo pieces from a given FIGURED BASS, providing extensive commentary on forty-eight practice pieces ('Prob-Stücke') of varying difficulty. His *Kleine General-Baß-Schule* (Hamburg, 1735) teaches accompanists how to realise a figured bass. Mattheson's most important book, *Der vollkommene Capellmeister* (Hamburg, 1739), distills his thoughts on musical theory and practice and includes several chapters addressing aspects of performance. The expressive gesturing of musicians, especially theatrical singers, is the subject of 'On the art of gesticulation' (part 1, chapter 6). 'Examination and the care of the human voice' (part 2, chapter 1) concerns vocal production and voice-care, including one of the earliest accounts of the vocal organs. A companion chapter, 'On the art of singing and playing with graces' (part 2, chapter 3), discusses the deficiencies of contemporary SINGING and the common ornaments that singers should know. 'On the art of playing' (part 3, chapter 25) advises the organist on accompanying singers and improvising preludes, fugues, chorale accompaniments and postludes. Finally, Mattheson provides remarks on the qualities of a good director and on vocal scoring in the book's concluding chapter, 'On conducting, direction, production and execution of a concert' (part 3, chapter 26).

FURTHER READING

J. Butt, *Music Education and the Art of Performance in the German Baroque* (Cambridge University Press, 1994).

E. C. Harriss, *Johann Mattheson's* Der vollkommene Capellmeister: *A Revised Translation with Critical Commentary* (Ann Arbor, MI: UMI Research Press, 1981).

F. Neumann, 'Mattheson on performance practice' and H. Turnow, 'Die Verzierungskunst aus Matthesons Sicht', in G. J. Buelow and H. J. Marx (eds.), *New Mattheson Studies* (Cambridge University Press, 1983), 257–68 and 269–89.

STEVEN ZOHN

Maugars, André (b. c1585; d. ?Paris, c1646) French viol player, writer and translator.

Maugars lived at least four years in England during the 1620s, probably not in royal service. He wrote of his indebtedness to English VIOL practices, in particular the various tunings ('accords'). He published two French translations of Francis Bacon and served Cardinal Richelieu and Louis XIII during the 1630s. Mersenne reports in his *Harmonicorum libri* (Paris: Baudry, 1635) that while Maugars and Nicolas Hotman both 'excel in diminutions and incomparably delicate, sweet bowing', Maugars 'executes by himself two, three, or more parts at the same time on his viol with so many ornaments and such dexterity of fingering ... that none have heard anything like it previously' ('Liber primus de instrumentis harmonicis', Propositio XXX, 47).

Visiting Rome in 1638–9, Maugars performed for Urban VIII and others. His 1639 letter about Roman music, published anonymously in Paris as *Response faite à un Curieux, sur le sentiment de la Musique d'Italie*, was among the first French comparisons of Italian and French music, describing performances in churches, oratorios and homes. He includes details on *cori spezzati* (ten choirs, each with an organ) for special Offices and Mass at Santa Maria sopra Minerva. For Maugars, Italian sacred music exhibits 'more art, science, and variety ... but also more license' (*Response*, 4) than French. He describes hearing recitative – unknown in France – performed during oratorios. A wide variety of instruments and styles lent to the grandeur of oratorio, but the pinnacle was hearing FRESCOBALDI play variations on the HARPSICHORD. Maugars also heard the harpist Orazio Michi and the singer-theorbist Leonora Baroni.

Maugars writes that Italians prize instrumental music over vocal; descriptions of instrumental practices and repertoires include his own, both studied and improvised (preludes, fantasias, divisions on a theme). Although his distinction between ARCHLUTES and THEORBOS seems muddled, his references to the latter imply that they were familiar in France by 1638. Maugars makes numerous mentions of embellishment practices, including archlutenists alternating divisions, and violinists and singers decorating melodies. Near the end of the *Response* he praises MONTEVERDI, aspiring to visit Venice and acquire some of the composer's music.

FURTHER READING

G. Cowart, *The Origins of Modern Musical Criticism* (Ann Arbor, MI: UMI Research Press, 1981).
A. Maugars, *Response faite à un curieux, sur le sentiment de la musique d'Italie* (Paris, 1639), facsim. edn, trans. and annotated by H. W. Hitchcock (Geneva: Minkoff, 1993).
E. Thoinan, *Maugars: Célèbre joueur de viole, musicien du Cardinal de Richelieu, conseiller, sécretaire, interprète du Roi en langue anglaise, traducteur de F. Bacon, prieur de Saint-Pierre Eynac* (Paris: Claudin, 1865; repr. London: Baron, 1965).

STUART CHENEY

McGegan, Nicholas (b. Sawbridgeworth, 14 January 1950) British keyboard player, flautist and conductor.

After studying at Oxford and Cambridge universities, McGegan was involved in early period-instrument projects in England in the 1970s, working both as a flautist and as a keyboard player with the ACADEMY OF ANCIENT MUSIC, among others. In 1979 he began an association with the English Bach Festival, CONDUCTING RAMEAU operas in historically informed staged productions and recordings, but in the early 1980s he moved to the USA, where in 1985 he became the first music director of the four-year-old California-based Philharmonia Baroque Orchestra, the USA's leading ensemble of its kind. He also worked and recorded frequently with the pioneer Hungarian period orchestra Capella Savaria in the 1980s and early 1990s.

Although he has conducted much concert repertoire with these and other ensembles both period and modern, it is largely in eighteenth-century opera (often in historical stagings) that his reputation has been built. In 1985 he conducted an influential staging of Handel's *Teseo* at the Boston Early Music Festival, and it is with Handel that he has become most closely associated, especially since his appointment in 1991 as artistic director of the Göttingen International Handel Festival, succeeding JOHN ELIOT GARDINER. In Göttingen he conducted annual Handel opera productions, of which *Ottone*, *Radamisto*, *Giustino* and *Ariodante*, all with the Freiburg Baroque Orchestra, were subsequently recorded by Harmonia Mundi, while for the same label he also conducted the Philharmonia Baroque in a number of Handel oratorios. He relinquished the Göttingen post in 2011. He has also conducted eighteenth-century opera for major international companies, including *Ariodante* at the English National Opera in 1993, and MOZART's *La clemenza di Tito* and Rameau's *Platée* for the Royal Opera in London.

McGegan's conducting combines intelligent musicianship and affinity for singers with instinctive understanding of the workings of the Baroque drama.

LINDSAY KEMP

Mechanical instruments The term 'mechanical' could be interpreted as applying to any instruments where mechanical systems contribute to sound production, such as the PIANO or ORGAN. The present discussion, however, is restricted to those that preserve a fixed musical repertory by mechanical means. The earliest account of such a device, apart from simple clock chimes, is from 1321, when one at the abbey of St Catherine near Rouen could apparently play the hymn 'Conditor alme siderum'. Other examples are documented from the fourteenth century, notably from Strasbourg and Lyons, and the earliest surviving instrument still in working condition dates from 1502.

The principle of storing the music by means of a pattern of pins and staples inserted into a rotating clockwork barrel – exactly as in a modern musical box – seems to have been established from the outset. Similar mechanisms also operated organs, such as the one built in the gardens of the Villa d'Este in Rome in 1548. This particular barrel, along with other mechanical details, was illustrated by Athanasius Kircher in 1650, who reported that it played a four-part hymn accompanied by moving figures.

By the eighteenth century, advances in technology allowed ever more sophisticated pieces of music to be performed by mechanical instruments and they became immensely fashionable. The most famous examples are those where a conventional instrument was played by a humanoid automaton, such as Jacques de Vaucanson's FLUTE player of 1737 (with a repertory of twelve songs) or the automaton dulcimer player by David Roentgen of 1784, which still survives and has been restored to working order. Spectacular though these may be, of much more interest musically are the organs that could play whole polyphonic sonata movements. Charles Clay built two such instruments in c1736 and each is programmed with ten pieces composed or arranged by Handel. Similarly MOZART, HAYDN and BEETHOVEN (among others) contributed pieces for comparable devices.

These have a particular significance for the history of performance in that they were meticulously programmed by musicians and preserve minute details of ORNAMENTATION and ARTICULATION so that they record an actual performance. This assumes of course that they sound as they did when they were first made, and it is also arguable that the slow process of barrel pinning may have encouraged ornaments different to those a live player would have used. Nevertheless these machines are still an invaluable resource for the understanding of historical performance.

The same principle was developed into more complicated machines known as orchestrions in the nineteenth century, beginning with the Panharmonicon invented in 1805 by Johann Maelzel. Mass production gave rise to a welter of competing brand names but the most significant development was the perforated paper roll, patented in 1883, which allowed the possibility of 'recording' specific performances with much more immediacy and ease, on the piano at least. Player pianos that used such rolls sold in huge quantities until they were eclipsed by the 78 rpm record in the 1920s.

FURTHER READING

J. Haspels, *Automatic Musical Instruments: Their Mechanics and Their Music 1580–1820* (Utrecht: Jan Jaap Haspels, 1987).
A. W. J. G. Ord-Hume, *The Musical Clock: Musical & Automation Clocks & Watches* (Asbourne: Mayfield Books, c1995).
R. Smith and D. Thompson, 'Vulliamy musical clocks for the Turkish market', *Antiquarian Horology*, 21/2 (1993), 118–31.

JON BANKS

Meifred, Pierre-Joseph Emile (b. Colmar, 22 November 1791; d. Paris, 28 August 1867) French HORN player, teacher and instrument designer.

Meifred won the *premier prix* in the PARIS CONSERVATOIRE's horn class in 1818 and gave the first French public performance on the valve horn at a concert in Paris on 9 March 1828. A low horn player like his teacher, DAUPRAT, he played in the orchestra at the Paris Opéra from 1822 to 1850, but it was his appointment to the Paris Conservatoire in 1833 which put him in the forefront of debate on the relative merits of the valve horn and hand horn. One major concern was that the development of valves would result in the loss of the wide tonal palette that was a by-product of the technique which hand horn players used to produce notes outside the harmonic series. In his *Méthode* for valve horn (Paris, 1840), Meifred advocates using the valves for playing chromatically in the lower compass to fill in the gaps in the instrument's range and to improve tuning. However, he also recommends using valves in combination with hand-horn technique to make heavily stopped notes more sonorous and to preserve the timbre of lightly stopped ones, particularly the characteristic tone of the leading note of the scale. Meifred also looked for other ways of addressing the perceived disadvantages of the valve horn, designing and playing a horn whose two Stölzel valves included tuning slides and allowed their use with crooks of different length. Later in his career he argued that players should be able to perform in all registers, ending the distinction between high and low players.

While Meifred's *Méthode* does not seem to have been disseminated widely outside Paris, the principles which it explains have potential as a key to performing the horn parts written by French and Italian composers up to Verdi.

FURTHER READING

P.-J. Meifred, *Méthode de cor chromatique ou à pistons* (Paris: Richault, 1840).
J. L. Snedeker, 'Joseph Meifred's *Méthode de cor chromatique ou à pistons (1840)*', *HBSJ*, 4 (1992), 87–105.

JOHN HUMPHRIES

Meiningen Town in Thuringia, Germany, founded c1000.

Meiningen's musical history is chiefly associated with the court of Saxe-Coburg-Meiningen from 1680, including the building of the palace Schloss Elisabethenburg in 1682, the establishment of the ducal orchestral by Duke Bernhard I in 1690, its expansion under Duke Bernhard II and visiting operatic performances leading to the building of the first Hoftheater by Duke Georg I in 1831. Meiningen's greatest fame as a performance centre is associated with the patronage of Duke Georg II (1826–1914). First known as the 'Theaterherzog', he later turned his attention to the orchestra, appointing HANS VON BÜLOW in 1880 to achieve new standards of performance (it had already provided players for the orchestra of the Bayreuth Festival). BRAHMS's close association with the orchestra, which von Bülow at an early stage invited him to conduct, was inspired as much by the flexibility possible with its ensemble of around only fifty players as by von Bülow's famed discipline: Brahms premiered his Fourth Symphony in the Hoftheater in 1885. It was Brahms's long familiarity with the playing of the principal clarinettist, Richard Mühlfeld, that inspired his later-composed clarinet works.

Von Bülow was succeeded by RICHARD STRAUSS for one year, 1885–6, which included the premiere of Strauss's First Horn Concerto. The orchestra's reputation burgeoned under FRITZ STEINBACH, who directed it during 1886–1903; he led the *Meiningische Landesmusikfeste*, beginning in 1895 with a chorus well in excess of 300 and an ORCHESTRA of over ninety in works by BACH, BEETHOVEN and BRAHMS, and extended the orchestra's touring.

Following his successor Wilhelm Berger, Max Reger directed between 1911 and 1914, including more modern programming, though he also championed BRAHMS. Artistic life continued following the abolition of the principality in 1914, and the now state theatre and orchestra have major reputations. The Schloss Elisabethenburg contains a museum containing the Max Reger archive, which includes his and von Bülow's marked scores of the Brahms symphonies, and musical instruments.

FURTHER READING

W. Blume (ed.), *Brahms in der Meininger Tradition. Seine Sinfonien und Haydn Variationen in der Bezeichnung von Fritz Steinbach* (author's typescript) 1933: repr. as *Brahms in der Meininger Tradition. Seine Sinfonien in der Bezeichnung von Fritz Steinbach*, with foreword by M. Schwalb (Hildesheim, Zurich and New York: Georg Olms Verlag, 2013).

MICHAEL MUSGRAVE

Meiningen Orchestra see MEININGEN

Melkus, Eduard (b. Baden, nr Vienna, 1 September 1928) Austrian violinist and violist.

Melkus was a VIOLIN pupil of Ernst Moravec (1943–53) and studied musicology at Vienna University (1951–3). The seeds of his interest in historical performance were sown in the late 1940s as a member of a VIOLA DA GAMBA quartet with Alice and NIKOLAUS HARNONCOURT and GUSTAV LEONHARDT. He furthered his violin studies with Firmin Touche (Paris), Peter Rybar (Winterthur) and Alexander Schaichet (Zurich) and was appointed violin and VIOLA professor at Vienna's Hochschule für Musik (1958). He formed the Vienna Cappella Academica (1965), which was ostensibly a period-instrument ensemble even if its performances espoused anachronistic elements – for example, Melkus himself used a chin-rest and modern wire and wire-covered strings rather than gut, played at modern PITCH, and consistently employed a continuous VIBRATO. Nevertheless, his performances and recordings of mid-seventeenth through to late eighteenth-century repertory with that ensemble, as well as with harpsichordist Huguette Dreyfus, organist Lionel Rogg and others, influenced audiences worldwide; these include concertos by Vivaldi, Pisendel, J. S. BACH, TELEMANN, HAYDN, Tomasini, Nardini and TARTINI, concerti grossi by CORELLI, trios by Haydn, sonatas by Biber, Ruggieri, Corelli, Handel, Bach, Leclair and MOZART, and various works by Caldara, Monn and COUPERIN.

Melkus's Viennese musicological grounding spawned collaborations with prominent contemporary scholars (notably with Marc Pincherle on the extempore ORNAMENTATION of CORELLI's Op. 5 sonatas) and inspired him to write a book about the construction, history and acoustics of the violin and violin playing (1973), as well as essays about Mannheim violin technique, vibrato, Bach and Handel interpretation, BOWINGS in Mozart, CADENZAS for Mozart's violin concertos and Schumann's Third Violin Sonata. Outside his own specialist field, Melkus premiered (1962) and recorded Egon Wellesz's Violin Concerto, Op. 84, of which he was the dedicatee, and served from 1982 as head of the University of Music and Performing Arts Vienna's transdisciplinary research institute Wiener Klangstil.

FURTHER READING

J. Creighton, *Discopaedia of the Violin* (University of Toronto Press, 1974), 477–9.

ROBIN STOWELL

Memory (performing from) Within different specialisms and genres, musicians have for centuries given performances from memory. For example, it is clear that much music making in the Renaissance took place without reference to NOTATION, leaving no written trace. As Jon Banks (304) has remarked, 'The informal, non-courtly contexts – fairs, village weddings, taverns – were the province of musicians whose lives and times are obscure to us now; many were itinerant outsiders who made the best part of their livings touring the festivals of Europe, as they had done in the Middle Ages.' A later example is seventeenth-century VIOLIN band music, which was evidently not improvised but first composed or arranged on paper and then committed to memory. Accounts of notable musicians performing without their scores abound. Handel performed from memory after 1751 because of his blindness. Evidence of W. A. MOZART's prodigious musical memory includes one of his own letters from 1777, and for first performances of violin sonatas in 1781 and 1784 he retained the PIANO part in his head, having committed only the violin part to paper. Mishra instances further examples from SPOHR (1811), Böhm (1816), and both Fanny and FELIX MENDELSSOHN (respectively 1818 and 1821), with reports of PAGANINI playing from memory as early as 1808. BEETHOVEN strongly disapproved of CZERNY (aged fourteen) playing his sonatas from memory, fearing inaccuracies. Indeed, artistic and critical opinion was generally against the practice, particularly in relation to solo performance. Mishra observes that performing from memory in public began in earnest in the 1830s and 1840s, spearheaded by Clara Wieck, Paganini and Mendelssohn. Liszt was soon to follow, performing most of his music from memory by 1840. This development may in part be ascribed to the commercialisation of music and the public thirst for virtuosity. The rise of the musical canon was also an important driver for memorisation to supplant IMPROVISATION as the favoured method of virtuosic display. Yet memorised performances continued to be described as ostentatious and in bad taste, with critics in London, for instance, famously heavily criticising Sir CHARLES HALLÉ in 1861 and HANS VON BÜLOW in 1870. CONDUCTING from memory remained controversial long after performing from memory on the piano and violin became commonplace.

By the end of the century, memorisation guides were being written, notably Frederick Shinn's *Musical Memory and its Cultivation* (London: Augener, 1898). Edwin Hughes ('Musical memory in piano playing and piano study',

MQ, 1/4 (1915), 592–603) was one of the first authors to make an explicit case in favour of performing from memory for the instrumental soloist, arguing that performing with 'a bundle of notes' obstructs 'absolute freedom of expression and the most direct psychological connection with the audience' (595). Since that time others have also justified the practice with claims that only by playing and singing 'by heart' can they create and communicate their insights and ideas effectively. While not all soloists have felt so strongly about performing from memory – and certainly the expectation to memorise seems not to extend uniformly to all instruments and repertoire nor to ensemble performance – the ability to learn and perform music from memory in public has become a measure of professional competence in most genres. During the 1920s and 1930s, the Kolisch Quartet generally performed from memory, not as a demonstration of special powers, but rather as a culmination of careful rehearsal which elevated the significance of eye contact within the ensemble. Larger group memorisation is even rarer, though the Aurora Orchestra has given performances of Mozart's 'Jupiter' Symphony and Beethoven's 'Pastoral' without a note of music on stage.

Apart from numerous anecdotal accounts of the merits of performing from memory, empirical evidence that it actually enhances performance is limited. In one study, audiences were asked to watch and evaluate videoed performances of a cellist playing the Preludes from BACH's Cello Suites I, II and III. Some of the performances were from memory and others were not, but in an experimental twist using an empty music stand as a prop and a side-facing camera angle, the performances were not always what they seemed. Some memorised performances looked as though the score was being used (i.e. an empty music stand was placed between the cellist and the camera), while some of the non-memorised performances looked memorised (i.e. with the camera positioned to the cellist's right so that the stand was out of video shot). Overall, AUDIENCES preferred the memorised to the non-memorised performances, whether or not they looked as though they were from memory. However, on closer inspection of the memorised performances, audiences most preferred those which complied visually with standard performance practice, where the view of the cellist was not obstructed by a music stand. This suggests that the value of performing from memory is closely intertwined with the visual information available to those watching the performance. Thus, with all being equal, research indicates that performing from memory can provide enhanced experiences for audiences, be it aurally, visually or both.

Scientific research into expert memory, initially undertaken outside the field of music, offers behavioural and psychophysiological evidence that musical memory is underpinned by 'retrieval cues' that combine into a mental representation (or retrieval structure) of a memorised work. These cues trigger recall of specific points in a composition identified by the musician as salient – aurally, visually, kinaesthetically and/or conceptually – when learning the piece. Once identified, the cues are reinforced and organised through practice. While there is scope for individual differences to emerge in the specific cues that musicians establish for a given piece, evidence suggests that identifying, rehearsing and relying upon retrieval cues to encode complex musical structures and to achieve secure recall under pressure are cornerstones of exceptional musical memory.

FURTHER READING

J. Banks, 'Performance in the Renaissance: an overview', in C. Lawson and R. Stowell (eds.), *The Cambridge History of Musical Performance* (Cambridge University Press, 2012), 297–317.
J. Mishra, 'Playing from memory', *American Music Teacher*, 65/6 (2016), 12–16.
A. Williamon, 'Memorising music', in J. Rink (ed.), *Musical Performance: A Guide to Understanding* (Cambridge University Press, 2002), 113–26.
'The value of performing from memory', *Psychology of Music*, 27/1 (1999), 84–95.

AARON WILLIAMON

Mendelssohn Bartholdy, Felix Jacob Ludwig (b. Hamburg, 3 February 1809; d. Leipzig, 4 November 1847) German composer and pivotal figure in the rise of musical historicism.

Mendelssohn grew up in a milieu in which the Old Masters were revered as a matter of course, really as part of a living tradition. His mother Lea and his grandfather Moses had both had piano lessons from J. S. BACH's pupil J. P. KIRNBERGER; and his composition teacher and mentor was C. F. Zelter, director of the Berlin Singakademie whose principal aim was the preservation and cultivation of model works of sacred polyphony from bygone eras. Mendelssohn was trained in strict counterpoint, and Zelter's method of teaching composition by making his pupil write practice works in the style of model composers resulted in a series of string symphonies after C. P. E. BACH, cantatas and ORGAN works after J. S. Bach, psalm settings and other sacred works after Handel, and *a cappella* sacred polyphony in the Italian *stile antico*. In 1827, he visited the jurist A. J. F. Thibaut, author of the seminal treatise *Über die Reinheit der Tonkunst*, advocating the primacy of *a cappella* sacred polyphony; in 1829, Zelter sent him to copy Handel autographs held at the Royal Collection in London; and during his brief sojourn in Catholic Düsseldorf in 1833 and 1834, he searched the local towns and monasteries for historic repertoire.

Most noteworthy, however, was the performance of Bach's *St Matthew Passion* on 11 March 1829. Sections of the passion had been sung by the Singakademie under Zelter since 1815, but to perform the work in its entirety in public was unprecedented. Despite Mendelssohn's declared intentions as an editor to present Bach's works 'absolutely as they were written' (preface to his edition of Bach's organ preludes, as cited in H. Haskell, *The Early Music Revival: A History* (London: Thames & Hudson, 1988), 16), there was little attempt at a 'historically accurate' rendition in making the work accessible to a modern audience. Mendelssohn applied substantial cuts (mostly regarding the arias), and adapted or reorchestrated much of what remained; in this, his approach was comparable to that of MOZART's adaptation of Handel's *Messiah* (a version that Mendelssohn himself performed several times). Mendelssohn profited from being at the right place at the right time: a generally growing historicist interest (tinged by Romanticism) coincided with growing numbers of amateur choral societies eager to perform such repertoire.

Mendelssohn himself arranged or annotated a number of further works, primarily by Bach (cantatas, orchestral suites, the concerto for three pianos and finally the chaconne from the D minor Violin Partita with piano accompaniment) and Handel (*Israel in Egypt*, *Acis and Galatea* and the *Dettingen Te*

Deum). Handel was a particularly strong presence at the grand music festivals which played a pivotal role for Germany's musical (and political) identity in the period, and Mendelssohn supported these festivals where he could. At the same time, as Gewandhaus *Kapellmeister* in Leipzig, he put together three series of 'Historical Concerts', with masterworks in roughly chronological sequence. Finally, wherever he went, he sought out and played on the local organs, here again focusing on J. S. Bach's works above all others.

Equally telling for Mendelssohn's attitude towards history is his editorial activity. In 1845-6, he edited Bach's organ preludes for Coventry & Hollier and Breitkopf & Härtel, as well as *Israel in Egypt* for the Handel Society Edition. In the former, he aimed to 'deviate as little as possible from Bach's original writing' (mistakenly believing himself to own an autograph); in the latter, he added an organ part and a PIANO reduction, but refused to add any DYNAMICS or other performance instructions not explicitly marked as his. As in his performances, he was keenly interested in bringing the works of the Old Masters into the present, but saw this as a process of explicit and as such documentable translation.

In general, therefore, Mendelssohn was one of the pioneers of a consciously historicist attitude towards early music. In contrast to his teacher Zelter, he saw Bach and Handel as belonging not to a living tradition, but to one removed from memory, yet to be revered, revived and reimagined, in contrast, for example, to the Cecilians and other romantically tinged movements of his time which made genuine attempts to turn the clock back. This extended to his compositions as much as to his activities as a collector, performer and editor.

FURTHER READING

A. Hartinger, Ch. Wolff and P. Wollny (eds.), *'Zu groß, zu unerreichbar': Bach-Rezeption im Zeitalter Mendelssohns und Schumanns* (Wiesbaden: Breitkopf & Härtel, 2007).

S. Reichwald (ed.), *Mendelssohn in Performance* (Bloomington and Indianapolis: Indiana University Press, 2008).

J. Thym (ed.), *Mendelssohn, the Organ, and the Music of the Past. Constructing Historical Legacies* (University of Rochester Press/Woodbridge: Boydell & Brewer, 2014).

THOMAS SCHMIDT

Mersenne, Marin (b. La Soultière, 8 September 1588; d. Paris, 1 September 1648) French mathematician, philosopher and music theorist.

Abbé Mersenne was one of the most celebrated French scholars of the early seventeenth century. Of his monumental *Harmonie universelle* (1636), the sections most relevant for historical performers are those dealing with vocal music and with some thirty instruments. Today's expanding bibliography on historical tunings and TEMPERAMENTS is reflected in the number of performing groups who are adopting different systems from the past. Book 2 of *Harmonie universelle* deals in detail with interval sizes, vibrating strings and tunings etc., and Mersenne's experiments form the basis of much of today's theories of acoustics. He contrasts meantone, well temperament and equal temperament systems, eventually favouring equal temperament. Mersenne was one of the first to follow up Baïf's concept of short and long syllables in the French language, which exerted a strong general influence over French vocal music for many decades. His views on ORNAMENTATION are in the context of musical EXPRESSION, yet his examples of vocal embellishment taken from singers of his day are much freer than in later times and give the impression of a rhapsodic variation of the simple lute airs; they are often quite virtuosic. One of the earliest to contrast French and Italian styles, Mersenne believed that French singers were better than others because of the delicacy and sweetness of their delivery (*Harmonie universelle*, Book 2, 42).

FURTHER READING

R. Chapman, *The Books on Instruments from Mersenne's* Harmonie universelle (The Hague: Martinus Nijhoff, 1957).
M. Lindley, 'Mersenne on keyboard tuning', *JMT*, 24/2 (Autumn, 1980), 166–203.

DAVID TUNLEY

Metronome A clockwork device intended to mark visually and sonically the initial pulse of a musical work.

Although the basic technology, which utilised a double-weighted pendulum, was invented by Dietrich Winkel, it was the entrepreneurial showman-engineer Johann Maelzel (1772–1838) who coined, developed and actively promoted the now-iconic TEMPO system. Maelzel's 1815 English patent described 'an instrument or instruments, machine or machines', suggesting his invention was not fully developed or perfected (*The Repertory of Arts, Manufacturers, and Agriculture* XXVIII, London, 1816, 127–8). The term 'metronome' continues to signify many tempo technologies, differing in precision, constancy and purpose, some of which include simple pendulums, handheld electronic components and digital sequencer programs with click-track features. The present definition concerns Maelzel's familiar nineteenth-century technology, an obelisk-shaped tempo clock, that automatically sounds and swings at a predetermined beats-per-minute rate.

Maelzel's purposes for the device changed to meet potential consumers' and collaborators' needs. For composers, its scale was meant to replace Italian time words, which were becoming ineffectual tempo standards. As Maelzel noted, Italian designations were an 'absurdity ... [since] no composer agrees with the other about the meaning of these words' (Albrecht, *Letters to Beethoven*, 1996, II, 137) in relation to the exact speed of a work. BEETHOVEN was troubled by the misleading and contradictory meanings in these basic terms, since *allegro*, for instance, did not accurately encapsulate the emotional qualities of certain energetic movements. He thus considered metronomic dictation a useful supplement to describe his more nuanced and complicated notions of musical movement and metre. Although Beethoven marked 135 metronome indications in total, he relied upon non-traditional verbal cues and customary Italian words throughout his career, despite his pledges to the contrary.

In 1818 Maelzel sent Beethoven instructional charts, detailing the ways MM numbers applied to metre, pulse and tempo words in various languages. Similar schemas appear later in HUMMEL's *Ausführliche theoretisch-practische Anweisung zum Piano-forte-Spiel* (1828). Because Maelzel's original number-ranges are contingent on a specified metre, a main note-pulse for that metre as well as a speed category for that note (*slow, moderate or quick*), these original MM calculations differ considerably from the simplified scale affixed to metronomes themselves, which hierarchically link beats-per-minute ranges to familiar Italian tempo designations.

Maelzel promoted the machine to the public mainly as a pedagogical apparatus. An endorsement in the *Wiener AMZ* (1818), signed by Beethoven and Salieri but assuredly drafted by Maelzel, claimed its value for 'all beginners and pupils' during lessons and even in the 'teacher's absence' as a rhythm training device (*Wiener AMZ* 2, No. 7, 14 February 1818, 58). Beyond a few high-profile endorsements, Maelzel's technology met with some opposition. Regardless of Maelzel's original intentions, a cultural consensus emerged in the nineteenth century around clockwork metronome usage: it was an initial reference, a limited indication of pulse-movement, which need not enforce a particular tempo-number across an entire composition, a phrase or even a single bar. In a lost song MANUSCRIPT, Beethoven stipulated his initial metronome marking 'can refer to the first measures only, for sentiment has also its peculiar rhythm; but this cannot be entirely expressed' by a single MM number (Marx, *Introduction to the Interpretation of the Beethoven Piano Works* (Berlin, 1863; trans. F. L. Gwinner (Chicago: Clayton F. Summy Co., 1895)), 74). MOSCHELES, a respected editorial 'metronomer' of Beethoven's works, recalled the presumption: 'The musical world knows that marking time by a metronome is but a slight guide for performers and conductors. Its object is to show the general time of a movement, particularly at its commencement; but it is not to be followed strictly throughout' (Schindler, 111fn).

Given the nineteenth-century metronome's slight referential utility, some argued that a simple pendulum was the more appropriate tempo tool. GOTTFRIED WEBER reverse engineered Maelzel's machine for those incapable of obtaining one or who found the 'designation of time written merely according to metronomical degrees ... unintelligible'. He suggested an inexpensive and easily built device, remarking, 'with what perfect convenience a mere simple thread pendulum can supply the place of a [Maelzel] metronome' (Weber, 76).

Maelzel's metronome did not garner universal admiration or employment, as some techno-centric tempo studies from the twentieth century have presumed. For its nineteenth-century proponents, the clockwork metronome was at best a novel pedagogical expedient, an educational convenience to help the unmusical improve incrementally. Playing in synchronicity with the metronome remained an uncustomary technique well into the second half of the nineteenth century. For its most vocal critics, the metronome actively damaged performance practices. Schindler observed a performance 'metamorphosis' caused by the metronoming of Beethoven's piano sonatas (Schindler, 97). The ninth edition of *Encyclopaedia Britannica* (1884) summarised many prevailing critiques:

> Maelzel's scale was needlessly and arbitrarily complicated ... the silent metronome and still more Weber's graduated ribbon are greatly to be preferred, for the clock-work of the other is liable to be out of order ... The value of the machine is exaggerated, for no living performer could execute a piece in unvaried time throughout, and no student could practise under the tyranny of its beat; and conductors of music, nay, composers themselves, will give the same piece slightly slower or quicker on different occasions, according to the circumstances of performance.
>
> (ENCYCLOPAEDIA BRITANNICA, XVI, 207)

Many, including Gottfried Weber and A. B. MARX, maintained that tempo knowledge was best served through imprecise verbal explanations and deeply considered interpretations, which accounted for metric accentuation, rhythmic gesture and harmonic motion. WAGNER, too, eventually found metronome data ineffectual indications of musical movement and opted instead to use verbal descriptions alone. 'I myself have never believed that my blood and a mechanical instrument go very well together', replied JOHANNES BRAHMS when conductor Georg Henschel requested metronome numbers (C. A. B., 'George Grove's analyses of Beethoven', *The Musical World* (3 November 1888), 850). Maelzel's metronome represented the antithesis of musical time for many iconic composers and pedagogues of the age. Its automated beat reflected the fundamental opposition between mechanical action, what NOTTEBOHM called 'soulless clockwork', and the vastly more complex, flexible and insufficiently notated musical intentions of nineteenth-century composers themselves.

FURTHER READING

T. Albrecht (ed.), *Letters to Beethoven and Other Correspondence*, 3 vols. (Lincoln, NE and London: University of Nebraska Press, 1996).
A. Bonus, 'Metronome', *Oxford Handbooks Online* (2014) www.oxfordhandbooks.com.
J. N. Hummel, *Ausführliche theoretisch-practische Anweisung zum Piano-forte-Spiel* (Vienna: Tobias Haslinger, 1828).
A. Schindler, *The Life of Beethoven*, ed. I. Moscheles (London: Henry Colburn, 1841).
G. Weber, *General Music Teacher: Adapted to Self-instruction, Both for Teachers and Learners; Embracing Also an Extensive Dictionary of Musical Terms*, trans. J. Warner (Boston: J. H. Wilkins & R. B. Carter, 1841).

ALEXANDER EVAN BONUS

Milchmeyer, Johann Peter (Philipp Jacob) (bap. Frankfurt am Main, 21 December 1749; d. Straßburg, 15 March 1813) German instrument maker (he worked with Dulcken for a while), composer, performer and teacher.

Milchmeyer's baptismal record and other sources refer to him as 'Philipp Jacob', but from the last decade of the eighteenth century he was sometimes referred to as Johann Peter – or simply J. P., as on the front cover of his most important work, *Die wahre Art das Pianoforte zu spielen* (Dresden: Carl Christian Meinhold, 1797).

Milchmeyer lived at various times in Munich, Mainz, Ochsstadt near Friedberg, Dresden, Straßburg, Paris and Lyon. His TASTES were very much of his time and he was fascinated by the possibilities of tonal variety offered by keyboard instruments of the later eighteenth century. His best known creation, described in the contemporary press in 1783, was a three-manual, HARPSICHORD-shaped instrument which boasted a total of 250 different tone colours, achieved by an array of sound-modifying devices. It had three manuals, two of which operated a harpsichord action, the third having a striking action of some sort – perhaps a *Tangentenflügel* mechanism, or a more conventional PIANO-type action. The 250 tone colours were achieved by the combined effects of the three manuals.

A similar fascination for tonal variation is found in his 1797 keyboard tutor which, he says, was written for amateurs following many years' residency in

Paris and Lyon, and in which he expresses a preference for French square pianos, with their four pedals. He bemoans the lack of attention previously given to the tonal capabilities of such instruments and praises Daniel Steibelt (the first composer to indicate PEDALLING in published music) for including their effects in his works. The pedals, he says, enables the instrument to imitate, for example, little bells, the launch of a rocket, the tambourine, HARP, mandolin, etc. Modern pedalling techniques are far from Milchmeyer's mind, but he offers rare insights into domestic piano performance of the 1790s.

Milchmeyer's tutor received a hostile reception when it was reviewed in the *Allgemeine musikalische Zeitung*, the author of the review preferring the approaches of C. P. E. BACH and TÜRK. Both of these authors wrote primarily for the CLAVICHORD, an instrument advocated by Milchmeyer only for the poor who could not afford a piano, but nevertheless preferable to the harpsichord, which he could not recommend at all. Nevertheless, the quiet finger technique required by Milchmeyer is similar to that described by the two earlier authors and he stresses the legato approach (sometimes an over-legato approach) espoused by many of his contemporaries. The wrist, he says, may be used in staccato performance. His tutor is very modern in its approach to ornaments, his descriptions of which include examples of main note trills and, most notable of all, a wealth of pre-beat realisations.

Milchmeyer's writing provides a fascinating insight into one strand of performance practice of the late eighteenth century. It does not represent a widely practised style, but nevertheless offers a valuable understanding of an often neglected moment in the history of the piano.

FURTHER READING

S. Berdux, 'Johann Peter oder Philipp Jacob Milchmeyer? Biographische und bibliographische Notizen zum Autor der Hammerklavierschule "Die wahre Art das Pianoforte zu spielen"', *Musica Instrumentalis: Zeitschrift für Organologie*, 2 (1999), 103–20.
M. Latcham, 'Jakob Spath and the "Tangentenflügel", an eighteenth-century tradition', *GSJ*, 57 (May 2004), 150–70.
D. Rowland, *A History of Pianoforte Pedalling* (Cambridge University Press, 1993).

DAVID ROWLAND

Military music From the eighteenth century, military musicians occupied the largest segment of the music profession: Jacob Kappey writing in the first edition of Grove's *Dictionary of Music and Musicians* (1878), and using a perfectly rational method of calculation, estimated that the number of full-time professional musicians employed in European military bands easily exceeded 52,000. These bands had distinctive idioms and conventions. Military music training schools were established in several countries. They were often much larger than civilian conservatories, and were more focused on the production of well-rounded working professionals. Consequently, military bands became a major source of training and supply for the civilian music profession. Furthermore, most of the main developments in wind (especially brass) instruments were aimed at improving military music.

Consequently, and because of its size and status, the military influenced musical practices more generally. Several genres that were incorporated into Western art and popular music imitated aspects of military music – the most obvious example is the march. It follows that the performance practices of military musicians are interesting in their own right, but they also have an important relevance to those practices and repertoires to which they provided a legacy.

Many forms of early DANCE were based on versions of military drill. THOINOT ARBEAU in his dance TREATISE *Orchésographie* (Lengres: Jehan des Preyz, 1588) wrote extensively of 'martial dances', which he illustrated with both musical extracts and choreographical drawings linked to advice about TEMPO. The association between music and the martial arts continued in later centuries in popular dance forms, equestrian ballets and other genres.

Some families of musical instruments are especially indebted to their history as military instruments. The practices of military drummers provide an important legacy for drumming more generally, and manuals aimed at training drummers to commit their skills to memory contain information on performance technique and the setting of tempo. The idea of soldiers marching in step was rejected in some countries (such as Britain) until late in the eighteenth century precisely because it resembled dancing. However, there was always a need to regulate an ordered movement of men so that the time taken to move troops between two determined points could be accurately calculated. Men marched (whether or not in step) to the sound of a beating drum. Tempo was calculated by a simple device called a 'plummet', a weight attached to a length of rope marked out with different tempo points. The speed of this pendulum functioned as a METRONOME long before the metronome itself was invented.

Books such as *The Art of Beating the Drum...* (London: H. Potter, 1817) by Samuel Potter, drum major with the British Coldstream Guards, are especially revealing about performance techniques, including the execution of the fundamental rhythmic patterns known as 'rudiments'. These rudiments became the basis for a significant part of PERCUSSION technique. Some appear to be imitations of the ARTICULATIONS employed by wind instrumentalists. For example, nomenclatures found in German sources include *Einfach Zungen* and *Doppel Zungen*: respectively, 'single-tonguing' and 'double-tonguing' stroke.

While military music can be regarded as a catch-all term for any music that had military connotations, there were differences between the ways the military (particularly the army) was organised in various countries and these impacted on the roles of military musicians. Before the seventeenth century, armies were mustered from groups of mercenaries as and when they were required. This changed late in the seventeenth century with the formation of professional 'standing armies'. By the late eighteenth century the main purpose of the groups known as military 'bands of music' was, in some countries, to be the private bands of the aristocratic officer class and royalty. Their performance of concerted music influenced their instrumentation and style. The groups formed for this purpose were analogous to the formations known in Germany as *Harmoniemusik*. These groups seldom numbered more than eight players with OBOES, HORNS, BASSOON or SERPENT and drum being prominent. In keeping with the modish regard for the exotic, janissary percussion instruments with native players were frequently added. CLARINETS became the principal treble instruments in the late eighteenth century.

During the early nineteenth century, the need to serve the social requirements of military officers continued, but it was also increasingly necessary to provide music that was appropriate for state ceremony and display. Consequently, military bands increased in size, and there was need to develop instruments and ways of playing them that would impress listeners in the open air. Among the instruments developed for this purpose were the keyed bugle, its bass counterpart the OPHICLEIDE, the upright metal SERPENT and the bass horn. Eventually the various species of brass valved instruments became prominent. The development of almost all these instruments was aimed at the improvement of military music.

The instrumentation of military bands has never been properly standardised, but attempts were made in several countries to create such standardisation. In Germany Wilhelm Wieprecht (co-inventor of the bass TUBA) was especially important, and in France ADOLPHE SAX was engaged to apply his ideas to the music of the military. These endeavours led to the production of a literature that cast light on wind and percussion instruments more generally. Prominent were J.-G. KASTNER's *Manuel général de musique militaire* (Paris, 1848), E. Neukomm's *Histoire de la musique militaire* (Paris, 1889), Wieprecht's *Die Militair-Musik und die militaire-musikalische Organisation eines Kriegsheeres* (Berlin, 1885), and C. Mandel's *Treatise on the Instrumentation of Military Bands* (London: Boosey and Sons, 1859).

From the mid-nineteenth century there was a preoccupation with the standardisation of PITCH caused by the need for bands to play together and for instrumentalists to move between regiments. This was manifest in different ways in different countries, but in most places there was a preference for a sharp pitch standard that was felt to make wind instruments more audible in the open air. In Britain a standard pitch was set in 1857, and each regiment was issued with a pitch fork to ensure consistency of intonation. Reference to this pitch standard was enshrined in the *Queen's Regulations for the Army*. This pitch was set at $a' = 452.4$ Hz and it endured until 1928 when instruments were standardised to the lower standard of civilian music, but amateur brass bands and those of the Salvation Army, which had always used instruments in military pitch, did not make the adjustment to $a' = 440$ Hz until 1966.

FURTHER READING

R. F. Camus, *Military Music of the American Revolution* (Westerville, OH: Integrity Press, 1975).
T. Herbert and H. Barlow, *Music and the British Military in the Long Nineteenth Century* (New York: Oxford University Press, 2013).
K. van Orden, *Music, Discipline and Arms in Early Modern France* (University of Chicago Press, 2005).

TREVOR HERBERT

Monachus, Guilielmus A late fifteenth-century theorist-musician, probably from northern Italy.

Monachus is known only from his rather chaotic TREATISE *De preceptis artis musicae*. This work is celebrated for its sections dealing with ensemble IMPROVISATION upon a pre-given line. An English and a local variant of three-part improvisation-technique is given, resulting in parallel $^6_3$ chords expanding into $^8_5$ chords for cadences. The former places the pre-given material at the bottom of the texture. The latter has it at the top, and offers also a technique for interspersing root-position chords within the extended $^6_3$ progressions. His most important contribution, though, is in his descriptions of two variants of four-part improvisation resulting in a progression of root-position chords avoiding parallel fifths and octaves. As the simplest and safest four-part setting technique, it became (perhaps subconsciously) ubiquitous in Western music for the next few centuries, perhaps most notably in choral settings and works based on ostinato basses.

FURTHER READING

E. Park, 'De preceptis artis musicae of Guilielmus Monachus: a new edition, translation, and commentary', PhD dissertation, Ohio State University (1993).
A. B. Scott, 'The beginnings of fauxbourdon: a new interpretation', JAMS, 24 (1971), 345–63.

URI SMILANSKY

Montéclair, Michel Pignolet (Pinolet) de (b. Andelot, Haute-Marne, bap. 4 December 1667; d. Aumont, 22 September 1737) French composer, theorist, cellist and teacher.

Montéclair was one of the first to perform on the *basse de violon* in Paris (1699) and was appointed 'symphoniste du *petit choeur*' at L'Opéra. He composed in most contemporary genres, influencing, amongst others, RAMEAU by including in his stage works detailed instrumental prescriptions for dramatic effect. His anonymous exchanges with Rameau (*Mercure de France*, 1729–30) about various musical/performance issues were also influential.

Montéclair's *Méthode facile pour aprendre [sic] à jouer du violon* (Paris, 1711–12), the first French VIOLIN TREATISE, is of modest content, but its recommended secure violin hold anticipates later developments. His three treatises (1709; c1735; 1736) on the application of musical theory to practice incorporate some significant material, notably his illustrations of 'Airs de dance sur toutes sortes de mouvements' in his *Nouvelle méthode pour apprendre la musique* (Paris: l'auteur, 1709); and a section on the '18 principal ornaments in singing' in his *Principes de musique* (Paris: l'auteur, 1736) is a valuable source on French vocal ORNAMENTATION of the time. His *Recueil de brunettes* (Paris: Boivin, c1730) adapts vocal music for the FLUTE, retaining the text as a flautist's guide to faithful reproduction of French style.

FURTHER READING

L. de La Laurencie, *L'école française de violon de Lully à Viotti*, 2 vols. (Paris: Delagrave, 1922–4).
M. Pincherle, 'Elementary musical instruction in the 18th century: an unknown treatise by Montéclair', MQ, 34 (1948), 61–7.

ROBIN STOWELL

Monteverdi, Claudio (b. Cremona, 15 May 1567; d. Venice, 29 November 1643) Italian composer and music director.

Although Monteverdi is rightly known as perhaps the most important composer of the early seventeenth century, it is easy to forget that he spent his entire life working as a practising musician: a decade as a rank-and-file singer and string player and then twelve years as *maestro di cappella* at the Gonzaga court in Mantua, and the remaining thirty years of his life in the equivalent role at St Mark's, Venice. He also wrote (and often directed) music for Venice's theatres, churches and confraternities, the Imperial court in Vienna, and other commissions. In all these jobs, he worked with some of the finest singers and instrumentalists in Europe, and it is his intimate 'hands on' knowledge of their particular skills, acquired through directing them daily in all kinds of repertoire that enabled him to write what, by any measure, is both extraordinarily refined and demanding music, conceived to be performed by elite professionals. Working at this level allowed him, in turn, effectively to redefine most of the principal musical genres, including the madrigal, concerted liturgical music and courtly music theatre, and to write three masterpieces of the newly invented public opera when he was already over the age of seventy.

Monteverdi's letters offer many insights into the practicalities of performance; for example, the detailed accounts of two vocal auditions, one of the duties he regularly undertook as part of his job. The first was a (male) contralto hoping to be employed as a court singer (Letter of 9 June 1610). The other was a high bass being considered for a role in the comic opera *La finta pazza di Licori*, a commission for Mantua, intended to star their comic actor-singer Margherita Basile in the title role (a project eventually abandoned (Letters of 7 May, 13, 20 June 1627)). In both cases, Monteverdi's audition reports succinctly evaluate each singer's sound, vocal technique and musicianship, benchmarking them against the precise requirements of the particular jobs each was trying for, and in the case of the contralto, even suggesting ways he could correct certain technical faults.

Although Monteverdi wrote both brilliantly and idiomatically for all kinds of instruments, including winds, keyboards, and plucked and bowed strings (he was probably a VIOLIN-family player himself), all his surviving compositions are primarily vocal. This reflects the requirements of the institutions that employed him, but also his lifelong commitment to devising music that effectively represents or expresses human emotional experiences, through the affective setting of poetry, liturgical and theatrical texts. Much of his music breaks new ground, not just compositionally, but also in his innovative NOTATION which directs the kinds of intervention that singers and instrumentalists are normally expected to make spontaneously. These include written-out *passaggi* and precise rhythmic notation of recitative for singers; continuo instrumentation (e.g. *Orfeo*, 1607); organ registrations (*Vespers*, 1610); and in the string parts of *Combattimento di Tancredi e Clorinda* (1638), two-fingered pizzicato, a sudden *sforzato* from *forte* to *piano* in a single BOW-stroke and an instruction to die away on the final note – instrumental effects never hitherto described in printed music.

FURTHER READING

T. Carter, *Monteverdi's Musical Theatre* (New Haven, CT and London: Yale University Press, 2002).
D. Stevens, *The Letters of Claudio Monteverdi* (Oxford University Press, 1980, rev. 1995).

R. Wistreich, 'Monteverdi in performance', in J. Whenham and R. Wistreich (eds.), *The Cambridge Companion to Monteverdi* (Cambridge University Press, 2007), 261–79.

RICHARD WISTREICH

Monteverdi Choir and Orchestra *see* GARDINER, JOHN ELIOT

Morley, Thomas (b. Norwich, 1557 or 1558; d. London, October 1602) English composer, editor, writer and organist.

Perhaps the most influential English composer and musical author of his day, Morley did more than any of his contemporaries to establish the Italian madrigal in England. As a writer, Morley is best known as the author of *A Plaine and Easie Introduction to Practicall Musicke* (London: Peter Short, 1597), a TREATISE of formidable scope and a testament to the breadth of his knowledge of music theory from several traditions as well as his scrutiny of a wide repertoire, from which many of his examples are drawn.

While many of the theoretical matters considered are abstruse, Morley's treatment is anything but – written as a thoroughly engaging imaginary dialogue between the would-be scholar, Philomathes and his erudite Master. The entire rationale for the treatise stems from a practical situation: Philomathes's inability to sight-sing and the social embarrassment that entailed. The instruction he receives – while grounded and expressed in notational concepts – is directed at developing his ability to make music in a live performance situation. The book's three sections are directed respectively at 'Teaching to Sing', 'Treating of Descant' and Composition. Towards the end of the third part Morley discusses music's expressive qualities (which a composer should observe in text-setting), including awareness of the rhetorical effect of certain intervals, chords, note values and rhythmic patterns – to be chosen according to the character of the text in order to avoid what he terms 'barbarism'. We may imagine that this practical advice applied also to Morley's good TASTE in matters of performance – a point reinforced by his earlier comment that 'the principal thing we seek in [music], is to delight the eare'.

FURTHER READING

A. Harman (ed.), *Thomas Morley: A Plain & Easy Introduction to Practical Music*, with a Foreword by T. Dart (New York: Norton, 1952).

JOHN IRVING

Moscheles, Ignaz (Isaac) (b. Prague, 23 May 1794; d. Leipzig, 10 March 1870) Bohemian-born pianist and composer.

After initial PIANO lessons in Prague, Moscheles moved in 1808 to Vienna, where he studied with ALBRECHTSBERGER and Salieri, and met his youthful inspiration, BEETHOVEN. From 1816 he toured Europe, quickly establishing a reputation as a brilliant virtuoso and composer. His display pieces, such as *La marche d'Alexandre* (1815), were taken up by other aspiring pianists including the young Robert Schumann. In 1825 he settled in London where, in addition to composing and dominating piano performance, he co-directed the Philharmonic Society, championing the music of Beethoven. A pioneer of the historical performance of earlier music, during the 1830s he established a concert series called the 'historical soirées' at which he performed a wide variety of earlier music, including by J. S. BACH, Handel and Scarlatti, on a 1771 HARPSICHORD. Moscheles's impact as a performer, teacher and pedagogue was enormous. He was considered the last of the Classical virtuosi for the precision, energy and delicacy of his playing and one of the first initiators of the Romantic epoch, with CLEMENTI, Field and HUMMEL, for his full tone and vocal *bel canto* sound. As a recitalist he was admired for his virtuosity of execution, the superiority of his touch and EXPRESSION and the excellence of his IMPROVISATIONS, especially of fugues. He taught the young MENDELSSOHN (who became a lifelong friend), played on occasions with Chopin and Liszt, and his pupils at the Leipzig Conservatory, where from 1846 he was principal professor of piano, included Thalberg, Litolff, Sullivan and Grieg. In addition to his piano studies, which found favour with Schumann and continued to be used into modern times, he wrote sonatas, fantasias, variations and eight concertos for piano, songs, chamber music, a symphony and numerous less demanding works for the amateur market.

FURTHER READING

M. Kroll, *Ignaz Moscheles and the Changing World of Musical Europe* (Woodbridge: Boydell & Brewer, 2014).

C. Moscheles (ed.), *Recent Music and Musicians as Described in the Diaries and Correspondence of Ignatz Moscheles, Edited by his Wife. Adapted from the Original German by A. D. Coleridge* (New York: Henry Holt and Co., 1873; repr. New York: Da Capo Press, 1970).

J. Roche, 'Ignaz Moscheles, 1794–1870', *MT*, 111/1525 (March 1970), 264–6.

TERENCE CHARLSTON

Mozart, (Johann Georg) Leopold (b. Augsburg, 14 November 1719; d. Salzburg, 28 May 1787) South German-Austrian composer, violinist and theorist, father of WOLFGANG AMADEUS MOZART.

Leopold Mozart studied philosophy and law in Salzburg. An accomplished organist and violinist, he became valet/musician to the Count of Thurn-Valsassina and Taxis (1739). Appointments followed in Archbishop Leopold Anton Freiherr von Firmian's court ORCHESTRA, including deputy *Kapellmeister* in 1763. Leopold compromised his career to support his son, Wolfgang, on his travels and assist him in composition (until c1770). Their correspondence records their fluctuating relationship and valuable insights into late eighteenth-century cultural history and musical performance.

Leopold's *Versuch einer gründlichen Violinschule* (1756) eclipsed all other eighteenth-century VIOLIN TREATISES in breadth and detail. Four editions appeared before 1800 (2/1769–70, 3/1787, 4/1800), Dutch (1766) and French (1770) translations were disseminated, and revisions of its text were published as late as 1817. Numerous German theorists were inspired by its example and some of its principles were adopted by, amongst others, JEAN BAPTISTE CARTIER (1798), Joseph Pirlinger (1799–1800), MICHEL WOLDEMAR (1801) and Johann Baptist Schiedermayr (c1818). Drawing on Italian influences, particularly TARTINI's theories, Leopold intended it to lay 'the foundation of good style'.

Incorporating copious musical examples, Leopold's treatise begins with a broad introduction to violin history and music in general. Descriptions of his recommended violin and BOW holds are followed by a brief chapter on keys, intervals and scales and important sections on bowing and tone-production, incorporating discussion of the rule of the down-bow and the four nuanced 'divisions' of the bow used to cultivate tonal purity, variety of EXPRESSION and skilful bow management. Leopold also nurtures controlled delivery of slow movements with an even-toned, slow bow stroke and uses the triplet as a vehicle for varied bowings to express different AFFECTS.

For Leopold, 'necessity, convenience and elegance' (148) justify the use of positions other than the first, elegance being aligned with timbral consistency and *cantabile* delivery. Contrary to the bold leaps prescribed by GEMINIANI, he advocates using adjacent fingers for upward shifts and making downward shifts when musically appropriate: on the beat or on repeated notes; by the phrase in sequences; after an open string; on a rest or pause between staccato notes; or within a dotted figure. He interconnects shifting and phrasing considerations and uses extensions and contractions (but HARMONICS rarely so) to avoid or facilitate shifts and preserve timbral consistency. He omits mention of PORTAMENTO, but some FINGERINGS suggest the introduction of slides, either as part of the shift mechanism or as a purposeful expressive device. He also includes observations on ARPEGGIANDO playing and Tartini's 'difference tones' for accuracy of tuning in double stopping.

Three chapters focus on ornaments, especially appoggiaturas, trills and VIBRATO ('tremolo'), and their affects. Leopold advocates selective application of vibrato, distinguishes three vibrato speeds (slow, accelerating and fast) and links its usage with bowing inflections, recommending variations in both speed and intensity. He cautions against over-embellishment, promotes appropriate ACCENTUATION and encourages fidelity to the composer's TEMPO and expressive indications and their intended affects. While neither comprehensive nor universally applicable as a guide to pan-European performing practices, Leopold's *Versuch* nevertheless represents the most informative guide to the performance of Wolfgang's music.

FURTHER READING

D. D. Boyden, *The History of Violin Playing from its Origins to 1761* (London: Oxford University Press, 1965).
C. Brown, 'Leopold Mozart's *Violinschule* and the performance of W. A. Mozart's violin music', in T. Steiner (ed.), *Bowed and Keyboard Instruments in the Age of Mozart* (Bern: Peter Lang, 2010), 23–50.
A. Rosenthal, 'Leopold Mozart's "Violinschule" annotated by the author', in C. Eisen (ed.), *Mozart Studies* (Oxford: Clarendon Press, 1991), 83–99.

ROBIN STOWELL

Mozart, Wolfgang Amadeus (b. Salzburg, 27 January 1756; d. Vienna, 5 December 1791) Austrian composer and pianist, son of LEOPOLD MOZART.

Mozart's acquaintance with, and performance of, earlier repertories is fairly well, if still incompletely, documented: during his childhood and adolescence in Salzburg he heard and played sacred works by Salzburg composers such as Eberlin and Italians such as Caldara, and in Italy he studied the *stile antico* fugues and canons of Giovanni Battista Martini and the Marquis de Ligniville (he may also have acquired a copy of Francesco Antonio Bonporti's *Invenzioni da camera*, Op. 10 of 1712). In Vienna, chiefly at musical gatherings at the home of the Imperial librarian, Gottfried van Swieten, he became acquainted with some works, chiefly fugues, by BACH and Handel (there is evidence to suggest he may have known some of Handel's works in Salzburg and it is documented that he came to know at least some of his works during his time in London in 1764–5).

The impetus to compose works in a similar style, however, and in particular a number of incomplete fugues or fugue transcriptions from the early 1780s, seems to have been 'social' rather than artistic: it was for van Swieten that he arranged fugues from *The Well-Tempered Clavier* (K405) and it was for his wife, Constanze, that he started, but did not complete, several fugal fragments. On 20 April 1782 he wrote to his sister that

> When Constanze heard the fugues she absolutely fell in love with them. Now she will listen to nothing but fugues, and particularly ... the works of Handel and Bach. Well, as she had often heard me play fugues out of my head, she asked me if I had ever written any down, and when I said I had not, she scolded me roundly for not recording some of my compositions in this most artistic and beautiful of all musical forms, and never ceased to entreat me until I wrote down a fugue for her.

There is little evidence that Mozart's exposure to Handel and Bach at the time had any direct influence on his own works except, perhaps, for a greater general awareness of counterpoint as an expressive gesture (e.g. in the finales of the String Quartet K387, the Piano Concerto K459 and the 'Jupiter' Symphony K551, whose finale is closer to later eighteenth-century traditions of symphonies with contrapuntal finales of a sort frequently composed by Michael Haydn rather than Baroque fugues). If at all, a Bachian kind of counterpoint is apparent only towards the end of his life, in the works for mechanical organ K594 and K608 or the chorale of the armed men in *Die Zauberflöte*, and a Handelian kind of counterpoint in parts of the Requiem (in particular the Introit, which appears to be based on HWV264, the 1737 funeral anthem for Queen Caroline, HWV 264). In all these cases, however, the contrapuntal gestures are intended to be outside the mainstream of contemporaneous style and to draw attention to themselves, for dramatic reasons, as archaic.

Mozart's arrangements of several works by Handel – *Acis and Galatea* K566 (1788), *Messiah* K572 (March 1789) and *Alexander's Feast* K591 and *Ode for St Cecilia's Day* K592 (both July 1790) – show that his concern was not to perform the works as Handel might have performed them but, rather, to update and modernise their textures for a late 1780s Viennese audience, as well as occasionally to add what he saw as meaningful expressive gestures. Accordingly, as STANLEY SADIE (208) points out, Mozart made minor changes in the vocal lines to accommodate the German texts, he re-arranged the TRUMPET parts (originally based on playing techniques no longer practised in the late eighteenth century), sometimes giving essential material to other instruments, and he added slurs, strokes and DYNAMICS in line with his own ideas about the central importance of an articulated surface as a key element of performance and, hence, EXPRESSION (compare 'Hush ye pretty warbling Quire' from *Acis and Galatea* in Handel's and Mozart's settings, Example 18 (a) and (b)). He also

Example 18: Handel: 'Hush ye pretty warbling Quire' (*Acis and Galatea*): (a) London: Walsh, 1734: (b) arr. Mozart (from *Neue Mozart-Ausgabe*).

substantially augmented the scoring, adding FLUTES, CLARINETS, independent BASSOON parts and HORNS, often writing new lines for them that served to bring the works more in line with his and contemporaneous ideas about orchestral and choral texture and to heighten the dramatic effect (see in particular his re-scoring of 'The people that walk'd in darkness' and 'All we like sheep' from *Messiah*). Some of the same kinds of changes, particularly the occasional rewriting of contrapuntal lines according to then-current ideas of voice-leading, are characteristic of his Bach TRANSCRIPTIONS as well. In both cases, then, Mozart largely left untouched the melodic and harmonic substance of the works, mostly limiting his changes to ARTICULATION and texture where, arguably, performance is key to expression.

It is unlikely that Mozart, who at various times in his career engaged with older music that remained in the repertory (particularly opera and church music) and was thus still 'current', heard these works as necessarily part of some grander (music) historical narrative that required preservation, at least with respect to performance conventions. Instead, one of his chief concerns seems to have been to distinguish between works in modern or old-fashioned styles (as early as 1755 Leopold Mozart described his own symphonies as 'modern' while in a letter of 5 June 1770 Mozart wrote to his sister from Mantua that 'The opera here is by Jomelli [*Armida abbandonata*], it is beautiful, but too ... old-fashioned for the theatre'). Whether of newer or older works, however, Mozart's performances were invariably grounded in the performance conventions of his own time and place.

FURTHER READING

R. L. Marshall, 'Bach and Mozart's artistic maturity', *Bach Perspectives*, 3 (1998), 47–79.
S. Sadie, 'Handel', in C. Eisen and S. P. Keefe (eds.), *The Cambridge Mozart Encyclopedia* (Cambridge University Press, 2006), 207–9.
C. Wolff, 'Mozart's Messiah: "The spirit of Handel" from van Swieten's hands', in E. Strainchamps et al. (eds.), *Music and Civilization* (New York: Norton, 1984), 1–14.

CLIFF EISEN

Muffat, Georg (b. Megève, Savoy, bap. 1 June 1653; d. Passau, 23 February 1704) German composer and organist of French birth.

Of French and Scottish ancestry, Muffat grew up in Alsace, studied music in Paris during LULLY's ascendancy, and worked as an organist and composer in Molsheim, Vienna, Prague, Salzburg and Passau. He died in Passau, following a military siege of that city.

Beginning at the age of ten, Muffat spent six years in Paris absorbing the distinctive French musical style, which he described variously in his writings as 'light', 'graceful' and 'lively'. As a musician at the court of Archbishop Maximilian Gandolf von Kuenberg in Salzburg, Muffat was sent to Rome to learn the Italian style; he studied with Bernardo Pasquini and became acquainted with ARCANGELO CORELLI. Muffat thought of the Italian style as rich, dark and full of surprises. In his compositions he deliberately sought to combine what he saw as the best aspects of the French, Italian and German styles. He wrote, 'I strove to moderate the melancholy Italian characters with the French festivity and beauty in such a way that the one might not be too dark and pompous, nor the other too free and boisterous' (Wilson, 69–70).

In 1690, Muffat became *Hofkapellmeister* at the court of Prince-Bishop Johann Philipp von Lamberg in Passau. Among Muffat's publications were two volumes of instrumental suites (called *Florilegia*), mostly in the French style, and a volume of Italian-style concerti grossi. Muffat included instructions about the performance of these NATIONAL IDIOMS as introductory material in each volume, the remarks appearing in French, Italian, Latin and German.

Muffat's remarks about French music included instructions about TEMPO ('One should not hurry in the Gavotte as one does in the Bourée' (Wilson, 17)), RHYTHMIC ALTERATION or NOTES INÉGALES ('one somewhat alters and accommodates the values of certain notes for greater grace' (Wilson, 42)), ORNAMENTATION ('Those who unreasonably hold forth that the Lullian ornaments only obscure the melody or are composed only of trills have not properly considered the matter' (Wilson, 46)) and rules of BOWING ('The first note of a measure which begins without a rest, whatever its value, should always be played down-bow' (Wilson, 34)). His remarks about the French style are in most cases quite detailed, and he makes extensive use of musical examples in the sections on bowing and ornamentation.

Regarding the Italian style, Muffat wrote that his five-part concerti can be played in a variety of configurations depending on one's preference and the number of musicians available, ranging from a trio sonata ensemble (the two solo VIOLIN parts and the BASSO CONTINUO part) to an ORCHESTRA with multiple players per *ripieno* part. Since his concerti were directly modelled on those of Corelli, this approach could potentially be applied broadly to Italian *concerti grossi*. Muffat also emphasised the importance of contrasts in Italian music: fast and slow, loud and soft, dissonance and resolution.

FURTHER READING

G. Muffat, *Exquisitioris Harmoniae Instrumentalis Gravi-Jucundae Selectus Primus*, ed. E. Luntz and E. Schenk, *DTÖ* vols. 23 and 89 (Passau: Maria Margaretha Höllerin, 1701).
Suavioris Harmoniae Instrumentalis Hyporchematicae Florilegium Secundum, ed. H. Rietsch, *DTÖ* vol. 4 (Passau: Georg Adam Höller, 1698).
D. Wilson, *Georg Muffat on Performance Practice: The Texts from* Florilegium Primum, Florilegium Secundum, *and* Auserlesene Instrumentalmusik. *A New Translation with Commentary* (Bloomington: Indiana University Press, 2001).

DAVID K. WILSON

Müller, Iwan (b. Reval (now Tallinn), 3 December 1786; d. Bückeburg, 4 February 1854) German clarinettist, BASSET HORN player, composer and inventor.

Iwan Müller was a brilliant and expressive virtuoso clarinettist, who found fame throughout all the major European cities. His playing was somewhat lacking in polish. An account of an 1810 concert in Vienna was especially critical of his tone quality; 'we heard some quite strong chirps (so to speak) – which can occur rather too easily on the clarinet if one does not take sufficient care'. In the 1830s Glinka commented on his 'harsh tone, like the screech of a goose'.

Müller moved to Paris in 1811 and conducted experiments which led to a radical new design of CLARINET constructed by the instrument-maker Gentellet. He boldly claimed for his new thirteen-keyed B♭ *clarinette omnitonique* that it would render C and A clarinets redundant. A panel at the PARIS

CONSERVATOIRE rejected the instrument on the grounds that its exclusive use would deprive composers of important tonal resources; whereas the C clarinet was brilliant and lively, the B♭ sounded sad and majestic and the A was 'pastoral'. However, FÉTIS remarked that there 'was not a word in the report about the greatly improved intonation, or the evenness of sound' and FRÖHLICH was similarly enthusiastic. Within two years the Conservatoire reversed its decision and the new design became highly influential, forming the basis for subsequent German system clarinets and for the so-called 'simple-system'. It also greatly influenced the development of the Boehm system widely in use today. All the keys on Müller's new instrument were mounted on pillars screwed to the body of the clarinet; the pads were made of soft thin leather stuffed with wool inserted into round, shallow cups. The pads achieved a much better seal than the old flat pieces of leather, closing against countersunk holes. These features soon influenced the manufacture of other woodwinds. Müller's *Méthode pour la nouvelle clarinette à 13 clefs et clarinette-alto* (Paris: Gambaro, 1821) reflects his various achievements in clarinet design, including the creation of the alto clarinet, which initially threatened the profile of the BASSET HORN.

FURTHER READING

E. T. Hoeprich, *The Clarinet* (New Haven, CT and London: Yale University Press, 2008).

COLIN LAWSON

Munclinger, Milan (b. Košice, Slovakia, 3 July 1923; d. Prague, 30 March 1986) Czech flautist, conductor and editor.

Munclinger studied FLUTE at the Prague Conservatoire and in 1948 he joined Václav Talich's CONDUCTING class where he began a lifelong friendship with CHARLES MACKERRAS. In 1951 Munclinger and his harpsichordist wife, Viktorie Švihlíková, founded Ars Rediviva (named in homage to Claude Crussard's Parisian Ars Rediviva, most of whose members were killed in an air crash in 1947), a flexible ensemble for Baroque repertoire. Several players were drawn from the Czech Philharmonic, and foreign guests included Jean-Pierre Rampal and Maurice André. Munclinger became the leading advocate of Baroque music in post-war Czechoslovakia, giving numerous concerts and making a series of recordings for Supraphon. He championed Bohemian composers, notably Benda, F. X. Richter and Zelenka, in his own EDITIONS. Munclinger also prepared performing versions of BACH's *Musical Offering* and *Art of Fugue* (he recorded both works twice), and with Ars Rediviva made the first Czech recordings of Bach's *Brandenburg Concertos* (in 1965) and orchestral suites. In 1958, he wrote the foreword and afterword to the Czech translation of DOLMETSCH's *The Interpretation of the Music of the Seventeenth and Eighteenth Centuries Revealed by Contemporary Evidence* (London: Novello & Co., 1915).

FURTHER READING

F. Sláma, *Z Herálce do Šangrilá a zase nazpátek* (Říčany: Orego, 2001).
'Milan Munclinger 1923–1986', www.frantiseklama.com.

NIGEL SIMEONE

Munrow, David (John) (b. Birmingham, 12 August 1942; d. Chesham Bois, Bucks, 15 May, 1976) English performer of early wind instruments.

A virtuoso RECORDER player and bassoonist, David Munrow was deeply influenced as a schoolboy by ANTHONY BAINES's *Woodwind Instruments and their History* (London: Faber & Faber, 1957). A year in South America offered him opportunities to collect and master a variety of folk wind instruments before he read English at Cambridge University, where he was lent a CRUMHORN by THURSTON DART and encouraged to seek parallels between his folk collection and early European instruments.

From Baines, Munrow absorbed the idea of a Medieval town band having roots in the Saracen military line-up met by Crusaders. Combined with Dart's persuasive promotion of an haut/bas binary in Medieval music and advocacy of folk music models for performance, Munrow created lively performances of *estampies* characterised by his own virtuoso solos on recorder or SHAWM and spiced with oriental percussion. These dances were also influenced by Michael Morrow for whom Munrow recorded with MUSICA RESERVATA.

With CHRISTOPHER HOGWOOD, Munrow also explored Renaissance and Baroque repertoire and in 1967 he founded The Early Music Consort (later THE EARLY MUSIC CONSORT OF LONDON), as its biography put it, 'with the intention of giving authentic but popularly attractive performances of pre-Classical music: Medieval, Renaissance and Baroque'.

Munrow held particular views about VIBRATO, especially vocal vibrato, recorded in an unpublished paper held in the archives of the ROYAL ACADEMY OF MUSIC, London and readily discernible from his recordings. In particular, he sought singers who could use vibrato as an ornament, rather than a ceaseless oscillation. In this regard he particularly admired the singing of ALFRED DELLER and Cleo Laine and once described JAMES BOWMAN's voice as 'the most fabulous "noise" I'd ever heard' (in E. Breen, 'Morrow, Munrow and Medieval music: understanding their influence and practice', *Early Music Performer*, 29 (2010), 7).

During 1974, Munrow began to move away from secular Medieval repertoire to focus on Renaissance vocal polyphony and Baroque repertoire. His plans to reform his consort along these lines were never fully realised.

FURTHER READING

A. Blyth, 'David Munrow talks to Alan Blyth', *Gramophone*, (May 1974), 2009–10.
E. Breen, 'The performance practice of David Munrow and the Early Music Consort of London: Medieval music in the 1960s and 1970s', PhD dissertation, King's College London (2014).
H. M. Brown, 'Instruments of the Middle Ages and Renaissance: in memoriam David Munrow', *EMc*, 4/3 (1976), 288–93.

EDWARD BREEN

Musard, Philippe (Napoléon) (b. Tours, 8 November 1792; d. Auteuil, 31 March 1859) French composer and conductor.

Apart from three string quartets and an unfinished composition method intended for publication in the *Revue Musicale* in the early 1830s, most of Musard's compositions were DANCE pieces: waltzes, polkas and especially quadrilles, often based on themes from operas then in vogue. These he performed at his own concert series based successively in various venues around Paris and London; he was also engaged to run the public ball at L'Opéra in the mid-1830s. His contribution to the history of nineteenth-century performance practice consists in aspects of these concerts, perhaps most obviously in the treatment of the ORCHESTRA. In 1837 Musard was CONDUCTING an ensemble of as many as ninety players in a marquee on the Champs-Elysées, and his orchestrations not only included an expanded role for instruments previously limited to harmonic and textural support (notably the TROMBONES), but also sound effects ranging from pistol-shots to breaking furniture. He was one of the first celebrity conductors in the concert culture of Paris and London, a role Louis Jullien was subsequently to take to still more extravagant heights of showmanship; through a combination of this and accessible pricing, his concerts brought new, more socially heterogeneous AUDIENCES to orchestral music. Critical reception of his own compositions included some of the earliest uses of the term 'light' in this context in English. Specifically, he was recognised at the time as the originator of the indoor promenade concert. The first examples seem to have taken place in 1833 in a hall on the Rue St Honoré in Paris, and within a few years the phrase *à la Musard* was being used as an advertising slogan both there and in London. A more or less unbroken tradition extended from these beginnings to 1895, when the still-running series of London Promenade Concerts was founded by Henry Wood and Robert Newman.

FURTHER READING

D. Scott, *Sounds of the Metropolis: The Nineteenth-century Popular Music Revolution in London, New York, Paris, and Vienna* (New York: Oxford University Press, 2008), esp. 41–3.

CORMAC NEWARK

Musica Antiqua Köln A German period-instrument ensemble of flexible constitution established in 1973 by REINHARD GOEBEL and fellow musicians from the Conservatory of Music in Cologne.

The group quickly acquired a reputation for its disciplined, thought-provoking, stylish and communicative performances, characterised by clean ARTICULATION, strong ACCENTUATION, detailed EXPRESSION, rhythmic precision and, often, fast TEMPOS. Starting as a chamber ensemble with a predilection for performing German and French music, the group developed into a period orchestra in the early 1980s, performing and recording works such as TELEMANN's *Wassermusik* and J. S. BACH's *Ouvertures* and *Brandenburg Concertos*. Its repertory became increasingly more orchestrally focused following the diagnosis of Goebel's career-threatening focal dystonia of the left hand, concentrating on works by Dresden-based composers, especially JOHANN DAVID HEINICHEN, Pisendel and Hasse. Telemann's string concertos, secular cantatas by J. S. Bach, and large-scale sacred choral works by Biber also featured on the wide-ranging agenda and there were forays, too, into France (COUPERIN, Clérambault, CHARPENTIER, Leclair, Rebel, Gilles), Italy (Veracini, Vivaldi) and England (Dowland). After about a decade, Goebel's return to orthodox VIOLIN playing coincided with the ensemble's brief reversion to chamber music performances (e.g. Biber's *Harmonia-artificioso ariosa*, Telemann's flute quartets and Gluck's trio sonatas); however, his dystonia returned in May 2006, forcing him to abandon violin playing forever and resulting in the ensemble's dissolution by the end of that year.

Musica Antiqua Köln toured widely during its prime, making appearances at principal venues and festivals worldwide, and recorded prolifically for Deutsche Grammophon's Archiv Produktion label, making valuable contributions to the revival of German music of the late seventeenth and early eighteenth centuries. Its recordings of sacred vocal music by members of the Bach family have also been widely acclaimed, along with its accounts of Telemann's *Musique de table*. Its final issue, *Meister: Il Giardino del Piacere*, originally recorded for television in 2004, was released in 2011. Many of its approximately sixty recordings received awards, including the Grand Prix International du Disque, Gramophone Award, Diapason d'or, and Grammy nominations.

FURTHER READING

R. Connolly, 'Starting over', *Early Music Today* (August/September 1994), 18–19.
F. Knights, 'A farewell to Musica Antiqua Köln', *EMc*, 41/1 (2013), 173–4.

ROBIN STOWELL

Musica ficta Literally, 'feigned' or 'imagined' music.

From the twelfth to the late sixteenth century *musica ficta* denoted extensions to the diatonic or *recta* set of natural, soft and hard hexachords (*ut–re–mi–fa–sol–la*) based on C, F and G respectively; the constituent steps are all whole tones except the *mi–fa* semitone in the middle.

Mutation from one hexachord to another, mentioned by Johannes of Afflighem c1100, almost inevitably arises from the overlapping of the three hexachords (in which C, for instance, can be *sol, fa* or *ut*) and by the tendency of plainsong melodies to exceed a six-note range. These mutations most conspicuously affect B, which can be flat or natural depending upon whether it is sung as *mi* or *fa* in either the soft or the natural hexachord. B *mi* and B *fa* could be signed with a square B (♮), forerunner of the modern natural sign, and round B (♭), which remains in use. An explicit flat sign was not always needed, however, where the need to sing *fa* could easily be deduced from the context; for instance, in the progression F–B.

The *mi–fa* relationship can be conceptually extended beyond the three diatonic hexachords. Flat signs invariably denote *fa*; so, for instance, E♭ *fa* denotes a fictive hexachord based on B♭ *ut*, a permutation very occasionally found in the form of a two-flat key signature. Exceptional in monophonic song, extreme hexachord mutations involving A♭ and even D♭ are sometimes found in polyphonic music – in cryptic PITCH spirals such as Willaert's well-known *Quid non ebrietas*, and sometimes in working repertories such as the *L'homme armé* masses of Johannes Regis and Marbrianus de Orto, or the D♭ chord found in a near-contemporary *Gaude virgo mater Christi* by Sturton (c1500).

If flat signs unambiguously denote *fa*; sharps are less clear-cut. Around 1430 Ugolino of Orvieto described the *diesis* or sharp sign (♯ and 𝄪), which can be used to cancel a flat or sharpen a 'white' note. Most frequently this sharpening applies to the leading notes at cadences, a tendency traceable to the thirteenth century and discussed by Johannes de Muris in the fourteenth. The sharpening of cadential leading notes, ubiquitous and seldom signed, had no impact on the solmisation status of a note: as seen in THOMAS MORLEY'S *Plaine and Easie Introduction to Practicall Musicke* (London: Peter Short, 1597), *fa* remained *fa* even if it sounded as a sharp. A sharp sign did not denote *mi*.

One of the principal applications of *musica ficta* in polyphonic music was in the emendation of 'bad' vertical intervals: as a general rule, achieving good vertical concords trumps the countervailing need for idiomatic linearity, a principle articulated in JOHANNES TINCTORIS's *Liber de Natura et Proprietate Tonorum* (1476) and re-iterated fifty years later by PIETRO AARON. The vertical discord between B and F rationalised as a choice between *mi* and *fa*, in which *fa* was increasingly the default choice from the mid-fifteenth century.

Musical sources convey only partial information on the application of sharps and flats. Sharps, seldom signed in sixteenth-century continental sources, are more frequently found in Tudor musical sources, along with the exclusively English 'f' cancellation sign. In some contexts, sharps and flats are used to indicate anomalous applications; in other cases, they re-affirm the reader's default assumptions, akin to a modern cautionary accidental. Because LUTE TABLATURE is pitch-specific, lute INTABULATIONS have been used by Anthony Newcomb and Robert Toft as evidence for sixteenth-century performers' habits of inflection.

A number of modern practices commonly described as *musica ficta* belong either to the tradition's conceptual fringes or its twilight. One example is the convention by which B is flattened when it lies melodically one step beyond *la*; the aphorism 'una nota supra *la* semper est canendum *fa* ' sounds Medieval but is found no earlier than 1618 (in the *Syntagma Musicum* of MICHAEL PRAETORIUS).

The modern usage of '*musica ficta* ' most commonly to describe a system for sharpening leading notes, with false relations as an occasional and gratifying by-product, would have been marginal to a Medieval musician's understanding of the term. The 'rules' of *musica ficta*, moreover, might better be understood as conventions or tendencies whose implementation varied according to time, place and TASTE.

FURTHER READING

M. Bent, 'Diatonic *ficta*', *Early Music History*, 4 (1984), 1–48.
K. Berger, *Musica ficta: Theories of Accidental Inflections in Vocal Polyphony from Marchetto da Padova to Gioseffo Zarlino* (Cambridge University Press, 1987).
A. Smith, *The Performance of 16th-century Music: Learning from the Theorists* (New York: Oxford University Press, 2011), 20–54.

MAGNUS WILLIAMSON

Musica reservata ('reserved music') The term *musica reservata* is found in about a dozen sources from the second half of the sixteenth century to 1625 (listed in the *NG* article), to indicate a musical work or repertory marked by a particular stylistic manner or manners (thus implying 'refined' or 'sophisticated' music), as well as the circumstances in which that repertory was customarily performed (thus implying 'exclusive' music conceived for an elite audience). The two meanings overlap to a considerable degree, since musical works conceived for expert or aristocratic ears typically featured somewhat idiosyncratic stylistic elements. Adrian Petit Coclico is the first documented author to use the term *musica reservata* in his TREATISE *Compendium musices* and in the motet anthology *Consolationes piae*, both from 1552. Because of their dramatic approach to text-painting and extensive chromaticism, the motets leave no doubt that he understood the term in a stylistic sense. An oft-cited reference to *musica reservata* in this musico-rhetorical sense is the one by the humanist Samuel Quickelberg in his well-known comments on Orlande de Lassus's cycle of *Penitential psalms* (from the 1560s). Quickelberg admires the composer's ability vividly to express the 'individual affections' of the texts with appropriately 'lamenting and plaintive tones', adding that 'this genre of music they call *musica reservata*'. Other authors associate the label with particular compositional styles and devices, such as avoided cadences (acts of the Synod of Besançon, 1559–71), chromaticism (Jean Tasnier, 1559; Eucharius Hoffmann, 1582), and solo instrumental performances (Reimundo Ballestra, 1611). More generally, the concept *musica reservata* appears to have carried connotations of novelty (thus operating as a virtual synonym of *musica nova* or *moderna*), even suggesting a tendency to rub against traditional modal and/or contrapuntal rules.

The 'sociological' meaning of the label is likewise well documented during the same period. One of the earliest and most significant sources in this regard is a passage from the treatise of Nicola Vicentino, *L'antica musica ridotta alla moderna prattica* (Rome: Antonio Barre, 1555) pointing out that in ancient cultures 'the chromatic and enharmonic music was fittingly reserved [*reservata*] ... for the pleasure of trained ears at private entertainments of lords and princes', unlike the diatonic genre that was conceived 'for the pleasure of ordinary ears' (10v). French poet and Pléiade member Pontus de Tyard echoed Vicentino in his *Solitaire second* ((Lyon: Jean de Tournes, 1555), 19) by observing that the diatonic *genus* continues to be best suited for the 'natural' musical settings of texts (*la naturelle prononciacion*), while the chromatic and the enharmonic require such 'diligent and well-trained perspicuity' and such 'exquisite and difficult artifice' (*tant exquiz et dificile artifice*) from their listeners that they seem to be the exclusive domain of the learned (*qu'elle semble estre reservee pour les doctes*), and have been practised only by the most excellent professional musicians.

The most sophisticated late Renaissance courts (Munich, Ferrara, Mantua) had an interest in fostering compositional styles and modes of performances inspired by the idea of *musica reservata*, as a way of cultivating an aura of exclusivity and refinement.

FURTHER READING

S. Cavicchioli, '"*Musica reservata*". Indagine sui concerti dipinti nell'Italia settentrionale del Cinquecento', in S. Macioce and E. De Pascale (eds.), *La musica al tempo di Caravaggio* (Rome: Gangemi, 2012), 133–47.

M. R. Maniates, *Mannerism in Italian Music and Culture, 1530–1630* (Chapel Hill: University of North Carolina Press, 1979), 260–74.

C. V. Palisca, 'A clarification of *Musica Reservata* in Jean Taisnier's *Astrologiae* 1559', in *Studies in the History of Italian Music and Music Theory* (Oxford: Clarendon Press, 1994), 239–81.

J. Winemiller, 'Lasso, Albrecht V, and the figure of Job: speculation on the history and function of Lasso's *Sacrae lectiones ex propheta Iob* and Vienna Mus. ms. 18744', *JMR*, 12 (1993), 273–302.

STEFANO MENGOZZI

Musica Reservata Pioneering, London-based early music group that flourished between c1965 and the 1980s.

Musica Reservata was jointly directed by Michael Morrow, who was responsible for the preparation and interpretation of performing editions, and the harpsichordist John Beckett, who led the group in concerts and recordings. Beckett left the group in the mid-1970s and his role was taken by ANDREW PARROTT. Its performances at London's South Bank and on several foreign tours (including one lengthy tour of the Soviet Union) provided important contributions to debates about early music performance.

Musica Reservata typically used four singers and five instrumentalists. Its approach was scholarly, but radically experimental. Key to the group's distinctiveness were Morrow's strident interpretations and his direction of the versatile vocal style of the mezzo-soprano Jantina Noorman. His approach was often controversial, but the group's recordings were highly praised, particularly those of sixteenth-century French and Italian dance music and the music of Josquin.

FURTHER READING

H. Haskell, *The Early Music Revival: A History* (London: Thames & Hudson, 1988).

TREVOR HERBERT

Mute (Fr. *sourdine*; Ger. *Dämpfer*; It. *sordino*) A device that transforms the timbre, muffles the tone and decreases the volume of musical instruments. Its application is normally indicated by *con sordino, avec sourdine* or *mit Dämpfer*.

Mutes have been employed for special effect on bowed string instruments since at least the seventeenth century. MERSENNE (*Harmonie universelle*, 1636–7) provided an early description; Schmelzer (*Memorie Dolorose*, 1679), LULLY (*Armide*, 1686), and Purcell (*The Fairy Queen*, 1692) employed it effectively; and QUANTZ (*Versuch*, Eng. trans., 233–4) claimed that muted strings 'express more vividly the sentiments of love, tenderness, flattery, and melancholy, and also . . . the more violent emotions, such as recklessness, madness and despair'. Mute usage was gradually extended from ensemble to solo playing during the course of the eighteenth century.

The traditional VIOLIN family mute resembles a three-pronged clamp (sometimes two- or five-pronged) made of metal (LEOPOLD MOZART mentions lead, tin, steel, or brass), ivory, wood (especially ebony and boxwood), or, latterly, bakelite. Among later models are some which are positioned on the strings between bridge and tailpiece and conveniently slid on to the bridge when required. 'Practice' mutes are exceptionally heavy versions of the traditional model; they decrease the instrument's volume considerably for quiet practice purposes and are rarely used in concert performance. Vivaldi, however, prescribes lead mutes ('con piombo') in some scores to mute the sound considerably (e.g. *Nisi Dominus* RV608). Once secured on the bridge, stringed-instrument mutes absorb some of the vibrations and veil the sound, the degree of muting and difference in tone-colour depending on the mute's material, mass and weight.

The exploitation of muted effects was rarer with woodwind instruments, especially FLUTES; but the high register of the piccolo has been tempered by covering the middle and foot joints with a tube with cloth-covered holes. OBOES were sometimes muted in the eighteenth century, particularly in melancholic pieces, by inserting cotton wool, paper, sponge or shaped wood into the bell. Nowadays, muting is generally achieved by stuffing a cloth/handkerchief into the bell, a method also used by saxophonists and bassoonists. German bassoonists sometimes use a mute made of a brass cylinder around which some soft material is wound. Bassoonists and clarinettists have also used bell-sized disc mutes made of a sound-absorbent material. Evidence suggests that CLARINET mutes were employed in military bands in the eighteenth century. Spontini (*Fernand Cortez*, 1809) muted both oboes and clarinets, tying a leather bag over the bell; BERLIOZ prescribed likewise for the clarinet (*Lélio*, 1831–2).

Brass instruments were muted as much for modifying timbre as for veiling the sound, as in early sixteenth-century funeral ceremonies. Mersenne describes and illustrates mutes for brass in his *Harmonie universelle* (1636–7) and *Harmonicorum libri XII* (Paris: Baudry, 1648). Mutes also raised pitch by between a semitone or tone; retuning to the original pitch was accomplished with an appropriate crook. The HORN technique of hand stopping probably developed from experiments with mutes by A.J. HAMPEL in the mid-eighteenth century (Domnich, *Méthode* (Paris: Le Roy, 1807)). ALTENBURG (1795) gave five reasons for muting the (natural) TRUMPET: secret military retreat; use at funerals; embouchure development; prevention of 'screeching'; and improving intonation.

Mutes for brass instruments either fit into the bell or (in the case of the metal 'bowler hat') are held over it. They may be made nowadays from aluminium, brass, copper, wood, papier-mâché, cardboard, fibre, composition, polystyrene or rubber and adopt many forms, particularly those for trumpet and, to a lesser extent, TROMBONE; each alters the tone in different ways and reduces the volume. Most common are the conical 'straight mute', the 'cup mute', the 'Hamon mute' for wah-wah effects, and the 'bucket mute'; among other types are practice mutes for all brass instruments and various specialist models ('mica', 'whispa', 'buzz-wow', 'plunger', 'bowler hat', 'double mute', 'hat', 'electronic') and techniques, some of which evolved in JAZZ circles. A cloth (Ives's *The Unanswered Question*, 1906–8, trumpet) or the player's hand (over or in the bell) may sometimes be used in lieu of a mute, especially in horn playing (indicated by 'stopped', *sons bouchés*, *gestopft*, or *chiuso*).

Muting was also applicable to various other instruments. With TIMPANI, it was formerly effected by placing a cloth over the parchment heads, opposite the striking point; sponge-headed sticks offer a modern alternative. Muted harp sounds are created by stopping the string as soon as the note is sounded (*sons étouffés*). With HARPSICHORDS and early PIANOS, the 'buff stop', operated by a hand-lever or a pedal, mutes the strings by pressing pads of felt or leather against the strings, veiling the tone and restricting its resonance. The 'soft' (*una corda*) pedal is the modern piano mute.

FURTHER READING

J. E. Altenburg, *Versuch einer Anleitung zur heroisch-musikalischen Trompeter- und Pauker-Kunst* (Halle, 1795/R; trans. E. H. Tarr as *The Art of the Trumpeter and Kettledrummer* (Nashville, TN: Brass Press, 1974)).

D. D. Boyden, *The History of Violin Playing from its Origins to 1761* (London: Oxford University Press, 1965).

R. Gregory, *The Horn* (London, 1961, 2/1969).

J. K. Page, '"To soften the sound of the hoboy": the muted oboe in the 18th and early 19th centuries', *EMc*, 21 (1993), 65–80.

ROBIN STOWELL

N

National idioms Stylistic identity and geography had particular relationships in the Baroque. Having been suppressed, small-scale decoration and extended embellishment flourished from the late seventeenth century in Italy (e.g. in da capo arias). QUANTZ observed that ORNAMENTATION was notated in France, and FRANÇOIS COUPERIN instructed performers to observe his *agréments*; JEAN-BAPTISTE LULLY had denounced excessive elaboration. Italian practice afforded the performer more freedom, especially in slow movements. French signs were also adopted elsewhere and, later, C. P. E. BACH's *Versuch* was significant in establishing more universal principles of ornamentation. Metrical concerns are relevant too. In the Italianate style, fantasias and toccatas offered opportunities for IMPROVISATION and flexibility; meanwhile German composers sometimes notated such effects. French DANCE styles tended to emphasise a need for discipline (and Lully is credited with establishing the coordinating beat of the conductor; the motoric style of some Italian music may have made timing more obvious). There has been controversy about the application of NOTES INÉGALES more generally, but it was in France that this RHYTHMIC ALTERATION was most frequently expected without NOTATION. Seventeenth-century and earlier Italian formulations identifying strong beats later became universal. But it was the French who developed mannered rhythmic inflection, and used the *reprise d'archet* to organise first-beat down-bows in three time. Dynamic contrast was a feature in Italy, where string sound was generally more robust. Changes in instrumental texture contributed to this variety, sometimes subject to performers' realisation (e.g. of BASSO CONTINUO). In contrast, dynamic variation could be considered distasteful in France. TELEMANN and J. S. BACH developed a cosmopolitan or 'mixed' German approach, incorporating aspects of French, Italian and other national styles. By the late eighteenth century carefully composed dynamic effects had become a feature of the MANNHEIM school.

Nineteenth-century violinists used a range of BOWING styles. RODE, BAILLOT, and KREUTZER followed Viotti in using the Tourte bow, and their *Méthode de violon* (1803) evinced a Parisian style. A German school is often associated with JOACHIM and AUER, although as the century progressed polar distinctions became more tenuous (Joachim teaching aspects of French bowing, for example). Interpretations of ARTICULATION were sometimes at variance: opposing definitions for staccato dots and wedges are found in DAVID's *Violinschule* (Leipzig: Breitkopf & Härtel, 1863) and Baillot's *L'art du violon* (1835). The use of gut for the upper strings prevailed through the nineteenth century. Willy Burmester (a Joachim pupil) was a proponent of steel alternatives; meanwhile Fritz Kreisler (sometimes associated with the Franco-Belgian school) was notable in continuing to use gut. Metal E strings were widely adopted from the 1920s. German ORCHESTRAS were apparently more likely to organise unanimous bowing than was usual in England.

The nineteenth century saw significant changes in wind and brass instrument making, with new key systems and valve designs. The foundations of mass production and distribution were established by makers such as SAX. BERLIOZ's treatise (1843) promoted new families of instruments, and Wieprecht's standardisation of German MILITARY MUSIC provided large-scale demand. There was extensive take-up of KLOSÉ and Buffet's Boehm CLARINET, apart from in Germany (where Oehler instruments endure). Simple-system clarinets were only gradually superseded in Britain; here and in Germany wooden FLUTES also found favour for longer. None the less, from OBOE to TROMBONE, a generalised division can be argued between narrower instruments favoured in France and Britain, and wider examples in Germany. Such differences crystallised in the early decades of the twentieth century, and intriguing diversity is captured on EARLY RECORDINGS. However, the homogenising forces of touring, powerful conductors and recording led to greater standardisation. Important foundations of the modern orchestra's instrumental character came to be derived from German practice. Whilst the metal flute gained ascendancy and in many places the shortening (but enlarging) TRUMPET retained piston valves, other distinct Anglo-French features waned from the 1930s (the piston-valve single F HORN being replaced by the German double in F/B♭; and the more powerful Heckel BASSOON replacing the reedier Buffet, sacrificing the ease in the high register that STRAVINSKY knew in Paris). American orchestras have been notable in synthesising local features with aspects of European style. From Pierre Monteux's time to Charles Munch's, the Boston Symphony was sometimes noted as one of the finest 'French' orchestras; German and Eastern European influences are discernible in Chicago, New York and Philadelphia orchestras.

There are then reasons why, in the current century, we might limit concepts of national idiom to particular historic periods and traditions. In post-Fordist societies, globalised markets and EXPRESSION have supplanted some of the control and identity of nation states. Latterly cultural artefacts arising from urban development, cities, particular institutions and individuals have shaped idiom; this observation suggests it may be fruitful to revisit earlier ideas of national style with a more discriminating eye for regional or other loci.

FURTHER READING

C. Brown, *Classical and Romantic Performing Practice 1750–1900* (Oxford University Press, 1999).
C. Lawson and R. Stowell, *The Historical Performance of Music: An Introduction* (Cambridge University Press, 1999).
R. Philip, *Early Recordings and Musical Style: Changing Tastes in Instrumental Performance, 1900–1950* (Cambridge University Press, 1992).

SIMON BAINES

Neidhardt, Johann Georg (b. Bernstadt, Silesia, *c*1680; d. Königsberg, 1 January 1739) German organist, theorist and composer.

Neidhardt's early years were spent in Altdorf and Wittenberg. He studied theology in Jena, a university city with a tradition for intellectual enquiry into the broader aspects of music, including physiology, acoustics and musical theory. He took part in a tuning competition with J. N. Bach, the university organist and cousin of J. S. BACH. Both tuned a different rank of ORGAN pipes and J. N. Bach was judged to have set the better TEMPERAMENT. They used different techniques: J. N. Bach set his temperament by ear while Neidhardt used a monochord, a method which he described in his first publication, *Beste und leichteste Temperatur des Monochordi* printed in 1706. Between 1710 and 1720 Neidhardt was in Bernstadt and Breslau before finally settling in Königsberg, where he held the post of *Kapellmeister* from 1720 until his death. In Königsberg he published three further surviving books on the theory of temperaments (1724, 1732 and 1734).

Like Werckmeister, Neidhardt's tuning methods provide practical solutions to the problems caused by the increasing use of more distant and less diatonic keys. An advocate of the circulating temperaments that favour the more commonly used keys, he devised over twenty widely differing temperaments which could be applied flexibly to specific uses; for example, for a village, a town and a city, and at court (for the last he recommended equal temperament). The principles behind Neidhardt's tuning methods have been studied and re-applied to keyboard instruments in recent times, especially for the performance of music by J. S. Bach.

FURTHER READING

M. Boyd (ed.), *Oxford Composer Companion: J. S. Bach* (New York: Oxford University Press, 1999), 313.
J. O'Donnell, 'Bach's temperament, Occam's razor, and the Neidhardt factor', *EMc*, 34/4 (2006), 625–33.

TERENCE CHARLSTON

Neumann, Frederick (b. Bielitz, 15 December 1907; d. Richmond, VA, 21 March 1994) Silesian socio-economist, musicologist, violinist and conductor.

Neumann obtained a doctorate in political science and economics from the University of Berlin in 1934, worked as a research analyst in Prague until 1937 and then moved to the USA. After the war he studied music and music education at Columbia University, receiving an MA in 1947 and a PhD in 1952. Neumann was an accomplished violinist and studied with some of the greatest pedagogues of his time, including František Ondříček, Otakar Ševčík, Henri Marteau, Carl Flesch, Max Rostal and Adolf Busch. After teaching at the Cornish School of Music and Arts in Seattle (1939–42) and as VIOLIN professor at the University of Miami (1948–51), Neumann was appointed professor of music at the University of Richmond in 1955, where he also led the Richmond Symphony Orchestra from 1957 until 1964. In addition, Neumann was visiting professor of music at Yale University. This varied activity as a violinist led to a collaboration with Ivan Galamian and a publication of their two-volume *Contemporary Violin Technique* (New York: Galaxy, 1963, 1966).

From the mid-1960s Neumann mainly occupied himself with research into performance practice, particularly of the seventeenth and eighteenth centuries. The book for which he is best known is *Ornamentation in Baroque and Post-Baroque Music, with Special Emphasis on J. S. Bach* (1978, 3/1983). In the introduction to this book he explains that it is the product of his research motivated by scepticism towards what he terms the prevailing theories of Baroque ORNAMENTATION, arguing strongly that all principal small graces such as the appoggiatura, the slide and the mordent must start exactly on the beat, taking their value from the following note, and must carry a metric-dynamic emphasis.

He wrote a highly acclaimed volume *Ornamentation and Improvisation in Mozart* (Princeton, 1989) and at the time of his death was researching performance practices in BEETHOVEN. Neumann also wrote critically about contemporary methodologies of historical performance, noting the dangers of the application of historical documents outside their legitimate pertinence through unjustified generalisations, and he published two volumes of thought-provoking articles on other topics, notably rhythmic conventions.

FURTHER READING

F. Neumann, *Ornamentation in Baroque and Post-Baroque Music, with Special Emphasis on J. S. Bach* (Princeton University Press, 1978).
New Essays on Performance Practice (University of Rochester Press, 1992).

ASHLEY SOLOMON

New York Pro Musica (Antiqua) American vocal and instrumental ensemble which specialised in Medieval and Renaissance music.

The New York Pro Musica Antiqua was founded in 1952, combining NOAH GREENBERG's Primavera Singers and Bernard Krainis's St Cecilia Players to form an ensemble with the mission of performing music from the Medieval through early Baroque periods. (The word 'Antiqua' was soon dropped from the name.) Under Greenberg's energetic and visionary leadership, the Pro Musica was soon recognised as the leading American exponent of early music through its concerts, recordings and EDITIONS. In addition to tours within the USA, Greenberg led tours to Europe, Latin America and Russia. The core group of ten musicians – the Concert Ensemble – was augmented for special projects, most notably the fully costumed and staged productions of the Medieval liturgical dramas *The Play of Daniel* (1957) and *The Play of Herod* (1963). Also performing under the aegis of the Pro Musica were a Motet Choir, VIOL Ensemble and Wind Ensemble.

Upon Greenberg's untimely death in 1966, the directorship was assigned to John Reeves White, who served until 1970; among White's achievements was the elaborate 1969 production of *An Entertainment for Elizabeth*, a masque written in Elizabethan style by John Hollander with period DANCES reconstructed by Julia Sutton. This show was subsequently taken on multiple tours, as *Daniel* and *Herod* also continued to be.

Paul Maynard (former keyboardist with the group) served for two years as interim director while a search took place for a permanent one. George Houle of Stanford University was named director in 1972. The ensemble continued to tour throughout the USA and Canada, as well as once more to Latin America. In 1973 Houle mounted a production of Marco da Gagliano's opera *La Dafne* (Mantua, 1608), which appeared in festivals in Spoleto and Corfu as well as on tour in America. Upon Houle's decision in 1974 to return to Stanford, the board of the Pro Musica chose to cease operations.

FURTHER READING

J. Gollin, *Pied Piper: The Many Lives of Noah Greenberg* (Hillsdale, NY: Pendragon, 2001).

HERBERT MYERS

Nicholson, Charles (b. Liverpool, bap. 12 August 1795; d. London, 26 March 1837) English flautist.

Following his arrival in London in the early part of the nineteenth century, Nicholson was soon engaged as a soloist at the Drury Lane Theatre, the Italian Opera and at the Philharmonic Society Concerts; he was appointed the first FLUTE professor at the ROYAL ACADEMY OF MUSIC when it opened in 1822. His major contribution to the development of the flute was his influence on flute design, introducing improved large tone holes for the eight-keyed model. Nicholson argued that the main advantage of these larger holes allowed for a more powerful tone as well as more EXPRESSION and delicacy. This flute broke away from the traditional German-style instrument by such London makers as Potter, Astor and Monzani. Over 4,500 of Nicholson's improved instruments were produced during the period 1820–45. As a flute virtuoso and builder he made an indelible mark on the history and development of the instrument, inspiring numerous solo compositions and methods. His outstanding tone enthralled Theobald Boehm after his visit to London in 1829, prompting him to redesign the flute.

Nicholson published three instruction books for the flute between 1816 and 1836, the last of which was his two-volume TREATISE *A School for the Flute*. He begins by offering the reader expert advice on the manner of holding the flute. In his chapter on tone he explains how to produce a strong bottom octave, suggesting that the ideal tone should be as reedy as possible, similar in sound to the OBOE. He discusses the challenges of the flute's second and third octave and on playing in soft DYNAMICS. His conclusion observes that the only way to achieve proficiency on the flute is through a strict and uniform attention to tone quality.

FURTHER READING

C. Nicholson, *Complete Preceptor for the German Flute* (London: Cocks & Co., 1826).
N. Toff, *The Flute Book* (Oxford University Press, 1996).
C. Welch, *History of the Boehm Flute* (London: Rudall Carte 1886/R1961).

ASHLEY SOLOMON

Niedt, Friedrich Erhard (b. Jena, bap. 31 May 1674; d. Copenhagen, 13 April 1708) German theorist and composer.

From 1694 Niedt studied (probably law) at Jena University. From 1695 he studied music with BACH's cousin Johann Nicolaus Bach, who was organist of the town church. He settled in Copenhagen in 1699 and remained there for the rest of his life.

His chief theoretical work is *Musicalische Handleitung* (facsim. edn (Buren, 1976); Trans. P. L. Poulin and I. C. Taylor as *The Musical Guide* (Oxford: Clarendon Press, 1989)). It was published in three parts. Part I (Hamburg, 1700, 2/1710) is subtitled 'Concerning the Thorough-Bass and how to play it with ease'. Part II (Hamburg, 1706; 2nd edn, rev. MATTHESON, 1721) was originally entitled 'Guide to Variation' and subsequently 'Musical Guide on the Variation of the Thorough-Bass'. It explains how to improvise over THOROUGHBASS and how to fill out a harmonic scheme with motives. Part III, left unfinished by Niedt due to his untimely death at the age of thirty-four, was edited and published posthumously by Mattheson (Hamburg, 1717). It is entitled 'Musical Guide on counterpoint, canon, motets, chorales, recitative style and cavatas'.

Niedt's *Handleitung*, in which he followed the precepts of his teacher J. N. Bach, offers valuable information about performance practice around 1700. Much of Part I is paraphrased in *The Precepts and Principles for Playing the Thorough-Bass or Accompanying in four parts ... by Mr. Johann Sebastian Bach at Leipzig, for his students in music, 1738*, a manuscript partly in the hand of Bach's pupil C. A. Thieme (facsim. edn, ed. P. L. Poulin (Oxford: Clarendon Press, 1994)).

Niedt also published *Musicalisches ABC zum Nutzen der Lehr- und Lernenden* (Musical ABC for the use of teachers and pupils (Hamburg, 1708)), an elementary manual that outlines the rudiments and philosophy of music.

FURTHER READING

P. L. Poulin, 'Niedt's *Musicalische Handleitung*, Part I, and Bach's *Vorschriften und Grundsätze*: a comparison', *MR*, 52 (1991), 171–89.
P. L. Poulin and I. C. Taylor, *The Musical Guide* (Oxford: Clarendon Press, 1989).

RICHARD D. P. JONES

Nivers, Guillaume Gabriel (b. ?Paris, c1632; d. Paris, 1714) French organist, composer and theorist.

A near contemporary of Louis XIV, Nivers held some of the most important positions in Paris and at court: organist of Saint-Sulpice (early 1650s until his death); one of four organists of the Chapelle Royale (from 1678); master of music to the queen (from 1681); director of music at the *Maison Royale de St Louis* at St Cyr (from 1686).

His first *Livre d'orgue* (1665), containing 100 pieces in all the eight church modes arranged into suites, was the first to establish the system of genres (*pleins jeux, fugues, diminutions, récits, duos, echos* and *grands jeux*) that were consistently developed for at least the next century. His second *Livre* (1667) established the same array of genres in the *alternatim* ORGAN mass and the principal hymns for the liturgical year. His third *Livre* (1675) retained the format of the first but with each piece somewhat developed. In the preface to his 1665 *livre*, Nivers made valuable remarks about the church modes and performance practice: organ touch, FINGERING, ORNAMENTS, metre and TEMPO, as well as registrational practices for each genre.

Nivers was also a composer of sacred vocal music, in particular for St Cyr, and he composed a cantata in honour of Mme de Maintenon. As organist of St Sulpice he was engaged in the reforms of PLAINCHANT, not only EDITING chants but also publishing his *Dissertation sur le chant Grégorien* (Paris: l'auteur, 1683) and *Méthode certaine pour apprendre le plain-chant de l'Eglise* (Paris: l'auteur, 1698). In addition, his *Traité de la composition de musique* (Paris: Chez l'auteur et Robert Ballard, 1667) ran to four editions, and his *L'art d'accompagner sur la basse continue*, published as part of his *Motets à voix seule* (Paris: Chez l'auteur, 1689), offered authentic advice for accompanying on both organ and HARPSICHORD.

FURTHER READING

G. Beechey, 'Guillaume Gabriel Nivers (1632–1714): his organ music and his *Traité de la composition*', *The Consort*, 25 (1968–9), 373–83.
C. Davy-Rigaux, *Guillaume-Gabriel Nivers: Un art du chant grégorien sous la règne de Louis XIV* (Paris: CNRS Éditions, 2004).
D. Ponsford, *French Organ Music in the Reign of Louis XIV* (Cambridge University Press, 2011).

DAVID PONSFORD

Norrington, Sir Roger (Arthur Carver) (b. Oxford, 16 March 1934) English conductor.

Roger Norrington is one of the most influential figures in historical performance, demonstrating flair and imagination alongside musical intelligence and practical scholarship. He has brought a radical approach to a huge range of repertoire that progresses way beyond mere use of period instruments to a rethinking of TEMPO, ORCHESTRAL PLACEMENT, bow speed and ARTICULATION. Norrington has said of his landmark BEETHOVEN symphony recordings from the 1980s with the London Classical Players (LCP) that he wanted to use everything that could be discovered about early nineteenth-century performance, style and tradition, supplemented by the information the composer left behind. With LCP his repertory moved through Schubert, Weber, MENDELSSOHN, Schumann and BRAHMS; there were further experiments with WAGNER and Bruckner.

In his work with the Stuttgart Radio Symphony Orchestra, he went on to assimilate the use of period principles on modern instruments. For Norrington, music is about GESTURE, colour, shape and form, and emotional intensity, rather than the mere material of sound. He plays the repertory from HAYDN to ELGAR without VIBRATO, arguing that this was what would have been expected. He has written that 'evidence-based playing with pure tone can make old music sound new, touching, innocent, profound'. He has argued that the 'glamorous' vibrato introduced by Fritz Kreisler was resisted by ORCHESTRAS through the 1920s and 1930s, analogous with the glamour of Hollywood, cocktails, slipstream car design, street make-up, radio, ocean liners and the early days of flight. Norrington has famously attracted criticism from RICHARD TARUSKIN, who regarded historical performance as 'the most modern sound around'; his stance on orchestral vibrato has been rebutted at some length by David Hurwitz.

Norrington's influence derives from a wide-ranging musical career. He made his CONDUCTING debut with the Schütz Choir of London, which he founded in 1962. He has since held positions with Kent Opera, Bournemouth Sinfonietta, Orchestra of St Luke's, Camerata Salzburg and the Zurich Chamber

Orchestra. He has appeared with the Vienna Philharmonic and Berlin Philharmonic and major orchestras throughout the world; he has conducted opera at Covent Garden and in Florence, Venice, Vienna, Berlin, Paris and Amsterdam.

FURTHER READING

D. Hurwitz, '"So klingt Wien": conductors, orchestras and vibrato in the nineteenth and early twentieth centuries', M&L, 93 (2012), 29–60.
R. Norrington, 'The sound orchestras make', EMc, 32 (2004), 2–5.
B. D. Sherman, 'Taking music off the pedestal: Roger Norrington on Beethoven', in *Inside Early Music* (Oxford University Press, 1997), 339–63.
R. Taruskin, *Text and Act* (Oxford University Press, 1995).

COLIN LAWSON

North, Roger (b. Tostock, Suffolk, 1651; d. Rougham, Norfolk, 1 March 1734) English lawyer, music historian and philosopher.

Son of Dudley, fourth Baron North, he studied briefly at Jesus College, Cambridge and took prominence in the law, becoming King's Counsel and a Bencher of Middle Temple. Due to his family's loyalty to strict Tory principles, in 1689 he retired from his offices to live in Covent Garden and then at his estate, Rougham. A variety of distinguished musicians participated in the North household, most notably John Jenkins and NICOLA MATTEIS, and in his youth, North played in an ensemble of amateurs and professionals. His extraordinary intellectual confrontation with music brought together science, philosophy and musical practice in idiosyncratic fashion. Amongst some two thousand pages on music written during the course of his life, North published most notably *Some Notes upon an Essay of Musick* (1677) and *The Musicall Grammarian being a scientifick essay upon the practise of musick* (1728), as well as *Notes of Me* (c1698). Kassler has observed that North's writings on music fall within the Augustan tradition of a wit who exercises judgement in commenting on the contemporary scene, and he indeed contributed important information about London's musical life during the early eighteenth century. In his philosophical wrings, North moved away from Platonic and Cartesian assumptions to speculate about how epistemological study helps understand how vibrations of sound contribute to mental aspects of musical experience. He saw music as a sensory process involved with movements of the body which stimulate the imagination, generating creative uncertainty as to emotional meaning. He also speculated about how chords and keys can function within a theory of harmony.

FURTHER READING

M. Chan, J. C. Kassler and J. D. Hine, *Roger North's* The Musicall Grammarian and Theory of Sounds: *Digests of the Manuscripts with an Analytical Index of 1726 and 1728 Theory of Sounds* (Kensington, NSW: University of New South Wales, 1988).
J. C. Kassler, *The Honourable Roger North (1651–1734): On Life, Morality, Law and Tradition* (Farnham: Ashgate, 2009).

WILLIAM WEBER

Notation If there is one consistent way of defining music in the 'Western art tradition' in all its diversity, and across over 1,000 years of historical and regional variety, it lies in the fact that at least some aspects of its practice are – or can be – notated. It is likely that the process of notation, in whichever of its many forms, inflects the repertories concerned, and – in some cases at least – renders the music more complex than it otherwise would have been. Nevertheless, the undoubted significance of notation should not be allowed to colour our judgement of those parts of the repertoire that were written without notation. In other words, music that is less 'fixed' is not necessarily inferior to that which is preserved in notation, and indeed, in much of the Medieval and Renaissance eras it was possible for certain elements of the repertory (e.g. Gregorian CHANT) to be 'fixed' or established as an authoritative text, without necessarily being notated. Large amounts of repertory could be memorised without the use of notation and, indeed, quite complex forms of polyphony could be composed and/or improvised in the mind.

These latter points also mean that early notation was not necessarily 'primitive' or uninformative, particularly if it interacted with a vast memorised repertory. It might have functioned as a mnemonic, a repository of variants, an indicator of only certain aspects of the music or verbal text, or as an aid for those less familiar with the repertory at hand. Nevertheless, there is an obvious sense in which notation developed from its inception to the end of the twentieth century. Given that the notion of scientific, political and industrial progress became established from around 1600, there is no doubt that many saw the ongoing development of notation (as of music in general) as progressive. According to this narrative, notation embraced an increasing number of elements in music and its performance, ranging from ever more accurate aspects of melody and rhythm, towards details of TEMPO, timbre, DYNAMICS and ARTICULATION. From this point of view, a piece of music by BACH is more precisely notated than one by MONTEVERDI, while MOZART's and HAYDN's contain more performance instructions than Bach's, but fewer than in most works of the nineteenth century. An indication of this increasing precision – almost mirroring that of technology – is the fact that composers such as Messiaen, Babbitt and BOULEZ could write music that serialised elements of rhythm, dynamic and attack in addition to the parameter of PITCH, as already developed by the Second Viennese School. Yet, it was also in the 1950s that JOHN CAGE began experimenting with notation that fell entirely outside the 'usual' conventions, often subverting the assumed tendency towards precision. Moreover, the advent of mechanical reproduction (whether in terms of gramophone record, tape or digital media) meant that notation was no longer necessarily the most precise way of preserving music. Its role as a range of 'instructions' or 'recipe' for performance rather than 'the work itself' has thus become clearer.

The advent of recording has also shown quite clearly that even in a period when notation was assumed to be most authoritative, it does not capture every aspect of performance (such as RUBATO or PORTAMENTI, for instance). Multiple recordings by composers such as STRAVINSKY also show that even composers are wont not to follow (or perhaps are not even capable of following) their own, seemingly inviolable, instructions to the letter, or with consistency from one recording to the next. All this goes to suggest that even at its most developed, notation might not be as directive of performance as its users, then or now, might believe. There is almost a sense that the 'finish' implied by an accurate notation is there partly for its own sake (perhaps indicating an ideal, Platonist, form for the piece) and not expected to correspond in every detail with its 'earthly' manifestations in performance. This idealist sense of notation may be even more intractable if there is also an overriding ideology of WERKTREUE – truth to the work – where the work, over and above its notation and every possible performance, is itself considered as an ideal form, one that might unfold in different, contingent ways for different peoples and generations. Here, then, there is a tripartite sense of existential status: ideal work, standing above all its possible instantiations; ideal notated instructions for the work, standing above all possible performances; ideal performance, somehow realising both notated letter and 'true' spirit. All three of these might be different things and have different relations to the human agents concerned.

Of course, the development of mechanical reproduction and romanticist theories of musical works and musical texts does not necessarily imply that notation has the same complex status in earlier periods (or indeed that all music relates to such heady ideologies), but it is entirely possible that some of these issues were always surreptitiously at work (e.g. a sense that the notation was devised partly 'for its own sake', above and beyond its function as a 'recipe'). What much of this suggests is that we should try to find out as much as possible about both the technical workings of any particular notation and the cultural context in which it functioned. For instance, was it exemplary of a type of music that would otherwise have been improvised (such as some liturgical music, and particularly that for ORGAN)? Was it one type of realisation among others (e.g. coloratura in *opera seria*)? A composer's mnemonic for a virtuoso solo part (e.g. some aspects of the keyboard concertos of Handel and Mozart)? An example for less advanced pupils (e.g. CORELLI's supposed ORNAMENTATION in his VIOLIN sonatas)? And was it aimed towards future performance or perhaps merely a souvenir of past performances?

None of these issues is of course certain, but they do imply that the idea of viewing notation as an unproblematic set of instructions (or even as a set of instructions to be decoded with the help of a historical TREATISE) is overly simplistic. Most crucially, any notation was created within a much larger context, one in which all the parameters were themselves in a state of flux. It is impossible to recapture the precise constellation of elements pertaining at a point when any particular notation was executed, but consideration of even a few of the variables could have a profound influence on the way we play and listen to this music today.

FURTHER READING

S. Boorman, 'The musical text', in N. Cook and M. Everist (eds.), *Rethinking Music* (New York: Oxford University Press, 1999), 403–23.
J. Butt, *Playing with History* (Cambridge University Press, 2002).

JOHN BUTT

Notes inégales In his *L'art de toucher le clavecin* (2/1717), FRANÇOIS COUPERIN alluded to *notes inégales* in the following passage:

> In my opinion there are faults in our manner of writing music, which correspond to the manner of writing our language. It is that we write differently to the

way we perform; it is this that causes foreigners to play our music less well than we play theirs. Conversely, the Italians write their music in the true time-values in which they conceive it. For example, we dot several conjunct quavers in succession, even though we notate them equally; our custom has enslaved us; and yet we continue.

Couperin is one of about forty mostly French writers between 1665 and 1775 to describe the practice of *notes inégales*, loosely defined as a rhythmic convention in which, under certain conditions, passages of music containing particular note values that are subdivisions of the metrical pulse were performed unequally, although notated equally. The purpose, expressed by SAINT LAMBERT (*Les principes du clavecin* (Paris: Christophe Ballard, 1702)) and others, was to give more grace to the music, and one of its purposes may have been to imitate the stylised theatrical declamation of literary texts as performed, for instance, by Molière. It can hardly be accidental that most of the descriptions and the advice concerning performance practice of *notes inégales* come from instrumental TREATISES, whereas singers declaiming poetic texts would have had little need for theoretical advice. Sources concerning details of the practice are frustratingly incomplete, and some descriptions (such as by ETIENNE LOULIÉ in his *Éléments ou principes de musique* (Paris: Christophe Ballard, 1696)) were acknowledged to be intended for children and amateurs rather than for professional performers. However, from as far back as Loys Bourgeois (*Le droict chemin de musique* (Geneva: Jean Gérard, 1550)) until the late eighteenth century, mostly consistent general principles for the practice were established under the following headings:

1 Time signatures:
   A full table of each composer's advice concerning time signatures and the note values eligible for *inégalité* is given in Hefling (1993), and which can be summarised as follows:
   - *Inégalité* applied to note values of one quarter of the metrical pulse in simple time:
     a) in time signatures 2 and ¢ (two beats), when quavers were eligible for *inégalité*;
     b) in 2/4, C (four beats) and 3/4, when semiquavers were eligible.
   - *Inégalité* applied to note values of one half of the metrical pulse in simple time:
     a) in 3/2, when crotchets were eligible;
     b) in 3 and 3/4, when quavers were eligible.
   - *Inégalité* applied to semiquavers in 3/8 and 4/8 and in compound time signatures of 6/8, 9/8 and 12/8.

The assumption that governs nearly all the written evidence is that, in a particular instance, there is only one note value that is eligible for *inégalité*, all other note values being deemed equal. Some writers suggested that *inégalité* descended to the shortest note value. Five authors (all later than 1728) specified cumulative *inégalité*, implying that inequality could operate at different levels simultaneously.

2   Degrees of *inégalité*
    In theory, the range of RHYTHMIC INTERPRETATION could vary from extreme long-short (LS) to extreme short-long (SL) through innumerable degrees of subtlety in between. Loulié described four manners of treating rhythm:
    a) they are sometimes equal, and used in melodies where the notes follow each other in disjunct motion ('*détachez les nottes*');
    b) the first half-beats are a little longer than the second ('*lourer*': mild LS inequality);
    c) the first half-beats are much longer ('*piquer*' or '*pointer*': extreme LS inequality);
    d) the first half-beats are shorter than the second (SL inequality); F. Couperin termed this manner '*coulés*', and gave an example in the ornament table published in his first book of HARPSICHORD music (1713). In Nicolas Gigault's *Livre de musique pour l'orgue* (1685), pervasive dotted rhythms (notated *inégalité*) give a good guide to where SL inequality is appropriate – normally in descending conjunct passages similar to F. Couperin's *coulés*.

3   Conjunct and disjunct motion
    Writers including Loulié, MONTÉCLAIR, F. Couperin and HOTTETERRE (and many others in their musical examples) associated *inégalité* with conjunct (scalic) motion and *égalité* with disjunct motion (intervallic leaps). Lacassagne (*Traité général des élémens du chant* (Paris: l'auteur, la veuve Duchesne, 1766)) mentioned that quavers were equal when mixed with semiquavers or with syncopated notes, and QUANTZ recommended no *inégalité* for repeated notes.

4   National styles
    F. Couperin's comment that 'the Italians write their music in the true time-values in which they conceive it' is supported by Loulié, J.-J. Rousseau and by musical examples in publications by N. Gigault (*Livre de musique pour l'orgue*, 1685), MARAIS (*Pièces de viole*, livre 2, 1701) and Montéclair (*Principes de musique* (Paris: l'auteur, 1736)). This evidence was the basis on which FREDERICK NEUMANN concluded that *inégalité* was limited to French music, although when French composers consciously adopted Italian styles, and Italian, German and English composers wrote in French styles, the situation became more complex.

5   Dotted rhythms as notation for *inégalité*
    In 1988, Neumann insisted that 'semantically and logically, the concept of *notes inégales* makes sense only in reference to notes that are written equal but rendered unequal'. However, G. G. NIVERS in his second *Livre d'orgue* (Paris: L'auteur & R. Ballard, 1667) did publish irrational dotted quaver/ quaver rhythms in his *récits* to suggest *inégalité*, and Gigault (1685) published most of his 183 ORGAN pieces with pervasive dotted rhythms, except (significantly) for his fugue '*à la manière italienne*'. Logically, it is hardly credible that Gigault would have demanded strict dotted quaver/semi-quaver rhythms in a precise 3:1 ratio for every piece. More likely, the required rhythmic ratio would have varied according to character and to the genre of each piece. Furthermore GEORG MUFFAT, who had spent some

time in Paris in his teens, later demonstrated the French style to Salzburg instrumentalists in *Florilegium secundum* (1698) by illustrating *inégalité* with notated dotted rhythms. The same is most likely the case with English and German composers when they adopted French styles and genres in their compositions. Henry Purcell's *Almand* from Suite 3 in G major was published in 1696 with dotted rhythms throughout, whereas the MANUSCRIPT version was written with equal semiquavers. One explanation is that the dotted version was intended for amateur musicians who had little knowledge of French styles, but who were desirous of learning, whereas the MS version had more limited circulation and could be taught by the composer. It is also possible that the pervasive dotted rhythms in J. S. BACH's Prelude in G minor (*The Well-Tempered Clavier*, vol. 2) represent *inégalité* for a prelude written in the style of a French *allemande*. Genre and style analysis, together with notational studies, can therefore suggest the extent of French musical styles, and hence their performance practices, in other countries.

Although the general principles of *inégalité* are well documented, particular problems occur when considering any one piece of music. Italian styles of composition were popular in late seventeenth-century Paris. Lalande wrote choral music heavily influenced by Italian styles, and in *L'Apothéose de Lully* (1725), F. Couperin attempted a mix of French and Italian styles to achieve 'la perfection de la Musique'. It is most likely that genre played a part: harpsichord *allemandes* and organ *récits* could be played with mild inequality, processional organ *grands plein jeux* and *loures* needed more extreme dottedness, and organ *basses de trompette* required no *inégalité* because of their military fanfare-like associations and prevailing disjunct movement.

Until recently the subject of overdotting in French overtures was discussed separately from *notes inégales*, although if genre was the key then the disparity was misguided. Neumann surmised that because there were no references to overdotting of French overtures before Quantz in 1752, French overtures in the time of LULLY were played with no overdotting. But if *inégalité* was genre-specific, then there was no need to make French overtures a special case any more than *allemandes* or *sarabandes*. Furthermore, Hotteterre's comment in 1737, 'in movements where quavers are *inégales*, the dot that is after the crotchet is equivalent to a dotted quaver, so that the quaver which follows the dotted crotchet is always short', links over-dotting to *notes inégales*. Thus, marked LS *inégalité* (over-dotting) may well have been appropriate for the first section of French overtures, whereas subtle *inégalité* would have been appropriate in sensitive vocal *airs de cour*. This approach was suggested by Montéclair in 1709 in relation to SINGING: 'it is very difficult to give general principles concerning the *égalité* or *inégalité* of notes, because it is the style of the pieces one is singing that decides it'. The final arbiter in respect of *notes inégales* was always that of '*goût*' ('TASTE' or 'style'), invoked by Saint Lambert in *Les principes du clavecin* (Paris: Christophe Ballard, 1702) and by many others.

Today, of course, we cannot fully recreate late seventeenth- and eighteenth-century *goût*, so authentic performance practice in this period is probably the most difficult to achieve. But performers need to consider the following topics relating to any particular piece of music in their quest for authenticity: national style, genre, time signature and TEMPO, note values eligible for *inégalité*, character of melodic line, degree of ORNAMENTATION, individual composer's notational habits. These considerations, backed up by intelligent reading of relevant treatises, will lead to a more informed interpretation.

FURTHER READING

J. Byrt, *An Unequal Music: Rhythmic Inequality from the 16th to the 18th Centuries* (Tiverton: John Byrt, 2016).
S. E. Hefling, *Rhythmic Alteration in Seventeenth- and Eighteenth-Century Music* (New York, NY: Schirmer Books, 1993).
D. Ponsford, *French Organ Music in the Reign of Louis XIV* (Cambridge University Press, 2011).

DAVID PONSFORD

Nottebohm, (Martin) Gustav (b. Lüdenscheid, Westphalia, 12 November 1817; d. Graz, Austria, 29 October 1882) German musicologist, editor, teacher, pianist and composer.

While Nottebohm is chiefly remembered for his innovative studies of BEETHOVEN's sketchbooks, he also edited some of the earliest collected EDITIONS and compiled important thematic catalogues. His teachers included Ludwig Berger, Siegfried Dehn, Friedrich Schneider and (in Leipzig) MENDELSSOHN and Schumann. He moved to Vienna in 1846, where he studied with Simon Sechter, remaining there the rest of his life. From 1862 until his death, he was colleague and friend to BRAHMS, with whom he performed PIANO duets and undertook editorial work. His *Nachlass* is preserved in the Gesellschaft der Musikfreunde in Vienna.

Nottebohm was the first to make a systematic evaluation of Beethoven's sketches, transforming them into materials both scholars and performers could utilise. His initial foray into this area, *Ein Skizzenbuch von Beethoven* (Leipzig: Breitkopf & Härtel, 1865), was followed by *Beethoveniana* (Leipzig: J. Rieter-Biedermann, 1872), a compilation of several earlier articles that he revised for publication. *Ein Skizzenbuch von Beethoven aus dem Jahr 1803* (Leipzig: Breitkopf & Härtel, 1880) covered the Landsberg 6 'Eroica' sketchbook. *Zweite Beethoveniana* (Leipzig: C. F. Peters, 1887) was published posthumously in an edition by his student Eusebius Mandyczewski.

Nottebohm is also remembered for his pioneering editorial work on three of the first collected editions. Breitkopf & Härtel invited him to edit Beethoven's and MOZART's works, and at the time of his death he was chief editor for J. S. BACH's *Gesamtausgabe*. He approached this task in systematic fashion with similar diligence, and for the first time both scholars and performers could now consult texts that reflected extant primary sources. He also assembled thematic catalogues of the works of Beethoven (1868) and Schubert (1874), both of which remained standard points of reference until well into the twentieth century. His other musicological work includes the monograph *Beethovens Studien* (Leipzig: J. Rieter-Biedermann, 1873), which outlines Beethoven's studies in counterpoint with HAYDN, ALBRECHTSBERGER and Salieri.

FURTHER READING

D. Johnson, A. Tyson, and R. Winter, *The Beethoven Sketchbooks: History, Reconstruction, Inventory* (Berkeley, CA: University of California Press, 1985).

L. Lockwood, 'Nottebohm Revisited', in J. Grubbs (ed.), *Current Thought in Musicology* (Austin: University of Texas Press, 1976), 139–91.

PAUL ELLISON

O

Oboe A conical-bore woodwind instrument played with a double reed.

The oboe was invented in France in the mid-seventeenth century as a less strident version of the SHAWM; it was the first woodwind instrument to find a place in the orchestra, playing along with the VIOLINS and then contrasting with them. Oboes replaced the shawm in military bands, where they remained the main melodic instrument until supplanted by CLARINETS, bugles and cornets in the mid-nineteenth century. The distinctive tone of the oboe derives from its narrow, conical tube; in recent times the distinctive timbres of Baroque, Classical and Romantic instruments have been explored, to revelatory musical effect. On each of these oboes, INTONATION, tone-colour and DYNAMICS are modified by the combined control of breath and embouchure pressure. Over the centuries reeds have varied in length and breadth, but they have consistently comprised two hollowed-out blades of thin cane bound face to face with thread to a narrow tapered metal tube, known as a staple.

By the early seventeenth century, the popularity of the shawm was in decline, since the new aesthetic, which required affective nuances and variety of dynamics, was not well served by its loud, even sound. Following attempts to modify the shawm between 1620 and 1660, the oboe had emerged by 1670, when it featured in LULLY's comédie-ballet *Le bourgeois gentilhomme*. It seems likely that prominent woodwind players at the French court were involved, notably members of the HOTTETERRE and PHILIDOR families. Precise dating is challenging because in France, both shawms and oboes (or hautboys) were called 'hautbois'. Subsequently, Lully used the hautbois as an obbligato instrument and (with BASSOON or *cromorne*) in the trios of orchestral movements. Shawms had been played in CONSORT, so Lully's combination of wind and strings was an innovation. At this stage the oboe was usually made of boxwood, less often of ebony, ivory and fruitwoods. Physical features, such as the shape of the keys, the type of wood and external profile, varied from one workshop to the next. One of the first oboe tutors was written by FREILLON-PONCEIN in 1700, by which time construction in three sections, united by tenon-and-socket joints, had become the norm. At this time the oboe had already been exported to other European countries such as Germany and Holland – and to England, where it was enthusiastically embraced by Purcell. These countries produced prominent makers such as the Hotteterres, the Denners, the Rottenburghs, Richard Haka and his followers and the Stanesbys. Initially the oboe had three keys for the lower little finger; the largest produced the lowest note c', while the others each produced eb' duplicated so that the instrument could be played either with the left hand above the right (as is today's practice) or vice versa. On the two-keyed oboe cross-FINGERINGS or half-holing provided chromatic notes and gave individual character to each tonality. In an age well before equal TEMPERAMENT was the norm, QUANTZ (1752) discusses enharmonic semitones on the FLUTE; for example, the difference between d♯ and e♭. The relatively lower pressure demanded of the player facilitated a rapid response to the musical gestures and dynamic nuance of Baroque style. The sensitivity of the double reed made the oboe especially responsive to cross-fingerings and so it was the last of the woodwind to gain a more complex mechanism to cope with new musical demands. In 1713 MATTHESON referred to the oboe's ability to emulate vocal nuance and dynamic contour because of its ability to articulate phrases as though speaking them. In trio sonatas the oboe was matched in relative volume with the VIOLIN, transverse flute and RECORDER. EISEL in 1738 noted its versatility in different contexts – in the battlefield, opera, social gatherings and churches.

During the first half of the eighteenth century, the oboe inspired a repertory of chamber works, concertos and operatic obbligati from such composers as Vivaldi, Sammartini, RAMEAU, BACH and Handel. Among the many hautboists at the French court were generations of family members, including Hotteterres and Philidors; in Germany court musicians were responsible for performing the burgeoning solo repertoire. From 1729 Giuseppe Sammartini settled in Handel's London, and made a great impression upon audiences and the wider musical community. Other Italian players such as the Besozzi brothers were highly influential in France and Germany. Bach's soloist at Leipzig was Caspar Gleditsch, who was featured extensively in the sacred works and in at least five concertos that survive only in arrangements for HARPSICHORD. Bach often scored for OBOE DA CACCIA, a tenor instrument with flared bell and sometimes curved shape, sounding a fifth lower than the oboe and often designated 'taille'. The OBOE D'AMORE was pitched a third lower than the oboe, so called because its bell was in the shape of a 'love foot' or *Liebesfuss*, resulting in exceptionally sweet lower notes. When the bulb bell was applied to the larger instrument, the COR ANGLAIS came into being; its name derived from Middle German *engellisch*, which meant English as well as 'angelic'. In relation to the latter meaning the bell of the oboe da caccia was reminiscent of angels' horns depicted in old religious imagery.

Later in the century the dimensions of the bore, the walls and tone holes became smaller, resulting in a softer, focused and agile sound, especially in the upper register. At the same time, as PITCH rose, reeds also tended to become narrower and shorter. Although additional keywork was added late in the century, the chromatic scale continued to involve forked fingerings and half-holing, which created an uneven quality from one note to the next. These covered, veiled sounds would have been expected by composers contemporary with HAYDN and MOZART. During the latter half of the eighteenth century, the practice of oboes doubling violins gave way to a more harmonic function for the winds, the two instruments assuming quite different functions. To counter this, travelling virtuosi wrote bravura solo pieces with ORCHESTRA, including Fiala, Druschetzky, Carlo Besozzi, Fischer, Lebrun and Ramm. Mozart's Oboe Quartet K370 typifies an increasing preference for a higher tessitura. The presence of more ambitious upward slurs in oboe repertory led eventually to the provision of a speaker key, as on the clarinet. German makers such as Grundmann and the GRENSERS were especially prominent, although there were also many celebrated makers in France, Italy, Austria and England.

By 1810 the oboe had acquired as many as eight keys; this eliminated cross-fingerings, enhanced tuning and increased fluency in a greater range of tonalities. But such developments changed the nature of the instrument, as a result of which some players were reluctant to abandon their two-keyed models. By comparison with the flute or clarinet, the oboe was never popular among amateurs or within the domestic market. However, the PARIS CONSERVATOIRE inspired a plethora of virtuoso concertos, fantasias and salon pieces. Having been used briefly by Haydn, Mozart and BEETHOVEN, the cor anglais found a place in Italian opera (notably Rossini) and was then vigorously espoused by BERLIOZ and WAGNER.

By 1825 Sellner had produced a thirteen-keyed oboe that was to remain the standard model in Austria and Germany for a century. The modern Viennese oboe that succeeded it retains the contraction rim at the end of the bell that is characteristic of the earliest Baroque instruments. Ease of playing in different tonalities was allied to a uniformity of sound, which was not universally welcomed. Schumann's *Drei Romanzen* of 1840 display the instrument's lyrical rather than virtuoso qualities, reflecting the context for most prominent orchestral solos. Although Buffet's attempt to apply the Boehm system from the flute to the oboe was not a success, Brod (with Triébert) sought to create a lighter, more sensitive instrument in the 1830s; at the hands of Lorée after 1878 this French 'conservatoire-system' oboe became the favoured instrument in the twentieth century and won the significant approval of RICHARD STRAUSS. The more complex key-systems meant that boxwood was gradually supplanted by more stable materials such as rosewood, grenadilla and ebony. By this time stability and volume had been achieved somewhat at the expense of closely nuanced dynamic and colour. However, the instrument's profile was radically enhanced by Léon Goossens (1897–1988), whose expressive style made extensive use of VIBRATO and inspired a number of English composers. French composers such as SAINT-SAËNS continued to write for professors and pupils of the Paris Conservatoire. Of large-scale solo repertory, the concerto (1945) by Strauss occupies a central position. In succeeding years, the oboist and composer Heinz Holliger (b. 1939) revolutionised the instrument's scope and profile, featuring breath noises, key clicks and other percussive effects in his music. In the latter half of the twentieth century multiphonics achieved wide currency, with Bruno Bartolozzi's *New Sounds for Woodwinds* (London, 1967) being an important point of reference. The narrow bore of the oboe has made it more stable in pitch than other wind instruments during fluctuations in temperature and the tradition of tuning the orchestra to the oboe dates from the beginning of the nineteenth century.

FURTHER READING

A. Baines, *Woodwind Instruments and Their History*, 3rd edn (London: Faber & Faber, 1967).
G. Burgess and B. Haynes, *Oboe* (New Haven, CT and London: Yale University Press, 2004).
B. Haynes, *Music for Oboe, 1650–1800: A Bibliography* (Berkeley, CA: Fallen Leaf Press, 1985).

The Eloquent Oboe: A History of the Hautboy 1640–1760 (Oxford and New York: Oxford University Press, 2001).

G. Joppig, *The Oboe and the Bassoon*, trans. A. Clayton (Portland: Amadeus Press, 1988).

COLIN LAWSON

Oboe d'amore *see* OBOE

Oboe da caccia *see* OBOE

O'Dette, Paul (b. Pittsburgh, PA, 2 February, 1954) American virtuoso of the LUTE and related instruments, generally regarded as the greatest player of modern times.

After pursuing the electric GUITAR while growing up in Columbus, OH, O'Dette encountered the lute and made it his passion. Following studies with Eugen Dombois and THOMAS BINKLEY at the SCHOLA CANTORUM BASILIENSIS, he was appointed at the age of twenty-two to the faculty of the Eastman School of Music in Rochester, NY. In addition to performance, his apparently insatiable appetite for research has advanced understanding of Renaissance and Baroque practice, and he is widely credited with rehabilitating the 'thumb-under' right-hand technique of the Renaissance lute. O'Dette's 140+ recordings as a solo and ensemble player have won numerous awards and opened up previously unexplored repertories. Since 1992 he has been artistic director (later co-director) of the Boston Early Music Festival, a highly influential position.

ROSS DUFFIN

Ophicleide *see* TUBA AND OPHICLEIDE

Ondes martenot *see* ELECTRONIC INSTRUMENTS

Oral tradition Oral tradition is the means by which knowledge is transmitted amongst contemporaries, individuals and/or groups, as well as from one generation to the next. This knowledge is manifest through various cultural artefacts and residue, often without any recourse to written or documentary modes.

Described by Peter Jeffery (124) as 'a universal characteristic of almost all music at almost all times', oral traditions continue to transmit individual pieces, whole repertories of music, performing practices and related contextual knowledge. These are as evanescent as the music itself, existing only in the moment of enactment or recreation. In contrast, we might think of literate traditions associated with musical notation and the written word, and the different ways these capture and preserve knowledge. TREATISES, methods and manuals make instrumental learning more readily available, but can one really learn both the *art* and *craft* of performance without recourse to a living practitioner? A greater awareness of orality enables a reading of documentary source materials which expects and even embraces contradictions and omissions, recognising that while *craft* might be relatively unambiguously explained and reconstructed by following written instructions, *art* is fundamentally grounded in orality, and, as such, eludes verbal and written explanation. Since MARTIN AGRICOLA's *Musica instrumentalis deudsch* (Wittenberg, 1545), those seeking musical knowledge have been advised to have recourse to a teacher in order more fully to understand principles and practices. In his early seventeenth-century songbook, the Roman musician Giovanni Domenico Puliaschi, celebrated as both a tenor and a bass, reports that the many aspects of the singing voice are better heard than described (*Musiche varie*... (Rome: Zanetti, 1618), 56), sentiments echoed over 150 years later in TÜRK's *Klavierschule* (Leipzig and Halle, 1789).

Walter Ong's *Orality and Literacy* remains the most celebrated exploration of the contrasting nature of those elements. Ong draws on research by Milman Parry and his student Albert B. Lord into the oral transmission of epic poems in the Homeric tradition, the distinctive characteristics of which were a direct result of the economy enforced by their oral methods of creation. Ong's exploration of how orality and literacy shape the acquisition and storage of knowledge facilitates a greater understanding of the complementary roles of oral and written traditions in the transmission of Western art music. For example, whilst both oral and literate cultures employ analytic thought, a literate mind's 'abstractly sequential, classificatory, explanatory examination of phenomena or of stated truths' is utterly reliant on writing and reading, whereas oral thought is shaped by ways in which learning occurs: through imitation, repetition and participation, as well as combination and recombination (9). An oral tradition fosters 'as many minor variants of a myth as there are repetitions of it, and the number of repetitions can be increased indefinitely' (42). Oral cultures conceive and articulate all knowledge by close reference to practice, through personal knowledge derived from participation or observation. Learning takes place through observation and imitation, and is empathetic and participatory.

One of the most significant consensuses reached in musicology during the last forty years concerns the symbiotic nature of oral and written modes of CHANT practices and transmission in Western music between the ninth and twelfth centuries. Through research by Leo Treitler, Helmut Hucke and others, which has also drawn on work by Parry and Lord, we now understand how the act of chant performance was more akin to reconstruction than reproduction. Through understanding and enacting various patterns, rules and principles, music was constructed from known elements in two ways: through its manifestation in performance, that is, an orally transmitted aural entity and/or by a mental recreation of the music which, by virtue of being notated, became a written transmission. The symbiosis between these two products is a result of their location within a culture which is not predicated on a pre-existing tradition of literacy. Jeffery (62–70) regards this as an 'oral/written continuum' and more recent research by Anna Maria Busse Berger explores how Western Medieval musical cultures operated with a 'predominantly pre-literate framework' (A. M. Busse Berger, *Medieval Music and the Art of Memory* (Berkeley: University of California Press, 2005), 130). Whilst this situation exists in stark contrast to most canonic historical repertoire reliant on more established and descriptive forms of NOTATION, it helps us further to liberate ourselves from any obligations to the composer, who becomes only one of those involved in the creation of a piece of music. Whilst practices were usually at a local or regional level and were far from fixed, during the Middle Ages oral and written transmission interacted in different ways. Most of what we now call books were initially created for purposes of private study instead of for use in performance. From the late fifteenth century onwards, however, with the publication of increasing numbers of didactic sources on music and other subjects, oral methods of transmission, particularly personal instruction *in situ*, continued to complement and support documentary materials. During the European Renaissance, the so-called dialogue form, first used by Plato, became a prevalent literary genre. Amongst such writing may be detected a more than passing resemblance to the master-apprentice mode of oral transmission, including GIROLAMO DIRUTA's *Il Transilvano* (Venice, 1593) and THOMAS MORLEY's *A Plaine and Easie Introduction* (London, 1597), both examples of a new kind of auto-didactic volume. Although the advent of moveable type in the fifteenth century enabled the printing of texts, vocal and much instrumental music, the intricacies of accurately representing keyboard music were not solved until well into the eighteenth century. Furthermore, before the mid-nineteenth century the majority of music was disseminated in MANUSCRIPT form. This situation ensured the co-existence and survival, often for posterity, of progenies of the same work, each containing vestiges of the oral tradition through which they were created and disseminated, as well as temporally and geographically distinctive performance practices. Whilst individual manuscripts appear to fix certain elements of music by virtue of their documentary preservation, the concept of a definitive version did not begin to appear until developments in commercial music publishing widened access to a greater range of repertoire. Until relatively recently our knowledge of seventeenth-century keyboard music from the Italian peninsula was drawn almost exclusively from commercially printed sources. For example, GIROLAMO FRESCOBALDI's use of printing to preserve a final version of only the music he most valued means that the many extant manuscript versions of his works, in his hand as well as those of his associates, offer a far more representative view of his output.

Since the emergence of the practitioner-as-primary-source phenomenon, first observed over twenty years ago by RICHARD TARUSKIN, historical performance has become more comfortable with orality. This contrasts a previously more formally literate approach in which documentary sources were the most respected remnants from which to recreate past performance styles. Postwar ethnomusicological and anthropological research has awakened practitioners of Western art music to synergies between aspects associated with a work's meaningful transmission or 'content' and those aspects which pertain to individual practices or 'style' (B. Nettl, *The Study of Ethnomusicology: Twenty-Nine Issues and Concepts* (Urbana: University of Illinois Press), 1983, 47–9, 115–17, 189–91). Despite the pitfalls of cross-cultural comparisons, evidence from indigenous and folk traditions has been particularly useful to performers of Medieval and Renaissance repertory. Indeed, the current positive reception of HISTORICALLY INFORMED PERFORMANCE derives from its ability to recognise the ongoing role of both oral and literate modes of mediation and transmission. Many historical performers are themselves second- and third-generation practitioners, bringing with them a rich variety of approaches manifest in performance and recording. They negotiate the theory/practice continuum with an ease and fluency impossible for previous generations. These musicians, in teaching future generations, draw upon the physicality and orality of their own learning, in combination with the literacy of documentary sources. They have acquired skills across both practice and theory, in both the *craft* and *art* of historical performance. In the early twenty-first century, technological advances in the creation and dissemination of audio and audiovisual materials have provided further access to a multiplicity of oral traditions.

FURTHER READING

P. Jeffery, *Re-Envisioning Past Musical Cultures: Ethnomusicology in the Study of Gregorian Chant* (University of Chicago Press, 1992).
W. J. Ong, *Orality and Literacy: The Technologizing of the Word* (London: Routledge, 1982/ R2002).
I. E. Pearson, 'By word of mouth: historical performance comes of age', *PPR*, 17/1 (2012), http://scholarship.claremont.edu/ppr/vol11/iss1/5/

INGRID E. PEARSON

Orchestra and orchestral placement Early orchestral equivalents might be argued through the sixteenth and seventeenth centuries, in dramatic, ceremonial and ecclesiastical settings. Diverse subgroupings of bowed and plucked strings, keyboards, wind and brass offered introductory sinfonias, or DANCE music; they might have supported polychoral music or been used between acts of a play. Instrumentation may not have been fixed, although some programmatic associations were recognised: common instrumental tropes included allusion to the gods or heaven with LUTES, VIOLS and HARPS; TRUMPETS and drums provided grand entrances and underlined status; FLUTES, OBOES and other winds depicted pastoral scenes; and TROMBONES suggested the underworld. Musicians may have been in costume, visible or out of sight, and divided into shifting groupings to provide narrative reinforcement or match prevailing circumstances. Employment often followed affiliations with church, state, or patronage, rather than as an orchestral collective (for instance, violinists at French courts, trombonists and cornettists at St Mark's Venice, and winds retained for military and ceremonial purposes throughout Europe). Even in more extravagant cases such as MONTEVERDI's *Orfeo* of 1607, in excess of thirty players were mostly divided into smaller functional groups playing one (or equal numbers) to a part. From the modern perspective, these varied practices do not constitute an orchestral entity, although gradual increase in music written for the string group (with multiple reinforcement of the bass) does prove significant.

A stabilising universal concept for the orchestra can be identified more readily as three important developments coincide from the end of the seventeenth century. First, the practical exigencies of providing music in public theatres saw ensembles numbering perhaps ten to fifteen players placed to the side or in front of the stage. Space was limited and, typically employed for a season, this 'symphonie' had to cover the range of diegetic functions, necessarily drawing together combined effects. Second, preference for the penetrating sound of the VIOLIN and the introduction of more than one player to a part grew from the model of French string bands, where five parts (including three inner parts for different sizes of VIOLA) might be doubled. LULLY institutionalised elements that predated his arrival, including standardised string scoring, coordinated BOWING, and carefully stylised ORNAMENTATION (e.g. in dance music for 'Les Vingt-quatre Violons du Roi', comprising six violins, twelve violas, and six basses). With larger groups, oboes and BASSOONS might double parts; trumpets and HORNS could be added from the 'Grande Écurie'. German courts emulated French ensembles (albeit often at a smaller scale or without doubling), as Charles's English court did briefly. In Italy CORELLI led groups in excess of forty players, although violins routinely made up half of the ensemble and violas were less numerous. This corresponded with the third important factor: in concerti grossi, a large *ripieno* group played all together, alternating with a smaller *concertino* of players (perhaps just two violins and bass). As numbers of violins increased and more instruments (including some at 16′ PITCH) doubled a unifying BASSO CONTINUO, string music came to be written in four parts (two treble voices in the violins, one viola alto line and a bass part). It is difficult to generalise numbers and balance: QUANTZ's recommendations range from four to twelve violins; in 1710 at the Haymarket Theatre, Handel had six firsts, five seconds, two violas, six CELLOS, double bass and HARPSICHORD, as well as two oboes, four bassoons and a trumpet. In general, violins came to equal or outnumber the rest of the strings. Exceptional circumstances witnessed much larger forces.

Placement followed function and occasion through the seventeenth and eighteenth centuries, but can be rationalised to a few typical situations. Balcony or raised gallery positions tended to put musicians in close rows, perhaps with little apparent principle of organisation. In church this may have afforded antiphonal *cori spezzati* effects, or musicians could be located out of the way of dancing or ceremony; and there were sometimes and acoustic advantages. In theatres, the space in front of stages had been called the 'orchestra' ever since Renaissance revivals of Greek drama; in such pit placements there could be two keyboards leading a continuo group on each side, with the *concertino* leader in close communication. As the eighteenth century progressed, violins were more frequently divided. At Turin's Teatro Regio c1790, violins faced each other in rows stretching between the two keyboards, those playing the first part with their backs to the audience. Oboes or flutes may have been placed amongst the violins, and any HORNS or trumpets at the extremities of the ensemble. Alternatively, the orchestra might itself be arranged on a stage (initially this was often outdoors and sometimes tiered for projection), or on the floor in a room with players facing inwards towards the keyboard or leader. Theatre venues predominated in professional situations; raised gallery positions tended to connote earlier musical practices; and occupation of floor or staged positions in larger halls presaged later focus on the orchestra as the centre of attention.

Formerly distributed and transitional histories achieved coherence with the advent of the Classical orchestra, and by 1800 it had an elemental form recognisable today. What has been termed a pan-European repertory endured, with Viennese music (HAYDN, MOZART and BEETHOVEN) at its heart, fostering transferability of musicians and musical roles across the continent's courts and cities. Pairs of oboes (players sometimes alternating with flutes), horns and bassoons earned greater parity with the string group, before what were initially occasional additions became more indispensable: these included separate parts for flute and bassoon (for instance, in Haydn's early Esterházy symphony 'Le Matin'), the addition of CLARINETS (popularised in the influential MANNHEIM ORCHESTRA, Mozart took the opportunity to write for them in *Idomeneo* and the 'Paris' Symphony), and trumpets and drums (evinced by Haydn's 'Military' and 'Drum Roll' symphonies).

Time beating (with a stick or similar) or leadership from the violin (QUANTZ's preference) or keyboard (which C. P. E. BACH recommended) had remained the principal means of coordinating orchestras through much of the eighteenth century. Although theorists such as Forkel and Rochlitz still favoured keyboard direction, larger violin groups made the HARPSICHORD less suitable (neither loud enough, nor quiet enough); meanwhile the FORTEPIANO was not incisive enough, and apart from supporting recitative, the continuo influence waned. Major orchestras had violin leaders (notably Cannabich in Mannheim, REICHARDT in Berlin, Salomon in London and Pugnani in Turin), fostering unanimity in matters of ARTICULATION, BOWING and INTONATION, and managing the business of rehearsing perhaps forty or fifty players. Beethoven was one of the earliest non-instrumentalist directors, and it was composers influential in orchestral development who also furthered a new type of leadership: MENDELSSOHN, Weber, BERLIOZ and WAGNER were all successful conductors.

Opera was a crucible for invention and experiment. Méhul (*Euphrosine* and *Ariodant* in the 1790s) and Spontini (*La vestale*, 1807) contributed additions we recognise more frequently via Beethoven's symphonies. They exploited extra horns crooked in different keys (as Haydn had in the 'Hornsignal' Symphony; Beethoven adds a third for the 'Eroica' in 1801, and has four for *Fidelio* in 1805; further potential is manifest in Weber's *Der Freischütz* (1817–21)). Trombones were not unusual in opera at the time Beethoven added them for his Fifth Symphony, nor was the piccolo new then (used for example in *Idomeneo*). Independence of the DOUBLE BASS part developed, its virtuosity celebrated in the Ninth Symphony, where extra PERCUSSION is also conspicuous (janissary music having been fashionable, for example, in Mozart's *Die Entführung aus dem Serail*).

The Romantic orchestra continued to be influenced by dramatically inspired works, as well as technological developments (notably woodwind keywork and valved brass). In his *Grand traité d'instrumentation et d'orchestration modernes*, Berlioz set about codifying diverse groupings unusual for their size and inclusion. Wagner's expansion of the orchestra's tonal resources was similarly ambitious: along with Schumann, he embraced the valve horn; for the *Ring*, the COR ANGLAIS became a solo voice and the sound of the BASS CLARINET assumed symbolic significance; in effect, orchestration in single-instrument families had evolved. This phase introduced manifold new possibilities within mainstream orchestral constitution. Infrequent examples most likely to be found subsequently in French- or Russian-influenced scoring include the cornet (from Berlioz to Franck, STRAVINSKY and Messiaen) and the saxophone (from Thomas's 1868 *Hamlet* and Bizet's 1872 *L'Arlésienne* onwards, or perhaps in jazz- or dance band-inspired roles). Wagner's specification for four *Tuben* can also be found in Bruckner. Bass and contrabass wind variants appear occasionally elsewhere too.

None the less, evidence of general augmentation is clear from Tchaikovsky to MAHLER, RICHARD STRAUSS and others. Together with larger string sections, triple or even quadruple woodwind more regularly included piccolo, cor anglais, bass (and/or small E♭) clarinet, and CONTRABASSOON. Exceeding a routine complement of four horns, three trumpets, three trombones (one covering the bass range fully) and TUBA became feasible. PERCUSSION might involve two or more players in addition to the timpanist; PIANO or celeste might complement one or more harps. Various seating solutions generally put strings closest to the conductor (first violins almost universally to the left, with the seconds either behind them or mirroring their position on the right). Benefits to tuning and ensemble saw the woodwind grouped in a central block, often raised, with brass and percussion to the sides and/or behind them. Other than operatic or choral contexts, placement more frequently came to establish the orchestra centrally, its institutional significance increasingly underlined by bespoke architecture: the Leipzig Gewandhaus moved to a new hall in 1885, the Concertgebouw in Amsterdam opened in 1883 and major halls were built in America (Carnegie Hall in 1891, Boston Symphony Hall in 1900). There has also been a trend of enlargement in orchestral sound, reflected in wire-wound strings, re-designed woodwind and brass, and larger TIMPANI.

In the last hundred years the orchestra has had a liminal existence, at once both museum and the site of reaction and innovation. New works for more modest forces might be divided into those related to SCHOENBERG's Chamber Symphony instrumentation (one player to a part, quartet plus principal wind), or those in formations similar to some of the Paul Sacher commissions (based around a string orchestra, and such groups sometimes also dedicated themselves to smaller scale performances of the Viennese classics). Those more closely concerned with historical performance and instruments formed groups such as CONCENTUS MUSICUS WIEN (1953), the ACADEMY OF ANCIENT MUSIC (1973) and MUSICA ANTIQUA KÖLN (1973).

FURTHER READING

D. J. Koury, *Orchestral Performance Practices in the Nineteenth Century: Size, Proportions, and Seating* (Ann Arbor, MI: UMI Research Press, 1986).

J. Spitzer and N. Zaslaw, *The Birth of the Orchestra: History of an Institution, 1650–1815* (Oxford University Press, 2004).

SIMON BAINES

Orchestra of the Age of Enlightenment The Orchestra of the Age of Enlightenment (OAE) gave its first concerts in June 1986, performing repertoire by Gossec, HAYDN, RAMEAU and TELEMANN, directed by SIGISWALD KUIJKEN. In the words of Michael Rose, who funded the OAE's incorporation, 'the Age of Enlightenment was as much the late 1980s as it was the period of the core repertoire' (Wallace, 12). By the mid-1980s historical performance in the UK was relatively localised. A consistent nucleus of players appeared with most of the established ensembles, such as the ACADEMY OF ANCIENT MUSIC,

ENGLISH BAROQUE SOLOISTS, THE ENGLISH CONCERT and the London Classical Players. With the founder/directors of these ensembles establishing independent reputations for themselves, their players wanted to collaborate with other musicians, particularly historical performers from the Continent as well as artists from the world of mainstream performance. The OAE was therefore founded as a self-governing ensemble, with a complement of between thirty and seventy-five players, depending upon the repertory. Musical directors are drawn from the ranks of conductors and instrumentalists and appointed on a project-by-project basis.

The orchestra made its Salzburg Festival debut in 1991 in music by MOZART conducted by FRANS BRÜGGEN and the following year appointed Brüggen and SIMON RATTLE as principal guest conductors. Other directors who have collaborated with the OAE include Marin Alsop, Harry Bicket, Ivor Bolton, Edward Gardner, PHILIPPE HERREWEGHE, CHRISTOPHER HOGWOOD, Monica Huggett, RENÉ JACOBS, TON KOOPMAN, GUSTAV LEONHARDT, Yannick Nézet-Séguin, Robin Ticciati and Bruno Weil. Currently Rattle and JOHN BUTT, Mark Elder, Iván Fischer and Vladimir Jurowski are principal artists, whilst ROGER NORRINGTON and WILLIAM CHRISTIE hold the title of emeritus conductor, a position formerly held by Brüggen and CHARLES MACKERRAS.

Partnerships account for some of the orchestra's success, particularly those with the Glyndebourne Festival, London's South Bank Centre and Virgin Classics. For example, since Rattle conducted *Le nozze di Figaro* in 1989 the OAE has appeared regularly at Glyndebourne. Other Glyndebourne productions have included music by J. S. BACH, BEETHOVEN, Gluck, Handel, MONTEVERDI, Purcell, Rameau, Rossini and Weber. The orchestra has been resident at London's South Bank Centre since 1992. Early recordings for Virgin included Schubert's Symphony No. 9 conducted by Mackerras (released in 1988), and symphonies and concertos of C. P. E. BACH directed by Leonhardt (1990). In 1996 the OAE appeared at the Royal Opera House, Covent Garden, in Verdi's *Alzira* under Mark Elder.

The orchestra's flexibility in functioning both with and without a conductor was reflected in its 1998 US debut at the Lincoln Center's 'Mostly Mozart Festival'. One concert, of music by Chopin and MOZART, was conducted by Paul Daniel; a second was presented by smaller forces performing Boyce, Vivaldi, Handel and J. S. Bach. Allan Kozinn in *The New York Times* (6 August 1998) noted a 'solidity and precision of its ensemble playing, and the sense of joy with which the musicians brought the music to life'.

Over its thirty-year history the OAE has performed music from Purcell, Bach and Handel, through the Viennese classics to BRAHMS and WAGNER. Its recordings encompass repertoire by C. P. E. and J. S. Bach, Beethoven, Bellini, Blow, Chopin, Crusell, Donizetti, Handel, Haydn, Kraus, MAHLER, MENDELSSOHN, Monteverdi, Mozart, Offenbach, Purcell, Rossini, Salieri, Schubert, Verdi and Vivaldi.

FURTHER READING

H. Wallace, *Spirit of the Orchestra* (London: Orchestra of the Age of Enlightenment, 2006).
Orchestra of the Age of Enlightenment. www.oae.co.uk.

INGRID E. PEARSON

Orchestra of the Eighteenth Century In co-founding the Orchestra of the Eighteenth Century in 1981, FRANS BRÜGGEN explicitly drew upon Dutch expertise in the arena of historical performance that had been established during the post-war years. Brüggen directed the orchestra until his death in 2014, establishing the ensemble's international reputation both on the platform and in the recording studio. The orchestra's co-founder, Sieuwert Verster (b. 1953), a record producer, musicologist and unofficial musical adviser to the Dutch royal family, continues to manage all aspects of the ensemble's activities. The orchestra is based in Amsterdam and numbers up to about sixty-five members, the majority of whom are Dutch. Unusually for a professional ensemble of international repute, entry is by invitation rather than audition. Brüggen formed the orchestra as a collective, once proudly exclaiming that he earned the same as the second clarinettist!

In his 2012 interview for *The Fryderyk Chopin Institute*, Brüggen described four ensembles within one: one for repertoire by J. S. BACH and his contemporaries, performing at $a' = 415$ Hz; another for the French Baroque, at $a' = 392$ Hz; an orchestra for later repertoire, at $a' = 430$ Hz, up to and including Chopin; and another embracing works as late as Schumann and BRAHMS, with appropriate instruments pitched at $a' = 440$ Hz.

Recordings for Philips include the complete BEETHOVEN symphonies (released 1988–93), major symphonic works by MOZART (1985–96) and HAYDN (1988–95), as well as music from Purcell to MENDELSSOHN. Demonstrating Brüggen's commitment to live music making, these recordings often include material captured during the act of performance itself. British critics have noted Brüggen's effective use of the anachronistic role of conductor in asserting his own musical imagination. The high level of technical accomplishment of Brüggen's musicians has certainly been a factor in producing what STANLEY SADIE described as 'stimulating, musicianly performances' (*Gramophone*, December 1986, 875). A second set of Beethoven symphonies was released in 2012 on the Glossa label. Combining the orchestra's legendary freshness and vitality with the idiosyncratic artistic vision of a single director, these interpretations manifest Brüggen's monumental and highly influential musical legacy.

FURTHER READING

D. J. Wakin, 'In Italy, "Eroica" energizes a frail fixture of period music', *The New York Times*, 30 June 2008.
Orkest van de Achttiende Eeuw. www.orchestra18c.com.

INGRID E. PEARSON

Orchestre Révolutionnaire et Romantique With a performance of BEETHOVEN's *Missa Solemnis* at London's Royal Festival Hall in November 1989 JOHN ELIOT GARDINER's Orchestre Révolutionnaire et Romantique (ORR) was founded. Although given under the ENGLISH BAROQUE SOLOISTS' name, this concert heralded Gardiner's foray into nineteenth- and twentieth-century repertory on period instruments. The following year, as ORR, the orchestra presented concerts of music by BRAHMS in Bremen and Schumann in London.

ORR proclaims its commitment to 'stylistic fidelity and intensity of expression' in seeking to recreate the vast and ever-changing palette of timbral colours available on historical instruments, and they often appear with Gardiner's Monteverdi Choir. Accordingly, their discography includes music by Beethoven, BERLIOZ, Bizet, BRAHMS, Fauré, Gluck, MENDELSSOHN, Schubert, Schumann, Verdi and Weber, for Decca, Deutsche Grammophon Archiv, EMI Classics, FRA Musica, Philips and Opus Arte. Since 2005 ORR has recorded for *Soli Deo Gloria*, the in-house label of Gardiner's ensembles, often releasing live concert performances on CD. For its recordings of Beethoven's nine symphonies (1994) ORR was hailed as 'a virtuoso band capable of astonishing feats of sonority and articulation'; and it was noted that some of the recordings were captured live in performance (*Gramophone*, November 1994, 64).

ORR has an affinity with the music of Hector Berlioz and in 1991 performed and recorded his *Symphonie Fantastique* in the same Parisian venue as the work's 1830 premiere. In 1993 the ORR gave the first performances since the composer's lifetime of Berlioz's recently rediscovered *Messe Solennelle*. The ORCHESTRA has also been particularly influential in its presentation of new productions of opera, in both the UK and Europe. Two Parisian residencies (at the Théâtre du Châtelet, 1999–2003, and the Opéra Comique 2007–11) saw fully staged productions of Gluck's *Orphée* and *Alceste*, Verdi's *Falstaff* and Weber's *Oberon* and the first complete performance of Berlioz's *Les Troyens*, as well as Chabrier's *L'Étoile*, Bizet's *Carmen*, Debussy's *Pelléas et Mélisande* and the Weber/Berlioz *Le Freischütz*.

FURTHER READING

'Orchestre Révolutionnaire et Romantique'. www.monteverdi.co.uk/about/orr.
B. Sherman, 'Reviving idiosyncrasies: John Eliot Gardiner on Berlioz and Brahms', in *Inside Early Music* (Oxford University Press, 1997), 364–77.

INGRID E. PEARSON

Organ A musical instrument consisting of a wind-raising mechanism that directs air pressure to a chest, in which the wind is contained, until admitted to one or more ranks of pipes by means of a keyboard.

Of all instruments, the organ is the most complex and its history is the most involved and wide-ranging in scope. Its extant repertory is both the oldest and the largest, comprising a huge range of styles and performance practices both chronologically and geographically. Despite an extensive but speculative history from Greek, Roman and Arab antiquity, Western European organs will be the focus here, particularly those on which the extant repertory was played. Further, rather than explaining issues of construction, the approach will be biased towards historical performance.

In Medieval times it was the Benedictines who cultivated the construction of organs. One such report from Wulfstan of Winchester claimed that the organ (built by about 990) had 400 pipes, ten ranks, forty notes and twenty-six bellows, although the instrument may well have functioned as a signal for summoning worshippers to services. The first illustration of organ keys played by individual fingers occurs in the Rutland Psalter (c1250–60). Two organs survive from the late fourteenth century: the now pipeless Positive *Norrlanda* organ (c1380, currently in Stockholm Museum), and that at Sion, Switzerland (c1380), although the latter has been much rebuilt and is less than reliable as historical evidence.

Organs became the norm in cathedrals in the fourteenth and early fifteenth centuries, initially used in alternation with singers in Lady Chapel Masses. HENRI ARNAUT DE ZWOLLE, writing in the 1440s, described several organs based on the *Blockwerk*: multiple ranks of octaves and fifths that all sounded together. The *Blockwerk* at Salins, for example, contained from six to fifteen ranks. At Amiens Cathedral in 1422, the four-octave keyboard contained a *Blockwerk* that began with nineteen ranks and ended at the top with ninety-one ranks per note. Later in the century, the development of wind chests enabled separate ranks to be drawn, so that by 1500 in northern Italy and southern France a chorus of ten or so separate stops could be expected. After 1500 organs could produce a greater variety of tonal colours than ever before, either with individual stops or multiple keyboards, or both. This made the organ suitable for liturgical services, most likely played in alternation with sung PLAINCHANT. Throughout the sixteenth century, regional characteristics began to emerge.

Italy

Separable *ripieno* stops, 4' flute ranks, half-stops, duplicated treble ranks, slider chests and spring chests were all known in the Italian states during the fifteenth century. Unlike organs in northern Europe, the Italian organ remained a relatively stable design, often with pairs of organs situated either side of the chancel, as in Milan Cathedral. Italian organs consisted essentially of one manual with an octave or so of pedals that pulled down the lowest notes of the keyboard. The most famous builders were the Antegnati family, from which Costanzo (1549–1624, son of Graziadio) wrote the most important TREATISE on instruments and registration, *L'arte organica* (Venice, 1608). The organ at the Old Cathedral in Brescia, built by G. G. Antegnati in 1536, is a good example:

Manual (50 notes, from FF 24'?)

Principale	16
Principale	16
Ottava	8
Decimaquinta	4
Decimanona	$2\,^{2}/_{3}$
Vigesimaseconda	2
Vigesimasesta	$1\,^{1}/_{3}$
Vigesimanona	1
Trigesima terza	$^{2}/_{3}$
Flauto in ottava	8
Flauto in decimaquinta	4
Vigesimaseconda	2
Pedal (C–c): *Principale*	16

The art of tonal variety lay in choosing different combinations of *ripieno* stops, described in *L'arte organica*. Reed ranks were exceptional to the norm, but one striking Italian combination was the *voce umana*: a pair of Principal ranks, one of which was de-tuned to produce an other-worldly tremolo effect, exploited particularly in FRESCOBALDI's Elevation toccatas. TEMPERAMENTS were based on ¼ comma meantone, with pure thirds and narrow fifths.

Spain and Portugal
The differing cultures in the Iberian peninsula suggest a range of organ traditions, but documentation is still incomplete. Organs could be found anywhere in the church, but mostly on one or both sides of the chancel. Short octave keyboards persisted until the 1840s; Pedal keys were very short; and at Toledo Cathedral the keys were small buttons played by the ball of the foot. Low wind pressures and a direct connection between keys and light pallets resulted in very light actions. The Flemish builder Gillis Brebos was commissioned to build four organs (1579–84) for the Escorial Palace, played by ANTONIO DE CABEZÓN, but only the cases survive today. Horizontal reeds can be dated only back to c1600, although they became a strong feature from then on. The organ in Seville Cathedral (1668–73) had four sets of reeds *en chamade*, as well as four manuals and a 32′ reed in the Pedal, but it was rebuilt beyond recognition in 1912. Nevertheless, the two organs either side of the chancel possess marvellously ornate cases.

France
Perhaps the most particular and consistent type of European organ was built in France from about 1670 up to the late eighteenth century. Both the consistency of design and the standard array of keyboards and stops enabled composers to develop a consistent range of genres that constituted their suites and organ masses. Further, each genre had a dedicated set of registration instructions (with alternatives) detailed in the prefaces to their *livres d'orgue*: *plein jeu, fugue, duo, récit au dessus, récit en taille, récit en basse, trio, fond d'orgue* and *grand jeu*. The design of the French Classical organ was based on the contrast between two manuals: *Grand Orgue* and *Positif*. Both departments had a similar complement of flues and reeds, although the *Positif* was based on a *Montre* (8′ or 4′ Principal) an octave higher than that on the *Grand Orgue* (16′ or 8′). Two further manuals, the *Récit* and *Écho*, were of a shorter compass, and provided solo stops such as the *cornet* and a *trompette*. Whereas the Pedal organ in Germany provided the bass of the musical texture, the French *Pédale* was based on 8′ pitch (whereas the GO was based on 16′ pitch), and served two purposes: first, as a solo keyboard for playing the plainchant on powerful reeds in the tenor (*en taille*); and second, as an 8′ flute bass for solo *récits*. An example of such an instrument was that played by Lebègue, one of the four *Organistes du roi*, at St Louis-des-Invalides in its rebuilt state (1679–87) by Alexandre Thierry, *facteur du roi*, and heard by Louis XIV.

Although this represents a large, ideal organ, the basic characteristics were consistent for all organs built and rebuilt throughout the period in France, with

Grand Orgue		Positif		Récit	
CD–c''', 48 notes		CD–c''', 48 notes		c'–c''', 25 notes	
Montre	16	Montre	8	Cornet	V
Bourdon	16	Bourdon	8	Trompette	8
Montre	8	Prestant	4		
Bourdon	8	Flûte	4	**Écho**	
Prestant	4	Nasard	2⅔	c–c''', 37 notes	
Flûte	4	Doublette	2	Bourdon	8
Grosse Tierce	3⅕	Tierce	1⅗	Flûte	4
Nasard	2⅔	Larigot	1⅓	Nasard	2⅔
Doublette	2	Fourniture	III	Quarte	2
Quarte de Nasard	2	Cymbale	II	Tierce	1⅗
Tierce	1⅗	Cromorne	8	Cymbale	II
Fourniture	V	Voix humaine	8	Cromorne	8
Cymbale	IV				
Cornet	V	**Pédale**		Tremulants: *'fort'*	
Trompette	8	AA, BB–f, 20 notes		and *'doux'*	
Clairon	4	Flûte	8	Coupler: *Positif* to	
Voix humaine	8	Trompette	8	*Grand Orgue*	

remarkably few differences. Two of the most important genres, which often began and ended suites and mass sections, were the *Plein jeu* and *Grand jeu*, typically registered thus:

Plein jeu: Pos. 8, 4, 2, *fourniture, cymbale*.
G.O. 16, 8, 4, 2, *fourniture, cymbale*.
Manuals coupled.

Grand jeu: Pos. bourdon 8, prestant 4, nasard 2⅔, quarte 2, tierce 1⅗, cromhorne 8.
G.O. trompette 8, clairon 4, cornet, prestant 4.
GO/Pos coupled
Récit: Cornet.
Echo: Cornet.
Tremblant à vent perdu.

Pertinent to performance practice are the physical dimensions of French organ consoles in this period. In contrast to the large-scale pedalboards of contemporary German pedalboards (encouraging alternate feet), French pedalboards are very small, necessitating a precise *detaché* toe technique.

England

Due to major political and religious events such as the Dissolution of the Monasteries, English Reformation and the Civil War, the early history of the organ in England has lacked continuity and detail. However, the discovery of the early sixteenth-century Wetheringsett soundboard and some extant contemporary contracts suggests that the organs were small and based on a

Principal 5′ or (for larger organs) 10′. In Durham Cathedral there were five organs in different parts of the building; these were used in a ritualistic manner according to particular liturgical functions and feast days in the church year.

Puritan opposition from about 1570 led to the wholesale removal of organs, but with William Laud's High Church movement in the early seventeenth century, organs were once again placed in cathedrals and college chapels. The organ in Worcester Cathedral, built by Thomas Dallam in 1613 for the organist Thomas Tomkins, contained the following specification:

Great Organ		Chaire Organ	
Open Diapason	10	Diapason	10
Open Diapason	10	Principal	5
Principal	5	Flute	5
Principal	5	Small Principal or Fifteenth	$2\frac{1}{2}$
Recorder	5	Two and Twentieth	$1\frac{1}{4}$
Twelfth	$3\frac{2}{3}$		
Small Principal or Fifteenth	$2\frac{1}{2}$		
Small Principal or Fifteenth	$2\frac{1}{2}$		

This was a transposing organ, with keys beginning on C that sounded as Choir pitch F.

At the start of the Civil War in 1642, Robert Dallam and his family emigrated to Brittany, where he and his sons built the organs at Quimper Cathedral, Lanvellec, Guimiliau, Ploujean and Ergué-Gaberic. At the Restoration in 1660, the family returned to England, and certain French characteristics can be observed in Dallam's proposal for an organ in New College, Oxford, in 1662, when he was requested to add some 'extraordinary stops, as the Trumpet Stop, the Cornet Stop, & some others'. This French influence was to permeate English organ building right through to the nineteenth century. In 1684, the celebrated 'Battle of the Organs' took place, after which the Benchers of the Temple chose between organs built by Renatus Harris and the Dutch/German organ builder Bernard Smith. Smith won the contract in 1688, building a three-manual organ ('Great', 'Chair' and 'Ecchos'), incorporating Dutch influences and split accidentals (D♯ and E♭, G♯ and A♭) to make it more versatile in meantone temperament.

One of the largest organs for the time in England was built by Richard Bridge in 1735 (recently restored). With three manuals, 'Great', 'Choir' and 'Swell', it possessed thirty-three stops, including doubled Principals, doubled Trumpets, Cornets and Sesquialteras, Bassoon, French Horn, Vox Humana and Drum pedal. Most English organs were much more modest, with no Pedals. The swell mechanism was introduced in an English organ in 1712, and the character of most English organs reflected the beautiful, gentle tone and sobriety that were fitting for Anglican worship. Registrations for the Georgian organ were specified in the works of John Stanley, and detailed registration instructions were printed in books of Voluntaries by JOHN MARSH (London, 1791) and Jonas Blewitt (London, c1795).

Following the discovery of the organ works by J. S. BACH, the visit of FELIX MENDELSSOHN, and tours in Europe made by prominent English organists, the English 'Classical' organ was displaced by the 'German System' in the 1840s. The old GG compass was replaced by a C compass, and the new Pedal organ was pitched at 16′, whilst unequal temperament remained. Such instruments as the William Hill organ (1841) in Great George Street Chapel, Liverpool, demonstrated new tonal ideals: the Swell became the principal second manual with reeds 16′, 8′ and 4′, the Choir was reduced to flutes, dulciana and solo reeds, the Tuba Mirabilis was introduced, and the small Pedal organ now contained a full chorus and 16′ Trombone.

North Germany and the Netherlands

The German organist ARNOLT SCHLICK, whose influence spread from South Germany to the Netherlands, is the most reliable source of knowledge about early sixteenth-century organs through his *Spiegel der Orgelmacher* (Speyer, 1511), the first work published in German about organ building and playing. His scheme for a two-manual and Pedal organ clearly reflects three independent and contrasting choruses, and was widely influential:

Hauptwerk: *principal, octave, gemshorn, zimbel, mixture, rauschpfeife* (probably a reed), *clapper* (possibly a glockenspiel or high flute stop), *zink, flageolet, regal.*
Rückpositif: *principal, small gemshorn, small mixture, small zimbel.*
Pedal: *principal, octave, mixture, trumpet or posaune.*

In Amsterdam, the three-manual Oude Kerk organ played by Sweelinck's father and known by the composer from 1580 to 1621, built by Niehoff from 1539 to 1542, was particularly influential in Holland. Its specification was:

Das Prinzipal: *Prinzipal 16, Oktav 8+4, Mixtur, Scharf.*
Oberwerk: *Prinzipal 8, Holpijp 8, Offenflöte 4, Quintadena 8 or 4, Gemshorn 2, Sifflöte 1 or 1 1/3, Terzzimbel, Trompete 8, Zinck 8.*
Rückpositiv: *Prinzipal 8, Octave 4, Mixtur, Scharf* ('these four shall make the *Prinzipal*'), *Quintadena 8, Holpijp 4, Krummhorn 8, Regal 8, Baarpijp 8, Schalmei 4.*
Pedal: *Trompete 8, Nachthorn 2.*

Such an organ offered many varied tonal colours, particularly facilitated by the *Oberwerk* and *Rückpositiv*, with the pedal designed for playing solo *cantus firmus* lines.

During the seventeenth century, organs in north Germany and the Netherlands became much larger in scale, with each department, *Hauptwerk, Ruckpositive, Oberwerk, Brüstwerk* and Pedal, having its own full complement of flue pipes and reeds, each department housed in a separate case. The mechanical layout of such organs necessitated a *Werkprinzip* design, with each department differing in both fundamental PITCH (Hw 16′, Rp 8′, Ow 4′, Ped 32′) and architectural placing against the west or east wall of the church.

Often these organs were owned by town councils and the *Werkprinzip* enabled enlargements and additions to be made throughout the century for both musical and status purposes. The number of tonal combinations was enormous, and the paradox is that for a composer such as Buxtehude (organist of the *Marienkirche*, Lübeck) no significant registration instructions survive. Some of his *Praeludia* were doubtless intended to demonstrate the huge resources of the organ, but appropriate stops for particular sections of any single piece are unknown.

Some registration instructions do survive for small organs by GOTTFRIED SILBERMANN, who was well known to J. S. Bach. Silbermann brought elements of French organ building to the Saxon tradition, and the specification of his first great organ at Freiberg (1710–14) is worth quoting:

Hauptwerk II		*Oberwerk* III		*Brustwerk* I	
Bourdon	16	Quintadena	16	Gedackt	8
Prinzipal	8	Prinzipal	8	Prinzipal	4
Rohrflöte	8	Gedackt	8	Rohrflöte	4
Viola da Gamba	8	Quintadena	8	Nasat	2⅔
Oktave	4	Oktave	4	Oktave	2
Quint	⅔	Spitzflöte	4	Tierce	1⅗
Superoktave	2	Superoktave	2	Quint	1⅓
Tierce	1⅗	Flachflote	1	Sifflöte	1
Mixtur	IV	Mixtur	III	Mixtur	III
Zimbel	III	Zimbel	II		
Cornet	V	Cornet	V		
Trompete	8	Krummhorn	8		
Clarin	4	Vox humana	8		

Pedal					
Untersatz	32	Posaune	16	Tremulants *fort* and *doux*	
Prinzipal	16	Trompete	8	Hw/Ow	
Oktave	16	Clarin	4	Hw/Bw	
Subbass	16				
Oktave	8				
Oktave	4				
Mixtur	VI				

Silbermann organs are known for their strong voicing, especially for the player at the console; but when heard in the nave with a full congregation in Freiberg Cathedral this organ sounds entirely 'normal' and is able to be heard by all when SINGING.

The 'Romantic' Organ

The invention of remote-control actions (pneumatic, Barker-lever, electro-pneumatic, direct electric) meant that large organs were no longer governed by mechanical linkages. Chests and consoles could be placed (in theory) anywhere and the gross size of any organ could be increased without creating a heavier keyboard action. The corollary was that players lost direct connection to the pipework. This enabled the organ to become a substitute for the symphony orchestra and many English town halls became venues for organ arrangements of orchestral works. With the Church of England's Oxford Movement, organs were taken down from west galleries and placed in spaces adjacent to chancels (thereby often emasculating the organ's acoustic properties) to accompany newly robed choirs. Tonal ideals included the capacity for infinitely subtle grades of *crescendo* and *diminuendo*, facilitated by EXPRESSION boxes, combination pedals and *crescendo* pedals. In England, the Swell organ became the principal second manual, and the 'Choir' (a linguistic corruption of 'Chaire') diminished into a resource for soft accompanimental effects. Individual key colour was destroyed by wholesale adoption of equal temperament.

In France from the 1840s, CAVAILLÉ-COLL's wide-scaled foundation stops resulted in rich, full-bodied 8′ sounds with a variety of orchestral and solo reeds, which inspired César Franck's organ music. The organ at St Denis (1841, restored 1987–8) was Cavaillé-Coll's first masterpiece, consisting of four manuals and sixty-nine stops:

Grand orgue: twenty stops – flues from 32′ to the highest mixtures, *Cornet* and reeds 8′ and 4′.
Positif: seventeen stops – flues from 16′ to *Cymbale* mixture, mutations, five reed stops.
Bombarde: twelve stops – flues 16′ to *Cornet VII*, five high-pressure reeds.
Récit: eight stops – flues 8′ to 2′, three reeds.
Pédale: twelve stops – flues from 32′ to 4′, seven reeds from 32′ to 4′.

In Germany, construction of Walcker's organs benefited from new industrial production techniques. His organ for the Paulskirche, Frankfurt (1827–33), had seventy-four stops and two pedalboards. In Italy, Serassi built on local traditions, producing organs with twenty or more stops based on 32′ ranks on the main manual, with the highest ranks of the old *ripieno* stops collected into mixtures. One or two secondary manuals provided echo effects, often in a swell box. The Pedal organ had six to eight bass stops, and could contain accessories such as bells, thunder and drums. New playing techniques were being taught. Lemmens's advocation of finger substitutions, note ties, and toe-and-heel pedal techniques were published in 1862.

In the early twentieth century, countless eclectic organs were built with the aim of doing justice to as many repertories as possible. Technology provided the means to combine Romantic and Baroque organs, and the enormous demand for organs in cathedrals, churches, concert halls, cinemas, department stores, restaurants, ballrooms, schools and even skating rinks encouraged factory-built organs inspired by mass-production techniques. This was the background against which the 'Organ Revival' ('*Orgelbewegung*') in c1930 reacted against contemporary trends to develop the idea of building historical copies, such as the 'Praetorius' organ built for Freiburg University in 1921. Steinmeyer's influential organ (1930) at Passau Cathedral was an attempt to combine German Romantic sections with French and Baroque departments, resulting in a huge organ with 208 stops.

In the past few decades, the building of both eclectic organs and historical models seems to have flourished in fairly equal measure. The 'new' Schnitger organ in Gothenburg, the result of a large-scale research project, has drawn enormous interest throughout Europe and America. Important organs in the UK based on historical principles include the 1965 Frobenius organ at The Queen's College, Oxford and the 1976 Metzler organ at Trinity College, Cambridge. The discovery of organ fragments at Wetheringsett and Wingfield enabled Gwynn & Goetze to build speculative reconstructions of early sixteenth-century English organs, and fine organs based on historical principles have been built by N. P. Mander, Peter Collins, Kenneth Tickell and William Drake. In Europe, notable builders include Ahrend, Flentrop, Garnier and Metzler, and in America, Fisk, Brombaugh and Taylor & Boody.

FURTHER READING

S. Bicknell, *The History of the English Organ* (Cambridge University Press, 1996).
F. Douglass, *The Language of the French Classical Organ* (New Haven, CT, and London: Yale University Press, 1969, 2/1995).
Q. Faulkner, *The Registrations of J. S. Bach's Organ Works* (Colfax, NC: Wayne Leupold, 2008).
F.-H. Gress, *Die Klanggestalt der Orgeln Gottfried Silbermanns* (Leipzig: VEB Deutscher Verlag für Musik, 1989).
W. L. Sumner, *The Organ, Its Evolution, Principles of Constructions and Use* (London: Macdonald, 1952, 4/1973).
N. Thistlethwaite, *The Making of the Victorian Organ* (Cambridge University Press, 1990).
P. Williams, *The European Organ 1450–1850* (London: Batsford, 1966).
A New History of the Organ (Cambridge University Press, 1980).
The Organ in Western Culture 750–1250 (Cambridge University Press, 1993).
C. Wolff and M. Zepf, trans. L. E. Butler, *The Organs of J. S. Bach: A Handbook* (Champaign, IL: University of Illinois Press, 2012).

DAVID PONSFORD

Ornaments, Ornamentation *see* IMPROVISATION AND UNWRITTEN PERFORMANCE PRACTICES

Ornithoparchus, Andreas (b. Meiningen, c1490; d. after 1521) German theorist.

Ornithoparchus's chief contributions to musical pedagogy and performance practices appear in *Musice active micrologus* (1517), an influential compendium that focuses on practical aspects of sacred monophonic and polyphonic SINGING. *Micrologus* builds upon the canon of Western music theorists, referencing BOETHIUS, GUIDO D'AREZZO, GAFFURIUS and TINCTORIS among others. Its longevity can be partially attributed to a logical organisational scheme, copious illustrations and memorable dictums, coloured throughout by Ornithoparchus's impassioned critical outlook, which remains undiminished in John Dowland's English translation, *Andreas Ornithoparchus His Micrologus* (1609).

Micrologus alternates between monophonic and polyphonic pedagogies in four books. It surveys principles of plainsong vocalisation, solfège, hexachord mutation and MUSICA FICTA, as well as monochord construction. Also addressed are the effects of modes and tone formulas upon auditors' psychological states (lib. I.13). Examples of mensural NOTATION, prolation and proportion signs are presented, some of which detail the subject of TACTUS dictation with unparalleled clarity (lib. II). Book III includes techniques for *accentus* delivery in epistles, gospels and prophecies, and Book IV illustrates principles of contrapuntal writing.

Ornithoparchus defines a true musician (*musicus*), in contrast to a *cantor*, as one who grasps intricacies of compositional theory beyond the attainment of vocal skill. Regarding instrumentalists, Ornithoparchus disdains those with fast fingers and little knowledge (lib. I. 1). He distinguishes contemporaneous styles of singing in England, France, Spain and Italy, reserving insult for Germans who often 'howl like wolves' (lib. IV.8) and degrade ecclesiastical music making. *Micrologus* concludes with ten rules for singing, wherein he stresses physical modesty in performance; consistent and clear PRONUNCIATION; equality of mensuration; suppressing ungainly loudness; and, in *concentus*, relating vocal EXPRESSION to textual meaning (lib. IV.8).

FURTHER READING

A. Ornithoparchus, *Musice active micrologus Andree Ornitoparchi Ostrofranci Meyningensis artium magistri, libris quattuor digestus: omnibus musice studiosis non tam utilis quae necessarius...* (Leipzig: V. Schumann, 1519).
G. Reese and S. Ledbetter, *Andreas Ornithoparchus and John Dowland. A Compendium of Musical Practice* (New York: Dover, 1973).

ALEXANDER EVAN BONUS

Ortiz, Diego (b. Toledo, ?1510; d. ?Naples, ?1570) Spanish theorist, composer and VIOL player.

Ortiz was resident in Naples by 10 December 1553, when he published his *Trattado de glosas sobre clausulas y otros generos de puntos en la musica de violones* (Treatise on Embellishments of Cadences and Other Sorts of Notes in Viol Music), which was produced simultaneously in Spanish and Italian. Addressing his readers, Ortiz declares his surprise that the viol, 'being such an important instrument and much in use', does not have the benefit of a TREATISE to assist amateur players 'to proceed in good order and play logically, and not haphazardly' despite the 'many skilled and practised [professional] players' (5). He divides his treatise into two 'books': the first is dedicated to embellishing CONSORT music in four or five parts and 'the second gives all the rules to be observed when descanting with another instrument' (5). He gives copious examples for breaking a melodic line, clarifying that 'grace' comes with variety, employing *passaggi* and different BOW strokes, and keeping the left-hand fingers down to sustain the harmony.

In the second book Ortiz explains that there are three ways to improvise with a keyboard instrument: fantasy, using a *cantus firmus* [ground] and embellishing a composition [in multiple parts]. The first method involves the keyboard playing some 'regular and ordered sequences of chords' while the viol plays 'some flourishes ... and when the viol settles on some long notes the keyboard replies in kind' (51). He then gives examples of four unaccompanied *recercadas* 'suited to loosen and exercise the hand ... and as examples of how to play the viol solo' (51). Playing divisions on a *cantus firmus* is illustrated by six examples embellishing *La Spagna*. Here the keyboard player is encouraged to use chords and imitative counterpoint. For those with different TASTES Ortiz provides eight *recercadas* on Italian 'tenors' such as *passamezzo*, *la Follia* and *la Romanesca*. He gives four embellished versions of both Arcadelt's 'O felici occhi miei' and Sandrin's 'Doulce memoire' to illustrate how to play divisions on any of the four parts or to add an extra voice. With their assured harmony, subtle relationship to the given ground, spectacular syncopation and dazzling virtuosity his compositions are a remarkable demonstration of the sophistication of mid-sixteenth-century string music.

FURTHER READING

D. Ortiz, *Trattado de glosas* (Rome, 1553), R/ed. A. Otterstedt (Kassel: Bärenreiter, 2003).

LUCY ROBINSON

Ozi, Etienne (b. Nîmes, 9 December 1754; d. Paris, 5 October 1813) French bassoonist and composer.

Ozi exercised an international influence as a virtuoso performer, teacher and composer of BASSOON music. After early tuition from a military ensemble, he settled in Paris in 1777, where his playing was praised for its freedom and confidence, its beautiful tone quality and the perfect accuracy of his INTONATION. He pursued an active and successful career as soloist and orchestral musician, and was appointed professor at the PARIS CONSERVATOIRE from its inception in 1795. His *Méthode nouvelle et raisonnée pour le basson* (Paris: Naderman, 1787) and *Nouvelle méthode de basson* (Paris: A l'imprimerie du Conservatoire de Musique, 1803) contain detailed principles for the study of the bassoon, including exercises, sonatas and caprices, as well as instructions on caring for the instrument and techniques of reed making. They are the most comprehensive and informative sources of instruction for playing the bassoon of their period and have achieved wider currency through their extensive attention to embellishment and extempore variation.

In his earlier treatise of 1787, Ozi identified an imperfect scale and lack of volume as major difficulties facing players. He warned against the undesirable practice of tilting the head to the right or left while playing. Central to his teaching was the imitation of a beautiful human voice through subtle fluctuations of volume. In the later treatise (commissioned by the Conservatoire), he aligned principles of breathing and phrasing with the art of SINGING and provided detailed advice on types of ARTICULATION. As both practitioner and theorist, he made an important contribution to expanding the expressive as well as the technical range of the instrument. Ozi was translated and quoted (often without attribution) throughout the nineteenth century. His 1803 treatise contains important discussion of reed-making: Ozi remarked that most bassoon reeds were made and sold by bassoon makers, but that a player might benefit from the independence afforded by learning to make individually tailored reeds.

FURTHER READING

J. B. Kopp, *The Bassoon* (New Haven, CT and London: Yale University Press, 2012).

COLIN LAWSON

P

Paganini, Nicolò (b. Genoa, 27 October 1782; d. Nice, 27 May 1840) Italian violinist and composer.

Paganini learnt the VIOLIN from his father and later Giovanni Cervetto and Giacomo Costa. He moved to Lucca (1801–9) and accepted a violin position in the republican ORCHESTRA (1805), but his desire to forge an independent solo career resulted in his undertaking extensive concert tours within Italy (from 1810), triumphing in most major centres, especially Milan, where he and Charles Lafont 'competed' in a double violin concerto by RODOLPHE KREUTZER (1815).

Paganini embarked on another lengthy tour of central and southern Italy in January 1825, gave numerous acclaimed concerts during a three-month stay in Vienna (from March 1828) and then performed throughout Europe, enjoying particular success in Germany (1829–31), Paris and London (1831–2). He commissioned a VIOLA concerto from BERLIOZ (1832); but, on examining the first sketches, he rejected them as unsuitable (Berlioz later rearranged them as *Harold en Italie*). By 1834 Paganini's career was in decline due to deteriorating health and injury. He returned to Italy and rarely performed in public; but he briefly became director and conductor at Parma's Teatro Ducale (1835), performed in Turin, Marseilles and Nice and backed a financially disastrous project to establish a Casino Paganini in Paris (1837). He sought immunity in Nice from the outcome of the resultant Parisian legal proceedings and resumed activity as a stringed instrument dealer. At his death, the Bishop of Nice refused him a religious funeral and interment in consecrated land. His remains were eventually moved and interred in a cemetery in Parma.

Paganini was often alluded to as a *maleficus* or an agent of the devil and he became a mystical cult figure. The idolatry of his audiences was constantly fuelled not only by his technical wizardry on the violin but also by his cadaverous appearance and public image (variously described as Satanic, ghostly, demonic or Mephistophelean), dark attire and contorted posture. His prison record for abduction and rape and anecdotes about his association with the underworld added to audience curiosity; that he possessed a strong psychical force became an integral part of the Paganini legend and has been given different shades of meaning and significance by various writers past and present.

Paganini's virtuoso achievements represent the summit of technical artistry in early nineteenth-century violin playing. Developing a manner of playing unique to his ungainly physique, advanced left-hand thumb position and remarkable finger extensibility (he probably had Marfan or Ehlers-Danlos syndrome), he revived and exploited to unprecedented degrees techniques such as SCORDATURA, left-hand pizzicato in combination with BOWING, HARMONICS (in single and double stopping), and *una corda* playing (especially on the G string), as well as various bowings, long before introduced into the violinist's vocabulary. CARL GUHR studied Paganini's idiosyncratic style in performances at Frankfurt and published his *Über Paganinis Kunst die Violine zu spielen* (Mainz: Schott, 1829), paying particular attention to the Italian's physique, technique and equipment.

Paganini's unique concert repertory also contributed substantially to his success. He rarely performed the works of others in public, preferring to present his own (sometimes including animal noises and unconventional sounds) to entertain his audiences. A composition pupil of Gnecco, Paër and Ghiretti, he wrote much music for violin and orchestra, showcasing his virtuosity in sets of variations on Italian operatic themes, arrangements of folk tunes and at least six concertos. Not one of his concertos was published during his lifetime, for a vital ingredient of the Paganini myth was his inaccessibility. He always performed from MEMORY and strictly controlled the distribution of his orchestral parts. His 24 Caprices, Op. 1 comprise a distillation of almost all his virtuoso techniques in remarkably challenging settings. Through his works for GUITAR, an instrument on which he was also very competent, he was influential in furthering the performance and appreciation of music in private circles.

Paganini skilfully integrated his extraordinary technical facility and bravura performing style, his challenging compositions specifically designed to showcase his virtuosity, and his emaciated spectral appearance and unusual mannerisms with his unique artistic and commercial aspirations. Even allowing for the rose-tinted memories of those who wrote about his playing, he was a legend in his lifetime. He raised the social status of instrumental soloists to the same level as opera singers and his performing ethos was imitated by several violinists, particularly Sivori, Ernst, Bériot, Vieuxtemps and Wieniawski; it also inspired executants of other instruments (e.g. pianists such as Liszt, Chopin and Thalberg) to acknowledge the significance of virtuosity as an element in art and emulate his technical feats. As Schumann aptly remarked, Paganini was 'the turning point in the history of virtuosity'.

FURTHER READING

A. Barizza and F. Morabito (eds.), *Nicolò Paganini: Diabolus in Musica* (Turnhout: Brepols, 2010).
C. Guhr, *Über Paganinis Kunst die Violine zu spielen* (Mainz: Schott, 1829?).
M. Kawabata, *Paganini: The 'Demonic' Virtuoso* (London: Boydell & Brewer, 2013).

ROBIN STOWELL

Page, Christopher (b. London, 8 April 1952) English musicologist, performer and professor of medieval music and literature in the University of Cambridge.

After reading English at Oxford University, Page became the leading advocate of the view that most Medieval polyphony, sacred and secular, was the exclusive domain of singers and that the music performed by instrumentalists formed a separate and largely unwritten repertoire. He developed this theory during work on Medieval stringed instruments, published in various issues of the *Galpin Society Journal* in the late 1970s and in *Early Music*, notably the article in the 1977 Machaut commemorative issue on the all-vocal performance of that composer's chanson repertoire.

Page has always grounded his performance practice research on literary sources, 'in which his expertise is unsurpassed' (E. Aubrey in *JAMS*, 66/1 (2013), 297). In 1981 he founded the ensemble Gothic Voices, which won three Gramophone Early Music Record of the Year awards. All twenty-five of its recordings have a close relationship to Page's simultaneously published work on performance, creating an unusually integrated body of work in text and sound. This is duly emphasised in the sustained account of the group given by DANIEL LEECH-WILKINSON (*The Modern Invention of Medieval Music* (Cambridge University Press, 2002)), who writes of its work as inducing a paradigm shift in the understanding of Medieval music.

In all his scholarship, Page has consistently maintained that the past is another country that it is possible to visit and that people in the Middle Ages had minds whose content it is possible in some measure to know. He has also championed the value of imagination in historical research and is a noted prose stylist. His most recent work has been devoted to the history of the early GUITAR in England; the first volume of his projected three-volume survey was published in 2015 as *The Guitar in Tudor England: A Social and Musical History* (Cambridge University Press).

FURTHER READING

C. Page, 'Around the performance of a fourteenth-century motet', *EMc*, 28 (2000), 343–56.
B. D. Sherman, 'The Colonizing Ear', in *Inside Early Music: Conversations with Performers* (Oxford University Press, 1997), 71–86.

JAMES WESTBROOK

Paris Conservatoire (Conservatoire de Paris) Several aspects of the Paris Conservatoire contribute to its paramount importance for historical performance, but perhaps the most important is its succession of teachers from its inception to the present. Born directly as a result of the Revolution, it was founded in 1795 to provide state-funded training for both classical and military musicians from all the regions of France, merging L'École royale de chant et de déclamation (founded 1783), which trained singers for the Paris Opéra, and L'École de musique municipale (founded 1792), which trained players for the Garde Nationale. Its early directorate included Gossec, Méhul and Cherubini. The emphasis on its military side ensured a particular expertise in wind and brass instruments running in tandem with their development; for example, the invention of metal FLUTES and improved key- and valve-systems. Many inventions and patents were showcased at the World Fairs and the Conservatoire continues to house an important collection of historic instruments.

A crucial aspect of its mission was to isolate a 'French tradition' and to ensure that it developed official TREATISES for every instrument, as well as for voice. Each teacher typically had a class of twelve pupils who were taught in groups rather than individually. Between 1800 and 1814 one official method was produced each year. These, and their successive re-editions, provide rich sources not only for French practice in the nineteenth century but also for established principles which lasted well into the twentieth. A catalyst to SINGING teaching in the early twentieth century was the appointment as director (1905) of Fauré, who insisted on more concentration on language and musicality.

Particular strengths of its teaching may be discerned in the flute and brass classes, the former under a succession of players from Tulou to Moyse, including the important players Gaubert and Taffanel. A tradition of increasingly demanding *Pièces de concours* ensured the development of tessitura, tone and ARTICULATION in many of the instruments, some of the teachers producing excellent compositions rather than mere *méthodes*, yet still with the aim of perfecting technique. One such composer-performer was the HORN player JACQUES-FRANÇOIS GALLAY, who wrote many caprices and preludes for solo HORN.

There was also a clearly delineated school of VIOLIN playing – often identified as the Franco-Belgian school – characterised by subtlety and a fleetness of BOWING but also allied to the developing TASTE for legato. PIERRE BAILLOT was perhaps the most important early pedagogue in this respect, bringing the subtleties of singing technique to lyrical string playing – particularly in the incorporation of both expressive VIBRATO and the *port de voix*. He even insisted on the presence of a singing teacher in examinations. Other early pedagogues were RODE and KREUTZER and the tradition continued through such players as DE BÉRIOT, Vieuxtemps and Ysaÿe into the recorded legacy of such players as Thibaut.

French pianism was also inseparable from the pianos of Érard and Pleyel: a frequently mentioned ideal was the *jeu perlé* (pearly touch). LOUIS ADAM had written the first *Méthode* in 1805, focused on twelve lessons on particular pieces. Other important professors were Marmontel, DIÉMER and Risler, the last two with recorded legacies. Alfred Cortot was a professor from 1907 to 1923, bequeathing EDITIONS of pieces with invaluable comments on interpretation. A succession of organists from Franck, through Widor and Tournemire, ensured that the special art of French ORGAN IMPROVISATION was preserved, inseparable from the organs of CAVAILLÉ-COLL.

In 1811 a concert hall was built, giving rise to the important series of *Concerts du Conservatoire*, inaugurated in 1825 by FRANÇOIS HABENECK, who played an important role in bringing the music of BEETHOVEN to France. Built in the shape of a narrow 'U', the hall was much admired for its acoustic. Perhaps its most famous premiere was BERLIOZ's *Symphonie fantastique*, which has been recorded there with its unusual orchestral layout. The ORCHESTRA, which later became the Orchestre de Paris, preserved the archetypal French sound, particularly of the wind section for which Debussy wrote so idiosyncratically in such pieces as his *Prélude à l'après-midi d'un faune*.

Its library houses a rich treasure-trove of materials – the *fonds du Conservatoire* – now preserved in the Music Department of the Bibliothèque Nationale. The Conservatoire also played a part in the publication of the ambitious *Dictionnaire de la Musique et Encyclopédie du Conservatoire*, whose first volumes were published in 1913.

In 1980 the Paris Conservatoire was supplemented by the establishment of a second National Conservatoire in Lyon; in 1990 it was rehoused in a purpose-built edifice in the Cité de la Musique at La Villette in the nineteenth *arrondissement*. In terms of the early music revival, it is noteworthy that a harpsichord professor (Robert Veyron Lacroix) was appointed in 1950 and an Early Music Department was established in 1984.

FURTHER READING

A. Bongrain, Y. Gérard and M.-H. Coudroy-Saghai, *Le Conservatoire de Paris, 1795–1995: Deux cents ans de pédagogie* (Paris: Buchet/Chastel, 1999).
D. K. Holoman: *The Société des Concerts du Conservatoire, 1828–1967* (Berkeley, CA: University of California Press, 2004).

RICHARD LANGHAM SMITH

Parrott, Andrew (Haden) (b. Walsall, 10 March 1947) English singer, conductor and scholar known for groundbreaking performance practices.

Parrott studied at Merton College, Oxford, during which time he worked with the Oxford Chamber Choir. MICHAEL TIPPETT's invitation to perform at the Bath Festival in 1973 led to the foundation of the Taverner Choir, Consort and Players. Around this time Parrott also played bass in a rock band and worked with the musicologist Michael Morrow and his pioneering ensemble MUSICA RESERVATA, with whom he later directed an album of music by Josquin.

At the first York Early Music Festival in 1977, Parrott gave an *a cappella* performance of MACHAUT's *Messe de Nostre Dame* with one voice per part, which became an important catalyst for the (re-)discovery of Medieval music in all-vocal performance. He also used high tenors rather than falsettists and thus his performance exemplified three important strands of his scholarship: questions of performance PITCH; investigations into the varying compositions of CHOIRS through the ages; and a deep-seated belief that the falsettist-countertenor was uncommon, possibly non-existent, before the age of Purcell.

Parrott has published a significant essay exploring the potential non-existence of the historical falsettist-countertenor entitled 'Falsetto beliefs: the "countertenor" cross-examined', which surveys evidence of vocal ranges to illustrate the low-pitched and high-pitched disposition of many late Medieval choirs, and then surveying occurrences of the word 'falsetto' in its many permutations from the 'falsitas' of *Instituta Patrum* (1210–20) to the 'fausset' of Dufay's will (1474). In each case he suggests an alternative reading to the modern use of 'falsetto'. This vexed question of falsetto is linked to performance pitch. This issue underlies his reasoning for downwards transposition of a fourth in the *Lauda Jerusalem* and *Magnificat a 7* of MONTEVERDI's *Vespers of 1610*. Here Parrott's arguments draw on an understanding that high clefs are not wedded to high tessitura. As for the varying compositions of choirs, he is author of *The Essential Bach Choir* (2000), which expanded JOSHUA RIFKIN's one per part theories.

FURTHER READING

A. Parrott, *Composers' Intentions: Lost Traditions of Musical Performance* (Woodbridge: Boydell Press, 2015).
The Essential Bach Choir (Woodbridge: Boydell Press, 2000).
'Falsetto beliefs: the "countertenor" cross-examined', *EMc*, 43/1 (2014), 79–110.

EDWARD BREEN

Partimento Known since 1634, this Italian term for 'division' was used in the late eighteenth and early nineteenth centuries for Neapolitan or Milanese compositional sketches, in which only the bass line was notated, often with FIGURED BASS symbols, as exercises in IMPROVISATION for keyboard players. The purpose was to develop such sketches into fully fledged pieces (including fugues). Examples include B. Pasquini's solo and duet figured bass sonatas.

FURTHER READING

R. Cafiero, 'La didattica del partimento a Napoli fra settecento e ottocento: note sulla fortuna delle "Regole" di Carlo Cotumacci', in M. Caraci Vela, R. Cafiero and A. Romagnoli (eds.), *Gli affetti convenienti all'idee. Studi sulla musica vocale italiana* (Naples: Edizioni Scientifiche Italiane, 1993), 549–79.

M. Panni, *Déchiffrage: Twelve Partimenti for One or More Performers* (London and New York: Peters, 1981).

G. Sanguinetti, *The Art of Partimento: History, Theory and Practice* (New York: Oxford University Press, 2012).

DAVID PONSFORD

Percussion In the thirteenth century, and beginning in the Iberian peninsula, a flood of new instruments came into Europe from the Maghrib, among them naqqereh, the nakers, and zil, the cymbals. At the same time the PIPE AND TABOR and the triangle also appeared. By the fourteenth century these instruments had spread throughout Europe.

The nakers were a pair of small kettledrums, usually less than a foot in diameter, and around the same in depth, that hung from the belt over the lower body, and were played with a pair of short, club-like beaters. They appear in MANUSCRIPT illuminations, church carvings and other sources, and are referred to in many documents. Sometimes we see larger versions, carried on the back by an acolyte, with the player walking behind him. Even more common, more often illustrated and referred to, was the pipe and tabor, the original one-man band. A three-holed pipe was played with the left hand and the tabor, a small drum, around a foot in diameter and perhaps six inches deep, held on the player's left shoulder, later on the arm or wrist, was played with a beater held in the right hand. This became the basic DANCE band combination, surviving into the twentieth century with our Morris sides. The tabor was always snared with a strand across the batterhead, playing simple dance rhythms.

By the sixteenth century, other percussion instruments had appeared. The side drum, a larger version of the tabor, slung at the player's side so that he could play it with both hands, had emerged with German and Swiss armies; larger kettledrums were carried on horseback, as they still are today in our cavalry regiments. These TIMPANI first appeared in the Turkish armies as they surged over the Balkans and as far as Vienna. They were eagerly adopted by many European courts, always in pairs, and served as the bass instruments for the TRUMPETS. They appeared at the court of Maximilian the Great by 1492, though did not reach Britain until 1540, and then only as visitors. It was not until 1660, with the return of Charles II, that they appear in English court records. Illustrations in such sources as PRAETORIUS show that they were tuned by a separate key on the square heads of bolts inserted, through holes in the iron hoop on which the head was lapped, into brackets on the shell. Since timpani played only the tonic and dominant of very few keys, most commonly D and A or C and G, the commonest keys then for the trumpets; such a tuning method sufficed as late as the second half of the eighteenth century.

Sticks were initially of wood or sometimes ivory and they were headed with a disc about 4 or 5 cm in diameter; these, sometimes covered in leather, remained the norm until the early nineteenth century. Timpani themselves were usually around 50 and 55 cm in diameter, increasing in size in the mid-eighteenth century when timpani became regular members of the ORCHESTRA. Salieri seems to have been the first to write parts for a set of three timpani in 1772, though this was not usual until late in the nineteenth century; even WAGNER wrote in pairs, with sizes of 60 and 70 cm, though often two pairs. Today sets of four or five are commonly seen, with diameters of around 80, 70, 60, 55, and 50 cm.

It was also not until the early nineteenth century that softer heads were used on the sticks, with soft leather or sometimes felt covering the wooden heads, or a wad of close-packed flannel discs. BERLIOZ specified sponge-headed sticks, though wooden heads still survived. Today felt is universal over a core of wood, cork, or balsa, and players keep a number of different hardnesses beside them, changing between passages to suit the character of the music and the acoustic of the hall or studio.

By the later eighteenth century, more freedom of PITCHES was required because the timpani became free from their role as bass trumpets, and also because composers were writing in a wider choice of keys. Changes of pitch within a work were required, especially in the opera orchestra where only a short recitative may allow time for retuning between arias. By around 1790 T-handles were adopted for the tuning screws, allowing players to retune within 20 or 30 seconds. Not until the mid-nineteenth century was even greater freedom required, and it was then that quick-tuning devices were invented, turning one handle to control all the tuning points round the drum, or altering skin tension by moving a drum up and down on a screw by rotating it. By the end of the nineteenth century a pedal mechanism had been introduced so that the timpanist could tune instantaneously.

Triangles and cymbals appeared in illustrations until the sixteenth century but then seem to have vanished into folk life and did not reappear until the rise of military bands in the late seventeenth century. Triangles, cymbals, and bass drums reappeared as pseudo-Turkish effects in operas and symphonies, and during the nineteenth century they gradually became regular members of all orchestras and bands. The side drum was a standard member of the military band but only appeared occasionally in the orchestra; it did not become a regular member until the late nineteenth century.

None of these instruments is capable of producing a sustained sound from a single stroke and the only way to achieve this is by a rapid reiteration of strokes, known as the roll. The side drum uses two bouncing strokes from each hand, called the dada-mama, a techique used also for shorter ORNAMENTS; the timpani also used this technique so long as they were played with wooden sticks, but when softer sticks became the norm, this was no longer possible, and so hand-to-hand playing became adopted. The speed of the strokes varies according to the dynamic level and also the tension of the heads. In the Baroque era, rather than rolls, players infilled long notes with rhythmic IMPROVISATION, especially at cadences. There is little written evidence for this; a rare exception is ALTENBURG's TREATISE, which gives examples of different techniques for *Schlag-Manieren* (*Versuch*... (1795), 129). Certainly this was customary in the Renaissance, from which survive written examples of tuckets and sennets where the bass parts are blank, or single tonic and dominant notes below elaborations of common chords by the trumpeters. Other instruments were added around the beginning of the twentieth century, such as the glockenspiel, a series of steel bars laid out like a keyboard, and the xylophone.

At much the same period, JAZZ bands appeared in the southern states of the USA among Afro-Americans, initially playing marches and similar music but evolving rapidly into improvisations around a basic melody. These used whatever percussion instruments they could improvise from ancestral memory, or recover from the detritus of the ex-military bands from the American Civil War, plus cheap imports such as Chinese woodblocks, temple blocks and small drums. Jazz bands spread all over America, not only among Afro-Americans, and gradually modified into larger combinations such as swing bands. Instrument makers started to improve the instruments and adapted them into the forms still used today – for example, drum sets with the bass drum played by a pedal, a similar technique for the cymbal (though that was soon freed with the introduction of the hi-hat and the suspended cymbal) and a set of tomtoms. Invention followed invention, with the introduction of plastic drumheads, ideal for military bands, which often have to play in the rain, and new instruments such as the rototoms.

Latin American bands became popular, introducing a whole new set of instruments such as bongos and timbales, as well as maraccas (pairs of vessel rattles) and scrapers. From Central America, modified in Chicago, came a much improved model of xylophone, and from it derived the vibraphone, a metal-barred version with rotors in the tops of the resonator tubes. More recently, instruments have been imported from all over the world, especially in the studio world of film and television, and also among small groups of young musicians. None of these instruments is confined to its own musical idiom; all migrate freely from one style to another, so that vibraphones have appeared in symphonies, timpani in swing bands, etc.

FURTHER READING

J. Altenburg, *Versuch einer Anleitung zur heroisch-musikalischen Trompeter- und Paukerkunst* (Halle: J. C. Hendel, 1795; facsim. Leipzig: Deutsche Verlag für Musik, 1972; trans. E. H. Tarr as *The Art of the Trumpeter and Kettledrummer* (Nashville, TN: Brass Press, 1974)).

E. A. Bowles, *The Timpani – A History in Pictures and Documents* (Hillsdale, NY: Pendragon, 2002).

J. Montagu, *Timpani and Percussion* (New Haven, CT and London: Yale University Press, 2002).

M. Praetorius, *Syntagma Musicum – de Organographia* (Wolffenbüttel: Elias Holwein, 1619; facsim. edn Kassel: Bärenreiter, 1958).

JEREMY MONTAGU

Performance Practice *see* HISTORICALLY INFORMED PERFORMANCE

Performance Practice Scholarship 'Nowhere is the connection between theoretical musicology and musical performance as close as in the field of historical performance practice', confidently opines the author of 'Aufführungspraxis' in *MGG*. The relationship between the scholarly study of music of the past and its realisation in performance, although fundamentally symbiotic, has always been complex and heterogeneous. The apparently porous interface between the more or less firmly established processes of musicological method and historiography, and the relatively open and imaginative interpretational field of contemporary early music performance, today gives the impression of having reached a reasonably mature stability. This is in contrast to the stormy adolescent decades of the early music revival in the 1970s and 1980s, that were characterised not least by the 'authenticity wars', which in retrospect seem of much less import than their bristling antagonists then thought. In reality, the settlement between scholarship and practice is perhaps less final than the impression conveyed by the markers of early music performance's hard-won institutionalisation in conservatoires and universities, international concert series and festivals, and academic journals and conferences. It is a fragility nicely encapsulated in the label 'historically informed', a badge self-awarded by performers to evidence their scholarly credentials, that on closer inspection turns out as often as not to be as tenuous now as it was in the nineteenth century.

The performance of music of earlier epochs as a consciously historicist endeavour can be traced back at least as far as John Pepusch's ACADEMY OF ANCIENT MUSIC, which successfully mounted performances of works by Palestrina, Victoria, Byrd, MORLEY, Purcell and other 'ancients' in London in the 1720s. A century later came the landmark moment on 11 March 1829, when the twenty-year-old FELIX MENDELSSOHN conducted his version of the *Matthäuspassion* at the Berlin Singakademie that is most often cited as the talismanic 'founders' day' for the early music revival. Above all, it set a precedent for the idea that the music of the great composers of the past (and especially *the* great composer) can be both practicably realised according to the professional standards of the day, and be relevant to AUDIENCES in the 'mainstream' musical present.

Mendelssohn's triumph certainly marked a key moment in the already well-established BACH revival, begun with the publication of Johann Nikolaus Forkel's hagiographic biography of the composer in 1802 that had established J. S. Bach as the 'father of German music'. In 1829 that genius was made manifest for a public audience, but Mendelssohn's Bach was unashamedly reinterpreted to suit contemporary Romantic sensibility. This contrasts sharply with the twentieth-century approach to the revival of early music, whose aesthetic focuses on the historical reconstructionist imperative of 'making strange' that which at first sight may appear familiar (e.g. on account of its readable NOTATION). Indeed, the antonymous metaphor of 'making familiar' can perhaps be applied to the totalising projects of EDITING and publishing the great 'complete' editions of the works of J. S. Bach, Handel, BEETHOVEN and Palestrina, and later of Mendelssohn,

MOZART, Chopin and Schumann, undertaken by Raymond and Hermann Härtel, beginning in the 1850s and 1860s. These 'monuments' (*Denkmäler*), and the rigorously scholarly editorial method that lay behind them, did more than anything to establish the credentials of the new discipline of musicology ('*musikalische Wissenschaft*'), particularly by the principal editor of the first *Händel-Gesamtausgabe*, Friedrich Chrysander. Along with a succession of scholars including Philipp Spitta and Otto Jahn, he helped extend the 'nineteenth-century's philological enthusiasm' to music, which, in turn, was 'the first serious and systematic attempt to establish the works of musical authors in a canonic way' (P. Brett, in Kenyon (ed.), 86). By the end of the nineteenth century, scholarly editions of the works of many more seventeenth- and eighteenth-century composers had been added to that canon, including RAMEAU, Buxtehude, Schütz, Purcell and Sweelinck, helping to extend to the pre-Romantic period an anachronistic normalisation of 'the composer' and the 'work' (not to mention the concept of a cohesive 'Baroque music') that to the present day doggedly persists in shaping much of the discourse – and, importantly, the commercial substructure – of pre-Classical music culture.

Further, although Chrysander appeared to yoke philology and execution together, based on the principle 'that the music of past ages should be edited and performed in a scholarly spirit, without introducing additions or modifications to cater to the tastes of the present' (F. Ll. Harrison, M. Hood and C. V. Palisca, *Musicology* (1963), 41), this *fiat* did not by any means guarantee a unitary purpose or direction for scholarship and performance despite Chrysander's own awareness of certain aspects of the challenges of realising Handel's scores in performance, such as ORNAMENTATION (which we would now recognise as a matter of performance practice), that found expression in his 'practical' editions of some of the oratorios. Likewise, the considerable advance towards allowing the music of the past to be heard on its own terms, made by FRANÇOIS-JOSEPH FÉTIS through his PARIS CONSERVATOIRE concerts in 1832 that included the significant step of using original instruments from the conservatoire's collections, was clearly not always based on rigorous scholarship of the kind that Chrysander was advocating. Indeed, such was not necessarily the primary purpose of Fétis's or of other performers' experiments with early repertoire and instruments; for example, IGNAZ MOSCHELES's concerts in London were played on an eighteenth-century HARPSICHORD, apparently with little or no concession to its pedigree. Rather, the historiographical impetus for much nineteenth-century performance of music of earlier ages was often a rather earnest didacticism aimed at bourgeois self-improvement through 'illustrated lecture recitals' featuring exotic music and instruments (paralleled by the underlying missions of the new great European public museums). Rather ironically – in view of the nineteenth-century's newfound reverence for Bach, Handel and Palestrina – this had the effect of promulgating 'a Darwinian evolution of musical forms and techniques, equated only too readily with the increasingly dated concept of artistic progress' (Haskell, 21), which led inexorably towards the pinnacle of Beethoven and its offspring: contemporary music. In other words, the idea of reconstructing the performance of early music in its own right through scholarly research with the aim of restoring its original sounds and style was not the principal motivation of its advocates much before the end of the century.

However, a different kind of transformation in the status of early music was underway elsewhere, as it became caught up in the sweeping programme of restructuring German academia in the latter decades of the century. This process led to the rise of the modern research-oriented university, and with it, the professionalisation of musicology as one of the Humanities. The origins of the idea of music history as a discipline requiring scientific study may go right back to the foundation in 1738 by Lorenz Christoph Mitzler of the *Societät der musikalischen Wissenschaften*, but the key moment for the founding of systematic study of music based on an objective attention to its evidential base is perhaps HUGO RIEMANN's inaugural lecture at Leipzig University in 1902. Its title, 'Musikwissenschaft im eigentlichen Sinn' ('Musicology in its truest sense'), blatantly aligned the history of music with Leopold von Ranke's programme for a historiography based on empirical sources, and his now iconic statement that history should aspire to reconstructing the past 'wie es eigentlich gewesen' – 'how it actually (or essentially) happened'. The prioritisation of a positivistic approach to musical texts as a class of 'documentary evidence', the disinterested forensic scrutiny of which becomes just a part of a dispassionate, 'scientific' piecing together of the massive jigsaw of 'the past', had deep implications for the realignment – and effective bifurcation – of the relationship between the study of historical musical texts (source studies, editing and analysis) and their realisation by performers as sound. Not that music historians were necessarily uninterested in musical performance; Riemann, for example, started his professional life as a choir conductor and later wrote his monumental *Musik-Lexikon* (Leipzig: Verlag des Bibliographischen Instituts, 1882) and *Opern-Handbuch* (Leipzig: Koch, 1887) while teaching piano and music theory at the Hamburg Conservatoire, and in 1908 he went on to found the first campus-based Collegium at the University of Leipzig. This weekly meeting of a group of musicologists and amateur players who gathered to perform Renaissance and Baroque music became a lasting tradition, successfully transplanted to universities in the USA, where it flourished thanks to the many eminent musicologists who fled Nazi Germany in the 1930s and 1940s. They included Willi Apel, Manfred Bukofzer, Otto Gombosi, Paul Henry Lang, Siegmund Levarie, CURT SACHS, Leo Schrade, Edward Lowinsky and Hans Tischler, who played such significant roles in shaping the great ascendancy of American musicology, which, in turn, helped foster the 'relaxed interaction between scholars and performers in the American academic world' (Haskell, 107–8). But this 'relaxed interaction' has always been based on a clear hierarchy: performance as an agreeable spin-off from the serious business of critical musicology.

In the world of performance, another 'red-letter day' for the period movement might well be 23 December 1879, when the young French violin student ARNOLD DOLMETSCH attended a concert in Brussels that featured instruments from Fétis's collection. It was a Damascene experience that would direct Dolmetsch – under the influence of the utopian artisanalism of William Morris and the neo-medievalist esotericism of the pre-Raphaelites – towards his embrace of historical music and its obsolete instruments as a means of communing with an imagined pre-modern world. Over a period of more than fifty years, Dolmetsch tirelessly pursued his project to bring back to sounding life the dead musical culture of the past by re-inventing it in the present, during which time he obstinately set his face against the cold march of modernism. As he wrote in his groundbreaking *The Interpretation of the Music of the Seventeenth and Eighteenth Centuries Revealed by Contemporary Evidence* (London: Novello & Co., 1915), 'It is advisable ... before beginning this study, to clear our mind of prejudice and preconceived ideas, and put aside intolerant modernity; or else we may, as others have done, corrupt and twist about the meaning of even the clearest statement ... We can no longer allow anyone to stand between us and the composer' (Dolmetsch, VIII, 470). Dolmetsch's book summed up his almost single-handed invention of a curriculum for HISTORICALLY INFORMED PERFORMANCE practice. It begins with the hand-building of modern copies of old instruments, according to (more or less) 'original' methods (which may include 'improvements'); learning to play them in a spirit of earnest craftsmanship that assiduously eschews any hint of 'Romantic' virtuosity; and filling the 'interpretational gaps' in laconic historical notation by reading TREATISES, but only in order to 'annotate ... difficult passages', otherwise leaving historical musical texts 'untouched' (470).

The book offered a template for recreationist performance practice that in some ways continues to characterise the early music project right up to the present. Indeed, the still influential *A Performer's Guide to Baroque Music* (London: Faber & Faber, 1973) by ROBERT DONINGTON, an erstwhile Dolmetsch pupil, is in many ways an updating of the original. The problem, though, was that Dolmetsch's progressive commitment to historicism, based on applying the evidence of contemporary treatises such as those of THOMAS MACE and CHRISTOPHER SIMPSON to English domestic music, was compromised by his tendency to ignore historical evidence if it did not suit him (encapsulated in Percy Grainger's fawning comment that 'Such conceptions as yours convince without proofs – the proofs merely confirm the basic impression of rightness, but are not needed to establish it') (Haskell, 41). Dolmetsch's sometimes casual attitude to the challenges of a rigorous attention to historiographical discipline earned him the scorn of numerous critics, including the younger generation of university-educated scholar-performers such as THURSTON DART. In a prickly defensive riposte to the charge that his father had had a cavalier attitude to scholarship, Carl Dolmetsch wrote in the introduction to the third edition of the book, published after Arnold's death in 1940: 'None of the rules for the correct performance ... laid down in this volume can be regarded as a matter of personal opinion, since all are supported by documentary evidence from the writings of musicians of the period' (Dolmetsch (1946), xvi).

While Dolmetsch's important (and it must be said, largely successful) contribution to the concept of an approach to performing music of the past based on historical evidence of organology, technique and style was dogged by the taint of amateurism in his own practical demonstrations of it, during the latter years of the nineteenth and the first decades of the twentieth century other more brilliant musicians gradually built the confidence of both the academics and the listening public in the idea that playing early music on appropriate instruments could be more than 'lifeless scholarship'. Performers such as WANDA LANDOWSKA and VIOLET GORDON WOODHOUSE did much to rehabilitate the harpsichord as more than just a quaint precursor of the PIANO, as a generation later AUGUST WENZINGER did for the VIOLA DA GAMBA, particularly by reviving so much of its high-quality, but forgotten, repertoire. It was Wenzinger, who in 1932, together with Paul Sacher, issued the manifesto for a new 'hybrid' institution, a mix of conservatoire and research institute, which would be solely dedicated to 'the study and practical exploration of all questions related to the revival of early music, with the goal of establishing a lively interchange between musicology and performance'; the following year, the SCHOLA CANTORUM BASILIENSIS was opened. Although it was (and remains) primarily a training school for performers, it was from the start based on the idea that musicians should learn for themselves the necessary musicological skills to be able 'to initiate interaction between critical scientific research and music-making' (*Gründungsprogramm der Schola Cantorum Basiliensis* (1932) www.scb-basel.ch).

A considerable number of the internationally leading performers of the most recent fifty or so years of the early music revival have been graduates of the Schola Cantorum or of the other conservatoires in Holland, Belgium, Germany, France, and elsewhere in Europe and latterly, in the USA, whose historical performance curricula have been more or less fashioned after the Basel model: the development of practical performance skills which, while deeply contextualised through the study of treatises and working from original NOTATION, is also firmly aimed at producing professional-standard musicians, rather than amateurs. Some leading British musicians also made the journey to Basel, den Haag, Brussels, Vienna and other cities in order to study with teachers steeped in the European 'scholar-performer' tradition such as NIKOLAUS HARNONCOURT, GUSTAV and Marie LEONHARDT, the KUIJKEN brothers, JORDI SAVALL and others. But most of those who went on to play leading roles in the British early music revival that burst into a riot of fecundity in the 1960s and 1970s were products of the universities of Cambridge or Oxford – RAYMOND LEPPARD, DAVID MUNROW, CHRISTOPHER HOGWOOD, ROGER NORRINGTON, JOHN ELIOT GARDINER, ANDREW PARROTT and CHRISTOPHER PAGE, to name just some of the most prominent. There was, in fact, a long tradition of experimental performance of early music at both universities going back to such events as the production in 1925 by JACK WESTRUP (while still an undergraduate) of MONTEVERDI's *Orfeo*. At the suggestion of J. M. Dent, Westrup prepared a new performing edition based on the original copy in the Bodleian Library and it was followed two years later by an apparently successful *Poppea*. In the 1950s and 1960s, THURSTON DART, who was both a musicologist and a fine keyboard player, set new standards for excellent performance based on rigorous research. While this combination of the theoretical with the practical was still viewed with distinct suspicion by plenty of successful performers of pre-Classical music including ALFRED DELLER, who famously remarked that 'musicology and the performance of music are two worlds best kept apart from one another' (Haskell, 163), the younger generation of players, singers and music directors were far more confident about the benefits that musicology could contribute to their adventurous re-explorations of Medieval, Renaissance, Baroque and later Classical, and Romantic music. Together, they created a new paradigm for professional early music ensemble performance and were able to undertake some truly experimental projects in public thanks to the propitious conditions that prevailed in London and other parts of Europe in the 1960s, 1970s and 1980s. These included supportive regimes at national radio stations (notably the BBC and West Deutsche Rundfunk in Cologne); a recording industry with the confidence to take risks; and a pool of highly talented players and singers eagerly looking for alternatives to the musical mainstream and ready both to do serious research themselves and to test its results in practice. This, in turn, provided optimal opportunities for dynamic and sustainable collaborations between scholars and professional performers, and generated the energy that for a time saw British early music taking the lead from its mainland European counterparts.

A final key landmark date for early music's newfound confidence and one that marked an extraordinary moment of rapprochement between the communities of organologists and post-Dolmetschian instrument builders, musicologists and 'historically-informed musicians', amateurs and professionals, is surely January 1973 and the first issue of *Early Music*. In his opening editorial the founding editor John Thompson declared that the JOURNAL would 'provide a link between the finest scholarship of our day and the amateur and professional listener and performer. At one end of the scale there will be practical help and guidance on techniques, interpretation and instruments: at the other authoritative articles written in such a way that they will stimulate and help the uninitiated as well as those more experienced' (*EMc*, 1/1 (1973), 1). The contents page of this first issue reads like a menu for the celebration of a new community, with scholarly performance practice articles on topics such as 'The performance of fifteenth-century chansons' and the history of early pianos, rubbing shoulders with 'An introduction to crumhorn repertoire' and tips on how to modify your RECORDER, as well as reviews of recordings, music editions and books, and advertisements for instruments, concerts and summer schools. For many years, the quarterly journal was required reading for performers, scholars and enthusiasts alike, and it is probably no exaggeration to suggest that many of those readers regarded themselves as being all three. 'Historical performance practice' had, over the course of a relatively short time, forged for itself an identity that was both a declaration of independence from – or at least, a new relationship with – the academy and simultaneously created the conditions for a new scholarly discipline within it. More specialised academic journals such as *Performance Practice Review* (founded in the USA in 1988) and a continuous stream of articles in journals of historical musicology continue to provide additional platforms for what has become a vast subject area. But it is also interesting that in the second decade of the twenty-first century, in which 'historically informed' music making is apparently obligatory for almost any repertoire before the early twentieth century, there is still as much debate about the optimal balance between 'history' and 'performance' as there has ever been.

FURTHER READING

J. Butt, *Playing with History: The Historical Approach to Musical Performance* (Cambridge University Press, 2002).

H. Haskell, *The Early Music Revival: A History* (London: Thames & Hudson, 1988).
N. Kenyon (ed.), *Authenticity and Early Music* (Oxford University Press, 1988).

RICHARD WISTREICH

Periodicals

Definition and Origins

The term 'music periodical' refers to any source (whether printed or electronic) published serially, and at regular or irregular intervals, whose principal contents consist of a collection of articles devoted to research and/or explanations of musical issues. Additionally, such publications may contain reviews, editorial commentaries, letters to the editor, notices of conferences and other events, and lists of recently published books and scores. An informal distinction exists between JOURNALS (in which the contributions have to be referee-approved before acceptance, supported by the full scholarly citation of sources and evidence, and focused on original research), and magazines (in which the style can sometimes be journalistic, subjectively opinionated, and more directed towards commentary and reviewing).

The interests and opinions of an epoch are strongly reflected in its periodicals and in that sense they not only present the most recent research but also become over time an important resource for musical and intellectual histories, often with a national orientation. Several important periodicals in the modern sense – featuring critical articles and reviews by a range of authors – became established in the early nineteenth century principally in Germany (*Allgemeine musikalische Zeitung*, Leipzig, 1798–1848), France (*Revue musicale*, Paris, 1827–35; *Le ménestrel*, Paris, 1833–1940) and England (*The Music World*, 1836–91, London; *The Musical Times*, 1844–, London). In America *The Euterpeiad*, 1820–3, covered events in Boston.

Access

Since journals are a principal source of ongoing research, it is essential that they can be searched comprehensively and easily. Several systems attempt to facilitate this formidable task, though none has yet achieved complete control of the material. Major searchable indexes of journal articles include the following:

1 *International Index to Music Periodicals* (IIMP)
This covers 430 periodicals from twenty-five countries in seventeen languages. It provides titles of articles with abstracts, but also exists in a full-text version (IIMPFT) which has a more limited range (120 titles available) (*see* http://iimpft.chadwyck.com). It is strong on performance and popular music.

2 *Music Index: A Subject-Author Guide to Music Periodical Literature*
This covers 800 journals from forty countries in twenty-two languages. It began in 1949 and so its early indexes up to the mid-1970s only exist in paper volumes. The electronic version can be found at www.harmonieparkpress.com/MusicIndex.asp. It does not include the full texts of articles, but has some links to JSTOR (*see* item 6 below) which does.

3 *Répertoire international de littérature musicale* (RILM)
This includes not only periodical articles but also books, conference proceedings, and articles in Festschriften, etc. RILM has the best international and non-English coverage, listing 740 journals and 300 languages. It provides abstracts of articles but not full texts (*see* www.rilm.org).

4 *Répertoire international de la presse musicale* (RIPM)
This covers historical sources no longer published dating between 1760 and 1966. The provision is normally of abstracts only, but full article texts are available depending on the level of subscription (*see* www.ripm.org).

5 *Bibliographie des Musikschrifttums* (Leipzig: F. Hoffmeister; Mainz: Schott, 34 vols., 1936–2001)
Available in printed format only, though an online version is planned. It is particularly useful for its coverage of German sources. It includes books as well as articles (abstracts only), and lists some 500 periodicals (some non-music).

6 *The Journal Storage Project* (JSTOR)
The JSTOR music collection is part of the JSTOR Arts and Sciences III collection. It provides downloadable, full-text versions of articles and covers thirty-two journals. Articles are not included on the site for between three to five years after their initial publication (*see* www.jstor.org).

Most of these sources are available via the public library system, or through academic institutions and their libraries, or by means of private subscription.

Performance-Related Journals
Articles on aspects of performance are now found in a vast range of journals. However, some publications have discernible orientations, and knowledge of these might help those with particular interests in issues such as historically aware performance, performance theory, organological investigation, historical recordings and the ICONOGRAPHY of musical performance.

Issues of historically aware performance and performance theory are frequently discussed in those journals that tend to situate scholarship along the axis of style and period. For example, *Early Music, Performance Practice Review*, and *Music Performance Research*. Performance matters also find their way into 'era-specific' journals such as the *Journal of Seventeenth-century Music, Eighteenth-century Music* and *Nineteenth-century Music*.

Some journals are dedicated to the histories, social functions, construction and repertories of specific musical instruments. These are designed to meet the demands of modern performers and the makers of period instruments. Examples include the *Galpin Society Journal*, the *Lute Society Journal*, the *Early Keyboard Journal* and the *Historic Brass Society Journal*.

There is no journal specifically dedicated to EARLY RECORDINGS, though two issues of *Musicae Scientiae* (vols. 11 and 14, 2007 and 2010) collect together work from the Centre for the History and Analysis of Recorded Music (CHARM). None of the major sound collections – for example, the British Library Sound Archive, or the Recorded Sound Research Centre of the Library of Congress in Washington – produces a journal as such, though some have occasional 'bulletins'. For the most part, articles of interest in this area are scattered throughout the musical periodicals, though reviews of what have become historical recordings can be found in *Gramophone*, which was founded in 1923.

The use of iconographic investigation as a method of musical research has become more important in recent times. Journals dedicated specifically to musical topics in art include *Imago Musicae* (the international yearbook of musical iconography, 1984–) and *Music in Art* (1998–), though more general art periodicals often have relevant articles. In particular, such journals deal with the research of pictorial representations of musical instruments and their decorations, occasions for music making and DANCE, the history of PERFORMANCE PRACTICE and the relationship between music and the visual arts in all historical periods. Some other journals such as *Early Music* also regularly carry articles on the iconography of music.

FURTHER READING

I. Fellinger, *Periodica Musicalica: 1789–1830* (Regensburg: G. Bosse, 1986).
L. Fidler and R. James (eds.), *International Music Journals* (New York: Greenwood, 1990).
L. Sampsel, *Music Research: A Handbook* (Oxford University Press, 2009).

ANTHONY PRYER

Perrine (d.? Paris, after 1698) Lutenist active in Paris during the second half of the seventeenth century about whom nothing is known apart from his publications.

Perrine aimed to revive the declining fashion for the LUTE by publishing pieces in staff NOTATION rather than TABLATURE. The first half of his *Livre de musique pour le lut . . . et une Table pour aprendre [sic] à toucher le lut sur la basse continuë* (Paris, 1682, 2/1698) addresses the issue and confirms that the standard tuning in France at that stage was notionally D minor. The second half is a tutor for *basse continue* on the lute, probably to provide an equivalent to tutors published in the 1660s for the newly fashionable THEORBO as an instrument for accompaniment. In common with most such tutors Perrine says little about artistic accompaniment, but explains chord shapes in terms of figures (in the sequence $\frac{5}{3}, \frac{6}{4}, \frac{6}{3}, \frac{6}{4}, \frac{6}{5}, \frac{7}{3}$, with subcategories of major and minor intervals). He then gives three cadence formulas (two perfect, with 4–3 suspension and $\frac{6}{4} - \frac{5}{3}$ appoggiaturas, and one imperfect with 7–6 suspension), repeated in various (including advanced) keys. There is no hint of RAMEAU's inversion theory, and little of Campion's *règle de l'octave*.

Perrine's *Pieces de luth en musique* (Paris, privilege dated 1680; ed. P. Erdas (Bologna: Ut Orpheus Edizioni, 1995)) was the first publication in France wholly dedicated to lute music in staff notation, with pieces exclusively by Ennemond and Denis Gaultier. Its *Advertissement* is important for explaining how fundamental the rhythmic *séparé* is for French *style brisé* lute music and gives a variety of arpeggiation patterns for different time signatures. Comparison of staff notation versions of pieces that Perrine gives in both volumes shows that rests were frequently used to avoid complicated ties (important also in the notation of keyboard music in this style) rather than literally as silences. In his *Pieces* he also sheds light on the allemande/gigue performance problem, giving two pieces by Ennemond Gaultier in both allemande and gigue versions.

FURTHER READING

D. Ledbetter, 'What the lute sources tell us about the performance of French harpsichord music', in P. Dirksen (ed.), *The Harpsichord and Its Repertoire* (Utrecht: STIMU, 1992), 59–86.

R. Zappulla, *Figured Bass Accompaniment in France* (Turnhout: Brepols, 2000).

DAVID LEDBETTER

Petrus de Cruce (Pierre de la Croix) (*fl. c*1290) French theorist, singer and composer, probably from Amiens (Picardy).

The primary source of information about Petrus is Book VII of the *Speculum musicae* by Jacobus de Ispania (also known as Jacques de Liège), who probably befriended him when they were both students at the University of Paris in the 1290s. Jacobus describes Petrus as a follower of the mensuration system of Franco of Cologne and as the creator of 'so many beautiful and good measurable songs' (Bent, 22). He credits Petrus with subdividing the perfect breve into an increasing number of semibreves in the *Tripla* of two of his motets, from four in *S'amour eust point* to as many as nine in *Aucun ont trouvé chant par usage*. Another contemporaneous theorist, Petrus Le Viser, argued that the TEMPO of performance would have to be comparatively slow in order to accommodate the higher number of fractional notes that could be found in a breve. Petrus de Cruce also appears to have introduced the 'dot of division', later to became a standard feature of polyphonic NOTATION, to indicate the groupings of breves and semibreves within the relevant *mensura* (Franco had used a different graphic symbol called *tractulus* for the same purpose).

Two TREATISES on mensural notation have been variously attributed to Petrus de Cruce, but his authorship remains doubtful because their content does not reflect the notational innovations for which he was celebrated in his time. On the other hand, he may be the same Petrus de Cruce Ambianensis who compiled a *Tractatus de tonis* with a sizeable tonary that includes CHANTS customarily used in Amiens.

FURTHER READING

M. Bent, *Magister Jacobus de Ispania, Author of the* Speculum musicae, *RMA Monographs 28* (Farnham: Ashgate, 2015), 21–43.
  Petrus de Cruce Ambianensi Tractatus de tonis, ed. D. Harbinson, Corpus scriptorum de musica, vol. 29 (n.p.: American Institute of Musicology, 1976).

H. Ristory, *Post-franconische Theorie und Früh-Trecento: Die Petrus de Cruce Neuerungen und ihre Bedeutung für die italienische Mensuralnotenschrift zu Beginn des 14. Jahrhunderts* (Frankfurt am Main: Peter Lang, 1988).

STEFANO MENGOZZI

Philidor French family of woodwind players and percussionists with important ties to the royal musical establishment.

Originally named Danican, according to LA BORDE (*Essai* (Paris: P. D. Pierres, 1780)), Louis XIII gave the name 'Philidor' to Michel Danican (b. Dauphiné, *c*1610; d.? Bordeaux, August 1659) as his shawm playing reminded him of the Italian player Filidori. Philidor probably played solo parts as well as in ensemble, documented in a manuscript by TRICHET. Over the course of

130 years, a further forty Philidors held posts as court musicians. The family played an important part in defining the French Baroque style of woodwind performance and was involved in the transition from Renaissance winds to their Baroque equivalents, although only Jacques Philidor *le cadet* (b. Paris, 5 May 1657; d. Versailles, 29 May 1708) appears to have been an instrument builder.

Two generations removed from Michel, André *l'aîné* (b. ?Paris, c1652; d. Dreux, 11 August 1730) is remembered for his activities as royal music librarian. Together with violinist François Fossard he oversaw the preservation of the music written for royal entertainments and ceremonies during the reigns of Henry IV to Louis XIV. In many cases Philidor's copy is the sole surviving source, the earlier material having been destroyed. His experience as a performer guided his editorial decisions for recent music, but it is unclear if he adapted earlier repertoires to modern practices and NOTATION. The *Partition de plusieurs Marches* (1705) includes examples of PERCUSSION practices in MILITARY MUSIC and ceremonial. Among André's own compositions, *Le mariage de la couture avec la grosse cathos* (1688) – a *divertissement* for singers, dancers and OBOE band – includes indications of stage movement and DANCE in Favier notation.

Of André's substantial progeny, Pierre (b. Paris, 22 August 1681; d. Versailles, 30 August 1731) played VIOL in addition to woodwinds, and had a significant impact on woodwind PERFORMANCE PRACTICE. His chamber music published in 1717–18 includes detailed ORNAMENTATION. His symbols differ from those used by contemporaries, and even though Philidor included no explanatory table, his intentions can still be extrapolated from context. This is one of the most informative sources for the use of *flattement* or finger VIBRATO (notated with a wavy line).

Composer, instrumentalist and entrepreneur Anne Danican Philidor (b. Paris, 11 April 1681; d. Paris, 8 October 1728) founded the *Concert Spirituel* concert series, which introduced foreign instrumental and sacred music to France from 1725, and two years later the *Concerts Français*.

Although more famous in his day as a chess player, François-André (b. Dreux, 7 September 1726; d. London, 31 August 1795) was one of the most gifted composers of French comic opera of his generation. His travels introduced him to a broad range of musical styles current outside France, and his sharp memory helped to cultivate fluency in Neapolitan and Handelian idioms that he mixed freely in his stage works with musical onomatopoeia, comic effects and occasionally the simultaneous use of different metres. His one instrumental opus, *L'art de la modulation* (1755), is remarkable for its advanced harmonic vocabulary, and a note regarding the observation of dynamic indications.

FURTHER READING

M. Benoit, *Versailles et les musiciens du roi, 1661–1733* (Paris: Picard, 1971).
J.-F. and N. Dupont-Danican Philidor, *Les Philidor: une dynastie de musiciens* (Paris: Zurfluh, 1995).
R. Harris-Warrick and C. G. Marsh, *Musical Theatre at the Court of Louis XIV* (Cambridge University Press, 1994).

B. Haynes, *The Eloquent Oboe* (Oxford University Press, 2001).
C. Pierre, *Histoire du Concert Spirituel 1725–1790*, ed. F. Lesure (Paris: 2000).

GEOFFREY BURGESS

Philip, Robert (b. Witney, Oxfordshire, 22 July 1945) English academic, broadcaster and writer about music.

Philip studied ORGAN and BASSOON at the ROYAL COLLEGE OF MUSIC, London, before reading music at Cambridge, where from 1964 to 1967 he was organ scholar at Peterhouse. His subsequent Cambridge PhD, 'Some changes in style of orchestral playing 1920–1950 as shown by gramophone recordings' (1975), was one of the first studies to treat EARLY RECORDINGS as evidence for historical performance.

From 1976 until his retirement in 2010 Philip worked in connection with the Open University, initially as an arts producer in the BBC's Open University Production Centre. From 1995 he worked for the OU as a visiting research fellow, lecturer (from 2000), and finally senior lecturer (from 2004). His association with the university has continued in retirement as a research supervisor. He has been a regular broadcaster on the BBC since 1971.

Philip has had a major influence on thinking about historical performance through his two monographs, *Early Recordings and Musical Style* (1992) and *Performing Music in the Age of Recording* (2004). The 1992 book, which grew out of his PhD thesis, was the first study of early twentieth-century PERFORMANCE PRACTICE and of the implications of recordings as documentation, drawing attention to the potential of recordings to upend assumptions about correct performance in a wide range of instrumental and orchestral repertoire. The second book looked in more depth at the interaction between recording and performance, and at the ways in which recording has changed performance.

Philip's research is characterised by comprehensive knowledge of the recorded evidence, meticulous listening and thoughtful, often groundbreaking commentary, drawing attention to features of musicianship lost during the age of recording. Together with his several JOURNAL articles and chapters in edited collections, his books initiated that field of musicological research that sees recordings as key evidence for understanding musical practice.

FURTHER READING

R. Philip, *Early Recordings and Musical Style: Changing Tastes in Instrumental Performance 1900–1950* (Cambridge University Press, 1992).
Performing Music in the Age of Recording (New Haven, CT and London: Yale University Press, 2004).

DANIEL LEECH-WILKINSON

Phonograph Invented in 1877 by THOMAS EDISON, the phonograph was the first device designed both to record and to playback sound. The invention emerged from Edison's simultaneous research on recording and repeating telegraph and telephone messages but soon became an independent device. The first phonographs were handcranked and recorded on a piece of tinfoil wrapped around a cylinder but they never became more than exhibition devices to demonstrate the feasibility of recording and reproducing sounds.

Alexander Graham Bell, assisted by Charles Sumner Tainter and Chichester Bell, took the next major step by replacing tinfoil with wax for recordings. By 1885 they had developed the graphophone (phonograph backwards), which recorded on removable wax cylinders. Edison rejected their offer to combine their patents with his and developed (1887-9) with his laboratory staff a much improved phonograph and wax cylinders. Both machines were marketed primarily for dictation, although Edison envisaged a music entertainment market if he could solve the problem of record duplication. During this same period, Emil Berliner began developing his gramophone, designed for listening to prerecorded discs, which proved easier to duplicate. In Britain the term 'gramophone' supplanted phonograph for record players.

A market for entertainment emerged in the early 1890s with the nickel-in-slot amusement phonograph. By the middle of the decade the use of small spring motors drove down the cost of phonographs for home use and created a growing market for recordings. Edison and his staff successfully resumed work on duplication technology for cylinder records and during the first years of the twentieth century he gained leadership in the new industry. However, Edison faced stiff competition from Victor Talking Machine, which improved Berliner's disc gramophone, and Columbia Phonograph, which also shifted to disc records. Discs were cheaper to duplicate and also capable of recording four minutes of music, twice as long as Edison's cylinders. Although he developed longer playing cylinder records in 1908 (and produced them until 1929), Edison was soon forced to develop his own disc phonograph, but his records, made from the plastic condensite rather than shellac, were not interchangeable with those of his competitors.

There were no major changes in phonograph technology until the mid-1920s when the emergence of broadcast radio created a need for improved audio fidelity. This forced a shift from acoustic to electrical recording. However, this was only a temporary counter to competition from the radio industry; by 1929 Edison had given up the phonograph business, while Victor was taken over by the Radio Corporation of America (RCA); a decade later Columbia became a subsidiary of the Columbia Broadcast System (CBS).

Over the next half century there were a few noteworthy changes in phonograph and record technology. The most significant during the 1930s and 1940s were the long play (LP) vinyl record and phonograph operating at $33\frac{1}{3}$ rpm. Although introduced initially by RCA in 1931, this new technology did not become commercially successful until the late 1940s when Columbia succeeded with its microgroove LP. RCA competed by introducing a 45 rpm phonograph and record. During the 1950s, the LP helped to create a boom in classical music records while the 45 became the primary medium for popular music. During the 1960s, the LP became more important for popular music and during the same decade high-fidelity stereo phonographs and records became common. While challenged by cassette and eight-track tape in the 1970s, phonograph record technology remained dominant until the introduction of the compact disc in the 1980s. None the less, phonographs have not entirely disappeared and there has been a resurgence of high-end phonographs and vinyl records in recent years.

FURTHER READING

R. Gelatt, *The Fabulous Phonograph*, 2nd edn (New York: Collier Books, 1977).
A. Millard, *America on Record: A History of Recorded Sound* (Cambridge University Press, 1995).
D. Morton, *Sound Recording: The Life Story of a Technology* (Baltimore: Johns Hopkins University Press, 2004).

PAUL ISRAEL

Pianoforte At the dawn of the nineteenth century, the two centres of pianoforte construction were Vienna and London. Viennese pianos underwent an evolution from double-stringing to triple-stringing – in the interest of creating greater projection and power – initially in the treble and later extending well into the bass range, whereas English pianos were triple strung from the outset (in the late nineteenth century makers reverted to double stringing in the lower bass and single stringing for the lowest register). Earlier Viennese instruments raised the dampers via hand stops, limiting the ability to sustain notes without an assistant. In the 1780s these were replaced by knee levers. Some Viennese pianos had separate knee levers which allowed the player to lift the dampers of either the entire range or only the lower half of the keyboard, enabling sustained bass-notes or octaves to resonate whilst avoiding blurring in right-hand passage work (MOZART's Walter piano in Salzburg has this feature). English instruments used pedals for this purpose. Until *c*1840 Viennese pianos had a so-called celeste stop, also known as the moderator, which when operated interposes a layer of felt between the hammerhead and the strings, creating a sonority of great delicacy. Earlier Viennese pianos controlled the moderator by a knob mounted at the centre of the fallboard, activating it by pulling the knob and deactivating it by pushing it back; the replacement of this mechanism with a further knee lever permitted instantaneous use.

Both types of piano allowed the shifting of the action to the right, thereby producing a gentler sonority by reducing the number of strings struck (from two to one in the double-strung register of Viennese pianos and from three to two in both types of piano – and to one in French and English pianos). English pianos pioneered the use of pedals for these functions, and French pianos such as those of Érard were quick to feature the shifting soft pedal. Although some REPLICAS of Viennese pianos activate the shifting soft pedal with a knee lever, this capability in historic Viennese instruments originates with six-octave pianos using pedals (*c*1808). The designations *una corda* and *tre corde* for the use of the shifting soft pedal have remained standard terminology despite the fact that Viennese instruments shifted only from three strings to two; Érard and Broadwood pianos allowed the player to choose to employ a full shift from three strings to one, and Broadwood's permitted limiting the shift to two strings through the use of a small wooden lever at the upper right of the keyboard that blocked shifting beyond two strings. Modern pianos shift only to two strings, and some makes (e.g. Bösendorfer) have a limited shift that causes a less-used portion of the hammerhead to strike the strings. Hence BEETHOVEN's prescriptions for the use of one, two and three strings – a possibility he discovered from the

Érard supplied to him by the maker – are not possible on modern instruments, nor were they possible as a rule during Beethoven's lifetime, save on Érard and English pianos. Some Viennese pianos of the early nineteenth century had additional stops, activated by pedals, including a BASSOON stop (which lowered a hollow tube of parchment paper close to the strings, producing a buzzing sonority somewhat redolent of the timbre of a bassoon of the time) and a 'Turkish' stop which operated a built-in drum and bells evoking the sonority of Janissary music (this effect was generally regarded as a device for amateur musicians and was not taken seriously by composers).

Damping on Viennese pianos was provided by V-shaped dampers for double stringing and flat felt dampers for triple stringing; these stopped the sound cleanly and instantaneously. English pianos initially used a damping method in which somewhat loosely overlaid felt strips descended onto the strings, preserving a residue of sonority after release of the key rather than an immediate cessation of the sound, but soon switched to felt dampers capable, like Viennese pianos, of instantaneous damping.

Hammerheads were small, made of wood, and covered by leather with the rough (suede) side outward. English piano makers switched to felt hammers long before Viennese builders and hammer size grew as part of the unstoppable trend towards more voluminous sonority and power.

A significant difference in Viennese and English actions is the layout of the hammershank. On Viennese pianos the hammershank was mounted towards the back of the key running forward, and the striking point was as close to the wrestplank (pin block) as possible. On English pianos the hammers were attached to a rail and the shanks ran from front to back, with a striking point further back than Viennese instruments. The Viennese action engendered a faster hammer velocity and somewhat greater focus in timbre; the English one had slower hammer velocity and a rounder sonority.

In the last two decades of the eighteenth century, the standard range of five octaves ($F'-f'''$) started to expand. During Beethoven's lifetime the range of pianos expanded more rapidly than at any other time in their history. He inherited the five-octave range and it is perhaps significant that the soloist's opening passage in the first movement of his Second Piano Concerto in B♭ major, Op. 19 (the earliest of the canonical five) starts with the highest note then available (f''') and concludes with chords on the dominant and tonic, the former using the lowest note (F'): the soloist takes command of the entire range of the instrument. From there the Viennese instruments first added two additional keys, $f\sharp'''$ and g''' – a range that Beethoven originally employed for his Third Piano Concerto in C minor, Op. 37 (and once again the soloist's opening bars in the first movement ascend to the newly acquired uppermost note, g'''). English pianos expanded the range sooner: HAYDN's Sonata in C major, Hob. XVI:50, calls for a''' – a pitch not available on Viennese pianos of the time. During the final reworking of his Third Piano Concerto, Beethoven obtained an instrument that went up to c'''', but he adapted a limited number of passages to the higher range, leaving others unaccountably constrained by the g''' upper limit. The Fourth Concerto (1805–6) does not exceed the Third's range of $F'-c''''$ but its middle movement requires a shifting soft pedal that can play three, two, or one string(s)(*see* above) – a capacity he demands in later works such as the Sonatas in

B♭ major, Op. 106 and A♭ major, Op. 110 and the Diabelli Variations, Op. 120, which prescribe changing from one to three strings, directly or incrementally. In his late period, Beethoven had at his disposal an instrument that extended from C' to f'''', and subsequent instruments extended further upwards to a'''' and downwards to A'', and finally up to c''''.

The genealogy of piano manufacture led from England to France, where Sébastien Érard expanded his HARP building firm to include pianos; Pleyel provided his chief competition. Érard invented the double escapement, which allowed a re-attack of a note without having to wait for the action to reset; his pianos damped the strings from below rather than above. Further developments in the evolution of construction came in the USA, spearheaded by the firms of Steinway and Chickering. Chief among these was Steinway's invention of overstringing, in which parallel stringing, taken over from HARPSICHORD design, was replaced by the bass strings running obliquely towards the right as they ran back, with baritone strings running slightly to the left. The narrow tail end of earlier pianos was thus replaced by a wider back to accommodate this change of design, whereas the shorter length of strings due to overstringing resulted in the need to introduce copper windings of increasing thickness in the bass to create the same pitches on shorter strings.

The evolution of pianoforte construction was prompted significantly by the desire for greater resonance and sustaining power. This led makers progressively to exert greater tension on the strings. Pianos had initially resembled harpsichords, employing parallel stringing and wood construction (except for the strings and certain details of the action); the gradual increase in power devolved from adding metal support bars and ultimately to a cast iron frame. Thus, whereas a late eighteenth-century pianoforte had approximately 2,000 kg of tension on the strings, that figure rose to 5,000 by the 1820s and 20,000 in later instruments. The quest for greater power of sonority also led to the introduction of larger and heavier hammers and dampers, engendering the use of lead weights embedded in the keys to maintain the action's equilibrium. Key depth and width grew, and dampers no longer extended to the full range of the treble (e.g. stopping at e''' on Steinway Bs and at g''' on Ds). These developments risked slowing hammer velocity and reliability of repetition, engendering design changes such as the aforementioned double escapement (invented by Érard) and the accelerated action (invented by Steinway). The tug of war between the quest for power and the need to overcome concomitant sluggishness anticipated the evolution of computers, where ever-faster processor speeds encouraged software programs of increasing complexity.

The manufacture of pianos originated in small workshops, where they were produced by a small number of workers, but over time the most successful makers expanded their operations to factories, employing the methods of mass production and technological innovation. Whereas early pianos were handcrafted and used materials primarily created on site, the development of the cast iron plate required a foundry, and keyboards were ultimately farmed out to specialised suppliers. Early nineteenth-century pianos used bone for the diatonic keys; later in the century this was supplanted by ivory until ecological concerns replaced ivory with plastic.

Just as the accretion of keys on wind instruments and the development of valves for brass instruments can be seen as efforts to make these more reliable technically, so analogous developments in pianoforte construction were driven by mechanical considerations as well as a desire for greater projection. None the less, it is inadvisable to regard such evolutions as progress, in which earlier instruments are considered primitive. This view has led some commentators to claim that composers wrote for idealised instruments rather than those at hand, and that they would undoubtedly prefer the instruments of today had they been available during their lifetimes.

Familiarity with the characteristics of eighteenth- and nineteenth-century pianofortes reveals the extent to which the effects created by composers reflected and, indeed, are dependent upon those characteristics. The lighter actions of eighteenth- and early nineteenth-century pianofortes, being extremely sensitive to touch, made them ideal for clarity of ARTICULATION. The shallower key dip made virtuoso passages possible at faster TEMPI, whereas the lighter sonority balanced effortlessly with other instruments in chamber music performance (a Beethoven cello sonata or a MENDELSSOHN trio on today's instruments demands accommodation to avoid an unbalanced outcome, whereas such compensation is unnecessary on period pianofortes). The fast decay of sound on earlier pianofortes makes the *sfp* or *sffp* encountered in Classic and early Romantic music – particularly in Beethoven and Schubert – explosive, given that the rapid decay makes it possible to continue in tempo, which is all but impossible on more recent pianofortes. The lesser string tension and faster decay confirms the validity of Beethoven's revolutionary pedal indications (among them the recitative in the first movement of the Sonata, Op. 31 No. 2, the principal theme of the finale of the 'Waldstein' Sonata, Op. 53 and many of the pedal indications in the Fourth Piano Concerto). In particular, the fastidious pedal indications of Chopin – who surpassed all other composers in his minute understanding of the critical nature of adroit PEDALLING – occasionally blur on pianofortes of the last 125 years but are utterly convincing on the Pleyels and Érards with which he was familiar (Chopin's use of the pedal through notes followed by rests shows that his NOTATION is geared towards touch, not merely duration – an aesthetic that particularly influenced later French composers).

Schubert calls for the use of the shifting soft pedal ('mit Verschiebung') but there can be little doubt that when he prescribes *ppp* he is calling for the moderator – whose exquisite sonority disappeared from Viennese pianos around 1840, by which time delicacy was far less important than sustaining power. As mentioned, the lack of true *una corda* on instruments manufactured outside of England in the early nineteenth century has rendered Beethoven's prescription for this sonority unattainable, but perhaps the most dramatic consequence of evolution in pianoforte construction was overstringing. There is no doubt that this innovation concentrated the power of the instrument and rendered passages such as the opening D♭ major chords in Tchaikovsky's First Piano Concerto with enormous resonance. A consequence of this fundamental design change was that a melodic line in the right hand on an overstrung piano necessitates 'quieting' the left hand; a performance of a Bach two-part invention with equal dynamics in the two hands creates the impression that the left hand is too loud. Pianists are taught from childhood to 'bring out the melody' and this seems completely natural; but it is revealing to play the opening of the 'Waldstein' Sonata on both a period instrument and a standard one. The thinner strings and the higher overtone spectrum of the early piano makes it possible to hear all four voices of the chords very clearly, and the passage crackles with vitality and energy. One can play all four voices equally. On today's instrument the thicker strings make the four-voiced sonority far less clear, and playing all voices equally causes the lower notes to dominate over the upper line. The solution is to bring out the top voice, as is commonly done. Carrying this practice back to the period piano is revealing, for it seems unnaturally to exaggerate the top voice at the expense of the totality of the texture. Overstringing has had a profound effect on the performance of polyphonic music, contributing to the oversimplification of bringing out every subject and answer in a fugue. Indeed, overstringing compels performers to choose the musical line they wish to feature and subordinate the rest of the texture – a choice that is unnecessary on parallel strung instruments.

These, and many other details, confirm the intimate connection between the acoustical and mechanical characteristics of earlier pianos and the music composed for them. Beethoven may have goaded piano manufacturers ceaselessly to address his agenda for pianofortes with greater range span and power, but his compositions are astutely calibrated to the instruments at his service. We cannot be certain if Beethoven would prefer the modern concert grand to the instruments he knew and loved; but one thing is certain, to the extent that he would have written exactly the music he created for a pianoforte of substantially different properties, he would be a less extraordinary composer.

FURTHER READING

C. Ehrlich, *The Piano: A History* (London: 1976; 2nd edn, Oxford University Press, 1990).
E. M. Good, *Giraffes, Black Dragons, and Other Pianos: A Technological History from Cristofori to the Modern Concert Grand* (Stanford University Press, 1982).
D. Rowland (ed.), *The Cambridge Companion to the Piano* (Cambridge University Press, 1998).
S. Sadie (ed.), *The Piano*. The New Grove Musical Instruments Series (London: Macmillan, 1988).
R. Winter, 'Keyboards', in H. M. Brown and S. Sadie (eds.), *Performance Practice: Music after 1600* (London: Macmillan, 1989), 346–73.

ROBERT D. LEVIN
(with acknowledgement to Edwin Beunk)

Pianoforte pedalling Mechanisms for modifying the sound exist from the earliest days of the PIANO. Cristofori's grands had a stop that caused the hammers to strike a single string (*una corda*), and SILBERMANN's grands incorporated stops for raising the dampers (sustaining) and for imitating the HARPSICHORD. A fondness for an array of effects is seen on smaller, later eighteenth-century German instruments, and the trend for special effects reached a peak in MILCHMEYER's harpsichord piano, which boasted 250 tone modifications, imitating the sounds of the CLARINET, BASSOON, FLUTE, HARP and the *pantalon* (*pantaleon*), among other instruments.

Eighteenth- and nineteenth-century English grands usually had an *una corda* and sustaining pedal (the latter sometimes divided into treble/bass early in the nineteenth century). English squares had no devices, a single sustaining stop/pedal, or sustaining and damping devices. On eighteenth-century 'Viennese' grands, knee levers replaced hand stops for the sustaining device c1780 (this was sometimes divided, as it was on MOZART's Walter piano of 1781) and some makers incorporated the *moderator*, which interposed a layer of felt between the hammers and strings and which was operated by a knee lever (rather than a hand stop) from c1790. Knee levers were replaced by pedals around 1800 and from then until c1840 'Viennese' pianos typically had four pedals (sustaining, *moderator*, *una corda* and bassoon, which pressed a strip of parchment or silk against the bass strings) and an occasional fifth which produced 'military' or 'Turkish' sounds such as drum, tambourine and cymbals, effects which were generally frowned upon by professional pianists. French grand and square pianos, having followed English designs for most of the eighteenth century, similarly had multiple pedals for the closing years of the eighteenth century and early decades of the nineteenth. From around 1840 two pedals (sustaining and a soft pedal of some sort) became the norm on all pianos, the only significant change being the introduction of selective sustaining devices from the 1840s culminating in Steinway's third, *sostenuto*, pedal, patented in 1875.

Pedal markings appeared in France in the early 1790s. The commercial pressure of publishing scores for both piano or harpsichord ensured that the date was later for British publications (1797) and slightly later still in Vienna. Prior to those dates, comments in tutors and the musical notation itself suggest that pianists/composers sometimes used tone-modifying devices, but it also appears that performances without them were usual (Mozart, for example, would have found it difficult to use knee levers at the same as playing on his piano's pedalboard, which he owned from 1785). The earliest pedal markings often indicate the pedal's uninterrupted use for whole sections or movements; hand stops would have made this inevitable, but the same effect is indicated in early BEETHOVEN works (such as Op. 27 No. 2), where 'senza sordini' and 'con sordini' mean without and with the dampers respectively. It is equally the case that sophisticated techniques, such as syncopated pedalling, were used from early in the nineteenth century. CZERNY declared that Beethoven used the pedal a good deal more than he indicated it and pedal markings are often missing where they are clearly needed in the works of his contemporaries. This should not surprise us, as we should expect composers as a rule to confine their pedal markings to those that are not axiomatic; an essential theorem of PERFORMANCE PRACTICE is that composers notate only that information that is not obvious to a well-trained musician of the composer's own time. While new NOTATIONS were invented for syncopated, half- and flutter-pedalling (Chaulieu, Lavignac, Grainger), they added significantly to the cost of music production and the use of these indications was never widespread. Indeed, few markings for anything other than the sustaining pedal exist in piano music of any period.

Mid-nineteenth-century debates about pedalling centred on the extent of blurring caused by the sustaining pedal and the use of the tone-changing *una corda* for *pianissimos*, Liszt representing an extravagant extreme with HUMMEL and the Schumann circle being more conservative.

FURTHER READING

M. Cole, *The Pianoforte in the Classical Era* (Oxford: Clarendon Press, 1998).
S. P. Rosenblum, *Performance Practices in Classic Piano Music* (Bloomington and Indianapolis: Indiana University Press, 1988).
D. Rowland, *A History of Pianoforte Pedalling* (Cambridge University Press, 1993).

DAVID ROWLAND

Pinnock, Trevor (b. Canterbury, 16 December 1946) British solo harpsichordist and conductor best known as the founder-director of one of the UK's first permanent period instrument orchestras, THE ENGLISH CONCERT.

Pinnock was a chorister at Canterbury Cathedral before studying ORGAN and HARPSICHORD at the ROYAL COLLEGE OF MUSIC in London. In 1966, with flautist Stephen Preston and cellist Anthony Pleeth, he founded the Galliard Trio, which played Baroque music on modern instruments, and two years later made his debut as a solo harpsichordist.

In 1973 the Trio gave way to The English Concert, a quintet and subsequently orchestra of period instruments which Pinnock directed from the keyboard. After a debut at the English Bach Festival in 1973 they were soon making recordings, at first for the British independent label CRD (including one of the first period versions of Vivaldi's *Le quattro stagioni*), and subsequently for Deutsche Grammophon's prestigious early music label Archiv Produktion, for whom during the 1980s they recorded much of the core Baroque orchestral repertoire – CORELLI, Vivaldi, J. S. BACH and Handel – as well as symphonies by C. P. E. BACH, HAYDN and MOZART (a complete cycle) and, with the Choir of The English Concert (formed in 1983), choral and stage works by Purcell, Handel and Haydn. Pinnock also made solo harpsichord recordings for both labels, including music by Scarlatti, Bach and RAMEAU. Pinnock retired from the directorship of The English Concert in 2003, since when he has focused his work on guest-conductor appearances and a revival of his solo and chamber career. In 2006 he celebrated his sixtieth birthday with concerts and a recording of J. S. Bach's Brandenburg Concertos with the specially convened European Brandenburg Ensemble.

From the start, Pinnock's performances with The English Concert were distinguished by a superior level of technical polish and textural clarity, allied to lively tempos and a naturally engaging musicality unfettered by musicological preconceptions which contributed much to their appeal. His reputation as a leading harpsichordist is likewise founded on an easy technique and elegant touch.

LINDSAY KEMP

Pipe and tabor A pair of instruments played by one musician.

The pipe is a duct FLUTE, typically a 'three hole pipe' (two finger-holes above, one thumb-hole below) as it is also known, which may include two to eight holes (such as Catalan and Mallorcan instruments with two finger-holes below for the thumb and little finger and five or six above, the top three covered by the remaining fingers. This allows the flute to be sometimes played with two hands in absence of the drum). The drum, either slung over the hand holding the pipe or over the shoulder, is played by a stick held in the free hand.

Figure 11: Mallorcan pipe and tabor player Tomas Salom. (photograph by Cassandre Balosso-Bardin)

Played widely in Europe and Latin America, historically and to this day, the pipe is known under many names (Basque *txistu*; Bolivia *waka-pinkillo*; Cat. *flabiol*; Columbia *gaita*; Eng. (Oxfordshire) *whittle*; Fr. *flûte à trois trous*; Ger. *Schwegel, Tamerlinpfeife*; Mestizo (Peru) *roncadora*; Provencal *galoubet*; Port. *pífaro*; Quichua *pingillu*) as is the tabor (Basque *tamboril, atabal*; Cat. *tamborí*; Eng. (Oxfordshire) *dub*; Fr. *tambourin*). Although the one-person duet is principally used for dancing, the variety of pipes and their repertoire differ widely from region to region.

European pipe and tabor traditions are mainly found in England, Spain, Portugal and southern France. The duet appeared suddenly in mid-thirteenth-century ICONOGRAPHY and spread from southern Spain to Germany. Early, shorter versions of the pipe have been affiliated to the Catalan/Balearic type of instrument, still in use today (Montagu, 22) (*see* Figure 11). Used in high social circles until the sixteenth century, it then remained more of a rural instrument. Like many other folk instruments, its popularity declined in the nineteenth century with the rise of the concertina and accordion. Cecil Sharp helped to revive the English pipe and tabor through the renewed Morris and folk dance tradition. Today, it is heard in many European countries as instrument makers have taken up its manufacture with its adoption in folk and early music revivals.

Pipe and tabor traditions are also found widely in Latin America, including Mexico, Ecuador, Peru and Bolivia. Although its wide dissemination and popularity was undoubtedly influenced by European colonisation, pre-Hispanic evidence exists of the pipe and drum played by a single musician (Olsen, 56–8).

FURTHER READING

C. L. Boilès, 'The pipe and tabor in Mesoamerica', *Anuario*, 2 (1966), 43–74.
J. Montagu, 'Was the tabor pipe always as we know it?', *GSJ*, 50 (1997), 16–30.
D. Olsen, *Music of El Dorado* (Gainesville, FL: University of Florida Press, 2002).

CASSANDRE BALOSSO-BARDIN

Pitch Once a subject primarily of academic interest, the history of musical pitch standards became one of practical concern in the last third or so of the twentieth century, when specialist performers of early music began to recognise the importance of the effect of pitch on timbre: both instruments and voices sound mellower at lower standards and more brilliant at higher ones. More recent research has in turn benefited from the findings of performers, builders and restorers, based upon their direct experience with surviving instruments. Groundbreaking studies by BRUCE HAYNES (1995, 2002) have made extensive use of these findings, superseding the work of Alexander Ellis ('The history of musical pitch', *Journal of the Society of Arts*, 28 (1880), 293-336) and Arthur Mendel ('Pitch in Western music since 1500, a re-examination', *AcM*, 1 (1978), 1–93). Haynes meshes the data from instruments with documentary evidence and offers a more complete picture of the history of pitch than has previously been available.

The first written discussions of pitch come from the sixteenth century, when the practice of mixing instruments of various kinds, as well as instruments with voices, caused the issue to become significant. The pitch standards of Continental Europe have tended to be at – or at least comparatively near – the pitches of a chromatic scale tuned to our modern standard of $a' = 440$ Hz, making it convenient to represent them with a scheme using numerals to specify their distance in semitones from modern pitch. Haynes thus uses 'A+0' to signify a standard near modern pitch; 'A+1', a semitone above; 'A-1', a semitone below; etc. Earlier English pitch standards also appear to have conformed to a grid of pitches separated by semitones, but in this case centred 'in the cracks' between the members of the Continental grid. They seem to have descended from a standard known as 'Quire [i.e. choir] pitch', standing at $a' \approx 474$ Hz (between A+1 and A +2). For the Quire pitch grid, Haynes uses 'Q-0' (for Quire pitch itself), 'Q-1' (for a semitone below that), etc. Some of the more important Continental standards from the sixteenth through to the eighteenth centuries include the following:

- A+3 ($a' \approx 522$ Hz): the pitch of a number of Renaissance-style recorders and some late fifteenth and early sixteenth-century Italian ORGANS. (This standard does not seem to have had a name.)
- A+2 ($a' \approx 494$ Hz): *Hoch Chorton* ('high choir pitch'). Pitch associated with far north Germany in the seventeenth and eighteenth centuries, including Dietrich Buxtehude's Lübeck. Sometimes referred to simply as *Chorton*.
- A+1 ($a' \approx 466$ Hz): *Cornet-ton* (or *Cornettenton*: 'cornett pitch'). Pitch associated with the majority of surviving CORNETTS (as well as the majority of other Renaissance winds). Prevailing pitch of German organs in the seventeenth and eighteenth centuries; also commonly called *Chorton* in north Germany throughout that period (and very occasionally *Kammerton* ('chamber pitch') there in the early seventeenth century).

Known as *tuon del cornetto di mezzo punto* ('halfway [down] cornett pitch'), or sometimes simply *mezzo punto*, in Italy from the mid-sixteenth century; also known as *corista di Lombardia* ('Lombard pitch') and *corista Veneto* ('Venetian pitch') until the early eighteenth century (at which time *corista Veneto* was lowered to A+0).

Apparently the pitch of most French woodwinds before the development of the Baroque forms in the latter half of the seventeenth century; probably known as *ton d'écurie* ('pitch of the (Royal) stable').

- A+0 (a′ ≈ 440 Hz): rare (but possible) level for *Chorton* in the early eighteenth century; more common by the latter part of the century. Ultimate meaning for *Kammerton*, beginning in the late eighteenth century.

Known as *tuon del cornetto di tutto punto* ('all the way (down) cornett pitch') in Italy from the mid-sixteenth century. The higher of the two *coristi di mezzo* ('intermediate pitch standards'), as described in the eighteenth century.

- A-1 (a′ ≈ 415 Hz): *Kammerton* ('chamber pitch'), sometimes distinguished as *hoch Kammerton* ('high chamber pitch'); standard level for much of the eighteenth century. Also known as *Chorton* in southern German-speaking areas in the seventeenth and early eighteenth centuries.

The lower of the *coristi di mezzo*, which were the typical pitches of indigenous Italian Baroque-style woodwinds of the early eighteenth century.

- A-1½ (a′ ≈ 403 Hz): *Ton de la Chambre du Roy* ('royal chamber pitch'); pitch of organs and woodwinds associated with the court of Louis IV.
- A-2 (a′ ≈ 392 Hz): *Tief Kammerton* ('low chamber pitch'); *Französischer Ton* ('French pitch'); *Operaton* ('opera pitch'): much in use in the early eighteenth century.

Corista di San Pietro ('pitch of St Peter's [Cathedral]'): pitch of Roman organs, c1600 to late nineteenth century. Standing at a′ = 384 Hz, actually on the low side of A-2.

Ton d'opéra ('opera pitch'); pitch of the French opera from late seventeenth through much of the eighteenth century. *Ton de chapelle* ('chapel pitch'); pitch of most French organs, from the sixteenth to the eighteenth century.

Among the most significant English standards were the following:

- Q-0 (a′ ≈ 473 Hz): 'Quire pitch' – the effective pitch for voices of early Restoration (and pre-Restoration) organs, found on surviving organs from 1660 to 1730 (on pre-Restoration organs this pitch was produced through TRANSPOSITION).
- Q-1 (a′ ≈ 448 Hz): probable pitch of English wind instruments (specifically cornetts and SHAWMS) in the early seventeenth century, when they were described as being a 'very little lower' than Continental ones at A+1. A common pitch of English organs before 1700.
- Q-2 (a′ ≈ 423 Hz): 'Chappell pitch' (late seventeenth century); 'new Consort pitch' (early eighteenth century); eventually simply 'Consort pitch' or 'Concert pitch'; dominant English orchestral pitch for much of the eighteenth century.
- Q-3 (a′ ≈ 400 Hz): 'Consort pitch' (late seventeenth century; probably of long standing by then; described as 'old' in 1746). Essentially identical to A-1½, allowing the use of French designs for Baroque woodwinds at this pitch.

As can be seen from the foregoing (far from exhaustive) listings, some of the terminology employed (particularly *Chorton*, *Kammerton*, *corista* and 'consort pitch') had multiple meanings, varying both geographically and temporally – a fact often unrecognised by researchers. Significantly, the one German term with a constant meaning seems to have been *Cornet-ton* (at A+1). By the end of the eighteenth century, pitches below A-1 had virtually disappeared, and A-1 itself was on the way out. By 1830 A+0 had become the orchestral norm across Europe; in the meantime, fluctuations to the high side have been driven by the quest for brilliance and to the low side, by reactions against its excessive height. (Again, England was the main outlier, with a standard about a quarter tone higher than that of the Continent throughout most of the nineteenth century.) Despite the international acceptance of $a' = 440$ Hz as a standard in 1939, modern orchestras regularly tune sharp to it by a few Hz.

As to modern conventions for early music, most specialist performers of Baroque music have adopted $a' = 415$ Hz (an exact semitone below $a' = 440$ Hz) as a standard, encouraged in no small part by the convenience of pitch-shifting keyboards on harpsichords and continuo organs. This choice is admittedly ideal for much eighteenth-century repertoire, but it does tend to shut out the use of other historical pitches (A-2, A-1½, Q-2 and A+0, specifically). A standard of $a' = 430$ Hz has considerable currency for period-instrument performance of music of the late eighteenth century, even though there is even less historical support for it as a universal standard at the time. A standard of $a' = 466$ Hz (A+1) is gaining ground among players of Renaissance and early Baroque music, but it is nowhere near having the same level of acceptance as the foregoing standards for eighteenth-century music.

FURTHER READING

B. Haynes, *A History of Performing Pitch: The Story of 'A'* (Lanham, MD: Scarecrow Press, 2002).

'Pitch standards in the Baroque and Classical periods', PhD dissertation, Université de Montréal (1995).

H. Myers, 'Pitch and transposition', in S. Carter (ed.), rev. and expanded J. Kite-Powell, *A Performer's Guide to Seventeenth-Century Music* (Bloomington, IN, and Indianapolis: Indiana University Press, 2012), 375–96.

HERBERT MYERS

Plainchant The performance history of plainchant is at least as old as – if not older than – Christianity itself, inasmuch as it inherited performing traditions from Judaic and polytheist rituals. Such history is inextricably linked with the development of musical NOTATION in the West and with the gradual transformation through time of liturgical practice and musical style. Our knowledge of the performance of chant in pre-modern times is and always will be vastly incomplete, due to the lack or loss of documentary sources. However, general information on the performance of plainsong may be gleaned from notated chant books and musical TREATISES. For the sake of convenience, one may identify the following related topics:

1. Manner of performance: most chant melodies were sung following two basic 'forms', responsorial and antiphonal. In the first – employed, for

instance, for responsories, antiphons and Mass Propers – one soloist (or more, depending on the solemnity of the ritual) alternates with the CHOIR; in the second – for psalms, hymns and sequences – two half choirs alternate, usually positioned behind the altar. As time went on, these performance schemes could also involve the alternation of plainchant and polyphony, with or without the use of the organ.

2   Accuracy of execution: even after staff notation had become widespread (in the twelfth century), *magistri* such as John Cotto and Pseudo-Guido lambasted the performances of chant melodies that did not follow the mode, or were marred by wrong intervals. Later authors (notably, CONRAD VON ZABERN) stressed the importance of SINGING chant in a devout and decorous manner.

3   Rhythm, TEMPO and EXPRESSION: the issue of the rhythmic profile of plainchant has long stirred controversy due primarily to the fact that the notated sources do not indicate the durations of the pitches other than in a few exceptional cases (Hiley, 48). A few post-Renaissance sources, most notably the *Editio Medicea* of 1614, clearly deploy different note shapes to indicate different long values (Hiley, 49), but they cannot be taken to represent earlier practices. Several contrasting approaches to the interpretation of rhythm in plainchant have been proposed in the twentieth century (Mahrt, 18–19). Notated sources provided indications about tempo and DYNAMICS by means of the 'significative letters' positioned next to the neumes, such as *c = celeriter* ('quickly'), *t = tenete* or *trahere* ('hold' or 'slow down'), *k = clange* ('ringing tone'), *p = pressionem* ('pressing forward') and others (Hiley, 46–7). Theorists such as Conrad von Zabern and GAFFURIUS recommend that tempos be slower on more solemn feasts.

The history of the PERFORMANCE PRACTICE of plainchant is intimately connected with that of sacred polyphony, which was often performed in alternation with plainchant throughout its history. Of course, most polyphonic genres – from the Notre Dame organum to the motets and masses of the sixteenth century and beyond – originated as contrapuntal elaborations of plainchant melodies, often during improvised performances (as shown, for instance, by the *fauxbourdon* practice in the fifteenth and sixteenth centuries). The liturgical practice of playing the organ *alternatim* with the *schola* (though not yet with the congregation) appears to have begun in the late thirteenth century.

FURTHER READING

D. Hiley, 'Chant', in H. M. Brown and S. Sadie (eds.), *Performance Practice: Music Before 1600* (London: Macmillan, 1989), 37–54.
  Western Plainchant: A Handbook (Oxford: Clarendon Press, 1993).
T. Karp, *Aspects of Orality and Formularity in Gregorian Chant* (Evanston, IL: Northwestern University Press, 1998).
T. F. Kelly (ed.), *Plainsong in the Age of Polyphony* (Cambridge University Press, 1992).
W. P. Mahrt, 'Chant', in R. Duffin (ed.), *A Performer's Guide to Medieval Music* (Bloomington, IN: Indiana University Press, 2000), 1–22.

STEFANO MENGOZZI

Playford Family As the predominant music publishers of the day, the Playford family was responsible for establishing commercial music printing in seventeenth-century England, largely through the entrepreneurship of John Playford (1623–87/8), followed by his son Henry (1657–1709). The elder Playford single-handedly created a market for music anthologies aimed at inexperienced amateurs, producing instrumental collections, vocal anthologies and a popular rudiments manual. The family's importance to our understanding of historical performance in seventeenth-century England is threefold.

First, both John and Henry Playford were skilled in appealing to the popular market, and their collections strongly reflect changing tastes in both instrumentation and repertory: early 1650s anthologies for cittern, gittern and lyra VIOL were soon replaced by books such as *Apollo's Banquet* for the VIOLIN, its successive EDITIONS between c1669 and 1701 demonstrating the instrument's sustained popularity. Anthologies from the 1680s conversely show the rise of the RECORDER, and those of the late 1690s the solo HARPSICHORD. Second, the Playfords constantly updated their anthologies, incorporating the most recent repertory. John Playford's close connections with London's professional musicians in particular allowed him access to the most up-to-date tunes. Recent studies have also revealed his creative role as editor, reflecting the varied interpretative possibilities that were open to seventeenth-century performers.

Third, in order to make their instrumental compilations accessible to inexperienced amateurs, the Playfords habitually began them with brief rudimentary instructions. Usually these included an explanation of the notation used – often a form of TABLATURE telling players where to place their fingers physically, thus removing the need to learn staff notation – basic technical advice, such as how to tune the instrument, and information on interpreting ornament signs. While such materials can barely have been sufficient for the books' users, today they provide important evidence of the technical features, FINGERINGS and playing techniques of the period's most common instruments.

More detail on performance practices is preserved in John Playford's *Introduction to the Skill of Musick*, the best-selling rudimentary instruction manual of its day. With nineteen editions published between 1654 and 1730, it was constantly updated to reflect changing approaches, and also exerted strong influence on other theoretical texts, being used both with and without acknowledgement. Interpreting its contents requires care, because John Playford (who produced the first ten editions, to 1683) was typical of his time in compiling the *Introduction*, sometimes tacitly, from a wide range of pre-existing writings, many written considerably earlier. Thus it is difficult to know, for example, whether the ORNAMENTATION instructions translated from the Preface to CACCINI's *Le nuove musiche*, of 1601 – included in the introduction from 1664 to 1694 – really had '*been used here in* England *by most of the Gentlemen of His Majesties Chappel above this 40 years*'. Henry Playford's approach when updating later editions was to commission current figures, most importantly Henry Purcell, who revised the twelfth edition of 1694. Despite its variable contents, comparing the introduction's main editions reveals important changes to performing practices – including those related to time signatures and metre as well as styles of rhythmic and melodic ornamentation.

Further Reading

G. Caccini, *Le nuove musiche* (Florence: Giulio Marescotti, 1601).
J. Playford, *A Breefe Introduction to the Skill of Musick for Song & Violl* (London: John Playford, 1654).
Apollo's Banquet: Short Rules and Directions for Practitioners on the Treble Violin, with a Collection of Old Country Dances (London: John Playford, c1669).

REBECCA HERISSONE

Popular music *see* JAZZ AND POPULAR MUSIC

Portamento The various terms used to indicate portamento (e.g. *portamento della voce*; *port de voix*; *Tragen der Töne*; glide or slur) had several different meanings, but central to each was the expressive practice of 'carrying' the sound. Carl Flesch described the effect (*Die Kunst des Violinspiels*, 1923–8) as 'the emotional connection of two notes' (I, 29). In SINGING, string playing and wind playing 'portamento' had two possible interpretations. Both required a smooth connection of one sound with another, that connection being realised either through a true legato or through a more or less audible slide through the intervening PITCHES. Portamento was cultivated by some late eighteenth- and nineteenth-century flautists, notably TROMLITZ (1791; 'das Durchziehen'), NICHOLSON (c1816; 'the glide'), Fürstenau (1826) and John Clinton (1843), by BERR (1836) on the CLARINET, and by Almenräder (1843) and Willent-Bordogni (c1844) on the BASSOON; it was also widespread in TROMBONE technique. However, as the incidence of expressive portamento with wind instruments was necessarily limited, this entry will focus on vocal and string portamento.

Vocal Portamento

The terms 'portamento della voce' and 'port de voix' appear in the literature from the early seventeenth century. Both Rognoni (*Selva de varii passaggi* (Milan, 1620)) and MERSENNE (*Harmonie universelle*, 1636) applied them to the seamless delivery of conjunct notes, though it is clear from Rognoni's examples that something more than legato is intended (Example 19).

For both TOSI and MANCINI, the term seems to have meant no more than legato. Tosi wrote of sliding and dragging ('scivolo e strascino'), translated by Galliard as 'gliding'; Galliard helpfully added that 'the gliding notes are like several notes in one stroke of the bow on the violin' (Tosi, trans. Galliard, ed. Pilkington, 1987, 20). Mancini described 'tying' one note to another: 'legando la voce' (*Pensieri e riflessioni pratiche sopra il canto figurato*, 1774, 91).

Example 19: Francesco Rognoni: *Selva de varii passaggi* (Milan, 1620), facing 2.

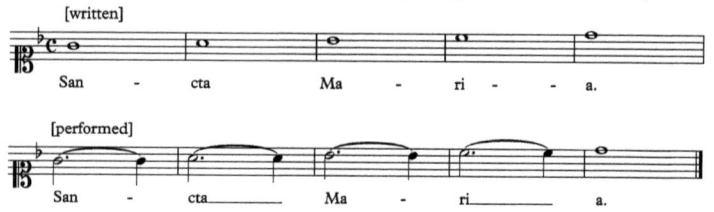

By the end of the eighteenth century the usage was still ambiguous. Even Corri, who defined portamento as 'the perfection of vocal music', provided no exercises that imply filling in the intervening notes when singing intervals of a third or more (*The Singers' Preceptor*, 2 vols. (London: Longman, Hurst, Rees and Orme, 1810), 3). But from the early decades of the nineteenth century, singing teachers put this practice beyond doubt by matching verbal instructions to vocal exercises. One of the first teachers to make this specific was Bernardo Mengozzi, head of singing at the PARIS CONSERVATOIRE from 1795. In his *Méthode de chant du Conservatoire de Musique*, published posthumously (Paris: A l'Imprimerie du Conservatoire de Musique, 1804), Mengozzi distinguished between the French style of portamento ('porter les sons'), which equates to simple legato, and what he called 'genuine Italian portamento', which involves 'sliding' between notes with an anticipation of the second note (Example 20).

Even greater precision is illustrated by MANUEL GARCÍA I, whose *Exercices pour la voix* (Paris: Petit, c1820) includes the following drill, accompanied by the direction to move from the low note to the high by passing rapidly through all the intermediate steps (Example 21).

His son, MANUEL GARCÍA II, reinforced this instruction, and suggested the slur as the definitive notation for portamento. In his *Traité complet de l'art du chant* (1840, rev. 1847), García jr analysed the emotional effect of portamento, and distinguished between a rapid run in vigorous passages and a slower, more lingering slide in tender contexts. He included a wealth of examples drawn not only from his contemporaries, Rossini, Bellini and Meyerbeer, but from Handel and MOZART, putting beyond doubt the fact that however little we know about the application of portamento in the eighteenth century, eighteenth-century music was regularly performed with portamento in the nineteenth (Example 22).

From the beginning of the twentieth century the recording industry provided a new type of evidence that cannot be ignored or misinterpreted. As an example of the extremes to which portamento could be taken, there is no better example than Adelina Patti's performance of 'Voi che sapete' (*Le nozze di*

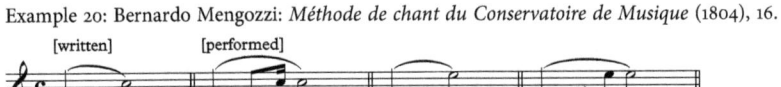

Example 20: Bernardo Mengozzi: *Méthode de chant du Conservatoire de Musique* (1804), 16.

Example 21: Manuel García I: *Exercices pour la voix* (c1820), 14.

Example 22: Manuel García II: *Traité complet de l'art du chant* (1840), 64.

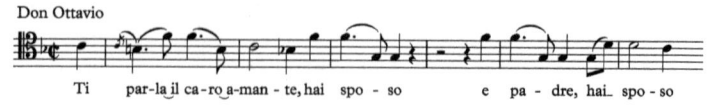

Don Ottavio

Ti par-la il ca-ro a-man - te, hai spo - so e pa - dre, hai. spo - so

Figaro), recorded in 1905: portamento is applied at almost every leap of a third, and even across the reprise. From this point forward there has been a steady diminution in the use of portamento; the decline is mapped in Potter (2006), who analyses ninety-seven recordings of Schubert's 'Ständchen' across the entire twentieth century.

String Portamento

Portamento gradually gained regular acceptance as an expressive colouring in string playing during the late eighteenth century and was executed most commonly in solo contexts during upward shifts in slurred BOWING, the relevant finger sliding rapidly but conspicuously between the appropriate notes. It is implied in some of LEOPOLD MOZART's (1756) FINGERINGS (Example 23(a) and (b)), and BURNEY (*A General History of Music from the Earliest Ages to the Present Period* (London, 1776–89, 1957), II, 992) wondered at the beautiful effects that can be produced by string players in shifting suddenly from a low note to a high, with the same finger on the same string.

Example 23: (a) and (b) Leopold Mozart: *Versuch* (1756), 241 and 178.

(a) (Adagio)

(b)

REICHARDT (*Ueber die Pflichten des Ripien-Violinisten* (Berlin and Leipzig: G. J. Decker, 1776)) permitted soloists to use the effect tastefully but warned orchestral players against introducing it; evidence suggests that his warnings were often ignored. Lolli and Mestrino used it exaggeratedly as an expressive device (e.g. the 'couler à Mestrino', illustrated in WOLDEMAR's *Grande méthode* (Paris: Cochet, c1800)). Mestrino's presence at Esterháza (1780–5) may have encouraged HAYDN to introduce fingerings suggestive of portamento in some of his string quartets (Example 24).

Portamento became a hallmark of the playing styles of KREUTZER, RODE and BAILLOT, and use of the effect increased during the nineteenth century. Baillot (1835) and HABENECK (c1840) recommended its tasteful introduction, either ascending (with *crescendo*) or descending (with *diminuendo*), particularly in slow movements and sustained melodies. SPOHR's instructions (1832), supplemented by copious examples, stipulate a rapid finger-slide with the cue-sized note inaudible (Example 25); some of his fingering indications, however, suggest the likelihood of any slide being audible (Example 26).

Example 24: Haydn: String Quartet in E flat major, Op. 33 No. 2, 2nd movement.

Example 25: Louis Spohr: *Violinschule* (1832), 120.

Example 26: (a) Louis Spohr: Violin Concerto No. 10 in A, Op. 62, 2nd movement; (b) and (c) Pierre Rode: Violin Concerto No. 7, 2nd movement, quoted in Spohr: *Violinschule* (1832), 209.

(a) **Adagio**

(b)

(c) **minore**
sopra la 4ta

His approach was shared by most important nineteenth-century schools of string playing. Some later writers interlinked the speed of the slide with considerations of character or mood. BÉRIOT (Paris: l'auteur, 1858), for example, emphasises the vocal nature of the effect and distinguishes three types of *port de voix*: *vif* (lively), *doux* (sweet) and *traîné* (drawn out); his various graphic markings indicate his suggested speeds and intensities of their execution according to the musical context.

The incidence and the more protracted execution of portamenti in both solo and orchestral contexts gradually increased and the effect became ever more freely employed up to c1930. A variety of portamento types became distinguishable, some of which were more acceptable than others. The most common was the slide made with the starting finger; sliding with the finger of arrival was generally frowned upon (Joachim and Moser, *Violinschule* (Berlin: N. Simrock, 1905)), as was gratuitous sliding down to an open string. Nevertheless, portamento played a prominent expressive role in early twentieth-century recordings such as Marie Hall's 1916 account of ELGAR's Violin Concerto, where examples are emphasised by increased bow pressure during the slides.

Example 27: (a) uninterrupted slide on one finger; (b) 'B-portamento'; (c) 'L-portamento'.

Flesch (*Die Kunst des Violinspiels*, 2 vols. (Berlin: Ries & Erler, 1923-8)), among others, reacted strongly against this trend, deploring the overuse of portamento, its slow execution, its introduction for convenient shifting rather than for expressive ends, and the false accents it created. He recommended that portamento usage should coincide as far as possible with the climax of a phrase and stressed the importance of sensitive dynamic shading, considering 'offensive' JOACHIM's frequent, generally slow portamenti with *crescendo*. Flesch, like Becker and Rynar (*Mechanik und Aesthetik des Violoncellspiels* (Vienna: Universal, 1929)), advocated three kinds of portamento: an uninterrupted slide on one finger (Example 27a); 'B-portamento', in which the beginning finger slides to an intermediary note and another finger stops the note of destination (Example 27b); 'L-portamento', in which the last finger slides from an intermediary note to the note of destination (Example 27c). Although Sarasate and Kreisler used the 'L-portamento' a little, it was rarely practised until the 1930s, when Jascha Heifetz introduced it frequently. Becker and Rynar (1929) aligned this kind of portamento as more 'for the heroic' and the other two types as 'for the lyrical' and, contrary to Joachim's frequent practice, advised that all portamenti should be accompanied by a *diminuendo*.

Non-uniform portamento usage in ORCHESTRAS varied by country but reached a crisis point by the first quarter of the twentieth century, especially in

Britain. Many writers warn against overusing and abusing the effect. A change to a more uniform and disciplined approach proved crucial and employment of portamento underwent a process of gradual refinement in both solo and ensemble performance, the consensus favouring its selective use as an expressive ornament and its rapid execution with minimum bow pressure. The move by, for example, Flesch (*Alta Scuola di diteggiatura violinistica* (Milan: Edizione Curci, 1960)) and Galamian (*Principles of Violin Playing and Teaching* (Englewood Cliffs, NJ: Prentice Hall, 1962)), and CASALS (*see* Alexanian, 1922) and Stutschewsky (*Die Kunst des Cellospiels*, 4 vols. (Mainz: Schott, 1929–38)), to reduce the incidence of formal shifts and cultivate cleaner, more subtle ARTICULATION by introducing novel extensions and contractions, also assisted this process. Katz (2006) contends that sound recording was the root cause of this transformation. Certainly recordings reveal the extent to which the frequency, speed and shading of portamenti changed during the early twentieth century. The onus of adding portamenti gradually passed from performer to composer.

FURTHER READING

C. Brown, *Classical and Romantic Performing Practice 1750–1900* (Oxford University Press, 1999).
M. Katz, 'Portamento and the phonograph effect', *JMR*, 25/3–4 (2006), 211–32.
D. Kauffman, 'Portamento in Romantic opera', *PPR*, 5 (1992), 139–58.
R. Philip, *Early Recordings and Musical Style: Changing Tastes in Instrumental Performance, 1900–1950* (Cambridge University Press, 1992).
J. Potter, 'Beggar at the door: the rise and fall of portamento in singing', *M&L*, 87/4 (2006), 523–50.
R. Stowell, *Violin Technique and Performance Practice in the Late Eighteenth and Early Nineteenth Centuries* (Cambridge University Press, 1985).

PATRICIA HOWARD AND ROBIN STOWELL

Praetorius, Michael (b. Creuzburg an der Werra, nr Eisenach, ?15 February 1571; d. Wolfenbüttel, 15 February 1621) German Lutheran organist, *Kapellmeister*, composer and music theorist.

Born Michael Schultze (or Schultheiss), he adopted the name 'Praetorius' (the conventional Latinisation of his German surname). He began his career as a church organist in Frankfurt an der Oder in 1587. From c1595 he served the Dukes of Brunswick-Wolfenbüttel as organist and (from 1604) as *Kapellmeister* as well; in 1613 he was invited to serve (concurrently) at the court of Elector Johann Georg I of Saxony in Dresden, where he worked with Heinrich Schütz and was exposed to the latest developments in Italian music.

Praetorius was a prolific and skilled composer, producing thousands of compositions, most of them sacred; they range from two-voice fantasies on psalm tunes to elaborate multi-choir concerted works. Perhaps somewhat ironically, he is best known nowadays for his simple four-part setting of the Christmas hymn *Es ist ein Ros entsprungen* ('Lo, how a Rose e'er blooming'). A number of the 312 French dances in his *Terpsichore* (1612 – his one secular publication) have also attained some popularity; for a large portion of the collection he himself was the arranger.

Most significant in its influence today, however, is his legacy of theoretical writings. Of primary importance are volumes 2 and 3 of his monumental *Syntagma musicum*, which are written (mostly) in German and consider numerous practical issues of concern to performers. Volume 2, *De organographia* ('On instruments' – Wolfenbüttel, 1618/19), provides descriptions of instruments 'old and new', with detailed information (including ranges, terminology, sizes and use) about those currently in vogue; the author's excursus on PITCH is of crucial importance to the history of that subject. It also presents a lengthy discussion of the history and design of the ORGAN. Its graphic appendix (the *Theatrum instrumentorum* ('Theatre of instruments') – Wolfenbüttel, 1620) provides forty-two plates with scaled representations of most of the instruments discussed in the text. Volume 3, *Termini musici* ('Musical terms' – Wolfenbüttel, 1619), does indeed start out as a dictionary of musical terminology (including forms, signs and descriptors) but then goes on to treat in depth a number of complex subjects (including modal theory, signs of proportion, TRANSPOSITION practices, figured bass realisation and choosing instrumentation according to ranges as indicated by clefs); it also contains a catalogue of the different approaches he had used in constructing his own polychoral compositions. In this volume in particular he demonstrates his passion for learning about Italian practices of both composition and performance and in bringing them into use in his Protestant Germany. While some scholars have questioned whether he should be counted as a primary witness concerning Italy, since he evidently never travelled there, it is quite clear his knowledge transcends what might be gleaned simply from reading; we should probably look to Schütz as his informant.

FURTHER READING

M. Praetorius, *Syntagma musicum II: De organographia* (Wolfenbüttel, 1618/19), Parts 1 and 2, trans. and ed. D. Z. Crookes (Oxford: Clarendon Press, 1986).
Syntagma musicum III: Termini musici (Wolfenbüttel, 1619), trans. J. T. Kite-Powell (New York: Oxford University Press, 2004).

HERBERT MYERS

Prelleur, Peter (Pierre) (b. ?London, ?December 1705, poss. bap. 16 December 1705; d. 25 June 1741) London-based English composer, organist and harpsichordist.

Prelleur is best known for compiling *The Modern Musick-Master or The Universal Musician* (London, 1730/31), a seminal compendium of TREATISES probably inspired by a similarly organised, anonymous volume, *The Compleat Musick-Master* (1704). Prelleur's publication comprises an introduction to SINGING, as well as separate instruction on playing the RECORDER, FLUTE, OBOE, VIOLIN and HARPSICHORD. It also includes a brief history of music, one of the earliest published in England, and a music dictionary. Its early EDITIONS were published anonymously and some portions continued to be printed for over sixty years.

The attribution of the compendium rests on HAWKINS's statement (*A General History of the Science and Practice of Music* (London, 1776) V, 373) that Prelleur was employed by publisher Cluer Dicey (c1730) to 'compile an Introduction to Singing, as also instructions for the practice of most instruments'. Prelleur's must have been an editorial role, as the instruction derives from others' publications. For example, Part III, for the 'German flute', is essentially an edited, abridged edition of an English translation (c1729) of HOTTETERRE's *Principes*... (1707) with an additional section on metre culled from Hotteterre's *L'art de préluder* (Paris: l'auteur, Foucault, 1719) and FREILLON-PONCEIN's *La véritable manière*... (Paris: Collombat, 1700); and the imprecise keyboard tuning instructions in Part VI were drawn from Godfrey Keller's *Compleat Method* (London: John Cullen, 1707). Because Part V, *The Art of Playing on the Violin*, bears a title identical to GEMINIANI's treatise for advanced violinists (1751), some commentators have mistakenly concluded that Geminiani was its anonymous author. However, the section was pirated largely from an anonymous method for amateurs, *Nolens volens* (1695).

The *Modern Musick-Master*'s six parts were also sold separately as pedagogical resources, as was some of its musical content. Each part contains guidance on how to play the instrument in question and includes scales, pieces and general notes on the instrument's history, as well as instruction regarding ORNAMENTATION.

FURTHER READING

D. D. Boyden, 'Geminiani and the first violin tutor', *AcM*, 31 (1959), 161–70; 'A postscript to "Geminiani and the first violin tutor"', *AcM*, 32 (1960), 40–7.
R. Donington, 'Geminiani and the gremlins', *M&L*, 51 (1970), 150–5.
P. Prelleur, *The Modern Musick-Master or The Universal Musician* (London, 1730–1); facsim. edn with introduction by A. H. King (Kassel: Bärenreiter, 1965).

ROBIN STOWELL

Preluding It has been a common practice since at least the fifteenth century for musicians to improvise a prelude at the start of a solo, and occasionally an ensemble performance. These IMPROVISATIONS introduce the tonality, give the opportunity to warm up the voice or to check the correct functioning and tuning of an instrument, and, where an audience is present, gain their attention for displays of musical and technical invention. The practice was most widely, but not exclusively, developed by VIOL, LUTE and keyboard players in the Baroque period and was continued by solo virtuosi until it largely died out in the early twentieth century.

Attempts to write down improvised preludes give only a limited impression of actual extemporisation. According to contemporary accounts, they were abstract in character and free from text or DANCE type, and renowned exponents achieved a spontaneous effect quite different to that of performing notated music. Organists regularly improvised service music (NIEDT, *Handleitung zur Variation* (Hamburg: Auff Kosten des Autoris ... bey B. Schillern, 1706)), often utilising complex counterpoint, and Handel famously preluded before his organ concerto performances. Non-keyboard preluding is described by ROUSSEAU (1768) for voice, HOTTETERRE (1719) for solo wind instruments, and Bordet (*Méthode raisonnée pour apprendre la musique* (Paris: l'auteur, Bayle, 1755)) for various instruments including the VIOLIN, musette and HURDY-GURDY, and by BROSSARD (1703) and FUHRMANN (1706) for groups of instruments. DENIS published a prelude to test his tuning system

(*Traité de l'accord de l'espinette* (Paris: Ballard and Jean Denis, 1643)), and a set of modulating preludes by W. A. MOZART survives.

Later tutor books include simple examples to instruct those unable to prelude extempore, particularly amateurs (Kollmann, *An Introduction to the Art of Preluding & Extemporising* (London: Wornum, 1792) and J. W. Hässler, *360 Preludes in all Major and Minor Keys*, Op. 47, 1817), and the sophisticated rhythmic ambiguity of the seventeenth-century French unmeasured prelude influenced the notation of later preludes (e.g. CZERNY, *Systematische Anleitung zum Fantasieren auf dem Pianoforte*, Op. 200 (Vienna: Diabelli, 1829)). BAILLOT's *L'art du violon* (1835) cites RODOLPHE KREUTZER as a rare successful practitioner of the improvised violin prelude. The great piano virtuosi (e.g. Clara Schumann and Liszt) preluded in their solo recitals and recommended doing so to their pupils. Sound recordings survive of improvised preludes and modulating transitions by Josef Hofmann (1938) and Dinu Lipatti (1957).

FURTHER READING

C. Hogwood, 'The practice of preluding', in B. Brauchli, A. Galazzo and J. Wardman (eds.), *De Clavicordio XI: Proceedings of the Eleventh International Clavichord Symposium*, Magnano, 2013 (Magnano: Musica Antica a Magnano, 2014), 109–36.

B. Mather and D. Lasocki, *The Art of Preluding 1700–1830, for Flutists, Oboists, Clarinettists and Other Performers* (New York: McGinnis and Marx, 1984).

D. Rowland, *Early Keyboard Instruments: A Practical Guide* (Cambridge University Press, 2001), 69–72.

TERENCE CHARLSTON

Programmes (annotated for concerts) Early eighteenth-century printed concert programmes and opera/oratorio libretti included similar types of basic information for the AUDIENCE – identification (not always very specific in concert handbills) of the work(s) to be heard, the names of the author(s) and of the principal performers, and the texts of vocal items – but they probably played a modest role in the formation of TASTE, which was fostered more by the later expansion of the daily press and specialist PERIODICALS such as the *Allgemeine musikalische Zeitung* (1799–1848).

By the end of the century public concerts were an important element in the musical life of Western Europe and after 1815 were rapidly professionalised as the repertoire shifted towards large-scale and complex instrumental music. Such extended, untexted works were challenging for listeners: influenced by BAILLOT and FÉTIS, John Ella (1802–88) established the Musical Union (London, 1845) as a select club that sought to cultivate the appreciation of the masterpieces of Classical chamber music. One crucial innovation was the provision of programme notes, combining information about each work, a partisan appreciation of its qualities, and guidance about how to listen to it (with appropriate musical examples). The notes were admired by visiting musicians (MENDELSSOHN and BERLIOZ included) and gradually imitated elsewhere in Europe and North America, most notably in the programmes of the Saturday Concerts at the Crystal Palace in South London under the guidance of George Grove, contributing to that building's ethos of providing popular education.

For professional events the simple handbill was thus gradually (but never wholly) replaced by much more substantial programme booklets, sometimes organised so that concert subscribers might have their programmes bound to form a reference resource: in Germany an ancillary form of publication, the *Konzertführer* (concert guide), short essays (with musical examples) on individual works in book form (exemplified by the examples by Herman Kretschmar) became popular and complemented or acted as a surrogate for programme notes.

The consumerisation of concert life encouraged new developments: advertising space in programmes was sold and by the end of the century the emergence of major artists' agencies (e.g. Hermann Wolff in Berlin) encouraged the growth of a celebrity culture that was reflected in the inclusion of artists' biographies and photographs in programmes. In the twentieth century, technology (sound recordings and film, radio and television and digital media) transformed access to and information about the canon, but also contributed to a decline in the domestic cultivation of musical skills. Except for new or unfamiliar music, the role of programme notes as a listener's guide was reduced – costly musical examples were dropped after WWII – and their original educational role was to some extent taken over by pre-concert talks, the booklets themselves becoming more substantially a marketing tool.

Surviving programmes are a rich source of cultural and social history that have formed the basis of important new insights about the history of concert giving: numerous projects concerned with their preservation, cataloguing, digitisation and data mining are designed to ensure they can be more comprehensively exploited for research (*see* www.concertprogrammes.org.uk/links/).

FURTHER READING

C. Bashford, 'Not just "G.": towards a history of the programme note', in M. Musgrave (ed.), *George Grove, Music and Victorian Culture* (Basingstoke and New York: Palgrave Macmillan, 2003), 119–42.
H.-W. Heister, 'Konzertwesen', *MGG* (Sach), v (1996), 686–710.
C. Richter, 'Musikpädagogischer Literatur', *MGG* (Sach), vi (1997), 1447–9.
www.concertprogrammes.org.uk/links/.

PAUL BANKS

Programmes (of concerts) At the earliest public concerts in late seventeenth-century London, there was little sense of co-ordinated planning, as ROGER NORTH bemoaned:

> the whole was without designe or order; for one master brings a consort with fuges, another shows his guifts in a solo upon the violin, another sings, and then a famous lutinist comes foreward, and in this manner changes followed each other, with a full cessation of the musick between every one, and a ga[b]ble and bustle while they changed places.
>
> (ROGER NORTH'S THE MUSICALL GRAMMARIAN 1728, ED.
> M. CHAN AND J. C. KASSLER (CAMBRIDGE UNIVERSITY PRESS, 1990), 266)

In the following decades a more rational succession emerged, but variety – whether of genre, performer, length or intensity – remained the essential characteristic of eighteenth-century programmes. At first this typically involved a loose alternation of songs and instrumental pieces (overtures, concerti grossi and solos); but the development of the symphony as a dedicated concert genre encouraged a more uniform structure. Thus at HAYDN's concerts of the 1790s the two halves were framed by overtures and symphonies, between which Italian arias alternated with concertos and quartets; the whole amounting to ten or twelve items. Elsewhere, there were variations in accordance with local TASTE and social function: thus arias might be replaced by vernacular songs or by ensembles and choruses, as at the Parisian *Concert Spirituel*, where *grands motets* by Lalande or newer sacred pieces were interwoven with the latest symphonies and concertos. Focus on a soloist naturally shifted the balance, so that at a Viennese concert in 1783 MOZART dispersed two piano concertos, a fugue and two sets of variations between orchestral and vocal pieces. Quite exceptional, therefore, were the early programmes of London's ACADEMY OF ANCIENT MUSIC, consisting purely of motets and madrigals in line with the society's particular ethos: otherwise, alternation of instrumental and vocal items was very much the norm.

Across the nineteenth century various factors broke down the general principle of miscellaneity, resulting in specialist concert types (symphony, chamber, choral) as well as a conspicuous fracture between 'high art' and popular programmes. Central here was what William Weber (2008, 86–7, 97–8) has identified as a musical idealism that derived its authority from the classics and demanded serious attentive listening based on prior learning. Complete symphonies and string quartets were elevated in more coherently planned programmes, while a high-minded reaction against the virtuoso practices of the 1830s and 1840s relegated opera arias and instrumental fantasies to lower genres.

A canonic repertoire solidified around Haydn, Mozart and BEETHOVEN, within which similarly orientated new music (as well as Handel and BACH) could gradually be absorbed. The transformation appeared at its most extreme at dedicated chamber music societies. Already in the 1820s the concerts of Beethoven's violinist Ignaz Schuppanzigh were restricted to a handful of instrumental masterworks, while two decades later London's similarly ascetic Musical Union added the idea of analytical programme notes, symbolising its intellectual and pedagogical aims. The pattern of three major works, presented without intervening distractions, was confirmed by the Berlin concerts of the Joachim Quartet, who assuredly sealed the canon as far as BRAHMS.

A similar trend towards more concentrated programming is perceptible at orchestral concerts, not least because the focus on long symphonies afforded them greater weight. At first the old structure was maintained, as at the marathon concert in 1808 when Beethoven's Fifth and Sixth Symphonies were premiered. But already the previous year the second half of a Leipzig Gewandhaus programme was given over to the 'Eroica', and by the end of the century leading symphony ORCHESTRAS restricted their programmes to four or five works; the overture–concerto–symphony format was sometimes preferred, though this was by no means a universal formula. Beethoven symphonies remained the touchstone against which new entrants were constantly compared, but it was the symphonic poem that best reflected shifting aesthetic tastes, sometimes directly responding to local national agendas. Meanwhile choral music became largely the preserve of amateur societies, whether festival oratorio CHOIRS or French Orphéons; and contemporary Italian arias disappeared from orchestral programmes altogether, although the WAGNER craze of the late nineteenth century returned opera into the concert hall in the guise of extended extracts.

Solo concerts underwent a similar transformation. Around the middle of the nineteenth century, miscellanies of opera selections, popular songs and instrumental fantasies began to give way to recognisable recital programmes. Critical here was Clara Schumann's emphasis on canonic PIANO repertoire (and appropriately serious new music), as interpretation became a defining feature of both performance and reception. Recital programmes might still interleave vocal and instrumental items, but there was a discernible trend towards coherent programming in the Beethoven sonata cycles of CHARLES HALLÉ and in solo recitals presenting a chronological survey of the repertoire (extending to whole series in the case of Anton Rubinstein).

Piano and VIOLIN recitals around 1900 often reached back into the late Baroque, and vocal recitals even earlier; but a much more explicit revivalism was embodied in the specialist 'early music' concerts of HENRI CASADESUS and ARNOLD DOLMETSCH, using reproductions of original instruments. A parallel development was the notion of the 'new music' concert, associated with a musical and political modernism reaching back to Liszt and Wagner, but becoming markedly more prominent in the 1900s, often with a nationalist agenda. More practically, in an increasingly over-crowded calendar performers were looking beyond the core Austro-German repertoire in search of a refreshingly distinctive variety. The challenge of creating a convincing and attractive programme had shifted from the miscellaneous medley to repertoire choices across the entire spectrum of musical history.

Turning outside the mainstream, the move towards classical programming in the 1830s was counterbalanced by the populist promenade concerts of PHILIPPE MUSARD in Paris, soon imitated by Louis Jullien in London, their purely instrumental programmes mixing quadrilles and cornet solos with the occasional lighter symphony movement. The Vienna concerts of Johann Strauss and his family were similarly focused around waltzes and potpourris, and in 1892 Sousa's band began to take military marches around the world. By contrast, London's ballad concerts consisted almost entirely of the latest sheet-music songs, while an evening at a music hall or Parisian café-concert was to venture into the unashamedly popular world of the variety show. Nor should we forget the quite different directions taken by amateur music making, whether in the convivial *Liedertafel* clubs of Germany or the brass bands of north England collieries.

It would be a mistake to exaggerate the divisions – arrangements of Wagner overtures were a common feature of the band repertory – but the gulf between 'art music' and the popular sphere had undoubtedly widened. It is true that the eighteenth century had recognised a split between expensive international culture and the vernacular; but around the middle of the nineteenth century the high-art idealism of the symphony concert and the string quartet society explicitly parted company with an alternative culture of popular concert programming, a legacy persisting to this day.

Reproducing early programmes comes with inevitable economic and practical obstacles, not least their length. The mixing of instrumental and vocal items was, however, a constant feature of concert programmes in the eighteenth century and well beyond. Towards the end of the nineteenth century examples of the 'complete' mentality surface in Beethoven piano sonata cycles and the like, with all the associated educational and moral overtones. The twentieth century has further encouraged this attitude, especially through the recording and publishing industries. But such obsessive programming was very much the exception, associated with particular individuals: variety of genre and musical idiom were much more prevalent guiding principles.

FURTHER READING

W. Weber, *The Great Transformation of Musical Taste: Concert Programming from Haydn to Brahms* (Cambridge University Press, 2008).

SIMON McVEIGH

Pronunciation (of vocal music) *see* RECONSTRUCTED PRONUNCIATION

Proportions (The system of) rhythmic proportions can be defined as the mathematically regulated transition between various divisions of a pre-given time unit. To a greater or lesser extent, this practice was integrated into most manifestations of measured music. In today's basic musical training, for example, triplets (i.e. 3:2 proportion) are presented as unremarkable components of musical language. Such relationships attracted greater interest within many earlier styles.

PETRUS DE CRUCE offers the first surviving examples of intense application of the phenomenon. In his late thirteenth-century theoretical system – and the handful of motets which use it – the durations of regular beats are shown by dots acting as barlines. The beat they outlined was to be divided into equal parts according to however many notes appeared between each pair of dots (up to – and including – seven). In the fourteenth century, the *Ars nova* motets often included a structural proportion, with the pre-given CHANT on which such works were constructed being repeated more quickly at the end of the piece. The contemporaneous Italian style and notational system included inbuilt 4:3 relationships between some of its time signatures, as well as an expectation for at least one change of time in each song. These changes, though, tended to occur between structural sections and in all voices simultaneously.

The greatest flowering of proportional behaviour is to be found in the francophone style straddling a few decades either side of the year 1400 and now referred to as the *Ars subtilior*. Indeed, it is often considered one of its main characteristics. Here we find pieces revolving around constant proportional friction between their voices, or songs such as 'Je prens d'amour', which integrate the proportions 4:1, 3:2, 5:2, 7:2, 2:3, 4:3, 5:3, 7:3, 10:3, 3:4, 9:6 and 9:8 within its melodies. Importantly, such complications are presented within a performative rather than a theoretical or educational context, and the rhythmical friction is heightened further by the use of complicated rhythms and syncopations within the proportional sections. Such behaviour led musicologists to remark that the degree of complexity achieved was not paralleled until the twentieth century, and that modern musicians lack the training to execute some of the surviving compositions. Theoretical writings of the time often try to keep up with practice rather than leading this preoccupation, and hint that 4:3 proportion was taken for granted for any trained musician (like triplets today).

Interest in proportions did not die out with the change of musical fashions. Later on in the fifteenth century we find more proportional behaviour in the motet and mass repertories, where their use tended more towards structuralism and decorativeness. Generally speaking, from this point on internal rhythms in proportional sections tend to be simpler, and such sections tend to occur over a background of a stronger and more stable sense of 'beat'. Nevertheless, interest in complex proportions regularly flared up in subsequent periods, notably in the late fifteenth-century theoretical and instrumental works of JOHANNES TINCTORIS (suggesting, perhaps, that they retained a central role in improvised practice) and the very late sixteenth-century works of John Baldwyn.

FURTHER READING

W. Apel, *The Notation of Polyphonic Music, 900–1600*, 5th edn (Cambridge, MA: The Medieval Academy of America, 1961).
A. M. Busse Berger, *Mensuration and Proportion Signs: Origins and Evolution* (Oxford University Press, 1993).

URI SMILANSKY

Prudenzani (Prodenzani), Simone de' (b. Prodo, nr Orvieto; *fl.* 1387–c1440) Italian poet.

Prudenzani wrote a cycle of eighteen *novelle* in ballata form (*Liber Solatii*, 'The Book of Sollazzo'), and a novel in four parts consisting of 176 sonnets (*Liber Saporecti*, or 'Il Saporetto', c1415). Sollazzo, the protagonist of the first two parts of *Il Saporetto*, is a fictitious character representing the ideal courtier: skilled musician, storyteller and a master in the arts of fencing and hunting. Invited by his father to entertain his court, Sollazzo plays musical works by famous composers of the time, such as Francesco Landini, Jaquemin de Senleches and Johannes Ciconia, named in the text; a number of DANCE forms (*chiarintana, striana, trotto, rigoletto*) and musical instruments (*piferi, viuole, liuti, orgheni*) are also mentioned. Thus, Prudenzani's *Saporetto* offers a rare glimpse into musical TASTES and practices in central Italy in the early fifteenth century.

FURTHER READING

J. Nádas, 'A cautious reading of Simone Prodenzani's *Il Saporetto*', *Recercare*, 10 (1998), 23–38.
S. de' Prodenzani, *Sollazzo e Saporetto*, ed. L. M. Reale (Perugia: Fabrizio Fabbri Editore, 1998).

STEFANO MENGOZZI

Q

Quantz, Joseph Joachim (b. Oberscheden, Hanover, 30 January 1697; d. Potsdam, 12 July 1773) German flautist and writer.

During his early training, Quantz played various stringed instruments, the OBOE and the TRUMPET, joining the Dresden town band in March 1716. He then studied counterpoint in Vienna with Zelenka and by 1718 had been appointed oboist in the Chapel of Augustus II, Elector of Saxony and King of Poland. By 1719 he had turned to the transverse FLUTE, studying briefly with the French flautist Buffardin and then further in France, Italy and England. Having met Prince Frederick in Berlin in 1728, he returned to the Prussian court twice a year to teach him the flute. After Frederick's accession as King of Prussia in 1740, Quantz dedicated himself to the supervision of his private evening concerts, for which he composed new works and at which he critiqued the King's playing. He also published numerous compositions including trio sonatas, concertos and numerous solo sonatas which tend to explore the emerging *galant* style. In 1752 appeared his celebrated TREATISE, *Versuch einer Anweisung die Flöte traversiere zu spielen* (Berlin: Voss).

Quantz's *Versuch* was more thorough than any previous instrumental treatise and has continued to be highly influential. It addresses many issues of general musicianship, including aspects of performance, from ORNAMENTATION and accompaniment to the evaluation of compositions and musicians themselves. As an essay it moves far beyond an introduction to the flute, offering a comprehensive programme of studies that is equally applicable to other instruments and singers. The treatise comprises three interrelated essays that deal with educating the soloist, the art of accompaniment and different styles and forms, but begins with an introduction explaining what is required of one who wishes to be a musician, including talent, a fiery but sympathetic nature, imagination, discernment, a good ear, eye and MEMORY, and a receptive mind, as well as of course a love for music. He also describes in detail various physical attributes that will suit a person to one instrument or another; for example, saying that a flautist's teeth must be neither too long nor too short.

In the first essay, Quantz sets out the history, structure and mechanics of the flute before writing about the basic forms of ornamentation and giving recommendations for individual practice; he finally expounds more advanced areas of performance, in particular characterisation, and gives detailed instructions for how to approach CADENZAS, the embellishment of Adagios and melodic variation. The second essay consists of a series of explanations of the duties of various accompanists, from the leader through each specific string player to the keyboard player, and then to accompanists in general. He also gives advice on the size, proportions and arrangement of ensembles. In the third essay Quantz discusses, compares and evaluates the different forms and styles of composition and performance in Germany, Italy and France. Throughout the treatise Quantz provides fine detail over a wide range of musical themes including ornamentation, phrasing, intensity, accents, cadenzas, stage deportment and techniques for performing DANCE movements. He provides a useful table that relates various TEMPOS to the speed of the pulse. Quantz distinguishes two principal types of ornamentation: essential graces (*wesentliche Manieren*), such as appoggiaturas and turns largely reflecting French influence, and arbitrary variation (*willkürliche Veränderungen*), reflecting the Italian practice of embellishing a melody, applicable only to certain types of Adagio movements.

Quantz takes care to embrace AESTHETICS but includes surprisingly little about technical details. Only fifty or so pages of the original 334 are solely applicable to playing the flute. He heavily criticises many of his contemporaries for various instances of bad TASTE and poor musicianship. He also discusses the amount of powder used on gentlemen's wigs and advises its use as an aid to prevent the flute slipping from the chin. Such considerations may be historically interesting but are not so relevant to informing PERFORMANCE PRACTICE, whereas of course his passages on technique remain a valuable resource.

Quantz's treatise contains the only contemporary account of the modifications made to the flute in the late seventeenth century, when referring to his own contributions to flute construction. He offers advice on the management of ORCHESTRAS, with discussions on tempos, seating plans and BOWING. His survey of the perceived characteristics of NATIONAL IDIOMS focuses on the notion of 'good taste' as an easily malleable tool of aesthetic judgement, here wielded to promote a proto-nationalist agenda where 'German' music was a synthesis of the best of the French and Italian styles.

FURTHER READING

M. ten Brink, *Der Flötenbauer Johann Joachim Quantz* (Hildesheim: Olms, 1995).
E. E. Helm, *Music at the Court of Frederick the Great* (Norman: University of Oklahoma Press, 1960).
A. Powell, *The Flute* (New Haven, CT and London: Yale University Press, 2002).

ASHLEY SOLOMON

Quarenghi, Guglielmo (b. Casalmaggiore, 22 October 1826; d. Milan, 3 February 1882) Italian cellist and composer.

Quarenghi studied with Vincenzo Merighi (who also taught Alfredo Piatti and Alexander Pezze) at the Milan Conservatory from 1839 to 1842, becoming principal cellist at La Scala in 1850 and a professor at the Conservatory in 1851. He became *maestro di cappella* at Milan Cathedral in 1879, but resigned due to ill health in 1881. Quarenghi composed much CELLO music, including 6 *Capricci* for solo cello (Milan: Ricordi, 1864), and several original pieces and TRANSCRIPTIONS. He also composed chamber music, church music and an opera.

His most important work is his *Metodo di violoncello* (Milan: Editoria Musicale, 1876), the largest cello method published in the nineteenth century, comprising five parts totalling some 550 pages. A preface traces the history of stringed instruments (referring to non-European folk instruments), and then lists the principal Italian luthiers. There are many references to much older sources and practices, such as obsolete clefs and chordal accompaniment of recitative on the cello. The latter is necessary, he explains, in order to perform older repertoire (he gives a long example from Rossini); Quarenghi also makes it clear that *secco* recitative is accompanied by cello, bass and keyboard. Quarenghi emphasises virtuoso technique, with complex BOWINGS and elaborate exercises in double stopping across the range of the instrument (including artificial HARMONICS, which are also found in GRÜTZMACHER's Op. 38 studies). Part 3 of the *Metodo* focuses on compositional techniques, mainly concerning harmony and counterpoint. Part 4 consists of twelve short pieces for cello and piano; part 5, of five substantial and increasingly virtuosic cello duets. Quarenghi does not refer to a tail-pin, which was only gradually coming into use at this time. He does not discuss VIBRATO, although he specifically indicates it in his *Capriccio* for cello and piano; PORTAMENTO is covered unusually with exercises that demonstrate its use over intervals as large as two octaves, combined with very fast scales.

FURTHER READING

G. Kennaway, *Playing the Cello, 1780–1930* (Farnham: Ashgate, 2014).

GEORGE KENNAWAY

Quatuor Mosaïques String quartet comprising violinists Erich Höbarth and Andrea Bischof, violist Anita Mitterer and cellist Christophe Coin.

These four performers first became acquainted as members of NIKOLAUS HARNONCOURT'S CONCENTUS MUSICUS WIEN and later of Coin's own Ensemble Mosaïques. After this latter group was dissolved in 1985, Coin invited its appropriate string-section principals to form the Quatuor Mosaïques. Despite their period-style label, these players have deliberately eschewed an unattainable ideal of 'authenticity' and used period instruments rather as a means for approaching the music afresh, consistently seeking to ensure that their performances retain close links with the European quartet tradition. Central to that tradition, and nurtured through Höbart's previous association with the Végh Quartet, has been their main interpretative goal of revealing in their performances the music's inner spiritual wealth. They have achieved this through their commendable technique and perceptive musical insights, especially evident in their performances of works by the Viennese Classical composers.

The Quartet performs regularly in the world's renowned festivals and concert halls, has toured extensively in Europe, the USA, Australia and Japan, and has collaborated with many international artists, including pianists András Schiff and Patrick Cohen, clarinettists Wolfgang Meyer and Sabine Meyer, oboist Peter Westermann and cellists Miklós Perényi and Raphael Pidoux. Its extensive discography includes works by HAYDN, MOZART, Arriaga, Boccherini, Jadin, BEETHOVEN, Schubert and MENDELSSOHN as well as more recent composers (works by Debussy, BARTÓK and WEBERN increasingly form part of its concert fare), and its recordings of the Viennese Classical repertory have received the prestigious *Diapason d'or*, the *Choc du Monde de la Musique* and two Gramophone Awards. Critics have praised the ensemble's lucid clarity, unique timbral palette, impeccable blend, wide expressive range, unaffected musicianship, variety of characterisation and instinctive rapport, all of which are consistently allied to a profound understanding of its repertory.

ROBIN STOWELL

Raguenet, François (b. Rouen? 1660; d. 1722) French writer on music.

Both medic and *abbé* (with an income from the Catholic church), Raguenet pursued a polymath life, writing a history of Cromwell as well as TREATISES on theology. As tutor to Cardinal Bouillon's nephews, he accompanied the diplomat to Rome in 1697. On his return to Paris he published a book on Rome's monuments and, anonymously, *Paralèle* [sic] *des italiens et des françois en ce qui regarde la musique et les opéras* (Paris: J. Moreau, 1702).

Raguenet's *Paralèle* is significant as an early contribution to musical AESTHETICS. He holds Italian music to be varied, bold and vivid; harmonic adventure, use of dissonance, interesting part writing and accompaniments are identified to support this view. In contrast, he suggests rule-bound French styles are likely to sound dull and insipid. He laments a lack of worthy successors to LULLY, but asserts the superiority of librettos and recitative in French opera, and the finesse of French violinists. Meanwhile Italian composers held to be first-rate are enumerated from successive generations (including Giacomo Carissimi, Francesco Bassani, Alessandro Scarlatti and Tomaso Albinoni). Italian TASTE for the dramatic is depicted by a particularly colourful account of ARCANGELO CORELLI's performing countenance, eyes rolling with the furies projected by his music.

VIÉVILLE published a reaction to the *Paralèle*, and Raguenet promptly issued a defence. This exchange set up what became known as 'The Great Querelle', a discourse between supporters of French and Italian style which continued through much of the eighteenth century. Noël-Antoine Pluche emphasised Enlightenment ideals of art and music conveying significant thoughts. Between Voltaire's support for Lully and JEAN-JACQUES ROUSSEAU's desire for change, a compromise combining the strength of French opera's poetry with Italian music was suggested by Jean le Rond d'Alembert. Despite being accused of incorporating barbarous Italianisms, RAMEAU became a champion of classicists opposing comic *buffa* in the 'Guerre des Bouffons'.

FURTHER READING

M. Cyr, *Style and Performance for Bowed String Instruments in French Baroque Music* (Farnham: Ashgate, 2012).

E. Fubini, *Music and Culture in Eighteenth-Century Europe: A Source Book*, trans. and ed. B. J. Blackburn (University of Chicago Press, 1994).

SIMON BAINES

Raison, André (b. before 1650; d. Paris, 1719) French organist and composer.

In a tax account concerning keyboard players in 1695, Raison was described as one of the highest-ranking organists in Paris. From 1666 he was organist of the royal abbey of St Geneviève and later held the post of organist at the college and convent of the Jacobins de St Jacques.

Raison's most important work was his *Livre d'orgue contenant cinq messes* (1688) in which the twenty-one ORGAN pieces in each of the five masses could also serve for three settings of the Magnificat (fifteen in total), and the five keys of the masses could be adapted to all eight church modes. The collection was the most significant publication following the organ books by Nivers (1665, 1667, 1675) and Lebègue (1676, c1678, c1685). Raison's *Second livre d'orgue* is less significant, but contains a cantus firmus setting and fugue on *Da pacem*, a prelude, fugues, an *Allemande grave* and some *noëls*.

The extensive preface to Raison's 1688 *livre* not only contains an important table of ORNAMENTS, registration instructions and advice on the '*mouvement et l'air*' of all the pieces, but includes the following advice: 'It is important to observe the time signature of the piece one is playing and to consider if it has some similarity to a *sarabande, gigue, gavotte, bourrée, canaris, passacaille* and *chaconne, mouvement de forgeron* etc., so that you give the same character that you would on the HARPSICHORD – except that it is necessary to set a slightly slower TEMPO because of the sanctity of the place' (Raison, *Livre d'orgue*, Preface ('Au Lecteur'), D [*sic*]). Analysis of all the pieces reveals an encyclopedia of different styles intended to refresh the traditional organ genres of *plein jeu, fugue, duo, récit, trio* and *grand jeu*, with a wider range of secular DANCES than was included in the books by NIVERS and Lebègue.

FURTHER READING

W. Apel, *The History of Keyboard Music to 1700*, trans. and rev. H. Tischler (Bloomington, IN and London: Indiana University Press, 1972).
F. Douglass, *The Language of the French Classical Organ* (New Haven, CT and London: Yale University Press, 1969, rev. 1995).
D. Ponsford, *French Organ Music in the Reign of Louis XIV* (Cambridge University Press, 2011).

DAVID PONSFORD

Rameau, Jean-Philippe (b. Dijon, bap. 25 September 1683; d. Paris, 12 September 1764) French composer and theorist.

Through his theoretical writings (see Jacoby (ed.), 1967–72), teaching and theatrical works, Rameau emerged as one of the most influential figures in French musical history. His interest in musical theories fascinated him throughout his life, those on harmony exerting a profound influence on modern pedagogy. This includes the now familiar concept of chord inversions and root movements – whether present or implied – which produce recognisable harmonic patterns through dominant/tonic chord progressions. Rameau was an aspirant to the *Académie des sciences*; much of his writing is couched in extremely erudite language (reminiscent of MERSENNE), for he was anxious that music should be regarded as being as much a science as an art.

For the modern performer the most useful information is contained in the very lengthy *Code de musique pratique ou Méthodes pour apprendre la musique* (1760; vol. 5 in Jacobi's EDITION), which ranges over advice on accompaniment (with or without FIGURED BASS, and including treatment of cadences) and modulations and NOTATION. The final volume of Jacobi's set includes Rameau's polemical writings defending his views and attacking those who disagreed with them. Like FRANÇOIS COUPERIN, he offers instruction on playing the HARPSICHORD, taking pains to describe the correct hand position: 'The fingers must be regarded as little springs attached to a shaft by pivots which give them complete freedom, from which it follows that the hand itself must be – so to speak – dead (*mort*) and the wrist as supple as possible so that the fingers moving independently can gain strength, lightness and overall equality' (*Code de musique pratique*, chapter 2). Rameau also provides a list of ORNAMENTS (*agréments*) to be employed in his harpsichord pieces. In the second chapter of the same book he discusses how to develop the voice (along the same lines as TOSI and others) and describes vocal ornamentation.

The complete modern edition of Rameau's musical compositions is still in progress, earlier attempts from 1877 having foundered. Unlike the earlier editions, the present one (from 1991, ed. S. Bouissou) aims to present Rameau's complete musical works in an authoritative way for performers and scholars. The subsequent revision of his stage works for modern performance is essential because, of the twenty-five extant works from his thirty titles, few, if any, were edited to the standards expected nowadays. As well as his operas and ballet scores, there are also seven extant secular cantatas (which may be regarded as 'apprentice-pieces' for his operas), some shorter works (airs and canons) and his suites for solo harpsichord and for instrumental ensemble. The first of these, his *Pièces de clavecin* (1706), includes a list of ornaments that make an interesting comparison with those published ten years later by François Couperin.

FURTHER READING

J.-P. Rameau, *The Complete Theoretical Writings of Jean-Philippe Rameau*, ed. E. Jacobi, 6 vols. (Wisconsin: American Institute of Musicology, 1967–72).
G. Sadler, *The Rameau Compendium* (Woodbridge: Boydell Press, 2014).

DAVID TUNLEY

Ramm, Andrea von (b. Pärnu, 8 September 1928; d. Munich, 30 November 1999) Estonian mezzo-soprano.

Andrea von Ramm was an influential singer, scholar, instrumentalist and teacher in the field of early music. Her repertoire encompassed music from early Medieval to late Baroque. Together with the lutenist THOMAS BINKLEY and Sterling Jones (vielle), she founded the STUDIO DER FRÜHEN MUSIK in Cologne. The group transferred to Munich in 1960, and expanded to include, successively, Nigel Rogers, Willard Cobb and Richard Levitt, frequently collaborating with the SCHOLA CANTORUM BASILIENSIS. Her work survives chiefly in the substantial output of recordings from this group. Besides SINGING, she also played the portative ORGAN, HARP and several woodwind instruments. Her dark-toned voice was not particularly powerful and had nothing lyrical about it, but it was remarkably expressive, with an exceptional precision of ARTICULATION and clarity in the enunciation of words. Her concern with language was reflected in her later work with recitation and phonetics.

FURTHER READING

D. Fallows and S. Morent, 'Andrea von Ramm' [obituary], *EMc*, 28/2 (2000), 325–6.
Ramm, A. von, 'Style in early music singing', *EMc*, 8/1 (1980), 17–20.
'Wandel der Wahrheit: Mittelalter-Aufführungen: Eine persönliche Meinung und Bestandsaufnahme', in D. Redepenning and A. Kreutziger-Herr (eds.), *Mittelalter-Sehnsucht? Texte des interdisziplinären Symposions zur musikalischen Mittelalterrezeption an der Universität Heidelberg*, April 1998 (Kiel: Vauk, 2000), 281–8.

PATRICIA HOWARD

Ramos de Pareja (Ramis de Pareia), Bartolomé (Bartolomeo) (b. Baeza, Andalucía, c1440; d. ?Rome, after 1490) Spanish theorist active primarily in Bologna (Italy) between c1470 and 1485.

In his only extant musical TREATISE (*Musica practica*, Bologna, 1482), Ramos proposed several theoretical innovations that directly affected the performance of instrumental and polyphonic music. His new method for tuning the keyboard was by far the most consequential one. Breaking with a timeless musical tradition, Ramos advocated a tuning system that pinned the major and minor thirds to the ratios of 5:4 and 6:5, rather than to the Pythagorean ratios of 81:64 and 32:27, thus introducing 'just INTONATION' in writing for the first time. Ramos's second proposal aimed at reforming the method of sight SINGING based on the *ut-la* syllables, first introduced by GUIDO D'AREZZO in the eleventh century. His goal was to formulate an alternative method based on the principle of octave equivalence, rather than on the major sixth, so that it would eliminate – or at least greatly reduce – the cumbersome 'mutations' from one set of syllables to the next. Although Ramos's new method, based on the syllables *psal-li-tur per vo-ces i-stas*, failed to establish itself in the world of musical practice, it may have inspired later, more successful sight-singing methods such as 'bocedization' and the 'Lancashire'. A section of the treatise is devoted to mensuration. Ramos was a proponent of the 'equal breve' approach to changes in mensuration, as he argued that the value of the breve should remain unchanged when transitioning from perfect to imperfect (effecting a change from triple to duple metre) and vice versa. Other theorists, such as JOHANNES TINCTORIS and FRANCHINUS GAFFURIUS, favoured the 'equal minim' interpretation (Busse Berger, 103). Finally, Ramos – again distancing himself from other theorists of his time – argued that the tritone was no more dissonant than the diminished fifth.

FURTHER READING

B. J. Blackburn, E. E. Lowinsky and C. Miller (eds.), *A Correspondence of Renaissance Musicians* (Oxford: Clarendon Press, 1991), 74–100, *passim*.
A. M. Busse Berger, *Mensuration and Proportion Signs: Origins and Evolution* (Oxford: Clarendon Press, 1993), *passim*.
B. Ramis de Pareia, *Musica practica*, ed. and trans. C. Miller (Neuhausen-Stuttgart: American Institute of Musicology, 1993), 11–38.

STEFANO MENGOZZI

Rattle, Sir Simon (b. Liverpool, 19 January 1955) British CONDUCTOR.
Rattle held assistant posts with several British ORCHESTRAS before becoming principal conductor of the City of Birmingham Symphony Orchestra

(CBSO) in 1979. With the CBSO he established a name for himself as one of the UK's brightest young conductors, known for his dynamic performances, adventurous repertoire choices and galvanising presence. He was knighted in 1994. After making numerous guest appearances with many of the world's leading orchestras, he became chief conductor and artistic director of the Berlin Philharmonic Orchestra (BPO) in 2002. In 2015 it was announced that he would take up the post of chief conductor of the London Symphony Orchestra in 2017.

Although always curious and open-minded in his programming, Rattle had not worked with period instruments before the ORCHESTRA OF THE AGE OF ENLIGHTENMENT (OAE), one year into its existence, invited him to conduct a performance of W. A. MOZART's *Idomeneo* at London's South Bank Centre in 1987. The success of that concert led to numerous return appearances, as well as productions at Glyndebourne Festival Opera of Mozart's *Le nozze di Figaro* (1989), *Così fan tutte* (1991), *Don Giovanni* (1994) and *Idomeneo* (2003) and BEETHOVEN's *Fidelio* (2001), all with the OAE. In 1992 the orchestra, which does not have music directors, named him as one of their principal guest conductors. He has also conducted the OAE in a staging of RAMEAU's *Les Boréades* at the 1999 Salzburg Festival and in WAGNER's *Das Rheingold* as part of the BBC Proms' concert *Ring*-cycle in 2004. He remains one of the orchestra's principal artists.

Rattle's approach to period instruments, realised almost entirely through his relationship with the OAE, is not primarily ideological but rather based on a TASTE for the sounds they make and for the way their players work. His experience of period style has, however, carried into his work with modern orchestras, for instance in the BPO's staged performances of J. S. BACH's *St Matthew Passion* in 2010.

FURTHER READING

A. Hartwig, *Rattle at the Door: Sir Simon Rattle and the Berlin Philharmonic 2002 to 2008* (Berlin: Evrei, 2009).
N. Kenyon, *Simon Rattle: The Making of a Conductor* (London: Faber & Faber, 1987).
  Simon Rattle: From Birmingham to Berlin (London: Faber & Faber, 2001).

LINDSAY KEMP

Reconstructed pronunciation Pronunciation does not change at a constant rate or in a fully linear fashion. Each language has its own trajectory, driven by social and linguistic influences. Furthermore, in the past even more than today, regional and class-based varieties of a language abounded. Consequently, there are significant challenges in reconstructing pronunciation accurately for compositions anchored to particular places, dates and/or performers. We have, of course, no recordings of speech or SINGING before the late nineteenth century, and reconstruction relies on indirect information.

For English, the Great Vowel Shift (c1400–1620), which considerably altered the long vowels, sparked contemporary attention to the changing relationship between spelling and speech. In addition to literary sources demonstrating the opportunities for rhymes and puns, we have rich information from many linguistic commentators, known as orthoepists, who either calmly described or vociferously berated the ways in which English pronunciation was changing. Some even proposed new alphabets, giving us, in effect, phonetic spellings, albeit not always accurate ones. With the exception of John Hart's *An Orthographie* (London: William Seres, 1569), which describes the physical movements for making the sounds associated with his phonetic spelling, it is difficult to know what the written symbols on the page sounded like. Compare a music score where one can see the relationship between the note pitches, but has no clef indicating the location of A on the stave, or knowledge of its Hz value.

French also changed considerably its consonant and vowel pronunciation, though a little earlier than English. Like English, French spelling did not keep pace, so that the text in an original score can include letters that were by then silent, and other misleading spellings. Reconstructions of German and Italian are less challenging in terms of historical change, but demand attention to regional standards, because of the many small kingdoms and states that existed at that time.

A further consideration is that singers moving from place to place would have brought their pronunciation with them, creating temporary microcosms of variation. It would have been most noticeable – and indeed possibly contentious – in relation to Latin. Because Latin had no native speakers by then, it tended to be pronounced like an extension of a user's own language. Generally, English Latin vowels changed in tandem with English, leaving it sounding very different from French, Dutch, German, Italian or Spanish Latin – all also contrasting with each other. The sound of some consonants, e.g. 'soft' <g> and <c>, also differed in local Latins. As today, singers from different places would have a strong sense that their Latin was the correct one.

Reconstructed pronunciation can be a mixed blessing for performers, with practical and technical challenges counterbalancing the intrinsic value of the endeavour. First, one cannot be truly 'authentic' by reconstructing pronunciation. The original performance achieved two things at the same time: a particular soundscape that must now be reconstructed; and an ease and immediacy for singers and AUDIENCE that resulted from using and hearing the sounds with which they were most familiar. Reconstructed pronunciation achieves the first at the expense of the second. Listeners will not easily understand the words, losing access to the meaning of the text. Singers can find themselves too anxious about the form to focus on interpretation as much as they would like.

Second, singers modify vowels according to where they fall in their vocal range. As with modern foreign languages, they must learn what modifications can be made to a sound without crossing the boundary into another. In practice, there can be tensions between the desire to be accurate to the reconstruction and the technical challenges of singing healthily and effectively (see Wray, 1999).

Third, a concert of early vocal music may feature works by several composers from different countries, regions and dates, in Latin as well as the local language. To sing or speak any language convincingly, the brain needs to settle into the inherent phonological palette of sounds; switching between pronunciations may disturb this process. In all these regards, then, restored pronunciation can inhibit the generation of a fully engaged holistic interpretation of the music.

All of that said, reconstructed pronunciation offers a compelling addition to HISTORICALLY INFORMED PERFORMANCE. It is the final piece in the performance jigsaw, removing an anachronism and giving both performer and hearer a closer approximation of what the composer envisaged, including vowel colour, the coincidence of consonants, and the sounds associated with different PITCHES. Although it requires specialist support from literary historians or historical linguists, it is an element of early music performance without which much is lost.

FURTHER READING

A. Wray, 'English pronunciation c1500–1700', in J. Morehen (ed.), *English Choral Practice c1450–1625* (Cambridge University Press, 1995), 90–108.
'The sound of Latin in England before and after the Reformation', in J. Morehen (ed.), *English Choral Practice c1450–1625* (Cambridge University Press, 1995), 74–89.
'Singers on the trail of "authentic" early modern English: the puzzling case of /æ:/ and /ɛ:/', *Transactions of the Philological Society*, 97/2 (1999), 185–211.

ALISON WRAY

Recorder A woodwind instrument with a thumbhole and (usually seven) fingerholes; the chief Western member of the class of duct FLUTES.

The instrument's name is inspired by the Latin verb *recordari* (to remember) and this etymology associates the recorder's sound with remembrance or recollection, qualities that are usually communicated with the voice. In English, the first known use of the word 'recorder' to denote an instrument was in 1388, while in most European countries the word for 'flute' referred to the recorder. Historical evidence points to a plurality of recorder types at each stage of its development, though today's period players prefer to opt for the 'GANASSI' recorder for music of the sixteenth century, and Bressan or Denner copies for the eighteenth-century repertory.

In the Bate Collection of Musical Instruments, Oxford, is one of the oldest known surviving woodwind instruments in the UK – a bone double-pipe dating from the fourteenth or fifteenth century, discovered in All Souls College, reputedly in a space under a floorboard. A fourteenth-century plumwood instrument is preserved in Göttingen, and a late fourteenth-century recorder was found in the former moat of the Huis te Merwede, near Dordrecht. Sylvestro di Ganassi offers a glimpse into sixteenth-century recorder construction in his *Opera intitulata Fontegara* (Venice, 1535), which provides detailed charts of FINGERINGS and ARTICULATIONS. There are two surviving instruments from this time, both probably made by members of the BASSANO family: a G-alto recorder in boxwood in the Kunsthistoriches Museum, Vienna, and a G-alto recorder in ivory, in the Musée de la Musique, Paris.

The first depiction of a recorder made in three parts appears in BARTOLOMEO BISMANTOVA's *Compendio musicale* (Ferrara, 1677; rev. 1694), and displays a cylindrical head joint, tapered middle joint up to the fourth hole, and a much steeper taper into the foot joint. From the eighteenth century there are a number of surviving instruments, of which some are still playable. The Bate Collection includes recorders by Peter Bressan, Urquhart, and R. Wijne, while the Grosvenor Museum in Chester, and Kunsthistoriches Museum in Vienna hold instruments by Bressan that feature double holes to facilitate the playing of the lowest two semitones, as mentioned by HOTTETERRE. At this time sizes and PITCHES of recorders were far from standardised – while F and C instruments tended to prevail, there is evidence of a variety of instruments in different keys. There is also mention of a double-recorder by an Amsterdam maker Michiel Parent (1692), and some scholars have suggested that J. S. BACH's 'fiauto d'echo' (Brandenburg Concerto No. 4, 1721) refers to an instrument such as the anonymous double recorder in the Grassi Museum, Leipzig, which consists of two differently voiced recorders joined together.

ARNOLD DOLMETSCH started to make recorders from 1919, after his son Carl had the misfortune to leave a bag containing an original eighteenth-century instrument at London's Waterloo station. Although Arnold did not attempt any radical modifications to the recorder's basic construction, Carl devised a series of patented 'improvements' including an echo key and tone projector. The first plastic recorders were produced by Dolmetsch in 1946. Similar in dimensions to the original wooden instruments, their INTONATION and tone quality were reliable and their affordability facilitated their introduction into schools, changing how music was taught for generations.

Shakespeare's Hamlet famously declared that playing the recorder was as easy as lying. He suggests that one simply has to cover the holes with one's fingers and thumb, blow into the headjoint and it will offer 'most eloquent music'. In the context of the play this forms a barbed comment to Rosencrantz and Guildenstern, equating the ease of recorder playing with lying and perhaps suggesting that, since they lie with such ease, they will find mastery of the instrument no trouble at all. This forms another example of the recorder's proximity to speech and text, while also highlighting its simultaneous characteristics of simplicity and eloquence.

The first composer to specify a recorder was G. B. Riccio in his *Primo libro delle divine lodi* (1612) and *Terzo libro* (1620). A few decades later in Amsterdam, Jacob van Eyck published the largest ever collection of solo woodwind music to this day, *Der Fluyten Lusthof* (1646–9), which contains over 140 sets of variations for unaccompanied descant recorder.

Later on in the eighteenth century there is a notable lack of French instrumental music specifically written for the recorder, with the exception of ANNE DANICAN PHILIDOR's *Sonate* (1712). However, Hotteterre invites recorder players to transpose his flute compositions a minor third higher and thus render them playable on an alto recorder, and this is a practice widely embraced today. Recorder sonatas from England, Italy and Germany also emerged at this time, and the instrument was also used in theatrical settings, particularly in pastoral or supernatural scenes.

TELEMANN wrote a vast amount of music for recorder, including solo sonatas, trio sonatas, concertos and vocal music with obbligato. J. S. Bach calls for recorder(s) in nineteen of his cantatas, also scoring recorder parts in Brandenburg Concerti No. 2 in F major BWV1047 and No. 4 in G major BWV1049.

From about 1750 to the beginning of the twentieth century, compositions for recorder are extremely scarce. The first new compositions for recorder tended to be largely tonal or modal, but from the start of the 1960s a new tradition of avant-garde music written for FRANS BRÜGGEN started to emerge, including Rob du Bois's *Muziek* (1961), Louis Andriessen's *Sweet* (1964), Luciano Berio's *Gesti* (1966) and Makoto Shinohara's *Fragmente* (1968). Through developing extended techniques and creating sounds that subverted the traditional view of the instrument, the recorder took on an almost counter-cultural identity, used by indie folk singers such as Vashti Bunyan (Rainbow River, 1969), and in *Adiemus*, a new-age project by Karl Jenkins. Experimentation, particularly with live electronics, continues to develop repertoire for the instrument to the present day.

FURTHER READING

A. Baines, *The Oxford Companion to Musical Instruments* (Oxford University Press, 1992).
E. O'Kelly, *The Recorder Today* (Cambridge University Press, 1990).
J. M. Thomson and A. Rowland-Jones (eds.), *The Cambridge Companion to the Recorder* (Cambridge University Press, 1995).

ASHLEY SOLOMON

Rehearsal A wide-ranging study of rehearsal has yet to be written. Historical documentation is uneven and reveals a wide variety of practice; it consists largely of evidence from diaries, reports, memoirs and other such sources, since formal records of rehearsal patterns and procedures have rarely been considered worth retaining. Among notable exceptions, LULLY's rehearsal technique – direct and with close attention to INTONATION – was recalled long after his death by Durey de Nonville (*Histoire du théâtre royale de musique en France* (Paris, 1757)). An account of preparations for Lully's stage ballet *Le triomphe de l'amour* of 1681 details a minimum of one daily rehearsal for singers, dancers and instrumentalists over a period of five weeks. Those dancers who were amateurs of noble birth needed special rehearsal time. Within the regulation of the Paris Opéra in 1714 were incorporated protocols for CONDUCTING and rehearsing; there is an equivalent document for the *Comédie-Italienne* dating from some sixty years later.

The evidence from eighteenth-century London probably reflects extremely variable standards of discipline and accuracy; McVeigh has observed that limited rehearsal for a skilled band, well used to playing together with familiar idioms, would certainly have been sufficient. For HAYDN's *Applausus* cantata of 1768, his first major commission from beyond the confines of Eszterháza, the composer proposed at least three or four rehearsals of the whole work so as to protect his own reputation and that of the performers. On the other hand, a report from Hamburg in 1792 stated that the ORCHESTRA's players were so strong and calm that they could correctly play at sight without error, but that when reinforced to play the latest repertoire, they would be heroes to venture to perform Haydn's symphonies (let alone MOZART's) at sight. Anton Schindler remarked of BEETHOVEN's experiences in Vienna that

> All German orchestras right up to the present day have this sin in common; they are insufficiently and poorly rehearsed ... If the composer was able to get them to play the correct notes in one, or at the most two, rehearsals, he had to be

satisfied with the results. As for ... deeper nuances, Viennese orchestras lacked both the capacity and the interest.

(A. SCHINDLER, *BIOGRAPHIE VON LUDWIG VAN BEETHOVEN* (MÜNSTER, 1860), TRANS. D. W. MACARDLE AS *BEETHOVEN AS I KNEW HIM* (LONDON: FABER, 1966), 142)

For opera, the amount of rehearsal varied widely until the late nineteenth century, practices reflecting the evolving roles of players, singers, conductors, composers, directors and patrons. At the Italian courts, rehearsal timings were set by the ruler and were sometimes protracted; by the mid-seventeenth century an opera company might rehearse intensively for a maximum of three weeks. Fenlon (168) has found documentary evidence relating to MONTEVERDI's *Orfeo* (Mantua, 1707), implying that singers would learn new music by memorising the notes first and then the text. Mozart's letters suggest that in the 1770s his *opera seria* productions would be assembled in no more than a week. By the 1820s the norm was fifteen days' rehearsal for *opera seria* and ten for *buffa*, with *Il Trovatore* rehearsed from scratch and premiered in seventeen days in 1853. The perfectionist and stern disciplinarian Spontini demanded as many as eighty rehearsals for his operas, achieving legendary control over DYNAMICS and unrivalled unanimity of ensemble. WAGNER instituted production rehearsals that involved collaboration between chief musical coach, conductor and stage director. When he went to London in 1855 to work with the Philharmonic Society, he complained that too much was expected of him in too short a time. His revolution of theatrical practice followed an experience in Paris which necessitated no fewer than 164 rehearsals for *Tannhäuser* (1861). An unprecedented regime of detailed rehearsal was instituted at the first Bayreuth Festival in 1875 and was highly influential elsewhere. In the years since Wagner, custom and practice in rehearsal has continued to vary across different countries, often influenced by the preferences of individual conductors and directors.

FURTHER READING

I. Fenlon, 'Monteverdi's Mantuan *Orfeo*: some new documentation', *EMc*, 12 (1984), 163–72.
S. McVeigh, *Concert Life in London from Mozart to Haydn* (Cambridge University Press, 1993).
A. Parrott, 'Composers' intentions, performers' responsibilities', *EMc*, 41 (2013), 37–43.

COLIN LAWSON

Reicha, Antoine (b. Prague, 26 February 1770; d. Paris, 28 May 1836) Czech composer, theorist and pedagogue.

Reicha left home at the age of ten and was eventually adopted by his musician uncle Josef Reicha. They moved to Bonn in 1785, where Reicha made friends with BEETHOVEN, played FLUTE and VIOLIN in the Bonn Orchestra, and began studying composition. He eventually settled in Paris, becoming a professor at the PARIS CONSERVATOIRE in 1818.

Reicha's best-known compositions remain the twenty-four wind quintets he composed for his colleagues at the Conservatoire. He also composed numerous didactic pieces, featuring advanced techniques of variation, modulation, form and counterpoint, as well as strange hybrids, such as his *fugues phrasées* (fugues with periodic phrasing). As a theorist, Reicha hoped to create a counterpart to

RAMEAU's work on harmony with his own *Traité de mélodie* (1814). In the more wide-ranging *Traité de haute composition musicale* (1824–6), he developed a model of sonata form conceived in terms of dramatic theory.

L'Art du compositeur dramatique, Reicha's TREATISE on the composition of opera (Paris: A. Farrenc et chez l'auteur, 1883), opens a rare window onto operatic PERFORMANCE PRACTICE in early nineteenth-century Paris. The main body of this work is an exhaustive treatment of every aspect of writing operas, from the versification of libretti to the composition of recitatives, arias, duos, trios, choruses and ensembles. In the last of its six main books, Reicha reports extensively on everything that pertains to the successful staging of an opera in Paris, including the various types of REHEARSALS required. He also discusses the changing TASTES of Parisian AUDIENCES and mentions specific productions and their fates.

During his tenure at the Paris Conservatoire, Reicha ultimately gained a reputation as an innovative, even revolutionary, teacher of composition, counting BERLIOZ, Liszt and Franck among his students.

FURTHER READING

P. Hoyt, 'The concept of *développement* in the early nineteenth century', in I. Bent (ed.), *Music Theory in the Age of Romanticism* (Cambridge University Press, 1996), 141–62.

SCOTT BURNHAM

Reichardt, Johann Friedrich (b. Königsberg (now Kaliningrad), 25 November 1752; d. Giebichenstein, nr Halle, 27 June 1814) German composer and writer.

After early studies with local musicians and at Königsberg University, Reichardt toured northern Germany as a violinist and keyboard player from 1771, meeting prominent musical and literary figures and involving himself in their various cultural activities. He spent two extended periods in Berlin, where he was eventually appointed (1776) *Kapellmeister* to Frederick the Great (and, from 1786, Frederick Wilhelm II); in this role, he became an influential exponent of north German music culture, steeped in Protestantism and the Enlightenment. He composed and conducted operas and other dramatic works, but also enjoyed freedom to travel and gain commissions. He founded the Berlin *Concert Spirituel* (1783), based on the Parisian model, to promote performances of neglected music. Dismissed from the court for his subversive views (1794), he travelled in Germany and Austria and, until the invasion of Napoleon's troops (1806), lived mostly in Hamburg and Giebichenstein as a political journalist, EDITING the JOURNALS *Frankreich* and *Deutschland*, and mixing with artists and intellectuals. The devastation of his Giebichenstein estate (1807) took him briefly to Kassel as music director (1808) and then to Vienna and other centres.

Reichardt's *oeuvre* includes several operas, *Singspiele*, symphonies, concertos, chamber and keyboard music and songs. He also pioneered the *Liederspiel*, a dramatic entertainment which combined simple songs with dialogue. His critical writings were significant, not least in the development of a German national opera (*Über die deutsche comische Oper* (Hamburg, 1774)), and his various travel diaries (notably his *Briefe eines aufmerksamen Reisenden die Musik betreffend* (Frankfurt and Leipzig, 1774, 1776) and *Vertraute Briefe geschrieben auf einer Reise nach Wien und den Oesterreichischen Staaten*

(Amsterdam: Kunst- und Industrie-Comtoir, 1810) and contemporary correspondence tell us much about society, culture, political and musical life and his musical/literary associates in the places he visited. His programme notes for the Berlin *Concert Spirituel* were among the first of their genre and his work as a writer for, and editor of, the *Musikalisches Kunstmagazin* and the *Berlinische musikalische Zeitung* was groundbreaking in influencing public musical TASTE during the Enlightenment. He insisted, for example, on fidelity to the composer in performance.

Reichardt's *Ueber die Pflichten des Ripien-Violinisten* (Berlin and Leipzig: G. J. Decker, 1776) preserves the German tradition of providing instruction for the orchestral violinist or amateur. He omits many basic technical principles and concentrates on the principal requisites of the orchestral violinist, notably tone production, flexible BOWING, facility and security in finger placement, knowledge and tasteful application of ORNAMENTATION, EXPRESSION and other general musical concepts. ACCENTUATION and ARTICULATION issues such as using detached playing in faster movements and smoother playing in slow movements (unless otherwise indicated), detaching the last note under a slur (especially in equal note-pairs) with a lifted bow stroke (*Abzug*) and matching bowing styles to TEMPO words are well summarised, as is the need from composers for more detailed dynamic, phrasing and expressive markings. VIBRATO is not mentioned, confirming the generally held view that it was not practised in ensemble situations; nor, according to Reichardt, was PORTAMENTO.

Reichardt also extensively revised a fourth edition (1797) of LÖHLEIN's *Anweisung zum Violinspielen,* making various 'improvements' and adding twelve DANCES from his operas *Andromeda* and *Brenno*.

FURTHER READING

T. Drescher, '"Die Pracht, diess schöne Ensemble hat kein Orchester": Johann Friedrich Reichardt als Leiter der Berliner Hofkapelle', *BJfhM*, 17 (1994), 139–60.
J. F. Reichardt, *Autobiographische Schriften,* ed. G. Hartung (Halle (Salle): Mitteldeutscher Verlag, 2002).
W. Salmen, *Johann Friedrich Reichardt: Komponist, Schriftsteller, Kapellmeister und Verwaltungsbeamter der Goethezeit* (Freiburg and Zürich: Atlantis Verlag, 1963).

ROBIN STOWELL

Reidemeister, Peter (b. Berlin, 1942) German musicologist, flautist and administrator.

Reidemeister studied the FLUTE under Aurèle Nicolet in Berlin and joined the Berlin Philharmonic Orchestra and, later, Helmut Winschermann's Deutsche Bachsolisten. He subsequently worked as Nicolet's assistant at Freiburg's Musikhochschule and undertook extensive concert tours. In c1970 he undertook doctoral studies in fifteenth-century Burgundian chanson with Thrasybulos G. Georgiades (Munich) and Carl Dahlhaus (Berlin), graduating in 1972. He was appointed deputy director (1973–8), and eventually director (1978–2005), of the SCHOLA CANTORUM BASILIENSIS (SCB), and became highly influential in furthering that institution's reputation as a dedicated centre of excellence for early music performance and scholarship, driving change in response to developments in early music study, creativity and reception. He facilitated numerous initiatives, collaborating with the publisher Amadeus Verlag Winterthur and the German branch of Harmonia Mundi and encouraging, for example, the publication of scholarly EDITIONS and texts (e.g. as general editor of the influential *Pratica Musicale* series), the creation of the SCB-Documenta series of recordings, established (1983) to combine the SCB's various study departments and raise its public profile, and the organisation of themed conferences about performance practices, as well as promoting the institution's everyday business and development.

Reidemeister's own scholarly writings about historical performance have been greatly valued in the discipline - his *Historische Aufführungspraxis: Eine Einführung* (Darmstadt, 1980), for example, has been a much cited text - as has also his unstinting service as editor of twenty-five volumes (1979–2003) of the Schola Cantorum's *Basler Jahrbuch für historische Musikpraxis*, each volume graced by an erudite editorial introduction. Other initiatives have included facilitating the establishment of La Cetra Barockorchester (1999), a 'period' ensemble of flexible constitution formed around graduates from the SCB, serving on international committees and juries, and lecturing widely. Since stepping down from his director's role, Reidemeister has continued to produce scholarly editions of music, taught at the University of Zurich (2008), organised early music concert series and fronted, as artistic director, a trilogy of themed early music festivals in Basle.

FURTHER READING

M. Quinn, 'A lighthouse for early music', *Gramophone Early Music*, 1/4 (Spring, 2000), 50–6.

ROBIN STOWELL

Repeats There can be fewer more vexed questions than the realisation of repeats in performance. Repetition of musical material on some level is basic to the narrative continuity of Western Classical music across many periods and genres. Among the simpler paradigms are found (schematically): A–B–A (da capo forms); A–A'–B–B' (simple binary form); and A–B–A–C–A (rondo designs) to list only the most common. In all these schemes, whether relatively simple or complex (and to which may be added classical sonata-form, best understood as an extension of the binary form), continuity is determined and made sensible to the listener through patterns of departure from, and return to, recognisable melodic and harmonic features. How repeated sections are handled by the performer - whether these are indicated by repeat signs, or else occur as reprises of a theme in the course of a phrase, section or musical structure - is a crucial ontological element of the piece. Both types offer the performer 'unnotated' opportunities for creative embellishment and open up questions of performance ethics in several dimensions, including appropriateness of stylistic approach, the violation of aesthetic norms (either 'then' or 'now'), performance as a strand of reception history and performance as recorded sound. For instance, many performers take the view that they should not creatively embellish repeats on recordings, because the very nature of a recording hangs on our desire for - even fetishising of - reproducibility (always the same), a scenario different from a 'live' performance in which the spontaneity of an embellished repeat succeeds precisely because of its irreproducibility. Hard and fast solutions are not easy to come by, nor are they imposed in the representative (though necessarily selective) case studies offered below.

In performing Renaissance chansons or LUTE songs, should the performer(s) repeat strophic verses identically, or add embellishments to successive verses? Perhaps in some circumstances instrumental accompaniment should be added or varied. Such accretions would be a viable way in which the performer could establish a narrative for the song in the act of performance (as opposed to its appearance on the printed page). Some early seventeenth-century variation sets by the English Virginalists (Byrd, Bull, Farnaby and others) treat the structure of the basic melody in such a way that its first phrase (or first half) is immediately embellished before continuing with the remainder (itself subsequently embellished). Farnaby's 'Woody Cock' variations (No. 141 in the Fitzwilliam Virginal Book) and Byrd's setting of 'Fortune my Foe' (copied into several contemporary sources) are cases in point. Does this practice represent contemporary performance expectations? Do these examples serve as models of how to approach internal repeats in these composers' pavans and galliards when these are indicated merely by repeat signs? Might we more generally experiment with embellishment devices straddling generic boundaries, for example, in secular vocal genres such as the madrigal?

And what of the historical dimensions to such a practice? It is easy enough to trace a line of influence from the English Virginalists, via Bull, Phillips, Sweelinck, Schein and their successors to J. S. BACH. Is the performer of Baroque dance suites to extemporise embellished repeats within these standard binary forms? Bach's NOTATION is generally precise (as is COUPERIN's), though always to be understood within existing norms of written EXPRESSION and expectation regarding note-length, tripletisation, synchronisation and so on. How far dare the performer go in deviating from Bach's notation in repeats? His son C. P. E. BACH had no hesitation in supplying written-out embellishments in many of his sonatas for the benefit of those who could not reliably improvise their own. MOZART's practice of varying what he committed to paper in his performances is well documented (including in his own letters). By contrast, BEETHOVEN and later composers normally expected their notated scores to be followed precisely. Here, the PERFORMANCE PRACTICE of repeats was reconsidered within an emergent romantic aesthetic in which a piece of music changed conceptually into something acquiring a cultural value: a work, of which a performance was a particular instantiation. Repeats lie at the intersection of composition and performance and are a useful gauge of stylistic change. An extreme illustration: it would be unusual for a performer of Ravel's *Sonatine* to add *extempore* decorations to the exposition repeat!

And what of repeating the second section in a sonata form? Within the eighteenth century's conception of a sonata (in which flexible attitudes towards melodic sequence were compensated by relatively strict handling of tonal succession), the second section (beginning after the central double bar) was normally marked for a repeat as well as the first section. By the 1820s sonata form was increasingly encoded as a textbook structure in three sections: exposition (normally repeated), development and recapitulation (the latter two not being repeated, and sometimes followed by a majestic coda). The performer's decision whether or not to repeat both sections in a first-movement sonata form, say by HAYDN, therefore takes place within a dynamically changing historical context of *Formenlehre* in the years after 1800. It also has an effect on the scale and internal proportion of the movement, not to mention the consequences for appreciating the whole three- or four- movement work.

Embellished repeats when written out by composers (e.g. Haydn's contrasting perspectives on the main and subsidiary themes in the Adagio e cantabile of his E♭ Sonata, Hob.XVI:49) richly repay study as exemplars to performers of what might be done in situations where no notated guidance survives, such as the Andante cantabile from Mozart's C major Sonata K330 (for which only a cursory da capo indication survives in the autograph MANUSCRIPT). But what of Beethoven? He emerged from the classical world of improvisatory practice (codified for pianists by his contemporary TÜRK) and made a reputation as an improviser. Should we treat works such as his thirty-two Variations in C minor as exemplars for decorated repeats in his early sonatas (especially rondo reprises)? He scolded his pupil CZERNY's interference with the letter of his scores (specifically in a private performance of the Quintet Op. 16). Yet Czerny's entire technique (learned from Beethoven and significantly influencing nineteenth-century pianism, not least through an extraordinarily large catalogue of pedagogic material) was founded on embellishment, appropriately decorating relatively simple underlying patterns of departure and reprise. Performers require solid grounds for ignoring his practice in approaching repeat sections in nineteenth-century music.

FURTHER READING

T. Beghin, 'Delivery, delivery, delivery!', in T. Beghin and S. Goldberg (eds.), *Haydn and the Performance of Rhetoric* (University of Chicago Press, 2007), 131–71.
J. Dunsby, 'The formal repeat', *JRMA*, 112/2 (1987), 196–207.
H. MacDonald, 'To repeat or not to repeat?', *PRMA*, 111 (1984–5), 121–38.

JOHN IRVING

Replicas (of instruments) *see* COPIES OF INSTRUMENTS

Rhetoric An art much developed and practised in the ancient world, rhetoric was to exert significant influence on Western Classical music (regarding both composition and performance) from the Renaissance through to the end of the Classical era, and perhaps a little beyond. The primary goal of the orator was to use language and its delivery skilfully to arouse the passions and move the feelings and thoughts of the listener. This was done by associative means, appealing to the idealised concepts of sadness, hatred, joy, love, anger, fear and so on shared by speaker and listener; by imitating such concepts subtly through language use, the orator held sway over those whom he wished to persuade, whether artistically, or legally (for in Roman Law, rhetoric was fundamental in addressing a jury).

Ancient Greek and Roman writers such as Aristotle, Cicero and Quintilian partitioned the different elements of a speech systematically, describing the various strategies for language use in great detail, raising parallels between music and speaking in relation to the shared ability of these art forms to control the emotional responses of an AUDIENCE. Quintilian's major

TREATISE *Institutio oratoria* (c60 AD) was rediscovered in 1416 and became a fundamental text in the ever-closer union of music and rhetoric. Riding on the back of humanistic thought, rhetoric became firmly entrenched within educational curricula, whether at school or university and across Catholic–Protestant divides. Such a framework for the understanding of the communicative powers of texts naturally led to theorisations of how music might also communicate, drawing on shared rhetorical models; against this background we might set certain generic and also historical musical trends such as the rise of the madrigal and, more broadly, the *seconda pratica*. Lassus's works were particularly singled out for their striking musical rhetoric in which the expressive intentions of the text were captured in appropriate music. *Musica poetica*, as this understanding of the union of words and music was broadly known from the mid-sixteenth century, radically reformulated music's theoretical context, effectively ousting the earlier standard that had been expressed in the Medieval *quadrivium* (setting music alongside geometry, arithmetic and astronomy) according to which music and number were counterparts. Joachim Burmeister's treatise, *Musica poetica* (Rostock: Myliander, 1606) positioned the expressive linkage of rhetoric and music within a theory of musical 'figures' (*figurae*), a concept that was to reign supreme in German compositional theory until the end of the Baroque.

Within the field of classical rhetoric, as codified by Aristotle, Cicero and Quintilian, the most effective tool at the orator's disposal – allowing him effectively to bend the feelings and thoughts of his audience to his will – was the *decoratio* (figures of speech) – that sometimes subtle, sometimes grandiose embellishment of language for emotional or dramatic effect. *Decoratio* was given extensive treatment by Quintilian and this may explain the codification of literally dozens of analogically musical *figurae* (*see* FIGUREN) in treatises following on from Burmeister, including CHRISTOPH BERNHARD's manuscript *Tractatus compositionis augmentatus* (c1650); Athanasius Kircher's *Musica universalis* (Rome, 1650); JOHANN GOTTFRIED WALTHER's *Musicalisches Lexicon* (Leipzig, 1732); JOHANN ADOLPH SCHEIBE's *Der critische Musikus*; Meinrad Spiess's *Tractatus musicus compositorio-practicus* (Augsburg, 1745 – a text known to LEOPOLD MOZART); and Johann Nikolaus Forkel's *Allgemeine Geschichte der Musik* (Leipzig, 1788–1801). Such *figurae* were primarily for the instruction of composers in relation to appropriate word setting but spoke equally to performers in terms of their representation of musical emotion to an audience in an age when composers were also singers and players, often of multiple instruments including high levels of competence across different instrumental families. Unsurprisingly, *figurae* are not restricted to vocal music, but (notably in J. S. BACH) cut across vocal–instrumental boundaries, similar representational decorative shapes occurring vocally in an aria, instrumentally in an obbligato part, as well as solo keyboard music such as chorale preludes. In such treatises, a rich language of Latin and Greek terms developed, many of these taken over by direct analogy from the figures of speech listed and described so precisely by Aristotle and Quintilian, including *anadiplosis*, *anaphora*, *epistrophe*, *gradatio* and *hyperbaton* (figures built from melodic repetition, and sometimes relying on a species of associative imitation described by the ancient writers as *mimesis*); *analepsis*, *congeries*, *hyperbole* (relating to the use of specific sounds for their own sake, rather than in a purely semantic sense and including *aposiopesis*, the use of dramatic interruption or total silence – a strategy particularly recommended by Burmeister); *ellipsis, syncope, prolongatio* (relating to strategies in which the orator plays against the expectations of his audience by unexpectedly juxtaposing or eliding successive thoughts, delays the arrival of an essential point or overly extends a point for effect). Others were newly invented terms stemming from purely musical situations such as the *passus duriusculus*, a figure described by Bernhard that is most often associated with falling semitonal steps signifying weeping, sadness or fear, but also applied to unusual chromatic intervals extending outside of normal tonal boundaries; unusually wide and typically ascending melodic intervals of a minor seventh or tritone (used for similar expressive effect) were termed *saltus duriusculus*; *suspiratio*, as its name implies, referred typically to the fragmenting of a melodic line by frequent interrupting rests, normally in illustration of the text, though this too was a figure transferred to instrumental music and helpfully contextualises for performers the opening of the F minor Prelude from Book 2 of J. S. Bach's *The Well-Tempered Clavier*.

For composers of the eighteenth century, such rhetorical figures gained an aesthetic dimension in the doctrine of the Affections (AFFEKTENLEHRE), not uniquely in German lands (though the principal treatises are by German authors), and most famously captured in JOHANN MATTHESON's *Neu-eröffnete Orchester* (Hamburg, 1713) and *Der vollkommene Capellmeister* (Hamburg, 1739). Underlying the doctrine was a rational, rather than intuitive, construction of musical EXPRESSION according to which discreet emotional states (especially those found in *opera seria* libretti) were each idealised and expressed through a musical setting whose melodic, harmonic and rhythmic elements (including also aspects such as melodic range and even key choices) were strictly coordinated, these elements remaining fundamentally unchanged throughout an aria in order that its stylised *Affekt* might be represented as a unity. In achieving such a stylised musical result, composers drew substantially upon rhetorical practices as enumerated in seventeenth- and eighteenth-century writings. In instrumental performance, such stylised effects benefit significantly from the use of appropriate equipment (most usually high-quality modern COPIES of historical originals) whose mechanics and manner of use (recoverable from contemporary performance treatises) naturally tend towards a direct, rhetorical style of delivery that strongly contrasts with later performance traditions from the second quarter of the nineteenth century broadly influenced by *bel canto*.

Already by the completion of Forkel's *Allgemeine Geschichte* in 1801, rhetoric was considered an old-fashioned approach to music, something perhaps no longer applicable to *galant* and Classical musical styles that superseded that typically practised by his revered master, J. S. Bach. Partly owing to emerging new aesthetic preferences for music and the arts more generally, and partly no doubt also to the rapid institutionalisation of musical instruction in conservatoires (and latterly in universities), rhetoric as a framework of musical understanding declined significantly and quite rapidly during the nineteenth century. Chopin may have been one of the latest musicians brought up in a system where rhetorical values were still strong. Their rediscovery as a foundational channel of communication for music of the later Renaissance, the Baroque and earlier Classical repertories (especially in North American higher education institutions) may have had much to do with patterns of emigration from mainland Europe to the USA during the inter-war years of German musicologists for whom this approach still had relevance and who passed it on through their university teaching to subsequent generations of scholars. In recent studies of eighteenth-century music, rhetoric has been strongly invoked as a hermeneutic approach to particular repertoires (Irving, 1997); composers (Beghin and Goldberg, 2007); and musical linguistics and meaning (Bonds, 1991; Mirka and Agawu, 2008; Mirka, 2014), sometimes focusing more specifically on one particular branch of rhetoric known as 'topics', which deals with associative bases for the construction of meaning. Rhetoric as an investigative framework for performance is still relatively nascent; Beghin and Goldberg (2007) offer the most extensive attempt to date in relation to HAYDN.

FURTHER READING

T. Beghin and S. Goldberg (eds.), *Haydn and the Performance of Rhetoric* (University of Chicago Press, 2007).

M. E. Bonds, *Wordless Rhetoric. Musical Form and the Metaphor of the Oration* (Cambridge, MA and London: Harvard University Press, 1991).

J. Irving, *Mozart's Piano Sonatas: Contexts, Sources, Style* (Cambridge University Press, 1997).

D. Mirka (ed.), *The Oxford Handbook of Musical Topic Theory* (New York: Oxford University Press, 2014).

D. Mirka and K. Agawu (eds.), *Communication in Eighteenth-Century Music* (Cambridge University Press, 2008).

J. Tarling, *The Weapons of Rhetoric: A Guide for Musicians and Audiences* (St Albans: Corda Music, 2004).

JOHN IRVING

Rhythmic Alteration *see* RHYTHMIC INTERPRETATION

Rhythmic Interpretation One of the presuppositions behind historical performance is the necessity to realise composers' musical intentions when the only evidence is the imprecise medium of NOTATION. When that notation is the only link with a composition written several centuries ago, misunderstandings as to precise meanings are magnified, especially given the difficulties of printing music in historical times and composers' 'less than precise' (sometimes very sketchy) handwriting of MANUSCRIPTS (e.g. Handel's autographs and BEETHOVEN's sketches). In addition, rhythmic notation was sometimes subject to 'period' conventions which need to be understood by modern interpreters. A strictly accurate attitude to rhythmic notation has the potential for serious misunderstanding of composers' intentions through history.

The earliest documents concerning rhythmic alteration come from Loys Bourgeois (*Le droict chemin de musique* (Geneva: Jean Gérard, 1550)), and TOMÁS DE SANTA MARÍA (*Libro llamado arte de tañer fantasia* (Valladolid: Francisco Fernandez, 1565)), which are often cited as the earliest evidence of what became known in France as NOTES INÉGALES. However, in a broader context, rhythmic interpretation can be divided into three categories:

1 Music in which no rhythm or metre is notated, such as French *préludes non mesurés*.

2. Rhythmic notation that was subject to certain 'shorthand' and interpretative conventions, such as *notes inégales* and the assimilation of binary rhythms into ternary rhythms.
3. Genre considerations subject to wholesale rhythmic alteration, such as in Froberger's and J. S. BACH's keyboard gigues, as well as first sections of French overtures.

In addition, the extensive history of TEMPO RUBATO, first described by PIER FRANCESCO TOSI in 1723, needs mention, although rubato can be regarded as a flexibility of rhythm and tempo rather than as a notational convention or a 'shorthand' per se. However, in practice the topics overlap, and Richard Hudson's survey of rubato from Gregorian chant to contemporary music is a very valuable resource.

Absence of Rhythmic Notation

Préludes non mesurés, written in the late seventeenth and early eighteenth centuries by composers such as LOUIS COUPERIN, Lebègue, D'ANGLEBERT and Gaspard Le Roux, appear to have been composed in order to avoid the metrical and rhythmic strictures of conventional time signatures and rhythmic notation, in order to reflect more accurately the improvisatory character of the HARPSICHORD *prélude*. Hence, these preludes are written in 'white' semibreves throughout, as shown in L. Couperin's Prélude in C major (Example 28).

Throughout, the continuous 'semibreves' (white notes) have no metrical or rhythmic significance whatsoever and are placed according to their spatial position along the stave as part of an intended continuum of sound. The music needs to be understood in terms of melodic motifs, ORNAMENTS and, most of all, arpeggiated chords that are an essential idiomatic technique for playing the harpsichord. Each 'white' note can therefore be a constituent part of a chord, an ornament or a melodic motif, with each note capable of being played at various speeds, depending on musical context. The challenge for the interpreter of these pieces is therefore to create musical *mouvement* and a metrical structure within a controlled improvisatory context. The notational experiment was not long-lasting, evidently having created problems in understanding the musical text. D'Anglebert's preludes are more visually intelligible, containing a combination of 'white' semibreves for the basic notation, but incorporating 'black' quavers and semiquavers for notes which are obviously intended to be played more quickly, such as flourishes between chords, auxiliary notes between harmonic notes of chords, fast chords and notes which are part of melodic motifs. In comparison, FRANÇOIS COUPERIN's *préludes* (*L'art de toucher le clavecin*, 2/1717) look conventional with their metrical notation (*see* Example 29), but the composer's advice implies an improvisational freedom which the notation per se cannot transmit:

> A prelude is a free composition, in which the imagination gives itself up to any fancy that occurs ... It is necessary that those who have recourse to these non-improvised preludes should play them in a free, easy style, without attaching too much importance to metrical precision, unless I have expressly indicated this by the word *mesuré*.

(*L'ART DE TOUCHER LE CLAVECIN*, 60)

Example 28: Louis Couperin: Prélude in C major.

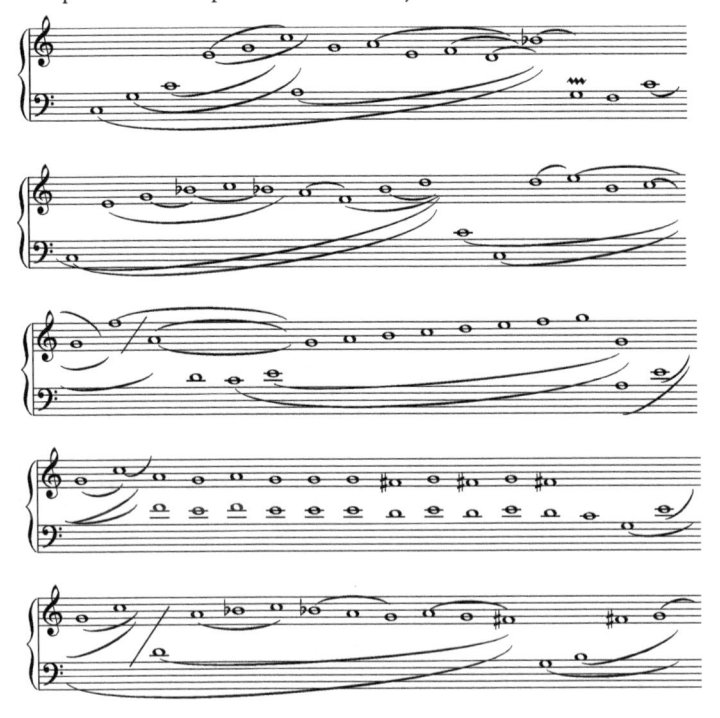

Example 29: François Couperin: Prélude (*L'art de toucher le clavecin*, 2/1717).

Although the notation of these two pieces looks completely different, the intended style of performance is not dissimilar. These *préludes* represent two different solutions to the problem of notating pieces that were conceived in an improvisatory style.

Example 30: Henry Purcell: Prelude from Suite No. 4 in A minor (1696).

Example 31: J. S. Bach: Corrente (Partita No. 1 (BWV825)), bars 1–5.

No other countries undertook such notational experiments, but it is quite possible that this French improvisatory style was adopted elsewhere. In England, Henry Purcell's Prelude from Suite No. 4 in A minor (1696), shown in Example 30, looks conventional in its notation, but makes little sense if played metrically. If one makes the paradigm shift of translating Purcell's semi*quavers* (Example 130) into semi*breves* (as in Example 28), then the unmeasured character of the Purcell prelude makes much more musical sense, given that French styles (as well as Italian) were thoroughly adopted in Restoration England.

Binary Rhythms as Shorthand for Triplets

The French convention of *notes inégales*, in which equal quavers are often performed unequally (in varying degrees on a scale from extreme short–long to extreme long–short, according to context), is discussed under its own discrete headword, but examples of notated dotted rhythms that imply ternary rhythms are common in CORELLI, Handel and particularly J. S. BACH (see Example 31).

Example 32: J. S. Bach: Organ Sonata No. 4 (BWV528), final movement, bars 14–15.

Example 33: J. S. Bach: Sonata in C minor for violin and harpsichord (BWV1017), 3rd movement, bars 9–12.

Performers will agree that the fast TEMPO of such a movement rules out any suggestion of non-synchronisation. This feature also occurs in the last movement of Bach's Organ Sonata No. 4 (BWV528), but in the same piece an alternative way of notating triplets occurs in which equal semiquavers imply triplets (Example 32).

Both equal and dotted note values may thus imply triplet rhythms, particularly at a time when alterations of rhythm courtesy of French *inégalité* were well known throughout Europe. Similar examples where notated dotted rhythms are a shorthand for triplet rhythms occur in the Gavotte from Bach's Partita No. 6 in E minor (BWV830), the Courante from French Suite No. 4 in E♭ (BWV815), Contrapunctus 13 from *The Art of Fugue* (BWV1080) and the third movement of Brandenburg Concerto No. 5 (BWV1050) amongst many others. Notated dotted rhythms that imply more sharply dotted rhythms occur in Variation 26 of Bach's *Goldberg Variations* (BWV988), where the dotted rhythms in 3/4 time synchronise with the last of the sextuplet semiquavers in 18/16 time.

The notated dotted rhythm in ratio 3:1 can therefore have a variable quality that synchronises with prevailing triplets. If this is true, then the Adagio of J. S. Bach's Sonata BWV1017 poses a conundrum with three different metrical notations occurring simultaneously throughout the movement (Example 33).

From previous arguments, both the dotted rhythms in the VIOLIN part and the equal quavers in the harpsichord LH could equate to triplets that synchronise with the harpsichord RH, as suggested by Howard Ferguson. But that entails both equal quavers and dotted rhythms being a shorthand for dotted rhythms consistently throughout the movement – a somewhat illogical position. Therefore the question needs to be addressed: 'Might Bach have intended three disparate metres simultaneously in this piece?' Subjectively, such an interpretation is effective, but the answer to this conundrum cannot be proved; both solutions are logically possible and the onus is therefore on the performers.

Genre Considerations
Overdotting in French overtures has been discussed elsewhere in this volume (*see* NOTES INÉGALES), but shortened upbeat flourishes call for comment here. An instructive example is the first movement of J. S. Bach's Overture in the French Style (BWV831). The manuscript (BWV831a in C minor, c1730) contains upbeat flourishes in semiquavers (Example 34a), whereas the published version in B minor (1735) has demisemiquavers (Example 34b).

Notwithstanding a (unlikely) change in performance practice between 1730 and 1735, it would appear that the published EDITION was more carefully notated than the manuscript version (for domestic use?), suggesting that the printed edition could be a model for similar rhythmic treatment of other (manuscript) French overtures.

Gigues written in binary metres (C or 4/4) also pose issues for the performer. Some gigues written in Froberger's *Libro Quarto* (1656) are written in common time, although one particular gigue (Partita No. 1 in E minor) also occurs in 3 time in the Bauyn MS with what we understand now as characteristic gigue rhythms. Both versions can be seen in Examples 35a and b.

Comparison between these examples has led some scholars to assume that Froberger's gigues need transliterating in performance to accord with the compound metres that we associate with 'normal' French and Italian gigues, but Siegbert Rampe (citing J. G. WALTHER) argues for the German tradition of composing gigues in common time. Certainly, there are common time gigues in the Fitzwilliam Virginal Book, but one definition of 'Jig' (apart from music for dancing) was a song or ballad of a frivolous nature, so care needs to be taken in avoiding semantic confusion. Incontrovertible proof of either performance solution concerning the Froberger gigues has yet to be presented convincingly.

Example 34: (a) and (b) J. S. Bach: Overture in the French Style (BWV831), bars 1–3.

Example 35: (a) and (b) Froberger: Gigue, Partita No. 1 in E minor ((a) Libro Quarto 1656 and (b) Bauyn MS).

Example 36: J. S. Bach: Gigue (French Suite No. 1 in D minor (BWV812)).

Further unresolved arguments concern Bach's gigues from the French Suite No. 1 in D minor (BWV812) and Partita No. 6 in E minor (BWV830) (*see* Examples 36 and 37(a) and (b)).

The number of notational alterations that are needed to convert the French Suite gigue into a compound metre is considerable, albeit possible, although one solution is to recognise that Bach was writing an example of a Frobergian gigue in common time and play the notation as written, which would be supported by J. G. Walther. Considering Partita No. 6, it is surely relevant that all five gigues in Bach's six partitas (Partita No. 2 lacks a gigue) are written in different time signatures: Partita No. 1, C with continuous triplets; No. 3, 12/8; No. 4, 9/16; No. 5, 6/8; No. 6, the proportional time signature ϕ. It is surely not

Example 37: (a) J. S. Bach: Gigue (Partita No. 6 in E minor (BWV830)); (b) J. S. Bach: Gigue (Partita No. 6 in E minor (BWV830)), translated into compound metre.

accidental that all six first movements were composed in different styles, genres and titles, suggesting an encyclopedic intention throughout the collection as a whole. In a similar challenge, Bach may well have been setting himself a metrical challenge in writing gigues in as many time signatures as possible, and adopting a proportional signature from the Renaissance for his final gigue. Certainly, proportional signatures indicated compound metres at some notational level, lending support to this gigue being intended to be played in a compound metre, as in Example 37(b).

* * *

Research into rhythmic interpretation has focused mostly on the Baroque period and with reference to J. S. Bach's music in particular, but Gwilym Beechey has drawn attention to many examples of notated dotted rhythms standing for triplet rhythms in music by MOZART, BEETHOVEN, Schubert and

Example 38: Beethoven: Sonata in E Op. 14 No. 1, Rondo, bars 1-5.

Schumann. Further, he raises the possibility that the convention also applied to certain passages in music by Chopin, BRAHMS, Wolf and Rachmaninov.

Certain exercises in LEOPOLD MOZART's *Versuch einer gründlichen Violinschule* (1756) make it clear (without explanation) that synchronisation of dotted rhythms with prevailing triplet movement was taken for granted. Further, the time signature of 2/4 implying 6/8 is evident in the last movement of Thomas Arne's keyboard Sonata No. 4 in D minor (also 1756) as well as in the first movement of C. P. E. BACH's Third Sonata in F minor (Wq. 57, 1781), where notated dotted rhythms in ratio 3:1 need integrating into triplet rhythms. Examples of the same convention can also be found in the first movements of Haydn's Sonatas Nos. 35 (Hob. XVI/43) and 36 (Hob. XVI/21), as well as in the Andante section (from bar 9) of W. A. Mozart's Prelude and Fugue in C (K394) where demisemiquavers should synchronise with the last note of the triplet semiquavers. Rhythmic synchronisation is also very probably intended in the last movement of Beethoven's Piano Sonata in E, Op. 14 No. 1 (Example 38).

The same convention probably also applies to the first movement of Beethoven's *Sonata quasi una fantasia* in C sharp minor, Op. 27 No. 2 (1801), whose title page mentions the *Clavicembalo* as well as the *Piano Forte* (possibly acknowledging earlier traditions). Unfortunately the extant autograph is incomplete and modern editions, which print the semiquaver in the repeated-note melody non-aligned with the last note of the accompanying triplets, may unwittingly be encouraging a false PERFORMANCE PRACTICE, although modern performing traditions of this movement differ. The three piano sonatas that Schubert composed in 1828 all contain similar examples where dotted rhythms need to be synchronised with accompanying triplet figures; similar examples are found in Schumann's *Humoreske*, Op. 20 and Romance in B minor, Op. 28 No. 1.

Such examples suggest that the variable rhythmic character of the standard dotted rhythm in ratio 3:1 lasted at least into the nineteenth century, and for such music a strictly forensic adherence to rhythmic notation may well be misplaced. Rather than being a notational detail, assimilation of duplet into triplet rhythms can markedly affect the character of certain pieces. Whether or not to align the dotted rhythms with the triplets in Schubert's 'Wasserflut' (*Winterreise* No. 6), shown in Example 39, is a major decision that every singer and pianist needs to consider.

Example 39: Franz Schubert: 'Wasserflut' (*Winterreise* No. 6), bars 1–4.

FURTHER READING

G. Beechey, 'Rhythmic interpretation: Mozart, Beethoven, Schubert, Schumann', *MR*, 33 (1972), 233–48.
M. Collins, 'The performance of triplets in the 17th and 18th centuries', *JAMS*, 19 (1966), 281–328.
L. Couperin, *Pièces de clavecin*, ed. D. Moroney (Monaco: L'Oiseau-lyre, 1985), Introduction.
H. Ferguson, *Keyboard Interpretation* (London: Oxford University Press, 1975).
J. J. Froberger, *New Edition of the Complete Keyboard and Organ Works. Vol. II: Libro Quarto (1656) and Libro di Capricci e Ricercati (c1658)* (Kassel: Bärenreiter, 1995), ed. S. Rampe, Preface.
R. Hudson, *Stolen Time: The History of Tempo Rubato* (Oxford: Clarendon Press, 1994).
R. McIntyre, 'On the interpretation of Bach's gigues', *MQ*, 51/3 (July 1965), 478–92.

DAVID PONSFORD

Riemann, (Karl Wilhelm Julius) Hugo (b. Gross-Mehlra, nr Sondershausen, 18 July 1849; d. Leipzig, 10 July 1919) German musicologist; one of the founders of modern musicology and the pre-eminent music scholar and teacher of his generation.

Riemann studied philosophy and musicology in Berlin and elsewhere, as well as PIANO and music theory in Leipzig. He gained his doctoral degree from the University of Göttingen with the thesis 'Ueber das musikalische Hören' ('On musical listening') in 1873, his post-doctoral qualification from Leipzig in 1878 and taught there from 1895. He was hugely influential as scholar and mentor to an entire generation of musicologists, influencing the subsequent development of the discipline. He was active throughout his career as a music theorist, historian, performer, editor, music lexicographer, critic and writer on AESTHETICS. He believed that musicology should explain 'the spiritual and expressive nature of the primitive elements of all musical experience ... to ascertain the physical properties of tones and the mechanical conditions governing their creation'. In examining the effects of tonal combinations on hearing and the imagination, the musicologist should study not only 'the simple, most basic manifestations of this tone material, but also the complex, richly differentiated formations into which it has miraculously evolved' (*Grundriss der Musikwissenschaft*, 4/1928, 8–9).

Riemann began historical research only after his theoretical system had been largely consolidated. He understood musical history as the gradual clarification of immutable laws; he regarded works primarily as milestones on a path to the full realisation of a timeless musical logic. Thus Riemann's musical theory complemented a view of history that postulated a gradual evolution of tonal consciousness culminating in the music of BEETHOVEN. It has been noted that

Riemann insisted as late as 1919 that music was still in the age of Beethoven and that although his concept of music history allowed for periods of growth, fruition and decay, he was at pains to forestall (or prevent) the arrival of this final phase. Whilst allowing for national differences, Riemann maintained a close affiliation with German music as the mainstream current of his musical logic, which was based on the principles of eighteenth- and nineteenth-century repertory.

FURTHER READING

A. Rehding (ed.), *Hugo Riemann and the Birth of Modern Musical Thought* (Cambridge University Press, 2003).
H. Riemann, *Grundriss der Musikwissenschaft* (Leipzig: Quelle & Meyer, 1908, rev. 4/1928).
M. Thiemel, *Tonale Dynamik – Theorie Musikalische Praxis und Vortragslehre seit 1800* (= Berliner Musik Studien XII) (Sinzig: Studio, 1996).

COLIN LAWSON

Rifkin, Joshua (b. New York, 22 April 1944) American musicologist, keyboard player and conductor.

During the 1960s Rifkin studied at the Juilliard School of Music, New York University, the University of Göttingen and Princeton University, and attended STOCKHAUSEN's summer courses at Darmstadt. Subsequently he taught at several universities in the USA, including Brandeis, Harvard, Yale and Boston. In 1970 he came to prominence with a very popular recording of Scott Joplin's piano rags informed by historical considerations, which resulted in TEMPI notably slower than had become the custom. It is as a BACH scholar and performer, however, that Rifkin has made the greatest impression, consequential on his research into the composer's vocal music. His argument that the choruses in J. S. BACH's church cantatas were written for ensembles of solo voices, first advanced publicly to the American Musicological Society in 1981, provoked a long-running controversy, including polemical exchanges involving supporters (such as conductor ANDREW PARROTT) and detractors (among them conductor TON KOOPMAN and musicologist Christoph Wolff) in the pages of the JOURNAL *Early Music*. Rifkin himself applied the principle on a practical level in his 1981 recording of Bach's Mass in B minor with the Bach Ensemble, a group that he had founded three years earlier. The recording (which won a Gramophone Award for choral music in 1983) proved influential, and despite continued debate the solo voice approach to Bach has since been adopted by conductors such as Parrott, Jos van Veldhoven, Paul McCreesh and JOHN BUTT. Rifkin later made several more recordings of Bach's cantatas. He has continued to be an active and influential Bach scholar, often challenging accepted theories regarding the provenance, dating and authorship of a number of the composer's works. Rifkin has also published on Josquin and Schütz, but his other musicological interests are wide-ranging and consistently applied. His lighter side is shown in his humorous Bach re-workings in the 1965 album *The Baroque Beatles Book*.

FURTHER READING

J. Butt, 'Bach recordings from 1980 to 1995: a mirror of historical performance', in D. Schulenberg (ed.), *Bach Perspectives 4* (University of Nebraska Press, 1999).

A. Parrott, *The Essential Bach Choir* (Woodbridge: Boydell Press, 2000).
J. Rifkin, 'Bach's chorus: a preliminary report', *MT*, 123 (November, 1982), 747–54.

LINDSAY KEMP

Rockstro, Richard Shepherd (b. London, 1826; d. Willesden, 1906) English flautist, teacher and instrument maker.

Rockstro's most celebrated work remains *A Treatise on the Construction, the History, and the Practice of the Flute, Including a Sketch of the Elements of Acoustics and Critical Notices of Sixty Celebrated Flute Players* (London: Rudall, Clark & Co., 1890). Earlier (c1864) he had designed the 'Rockstro model FLUTE', a cylindrical bore instrument, which was for a time manufactured by Rudall, Carte & Co. In the second part of his treatise Rockstro describes pre-Victorian instruments as 'primitive' and only 'quasi-musical' (399).

Rockstro's work was contemporaneous with that of Theobald Boehm (1794–1881), with whom he became involved in the so-called 'Boehm–Gordon' controversy of 1838; Boehm was accused of taking false credit for the invention of the ring-key flute away from Captain James Gordon and Rockstro supported this claim. Writing about this contention, flute virtuoso Leonardo De Lorenzo (1875–1962) later claimed that Rockstro's accusation against Boehm undermined the real value of his TREATISE. Rockstro's account was unnecessarily prejudiced, even referring to Boehm's 1847 cylinder flute as 'Gordon's flute'. While it seems that contemporary popular opinion on Rockstro was influenced and affected by his views on Boehm, Lorenzo may well be exaggerating the extent to which Rockstro's treatise was marred by this one opinion. What emerges clearly, however, is that Rockstro's work (and that of Captain Gordon) challenges the received notion of Boehm as a unique and isolated inventor, situating him within a diverse context of change and development in flute making. It is also interesting that, while advocating innovation in the design of the instrument, he takes pains to defend well-established ways of holding and playing it, deploring more modern approaches taken by some of his contemporaries and referring back to writers such as QUANTZ and Drouet.

FURTHER READING

L. de Lorenzo, *My Complete Story of the Flute: The Instrument, the Performer, the Music* (New York: Citadel Press, 1951).
S. J. Maclagan, *A Dictionary for the Modern Flutist* (Lanham, MD: Scarecrow Press, 2009).
A. Powell, *The Flute* (New Haven, CT and London: Yale University Press, 2002).

ASHLEY SOLOMON

Rode, (Jacques) Pierre (Joseph) (b. Bordeaux, 16 February 1774; d. Château de Bourbon, nr Damazon, 25 November 1830) French violinist and composer.

Rode studied the VIOLIN with Gaviniès's pupil André-Joseph Fauvel *l'aîné* and Viotti and made his Paris debut in 1790. After a short period in the Théâtre de Monsieur (Feydeau) Orchestra, he became violin professor at the PARIS CONSERVATOIRE (1795). He toured extensively in the Netherlands, Spain, Germany and Russia, where he served as solo violinist to the Tsar in St Petersburg (1804–8), resuming his European travels in 1811. In Vienna he premiered BEETHOVEN's Violin Sonata in G, Op. 96 (1812), composed with his playing style in mind, but his performing skills were by then in decline. He married and settled in Berlin (1814–19) but later returned to Bordeaux, composing but rarely performing.

Rode was the most finished representative of the French violin school, having absorbed Viotti's style from first hand; REICHARDT (1802) described Rode's mastery of the instrument, precise INTONATION, penetrating tone and good TASTE (*Vertraute Briefe aus Paris*, 3 vols. (Hamburg: B. G. Hoffmann, 1804), I, 389–90, 448–9). Evidently one of Rode's idiosyncrasies was his frequent use of PORTAMENTO; Reichardt criticised SPOHR for emulating the Frenchman in this respect (*Berlinische Musikzeitung*, I (1805), 95). Although his peripatetic career was not conducive to long teacher–pupil associations, Rode disseminated the French school's principles in Russia, taught Eduard Rietz and, briefly, Joseph Böhm and Charles Lafont, and influenced Spohr (and hence his disciples) and GUHR. He played an invaluable pedagogical role at the Conservatoire and collaborated with BAILLOT and KREUTZER in compiling that institution's *Méthode de violon* (1803; see KREUTZER, RODOLPHE). His twenty-four *Caprices* (c1815) balance the student's technical and artistic needs and have become a staple of violin training. His other significant compositions include thirteen violin concertos, twelve *quatuors brillants*, twenty-four violin duos, twelve études and several popular *airs variés*. His *Air varié*, Op. 12 was adopted by celebrated singers, including Angelica Catalani, Maria Malibran and Pauline Viardot, to display their coloratura.

FURTHER READING

M. F. Boyce, 'The French school of violin playing in the sphere of Viotti: technique and style', PhD dissertation, University of North Carolina, Chapel Hill (1973).

A. Pougin, *The Life and Music of Pierre Rode, Containing an Account of Rode, French Violinist* (1874), trans. and with an introduction by B. R. Schueneman (Kingsville, TX: Lyre of Orpheus Press, 1994).

B. Schwarz, *Great Masters of the Violin* (London: Robert Hale, 1984).

ROBIN STOWELL

Roeser, Valentin (b. Germany, c1735; d. Paris, probably 1782) German composer and clarinettist.

Roeser was active in Parisian musical life from the mid-1750s, largely as a teacher and composer. His significance lies primarily in his didactic works. His *Essai d'instruction à l'usage de ceux qui composent pour la clarinette et le cor* (Paris: Mercier, 1764) is the first theoretical study of the CLARINET and the earliest treatise on instrumentation, focusing on timbre and expression; and his *Gamme de la clarinette* (Paris, 1769) is the first work to include a FINGERING chart for the four-keyed clarinet. FÉTIS records (*Biographie universelle des musiciens*, 2nd edn, 8 vols. (Paris: Firmin-Didot frères, fils et cie, 1860–5), VII, 291–2) that Roeser authored similar works for BASSOON and OBOE as well as a FLUTE TREATISE.

Roeser also published anonymously (1764) an abridged and reorganised version of MARPURG's *Principes du clavecin* (1756), the French translation of the German's *Die Kunst das Clavier zu spielen* (1750), under the Couperinesque title *L'art de toucher le clavecin selon la manière perfectionnée des modernes*. He is best known for his translated version, evidently unauthorised, of LEOPOLD MOZART's *Versuch* (1756), published as *Méthode raisonnée pour apprendre à jouer du violon* (Paris: Naderman, s.d. [1770]). Divided into three main sections comprising five chapters of BOWING rules, three chapters dealing with position-work and four chapters concerning ORNAMENTATION, his EDITION incorporates numerous amendments to Mozart's original script. Much textual material is omitted, including Mozart's introduction and short history of music, and the whole is more succinct; however, the informal pedagogical approach so important to Mozart's original conception of the treatise is compromised. Roeser added twelve duos and a caprice of his own composition and he even amended some of Mozart's musical examples, adding or deleting bars or sections. With only one exception – the manner of holding the violin – Roeser's version is a faithful and accurate translation of those sections of Mozart's original which he considered particularly relevant to contemporary technique and performance.

FURTHER READING

D. Moroney, 'Couperin, Marpurg and Roeser: a Germanic Art de toucher le clavecin, or a French wahre Art?', in C. Hogwood (ed.), *The Keyboard in Baroque Europe* (Cambridge University Press, 2003), 111–32.

A. R. Rice, 'Valentin Roeser's Essay on the Clarinet (1764): background and commentary', MA dissertation, Claremont Graduate School, CA (1977).

'Clarinet fingering charts, 1732–1816', *GSJ*, 37 (1984), 16–41.

ROBIN STOWELL

Rognoni (Taeggio), Francesco (b.? Milan, second half of sixteenth century; d. *c*1626) Italian composer and writer.

Francesco Rognoni is best known for his *Selva di varii passaggi secondo l'uso moderno per cantare e suonare con ogni sorte di stromenti* (Milan, 1620), a diminution manual in the tradition of GIROLAMO DALLA CASA's *Vero modo di diminuir* and Rognoni's father Riccardo's *Passaggi per potersi essercitare nel diminuire* (Venice, 1592). The *Selva* is in two parts: the first devoted to SINGING, the second to instrumental practices. In typical late Renaissance fashion, Rognoni offers numerous ways to vary scalar passages, cadential patterns and simple intervals; in one instance he offers 225 variations on a single pattern. His ornament table includes illustrations of embellishments in early Baroque style, including the *gruppo, tremolo, esclamatione, portar la voce* and *trillo*; some of his illustrations were borrowed from CACCINI's *Nuove musiche*. Figure 12 shows one of his elaborate ORNAMENTATIONS for a simple interval, combining the repeated-note *trillo* with a Renaissance-style *passaggio*.

Part II of the *Selva* includes a description of slurring for stringed instruments, which he calls *lireggiare*, and a related technique, *lireggiare affettuoso*, in which the player 'almost leaps' with the BOW (Figure 13).

His instructions for down-bow and up-bow are accompanied by musical examples in which T (for *tirar*, 'to pull') is indicated but P (for *pontar*, 'to push') is usually only implied. His TONGUINGS for wind instruments are based on those of Dalla Casa.

The *Selva* is also an important source for the *bastarda* technique, in which the player skips from one part of an existing polyphonic composition to another, embellishing continually. The technique is usually associated with the *viola bastarda*, but Rognoni provides a complete *bastarda* part for Lassus's

Figure 12: Francesco Rognoni, *Selva de varii passaggi* (Milan, 1620), pt 1, p. 29.

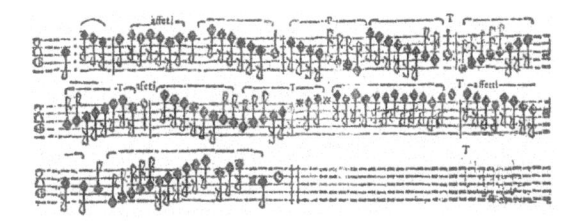

Figure 13: Francesco Rognoni, *Selva de varii passaggi* (Milan, 1620), pt 2, p. 5.

Susanne un jour, designated for *Violone Over Trombone alla Bastarda*, and another for Palestrina's *Pulcra es amica mea*, 'to sing in the *bastarda* style' (*da Cãtar all Basstarda*).

FURTHER READING

S. Carter, 'Francesco Rognoni's *Selva de varii passaggi* (1620): fresh details concerning early-Baroque vocal ornamentation', *PPR*, 2/1 (Spring 1989), 5–33.
F. Rognoni, *Selva de varii passaggi, 1620, Parte prim.*, ed. R. Erig, trans. H. Weiner (Zurich: Hug, 1987), 'Epilogue', 50–1.
Selva de varii passaggi (Milan, 1620), facsim. edn with intro. by G. Barblan (Bologna: Forni, [1970]).

STEWART CARTER

Romberg, Bernhard (b. Dinklage, Oldenburg, 13 November 1767; d. Hamburg, 13 August 1841) German cellist and composer.

Romberg was the most celebrated cellist of the early nineteenth century. He toured in Holland, Germany and France until 1799, playing for the Paris *Concert Spirituel* and ORCHESTRAS in Bonn and Hamburg. In 1796 he gave the first performance in Vienna of BEETHOVEN's Cello Sonatas, Op. 5 with the composer. Romberg taught at the PARIS CONSERVATOIRE (1801–3) and then joined the Berlin court orchestra (1805), sitting alongside JEAN-LOUIS DUPORT. He left in 1806, touring widely for the next three decades. He was a prolific composer, writing symphonies, overtures, chamber works for strings including eleven string quartets, music for operetta and ballet, and a small number of vocal works. He wrote ten cello concertos and many other smaller works for CELLO such as potpourris, fantasias and sets of variations.

In 1840 Romberg published a *Violoncellschule* simultaneously in German, French and English (Berlin: Trautwein; Paris: Lemoine; London: Cocks & Co.). This was one of the largest and most extensive cello TREATISES to date, covering a wide range of practical and aesthetic topics. There are many musical examples, mostly cello duets, and some longer compositions. Romberg held the BOW close to the frog with the right thumb placed roughly centrally, like Duport, but it was some time before this became standard practice. He was influential in the adoption of the Tourte bow, and redesigned the fingerboard with a groove below the C string to help it vibrate more freely – a striking passage in his Second Cello Concerto exploits this. Romberg was one of the earliest soloists to play from MEMORY and his concert demeanour was much admired. In some respects he was idiosyncratic. His sloped left hand, used by a small number of eighteenth-century cellists, was not recommended by any other teacher (Olive-Charlier Vaslin only used it to correct hypermobility) and it was positively discouraged by GUNN. He kept the right wrist low even when playing at the tip of the bow, and his posture was notably more 'square' than any of his contemporaries recommended. Romberg used occasional VIBRATO (mostly with the second finger) but restricted its use, describing its abuse as 'Jammer-musik'; he was more positive about PORTAMENTO, giving several exercises and examples. He deprecated staccato effects, a trait of German cellists for some decades afterwards. Romberg's concertos were deemed unfashionable by the mid-nineteenth century (a few cellists kept No. 2 in their repertoire), but were standard teaching material well into the twentieth century, in the detailed editions by GRÜTZMACHER.

FURTHER READING

G. Kennaway, *Playing the Cello, 1780–1930* (Basingstoke: Ashgate, 2014).
V. Walden, *One Hundred Years of Violoncello* (Cambridge University Press, 1998).

GEORGE KENNAWAY

Rousseau, Jean (b. Moulins, 1 October 1644; d. Paris, 1 June 1699) French VIOL player, teacher, theorist.

Rousseau dedicated his *Méthode claire, certaine, et facile pour apprendre à chanter* to Michel Lambert. According to FÉTIS, the first EDITION (now lost) appeared in 1678. Ballard published three subsequent Paris editions up to 1691, the same year in which the first of three Amsterdam editions appeared. Like other contemporaneous SINGING manuals, the *Méthode* introduces fundamentals of music and singing. Rousseau explains metres, their relation to TEMPO, and introduces some newer Italianate time signatures (3/4, 3/8, 6/4, 6/8). Coverage of *agréments* concentrates on the *cadence* (trill) and *port de voix*. Unlike BACILLY's TREATISES on singing, Rousseau based his principles of ORNAMENTATION on purely melodic considerations, irrespective of the EXPRESSION of the text.

Rousseau's *Traité de la viole* (Paris: Christophe Ballard, 1687) appeared in the same year as the viol method of another Sainte-Colombe pupil, Danoville. These joined a flurry of Parisian publications from the mid-1680s aimed at the viol, including De Machy's *Pieces de Violle* (1685) and MARAIS's *Premier livre de pièces à une et à deux violes* (1686). More thoroughly than Danoville, Rousseau introduced methods of holding the instrument, FINGERING, BOWING and interpreting ornaments. His advice for placing the left thumb opposite the middle instead of the index finger broke with earlier LUTE-based techniques (including the advice in De Machy's *avertissement*), demonstrating that by the 1680s fewer viol players came from the ranks of lutenists. Until then, many prominent French instrumentalists played both instruments, including Nicolas Hotman and Germain Pinel. French solo viol music had emphasised the instrument's self-accompanimental chordal abilities, akin to lute and keyboard repertories, but Rousseau's emphasis on melodic playing reflects the influence of vocal music and the introduction of continuo accompaniment. In his discussion of over a dozen ornaments (including *cadence/tremblement, port de voix, martellement, cheute, batement, plainte* and *coulé de doigt*), he borrows some terminology and execution from vocal music.

FURTHER READING

H. Bol, *La basse de viole du temps de Marin Marais et d'Antoine Forqueray* (Bilthoven: A. B. Creyghton, 1973).
R. A. Green, 'Annotated translation and commentary of two works of Jean Rousseau: a study of late seventeenth-century musical thought and performance practice', PhD dissertation, Indiana University (1979).
'Jean Rousseau and ornamentation in French viol music', *JVdGSA*, 14 (1977), 4–41.

STUART CHENEY

Rousseau, Jean-Jacques (b. Geneva, 28 June 1712; d. Ermenonville, nr Paris, 2 July 1778) Genevan philosopher, music theorist and composer.

Rousseau had little musical training but considered music copying his profession. A year in Venice (1743–4) advanced his knowledge of Italian opera, then rarely performed in France: he especially admired the works of Leo, Vinci and Pergolesi. He claimed Italian influence in the recitative of *Le devin du village* (1752), a comic *intermède* entirely sung, with innovative use of pantomime (performed at the Paris Opéra 1753–1829). Despite Rousseau's hostility to mixing speech with song, *Le Devin* influenced the evolution of French *opéra-comique* in style and theme.

Rousseau's significance for historical performance lies principally in his theoretical writings. He devised a moveable cipher NOTATION system (*Dissertation sur la musique moderne* (Paris: Chez G. F. Quillau *père*, 1743)). Initially ignored, it influenced later simple notation methods (Galin-Paris-Chevé, 1818). In 1748–9 Rousseau wrote about 430 articles on music (excluding instruments) for Diderot and D'Alembert's *Encyclopédie* (published 1751–65). He criticised JEAN-PHILIPPE RAMEAU (despite constant recourse to his harmonic theory) and vigorously promoted Italian over French opera. Rameau's full harmonies were a constant target, Rousseau claiming that the result was just noise. In the 'Querelle des Bouffons' (1752–4), his 'Lettre sur la musique française' (1753, written 1752), attacked LULLY's monologue 'Enfin il est en ma puissance' (*Armide*) for failing to express the emotions of Quinault's text. Following Friedrich-Melchior Grimm, Rousseau satirised CONDUCTING and instrumental standards at L'Opéra. His principle of 'unité de mélodie', stating that melody should have primacy over all other musical parameters, favoured the Italian style, championing as an ideal a clear melodic line, light harmonies and few duets and trios.

Rousseau's *Dictionnaire de musique* (Paris: Chez la veuve Duchesne, 1768, Eng. trans. 1779 or earlier) expanded his *Encyclopédie* contribution, asserting music's mimetic character: in *la musique imitative* – essentially, Italian opera – the voice moves listeners by imitating situations of intense feeling. French music, dominated by harmony and with no clear melodic line, cannot arouse feeling, Rousseau claims. Fascinated by enharmonicism, he was wary of modern systems of TEMPERAMENT, especially those of Rameau. Rousseau praised the Dresden Opera ORCHESTRA PLACEMENT under Hasse. He claimed only women and CASTRATI could sing *haute-contre* properly and favoured the tenor/*taille* (common in Italy) over the bass (France). Recitative is said to be close to speech in musical languages (Italian) but is an unsatisfactory form of song in French. The posthumous *Essai sur l'origine des langues* (completed c1761–62) gave a historical basis to Rousseau's musical preferences. Gluck's operas in French seem to have attenuated his anti-French views late in life.

FURTHER READING

D. Charlton, *Opera in the Age of Rousseau: Music, Confrontation, Realism* (Cambridge University Press, 2012).
C. Kintzler, *Poétique de l'opéra français de Corneille à Rousseau* (Paris: Minerve, 1991).
J.-J. Rousseau, *Le devin du village*, ed. J. Waeber (Paris: Classiques Garnier, forthcoming).

MICHAEL O'DEA

Royal Academy of Music (London) A Royal Academy of Music (RAM), modelled on the Schools of the Royal Academy of Arts, constituted part of the Royal Philharmonic Society's original (1813) vision. Although unrealised, it gave impetus to the scheme to establish the present RAM in 1822, under the patronage of the Earl of Westmorland. The Academy opened in March 1823 in rather ramshackle premises at Tenterden Street, off Hanover Square, and its award of a Royal Charter (1830) was more a compliment to its aristocratic supporters than testimony to its effectiveness. Although the early Academy did train some significant musicians such as William Sterndale Bennett and Arthur Sullivan, its lack of a secure financial basis made it a mainly hand-to-mouth operation. There were no formal courses of study (students generally entered in their pre-teen years, leaving as soon as they began earning an income from music) and the institution was roundly criticised in a famous 1866 Society of Arts Report. This report effectively cost the RAM its meagre £500 Treasury grant, and in 1868, with just sixty-six students, its closure was prevented only by the willingness of its staff virtually to donate their services and the determination of its principal, Sterndale Bennett. From this low point, the RAM turned itself around, increased its student numbers and by 1879 was in a strong enough position to reject the offer of £3,000 to cede its Royal Charter and relocate to South Kensington to merge with the Society of Arts-sponsored National Training School for Music. In the subsequent fund-raising campaign for the ROYAL COLLEGE OF MUSIC (RCM), the RAM mounted a spirited defence of its position while denying any necessity for the college's foundation; only with the establishment of the Associated Board of the Royal Schools of Music (1889) to hold joint music exams did friendly rivalry replace bitter resentment.

The stimulus of institutional competition with the RCM, combined with Sir Alexander Mackenzie's energising and reforming principalship, transformed the RAM. It began to attract significant capital donations and in 1911 moved to its present building on Marylebone Road. Subsequent expansion took place in the 1970s (including the Sir Jack Lyons opera theatre) and the 1990s when it acquired 1–5 York Gate and the David Josefowitz recital hall as part of the underground interconnection between these buildings. The RAM Museum

(2001) in York Gate houses the permanent collections of the RAM's history, the Strings Gallery (including important instruments by Stradivarius and Amati) and the PIANO Gallery, as well as temporary exhibitions of other materials from the RAM's extensive historical holdings. These include collections and archives from conductors such as Sir John Barbirolli, Otto Klemperer and Sir Henry Wood as well as two significant early music pioneers, DAVID MUNROW and ROBERT SPENCER. The RAM's Historical Performance Department provides wide training in the field. A major project is the BACH cantata series to perform all of J. S. Bach's sacred and secular choral works. The RAM, sponsored by the Kohn Foundation, also presents an annual Bach Prize for outstanding contribution to Bach scholarship or performance.

FURTHER READING

W. Cazalet, *The History of the Royal Academy of Music, Compiled from Authentic Sources* (London: T. Bosworth, 1854).
F. Corder, *A History of the Royal Academy of Music from 1822 to 1922* (London: F. Corder, 1922).
L. Langley, 'A place for music: John Nash, Regent Street and the Philharmonic Society of London'. www.bl.uk/eblj/2013articles/pdf/ebljarticle122013.pdf, 15, 16.
Society for the Encouragement of Arts, Manufactures and Commerce, *First Report of the Committee ... on the State of Musical Education at Home and Abroad* (London: Bell & Daldy, 1866).
D. Wright, 'The South Kensington music schools and the development of the British conservatoire in the late nineteenth century', *JRMA*, 130/2 (2005), 236–82.
The Associated Board of the Royal Schools of Music: A Social and Cultural History (Woodbridge: Boydell Press, 2013).

DAVID WRIGHT

Royal College of Music (London) The Royal College of Music (RCM) opened on 7 May 1883 following a campaign for public donations led by its first director, George Grove, editor of the eponymous dictionary, actively supported by the then Prince of Wales (the future King Edward VII). This call for subscriptions was prompted by government refusal of Treasury funding to establish the college, despite the significant growth in musical life and pressures to provide systematic training for British composers and performers. The Prince of Wales's involvement added significant status to the college, as did its royal charter (tasking the RCM to cultivate the art and teaching of music in Britain and across the Empire). The quality of its training (including orchestral and opera classes) and the musical distinction of its staff and students quickly established the RCM's national standing, its image significantly enhanced by the imposing building donated by the industrialist Samson Fox (1894).

In consequence, the RCM received several important collections of historical material (including autographs of major works) and instruments, access to which stimulated ARNOLD DOLMETSCH (a founding student) in his pioneering work on the performance of early music. A major donation of historical instruments (including a clavicytherium dated c1480, VIRGINALS by Celestini and a HARPSICHORD by Trasuntino), the autograph MANUSCRIPT of MOZART's C minor Piano Concerto K491, composer portraits and sculptures was gifted by George Donaldson in 1894. The RCM's collections, now housed in the Museum of Instruments, the Library and the Centre of Performance

History, have international significance and are an exceptional resource for historical performance training within the college.

For much of its history the RCM, in common with other British conservatoires, focused on the core Romantic and Classical repertory as played in essentially nineteenth-century performance traditions. The adherence to a received musical tradition constrained much interest in repertories of other types. It helps to explain the prominence of university- rather than conservatoire-trained British musicians in the early 'authentic' phase of the historical performance movement as well as in avant-garde repertoire. This gradually changed. Edwin Roxburgh's work with the RCM's Twentieth-Century Ensemble (established in 1968) and a strikingly talented new generation of RCM composers helped to establish the importance of modern contemporary music within the college's artistic life. As HISTORICALLY INFORMED PERFORMANCE became more of a mainstream aspect of professional musical life, creating more demand for skilled performers, so training in that specialism began to be viewed more seriously; in 1985 an 'Adviser for Early Music' was appointed to coordinate the work of the early music department. The arrival of the period clarinettist COLIN LAWSON as the RCM's director in 2005 gave fresh impetus to this area, and in 2006 Ashley Solomon became head of historical performance with the brief to expand the scale and scope of the faculty's work in the college. This has resulted in major projects including the International Festival of Viols (an annual focus on VIOL performance and its repertory, together with associated research papers), involvement with FLORILEGIUM's (the RCM's Ensemble in Association) Bolivian Baroque Project and a collaboration with *Le Centre de musique baroque de Versailles* and ROGER NORRINGTON in repertoire of Louis XIV's *24 Violons du Roi* presented on recreations of the original instruments.

FURTHER READING

H. C. Colles and J. Cruft, *The Royal College of Music: a Centenary Record 1883–1983* (London: Prince Consort Foundation, 1982).

G. Warrack, *The Royal College of Music: The First Eighty-five Years 1883–1968* (Unpublished [1968]).

N. Wilson, *The Art of Re-Enchantment* (Oxford University Press, 2014).

D. Wright, 'The South Kensington music schools and the development of the British conservatoire in the late nineteenth century', *JRMA*, 130/2 (2005), 236–82.

DAVID WRIGHT

Royal Conservatory of The Hague Founded in 1826 by King William, the Royal Conservatory is the oldest conservatoire in the Netherlands, providing higher education in music and DANCE. Its primary aim is to equip young talent with the highest artistry, technical skill and flexibility in order to be able to perform in a highly demanding and constantly changing professional environment. The Early Music Department enjoys a worldwide reputation as one of the largest and most important faculties of its kind. Opportunities for student participation in practical projects are unusually wide, ranging across chamber music, opera, symphonies and oratorios.

Following a series of student-driven protests against the conservative programming of Dutch orchestras in the late 1960s, there arose widespread commitment to the renewal of musical life in the Netherlands and to more socially engaged forms of music making; this coincided with a period of increased government spending on the arts and arts education. Composer Jan van Vlijmen became the Conservatory's director in 1971 and proved to be a strong advocate of historical performance, though his institutional reforms extended much more widely. He soon expanded the curriculum beyond RECORDER and HARPSICHORD to the Baroque VIOLIN, SIGISWALD KUIJKEN joining the faculty in 1971. It was not long before courses in Baroque CELLO, OBOE, TRUMPET and LUTE were added, followed shortly afterwards by the FORTEPIANO. HARNONCOURT was invited to direct highly influential MONTEVERDI and BACH projects, justifying Van Vlijmen's innovative policy of having students focus on a particular topic for a discrete period of time. By the mid-1970s the Dutch conservatoires had an unrivalled reputation for the study of historical performance; by 2004 between 85 per cent and 91 per cent of the early music students in Amsterdam and The Hague were international, compared to 29 per cent of the general conservatory population in the Netherlands.

In 1990 the Royal Academy of Art and the Royal Conservatoire were fused into the Academy of Fine Arts, Music and Dance, which in 2010 was renamed the University of the Arts, The Hague.

FURTHER READING

K. R. Rubinoff, 'Cracking the Dutch early music movement: the repercussions of the 1969 Notenkrakersactie', *Twentieth-Century Music*, 6/1 (2009), 3–22.

COLIN LAWSON

Rubato *see* TEMPO

S

Sachs, Curt (b. Berlin, 29 June 1881; d. New York, 5 February 1959) German-born but American-domiciled musicologist and organologist.

Sachs studied composition, history of music and history of art in Berlin, and was strongly influenced by the cultural–historical theories that were being developed by Friedrich Ratzel, Fritz Graebner and Wilhelm Schmidt. His life and activity were divided between Berlin (until 1933), Paris (1933–7) and New York. His 200+ publications played a major role in the development of the study of musical instruments, of comparative musicology and in the attempt to integrate music into a holistic history of the arts.

From 1913 his work focused specifically on the history and symbolism of musical instruments, leading to the first systematisation of this area of study. Milestones include his *Reallexikon der Musikinstrumente* (1913), his *Systematik der Musikinstrumente* (1914), which introduced the classification system still widely used today, and his *Geist und Werden der Musikinstrumente* (1929). The second part of his *oeuvre*, published during his period in the USA, moves to wider cultural issues, including a comparative history of the arts (*The Commonwealth of Art*, 1950), and *Rhythm and Tempo* (1953).

A major contribution to the popularisation of early repertory resulted from his direction of two pioneering recording projects. His *2,000 Years of Music: A Concise History of the Development of Music from the Earliest Times through the 18th Century* (Parlophone 1931–3, reissued by Decca, 1950) was the earliest attempt of its kind. It was followed by *L'anthologie sonore*, a series of 140 records, half of which were directed by Sachs, aimed at presenting an enjoyable, systematic introduction to the repertory from the ninth to the eighteenth century, performed to a high standard of scholarly accuracy on 'authentic' instruments.

As museum curator in Berlin and consultant in New York, Sachs's activities often promoted radical restoration, which, although controversial by today's standards, were instrumental in the dissemination of interest in PERFORMANCE PRACTICE on historical instruments.

FURTHER READING

E. Hertzmann, 'Curt Sachs (1881–1959): a memorial address', *JAMS*, 11/1 (1958), 1–5.
R. Meucci, 'The foundations of musical organology', in J. H. van der Meer (ed.), *In Search of Lost Sounds* (Briosco: Villa Medici Giulini, 2006), 598–617.
P. Roberge, *L'anthologie sonore*. www.medieval.org/emfaq/cds/ans99999.htm.

GABRIELE ROSSI ROGNONI

Sadie, Stanley (John) (b. Wembley, 30 October 1930; d. Cossington, Somerset, 21 March 2005) British musicologist, critic and editor.

Sadie read music at Gonville and Caius College, Cambridge, under THURSTON DART and gained a PhD in 1958. His doctoral dissertation was on eighteenth-century British chamber music. He taught at Trinity College of Music, London (1957–65) before being appointed music critic for *The Times* (1964–81) and assistant editor of *The Musical Times* (1966–8), of which he was then editor until 1986. He also reviewed for *Gramophone*. His career as a journalist and reviewer flourished alongside the growth of early music and HISTORICALLY INFORMED PERFORMANCE and many of his writings show a deep fascination with this area, as well as a keenness to view such performances equally alongside the mainstream.

From 1970 Sadie was the editor of *The New Grove Dictionary of Music and Musicians*, which appeared a decade later. He oversaw major changes to the dictionary, which more than doubled in size and included many new topics to reflect the musicological climate of the time. These new entries included Medieval music, sources, analysis, world music, ethnomusicology and popular music, each written by a specialist. Sadie also edited many related Grove publications, relating to instruments, composers and PERFORMANCE PRACTICE.

Sadie's own scholarship focused on MOZART and Handel; in 1993 he founded the Handel House Trust, to create a museum in the Mayfair house where Handel once lived. In 1987 he and Anthony Hicks co-edited the Handel Tercentenary Collection. He published many monographs, notably *Mozart: The Early Years, 1756–1781* (Oxford University Press, 2006), which was to be his final project.

FURTHER READING

D. Link and J. Nagley (eds.), *Words about Mozart: Essays in Honour of Stanley Sadie* (Woodbridge: Boydell Press, 2005).
B. Millington, 'In memoriam: Stanley Sadie', *MT*, 146/1891 (2005), 4–6.

EDWARD BREEN

Saint Lambert, Monsieur de (*fl.* early 1700s) French harpsichordist, composer and pedagogue.

Nothing is known of Saint Lambert's life other than that he was probably from Paris. He has frequently been confused with the more celebrated Michel Lambert (1610–96), singer, composer of vocal music at the court of Louis XIV, and father-in-law of LULLY. Nevertheless, Saint Lambert seems to have been a respected teacher (probably of children for the most part) and is now principally remembered for two TREATISES: *Les principes / du / clavecin / Contenant une explication exacte de tout ce qui concerne / la tablature & le clavier. / Avec des remarques nécessaires pour l'intelligence de plusieurs difficultées / de la musique. / Le tout divisé par chapitres selon l'ordre des matières*; and *Nouveau traité / de l'accompagnement / du clavecin, / de l'orgue, / et des autres instruments*. There is some uncertainty as to their publication dates, although the consensus is that they were published in Paris by Christophe Ballard in 1702 and 1707 respectively.

Rebecca Harris-Warrick considers *Les principes* 'the first true method for the harpsichord, its only predecessors being books about other keyboard instruments or large works about music and instruments with subsections on the harpsichord' (*Principles*, translator's intro, vii). Both of Saint Lambert's treatises were reprinted and continued to be known well into the eighteenth century. Although he sometimes labours the point, Saint Lambert's *Les principes* shows him to be a practical teacher who addresses both the grammar of music, particularly with respect to his proposed simplifications to the system of clefs, and the practicalities of FINGERING. His important discussion of ORNAMENTATION reproduces ornament tables from the keyboard works of composers such as CHAMBONNIÈRES, NIVERS and D'ANGLEBERT, compares their symbols and terminology, highlights their inconsistencies and includes his own views on contemporary ornamental practice. His *Nouveau traité* is equally practical and incorporates a discussion about recitative accompaniment and how to read from both FIGURED (and unfigured) BASS parts. It also addresses ornamentation in the bass and differentiates between continuo realisation on the HARPSICHORD and the ORGAN. Interestingly, Saint Lambert allows the use of parallel fifths and octaves when playing in large ensembles and shows how one can play on the offbeat in triple metre in order to maintain sonority and rhythmic vitality.

FURTHER READING

Saint Lambert, Monsieur de, *Principles of the Harpsichord by Monsieur de Saint Lambert*, trans. and ed. R. Harris-Warrick (Cambridge University Press, 1984).
A New Treatise on Accompaniment. With the Harpsichord, the Organ, and with Other Instruments / by Monsieur de Saint Lambert, trans. and ed. J. S. Powell (Bloomington, IN: Indiana University Press, 1991).

JULIAN PERKINS

Saint-Saëns, (Charles-) Camille (b. Paris, 9 October 1835; d. Algiers, 16 December 1921) French composer, pianist, organist and writer.

Saint-Saëns was a child prodigy as a pianist, performing worldwide right up to his death. He gave his first recital aged eleven in Salle Pleyel in Paris, playing J. S. BACH, MOZART and BEETHOVEN. His love of older music outweighed his admiration for his contemporaries, especially WAGNER, Franck and Debussy. His many arrangements of Bach's music for the PIANO added texture but never altered the harmonies. Lesser known are his arrangements of movements from Bach's cantatas and extracts from *Grand siècle* French operas, regularly programmed at the *Société des Concerts du Conservatoire*. Several of his compositions are indebted to Bach, particularly his Second Piano Concerto.

Saint-Saëns's EDITIONS of LULLY, Gluck and RAMEAU testify that it was with his editorial work that he made his strongest contribution to historical performance. Most important was his appointment by Durand as overall editor of the Rameau *Œuvres Complètes* in 1893. In an essay on Rameau, he summed up his attitudes to editing. From a marking in Rameau's harpsichord piece 'L'enharmonique' indicating a rigid TEMPO, he concluded that the norm in Baroque music was to be free from rigidity. His edition of Rameau's *Pièces de clavecin* leaves the Unmeasured Prelude exactly as it was printed, entirely without the anachronistic expressive markings added; for example, in the

German editions of Bach, which he considered 'puffed-up', employing 'the parasitical luxury of added markings'. His view of the status of the score was one with which present-day musicians might not disagree. Faithfulness to the original score in an edition was a principle he adhered to resolutely but he did not advocate its slavish following, prescribing flexibility of interpretation.

His writings on many musical subjects became celebrated both in English and in French, the title of his *Outspoken Essays on Music* most aptly summing up his critical approach. He qualified his ideas on historical performance in his prefaces, writings and a key series of lectures given in San Francisco in 1915. He counsels against modern tempi: very fast Allegros and very slow Adagios. He reminds the player of the inability of the HARPSICHORD to 'nuance' and of its charm and delicacy, advising against the use of 'the formidable explosions that emerge from the cases of our concert grand pianos'. He drills down to detail in these *Outspoken Essays*, protesting at slurred phrasings across the beat and ironing over ARTICULATION in Mozart to form a seamless legato: details he regards as 'disfigurement'. His knowledge is consistently based on TREATISES: the interpretation of appoggiaturas he claims is 'not a matter of taste but of erudition' (93), referring the reader to LEOPOLD MOZART.

In 'A note on Rameau', he isolates another dilemma of modern performance practice concerning the changes in choruses and its former reliance on the *haute-contre*. He writes: 'If this part is entrusted to tenors, we have, as the result, intolerable screams and cries. Sung by contraltos, all its dash and brilliancy depart and it loses whatever value it possessed' (91). He goes on to point out the differences between French low PITCH, modern pitch and Baroque pitch elsewhere. One wise statement sums up the acute perception on historical performance Saint-Saëns bequeathed to the knowledge of the early twentieth century: 'When performing ancient music as it was written, we are like a man spelling out the words of a foreign language which he is unable to pronounce' (Saint-Saëns, 1922).

FURTHER READING

K. Ellis, 'Saint-Saëns and Rameau's keyboard music', in J. Pasler (ed.), *Camille Saint-Saëns and His World* (Princeton University Press, 2012), 266–74.

S. T. Ratner: *Camille Saint-Saëns 1835–1921: A Thematic Catalogue of his Complete Works*, 2 vols. (Oxford University Press, 2002).

C. Saint-Saëns, 'A note on Rameau', in *Outspoken Essays on Music*, trans. F. Rothwell (London: Kegan Paul, Trench, Trubner, 1922), 89–96.

RICHARD LANGHAM SMITH

Santa María, Tomás de (b. Madrid; d. Ribadavia, 1570) Spanish organist, composer and theorist.

As a Dominican friar, Santa María served as organist in monasteries in Madrid and Valladolid, where his *Arte de tañer fantasia* was published in 1565; it had been started c1541 and was first licensed in 1557. The sixteenth century was the period in which practical tutors for singers and players first appeared, and Santa María's *Arte* was the first to discuss keyboard technique in detail. Its aim was to teach IMPROVISATION of imitative *fantasias* in a style reminiscent of Josquin, and is divided into two parts. The first discusses rudiments and keyboard techniques, including essential requirements for elegant performance, hand position, touch, ARTICULATION, playing runs, FINGERING, ORNAMENTS, use of the pointed or dotted style, and concluding with the playing of divisions. The second part is a systematic TREATISE on harmony, followed by procedures for constructing four-part *fantasias*. The treatise concludes with advice to beginners and tuning instructions.

Of prime importance are the chapters on keyboard technique, particularly relevant to CLAVICHORDS. The principal fingers were the third (middle) for the RH, and second and third for the LH, so that they begin and end ornaments elegantly. Santa María gave a wide range of alternative fingerings, from paired fingerings (RH: 3–4, 3–4; LH: 1–2, 1–2) to a variety of other methods involving all the fingers. On the subject of playing stylishly, there is one of the first demonstrations of playing crotchets unequally (in a minim beat): long–short and short–long, as well as rhythmic inequality over four quavers. Although he mentioned only two types of ornament, *redoubles* and *quiebros*, the range of interpretations are familiar in some of the ornaments illustrated by J. S. BACH, C. P. E. BACH and HAYDN, including the upper-note trill played before the beat, which Santa María found very stylish.

FURTHER READING

D. Poulton, 'How to play with good style by Thomas de Sancta María', *Lute Society Journal*, 12 (1970), 23–30.
A. Silbiger (ed.), *Keyboard Music before 1700* (New York and London: Routledge, 2004).

DAVID PONSFORD

Savall, Jordi (b. Igualada, Catalunya, 1 August 1941) International VIOLA DA GAMBA virtuoso and ensemble director.

Jordi Savall has achieved international recognition perhaps unique amongst performers of early music. Annual festivals in Fontfroide (Languedoc-Roussillon) and Poblet (Catalunya) and the record label AliaVox (founded 1998) are devoted solely to his and his family's performances.

Savall and his first wife, soprano Montserrat Figueras (d. 2011), met as CELLO students at Barcelona's Conservatori del Bruc. Following their studies at the SCHOLA CANTORUM BASILIENSIS, where Savall succeeded his teacher August Wenzinger as gamba professor (1973), they founded Hespèrion XX (1974). The ensemble's first recording (1976) explored *Music from Christian and Jewish Spain 1450–1550*; the next eight recordings were released within just three years. Of these, four LPs were dedicated to Spanish repertories, including a double album of *Music from the Armada Years* also featuring the ACADEMY OF ANCIENT MUSIC and Sneak's Noyse playing Elizabethan favourites. Before the establishment of Hespèrion XX, Savall had already appeared as gamba soloist in recordings with Jean-Pierre Rampal, Trevor Pinnock and others. Three Hespèrion XX recordings from the 1970s combine the viol CONSORT with an ensemble of CORNETT, SHAWM, sackbut and dulcian, changing frequently between strings and winds; fast-changing re-orchestrations became a permanent hallmark of Savall's personal style.

These ensemble recordings together with solo releases of *pièces de viole* (e.g. by Marais) consolidated Savall's worldwide position as the leading exponent of the viola da gamba and established Hespèrion XX's reputation for Spanish exoticism (a distinctive mix of strings, winds, percussion and the unique timbre of Figueras's voice) and Renaissance divisions. A certain sense of barely controlled anarchy stood out against the background of cool, well-drilled English, German and Dutch ensembles.

Returning to Barcelona, Savall and Figueras created the vocal ensemble *La Capella Reial de Catalunya* (1987) and the Baroque orchestra *Le Concert des Nations* (1989). Their choice of singers and approach to vocal scoring reflected their concept of 'Mediterranean voices' as an alternative to the *voci bianchi* of British and northern European choirs.

It was Savall's recording of the soundtrack to the film *Tous les matins du monde* (1991) that brought him to unprecedented worldwide attention. Savall seized the moment with effective image management and further expansion of his recording activities. His production of MONTEVERDI's *Orfeo* at Barcelona's Liceu theatre was filmed for the BBC in 2003. Beginning with *Don Quixote* in 2005, AliaVox released a series of CD-books of historical narratives in parallel with musical selections, a format presented also in Savall's concerts. Many of these projects combined Baroque and world music, notably Savall's vision of *Jerusalem* (2008) as a 'city of heavenly and earthly peace', which brought Arabic, Israeli, Turkish and Western musicians together with an archive recording of *El Male Rahamim* (*Hymn to the Victims of Auschwitz*, 1941). Among their many awards, Savall and Figueras were named as UNESCO Artists for Peace (2008).

ANDREW LAWRENCE-KING

Sax, Adolphe (Antoine-Joseph) (b. Dinant, 6 November 1814; d. Paris, 4 February 1894) Belgian inventor, instrument designer and musician.

The major legacy of Adolphe Sax is his invention of the saxophone, whose profound influence on musical life has been greater than even he or any of his contemporaries could have predicted, especially its contribution to the development of JAZZ. Yet his talent as an inventor was prodigious across a wide range of instruments (see Sax's *Prospectus* of 1867 reproduced in Haine and De Keyser, 152). His parents were themselves instrument designers and Sax, having studied FLUTE, CLARINET and voice at the Royal Conservatory in Brussels, patented at the age of twenty-four an improvement of the BASS CLARINET. In 1834 he made a bass clarinet with no fewer than twenty-four keys, which he exhibited the following year; in 1838 he patented a further improved model. This latter design established the now familiar upturned bell; FÉTIS ascribed Sax's success to his research on the proportions between bore size and tonehole size and location.

Sax's clarinet patents in 1840 and 1842 removed some inequalities of tone and problems of INTONATION; BERLIOZ praised his improvements and but for the arrival of the Klosé-Buffet model its usage would clearly have become widespread. Having moved to Paris in 1842, Sax exhibited in 1844 a set of valved bugles, which were a substantial improvement on existing instruments. Known as the saxhorn, the instrument influenced the development of the flugelhorn and also paved the way for the euphonium. Its valve design has been widely influential and saxhorns have been used throughout the world, not least in the British brass band movement. Among other inventions was the saxotromba family with narrower bore than the saxhorns, which was less successful in the longer term. Around 1840 Sax invented the clarinette-bourdon, an early short-lived attempt at a contrabass clarinet. He patented the saxophone in June 1846 for use in ORCHESTRAS, having some four years earlier won the approbation of Berlioz, who described him as 'skilled beyond words'. In essence, the saxophone was based on the application of a clarinet mouthpiece to the OPHICLEIDE. By the time of the patent, Sax had designed a full range of saxophones, from sopranino to contrabass. His reputation secure, Sax was appointed to the PARIS CONSERVATOIRE in 1857, where he presided over a new saxophone class from the following year. The class was suspended in 1871 and reconstituted under the virtuoso Marcel Mule only in 1942.

From the 1840s, Sax manufactured standard brass and woodwind instruments of very high quality, adding a chromatic attachment to the military bugle (1849), a 'rational' BASSOON (1840, 1851), an improved TROMBONE (1852) and a radical system of six independent valves for brass instruments (1852). Among other improved instruments were kettledrums without shells, a DOUBLE BASS tuned in fifths and an improved PIANO. The official adoption of Sax's instruments in French MILITARY MUSIC from 1845 gave him an effective monopoly, to the detriment of other well-known makers. Sax suffered attacks from his rival makers and was driven into bankruptcy in 1856 and again in 1873 as a result of various lawsuits disputing the originality of his patents. Press campaigns, poaching of his best workers, an unexplained fire at his factory and even physical attacks were part of the campaign against him. Sax himself combined enthusiasm with combativity and was clearly quarrelsome, conceited and excessively suspicious of competitors. On the other hand, his many influential supporters in Paris numbered Auber, Rossini, HABENECK, Halévy, Meyerbeer and Fétis.

Having already praised the saxophone in 1842, Berlioz expressed even greater enthusiasm in the 1860 revision of his *Grand traité d'instrumentation* (284): 'It is in short, a timbre *sui generis*, offering vague analogies with that of the cello, the clarinet and the English horn, and taking on a brassy hue, that gives it a particular tone.' Bizet's *L'Arlésienne* (1872) provides an early example of the saxophone's occasional assimilation into the ORCHESTRA. Cottrell charts the instrument's role in European and American light classical music and bands, variety acts, saxophone ensembles, virtuoso solo music and the dance band. Among prominent JAZZ soloists he cites Sidney Bechet, Coleman Hawkins, Lester Young, Charlie Parker, John Coltrane and Ornette Coleman as representing a wide variety of styles and sound-worlds. Cottrell's insightful chapter 'The saxophone as symbol and icon' (306–42) provides an excellent survey of the saxophone's colourful cultural trajectory. He observes that in the 1920s and 1930s the saxophone's close association with DANCE music and jazz, while responsible for its widespread familiarity, associated it with what the moral majority regarded as every kind of youthful dissolution. A conservative musical establishment believed that the inherent merit of the Western art tradition was threatened by the alleged worthlessness of jazz. For certain others, the welfare of society itself was threatened by the evil nature of dance music and jazz; the principal architect of such depravity was the saxophone.

FURTHER READING

S. Cottrell, *The Saxophone* (New Haven, CT and London: Yale University Press, 2012).
M. Haine and I. De Keyser, *Catalogue des instruments Sax au musée instrumental de Bruxelles* (Brussels: Museum of Musical Instruments Bulletin, 1980).
E. Mitroulia and A. Myers, 'Adolphe Sax: visionary or plagiarist?', *HBSJ*, 20 (2008), 93–141.

COLIN LAWSON

Scheibe, Johann Adolph (b. Leipzig, 5 May 1708; d. Copenhagen, 22 April 1776) German composer and writer on music.

Scheibe matriculated at Leipzig University in 1725, studying law. A testimonial that J. S. BACH wrote on his behalf in 1731 strongly suggests that he had been a pupil of Bach, who 'gladly witnessed to his knowledge in *musicis* ' and testified that 'he is thoroughly at home not only on the clavier and violin but also in composition' (in H. T. David and A. Mendel (eds.), *The Bach Reader* (New York: Norton, 1945, 2/1966), 237–52).

In 1736, after teaching in Leipzig for some years, Scheibe moved to Hamburg, where he was active as composer and music critic. In 1737 he founded the JOURNAL *Der critische Musicus*, which appeared regularly in 1737 to 1740. In 1740 he settled in Denmark, finding employment as *Kapellmeister* to the Danish court in Copenhagen; and in 1749 he moved to Sønderborg, where he opened a music school for children. He returned to Copenhagen during the 1760s, working as court composer until 1769.

In Leipzig, Scheibe was strongly influenced by the poet and philosopher J. C. Gottsched, a university teacher there and the most prominent figure in the early German Enlightenment. This partly explains his notorious attack on the music of J. S. Bach in the sixth issue of *Der critische Musicus* (14 May 1737). Bach is accused of writing in a style that was too artificial, complicated and old-fashioned. By contrast, Scheibe – like the composers he most admired, TELEMANN, Hasse and Graun – subscribed to the progressive Enlightenment principles of the imitation of nature, the guidance of reason and the leading role of melody. In a copy of Scheibe's journal recently discovered in Jena, the composers criticised – left anonymous by Scheibe – are identified by J. G. WALTHER. It is clear from this source that Bach was neither the only prominent composer taken to task nor the most sharply criticised.

FURTHER READING

G. J. Buelow, 'In defence of J. A. Scheibe against J. S. Bach', *PRMA*, 101 (1974–5), 85–100.
M. Maul, 'Johann Adolph Scheibes Bach-Kritik: Hintergründe und Schauplätze einer musikalischen Kontroverse', *BJb*, 96 (2010), 153–98.
G. Wagner, 'J. A. Scheibe – J. S. Bach: Versuch einer Bewertung', *BJb*, 68 (1982), 33–49.

RICHARD D. P. JONES

Schlick, Arnolt (b. ?Heidelberg, c1460; d. ?Heidelberg, after 1521) German organist and composer.

Heidelberg, where Schlick lived, was the central palatinate court town. In 1486 Schlick played for the election of Maximilian I to the Imperial throne, and in 1509 he was given an appointment for life. Maximilian's recognition of Schlick's esteem is illustrated by his granting him the copyright for his *Spiegel der Orgelmacher und Organisten* (Speyer, 1511) and *Tabulaturen etlicher*

Lobgesang (Mainz, 1512). No doubt his travels from south Germany to the Netherlands as a consultant and tester of ORGANS were facilitated by the emperor's wide-ranging political and geographical influence. *Spiegel der Orgelmacher* was the first work in German about organ building and organ playing. Comprising ten chapters, it deals with pipe construction, choice of registers, wind chests, bellows, PITCH, tuning, compass, composition of mixtures and suitable positions for organs. Records of Schlick's consultations and testing of organs in Haguenau (Alsace), Speyer and Neustadt an der Haardt reveal something of the extensive influence that he commanded.

Equally important were his organ compositions, published in *Tabulaturen etlicher Lobgesang* (the first book of printed German organ TABLATURES), which contained nine works for organ in three to five parts plus a number of LUTE pieces. Pieces such as the five-part *Salve regina* reveal extensive sections using imitative techniques, procedures which anticipate composers such as Sweelinck. *Maria zart*, based on a German hymn, demonstrates characteristics of the later chorale prelude, with each phrase of the melody being treated contrapuntally. Schlick's two settings of *Ascendo ad patrem meum* represent two extremes of texture: one setting for two voices, the other for ten voices arranged as four RH parts, two LH parts and four pedal parts with parallel thirds for each foot. Such a piece breaks new ground in the history of organ music, demonstrating the importance of Schlick in both organ design and composition.

FURTHER READING

W. Apel, *The History of Keyboard Music to 1700*, tr. and rev. H. Tischler (Bloomington, IN and London: Indiana University Press, 1972).
P. Williams, *The European Organ, 1450–1850* (London: Batsford, 1966).

DAVID PONSFORD

Schoenberg, Arnold (b. Vienna, 13 September 1874; d. Los Angeles, 13 July 1951) Composer and theorist, of Hungarian, Czechoslovak and, from 1941, American nationalities.

Schoenberg's theoretical views about 'creative' music composition were the basis of his approach to 'reproductive' performance. Interpretation was needed, Schoenberg claimed, 'to bridge the gap between the author's idea and the contemporary ear' (Stein, 326–30). Through rigorous analysis, based on his idea of *Grundgestalt* (basic shape), the interpreter formed a complete image of the work. Schoenberg's frequent collaborator RUDOLF KOLISCH explained (1924) that Schoenberg's manner of performing 'is guided by the mind and not by sentimentality; it is full of ideas and not of feelings ... What a triumph of fantasy over technique!' (1995, 34–5). The Society for Private Musical Performances, overseen by Schoenberg in Vienna during 1919–21, exemplified this analytical approach through 117 carefully prepared concerts, all featuring recent works, including by Debussy, Skryabin, BARTÓK, STRAVINSKY, Reger and Schoenberg himself.

Schoenberg's views were notably inconsistent, however: between his many theoretical tracts, between what he expected of theory and of performance, and between his exacting approach while in Europe and more liberal interest in the 'expression of the performer' in America. He occasionally wrote about specific performing techniques. *Style and Idea* contains many short essays on such topics as DYNAMICS, TEMPO, phrasing, VIBRATO, TRANSPOSITION, instrumentation, and NOTATIONAL meanings.

Five recordings exist of his CONDUCTING (from 1927 to 1940); he also endorsed or sanctioned several recordings by others. They show that Schoenberg did accommodate to changing performing trends; for instance, in string playing, with more regular vibrato, less frequent PORTAMENTO and more assertive BOWING. His 1940 recording of *Pierrot Lunaire* is problematic because of its highly 'spoken' realisation of SPRECHSTIMME, in contrast to his own published instructions.

FURTHER READING

R. Kolisch, 'Schoenberg as a performing artist', *Tempo*, 193 (July 1995), 34–5.
L. Stein (ed.), *Style and Idea: Selected Writings of Arnold Schoenberg* (London: Faber & Faber, 1975), Part VII: 'Performance and Notation'.

MALCOLM GILLIES

Schola Cantorum Basiliensis Founded by a group of musicians headed by Paul Sacher in 1933, Schola Cantorum Basiliensis (SCB) is dedicated to the teaching and research of early music and HISTORICALLY INFORMED PERFORMANCE. First faculty members included AUGUST WENZINGER (CELLO and VIOLA DA GAMBA), Ina Lohr (Gregorian CHANT) and Max Meili (vocal music). Sacher's vision was that 'early music should not be an elitist pursuit, open only to a guild of professionals, but part and parcel of everyday life' (Haskell, 63). In 1954 the Schola merged with two other schools to form the City of Basel Music Academy while still retaining its own identity.

Through the 1960s the core curriculum was conceived and instructed by Ina Lohr. Her musical philosophy evolved from a conglomeration of ideas stemming from the Caecilian movement and the *Singbewegung* and focused on creating communal bonds through music, particularly within church congregations. Conversely, Wenzinger, through his *Konzert-Gruppe* and Gamba ensemble, promoted the professionalisation of early music performance. This approach received additional support from Hans Martin Linde (RECORDER) when he joined the staff in 1957. Following Lohr's retirement, Sacher invited the young musicologist Wulf Arlt to restructure the Schola in 1971. Arlt's new curriculum reflected the founding maxims of the institution through practical study and research, but also anticipated future needs of the early music performer in the rapidly evolving cultural environment.

Not only did Arlt create a new programme of theoretical instruction that still serves as the foundation of the Schola today, but he also sought to bring new life into the practical side of the Schola by hiring some of the most innovative performers of early music, such as THOMAS BINKLEY'S *STUDIO DER FRÜHEN MUSIK* and JORDI SAVALL (viola da gamba).

The subsequent directors, including PETER REIDEMEISTER, Regula Rapp and Pedro Memelsdorff, built upon Arlt's framework. They developed an internationally recognised faculty while maintaining the coordinated theoretical programme, designed to give students the means both to support their interpretations through discerning dialogues with musical texts and to bridge the traditional gap between theoretical instruction and practical execution.

FURTHER READING

W. Arlt, 'Zur Idee und Geschichte eines "Lehr- und Forschungsinstituts für alte Musik" in den Jahren 1933 bis 1970', in P. Reidemeister and V. Gutman (eds.), *Alte Musik: Praxis und Reflexion* (Winterthur: Amadeus, 1983), 29–76.

H. Haskell, *The Early Music Revival: A History* (London: Thames & Hudson, 1988).

M. Kirnbauer, 'Paul Sacher und die alte Musik', in U. Mosch (ed.), *Paul Sacher: Facetten einer Musikerpersönlichkeit* (Mainz: Schott, 2006), 25–56.

EDWARD BREEN

Schröder, Jaap (b. Amsterdam, 31 December 1925) Dutch violinist, conductor and pedagogue.

A pioneer of historical performance since the early 1960s, Schröder has played period and modern instruments, recorded works from the Baroque to the twentieth century both as a soloist and as a chamber musician, directed or led various ensembles, and enjoyed a long career as a teacher in Europe and the USA.

Schröder combined VIOLIN studies in Amsterdam and Paris (École Jacques Thibaud) with musicological study at the Sorbonne and considered himself an exemplar of the French violin tradition perpetuated by his teachers Joseph Calvet and Jean Pasquier. He became concertmaster of the Hilversum Radio Chamber Orchestra (1950–63) and joined the Netherlands String Quartet (1952–69). He founded his own chamber ORCHESTRA (Concerto Amsterdam, 1960) originally to give HISTORICALLY INFORMED PERFORMANCES on modern instruments, but this ensemble transferred to period instruments from the late 1960s. Quadro Amsterdam (Schröder, FRANS BRÜGGEN, GUSTAV LEONHARDT and ANNER BYLSMA) was formed in 1962 to perform and record some of the Baroque repertory for violin, FLUTE and continuo (again using modern instruments), but Schröder explored the eighteenth- and early nineteenth-century string quartet literature on period instruments as leader of Quartetto Esterházy (1972–82), the Smithson String Quartet (1982–96) and latterly the Iceland-based Skálholt Quartet. He was concertmaster of the ACADEMY OF ANCIENT MUSIC (1980–4), co-directing (with CHRISTOPHER HOGWOOD) the Academy's acclaimed recordings of MOZART's symphonies.

Schröder has directed various European and American Baroque orchestras and been pro-active as an articulate and knowledgeable teacher, holding several prestigious appointments (including at Yale University, the Smithsonian Institution, the SCHOLA CANTORUM BASILIENSIS and the Amsterdam Conservatoire). His c150 recordings have included Baroque standards such as J. S. BACH's works for unaccompanied violin and Vivaldi's *Le quattro stagioni* as well as lesser-known solo literature by Biber, Veracini, Uccellini and others and several examples of the Classical and nineteenth-century solo and chamber ensemble repertory. Principal among his writings is his monograph *Bach's Solo Violin Works: A Performer's Guide* (New Haven, CT and London: Yale University Press, 2007), which combines practical and imaginative advice about Baroque performance practice with musical judgement informed by a wealth of knowledge and professional experience.

ROBIN STOWELL

Schubert, Johann Friedrich (b. Rudolstadt, 17 December 1769; d. Mülheim am Rhein, 13 October 1811) German violinist, composer, director and SINGING teacher.

After studying the VIOLIN and the BASSOON, Schubert rose quickly through the ranks at various opera houses in north Germany, from second violinist to concertmaster. The success of his only opera, *Die nächtliche Erscheinung*, performed at Stettin in 1798, led to his first appointment as musical director there. He subsequently directed the opera at Glogau (from 1801) and, briefly, at Ballenstedt (in 1804). As opera director, he insisted on coaching his soloists himself, and also undertook private teaching. The result of these experiences informed his influential vocal TREATISE, *Neue Singe-Schule* (1804). Finally he moved to Mülheim, where he directed the concerts and composed numerous instrumental pieces including a violin concerto (1805).

In his Preface to the *Neue Singe-Schule*, Schubert acknowledges his debt to past vocal teachers, including TOSI and J. A. HILLER, and announces his intention of bringing their advice up to date, drawing on his twelve years of theatrical experience. The *Singe-Schule* breaks new ground in the attention it gives to the falsetto register, recommending its cultivation to both tenors and sopranos; his advocacy of a smooth transition from chest register to falsetto, however, raises the possibility that (in common with other singing teachers) he confuses falsetto with head voice. His treatise is imbued with the result of his practical experience in the opera house. He pays considerable attention to PRONUNCIATION and the interpretation of the text, and deals with problems such as the division of responsibility between the singer and the director in setting the TEMPO of an aria, addressing points of potential friction between a singer and the orchestra.

Schubert illustrates the usual ORNAMENTS including trills, turns and mordents, and provides a compendium of sample CADENZAS, with and without obbligato instruments. His advice on the performance of the cadential appoggiatura in recitative is often cited; he allows the singer complete freedom to choose between the performance options shown in Example 40.

Example 40: J. F. Schubert: *Neue Singe-Schule* (1804).

FURTHER READING

J. F. Schubert, *Neue Singe-Schule, oder Gründliche und vollständige Anweisung zur Singkunst* (Leipzig: Breitkopf & Härtel, 1804).

PATRICIA HOWARD

Scordatura (descordato, discordato) (It., from *scordare*: 'to mistune'; Fr. *discordé, discordable, discordant, à cordes ravallés (avallés)*; Ger. *Umstimmung, Verstimmung, mit der gebundenen Violine*) A term applied to the VIOLIN and VIOL families, LUTES, GUITARS, some early HARPS and folk instruments and instruments with no standard tuning (e.g. the VIOLA D'AMORE (before c1750) and lyra viol) to designate a tuning in which one or more strings is pitched unconventionally.

Violin/viola *scordature* can: offer novel sonorities and alternative harmonic possibilities; extend an instrument's PITCH-range; assist in imitating other instruments; facilitate execution (e.g. PAGANINI's First Violin Concerto); make possible passages involving wide intervals, intricate string crossing or unconventional double stopping; increase tonal resonance (e.g. solo viola, MOZART's *Sinfonia Concertante* K364/320d); and enable the realisation of drone effects (e.g. the a–e′–a′–e″ 'open' tuning of North American and Scottish fiddlers).

The requisite tuning is usually specified and, with only few exceptions (e.g. Marini's Sonata, Op. 8 No. 2), the player reads the music as if the instrument were tuned normally, using open strings and first position unless otherwise indicated. Accidentals in key signatures apply only to that specific pitch. Retuning during a piece is rare.

Scordatura was popular with seventeenth-century German violinists, notably Strungk, Kindermann, Hunger, Schmelzer and Biber ('Rosary' sonatas; *Sonatae violino solo*; *Harmonia artificiosa-ariosa*). Baltzar, Mell and JOHN PLAYFORD employed it in seventeenth-century England. CORRETTE's *L'école d'Orphée* (1738) exploits four different tunings in *Pièces à cordes ravallées*; other compatriots who employed variant tunings include Le Maire, Tremais and Berthaume. BAILLOT (*L'art du violon*) provides a comprehensive survey, discussing nine tunings. Following the adoption of scordatura by Marini, Bononcini and Lonati in Italy, Vivaldi, TARTINI, Castrucci, Lolli, Barbella, CAMPAGNOLI and Nardini also used it, Barbella's and Campagnoli's tuning (a–d′–f′–c″) being used to imitate the viola d'amore. Lolli prescribed lowering the G string to d for self-accompanimental purposes, as did Nardini (*Sonate énigmatique*).

Paganini commonly raised the G string to B♭ for his 'sul G' violin pieces. Other nineteenth-century examples of scordatura include those by Mazas (*La cloche fantaisie*, Op. 76), SPOHR (some violin/harp duets) and BÉRIOT, Prume and Vieuxtemps (all of whom raised the violin G string a tone). Winter occasionally tuned the violin G string down to f; Baillot does likewise in his Fifteenth Etude but requires that string to be lowered by semitones to d in Etude No. 23. The solo violinist in SAINT-SAËNS's *Danse macabre* tunes the E string down a semitone; and STRAUSS introduces *scordature* in *Ein Heldenleben* (violin) and *Don Quixote* (lowering the solo viola's C string to B). MAHLER (Fourth Symphony), Bax (First Symphony), HINDEMITH (*Symphonische Tänze*), BARTÓK (*Contrasts*) and Scelsi (String Quartets Nos. 3 and 4, and *Xnoybis*), among others, later exploited the novel sonorities of alternative tunings. Ligeti's *Ramifications* (1968–9) for twelve solo strings, which requires half the ensemble to be tuned a quartertone higher than normal pitch, reflects twentieth-century interest in microtones.

Two *scordature* were routinely associated with the CELLO: the 'bass violin' tuning B♭′–F–c–g and the 'Italian' tuning C–G–d–g employed by Domenico Gabrielli, Marcello, Torelli and others in the late seventeenth century. Interestingly, Taglietti describes C–G–d–g as a 'discordatura' (Sonata, Op. 1 No. 2). Notable eighteenth-century examples are Klein's D–A–e–b tuning in his Op. 1

sonatas and C–G–d–g in Op. 2 No. 6 and J. S. BACH's C–G–d–g in his Fifth Cello Suite (BWV1011). Alternative tunings, employed sparingly, have since included: B♭'–G–d–a (Schumann: Piano Quartet, Op. 47; Sculthorpe: *Requiem*), B'–G–d–a (BERG: *Lyric Suite*; Respighi: *Pini di Roma*), C–G–d–g♯ (STRAVINSKY: *The Rite of Spring*), B'–F♯–d–a (Kodály: Sonata, Op. 8), A'–G–d–a (Shapey: *Krosnick Soli*), C–G♯–d–a (Berio: *Sequenza XIV*), B♭'–G–c♯–a (Saariaho: *Spins and spells*) and B♭'–F♯–d–a (Dutilleux: *Trois strophes*).

The DOUBLE BASS has evolved as a three-, four- or five-stringed instrument associated with various tunings. The common orchestral four-string tuning is E'–A'–D–G, but soloists have used F'–B'–E–A to enhance sound projection and clarity. C'–G'–D–A is popular with JAZZ bassists.

LUTES use *scordature* widely, whether *à cordes avallées* (the lowering of one course, usually the lowest, to achieve a wider open-string range) or as actual 'mistunings', to enhance resonances in certain keys or realise drones and other effects. The standard tuning throughout the sixteenth century (and until the eighteenth in Italy) employed the interval pattern (from lowest to highest main fingered courses) fourth–fourth–major third–fourth–fourth (commonly G–c–f–a–d'–g'). Significant examples of altered tunings include Dalza's fourth–fifth–major third–fourth–fourth (1508), Francisque's minor third–fifth–fourth–major third–fourth (1600) and Besard's fourth–fifth–fourth–major third–fourth (1603).

Melli's *Intavolatura di liuto* (4 books (Venice: Giacomo Vincenti, 1614–16)) was the first Italian publication to feature scordatura exclusively (fourth–major third–minor third–major third–fourth). Ballard's *Tablature de luth* (Paris: Pierre Ballard, 1631) was the equivalent French collection, utilising the two most common of over thirty seventeenth-century *scordature*: fourth–fourth–major third–minor third–major third and fourth–fourth–minor third–major third–minor third. The fourth–minor third–major third–fourth–minor third pattern became standard in French and German high-Baroque usage.

The early GUITAR's variant tunings were complicated by re-entrant stringings and octave dispositions. The five-course instrument's normal tunings were predominantly: a/a–d'/d'–g/g–b/b–e' (entirely re-entrant) or a/a–d/d'–g/g–b/b–e' (with a low *d* on the fourth course). Additionally, some players used a high g' on the third course, and others, a low A on the fifth. With the re-entrant stringing, resonance was enhanced by using open strings whenever possible and/or adopting another of about twenty variant tunings, of which major third–fourth–fourth–fourth was most common. Examples of *scordature* appear in Foscarini's *I quatro libri della chitarra spagnola* (c1632), Corbetta's *Varii capricci* (1643), Granata's *Soavi concenti* (1659), Bottazzari's *Sonate nuove* (1663), Kremberg's *Musicalische Gemüths-Ergötzung* (1689) and Campion's *Nouvelles découvertes sur la guitarre* (1705).

Better suited to TABLATURE than staff NOTATION, *scordatura* is rare in the six-string guitar's repertory. The most common variant involved lowering the sixth string a tone (Castelnuovo-Tedesco: Sonata, Op. 77).

In addition to several six-string viol tunings based on the standard interval pattern (fourth–fourth–third–fourth–fourth), PRAETORIUS (*Syntagma musicum*, II, 1619) records tunings with a fourth–third–fourth–fourth–fourth pattern, two entirely in fourths, and some for three-, four- and five-string viols.

Otherwise, apart from the approximately fifty-five alternative tunings known for the lyra viol in seventeenth-century England, viol *scordature* were rare. Nevertheless, examples of tuning the lowest string down a tone appear in pieces by, among others, Hume, SIMPSON, Finger and MARAIS.

FURTHER READING

E. Schulze-Kurz, *Die Laute und ihre Stimmungen in der ersten Hälfte des 17. Jahrhunderts* (Wilsingen: Tre Fontane, 1990).
R. Stowell, *Violin Technique and Performance Practice in the Late Eighteenth and Early Nineteenth Centuries* (Cambridge University Press, 1985).
J. Tyler, *The Early Guitar: A History and Handbook* (Oxford University Press, 1980).

ROBIN STOWELL

Sequentia Ensemble for Medieval music.

Founded in 1977 at the SCHOLA CANTORUM in Basel by two American students, Benjamin Bagby and Barbara Thornton, Sequentia has emerged as one of the most influential and important Medieval ensembles of modern times. Based in Cologne for twenty-five years, it undertook its first North American tour in 1979 with a programme of Latin monophony that became its first of more than thirty recordings. Sequentia has performed and recorded much significant Medieval repertory, both monophonic and polyphonic, including the complete works of Hildegard von Bingen, a particular passion of Thornton. Several distinguished musicians performed with Sequentia over the years, including Margriet Tindemans, Mary Springfels, Crawford Young, David Hart, Elizabeth Gaver, Lena Susanne Norin, Norbert Rodenkirchen and others. After Thornton's death (1998) and a move to Paris, the repertory focus has been on extended narrative works, including the Icelandic *Edda*, earlier Medieval song and Bagby's self-accompanied performance of the Anglo-Saxon epic *Beowulf*.

ROSS DUFFIN

Serpent A bass wind instrument most commonly made of wood with a metal lead pipe and sounded through a mouthpiece similar in size and shape to that used on a bass TROMBONE.

The serpent was developed in France late in the sixteenth century specifically to accompany plainsong in cathedrals. The instrument is not mentioned by PRAETORIUS in his *Syntagma Musicum* and appears to have had little use in Germany in the seventeenth century, but serpents of various types were used in most parts of Europe, particularly France and England, until the mid-nineteenth century. The serpent has similarities with instruments of the CORNETT family, but is distinguished from them by not having a rear thumb-hole. Early instruments had six finger-holes, but from two to eight further holes, some with keys, were added during the nineteenth century. The acoustical quality of the serpent is such that performance on it requires specialist skills and musicianship. Some early FINGERING charts show identical finger positions for adjacent notes, with the obvious implication that notes are differentiated by embouchure adjustment alone. The instrument was originally held in a vertical position before many players adopted a horizontal or diagonal grip.

MERSENNE's description of the instrument in his *Harmonie universelle* (Paris, 1635) indicates that he knew of serpents that were made from metal.

The serpent is also one of the instruments described with measurements in the unpublished writings of the English scholar JAMES TALBOT (c1695 (GB-Och)). The instrument he examined was made of walnut with 'a ring for which a ribband is fastened'. In 1814 a *Méthode de serpent* was included as one of the fourteen instruction books that formed the basis for the curriculum of the PARIS CONSERVATOIRE. Though the publication carries no author attribution, it was written by Jean-Baptiste Métoyen and edited by the Conservatoire's librarian Abbot Nicolas Roze. The inclusion of a serpent *méthode* in the official literature of the Conservatoire is indicative of the importance of the instrument in French culture at that time, and the inscription on the title page, '*Pour la service du culte et la service militaire*' ('for the service of worship and the service of the military'), conveys both a continuance of the instrument's traditional role in sacred music and its more recent purpose in military bands.

The serpent had similar functions in Britain. It was frequently included in the bands that played in the west galleries of rural churches (rather than Anglican cathedrals), but was particularly prominent in military bands, which were then primarily the private bands of the officers' mess. Some of the repertory for these bands included serpent parts along with parts for CLARINETS, OBOES and HORNS. The instrument has also been specified in works by major composers such as MENDELSSOHN, Rossini and BERLIOZ. It survived the longest in church bands but gradually lost favour elsewhere, mainly because other instruments such as the bass horn and OPHICLEIDE were considered to offer greater efficiency and versatility. It was the French serpentist Louis Alexandre Frichot, working in London around 1799, who is credited with the invention of the 'English' bass horn, which was regarded by many as a better alternative for the bass part in military bands.

The serpent, bass horn, ophicleide and TUBA appeared in various shapes and sizes in the nineteenth century, often with different or amended names. They were all intended to provide an appropriate lip-vibrated bass voice for the variety of contexts in which they were required. The key PERFORMANCE PRACTICE decision about which instrument to employ depends largely on considerations of geographical, cultural and musical context.

FURTHER READING

A. Baines, 'James Talbot's manuscript. (Christ Church Library Music MS 1187). I. Wind instruments', *GSJ*, 1 (1948), 9–26.

C. Bevan, *The Tuba Family* (Winchester: Piccolo Press, 2000).

TREVOR HERBERT

Shawm (From Latin *calamus*. Alternative English names: 'waits (pipe)', 'hoboy', 'shalemele'. French *chalemie, hautbois*; German *Schalmei*; Italian *piffaro* (or *piffero*), *ciaramella*; Spanish *chirimía*.) Double-reed instrument with conical bore; ancestor of the OBOE.

The shawm came to Europe in the thirteenth century with the adoption of the ceremonial loud band of the Arabic world. By the fourteenth century the instrument had begun to develop into a 'family' capable of polyphonic performance. To the treble shawm (already enlarged from its Arabic progenitor) was added a tenor (known as a *bombarde* in French, apparently because of its visual resemblance to the cannon). A salient feature of the *bombarde* is its key (with barrel-shaped cover or *fontanelle*), extending the reach of the bottom finger. Both sizes were provided with a *pirouette*, a vase-shaped appurtenance surrounding the base of the reed, both supporting the lips and allowing them to control it.

Near the beginning of the fifteenth century, the shawms began to be joined by brass instruments which were able to play melodically: at first by a form of (?slide) TRUMPET and, by the end of the century, the TROMBONE. This coupling with brass continued throughout the period of the shawm's use (generally through the seventeenth century and, in some areas, beyond). By the early seventeenth century, the shawm family had greatly expanded, producing three sizes below the original tenor (including a greatbass, almost three metres in length). Nevertheless, the two most common sizes remained the original treble and tenor (the latter is now generally known as an 'alto' in light of later developments). Eventually the CORNETT and DULCIAN (or CURTAL) were often used in combination with the shawms.

The shawm band had an important role in both noble and civic life, its members acting as watchmen as well as performing for dances, banquets, wedding celebrations and other public entertainments.

FURTHER READING

H. Myers, 'Reeds & brass', in R. Duffin (ed.), *A Performer's Guide to Medieval Music* (Bloomington and Indianapolis: Indiana University Press, 2000), 384–98.

'Woodwinds', in J. Kite-Powell (ed.), *A Performer's Guide to Seventeenth-Century Music*, 2nd edn (Bloomington and Indianapolis: Indiana University Press, 2012), 71–99.

HERBERT MYERS

Silbermann, Gottfried (b. Kleinbobritzsch, 14 January 1683; d. Dresden, 4 August 1753) German ORGAN builder.

Saxon by birth, Gottfried studied French-Alsatian organ building with his elder brother Andreas in Strasbourg. In 1710 he won his first major contract to build the now famous three-manual, forty-four-stop organ in Freiberg Cathedral, where he settled permanently in 1711. Gottfried dispensed with *Rückpositiv* organs, building the *Oberwerk* and *Brustwerk* as well as the *Hauptwerk* within one large case. His organs have prominent French influences (Silbermann's *Grand jeu* in Freiberg's Petrikirche is particularly fine) and there were five basic designs:

1 Small single manual organs based on Principal 4' or 2' (5–8 stops).
2 Single-manual organs based on Principal 8' (9–15 stops).
3 Small two-manual organs without 16' manual stop (17–21 stops).
4 Large two-manual organs with 16' manual stop (22–32 stops).
5 Three-manual organs with full pedal specification (43–7 stops).

Silbermann built forty-six organs in middle Germany, many of which survive today. At the console, the organs sound powerful, with wind pressures of 97/109 mm at Freiberg. The voicing seems to have been designed so that the organ sounded clear and audible in the naves of churches packed with people. PITCH was $a' = 460$–5 Hz, and Silbermann's strong conservative personality retained meantone tuning, including the four 'bad' triads that J. S. BACH criticised as barbaric and intolerable to a good ear. Bach and Silbermann were colleagues examining Hildebrandt's organ at Naumburg and Bach played many organ recitals on Silbermann's instruments. Fortunately, authentic registration instructions survive from Grosshartmannsdorf (1741) and Fraureuth (1742). Pupils and colleagues include Joachim Wagner and Zacharias Hildebrandt, the latter completing Silbermann's last and greatest organ in the Hofkirche (now the Cathedral) in Dresden.

Silbermann built Hebenstreit's pantaleons and is credited with building the *cembalo d'amour*. His CLAVICHORDS were renowned and were especially praised BY C. P. E. BACH. Although J. S. Bach criticised Silbermann's earlier pianos for weak trebles and heavy action, he approved of his later models.

FURTHER READING

F.-H. Gress, *Die Klanggestalt der Orgeln Gottfried Silbermanns* (Leipzig: Deutscher Verlag für Musik, 1989).

DAVID PONSFORD

Simpson, Christopher (b. ?Egton, N. Yorks., ?1602–6; d. Holborn, London, between 5 May and 29 July 1669) English VIOL player and composer and the most significant writer on English music of the mid-seventeenth century.

Simpson wrote the seminal English TREATISE on viol playing and on playing divisions: *The Division-Violist: or an Introduction to the Playing upon a Ground* (London, 1659). He issued a second, revised and extended edition in 1665 (second state 1667) with parallel English and Latin texts 'that it might be understood in Foreign Parts' (dedication), and a useful nomenclature of the parts of the viol in four languages: Latin, English, French and Italian. He renamed the second edition *The Division-Viol, or the Art of Playing* Ex tempore *upon a Ground* in English and called it *Chelys...* in Latin. It is divided into three parts: 'Of the Viol it self, with Instructions how to Play upon it', 'Use of the Concord, or a Compendium of Descants' and 'Of Division, and the manner of performing it'. The first part discusses a viol suitable for division, its bridge, the relationship between the bridge and the fingerboard, and the BOW. Simpson explains how to hold the viol and play it, and gives six carefully fingered exercises to develop the left hand (one of which reaches a''), 'Swift Division' and playing chords. He then examines 'the Gracing of Notes' including DYNAMICS and VIBRATO, noting the importance of responding to 'the humour of the Musick'.

The third and most substantial section is devoted to a detailed analysis of the art of playing divisions on a ground bass. Simpson explains that division playing uses the whole compass of the instrument: 'acting' alternatively the bass, treble and other parts. He identifies two basic methods: 'breaking' the ground and 'descanting' on it; these two methods can be mixed. He also gives advice on how to plan divisions and extensive examples of divisions 'for the practice of Learners' (54). Jenkins declared that '*Simpsons* great *Work* will teach the *World* to *Play*' (prefatory material to *The Division-Violist*) and L'Estrange rated it 'a work of exceeding use in all sorts of Musick whatsoever' (prefatory remarks to *The Division-Viol*).

In 1665 Simpson published *The Principles of Practical Musick* (London), which he enlarged as *A Compendium of Practical Musick* (London, 1667). He draws attention to the importance of accurate time keeping and recommends beating the pulse with 'a constant Motion of the Hand' or foot, 'if the Hand be otherwise employed' (14). Examining the role of discords to give variety, he describes how they require emphasis 'with a disproportionate Sound, to beget a greater Attention to that which follows' (66). Simpson discusses the need to express the appropriate AFFECT; in his consideration of instrumental forms he notes that the pavan, once 'a grave and stately manner of Dancing ... [is] now grown up to a height of Composition, made only to delight the Ear' (116). In prefatory material to the first edition Locke praised the work as 'new, plain and rational: omitting nothing necessary, nor adding anything superfluous'; in the 1694 EDITION Purcell recommends it as 'the most Ingenious Book I e're met with upon this subject'.

FURTHER READING

C. Simpson, *The Division-Viol*, 2nd edn (London: W. Godbid for Henry Brome, 1665/7).
A Compendium of Practical Musick (London: W. Godbid for Henry Brome, 1667).

LUCY ROBINSON

Singing That the anatomy of the vocal apparatus is the same in all humans and has not changed through evolution for tens of thousands of years is the truism that sets the voice apart from man-made musical instruments. What varies is the way the vocal tract is manipulated to produce speech and singing; this can result in an extraordinary range of different sounds, evident in the multiplicity of spoken languages and ways of singing that exist simultaneously in the world. Although we have no way of recovering the actual sounds of vocal music before the invention of recording and playback, there is nevertheless a substantial body of evidence that can contribute to reconstructing in very broad terms the prevailing AESTHETICS of voice production in Western art singing in different times, places and circumstances in history. What is harder to know are the degrees of variability in how vocal music sounded in practice, even within what one might expect to be relatively homologous repertories. Twenty-first-century expectations of vocal sound in, say, MOZART opera performance remain pretty consistent from day to day, theatre to theatre and city to city, from Los Angeles to Beijing; but such normalisations can be shown to be both historically contingent and unstable (not least from the evidence of EARLY RECORDINGS that capture the singing of celebrated performers of the late nineteenth century). How much more variation might there have been in a world that, until the modern tendency towards homogenisation (whether in *Lieder* singing or the performance of fifteenth-century polyphony, which recording above all has cemented), prized individualism above all else in vocal performance?

The basic functioning of the vocal tract is equally constrained in all humans; everyone's singing voice has two basic 'registers': the modal (or chest voice) and the falsetto. All singers are limited in how low they can get – the length of the vocal folds determines the pitch range of the voice (the longer, the deeper); but the point at which the modal voice gives out at the top and the falsetto naturally cuts in is remarkably similar in men, women and children, occurring in the PITCH range around d′ to f′. It is possible to push the modal voice above this so-called *passaggio*: children, for example, can get up to b′ or c″ or even higher by pressuring the larynx upwards, as many singers outside Western art music (rock singers, for example) also do as a matter of course. The lightly placed 'head voice' of which modern trained tenors, baritones and sopranos speak is sometimes described as a third, 'intermediate' register; but it is, in fact, part of the modal (men) or falsetto (women) voice register (Sundberg, in Potter (ed.), 2000, 239). Singing (or speaking) in one or other, or in a combination of the two registers, is a matter of choice and, above all, convention. Nevertheless, the overwhelming evidence of musical NOTATION and PERFORMANCE PRACTICE suggests that most singers of both liturgical and secular polyphony sang either in the modal or in the falsetto range, at least up to the early seventeenth century. Only with the development in the early sixteenth century of solo vocal performance of arrangements of polyphonic music, in which a chordal instrument such as the ORGAN or LUTE filled in the missing parts, did 'mixing registers' become part of the technical armoury of elite singers. From the 1560s onwards there are references to male singers who could sing sections of the bass, tenor, alto and even the soprano parts within one piece of music (called singing *alla bastarda*).

The perennial reiteration in every generation of the mantra that the principal object of expressive singing is the perfect enunciation and audibility of the text, most easily achieved by singing in the same register as we use for speaking (i.e. the modal voice), meant that 'mixed-register singing' was resisted for a long time, especially in refined chamber song; for example, GIULIO CACCINI famously remarked that 'the falsetto voice cannot give rise to nobility of good singing' (*Le nuove musiche* (Florence, 1602), 11). It is only with the first TREATISE on the training of CASTRATI, PIER FRANCESCO TOSI's *Opinioni* (1723), that we find described a systematic method for learning to pass seamlessly from modal to falsetto voice. This became the basis of the *bel canto* technique learned by operatic singers – male and female – to the present day. As Tosi explained, castrati had to be able to utilise both registers, otherwise they would be 'constrained to sing within the narrow compass of a few notes' (Tosi, trans. Galliard (1743), I, 23). Blending the break between the registers (achieved by years of patient, incremental practice) allowed singers to extend their overall range beyond the limit of the notes of one stave (about a tenth) that had characterised almost all written Medieval and Renaissance vocal music. The technique, first used by CASTRATI, led to the development of a completely 'new' vocal type in the eighteenth century, the operatic tenor, capable of singing to extraordinary heights by seamlessly passing into falsetto. As a result, HAYDN could call on Karl Friberth to sing top d″ and baritone low A in the same aria (*Il ritorno di Tobia*, 1784), and Bellini could rely on the phenomenal Giovanni Battista Rubini to reach f′ in *I Puritani* in 1834/5 (Potter, 2009, 27, 117).

Sensibility to individual vocal difference was highly attuned in the Medieval and early modern eras thanks to the ubiquity of the ancient 'pseudo-science' of physiognomy. Nowadays we think of physiognomy as an arbitrary and distinctly unscientific system of classification of human 'types' according to visible bodily features; but until well into the eighteenth century a person's voice was also considered a precise signifier of character, which permeated everyday understanding of everything from medical diagnosis to social relations. Voices were categorised as naturally 'hard' or 'soft', 'rigid' or 'flexible', 'high', 'low', 'nasal', 'guttural' and so on, and in turn recognised – among other things – as either conducive or unfavourable to artful singing. Perhaps unsurprisingly, we find different aesthetic ideals championed in different eras. Thus, for Isidore of Seville in the seventh century the desirable voice was 'high, sweet and strong'. It is possible to extrapolate from this oft-repeated maxim to explain an apparently consistent preference for high voices over low that arguably prevails from the Medieval church, with its emphasis on clarity and fervour in the ARTICULATION of the text, to Italian high-Baroque opera, in which castrati rather than tenors or basses were normally cast in the role of the male hero. In 1636, the French philosopher MARIN MERSENNE reflected on the fact that 'sopranos ... come much nearer to heaven and to life than basses ... and many maintain that high sounds are more pleasant than low sounds, and that they derive more pleasure hearing a soprano than a bass' (*Harmonie universelle*, I, 24, 26). Children's voices were thus considered especially desirable for the adornment of both worship and chamber music. The 1533 regulations of the *maîtrise* (choir school) at Reims cathedral, for example, specified that 'choirboys must be chosen for their clear, sweet and harmonious voices ... so that they resemble little angels in the service of God and excite each one to devotion' (cited in C. Herr, 'Zur Ästhetik der Knabenstimme', *Trossinger Jahrbuch für Renaissancemusik*, 10 (2011), 188). Until well into the eighteenth century the voice-label 'cantus' or 'soprano', apart from signifying the highest-sounding part, could be occupied by a boy, a girl, a woman, or an adult man – either a castrato, or a falsettist, all singing the same pitches. Indeed, it is a common misconception that vocal classifications are absolutes that correlate with a particular vocal type or pitch range, irrespective of the era, genre or geographical origin of the notated part that bears a particular voice name: e.g. 'bassus' simply means the lowest sounding part, but not necessarily that it has to be performed by a 'bass singer'.

In fact, men singing in their falsetto voice seems to have been quite normal in secular and church music practice, both solo and choral, until the late seventeenth century, although not, as far as we know, on the opera stage. Male falsetto singing 'survived' as a professional practice, albeit in relative obscurity, in English cathedral choirs throughout the nineteenth century and beyond (and is widely practised in popular music and in many kinds of non-European singing). Its vigorous 'revival' in modern times as the so-called countertenor voice (something of a misnomer, as this term – like its synonym, 'contralto' – signified merely 'the voice that sings against the tenor') presents, rather paradoxically, a good example of the anachronism that runs deep in most manifestations of the modern 're-invention' of historical singing.

Perhaps the most famous falsettist of the late sixteenth century was GIOVANNI LUCA CONFORTI, remembered as a 'great singer of *gorge* and *passaggi*, who could sing as high as the stars' (Pietro della Valle, 'Della musica dell'età nostra' (1640), 255). *Gorge* (from the Italian for 'throat') is a generic term for a style of vocal ORNAMENTATION that involves very accurate control of extremely fast articulations of the vocal folds. It was regarded as intrinsic to refined singing by both men and women from at least the early sixteenth century and was still a critical element of *bel canto* technique well into the nineteenth (i.e. 'coloratura' – derived from the Latin *colorare*, 'to colour or embellish'). One of the first to describe both how *gorge* are done, and how they should be applied spontaneously in the decoration of the basic vocal line of a written song (*cantar di gorga*) was the courtier GIOVANNI CAMILLO MAFFEI, who was both a physician and an amateur singer. Invoking the terminology of vocal physiognomy, he explains that only those endowed with 'smooth and pleasing throats are apt for singing *passaggi* (runs of fast ornamental notes)' (*Discourse on the Voice* (1562), 17). The only way to achieve the almost unbelievable speed of articulation of *cantar di gorga*, of which there are a few written-down examples from the period such as in the aria 'Possente spirto' as sung by the tenor Francesco Rasi in the title role of MONTEVERDI's *Orfeo* (1607), is to maintain very low sub-glottal breath pressure and allow the larynx to move freely within the vocal tract. And this is key to understanding the essential difference between 'pre-Romantic' and modern art singing. All available evidence points to the fact that until the early nineteenth century singers allowed the larynx to rise and fall as the notes went up or down in pitch, which is what the 99.99 per cent of singers in the world who have not been trained in Western art-singing do naturally. The need to make the voice loud enough to be heard in big theatres and against ever larger ORCHESTRAS led to singers depressing the larynx while singing, in order to optimise one particular frequency of the vocal tract, the so-called 'singers' formant' (Wistreich, in Potter, 2000, 180). Consciously dropping the larynx and elongating the vocal tract by expanding the pharynx allowed the now mythicised moment in 1837 when the French tenor Gilbert-Louis Duprez famously produced a top c' in full chest voice during a performance of Rossini's *Guillaume Tell* (to the apparent disgust of the composer). Depressing the larynx is a fundamental feature of modern operatic voice production, and although Duprez's top c' may have opened the way to *verismo* singing later in the century, his vocal technique was, like that of his peers, a natural outcome of the so-called 'golden age of bel canto'.

Bel canto singing claims direct lineage from the age of Baroque opera and the methods of pedagogues including Tosi (who looked back to the seventeenth century), AGRICOLA, MANCINI and Porpora. With the advent of institutionalised conservatoire training based on 'scientific principles', its pedagogy was subsequently codified in systematic training manuals by perhaps the most influential singing teachers of the nineteenth century: ALEXIS DE GARAUDÉ, who taught at the PARIS CONSERVATOIRE (1816–41) and summed up his life's work in his *Méthode complète de chant* (2nd augmented and improved edn (Paris: Chez l'auteur, 1841)); and the two MANUEL GARCÍAS (father and son). García the younger's *Traité complet de l'art du chant* was published in two parts in 1840 and 1847 (Paris: Chez l'auteur) and later translated as *García's New Treatise on the Art of Singing* in 1857; he died in 1906 at the age of 101, having been singing professor at the ROYAL ACADEMY OF MUSIC in London for fifty years (Potter and Sorrell, 122). The durability of the 'conservatoire method' that is the legacy of García's and Garaudé's teaching (neither of whom, incidentally, had singing careers before becoming teachers) means that almost all trained singers today have learned a technique optimised for efficiency, which maximises volume, 'ring' and evenness across the range (and this includes countertenors); particularly designed for the operatic stage, it naturally tends to iron out differences between individual voices. Such recognisable integers of 'proper' art singing necessarily come at the expense of certain fundamental and very long-lived aesthetic priorities expressed from the Middle Ages until the early nineteenth century, including clarity of diction, flexibility, 'sweetness', and the ability to sing appropriately (and differently) – in the words of LUIGI ZENOBI written c1600, 'in one way in church, in another in the chamber and in a third in the open air, whether it be daytime or at night' ('Letter on the Perfect Musician', in B. Blackburn and E. Lowinsky, 'Luigi Zenobi and his letter on the perfect musician', *Studi Musicali*, 22/1 (1993), 61–114 (101–2)) – and also to vary the sound according to the genre of the piece being sung. And yet, in contrast to instrumentalists who now recognise that 'historically informed performance' includes close attention to the sounds of the instruments for which the music was conceived, when it comes to the professional performance of most vocal music of the past, whether a mass by Ockeghem, a madrigal by Marenzio, a cantata by J. S. BACH or an opera by Bellini, even the apparently most dedicated historicists seem to have acquiesced to what are portrayed as inevitable compromises, and the question of 'historical singing' remains, to a greater or lesser extent, 'the elephant in the room'.

FURTHER READING

C. Lawson and R. Stowell (eds.), *The Cambridge History of Musical Performance* (Cambridge University Press, 2012), especially chapters 9, 13, 17, 21 and 25.

J. Potter, *Tenor: History of a Voice* (New Haven, CT and London: Yale University Press, 2009).

J. Potter (ed.), *The Cambridge Companion to Singing* (Cambridge University Press, 2000), especially chapters 14, 15, 17 and 19.

J. Potter and N. Sorrell, *A History of Singing* (Cambridge University Press, 2012).

RICHARD WISTREICH

Spataro, Giovanni (b. Bologna, ?26 October 1458; d. Bologna, 17 January 1541) Italian composer and music theorist.

Spataro's surviving music is competent but undistinguished. He studied music theory under Bartolomeus Ramis de Pareia. His printed writings are controversial; the longest, *Tractato di musica* (Venice, 1531), is a defence of perfect mensuration under sesquialtera proportion (3:2) and of breve equivalence between mensurations. An introduction to mensural NOTATION survives in MANUSCRIPT, but TREATISES on counterpoint and proportions have been lost. Spataro's letters to PIETRO AARON and others are especially important. He recognised that Adrian Willaert's *Quid non ebrietas* required equal semitones, and he defended Ramis's eccentric division of the monochord, with its pure thirds (6:5 and 5:4 rather than the Pythagorean 32:27 and 81:64), as representing the intervals used in practice rather than theory.

FURTHER READING

B. J. Blackburn, E. E. Lowinsky and C. A. Miller (eds.), *A Correspondence of Renaissance Musicians* (Oxford: Clarendon Press, 1991), *passim*.

JEFFREY J. DEAN

Spencer, Robert (b. Ilford, 9 May 1932; d. Woodford Green, 8 August 1997) English lutenist, guitarist, teacher and singer.

One of the most influential figures in the modern LUTE revival, Spencer is also remembered as a musicologist who assembled a unique collection of MANUSCRIPTS and early printed EDITIONS which was made freely available to scholars (now housed in the ROYAL ACADEMY OF MUSIC, London). His articles and FACSIMILE editions of lute and GUITAR music are seminal works in their field. Spencer was regarded as a most sensitive and inspirational teacher, particularly of students of historical PERFORMANCE PRACTICE. His interest in organology and his important and diverse collection of early guitars encouraged his constant experimentation with historical string-materials, tensions and spacing, chiefly in respect of his lutes. He was deeply involved in the philosophy of performance and found it particularly important to recreate the intimacy of domestic music making, whether his AUDIENCES were from the Royal Shakespeare Company, Glyndebourne or schools.

FURTHER READING

The Burwell Lute Tutor, with an introductory study by Robert Spencer (Leeds: Boethius Press, 1974).

R. Spencer, 'Nineteenth-century music: the type of edition we should play from', *Guitar Journal*, 6 (June 1995), 15–18.

JAMES WESTBROOK

Speth, Johann (b. Speinshart, Upper Palatinate, 1664; d. Augsburg, c1720) German organist and composer.

Speth was organist of Augsburg Cathedral 1692–4. His *Ars magna* (Augsburg, 1693) consists of ten toccatas, eight Magnificats and three variation sets. The toccatas are mostly shorter than those in MUFFAT's *Apparatus musico-organisticus* (Salzburg, 1690) and Speth's *alternatim* Magnificats show similarity with those in Kerll's *Modulatio organica* (Munich, 1686).

FURTHER READING

W. Apel, *The History of Keyboard Music to 1700*, trans. and rev. H. Tischler (Bloomington, IN, and London: Indiana University Press, 1972).

G. Beechey, 'A 17th-century German organ tutor', *MT*, 113 (1972), 86–9.

DAVID PONSFORD

Spinet (Fr. *épinette*; Ger. *Spinett, Querflügel*; It. *spinetta, spinettone, spinettina, cembalo traverso*) A small wing-shaped plucked keyboard instrument of the HARPSICHORD family in which the strings run obliquely to the line of the keys, with the bass strings furthest from the player.

The spinet is usually single-strung (i.e. with one keyboard and one set of strings and jacks) and like the VIRGINAL, the strings run in widely spaced pairs with two jacks between each pair, each jack plucking in opposite directions. The sound is closer to a small harpsichord than a virginal, however. Double-strung instruments such as the double-manual octave spinet by Gellinger and the *cembalo traverso* or *spinettone*, an invention of Cristofori with 8' and 4' strings, are very rare attempts to vary volume and tone colour.

The name 'spinet' comes from Italy, where it originally denoted a rectangular or polygonal virginal (*spinetta*), in which the bass strings are closest to the player. The term is now reserved for the elegant wing-shaped or bent-side spinet, which replaced the substantial and richly decorated rectangular virginal in Britain in the last quarter of the seventeenth century. These instruments evolved naturally from smaller octave spinets (called *ottavino*, *spinettino* or *spinetta ottavina*) and the first recorded maker is the Italian Girolamo Zenti. Large numbers survive today, notably more than fifty by the Hitchcock family, and although more compact than the harpsichord, they had an equivalent range (up to five octaves) and suited similar repertory.

'Spinet' and its non-English equivalents have been used in conflicting descriptive contexts. These include not only different types of instruments but also a maker's name (Giovanni Spinetti) and parts of the mechanism (plectra, lute stop). In sixteenth- and seventeenth-century France *épinette(s)* was a generic term for all plucked keyboard instruments, and was used similarly to 'virginals' in England.

FURTHER READING

E. L. Kottick, *A History of the Harpsichord* (Bloomington and Indianapolis: Indiana University Press, 2003).
P. Mole, 'The English spinet with particular reference to the schools of Keene and Hitchcock', PhD dissertation, Edinburgh University (2009).
R. Russell, *The Harpsichord and Clavichord: An Introductory Study*, 2nd edn, rev. H. Schott, (London: Faber & Faber, 1973).

TERENCE CHARLSTON

Spohr, Louis (Ludewig, Ludwig) (b. Brunswick, 5 April 1784; d. Kassel, 22 October 1859) German composer, violinist, conductor and pedagogue.

Spohr studied the VIOLIN with J. A. Riemenschneider, Dufour, Gottfried Kunisch and Charles Maucourt before Duke Carl Wilhelm Ferdinand appointed him *Kammermusicus* of the Brunswick *Hofkapelle* (1799) and assisted him in furthering his violin studies with Franz Eck (1802–3). Eck's instruction and the experience of hearing PIERRE RODE's performances in Brunswick (1803) were lifelong influences. He was appointed *Konzertmeister* in Gotha (1805) and Vienna (Theater an der Wien; 1812) and *Kapellmeister* at the Frankfurt theatre (1817–19) and made the first of his six successful visits to England in 1820 (others followed 1839–53), conducting for the London Philharmonic Society. He settled in Kassel as *Kapellmeister* (1822), directing the opera and the established subscription concerts series and founding the choral music-orientated *Cäcilienverein*. He eventually fell out with his employer, the Elector of Hesse (1851), by taking ungranted leave, and was pensioned off in 1857; a broken arm that same year ended his violin playing.

Spohr cultivated refined technical and expressive vocal ideals and a noble artistic integrity, despising empty virtuosity. His tripartite *Violinschule* (1832) is addressed to teachers, parents and advanced pupils. Its first section is devoted to the violin's construction and maintenance, its set-up and accessories, and the BOW. Its central section embraces musical rudiments and violin technique. Spohr's chin-braced grip, using his invention the chin-rest, and his advanced position of the left shoulder offer the requisite stability to facilitate shifting, bowing and VIBRATO. He emphasises the expressive and tonal benefits of shifting, recommending the use of (unsounded) anticipatory notes for its mastery, and promotes a systematic approach to the FINGERING of three-octave diatonic scales.

Spohr's bow hold approximates modern principles but his slightly raised wrist and position of the elbow close to the body belong to the early nineteenth century. Favouring a Classical on-the-string bowing technique and sonorous tone, he stresses the non-participatory role of the upper arm in the execution of short strokes in the bow's upper third. His extensive catalogue of bowings ignores 'thrown' or springing varieties other than *fouetté* but includes lifted strokes, slurred staccato and the so-called 'Viotti' and 'Kreutzer' bowings. He was the first writer to recommend the modern practice of breaking bowed four-note chords upwards in twos, as opposed to the previous rapid upward or downward ARPEGGIANDO spreading. He favours holding the violin in 'guitar position' for pizzicato chords, with the right thumb performing the pizzicato. He ignores left-hand pizzicato and is reserved about the use of HARMONICS, only rarely employing them in shifting. He distinguishes four VIBRATO speeds: fast for sharply accentuated notes; slow for sustained notes in impassioned melodies; accelerating for *crescendos*; and decelerating for *decrescendos*; and he demonstrates the selective application of vibrato at speeds appropriate to its context.

Part three focuses on style and interpretation; its four sections embrace interpretation in general, concerto playing, quartet performance and orchestral playing. He distinguishes between a correct interpretation (a faithful account of the prescribed performance details) and a fine one that combines accuracy, technical mastery, subtlety of EXPRESSION, PORTAMENTO, TEMPO flexibility, vibrato and refined TASTE. The section on concerto performance incorporates a detailed commentary on the interpretation of the solo passages of RODE's Violin Concerto No. 7 and an explicitly annotated EDITION of his own Violin Concerto No. 9, both presented in duo format with an accompanying violin part.

Spohr's pedagogical principles were widely influential, especially in Germany and Britain. Many were perpetuated through the performances and teaching of his most renowned pupil, FERDINAND DAVID, and some were cited verbatim by later writers, notably in JOSEPH JOACHIM and Andreas Moser's *Violinschule* (3 vols. (Berlin: N. Simrock, 1905)). Among other notable pupils were August Wilhelmj and Hubert Ries.

Spohr was a prolific composer in a wide range of genres: operas, oratorios, songs, symphonies, concertos, string quartets, double string quartets and much other chamber music. His style combined the formalism and clarity of the Classical tradition with the structural and harmonic experimentation of Romanticism. He was the first major conductor to use a baton (although he also conducted with his violin bow) and to add rehearsal letters to sheet music, thereby increasing efficiency in REHEARSALS. He was also among the first to annotate many of his compositions with METRONOME and/or chronometer markings, in addition to ARTICULATION, bowing and vibrato indications, in order to guide performers in realising the composer's intentions. His autobiography (completed by family members using materials provided by his wife), travel diaries and letters provide lively (but not necessarily always accurate) insights into various aspects of musical life. His correspondence with MENDELSSOHN is especially informative, including discussions of some of their works and comment about recommending and hiring performers, concert programming and arranging for the performance of new music, libretto creation and the early music revival.

FURTHER READING

J. M. Cooper and R. L. Todd, '"With true esteem and friendship"; the correspondence of Felix Mendelssohn Bartholdy and Louis Spohr', *JMR*, 29/2–3 (2010), 171–259.

L. Spohr, *Louis Spohr's Autobiography. Translated from the German* (Cambridge University Press, 2010).

M. Wulfhorst, 'Louis Spohr and the metronome: a contribution to early nineteenth-century performance practice', in M. Jabłoński and D. Jasińska (eds.), *Henryk Wieniawski. Composer and Virtuoso in the Musical Culture of the XIX and XX Centuries* (Poznań: Rhytmos, 2001), 189–205.

ROBIN STOWELL

Sprechstimme (German, 'spoken voice') An extended vocal technique combining SINGING and speech, often now used synonymously with *Sprechgesang* ('spoken singing').

Sprechstimme is most associated with expressionist works of the Second Viennese School, above all ARNOLD SCHOENBERG's melodrama *Pierrot Lunaire*, Op. 21 (1912), where the female *Rezitation* part uses the technique almost continuously. Earlier examples of speech-like declamation occur in works by Humperdinck (*Königskinder*, 1897), RICHARD STRAUSS (*Enoch Arden*, 1897) and Schillings (*Das Hexenlied*, 1902). The technique existed also in French and German cabaret of the period.

In his Preface to the score of *Pierrot Lunaire* (UE, 1914), Schoenberg called for 'a speech melody [*Sprechmelodie*], taking into account the given pitch'. This was achieved by 'maintaining the rhythm as accurately as if one were singing', and 'becoming acutely aware of the difference between singing tone and speaking tone', without adopting 'a *singsong* speech pattern'. Exactly where the performer locates such *Sprechstimme* between singing and speaking and between hitting or hinting at notated pitches remains a key question of interpretation. Other unresolved questions include the representation of different vocal registers, adaptation to the individual performer's singing and speaking range, the 'mutual relations' between notated pitches (including harmonic representation) and the appropriate rendition of longer notes.

Schoenberg conducted a technically indifferent Columbia Records recording of *Pierrot Lunaire* in 1940, with Erika Stiedry-Wagner as reciter. It is a 'spoken' rather than 'sung' interpretation; the voice frequently ignores not only the notated pitches but also sometimes the prevailing direction of the melody.

Variants of *Sprechstimme*, with distinctive NOTATIONS, occur across Schoenberg's output, including *Gurre-Lieder, Die glückliche Hand, Ode to Napoleon Buonaparte, A Survivor from Warsaw* and the incomplete *Die Jakobsleiter, Moses und Aron* and *Modern Psalm*. Other composers using the technique include BERG (*Wozzeck, Lulu*), Weill (*Mahagonny*), BOULEZ, Kagel, BRITTEN, Berio and Rihm.

MALCOLM GILLIES

Stadler, Anton Paul (b. Bruck an der Leitha, 28 June 1753; d. Vienna, 15 June 1812) Austrian CLARINET and BASSET HORN player.

Anton Stadler was the virtuoso for whom MOZART wrote his great clarinet works. A Viennese critic of the time remarked, 'Never would I have thought that a clarinet could imitate the human voice as deceptively as it was imitated by you. Your instrument has so soft and delicate a tone that no-one with a heart can resist it.' Spitzer and Zaslaw have observed that Anton and his brother Johann serve as fine examples of Viennese instrumentalists during the transition from the Kapelle to the free-market system. They came from modest origins: their father was a shoemaker, their mother a midwife. They lived in crowded conditions in rented lodgings in poor neighbourhoods; they were constantly in debt and died in poverty. Yet in the Masonic lodges, they interacted with a broad social spectrum and came into contact with aristocracy at private concerts. Significantly, Anton Stadler specialised in second clarinet parts and this, together with his experience of the basset horn, may have led to his collaboration with the maker Theodor Lotz. They added two and four notes to the low register of his clarinets in B♭ and A respectively, creating what was initially known as the BASS CLARINET and is now called the basset clarinet. Mozart's Quintet K581 and Concerto K622 were written for it, as was the concerto by Süssmayr, which survives in two incomplete MANUSCRIPTS. Stadler premiered Mozart's Clarinet Concerto in Prague on 16 October 1791; on his subsequent Baltic tour he played the Concerto at a Riga concert on 5 March 1794. The programmes for his Riga concerts contain an engraving of his own special instrument with protruding bulb bell, which Stadler himself described as 'a new kind of *clarinette d'amour*'. Frustratingly for later generations, the autographs of Mozart's Quintet and Concerto have not survived Stadler's death, nor have his basset clarinets.

In 1799 Stadler prepared a fifty-page 'Musik Plan' for a new music school that Count Georg Festetics intended to establish in an abandoned monastery on his Hungarian estate. The scope is ambitious: 'Whoever wants to achieve genuine mastery of music must acquire a broad knowledge of the world, plus mathematics, poetry, RHETORIC and several languages.' Pamela Poulin has summarised its value with regard to eighteenth-century musical life and education. Stadler recognised three areas of music – theory, performance and composition – the absorption of which would require a six-year course. All students would participate in SINGING, PIANO, ORGAN or THOROUGHBASS, VIOLIN and wind instruments. The bibliography promises a clarinet tutor by Stadler which appears never to have materialised. His advice ranges across purely practical matters such as reed making; he also offers more general comments; for example, on the unpredictability of the mood of an AUDIENCE on any particular evening. Amongst other areas represented in Stadler's text is the importance of following one's calling, whether or not it be music. Conductors should remember that instrumentalists 'are not to be shouted at when they make a mistake, or made [to look] ridiculous, or treated with sarcasm, because then they lose their composure'.

FURTHER READING

C. Lawson, *Mozart: Clarinet Concerto* (Cambridge University Press, 1995).
P. L. Poulin, 'A view of eighteenth-century musical life and training: Anton Stadler's "Musik Plan"', *M&L*, 71 (1990), 215–24.

H. Strebel, *Anton Stadler: Wirken und Lebensumfeld des 'Mozart-Klarinettisten': Fakten, Daten und Hypothesen zu seiner Biographie* (Vienna: Hollitzer Verlag, 2017).

COLIN LAWSON

Steinbach, Fritz (b. Grünsfeld (Baden Württemberg), 17 June 1855; d. Munich, 13 August 1916) German conductor and composer.

Following studies with his brother Emil and at the Leipzig Conservatoire (when he received a stipend recommended by BRAHMS), Fritz Steinbach studied in Vienna in 1877 (with GUSTAV NOTTEBOHM and Anton Door) and Karlsruhe in 1878 (with Vincenz Lachner and Otto Dessoff). He became assistant *Kapellmeister* in Mainz in 1880. With his appointment in 1886 by Duke Georg II to succeed HANS VON BÜLOW (who directed 1880–5, with an interregnum by RICHARD STRAUSS (1886)) as *Hofkapellmeister* (later GMD and Intendant) of the Meiningen *Hofkapelle* (until 1902), he led the *Meiningenschen Landmusikfeste* in 1895, 1899 and 1903, and increased the orchestra's touring, including visits to Paris, London and New York. He moved to Cologne in 1903, where he was civic *Kapellmeister*, director of the Gürzenich Concerts and director of the Conservatory, retiring in 1914 to Munich.

Steinbach's greatest fame as a performer relates to his CONDUCTING of the works of BRAHMS, to whom he became close at Meiningen. By the time of his Meiningen tour to London in 1902, Steinbach's Brahms performances had come to be regarded as embodying a definitive Brahmsian performance style in both their understanding and their standard of execution. Although he did not make recordings, Steinbach's performances of Brahms's symphonies and St Antoni Variations were described and illustrated in detail with numerous music examples by his Munich pupil Walter Blume in a typescript book published in the Brahms centenary year of 1933. Stressing Brahms's total approval of Steinbach's readings, Blume claims that his markings are authentic in showing rhythmic continuity yet elasticity of TEMPO and phrasing, in contrast to the radical changes he claims in music making since Brahms's time towards speeds that were too fast and metronomic.

FURTHER READING

W. Blume (ed.), *Brahms in der Meininger Tradition. Seine Sinfonien und Haydn Variationen in der Bezeichnung von Fritz Steinbach* (author's typescript, 1933); repr. as *Brahms in der Meininger Tradition. Seine Sinfonien in der Bezeichnung von Fritz Steinbach*, with foreword by M. Schwalb (Hildesheim, Zurich and New York: Georg Olms Verlag, 2013).

MICHAEL MUSGRAVE

Stockhausen, Karlheinz (b. Burg Mödrath, nr Cologne, 22 August 1928; d. Kürten, 5 December 2007) German composer.

Stockhausen studied with Frank Martin and Olivier Messiaen, was strongly influenced by Werner Meyer-Eppler at Bonn University and became the leading composer of the post-1945 avant-garde. His compositional innovations and philosophy were groundbreaking – by the late 1950s he was central (with BOULEZ and Nono among others) to a new radical post-serial composition that was pre-eminent in post-War European music; he was also an influential teacher (including at the Darmstadt summer school (from 1956) and the Cologne Musikhochschule (1971–7)) and performer (with his ensemble, established in the 1960s), bringing together younger composers (e.g. Cornelius Cardew and Tim Souster), established performers (e.g. Aloys Kontarsky, Rolf Gehlhaar and Peter Eötvös) and eventually some family members to work as assistants or play his music. Among his pupils were Klarenz Barlow, Wolfgang Rihm and Kevin Volans, who in turn became influential at the Darmstadt Summer Courses.

Stockhausen's reputation and influence developed globally beyond the specialist audience for contemporary art music, gaining acknowledgement from popular culture artists such as Kraftwerk, Pink Floyd and Björk; his photograph also appeared on the record cover for the Beatles' *Sergeant Pepper* (1967). From the later 1970s he worked mostly from his home in Kürten, setting up his own publishing house, Stockhausen-Verlag, after a long association with Universal Edition, and concentrating on the *Licht* cycle of seven operas, each named after a day of the week. *Licht*'s conception differed from traditional operatic writing: characters and roles were given to instrumentalists. The work spawned some solo and duo pieces, which are available in versions for different instruments.

Stockhausen's earlier music continues to be influential in terms of the extension and redefinition of serial technique, the development of form and structure, the use of fragmentation, indeterminacy and the Fibonacci series and, during the 1960s, the development of 'moment form', his radical departure from conventional NOTATION using plus and minus signs together with text-only scores such as *Aus den sieben Tagen* (1968), most with prefaces detailing performance instructions. From c1952 he developed a particular performance practice for his works involving sound diffusion employing instrumental microphones and amplification, for example, to avert balance problems between the three percussionists and the OBOE, BASS CLARINET and PIANO in *Kreuzspiel* (1951). His detailed prefaces to most stipulate the number and placement of the loudspeakers, microphones and contact microphones. In a 1991 lecture he described six areas of electro-acoustic PERFORMANCE PRACTICE of which the second two, amplification and transformation techniques, are the most significant because they transform, enhance and extend works originally conceived as purely acoustic instrumental works. In his *Kreuzspiel*, the piano, oboe and bass clarinet are amplified and the sound diffusion is through a stereo spread of four speakers, paired left and right next to the oboe and bass clarinet, the piano being central and the PERCUSSION behind the piano. This arrangement allows listeners to hear not only an even stereo image from anywhere in the hall but also the sound directly from where it is being produced. Stockhausen also uses amplification for his series of *Klavierstücke* so that listeners can hear the piano as the pianist hears it. Sound projection therefore becomes integral to the performance, as is often the performance venue.

In 1978 Stockhausen composed cadenzas for MOZART's Clarinet Concerto K622; that for the slow movement, headed 'langsamer als Adagio', is particularly striking for its dynamic and timbral contrasts, VIBRATO annotations and specific FINGERINGS for playing b'' and c''' as unconventional HARMONICS.

FURTHER READING

J. Kohl et al., 'A Gedenkschrift for Karlheinz Stockhausen', *Perspectives of New Music*, 50/1–2 (2012), 306–523.

K. Stockhausen and J. Kohl, 'Electro-acoustic performance practice', *Perspectives of New Music*, 34/1 (1996), 74–105.

S. Williams, 'Interpretation and performance practice in realising Stockhausen's *Studie II*', *JRMA*, 141/2 (2016), 445–81.

ROGER HEATON

Stowell, Robin (b. Exeter, England, 30 August 1949) English historical and modern violinist, academic, administrator and pedagogue.

Born into a musical family, Stowell read music at St Catharine's College, Cambridge, before undertaking post-graduate VIOLIN studies at London's ROYAL ACADEMY OF MUSIC. Returning to Cambridge University, he completed his PhD in 1978 under the supervision of Peter le Huray. His thesis, 'The development of violin technique from L'Abbé le fils (Joseph Barnabé Saint-Sevin) to Paganini', served as the basis for his 1985 monograph *Violin Technique and Performance Practice in the Late Eighteenth and Early Nineteenth Centuries*, beginning a fruitful association with Cambridge University Press.

Stowell's research concerns string PERFORMANCE PRACTICES, instruments, players and repertory. In addition to his many JOURNAL articles, book chapters and conference presentations, his publications include an authoritative yet approachable study of BEETHOVEN's Violin Concerto (1998) and three edited *Cambridge Companion* volumes (Violin (1992); CELLO (1999); String Quartet (2003)). His 2001 monograph *The Early Violin and Viola*, part of the *Cambridge Handbooks to the Historical Performance of Music*, takes a pragmatic approach characteristic of those who move fluently between practice and theory. More recently, Stowell collaborated with colleagues at the University of Leeds in the AHRC-funded *CHASE Research Project* investigating nineteenth- and early twentieth-century annotated EDITIONS of string music. His three major publications with COLIN LAWSON have made a significant impact on the wider understanding of historical performance.

In tandem with his long-standing leadership role in the School of Music at Cardiff University, Stowell has maintained an active performing career across solo, chamber and orchestral repertory. He made his London solo debut at the Purcell Room in 1974. During the 1970s and early 1980s, as a member of CHRISTOPHER HOGWOOD'S ACADEMY OF ANCIENT MUSIC and other period ensembles, he was in the vanguard of historical performance internationally, performing, broadcasting and recording widely.

In 2004 Stowell established Cardiff University's Centre for Research into Historically Informed Performance; he continues to be affiliated with Cardiff University as emeritus professor.

INGRID E. PEARSON

Strauss, Richard (Georg) (b. Munich, 11 June 1864; d. Garmisch-Partenkirchen, 8 September 1949) German composer and conductor.

In parallel with his career as one of the most successful composers of his time, Strauss was also a busy conductor, prompting him to produce his own versions of several works. Among these was a German performing EDITION of Gluck's *Iphigenie auf Tauris* made in 1890, published the following year and used for the Metropolitan Opera premiere of the work in 1916. Strauss was devoted to MOZART and in 1885 he composed CADENZAS for the C minor

Piano Concerto K491. He became a tireless advocate for *Così fan tutte*, contributing significantly to its rehabilitation in the early twentieth century. Before a 1910 production in Munich, Strauss wrote of the need to rescue *Così* from neglect and from ruinous cuts. His own performances were largely uncut, and he is reported to have accompanied the recitatives himself. For the 150th anniversary of Mozart's *Idomeneo*, Strauss sought to revive its fortunes with an interventionist new edition (including some interpolations of his own), first performed in Vienna in 1931. Earlier, in 1924, Strauss and Hofmannsthal reworked BEETHOVEN's incidental music from *Die Ruinen von Athen*. Their version incorporates borrowings from *Prometheus* as well as a melodrama for which Strauss composed an accompaniment derived from Beethoven's Third and Fifth Symphonies.

Strauss's enthusiasm for the French Baroque led him to quote from LULLY's music for *Le bourgeois gentilhomme* in the original version of *Ariadne auf Naxos* and in the suite *Die Bürger als Edelman*. He arranged a Suite of Dances (1923) and a Divertimento (1941) from keyboard works by FRANÇOIS COUPERIN and his last opera, *Capriccio*, includes a quotation from the 'Air italien' in RAMEAU's *Les Indes galantes*.

As a conductor, Strauss was especially admired for his Mozart and he was the first conductor to record all three of the last symphonies. Despite some rough playing, what stands out in these Mozart recordings is Strauss's clearheaded and unsentimental interpretation, enlivened by fluid speeds and subtle placement of ACCENTS.

FURTHER READING

N. Del Mar, *Richard Strauss: A Critical Commentary on his Life and Works*, 3 vols. (London: Barrie and Rockliff, 1962–72).
M. Kennedy, *Richard Strauss: Man, Musician, Enigma* (Cambridge University Press, 1999).

NIGEL SIMEONE

Stravinsky, Igor (b. Oranienbaum (now Lomonosov), 5/17 June 1882; d. New York, 6 April 1971) Russian, later French, from 1945 American, composer, conductor and pianist.

Stravinsky was a pivotal figure in PERFORMANCE PRACTICE of the twentieth century, raised in a Rimsky-Korsakovian tradition yet living to influence post-modern, even minimalist, practice. Nicholas Cook speculates that Stravinsky's most effective legacy, even more than his modernist or neo-classical scores, may have been 'his fusion of the power of the baton and the word ... to create, through performance, a new musical past' (191). In such a view, Stravinsky's espousal of objectivity in music, in association with his belief that 'interprétation' needed to be replaced by a faithful 'exécution' of the score, led to a strict, so-called 'machine aesthetic'. That aesthetic then came to affect the emerging historical performance practices of early, Baroque and Classical musics, as well as compositional and performance styles of his own day.

Primary sources informing how Stravinsky wanted his own music performed, in addition to the scores themselves, include many gramophone recordings made across five decades from the 1920s. These recordings mostly feature Stravinsky as conductor, though occasionally as pianist (*see*, for instance, *Works of Igor Stravinsky*, twenty-two CDs (Sony, 2007)). There are also many hand-cut pianola rolls, mostly from the 1920s, which Stravinsky likened to 'lithographs' that 'reconstituted' his works. Essays, sometimes co-authored with Robert Craft, many thousands of letters and occasional forays into criticism also illuminate the topic.

Over his long career, however, Stravinsky changed his views and practices, thereby confounding rather than clarifying attempts to isolate a definitive Stravinskyan reading of a particular work. Later in life he resiled from his long-asserted faith in 'exécution', having come to believe that 'one performance presents only one set of circumstances, and that mistakes and misunderstandings are cemented into traditions as quickly and canonically as truths' (Stravinsky, 139). Despite making his own recordings explicitly as performing models for others, and often being dogmatic about correct TEMPI, RHYTHMIC INTERPRETATIONS and nuances, his own practice was frequently as variable as those, particularly conductors, whom he criticised. He even came to recognise that 'the speeds of everything in the world and in ourselves' had changed, in justification of his own wide deviations from original METRONOME markings in his works (Stravinsky and Craft, 122).

The Rite of Spring remains the most intense battleground over Stravinsky's performance AESTHETICS, not just by virtue of his several revisions of its score and four conducted recordings (1929, 1940, 1958, 1960), but also his own detailed criticism in 1964 of recordings of the work by Karajan, BOULEZ and the Russian P. Kpaøt. That late review addressed, comparatively, such issues as tone, ARTICULATION, ACCENTUATION, volume, rhythmic realisation, pauses and instrumental balance, as well as tempo, before concluding that 'None of the three performances is good enough to be preserved' (Stravinsky, 241).

The Rite, too, stands centrally among attempts to recreate particular performances. The recreation of Nijinsky's choreography at its premiere in 1913, by Millicent Hodson and Kenneth Archer with the Joffrey Ballet in 1987, preceded the centenary recreation of its musical performance, by LES SIÈCLES, conducted by François-Xavier Roth. Roth gained special permission from Boosey & Hawkes to perform and record his recreation of the score 'as it might have been heard on the evening of 29 May 1913', rather than use the authorised 'final' edition of 1967 (I. Stravinsky, *Le Sacre du Printemps, Petrouchka*, Les Siècles, cond. F.-X. Roth, CD (Les Siècles, 2014)). That recreation notably re-introduced DYNAMICS, articulations and rhythmic arrangements not heard since the *Rite*'s earliest performances. Roth's work also involved a reconstruction of the Ballets Russes ORCHESTRA, with much use of French-made instruments from the 1911–13 period, including original-sized TUBAS and TROMBONES, piston-valved HORNS, period PERCUSSION and uniform use of gut in the string section. Les Siècles have similarly recorded *Petrushka* and *Firebird*. Other works attracting rehabilitation or HISTORICALLY INFORMED PERFORMANCE include *L'Histoire du soldat, Pulcinella, Les Noces* and the late ballet, *Agon*.

FURTHER READING

N. Cook, 'Stravinsky conducts Stravinsky', in J. Cross (ed.), *The Cambridge Companion to Stravinsky* (Cambridge University Press, 2003), 176–91.

H. Danuser and H. Zimmermann (eds.), *Avatar of Modernity: The Rite of Spring Reconsidered* (London: Boosey & Hawkes, 2013).
I. Stravinsky, *Themes and Conclusions* (London: Faber & Faber, 1972).
I. Stravinsky and R. Craft, *Dialogues and a Diary* (London: Faber & Faber, 1968).

MALCOLM GILLIES

Studio der frühen Musik (Early Music Quartet) Early music ensemble founded in Munich in 1960, directed by American musicologist and lutenist THOMAS BINKLEY.

Binkley formed the Studio der frühen Musik (Early Music Quartet) with American string player Sterling Jones, Estonian mezzo-soprano ANDREA VON RAMM and English tenor Nigel Rogers. Rogers was succeded by two Americans: first, tenor Willard Cobb, then countertenor Richard Levitt. From the outset, the goal was to 'award professional attention to that vast repertory which lay chronologically before the Baroque'. Binkley was disappointed at the quality of Medieval instruments previously used in performance, concerned that not enough research went into reconstructions of the music and dismayed that some performances never achieved anything beyond a dry documentation of the NOTATION.

At von Ramm's suggestion, the group's first Medieval project was a reconstruction of the songs in the thirteenth-century *Carmina Burana* MANUSCRIPT, whose lyrics were used by Carl Orff for his famous work. Binkley was inspired by Arabic and other north African music making, in terms of the unique 'voices' of the different instruments available and how they helped to shape the vocal music. Finding that essence became the task for each successive project for the group. The use of improvised preludes, interludes and postludes became a distinctive feature, as did entirely memorised performances and the characteristic voice of Andrea von Ramm.

Recordings of several monophonic repertories ensued, from Germany, France and Iberia, followed by recordings devoted to major Medieval composers, including Oswald von Wolkenstein, MACHAUT, Landini, Ciconia and Dufay. In many cases, these were the first recordings of the repertory and were extremely influential on subsequent work.

In 1973, the ensemble began a residency at the SCHOLA CANTORUM in Basel and helped to train an important cadre of new professionals, even while issuing several recordings per year until c1976. While some of its members remained in Basel, Binkley moved back to the USA and established the Early Music Institute (now the Historical Performance Institute) at Indiana University in 1979.

FURTHER READING

T. Binkley, 'Zur Aufführungspraxis des einstimmigen Musik des Mittelalters: Ein Werkstattbericht', *BJhM*, (1977), 19–76.
S. S. Jones, *The Story of an Early Music Quartet (as revealed through the Personal Experiences of a Founding Member)* (Munich: privately printed, 2005).
K. Yri, 'Thomas Binkley and the Studio der Frühen Musik: challenging "the myth of Westernness"', *EMc*, 38 (2010), 273–80.

ROSS DUFFIN

Sulzer, Johann Georg (b. Winterthur, 16 October 1720; d. Berlin, 27 February 1779) Swiss aesthetician and lexicographer.

Sulzer was not by training a musician. Having studied theology in Zurich, he initially joined the clergy, pursuing further study in mathematics, sciences and AESTHETICS. Becoming professor of mathematics at the Joachimsthal Gymnasium in Berlin (1747), Sulzer began to establish a name for himself in lexicography and aesthetics, writing numerous articles and beginning the work for which he would become most famous, the *Allgemeine Theorie der schönen Künste*. This conservative and widely influential encyclopedia ranging broadly across the arts (Leipzig, 1771–4) was reprinted twice in enlarged formats before the end of the eighteenth century, despite failing to keep abreast of developing stylistic and generic benchmarks (for which it was criticised by Goethe). Sulzer believed art (and most especially music) served the principally moral purpose of making natural truths manifest not through rational reflection but by awakening emotional responses that equate to virtuous thoughts or actions. Thus, the experience of a work of art (meaning, in the case of music, a performance) was not purely mimetic, but served as a catalyst for moral sentiment.

The musical articles in Sulzer's *Allgemeine Theorie* were heavily indebted to two collaborators: J. S. BACH's pupil, JOHANN PHILIPP KIRNBERGER and Johann Adolph Peter Schulz. Despite his rather limited musical knowledge, Sulzer was involved in some of the earlier articles, though the vast majority were the work of Kirnberger and Schulz. Sulzer advocated a three-stage plan to musical creation: a plan (*Anlage*); its realisation (*Ausführung*); and subsequent elaboration (*Ausarbeitung*). This model was to influence HEINRICH KOCH significantly in conceptions of musical form.

FURTHER READING

N. K. Baker and T. Christensen (trans. and eds.), *Aesthetics and the Art of Musical Composition in the German Enlightenment: Selected Writings of Johann G. Sulzer and Heinrich C. Koch* (Cambridge University Press, 1995).

JOHN IRVING

Suzuki, Masaaki (b. Kobe, 29 April 1954) Japanese conductor, organist and harpsichordist.

Suzuki graduated in composition and ORGAN performance at the Tokyo National University of Fine Arts and Music and went on to study at the Sweelinck Conservatory in Amsterdam under TON KOOPMAN (HARPSICHORD), Piet Kee (organ) and Klaas Bolt (IMPROVISATION). He twice competed in the Flanders Early Music Festival in Bruges, winning prizes in improvisation (1980) and organ performance (1983). From 1981 to 1983 he taught harpsichord in Duisburg, Germany before returning to Japan in 1983, where he began teaching at Kōbe Shōin Women's College.

In 1990 he founded the Bach Collegium Japan with whom he has established himself as a leading authority on the works of J. S. BACH. Under his direction this ensemble has recorded Bach's major choral works, all the church cantatas and much of the instrumental music for the Swedish label BIS. Suzuki has also recorded all Bach's harpsichord music. Critically acclaimed for their high standards of recorded sound and balance, carefully chosen historical instrumental timbres and meticulously realised vocal EXPRESSION, these recordings redefine the performance tradition established in the 1970s and 1980s by HARNONCOURT and LEONHARDT and are interpretatively clearly distinguishable from the work of other contemporary directors such as GARDINER and Koopman.

Suzuki's recent guest conducting engagements have included later repertory with leading modern ORCHESTRAS. The founder and head of the early music department at the Tokyo University of the Arts, he is currently visiting professor of choral conducting at Yale University and the conductor of Yale Schola Cantorum. He is one of the first pioneers of historical PERFORMANCE PRACTICE in Japan to be internationally recognised and has received a number of prestigious awards, including the Leipzig Bach Medal in 2013 and an honorary doctorate from the Theological University of the Reformed Churches in Kampe in 2015.

TERENCE CHARLSTON

T

Tablature A term which usually refers to a notational system that uses letters, numbers, or means other than mensural or staff systems to designate PITCHES and rhythms. Historically, musicians have sometimes used the term for condensed scores such as keyboard or short scores, or diagrams of DANCE choreographies.

Tablature occurs most frequently in plucked string and keyboard sources. Most versions specify the physical actions on instruments required to perform pitches and are more condensed than staff NOTATION, saving time and space. Most tablature systems are vague about some aspects of duration, since they normally prescribe the beginnings of notes but rarely their endings. On the other hand, metrical clarity results when regular barring occurs in TABLATURES well before the practice is common in staff notation.

Tablature made music more accessible to many by offering a notation system easier to implement than the more complex mensural notation, which required some prior theoretical knowledge. However, owing to a modern lack of familiarity with the notation, vast amounts of music in tablature remain practically unknown today.

The earliest examples are fourteenth- and fifteenth-century keyboard tablatures, with the top voice appearing in staff notation and letters for lower voices written below. This so-called 'old German keyboard tablature' dominates the Buxheim Organ Book (c1470) and accounts for most keyboard sources from Germany and central Europe until the middle of the sixteenth century, when the top line also began to appear in letter notation. Use of this 'new German keyboard tablature' (Figure 14) persisted well into the eighteenth century.

Three systems of Spanish keyboard tablature, or *cifras*, using numbers appeared between the 1550s and 1700; some were advocated for HARP as well. The significant advantage of these systems was that normal print type could be used instead of special music types.

Since the sixteenth century, tablatures have been most common among stringed instruments: LUTES (including THEORBO, mandore and others), GUITAR, cittern, harp, VIOL and even the VIOLIN family. Notwithstanding interesting but rare examples, the vast majority of the enormous repertories for plucked strings resides in tablature, whether solo music or ensemble parts. For instruments with necks and (usually) frets, horizontal lines represent courses, and numbers or letters on or above those lines designate frets. Rhythmic signs appear above. Special symbols were developed to indicate details of FINGERING for both hands, ORNAMENTATION and various types of ARTICULATION, including arpeggiation. Tablature proved useful when performers used a

(a)

(b)

Figure 14: a, b and c New German keyboard tablature.
(in Johann Woltz, *Nova musices organicae tabulatura* (Basle: Johann Jacob Genath, 1617))

Figure 15: Italian lute tablature.

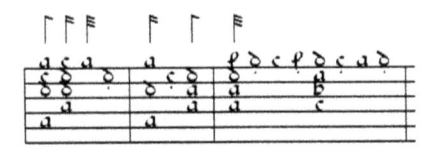

Figure 16: French lute tablature.

variety of tunings for open courses, since knowledge of all the notes in each tuning was unnecessary.

In the Italian system the bottom line represents the highest-pitched course, and numbers indicate frets (Figure 15); this system was also most common in VIHUELA sources. The French system, in which letters indicate frets and the top line is the highest-pitched course, became the most popular system by the early seventeenth century, lasting until the end of the eighteenth (Figure 16).

The earliest known lute source is a German tablature from the Brunswick area probably notating repertoire for plectrum lute from c1460; its eight-line staff indicates pitches (not courses) across a two-octave range, similar to ORGAN tablature from this era. The settings of secular songs preserved in this source alternate between two voices and strummed chords.

A more common German lute tablature system probably began slightly later in the fifteenth century; this system, attributed to Conrad Paumann, was common in central Europe in the sixteenth and early seventeenth centuries and stood apart from the other traditions in that each intersection of course and fret had its own letter symbol, eliminating the need for depicting all courses.

Guitar music adapted Italian or French lute tablature in the sixteenth century, sometimes adding abbreviations in the seventeenth for the most common chords. These chords are represented by large numbers in Spain and capital letters (*alfabeto*) in Italy, frequently combined with standard lute tablature.

All three prevalent lute systems were adapted for the viol, but ensemble parts appear most often in mensural notation after the mid-sixteenth century. Solo repertories, especially for lyra or bass viol, retained tablature the longest. Viol players still used and advocated for French tablature during the latter third of the seventeenth century (e.g. Mace (*Musick's Monument* (London: T. Ratcliffe & N. Thompson, 1676)), Machy (*Pièces de violle en musique et en tablature* (Paris: L'autheur [*sic*], 1685)).

Many modern string players play from tablature, whether in historic repertories or in recent popular music for guitar, bass guitar, mandolin, banjo, ukulele and other instruments. The evolution of notation for aerophones sometimes incorporated types of tablature, including for RECORDER, FLUTE, flageolet and OBOE and normally prescribing fingerings and rhythms. Notating signals for hunting HORN inspired a variety of innovative solutions, all of which were short-lived and regional until staff notation became common *c*1700.

FURTHER READING

M. Lewon, 'The Wolfenbüttel lute tablature', *mlewon: Research News from Marc Lewon*. mlewon.wordpress.com/2014/02/22/wolfenbuettel-lute-tablature/.

R. Rastall, *The Notation of Western Music* (London: J. M. Dent & Sons, 1983).

P. Vendrix, J. Griffiths and D. Dolata (eds.), *Encyclopedia of Tablature* (Turnhout: Brepols, forthcoming).

STUART CHENEY

Tactus (beat) Most Western art music is 'measured', in the sense that it relies on sounds whose durations are not only precisely quantified, but also proportionally related to one another, so that, for instance, a modern semibreve corresponds to four crotchets and a dotted crotchet equals three quarters of a minim. In the polyphonic practice of pre-modern times, the tactus (from the Latin *tangere*, to touch) referred to a referential unit of time, typically marked by the up and down motion of the director's hand – the 'beat' – against which performers measured the notated rhythmic values. The referential unit of time was usually labelled *mensura*, and expressly indicated through a dedicated sign (the *tempus*, now called 'metre') placed at the beginning of the musical NOTATION. For instance, in standard mensural practice a 'cut C' sign called for the *breve* to be used as tactus (*tempus imperfectum diminutum*, with two semibreves per tactus), whereas uncut *tempora* equated the tactus with the semibreve. Modern scholars and performers generally agree that a change of metre in the course of a composition calls for the adoption of a new tactus that is proportionally related to the old one, though at times there is ambiguity as to just what that PROPORTION should be; in many instances the tactus itself may not change, but only its internal subdivision. These cases highlight the fact that the problem of tactus/beat is indistinguishable from considerations of TEMPO, which Sherr (1987) describes as perhaps the most frustratingly elusive aspect of pre-modern music.

The adoption of increasingly shorter rhythmic values in musical practice through time led to the demise of the time-worn practice of equating the tactus with the semibreve (Houle, 32). In the modern era the beat usually corresponds to the crotchet (the standard beat in 'common time', marked 4/4 or 'C'), and sometimes even to the quaver, though works or individual movements marked 'alla breve', with the minim indicating the beat (marked 2/2 or 'cut C'), persisted into the eighteenth century and beyond. Thus, the semibreve, the tactus of the pre-modern era, came to indicate a four-fold grouping of 'beats', or a bar (or measure) separated out by bar lines.

FURTHER READING

R. DeFord, *Tactus, Mensuration, and Rhythm in Renaissance Music* (Cambridge University Press, 2015).
G. Houle, *Meter in Music, 1600–1800: Performance, Perception, and Notation* (Bloomington, IN: Indiana University Press, 1987).
R. Sherr, 'Tempo to 1500', in T. Knighton and D. Fallows (eds.), *A Companion to Medieval and Renaissance Music* (London: Dent, 1992), 327–36.

STEFANO MENGOZZI

Tafelmusik Canadian period-instrument orchestra specialising in Baroque and Classical repertoire.

Founded in Toronto as a chamber group in 1979 by RECORDER player Kenneth Solway and bassoonist Susan Graves (both of whom had trained in the Netherlands), Tafelmusik was one of Canada's first period ensembles and originally gave concerts in the city's Church of Holy Trinity before finding a new regular home at Trinity-St Paul's United Church. The ensemble quickly expanded into an ORCHESTRA, and in 1981 it moved away from working with guest directors by appointing American-born violinist Jeanne Lamon as concertmaster and music director. Under Lamon's leadership Tafelmusik built a reputation for precise ensemble, polished sound and strong group ethic.

In 1981 the orchestra toured the USA and in 1984 was the first North American period orchestra to visit Europe. It made a small number of commercial recordings in the 1980s, but the signing of a forty-CD contract for Sony Classical's newly established early music label Vivarte in 1990 was a major boost to the orchestra's international fame. In addition to core BACH, Handel and Vivaldi directed by Lamon, it recorded orchestral and choral works by HAYDN, MOZART, BEETHOVEN and Schubert with German conductor Bruno Weil.

The Tafelmusik Chamber Choir was formed to complement the orchestra's work in 1981; and since 1982 it has been under the directorship of Ivars Taurins. In 1985 the orchestra began a collaboration with Toronto's Opera Atelier, participating in productions of operas by MONTEVERDI, LULLY, CHARPENTIER, Gluck and Mozart. It has also performed in the multimedia productions *The Galileo Project* (2009), *House of Dreams* (2012) and *Tales of Two Cities: The Leipzig-Damascus Coffee House* (2016), devised by the orchestra's DOUBLE BASS player Alison Mackay, in which live musical performance mixes with narration, DANCE, film and photography.

Lamon stood down as music director in 2014, a year after the orchestra's renovated home venue had been renamed the Trinity-St-Paul's, Jeanne Lamon Hall. She was succeeded in 2017 by the violinist Elisa Citterio.

LINDSAY KEMP

Talbot Manuscript The 'Talbot Manuscript' is a source of informative notes on the history, appearance and measurements of musical instruments in the hand of James Talbot (1664–1708), professor of Hebrew at Cambridge University (1699–1704). It comprises a series of fascicles, which have been numbered one to eleven somewhat indiscriminately by a librarian at Christ Church, Oxford. Two further fascicles, though unnumbered, clearly belong to the whole, which forms part of a 'Collection for a Treatise upon Musick by Dean Aldrich' (*GB-Och* Music MS 1187), incorporating an undistinguished TREATISE by Aldrich about Greek music theory. Because Mus.1187 is unbound and has never been systematically foliated or paginated, its constituent sheets and fascicles have been vulnerable to re-organisation over the years, hence the librarian's version, BURNEY's subdivision of its contents into fifteen sections (*A General History of Music from the Earliest Ages to the Present Period* (London, 1776–89, 1957), II, 602, footnote d) and the various other arrangements through history summarised in Christ Church library's online documentation.

Talbot's contribution comprises 241 pages (of three different sizes) on which some text appears, whether simply headings (suggesting that his task was incomplete) or measurements, TABLATURES, tunings, FINGERINGS and other relevant details about various keyboard, stringed and wind instruments. Much of his material was obtained first-hand from leading players and makers (notably Gottfried Finger, John Blow, John Banister (ii), James Paisible, John Shore, Peter Bressan, William Bull, Ralph Agutter, Renatus Harris and Father Smith) and from his own examination of instruments loaned to him. Other pages record quotations from PRAETORIUS's *Syntagma musicum* (1619), Talbot's principal model, MERSENNE's *Harmonie universelle* (1636–7) and KIRCHER's *Musurgia Universalis* (2 vols. (Rome: Lodovico Grignani, 1650)) and refer to early sixteenth-century publications by AGRICOLA and VIRDUNG.

Talbot was not primarily a musician, composer or instrument maker, but his copious corrections to his manuscript demonstrate his intention to be as accurate as possible. However, his recorded measurements are sometimes ambiguous or inconsistent – comparing the thickness of a VIOLIN soundpost to a 'goosequill', for example, is unhelpful – and some are almost certainly inaccurate (e.g his 3.5 inches violin belly-to-back measurement under the bridge). Nevertheless, his manuscript is the most detailed document concerning the violin and BOW c1700 and the only surviving information source about ORGAN mutation-stop registrations in late seventeenth-century England; amongst its many other attributes it contains illustrations and descriptions of organ tracker actions of the time and provides contemporary evidence about the arrival in England of 'French woodwind' instruments.

FURTHER READING

A. C. Baines, R. Donington, W. A. Cocks, M. Prynne, D. Gill, J. Rimmer and C. Mould, 'James Talbot's Manuscript', *GSJ*, 1 (1948), 9–26; 3 (1950), 27–45; 5 (1952), 44–7; 14 (1961), 52–68; 15 (1962) 60–9; 16 (1963), 63–72; 21 (1968), 40–51.

R. Unwin, 'An English writer on music: James Talbot 1664–1708', *GSJ*, 40 (1987), 53–72.

http://library.chch.ox.ac.uk/music/page.php?set=Mus.+1187; and http://library.chch.ox.ac.uk/music/page.php?page=Mus.+1187%3A+James+Talbot's+papers.

ROBIN STOWELL

Tartini, Giuseppe (b. Pirano, 8 April 1692; d. Padua, 26 February 1770) Italian composer, violinist, teacher and theorist.

Tartini is of threefold importance in the history of eighteenth-century music: as a violinist and influential teacher, as a composer of a rich corpus of concertos and sonatas, and as a theorist both of VIOLIN playing and of more abstruse scientific concepts. Largely self-taught, though greatly inspired by hearing Veracini in 1716, he was appointed five years later to the prestigious post of *primo violino e capo di concerto* at Sant'Antonio in Padua, a position he retained for almost the whole of his life. In 1727 he formalised his teaching practice into what became known as his 'Scuola delle Nazioni', attracting selected students from across Europe to a programme that extended beyond violin playing into composition, musical theory and AESTHETICS.

Motivated by the discovery of the 'terzo suono' (the lower note perceived when a double-stop is perfectly in tune), he published several theoretical TREATISES and also wrote a practical guide to ORNAMENTATION, the *Regole per arrivare a saper ben suonar il violino*, published in Paris only in 1771. The first part (already purloined in LEOPOLD MOZART's 1756 treatise) explains the subtle nuances attached to the performance of individual ornaments; while the second discusses free ornamentation, made manifest in his set of CORELLI variations entitled *L'arte del arco*. For Tartini, BOWING was at the heart of expressive violin playing, as he emphasised in a famous letter to his pupil Maddalena Lombardini, with its invaluable advice on how to practise long notes and fast semiquaver passages.

Here lies a fundamental aspect of Tartini's musical aesthetic: the distinction between the vocal 'cantabile' and the instrumental 'suonabile'. The former was by far the more important, representing principles of nature rather than human artefact: 'the highest perfection of good taste lies in the voice, and in expression' (trans. from G. Tartini, *Trattato di musica secondo la vera scienza dell'armonia* (Padua, 1754), 149). He sought to reproduce not only the sound of the human voice but also its natural way of inflecting musical phrasing; while ornamentation, far from being mere superficial decoration, was essential in bringing out the affect of the vocal line.

Tartini's own compositions, yet to be fully appreciated in the absence of a complete EDITION, include around 160 violin concertos and numerous sonatas. The concertos describe a trajectory from the early large-scale, Vivaldian structures through a more elegantly ornamented *galanterie* to the much sparer late works, where the musical elements seem reduced to their very essence. The expressive *cantabile* is revealed in poetically regular melodies, devoid of chromaticism and laid out in the simplest structures with only light accompaniment. The sonatas follow a similar path from Corellian beginnings to the final *piccole sonate*, where pure vocal EXPRESSION is taken to its ultimate extreme, and the violin alone is sufficient: 'I play them without bass, and this is my true intention' (trans. from letter to Algarotti dated 24 February 1750, in Petrobelli, 82). The work by which Tartini is still best known, the demanding 'Devil's Trill' Sonata, is usually heard in melodramatic nineteenth-century arrangements, the antithesis of the natural melodic simplicity towards which his whole life aspired.

FURTHER READING

Ad Parnassum, 11/22 (October, 2013) (Tartini special issue).
P. Petrobelli, *Tartini, le sue idee e il suo tempo* (Lucca: Libreria musicale italiana, 1992).
G. Tartini, *Traité des agréments de la musique*, ed. E. R. Jacobi (New York: Celle, 1961).

SIMON McVEIGH

Taruskin, Richard (Filler) (b. New York, 2 April 1945) American musicologist and critic.

One of the most significant musicologists in the decades spanning the turn of the twenty-first century, Richard Taruskin has produced work and critical commentary in a remarkable variety of musical areas, ranging from Renaissance studies to Russian modernism. He also had considerable experience working as a violist and choral director during the 1970s and 1980s.

Taruskin's approach to the 'authenticity debate' inaugurated an entirely new way of looking at the issues. Critiques hitherto tended to centre on internal disputes (simply put, as to who was the more 'authentic' in recreating past practice) or on external ones, which saw the movement as killing off all 'expressive' elements or as a sad reflection on the decline of the supposedly unbroken classical tradition. While Taruskin shared at least some of these latter misgivings, he turned the entire discourse on its head by affirming that historical performance was no real recreation of a past at all, but the most 'authentic' performance practice of the age. It was, namely, an archetypal form of 'modernist' performance. His profoundly ambivalent attitude towards historical performance practice (sometimes mistaken for outright and unrelenting antipathy) clearly related to his view of STRAVINSKY, and the latter's inauguration of a 'geometrical' style of performance.

By the 1990s Taruskin perceived more promising directions in historical performance. For him, a future for historical performance was possible if only performers used their historical awareness as a pretext for deviating from the letter of the score or from the assumed 'sanctity' of the musical work. The title of his 1995 compendium of essays on historical performance, *Text and Act*, underlines his analysis of what he saw as the essential problem with historicist performers, namely that the act of performance was being reduced to the status of a text, thus conflating the roles of scholarly EDITING and performance.

FURTHER READING

R. Taruskin, *Text and Act – Essays on Music and Performance* (New York: Oxford University Press, 1995).

JOHN BUTT

Taste/s The notion of 'taste' (Fr. *goût*; Ger. *Geschmack*; Ital. *gusto*) has played a central role in discussions of music, particularly those from the seventeenth and eighteenth centuries. This brief entry cannot provide a full analysis of those debates. Instead it offers an introductory taxonomy of the uses of the term as applied to music under four main headings: 1) Taste as subjective preference; 2) Taste as a systematic type of judgement; 3) Taste as a refined and alert sensibility; and 4) Taste as a description of the norms of fashions, practices or styles. In writings on music these types often overlap in confusing ways.

The most relativistic notion of taste derives by metaphor and extension from our subjective preferences for certain types of food and drink. Such appetites, according to QUANTZ (*Versuch*, 279), also occur in relation to music in those ruled by ignorance, prejudice and passion, where the diversity of tastes 'depends upon differences in temperament'. A more subtle aspect of subjective taste concerns those habits of musical EXPRESSION and display which we take to be 'instinctive' or 'natural', but which are largely acquired through a process of unconscious acculturation. Much of the historical performance movement has been concerned with undoing or modifying our historically situated 'natural' tastes for certain types of intensification and expression in music.

Although unthinking preferences can bring pleasure, most art works require something beyond raw appetite for their full appreciation and understanding. In the eighteenth century, philosophers such as Hume and Kant explored the processes involved in making judgements of taste with great subtlety. For Kant (*Critique of Judgment* [1790], trans. W. Pluhar (Indianapolis: Hackett Publishing, 1987)), 'taste' was not just an attitude of the right sort, but a complex perception that arose from a particular procedure – the free play of the imagination and understanding (62) while contemplating the artwork for its own sake (45–6). It was the presence of this phenomenological 'pathway' that allowed Kant to distinguish between a judgement of 'taste', and a judgement of the merely 'agreeable' (47–8: the claim that we simply find something pleasant or useful). This construal of 'taste' arose not so much from uniformity in the final verdicts asserted by those 'of taste', but rather from the similarity of the processes and experiences sought by them in pursuit of their verdicts – even if those final verdicts might differ. Nor were such mental experiences to be seen as merely intellectual ones, for it was agreed that concepts and feelings frequently acted in combination ('fascination', for example, could be seen as an emotion of the intellect). Thus we find the music theorist JOHANN MATTHESON defining taste as 'that internal sensibility, selection and judgement by which our intellect reveals itself in matters of feeling' (*Die neueste Untersuchung der Singspiele, nebst beygefügter musikalischen Geschmacksprobe* (Hamburg: Christian Herold, 1744), 123).

The role of 'sensibility' in relation to the concept of taste was complex. Sometimes it signalled an attribute of a person – one who was in possession of a discriminating and alert receptivity. Elsewhere it indicated a quality found in certain performances executed with 'good taste' (*le bon goût*); that is, with poise, intelligent sensitivity and refinement, as described by FRANÇOIS COUPERIN in the Preface to his *Pièces de clavecin: troisième livre* (Paris, 1722). Such delicacy of technique was usually linked to the problem of musical expression, where it was seen as necessary for the graceful and elegant display of feelings. It was recognised that such elegance retained a certain intensification or radiance, but it was a radiance that was infused with sensibility rather than overt passion. These notions arose largely from an admiration for the French courtly manner filtered through the rationalist philosophy of Descartes with its concern for clear and distinct ideas.

The most extended debates on taste in the eighteenth century concerned the description and relative merits of NATIONAL IDIOMS. In France, for example, RAGUENET in 1702 and LE CERF (DE VIÉVILLE) in 1704 argued respectively for Italian and French tastes, a debate that led more broadly to the conscious combination of both styles by later composers (François Couperin, J. S. BACH, etc.). In England, observations on Italian opera by, among others, Joseph Addison in *The Spectator* brought the notion of taste firmly into the arena of fashion, and thence into a growing awareness of how tastes change and whether or not there might be 'progress' in the arts. BURNEY commented (*A General History of Music from the Earliest Ages to the Present Period* (London, 1776–89)) that GEMINIANI's writings on taste (c1748, 1749) were no longer applicable in the 1780s, while TOSI in his treatise on SINGING (1723) did not hesitate to prefer certain traditional practices over those of his own time. It was soon recognised, too, that preferences for certain styles and tastes could be taken as fashionable indicators of social position, and therefore could be manipulated for that purpose. Hence William Hazlitt's contention that 'fashion is gentility running away from vulgarity and afraid of being overtaken' (A. Waller and A. Glover (eds.), *The Collected Works of William Hazlitt: Table Talk and Conversations of James Northcote, Esq., R. A.* (London: J. M. Dent, 1903), Bk VI, no. 19, 439) – a warning that tastes could not only change but also degenerate into the kitsch and commonplace. Translated into the concerns of musical performers this means that unthinking tastes run the risk of becoming empty mannerisms.

FURTHER READING

R. Donington, *The Interpretation of Early Music* (London: Faber & Faber, 1963/R 1974).
I. Kant, *Critique of Judgment* [1790], trans. W. Pluhar (Indianapolis: Hackett Publishing, 1987).
L. Treitler (ed.), *Strunk's Source Readings in Music History* (New York: W. W. Norton, 1998).

ANTHONY PRYER

Telemann, Georg Philipp (b. Magdeburg, 14 March 1681; d. Hamburg, 25 June 1767) German composer.

Following Gymnasium studies in Hildesheim (1697–1701), Telemann studied law at the university in Leipzig (1701–5), where he also founded a Collegium Musicum, directed the opera and music at the Neukirche, and wrote vocal works for the Thomaskirche. Following court appointments at Sorau (1705–8) and Eisenach (1708–12), he held the post of city music director at Frankfurt (1712–21) and then at Hamburg (1721–67), directing Collegia Musica and giving public concerts in both cities.

During the early decades of his career, Telemann remained professionally active as a singer (baritone) and player of the VIOLIN (his principal instrument), keyboard, RECORDER, CHALUMEAU, CELLO and calchedon. Although he never followed through on plans to write a TREATISE on performance (in 1733 he listed a *Traité du récitatif* among his projected publications, and in the mid-1740s he contemplated issuing serially a treatise called *Musicalischer Practicus*), several of his publications include extensive remarks on continuo playing and the performance of recitative, as well as important examples of free ORNAMENTATION. The preface to his first published cantata cycle, the *Harmonischer Gottesdienst* (Hamburg, 1725–6), includes discussions of the so-called 'prosodic' appoggiatura in recitative and the TRANSPOSITION of *Kammerton* ORGAN continuo parts to accommodate *Chorton*. In the 'lesson'

(*Unterricht*) concluding his 'nearly universal hymnal', the *Fast allgemeines evangelisch-musicalisches Lieder-Buch* (Hamburg, 1730), Telemann instructs on realising a FIGURED BASS, provides tonal plans for improvised organ preludes to chorale singing and advises on the use of the cadential Picardy third. With few exceptions, each of the forty-eight songs of the *Singe- Spiel- und General-Bass-Übungen* (Hamburg, 1733–4) is accompanied by instructions for realising the figured bass accompaniment. Telemann offers further remarks on figured bass realisation in the preface to his cantata cycle *Musicalisches Lob Gottes* (Nuremberg, 1744). And the *Avertissement* to the *Nouveaux quatuors* (Paris, 1738) introduces the new bass figure of a half circle for the diminished triad (dubbed the 'Telemannischer Bogen' by C. P. E. BACH). Each opening slow movement in the *Sonate metodiche* (Hamburg, 1728) and *Continuation des sonates méthodiques* (Hamburg, 1732) presents the flute/violin part in plain and ornamented versions. The ornaments, like those for the slow movements in the first three trios of the *III Trietti methodichi e III scherzi* (Hamburg, 1731), are predominantly Italianate and feature an attractive rhythmic variety. Studies of Telemann's performing forces at Frankfurt and Hamburg indicate that he ordinarily performed his sacred and occasional vocal works with four singers, sometimes supplemented by four ripienists.

FURTHER READING

D. Gutknecht, W. Hobohm and B. Reipsch (eds.), *Freiheit oder Gesetz? Aufführungspraktische Erkenntnisse aus Telemanns Handschriften, zeitgenössischen Abschriften, musiktheoretischen Publikationen und ihre Anwendung* (Hildesheim: Olms, 2007).

J. Neubacher, *Georg Philipp Telemanns Hamburger Kirchenmusik und ihre Aufführungsbedingungen (1721–1767): Organisationsstrukturen, Musiker, Besetzungspraktiken* (Hildesheim: Olms, 2009).

S. Zohn, *Music for a Mixed Taste: Style, Genre, and Meaning in Telemann's Instrumental Works* (New York: Oxford University Press, 2008).

STEVEN ZOHN

Temperament A system of tuning whereby some or all of the concords of the scale are deliberately widened or narrowed from their corresponding pure intonation (hence 'tempering'). Western musical culture has produced a number of methods of tuning and temperament (some practical but many purely theoretical) which attempt to reconcile the harmonic needs of different styles of music with the physical laws which govern sound.

Considered acoustically, the pure intervals which make a scale of twelve notes cannot be used to form a pure octave. In practical terms, a unison tuned from twelve pure perfect fifths (C–G–D–A ... C) is almost a quarter-tone sharp of pure. This mathematical anomaly is known as the Pythagorean or ditonic comma. To make the two C's coincide, the twelve fifths must be narrowed by the total amount of the ditonic comma. If each fifth is reduced by exactly $\frac{1}{12}$ of the comma, the resulting tuning is known as equal temperament, the standard Western temperament today. Similarly, a major third tuned from four pure perfect fifths (C–G–D–A–E) is also almost a quarter-tone sharp of pure, though by a slightly smaller fraction than the ditonic comma. This new anomaly is known as the comma of Didymus or syntonic comma. Whilst a singer, trombonist or violinist can adjust their intonation for harmonic or expressive (*notes sensibles*) reasons, fixed-pitch instruments (keyboard and harp), fretted instruments and many wind instruments required the tuner or maker to adopt a single system of temperament.

The history of temperaments since the Middle Ages is closely allied to the development of harmony, composition and performance. Medieval tunings used pure fifths and were called Pythagorean. The comma was placed between G♯ and E♭ rendering this fifth too narrow for use (the 'wolf') but leaving the remaining eleven fifths pure. Major thirds on the natural notes were uncomfortably wide in this tuning and, reflecting contemporary musical style, were considered dissonances to be resolved onto pure fifths and fourths. As harmony developed and the major third became more frequently used, singers began to soften this interval by narrowing it. For keyboard music, the 'wolf' fifth was moved round the circle of fifths to a new position between B and F♯, giving almost pure major thirds above the notes D, E, A and B. This solution, first recorded by HENRI ARNAUT DE ZWOLLE (*c*1440), anticipates the next widely adopted tuning method, the regular meantone systems, which produce pure (or nearly pure) major thirds on all the natural notes by compromising the purity of the fifths.

The most common form of meantone was quarter-comma, in which eleven fifths were made very narrow – a quarter of a comma narrower than pure – and the remaining fifth was a 'wolf', so harshly dissonant as to be unusable. In this tuning, there were eight pure major thirds, and four wide 'wolf' thirds. Other kinds of meantone – for example, fifth- and sixth-comma – balanced the impurity of both thirds and fifths while taming slightly the harshness of the 'wolves'. While all the diatonic whole-tone steps were equal in size (hence meantone) the unequal semitone steps heightened the expressive intonation of chromatic melodies and progressions; moreover, the existence of genuine diminished fourths and sevenths heightened harmonic contrasts. The presence of 'wolf' fifths and thirds, however, limited modulation. This was partly overcome by keyboards with divided keys to provide enharmonic equivalents; for example, separate keys for E♭ and D♯ (e.g. the organ at San Martino, Lucca, 1484). In the late Renaissance, the limitations of meantone were in any case being circumvented by equal temperament on fretted instruments (LUTES, citterns and VIOLS) and just intonation in advanced vocal writing (Willaert (1530) and Orso (1567)). Keyboard compositions using remote keys (e.g. Bull's 'Ut, re, mi, fa, sol, la') may have been written for the experimental *arcicembali* (Vicentino (1555) and Trasuntino (1606)) with more than twelve notes per octave.

By the seventeenth century new systems of irregular temperaments developed to accommodate the remoter keys not available in meantone. These new methods took two general forms. The first were irregular circulating temperaments which gradually absorbed the 'wolf' across the remote keys, leaving the natural keys more concordant. Each key was differentiated by its own pattern of intervals and 'KEY CHARACTER'. In France these schemes went under the generic term *tempérament ordinaire*, but were widely used all over Europe. The other group of temperaments abandoned meantone and tuned most of the fifths pure. Werckmeister's third temperament (1681) is a typical example. These are closely associated with organ building in German-speaking countries, and are related to 'Vallotti' and Thomas Young's second temperament, the temperaments most frequently encountered in the performance of Baroque music today.

The title *The Well-Tempered Clavier* (1722) refers to some kind of temperament suitable for J. S. BACH's two cycles of twenty-four preludes and fugues in every key: either equal temperament (Rasch, 1985) or an irregular temperament (Lindley, 1977). Bach's choice of temperament is not known and was keenly debated in the eighteenth century. His practical tuning, however, was fast and set by ear, and (according to KIRNBERGER) used no pure thirds. Recent suggestions that the decorative loops on the title page of Bach's autograph of the first part of the '48' may reveal the answer has led to renewed speculation (Lehman, 2005).

Equal temperament was used on fretted instruments from the sixteenth century (GALILEI, 1581), and its early advocates as a keyboard temperament include FRESCOBALDI (1630s) and MERSENNE (1636). It did not gain general acceptance, however, until the late eighteenth and nineteenth centuries. While the equivalence of all keys in equal temperament had utilitarian advantages for modulation and general intonation (C. P. E. BACH, 1762 and MARPURG, 1776), it lacked the key colour, variety and ingenuity of all other eighteenth-century (irregular) temperaments (MATTHESON, 1713 and NEIDHARDT, 1724 and 1732). In practice, equal temperament was adopted by degrees and in parallel with changing string and wind intonation. The music of HAYDN and MOZART remained tonally relatively conservative and, like BEETHOVEN, these composers continued to exploit the late Baroque understanding of the emotional associations of certain keys. The early Romantic composers, Chopin, for example, utilised a fuller range of keys, although non-equal temperaments were still in use in the middle of the nineteenth century.

FURTHER READING

A. Baines (ed.), *The Oxford Companion to Musical Instruments* (Oxford University Press, 1992), art. 'Temperament', 331–3.
P. Bavington, *Clavichord Tuning and Maintenance* (London: Keyword Press, 2010), 22–34, 192–5.
B. Haynes, 'Beyond temperament: non-keyboard intonation in the 17th and 18th centuries', *EMc*, 19/3 (1991), 357–81.
C. Kent, 'Temperament and pitch', in N. Thistlethwaite and G. Webber (eds.), *The Cambridge Companion to the Organ* (Cambridge University Press, 1999), 42–51.
D. Ponsford, 'Instrumental performance in the seventeenth century' in C. Lawson and R. Stowell (eds.), *The Cambridge History of Musical Performance* (Cambridge University Press, 2012), 446–7.
P. Walls, 'Instrumental performance in the "long eighteenth century"', in C. Lawson and R. Stowell (eds.), *The Cambridge History of Musical Performance* (Cambridge University Press, 2012), 533–40.

TERENCE CHARLSTON

Tempo Tempo is one of the most problematic concepts in performance. MONSIEUR DE SAINT LAMBERT, writing in his *Principes de Claveçin* (1702), devotes considerable attention to matters of tempo, noting how musical NOTATION, and specifically time signatures (the systems of indicating the quantity and nature of beat-units within a bar by means of numerical fractions), could never hope to convey correct tempo adequately without the further help of descriptive words. Saint Lambert was writing at a time when such fractional time signatures had only recently ceased to function as indicators of proportional tempo relationships (*see* PROPORTIONS, THE SYSTEM OF). Since the late fourteenth century at least, their application had principally been one of relative time-measurement (mensuration signs), originally a musical shorthand for guiding singers towards the correct subdivision of one note value into multiple values on a lower hierarchy (e.g. a semibreve into either three or two minims). Such mensural indications frequently expressed quite complicated interrelations: one might, for instance, encounter signs denoting the simultaneous division of two hierarchies (the highest level unit being divided into three smaller units, and the next level down from that into two); or else the subdivision of a unit into two during one section might be followed immediately by another in which the division is into three, those three being performed strictly in the same length of time formerly taken by two (a relationship known as *sesquialtera* – a practice regularly encountered in English VIRGINALS and string CONSORT music from the Elizabethan era). Yet more complicated proportionate relations existed, and one encounters MANUSCRIPT sources – especially of Medieval secular song – in which the musical, intellectual and calligraphic aspects (extending even to different-coloured inks) appear to merge in a tour de force of representational AESTHETICS for its own sake.

But for all this complexity of representation, while the proportionate designations might be expressed definitively, the actual tempo could only be achieved conventionally and by agreement by performers in the act of rehearsal. This was still the case once fractional time signatures had become embedded in musical practice – largely by the end of the seventeenth century – though Saint Lambert (*Les principles du clavecin* (Paris: Christophe Ballard, 1702)) still explains certain aspects of the fractional system proportionally, noting, for instance, that a denominator of 4 indicated an absolute speed twice that indicated by 2 (likewise a denominator of 8 was to be performed at twice the speed indicated by 4). Such claims are found also at around this time in other writings (MUFFAT, for instance). Careful distinction was conventionally observed between these hierarchical levels: a tempo notated in 3/4, for example, must not sound so fast that it could be mistaken for 3/8, and vice versa. The degrees of permissible tempo inflection, however, required the addition of specific tempo words; thus a movement in 3/4 marked *légèrement* would indicate a swiftness of movement that veered towards, without exceeding, the 3/8 boundary.

But how might such a boundary between a 3/4 tempo and a 3/8 tempo achieve universal agreement? In the pre-industrial age, Saint Lambert attempted to codify his tempo suggestions in relation to the time taken by a male of average height walking a distance of 1.25 French leagues at a normal pace; previous standards of measurement (against which, for example, a choirmaster might indicate the TACTUS by beating his hand) included the speed of an average human heartbeat or the swing of a pendulum – though clock pendulums were widely conceded to be inconsistent (LOULIÉ had evidently invented a more accurate pendulum for this purpose, the *chronomètre*, around 1694, apparently unknown to Saint Lambert).

It was not until the appearance of Maelzel's METRONOME in 1816–17 that a notional standard (capable of being represented numerically in print) was achieved. This ideal standard required but one constant: the provision of a mechanical metronome expertly and identically calibrated everywhere according to the same standard. Thus achieved, composers could indicate the desired tempo by a metronome mark (expressed as the number of beats per minute) in their scores, and the purchasers of the EDITION could select this same number along the pendulum of their metronome and replicate the exact number of beats per minute (the 'tempo') to guide their performance. This apparently desirable situation (emblematic, perhaps, of a newly progressive spirit of industrialisation in the early nineteenth century) nevertheless falls foul of two inescapable variables: the involvement of human performers and different acoustic spaces for musical performance, both of which impact significantly on actual realisable tempos, from both performer and audience perspectives.

BEETHOVEN's metronome marks (which he sometimes applied retrospectively to his earlier chamber music, including the Septet, Op. 20) have been the subject of much debate, as they not infrequently appear to indicate a tempo rather too quick for sensible execution. Interestingly, Beethoven (at all stages of his career) offered detailed nuancing of tempo. The breathless intention that may underlie the first-movement Allegro of the G minor Cello Sonata, Op. 5 No. 2 is captured in his character description (*Allegro molto più tosto presto*); while the opening *Allegretto ma non troppo* of the late A major Piano Sonata, Op. 101 is qualified by 'Etwas lebhaft und mit der innigsten Empfindung'.

Historical instruments and historical documents of playing styles offer further significant clues regarding choice of tempo. The held chord at the start of Beethoven's 'Pathétique' Sonata, Op. 13 is a case in point. Played on a modern concert grand, the chord can bear significant elongation because of the instrument's mechanics of sound production, featuring extended sound delay; by contrast, a Walter five or five-and-a-half octave grand from the 1790s (or a modern copy) will suggest a rather swifter tempo for this Grave because of the more rapid decay of the opening chord (affecting also the likely ARTICULATION of the dotted chords that follow). The lighter tension of a Baroque BOW, compared to its modern counterpart (fashioned for an altogether heavier legato concept of sound and a broader repertory of strokes), immediately suggests relatively short strokes and brisk tempos in Italianate concerti grossi from the early eighteenth century, rather than the ponderous 'on the string', VIBRATO-laden accounts that have characterised certain schools of twentieth-century performance practice on modern instruments. The shorter bow, combined with the 'chin off' approach to holding the instrument, recaptures physically as well as sonically the close connection of Baroque music with DANCE, and with it, something of its spirit; indeed, an understanding of Baroque dance, informed by historical choreography, can play an important part in determining tempo, including a delight in flexibility of pulse – mimicking temporally the elegant definition of space that once unified the arts of music and dance.

Genre can have wide-ranging implications for tempo in vocal music: the liturgical requirements of Cranmer's original *Book of Common Prayer* (1549/

rev. 1552), alongside various contemporary statutes, for clear audibility of the words in an anthem such as Tallis's *If Ye Love Me* will impact on the speed of delivery to an important degree, especially in intimate devotional settings; motets from the late fifteenth-century Eton Choirbook by contrast reflect no such liturgical stipulation and speak to a wholly different aesthetic in which the extension of individual vowels in elaborate polyphonic tracery seems deliberately to reflect the magnificent vaulted ceilings of contemporary perpendicular architecture of the chapels for which this music was written. In such a context, a hurried tempo makes little sense. The internal musical factors involved in deciding upon a tempo are, of course, legion, and far too great in number to receive anything more than exemplary illustration here. FRESCOBALDI, writing in the Preface to his *Toccate e partite* (1615–16), advised that cadences be approached in a rather leisurely way, emphasising marker-points within the musical narrative presumably as an aid to comprehensibility in a style that was new, unfamiliar and perhaps unsettling. It would perhaps be mistaken to apply his advice to all genres and styles of music (including national styles) across the whole of the Baroque era. Nevertheless, a careful consideration of the harmonic trajectory of the bass line (and where appropriate, its relation to prevailing dance metres, whether functional or associative) will often suggest the need for cadences to be marked a little more clearly than is apparent from the notation, and consequently have an effect on tempo, whether globally or locally. The question of local tempo variation is related, from the later Renaissance through to the early nineteenth century, to conceptions of music as analogous to rhetoric. Effective rhetorical speech depended in large part on convincing delivery, and that in turn depended crucially on the management by the speaker of the flow of both ideas and the time in which those ideas were delivered. Convincing musical delivery hangs no less on management of the tempo, and historically informed approaches, taking into account the advice of many TREATISES linking RHETORIC and music, will continue to provide fresh and challenging contributions to the art of performance.

Tempo Flexibility

Writing in c1782, DOMENICO CORRI noted that performing a piece of music 'exactly as it is commonly noted, would be a very inexpressive, nay, a very uncouth performance' (*A Select Collection*, 3 vols. (Edinburgh: printed for John Corri, c1782), I, 2). Nowhere is this more true than in the case of tempo flexibility. MOZART himself described *rubato* playing at the keyboard as consisting of a strictly maintained tempo for the left hand (ensuring coherence of harmonic progressions, for instance) against which the right hand might subtly deviate; he notes that most players (wrongly) deviated from a pulse in both hands simultaneously. Something like the effect Mozart had in mind might still be present in the piano roll recordings of his keyboard works made by Carl Reinecke (1824–1910) towards the end of his life, in which (typically for the early twentieth century) the left hand arrives noticeably ahead of the right on the main downbeats, while the right hand meanders significantly. Reinecke's approach to *rubato* may have been absorbed during his early training during the 1830s (he was performing publicly from the age of twelve); assuming minimal deviation from those fundamentals during his career, his recordings might plausibly therefore reflect a tradition of Mozart performance from an age when Mozart's pupils were still active. At any rate, Reinecke's playing is notable overall for its TEMPO FLEXIBILITY and, on a local level, for its modification of notated rhythms, for instance through the application of inequality in slurred note-pairs, and typically incorporating a marked accelerando in rising semiquaver scale passages, exaggerating the gestural peaks and troughs of the leading melodic strand.

Such flexibility seems to have been axiomatic of the nineteenth-century approach to performance. An early reference point is Weber, who equated the underlying beat in a performance to the naturally varying human heartbeat. While Weber himself advocated the use of the metronome, the beat thus prescribed was 'not a tyrannically impeding hammer'. For Weber, slower tempos required, from time to time, a quicker motion, and prestos a 'quieter delivery' in order to retain expressiveness; such things could not be conveyed through notation alone. Nevertheless, he was quick to point out that flexibility was not an excuse for extreme deformation of the tempo. It was perhaps this aspect that drew criticism in some quarters: for instance, REICHARDT's unflattering review of SPOHR's playing in the *Berlinische musikalische Zeitung* following a performance on 3 March 1805, in which he castigated Spohr's wayward tempi; and BERLIOZ's reports of Liszt's BEETHOVEN performances during the 1830s which took the most extraordinary liberties with Beethoven's texts. Issues of TASTE aside, tempo flexibility seems to have played a defining role throughout the nineteenth century. Stanford's reports of BRAHMS's conducting of his own works notes that 'his tempo was very elastic' (though a little more restrained than that of HANS VON BÜLOW), and recordings of JOACHIM's performances of Brahms confirm this overall approach. Reinecke's 1905–6 piano rolls of Mozart thus take their place within a long-established tradition.

While the recording studio is not the concert stage, the sheer numbers of EARLY RECORDINGS (across many different genres) prominently featuring expressive tempo shifts offer strong evidence of a widespread practice that had little or no notational presence. This holds true even when composers themselves are responsible for the recordings. ELGAR's many recordings of his orchestral works include a 1926 version of the 'Enigma' Variations with the Royal Albert Hall Orchestra. As ROBERT PHILIP has noted, Elgar frequently ignores his published metronome markings, sometimes taking a generally quicker, sometimes a generally slower speed, and nearly always varying the absolute tempo markedly, sometimes from phrase to phrase. 'Nimrod' is a classic case. Despite the fact that Elgar had several times reconsidered the metronome mark since 1899 (for which some correspondence with Jaeger survives), he starts his recording much more slowly than the notated crotchet = 52, speeds up to something still considerably slower, then overrides it (to crotchet = 56) at the climax. Shortly before the recording, reports of a live performance by Elgar refer to his 'unsteady beat' and 'wilful *rubato*'. Elgar would perhaps have approved: he had told Jaeger in 1903 that he did not want his music to be played 'squarely ... like a wooden box'.

FURTHER READING

C. Brown, *Classical & Romantic Performing Practice 1750–1900* (Oxford University Press, 1999).
R. Donington, *Baroque Music: Style and Performance* (London: Faber & Faber, 1982).
R. Harris-Warwick (trans. and ed.), *Principles of the Harpsichord by Monsieur de Saint Lambert* (Cambridge University Press, 1984).
R. Hudson, *Stolen Time: The History of Tempo Rubato* (Oxford University Press, 1994).
R. Philip, *Performing Music in the Age of Recording* (New Haven, CT, and London: Yale University Press, 2004).
J. Tarling, *Baroque String Playing for Ingenious Learners* (St Albans: Corda Music, 2001).

JOHN IRVING

Tempo Flexibility *see* TEMPO

Tempo Rubato *see* TEMPO

Text Underlay As with many other parameters, text-underlay technique was a continuously shifting entity, reliant upon changing aesthetic expectations, generic conventions, manuscript production technique and the more personal interests and efforts of individual scribes. As a result, its practical manifestations can range from notational clarity and precision to a complete lack of instruction, where stable performance practice conventions replaced the need for scribal accuracy. None the less, some general tendencies can be detected. As with any other notational or expressive parameter, their development is not linear, and is often irreconcilable with our expectations.

Modern notions of 'good' text underlay may be said to hark back to the Renaissance's conceptual linking of specific rhythmic and melodic behaviour with word ACCENTUATION and text declamation patterns. Such clarity became established practice probably with Willaert's generation. Perhaps counterintuitively, these notions were strong enough to obviate the need for their actual NOTATION. Underlay thus became part of performance practice, rather than necessarily of notation. This, though, was not always the case. From the very earliest neumatic notations, musical signs were designed to show text–music relationships. The ligating of notes into multi-note neumes (or later, ligatures) enabled the signalling of melodic relationships between the notes in question, but, just as importantly, it signalled the formation of a melismatic group which could not be separated through syllable change. Indeed, in more syllabic passages adiastematic notations are not good for much other than showing text–music alignment.

Most forms of monophony and early polyphony are, therefore, clear in terms of text underlay. Occasional problems only occur when a succession of melismas are matched by particularly careless copying. This is even true for sources which supply the music and text separately, as happens in some chant manuscripts (e.g. the Sankt Gallen manuscripts) or some anthologies of German song (the Riedsche and Lochamer songbooks or the works of Michel Beheim). All that is required for precise underlay is a match between syllable count and number of groupings, along with the occasional appreciation of typical melisma locations and melodic cadential formulae. In this context, one should remember that a lack of music in a collection of lyric poetry does not mean the contents were not to be sung, and that the presentation of all strophic songs (other than some *Lay* types) involves more texts written away from the music than under it. Alignment systems were, therefore, very useful for a successful practice. In *Notre Dame* polyphony, where extended melismas are an integral part of the style, dashes with no rhythmic or musical effect other than signalling the coordination of syllable-change were introduced. In this PITCH-specific context, underlay groupings are often clearer than RHYTHMIC INTERPRETATION, especially in the text-rich and homophonic *conductus*.

The notation of text–music relationships become more complex with the introduction of the notational habits (making ligatures less useful) and florid secular styles of the *Ars nova*. Still, many early Italian genres involved an expectation for each line of text to have a melisma-syllabic declamation-melisma structure, making alignment easy regardless of scribal precision. The increased interest in non-standardisation and enhanced compositional control noticeable during the later fourteenth and early fifteenth centuries demanded freer underlay patterns and thus a way to notate them. Scribes, therefore, fine-tuned their copying technique, settling on a time consuming but ultimately successful system of text-first copying that allowed for careful musical overlay. From countless emendations of both text and music in such MANUSCRIPTS it becomes clear scribes took underlay seriously and were precise in their indications. This precision, though, does not equate to the matching of musical and textual ACCENTUATION patterns, or to 'natural' declamation. Indeed, the arrangements of text and music often work to undermine each other in order to propel the music on, bridging over ends of syntactical or musico-structural units.

The early to mid-fifteenth century saw a stylistic simplification that gradually re-established stronger underlay expectations. The same period also saw an expansion of manuscript production, leading to a transition towards the time-saving technique of equidistant, music-first copying. The combination of these two processes resulted in a near complete disinterest in notating underlay in the post-1450 chansonniers. As long as the positioning of verse beginnings was clear, each line of text was to be underlaid more or less syllabically (avoiding syllable changes on small rhythmic values), ending with a melisma, usually on the penultimate syllable. From here, the humanist interest in classical declamation and accentuation systems made it a small step to replace structural guidelines with rhythmic and accentual ones, arriving at the performance practice of text underlay with which we began.

FURTHER READING

H. M. Brown, '"Lord, have mercy upon us", early sixteenth-century scribal practice and the polyphonic Kyrie', *Text Transactions of the Society for Textual Scholarship*, 2 (1985), 93–110.

L. Earp, 'Texting in 15th-century French chansons: a look ahead from the 14th century', *EMc*, 19 (May, 1991), 195–210.

D. Harrán, *Word-Tone Relations in Musical Thought From Antiquity to the Seventeenth Century*, Musicological Studies and Documents 40 (Middleton, WI: A-R Editions, 1986).

URI SMILANSKY

The Consort of Musicke British early music ensemble, founded in 1969 by lutenists Anthony Rooley and James Tyler.

Tyler left the group at an early stage and Rooley became sole director. From the beginning the Consort focused its activities on the English and Italian secular repertories of the sixteenth and seventeenth centuries, and carefully constructed concert programmes (often enthusiastically introduced from the stage by Rooley) and numerous recordings for the early music label Decca L'Oiseau-Lyre quickly made it one of the most internationally influential ensembles of the British early music boom of the 1970s and 1980s. Early projects exposed repertories by relatively little-known composers such as John Ward, Sigismondo d'India and the fifteenth-century masters of the *Chansonnier Cordiforme*, but also brought new insights to more familiar names such as Byrd, Lawes and Dowland (whose complete works were recorded between 1976 and 1981). In 1987 the group began a recorded cycle of MONTEVERDI's eight books of madrigals for L'Oiseau-Lyre, completing it on Virgin Classics in 1993 while also recording works by lesser-known Italian madrigalists on Musica Oscura, the label Rooley had himself founded. Rooley's interest in English seventeenth-century theatre music also led to imaginative realisations of the 1653 *Cupid and Death* (staged in Bruges, London and Basle), and the 1694 *Don Quixote* with music by Purcell, Eccles and others (recorded in 1995).

Although in its early years the Consort performed instrumental music, the emphasis has since been mostly on vocal repertoire, with the group's personnel including leading British-based early music singers including (at various times) EMMA KIRKBY, Evelyn Tubb, Mary Nichols, Andrew King, Paul Agnew, Rufus Müller, Richard Wistreich, Alan Ewing, Simon Grant and David Thomas. In concert their performances could be boldly theatrical, often involving movement and gesture. The turn of the century saw a relaxation in the group's activities as Rooley became increasingly involved in teaching (notably at the SCHOLA CANTORUM BASILIENSIS) before eventually retiring from performance in 2014.

FURTHER READING

A. Rooley, *Performance: Revealing the Orpheus Within* (Shaftesbury: Element Books, 1990).

LINDSAY KEMP

The Handel and Haydn Society The Handel and Haydn Society (H+H) first met in Boston in March 1815, with the aim of bringing concerted European choral music to the city. The first performance was on Christmas Day, 1815, making H+H the oldest continuously performing arts organisation in the USA. Among its American premieres were Handel's *Messiah* (1818), HAYDN's *Creation* (1819), Handel's *Jephtha* (1867), and J. S. BACH's *St Matthew Passion* (1879). The group began its annual and unbroken series of *Messiah* performances in 1854, and gave its first performance in its current home, Boston's Symphony Hall, just six days after the venue opened in October 1900. For its first 150 years, H+H was a choral society, featuring a large ensemble of amateur singers (initially only men), but in 1967 Artistic Director Thomas Dunn hired a small professional chorus and began paying attention to recent scholarship in performance practice. In 1986, CHRISTOPHER HOGWOOD became artistic director and converted the orchestra to a period instrument ensemble. Also under Hogwood, the ensemble first performed outside the USA, with a visit to the Edinburgh Festival in 1996.

Following Hogwood, Artistic Director Grant Llewellyn extended the group's repertoire to the secular realm with operas by MONTEVERDI and Purcell. After he stepped down in 2006, the group used guest conductors such as ROGER NORRINGTON, who led the ensemble in a performance at the Proms in 2007. Another guest conductor during this time was Harry Christophers, who led H+H in its first performance on the continent, at the Esterházy Palace in 2006. By 2008 Christophers had been named as the incoming artistic director and has served since 2009. Recent concertmasters have included Daniel Stepner, who served for a quarter of a century until 2006 and (since 2011) the Canadian violinist Aisslinn Nosky.

FURTHER READING

T. Neff and J. Swafford, *The Handel and Haydn Society: Bringing Music to Life for 200 Years* (Boston: Godine, 2014).

ROSS DUFFIN

The Hanover Band The Hanover Band was founded in London by its artistic director Caroline Brown in 1980 on the Viennese Classical model. The ORCHESTRA has an international reputation for the excellence of its performances and recordings of eighteenth- and nineteenth-century music. It has performed throughout the UK, Europe, USA, Canada and Mexico, appearing in prestigious festivals and venues such as Carnegie Hall, Concertgebouw Amsterdam, Royal Albert Hall and Berlin Philharmonie. It has an impressive discography of over 170 recordings for Hyperion, EMI, Nimbus, BMG, CPO and other labels. The orchestra's list of directors has included Monica Huggett, CHARLES MACKERRAS, Roy Goodman, NICHOLAS MCGEGAN and Anthony Halstead. It was the first period orchestra to record the complete symphonies of BEETHOVEN, Schubert and Schumann and has simultaneously expanded its repertory back to the Baroque and forward to Dvořák, BRAHMS and Sullivan.

The Hanover Band and Caroline Brown generated a pioneering spirit from the start; in language characteristic of the early 1980s their first disc was described by *Early Music News* as 'The most original Beethoven yet recorded', *The Guardian* remarking that the recording 'puts us in a new generation of authentic performance'. While Goodman and The Hanover Band recorded a great number of HAYDN symphonies for Hyperion, it was their fruitful but sometimes difficult association with the label Nimbus that defined the partnership. Nimbus proudly declared its house policy of 'encouraging artists who were willing and able to approach recording in the same spirit as live performances ... without recourse to the edit'. The Nimbus sound was also controversial, given the use of a single 'soundfield' microphone. Ever since those pioneering days, The Hanover Band's ethos has been that the use of period instruments must be complemented by musical understanding, an awareness of social and cultural context and recourse to a rich variety of historical evidence. Even within the burgeoning marketplace of period orchestras it has thus contrived to retain a distinctive voice.

FURTHER READING

J. Griffiths, *Nimbus: Technology Serving the Arts* (London: André Deutsch, 1995).

COLIN LAWSON

The King's Consort British period-instrument ensemble specialising in Baroque and early Classical choral and orchestral repertoire, founded in 1980 by English conductor Robert King.

The Consort, augmented where necessary by the Choir of The King's Consort, became one of the world's best-known period ensembles, due in part to extensive international touring but perhaps above all to a wide-ranging discography of nearly ninety-five discs for the British independent label Hyperion. These recordings ranged from popular works such as Handel's *Water Music*, Vivaldi's *Le quattro stagioni* and J. S. BACH's violin concertos and B minor Mass to unfamiliar corners of the repertoire, including Astorga, Zelenka and Bach's Leipzig predecessors, as well as lesser-known Handel oratorios such as *Alexander Balus*, *Deborah* and the *Occasional Oratorio*. They also embarked upon major projects such as the complete church music, secular songs and odes of Purcell, and the complete sacred outputs of MONTEVERDI and Vivaldi. Among other distinctive releases were reconstructions of the music for the Venetian celebration *Lo Sposalizio* and for the Coronation of George II. King's directing was brightly efficient if not greatly individual, but as a group The King's Consort was able to field many of the UK's finest players, while shrewd choices of vocal soloist allowed early opportunities for singers such as Susan Gritton, Deborah York and Carolyn Sampson at the same time as providing a rich showcase for the countertenor JAMES BOWMAN in the final maturity of his career.

In 2007 Robert King began a prison sentence for sexual assault, during which the Consort was conducted by its recently appointed associate director, Matthew Halls. The Consort was later renamed the Retrospect Ensemble with Halls as artistic director, but on his release in 2009 King relaunched the group separately under its original name. He also founded a new CD label, Vivat, on which the reconstituted King's Consort's recordings include Purcell's two sets of trio sonatas, a disc of choral works by Parry and Stanford and Handel's *Israel in Egypt* in Mendelssohn's arrangement.

LINDSAY KEMP

The Music Party The Music Party was founded in 1972 by clarinettist Alan Hacker (1938–2012) to play chamber music from the Classical era on period instruments. Other founder members were Duncan Druce (violin), Simon Rowland-Jones (violin/viola), Jennifer Ward Clarke (cello) and Richard Burnett (piano). Their repertoire often had a string accompaniment but the group's sound was always characterised by Hacker's colourful and virtuosic CLARINET playing.

Early performances took place in venues such as the Victoria and Albert Museum and Wigmore Hall and a twenty-one-piece ensemble played HAYDN's Symphony No. 18 at St John's, Smith Square in 1974. Later the group performed works for wind alone, often with Lesley Schatzberger as second clarinet. Other repertory included Mozart's *Gran Partita* K361 (Wigmore Hall, 1981), his Serenade K375 and the Quintets for Piano and Wind by both BEETHOVEN and MOZART (Wigmore Hall and Holywell Music Room, Oxford), Beethoven's Septet, Op. 20 (York, 1978) and Handel's *Ouverture* for two clarinets and HORN. The group made three recordings for Decca's L'Oiseau Lyre label: Weber's Clarinet Quintet and HUMMEL's Clarinet Quartet (1973); Weber's *Grand Duo Concertant*, Op. 48, Schumann's *Märchenerzählungen*, Op. 132 and Glinka's *Trio Pathétique* (1976); Haydn's 8 *Notturni*, Hob. II:25–32 (1976). It also recorded Mozart's *Gran Partita* in 1987.

Hacker's appointment as a lecturer at York University in 1976 led to frequent performances by The Music Party in the vicinity and, in particular, at the York Early Music Festival which he helped to found. A significant offshoot, The Classical Orchestra, was founded in 1978 and performed in the University, Minster, Assembly Rooms and in London at St John's, Smith Square. Hacker conducted it in Mozart's Symphony No. 39 K543, MENDELSSOHN's *Hebrides* Overture, Beethoven's Symphonies Nos. 2, 3 and 7, probably the first English performance of Beethoven's Ninth Symphony using period instruments and Mozart's Clarinet Concerto K622, in which he also played the solo part.

JOHN HUMPHRIES

Theorbo (Fr. *théorbe* or *tuorbe*; It. *tiorba*) A large plucked instrument that evolved from the bass LUTE. It was also known in Italy as *chitarrone*, but this name rarely appears in any source after 1650.

During the late sixteenth century a group of poets, musicians and scholars in Florence met to discuss how best to revive the classical Greek dramas of antiquity. This *camerata* aimed to promote a new musical style, later termed *stile recitativo*, where the text was the most important element. The lute was considered an ideal instrument to accompany a singer but this new style required a stronger bass line to act as a foundation to the harmonies supporting the voice. The largest member of the lute family, the bass lute, was restrung to enhance its resonance. Thinner strings were mounted and the PITCH was raised by as much as a fifth. The two top courses, unable to withstand tuning to this high pitch, were tuned an octave lower, resulting in a 're-entrant' tuning where the third course was the highest. This new instrument first became known as the CHITARRONE. It was probably named after the ancient Greek instrument the *kithara* and one of the earliest references to it in performance is found in the detailed descriptions of the Florentine *Intermedi* of 1589.

The initial appearance of the chitarrone was similar to that of the bass lute with its bent-back pegbox. However, a straight extended neck to hold the lowest courses was soon added. Alessandro Piccinini (1566–c1638) describes this development in his *Intavolatura di liuto et di chitarrone, libro primo* (Bologna, 1623) and claims that he was himself responsible for it (see Figure 17).

Giovanni Girolamo Kapsperger (c1580–1651) and Bellerofonte Castaldi (1581–1649) also wrote solos for the chitarrone (or theorbo) and each developed a unique style of his own. However, the theorbo was conceived for accompaniment and became indispensable for Italian monody and early opera. Its use spread to most parts of Europe and it was used as a continuo instrument for vocal and instrumental music well into the eighteenth century, with variations in design and tuning (*see* Examples 41–3).

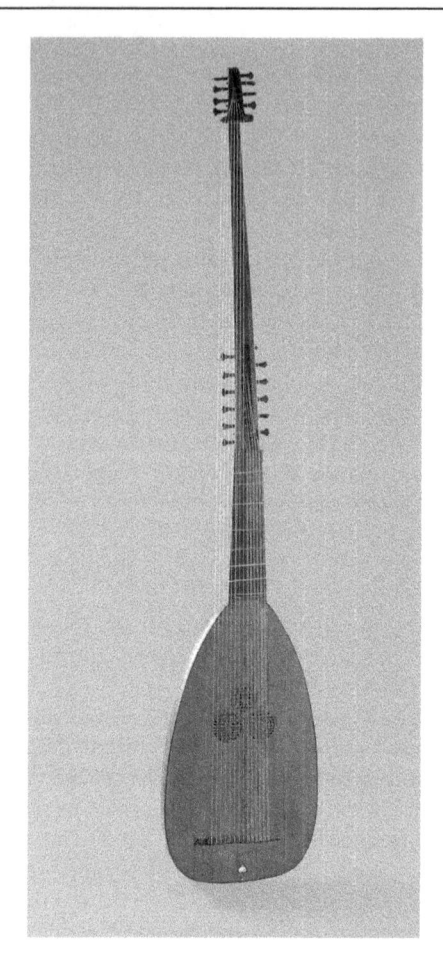

Figure 17: Fourteen-course chitarrone by Magno Dieffopruchar, Venice 1608. String lengths 930 mm and 1703 mm (by kind permission of the Royal College of Music, London).

Example 41: Chitarrone tuning (the top six courses were often double).

Example 42: English theorbo tuning (the courses seem to have been double throughout).

Example 43: German theorbo tuning (the distribution of double courses is unknown).

FURTHER READING

T. Mace, *Musick's Monument* (London, 1676; facsim. edn, Paris: Editions du Centre National de la Recherche Scientifique, 1966).

K. Mason, *The Chitarrone and its Repertoire in Early Seventeenth-Century Italy* (Aberystwyth: Boethius Press, 1989).

R. Spencer, 'Chitarrone, theorbo and archlute', *EMc*, 4/4 (October 1976), 407–23.

JAKOB LINDBERG

Thoroughbass *see* BASSO CONTINUO

Thuringus, Joachim (b. Fürstenberg, Brandenburg, late sixteenth century). German theorist.

Thuringus's *Opusculum bipartitum de primordiis musicis* (Berlin, 1624, 2/1625), a music TREATISE drawing on contemporary and past theorists and composers, lists the following sources: Alsted, Burmeister, Calvisius, Dedekind, Deucerus, Eichmann, Faber, Galliculus, Glarean, Gantzschovius, Hoffmann, Josquin, Listenius, Meilandus, Nucius, Orlandus (Lassus), Praetorius, Rhau, Senfl, Spangenberg, Vulpius, Weisensee and Zangius. Thuringus's most significant source is Johannes Nucius's *Musices poeticae* (Neisse, 1613).

In the first part of his treatise, Thuringus focuses on modal theory. He systematically deals with each of the modes according to nine aspects: name, ambitus, repercussions, TRANSPOSITIONS, cadential notes, finals, nature or AFFECT, terminations for psalm tones, and musical examples from chorales and polyphonic compositions. In identifying specific affections with particular modes, Thuringus aligns himself with Nucius and Hoffmann (*Doctrina de tonis seu modis* (Greifswald: Ferberi, 1582)) – the latter also being the source for Thuringus's discussion of *musica reservata* – in contrast to Burmeister and Calvisius, who held that composers could express various affections using the same mode.

The second part focuses on the art of composition, which Thuringus identifies as *musica poetica* in keeping with contemporary treatise titles, and discusses in its first two chapters the meaning and the uses of *musica poetica*. He follows this with a discussion of the various styles of counterpoint and the fundamentals of composition, before turning his attention to musical-rhetorical FIGURES. Like Nucius, Thuringus proposes that the role of the figures is one of embellishment, just as painters embellish their paintings, and that it would not be difficult to assemble a large catalogue of musical figures in imitation of RHETORIC. In keeping with this point, Thuringus renames a number of Burmeister's figures with terms borrowed directly from rhetoric. It would be Athanasius Kircher (*Musurgia Universalis*, 2 vols. (Rome: Lodovico Grignani, 1650)) who would then adopt Thuringus's list of figures, highlighting their role as affection-arousing rhetorical devices.

FURTHER READING

D. Bartel, *Musica Poetica: Musical-rhetorical Figures in German Baroque Music* (Lincoln, NE: University of Nebraska Press, 1997).

F. Feldmann, 'Das "Opusculum bipartitum" des Joachim Thuringus (1625) besonders in seinen Beziehungen zu Joh. Nucius (1613)', *AMw*, 15 (1958), 123–42.

DIETRICH BARTEL

Tillière, Joseph Bonaventure (b. before 1750; d. after 1790) French cellist and composer.

Little biographical information is available for Tillière. Like JEAN-PIERRE DUPORT, he was a pupil of Martin Berteau in Paris. He was a member of the *Académie Royale de Musique* and performed in the Paris Opéra Orchestra.

Tillière's *Méthode pour le violoncelle* (Paris: Jolivet, 1774 – this publication is not extant; Bailleux, c1775) appeared in English as *New and Compleat Instructions for the Violoncello* (London: Longman & Broderip, c1790). There were subsequent reissues of the English version until the 1820s, and a heavily revised and shortened French edition was published in the later nineteenth century (Paris: Ikelmer Frères, c1879). Tillière's is the first tutor to treat the CELLO as a solo instrument. In the course of his twenty-seven *leçons* he begins with simple scales and BOWING exercises, but quickly moves to complex ARPEGGIO bowings, bariolage and extreme string-crossing exercises, scales and chords in thumb position, scales in thirds, double stops and other examples of more advanced writing. The last lesson consists of a complex cello solo and a sonata in three movements for two cellos, of which the upper part exploits almost all the advanced techniques previously discussed. His published compositions include over twenty sonatas (some more of which were included in some editions of the *Méthode*), and sets of cello duos including collections of *ariettes* and minuets for two cellos. These arrangements are less technically demanding but exploit textures such as pedal points on open strings. One of Tillière's sonatas was edited by Carl Schroeder (Mainz: Schott, 1900).

FURTHER READING

S. Milliot, *Le violoncelle en France au XVIII siècle* (Paris and Geneva: Champion-Slatkine, 1985).
V. Walden, *One Hundred Years of Violoncello* (Cambridge University Press, 1998).

GEORGE KENNAWAY

Timpani *see* PERCUSSION

Tinctoris, Johannes (b. Braine-l'Alleud, nr Nivelles, c1435; d. before 12 October 1511) Franco-Flemish composer, singer and performer on stringed instruments.

Tinctoris spent much of his career in Naples. He is best remembered for his writings on music, which are notable for their direct commentaries on contemporary composers and their compositions, as well as some provocative cultural observations. There is much that is of direct interest to performers, in particular in *Ars contrapuncti* (1477) and the unfinished *De inventione et usu musicae* (early 1480s). It is in *Ars contrapuncti* that the first use of the term 'cantare super librum' (literally 'singing on the book') appears, which Tinctoris seems to distinguish from composed polyphony; this has been interpreted to indicate some kind of improvisatory practice, although the matter remains controversial. The fourth book of *De inventione* contains much on the variety and origins of the instruments in use in his time and also the manner in which they were played; he documents the way in which a low brass instrument was used with the SHAWMS in the *alta* band, praises the lutenist Pietrobono del Chitarino as an improviser and stresses the novelty of playing all parts of a polyphonic composition together on the LUTE. The same passage also describes the performances of two blind brothers whose virtuosity on stringed instruments astonished the courts of Europe and who can be connected with a long and enigmatic composition by Alexander Agricola. Tinctoris's interest in the performative sound of music is also evinced by several references in *De inventione* to 'Turkish' music, which although disparaging in tone are meticulously observed.

FURTHER READING

A. Baines, 'Fifteenth-century instruments in Tinctoris's *De inventione et usu musicae*', *GSJ*, 3 (1950), 19–27.
M. Bent, *Counterpoint, Composition and Musica Ficta* (New York and London: Routledge, 2002).

JON BANKS

Tippett, Sir Michael (Kemp) (b. London, 2 January 1905; d. London, 8 January 1998) English composer.

Although known primarily as a composer, Michael Tippett was also an enthusiastic advocate of early music. He was self-confessedly musically ignorant when he arrived at the ROYAL COLLEGE OF MUSIC in 1923, but set about teaching himself the history of music, starting at what he considered 'the beginning', the polyphony of Palestrina. Despite some early forays into performing early music (particularly madrigals) with the Oxted and Limpsfield Players, his most intense engagement with it began in 1940, when he took over the choir of the very recently bombed Morley College. Over the next eleven years under Tippett's direction, the Morley College Choir revived a large number of early works, starting with the madrigals of MONTEVERDI and the 'Elizabethans' (actually MORLEY, Gibbons, Dowland, Weelkes and Wilbye) and with a particular focus on Purcell. Purcell's music was not entirely unknown at the time, but the larger choral works were rarely performed. In 1941, Tippett and his choir gave the first of many performances of Purcell's 1692 *Ode to Saint Cecilia*, accompanied by a string quartet, OBOES, RECORDER and PIANO. Over the next few years, Tippett and his choir gradually developed a greater historical awareness; CONTINUO parts were soon played on the HARPSICHORD and, from 1944, ALFRED DELLER often sang countertenor solos. Morley College became known as a place where Purcell could be heard 'as written'. Tippett's interest in Purcell and the 'Elizabethans' was reflected in a series of eight radio talks broadcast by the BBC in 1947, illustrated by the Morley College Choir.

One of the keys to Tippett's success at Morley was his ability to bring together talented musicians, many of whom were European refugees. He was particularly indebted to the expertise of Walter Bergmann, who fled the Gestapo in 1939. Bergmann was considered an expert on the music of TELEMANN, which, together with 'the Bachs' appeared frequently in Morley College programmes. He taught recorder at the College, played continuo, and acted as a mentor to Tippett. Together, they produced a number of restrained and scholarly EDITIONS of early music, particularly by Purcell, with Bergmann reportedly doing the lion's share of the editing.

After WWII, Tippett's choir began to tackle more ambitious programmes. In 1946, with the assistance of Walter Goehr and Hans Redlich, who had both fled Nazi Germany in the 1930s, Morley College gave the first London performance of Monteverdi's *Vespers* of 1610, followed in 1948 by *L'Incoronazione di Poppea*, also in an edition by Redlich. In 1949, Tippett conducted the choir in the first recording of Tallis's forty-part motet, *Spem in alium*, which they also performed at the Festival of Britain in 1951.

During his time at Morley, Tippett had developed a growing reputation as a composer, and in 1951 he resigned his position in order to focus more on composition. He was never again as active in the performance of early music, but compositions such as the *Fantasia Concertante on a Theme of Corelli* (1953) and the *Divertimento on Sellinger's Round* (1953–4) indicate his lifelong interest in the area.

FURTHER READING

S. Cole, '"Musical trail-blazing and general daring": Michael Tippett, Morley College and Early Music', in S. Robinson (ed.), *Michael Tippett: Music and Literature* (Aldershot: Ashgate, 2002), 151–73.

'"Things that chiefly interest ME": Tippett and Early Music', in K. Gloag and N. Jones (eds.), *The Cambridge Companion to Michael Tippett* (Cambridge University Press, 2013), 48–67.

SUZANNE COLE

Tolbecque, Auguste (b. Paris, 30 March 1830; d. Niort, Deux Sèvres, 8 March 1919) French cellist, composer, instrument maker and organologist.

Tolbecque studied CELLO with Olive-Charlier Vaslin and composition with Napoléon Henri Reber. In the early 1870s, he apprenticed as a violin maker with Claude Victor Rambaux, and was influenced by the latter's innovations. After making VIOLINS, VIOLAS and cellos for several years and gaining a strong reputation as a restorer, he developed an interest in the reconstruction of Medieval and Renaissance instruments based on iconographical sources. Among his REPLICAS are several stringed instruments including Greek lyres, rebecs, crwths, but also RECORDERS and crumhorns.

After 1879, when his collection of early instruments was acquired by the Belgian government for the *Musée Instrumental*, Tolbecque's replicas enjoyed increasing success and public visibility, effectively building a widespread public interest in early music in France. VICTOR CHARLES MAHILLON commissioned several reproductions to fill the gaps in the Brussels collection, and Tolbecque's instruments were also displayed at the *Exposition Universelle* (1889), the *Exposition de Tours* (1892), where they gained the *Grand Prix*, and at the *Palais de l'Industrie* in Paris (1898), where again they were awarded the highest prize. Over thirty more of his copies are preserved at the *Musée de la Musique* in Paris.

Tolbecque's *Notice historique sur les instruments à cordes et à archet* (Paris: Chez Gustave Bernardel et chez l'auteur, 1898) describes his sources (paintings, sculptures and texts), which are often directly referable to some of his surviving instruments. It offers a rare insight into the process of understanding the instruments of the past and their construction at the beginning of the early music revival.

FURTHER READING

J. Dilworth, 'Tolbecque, Auguste', in *Brompton's Book of Violin and Bow Makers* (London: Usk Publishing, 2012).
A. Tolbecque, *L'art du luthier* (Niort: Mercier, 1903; repr. Marseille: Laffite, 1978).

GABRIELE ROSSI ROGNONI

Tonguing *see* ARTICULATION

Tosi, Pier Francesco (b. Cesena, 13 August 1654; d. Faenza, c16 July, 1732) Italian CASTRATO, teacher, composer and writer.

Tosi's method for producing fine SINGING, *Opinioni de'cantori antichi e moderni* (Bologna, 1723; trans. and ed. J. E. Galliard, 1742 as *Observations on the Florid Song*; ed. M. Pilkington, 1987), looks back to the mid-seventeenth-century vocal style, the purity of which he believed in his later years was being diluted by excessive ORNAMENTATION and fast TEMPI. The notes in Pilkington's EDITION both clarify and – at times – abbreviate some of the original eighteenth-century English. A further glimpse into Tosi's methods was offered by the German composer JOHANN FRIEDRICH AGRICOLA's translation of the Italian's text, entitled *Anleitung zur Singkunst* (1757; trans. and ed. J. Baird, 1995 as *Introduction to the Art of Singing*).

It should be noted that the term *bel canto* popularly associated with Tosi's style appears neither in the original publication, nor in Galliard nor Agricola, but was invented and applied much later. The art of singing with a consistently pure tone throughout the vocal compass was cultivated by Italian singers, who were imitated throughout Europe for many years. It commenced with CACCINI (*Le nuove musiche* (Florence: Giorgio Marescotti, 1602)) whose insistence on single-note exercises maintaining long *crescendos* and *diminuendos* has remained standard to the present day. Tosi's development of consistent vocal tone is through the imperceptible merging of the so-called 'chest tone' and 'head tone'. Also fundamental to the style is a mastery of ornaments, particularly the appoggiatura and the trill. So-called 'divisions' (or *passaggi*), in which the notes of a melody are dissolved into more improvised coloratura style, became essential elements of the new vocal technique, much of it borrowed from sixteenth-century practice, but more closely aligned than before to the text. Descriptions and performance instructions of ornaments additional to Tosi's are found in the texts cited above. An example of an amplification of Tosi's comments may be seen in the discussion of the appoggiatura. 'Among all the Embellishments in the Art of Singing there is none so easy for the Master to teach, or less difficult for the Scholar to learn' declared Tosi (1742, 15). His ten pages of instructions are extended by Agricola into thirty-eight pages of rules and examples, so it is advisable to study all the texts cited above. Tosi demanded that his students must be expert sight-readers and develop keen aural acuity and it may have been the influence of Caccini's teaching and his famous book which led to Tosi's concern for clear PRONUNCIATION and correct vowel sounds. This sure vocal foundation enabled his students to develop the expressive and dramatic side of singing so essential to the cultivation of opera and cantata in the Baroque period.

FURTHER READING

M. Bovolenta, 'La cantata in Pier Francesco Tosi, teorico e compositore', in 'Studi e ricerche sulla cantata da camera nel barocco italiano', *I Quaderni della Civica Scuola di Musica* (special issue, ed. L. Zoppelli), 19–20 (December, 1990).

J. Rosselli, 'The castrati as a professional group and a social phenomenon, 1550–1850', AcM, 60 (1988), 143–79.

DAVID TUNLEY

Transcription Transcription of music from one mode of performance to another reflects an enduring desire to accommodate repertoire within a variety of settings, transgressing geographical, social, institutional, generic and organological boundaries. It provides strong evidence of the flexibility with which musicians have historically approached notated musical texts and the works they seek to encode. The practice has proved to be an important indicator of changing musical TASTES across the centuries; likewise in establishing the canonicity of certain composers or particular pieces.

Transcriptions during the late Renaissance of madrigals and chansons (such as Lassus's 'Susanne un jour') for solo keyboard and LUTE document both fluidity across vocal and instrumental boundaries and a healthy environment of MANUSCRIPT exchange, whether diplomatic or mercantile. John Dowland's *Lachrimae or Seaven Teares Figured in Seaven Passionate Pavans* 'set forth for the lute, viols, or violons, in five parts' is illustrative. Originally a reworking of his lute song 'Flow my Teares' (1597), the *Lachrimae* pavan (1604) spawned numerous transcriptions, establishing both work and composer on the international stage. Numerous keyboard transcriptions were prepared in England, including two found in William Tisdale's Virginal Book and three more (by Byrd, Farnaby and MORLEY) in the Fitzwilliam Virginal Book; Melchior Schildt's setting of it in the Anders von Düben Keyboard Tablature (1641) is one of many continental texts to survive.

Transcription continued to occupy a central place throughout the eighteenth and nineteenth centuries. J. S. BACH's transcriptions of concertos by Albinoni and Vivaldi for one or more HARPSICHORDS are among the best known; GEMINIANI's radical reworking of CORELLI's Op. 5 Violin Sonatas as concerti grossi, less so. Bach frequently transcribed his own music for alternative forces (e.g. the E major Violin Concerto BWV1042 for keyboard), and later in the century his own works served as transcription models for others, among the most notable examples being MOZART's reworkings of certain fugues from *The Well-Tempered Clavier* (WTC) for string quartet K405, the fruits of his serious study of manuscript copies of Bach's works collected by Baron Gottfried van Swieten (one of Mozart's staunchest patrons). BEETHOVEN also absorbed Bach's music through copies in Swieten's library, and made a transcription for string quintet of the B♭ minor fugue from Book 1 of WTC. On rare occasions Beethoven transcribed his own works. Among the most creative examples are his versions of the Quintet for Piano and Winds, Op. 16 for piano quartet (incorporating in the slow movement an object lesson in how to elaborate an already-elegant HORN solo as a piece of coloratura for VIOLA), and his Trio, Op. 38 for CLARINET, CELLO and piano (a reworking of the Septet, Op. 20).

Opera also proved fertile territory for transcriptions. During the last quarter of the eighteenth century, transcriptions of excerpts from favourite operas were frequently made for wind sextet (or octet), sometimes with an additional 16' bass instrument. *Harmoniemusik* of this kind became a popular public mode of dissemination for operatic repertory in Vienna, Prague and Budapest, and especially for music by Mozart. Among the many examples of the practice are transcriptions by Georg Kaspar Sartorius (1754–1809) of arias from *Le nozze di Figaro, Don Giovanni* and *La Clemenza di Tito*.

The increasingly virtuosic quality of opera transcriptions by nineteenth-century piano virtuosi is no doubt bound up with the advancing mechanical possibilities of the instrument after the mid-1820s. Liszt's transcriptions are perhaps the most famous; examples of his work include a concert paraphrase on Verdi's *Rigoletto*; a waltz from Gounod's *Faust*; a polonaise from Tchaikowsky's *Eugene Onegin*; the 'Spinning Song' from WAGNER's *Flying Dutchman*; and the 'Liebestod' from *Tristan und Isolde*. Later composers continued to build on this legacy (notably BUSONI). For SCHOENBERG, transcription remained a fundamental element of compositional craft and reveals the surprising extent of his musical TASTE (including delightful chamber transcriptions of waltzes by Johann Strauss II).

FURTHER READING

M. Boyd, *Bach* (London: Dent, 1983).
R. Hellyer, 'Wind music', in C. Eisen and S. P. Keefe (eds.), *The Cambridge Mozart Encyclopedia* (Cambridge University Press, 2006), 532–6.
J. Irving, *The Anders von Düben Tablature* Corpus of Early Keyboard Music 28 (Holzgerlingen: American Institute of Musicology, 2000).
D. Lumsden, 'The sources of English lute music (1540–1620)', PhD dissertation, University of Cambridge (1955).

JOHN IRVING

Transposition A widespread musical practice by which either an entire musical piece, or select portions of it (as happens in select CHANT melodies, for instance), are notated or performed at a PITCH that is higher or lower in relation to an earlier standard (such as a different performance or NOTATION).

Exact transposition requires that the intervallic distances that are constitutive of the piece (or of a portion of it) remain unaltered, but various forms of partial or modified transposition are also common in Western musical practice. An early, if not the earliest, documented case of polyphonic transposition is found in the Robertsbridge fragment (for keyboard, *c*1360), where the *Fauvel* motet *Tribum quem - Quoniam secta - Merito* is notated a step higher than its original vocal version, from F to G, probably for tuning considerations. Throughout the pre-modern era, vocal music as a rule was not anchored to the notated pitch (which in any case was conceived as a relative, not absolute value as it came to be regarded in the modern era). For instance, polyphonic works of the sixteenth century were routinely notated in 'high clefs' (the so-called *chiavette*, such as g2–c2–c3–c4, respectively for cantus, alto, tenor, and bass) as a way of coordinating the vocal ranges with the notational conventions of the time regarding the use of ledger lines, accidentals and original chant notation (Kurtzman, 1994; additional complications ensued when the voices began to be doubled by instruments with some regularity towards the end of the sixteenth century in the practice of sacred music). Most scholars now agree that works set in the *chiavette* were expected to be performed a third or a fourth lower than notated, though the actual interval of transposition is certainly amenable to different interpretations (for instance, the question whether MONTEVERDI's *Lauda Jerusalem*, from the 1610 *Vespers*, should be performed a fourth or a second lower than notated has been the object of a prolonged debate in the scholarly literature). In similar fashion, transcriptions of polyphonic music for voice and LUTE were de facto PITCH neutral because lutes came in a variety of sizes and nominal tunings (typically in G, A, D and E): since lute notation (TABLATURE) did not indicate pitches, but positions on the fingerboard, the 'key' of a piece changed with the tuning. For the same reason, the musical NOTATION instructed singers performing to lute accompaniment to take their pitch from a particular string of the lute (*see*, for instance, Adrian Willaert's transcriptions for voice and lute of Verdelot's madrigals, discussed in Brown, 1989). The practice of transcribing vocal music for VIOL ensemble (as illustrated in several Renaissance TREATISES, for instance by SILVESTRO DI GANASSI) followed similar principles.

The ability to transpose a musical work at sight was expected of professional organists for much of the pre-modern and modern eras (as shown, for instance, by the test for becoming organist at St Mark's in Venice in the sixteenth century, and by the lengthy section on this topic in GIROLAMO DIRUTA's *Il transilvano* (1593 and 1609)). In the Baroque era, the use of different pitch standards for sacred and chamber music (known as *Chorton* and *Kammerton*) forced performers to transpose the notation up or down when playing in large ensembles involving winds, strings and ORGAN. The scoring of modern symphonic music takes into account the pitch of particular 'transposing' instruments: thus CLARINET parts when destined for instruments pitched in A are notated a minor third higher than they sound; parts for HORNS in F are notated a fifth higher, and so on. Transposition was also practised routinely in the seventeenth and eighteenth centuries in order to accommodate the music to the vocal range of a particular singer (the practice continues to the present day). In modern times there is evidence suggesting that the composers themselves may have occasionally changed the key of sections of previously composed works (for instance, Puccini in *Il tabarro* and *La bohème*; see Greenwald, 1998) for dramatic or large-scale structural reasons.

FURTHER READING

H. M. Brown, 'Bossinensis, Willaert, and Verdelot: pitch and the conventions of transcribing music for lute and voice in Italy in the early sixteenth century', *RM*, 75 (1989), 25–46.

H. Greenwald, 'Puccini, *Il tabarro*, and the dilemma of operatic transposition', *JAMS*, 51 (1998), 521–58.

J. G. Kurtzman, 'Tones, modes, clefs, and pitch in Roman cyclic Magnificats of the 16th century', *EMc*, 22 (1994), 641–64.

STEFANO MENGOZZI

Treatises Instrumental and vocal treatises offer the most direct access to information about the preferred technical and interpretative practices of approximately their times; some also discuss more general musical issues such as NOTATION,

EXPRESSION, TASTE and AESTHETICS, embraced also by specialist theoretical and other dissertations. Care should be taken in interpreting and using treatises as evidence, for their content can easily mislead; several present the fruits of many years' thought, experience and observation and incorporate instructions that may lag behind actual practice.

Instrumental/Vocal Treatises
Most instrumental/vocal treatises up to the mid-eighteenth century were addressed to educated amateur musicians or provincial music teachers. They focused on matters pertinent to a single instrument or family of instruments but few discussed technique in detail. Nevertheless, CONRAD VON ZABERN's *De modo bene cantandi* (1474) far outstrips for detail any account of CHANT SINGING before or since. SIMPSON's *The Division-Violist* (1659) documents the growing interest in CONSORTS and ensembles and the emerging recognition of instrumental music, and MACE's *Musick's Monument* (1676) specialises in the needs of lutenists and THEORBO players. Keyboard instruments are the principal focus of attention for writers such as BANCHIERI (1605), AGAZZARI (1607), Werckmeister (1698), FRANCESCO GASPARINI (1708), HEINICHEN (1728) and MATTHESON (1731), who incorporate discussion of CONTINUO playing.

On a generally higher technical level are treatises such as FRANÇOIS COUPERIN's more independent approach to solo keyboard performance, *L'art de toucher le clavecin* (1716, 2/1717), and JACQUES HOTTETERRE's *Principes de la flûte traversière* (1707), which includes instructions for playing the FLUTE, RECORDER and OBOE, and is an important information source about early woodwind practice. TOSI's *Opinioni de' cantori antichi e moderni* (1723) reflects the growth in popularity of opera, incorporating significant instruction about ORNAMENTATION, expression and TEMPO RUBATO.

GEMINIANI's progressive *The Art of Playing on the Violin* (1751) was the first treatise addressed to advanced violinists. Three other major treatises of the 1750s combined comparatively advanced technical instruction with copious details regarding performance practice and style: QUANTZ's *Versuch einer Anweisung die Flöte traversiere zu spielen* (1752), C. P. E. BACH's *Versuch über die wahre Art das Clavier zu spielen* (1753, 1762) and LEOPOLD MOZART's *Versuch einer gründlichen Violinschule* (1756). The establishment of the PARIS CONSERVATOIRE (1795) prompted the production of faculty-based treatises offering systematic courses of technical and interpretative instruction for aspiring professionals.

Instrumental/vocal treatises also provide significant information about NATIONAL IDIOMS of composition and performance. Like RAGUENET and other writers, Quantz compares the Italian and French styles at length, directly contrasting their approaches to composition, singing and playing, and especially to ornamentation. He advocates cultivating 'a good style that is universal' (*Versuch*, trans. Reilly, 342), a 'mixed' German style which makes 'use of the good things in all types of foreign music' (338).

Among the most significant instrumental treatises published since c1760 are those of TÜRK (1789), MILCHMEYER (1797), CLEMENTI (1801), ADAM (1804), HUMMEL (1828) and CZERNY (1839) for keyboards, and L'ABBÉ LE

FILS (1761), GALEAZZI (1791), CARTIER (1798), RODE, BAILLOT and KREUTZER (1803), SPOHR (1832), BAILLOT (1835), HABENECK (c1840), BÉRIOT (1858), DAVID (1864), JOACHIM and Moser (1905) and FLESCH (1923-8)) for the VIOLIN. The works of Baillot, Levasseur, Catel and Baudiot (1804), DUPORT (c1806), DOTZAUER (1825), Kummer (1839), ROMBERG (1840) and PIATTI (1878) best represent the CELLO, as does that of LABARRE (1844) for the HARP. TROMLITZ (1791), LEFÈVRE (1802), OZI (1803), Hugot and Wunderlich (1804), Brod (1825-35), KLOSÉ (1843), SELLNER (1825), MÜLLER (1825), BERR (1836), BAERMANN (1864-75), Almanraeder (1843) and Jancourt (1847) were among those who bolstered the market for woodwinds. Prominent contributors to instruction materials for brass instruments were ALTENBURG (1795), DAUPRAT (1824), MEIFRED (1840), GALLAY (c1845) and ARBAN (1864), and MANCINI (1774), HILLER (1774), CORRI (1810) and GARCÍA II (1840, 2/1847) authored influential methods for the voice. Vocal treatises are especially helpful for guidance on issues of ornamentation, extempore embellishment and improvisation, but few other than García's include detail about the physiology of voice production.

Theoretical Treatises
Numerous treatises on theoretical musical issues appeared through history, ranging from the writings of Lanfranco (1533), ZARLINO (1558), PRAETORIUS (1614-18), MERSENNE (1636-7), ZACCONI (1592, 1622) and KIRCHER (1650) to those of Mattheson (1739), AVISON (1752), ADLUNG (1758) and Mosel (1813). Prepared largely for academicians, they broadly explain the rules and aesthetics of composition, provide inventories or descriptions of existing (or at least theoretically possible) instruments, or discuss mathematical and somewhat idealised historical aspects of music. They help to exclude some potential interpretative issues, but rarely offer straightforward advice of immediately practical assistance. Nevertheless, the works of Lanfranco and Zarlino incorporate important rules for the satisfactory realisation of TEXT UNDERLAY; aestheticians provide useful descriptors of the character and 'colour' of specific tonalities; and the treatises of Praetorius, Mersenne and Adlung, among others, give vital clues regarding tuning and PITCH. Several specialist publications were also devoted to these latter issues, different TEMPERAMENTS having the potential to inflect a performance with a variety of nuances.

Evidence for the vocal or instrumental forces available in various centres of creativity through history is often obtainable from practical and theoretical treatises. Quantz's recommendations range from an ORCHESTRA with four violins to one with twelve; there were doubtless occasions when equivalent instruments were freely substituted, according to what was available. The orchestration manuals of KASTNER (1837, 1839), BERLIOZ (1843), STRAUSS (1905), Rimsky-Korsakov (1913) and others are invaluable reference material for the technique and potential of orchestral instruments, ORCHESTRAL PLACEMENT and other performance details, as are the CONDUCTING treatises of Berlioz (1856), WAGNER (1869) and Weingartner (1895), and many lesser studies. Iconographical evidence also survives for a variety of orchestral layouts, and further commentary is provided by Quantz, JUNKER, Petri, REICHARDT, Galeazzi and KOCH, as well as in dictionaries, autobiographies, letters and more general musical literature. The role of the concertmaster is also described in some of these publications.

Other Relevant Treatises
A wide variety of other treatises holds clues as to performance-related issues of their times, even as far back as philosophers such as Aristotle, BOETHIUS and Plato, the latter providing interesting insights into attitudes towards number theory, *harmonia*, rhythm, the modes and musical instruments. One of the most influential early treatises on instruments appears in the second volume, *De Organographica* (1618), of Praetorius's *Syntagma Musicum* (1614–18). Following almost a century after AGRICOLA's pioneering *Musica instrumentalis deudsch* (1529), its clear, detailed information and accurate scaled drawings have enabled instrument makers to model their REPLICAS precisely on its evidence. However, so authoritative a source is exceptional, and conclusions from similar publications should be corroborated from literary, archival or other sources, and by direct comparison with surviving instruments; further, illustrations of instruments cannot reveal the impossible regarding, for example, the materials used, the size and shape of a bore, the thickness of a soundboard or the tension of a string.

Evidence for achieving period accuracy in RECONSTRUCTED PRONUNCIATION of texts in vocal music may be found in linguistic sources such as Hart's *An Orthographie* (1569) or Palsgrave's *Lesclarissement de la langue francoyse* (1530); and the implementation of accurate period pronunciation can have important consequences for tuning, rhythm and expressive effect. Familiarity with characteristic steps and patterns notated in DANCE treatises may also provide clues regarding tempo and performance style in various dance-inspired movements. However, performers should exercise caution in using such evidence for the determination of precise tempos for specific dances. Dance steps and figures (and with them tempos) varied widely at different times and places; and dances often underwent considerable transformation in the instrumental domain.

The Need for Circumspection
The need for circumspection applies when using all treatises. Many have led performers to devise theories mistakenly, make inferences from sources too hastily and use performing conventions erroneously, the problems generally arising from the use of wrong sources or the wrong use of sources. Care should therefore be taken in the application of, say, Quantz's instructions, published in his mid-fifties and beholden to practices fashionable in his formative years, to performances of works by the young MOZART. Similarly, LEOPOLD MOZART's violin treatise may not be an infallible guide to the performance of Wolfgang's later works, following his absorption of an increased range of influences.

FREDERICK NEUMANN (316) regards treatise writers not as 'prophets who reveal infallible verities', but rather as 'very human witnesses who left us an affidavit about certain things they knew ... believed in, [and] ... wished their readers to believe'. A sense of context is vital. Neumann claims that historical treatises cannot be used safely without thorough and satisfactory assessment of the personality, background, knowledge, status and influence of the writer, the credibility, reliability and consistency of each treatise's textual content and the musical style and aesthetic it propounds, the readership to whom it is addressed, its relationship to other sources, its geographical and temporal limitations, and its relationship to the repertory (and the composers) to which it is applicable. Further, historical performance should never be governed by rigid rules, whatever their derivation. As MARPURG remarks about the art of embellishment, 'it is impossible to derive rules suitable to all possible occasions as long as music remains an inexhaustible sea of change, and one person's feelings differ from another's' (*Anleitung zum Klavierspielen*, 43). Indeed, performers may well need to consult other kinds of evidence besides treatises (such as ICONOGRAPHY, instruments, historical archives, critiques and other literary sources) to determine appropriate technical and interpretative solutions with assurance and authority.

FURTHER READING

H. M. Brown and S. Sadie (eds.), *Performance Practice: Music after 1600* (London: Macmillan, 1989).
T. J. McGee, *The Sound of Medieval Song: Ornamentation and Vocal Style According to the Treatises* (Oxford: Clarendon Press, 1998).
F. Neumann, 'The use of Baroque treatises on musical performance', *M&L*, 48/4 (1967), 315–24.
R. Stowell, 'The evidence', in C. Lawson and R. Stowell (eds.), *The Cambridge History of Musical Performance* (Cambridge University Press, 2012), 63–104.
T. E. Warner, 'Indications of performance practice in woodwind instruction books of the 17th and 18th centuries', PhD dissertation, New York University (1964).

ROBIN STOWELL

Tremolo For modern string players, 'tremolo' refers to the rapid reiteration of a note in separate BOW strokes, but this was not its customary meaning prior to the nineteenth century. In pre-Romantic music, three different gestures were associated with this label. The first involves the rapid alternation of a note with its upper neighbour – essentially a main-note trill, as described in the preface to the *Capirola Lutebook* (MS, n.d. [c1517]) and also in SYLVESTRO DI GANASSI's *Fontegara* (Venice: S. Ganassi, 1535), a method book for the RECORDER. GIROLAMO DIRUTA offers an illustration of this ornament for keyboardists in part I of *Il Transilvano* (1593; see Example 44), in which the alternations take up half the value of the original note.

'Tremolo' could also refer to the tremulant stop on an ORGAN, which creates undulations in the wind supply, and to the imitation of this effect on stringed instruments, playing repeated notes of relatively short value in a single bow stroke. Carlo Farina clearly connects the organ tremulant and the string tremolo in his *Capriccio stravagante* (*Ander Theil newer Paduanen, Gagliarden,*

Example 44: Girolamo Diruta: *Il Transilvano*, part I (1593), 10.

Example 45: Antonio Cesti: *Il pomo d'oro* (1666), Act IV, scene 4, violin I.

Couranten, französischen Arien, 1627) when he states, 'The tremolo is made with a pulsating of the hand that holds the bow, imitating the manner of the organ tremulant' ('So wird das Tremulieren mit pulsierenden Hand / darinnen Man den Bogen hat / auff Art des Tremulanten in den Orgeln imitiret'). Typically reserved for slow, affective passages, this gesture was sometimes marked with a wavy line (*see* Example 45), at other times with slurs over groups of repeated notes.

'Tremolo' could also refer to left-hand VIBRATO on a stringed instrument. Ganassi specified this type of tremolo for viola da gamba, used in conjunction with the bowed tremolo, in his *Regola rubertina* (1542). Alessandro Piccinini equated 'tremolo' with left-hand vibrato in the preface to his *Intavolatura di liuto, et di chitarrone* (Bologna: Gio Paolo Moscatelli, 1623).

FURTHER READING

S. Carter, 'The string tremolo in the seventeenth century', *EMc*, 19 (1991), 42–59.
O. Gombosi, *Compositione di meser Vincenzo Capirola: Lute-book (c1517)* (Neuilly-sur-Seine: Société de musique d'autrefois, 1955; R/New York: Da Capo, 1983).
G. Moens-Haenen, *Das Vibrato in der Musik des Barock: ein Handbuch zur Aufführungspraxis für Vokalisten und Instrumenten* (Graz: Akademische Druck- und Verlagsanstalt, 1988).

STEWART CARTER

Trichet, Pierre (b. Bordeaux, 1586–7; d. Bordeaux, before 1649) French collector, author and lawyer.

Trichet was a lawyer in the parliament of Bordeaux, the city where he spent his whole life. He showed a breadth of humanistic interests and published tragedies, epigrams and a book on witchcraft. He was a very active collector in several areas, including books, printed portraits, medals, naturalia, ethnographic objects and mathematical and musical instruments.

Around 1630 he began working on a *Traité des instruments de musique*, which remained unpublished until 1950. For each instrument it includes a discussion of the etymology of the name, some historical notes and a discussion of current use, sometimes relying on information taken from the work of MERSENNE – with whom he corresponded extensively – but often based on personal experience. While his work is not as systematic as other TREATISES of the time, his comments – often personal and outspoken – offer a rare insight into the TASTE and reception of many instruments in France in the early seventeenth century.

FURTHER READING

F. Lesure, 'Pierre Trichet's *Traité des instruments de musique: supplement*', *GSJ*, 15 (March 1962), 70–81.

P. Trichet, *Traité des instruments de musique*, ed. F. Lesure (Neuilly sur Seine: Société de Musique d'autrefois, 1955–7).

GABRIELE ROSSI ROGNONI

Trombone A brass lip-reed aerophone with a predominantly cylindrical bore.

The slide trombone was developed in the middle of the fifteenth century. The earliest image of the instrument is in a fresco by Filippino Lippi and has been dated 1488–93. It was called *trombone* in Italy, *Posaune* in German-speaking countries and words such as sagbut and *sacqueboute* (there are a multitude of spellings) in England, France, Spain and Portugal. In modern times 'sackbut' has routinely denoted the early form of the trombone.

The trombone was preceded in the fifteenth century by an instrument referred to in modern times as the 'slide trumpet'. It had a *single* telescopic slide, so a more limited range of notes could be played on it. No specimens of this instrument survive, but iconographical and other contextual sources are sufficiently abundant and convincing to extrapolate that this instrument was used to play the tenor, *cantus firmus*, lines in dance ensembles such as *alta* bands.

The earliest trombone to have survived (though not in its original condition) was made by Erasmus Schnitzer of Nuremberg and is dated 1551. Several Baroque instruments survive which are broadly similar to those of the previous century and have been successfully copied. Typically they have a narrower bore and produce a smaller and much more focused sound than their modern counterparts. In *Syntagma musicum*, PRAETORIUS shows the alto, tenor, bass and contra bass instrument, but though each of these sizes was used, it was the tenor that was most common in the sixteenth and seventeenth centuries.

No labelled lines for trombone survive from the sixteenth century (in any language), and few from the seventeenth, but there is enough contextual evidence for important generalisations to be made about the utility and performance conventions of the Renaissance instrument. Mainly (but not exclusively) trombonists were professionals. The instrument had a wide dynamic range, so it could be played loudly with TRUMPETS, but its comparatively wide range and expressive capability meant that good professional players could use highly nuanced ARTICULATIONS that matched those of other instruments and especially of the human voice. Thus, as well as being used in homogeneous groups, the trombone was used as a quiet instrument in mixed CONSORTS and for the accompaniment of voices in sacred music.

The instrument is mentioned and illustrated by early writers such as AGRICOLA and VIRDUNG, but the first informative source about the way it was played is the unpublished *Il dolcimelo* by Aurelio Virgiliano (MS, n.d. [c1592]). It shows that players used four slide positions with the highest (closest to the mouthpiece) producing a harmonic series on A. The scheme of slide positions is laid alongside FINGERING charts for the CORNETT, confirming what is known from many other sources, that these instruments were combined in sacred and secular contexts. Virgiliano's scheme for slide positions seems to have been consistent across Europe for at least a century, for similar information is found in Daniel Speer's *Grund-richtiger, kurtz- leicht- und nöthiger, jetzt wol-vermehrter Unterricht der musicalischen Kunst* (Ulm, 1697).

Despite such consistency, a cautionary point should be made that is applicable to all performance practice decisions relating to trombones up to the mid-twentieth century. While the evidence allows generalisations, there were also pronounced differences between and sometimes within countries. These differences applied to the types of instruments that were favoured, the unwritten conventions that were applied and the ways in which instruments were deployed. A vivid illustration of this can be found in the status of the instrument between the late seventeenth and late eighteenth centuries.

In many countries the instrument fell into disuse completely at the end of the seventeenth century. There were important exceptions, particularly in German-speaking countries and especially Austria, where alto, tenor and bass instruments, in continuation of an established tradition, were used *ad libitum* to support vocal lines in sacred music. Furthermore, there were sufficient players of stature to stimulate the creation of a solo repertory and some virtuosic, *obbligato* solos, many for the alto trombone. It is therefore no coincidence that the re-emergence of the trombone in art music occurred in Austria, and equally no coincidence that attempts to assemble players in London for the Handel commemoration in 1784 included some debate about what the words 'trombone' and 'sackbut' actually meant.

Another change seems to have taken place at about this time. Late in the eighteenth century André Braun, in his *Gamme et méthode pour les trombonnes* (Offenbach s/M: Jean André, [s.d.]), indicated that the instrument was then understood to have seven slide positions separated by a semitone: trombonists were therefore thinking in chromatic rather than diatonic terms. Furthermore, he gave B♭ as the series produced in the closed position. The focus on chromaticism was consolidated from the 1830s when the valve trombone was introduced, a development that also seems to have occurred in Austria. The valve trombone was extremely popular in some countries in the nineteenth century. For example, the Vienna Philharmonic used only valve trombones between 1862 and 1883, and the idiom of trombone parts in Italian opera scoring, as well as some concerted music, clearly signifies that valve trombones were used.

The slide trombone did survive, mainly at the behest of symphonic composers, but performance preferences in the nineteenth century varied significantly. Wider-bored instruments were favoured in German-speaking countries. French ORCHESTRAS usually used three tenor trombones (with no bass trombone), a practice that may have begun through the advocacy of BERLIOZ. English players in the first part of the century often used instruments pitched in C for the tenor (rather than B♭) and G (rather than F) for the bass. There was hardly any consistency in the use of the alto instrument and by the end of the century many writers were reporting its demise.

From the 1950s, wide-bore instruments designed in the USA (later also in Japan and elsewhere) became increasingly popular and eventually ubiquitous, but within the USA the demands of JAZZ musicians ensured that some smaller-bore, lighter-sounding instruments were also in circulation. It was the advent of jazz that caused the greatest changes to the idiomatic palette of the trombone, and this extended emphatically to the way the instrument was written for in modern art music.

Increasing globalisation impacted on performance practice from the second half of the twentieth century as diversity gave way to sameness. Some important performance characteristics were dissipated in this process. For example, VIBRATO, which is evidenced in EARLY RECORDINGS of many European orchestras, became *passé*. But perhaps the more important change concerned instrument designs. On the older, narrow-bore instruments the timbre changed at different dynamic levels: a highly focused softness in *pianissimo* gave way to a brassy-edged sound in *fortissimo*. Modern American instruments were designed to obtain a common timbre across all parts of the range and irrespective of dynamic level.

FURTHER READING

S. Carter, *The Trombone in the Renaissance* (Hillsdale, NY: Pendragon Press, 2012).
T. Herbert, *The Trombone* (New Haven and London: Yale University Press, 2006).

TREVOR HERBERT

Tromlitz, Johann George (b. Reinsdorf, 8 November 1725; d. Leipzig, 4 February 1805) German flautist, teacher and flute maker.

In 1750 Tromlitz received the degree of Imperial Public Notary at Leipzig University, and shortly afterwards began to make FLUTES. He was appointed principal flautist of the Grosses Konzert (a forerunner of the Gewandhaus Orchestra) in 1754, with which he undertook solo tours as far afield as St Petersburg. He eventually left the ORCHESTRA in 1776 in order to pursue teaching, writing, composing and flute manufacture. As an instrument maker he contributed greatly to the flute's development from 1781 through to the beginning of the nineteenth century, most importantly by adding a number of keys to facilitate tuning.

In 1786 Tromlitz published his first TREATISE in Leipzig: the *Kurze Abhandlung vom Flötenspielen*, which set out to reject merely average standards of performing and instrument making, focusing on the central ideas of clarity in ARTICULATION and EXPRESSION, perfect INTONATION in a system having both large and small comma semitones (for which the E♭ and D♯ flute keys invented by Quantz in 1726 were essential), concert PROGRAMMES that took into consideration the space and audience in question, and the total technical control and emotional involvement of the performer. These themes were developed in the work for which he has become best known, the *Ausführlicher und gründlicher Unterricht die Flöte zu spielen* (Leipzig, 1791), designed to instruct students in all aspects of flute playing. This is particularly significant because of his extremely thorough instructions on articulation and TONGUING; two whole chapters are devoted to this subject. He also gives detailed advice on FINGERING, intonation, VIBRATO, flute maintenance, posture and breathing, DYNAMICS, ornaments, musical style and CADENZAS, as well as the flute's construction. In 1800 Tromlitz published *Über die Flöten mit mehrern Klappen* as a supplement to the 1791 tutor, offering a practical guide to the flute of his own design.

FURTHER READING

R. Brown, *The Early Flute: A Practical Guide* (Cambridge University Press, 2002).
A. Powell, *The Flute* (New Haven and London: Yale University Press, 2002).

ASHLEY SOLOMON

Trumpet A lip-blown aerophone, ubiquitous in many different forms in most civilisations and societies throughout history.

The earliest trumpets were made from wood, stone, bone and shell. Early examples of metal trumpet-like instruments come from the Oxus civilisation (3200 BC) in northern Afghanistan. Short and ornate, their conjectured use was imitating animal calls in hunting, and from earliest times both trumpets and HORNS were used to signal over distance. The Ancient Egyptians, Greeks and Romans used trumpets in military manoeuvres, the Israelites and the Celts in religious ritual as well as warfare. Both uses – military and religious – became core to the symbolic idiom attached to the trumpet's sound. Medieval and Renaissance use elevated the trumpet to represent royal and spiritual authority. This heraldic character became central to the trumpet's idiom in the Baroque period. The trumpets depicted in ICONOGRAPHY from the late Medieval period were constructed from folded brass cylindrical tubing with a flared bell and a mouthpiece at the other. The player's lips formed an embouchure and the stream of air blown into the instrument was excited into sympathetic vibration. The PITCHES produced were part of the natural HARMONIC series playable on any particular length of trumpet. The embouchure controlled the pitch, fulfilling the same function as a singer's vocal cords; it is unsurprising that the earliest TREATISES stress the analogy with SINGING.

Iconographic evidence from the early Renaissance points to the slide trumpet being the bass instrument of the Alta Band. This instrument played in the low register, its single slide moving along the mouthpipe. Evidence of what it played comes from a MANUSCRIPT (c1444–9), containing contratenors to Dunstable's *Puisque m'amour*, compiled by Venetian musician Zorzi Trombetta da Modon. The more agile double-slide TROMBONE evolved and superseded this instrument during the second half of the fifteenth century. Whereas the trombone was played commonly in consort with the CORNETT to accompany church choirs, trumpets played outside together with kettledrums in a repertory that was committed to MEMORY. We know the structure of late Renaissance and early Baroque trumpet ensemble music from two of the earliest trumpet tutors – by Cesare Bendinelli (1614) and GIROLAMO FANTINI (1638). The earliest-known example of fully written-down trumpet ensemble music is the Toccata preceding MONTEVERDI's opera *Orfeo* (1607). The two lowest trumpets (*basso* and *vulgano*) of the five play drones on C and G, the highest (termed *clarino*) plays florid passagework in the upper register whilst the middle parts (*Quinta* and *Alto e basso*) play energetic military trumpet calls, to brilliant effect.

Natural trumpet playing flourished during the seventeenth and eighteenth centuries, as new levels of artistry within the upper register developed in Italy. From c1580, Bendinelli was active north of the Alps at the Munich court of Albrecht V, Duke of Bavaria, where Orlande de Lassus was *Kapellmeister* of an influential proto-orchestral ensemble. Powerful courts employed great trumpet ensembles. In Copenhagen, at Christian IV's court in the 1590s, trumpeters Henrich Lübeck and Magnus Thomsen notated over 300 pieces of trumpet ensemble repertoire, writing down, as a form of shorthand, only the middle *Sonata* part, around which the drones and *clarini* improvised. Knowledge of the performance practice of solo and ensemble trumpet sonatas of this period derives from Bendinelli and Fantini. Their learning methodology, and advice on ARTICULATION and phrasing, is derived from voice teaching. The other major surviving publication on Baroque trumpet playing practice is ALTENBURG's *Versuch* (Halle, 1795). Altenburg's trumpet pedagogy is remarkably consistent with the earlier tracts, demonstrating an accepted orthodoxy throughout these two centuries.

Pedagogy was predicated on a master-apprentice system of teaching. An Imperial Privilege of 1623, revised in 1653 and 1747, established the Imperial Guild of Trumpeters and Kettledrummers in the Holy Roman Empire. While this regulation attempted to restrict trumpet playing to aristocratic service, it carried little authority in many cities. In Leipzig, some of the most adventurous trumpet music of the Baroque was written by J. S. BACH for performance by Gottfried Reiche, a *Stadtpfeifer* who also played VIOLIN and horn. Solo trumpet writing became popular in later seventeenth-century Italy. Bologna's San Petronio Basilica supported a large ORCHESTRA, for which Torelli and his contemporaries wrote many sonatas and concertos for multiple trumpets. The Italian style of writing was diatonic and florid, with fast, running semiquaver passages. Francheschini, CORELLI and Alessandro Scarlatti also wrote music representative of this approach. From the 1660s other prominent centres were Moravia and Austria. Vejvanovský and Biber, who knew one another, were active in Kroměříž and Salzburg, respectively. A trumpeter himself, Vejvanovský was adventurous in his use of non-harmonic notes and the minor mode. The Moravian composer Gottfried Finger took this style of trumpet writing to England in 1687. Purcell's angular, idiosyncratic trumpet writing shows the influence of both Italy and Moravia. Finger wrote the 1691 St Cecilia's Day music featuring 'flatt' trumpets – the English slide trumpets used to great effect by Purcell in *Queen Mary's Funeral Music* (1695).

NATIONAL IDIOMS of writing for trumpet become discernible around this time. For example, the French style emphasised strongly diatonic melody, Michel-Richard de Lalande's *Concerts de trompettes* and *Les symphonies pour le soupez du roy* showing the influence of Lully. Marc-Antoine Charpentier's Prelude to the D major *Te Deum* (c1690) is a supreme example of the celebratory use of trumpet in sacred music. This French style influenced English theatre composers such as Jeremiah Clarke, whose confidence-inspiring trumpet tunes such as *The Prince of Denmark's March*, benefit from being played *inégale* in the French manner. In 1711 Handel's first London opera *Rinaldo* uses four trumpets and the soprano aria in this work, 'Or la tromba', uses them all in Italian virtuoso style. Throughout the half-century of his career in England, Handel's solo trumpet writing for Valentine Snow became increasingly noble and majestic in *obbligatos* to the arias, as 'The trumpet shall sound' (*Messiah*, 1742) and 'Let the bright seraphim' (*Samson*, 1743), demonstrate.

German and Austrian composers such as J. S. Bach, Fux and Caldara wrote the most complex and demanding music for trumpet in the Baroque period, requiring both facility and stamina. Non-harmonic notes, rapid articulations and extended passages in the highest tessitura were commonplace. By the 1720s Bach's Brandenburg Concerto No. 2 in F and Caldara's *I due dittatori* extend the range to g'''. One commentator noted that the Viennese trumpeter Johann

Heinisch could play the trumpet so artfully and high that it seemed almost beyond human capability. Georg Reutter II's *Il Parnasso* (1738) provides evidence of this exceptional virtuosity, with g''' again the highest note. Trumpets were built in different lengths from 6 ft F to 9 ft B♭. C and D were the most common pitches, with D major the key of alleluyahs and rejoicing and C major representing the heroic; B♭ was dark, and F the key of the hunt. Baroque pitch varied. It was both lower and higher than modern pitch. Solo natural trumpet writing in the *clarino* register persisted into the early Classical period in Austria and Germany. Michael Haydn and LEOPOLD MOZART wrote virtuoso works in the early 1760s for Salzburg court trumpeter Johann Schachtner, with Michael Haydn ascending to the D trumpet's twenty-fourth harmonic, a'''. Contemporaries F. X. Richter in Mannheim, Joseph Riepel in Regensburg, and J. S. Endler in Darmstadt also wrote significant solo works for trumpet. The *clarino* register fell out of use in the later eighteenth century, as trumpets in the Classical ORCHESTRA rarely ventured above the twelfth natural harmonic. In partnership with kettledrums, their function was to add ceremonial gravitas to orchestral sonority. Towards the century's end, the first keyed trumpets appeared. The Viennese trumpeter ANTON WEIDINGER inspired a series of solo works by Joseph HAYDN, HUMMEL, Koželuch, Weigl and Neukomm for his own *Inventionstrompete*. Charles Clagget patented a valve mechanism in London in 1788; Irish bandmaster Joseph Halliday invented the keyed bugle in 1806; in Berlin Stölzel and Blühmel patented valve designs in 1818. A plethora of new inventions – keyed bugles, keyed trumpets, slide trumpets, valve trumpets, cornets, flügel horns – co-existed. The cornet became a popular virtuoso solo instrument in promenade concerts, brass and military bands.

The valve trumpet was championed at the Prague Conservatory in the 1820s. Its director, Bedrich Diviš Weber, wrote *Variations in F* for trumpet and orchestra, while Josef Kail and Conradin Kreutzer wrote competition pieces. The new instruments were around 6 ft long, crooked into G, F and E, and became the chief orchestral trumpets of the second half of the nineteenth century. Shorter trumpets in B♭, the same length as, but coiled differently from, the cornet, became more widespread later in the century. This trumpet was easier to play in the high register, which came back into vogue through a generation of composers headed by RICHARD STRAUSS and MAHLER. In the late nineteenth century there was a Bach revival, and German player Julius Kosleck popularised the 'Bach Trumpet' in A, with valves, but wrapped to look very long and impressive, to play difficult works such as the Mass in B minor.

The valve trumpet arrived at its fully recognisable modern form in the 1920s. Solo trumpet writing become more prevalent from the early twentieth century. Belgian trumpeter Théo Charlier played Bach's Brandenburg Concerto No. 2 in 1898 on a short valve trumpet in F, 3 ft long. In 1906, Merri Franquin introduced the Georges Enesco *Légende*, requiring woodwind-like flexibility on C trumpet, as a *morceau de concours* at the PARIS CONSERVATOIRE. STRAVINSKY required an extended trumpet section, from bass to piccolo, in *Le Sacre du Printemps* (1913). Although Franz Rossbach revived Haydn's Trumpet Concerto in E♭ with the Vienna Philharmonic in 1908 after a gap of a century, the concerto entered the core repertory only after WWII, popularised through gramophone records by Helmut Wobisch and George Eskdale.

Brandenburg Concerto No. 2 became accessible to more players with the proliferation of piccolo B♭/A trumpets by makers Scherzer and Selmer. Maurice André became the most imitated piccolo trumpet exponent, playing transcriptions of Baroque OBOE and VIOLIN concertos. From the 1960s players such as Walter Holy, Don Smithers and Edward Tarr played Baroque music on reproduction natural trumpets. Tarr taught natural trumpet at the SCHOLA CANTORUM BASILIENSIS, and Michael Laird similarly at the ROYAL COLLEGE OF MUSIC, London. Natural trumpet making and playing developed rapidly in the context of a heightened interest in period instrument ensembles. Twentieth-century reproduction natural trumpets usually had three or four finger-holes bored at nodal points. When uncovered, these holes enabled certain natural harmonics to sound more approximate to equal TEMPERAMENT. During the first decades of the twenty-first century, influential players, notably Crispian Steele-Perkins in Britain and Jean-François Madeuf in France, led a vogue for 'hole-less' natural trumpets and large-diameter reproduction period mouthpieces, to recreate the sound world of the authentic natural trumpet.

The average bore size of valve trumpets increased during the twentieth century. Mouthpieces became shallower. Trumpets became louder, with a more penetrating timbre. These changes caused many twenty-first-century orchestras, otherwise playing modern instruments, to use natural trumpets, horns and small kettledrums in Classical repertory, for their sound quality. The ORCHESTRA OF THE AGE OF ENLIGHTENMENT plays nineteenth-century repertory on period instruments. Within a softer aesthetic, the brass section sounds more 'brassy' when playing loudly. The warm sounds of late nineteenth- and early twentieth-century brasses have been recreated in period orchestras such as the New Queen's Hall Orchestra. The sound world of brass has changed so much during the past century that period instrument performances of STRAVINSKY's *Le Sacre*, which began in the centenary year of 2013, are likely to set future trends for twenty-first-century historic brass performance.

FURTHER READING

J. E. Altenburg, *Versuch einer Anleitung zur heroisch-musikalischen Trumpeter- und Pauker-Kunst* (Halle: J. C. Hendel, 1795/R Dresden: Bertlling, 1911; trans. E. H. Tarr, Nashville, TN: Brass Press, 1974).

C. Bendinelli, *Tutta l'arte della trombetta* (MS, 1614); facsim. edn, with commentary by E. H. Tarr in DM, 2nd ser., Handschriften-Faksimiles, v (1975); Eng. trans. (Nashville, TN: Brass Press, 1975).

G. Fantini: *Modo per imparare a sonare di tromba* (Frankfurt: D. Watsch, 1638); facsim. edn with trans. and commentary by E. H. Tarr (Nashville, TN: Brass Press, 1978).

J. Wallace and A. McGrattan, *The Trumpet* (New Haven and London: Yale University Press, 2011).

JOHN WALLACE

Tuba and ophicleide The tuba and ophicleide were developed entirely independently, but like the SERPENT and the bass horn were both aimed at providing an effective bass voice for the brass instrument (lip-vibrated) family. The ophicleide was used in many musical genres before the tuba was invented, and although the tuba was to endure to modern times, the two instruments overlapped and led parallel lives for much of the nineteenth century. The ophicleide was invented in France by Halary (Jean Hilaire Asté) and patented in 1821. It is a conical, keyed, brass-wind instrument played with a mouthpiece similar to that of a TROMBONE and is the bass equivalent of the keyed bugle. The tuba was patented in Germany as the bass tuba in 1835 by Wilhelm Wieprecht and Johann Moritz. Several designers, most notably ADOLPHE SAX, introduced improvements, particularly aimed at valve designs and ways of assuring good intonation. Manufacturers have experimented with a variety of shapes for the tuba, and some designs have acquired distinctive nomenclatures such as bombardon, helicon and sousaphone, but each is a type of tuba and they are usually pitched at 8 ft C or lower. The euphonium (called baritone horn in the USA) is, in effect, a tenor tuba.

The ophicleide flourished for a relatively short period and had fallen out of use by the 1870s; but in the half century when it was in common use it held an important place in several musical contexts. Many photographs of early British brass and military bands show the ophicleide alongside euphoniums and tubas; although there were mixed opinions about the instrument, it was incorporated into several large-scale orchestral works and taught at the major conservatoires, and a body of musical sources survives that casts a significant light on its idiom.

Many early method books for the ophicleide were expediently assembled in the decades immediately after the instrument was invented, but only two were written by authors who were also known to be ophicleide players: Victor Cornette's *Méthode d'ophycléide alto et basse* (Paris, 1835) and Joseph Caussenus's *Solfège-méthode pour l'ophicléide basse, en 2 parties* (Paris, 1836). Equally interesting are handwritten ophicleide band parts copied for particular players. None are more important than those written for the virtuoso Sam Hughes when he was a member of the private band of R.T. Crawshay at Cyfarthfa Castle, South Wales. These parts, which require astonishing virtuosity, reveal an idiom that contradicts what some writers (including BERLIOZ) say of the instrument's turgid capacity in the middle register.

The late 1840s seem to have seen the beginning of the final transition from the ophicleide to the tuba as the instrument of preference. Berlioz, despite his reservations about the ophicleide, introduced it into several of his works. By this time, new species of MILITARY and brass BANDS were starting to flourish, using valve instruments that were easier to play than the ophicleide, with a more consistent timbre across their range, and easier to make under factory conditions. The tuba quickly became the default bass instrument for the brass family, but its main use continued to be in military and brass bands.

The method books written for the tuba in the nineteenth and early twentieth centuries were formulaic in nature, as was the didactic literature of most valve instruments other than the cornet and French HORN; they explained a common approach to technique, irrespective of the register at which the instrument was pitched, so publications disseminated as tuba method books contain a significant overlap with books in the same series for other brass instruments.

As with most brass instruments that were to survive to modern times, performance idioms and the preference for particular types of instrument design showed considerable regional diversity until the late twentieth century when globalisation encouraged commonality. It is important to stress, however, that throughout its history the idiom of the tuba has been influenced by forms of music making that emerged outside the central domain of art music – particular military music, brass bands, JAZZ and other popular forms.

The term 'cimbasso', a designation frequently encountered in Italian opera scores for the bass voice line below the trombones, does not consistently refer to a specific instrument; rather, it came to be what Meucci calls a 'jargon' for the part or voice below the trombone section. Nevertheless, there is some dispute among scholars about what, at any given time, this designation was intended to signify: the serpentone (SERPENT), ophicleide and even the bass horn were sometimes used. Clifford Bevan has pointed out that the tuba was not regularly encountered in Italian ORCHESTRAS until the 1920s, and it is clear that many different solutions were implemented. Verdi recognised a lack of homogeneity between the trombone section and the tuba, and in 1881 approached the Milan instrument maker Pelitti to solve this problem. His solution was a contrabass valve trombone in B♭ and E♭, and though it was specified only in Verdi's last two operas, there are grounds for believing that he would have used this instrument earlier had it been available. However, the indiscriminate use of Verdi's 'trombone basso' for the cimbasso line is contentious. In modern times instruments marketed as 'cimbasso' have been designed, and while not wholly accurate historically have been used successfully by opera orchestras to achieve the effect for which Verdi was searching, probably along with other Italian opera composers. However, as is the case with many performance practice decisions concerning the lowest brass voice in the nineteenth century, the choice of instrument (when not specifically designated in the original source) depends on the musical, regional and cultural context.

FURTHER READING

C. Bevan, *The Tuba Family* (Winchester: Piccolo Press, 2000).
T. Herbert and J. Wallace (eds.), *The Cambridge Companion to Brass Instruments* (Cambridge University Press, 1997).
R. Meucci (trans. W. Waterhouse), 'The cimbasso and related instruments in 19th-century Italy', *GSJ*, 49 (1996), 143–79.

TREVOR HERBERT

Tuning fork A U-shaped metal bar with a stem projecting from the base, used by musicians as a convenient and reliable standard PITCH source.

Although Stradner (1994) has suggested that a tuning fork was depicted by Michael Pacher in his 1486 *Kirchenväteraltar*, there is no reliable evidence of its musical use before the eighteenth century. Writing in 1776, HAWKINS describes the trumpeter and lutenist John Shore as the original inventor of the tuning fork. The date commonly given for the invention is 1711, but Hawkins (*A General History of the Science and Practice of Music*, 5 vols. (London: T. Payne, 1776, R/1875, II, 752)) states only that Shore had a place in the Queen's band that year. Certainly Shore was well known for using the tuning fork for some time before his death in 1752: Hawkins records that 'At a concert he would say, "I have not about me a pitch-pipe, but I have what will do as well to tune by, a pitch fork."' In fact, the tuning fork was a great improvement on the pitch-pipe, a small RECORDER-like whistle with a sliding piston to adjust the sounding length, because its PITCH was much less sensitive to changes in temperature.

Tuning forks surviving from the eighteenth and nineteenth centuries provide valuable evidence of contemporary pitch standards, although links which have been claimed between specific forks and composers such as Handel and MOZART are unsubstantiated. The first systematic survey of tuning fork frequencies was made by Ellis (1880); his work has been critically reviewed by Mendel (1978), who notes that the historical significance of a tuning fork is often limited by uncertainty about where, when and by whom it was used. It should also be borne in mind that although the frequency of an unmodified fork is very stable, it may have been significantly changed over time by small mechanical adjustments such as bending or filing.

FURTHER READING

A. J. Ellis, 'On the history of musical pitch', *Journal of the Society of Arts*, 28 (1880), 293-336 and 400-6.
A. Mendel, 'Pitch in Western music since 1500: a re-examination', *AM*, 50 (1978), 1-93, 328.
G. Stradner, 'Stellt Michael Pacher 1486 eine Stimmgabel dar?', in M. Nagy (ed.), *'Musik muss man machen', eine Festgabe für Josef Mertin* (Vienna: Vom Pasqualatihaus, 1994), 127-41.

MURRAY CAMPBELL

Türk, Daniel Gottlob (b. Claussnitz, nr Chemnitz, 10 August 1750; d. Halle, 26 August 1813) German theorist and composer.

Early in his life Türk learned to play the VIOLIN and a variety of wind instruments. In Leipzig he studied composition with HILLER and was introduced to C. P. E. BACH's keyboard method by J. W. Hässler. From 1774 to the end of his life he held organist's positions in Halle, where he lectured at the university in the theory and composition of music. He was an influential conductor and keyboard performer (he is regarded as the founder of the Halle Handel tradition), but he is mostly known for his theoretical works, which are among the most detailed of their kind.

His comprehensive *Klavierschule, oder Anweisung zum Klavierspielen für Lehrer und Lernende* (Leipzig and Halle: Hemmerde & Schwickert, 1789, enlarged 2/1802/R; trans. R. Haggh, 1982) is acknowledged to be intended primarily for CLAVICHORD players. Both EDITIONS regard the clavichord as the best keyboard instrument on which to learn on account of the finesse required to play it, but nevertheless comment on a wide range of around twenty keyboard instruments. Türk also discusses performance matters of relevance well beyond the sphere of keyboard playing. Like many of his German predecessors, he says much about RHETORIC, advocating an expressive performing style including close attention to the declamation of melody. He has much to say about appropriate ACCENTUATION, phrasing, ARTICULATION and touch, and lays great stress on the careful and expressive use of DYNAMICS. He also advocates a very flexible approach to dotted notes, although he observes that they are usually held longer than their NOTATION literally requires. Türk's definition of TEMPO RUBATO is of the displaced kind, in which the duration of a note can be shortened or lengthened, and compensated for in the value of surrounding notes (although in the 1802 edition of his *Klavierschule* he acknowledges that composers generally notate the effect when it is required). In the 1789 edition Türk already permits a degree of TEMPO fluctuation, recommending the occasional slackening of tempo for expressive effect at the end of sections. His comments on individual ornament signs are comprehensive, and in some instances he offers a critique of earlier writers' interpretations. His approach to improvised ORNAMENTATION is cautious; it is clearly appropriate at fermatas, in rondos and other works where passages would otherwise become tedious on repetition, but generally it is best reserved for slower music. Like many of his contemporaries, Türk espouses the non-legato style. His FINGERING instructions emphasise the thumb as a pivot, but acknowledge circumstances where older patterns of paired fingerings may still be useful. The 1789 *Klavierschule* is acknowledged as one of the most important sources of performance practice in the late eighteenth century and the re-organised 1802 edition provides updated material on matters such as dynamics, REPEATS and ornamentation. The later edition also provides occasional commentary on keyboard TREATISES published since the first edition.

In his *Kurze Anweisung zum Generalbassspielen* (Leipzig and Halle: Author, 1791, enlarged 2/1800/R as *Anweisung zum Generalbassspielen*, enlarged 5/1841 by F. Naue), the last major treatise of its kind, Türk acknowledges a contemporary neglect of FIGURED BASS. He advocates a simple style, especially on the ORGAN, commenting, for example, that repeated bass notes in orchestral music do not all have to be played and that keyboard parts in recitative should be restrained, with short chords recommended, especially in organ accompaniment.

Organists in Türk's time relied on their knowledge of figured bass, since many hymnals were published with melody line and continuo accompaniment only. Hence his *Von den wichtigsten Pflichten eines Organisten: ein Beytrag zur Verbesserung der musikalischen Liturgie* (Halle: Hemmerde & Schwickert, 1787/ R, rev. 2/1838 by F. Naue; trans. and commentary M. Woolard, 1987) also deals with the subject. In addition, Türk shows himself to be a relatively early proponent of the heel and toe method of organ pedalling. His treatise also offers advice on IMPROVISATION for preludes and postludes, modulation, how to accompany hymns sensitively, without over-embellishment, and organ maintenance. In his last theoretical work, *Anleitung zu Temperaturberechnungen* (Halle, 1808/R), Türk advocates equal TEMPERAMENT.

FURTHER READING

F. T. Arnold, *The Art of Accompaniment from a Thorough-bass*, 2 vols. (Oxford University Press, 1931).

S. P. Rosenblum, *Performance Practices in Classic Piano Music* (Bloomington and Indianapolis: Indiana University Press, 1988).

P. Williams, *Figured Bass Accompaniment* (Edinburgh University Press, 1970).

DAVID ROWLAND

U

Urtext *Urtext* ('original text') is a term coined by German publishers around 1900. It refers to EDITIONS prepared to make available 'authentic', 'reliable', and 'objective' versions to educated performers. The earliest use of the term *Urtext* is found in the editions of canonic works (by J. S. BACH, BEETHOVEN, MOZART and others) published through the Akademie der Künste in Berlin in 1895–9; but it did not become common currency until after WWII, most notably through Günter Henle, who in 1948 established a publishing house entirely devoted to the cause.

In the spirit of nineteenth-century positivism and historicism, and roughly concurrently with the rise of HISTORICALLY INFORMED PERFORMANCE, *Urtext* editions purported to be based on the earliest and most clearly authorised sources (ideally on autographs), in order to cleanse musical practice from the layers of additions, modifications and arrangements based on latter-day performing traditions that had pervaded practical or pedagogical editions. The association of *Urtext* with idealist concepts of authority and originality has meant that the term has rarely been used for editions of pre-Baroque music, given the much more radical process of translation from original sources into modern editions in this repertory (regarding the NOTATION itself, but also scoring, clefs, TEXT UNDERLAY, etc.), coupled with the fact that the extant sources are rarely 'authorised' in a way that would make them *Urtext*-compliant in the strict sense.

Although still in wide use, not least as a marketing tool for publishers who like to promote the credibility of their products, the term is far from unambiguous, even apart from the fact that it relies on concepts of authenticity and authorial intent which themselves have come into question in recent textual scholarship. On the one hand, *Urtext* is often used virtually synonymously with 'critical', referring to editions applying philological standards similar to those of Complete Editions, based on a full documentation, examination and comparison of all extant original sources (autographs, first editions, etc.), only distinguished by the comprehensiveness of the critical apparatus. Indeed, publishing houses often market performing editions derived from critical editions with a reduced commentary as 'Urtext based on the Complete Edition'. In a more purist interpretation, *Urtext* has also been taken to imply a reversion to a single 'Ur'-source (ideally the autograph) in near-diplomatic TRANSCRIPTION, even where a later authorised version (a 'Fassung letzter Hand') exists. Here, the concept of *Urtext* can overlap with that of the 'Urfassung' ('original version'), feeding into the unabated desire by scholars and performers to unearth and disseminate earlier versions of well-known works.

In terms of editorial practice, the objective of *Urtext* publishers to address performers – rather than scholars – has often implied the addition of some non-original features aiding execution, such as FINGERINGS, BOWING directions in string music or the realisation of a FIGURED BASS. Along with the rise of historically informed practice in recent decades, and with the concomitant attitude that educated performers should not require such editorial assistance, these additions have tended to become less frequent and less elaborate. Many *Urtext* editions now present a non-interventionist text that aims to reflect as closely as possible the notation of the chosen original source(s). In the end, however, there is no hiding behind the *Urtext* label: every edition is a translation from one medium into another, based on many decisions on many levels, and the editor has to take ownership of that process.

FURTHER READING

M. Caraci Vela, *Musical Philology. Institutions, History, and Critical Approaches, I: Historical and Methodological Fundaments of Musical Philology* (Pisa: ETS, 2015).

G. Feder (with H. Unverricht), 'Urtext und Urtextausgaben', *Die Musikforschung*, 12 (1959), 432–54.

J. Grier, *The Critical Editing of Music: History, Method, and Practice* (Cambridge University Press, 1996).

THOMAS SCHMIDT

V

Vaccai, Nicola (b. Tolentino, 15 March 1790; d. Pesaro, 5 August 1848) Italian singing teacher and composer.

Only after a series of disappointments and outright failures as an opera composer did Vaccai find his true vocation as a SINGING teacher. He began his teaching career in Paris in 1830 and pursued it in London where he published his *Metodo pratico* (1832), which found immediate popularity; it has rarely been out of print. He subsequently became head of singing at the Milan Conservatory.

Vaccai's *Metodo* contains no exercises as such, but comprises a series of short lyric pieces, arranged in fifteen lessons, devised to build technique, working systematically through all the interval leaps, and introducing common ornaments. Instead of the usual wordless vocalisations, these studies set words by Metastasio, whom Vaccai greatly admired; they are devised for practising elisions and 'unusual syllable combinations' (5) to assist non-Italian students to acquire good PRONUNCIATION. His definition of PORTAMENTO is restricted to legato, excluding 'the incorrect practice of dragging the voice from one interval to another through the intermediate steps' (27); despite this the second note is invariably anticipated with a grace note. In recitative he advocates a liberal use of appoggiaturas, insisting that the penultimate note of a phrase should always be taken as an appoggiatura, with similar treatment for repeated notes within a phrase (30). In Example 46, 'A' denotes appoggiatura.

Example 46: Nicola Vaccai: *Metodo pratico* (1832).

FURTHER READING

G. Vaccai, *La vita di Nicola Vaccai, scritta dal figlio Giulio* (Bologna: Zanichelli, 1882).

N. Vaccai, *Metodo pratico di canto italiano* (London: Bowerman, 1832).

PATRICIA HOWARD

Vaillant (Vayllant), Jehan (Johannes) (fl ?1360–90) French composer and theorist.

Vaillant stands at the centre of a number of important yet elusive strands of fourteenth-century music making. As a composer, he exhibits direct links with practitioners including GUILLAUME DE MACHAUT, Grimace, Franciscus, Guilot and Guido, thus bridging mid-century practices and the later, more complex style now referred to as the *Ars subtilior*. The influence of his work, though, reached much further afield, as one of his songs 'Par maintes fois' was integrated into the so-called 'international repertory' circulating throughout Europe. It was popular enough to survive in multiple copies and versions, including elaborations, simplifications and retextings in German and Latin. Furthermore, Vaillant stands out as having a direct and documented link with musical education. The *Règles de la seconde rhétorique* mentions him as running a music school in Paris, a theory TREATISE has tentatively been ascribed to him, and, most unusually, there survives a mid-fifteenth-century Hebrew MANUSCRIPT that contains what appears to be student notes from his classes. This source makes clear that in addition to the customary discourse on the philosophy and mythical history of music, Vaillant directed his teaching towards practical musicianship and integration within the prevailing musical context. Thus, he enumerates 'a pleasant voice' as one of the three basics of a musician's knowledge, describes in great detail the various PROPORTIONS that musicians were expected to be able to execute, and occasionally illustrates them by reference to specific pieces (one of which survives to this day). In mentioning a song containing the demanding 9:8 proportion, he remarks not on technical rectitude but on how refined and delicate the use of the device is, showing that his interest is in a living musical culture and not in academic sophistries.

FURTHER READING

C. Page, 'Fourteenth-century instruments and tunings: a treatise by Jean Vaillant? (Berkeley, MS 744)', *GSJ*, 33 (1980), 17–35.

Y. Plumley, *The Art of Grafted Song: Citation and Allusion in the Age of Machaut* (Oxford University Press, 2013).

A. Stone, 'The *ars subtilior* in Paris', *Musica e storia*, 10/2 (2002), 373–404.

URI SMILANSKY

Van, Guillaume de (William Carrolle Devan) (b. Memphis, TN, 3 July 1906; d. Amalfi, Italy, 2 July 1949) American musicologist.

After studies at Princeton, Devan attended courses in Berlin (1927–8) before studying Gregorian CHANT in Rome for several years. By 1935 he had settled in Paris and styled himself Guillaume de Van. In 1936, he founded Les Paraphonistes de Saint-Jean des Matines with Abbé François Ducaud-Bourget. This ensemble specialised in Medieval music and de Van's pioneering recordings included four movements from Machaut's *Messe de Nostre Dame*, recorded for

L'Anthologie sonore in 1936. In the late 1930s, de Van also recorded for Editions de l'Oiseau-Lyre.

De Van joined the staff at the Bibliothèque nationale in 1937 and became head of the music department in 1942, during the years of Nazi occupation. He gave concerts of Medieval music at the library that were praised by critics, including André Jolivet who noted that the best way to bring these works back to life was by performing them (*Écrits*, ed. C. Jolivet-Erlih, 2 vols. (Paris: Delatour, 2006), I, 130). But there was a darker side to de Van's activities, summarised by Catherine Parsoneault (347): 'De Van was an enthusiastic collaborator with the Nazis in their efforts to confiscate musical instruments, materials and manuscripts, as well as to identify Jewish musicians in Paris. So egregious was de Van's cooperation with the *Sonderstab Musik* that he was eventually arrested.' De Van was suspended from his duties when Paris was liberated in August 1944. After the war, he edited the first volumes of the Dufay complete edition for Corpus Mensurabilis Musicae (1947, 1948), as 'Guglielmus de Van'.

FURTHER READING

S. Iglesias, *Musicologie et Occupation. Science, musique et politique dans la France des 'années noires'* (Paris: Éditions de la Maison des sciences de l'homme, 2014), 257–61.

C. Parsoneault, 'Aimer la musique ancienne: Yvonne Rihouët Rokseth (1890–1948)', in J. Chance (ed.), *Women Medievalists and the Academy* (Madison, WI and London: University of Wisconsin Press, 2005).

NIGEL SIMEONE

Vandenbroek, Othon-Joseph (b. Ypres, 20 December 1758; d. Passy, 18 October 1832) Flemish composer, conductor and HORN player.

Vandenbroek studied at The Hague and in Amsterdam, and worked in ORCHESTRAS in Brussels and Maastricht before moving to Paris in 1783. He made his Parisian debut as a HORN player in 1784 at the *Concert Spirituel*, and subsequently played at the Théâtre de Monsieur and then from 1793 to 1816 was the fourth horn player at L'Opéra. In 1812 he was appointed 'attaché à la chapelle de l'Empereur et Roi'. His stage works and operas were mounted at theatres in Paris including the new Théâtre des Beaujolais; they are now considered to be of little consequence and were for the most part cast in the 'sentimental' operatic style then in vogue.

He wrote two pedagogical treatises, *Méthode nouvelle pour apprendre à sonner du cor* (Paris, 1789) and *Traité général de tous les instruments à vent, à l'usage des compositeurs* (Paris, 1795). Despite the title of this second TREATISE, succinct overviews are given of the OBOE, FLUTE, BASSOON, SERPENT, CLARINET, TRUMPET, TROMBONE and TIMPANI, whilst extensive discussion is made of the horn, with forty-four of its sixty-five pages concerning this instrument. He writes exhaustively of the capabilities of the horn, setting out all the runs and melodic passages that can be performed on it, as well as its range in every key when playing in unison with a VIOLIN. This treatise was intended to help composers write effectively for wind instruments, so throughout the book he focuses on the mechanisms of the instruments (i.e. range and chromatic ability), rather than describing their character or tone quality.

Exceptionally, he compares the oboe with the human, especially female, voice. He also recommends that all instruments of the orchestra should tune to the horn. Vandenbroek was professor at the PARIS CONSERVATOIRE from 1795 to 1800.

FURTHER READING

E. I. Dolan, *The Orchestral Revolution, Haydn and the Technologies of Timbre* (Cambridge University Press, 2013).

D. M. Guion, *Trombone: Its History and Music, 1697–1811* (Newark, NJ: Gordon and Breach, 1988).

ASHLEY SOLOMON

Vanderhagen, Amand (Jean François Joseph) (b. Antwerp, 1753; d. Paris, July 1822) Flemish clarinettist, composer and pedagogue.

A prolific composer and arranger of military and wind music, Vanderhagen wrote didactic works of lasting significance. His *Méthode nouvelle et raisonée pour la clarinette* (Paris, 1785) is essentially the first tutor for the Classical CLARINET and was in scope and design far in advance of the jejune methods published for other woodwind instruments. Vanderhagen summed up the character of the instrument by noting that the beauty of the clarinet lay in its sweet sound; and that even a mediocre player could delight the listener with the instrument. His title page claimed to offer a clear and succinct explanation of the manner in which the clarinet is held. He advised at the outset that the head not be held too high as this would hinder the breathing; it must be held naturally and without affectation. He is an important source for ARTICULATION of the period, making an exception to tongue stroke for the performance of triplets slurred in threes, where (to avoid undue emphasis) he recommended the throat be used to mark off the first note. One of the earliest commentators on the subject of reeds, Vanderhagen advised beginners to choose a reed that is neither too hard nor too soft. Regarding choice of cane, he warned against that which is too spongy. His more specific instructions concerning the actual manufacturing process imply that once the reed was finished it was subjected to considerable fine-tuning for days afterwards. Vanderhagen's method proved extremely popular and he himself revised it in 1796. A further update from 1819 addresses the new twelve-keyed clarinet and is important for its depiction of the instrument used by Weber's clarinettist Heinrich Baermann. It is shown with reed above, although Baermann is known from other sources to have played with reed against the bottom lip. Vanderhagen's methods for the OBOE and FLUTE date respectively from 1792 and 1798.

FURTHER READING

B. François-Sappey, 'Le personnel de la musique royale de l'avènement de Louis XVI à la chute de la monarchie (1774–1792)', *Recherche sur la musique française classique*, xxvi (1988–90), 133–72.

T. E. Hoeprich, *The Clarinet* (New Haven and London: Yale University Press, 2008).

COLIN LAWSON

Vaughan Williams, Ralph (b. Down Ampney, 12 October 1872; d. London, 26 August 1958) English composer, teacher, writer and conductor.

Vaughan Williams studied at the ROYAL COLLEGE OF MUSIC (1890–3 and 1895–6) and Trinity College, Cambridge, and subsequently took lessons from Max Bruch and Ravel. As a composer he was slow to develop and not until 1909–10 did his personal voice fully emerge. His style owed much to the influence of English folksong and sixteenth- and early seventeenth-century music; the latter inspired one of his earliest masterpieces, the *Fantasia on a Theme by Thomas Tallis* (1910). In 1904 he was instrumental in the establishment of the Leith Hill Musical Festival and for forty-eight years (1905–53) conducted its concerts. Here, and with the Bach Choir (which he conducted from 1921 to 1928), he was able to indulge his devotion to the music of J. S. BACH and his predecessors. The 300 voices of the Bach Choir necessitated a contemporary rather than period-style performance which Vaughan Williams justified on the grounds that it was better for Bach's music to be sung by a large choir than not at all, in a language (English) that the audience understood, and with 'a slight modification of the instrumental detail' (Keen, 110), in the form of minor re-orchestration and the use of a PIANO as the CONTINUO instrument. As he wrote, 'The harpsichord is all right with a small band and a small choir – but 350 in the Q.H. [Queen's Hall]?' (Cobbe, 142). A critic noted that although the choir's 1924 performance of Bach's Mass in B minor 'did not attain to faultlessness or great splendour, it possessed a peculiar spiritual interest' (*MT*, 65 (1924), 552). As recordings demonstrate, although the performances may sound ponderous to contemporary ears, they evince great sincerity. In addition to Bach's two passions, Mass in B minor and a selection of cantatas, Vaughan Williams conducted many shorter choral works by composers of the sixteenth to eighteenth centuries.

FURTHER READING

H. Cobbe (ed.), *Letters of Ralph Vaughan Williams, 1895–1958* (Oxford University Press, 2008).
B. Keen, *The History of the Bach Choir: The First Hundred Years* (Aldershot: Ashgate, 2008).
U. Vaughan Williams, *R.V.W.: A Biography of Ralph Vaughan Williams* (London: Oxford University Press, 1964).

PETER HORTON

Venues and functions The establishment of venues for musical performance has tended to follow the development of particular genres. The earliest operas were entertainments given in noble houses or at court, but as the repertory grew, the first opera house for the paying public opened for business in 1637: the Teatro San Cassiano in Venice (demolished in 1812). Over the next two centuries, opera houses were built in most of Europe's cultural centres (Vienna in 1653, Paris in 1671), though the perils of operatic production meant that many of them were also destroyed in fires. The first theatre on the site of Covent Garden in London opened in 1732, but following fires in 1808 and 1856, the present Royal Opera House dates from 1858. The Teatro San Carlo in Naples opened in 1737. It burned down in 1816 but reopened the following year. La Scala, Milan, opened in 1778. In the USA, one of the earliest centres of opera was New Orleans, with regular performances as early as 1796. After fleeing from bankruptcy in Europe to New York, Lorenzo da Ponte campaigned for an opera house in the city, and in 1833 the Italian Opera House became one of the first purpose-built opera theatres in America.

Concerts of instrumental and vocal music were customarily given in the homes of aristocrats, and occasionally in court theatres, until the end of the eighteenth century. A few early concerts in London took place in churches. John Evelyn's diary for 21 December 1662 describes a service at the Chapel Royal after which 'was introduced a concert of twenty-four violins betweene [sic] every pause ... better suiting a tavern or playhouse than a church'. The earliest 'music-houses' – taverns with a performance space – included Thomas Smith's *Blew Bell* at London Wall (1658) and Robert Hubert's *The Mitre* near St Paul's Cathedral, which was destroyed in the Great Fire of 1666. In 1672 John Banister the elder – previously one of the King's Violins – announced Monday afternoon concerts at his 'Musick-School' in Whitefriars, events that were among the first public concerts in London. Banister was soon followed by the coal merchant Thomas Britton, who put on a series of concerts above his shop in Clerkenwell from 1678 to 1714. The earliest concert hall in London was probably the 'Music Meeting' located in York Buildings, Villiers Street (near the present-day Charing Cross station), built in about 1675. It was described as 'a great room ... with proper decorations'. It was used for more than half a century: the last known concert there was Handel's *Esther*, given on the composer's birthday in 1732.

'Change of use' is not an exclusively modern phenomenon. One of London's most famous musical series of the eighteenth century began in a 'Great Room' that had originally been a Huguenot chapel. The concerts put on by JOHANN CHRISTIAN BACH and CARL FRIEDRICH ABEL were inaugurated there in February 1764, and the first season featured the London debut of 'Master Mozart of seven years of age'.

In Leipzig, the Zimmermann Coffee House (built in about 1715) was the venue from 1720 for performances by the Collegium Musicum, led by TELEMANN and J. S. BACH. The city's first concert hall, the original Gewandhaus, was built in 1781. Public concerts were given in Hamburg and Frankfurt am Main from the early 1700s onwards. It was not until towards the end of the century that regular public concerts took place in Vienna. As elsewhere, the custom had been for concerts to be given in Lent (when theatres were closed), either in the Burgtheater or in the homes of aristocrats. The impresario Philipp Jakob Martin (originally from Regensburg) established a series of Sunday concerts in the Augarten (a park opened by Josef II in 1775) at which MOZART performed in May 1782.

The era of the great concert halls went in tandem with the establishment of permanent symphony orchestras. An early example was the Argyll Rooms in London, which housed the Philharmonic Society from 1813 until 1830, when it was destroyed in a fire. Concerts were given by, for example, MENDELSSOHN, Liszt and SPOHR, and the first London performance of BEETHOVEN's Ninth Symphony took place there in 1825. The Vienna Philharmonic was established in 1842 and its home in the Musikverein was opened in 1870. In Amsterdam the opening of the Concertgebouw in April 1888 was followed by the inaugural concert of the Concertgebouw Orchestra in November that year. Carnegie Hall in New York opened with a five-day festival in 1891 at which Tchaikovsky appeared as a guest conductor. In Paris, the Cirque d'Hiver (originally the Cirque Napoléon) opened in 1852 and became the home of the Concerts Pasdeloup in 1861. It was an early example of a multi-purpose *salle polyvalente*: alongside concerts, circus performances, wrestling and equestrian events were all part of the hall's programme during the nineteenth century. The Royal Albert Hall in London opened in 1871 and as well as concerts (among those appearing in its early seasons were SAINT-SAËNS and WAGNER), the hall was also used for exhibitions, party political conferences and sporting events including London's first indoor marathon in 1909 (524 laps of the auditorium), and the Chelsea Arts Club Balls. From its opening in 1893 until it was bombed in 1941, London's main concert hall was the Queen's Hall in Langham Place, which had better acoustics (George Bernard Shaw described it as 'a happy success acoustically').

Symphony Hall Boston opened in 1900 and boasted 'the first auditorium in the world to be built in known conformity with acoustical laws' (commemorative plaque). Though it was also clearly modelled on European halls such as the second Leipzig Gewandhaus (1884, bombed 1944), and the Concertgebouw, the architects of Symphony Hall employed the Harvard physicist Wallace Clement Sabine (1868–1919) as an acoustical consultant. Sabine is credited with creating the science of architectural acoustics, and his lasting memorial in Boston is widely recognised as one of the world's best-sounding concert halls. Half a century later, the science of acoustics was much less successfully applied to London's Royal Festival Hall (1951) and Philharmonic Hall at New York's Lincoln Center (1962). Both have been criticised for the dryness of the sound despite the involvement of acousticians. Some recent halls have been far more successful in terms of acoustics, including Symphony Hall in Birmingham (UK), opened in 1991, and the Philharmonic de Paris, opened in 2015.

Churches and cathedrals have been popular concert venues since at least the nineteenth century. The development of festivals such as the Three Choirs Festival (which dates back to c1715) meant that not only major choral works were performed in the three cathedrals of Gloucester, Hereford and Worcester, but so were the premieres of pieces such as ELGAR's *Froissart* (1890) and VAUGHAN WILLIAMS's *Fantasia on a Theme by Thomas Tallis* (1910). BRITTEN used local parish churches for many events in the Aldeburgh Festival from 1948 onwards. *Noye's Fludde* was first performed in Orford Parish Church in 1958. This was followed by the three Parables, subtitled 'for church performance', which were also given in Orford: *Curlew River* (1964), *The Burning Fiery Furnace* (1966) and *The Prodigal Son* (1968). These are interesting examples of works for which the composer specified a particular kind of venue.

Venues specifically designed for chamber music and recitals have often been built alongside larger halls (such as the Brahms-Saal in Vienna's Musikverein), while a few have been purpose built. The Bechstein Hall in London's Wigmore Street is an outstanding example. Opened in 1901 (with an inaugural concert in which BUSONI and Ysaÿe were performers), it was renamed Wigmore Hall in 1917. It has always been considered to have some of the finest acoustics of any small hall in Europe, and has been a favourite among singers as well as instrumentalists. During the twentieth century, composers such as Ravel,

Fauré, Scriabin, Prokofiev, Poulenc, HINDEMITH and Britten all appeared there as performers.

FURTHER READING

R. Elkin, *The Old Concert Rooms of London* (London: Edward Arnold, 1955).
M. Forsyth, *Buildings for Music* (Cambridge University Press, 1986).

NIGEL SIMEONE

Vibrato (It., from Lat. *vibrare*: 'to shake') Most commonly a regular oscillation of PITCH and/or intensity, either more or less pronounced and more or less rapid.

Introduced by players of stringed and wind instruments and singers (as well as clavichordists), vibrato has been described through history by a wide range of terminology (including *flattement, flatté, balancement, balancé, ondulation, plainte, langueur, verre cassé, sons vibrés; tremolo, tremolo sforzato, ardire, trilletto, ondeggiamento;* Bebung, Schwebung, Tremulant, Zittern; sting and sweetening), depending on the effect or timbre desired and the instrument and technique employed. Some of these terms were used to describe contrasting techniques, a particular kind of ACCENTUATION, or even a style of EXPRESSION or (especially in opera) dramatic delivery; in fact, the term 'vibrato' was employed rarely with its present meaning of an expressive pitch fluctuation until well into the nineteenth century. 'Measured vibrato', a regular oscillation of intensity often described as TREMOLO executed in string playing by controlled pressure bow changes and in wind playing and singing by a measured breath vibrato, was occasionally employed from the seventeenth through to the early nineteenth centuries, most significantly in opera.

Vibrato, discussed as early as the sixteenth century by theorists such as GANASSI and AGRICOLA, has passed in and out of fashion. Broadly, its introduction was regarded as one of the solo performer's expressive responsibilities up to the early twentieth century. Other than in solo contexts, orchestral string players generally refrained from using vibrato, as GEMINIANI (1751), LEOPOLD MOZART (1756), BREMNER (1777), W. A. MOZART (1778), C. F. Cramer (1783), GALEAZZI (1791–6) and SPOHR (1832) indicate. For guidance, some composers and theorists notated where the effect should be implemented, using various methods and causing some ambiguity and misinterpretation; for example, the 'wavy line' (⌇⌇⌇⌇) had several possible realisations, ranging from trills to octave displacements and VIBRATO. WALTHER indicates vibrato by 'm' (*Hortulus Chelicus*, 1688), and MARAIS includes signs for two vibrato types (*Pièces de viole*, Bk. 2, 1701). In LUTE playing, vibrato may be indicated by a cross (×), a red dot placed over the relevant note(s) (Capirola, *c*1517), a symbol similar to a mordent sign, and by < on the higher strings. With other instruments the effect may also be notated by a series of dots under a slur. Spohr uses the wavy line (⌇⌇⌇⌇) (e.g. in his String Quartets Opp. 146 and 152), and the common nineteenth-century use of the *messa di voce* sign (<>) often implied the introduction of vibrato during the swell (*see*, for example, the violin treatises of BAILLOT, CAMPAGNOLI, and JOACHIM and Moser). Composers such as WAGNER and ELGAR occasionally spell out vibrato incidence in their scores, as do Donizetti, Halévy, Meyerbeer and others. These annotations would clearly be redundant if anything like a continuous vibrato were envisaged.

Broadly, selective, ornamental use of vibrato (on long notes, or for purposes of accentuation) was the norm in instrumental playing and (to a certain extent) singing until the early twentieth century, when most performers began to apply the effect continuously as a fundamental element of tonal character and sonority. With some instruments, especially strings, the normal cultivation of a continuous vibrato resulted in an increased vibrato vocabulary promoted by a perceived need for contrast.

FURTHER READING

G. Moens-Haenen, *Das Vibrato in der Musik des Barock: Ein Handbuch zur Aufführungspraxis für Vokalisten und Instrumentalisten* (Graz: Akademische Druck- und Verlagsanstalt, 1988).

C. E. Seashore (ed.), *The Vibrato* (Iowa City, IA: University of Iowa Press, 1932).

String Playing

On unfretted stringed instruments the most common vibrato type is produced by rocking the finger back and forth on the string, aided by the wrist and sometimes the forearm. The amount of wrist/arm movement differs according to musical context, individual preference or heritage. The equivalent effect on fretted stringed instruments such as VIOLS is generally a 'two-finger' variety (close shake or *battement*), for which one finger stops the string firmly and another performs a trilling movement close by, thus creating a narrow oscillation in the pitch of the stopped note (see Demachy, *Pièces de violle* (Paris, 1685); Rousseau, *Traité de la viole* (Paris, 1687)). Players occasionally had to use the little finger alone for vibrato purposes, known as *langueur* (Rousseau, 1687) or sting (Mace, *Musick's Monument* (London, 1676)). Both one- and two-finger types are similarly produced on most plucked instruments, but the lower strings of the lute require a different technique involving pulling the string back and forth (Piccinini, *Intavolatura di liuto et di chitarrone* (Bologna, 1623); Basset, in MERSENNE, 1636–7).

GANASSI (1542) recommends a trembling of the bow arm and a shaking of the fingers to portray sad music, but most seventeenth- and eighteenth-century string players used pitch vibrato sparingly and discreetly as an expressive ornament linked inextricably with the inflections of the BOW. Sometimes indicated but generally freely added by the performer, it was generally applied fairly discreetly and largely to enhance special moments in the music (particularly long sustained or final notes in a phrase), and at a speed and intensity appropriate to the music's dynamic, TEMPO and character. It also served to articulate melodic shape or to assist in the cultivation of *cantabile* playing. Baroque vibrato, executed with the fingers and wrist but without lower arm participation, was generally narrower, tighter and less intense than its modern counterpart. Muffat (Passau, 1698) warns that vibrato should never be allowed to prejudice tuning issues.

ROGER NORTH's liberal approach to vibrato usage is reflected in Geminiani's recommendation (1751) for soloists to introduce it 'as often as possible', even on 'short notes', specifically for tonal enhancement. However, although some players of the period evidently utilised something approximating a continuous vibrato – Leopold Mozart's condemnation (1756, 203) of those 'who tremble consistently on each note as if they had the palsy' is a case in point – Geminiani's recommendation was by no means general practice; indeed, BREMNER suppressed it in later eighteenth-century EDITIONS of Geminiani's treatise.

Most eighteenth-century string players probably employed a fairly slow and narrow left-hand vibrato, but TARTINI (*Trattato di musica* (Padua, 1754)) describes vibrato with slow, accelerating, or rapid oscillations according to the needs of the affect, and Leopold Mozart (1756) describes three vibrato speeds (slow, accelerating and rapid) for variety of effect (Example 47(a)), associating the slowest movement with a soft dynamic and the fastest with a loud dynamic and emphasising the importance of preserving a regular metrical stress in the vibrato (Example 47(b)).

In Example 47(a), Leopold Mozart comments that 'the larger strokes can represent quavers, the smaller semiquavers, and as many strokes as there be, so often must the hand be moved' (*Versuch*, trans. Knocker, 204). The hand movement is made 'with strong after-pressure of the finger . . . applied always on the first note of every crotchet' [quaver in rapid movement] (*see* Example 47(b)). He further explains:

> In the two examples [Example 47(b)], in No. 1 the strong part of the movement falls ever on the note marked by the numeral (2), for it is the first note of the whole or half-crotchet. In example No. 2, on the contrary, the stress falls, for the same reason, on the note marked with the numeral (1).
>
> (*VERSUCH*, TRANS. KNOCKER, 205)

Example 47: (a) Leopold Mozart: *Versuch* (1756), 239; (b) Leopold Mozart: *Versuch* (1756), 240, trans. Knocker, 204–5.

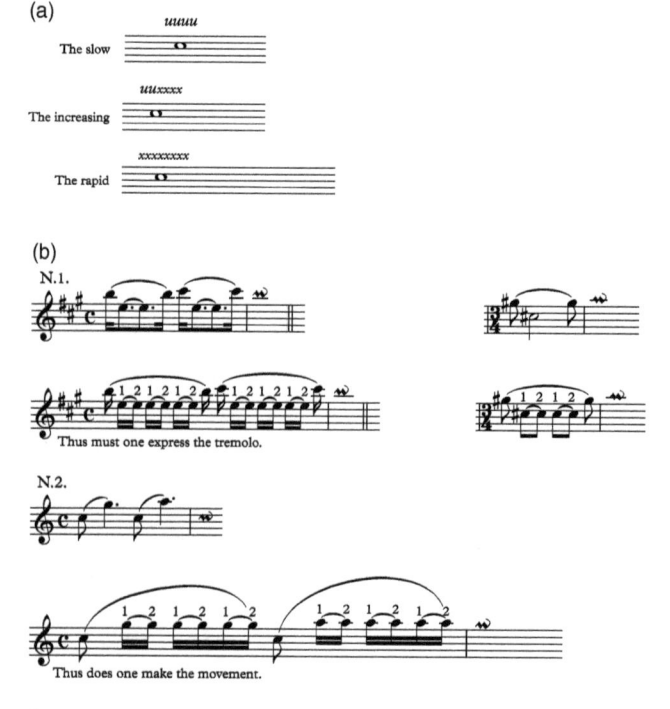

Example 48: Pierre Baillot: *L'art du violon* (1835), 138.

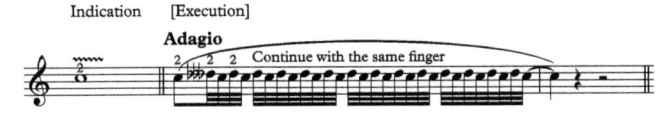

Example 49: Louis Spohr: *Violinschule* (1832), 176.

Other theorists (e.g. LÖHLEIN (Leipzig and Züllichau, 1774)) indicate an approximate vibrato speed by equating the number of dots used with the appropriate number of pulsations.

Many early nineteenth-century TREATISES, including those of WOLDEMAR (Paris, c1800), RODE, BAILLOT and KREUTZER (Paris, 1803), HABENECK (Paris, c1840) and ALARD (Paris, 1844), omit discussion of pitch vibrato altogether. Others including Spohr (1832), DOTZAUER (Mainz, [1825]), BAILLOT (Paris, 1835), Kummer (Leipzig, 1839) and BÉRIOT (Paris, 1858) warn against its overuse. In the interests of purity of intonation some writers (e.g. Baillot, 1835; ROMBERG (Berlin and Paris, 1840)) recommend that the beginning and end of a note with vibrato should be free of any pulsation (Example 48); however, these are exceptions rather than the rule.

Baillot expanded the vibrato concept to include three types of 'undulated sounds': left-hand vibrato; a wavering effect caused by variation of pressure on the bowstick; and a combination of the two.

The violinist's/violist's chin-braced grip and the development of accessories such as the chin-rest and shoulder pad (and the cellist's end pin) freed the left hand somewhat to cultivate a more fluid vibrato movement. Evidence (e.g. Baillot's METRONOME markings for vibrato as performed by Viotti) suggests that left-hand vibrato speeds generally became faster during the nineteenth century, although variety and fidelity to the musical context and desired effect were prime concerns. Vibrato speed was also associated with volume, a *crescendo* being accompanied by an accelerating pulsation and a *diminuendo* by a decelerating one.

Spohr (1832) distinguishes four types of violin vibrato – fast, for sharply accentuated notes; slow, for sustained notes in impassioned melodies; accelerating, for *crescendos*; decelerating for *decrescendos* (Example 49) – and demonstrates their selective implementation (Example 50). Like Baillot (1835), he emphasised that deviation from the note should be scarcely perceptible, but he does not share Baillot's view about the beginnings and ends of notes involving vibrato. Spohr's views held sway in Germany for well over seventy years; they are cited in Joachim and Moser's *Violinschule* (Berlin, 1905), which recommends extreme restraint in the use of vibrato, recognising that the 'steady tone' should be 'the ruling one' and that vibrato should be introduced 'only where the

Example 50: Louis Spohr: *Violinschule* (1832), 228.

expression seems to demand it' (II, 96a). Recommended FINGERINGS (by Spohr, DAVID and others), including examples incorporating natural HARMONICS and open strings within *cantabile* passages, endorse the attitude of restraint towards vibrato broadly practised by nineteenth-century string players. Nevertheless, there was an increasing trend towards more frequent and prominent employment of vibrato during the second half of the nineteenth century. While Vaslin (*L'art du violoncelle* (Paris, 1884)) disliked the monotony produced by the constant vibration of the left hand, writers such as Broadley (*Chats to Cello Students* (London, 1899)) and van der Straeten (*Technics of Violoncello Playing* (London, 1898)) were more sensitive to the need for vibrato in sustained passages, and at speeds adjusted to dynamic levels and sonority.

Brown (1999) claims that there was a division, increasingly apparent around the turn of the century, between those trained in the German and Franco-Belgian 'schools'. Joachim and his followers, who favoured a broader style of BOWING, with the elbow held low, represented the older views regarding tasteful, selective employment of the effect; Kreisler, trained in the newer aesthetic, anticipated by Massart, Wieniawski, Vieuxtemps and Ysaÿe, regarded vibrato as an essential element of tone.

EARLY RECORDINGS reveal a variety of vibrato widths and intensities, ranging from Kreisler's constant and fairly intense vibrato, to Paris-trained Sarasate's more discreet, slower vibrato applied on most but not all longer notes, and Joachim's strikingly varied approach. Joachim-pupil LEOPOLD AUER (New York, 1921) described continuous vibrato as inartistic and monotonous, claiming that it served only to conceal poor tone and inaccurate intonation. Nevertheless, some of his distinguished pupils, including Heifetz, Elman and Zimbalist, introduced continuous vibrato into their playing, considering it, like Siegfried Eberhardt (*Violin Vibrato* (New York, 1910)), more as a constituent of a pleasing tone than as an embellishment.

The general progression towards greater tonal power and intensity, the substitution of metal strings for gut, and consequent modifications in bowing technique (particularly the general adoption of a higher right elbow and adjustments to the bow hold) expedited the demand for a continuous left-hand string vibrato and the introduction of the forearm into the vibrato mechanism. Most theorists advocated a combination of finger, hand and arm movements for optimum vibrato production, but Rolland even included the shoulder.

Violist Lionel Tertis (*Beauty of Tone in String Playing* (London, 1938)) considered continuous vibrato vital for tonal beauty, urging players to 'keep [their left-hand] fingers alive'. In CELLO playing, Alexanian (Paris, 1922) articulates CASALS's espousal of a continuous, yet flexible and varied vibrato, and other cellists such as Suggia (*M&L*, 2/2 (April 1921), 130-4), Becker and Rynar (Vienna and Leipzig, 1929) align vibrato usage with the spiritual enlivenment of tone. Stutschewsky (Mainz, 1932-7) later emphasises the importance of varying vibrato speeds and intensities, and Eisenberg ([with Stanfield] London, 1957) considers that vibrato should produce as many shades and nuances as in a painting.

As the century progressed, the role of vibrato gradually underwent further change, becoming not only an integral part of each player's individual tone quality but also serving as an intensifying device, an ornament and an independent expressive technique occasionally separate from traditional musical phrasing. Customary usage of vibrato was often reversed in the twentieth century, with demand for an intense, fast vibrato in soft passages, a wide slow vibrato in loud passages, or even a requirement for *senza vibrato* to emphasise steady-state pitch precision for contrast or special effect. Other extreme applications of vibrato have also been prescribed, among them the ornamental vibrato-glissando, the extremely wide, pulsated vibrato specified by Scelsi in his *Triphon* (1957) for solo cello and the very slow vibrato over a quarter tone required in Penderecki's First String Quartet.

FURTHER READING

C. Brown, *Classical and Romantic Performing Practice 1750-1900* (Oxford University Press, 1999), 517-57.
G. Kennaway, *Playing the Cello, 1780-1930* (Farnham: Ashgate, 2014), 123-70.
R. Stowell, *Violin Technique and Performance Practice in the Late Eighteenth and Early Nineteenth Centuries* (Cambridge University Press, 1985).

Wind Playing
AGRICOLA (1529) writes that one should play with vibrato, advising that one should learn to pipe with trembling breath, for it greatly embellishes the melody. He is alone in mentioning the use of a diaphragmatic vibrato, as opposed to finger vibrato, in the sixteenth century. RECORDER players clearly used trills to make tremolo, at least from the time of Ganassi (1535), who gives FINGERINGS for *tremoli suavi* and *tremoli vivaci*, varying in intervals from microtones for the sweet ones to major thirds for the lively ones. PRAETORIUS (1619) discusses vibrato created by diaphragm action. Mersenne (1636) talks of 'certain tremolos which intoxicate the soul' and specifies that organ tremolo has a frequency of four vibrations per second, which he suggests as a model for wind players. HOTTETERRE, in his *Principes de la flûte* (1707), discusses a finger vibrato, called a *flattement*, which also appears in the methods of Corrette (Paris, c1735) and MAHAUT (Amsterdam and Paris, 1759). QUANTZ's *Versuch* (1752) discusses a *messa di voce*, a swelling and diminishing of volume within a single note, produced by a finger *flattement* on the nearest open hole. (Because

this procedure also lowers the pitch, Quantz advised flautists to compensate with the embouchure.) Delusse (Paris, c 1761) speaks of a breath vibrato, used in imitation of the ORGAN tremulant, as a measured expression of 'solemnity and terror'. And TROMLITZ (1791) discusses the *Bebung*, a finger vibrato, recommending it exclusively, advising against breath vibrato, which makes a wailing sound and militates against a firm and pure tone. Most vibrato on wind instruments before 1800 was thus normally produced by a trill movement over a hole some distance from the ones covered, producing rapid pitch movement. Yet MOZART (letter to his father 4 April 1787) described the oboist J. C. Fischer as having an entirely nasal tone and held notes like the tremulant of the ORGAN. This may have been produced by the breath or perhaps aligns with the description of a 'shaking' (*frémissement*) of the lips to make a vibrato described by Joseph François Garnier, the first OBOE professor at the PARIS CONSERVATOIRE. A rare early direction to employ vibrato on the CLARINET occurs in the Largo of Glinka's *Trio Pathétique* (1832). In 1830 James Alexander's *Improved Preceptor for the Flute* described a tremulous or panting motion of the breath, while acknowledging two types of fingered vibrato. By 1844 the virtuoso Anton Bernhard Fürstenau identified two forms of breath vibrato, of which he preferred rapid alternation of lung pressure over causing the jawbone to move in trembling fashion.

Notwithstanding Maximilian Schwendler's advocacy of vibrato originating in the throat in imitation of well-trained singers (*Flöte und Flötenspiel* (Leipzig 1910)), the consensus of most wind players since then has been for a vibrato produced by rapid pulsation of the diaphragm. Arthur Weisberg (*The Art of Wind Playing* (New York and London, 1975)) propagated this view, while others such as James Galway (*Flute* (London, 1982)) have insisted that the muscles of the throat are responsible for controlling the fluctuating air pressure. Bringing together elements of French and German national schools, the oboist Léon Goossens made a feature of adopting a rich vibrato, which was both controversial and highly influential at the time. He reported the considerable abuse and jibing he received from colleagues, but regarded a well-modulated vibrato as an expressive inflection of musical personality and sensibility. Goossens was a particular influence on Reginald Kell, who greatly advanced the cause of clarinet vibrato outside jazz, though clarinettists in Germany have resolutely resisted it, as have many players in the USA and Great Britain. None the less, evidence of persistent vibrato in clarinet playing extends back at least as far as BRAHMS's inspiration Richard Mühlfeld (1856–1907). During the early years of the twentieth century, vibrato became increasingly pronounced in JAZZ and played a distinctive role in the make-up of each individual player's tone-quality. On jazz saxophone, jaw vibrato is the norm, while other instrumental effects include cultivation of slide vibrato on the trombone. HORN vibrato has long characterised the orchestral sound-world of Russia and Eastern Europe, for example the Czech Philharmonic.

FURTHER READING

D. Manning, 'Woodwind vibrato from the eighteenth century to the present', *PPR*, 8 (1995), 67–72.

Singing
Many contend that vibrato is omnipresent in SINGING, not least because the physiological process of producing vocal sound requires the vocal chords to vibrate. Supplementary vibrato, often referred to as 'tremolo' (signifying either a pitch oscillation stemming from the diaphragm or a rhythmic pulsation originating in the throat), has been documented in Western music since the Middle Ages. Towards the end of the thirteenth century, for example, JEROME OF MORAVIA described various vibrato types for use as appropriate on specified long notes in Gregorian chant, slow and accelerating, through an upper semitone or whole tone.

Vibrato became fashionable as a mannerist ornament during the sixteenth and seventeenth centuries, some writers (including Agricola (Wittenberg, 1529); Ganassi (Venice, 1542); ZACCONI (Venice, 1592); Friderici (Rostock, 1618); PRAETORIUS (Wolfenbüttel, 1619); and Herbst (Nuremberg, 1642)), accepting it as a natural component of singing, and particularly as the basis of trilling ornaments. Zacconi suggests the ornamental use of a 'slight', unforced, yet rapid vibrato (probably meaning the throat variety). Quitschreiber (Jena, 1598) may intend an effect closer to a narrow continuous vibrato when he claims that singers perform best with a trembling voice (*tremula voce*); and in his training manual for choirboys, *Die Musica Figuralis* (Rostock, 1624/1649), Daniel Friderici encourages the cultivation of a gentle 'shaking, wavering or trembling in the throat or neck' (ed. E. Langelütje (Berlin: Gaertner, 1901), 17), ensuring that the voice is free and unforced.

Any kind of more or less continuous vibrato was rejected first by practitioners of solo singing and the new style in Italy, and later gradually elsewhere so that vibrato became used sparingly as an expressive ornament, in association with the prevalent AFFEKT. Singing methods generally distinguish between the small 'natural' vibrato of the well-placed voice and the audible ornamental vibrato, used sparingly for emphasis on long notes and in other appropriate musical contexts. However, some authors (e.g. BERNHARD, c1650; TOSI, 1723) objected to its use; some describe vibrato of less than a semitone as an ornament similar to a trill; and others recommend continuous use of 'tremolo' (which may signify rhythmic pulsation rather than pitch undulation).

As singers began pulling the chest voice up into the head register in the Classical era, pitch vibrato was a more natural outcome, especially for women's voices. Bérard (Paris, 1755), for example, favoured a narrow vibrato, but HILLER (Leipzig, 1774 and 1780) treats vibrato as an ornament to be employed with good taste. Mozart described (12 June 1778) Joseph Meissner's 'bad habit of intentionally vibrating his voice' as 'contrary to nature', since 'the voice has its own natural vibrations'. Most early nineteenth-century singing tutors omit mention of vibrato as an element of normal tone production (e.g. GARCÍA I (London, [c1820])). However, some mid-nineteenth-century writers (e.g. GARCÍA II (Paris, 1840, 1847)) permit tasteful use of tremolo or vibrato as an occasional effect or expressive ornament, describing how it can portray poignant sentiments (anguish, tears), and it appears that such vibrato usage gradually increased as the century progressed; indeed, it was specifically indicated with symbols by CINTI-DAMOREAU (*Nouvelle méthode de chant* (Paris, 1855)) and spelt out ('vibrée', 'vibrato' or 'canto vibrato') in some scores by Donizetti,

Halévy, Meyerbeer and others. By mid-century, some Italians appear to have performed with an audible vibrato on nearly every sustained note; and it seems that many late nineteenth-century opera singers developed voices with vibrato of a width that would never previously have been tolerated.

NATIONAL IDIOMS of vibrato production are detectable with many early twentieth-century singers. Crutchfield distinguishes between the narrow, regular and almost imperceptible vibrato of English, Scandinavian and German singers at the turn of the century, and the 'quick, intense, flickering' vibrato of the Spanish and Italians (in Brown and Sadie (eds.), 453). He stresses that no recorded singer born before 1870 developed anything like the slow, wide vibrato of modern times. Some (e.g. Nellie Melba or Emma Calvé) may give the impression of using almost no vibrato at all, though analysis (e.g. Seashore (University of Iowa, 1932); Sundberg, 1994) confirms that a fairly fast, narrow, yet continuous vibrato in the modern sense is always present, except on occasional short notes. As attitudes to vibrato changed from about the 1920s, writers such as J. H. Allen (*The Technique of Modern Singing* (London, 1935), 64) described vibrato as being 'as essential to the tone colour of the voice as to the violinist'. However, continuous vibrato in singing does not seem to have been accepted universally until at least the 1930s, some theorists doubting its expressive qualities and considering that it affected adversely tonal quality and accuracy of intonation. This may explain the dichotomy noted between Lilli Lehmann's instructions to avoid vibrato in her *How to Sing* (Berlin, 1902; trans. R. Aldrich (New York, 1914)) and the wide vibrato that she uses in her recordings. Period performers excepted, sung vibrato nowadays tends to be fairly wide, partly due to the increased volume required for performers to be heard in large concert halls and opera houses.

FURTHER READING

H. M. Brown and S. Sadie (eds.), *Performance Practice: Music after 1600* (London: Macmillan, 1989).
P. Reidemeister, 'Zur Vokalpraxis', *Historische Aufführungspraxis: eine Einführung* (Darmstadt: Wissenschaftliche Buchgesellschaft, 1988), 91ff.
J. Sundberg, 'Acoustic and psychoacoustic aspects of vocal vibrato', *STL-Quarterly Progress and Status Report*, 35/2–3 (1994), 45–68.

ROBIN STOWELL AND COLIN LAWSON

Viéville, Jean Laurent le Cerf de la (b. Rouen, 1674; d. Rouen, 10 November 1707) French writer of musical polemic.

Viéville was trained in philosophy and law, and succeeded his father as keeper of the provincial parliament. His *Comparaison de la musique italienne et de la musique françoise* was published as a reaction to RAGUENET's promotion of Italian opera and musical style, amongst controversy about the growing popularity of Italian sonatas and cantatas in Paris. The first part of Viéville's *Comparaison* (1704) was a refutation of Raguenet's argument; a later part contained ideas on good TASTE in music, the life of LULLY and the history of opera (Brussels, 1705). Raguenet defended his views in *Défense du parallèle des italiens et des françois en ce qui regarde la musique et les opéra (sic)* (Paris, 1705). Viéville uses cuisine as an analogy to suggest that the piquant variety in Italian music is overdone.

FURTHER READING

G. Cowart, *The Origins of Modern Musical Criticism: French and Italian Music 1600–1750* (Ann Arbor, MI: UMI Research Press, 1981).
C. B. Schmidt (ed.), *Jean Laurent Le Cerf de la Viéville: Comparaison de la musique italienne et de la musique françoise: Index* (Geneva: Minkoff, 1993).

SIMON BAINES

Vihuela A plucked chordophone.

There is much to suggest that the vihuela, in its earliest form, was morphologically interchangeable with other waisted instruments which could be plucked, strummed or bowed, including the proto-VIOL and the early GUITAR. Such instruments with a curved bridge could be used for polyphonic music, as could those that were plucked where the bridge could be flat. The repertoire of both comprised narrative songs, popular songs and simple DANCE music, while bowed examples with round bridges, and those associated with plucking, might also be used to perform elaborate composed polyphony. It was especially in Italy during the fifteenth century that there was a move away from Medieval traditions of counterpoint towards block-chord textures, which accommodated themselves so well to bowed examples with flat bridges and to strumming.

The vihuela in Spain was tuned like a LUTE, and in every respect was the equivalent of the lute north of the Pyrenees. It was associated with a delicate plucked technique, with very little or no strumming, save when this was required for very full chords. It was used to produce intabulations of music by great masters of the period of Spanish and Franco-Flemish counterpoint, in a series of vihuela books such as Luis de Narváez's *Los seys libros del delphín* (Valladolid, 1538), Alonso Mudarra's *Tres libros de música* (Seville, 1546) and Juan Bermudo's *Declaración de instrumentos musicales* (Osuna, 1555). The serious vihuelist should obtain FACSIMILE editions of the original tutors and writings, and explore the techniques composers used for their own compositions.

The guitar and the vihuela had a complex relationship: both had figure-of-eight-shaped bodies, but if an instrument seemed relatively large and was used to play elaborate plucked music on five courses or more, it was liable to be called a 'vihuela', but if it was relatively small (in comparison with what one would term a 'vihuela') had fewer courses and was associated with music that was largely or entirely strummed, it was called a *guitarra*.

The surviving repertoire for the vihuela is not large and can be extremely demanding, for (unlike the *guitarra*) it was regarded as a serious instrument. Milán gives indications of regular tempi, yet Narváez expected the player to vary the speed of each variation. Extemporisation is an important component of vihuela playing. Narváez, for example, was known to be an accomplished improviser and therefore this should be an important skill to develop, recognising the ability and TASTE of the individual player.

Many aspects of vihuela performance remain ambiguous: Should one double the melodic line when accompanying singers? Was unison tuning for the bass strings universally employed? Although Luis Milán (*El maestro* (Valencia, 1536)) discusses where to use the *dedillo* technique (the alternation of up and down strokes with the index finger), there is much debate as to how this should be executed.

FURTHER READING

L. Gássar, *Luis Milán on Sixteenth-Century Performance Practice* (Bloomington: Indiana University Press, 1996).
J. Griffiths, 'The vihuela: performance practice, style, and context', in V. Coelho (ed.), *Performance on Lute, Guitar, and Vihuela: Historical Practice and Modern Interpretation* (Cambridge University Press, 1997), 158–79.

JAMES WESTBROOK

Viol (viola da gamba, gamba) (Fr. *viole de gambe*; Ger. *Gambe*; It. *viola da gamba*) A family of bowed, fretted stringed instruments, held downwards between the knees.

Evolution and Development

The early Valencian viol or *vihuela de arco*, which combined the characteristics of the plucked VIHUELA with the downwards playing position of the Moorish *rabāb*, first appears in paintings in the Aragonese province of Valencia around 1475. By 1500 angelic CONSORTS playing the viol are frequently portrayed by Valencian, Majorcan and Sardinian artists. This early tenor-sized, fretted instrument already had a characteristic viol form, waisted with marked corners; but it lacked an arched bridge. The viol soon arrived in Italy and by 1495 Isabella d'Este had a consort of three viols at Mantua. Raphael's *Allegory of St Cecilia* (?1516) includes a tenor viol with a carved lion's head and most of the characteristics of a seventeenth-century viol: six pegs, a rounded finger board with frets, an arched bridge, deep ribs meeting flush with the table and back, sloping shoulders and a flat back bending in towards the neck.

Lanfranco's *Scintille di Musica* (Brescia, 1533) is the first published source of Italian viol tunings. He uses the standard tuning of two fourths, followed by a third and then two more fourths. He tunes his tenor viol like a LUTE: A, d, g, b, e', a'' and pitches the treble a fourth higher: d, g, c', e', a', d'' and the bass a fifth below the tenor: D, G, c, e, a, d'. Alternatively he says the bass may be tuned a fourth below the tenor: E, A, d, f♯, b, e', thus with the treble a seventh above the bass. GANASSI (1542, 1543) gives four rules of tuning, the first of which is the standard d–g–d used today. By the turn of the century two methods of tuning a consort were in use, one a fifth lower than the other; the higher d–g–d' tuning was to prevail. The earliest printed collections of viol consort music are vocal transcriptions by GERLE (Nuremberg, 1532, 1546) whilst Ganassi composed the earliest printed solo compositions. Improvising divisions was an essential skill for viol players until at least the mid-seventeenth century. ORTIZ (1553) devotes his TREATISE to the topic, covering both IMPROVISATION in consort playing and for solo viol with keyboard accompaniment; he gives examples of how to embellish a madrigal or chanson. This laid the ground for the important virtuosic viola bastarda school favoured in Italy between 1580 and 1630. Here a bass violist condensed a polyphonic composition to a single line, leaping between the voices at their original PITCH and adding highly elaborate diminutions. The young MONTEVERDI was a viola bastarda player, a style he transferred to the VIOLIN in *Orfeo* (1607) and the *Vespers* (1610).

The viol crossed the Alps in the early 1600s and the profusion of German pictures of the viol from about 1510 pays homage to the instrument's instant popularity. By 1529 François I had a consort of four viols, which performed at the conference of Cambrai, and in ?1546 Gervaise's *Premier Livre de Violle* (now lost) was published. JAMBE DE FER (Lyon, 1556) writes that the French viols had five strings tuned throughout in fourths. In 1517 Matthew de Weldre appears in the English court accounts as a viol player and by 1540 with the arrival of Henry VIII's 'newe vialles' (from Italy) the viol's position was firmly established. Throughout Europe during the sixteenth century consorts of viols played textless contrapuntal music and dances; they were also regular performers in large state spectacles.

Very little is known about sixteenth-century English viols, but with the instruments of Rose the younger (d. 1611) the viol found its classic outline. By the time of Jaye (?1610), the viol had also adopted a soundpost, from the violin family. Playing consort music by Coprario, Ferrabosco, Gibbons, Jenkins, Lawes and Locke was greatly in vogue in Britain during the seventeenth century until the Restoration. Inspired by lute music and the Italian bastarda style, the bass viol found its solo voice in England playing 'lyra-way'. PLAYFORD (London, 1667) defines the lyra viol as the smallest of the three kinds of bass – lyra viol, division viol and consort bass. Lyra viol music was written in TABLATURE and nearly sixty different tunings were used in England during the seventeenth century. Sympathetic strings were used on some lyra viols. SIMPSON (London, 1659) gives precise details about the sound of a division viol, its shape, size and set up, before giving extensive information on how to improvise divisions. Until the 1650s most viol strings were made of gut. Sometimes a high-twist was used; for bass notes this gave the appearance of rope. In 1664, Playford advertises silver-covered gut or silver strings. Charles II's taste for the violin and French DANCE music led to the demise of the consort, but the bass viol was valued both as a CONTINUO instrument and in solo music and trios introduced by Continental émigrés. The solo bass viol saw a short-lived revival in the 1760s and 1770s, when ABEL made London his home and inspired the cultured élite to take up the viol.

Monteverdi employs three *bassi da gamba* in *Orfeo* (1607) and he underpins the texture with a *contrabasso da gamba* in *Il Combattimento* (1624). The bass viol is specified in two Venetian operas in the 1670s, and ten patterns by Stradivari (1701) survive for a 'Viola da Gamba in French form'. In Rome, Handel wrote virtuoso bass viol parts in *Tra le fiamme* (1707) and *La Resurrezione* (1708).

Maudit is credited with adding the sixth string to the French viol, and around 1589 he brought the viol consort into fashion with Parisian society. MERSENNE (1636) has a clear illustration of a classical six-string bass viol. TRICHET (?1640; ed. F. Lesure (Neuilly sur Seine, 1955–7) 18) recommends the viol as 'highly appropriate for consorts'. The celebrated French virtuoso bass viol school can be traced from MAUGARS through Hotman to Sainte-Colombe, who is attributed with adding the seventh low A' string to the bass viol and introducing silver-covered gut for the lowest three strings – A', D, G. The most famous makers were Colichon, Bertrand and Barbet. Sainte-Colombe's pupil MARAIS published five books of carefully bowed and fingered works for bass viol and continuo, which represent the zenith of the French school. Antoine and Jean-Baptiste Forqueray emulated the virtuosity of the Italian violinists (who arrived in Paris after the death of LULLY), marrying rich French harmony with the Italian sonata style. Jean-Baptiste Forqueray (Paris, 1747) bemoans the viol as 'a forgotten species' (*Avertissement*). He recommends (Paris, ?1767) using a gut half-covered (*demi-filée*) with silver C string. In France, unlike the rest of Europe, the treble viol (*dessus de viole*) remained popular long after the disappearance of the consort. The popularity of the Italian sonata led to the development of the *pardessus de viole* (tuned g, c′, e′, a′, d″, g″) so that women were given the opportunity to play VIOLIN sonatas on a viol which reached d‴ in first position. By the 1760s a four-stringed *pardessus* had been developed tuned like a violin; Brijon (Paris, 1766) remarks that many Parisians play it.

Around 1600 a number of English viol players took up employment in Germany, Austria and the Low Countries and had a major effect on the development of Continental viol playing. Consort music was published by both English and German composers. The viol, symbolising death and resurrection, is frequently found in the scoring of Lutheran church music particularly around Holy Week. Schütz uses a consort of bass viols in his *Historia* (1623) and the instrument appears in Passions from the 1640s until the works of J. S. BACH and C. P. E. BACH. Viols also played a prominent role in the Roman Catholic Viennese Passiontide genre, the *sepulcro*. The German-Netherlandish virtuoso bass viol school led by Kühnel and Schenck was influenced by the brilliance of the Italian-inspired violin school. Schenck's cultivation of virtuosity – multiple stopping, polyphonic writing and high positions up to b″ – is a parallel to the dazzling technique demanded by WALTHER. Gottfried Finger made use of SCORDATURA. The viol featured strongly in chamber music such as trios for violin, bass viol and continuo, notably by Buxtehude (?1694, 1696); TELEMANN wrote over sixty works which include the viol. Germany's most celebrated viol maker, Tielke, developed an Anglo-German model and later carved solid, gently arched backs. His instruments are particularly noted for their exceptional decoration. The viol saw its final flowering at the Berlin court, where there was a strong tradition of virtuoso viol playing led by the court viol player, L. C. Hesse, with his pupil, crown-prince Friedrich Wilhelm; at least eight concertos were written by J. G. Graun, and others survive by Telemann and TARTINI.

A thin thread of interest in the viol was maintained throughout the nineteenth century both on the Continent and in England. FÉTIS included it in his *Concerts historiques in* the 1832–3 season and by the last quarter of the nineteenth century the cellists de Wit, Delsart and TOLBECQUE played the viol professionally; Tolbecque, a fine *luthier*, made viols. In 1890, DOLMETSCH formed a viol consort playing 'original instruments', and went on to make viols. Today viols are played all round the world; a wide range of REPLICAS is made, based on models from the early Renaissance to the high Baroque.

Pedagogical Treatises
Ganassi's tutor (Venice, 1542, 1543) is the first dedicated to the viol and its technique, but Ortiz (Rome, 1553) examines diminutions in remarkable detail and DALLA CASA (Venice, 1584) and FRANCESCO ROGNONI (Milan, 1620) are important studies on bastarda playing. Jambe de Fer (Lyon, 1556) provides an enlightening French perspective.

In England, Thomas Robinson (*The School of Musicke* (London, 1603)) gives brief instruction on playing the viol. Playford (*An Introduction to the Skill of Musick* (London, 1654), addresses consort players and the final 1730 edition retains a section on the viol. Playford (*Musicks Recreation* (London, 1652)) examines playing the viol lyra-style. Simpson's *The Division-Violist* (London, 1659) is remarkably comprehensive. The third section of MACE (London, 1676) has useful material. Hely (*The Compleat Violist* (London, 1699)) gives concise guidance on viol playing.

French TREATISES provide a mine of information. De Machy (Paris, 1685), Danoville (*L'art de toucher le dessus et le basse de violle* (Paris, 1687)) and especially ROUSSEAU (*Traité de la viole* (Paris, 1687)) give detailed information on holding the instrument, left-hand and right-hand technique. LOULIÉ (*Éléments, ou principes de musique* (Paris, ?1690)) describes a remarkable range of bow strokes. Roland Marais (Paris, ?1730) gives advice on continuo playing, and Le Blanc (Amsterdam, 1740) assesses the playing of Marais and Antoine Forqueray and compares it with new developments. Forqueray (?1767) is a fascinating source on mid-eighteenth-century viol playing. CORRETTE (Paris, 1748) and Brijon (Paris, 1766) provide treatises for the *pardessus de viole*.

With the viol's revival came modern treatises by players such as Grümmer (*Viola da Gamba-Schule* (Hamburg, 1928)) and WENZINGER (*Gambenübung*, 2 vols. (Kassel, 1935, 1938)), and more recently by Biordi and Ghielmi (*Complete and Progressive Method for Viol* (Bologna, 1998)).

Technique

The viol is held between the legs, firmly enough so that it would not fall if the left hand is removed, and so that the bow is not impeded by the player's legs. (Ganassi, 1542; Simpson, 1659; Rousseau, 1687). Some early players experimented with a horizontal position. The viol BOW was held between the thumb, index and middle fingers (Ganassi). Simpson stresses that it should be held near the nut, with the middle finger (and the ring finger if necessary) pressed on the hair. Forqueray (?1767, 6) emphasises that the bow 'expresses all the passions' and Rousseau claims that it gives music its soul and all the characters. Ganassi teaches the use of separate bows with the strong (push) bow on the strong beat, tucking in if necessary. Ortiz (1553) says that some fast notes can be slurred, but the first beat should be articulated. Mersenne (1636) and Le Blanc (1740) define the French seventeenth-century sound as 'percussive' and 'resonant', like the GUITAR. A wide variety of bow strokes are described: dry, nourished, thrown, swelling, sustained (Marais, Loulié ?1690). By the mid-eighteenth century the stroke had become more legato (Le Blanc). Hume (1605) indicates pizzicato and *col legno*. Left-hand technique was strongly influenced by the lute, thus Simpson describes placing the thumb on the back of the neck opposite the forefinger; Marais and Rousseau recommend that the thumb should be opposite the middle finger. The system of 'holds' (*tenue*), keeping the fingers down to preserve the harmony, is integral to good technique (Ganassi, Ortiz, Simpson, Mace, Marais, Rousseau). Viol players used two forms of VIBRATO – with one or two fingers – as ORNAMENTATION (Marais). Generally players (including Marais) liked the bright sound of the top string; by the mid-eighteenth century Forqueray recommends utilising *le petit manche* – the practice of using the top three strings on the top fret and above by laying the first finger across the strings to function like the nut. He explains that this produces 'a beautiful sound', gives greater facility and is 'much less tiring'.

FURTHER READING

P. Holman, *Life after Death: The Viola da Gamba in Britain from Purcell to Dolmetsch* (Woodbridge: Boydell Press, 2010).
M. O'Loghlin, *Frederick the Great and his Musicians: The Viola da Gamba Music of the Berlin School* (Aldershot: Ashgate, 2008).
L. Robinson, 'Forqueray *Pieces de Viole* (1747): a rich source of mid-eighteenth-century French string technique', *Viola da Gamba Society of America*, 43 (2006), 5–31.
I. Woodfield, *The Early History of the Viol* (Cambridge University Press, 1984).

LUCY ROBINSON

Viola (Fr. *alto*; Ger. *Bratsche*) Alto-tenor member of the VIOLIN family.

The viola evolved concurrently with the violin in northern Italy, the earliest known representation being Gaudenzio Ferrari's fresco (1535) in the cupola of the church of Santa Maria delle Grazie, Saronno. It became a middle (alto-tenor) voice in sixteenth-century instrumental ensembles in pieces such as GIOVANNI GABRIELI's *Sonata pian e forte* (1597), in which one part confusingly headed 'violino' descends lower than the violin's range. Such confusions, along with the various early sixteenth-century interpretations of the term 'viola', have clouded the instrument's early history; interpretations range from a general denotation of any stringed instrument, plucked or bowed, to one specifying a particular family or instrument, notably *viola da braccio* ('viola of the arm', hence violin family) or *viola da gamba* ('viola of the leg', hence VIOL family). The term was also qualified to distinguish between registers within the instrument's range, thus explaining the occasional use of 'Alto Viola' and 'Tenor Viola' parts (e.g. in Handel's Concerto Grosso Op. 3 No. 1, Walsh edition, 1734), the common incorporation of three viola lines exploiting different registers in seventeenth-century French five-part ensembles, and the naming of the three parts for the twelve violas in Louis XIII's *Vingt-quatre Violons du Roi* as *haute-contre* (or *haute-contre taille*), *taille* and *quinte* (or *cinquiesme*) (MERSENNE, 1636–7). This differentiation also explains the availability of instruments of various sizes, body lengths ranging from *c*38 to 45 cm (the modern viola ranges from *c*41 to 44 cm). Some 'tenor violas' were so large that they were almost unplayable 'on the arm' – Antonio Stradivari's enormous 1690 'Medici' instrument (48.3 cm) contrasts strikingly with his smaller models (41.3 cm). Most of the larger models have since been 'cut down' for ease of playing under the chin in the modern position.

The Amati family was pre-eminent in viola making in sixteenth-century Italy, producing small and large models. Gasparo da Salò's instruments were also in demand for their sonorous tone, as well as those of de Micheli, Linarol, Mariani and Maggini. From *c*1600 viola production hit a barren patch owing to musical preferences for four- as opposed to five-part ensembles and the popularity of the emergent trio sonata. Violas of varying sizes continued to be produced throughout the seventeenth and early eighteenth centuries but the success of smaller models made in England, the Netherlands and elsewhere prompted Italian makers such as Guadagnini, Storioni and Bellosio to produce violas of 40.6 cm or less in body length. Violas underwent similar (but proportionate) modifications of the neck, fingerboard and internal fittings as the violin in the late eighteenth century, to increase string tension, tonal brilliance and left-hand facility.

Some compromise instruments between the violin and viola were introduced towards the end of the eighteenth century in order to alleviate the contemporaneous dearth of good violists. These included WOLDEMAR's *violon-alto* (c1788), which added a fifth c string to what was essentially a violin body, the *viola alta*, and Friedrich Hillmer's five-string *violalin*. Experiments continued in the following century to resolve the problems of the viola's optimum size and sonority (see Stowell, 177–9). Scientists such as Savart were adamant that the instrument's body was much too small for its intended tonal range. Subsequent investigations spawned various instruments with lengthened or enlarged bodies, including Vuillaume's viola with extremely wide bouts, Henri's lop-sided instrument (with its left side larger than the right), and designs by Dessauer, Sprenger and Ritter, whose *viola alta* (c48 cm in body length) captured WAGNER's interest. Lionel Tertis later proposed a design similar to a small CELLO or tenor violin, but his compromise 'Tertis model', developed in collaboration with Arthur Richardson in the 1930s, had an average body length of 42.5 cm.

Acoustical experiments by Carleen Hutchins and her associates in the 1960s determined that the ideal viola body length should be c53 cm. Her 'New Violin Family' of eight acoustically balanced instruments in graduated sizes and tunings includes an alto (body length 50.8 cm), tuned as a viola but normally held cello-fashion with an endpin, and a tenor violin of approximately half-size cello length. Erdesz's asymmetrical viola has afforded greater left-hand facility in the higher positions, as has Rivinus's ergonomic Pellegrina viola with expanded upper left and lower right bouts, tilted fingerboard and off-centre neck. Electric and MIDI violas have also been produced worldwide in various shapes and sizes.

Other related instruments include the viola d'amore, the *viola di fagotto* (with the tuning range of a cello but played on the arm) and the *viola pomposa*, a five-stringed instrument used c1725–70, tuned c–g–d′–a′–e″ (or possibly d–g–d′–d′–c″), and presumably played on the arm. The viola d'amore, employed mostly in the late seventeenth and the eighteenth centuries, normally had a flat viol-like back, wide ribs, sloping shoulders, 'flaming sword' soundholes and a carved head instead of a scroll. Eighteenth-century models normally had a fretted fingerboard, seven principal gut and seven resonating metal strings; Majer (*Museum musicum* (Schwäbisch Hall, 1732)) gives what became the standard tuning (A–d–a–d′–f♯′–a′–d″) but various *scordature* were also adopted. The instrument was later employed by, among others, Meyerbeer (*Les Huguenots*), Puccini (*Madama Butterfly*) and HINDEMITH (*Kleine Sonate*). The *violetta marina*, a larger instrument with seven principal and fourteen sympathetic strings, was the brainchild of Pietro Castrucci, for whom Handel composed obbligato parts in some of his operas.

Viola strings were originally of gut. However, by the early eighteenth century, gut (or silk) strings wound with silver (or copper) gained preference for their superior tonal potential for the viola's C and (later) G strings, allowing for an increase in mass without an increase in diameter or consequent loss of flexibility. During the course of the twentieth century, strings wound with metal over gut, synthetic or metal cores found favour across the instrument, assisting their capacity to 'speak', improving uniformity of tone and response, and offering greater reliability. Like violinists, most violists gradually adopted the chin-rest (see VIOLIN) and shoulder pad during the first half of the nineteenth century.

Several all-purpose TREATISES were published in Germany in the late seventeenth and early eighteenth centuries, but these offered little instruction regarding viola playing. QUANTZ (1752) bemoaned the musical establishment's neglect of violists and the earliest treatises devoted specifically to the instrument, by CORRETTE (*Méthodes...* (Paris, 1773)), Woldemar (*Méthode d'alto* (Paris, c1800)) and Cupis (*Méthode d'alto* (Paris, ?1803)), were soon superseded by the more substantial and sophisticated methods of Gebauer (*Méthode d'alto* (Paris, c1805)), Bruni (*Méthode pour l'alto-viola* (Paris, c1820)) and MARTINN (*Nouvelle méthode d'alto* (Paris, 1823)). GIORGETTI's *Metodo* (Milan, 1854) and Klingenfeld's *Viola-Schule* (Leipzig, 1897) addressed the dearth of specialist violists by encouraging talented violinists to make the transition to the viola. Tours and Sitt were among those who published treatises purposefully designed for beginner violists and Firket (*Méthode pratique*, 2 vols. (Brussels, 1873)) and Brähmig (*Praktische Bratschenschule* (Leipzig, c1885)) provided the most notable advanced nineteenth-century publications. The instrument's more prominent role in music making from the twentieth century onwards is reflected in the repertory and the methods of Dolejši (*Modern Viola Technique* (University of Chicago Press, 1939)) and Primrose (*Technique is Memory* (Oxford University Press, 1960)).

Viola left-hand techniques have developed in parallel with the violin, any differences being related to the viola's larger size. In their heyday large-bodied violas were probably played with the lower bouts resting against the player's chest; and throughout history the viola's greater weight and size have resulted in its being held with the scroll slightly lower than the violin norm. Developments in FINGERING were broadly similar to those for the violin, but viola VIBRATO tended to be wider and less intense. SCORDATURA was occasionally used to advantage. MOZART, for example, prescribed raising all the viola strings a semitone in his *Sinfonia Concertante* (K364), in order to gain greater facility (through 'fingering' in D major) and additional tonal brilliance and clarity. Concertante works by Carl Stamitz, Sperger, Amon, Vanhal, Druschetsky and Voigt similarly demand 'brighter' tunings (for right-hand technique, see BOWING).

Viola playing developed into a more specialist activity during the twentieth century, violists, like violinists, increasingly being required to master a wide range of specifically prescribed techniques in rapid succession.

FURTHER READING

M. W. Riley, *The History of the Viola*, 2 vols. (I, Ypsilanti, MI: Braun-Brumfield, 1980; II, Ann Arbor, MI: Braun-Brumfield, 1991).
R. Stowell, *The Early Violin and Viola: A Practical Guide* (Cambridge University Press, 2001).
L. Tertis, *My Viola and I* (London: Paul Elek, 1974).

ROBIN STOWELL

Violin (Fr. *violon*; Ger. *Violine, Geige*; It. *violino*; Sp. *violín*) Soprano member of a family of string instruments also including the VIOLA, CELLO and DOUBLE BASS.

The violin evolved in northern Italy, probably combining characteristics of the Medieval fiddle, usually with five strings or more (including at least one unstopped drone), and the small, pear-shaped two- or three-string rebec. Late fifteenth-century Italian frescoes suggest the existence of three-stringed quasi-violins well before Ferrari's examples (1535) in Saronno, which represent the earliest known illustration of the complete violin family. JAMBE DE FER (*Epitome musical* (Lyons, 1556)) gave the first description of the violin as a four-stringed instrument tuned g, d′, a′, e″.

Full-size violins were made initially in small and large models, body lengths varying from *c*33 cm to *c*36.9 cm. Not until the classical model of Antonio Stradivari (e.g. the 'Betts', 1704) did the current *c*35.5 cm body length become standard. Among the violin's relatives, though differing in size, shape, tuning and often function, were the KIT (dancing master's fiddle, *pochette, canino, Taschengeige*) and *violino piccolo*. The latter (*c*27 cm in body length) was commonly tuned c′–g′–d″–a″, but J. S. BACH used b♭–f′–c″–g″ (Cantatas Nos. 96 and 140; Brandenburg Concerto No. 1).

The decisive evolutionary step for the violin was the creation (probably *c*1505) of a CONSORT of three sizes (soprano, alto or tenor (tuned in unison), bass) modelled on the VIOL consort, thus differentiating it from the *vielle* and rebec. Holman (1993) has convincingly linked the spread of this 'consort principle' with that of polyphony into secular music. The depiction in Ferrarese wall paintings (*c*1506–10) of a three-string violin and a four-string viola-like instrument and entries in the court inventories suggest that a violin consort existed in Ferrara by 1511. The violin's penetrating tone and flexible intonation led to its increasing use in northern Europe in four- or five-part consorts (one or two violins, two to three violas and bass) for polyphonic DANCE music, outdoor entertainments and (occasionally) doubling vocal music. Several violin bands were formed by the end of the sixteenth century, including at the courts of England, France and the German-speaking areas of Europe. Although these bands did not normally displace the LUTES and viols in *MUSICA RESERVATA*, they provided music for court ballets, ceremonies, theatrical entertainments and concerts. Especially notable are the *Violons Ordinaires de la Chambre du Roy* (est. 1609) and its immediate successor, the *Vingt-quatre Violons du Roi* (a five-part string ensemble with three 'viola' lines) established (1626) by Louis XIII.

The advent of the *stile moderno* after *c*1600 and its consequent expressive, soloistic requirements resulted in the violin's increased social esteem and cultural credibility. The instrument was employed in mixed or 'broken' consorts (with winds, keyboards and hand-plucked instruments) first in Italy and later in English aristocratic households. It also became involved in Italian contrapuntal and church music, secular mixed ensembles, such as those accompanying *intermedi* at the Florentine court, and in the virtuoso sets of *passaggi* or variations on the soprano parts of vocal music by, for example, DALLA CASA (*Il vero modo di diminuir* (Venice, 1584)) and BASSANO (*Motetti, madrigali et canzone francese* (MS Chrysander, 1890) after 1st edn (Venice, 1591)).

MONTEVERDI (*L'Orfeo*, 1607; *Vespers*, 1610; *Il combattimento*, 1624) was particularly significant in developing a true violin idiom and exploiting the instrument for dramatic EXPRESSION. Italian composers such as Marini, Fontana, FARINA, Castello, Legrenzi, Vitali and Stradella and south German and Austrian composers such as Schmelzer (*Sonatae unarum fidium*, 1664), Biber ('Mystery' Sonatas, c1676; *Sonatae violino solo*, 1681), WALTHER (*Scherzi da violino solo*, 1676; *Hortulus chelicus*, 1688) and Westhoff further expanded the instrument's solo idiom in the seventeenth century, disseminating their developments widely. However, not until CORELLI's twelve Concerti Grossi, Op. 6, published posthumously in 1714, was the violin family finally established as the ORCHESTRA's mainstay and liberated from accompanying dance music or prefacing vocal music.

The viol remained in favour well into the seventeenth century in Britain and France, but the Renaissance violin consort proved a durable ensemble in England until Purcell's time. It reached orchestral proportions by 1612 – a total of twenty-five to thirty is reported in 1618. A small fourteen-piece string orchestra was formed at the English court in 1631, but the introduction of violins at the Chapel Royal was a significant forward step, as was Charles II's establishment (1661) of his 'Twenty Four Violins', based on the French model. Significantly, this group's repertory, composed by Locke, Banister and others, comprised four (mostly a string quartet arrangement with two violins) rather than five parts. LULLY influenced change at the Paris Court. Although his relationship with the *Vingt-quatre violons* was variable, he eventually headed the small group called *Petits violons* (sixteen players, later enlarged to twenty-one) and formed the first ORCHESTRA (known from 1702 as *Violons du cabinet*) renowned for its precision and discipline (*see* MUFFAT, *Florilegium Secundum* (Passau, 1698)).

The distinct German 'school' of violin playing, centred in Mannheim and developed by Johann Stamitz, his sons Carl and Anton, and Cannabich, Fränzl and others, had a powerful influence on musical life in the mid-eighteenth century; the MANNHEIM ORCHESTRA became celebrated for its disciplined ensemble and expressive vocabulary. Nevertheless, Italian musicians were pre-eminent well into the eighteenth century (latterly through Corelli, Albinoni, Vivaldi, GEMINIANI, Somis, Veracini, TARTINI, Locatelli, Pugnani and others); their influence ignited a groundswell of activity in England, where, following Geminiani, Giardini, Castrucci and Carbonelli made their mark, and especially in France, where Leclair, Guillemain, Gaviniès and others progressed the violin's idiom and repertory.

By the 1780s Paris was the violin capital of Europe, hosting significant makers (e.g. Lupot, Pique, Gand, Bernardel, Chanot, Lété and Vuillaume) and performers, most notably Pugnani's pupil Viotti, whose debut at the *Concert Spirituel* (1782) met with considerable acclaim. Viotti championed Stradivari's violins, facilitated Tourte's BOW developments, and influenced late eighteenth-century sound ideals with his powerful tone and singing legato. These ideals, together with rising PITCH standards and a desired increase in string playing length, resulted in most extant violins undergoing constructional modifications to address the additional tensions thus caused. Broadly, luthiers lengthened the neck (by 0.64–1.27 cm to 12.86–13.02 cm) and tilted it back at a

4–5° angle to the instrument's body, rendering redundant the wooden wedge between the neck and fingerboard formerly employed to align the fingerboard and strings. Consonant with the longer, narrower neck, the fingerboard was lengthened (by 5.08–6.35 cm) to c26.7 cm, thus facilitating high passagework, narrowed at the peg-box end, affording the player greater left-hand agility, and broadened somewhat towards the bridge. The consequent increased pressures on the instrument led to the neck being mortised (rather than glued and nailed) into the top-block for greater strength and the introduction of a longer, thicker bass-bar and a more substantial soundpost. These modifications, first introduced by French makers, resulted in the flat-model Stradivari flourishing as concert instruments at the expense of the highly arched, smaller-toned Stainers and Amatis.

The violin has since remained largely unaltered, despite further attempts at 'improving' its volume, tone, playability, recording potential or acoustical credibility. Makers have: used different materials (e.g. metals, glass, leather, plastics and ceramics); experimented with various designs (e.g. Savart's trapezoidal violin (1817) or Chanot's guitar-shaped model (1817)) for acoustical reasons; created new related instruments for specific purposes (Stroh's violin (c1900) for early gramophone recording, dance band or al fresco performance, Hutchins's 'concert violin' with a longer, revamped body and larger f-holes, or string octet); widened its range downwards (e.g. the *violectra*, exploited by John Adams (*The Dharma at Big Sur*), and in JAZZ circles, sounds an octave below the conventional violin); introduced electronic amplification, developing from the crude electromagnetic pickups or contact microphones of the 1920s to more sophisticated modern instruments, which allow their signal to be amplified, modified or altered through changes in frequency response, rapid changes in amplitude, harmonic alteration (of overtones), echo and reverberation effects, and distortion; and increased the instrument's stringing to five (tuned c–g–d'–a'–e''), six (F–c–g–d'–a'–e''), seven (B♭–F–c–g–d'–a'–e'') or more or sometimes adding sympathetic strings (e.g. the Norwegian Hardanger fiddle). Lakshminarayana Shankar designed and plays a ten-string violin with two necks. Significantly for historical performance, makers worldwide have been encouraged to restore fittings of appropriate violins to their original lightness or construct reproduction instruments to Baroque/Classical dimensions.

Although metal strings were preferred by some (e.g. PRAETORIUS, II, 2/ 1619) for their softer tone – silk strings were another option (Kircher, *Musurgia Universalis* 2 vols. (Rome: 1650)) – most early Baroque violins were strung with gut. Some violinists (especially in Italy and Germany) persevered with all-gut stringing, but others (notably in England from the 1660s) favoured the response from a gut G wound with silver wire; French sources (e.g. BROSSARD, *Fragments*, MS, c1712) mention D strings which are half covered (*demi-filée*), wound with a single open spiral of metal thread. Despite Welcker von Gontershausen's (*Neu eröffnetes Magazin musikalischer Tonwerkzeuge* (Frankfurt, 1855)) powerful support for all-gut stringing, the combination of plain gut E and A, high-twist gut D and a G with copper, silver-plated copper or silver round wire close-wound on a gut core was the norm throughout the nineteenth century.

The gut E string was gradually replaced in the twentieth century by a more durable and responsive steel variety (with metal fine-tuning adjuster). Only a few performers (e.g. Fritz Kreisler) persevered with a gut E string as late as 1950. Carl Flesch (*Die Kunst des Violinspiels*, 2 vols. (Berlin, 1923, 1928)) documents the use of an overspun A string, while the high-twist D was replaced by gut with aluminium winding. The development of more flexible woven core later led to some players adopting all-steel stringing, because of their longer wear, easier tuning with adjusters (usually on specially designed tailpieces), minimal stretching and precise moderation of thicknesses for true fifths. However, these strings' perceived tonal inferiority and the additional pressures they place on the instrument have encouraged a preference for metal-wound strings with a gut or nylon core.

MUTES of various types and weight have been employed through history. The three-pronged, wood, metal, or ivory clamp model began as the norm, some composers occasionally specifying the use of a particularly heavy variety (e.g. Vivaldi's requirement of lead mutes (*piombi*)) for special effect. Apart from the appearance of some two- or five-pronged varieties, it remained virtually unchallenged until the mid-nineteenth century, when Bellon, Vuillaume and others attempted (with little success) to introduce models which could be applied more quickly and conveniently in play. Made also from bakelite or rubber in the twentieth century, it has been supplemented by models which are stored between the bridge and tailpiece for convenient application.

SPOHR's invention, the chin-rest (c1820), ensured the instrument's stability and facilitated left-hand mobility, including the application of VIBRATO. Originally of ebony, it was positioned centrally over the tailpiece, not to the bass side as later became customary. It only gradually achieved general approbation; however, later made from ebony, rosewood or vulcanite (and available in various sizes and designs), it has become a standard accessory for all but Baroque/Classical historical performance.

BAILLOT's recommendation (*L'art du violon* (Paris, 1835)) of using a thick handkerchief or cushion to assist supporting the instrument comfortably also took time to catch on. Gradual acceptance (though not exclusively) of its benefits has led to the production of a plethora of different shoulder pads for attaching to the underside of the instrument. Their detractors point to their perceived adverse effect on tone-quality and their causing undesired body tensions.

JOHN LENTON's *The Gentleman's Diversion, or the Violin Explained* (London, 1693) is the first extant TREATISE devoted specifically to the violin. Earlier encyclopedic, multi-purpose works by, for example, Praetorius (*Syntagma Musicum* (Wolfenbüttel, 1618–20)), MERSENNE (*Harmonie universelle* (Paris, 1636–7)), ZANETTI (*Il scolaro...* (Milan, 1645)), Prinner (*Musicalischer Schlissl* (MS, 1677)), Speer (*Grund-richtiger, kurtz, leicht und nöthiger Unterricht der musicalischen Kunst* (Ulm, 1697)) and Falck (*Idea Boni Cantoris* (Nuremberg, 1688)) had begun to reflect the liberation of instruments from their subordination to the voice and the violin's improved social position by incorporating descriptions of contemporary instruments, sometimes with rudimentary technical information for amateurs. A steady stream of self-instructor books for amateurs continued well into the eighteenth century, whether instrumental compendia (e.g. Merck, 1695; MAJER, 1732; EISEL, 1738; Tessarini, 1741?) or tailored to specific instruments (e.g. *Nolens Volens* (1695)) or the modest French violin tutors by MONTÉCLAIR (*Méthode facile pour aprende* [sic] *à jouer du violon* (Paris, 1711–12)) and CORRETTE (*L'école d'Orphée* (Paris, 1738)). Much of their technical instruction was suspect and most publications comprised little more than a fingerboard guide and some simple pieces.

The first books to reflect more advanced practices appeared from the mid-eighteenth century. Geminiani disseminated the technique and style of his mentor, Corelli (but with some French seasoning!), through his compositions, teaching, performance and *The Art of Playing on the Violin* (London, 1751). Tartini's treatise on ornaments, first printed posthumously as *Traité des agrémens* (Paris, 1771), was certainly in circulation in manuscript by c1750, as LEOPOLD MOZART 'borrowed' from it for his comprehensive violin treatise (*Versuch* ... (Augsburg, 1756)). CAMPAGNOLI's violin method (*Nouvelle méthode de la mécanique du jeu de violon* (Leipzig, 1824), but possibly in preparation in the 1790s) reflects the influence of Nardini's instruction, and GALEAZZI's *Elementi teorico-pratici* (Rome, 1791–6) provides a detailed, methodical survey of violin playing technique and general solo and orchestral performing practices.

In Germany, in addition to Leopold Mozart's method, QUANTZ's flute treatise (Berlin, 1752) includes some invaluable instruction (mostly regarding bowing) for orchestral violinists (*Ripienisten*), who also form the target audience for the technically limited tutors of KÜRZINGER (1763), Petri (1767), LÖHLEIN (1774), REICHARDT (1776), HILLER (1792), Schweigl (1786 and 1795) and Fenkner (1803).

HERRANDO's violin treatise (*Arte y puntual explicación del modo de tocar el violin* (Madrid, 1757)) was first engraved in Paris, where the appearance of L'ABBÉ LE FILS's *Principes du violon* (1761) confirmed the ascendancy of a French violin school. The methods of Corrette (*L'art de se perfectionner dans le violon* (Paris, 1782)), CARTIER (*L'art du violon* (Paris, 1798)) and WOLDEMAR (*Grande méthode* (Paris, c1800)) are significant principally for their musical content. Baillot, RODE and KREUTZER, professors at the PARIS CONSERVATOIRE from its establishment (1795), were either taught or inspired by Viotti; together they produced the Conservatoire's official *Méthode de Violon* (Paris, 1803), offering systematic technical and interpretative instruction for aspiring professionals. The method was widely influential – Fauré (c1820) and Mazas (1830) include extracts verbatim – but it was superseded by Baillot's own *L'art du violon* (Paris, 1835), the fruits of which were perpetuated by his pupils HABENECK (*Méthode théorique et pratique de violon* (Paris, c1840)), ALARD (*École du violon* (Paris, 1844)) and DANCLA (*Méthode élémentaire et progressive pour violon* Op. 52 (Paris, 1855) and *École de mécanisme* Op. 74 (Paris, 1844)). The Belgian school's debt to Viotti is evident in the contents of Bériot's (*Méthode de violon* Op. 102 (Paris, [1858])) and Léonard's (*Méthode de violon* (Paris, 1877)) treatises, both committed to 'imitating the accents of the human voice' as opposed to cultivating virtuosity for its own sake.

Such virtuosity is described in GUHR's account of PAGANINI's performing style (*Ueber Paganinis Kunst* (Mainz, 1829)). By contrast, Spohr's *Violinschule* (Vienna, 1832) is more typically German, constrained by his own technical and stylistic TASTES. Nevertheless, his principles were widely influential, particularly on his pupil DAVID (*Violinschule* (Leipzig, 1863)); some were later quoted verbatim by JOACHIM and Moser (*Violinschule*, 3 vols. (Berlin, 1905)). Among other notable Austro-German writers of violin treatises in the second half of the nineteenth century were Dont (1850), Kayser (1867), Courvoisier (1873 and 1878) and Schradieck (1875).

AUER upheld the Franco-Belgian tradition in his various writings and at the St Petersburg Conservatory. Among other twentieth-century pedagogical literature appropriate for historical performers, Flesch's *Die Kunst des Violin-Spiels* (1923-8) and treatise on FINGERING (1960) are foremost, synthesising the techniques and artistic priorities of the principal violin schools in the nineteenth and early twentieth centuries.

Central to the advancement of violin technique through history have been the various modifications to the manner of holding the instrument, as this directly affects approaches to fingering and shifting (including PORTAMENTO), holding the BOW and BOWING, HARMONICS and other effects, and expressive factors such as VIBRATO. Initially the violin was normally held against the chest or the shoulder just beneath the collarbone (Playford, *Apollo's Banquet* (London, c1699); Geminiani, 1751), as has often been the practice in some national folk styles. However, some players chose to rest the instrument on the collarbone with the option (not always taken) of using their chins (positioned on either side of the tailpiece) to stabilise it, particularly when shifting (Corrette, 1738; Bailleux, *Méthode raisonné* (Paris, 1779)); others (Prinner, 1677; Herrando, 1757) advocated a chin-braced grip in order to liberate the left hand. The 'Geminiani grip' (*see* Example 11) remained the most common guide to correct elbow, hand, wrist and finger placement (in first position) until well into the twentieth century.

Not until the early nineteenth century were posture and the violin hold substantially standardised. Rode, Baillot and Kreutzer (1803) state unequivocally that the violin should be placed on the collarbone, held by the chin on the left-hand side of the tailpiece, and inclined a little to the right. Baillot later recommends (1835) a 'noble' and relaxed position, with head upright, feet normally in line but slightly apart, and body-weight distributed slightly towards the left side, and Spohr (1832) extols the virtues of his central chin-rest for a 'firm and unconstrained' violin hold and greater bowing freedom. The right arm, closer to the player's side than formerly, required the violin to be inclined to the right (Baillot proposed 45°, Spohr 25-30°) for optimum bowing facility on the lowest string. Some nineteenth-century violinists (most notably Paganini) advanced their thumb position to achieve greater mobility and facility in extensions, often liberating the hand from its customary position-sense.

Twentieth-century attitudes towards posture and the violin hold have generally been flexible, emphasising comfort and ease but disdaining exaggerated body movement. Flesch (1923-8) stresses the importance of feet placement, recommending a 'rectangular' leg position in which the feet are close together;

an 'acutangular' position in which the feet are separated, with either the right or left foot advanced and the body-weight on the rear foot; and his favoured 'spread-leg' position. He and most twentieth-century pedagogues recommend that the violin be held almost parallel to the floor.

As the century progressed, increased chromaticism, whole-tone, microtone and other scale patterns, and non-consonant double and multiple stopping necessitated the cultivation of a thumb position that totally liberated the left hand. Technical demands resulted not so much from the need to familiarise with new techniques as to adapt to the intensity of known ones, their specific prescription (e.g. for pizzicato locations, plucking agents, snap pizzicatos, etc.) and often their rapid interchange.

FURTHER READING

D. D. Boyden, *A History of Violin Playing from its Origins to 1761* (London: Oxford University Press, 1965).
C. Brown, *Classical and Romantic Performing Practice 1750–1900* (Oxford University Press, 1999).
P. Holman, *Four and Twenty Fiddlers: The Violin at the English Court, 1540–1690* (Oxford University Press, 1993, 2/1995).
D. Milsom, *Theory and Practice in Late Nineteenth-Century Violin Performance: An Examination of Style in Performance, 1850–1900* (Aldershot: Ashgate, 2003).
R. Stowell, *Violin Technique and Performance Practice in the Late Eighteenth and Early Nineteenth Centuries* (Cambridge University Press, 1985).

ROBIN STOWELL

Virdung, Sebastian (b. Amberg, c1465; d. after 1511) German singer, theorist and teacher of composition, based largely in Heidelberg.

Virdung's interest in contemporary performance is evidenced in his requesting, among other musical items, copies of Ockeghem's masses for the Elector Palatine's chapel library. His most important legacy to performers is a book known as *Musica getutscht* (1511), whose full title explicitly offers instructions for transcribing music into TABLATURE for three instruments, the ORGAN, LUTE and RECORDER; it is notable as the first printed TREATISE devoted to musical instruments and the way they are played.

Musica getutscht opens with an encyclopedic picture gallery of over sixty instruments, again the first of its kind in a printed book. These include dulcimer, BAGPIPE, HURDY-GURDY and a variety of folk and PERCUSSION instruments; the images are not always technically accurate but some of them yield useful information such as the constitution of the recorder family as three sizes pitched nominally in F, C and G.

Virdung goes on to give details of three kinds of tablature, along with other playing instructions, for keyboards, fretted strings and recorder. For keyboards he gives the standard German tablature and Virdung attributes its invention here to the blind Nuremberg organist Conrad Paumann. As well as conventional tablature, the section on fretted stringed instruments includes diagrams to instruct the performer in matters of stringing and fretting. Comparable diagrams are provided for the recorder and here the tablature may well have been of Virdung's own devising; it does not seem to have been adopted elsewhere. The tablature examples that Virdung gives for keyboard and lute are not actually playable, being demonstrations of how to transcribe literally from polyphonic originals, with no attempt to render the music idiomatic for the instrument. However, Virdung is aware of this and promises to provide better in a later work.

FURTHER READING

B. Bullard: *Musica getutscht: A Treatise on Musical Instruments (1511) by Sebastian Virdung* (Cambridge University Press, 1993).

JON BANKS

Virginal (Fr. *virginale, épinette*; Ger. *Virginal, Instrument*; It. *arpicordo, spinetta, spinettina*) A plucked keyboard instrument of the HARPSICHORD family in which the strings run at right angles to the line of the keys, with the bass strings closest to the player.

It is usually single-strung (i.e. with one keyboard and one set of strings and jacks). The strings run between two bridges, both attached to the sound board, and are arranged in widely spaced pairs with two jacks between each pair, each jack plucking in opposite directions. The jacks protrude through rectangular slots cut into the soundboard. The bass key levers are shorter than the treble so that the touch changes over the compass.

From its first use (Paulus Paulirinus, c1460), the term 'virginal' has implied female gender. In England 'virginals' was applied generically to all plucked keyboard instruments up to the mid-seventeenth century (the use of the plural form – as in a 'pair of virginals' – denotes a single instrument). In Italy and France, however, the equivalent term (*virginale*) was not used until modern times. In Italy, *spinetta* first denoted the rectangular virginal and then later came to mean any plucked keyboard instrument smaller than a harpsichord, while *arpicordo* was used for polygonal instruments and *clavicordio* could mean any kind of plucked keyboard instrument (the true CLAVICHORD usually being known as *manicordo* or similar).

The earliest virginals, described by Paulirinus and illustrated by SEBASTIAN VIRDUNG (*Musica getutscht*, 1511), were rectangular, but later depictions portray its polygonal form, as in the lid painting of the otherwise lost Paul Wismayer Virginal (*see Figure 18*).

This image shows a virginal used in ensemble performance, and placed above a simultaneously operated chest ORGAN. In Italy, virginals tended to be polygonal (usually five- or six-sided) and were similar to Italian harpsichords with thin case-sides, often with an additional protective outer case, and typical mouldings and decoration. The keyboard generally projected from the case front and the sound varied greatly from bass to treble as the plucking point moved progressively closer to the end of the string.

Flemish virginals had a thicker case into which the keyboard was set and were mostly rectangular in shape. Instruments with the keyboard placed to the left of centre were called *spinetten* and made a bright and nasal sound. Those with the keyboard placed to the right, called *muselaars*, were more popular. The jacks of the *muselaar* plucked the string somewhere between a half and about one-third of its length, resulting in a distinctively sonorous and flute-like quality. *Muselaars* included a *harpsichordium* stop whereby small metal hooks could touch the bass strings causing a buzzing sound. The famous Ruckers family of Antwerp made many virginals in a great variety of sizes and

Figure 18: Detail from lid painting by Frederik van Valckenborch or Falckenberg (c1570–1623), *The Four Seasons* (1619). Paul Wismayer Virginal, Germanisches Nationalmuseum, Nürnberg. (photograph by Malcolm Rose)

PITCHES, including an enlarged harpsichord case with incorporated virginal and the so-called 'double' or 'Mother and Child' virginal which combined a standard-pitch and octave-pitch instrument.

The virginal was a more popular domestic instrument than the harpsichord throughout Europe in the sixteenth and seventeenth centuries. In England large rectangular virginals, commonly of oak with coffered lids, were made for nearly a century from about 1570 until they were superseded by the 'bent-side' SPINET. Keyboard composers of the era have been referred to as the 'English Virginalist School' and their works have been preserved in sumptuous MANUSCRIPT collections such as the Fitzwilliam Virginal Book. Although virginal making has been revived in recent times, the instrument is less frequently heard than the harpsichord.

FURTHER READING

E. L. Kottick, *A History of the Harpsichord* (Bloomington and Indianapolis: Indiana University Press, 2003).
G. O'Brien, *Ruckers: A Harpsichord and Virginal Building Tradition* (Cambridge University Press, 2008).
R. Russell, *The Harpsichord and Clavichord: An Introductory Study*, 2nd edn, rev. H. Schott (London: Faber & Faber, 1973).

TERENCE CHARLSTON

Vitry, Philippe de (b.? Champagne, 31 October 1291; d. 9 June 1361) French musician, theorist, author, bishop and high-rank adviser.

During his extraordinary career Vitry was close to the leading political and ecclesiastical figures of the early fourteenth century. According to the *Règles de la seconde rhétorique* (early fifteenth century), Vitry was the inventor of the ballade, but no musical setting survives for the one extant text by him in this form, *De terre en grec Gaulle appellee*. However, Vitry may have authored at least some of the (monophonic) ballades in the 'interpolated' version of the *Roman de Fauvel*, just as he almost certainly authored some or most of the motets. Vitry was also likely connected with the practice of intoning in measured rhythms – that is, with the same patterns used in the motets – the *Fauvel* monophonic songs cast in the fixed forms.

The *Fauvel* motets are the earliest examples of the rhythmic and notational innovations illustrated in the TREATISE *Ars nova* (early 1320s), once thought to be by Vitry himself and now regarded as merely a repository of his teaching. Chapters 15–24 set forth several notational innovations for rhythmic patterns that were already part of musical practice. They officially recognised both perfect (triple) and imperfect (duple) divisions of the longa, breve and semibreve (respectively *tempus, modus,* and *prolatio*); they recognised four basic *tempus/modus* combinations of those rhythmic patterns: perfect-perfect (corresponding to the modern metre of 9/8); perfect-imperfect (3/4); imperfect-perfect (6/8); and imperfect-imperfect (2/4); for the first time in Western music they contemplated divisions of the semibreve into *minimae*; and they introduced red notes in musical notation, effecting rhythmic and/or metrical changes. These notational changes characterised the period of the so-called *Ars nova*, in contrast with the earlier *Ars antiqua* based on the teaching of Franco of Cologne.

FURTHER READING

M. Bent, 'Early Papal motets', in R. Sherr (ed.), *Papal Music and Musicians in Late Medieval and Renaissance Rome* (Oxford: Clarendon Press, in association with Library of Congress, Washington, DC, 1998), 5–43.
S. Fuller, 'A phantom treatise of the fourteenth century? The *Ars nova*', *JM*, 4 (1985–6), 23–50.
D. Leech-Wilkinson, 'The emergence of *ars nova*', *JM*, 13 (1995), 285–317.

STEFANO MENGOZZI

Vocal performance It is now widely accepted that SINGING, in the form of calls and other non-verbal sounds, was the earliest means of structured human communication, predating language and speech. But anthropologists also report that almost all humans sing for more complex reasons, principally to express happiness (we tend to prefer to listen to others sing when we are sad), or because they must, as part of rituals 'which could not take place without [singing]' (Potter and Sorrell, 15). These three fundamental motives – communication; the EXPRESSION of feelings; and as a means of interceding with gods – provide the basis for exploring a history of vocal performance since the Middle Ages that focuses on how the *act of singing* makes potent *what is sung*.

The earliest surviving NOTATIONS of 'Western' vocal performance are from Classical Greece, but it is the development of a conveniently stable means for the dissemination of standardised patterns for intoning the liturgical offices of the Christian church across Europe in the form of Gregorian CHANT notation that provides the earliest evidence for a source-based history of modern vocal performance. From its earliest surviving ninth-century manifestations in the form of unheightened neumes to later forms featuring notes arranged on staves, Gregorian chant is, by comparison with later more sophisticated notational systems, seemingly very 'open' about what it conveys to the reading singer about performance, beyond basic matters of PITCH relationships and text. But even this music nevertheless 'requires performers to exhibit a wide range of expression, as dictated by the subject matter, its context, the meaning of the words and the character of the melodic line' (J. Summerly, in Lawson and Stowell, 254). It is now widely accepted that chant notation is primarily 'descriptive' of vocal performance, an aid to recalling already memorised musical lines, rather than 'prescriptive', in the more modern sense of the medium through which a composer to a greater or lesser extent 'instructs' the singer when, how and what notes to sing in order to produce a self-sustaining performance of a pre-constructed work. Song that is on the one hand generated by the singer from autonomous thoughts interacting directly with the vocal mechanism of his or her body, and, on the other, which results from the highly-specialised form of 'reading aloud' entailed by singing from notation, are two distinct manifestations of musical skill that were nevertheless both required of 'literate' singers of Western art music for centuries, from the later Medieval period until at least the mid-nineteenth century.

Thus the training of boy choristers recruited into the elite cathedral and monastic choir schools established across Europe from the later fourteenth century onwards began, as it had done for at least the previous five hundred years, with memorising enormous amounts of Gregorian chant taught by rote (as children in the Islamic tradition continue to learn the Koran to this day). But it then continued with learning how to imagine and simultaneously sing increasingly complex melodies 'against' sections of chant already deeply embedded into the mind (i.e. counterpoint; in English, 'descant'), which produces more-or-less structurally robust polyphonic music. This formed the basis of the principal style of polyphonic singing performed by professional church musicians in most parts of Europe until well into the seventeenth century (and still being taught in some French choir schools in the nineteenth): namely, *cantus super librum* ('singing upon the book'), otherwise known as improvised multi-voiced counterpoint on a *cantus firmus*. It is quite difficult for us even to imagine today that most of the polyphony heard in these centuries in those European Catholic churches sufficiently grand to sustain a choir of professional singers was composed on the spot, using just the ear and voice and without recourse to the reading eye, according, of course, to strict rules and conventions (not unlike JAZZ). Singers also learned to read polyphonic music written down by composers ('*res facta*'), which allowed for works constructed (and thus 'polished') in one place to be performed in another.

That the ability to do both kinds of singing – improvised counterpoint and reading from notation – was still an absolute requirement for professional singers in the late sixteenth century is clear from LUIGI ZENOBI's 'Letter on the perfect musician' description (c1600) of the ideal music director as a singer capable of controlling group improvisations and being ready to jump in to rescue any of the other singers in danger of losing his way, while the rank-and-file singers must also be capable of reading any kind of notated music at sight, however difficult (in B. Blackburn and E. Lowinsky, 'Luigi Zenobi and his letter on the perfect musician', *Studi Musicali*, 22/1 (1993), 61–114 (96–8)). Zenobi (100–2) also insisted that when performing solo, singers (especially sopranos) must be able to apply a wide variety of ORNAMENTATION to a melodic line, both spontaneously and appropriate to the genre of music, to the place of its performance and even the time of day. He was in effect summarising the legacy of practices of improvised ornamentation of song that had been prevalent in Europe for two hundred years or more, attested to by a steady succession of TREATISES and the evidence of instrumental INTABULATIONS of songs. The vocal treatises of the sixteenth, seventeenth, eighteenth and early nineteenth centuries are essentially successive attempts to codify the parameters of this continuing art of spontaneous 'co-composition' by the singer, which in turn is what makes true art singing individual, powerfully affective and thus 'authentic'.

The 'methodisation' of what was clearly a ubiquitous improvisatory singing practice reached its first apogee in GIULIO CACCINI's two volumes of *Le nuove musiche* (Florence, 1602 and 1614). This famous singer-composer described in both words and notated examples a style of solo singing that places every aspect of subtle vocal expression, from the initiation of a phrase (*intonazione*), through ornamentation (*trilli e gruppi*) and dynamic shaping of notes (*crescere e scemare della voce*), to controlled rhythmic freedom (*sprezzatura*), in the service of the intelligent ARTICULATION of poetry, in songs characterised by simple strophic or through-composed melodies over basic harmonisations (Caccini (Florence, 1602), 4–6; (Florence, 1614), *ai lettori*). At the same time, Caccini and his contemporaries in Florence were pioneering a more austere style of sung text declamation, which subjugates all vocal ornament to *recitar cantando* ('singing recitation') for extended narrative passages, and thereby enabling through-sung drama – opera. From its 'standing start' in Florence in 1600, opera rapidly developed into perhaps the principal arena in which great singers could harness their voices to the affective expression of the extreme human passions within the context of theatrical narratives that dramatised the widest range of mythology, history, tragedy and comedy.

As 'art singing' became an increasingly specialised practice, particularly with the development of techniques for elaborating chant and other pre-existing melodic materials to make polyphony, the relationship between what the singer does in performance, and the notation that connects the totality of the vocal act to the logic of abstract musical structures, remained a complex one, subject to negotiation. The evidence the on one hand of evolving notational systems and on the other of vocal treatises, which work to standardise and impose rules for 'in-performance interventions' or elaborations of the notated text by the singer (and usually written reactively, fighting rearguard actions against changing TASTES), demonstrates the almost continuous attempts by theorists, composers and pedagogues to 'fix' the unstable relationship between prescription and interpretation, by making notation more specific and improvisation more systematic. These include, for example, the introduction of mensural and proportional signs in monophonic songs in the years around 1300 that later allowed the construction of complex polyphony in the fifteenth century; or the representation of the very short note values that can describe the traditionally highly individualistic practice of making ornamental diminutions produced in the throat (*gorgie*), made possible in the age of Caccini by the earlier invention around 1520 of printing music on an industrial scale using moveable type. It would, however, be a mistake to assume that these changes over the course of the Medieval and early modern periods necessarily suggest a historiography of some kind of endless 'war of attrition' in which 'autonomous composers', particularly in the Baroque and Classical periods, were in a continual struggle to retain control in the face of insurgent singers' attempts to stymie them through misplaced and egotistical performative incontinence, a 'war' finally won by Verdi and WAGNER.

In the eighteenth-century opera theatre, for example, AUDIENCES came first and foremost to hear the singers rather than the 'work', and the role of the composer of operatic music, essentially subordinate to that of the singer, was to provide a scaffold which could function as the basis for spontaneous elaborations in the moment of performance. The vocal performances were judged according to their virtuosity and ability to excite and move the audience's emotions. *Bel canto* virtuosity consisted in a combination of the perfection of the singer's technique: quality of sound, breath control (demonstrated through the *messa di voce*) and dynamics, and the singer's inventiveness and bravura in ORNAMENTATION and melodic variation. Careful exposition of the text appears to have been of only secondary importance to the success of the performance for most of the audience. BURNEY's account of FARINELLI's signature opening of an aria with an almost impossibly extended and perfectly controlled *messa di voce* on the first note is illustrative of this: 'the first note he sung was taken with such delicacy, swelled by minute degrees to such an amazing volume, and afterwards diminished in the same manner, that it was applauded for full five minutes' (C. Burney, *The Present State of Music in France and Italy* (1771), 208). The balance between such virtuosity (or vulgarity?) and restraint was both a fine one and subject to changes in taste over time.

Even in the age of Gluck and MOZART and well into the early nineteenth century, the success of the operatic experience rested almost entirely on the spontaneous nuance of individual singers' performances, and this in turn hinged on their own judgements about how to harness their prodigious technical accomplishments, in the words of CACCINI at the start of the seventeenth century, 'to move the affect of the soul' of their listeners (Caccini (Florence, 1602), 5). One of the last great exponents of the golden age of eighteenth-century *bel canto* castrato singing was Gasparo Pacchierotti, who died in 1821. The Earl of Mount Edgcumbe recalled in his *Reminiscences* (1834) that Pacchierotti confined his virtuoso bravura singing to one aria only in each opera, 'conscious that the chief delight of singing, and his own supreme excellence, lay in touching expression and exquisite pathos' (J. Potter, 'Vocal performance in the long eighteenth century', in Lawson and Stowell, 526).

The degrees of individuality expected from singers in the interpretation of composers' 'blueprints' in performance, ranging from matters of timbral, articulatory and dynamic features of vocal production to questions of creativity in rhythm and TEMPO, as well as variation of basic melodic material, remain remarkably audible in the earliest surviving recordings of singers, some of whom were schooled within their teachers' living memory of the pre-Romantic era. The potential value of this large body of evidence to a re-thinking of the nature of pre-modern vocal performance is only now becoming evident, and it remains to be seen whether it will have a fundamental effect on the way that vocal music of the past is performed in the present. But one thing is certain: in order to begin to reconstruct a historically contextualised understanding of the relationship between vocal compositions as they appear to us as writing, and their intended manifestation in performance, will entail a renegotiation of some currently deeply embedded assumptions about the normally elevated hierarchical status of the former over the latter.

Nevertheless, if there is one enduring and consistent characteristic of the relationship between the 'composition' of song and its vocal performance that persists right up to the present day, it is the rhetorical challenge of *ethopoeia* ('the simulation of character'). Its implication for the role of the composer is, as Quintilian observed, the fact that 'assuredly a speech cannot be conceived without being conceived as the speech of some person' (*Institutio Oratoria*, 12 books (Rome: c60AD); trans. H. E. Butler as *Institutes of Oratory* (London: Heinemann, 1922), Bk. 9, Ch. 2). At its most basic, the singer's responsibility is to embody the 'person' and convey the full import of the words of the 'speech' in such a way that they are sufficiently efficacious to affect and change the listener's psychosomatic state, employing whatever means this may take in terms of the AESTHETICS of vocality pervading at the particular time and place of the performance. In the words of Ottavio Durante, the singer's task is to 'seek to understand well what they have to sing – in particular if they are singing solo – so that understanding it well *and making it their own* [my emphasis], they are able to make others who are listening understand it, which is their principal purpose' (Durante, *Arie devote* (Rome: Verovio, 1608), *ai lettori*).

Thus, although a purely paper-based comparison of the apparent 'openness' of, say, the notation of a trouvère song with the apparently prescriptive written-out *passaggi* in a MONTEVERDI madrigal or BACH aria seems to suggest a gradual reduction in the autonomy of vocalists through the early modern era, the very fact that *bel canto* treatises as recent as the early nineteenth century are still insisting that the key to becoming a successful singer is the mastery of IMPROVISATION during the performance of pre-composed operatic arias, only underlines the profundity of the changes that occurred in art music in the mid-nineteenth century, which gradually but inexorably did eventually lead to the removal of co-compositional responsibility from art-music singers. It did not die, though, but merely continued in the mainstream of singing; to find it still alive and well in vocal performance practice today, one must look to jazz and popular music.

FURTHER READING

P. Canghuilem, '"Singing upon the book" according to Vicente Lusitano', *Early Music History*, 30 (2011), 55–103.
M. Elliott, *Singing in Style: A Guide to Vocal Performance* (New Haven and London: Yale University Press, 2006).

C. Lawson and R. Stowell (eds.), *The Cambridge History of Musical Performance* (Cambridge University Press, 2012), chs. 9, 13, 17, 21 and 25.

J. Potter and N. Sorrell, *A History of Singing* (Cambridge University Press, 2012).

RICHARD WISTREICH

Vogl, Johann Michael (b. nr Steyr, 10 August 1768; d. Vienna, 20 November 1840) Austrian baritone.

Vogl studied law at the University of Vienna but was persuaded into music by his schoolboy friend Süssmayr. In 1794 he joined the Vienna Hofoper and became known for his commanding stage presence and vocal technique, taking leading roles in Italian and German opera, including Count Almaviva (*Le nozze di Figaro*) and Pizarro (*Fidelio*). He met Schubert in 1817 and gave many performances of his songs, including *Erlkönig* in 1821. Following his retirement from the stage the following year, he dedicated himself to promoting the music of Schubert, becoming a close friend of the composer. Vogl's approach to the songs was operatic and dramatic, incorporating improvised embellishments. By mid-century such practices were outdated and were described in Heinrich Kreissle von Hellborn's 1865 biography of Schubert as 'detestable alterations' (Vienna, 1865, 125). In 1893 Max Friedländer encouraged the view that Vogl's interpretations and alleged influence on Schubert had been harmful. Only recently has Walther Dürr (1979) shown that Vogl was greatly admired within the Schubert circle; his versions of the songs 'should serve only as models for individual creation of improvised, non-essential embellishments' and the alterations should not be raised to the status of composed ones.

FURTHER READING

W. Dürr, 'Schubert and Johann Michael Vogl: a reappraisal', *19CM*, 3/2 (1979), 126–40.

M. Friedländer, 'Fälschungen in Schubert's Liedern', *Vierteljahrschrift für Musikwissenschaft*, 9 (1893), 166–85.

COLIN LAWSON

W

Wagner, Richard (b. Leipzig, 22 May 1813; d. Venice, 13 February 1883) German dramatic composer of almost unparalleled influence, a conductor, opera director, writer and polemicist, and a pivotal figure for nineteenth-century performance practice.

Wagner, along with BERLIOZ and Liszt, was fundamental to the development of the interpretative or virtuoso orchestral conductor, in contrast to earlier ideas of the role as a leader largely concerned with cohesion of ensemble and the general setting of tempi. In his operas or 'music-dramas' Wagner pioneered original approaches to staging; with his founding of the Bayreuth Festival he realised a new approach to the design of the theatre itself.

In *On Conducting* (trans. E. Dannreuther (London, 1897)) Wagner set forth his ideas, in typically trenchant and verbose fashion, on the faults he perceived in contemporary ORCHESTRAS and conductors. He regarded German orchestras as far behind those of France, advocating more frequent and, where necessary, sectional REHEARSALS (at the time a far from routine approach). He believed that the increasingly complex nature of music from BEETHOVEN onwards required a new type of conductor, one who would not only set 'correct' tempi, but also indicate the necessary modifications of tempi within movements themselves. These modifications ('of which our conductors know nothing') – many of them subtle nuances impossible to achieve without the thorough rehearsals now required – constitute the core of Wagner's new approach, along with the increasing cultivation of long, linear phrasing, in contrast to the more articulated style of earlier eras.

Wagner believed that most eighteenth-century music could be successfully performed in the basic TEMPO indicated by the composer, or implied by the genre of the piece, but that the music of Beethoven and his successors demanded a more sophisticated and flexible interpretation. The difference, he claimed, was akin to Schiller's famous distinction between 'naïve' and 'sentimental' poetry. Using specific examples largely taken from Beethoven's symphonies, Weber's overtures and his own overture to *Die Meistersinger*, Wagner argued that the conductor's role was to identify the 'melos' of a piece, which is 'the sole guide to the true tempo' and therefore to its necessary modifications (*On Conducting*, 19). This 'melos' appears to be a combination of the melody itself, and what eighteenth-century theorists might have called the AFFECT of the music. According to Wagner, only a conductor sensitive to the interpretative nuances of great singers – the prime example is his idol Wilhelmine Schröder-Devrient – will unerringly identify the melos of a piece.

Wagner's approach was thus similar to that of Liszt, who imported the TEMPO flexibility and subtle dynamics of his piano playing into his CONDUCTING and into the performance directions of his orchestral scores. Of the next generation of conductors, HANS VON BÜLOW, a student of both Wagner and Liszt, most successfully embodied their ideas, which have been followed by a host of subsequent conductors and remain the predominant concept of interpretative conducting today. During the nineteenth century, however, the change in performance style was hardly welcomed by all. The Viennese Eduard Hanslick, for example, in reviews of the conducting of both Wagner and von Bülow, condemned what he regarded as the imposition of jarring soloistic effects onto orchestral playing. 'If this becomes universal', he claimed, 'it will destroy the last healthy element of our concert life.'

Wagner's influence on opera production was no less remarkable. In keeping with his intention to create a *Gesamtkunstwerk* or 'complete work of art', he not only composed music and text, and provided copious instructions for the performance of his works, but also took on the role of stage director for the Bayreuth Festival premieres of *Der Ring des Nibelungen* (1876) and *Parsifal* (1882). His expansion of orchestral forces for the *Ring* even included the development of a new type of brass instrument, the so-called 'Wagner tuba', which features in later repertoire by Bruckner and RICHARD STRAUSS, and makes an occasional appearance in film music scores.

The Bayreuth theatre itself was built to a novel design of Wagner's own devising. Inspired by ancient Greek theatres, it has a raked, fan-shaped auditorium designed to ensure satisfactory sightlines from every seat, a double proscenium stage and a covered, sunken orchestral pit. The stage action thus appears distant (owing to the shift in perspective produced by the double proscenium) yet clearly visible; the orchestra audible but invisible. According to Wagner, this results in a 'mystic gulf' between performers and audience, allowing audience members to concentrate upon the drama without distraction. The effect was enhanced by complete darkness in the auditorium itself (in many nineteenth-century theatres the auditorium was as brightly lit as the stage), use of the very latest stage lighting technology and several other technical innovations, including the employment of a 'steam curtain' (jets of steam covering changes of scene from the sight of the audience) and (in *Parsifal*) rolling scenery to effect 'transformation scenes'. For *Parsifal*, Wagner even attempted to prohibit APPLAUSE until the end of the final act, in order not to break the spell of the drama.

With the extravagantly fantastical stage directions of his music dramas, and the design of the Bayreuth theatre itself, Wagner seemed to have been striving for effects fully realisable only in modern cinema. Although the *Prinzregententheater* in Munich was closely modelled on Bayreuth, and also originally intended for the production of Wagner's works, the design is less suited to performances of operas by other composers. For this reason, and owing to the difficulties of instrumental performance and coordination with the stage occasioned by the covered orchestral pit, the Bayreuth theatre remains iconic but atypical.

FURTHER READING

T. Grey (ed.), *Richard Wagner and His World* (Princeton University Press, 2009).
N. Heinel, *Richard Wagner als Dirigent* (Vienna: Praesens Verlag, 2006).

B. Millington and S. Spencer (eds.), *Wagner in Performance* (New Haven and London: Yale University Press, 1992).

KENNETH HAMILTON

Walther, Johann Gottfried (b. Erfurt, 18 September 1684; d. Weimar, 23 March 1748) German organist, composer, theorist and lexicographer.

After studying the ORGAN and SINGING, Walther attended Erfurt's Ratsgymnasium before briefly working as an organist at the Thomaskirche. During subsequent travels he befriended the organist and writer Andreas Werckmeister and studied organ with Johann Pachelbel's son, Wilhelm Hieronymus. In 1707 he was appointed organist of Weimar's Stadtkirche, a position he retained to the end of his life, and simultaneously became music teacher to Prince Johann Ernst until the young man's untimely death in 1715. He established a close relationship with his cousin, J. S. BACH, who joined the Weimar court in 1708, and was himself appointed as a court musician in 1721.

Walther's landmark dictionary of musicians and musical terms, the *Musicalisches Lexicon oder musicalische Bibliothec* (Leipzig, 1732), contains numerous entries relating to aspects of performance, including ARTICULATION (*see* especially 'détaché' and 'legato'), tempo (sometimes recognising fine gradations such as 'Allegro', 'Allegro allegro', 'Allegro assai' and 'Allegrissimo'), ORNAMENTATION (often illustrated with musical examples, as with 'Groppo', 'Port de Voix' and 'Tirata'), vocal scoring (e.g. the distinction between 'Alto concertante' and 'Alto ripieno') and instruments (occasionally addressing their use in performance, as with 'Violoncello'). Among Walther's organ works, of special performance-practical interest are his organ arrangements of concertos and other instrumental ensemble works by Italian and German composers (fourteen survive of the seventy-eight he claimed to have fashioned), some of which contain instructive examples of free ornamentation.

FURTHER READING

A. Aalgrimm and H. Scholz-Michelitsch (eds.), *Ornamentik der Musik für Tasteninstrumente: Ein Kompendium aus Originalquellen vom 16. bis zum ersten Drittel des 19. Jahrhunderts*, vol. 1: *Deutschsprachige Quellen* (Graz: Akademische Druck- und Verlagsanstalt, 2005).

D. Bartel, *Musica Poetica: Musical-Rhetorical Figures in German Baroque Music* (Lincoln, NE: University of Nebraska Press, 1997).

STEVEN ZOHN

Weber, (Jacob) Gottfried (b. Freinsheim (Pfalz), 1 March 1779; d. Bad Kreuznach, 21 September 1839) German theorist, composer and writer.

Weber undertook professional training as an attorney; he held posts in that capacity at Mannheim, Mainz and finally Darmstadt. His musical training began in childhood, with instruction in PIANO and FLUTE. While in Mannheim, Weber studied ORGAN and became an accomplished cellist. It was during this period that he initiated his activities as a composer and, more importantly, as a writer on a wide variety of music-related subjects, including acoustics, instrument construction, AESTHETICS and theoretical issues. Between 1803 and 1839 Weber contributed articles to several journals and encyclopedias. The preponderance of these articles appeared either in the journal *Cäcelia*, which Weber founded in 1824, or in the *Allgemeine musikalische Zeitung*. Articles in the *AMZ* often reported on technical advancements in performance practice; representative are 'Wichtige Verbesserung des Horns' (*AMZ* XIV/47, 1812), in which Weber describes the advantages of a new slide mechanism for French HORNS and 'Ueber Instrumentalbässe bey vollstimmigen Tonstücken' (*AMZ* XIV/47, 1812), which introduced his own concept of a double slide for the bass TROMBONE in F. Drawing on essays originally published in *Cäcelia* (1825), Weber issued two independent publications challenging for the first time the intrinsic authenticity of MOZART's *Requiem* on both historical and aesthetic grounds.

Weber also advocated for the use of his innovative musical chronometer, a simple pendulum device that he felt would facilitate the contemporary interpretation of TEMPO markings. He outlined his system for its use in an 1813 *AMZ* article. He later included much of this information in his *Versuch einer geordneten Theorie der Tonsetzkunst* (Mainz: Schott, 1817–21), and derived a separate publication (*Ueber chronometrische Tempobezeichnung* (Mainz: Schott, 1817)) from the material therein. This latter effort attests to the continued popularity of Weber's chronometer, notwithstanding the patenting of Maelzel's METRONOME in 1815.

Material contained in the third edition of the *Versuch* (1832) formed the basis for Weber's *Generalbaßlehre* (Mainz: Schott, 1833). Despite his recognition of the value of FIGURED BASS NOTATION as a compositional and pedagogical tool, Weber was an early advocate for the abandonment of *Generalbass* accompaniment in concerted works. In an 1813 article ('Ueber das sogenannte Generalbass-Spielen bey Aufführung von Kirchen-Musiken', *AMZ* XV/7), Weber contends that *Generalbass* notation had by this time become an inadequate method for realising 'intricate ... current harmonic materials', and thus the performer of figures can 'no longer ... provide an effective accompaniment'.

FURTHER READING

L. Holtmeier, '[Jacob] Gottfried Weber', *MGG (Personenteil)*, xvii (2007), 574–7.
A. Lemke, *Jacob Gottfried Weber: Leben und Werk*. Beiträge zur mittelrheinischen Musikgeschichte, nr 9 (Mainz: Schott, 1968).
J. K. Saslaw, 'Gottfried Weber and the concept of Mehrdeutigkeit', PhD dissertation, Columbia University (1992), 1–24.

DAVID F. CHAPMAN

Webern, Anton (Friedrich Wilhelm von) (b. Vienna, 3 December 1883; d. Mittersill, 15 September 1945) Austrian composer, conductor and musicologist.

Webern was the only member of the Second Viennese School to pursue an active professional career as a conductor. Having garnered experience in a variety of opera houses in central Europe, he directed the Vienna Workers' Symphony Orchestra and Vienna Workers' Chorus from 1922 to 1934, and also gave occasional concerts with the BBC Symphony Orchestra from 1929 to 1936.

Despite a somewhat limited baton technique, Webern sustained a painstaking and fervent approach to REHEARSAL, focusing on the power of his conviction and spiritual intensity to put his ideas across. Such qualities rendered his performances of MAHLER's symphonies particularly memorable and emotionally overwhelming. He was a devoted interpreter of J. S. BACH's choral and instrumental works, combining a projection of motivic structure with a sense of line which was always supported by simple and clear dynamics faithfully adhering to the markings in the original scores. His conducting of BEETHOVEN symphonies was equally direct, placing the greatest emphasis on achieving an ideal basic TEMPO for each movement without inhibiting any capacity for contrasts.

A surviving recording of Webern conducting the BBC Symphony Orchestra in the first British performance of ALBAN BERG's Violin Concerto (with violinist Louis Krasner) in 1936 (Testament CD SBT1004 first issued in 1991) gives a very good indication of his interpretative approach to the music of the Second Viennese School. The performance manifests an extremely fluid and hyper-Romantic interpretation, with broadly paced tempo. Despite inferior sound quality, Webern none the less secures a clear orchestral texture, highlighting the all-important melodic lines.

The most significant document relating to Webern's ideas regarding the performance of his own music remains the publication in 1979 of a FACSIMILE EDITION of a copy of the *Variationen für Klavier*, Op. 27 owned by the pianist Peter Stadlen. Stadlen, who gave the first performance in 1937, had benefited from intensive study of the work under the composer's direction, and the edition reproduces all the details of this invaluable experience. On the left-facing page, the score is presented with the pencil annotations made by Webern as he coached Stadlen. On the right, the same music is printed with Webern's lines, arrows and other indications superimposed on the musical text in red alongside Stadlen's memories of Webern's instructions, including verbatim quotations from the composer, printed in green. Amongst the most fascinating additions to the published score are the brackets presented around individual notes intended to demonstrate their melodic connection to each other, and further directions for voicing, phrasing, ARTICULATION, tempo fluctuation, dynamic surges and PEDALLING. Above all, Webern's annotations incorporate detailed expressions of emotional and poetic imagery suggesting that powerful tensions exist between the seemingly autonomous structural logic of the musical argument and the composer's suggested extra-musical content which relates more strongly to music of the Romantic era. Explaining this dichotomy, Stadlen suggests that Webern's sparing notational instruction 'points to an enigmatic dialectic of emotive and constructive intent, at any rate at the moment of composition' and that contrary to the generally ascetic nature of the music as it is presented on the page, a 'fervently lyrical mind bent on expressiveness has been at work' (*Variationen*, 1979, Preface, v).

FURTHER READING

H. Moldenhauer, *Anton von Webern: A Chronicle of His Life and Work* (London: Gollancz, 1978).
A. Webern, *Variationen für Klavier*, Op. 27, ed. P. Stadlen (Vienna: Universal Edition, 1979).

ERIK LEVI

Weidinger, Anton (b. Vienna, 9 June 1766; d. Vienna, 20 September 1852) Austrian trumpeter.

Through his early adoption of a new form of TRUMPET, with holes in the tubing covered by keys like a woodwind instrument, Weidinger was central to the development of the chromatic trumpet. The most important solo works of the Classical period were written for him. He served a traditional natural trumpet apprenticeship with chief court trumpeter Peter Neuhold at the Vienna Imperial Court. This ended in 1785 with his entry into military service as a field trumpeter, first with the *cuirassier* regiment of Prince Adam Czartorisky and later with Archduke Joseph's dragoon regiment. In 1792, he left military service to join the ORCHESTRA of the Royal Imperial Theatre in Vienna. Although initially grounded in natural trumpet, he became the keyed trumpet's first great exponent. After much success around the turn of the nineteenth century, Weidinger's career as a keyed trumpeter was eclipsed by the fast pace of other brass developments, including valve mechanisms, their application to the trumpet and newly invented instruments such as the cornet.

Although often credited as inventor of the keyed trumpet, it is more likely that Weidinger developed his *organisierte Trompete* around 1793 from an idea which had currency at the time. JOSEPH HAYDN wrote his Concerto in E♭ Hob. VIIIe:1, his last purely orchestral composition, for Weidinger in 1796. The concerto made exceptional demands on trumpet technique of that time. It is the first known solo work to exploit the range and modulating capacity of a chromatic trumpet. Weidinger did not present the new concerto until 1800, in the Imperial Royal National Court Theatre. In the interim, he performed concertante works with less adventurous keyed trumpet parts but with exotic instrumentation by Leopold Kozeluch (1798) and Joseph Weigl (1799).

Weidinger was well received by audiences in Vienna and on concert tours to Germany, France and England. In 1802, the *AMZ* reviewed a concert he gave in Leipzig, describing his 'masterful playing' of 'his significant invention concerning the perfection of the trumpet', his 'full, penetrating tone' and his capacity to play as gently and delicately as a CLARINET. HUMMEL's Trio for Piano, Violin and Keyed Trumpet, now lost, is referred to in the same publication. Hummel went on to write a Concerto in E major for Weidinger, which was premiered at a New Year's Day banquet at the Hapsburg Court in Vienna in 1804. The last major work in which Weidinger played a key solo role was Sigismund Neukomm's *Requiem*, composed for performance at the Congress of Vienna in January 1815. Although Weidinger did not retire from the orchestra in the Court Theatre until 1850 (then aged 83), his solo career went no further, despite his introduction of a new, improved keyed trumpet in 1829.

FURTHER READING

R. Dahlqvist, *The Keyed Trumpet and Its Greatest Virtuoso, Anton Weidinger* (Nashville: Brass Press, 1975).

E. H. Tarr, *Die Trompete* (1977), trans. S. E. Plank and E. H. Tarr as *The Trumpet* (Portland, OR: Amadeus, 1984/R1988; London: Batsford, 1988).

JOHN WALLACE

Weigl, Joseph Franz (b. Bavaria, 19 May 1740; d. Vienna, 25 January 1820) Austrian cellist.

Weigl was principal cellist in the ORCHESTRA of Prince Paul Esterházy at Eisenstadt, joining that establishment in 1761 at the same time as HAYDN and the VIOLIN virtuoso Aloisio Tomasini. Haydn and Weigl were already friends in Vienna, and Haydn was also godfather to Weigl's son Joseph, an opera composer (the two Weigls are frequently confused). He remained there until 1769 when he became principal cellist at the Kärntnertortheater in Vienna, where in 1771 he publicly quarrelled with Ignaz Küffl, another cellist, over who should sit next to the keyboard player and accompany recitatives. Weigl also played in Leopold Hofmann's orchestra at the Peterskirche until at least 1783. In 1792 Weigl entered the Hofkapelle, and often appeared as soloist in Vienna; Salieri frequently suggested him as a soloist for music at court banquets. CHARLES BURNEY heard Weigl playing Haydn string quartets 'executed in the utmost perfection' at the house of the British ambassador, and described him as 'an excellent performer on the violoncello' (*The Present State of Music in Germany, the Netherlands, and United Provinces* (3 vols. (London, 1773), I, 294).

As principal cellist at Eisenstadt, Weigl was the intended soloist in Haydn's Symphonies nos. 6–8, 'Le matin', 'Le midi' and 'Le soir', and his Cello Concerto in C, Hob.VIIb:1 (rediscovered in 1961). Weigl's playing appears to have also interested Leopold Hofmann, who wrote more for the CELLO after Weigl moved to Vienna. In the period 1770–82 Hofmann wrote concertos, concertinos and other chamber and orchestral works with prominent solo cello parts, several of which were more demanding of the soloist than Hofmann's earlier works. It has been suggested that a recently discovered anonymous concerto in B♭ major, attributed to Michael Haydn, may have been partly composed by Weigl; he is not otherwise known to have composed for the instrument.

FURTHER READING

G. Kennaway, 'Haydn's (?) cello concertos, 1860–1930: editions, performances, reception', *Nineteenth-Century Music Review*, 9 (2012), 177–211.

GEORGE KENNAWAY

Wenzinger, August (b. Basel, 14 November 1905; d. Basel, 25 December 1996) Swiss VIOL player, cellist and musicologist.

Wenzinger was principal cellist of the Basel Orchester Gesellschaft (1936–70), cellist of the Basel String Quartet (1929–34) and a member of the Basel Gesellschaft für Kammermusik until 1968. He began playing the viol as a schoolboy in Basel because his CELLO teacher, Treichler, also played the viol. When he went to Cologne in 1927 to complete his cello studies with Grümmer, his new teacher encouraged him to continue his viol playing and sent him to Darmstadt library to copy works with viol by TELEMANN. Whilst there, Wenzinger found the concertos by J. G. Graun and was amazed by the viol's range of technical and musical possibilities. In 1929, an invitation by the owner of Bärenreiter Verlag to give a course on stylistically correct viol playing led Wenzinger to study original TREATISES (GANASSI, ORTIZ, SIMPSON, ROUSSEAU) and to examine early viol paintings. Through scrutiny of these sources Wenzinger (1994, 136) 'developed a physiologically correct technique which could meet all the technical and musical requirements of different styles'. He also realised that viol technique was equivalent to the art of VIOLIN playing. In 1933 Wenzinger became a founder member of the SCHOLA CANTORUM BASILIENSIS, teaching the viol, ensemble playing and ORNAMENTATION and publishing a viol tutor (1935, 1938). He persuaded some of his colleagues from the violin department to play the viol and they set up a professional CONSORT. In 1938 Wenzinger recorded Telemann's D major Suite (for Electrola) and went on to make many recordings, particularly for Deutsche Grammophon's Archiv Produktion. He was a respected conductor and in 1953 made the first complete recording of J. S. BACH's Brandenburg Concertos partially on original instruments, followed in 1955 by the first recording of MONTEVERDI's *Vespers*. In 1973 Wenzinger retired from the Schola Cantorum; his position was taken by his student JORDI SAVALL.

FURTHER READING

A. Wenzinger, 'The revival of the viola da gamba: a history', in J. Boer and G. van Oorschot (eds.), *A Viola da Gamba Miscellany: Proceedings of the International Viola da Gamba Symposium* (Utrecht: STIMU, 1994), 133–9.

LUCY ROBINSON

Werktreue The ideal of *Werktreue* – 'faithfulness to the work' – became a particular issue in the mid-twentieth century for performers and musicologists concerned with AUTHENTICITY (see Fabian, 2001). Regarded by many as disastrously harmful, even 'the musical analogue of religious fundamentalism' (Nicholas Cook, in Haynes, 90), *Werktreue* is a contentious concept. On the one hand, there is the difficulty of accounting for the 'work' – whether as musical score (*Notentexttreue*), composition, (fetishised) text, musical sense, real meaning, work-concept or intentions (musical and otherwise) of the composer. On the other hand, there is the question of remaining 'faithful', whether this involves removing one's own personality from performance, being transparent, demonstrating fidelity towards the 'URTEXT imperative' or the work's 'untouchability', or, perhaps, following MOZART's advice, performing 'so that one believes that the music was composed by the person who is playing it' (Mozart, letter of 17 January 1778).

FURTHER READING

D. Fabian, 'The meaning of authenticity and the early music movement: a historical review', *International Journal of the Aesthetics and Sociology of Music*, 32/2 (2001), 153–67.
L. Goehr, *The Imaginary Museum of Musical Works* (Oxford University Press, 2007).
B. Haynes, *The End of Early Music* (Oxford University Press, 2007).

NICK WILSON

Westrup, Sir Jack Allan (b. London, 26 July 1904; d. Headley, Hants., 21 April 1975) English musicologist and conductor.

Educated at Dulwich College and at Balliol College, Oxford, Westrup was co-founder and musical director of the Oxford Opera Club (1927), notable for its first complete modern performance of MONTEVERDI's *L'Orfeo* and first British performance of Monteverdi's *L'incoronazione di Poppea*, both edited by Westrup. In 1926 Westrup won a research grant to collect 'Noëls provençaux' in Avignon, after which he conducted the London Opera Festival (1929–30) where his edition of Locke and Gibbons's *Cupid and Death* was performed in 1929.

Westrup was a music critic of the *Daily Telegraph* (1934–9), during which time his book on Purcell (London: Dent, 1937) was published. He taught at the

ROYAL ACADEMY OF MUSIC in London before becoming lecturer in music at King's College, Newcastle upon Tyne (1941-4) and then Peyton and Barber professor of music at the University of Birmingham (1944-7). Finally, he was appointed to Wadham College, Oxford (1947-71) as Heather professor. In 1950 he helped design a new honours syllabus for music emphasising the application of historical method, a philosophy outlined in his *An Introduction to Musical History* (London: Hutchinson, 1955).

Active in many key musicological areas, Westrup became chairman of the editorial board of the *New Oxford History of Music* in 1947, editor of *Music & Letters* in 1959 and chairman of the Purcell Society from 1957. His research embraced many subjects, including the performance of late Medieval music, but the majority of his writings and musical EDITIONS focus on opera and English music from the seventeenth to nineteenth centuries. Anglo-centric interests led to work with *Musica Britannica*, of which he was a co-founder and trustee. This collection was designed to appeal to both scholars and performers and neatly demonstrates Westrup's commitment to performance underpinned by strong scholarship. In 1966 he was one of the first advisers to *Répertoire International de Littérature Musicale* (RILM).

FURTHER READING

F. W. Sternfield and M. Marx-Weber, 'Sir Jack Westrup (1904-1975)', *Die Musikforschung*, 29/2 (1976), 129-30.

F. W. Sternfield, N. Fortune and E. Olleson (eds.), *Essays on Opera and English Music in Honour of Sir Jack Westrup* (Oxford University Press, 1975), Preface, ix-x.

EDWARD BREEN

Williams, Peter (Frederic) (b. Wolverhampton, 14 May 1937; d. Cheltenham, 20 March 2016) English musicologist, harpsichordist and organist.

Williams was an internationally renowned scholar in historical performance, informed by his skills as an organist and harpsichordist. Formative influences were studies with THURSTON DART (Cambridge) and GUSTAV LEONHARDT (Amsterdam). As professor and first director of the Russell collection of harpsichords at the University of Edinburgh, it was first-hand experience of performing on historical HARPSICHORDS and ORGANS (particularly organs by GOTTFRIED SILBERMANN) that inspired his writings. His first major publication, *The European Organ, 1450-1850* (London: Batsford, 1966), described the major European organ-building traditions that were little known in England at the time. Performing as harpsichordist in concerts at St Cecilia's Hall led him to write *Figured Bass Accompaniment* (Edinburgh University Press, 1970), and the installation of the Ahrend organ in the Reid Concert Hall was a catalyst for *The Organ Music of J. S. Bach* (Cambridge University Press, 1980 and 1984, 3 vols.; later revised in 2003). Further books include: *A New History of the Organ* (Bloomington, IN and London: Indiana University Press, 1980); *Bach: The Goldberg Variations* (Cambridge University Press, 2001); *The Organ in Western Culture 750-1250* (Cambridge University Press, 1993); *The Chromatic Fourth During Four Centuries of Music* (Oxford: Clarendon Press, 1998); *J. S. Bach: A Life in Music* (Cambridge University Press, 2007); and *The King of Instruments* (London: S. P. C. K., 2012). His mission to elevate organology and performance practice to new critical levels is enshrined in *The Organ Yearbook*, the annual journal that he edited from its inception in 1970. His EDITIONS, for example of Handel's keyboard music (Wiener Urtext), are full of information concerning sources and performance practice considerations that inspire enthusiastic engagement. Following Edinburgh, he was appointed arts and sciences distinguished professor at Duke University, North Carolina, and later John Bird professor at Cardiff University.

Williams's writings on both organological and performance practice issues were all based on historical sources, and characterised by intellectual precision and literary conciseness. In reaction to 'posivitist' musicology, he analysed and deconstructed historical sources, which led more to the framing of questions rather than the defining of answers regarding authenticity, chronology, context, style and performance practices. As a teacher, his breadth of knowledge and wealth of stimulating ideas, combined with constructive criticism, made him extremely effective in developing the skills of the next generation of scholars and performers.

FURTHER READING

D. Ponsford and A. Thomson, 'In memoriam Peter Williams', *MT*, 157/1935 (Summer 2016), 4–7.
P. Williams, 'Organs and organ music: one BIOS member's involvement', *Journal of the British Institute of Organ Studies*, 40 (2016), 10–26.

DAVID PONSFORD

Willman, Thomas Lindsay (b. London, 1784; d. London, 28 November 1840) English clarinettist, basset horn player and teacher.

Thomas Willman was the idol of the British public during the first half of the nineteenth century. Following his benefit concert in 1836 the *Musical World* recorded: 'Mr. Willman's tone, execution, feeling and expression were perfectly satisfactory. We never expect to hear them surpassed – and we can very contentedly wait for that event. His power too in sustaining his breath is very extraordinary.' Two years later Willman's London premiere of MOZART's Clarinet Concerto was described in the same journal as a novelty '*said to be the composition of Mozart* ... We look with great suspicion on those novelties from the pens of older composers long deceased.' The reviewer remarked that there was nothing in the concerto which internally stamped it as the production of Mozart, except for the *Andante*: 'The first movement is "the music of the peruke"; in its terse and sententious phrases we discover the wig-tailed *maestro* of the last century; but there is nothing which [Mozart's publisher] André could not have written himself ... The *finale* of the present concerto is decidedly vulgar, and ... affords evident traces of haste and inexperience.' Reflecting the vagaries of Mozart reception in the nineteenth century, Oscar Street noted in 1916 that the concerto had not been played at a Philharmonic concert in London since the 1838 premiere. Willman's fifty-page *A Complete Instruction Book for the Clarinet* (London: Goulding D'Almaine & Co., 1826) assumes an embouchure with reed against the top lip and ARTICULATION with the tongue rather than chest or throat. Placing considerable emphasis on the correct way to hold the instrument, Willman proposes a distance of 9.5 inches between bell and the player's body, adding 'The beginner should avoid any contortion of the Head or Features, a graceful attitude of body and a natural expression of the Countenance being essentially requisite to constitute a good performer' (see the lithograph illustrations reproduced in Lawson (ed.), 141–2).

FURTHER READING

T. E. Hoeprich, *The Clarinet* (New Haven and London: Yale University Press, 2008).
C. Lawson (ed.), *The Cambridge Companion to the Clarinet* (Cambridge University Press, 1995).

COLIN LAWSON

Woldemar, Michel (bap. Orléans, 21 September 1750; d. Clermont-Ferrand, 19 December 1815) French violinist, composer and teacher.

Woldemar described himself as 'a pupil of Lolli'; he certainly shared some of Lolli's eccentricities and virtuoso proclivities. His *Grande méthode, ou Etude élémentaire pour le violon* (Paris, c1800) is scarcely an 'elementary study'; it soon demands an advanced technique. Notable for its information about the history of the BOW, HARMONICS, its exhaustive study of scales and its extensive musical content, it considers various violinists' playing styles, showcases the *couler à Mestrino* (a glissando using one finger) and concludes with a collection of challenging exercises, studies, *Le nouvel art de l'archet* (variations on a polonaise, incorporating varied bowings), three *fugues en caprices*, another polonaise with variations, CADENZAS in various keys and examples of varying degrees of melodic elaboration. Woldemar's focus on BOWING, scales, double stopping and ORNAMENTATION is followed up in publications such as his *Etude élémentaire de l'archet moderne* (1802), *Le nouveau Labyrinthe harmonique*, Op. 10 (c1800), and his *Six caprices ou points d'orgue* (c1804).

Woldemar also published 'EDITIONS' of the VIOLIN TREATISES by LEOPOLD MOZART and RODE, BAILLOT and KREUTZER. His version of Leopold Mozart's work (1801) is much abridged and reflects considerable technical change since the mid-eighteenth century, particularly regarding the violin hold and FINGERING and bowing principles. Concluding with various caprices, its musical and textual revisions totally transform the presentation and content of Mozart's original.

Woldemar's *Méthode d'alto* (Paris, c1800) is a strange, unsystematic study of musical rudiments, scales, artificial and natural harmonics, and varied bowings, concluding with duets for VIOLA and violin. His other compositions include caprices, variations, sonatas, duos, three violin concertos, and a concerto (1787) for a five-stringed 'violon-alto' (tuned c–g–d′–a′–e″) similar to an instrument also cultivated by HERRANDO. Among his curiosities are his four *Sonates fantômagiques*, which imitate the styles of Lolli, Mestrino, Pugnani and TARTINI, his parody of the Ten Commandments (*Les Commandemens du violon*) and his 'Tableau mélo-tachygraphique' system of musical stenography. Controversial opinions expressed in his published letters and articles confirm his idiosyncratic character.

FURTHER READING

F. Hellouin, 'La sténographie musicale', *Feuillets d'histoire musicale française*, 1st ser. (1903), 155–67.

N. K. Nunamaker, 'The virtuoso violin concerto before Paganini: the concertos of Lolli, Giornovichi, and Woldemar', PhD dissertation, Indiana University (1968).

R. E. Seletsky, '18th-century variations for Corelli's Sonatas, op. 5', *EMc*, 24/1 (1996), 119–32.

ROBIN STOWELL

Woodhouse, Violet Gordon *see* GORDON WOODHOUSE, VIOLET

World Music: Historical Dimensions Ethnomusicology has encouraged an understanding of world music – that is to say, all music – as a process of human social behaviour, a complex process that frequently transcends such familiar dichotomies as text and performance, composition and IMPROVISATION, individual and group creativity, written and oral transmission. It is consequently challenging to rethink the notion of 'historical performance' in a global context, implying as it does some disjunction between a 'work' and its performance, between the present and an unspecified past. Most music in the world is not written. It may be more or less memorised, more or less improvised, more or less susceptible to change at every performance, more or less dependent on individual initiative, oral instruction or group interaction. Its pasts may be captured in sound recordings, documented in written records or archaeological artefacts, known through ORAL TRADITION, or distant beyond recall. Where tangible evidence for music history exists, it portrays both continuity and change, though ideology may emphasise one at the expense of the other. The only safe generalisation is that performance of music is constantly in dialogue with the past, however that dialogue is conducted or conceived.

For the sake of clarity we might wish to confine the notion of 'historical performance' to repertories where documentary evidence allows scope for the reconstruction of pre-modern repertories, styles of performance, instruments or ensembles. In principle this is possible for some of the historical repertories of Asia, where NOTATIONS, historical documentation of performance practice, ICONOGRAPHY and instruments survive from pre-modern periods. Across Asia, prestigious musical repertories have been recorded in indigenous notation systems, either through the influence of Western music, as in the case of Turkish, Iranian and Central Asian art-musics, or independently of Western models, as in the traditional tablature notations of Chinese, Korean and Japanese court musics, the graphic neumes of Tibetan and Japanese Buddhist chant, or the syllabic oral notations of South Asia. The realisation of such notations depends on knowledge of performance style that is learned implicitly through acculturation, or explicitly through oral instruction, and may be embellished with interpretative or improvisatory variation and expansion. For example, the Chinese seven-stringed long zither *qin* has a repertory notated in TABLATURE dating from the third century onwards; the notation explicitly determines playing techniques, sonorities and ornamental detail as well as PITCH, but is indeterminate as to rhythm, with the result that learning any piece requires a teacher's instruction and example. Compositions of Indian classical vocal music have been collected in didactic anthologies with notation, but performers learn them through oral transmission, often without reference to written versions, and render them with unwritten ornamentation and with extensive improvisatory expansion based on the underlying mode and metre. Notations can be taken as a guide to musical content but not to performance style.

The pace of change is often assumed, rightly or wrongly, to be slower in Eastern than in Western cultures, and traditional music is often believed to be 'ancient', in which case its performance style might be thought of as intrinsically 'historical'. The north Indian vocal tradition of *dhrupad* is popularly associated with the oldest traditions of Hindu religion; while such remote ancestry would be hard to document, some features of the genre can be recognised in theoretical texts from as far back as the thirteenth century, and in descriptions of performance at the seventeenth-century Mughal court. Documentary evidence shows that the *Gagaku* repertoire of Japan, performed at the Imperial Court and in temples today, was transmitted from the courts of Tang China, Korea and Central Asia in the seventh to ninth centuries AD, and is believed to be performed 'unchanged for a thousand years' by the current bearers of the tradition. Notated records of Korean court and ritual music survive from the fifteenth century onwards, and parts of the historic repertory survive in performance today. Compositions notated in the seventeenth to nineteenth centuries by musicians at the Ottoman court are still performed in the Turkish classical tradition. National ideologies sometimes encourage the reconstruction of historic practices, instruments or repertories, and typically resist the notion that ancient musical traditions may have changed over time. Apparently common to several such ideologies is the belief that 'old', prestigious music is necessarily slower in TEMPO than 'new'.

Evidence for continuity in some aspects of music, however, has to be balanced with evidence for change in others. Music that has apparently survived over long periods of time has usually undergone not only gradual change but also interruption, expansion, contraction, re-organisation, standardisation or reconstruction at particular historical junctures, whether in response to political events, social requirements, or artistic preferences. In contradiction to the nationalistic myth of continuity over millennia, some scholars have suggested that Indian classical music in general was 'invented', that is, standardised, only in the nineteenth and early twentieth centuries, as a response to colonialism and modernisation; but others have argued that such processes had already occurred at the Mughal court in the seventeenth century, and at other places and times throughout history. Similarly conscious processes of reconstruction, appealing to ancient texts and temple sculptures rather than to hereditary exponents, underlie the 'classical' traditions of Indian dance, especially Bharatanāṭyam and Oḍissī. In Japan, lively entertainment music from the Tang Court of China (seventh to ninth centuries) was transformed into august ceremonial music (*Gagaku*); further transformations of this tradition included loss of repertory during the civil wars of the fifteenth and sixteenth centuries, and reconstruction of performance in the late nineteenth century, as an emblem of nationalism under the newly restored Meiji dynasty. Occasional attempts to reconstruct instruments, pieces and performance styles of the Nara and Heian periods, and the view of some scholars that this music would originally have been played (and danced) much faster than today, contrast with the 'traditional', largely nineteenth-century performance style, in very slow tempi, associated with the Imperial Court.

Further examples abound of historically rooted traditions where the relationship between contemporary and historical performance styles is contested, uncertain, or unknowable. That does not necessarily prevent explicit attempts to revive or reconstruct instruments, repertories and performance styles of the pre-recording era. Such attempts may reflect evolving geo-political perspectives. In parts of the Middle East, where the use of large ensembles including Western instruments became prevalent during the twentieth century, there is now a post-colonial trend towards smaller ensembles, using indigenous instruments only, and hence a more historically 'authentic' sound. The revival of Central Asian *makam* repertories can be linked to the emergence of post-Soviet national identities in search of historical roots and artistic EXPRESSION. In Iran, a conscious, modernising standardisation of the classical music repertoire (*radif*) in the mid-twentieth century is challenged through exploration of earlier performance styles, and creative experimentation with modes and rhythmic cycles defined in Medieval music-theory texts. In Turkey, performers of the Ottoman classical repertory increasingly turn to seventeenth-, eighteenth- and nineteenth-century notated collections. Having suffered nationalist disapproval in twentieth-century Turkey, Ottoman musical culture (like that of the Chinese Tang dynasty) is now seen as a cosmopolitan heritage, with compositions by musicians of Turkish, Greek, Armenian, Jewish, European and other ethnic origins, some of which now feature on recordings by Turkish and European 'early music' ensembles. This trend reflects the growing awareness of a rich trans-national musical culture circulating throughout the eastern Mediterranean in the nineteenth century and earlier.

Meanwhile, groups such as Fong Naam in Thailand and Reigakusha in Japan combine historical reconstructions and new compositions in their programmes; the Silk Road Ensemble's pipa player Wu Man breathes new life into melodies transcribed from Medieval Japanese scores; and in Mali, Bassekou Kouyate's group Ngoniba – modelled on the pre-colonial ensemble of the Bamana Segu empire (1712–1867) – secured a Grammy nomination for exploring old repertories and possible connections with the roots of the blues. Creative engagement with the past, sustained by whatever ideals and ideologies, remains a meaningful and richly variable facet of the global human social behaviour that we call music.

FURTHER READING

J. Bor, F. Delvoye, J. Harvey and E. te Nijenhuis (eds.), *Hindustani Music: Thirteenth to Twentieth Centuries* (New Delhi: Manohar, 2010).
M. Church (ed.), *The Other Classical Musics: Fifteen Great Traditions* (Woodbridge: Boydell & Brewer, 2015).
J. McCollum and D. G. Hebert (eds.), *Theory and Method in Historical Ethnomusicology* (Lanham, MD: Rowman and Littlefield/Lexington Books, 2014).
R. Sanyal and R. Widdess, *Dhrupad: Tradition and Performance in Indian Music* (Aldershot: Ashgate, 2004).
A. M. Tokita and D. W. Hughes (eds.), *The Ashgate Research Companion to Japanese Music* (Aldershot: Ashgate, 2008).
R. Widdess, 'Historical ethnomusicology', in H. Myers (ed.), *Ethnomusicology: An Introduction* (London: Macmillan, 1992), 219–42.

RICHARD WIDDESS

XYZ

Zabern, Conrad von (b. c1405; d. c1481) Probably the priest Conradus Zabern, who taught at the University of Heidelberg and published *De modo bene cantandi* in 1474, the earliest known set of SINGING directions intended for church choir.

Zabern's stated motivation was from observation of 'rustic' singing practices in the area from Frankfurt to Koblenz and Trier (i.e. western Germany). He instructs choir members to enter in unison; blend the voices; observe rhythmic values accurately and uniformly; and not to add notes or harmonies to the melody. He stresses the need for a cultivated vocal delivery which he contrasts with undesirable 'rustic' practices such as adding consonant sounds for the purpose of ARTICULATION during a melisma; extreme nasal sound; inattention to pure vowel sounds; wavering PITCH on long notes; continuous VIBRATO; forced vocal sound; bellowing on high notes and singing faintly on low notes; and making elaborate facial and body gestures.

FURTHER READING

J. Dyer, 'Singing with proper refinement from *De modo bene cantandi* (1474) by Conrad von Zabern', *EMc*, 6/2 (1978), 207–29.

K. W. Gümpel, *Die Musiktraktate Conrads von Zabern* (Mainz: Verlag der Akademie der Wissenschaften und der Literatur, 1956).

TIMOTHY J. MCGEE

Zacconi, Lodovico (b. Pesaro, 11 June 1555; d. Fiorenzuola di Focara, nr Pesaro, 23 March 1627) Italian singer and theorist.

Based on his own experience as a professional choral singer, including under Lassus in Munich, the first volume of Zacconi's encyclopedic *Prattica di musica* (1592) is a huge compendium of both technical and cultural information about SINGING style in the late Renaissance that repays close study. While it contains extensive discussion of *gorgie* (improvised embellishments made in the throat), including short, passing-note *accenti* and *passaggi* (divisions of the note), with many pages of examples of ways of 'breaking' standard intervals that are not dissimilar to those in the TREATISES by his contemporaries, such as BOVICELLI and DALLA CASA, Zacconi also gives considerable additional information about just how to execute them in practice. He explains, for example, how to develop throat ARTICULATION, working up from 'the tremolo, that is, the trembling voice, [which] is the true door for entering into the *passaggi* and for mastering the *gorgie*, because a ship sails more easily once it is already in motion' (1592, I, 60^r), but advises against showing off in company before having mastered the style (I, 59^r). There are extensive chapters, too, on such matters as who should and should not practise singing (not women, 'because they must be accompanied and mixed with young boys and men' – Zacconi was a priest) (I, 54^r); and the social and acoustical differences between church and chamber singing ('many learn to sing by singing softly and in chambers, where loud singing is abhorred, and here sing those gentlemen and others who are not forced by necessity to sing in the churches and in the chapels where hired singers sing') (I, 52^v).

FURTHER READING

H. M. Brown, *Embellishing 16th-Century Music* (Oxford University Press, 1976).
L. Zacconi, *The Practice of Singing. Book I Chapters LVIII–LXX* [1592], trans. in E. Foreman (ed.), *Late Renaissance Singing* (Minneapolis, MN: Pro Music Press, 2001).

RICHARD WISTREICH

Zanetti (Zannetti), Gasparo (*fl* Milan, 1626–45) Italian music editor and violinist.

Zanetti uses VIOLIN TABLATURE in tandem with staff notation in his *Il scolaro ... per imparar a suonare di violino, et altri stromenti* (Milan, 1645), a collection of anonymous DANCES in four parts (mostly violin, two VIOLAS and CELLO) designed for violin students. Each dance is accompanied by an INTABULATION, which prescribes FINGERINGS (all in first position and with the extended fourth finger indicated by the figure '5') and BOWINGS and provides clues as to the tuning/PITCH of the open strings of the various string instruments employed (the cello, for example, uses the 'Italian' tuning B$\flat'$–F–c–g). Following FRANCESCO ROGNONI's lead (*Selva di varii passaggi* (Milan, 1620)), Zanetti uses the letter 'P' for an up-bow ('pontar in sú') and 'T' for a down-bow ('tirare in giù') and subscribes essentially to the ACCENTUATION principles of the rule of the down-bow, whereby strong beats are played with the naturally weighted down-bow.

FURTHER READING

D. D. Boyden, *The History of Violin Playing from its Origins to 1761* (London: Oxford University Press, 1965).

ROBIN STOWELL

Zarlino, Gioseffo (b. Chioggia, ?31 January 1517; d. Venice, 4 February 1590) Italian singer, organist, theorist and composer.

Zarlino studied with Adrian Willaert in Venice, where he became *maestro di cappella* at the cathedral of San Marco in 1565. His reputation in posterity has rested not so much on his accomplishments as a performer or composer, though both were considerable, as on his writings about music, particularly his *Le istitutioni harmoniche* (Venice: the author, 1558). Much of this work discusses music from a theoretical or compositional perspective, but of particular interest to performers are the comments he makes in the second part about tuning.

In chapters 40–4 of *Le istitutioni*, Zarlino gives the first numerically precise definitions of meantone TEMPERAMENT and its application to keyboard instruments, though it is questionable whether the systems he advocates, most famously his 2/7-comma meantone, were ever practical and they are rarely used today. Zarlino follows this discussion with a chapter on vocal INTONATION where he is emphatic that unaccompanied singers follow the 'true form' (i.e. just intonation) of intervals rather than any kind of temperament, again a problematic assertion but one that recognises the practical difficulties that arise when singers are accompanied by a keyboard.

In chapter 47 Zarlino illustrates a keyboard with nineteen notes to the octave rather than the usual twelve. He asserts that this instrument was actually built for him in 1548, by Domenico Pesarese; although it has not survived, it was described as late as 1773. This connects Zarlino with the vigorous Renaissance microtonal performing tradition most commonly associated with Nicola Vicentino. He is also an early witness to a diversity of performing traditions other than his own, such as monophonic music in Crete and Cyprus or the unconventional (by his standards) Greek polyphony that he heard in Venice.

FURTHER READING

A. Moyer, *Musica Scientia: Musical Scholarship in the Italian Renaissance* (Ithaca, NY: Cornell University Press, 1992).

JON BANKS

Zaslaw, Neal (b. New York, 28 June 1939) American musicologist.

After graduating from Harvard and Juilliard, Zaslaw played the FLUTE in the American Symphony Orchestra under Stokowski (1962–5). During postgraduate study at Columbia University (MA, 1965; PhD, 1970) he was editor-in-chief of *Current Musicology* (1967–70) and taught at the City College of CUNY (1968–70). In 1970 he joined the faculty at Cornell University, where he became Herbert Gussman professor of music in 1995. He was also a member of the graduate faculty at Juilliard (1988–91), served as book reviews editor for *Notes* (1971–5) and was musicological adviser and scholar-in-residence for Lincoln Center's celebration of the Mozart bicentennial.

The first of his many contributions to the study of historical performance was *Performance Practice: A Bibliography* (New York: W.W. Norton, 1971), with Mary Vinquist. His interest in early orchestral practices led to the groundbreaking studies 'Toward the revival of the classical orchestra' (*PRMA*, 103 (1976–7), 158–87) and 'The compleat orchestral musician' (*EMc*, 7/1 (1979), 46–57; 8/1 (1980), 71–2), and to his position as 'musicological supervisor' to a recording of the complete MOZART symphonies by the ACADEMY OF ANCIENT MUSIC under CHRISTOPHER HOGWOOD and JAAP SCHRÖDER (1978–82). Subsequent studies include: 'Improvised ornamentation in eighteenth-century orchestras', with John Spitzer (*JAMS*, 39/3 (1986), 524–77), 'Lully's orchestra' (*Jean-Baptiste Lully: Actes du colloque/Kongressbericht*, Laaber: Laaber Verlag, 1990, 539–79) and 'The origins of the classical orchestra' (*BJhM*, 17 (1994), 9–40) and two widely praised books: *Mozart's Symphonies: Context, Performance Practice, Reception* (Oxford: Clarendon Press, 1989) and (with John Spitzer) *The Birth of the Orchestra: History of an Institution, 1650–1815* (Oxford University Press, 2004). Especially influential among his writings on other performance-related issues is 'Ornaments for Corelli's violin sonatas' (*EMc*, 24/1 (1996), 95–115) and a sequel study, '"Curling graces" and "vermin": problems with the ornaments for Corelli's op. 5' (*BJhM*, 37 (2013), 179–92).

FURTHER READING

J. Spitzer, 'Musicology and performance: a conversation with Neal Zaslaw', in C. Eisen (ed.), *Coll'astuzia, col giudizio: Essays in Honor of Neal Zaslaw* (Ann Arbor: Steglein, 2009), 428–43.

STEVEN ZOHN

Zenobi, Luigi (b. Ancona, 1547/8; d. Naples, after 1602) Italian musician.
 Known as the 'Cavaliere del Cornetto', Zenobi was a virtuoso who worked at various major musical centres in the later sixteenth century, including Ferrara and the Imperial court in Vienna. In a letter *c*1600 to an unidentified prince describing the ideal musical establishment, he provided unprecedented information about the qualities and practical skills required of each of its members. The music director must be able to lead 'mediocre singers in difficult music' and be a 'true musician', capable of creating and leading spontaneous composition of counterpoint, both simple and 'artful'. He needs a good ear to anticipate if a singer is about to fall off, and have a 'voice that ranges from high to low' so he can jump in to rescue any of the parts. Rank-and-file singers of the four vocal parts (all male) must be able to perform any written music at sight, however syncopated or dissonant, including quavers and semiquavers, difficult leaps, and complex time signatures and proportions. Basses should have a range of twenty-two notes (three octaves!) with full and even tone; tenors and altos should only embellish sparingly in ensembles, but may do more when performing solo. The most space by far is devoted to sopranos – 'truly the ornament of all the other parts' – who have 'the obligation and complete freedom to improvise diminutions, to indulge in playfulness, and, in a word, to ornament a musical body' (Blackburn and Lowinsky, 100). Players of foundation instruments 'such as the harpsichord, lute, harp, theorbo, cittern, and Spanish guitar or vihuela' must 'show taste and skill when playing in ensemble or accompanying a solo singer' (105). Zenobi distinguishes between ideal court musicians and mere 'singers', above all on account of their refined sensibilities, declaring that 'true musicians are those who bring the harmony of their manners into perfect accord with the harmony of their music' (105).

FURTHER READING

B. Blackburn and E. Lowinsky, 'Luigi Zenobi and his letter on the perfect musician', *Studi musicali*, 22 (1993), 61–114.

RICHARD WISTREICH

Zwolle, Henri Arnaut de (b. Zwolle, late fourteenth or early fifteenth century; d. Paris, 6 September 1466) Franco-Flemish physician, astrologer, astronomer and author of a TREATISE on musical instruments.
 A few autograph folios in manuscript F-Pn 7295 bear witness to Zwolle's accomplishments in the field of organology. The folios contain drawings and many technical details for constructing the LUTE and several keyboard instruments (the HARPSICHORD, the CLAVICHORD and the *dulce melos*, a kind of 'keyed dulcimer'). Because Zwolle appears to describe standard organological practices of the time, his manuscript is an invaluable source of information about fifteenth-century instruments. Zwolle may also have introduced a

transposed version of Pythagorean tuning that soon became common, one that positioned the pure major thirds on the 'right' steps of the gamut (such as D–F♯, A–C♯ and E–G♯), i.e. those that were commonly altered in the compositional practice of the time (*see* TEMPERAMENT).

FURTHER READING

E. Bowles, 'On the origin of the keyboard mechanism in the Late Middle Ages', in T. McGee (ed.), *Instruments and their Music in the Middle Ages* (Farnham: Ashgate, 2009), 87–104.

G. Le Cerf and E.-R. Labande (eds.), *Instruments de musique du XVe siècle: les traités d'Henri-Arnaut de Zwolle et de divers anonymes* (Paris, 1932; repr. Kassel: Bärenreiter, 1972).

STEFANO MENGOZZI

Index

Aaron, Pietro, 1, 106, 425, 580
Abbado, Claudio, 194
Abel, Carl Friedrich, 1, 310, 648, 661
Abraham, Gerald, 95
Academy of Ancient Music (18th C), 2, 142, 188, 194, 293, 304, 306, 476, 512
Academy of Ancient Music (20th C), 2, 192, 308, 347, 368, 398, 454–5, 562, 568, 588, 698
Academy of St Martin in the Fields, 191
Academy of Vocal Musick, 2
Accademia Bizantina, 193
Accademia Monteverdiana, 3, 82
Accent, 4
  see also Accentuation
Accentuation, 73, 129, 212, 264, 292, 301, 339, 371, 395, 416, 423, 531, 590, 610–11, 639, 650, 697
Accordion, 42, 51, 496
Adam, Louis, 7, 343, 471, 625
Adams, John
  Dharma at Big Sur, The, 669
Adams, Nathan, 312
Adderley, Cannonball, 336
Addison, Joseph, 602
Adler, Frédérique Guillaume, 68
Adler, Guido, 7
Adlung, Jakob, 8, 137, 626
Adorno, Theodor W., 8, 12, 352
  Aesthetic Theory, 8
  Negative Dialectics, 8
  Philosophy of New Music, 8
Aesthetics, 9, 102, 249, 326, 351, 373, 517, 520, 546, 576, 590, 592, 599, 606, 625, 680, 684
  identity and definition, 10
  interpretation and value, 13
  musical meanings, 11
  performing arts and, 9
Affect/Affekt, 264, 657
  see also Affections/*Affektenlehre*
Affections/*Affektenlehre*, 14, 44, 56, 226, 255, 297, 324, 536
Agazzari, Agostino, 17, 62, 284, 625
Agnew, Paul, 366, 612
Agnew, Vanessa, 101
Agricola, Alexander, 619
Agricola, Johann Friedrich, 8, 17, 30, 107, 301, 580, 621

Agricola, Martin, 18, 118, 241, 598, 627, 650, 655
  Musica instrumentalis deudsch, 19, 31, 448, 627
Aguado, Dionisio, 276
Agutter, Ralph, 598
Ahle, Johann Georg, 227
Ahle, Johann Rudolph, 91
Aichinger, Gregor, 253
Akademie für Alte Musik Berlin, 193
Akademische Bande, 249
Al Ayre Español, 193
Alamire, 197
Alard, Benjamin, 361
Alard, Delphin, 19, 114, 171, 279, 653, 672
Alarius Ensemble, 355
Alberghi, Paolo, 112
Albert, Eugène d', 20
Alberti bass, 28
Albinoni, Tomaso, 520, 668
Albrecht, Johann Lorenz, 8
Albrechtsberger, Johann Georg, 20, 127, 341, 343, 414, 443
Aldeburgh Festival, 94–5, 649
Aldrich, Putnam, 199
Alessandrini, Rinaldo, 193
Alexander, James, 656
Alexandre *père et fils*
  orgue-mélodium, 74
Alexanian, Diran, 94, 115, 122, 237, 272, 655
Alfonso I, Duke of Ferrara, 241
Allegri, Gregorio
  Miserere, 389
Allen, J. H.
  The Technique of Modern Singing, 658
Almenräder, Carl, 68, 502, 626
'Almenraeder u Heckel', 68
Alsop, Marin, 455
Alsted, Johann Heinrich, 617
Alta Villa, Count of, 382
Alte Musik, 185
Altenburg, Johann Caspar, 21
Altenburg, Johann Ernst, 21
  Versuch, 79, 475, 626, 634
Altès, Joseph Henry, 22
Alvars, Elias Parish, 286
Amati, Andrea, 119
Amati family, 664
Ambros, August Wilhelm, 158

INDEX

Ambrosian Singers, 3
American Bach Soloists, 195
American Recorder Society, 194
Amherst Early Music Festival, 195
Ammerbach, Elias Nikolaus, 22, 228
Amon, Johann Andreas, 666
Amsterdam Baroque Choir, 353
Amsterdam Baroque Orchestra, 192, 352–3
Anderson, Kinloch, 3
André, Maurice, 421, 636
Andriessen, Louis
    Sweet, 528
Andrijeski, Julie, 197–8
Anet, Jean-Jacques-Baptiste, 65
Anonymous IV, 198, 331
Ansani, Giovanni, 259
Ansermet, Ernest, 170
Antegnati, Costanzo, 64, 458
Antegnati, Gian Giacomo, 458
Antonini, Giovanni, 193
Apel, Willi, 478
Apollo's Fire, 197
Applause, 23, 683
Arakaendar Bolivia Choir, 240
Arban, Jean-Baptiste, 25, 626
Arbeau, Thoinot, 25, 163, 410
Arcadelt, Jacques
    'O felici occhi miei', 467
Arcas, Julián, 276
Archer, Kenneth, 590
Archlute, 64, 397
Arezzo, Guido d', 26, 465, 523, 644
    'Ut queant laxis', 26
Argyll Rooms, London, 648
Ariosti, Attilio, 131, 302
Aristotle, 9, 382, 534–5, 627
    De Anima, 9
Aristoxenus (of Tarentum), 255
Arlt, Wulf, 567
Arne, Thomas, 3, 101, 131
    Sonata No. 4 in D minor (keyboard), 545
Arnulf of St Ghislain, 27
Arpeggiando, 27, 114, 231, 280, 416, 583
Arpeggio, 27
Ars antiqua, 676
Ars nova, 514, 611, 676
Ars Rediviva, 191, 421
Ars subtilior, 514, 644
Arte dei Suonatori, 193
Articulation, 27–8, 41–2, 44, 46, 72–3, 75, 77, 84, 95, 100, 102, 129, 149, 152, 160, 173–4, 206, 214–16, 219, 222, 228, 242, 246, 248, 258, 263, 269, 281, 286, 316, 351, 353, 363, 365, 370, 385–6, 393, 399, 419, 423, 430, 436, 438, 467, 471, 492, 507, 522, 531, 561–2, 578, 583, 590, 594, 607, 632, 634, 639, 646, 678, 684, 686, 691, 696
Artôt, Alexandre, 130
Artusi, Giovanni Maria, 33–4
Aruspix, 201

Asioli, Bonifacio, 305, 341
Asociación pro Arte y Cultura, 240
Asplmayr, Franz, 131
Associated Board of the Royal Schools of Music, 554
Aston Magna Foundation, 195, 198
Astorga, Emmanuele d', 614
Attaingnant, Pierre, 137, 163, 375
Auber, Daniel, 25, 564
    La muette de Portici, 36
Audiences, 34, 312, 367, 403, 423, 476, 510, 530, 581, 679
Auer, Leopold von, 36, 272, 339, 430, 654, 672
    Graded Course of Violin Playing, 37
    My Long Life in Music, 38
    on 'rhythmic' vs 'antirhythmic' (off-beat shifting) fingering, 235
    Violin Masterworks and their Interpretation, 37
    Violin Playing as I Teach it, 37
Aurelian of Réôme, 38
    Musica disciplina, 38
Aurora Orchestra, 403
Austrian Radio, 96
Authenticity, 8, 38, 172, 335, 365, 689
Autograph scores, 388
Aveling, Valda, 268
Avison, Charles, 40, 263, 626
Ax, Emanuel, 24
Axelrod, Herbert and Evelyn, 196
Azéma, Anne, 196

Babbitt, Milton, 438
Babitz, Sol, 235
Bach, Anna Magdalena, 63
Bach, Carl Philipp Emanuel, 43, 47, 63, 91, 137, 217, 245, 326, 349, 395, 453, 562, 575, 603, 605
    on articulation, 32
    on the clavichord, 138
    fantasies, 246
    on fingering, 44, 230
    on keyboard leadership, 143
    keyboard sonatas, 322, 545
    Sonaten mit veränderten Reprisen Wq50, 322, 327
    Versuch, 29, 43–5, 160, 286, 322, 324, 370, 430, 625, 639
    on written-out embellishments, 533
Bach, Johann Christian, 43, 68
    collaboration with Abel, 1
Bach, Johann Ludwig, 131
Bach, Johann Nicolaus, 432, 434
Bach, Johann Sebastian, 45, 189, 208, 247, 252, 281, 302, 349, 364, 430, 535, 562, 565, 575, 684
    Art of Fugue, The, BWV1080, 268, 294, 393, 541
    on articulation, 33
    Brandenburg Concertos, BWV1046–51, xiv, 115, 141, 167, 307, 421, 423, 689

INDEX

No. 1 in F major, BWV1046, 180
No. 2 in F major, BWV1047, 527, 634–5
No. 4 in G major, BWV1049, 527
No. 5, in D major BWV1050, 108, 541
cadenzas, 108
Cantatas, 67, 95, 547
  Christ lag in Todesbanden, BWV4, 96
  Gott fähret auf mit Jauchzen, BWV43, 217
  Es ist genug, BWV60, 91
  Herr Christ, der einige Gottesohn, BWV96, 667
  Nach dir, Herr, verlanget mich, BWV150, 92
  Wachet auf, BWV140, 667
Cello Suites, BWV1007–12, 103, 115, 122, 179, 283, 323, 355, 403
  No. 5 in C minor, BWV1011, 120, 571
  No. 6 in D major, BWV1012, 119
chorus size, 319
Chromatic Fantasia and Fugue, BWV903, 91, 303
on the clavichord, 138
Clavier-Übung, 322
continuo playing, 63
Eichentopf and, 208
English Suites, BWV806–11
  No. 2 in A minor, BWV807, 322
  No. 3 in G minor, BWV808, 322
fingering in, 29, 230
French Suites, BWV812–17, 309
  No. 1 in D minor, BWV812, 543
  No. 4 in E flat major, BWV815, 541
Goldberg Variations, BWV988, 268, 303, 348, 360, 541
on improvisation, 46
keyboard suites, allemandes in, 163
Klavierbüchlein für Wilhelm Friedemann Bach, 47, 322
  Applicatio, BWV994, 322
  Explicatio, 166
Mass in B minor, BWV232, 189, 194, 215, 298, 547, 614, 635, 647
Musical Offering, The, BWV1079, 421
natural trumpet tuning, 217
notation, 533
Organ Sonata No. 4 in E minor, BWV528, 541
ornament table, 166
Ouvertures (Orchestral Suites), BWV1066–9, 423
Overture in the French Style, BWV831, 542
Partitas, BWV825–30, 543
  No. 1 in B flat major, BWV825, 540
  No. 6 in E minor, BWV830, 540, 541, 543
Sinfonia in E flat major, BWV791, 323
Sonata in G minor for viola da gamba and harpsichord, BWV1029, 183
Sonata in B minor for flute and harpsichord, BWV1030, 64

Sonata in C minor for violin and harpsichord, BWV1017, 541
Sonatas and Partitas for unaccompanied violin, BWV1001–6, 42, 169, 213, 323, 341
  Partita No. 2 in D minor, BWV1004, 302
  Sonata No. 3 in C major, BWV1005, 113
St John Passion, BWV245, 65, 217
St Mark Passion, BWV247, 353
St Matthew Passion, BWV244, 64, 114, 126, 189, 404, 524, 612
transcriptions, 419, 622
trumpet range, 281
Violin Concertos, 614
  Violin Concerto in E major, BWV1042, 108, 622
Well-Tempered Clavier, The, BWV846–93, 44, 102, 161, 208, 268, 303, 323, 360, 417, 442, 536, 605
Bach, Maria Barbara, 302
Bach, Michael (Bachtischa), 43
Bach, Wilhelm Friedemann, 43, 46–7, 91, 322
'Bach' bow, 42, 90
  Vega Bach bow, 42
Bach Choir, 647
Bach Choir of Bethlehem (PA), 194
Bach Collegium Japan, 592
BACH Digital, 200
Bach Ensemble, 547
Bach Gesellschaft, 91, 206, 292, 443
Bach harpsichord, 95
Bach trumpet, 491, 548
Bacilly, Bertrand 'Bénigne' de, 48, 372, 552
Backofen, Johann Georg Heinrich, 48
Badura-Skoda, Eva, 49
Badura-Skoda, Paul, 49, 110, 142
Baermann, Heinrich, 133, 239, 626, 646
Bagby, Benjamin, 197, 572
Bagpipes, 50–1
  Highland bagpipes, 51
Bailleux, Antoine, 672
Baillot, Pierre, 19, 52, 73, 113, 121, 165, 219, 234–6, 278, 341, 354, 368, 394, 430, 471, 504, 510, 549, 626, 653, 670–2, 692
  Études, 570
  L'art du violon, 29, 53, 430, 510, 570, 671
  metronome markings for vibrato, 653
  on *ports de voix* and expressive fingering, 235
  on vibrato, 653
Baines, Anthony, 54, 422
Baird, Julianne, 198
Baker, David, 336
Baker, Theodore, 356
Bakfark, Valentin Bálint, 330
Baldwin Wallace Bach Festival, 194
Baldwyn, John, 515
Ballard, Christophe, 559, 571
Ballestra, Reimundo, 426
Ballet, 163

INDEX

Baltimore Consort, 197
Baltzar, Thomas, 570
Banchetto Musicale, 197
Banchieri, Adriano, 55, 176, 228, 625
Banister, John, I (the elder), 309, 648, 668
Banister, John, II, 309, 598
Banks, Jon, 402
Banzo, Eduardo López, 193
Barbella, Emanuele, 570
Barbirolli, Sir John, 555
Barclay, Robert, xvii
Bardi, Giovanni, 255
Baritone horn, 637
Barlow, Klarenz, 587
Barnes, Eric, 172
Barnes, Harry, 172
Baroni, Leonora, 397
Baroque gesture, 55
Barrel organ, 58
Barrère, Georges, 244
Barrière, Jean-Baptiste, 160
Barto, Robert, 198
Bartók, Béla, 58, 71
   Contrasts, 570
   Eight Hungarian Folksongs, 59
   Five Hungarian Folk Tunes, 59
   Mikrokosmos, 59
   Miraculous Mandarin, 82
   piano playing of, 219
Bartolozzi, Bruno, 133, 245, 447
Baryton, 60
Basbas, Louise, 195
Basevi, Abramo, 266
Basie, Count, 336
Basile, Margherita, 413
Basler Kammerorchester, 191
Bass clarinet, 133, 453
Bass horn, 573, 636
Bassani, Francesco, 520
Bassano, Giovanni, 61, 107, 162, 242, 667
Bassano family, 67, 526
Basset, Jehan, 651
Basset clarinet, 132, 585
Basset horn, 21, 132
Basso continuo, 29, 61, 143, 154, 288, 321, 368
Bassoon, 66, 295
   Eichentopf, 208
   French, 74
   substitutions for, 146, 163
Bass-tuba, 637
Bate, Philip, 54
Bate Collection of Historical Woodwind Instruments, 55
Baton, 144
Bâton, Henri, 316
'Battle of the Organs', 461
Baudiot, Charles, 52, 183, 236–7, 368, 626
Baumann, Hermann, 313
Baumgart, Hans, 42
Baumgarten, Alexander
   Aesthetica, 10

Baumgartner, Johann Baptist, 69, 236
   Fuga for solo cello, 70
Bax, Arnold
   First Symphony, 570
Bayerische Staatsbibliothek, Munich, 199
Bayreuth Festival, 400, 529, 682–3
Bazelaire, Paul, 183
Beard, John, 117
Beatrice of Aragon, 140
Bechet, Sidney, 133, 564
Bechstein Hall, Wigmore Street (London), 649
Beck, Jean, 279
Becker, Hugo, 121, 179, 183, 655
Beckerath, Willy von, 91–2
Beckett, John, 427
Bédier, Henri, 206
Bédos de Celles, François, 216
Beecham, Sir Thomas, 268
Beechey, Gwilym, 544
Beethoven, Ludwig van, 70, 122, 321, 406, 414
   on cadenzas, 109
   Cello Sonatas, 109, 169, 551
      Cello Sonata in G minor, Op. 5 No. 2, 551
   clavichord and, 138
   conducting and, 70
   on Czerny, 160, 402
   Diabelli Variations, Op. 120, 491
   Die Ruinen von Athen, Op. 113, 589
   Fantasy, Op. 77, 326
   Fidelio, Op. 72, 453, 524
   fidelity to notated scores, 533
   Grosse Fuge, Op. 133, 101
   Horn Sonata Op. 17, 98, 311
   legato tone, 230
   Materialien zum Generalbass, 66
   metronome markings, 70, 161, 406, 607
   Missa Solemnis, Op. 123, 66, 456
   Piano Concertos
      No. 2 in B flat major, Op. 19, 490
      No. 3 in C minor, Op. 37, 161, 490
      No. 4 in G major, Op. 58, 141, 490, 492
      No. 5 in E flat major ('Emperor'), Op. 73, 66, 109, 300
   piano pedal indications, 492
   Piano Sonatas, 109, 407
      No. 8 in C minor ('Pathétique'), Op. 13, 607
      No. 9 in E major, Op. 14 No. 1, 545
      No. 14 in C sharp minor, Op. 27 No. 2, 494, 545
      No. 17 in D minor, Op. 31 No. 2, 492
      No. 21 in C major ('Waldstein'), Op. 53, 246, 492–3
      No. 28 in A major, Op. 101, 491, 607
      No. 29 in B♭ major ('Hammerklavier'), Op. 106, 490–1
      No. 31 in A flat major, Op.110, 491
   on piano strings, 489–90

Quintet for piano and wind, Op. 16, 312, 534
  arranged for piano quartet, 622
Septet in E flat major, Op. 20, 6, 133, 141, 607, 615, 623
String Quartets, 340
studies in counterpoint, 443
Symphonies, 306
  No. 3 in E flat major ('Eroica'), 23, 97, 141, 392, 453, 512, 589, 615
  No. 5 in C minor, Op. 67, 146, 453, 512, 589
  No. 6 in F major ('Pastoral'), Op. 68, 403, 512
  No. 7 in A major, Op. 92, 141, 615
  No. 9 in D minor ('Choral'), Op. 125, 11, 126, 144, 185, 389, 453, 615, 648
32 Variations in C minor, WoO80, 534
Trio for clarinet, cello and piano, Op. 38, 622
Triple Concerto in C major, Op. 56, 141
Violin Concerto in D major, Op. 61, 109, 339
Violin Sonatas, 341
  No. 9 in A major ('Kreutzer'), Op. 47, 354
  No. 10 in G major, Op. 96, 548
Beheim, Michel, 610
Beidler, George C., 221
Bel canto, 18, 27, 73, 154, 208, 260, 299, 377, 386–7, 415, 536, 577–9, 621, 679–80
Bell, Alexander Graham, 488
Bell, Chichester, 488
Bellini, Vincenzo
  cadenzas, 110
  I Capuleti e i Montecchi, 216
  I Puritani, 577
Bellon, Jean-François-Victor, 670
Bellosio, Anselmo, 665
Benda, Franz, 71, 421
Bendinelli, Cesare, 222, 633
Beowulf, 572
Bérard, Jean-Antoine, 72
  L'art du chant, 72
  on vibrato, 657
Berg, Alban, 5, 8, 72
  Drei Orchesterstücke, 72
  Lulu, 73, 584
  Lyric Suite, 72, 571
  Violin Concerto, 686
  Wozzeck, 72, 82–3, 584
Berger, Ludwig, 138, 443
Berger, Wilhelm, 401
Bergmann, Walter, 619
Berio, Luciano, 584
  Gesti, 546
  Sequenza XIV, 571
Bériot, Charles-Auguste de, 52, 73, 234, 339, 469, 471, 506, 570, 626, 653, 671
Berkeley Early Music Festival, 195
Berkowskis, Hermann, 42
Berlin *Concert Spirituel*, 530–1

Berliner Barock Solisten, 194
Berliner, Emil, 488
Berlioz, Hector, 74, 117, 134, 145, 171, 278, 306, 344, 351, 431, 453, 474, 564, 626, 631, 637
  Benvenuto Cellini, 278
  on conducting, 626
  Grand traité d'instrumentation et d'orchestration modernes, 74
  Grande messe des Morts, Op. 5 ('Requiem'), 127, 278
  Harold en Italie, 468
  La Damnation de Faust, 74
  Le Freischütz, 457
  Lélio, 428
  Les Nuits d'été, 75
  Les Troyens, 457
  Marche Funèbre (*Hamlet*), Op. 18 No. 3, 125
  Messe Solennelle, 457
  Roméo et Juliette, 74
  Symphonie fantastique, 74, 278, 287, 457, 471
  on valve horn, 312
Bermudo, Juan, 62, 107, 229, 273, 284, 659
Bernhard, Christoph, 75, 227, 535–6
  Coloraturen, 75
Bernstein, Leonard, 12, 359
Berr, Frédéric, 75, 502, 626
Berry, Walter, 117
Berteau, Martin, 93, 618
Berthaume, Isidore, 570
Bertoli, Giovanni Antonio, 67
Berton, Henri-Montan, 171
Besard, Jean-Baptiste, 571
Besozzi, Carlo, 446
Besozzi family, 67, 446
Bevan, Clifford, 638
Bevan, Maurice, 172
Biber, Heinrich Ignaz Franz, 142, 302, 568, 634
  Harmonia-artificiosa ariosa, 424
  'Mystery' ('Rosary') sonatas, 267, 570, 668
  Requiem in A major, 353
  Sonatae violino solo, 570
Bibliographie des Musikschrifttums, 483
Bibliothèque Nationale, Paris, 199, 471
Bicket, Harry, 455
Bigaglia, Diogenio, 305
Billings, William, 126
Bilson, Malcolm, 29, 76, 193, 215, 372
Bindig, Susan, 198
Binkley, Thomas, 76, 192, 196, 448, 522, 567, 591
Biondi, Fabio, 193, 216
Biordi, Paolo, 663
Birnbaum, Johann Abraham, 76
Bischof, Andrea, 142, 518
Bischoff, Hans, 356
Bismantova, Bartolomeo, 62, 76, 235, 526
  Compendio musicale, 31, 77

INDEX

Bizet, Georges
  Carmen, 457
  L'Arlésienne, 454, 564
Blachly, Alexander, 198
Black, Andrew, 213
Blanc, Serge, 214
Blanton, Jimmie, 182
Blasius, (Mathieu-)Frédéric, 78
Blewitt, Jonas, 462
Bloch, Ernest, 194
Bloch, Suzanne, 194
Blow, John, 598
Blue Heron, 198
Blühmel, Friedrich, 311, 635
Blume, Friedrich, 185
Blume, Walter, 586
Boccherini, Luigi
  Cello Concerto in B flat major, G482, 272
Böddecker, Philip Friedrich, 67
Bodky, Erwin, 195
Boehm, Joseph, 339
Boehm, Theobald, 239, 243–4, 350, 434, 548
Boehm clarinet, 350, 431
Boehm flute, 22, 245, 548
'Boehm-Gordon' controversy, 548
Boehm system, 350, 421, 447
Boeke, Kees, 99
Boethius, Anicius Manlius Severinus, 78, 134, 465, 627
  De institutione musica, 78
Böhm, Joseph, 549
Bois, Rob du
  Muziek, 528
Boismortier, Joseph Bodin de, 51, 316
Bol, Hans, 231
Bolt, Klaas, 592
Bolton, Ivor, 455
Bonanni, Filippo, 58
Bonaparte, Elisa, 266
Bond, Capel, 67
Bonifacio, Giovanni, 56
Bononcini, Giovanni Maria, 570
Bononcini brothers, 131
Bonporti, Francesco Antonio, 416
Boody, John, 196
Book of Common Prayer, 607
Boomkamp, Carel van Leeuwen, 103
Boracchi, Carlo Antonio, 79
Borchgrevinck, Melchior, 253
Bordes, Charles, 80, 190, 328
Bordet, Toussaint, 509
Bordoni, Faustina, 262
Borghese, Antonio
  L'art musical, 277
Borghese, Cardinal, 222
Borjon de Scellery, 313
Boston Baroque (originally Banchetto Musicale), 197
Boston Camerata, 196
Boston Early Music Festival, 195, 197

Bottazzari, Giovanni
  Sonate nuove, 571
Bottesini, Giovanni, 80, 181, 238
Bottesini bow, 81
Bottrigari, Ercole, 34
Boufil, Jacques-Jules, 363
Boulanger, Nadia, 3, 81, 97, 261, 348, 369
Boulez, Pierre, 36, 82, 111, 220, 438, 584, 586, 590
  Le marteau sans maître, 82
  Piano Sonata No. 3, 82
  Pli selon pli, 82
Boult, Adrian, 95
Bour, Ernest, 82
Bourdelot, Pierre, 222
Bourdieu, Pierre, 14
Bourgeois, Loys, 440, 537
Bovicelli, Giovanni Battista, 83, 696
Bowing, 29, 37, 69, 77, 84, 94, 103, 115, 165, 184, 214, 224, 250, 254, 258, 267, 272, 277, 364, 368, 371, 373, 390, 420, 430, 452–3, 469, 471, 504, 517, 531, 550, 552, 567, 599, 618, 642, 654, 666, 672, 692
Bowman, James, 89, 188, 422, 614
Bows, 84
  early nineteenth-century, 87
  longer 'High Baroque', 86
  short 'Early Baroque', 84
  transitional/Classical, 86
  types:
    'Bach', 43–4, 90
    Bottesini, 81
    Butler, 180
    'cello, 85, 120
    Corelli, 167
    Dodd, 88
    Dragonetti, 81, 181
    French, 81, 85, 181
    German, 180–1
    long, 86
    'pike-head', 84
    Simandl, 180–1
    'swan bill', 86
    Tourte, 53, 85–8, 120, 184, 430, 551–2, 665
    Vega Bach, 42
    viola, 85
    viola da gamba, 85
Boyd Neel Orchestra, 167, 191
Boyden, David Dodge, 42, 84, 90, 265
Brähmig, Bernhard, 666
Brahms, Johann Jacob, 90
Brahms, Johannes, 90, 122, 189, 339, 400, 408, 443, 586
  Clarinet Quintet, Op. 115, 133
  Clarinet Sonatas, Op. 120, 133
  Clarinet Trio, Op. 114, 133, 170
  conducting of his own works, 609
  Ein deutsches Requiem, Op. 45, 91–2, 175
  early recordings of, 204
  51 Übungen, 91

INDEX

Piano Concertos
  No. 1 in D minor, Op. 15, 91, 101
  No. 2 in B flat major, Op. 83, 91
Piano miniatures, Opp. 116 and 117, 170
piano playing (recording), 202
Piano Quartets, Opp. 25 and 26, 90
Piano Trios
  Op. 8, 170
  Op. 101, 170, 250
'St Anthony Chorale' Variations, Op. 56, 91
Symphonies
  No. 1 in C minor, Op. 68, 92
  No. 4 in E minor, Op. 98, 92, 101, 132, 400
Triumphlied, Op. 52, 92
Variations and Fugue on a Theme of Handel, Op. 24, 90–1
Variations on a Theme of Paganini, Op. 35, 91
Violin Concerto in D major, Op. 77, 109–10, 340
Brainard, Ingrid, 198
Branscombe, Peter, 50
Braun, André, 631
Bream, Julian, 92
  see also Julian Bream Consort
Brebos, Gillis, 459
Brée, Malwine, 367
Breitkopf & Härtel, 443
Bremner, Robert, 93, 263, 265, 650
Bressan, Peter, 526, 598
Bréval, Jean-Baptiste Sébastien, 93, 368
  Traité du violoncelle, Op. 42, 94
Brewer, John, 394
Bricqueville, Eugène de, 190
Bridge, Richard, 461
Brijon, C. R., 662–3
British Broadcasting Corporation (BBC), xiv, 35, 95, 188, 481
British Library's Early Music Online, 200
Britten, Benjamin, 94, 584, 649
  Burning Fiery Furnace, The, 649
  Curlew River, 649
  Death in Venice, 89
  Fanfare for St Edmundsbury, 14
  Midsummer Night's Dream, A, 89, 172
  Noye's Fludde, 649
  Prodigal Son, The 649
Britton, Thomas, 34, 648
Broadcasting, 95, 187, 191
Broadley, Arthur, 654
Brod, Henri, 447, 626
Broderip, Robert, 230
Brodersen, Friedrich, 299
Brodsky Quartet, 250
Broken consort repertoire, 197
Brombaugh, John, 196
Brookes, Oliver, 188
Brossard, Sébastien de, 97, 509, 669
Brown, Caroline, 613
Brown, Clive, xviii, 87, 98

Brown, Howard Mayer, 39, 71, 98, 196, 198, 317
Brown, Ryan, 197
Brown family, 196
Browne, James, 244
Bruch, Max, 305, 647
Bruckner, Anton, 454, 683
  Symphony No. 4 in E flat major, 385
Brückner, Oskar, 272
Brüggen, Frans, 71, 99, 103, 192, 295, 355, 365, 455–6, 528, 568
Brunelli, Antonio, 99
Bruni, Antonio, 305, 666
Brunold, Paul, 100
Bry, Théodore de, 163
Buchner, Hans, 100, 228, 230
  Fundamentum, 62, 100
Buffardin, Pierre-Gabriel, 516
Buffet Crampon, 68
Buffet, Jean-Louis, 68, 132–3, 350, 431, 447
Bukofzer, Manfred, 478
Bull, John
  Fantasia, 229
Bull, William, 598, 604
Bullokar, John, 147
Bülow, Hans von, 71, 92, 101, 373, 384, 400, 402, 586, 609, 683
Bulwer, John, 56–7
Bunting, Christopher, 122, 286
Bunyan, Vashti, 528
Burgess, Geoffrey, 295
Burgess, Grayston, 192
Burmeister, Joachim, 226–7, 535, 617
  Musica poetica, 535
Burmester, Willy, 431
Burnett, Richard, 614
Burney, Charles, 41, 44, 101, 223, 293, 387, 389, 391, 396, 504, 598, 602, 679, 688
Busch, Adolf, 432
Busoni, Ferruccio, 5, 102, 217, 268, 623, 649
  cadenzas, 110
  Clavierübung, 102
  edition of Liszt's *Reminiscences de Don Juan*, 102
  Entwurf einer neuen Aesthetik der Tonkunst, 102
Busse Berger, Anna Maria, 449
Butt, Clara, 213
Butt, John, xviii, 33, 102, 455, 547
Buxheim Organ Book, 594
Buxtehude, Dietrich, 250, 396, 463, 497, 662
  Ad cor: Vulnerasti cor meum, 148
Bylsma, Anner, 99, 103, 142, 160, 192, 365, 568
Byrd, William, 93, 252, 304, 612, 622
  'Fortune my foe', 533

Cabezón, Antonio de, 104–5, 459
Cabezón, Hernando de, 104, 229
Caccini, Giulio, 62–3, 83, 99, 105, 107, 216, 501, 550, 577, 621, 678–9
  Le nuove musiche ('New Songs'), 62, 83, 105, 501, 550, 577, 621, 678

707

cadenza, 18, 37, 45, 71, 106, 168, 173, 209, 223, 569, 588
Cage, John, 43, 82, 438
  4′ 33″, 111
  Music of Changes, 111
  Perilous Night, The, 111
  Sonatas and Interludes, 111
  use of shortwave radio, 212
Caldara, Antonio, 131, 416
  I due dittatori, 634
Caldwell, James, 195
Calvé, Emma, 658
Calvet, Joseph, 568
Calvisius, Seth, 345, 617
Cambini, Giuseppe Maria, 111, 258
Cambridge (MA) Society for Early Music, 195
Cambridge Court Dancers, 198
Camerata, 105
Campagnoli, Bartolomeo, 112, 266–7, 570, 671
Campanellas, 274
Campion, François, 276, 571
  règle de l'octave, 484
Campra, André, 51
  L'Europe galante, 361
Cannabich, Christian, 453, 668
Cantabile style, 30
Cantelo, April, 172
Canteloube, (Marie-)Joseph, 80
Cantigas de Santa Maria, 51, 240
Cantus Cölln, 193
Cape, Safford, 191, 196
Capella Academica Wien, 192
Capella Antiqua München, 192
Cappella Savaria, 193, 398
Caplan, Ben, 11
Cappella Coloniensis, 96
Capuzzi, Antonio, 181
Carbonelli, Giovanni Stefano, 668
Cardew, Cornelius, 587
Cardinall's Musick, The, 193, 197
Cardozo, Félix Pérez, 287
Carestini, Giovanni, 390
Carissimi, Giacomo, 520
  Jephte, 81
Carl Augustin I, 271
Carl Augustin II, 271
Carl, Johann Christian, 648
Carlson, Chester, 221
Carmel (California) Bach Festival, 194
Carmignola, Giuliano, 2
Carmona, Manuel Salvador, 298
Carnegie Hall, New York, 649
Cartier, Jean-Baptiste, 160, 171, 415, 626, 671
Carwood, Andrew, 193
Casadesus, Francis, 114
Casadesus, Henri, 114, 190, 305, 513
Casals, Marta, 115
Casals, Pablo, 115, 122, 213, 237, 268, 372, 655
Cassadó, Gaspar, 94
Castaldi, Bellerofonte, 63, 615

Castello, Dario, 668
Castelnuovo-Tedesco, Mario,
  Guitar Sonata in D major, Op. 77, 571
Castil-Blaze, François Henri Joseph, 116
Castrato, 90, 116, 223, 391, 577
Castrucci, Pietro, 570, 665, 668
Catalani, Angelica, 30, 130, 549
Catel, Charles-Simon, 52, 236, 368, 626
Caudle, Mark, 309
Caus, Salomon de, 58
Caussenus, Joseph, 637
Cavaillé-Coll, Aristide, 118, 464, 471
Cavalieri, Emilio de', 62–3
Cavalli, Francesco, 304, 358
  La Calisto, 90, 365
  Le Nozze di Teti e di Peleo, 310
  L'Ormindo, 365
Cavallini, Eugenio, 267
'Cello, 118
  Baroque, 355
  bow, 85
  tuning, 571
  see also Violoncello
Centre for Musical Performance as Creative Practice (CMPCP), 363
Centre for the History and Analysis of Recorded Music (CHARM), 363, 483
Cerone, Pietro, 106
Cervetto, Giovanni, 468
Cesti, Antonio, 629
Chabrier, Emmanuel,
  L'Étoile, 457
Chailley, Jacques, 190
Challis, John, 195
Chalumeau, 131, 210, 361
Chamber Orchestra of Europe, xv
Chambers, Paul, 182, 336
Chambonnières, Jacques Champion, Sieur de, 100, 123, 157, 173, 291, 560
Chansonnier Cordiforme, The, 612
Chant scholarship, 206
Chapel Royal, 648
Chaplin sisters, 95, 123, 164
Charlier, Théo, 635
Charpentier, Marc-Antoine, 65, 67, 124, 129, 345
  Mélanges (Meslanges) *autographes*, 124
  Pestis Mediolensis, 81
  Te Deum in D major, 634
Charvet, Pierre, 97
CHASE (Collection of Historical Annotated String Editions), 98
Chaulieu, Charles, 494
Chausson, Ernest,
  Poème, 213
Chelard, André Hippolyte, 278
Chéreau, Patrice, 36, 83
Cherubini, Luigi, 128, 258, 354, 470
Chiavette, 623
Chickering Piano Company, 176, 195, 491
Children's Salon, 164

Chilperic I, 270
Chinnery, Mrs Caroline, 278
Chiroplast, 343
Chitarrone, 64, 615
Choir, 125
  a cappella, 192
Choir of the English Concert, 495
Chopin, Fryderyk Franciszek [Frédéric François], 6, 303, 343, 536
  ballades, 326
  bibliography, 208
  on fingering, 230
  Mazurka, Op. posth. 67 No. 4, 209
  on piano pedalling, 492
  Prelude, Op. 28 No. 1, 324
Choral Public Domain Library, 200
Choron, Alexandre, 114, 127, 189, 278
Chorton, 66, 497–9, 602, 624
Christiane Eberhardine, Queen and Electress, 65
Christiani, Adolph Friedrich, 5, 128
Christie, William, xv, 129, 192, 197, 366, 455
Christophers, Harry, 193, 613
Chronomètre, 359, 371
Chrysander, Friedrich, 7, 61, 477
  Denkmäler der Tonkunst, 91
  Händel Werke, 91
Chrysostom, Dio
  Orationes LXXI, 51
Ciaramella, 197
Cicero, 56, 216, 534–5
Ciconia, Johannes, 515, 591
Cimbasso, 638
Cinti-Damoreau, Laure, 30, 130, 657
Cirque d'Hiver (originally Cirque Napoléon), Paris, 649
City of Bath Festival, 3
Clagget, Charles, 635
Clarinet, 130, 318, 350, 410, 420, 453
  bass, 133, 453, 563, 585
  basset, 132, 585
  Boehm, 350, 431
  vs. chalumeau, 210
  in 18th and 19th centuries, 318, 410, 445
  mutes, 428
  vibrato on, 656
Clarion Concerts Orchestra, 197
Clarke, Jennifer Ward, 614
Clarke, Jeremiah
  Prince of Denmark's March, The, 634
Classification of instruments, 133
Clavichord, 29, 44, 136, 245, 250, 309, 409, 562, 674
Clavicytherium, 289
Clay, Charles, 399
Clementi, Muzio, 138, 160, 230, 314, 625
  1781 pianistic duel with Mozart, 138
  Sonatas for Piano Forte or Harpsichord, 138

Cleobury, Stephen, 2
Clérambault, Louis-Nicolas, 65, 100
Clerkes of Oxenford, 192
Cleveland's Chapel, Court, & Countryside Concert Series, 195
Clinton, John, 502
Cobb, Jimmy, 336
Cobb, Willard, 76, 196, 522, 591
Coclico, Adrian Petit, 426
Codex, 139
Cogliati, Carlo, 80
Cohen, Joel, 196
Cohen, Patrick, 518
Coherence theories, 11
Coin, Christophe, 142, 518
Cole, Robert, 195
Coleman, Ornette, 564
Collegium 1704, 193
Collegium Aureum, 141, 172, 193
Collegium Musicum, 99, 190, 198, 303, 329, 602, 648
Collegium Vocale Gent, 193, 298
Collins, Peter, 465
Colonna, Giovanni, 180
Coltrane, John, 336, 564
Columbia Phonograph, 488
Colver, Michael, 152
Combattimento, 194
Computerised Mensural Music Editions, 201
Comte, Auguste, 225
Concentus Musicus Wien, 142, 172, 191, 282, 365, 454, 518
Concert d'Astrée, Le, 193
Concert Royal, 198
Concert Spirituel, 34, 78, 111, 353, 486, 512
Concert Spirituel, Le, 193
Concertgebouw
  Amsterdam, 454, 648
  Leipzig, 649
Concertina, 496
Concerto Castello, 197
Concerto Copenhagen, 194
Concerto Italiano, 193
Concerto Palatino, 174, 197
Concerto Vocale, 129, 192, 334
Concerts Français, 486
Concerts Historiques, 225, 278, 304
Concerts of Antient Music, 2, 142, 188, 304, 306
Concerts Pasdeloup, 649
Conducting and direction, 143
Conforti, Giovanni Luca, 147, 578
Consolo, Federico, 266
Consort, 123, 147, 176, 241, 625
  viol, 309
Consort of Musicke, The, 192, 347, 612
Consort principle, 19
Contenance angloise, 331
Context, 372
Conti, Francesco Bartolomeo, 131

709

INDEX

Contrabassoon, 69, 454
Cook, Captain James, 101
Cook, Nicholas, 589
Cooke, Benjamin, 2
Cooke, Derycke, 12
Coomaraswamy, Ananda Kentish Muthu, 111
Co-op Piccionaia of Vicenza, 347
Cooper, Frank, 4, 195
Coperario (Coprario), Giovanni, 63, 661
Copies of instruments, 149, 247
Copyist scores, 389
Cor anglais, 446, 453
Corbetta, Francesco, 166, 274
   Varii capricci, 571
Cordier, Baude, 319
Corelli, Arcangelo, 90, 122, 150, 156, 255, 262–3, 297, 302, 321–2, 419–20, 439, 452, 520, 634, 668, 671
   Corelli's orchestra, 150–1, 452
   ornamentation, 439
   Concerti Grossi, Op. 6, 361, 668
   Trio Sonatas, Opp. 1 and 3, 64, 263, 340
   Violin Sonatas Op. 5, 151, 263, 322, 364, 402, 622
Corelli bows, 167
Cornett, 77, 151, 344
Cornette, Victor, 637
Correa de Arauxo, 229
Corrette, Michel, 51, 121, 152, 231, 233, 242, 316, 655, 663, 666, 671–2
   fingerings, 236
   Concertos comiques, Op. 8, 152
   dons d'Apollon, Les, 153
   école d'Orphée, L', 153, 570
   Méthode théorique et pratique, 153
   Parfait maître à chanter, Le, 153
Corri, Domenico, 154, 277, 503, 608, 626
Corri, John, 608
Cortot, Alfred, 471
Cossel, Otto, 90
Cossmann, Bernhard, 154–5, 249
Costa, Giacomo, 468
Costa, Sir Michael, 145
Cosyn, Benjamin, 252
Cotgrave, Randle, 147
Cotto, John, 500
Cottrell, Stephen, 564
Countertenor, 117, 472, 578
Couperin, François, 100, 139, 155, 157, 229–30, 291, 314, 393, 430, 439, 441, 522, 533, 589, 601, 625
   ornamentation, 155
   Allemande la laborieuse, 156
   L'Apothéose de Lully, 156, 442
   Leçons de ténèbres, 156
   Ordres, 155
   Pièces de clavecin, 32, 91, 156
   Préludes, 538–9

Couperin, Louis, 100, 123, 157, 309, 319, 365, 538, 540
   on notation, 166
   Prélude in C major, 538
Courvoisier, Karl, 169, 672
Cousin, Victor, 225
Covent Garden, London, 647
Covey-Crump, Rogers, 302
Cowell, Henry, 111
Craft, Robert, 590
Cramer, Carl Friedrich, 93, 650
Cramer, David, 223
Cramer, Wilhelm, 86
Cranmer, Thomas, 607
Crawshay, Robert Thompson, 637
Crescentini, Girolamo, 258
Cristofori, Bartolomeo, 29, 245, 382, 581
   Cristofori piano, 493
Criticism of music, 157
Crome, Robert, 121
Crompton, Bernhard, 164
Crompton, Robert, 163
Crumb, George
   Vox Balaenae, 120
Crumhorn, 19, 159, 422
Crusell, Bernhard, 270, 363
Crussard, Claude, 421
Crutchfield, Will, 658
Cunningham, Merce, 111
Cunningham, Sarah, 197
Cupis, Jean-Baptiste, 93, 367, 666
Curtal, 66, 574
Cuvillon, Jean-Baptiste de, 279
Cyr, Mary, 159
Czerny, Carl, 6, 129, 139, 160, 218, 230, 366, 370, 402, 494, 510, 534, 625
   on cadenzas, 109
   Systematische Anleitung zum Fantasieren auf dem Pianoforte, Op. 200, 160–1
   Vollständige theoretisch-praktische Pianoforte-Schule (Grand Piano School), Op. 500, 160–1, 356

Dahlhaus, Carl, 12, 531
D'Alembert, Jean le Rond, 173, 393, 520, 553
Dalla Casa, Girolamo, 106, 152, 162, 550, 662, 667, 696
Dallam, Robert, 461
Dallam, Thomas, 461
Dalza, Joan Ambrosio, 571
Dance, 162, 594
   music, 163
   re-creation, 163
   sources, 162
   treatises, 627
Dancla, (Jean-Baptiste) Charles, 52, 165, 671
   20 études brillantes et caractéristiques, Op. 73, 165
   36 études mélodiques et très faciles, Op. 84, 165
   L'école de l'archet, Op. 110, 165

L'école de mécanisme, Op. 74, 165
L'école des cinq positions, Op. 193, 165
Petite école de la mélodie, Op. 123, 165
Le Semainier du jeune violoniste, Opp. 144 and 150, 166
Dancla, Léopold, 52
Dancla family, 165
Dandrieu, Jean-François, 290, 305
Daneman, Sophie, 366
D'Anglebert, Jean Henry, 63, 123, 166, 291, 538, 560
   five organ fugues, 166
   harpsichord transcriptions, 166
   Pièces de clavecin, 166
Danican, Michel, 485
Daniel, Paul, 455
Daniels, David, 117, 198, 216
Dannreuther, Edward, 177, 251
Danoville, Le Sieur, 231, 552, 663
Danzi, Franz, 236
Dark Horse Consort, 197
Dart, Thurston, xiii–xiv, 96, 166, 185, 191, 261, 292, 307–9, 369, 422, 479–80, 559, 690
Dauprat, Louis François, 167, 256, 311, 400, 626
   Sextet, Op. 10, 168
Davenport, LaNoue, 269
David, Ferdinand, 168, 171, 235, 272, 339, 583, 626, 672
   Concertino, Op. 34, 168
   Hohe Schule des Violinspiels, 20, 114
   Vorstudien zur Hohen Schule des Violinspiels, 114
   Zur Violinschule, 169, 430
Davidov, Carl, 237, 249
Davies, Fanny, 170
Davies, Iestyn, 117
Davies, Stephen, 12, 39
Davies, Sir Walford, 369
Davis, Miles, 336
Davis, Robert Aubrey, 199
De Machy, Le Sieur, 552, 663
De' Medici, Lorenzo, 328
De Wit, Eric, 662
Dean, Winton, 24
Debroux, Joseph, 305
Debussy, Claude, 220
   Danse sacrée et danse profane, 287
   Pelléas et Mélisande, 83, 457
   Prélude à l'après-midi d'un faune, 471
Dedekind, Henning, 617
Dehn, Siegfried, 443
Deldevez, Edmé (Édouard) Marie Ernest, 170
   26 Pièces diverses, 114
Delius, Frederick, 268
Della Valle, Pietro, 147
Deller Consort, 171–2, 192
Deller, Alfred George, 89, 171–2, 364, 422, 480, 619
Deller, Mark, 172
Delsart, Jules, 175, 662

Delusse, Charles, 172, 656
   L'amant statue, 173
Demus, Jörg, 49
Denis, Jean, 173, 509
Denisov, Edison
   Ode, 327
Denner, Jakob C., 67, 295, 386
Denner, Johann Christoph, 131
Denny, Dene, 194
Dent, J. M., 480
Désargus, Xavier, 286
Descartes, René, 15, 601
Désormière, Roger, 82, 97
Dessauer, Heinrich, 665
Dessoff, Otto, 586
Destouches, Cardinal André, 305
Deucerus, 617
Deutsche Vereinigung für alte Musik, 190
Devienne, François, 68, 112, 173, 243
   Les Visitandines, 173
Dewey, Melvil, 135
Dhrupad, 694
Diaghilev, Sergei, 268
Diamond, Neil, 337
Dibdin, Charles, 341
Dicey, Cluer, 508
Dickey, Bruce, 152, 197
Dickinson, Peter, 188
Diderot, Denis, 173, 553
DiDonato, Joyce, 216
Dieffopruchar, Magno, 616
Diémer, Louis-Joseph, 175, 177, 189, 292, 471
Dies, Albert Christoph, 294
Dietrich, Albert, 175
Dieupart, Charles, 100
   Six suites pour le clavecin, 65
Digital Image Archive of Medieval Music, 199
Digitisation, 199
Dilworth, John, 88
D'India, Sigismondo, 612
Diruta, Girolamo, 55, 62, 175, 228, 291, 450, 628
   Il Transilvano, 29, 622
Dittersdorf, Carl Ditters von, 131, 176, 181
Dixon, William
   manuscript for border bagpipes, 52
Döbereiner, Christian, 190
Dodd, Edward, 87
Dodd, John, 87–8
Dolejši, Robert, 666
Dolmetsch, Arnold, xiii, xvi, 39, 88, 138, 146, 149, 164, 176–8, 186, 189, 195, 198, 268, 292, 305–6, 348, 421, 478, 513, 527, 555, 662
Dolmetsch, Carl, 177, 479, 527
Dolmetsch, Cécile, 177
Dolmetsch, Élodie, 177
Dolmetsch, Hélène, 177
Dolmetsch, J & M, 177
Dolmetsch, Jeanne, 177

INDEX

Dolmetsch, Mabel, 164, 177
Dolmetsch, Marguerite, 177
Dolmetsch, Nathalie, 177
Dolmetsch, Rudolph, 177, 292
Dolmetsch Foundation, 177
Dolmetsch Historical Dance Society, 177
Dombois, Eugen, 448
Domenico da Piacenza, 162
Domnich, Heinrich, 280
Donaldson, George, 555
Donington, Margaret, 178
Donington, Robert, xiii, xvi, 177, 185, 479
Donington Consort, 178
Donizetti, Gaetano, 316
  Lucia di Lammermoor, 381
Donne, John, 56
Dont, Jakob, 37, 169, 672
Door, Anton, 586
Dotzauer, Justus Johann Friedrich, 121, 155, 178, 184, 236, 626, 653
Double bass, 180, 453, 571
  five-stringed, 101
  Gibson electric, 182
  tunings, 210, 564
Double horns, 312
Douglass, David, 197
Dowd, William, 195, 292
Dowland, John, 63, 93, 376, 465, 612, 619
  Lachrimae or Seaven Teares Figured in Seaven Passionate Pavans, 622
Downes, Olin, 24
Dräger, Hans Heinz, 135
Dragonetti, Domenico, 181
  Dragonetti bow, 81, 181
Drake, William, 465
Drechsler, Karl, 155, 179, 271
Dresden School, 155
Drexel family, 196
Dreyfus, Huguette, 401
Dreyfus, Laurence, 182, 307
Drottningholm Court Baroque Ensemble, 194
Drouet, Louis François Philippe, 548
Druce, Duncan, 614
Druschetzky, Jiri, 446, 666
Du Mont, Henri
  Cantica sacra, 65
Düben, Anders von
  keyboard tablature, 622
Düben Collection Database Catalogue, 200
Dubourg, Matthew, 151, 263
Ducaud-Bourget, Abbé François, 644
Duchaine family, 87
Dufaut, François, 377
Dufay, Guillaume, 472, 591
  Missa 'Se la face ay pale', 188
Dufay Collective, 193
Duffin, Ross, 195
Dufour, (Lieutenant), 582
Dukas, Paul, 360
Dulcian, 69, 574

Dunn, Thomas, 612
Dunstable, John
  Puisque m'amour, 633
Duport, Jean-Louis, 52, 87, 120–1, 183, 367, 551
  Essai, 120–1, 179, 236, 277, 551, 625
Duport, Jean-Pierre, 178, 183, 618
Duport system, 236
Dupré, Desmond, 172, 364
Duprez, Gilbert-Louis, 579
Dupuits, Jean-Baptiste, 316
Durand, 560
Durante, Ottavio, 680
Durey de Nonville, Jacques-Bernard, 528
Dussek, Jan Ladislav, 315
Dutilleux, Henri, 369
  Trois strophes, 571
Duvernoy, Frédéric Nicolas, 31
Dvořák, Antonín
  Cello Concerto in B Minor, Op. 104, 36, 250
Dyer, Louise, 167
Dylan, Bob, 337
Dynamics, 9, 41, 59, 64, 70, 90, 112–13, 118, 139, 160–1, 173, 203, 206, 214, 217, 263–4, 272, 279, 290, 354, 373, 385, 405, 417, 434, 438, 445, 500, 529, 567, 575, 590, 632, 639
  in early recordings, 202

Eagan, John, 287
Early English Books Online, 199
Early music
  concepts of, 185
  in Europe, 188
  in North America., 199
  in the digital age, 199
Early Music America, 194
Early Music Consort of London, xiv, 89, 97, 186, 188, 192, 307–8, 369, 422
Early Music Guild of Seattle (EMG), 195
Early Music New York (former the New York Ensemble for Early Music), 196
Early Music Quartet, 76
Early Music Shop, The, 186
Early Music Vancouver (EMV, Vancouver Society for Early Music), 195
Early recordings, 202
Eberhardt, Siegfried, 654
Eberlin, Johann Ernst, 416
Eck, Franz, 86, 582
Edda, 572
Edison, Thomas Alva, 202, 205, 487
Editing/editions, 205
Egarr, Richard, 2
Eggington, Tim, 304
Eichentopf, Andreas, 69
Eichentopf, Johann Heinrich, 67, 207
Eichmann, Peter, 617
Eichner, Ernst
  Concerto in C major (for harp or harpsichord), 286
Eigeldinger, Jean-Jacques, 208

712

Eingang, 209, 323
Eisel, Johann Philipp, 48, 210, 446
Eisenberg, Maurice, 122, 237, 655
Elder, Sir Mark, xiii, 455
Electronic Corpus of Lute Music, 201
Electronic instruments, 211
Electronic keyboard instruments, 282
Elgar, Sir Edward, 212
  Overture: *Froissart*, Op. 19, 649
  Overture: *In the South (Alassio)*, Op. 50, 213
  Piano Quintet in A minor, Op. 84, 212
  Sea Pictures, Op. 37, 213
  Symphony No. 1 in A flat major, Op. 55, 23, 213
  Variations for Orchestra ('Enigma'), 212–13, 609
  Violin Concerto in B minor, Op. 61, 110, 213, 506
Ella, John, 510
Ellington, Duke, 336
Elliot, Moppa, 336
Elliott, Paul, 302
Ellis, Alexander, 303, 497, 639
Ellis, Katharine, 304
Elman, Mischa, 37, 654
Endler, J. S., 635
Enescu, George, 213
  Impressions d'enfance, 213
  Légende, 635
  Sonata No. 3 for violin and piano (*dans le caractère populaire roumain*), 213
Engel, Carl, 214, 303, 329
English Bach Festival, 359, 398, 495
English Baroque Soloists, 192, 214, 261, 368, 455–6
English Concert, The, 192, 361, 455, 495
English Consort, The, 54
English Consort of Viols, 178
English Opera Group, 94
English Singers, 190
Engramelle, Marie Dominique Joseph, 215
Ensemble Clément Janequin, 193
Ensemble Intercontemporain, 83
Ensemble La Romanesca, 193
Ensemble Micrologus, 193
Ensemble Mosaïques, 193, 518
Ensemble Mozart, 194
Ensemble Organum, 193
Ensemble Sarband, 194
Eötvös, Peter, 587
Epstein, David, 220
Érard (Company), 175, 287
Érard, Pierre-Orphée, 286
Érard, Sébastien, 286, 491
Erdesz, Otto, 665
Erlebach, Philipp Heinrich, 302
Ernst, Heinrich Wilhelm, 469
Ersch, Johann Samuel, 249
Eskdale, George, 636
Este, Ercole d', Duke of Ferrara, 241

Esterházy Quartet, 193
Eton Choirbook, 608
Euphonium, 637
Europa Galante, 193, 216
Evans, Bill, 336
Evelyn, John, 648
Ewing, Alan, 612
Expression, 9, 28, 40, 53, 73, 75, 114, 153, 169, 184, 216, 224, 231, 246, 254–5, 257, 264, 268, 279, 336, 339, 342, 348, 354, 373, 406, 415–17, 423, 431, 434, 464, 466, 500, 531, 533, 536, 549, 552, 583, 592, 599, 601, 625, 632, 650, 668, 676, 695
Expressive intonation, 115
Eyck, Jacob van, 527

Faber, Heinrich, 617
Facsimile, 221, 265, 303, 348, 369, 581, 659, 686
Faenza Codex, 140
Fairlight CMI, 211
Falck, Georg, 670
Falckenhagen, Adam, 377
Falcon, Cornélie, 130
Falla, Manuel de, 276, 360
Fallamero, Gabriel, 330
Fallis, David, 197
Fantini, Girolamo, 222, 633–4
Farina, Carlo, 222, 628, 668
  Capriccio stravagante, 222
Farinelli [Carlo Broschi], xvii, 107, 154, 223, 297, 679
Farnaby, Giles, 622
  'Woody Cock' variations, 533
Farnell-Watson, Anne E., 95
Fasano, Renato, 191
Fasch, Johann Friedrich, 67
Fauré, Gabriel, 360, 471, 671
  Requiem, Op. 48, 23
Fauvel, André-Joseph, 548
Feldlen, Magnus, 60
Feldman, Grace, 197
Feldman, Jill, 366
Feldman, Morton, 111
Fellowes, Edmund H., 166, 190, 224, 369
Fender, Leo, 182
Fenkner, Johann August, 224, 671
Ferguson, Howard, 541
Fermate, 210
Ferrabosco, Alfonso, 661
Ferrari, Gaudenzio, 118, 664, 667
Ferras, Christian, 214
Festetics, Count Georg, 585
Festing, Michael, 263
Festival Music Society (now Indianapolis Early Music), 195
Fétis, François-Joseph, 19, 75, 84, 112, 114, 126, 177, 189, 224, 247, 278, 304, 306, 356, 421, 477, 510, 552, 563–4, 662
Feuermann, Emanuel, 115
Fiala, Joseph, 446
Figueras, Montserrat, 562–3

713

INDEX

Figured bass, 17, 43, 62, 171, 206, 263, 393, 396, 473, 522, 603, 640, 642, 685
Figurenlehre, 16, 225
Filidori, 485
Filtz, Anton, 236
Finger, Gottfried, 598, 634, 662
Fingering, 19, 22, 29, 37, 44, 47, 49, 52, 77–8, 104–5, 114, 153, 175, 183, 214, 224, 227, 248, 258, 264, 273, 286, 314, 338, 341, 362, 370, 386, 390, 435, 549, 552, 560, 562, 572, 582, 594, 630, 632, 640, 666, 672, 692
   bowed stringed instruments, 231
   cello, 69, 236, 277
   chromatic scales, 264
   clarinet, 363
   cornett, 152
   double bass, 181, 237
   keyboard instruments, 228
   organ, 22
   viol, 231
   violin, 232
   viola, 232
   wind instruments, 238
Firket, Leon, 666
Fischer, Ivan, xv, 446
Fischer, Johann Caspar Ferdinand, 137, 446, 656
Fischer-Dieskau, Dietrich, 117
Fisk, Charles, 195
Fitzenhagen, Wilhelm, 272
Fitzwilliam Virginal Book, The, 252, 309, 533, 542, 622, 675
Flageolet, 77
Flamenco guitar, 274
Flauto italiano, 77
Fleet Street Choir, 190
Flelle, Jean le, 285
Flesch, Carl, 235, 432, 502, 506, 626, 670, 672
   Die Kunst des Violin-Spiels, 672
Florence 229, 141
Florentine Camerata, 255
Florilegium, 239, 556
Flothius, Marius, 110
Fludd, Robert, 58
Flugelhorn, 563
Flute, 31, 148, 240
   Boehm, 350
   metal, 471
   muting, 428
   national styles, 203
   Rockstro model, 548
   Tromlitz, 632
   wooden, 431
Foley, Madeleine, 115
Folkers, Cathy, 196
Fontana, Giovanni Battista, 668
Forde, W., 341
Forkel, Johann Nikolaus, 227, 453, 476, 535
   Allgemeine Geschichte, 536
Forqueray, Antoine, 231, 661, 663

Forqueray, Jean-Baptiste, 236, 662, 663
Forqueray family, 160
Fortepiano, 65, 76, 245, 288
Foscarini, Giovanni Paolo, 274
   I quatro libri della chitarra spagnola, 571
Fossard, François, 486
Foster, Muriel, 213
Foster, Pops, 182
Fouchécourt, Jean-Paul, 366
Fowkes, Bruce, 196
Fox, Samson, 555
Fox, Steven, 197
Franceschini, Petronio, 119, 634
Francesco da Milano, 330, 376
Franciscus, Magister, 644
Francisque, Antoine, 571
Franck, César, 230, 326, 471
   organ music, 464
   Symphonic Variations, 175
Franco of Cologne, 106, 485, 676
Francoeur, François, 234
Franquin, Merri, 635
Fränzl, Ignaz, 668
Frauenchor Hamburg, 91
Frei, Hans, 374
Freiburg BarockConsort, 247
Freiburger Barockorchester, 247
Freillon-Poncein, Jean-Pierre, 247, 445, 509
French bow, 81, 85, 181
Frescobaldi, Girolamo Alessandro, 222, 248, 291, 365, 397, 450, 459, 605
   Fiori musicali, 248
   Il primo libro di capricci, 248
   Il primo libro di toccate, 248
   Toccate e partite, 608
Fretwork, 192
Frey, Georges, 42
Friberth, Karl, 577
Frichot, Louis Alexandre, 573
Friderici, Daniel, 657
Friederici, Christian Ernst, 137
Friedländer, Max, 681
Fritts, Paul, 196
Frizzi, Benedetto, 391
Froberger, Johann Jakob, 248, 365
   Libro Quarto, 542
   Partita No. 1 in E minor, 543
Fröhlich, Joseph, xvii, 238, 249, 421
Fuchs, Carl, 120, 155, 249
Fuenllana, Miguel de, 330
Fuhrmann, Martin Heinrich, 250, 509
Fulda, Adam of, 251
   'Ach hülf mich leid', 251
Fuller, Albert, 195, 198
Fuller-Maitland, John Alexander, 177, 251
Fürstenau, Anton Bernhard, 271, 502, 656
Furtwängler, Wilhelm, 24, 49, 74, 146
Fux, Johann Joseph, 21, 127, 131, 142, 634

Gabrieli, Andrea, 175–6, 253
Gabrieli, Giovanni, 176, 253, 664

Symphoniae Sacrae, 303
Gabrieli Consort & Players, 192
Gabrielli, Domenico, 119, 570
   Ricercari, 119
Gabrilovitsch, Ossip, 366
Gaffurius, Franchinus, 254, 465, 500, 523
Gaffurius Codices, 140
Gagaku, 694
Gagliano, Marco da, 62
   La Dafne, 434
Gähler, Rudolf, 42
Gainsborough, Thomas, 1
Gaisberg, Fred, 23
Gaius Suetonius Tranquillus
   De vita Caesarum, 51
Galamian, Ivan, 235, 371, 432
Galeazzi, Francesco, 233, 254, 626, 650, 671
Galen (of Pergamon), 382
Galeotti, Stefano, 368
Galilei, Vincenzo, 34, 330, 605
Gallay, Jacques François, 256, 311, 471, 626
   Grand Quartet, Op. 26, 256
Galliard, John Ernest, 502
Galliard Trio, 495
Galliculus, Johannes, 617
Galpin, Francis William, 135, 149, 164, 177, 196, 256
Galpin Society, 54, 178
Galuppi, Baldassare, 262
Galway, James, 656
Ganassi, Sylvestro di, 31, 86, 106, 162, 180, 231, 257, 526, 624, 628–9, 650, 655, 660, 663, 688
   on vibrato, 651
   Opera intitulata la Fontegara, 30, 152
   Regola rubertina, 29
'Ganassi' recorder, 526
Ganswindt, 302
Gantzschovius, Johannes, 617
Garat, Pierre-Jean, 258
Garaudé, Alexis de, 112, 258, 579
Garbarek, Jan, 302
Garcia, José, 115
García, Manuel (I), 259–60, 503, 657
García, Manuel (II), 260, 503, 580, 626
   Traité complet, 30
García, Pauline Viardot, 73, 117
Garcin, Jules, 19
Garcin-Marrou, Michel, 313
Garden, Mary, 220
Gardiner, John Eliot, xv, 76, 82, 192, 214, 261, 307, 359, 368, 398, 456, 480, 593
Gardner, Edward, 2, 455
Garnier, Joseph François, 656
Garratt, Elizabeth, 164
Garrick, David, 101, 293
Gasparini, Francesco, 62, 262, 625
Gasparini, Michelangelo, 262
Gasparini, Paolo Lorenzo, 262
Gasparo da Salò, 90, 180, 664
Gassmann, Florian Leopold, 131

I rovinati, 131
Gaubert, Philippe, 471
Gaultier, Denis, 484
Gaultier, Ennemond, 484
Gaver, Elizabeth, 572
Gaviniès, Pierre, 113, 357, 668
Gawriloff, Saschko, 267
Gay, John
   Beggar's Opera, The, 124
Gebauer, Michel, 666
Gehlhaar, Rolf, 587
Gellinger, Israel, 581
Geminiani, Francesco, 40, 90, 93, 114, 150–1, 232–5, 263, 298, 341, 358, 362, 416, 509, 602, 622, 625, 650, 668, 671–2
   Geminiani grip, 37, 53, 169, 264, 297, 672
   one-finger-per-note chromatic scale, 234
   on vibrato, 652
   The Art..., 265
Genlis, Comtesse de, 286
Gens, Véronique, 366
Gentellet, 420
Georg II, Duke, 400
Georgiades, Thrasybulos G., 531
Gerald of Wales, 283
Gerber, Heinrich Nikolaus, 323
Gerle, Hans, 265, 660
German bow, 180
Gerstenbüttel, Joachim, 396
Gervaise, Claude, 661
Gesner, J. M., 46
Gesualdo, Carlo, 216, 303
Ghielmi, Vittorio, 663
Ghiretti, Gasparo, 469
Giardini, Felice, 40, 668
Gibbons, Orlando, 180, 619, 661, 689
Gigault, Nicolas, 441
Gilbert, Adam and Rotem, 197
Gilbert, Kenneth, 156, 198–9, 292
Gillespie, Dizzy, 336
Gillespie, Wendy, 197
Giorgetti, Ferdinando, 266, 666
Giovacchini Giovacchino, 166
Giuliani, Francesco, 266
Giuliani, Mauro, 275
Glarean, Heinrich, 617
Gleditsch, Caspar, 446
Glenn, George, 194
Glinka, Mikhail, 420
   Trio Pathétique, 615, 656
Glockenspiel, 475
Gluck, Christoph Willibald, 358, 554
   Alceste, 131, 457
   Iphigénie auf Tauris, 588
   Orfeo e Euridice, 117, 131, 286, 457
   Trio Sonatas, 424
Glyndebourne Festival, 186, 455
Gnecco, Francesco, 469
Goebel, Reinhard, 192, 267, 423
Goehr, Walter, 261, 620
Goff, Thomas, 268

Goldberg, Laurette, 197
Goldsbrough, Arnold, 96, 166
Goldsbrough Orchestra (later English Chamber Orchestra), 191
Goltz, Gottfried von der, 247
Gombosi, Otto, 478
Goodman, Benny, 133
Goodman, Nelson, 11
Goodman, Roy, 309, 613
Goodwin, Paul, 3
Goossens, Léon, 213, 447, 656
Gordon, Captain James, 244, 548
Gordon Woodhouse (née Gwynne), Violet, 95, 268, 292, 480
Gorge, 578
Gorzanis, Giacomo, 375
Gossec, François-Joseph, 470
Gothic Voices, 470
Göttingen Festival, 190
Gottsched, Johann Christoph, 227, 565
Gough, Hugh, 292
Gould, Glenn, 13, 268
Gounod, Charles
 Faust, 623
Graebner, Fritz, 558
Graf von Rothenburg, Friedrich Rudolph, 392
Grainger, Percy, 479, 494
Granata, Giovanni Battista
 Soavi concenti, 571
Grandjany, Marcel, 287
Grant, Simon, 612
Graphophone, 488
Graun, Johann Gottlieb, 662, 688
Graupner, Christoph, 131, 243
Graves, Susan, 597
'Great *Querelle*', The, 520
Great Vowel Shift, 524
Greenberg, Noah, 97, 196, 269, 433
Greer, Lowell, 313
Gregorian chant, 89, 97, 328, 331, 438, 538, 657, 677
Gregory of Tours, 269
 De cursu stellarum, 269
Grenser, August, 68, 270
Grenser, Heinrich, 68, 238, 270
Grenser family, 270, 447
Grétry, André-Modeste, 305
Greville, Fulke, 101
Grieg, Edvard, 415
Griesinger, Georg August, 294
Grimace, Magister, 644
Grimm, Friedrich-Melchior, 553
Gritton, Susan, 614
Grocheio, Johannes de, 271
Gröninger, Eduard, 96
Grove, George, 35, 510, 555
Gruber, Johann Gottfried, 249
Grumiaux, Arthur, 214
Grümmer, Paul, 663, 688
Grundmann, Jakob, 68, 447

Grützmacher, Friedrich Wilhelm Ludwig, 115, 155, 179, 183, 237, 271–2, 552
 Höhe Schule, 70
 Studies, Op. 38, 518
Grützmacher, Leopold, 272
Guadagnini, Giovanni Battista, 665
Guastarobba, Paolo, 112
Guérin, Paul, 165
Guhr, Carl, 234, 273, 469, 549, 672
 Violin Concerto in E minor ('Souvenir de Paganini'), 273
Guignon, Jean Pierre, 65, 362
Guillemain, Louis-Gabriel, 668
Guilmant, Alexandre, 80, 190
Guilot, 644
Guitar, 64, 92–3, 152, 166, 263, 273, 285, 330, 342, 350, 448, 469–70, 571, 581, 594, 659, 663
Güldenlöw, Count von, 396
Gunn, John, 94, 121, 183, 236, 277, 368, 552
Gunn/Duport system, 179
Gurlitt, Wilibald, 190
Gutmann, Friedrich, 217
Gwynn & Goetze, 465

Haas, Robert, xiii
Habeneck, François-Antoine, 19, 52, 74, 144, 170, 234, 278, 471, 504, 564, 626, 653, 671
 Société des Concerts du Conservatoire, 165
Hacker, Alan, 193, 614
Hagen, Bernard, 377
Hagen, Oskar, 117
Hagenauer, Lorenz, 388
Haïm, Emmanuelle, 193, 366
Haitink, Bernard, xv
Haka, Richard, 67, 445
Halary (Jean Hilaire Asté), 637
Halévy, Fromental, 171, 564
Hall, Marie, 506
Halle, Adam de la, 279
 Le Jeu de Robin et de Marion, 279
Hallé, Lady Wilma Neruda, 250
Hallé, Sir Charles, 145, 170, 250, 280, 402, 513
Halliday, Joseph, 635
Halls, Matthew, 614
Haloid Company, 221
Haloid Xerox, 221
Halstead, Anthony, 313, 613
Haltenhoff, J. G. (of Hanau), 311
Hambourg, Mark, 366
Hammerschmidt, Andreas, 250
Hammond organ, 211–12
Hampel, Anton Joseph, 280, 311, 428
Hand horn, 312
Handel, George Frideric, 45, 122, 302, 304, 310, 322, 389, 396
 Acis and Galatea, 96, 172, 214, 405, 418
 Alcina, 96
 Alexander Balus, 614

INDEX

Athalia, 23
Ariodante, 117, 390, 398
Concerti Grossi, Op. 6, 141
Concerto Grosso, Op. 3 No. 1, 664
Concerto in B flat for harp, Op. 4 No. 6, 285
Deborah, 614
Dettingen Te Deum, 405
Esther, 2, 23, 648
Fireworks Music, 34
Giulio Cesare, 117, 129, 381
Giustino, 398
Il pastor fido, 117
Israel in Egypt, 405, 614
Jephtha, 305, 612
La Resurrezione, 661
Messiah, 3, 95, 308, 419, 612, 634
Music for the Coronation of King George II, 126
Occasional Oratorio, 614
Orlando, 117
ornamentation, 477
Ottone, 398
Ouverture for 2 clarinets and horn, 131, 615
Radamisto, 398
Rinaldo, 634
　'Or la tromba', 634
Rodelinda, 95, 129, 190
Samson, 365, 634
Saul, 117
Semele, 381
Suites, 268
Water Music, 614
Teseo, 398
Theodora, 129
Tra le fiamme, 661
Xerxes, 381
Handel and Haydn Society, The, 194, 308, 368, 612
Handel Commemoration (1784), 126, 142, 188, 631
Handel House Trust, 559
Hanover Band, The, 361, 613
Hansen, Cäcilia, 37
Hanslick, Eduard, 91, 683
Hardel, Jacques, 123
Harding, Daniel, xv
Hargis, Ellen, 198
Harich-Schneider, Eta, 292
Harmonic clavichord, 137
Harmonics, 52, 60, 94, 114, 121, 149, 165, 169, 179, 181, 184, 232, 254, 273, 279, 281, 286, 339, 357, 368, 416, 469, 583, 587, 654, 672, 692
Harmoniemusik, 410, 623
Harnoncourt, Alice, 142, 401
Harnoncourt, Nikolaus, xiv–xv, 96, 142, 172, 185, 282, 298, 307, 359, 364–5, 401, 480, 518, 593
Harp, 283
　Clark blade harp, 287

Dital Harp, 287
　troubadour lever harp, 287
Harp Consort, The, 194
Harper, Charles, 312
Harpsichord, 63–4, 195, 246, 287
　'Bach harpsichord', 292
Harrer, Gottlob, 131
Harris, Renatus, 461, 598
Harrison, May, 37
Harris-Warrick, Rebecca, 560
Harrold, Steven, 302
Hart, David, 572, 627
Hart, John
　Orthographie, An, 525
Härtel, Raymond and Hermann, 477
Harvey, Jonathan
　From Silence, 211
Harwood, Ian, 196
Haskell, Harry, xiv, 186, 305
Haslemere Festival, 177
Hass, H. A., 291
Hass family, 137
Hasse, Johann Adolf, 131, 305, 310, 423, 554
Hassler, Hans Leo, 253
Hässler, Johann Wilhelm, 510, 639
Hatten, Robert S., 219
Haulteterre, Loys de, 313
Hauptmann, Moritz, 292, 339
Hauptstimme, 72
Hause, Wenzel, 181
Hausmann, Robert, 120, 170, 179, 183
Hausmusik, 193
Hautbois, 445
Hauwe, Walter van, 99
Hawkins, Coleman, 564, 638
Hawkins, John, 2, 101, 293
Haydn, Franz Joseph, 6, 60, 294, 443, 512, 562, 688
　8 Notturni, Hob. II:25–32, 615
　'Applausus' Cantata Hob.XXIVa:6, 390, 528
　'Applausus' letter, 294
　Cello Concerto in C major Hob.VIIb:I, 688
　clavichord and, 138
　Die Jahreszeiten (The Seasons) Hob.XXI:3, 247
　Die Schöpfung (The Creation) Hob.XXI:2, 65, 144, 247, 612
　on fortepiano, 65
　Horn Concerto in D major Hob.VIId:3, 311
　Il ritorno di Tobia Hob.XXI:1, 577
　keyboard leadership, 144
　Keyboard Sonatas
　　E flat, 'Adagio e cantabile' Hob.XVI:49, 534
　　C major ('English') Hob.XVI:50, 246, 490
　　No. 35 Hob.XVI:43, 545
　　No. 36 Hob.XVI:21, 545
　L'anima del filosofo Hob.XXVIII:13, 286
　Sinfonia concertante in B flat major Hob. I:105, 106

717

Haydn, Franz Joseph (cont.)
  String Quartets
    E flat major, Op. 33 No. 2 Hob.III:38, 505
    C major, Op. 64 No. 1 Hob.III:65, 388
  Symphonies
    No. 6 'Le matin' Hob.I:6, 453, 688
    No. 7 'Le midi' Hob.I:7, 688
    No. 8 'Le soir' Hob.I:8, 688
    No. 18 Hob.I:18, 614
    No. 31 'Hornsignal' Hob.I:31, 453
    No. 100 'Military' Hob.I:100, 453
    No. 103 'Drum Roll' Hob.I:103, 453
  Trumpet Concerto in E♭ Hob.VIIe:I, 635, 687
  use of *lira organizzata*, 316
Haydn, Michael, 417, 635, 688
Haynes, Bruce, xviii, 40, 295, 497
Hazlitt, William, 602
Heaton, Roger, 133
Heckel, Johann Adam, 68
Heckel, Wilhelm, 68
  Heckel model, 69
Hefling, Stephen, 440
Hegar, Emil, 272
Hegel, Georg Wilhelm Friderich, 11
Heifetz, Jascha, 37, 506, 654
Heinichen, Johann David, 16, 262, 296, 423, 625
Heinisch, Johann, 635
Helfer, Charles d', 358
Hellborn, Heinrich Kreissle von, 681
Heller, Stephen, 208
Hellmesberger, Georg, 339
Hellmesberger, Josef jr, 213
Hellwig, Günther, 42
Hely, Benjamin, 663
Hemy, Henri, 341
Hendrix, Jimi, 337
Henle, Günter, 641
Henri, Charles, 665
Henschel, Georg, 92, 408
Heras-Casado, Pablo, 247
Herbage, Julian, 95
Hermann, Friedrich, 168
Hermstedt, Simon, 133
Herrando, José, 232, 297, 671–2, 692
  El Jardín de Aranjuez, 297
Herreweghe, Philippe, 193, 298, 359, 455
Herschel, William, 40
Hespèrion XX, 193, 562
Hespèrion XXI, 193–4
Hesse, Ludwig Christian, 662
Hesselbein, 165
Hey, Hans, 299
Hey, Julius, 298
Heyde, Herbert, 135
Hicks, Anthony, 559
Hidalgo, Juan, 285
Hildebrandt, Zacharias, 575
Hildegard von Bingen, 193, 572
Hilf, Arno, 168

Hiller, Ferdinand von, 299, 315
Hiller, Johann Adam, 30, 300, 370, 569, 626, 639, 671
  on vibrato, 657
Hilliard Ensemble, 193, 301
Hillier, Paul, 301
Hillmer, Friedrich, 665
Hilton, Wendy, 198
Himmel, Friedrich Heinrich, 316
Hindemith, Paul, 96, 198, 302
  Kleine Sonate for viola d'amore and piano Op. 25 No. 2, 665
  Symphonische Tänze, 570
Hipkins, Alfred James, 177, 251, 292, 303
Historic Brass Society, 194
Historical concerts, 304
Historically informed performance, 40, 95, 146, 158, 186, 189, 239, 261, 305, 308, 313, 359–60, 367, 380, 450, 479, 526, 556, 559, 567–8, 590, 641
Hitchcock family, 582
Höbarth, Erich, 142, 518
Hodson, Millicent, 590
Hoeprich, Eric, 197, 350–1
Hoffmann, E(rnst) T(heodor) A(madeus), 346, 395
Hoffmann, Eucharius, 426, 617
Hoffmann, Johann Christian, 208, 355
Hofhaimer, Paul, 100
Hofmann, Josef, 326, 510
Hofmann, Leopold, 688
Hofmannsthal, Hugo von, 589
Hogwood, Christopher, xiii–xv, xvii, 2–3, 40, 188, 193, 305, 307–8, 368, 422, 455, 480, 568, 588, 612, 698
Hollander, John, 433
Holliger, Heinz, 447
Hollingworth, Robert, 193
Holman, Peter, 192, 309, 667
Holst, Imogen, 95
Holt, Ardern, 164
Holy, Walter, 636
Hood, Mantle, 135
Horn, 310
  hand stopping, 74, 428
  hunting, 596
  slide mechanism, 685
  vibrato, 656
Hornbostel, Eric von, 134, 384
Hornbostel-Sachs classification, 135
Horst, Louis, 164
Hotman, Nicolas, 397, 552, 661
Hotteterre family, 313, 445
Hotteterre, Jacques(-Martin) ['le Romain'], 32, 51, 242, 248, 314, 441–2, 509, 625, 655
Hotteterre, Jean *fils* II, 314
Hotteterre, Louis *fils*, 314
Hotteterre, Martin, 51
Hotteterre, Nicolas, 67
Houle, George, 433
Howells, Herbert

Lambert's Clavichord, 138
Hrabě, Josef, 181
Hubbard, Frank, 195, 292
Hubbard & Dowd, 348
Hubermann, Bronislav, 339
Hubert, Robert, 648
Hucke, Helmut, 449
Hudl, J. J., 341
Hudson, Richard, 538
Huelgas Ensemble, 193
Huene, Friedrich von, 295
Huggett, Monica, 455, 613
Hughes, Edwin, 402
Hughes, Sam, 637
Hugo, Antoine, 31, 174, 626
Hume, Tobias, 663
Hummel, Johann Nepomuk, 68, 109, 214, 299, 314, 324, 406, 625
   metronome markings, 161
   Clarinet Quartet, 615
   Piano Concerto No. 3 in B minor, Op. 89, 218
   Trumpet Concerto in E major, 687
   Trio for piano, violin and keyed trumpet (lost), 687
Humperdinck, Engelbert
   Königskinder, 584
Hunger, Christoph Friedrich, 570
Hunkins, Sterling, 119
Hunt, Edgar, 55
Hunter, George, 198
Hunt Lieberson, Lorraine, 366
Huray, Peter le, 588
Hurdy-gurdy, 284, 315
Huré, Jean, 97
Hurst, George, 261
Hurwitz, David, 436
Hutchins, Carleen, 119, 665

I Fagiolini, 193
I Musici, 191
I Solisti Veneti, 191
I Virtuosi di Roma, 191
Icking, Werner, 200
Iconography, 162, 214, 284, 317, 496, 633
Iconology, 318
Il Giardino Armonico, 193
Imperial Music Society, 37
Improvisation, 8, 44, 46, 61–2, 83, 157, 161, 173, 212, 254, 315, 319, 336, 386, 402, 411, 430, 471, 473, 475, 561, 592, 640, 660, 680, 693
   vocal, 125
Indy, Vincent d', 80, 81, 190, 328
Ingarden, Roman, 11
Ingles, Greg, 197
Instrument collections, historical, 328
Instrumental/vocal treatises, 625
Intabulations, 22, 266, 329
International Index to Music Periodicals (IIMP), 482
International Music Score Library Project, 200
Intonation, 363
Intonation systems, 331
Inventionshorn, 311
Ireland, John
   Cello Sonata in G minor, 250
Isabella d'Este, 660
Isserlis, Annette, 215
Ivrea Codex, 31

Jacchini, Giuseppe Maria, 119
Jackson, Christopher, 198
Jacobean Consort, 167
Jacobs, René, 129, 192, 247, 334, 455
Jacobus de Ispania (Jacques de Liège), 485
Jacoby, Erwin, 522
Jacquemin de Senleches, 515
Jacquet de La Guerre, Elisabeth-Claude, 160
Jacquet of Mantua, 126
Jaffee, Michael and Kay, 196
Jahn, Otto, 477
Jambe de Fer, Philibert, 242, 334, 661–2, 667
James, David, 301–2
Janáček, Leoš,
   Kát'a Kabanová, 380
Jancourt, Louis-Marie-Eugène, 68, 626
Janitschek, 273
Janowka, Thomas, 143
Jansen, Simon, 353
Jaques-Dalcroze, Émile, 374
Jardin des Voix, Le, 129
Jaroussky, Philippe, 216
Javault, Louis Marie Charles, 165
Jazz, 182, 321, 335, 475, 564, 631, 656, 669
'Je prens d'amour', 514
Jean-François Paillard Chamber Orchestra, 191
Jeffery, Peter, 448–9
Jenkins, John, 63, 437, 575, 661
Jenkins, Karl, 528
Jenkins, Newell, 197
Jerome of Bologna, 289
Jerome of Moravia, 338, 657
Joachim, Joseph, 37, 90, 110, 168, 170, 175, 189, 203, 213, 219, 235, 272, 338, 340, 430, 506, 583, 609, 626, 654, 672
   Romance, Op. 2, 339
Joachim Quartet, 339, 512
Joglaresa, 194
Johann Ernst, Prince, 684
Johannes de Muris, 425
Johnson, Dr. Samuel, 293
Jolivet, André, 645
Jomelli, Niccolò
   Armida abbandonata, 419
Jones, Gordon, 302
Jones, Sterling, 76, 196, 522, 591
Joplin, Scott, 547
Jorgensen, Owen, 347
Joseph I, Emperor, 131

Josquin (des Prez), 427, 472, 547, 561, 617
Journal Storage Project (JSTOR), 483
Journals, 482
Jousse, Jean, 341
Julian Bream Consort, The, xiv, 92, 192
 Guitarra!, 659
Jullien, Louis, 423, 513
Junghänel, Konrad, 193
Junker, Carl Ludwig, 341, 626
Jurowski, Vladimir, xv, 455

Kabisch, Thomas, 219
Kagel, Mauricio, 584
Kail, Josef, 312, 635
Kalkbrenner, Friedrich, 218
Kammerton, 67, 497–9, 602, 624
Kant, Immanuel, 14, 601
 Kritik des Urtheilskraft, 10
Kappey, Jacob, 409
Kapsberger, Giovanni Girolamo, 63, 376, 615
Karajan, Herbert von, 24, 49, 590
Karest, Joes, 289
Karr, Gary, 182
Kartomi, Margaret, 135
Kassler, Jamie C., 437
Kastner, Jean-Georges, 343, 411, 626
Kauer, Ferdinand, 121
Kayser, Heinrich Ernst, 672
Kee, Piet, 592
Keeffe, Bernard, 97
Keiser, Reinhard, 131, 304
Kell, Reginald, 656
Keller, Godfrey, 509
Kelway, Joseph, 263
Kendrick, Robert, 317, 319
Kennaway, George, xviii
Kenyon, Sir Nicholas, xv, 39, 308, 344, 360
Kerll, Johann Caspar,
 Modulatio organica, 581
Kersey-Phillips Dictionary, 4
Key character, 16, 345, 604
Khachaturian, Aram
 Violin Concerto in D minor, 109
Kiesewetter, Raphael G., 189, 304
Kimball, Joan, 197
Kincaid, William, 245
Kindermann, Johann Erasmus, 570
King, Andrew, 612
King, Robert, 90, 614
Kingma, Eva, 245
King's Consort, The, 90, 192, 614
King's Music, 353
King's Noyse, The, 197
Kinsky, Georg, 317
Kircher, Athanasius, 16, 58, 227, 399, 535, 598, 617, 626, 669
Kirkby, Dame Emma, 347, 612
Kirkland, Joseph, 95
Kirkman, Jacob, 251, 290
Kirkpatrick, Ralph, 129, 198, 292, 348

Kirnberger, Johann Philipp, 332, 349, 392, 404, 592, 605
Kit, 349, 667
Kivy, Peter, 12, 39
Klausner, David, 197
Kleczynski, Jan, 6
Kleiber, Carlos, 36
Klein, Jacob
 Sonatas Op. 1 and Op. 2 No. 6, 571
Klemperer, Otto, 555
Klezmer, 133
Klindworth, Karl, 373
Klingenberg, Johannes, 179, 272
Klingenfeld, Heinrich, 666
Klingler, Karl, 339
Klosé, Hyacinthe-Eléonore, 76, 132, 350, 431, 626
Klosé-Buffet model, 563
Knappertsbusch, Hans, 146, 230
Knecht, Justin Heinrich, 230
Knorr, Julius, 370
Koch, Heinrich Christoph, 4–5, 16, 143, 351, 592, 626
Kocsis, Zoltán, 59
Kodály, Zoltán
 Solo Cello Sonata, Op. 8, 120, 571
Koenig, Adolphe, 312
Kohaut, Karl, 378
Köhler, Louis, 129
Kohn Foundation, 555
Kohne, Ridley, 37
Kohnen, Robert, 355
Kolisch, Rudolf, 8, 352, 566
Kolisch Quartet, 59, 352, 403
Kollmann, Augustus Friedrich Christian, 510
König, Johann Balthasar, 131
Kontarsky, Aloys, 587
Koopman, Ton, 192, 352, 359, 455, 547, 592
Köpp, Kai, 88
Kosleck, Julius, 635
Koussevitzky, Serge, 24
 Double Bass Concerto, Op. 3, 182
Kozeluch, Leopold, 687
Kozinn, Allan, 455
Kpaøt, P., 590
Krainis, Bernard, 269, 433
Kramer, Lawrence, 12
Krasner, Louis, 686
Kraus, Felix von, 299
Kreisler, Fritz, 213, 219, 431, 436, 506, 654, 670
Kremberg, Jacob, 571
Kreutzer, Auguste, 52, 354
Kreutzer, Conradin, 635
Kreutzer, Rodolphe, 52–3, 73, 234, 278, 340–1, 353, 430, 468, 471, 504, 510, 549, 626, 653, 671–2, 692
 42 [40] *Etudes ou caprices*, 354, 394
 Grande Sonate for violin and piano, 354
 Violin Concerto No. 1, 353
Kriegck, J. J., 178

Krumpholz (Krumpholtz), Jean-Baptiste, 286
Kruspe, Edward, 312
Küffl, Ignaz, 688
Kuhnau, Johann, 16
Kühnel, August, 662
Kuijken, Barthold, 354
Kuijken, Sigiswald, 192, 354, 360, 454, 557
Kuijken, Wieland, 160, 182, 354–5
Kuijken brothers, 142, 354, 365, 480
Kullak, Adolph, 129, 356
Kullak, Theodor, 160, 356, 395
Kummer, Friedrich, 121, 155, 179, 272, 626, 653
Kunisch, Gottfried, 582
Kürzinger, Ignaz Franz Xaver, 356, 671
Kytte, 349

La Barre, Michel de, 242
La Borde (or Laborde), Jean Benjamin de, 358
La Cetra Barockorchester, 532
La Couperin, 190
La Grand Écurie et la Chambre du Roy, 192
La Petite Bande, 103, 192, 355, 360, 365
La Petite Scène, 190
La Scala, Milan, 35–6, 647
Labadie, Bernard, 3
Labarre, Théodore, 626
L'Abbé le fils, 84, 114, 232, 341, 626
  Principes du violon, 671
  Violin Sonatas Opp. 1 and 8, 357
Lacassagne, Joseph, 441
Lachenmann, Helmut Friedrich
  Pression, 122
Lachner, Vincenz, 586
Lachnith, Ludwig-Wenzel, 7
Lacroix, Robert Veyron, 472
L'Affilard, Michel, 359
Lafont, Charles, 354, 468, 549
Laird, Michael, 636
Lalande, Michel-Richard de, 442, 634
Lalandi, Lina, 359
Lalo, Édouard, 52
  Cello Concerto in D minor, 250
Lam, Basil, 96
Lamare, Jacques-Michel Hurel de, 368
Lambert, Michel, 552, 559
Lamon, Jeanne, 197, 597
Landini, Francesco, 515, 591
Landowska, Wanda, 190, 198–9, 292, 348, 360, 480
Laine, Cleo, 422
Lanfranco, Giovanni Maria, 180, 626, 660
Lang, Paul Henry, xv, 478
Lange, Daniël de, 189
Lanzetti, Salvatore, 236
L'Arpeggiata, 194
Larsson, Lars-Erik, 182
Lassus, Orlande de, 126, 253, 358, 535, 617, 633
  Penitential Psalms, 426
  'Susanne un jour', 551, 622
Laud, William, 461
Lauffensteiner, Wolff Jacob, 377

Laurens, Guillemette, 366
Lavignac, Albert, 100, 494
Lawes, William, 63, 612, 661
  Harp Consorts, 285
Lawrence of Arabia, 268
Lawson, Colin, 361, 369, 556, 588
Layolle, Francesco de
  'Lasciar il velo o per sol' o per ombra', 382
Layton, Stephen, 3
Le Blanc, Hubert, 362, 391, 663
Le Châtelain de Coucy, 358
Le Gallois, Jean, 123
Le Gros (Legros), Joseph, 117
Le Jeune, Claude
  Fantaisies, 148
Le Maire, Louis, 570
Le Roux, Gaspard, 538
Le Roy, Adrian, 63, 330
Le Sueur, Jean-François, 126
Lebègue, Nicolas, 521, 538
Lebrun, Ludwig August, 446
Leclair, Jean-Marie, 234, 668
  sonatas, 357
Leech-Wilkinson, Daniel, 362, 470
Lefèvre, Jean Xavier, 31, 363, 626
Legato style, 29–30, 32–3
Legnani, Luigi, 275
Legrenzi, Giovanni, 668
Lehmann, Lilli, 658
Leichnamschneider, Michael, 310
Leinsdorf, Erich, 24
Leipzig Thomanerchor, 190
Leitner, Ferdinand, 96
Lemmens, Jacques-Nicolas, 464
Lenton, John, 363, 670
Léonard, Hubert, 279, 671
Leonhardt, Gustav, xiv, 99, 103, 142, 172, 192, 282, 292, 295, 298, 307–8, 353, 355, 359–60, 364, 401, 455, 480, 568, 593, 690
Leonhardt, Marie, 267, 480
Leonhardt Consort, 103, 142, 191, 282, 295, 364–5
Leopold Anton Freiherr von Firmian, Archbishop, 415
Leopold I, Holy Roman Emperor, 389
Leppard, Raymond, 191, 308, 365, 480
Leroux, Xavier, 100
Les Arts Florissants, 129, 192, 197, 366
Les Délices, 197
Les Filles de Sainte Colombe, 197
Les Paraphonistes de Saint-Jean des Matines, 644
Les Siècles, xv, 367, 590
Les Talens Lyriques, 193
Les Voix Humaines, 197
Leschetizky, Theodor, 160, 366
Leutgeb, Joseph, 311
Levarie, Siegmund, 478
Levasseur, Auguste, 24
Levasseur, Jean Henri, 52, 236, 367, 626
Levasseur, Pierre François, 367
Levi, Hermann, 384

721

INDEX

Levin, Robert D., 3, 29, 108, 110, 368
Levinson, Jerrold, 12
Levitt, Richard, 76, 196, 522, 591
Lewis, Sir Anthony Carey, 191, 369
Lewy, Eduard, 311
Lewy, Joseph, 311–12
Libin, Laurence, 196
Liederspiel, 530
Ligeti, György
   Ramifications, 570
Ligniville, Marquis de, 416
Linarol, Francesco, 664
Lind, Jenny, 30, 261
Linde, Hans-Martin, 142, 567
Lindner, August, 183
Lipatti, Dinu, 510
Liphart, Karl von, 168
Lippi, Filippino, 630
Listenius, Nikolaus, 617
Liszt, Franz, 101, 300, 320, 326, 343, 402
   on conducting, 145
   transcriptions, 71, 623
Litolff, Henry, 415
Little, Margaret, 197
Llewellyn, Grant, 613
Lloyd, Edward, 213
Loar, Lloyd, 182
Lobe, Johann Christian, 214
Locatelli, Pietro, 108, 113, 232, 668
Lochamer songbook, 610
Locke, Matthew, 661, 668
   Cupid and Death, 689
Loewe, Carl, 214
Logier, Johann Bernhard, 343
Löhlein, Georg Simon, 370, 531, 653, 671
Lohr, Ina, 567
Lolli, Antonio, 114, 504, 570, 692
Lombardini, Maddalena, 599
Lonati, Carlo Ambrogio, 570
London Baroque, 192
London Classical Players, 192, 361, 368, 436, 455
London Consort, 178
Long bows, 86
Long play (LP) vinyl record, 488
Lonsdale, Roger, 101
Lord, Albert B., 449
Lorée, F. (François), 447
Lorenzo, Leonardo de, 548
Lost Voices project, 201
Losy von Losinthal, Graf Johann, 377
Lot, Marie-Anne, 314
Lotz, Theodor, 21, 585
Loughran, James, 96
Loulié, Etienne, 248, 359, 371, 440–1, 663
Loveday, Alan, 96
Lowinsky, Edward, 478
Lübeck, Henrich, 633
Luca, Sergiu, 371
Ludus Danielis, 283
Luis de Narváez, 659

Lully, Jean-Baptiste, 51, 65, 67, 129, 150, 156, 304, 316, 372, 390, 419, 430, 442, 452, 520, 553, 559, 668
   audible time-keeping, 144
   five-part string orchestra, 163
   rehearsal technique, 528
   Armide, 427
   Atys, 129, 366
   Ballet d'Alcidiane, 65
   Concerto Op. 6 No. 3, 150
   Le bourgeois gentilhomme, 360, 445, 589
   Le triomphe de l'amour, 528
Lussy, Mathis, 129, 373
Lute, 374, 448, 571
Lute Society of America, The, 194
Luther, Martin, 226
Lutyens, Elisabeth, 188
Luzzaschi, Luzzasco, 176

Mace, Thomas, 148, 379, 479, 625, 663
Machaut, Guillaume de, 279, 284, 362, 380, 591, 644
   La Prise d'Alexandrie, 240–1
   Mass/*Messe de Nostre Dame*, 331, 472, 644
Mackay, Alison, 197, 597
Mackenzie, Sir Alexander, 554
Mackerras, Sir Charles, xiii, 96, 191, 380, 421, 455, 613
Maderna, Bruno, 82
Madeuf, Jean-François, 636
Maelzel, Johann, 399, 406–7, 607
Maffei, Giovanni Camillo, 382, 579
Maffei, Scipione, 150, 245, 382
   Casini, Signor (of Florence), 382
Magazines, 482
Maggini, Giovanni Paolo, 180, 664
Mahaut, Antoine, 383, 655
   Six Duets for German Flutes or Violins, 383
Mahillon, Victor-Charles, 134, 149, 257, 383, 620
Mahler, Gustav, 24, 146, 245, 384, 635, 685
   on Wagner singers, 219
   Kindertotenlieder, 23
   revised Beethoven's Symphony No. 9, 71
   Symphonies
      No. 4 in G major, 570
      No. 9 in D major, 23
Mahler Chamber Orchestra, xv
Maier, Franzjosef, 141, 267
Maintenon, Mme de (Françoise d'Aubigné), 435
Majer, Joseph Friedrich Bernhard Caspar, 210, 385, 665
Makam, 695
Malcolm, George, 178, 292
Maler, Laux, 374
Malgoire, Jean-Claude, 192
Malherbe, Charles, 372
Malibran, Maria, 73, 260, 549
Malipiero, Gian Francesco, 81

722

Malraux, André, 83
Mancini, Giovanni Battista, 107, 260, 301, 386, 502, 579, 626
Mandel, Charles, 411
Mander, Noel Percy, 465
Mandyczewski, Eusebius, 443
Mannheim, 430
Mannheim Orchestra, 387, 668
Mannheim School, 131
Manns, August, 35
Mantel, Gerhard, 122
Manuscript parts, 389
Manuscripts, 388
Marais, Marin, 160, 231, 242, 362, 390, 441, 552, 661, 663
  Pièces de violes, 231, 650
  on vibrato, 650
Marais, Roland, 663
Marbrianus de Orto, 424
Marcello, Benedetto, 262, 570
Marchand, Louis, 76
Marchesi, Luigi, 391
Marchesi, Mathilde, 261
Marcón, Andrea, 193
Marenzio, Luca, 304
Mariani, Angela, 199
Mariani, Angelo, 392
Marini, Biagio, 570, 668
  Sonata, Op. 8 No. 2, 570
Marmontel, Antoine, 100, 175, 471
Marpurg, Friedrich Wilhelm, 15, 21, 30, 301, 392, 395, 549, 605, 628
  Anleitung, 30
Marriner, Neville, 167, 191
Marsalis, Wynton, 336
Marsh, John, 393, 462
Marteau, Henri, 432
Martin, Dean, 337
Martin, Frank, 586
Martin, Philipp Jakob, 648
Martini, Giovanni Battista, 127, 416
Martinn, Jacob-Joseph-Balthasar, 394, 666
Marvin, Bob, 196
Marx, Adolf Bernard, 6, 394, 408
Marxsen, Eduard, 90
Massart, Joseph Lambert, 354, 654
Masson, Charles, 345
Masters, Robert, 3
Matheson, Carl, 11
Matteis, John-Nichola, 396
Matteis, Nicola, 364, 396, 437
Mattheson, Johann, 5, 15–16, 32, 67, 137, 227, 294, 296–7, 301, 345–6, 355, 396, 446, 536, 601, 605, 625–6
  Naturlehre, 15
Maucourt, Charles, 582
Maudit, Jacques, 148, 661
Maugars, André, 397, 661
Maurer, Ludwig Wilhelm, 52
Maxwell Davies, Peter
  Taverner, 89, 188

May, Florence, 91
Maynard, Paul, 433
Mazas, Jacques-Féréol, 52, 570, 671
  La cloche fantaisie, Op. 76, 570
McCarthy, John, 3
McClary, Susan, 12
McCreesh, Paul, 192, 547
McGee, Timothy, 197
McGegan, Nicholas, 197, 247, 398, 613
McLoughlin, Eileen, 172
McVeigh, Simon, 528
Mealy, Robert, 197, 199
Meauchand, Jean-Jacques, 87
Mechanical instruments, 215, 398
Mediolani, Maria Anciuti, 69
Méhul, Étienne, 470
  Euphrosine, 453
  Ariodant, 453
Mei, Girolamo, 255
Meifred, Pierre-Joseph Emile, 168, 311, 400, 626
Meilandus, Jacobus, 617
Meili, Max, 567
Meiningen, 400
Meiningen Orchestra, 133
Meints, Catharina, 195
Meissner, Joseph, 657
Melanchthon, Philipp, 226
Melba, Nellie, 658
Melkus, Eduard, 192, 401
Mell, Davis, 570
Melli, Pietro Paulo, 571
Mellon, Agnès, 366
Mellon Chansonnier, 140
Mellotron, 211
Memelsdorff, Pedro, 567
Memory, 402
  see also Performing from memory
Mendel, Arthur, 497, 639
Mendelssohn, Felix, 144, 168, 189, 300, 339, 402, 404, 415, 443, 462, 583
  J. S. Bach's *St Matthew Passion* (1829 performance), 114, 126, 185, 476
  use of baton, 145
  Hebrides Overture Op. 26, 615
  Piano Concerto No. 1 in G minor, Op. 25, 326
  Symphonies
    No. 1 in C minor, Op. 11, 23
    No. 4 in A major ('Italian'), Op. 90, 381
  Violin Concerto in E minor, Op. 64, 23, 109, 168, 340
Mengelberg, Willem, 146
Mengozzi, Bernardo, 258, 503
Menuhin, Yehudi, 3, 178, 213–14
Merighi, Vincenzo, 517
Merrick, Arnold, 368
Mersenne, Marin, 123, 148, 173, 222, 232, 242, 405, 427–8, 502, 521, 572, 578, 598, 605, 626, 629, 655, 661, 663–4, 670
Merulo, Claudio, 175–6, 228, 253

Mesomedes (of Crete), 255
Messiaen, Olivier, 211, 359, 438, 586
Mestrino, Niccolò, 504, 692
Metastasio, Pietro, 643
Metcalfe, Scott, 198
Métoyen, Jean-Baptiste, 573
Metronome, 70, 161, 315, 359, 406, 607, 685
    electric metronome, 75
Meucci, Renato, 638
Meyer, Edgar, 182, 286
Meyer, Philippe-Jacques, 286
Meyer, Sabine, 518
Meyer, Wolfgang, 518
Meyerbeer, Giacomo, 110, 392, 564
    L'Africaine, 224
    Les Huguenots, 24, 133, 665
Meyer-Eppler, Werner, 586
Meyers Großes Konversations-Lexikon, 4
Meyerson, Mitzi, 198
Micheli, Giulio de, 664
Michi, Orazio, 397
Mikrokosmos Quartet, 59
Mikuli, Karl, 300
Milán, Luis, 659
Milchmeyer, Johann Peter, 408–9, 493, 625
Military bands, 573, 637
Military music, 344, 409, 431, 564
Miller, Dayton C., 196
Milsom, David, xviii
Milstein, Nathan, 37
MIMO project, 329
Minguet y Yrol, Pablo, 242
Mingus, Charles, 182, 336
Minkowski, Marc, 193
Minuet, 164
Mitchell, William, 317
Mitteldeutscher Rundfunk AG (MIRAG), 96
Mitterer, Anita, 142, 518
Mitzler, Lorenz Christoph, 478
Moffatt, Alfred, 94
Moiseiwitsch, Benno, 366
Molière, 440
Molinaro, Simone, 376
Molter, Johann Melchior, 131, 210, 243
Momigny, Jérôme-Joseph de, 374
Monachus, Guilielmus, 411
Mondonville, Jean-Joseph Cassanéa de, 232
Montéclair, Michel Pignolet de, 412, 441–2, 671
Monteux, Pierre, 24, 431
Monteverdi Choir, 214, 261, 457
Monteverdi Orchestra, 192, 214
Monteverdi, Claudio, 63, 81, 188, 282, 304, 358, 398, 412, 612, 619
    seconda pratica concept, 296
    Eighth Book of Madrigals, 23
    Il ballo delle ingrate, 81
    Il Combattimento di Tancredi e Clorinda, 64, 413, 661
    Il ritorno d'Ulisse in patria, 95
    La finta pazza di Licori, 413

L'incoronazione di Poppea, 117, 365, 480, 620, 689
Orfeo, xiv, 56, 63, 96, 100, 191, 284, 307, 321, 365, 413, 451, 480, 529, 563, 579, 621, 633, 661, 689
Vespro della Beata Vergine, 3, 63–4, 96, 261, 369, 413, 472, 620, 660, 668, 689
Moog synthesiser, 211
Móor, Emanuel, 115
Moravec, Ernst, 401
Moreno, José Miguel, 193
Moria, 113
Moritz, Johann, 637
Morley, Thomas, 62–3, 93, 147, 414, 425, 450, 619, 622
    Philomathes, 414
Morley-Pegge, Reginald, 55
Morris, William, 176, 478
Morrow, Michael, 422, 427, 472
Moscheles, Ignaz, 139, 189, 280, 292, 324, 356, 407, 414, 477
    metronome markings, 161
Mosel, Ignaz Franz, 145, 626
Moser, Andreas, 169, 235, 339–40, 583, 626, 672
Mostly Other People Do The Killing, 336
Moule, Henry, 166
Moulinié, Étienne, 63
Mount Edgcumbe, Earl of, 679
Mouton, Charles, 377
Mozart, Leopold, 5, 85, 114, 217, 232–3, 270, 282, 316, 326, 341, 358, 370, 388, 415, 419, 535, 545, 561, 635, 650, 671, 692
    on articulation, 32
    on cadenzas, 107, 110
    on fingering, 234, 504
    on the bow, 113
    on vibrato, 651
    on violin leadership, 144
    on violin mute, 427
    Versuch, 264, 357, 415–16, 504, 549, 625, 627, 652
Mozart Nannerl (Maria Anna), 323
Mozart, Wolfgang Amadeus, 21, 189, 314, 316, 321, 415–16, 510, 512, 650
    Adagio and Allegro in F minor for mechanical organ, K594, 417
    on applause, xvii
    arrangements of Handel
        Acis and Galatea, 417
        Messiah, 404, 417
        Alexander's Feast, 417
        Ode for St Cecilia's Day, 417
    Bassoon Concerto, K191, 68
    on cadenzas, 108
    Clarinet Concerto, K622, 132, 585, 587, 615, 691
    Clarinet Quintet, K581, 132, 585
    Clarinet Quintet fragment, K516c, 369
    Clarinet Trio, K498, 132
    clavichord and, 138
    Concerto for flute, harp and orchestra, K299, 285

continuo in piano concertos, 66
Così fan tutte, 381, 524, 589
detached style of playing, 230
Die Entführung aus dem Serail, 78, 453
Die Zauberflöte, 132, 301, 381, 417
Divertimento in C major, K187/159c, 131
Don Giovanni, 259, 524, 623
on expression, 218
Fantasia in F minor for a mechanical organ, K608, 417
Gran Partita, 132, 614–15
Horn Quintet, K407, 311
horn writing, 281
Idomeneo, 387, 453, 524, 589
improvisation, 533
La clemenza di Tito, 398, 623
Le nozze di Figaro, 259, 326, 334, 381, 455, 524, 623
Mass in C minor, K427, 369
Oboe Quartet, K370, 446
pianistic duel with Clementi, 138
Piano Concertos, 193, 323
  No. 5 in D major, K175, 323
  No. 9 in E flat major, K271, 323
  No. 19 in F major, K459, 417
  No. 20 in D minor, K466, 109–10
  No. 22 in E flat major, K482, 132
  No. 23 in A major, K488, 109, 132
  No. 24 in C minor, K491, 132, 369, 555, 589
Piano Quartet, K493, 96
Piano Quintet, K452, 106
Piano Sonatas
  C major, K330, 534
  A major, K331, 13
  F major, K332, 388
Prelude and Fugue in C, K394, 545
Four Preludes, K284a (formerly known as the Capriccio K395), 326
rehearsal time for operas, 529
Requiem, K626, 132, 215, 369, 417, 685
Rondo in A, K581a, for Clarinet Quintet, 369
rubato playing at the keyboard, 608
Serenades
  K203, 96
  K375, 132
Sinfonia Concertante in E flat major, K297b, 369
Sinfonia Concertante in E flat major, K364, 112, 570, 666
String Quartets
  K387, 417
  K405, 622
Symphonies
  No. 31 in D major ('Paris'), 23, 453
  No. 39 in E flat major, 615
  No. 41 in C major ('Jupiter'), 403, 417
on vibrato, 657
Violin Concertos, 209
Walter piano of 1781, 494
Wind Serenades, 132, 141

Mudarra, Alonso, 659
Muffat, Georg, 64, 239, 361, 373, 419, 441
  Apparatus musico-organisticus, 581
  Florilegium Secundum, 86
  on vibrato, 651
Mühlfeld, Richard, 133, 170, 401, 656
Mule, Marcel, 564
Müllejans, Petra, 247
Müller, August, 370–1
Müller, Iwan, 48, 132, 270, 420, 626
Müller, Rufus, 612
Müller, Theodore, 155
Munch, Charles, 431
Münchinger, Karl, 191
Munclinger, Milan, 191, 421
Munrow, David, xiv, 89, 97, 167, 186, 188, 192, 307–8, 369, 422, 480, 555
Murcia, Santiago de, 274
Musard, Philippe, 422, 513
Museo internazionale e biblioteca della musica, Bologna, 200
Musette, 51
Music Antiqua Amsterdam, 353
Music Before 1800 series, 195
Music Encoding Initiative, 201
Music Index, 482
Music Party, The, 193, 614
Musica Aeterna, 193
Musica Antiqua Köln, 192, 267, 423, 454
Musica da Camera, 353
Musica ecclesiastica, 271
Musica ficta, 331, 424, 465
Musica mathematica, 38
Musica mensurata, 271
Musica poetica, 535, 617
Musica reservata, 425, 617, 667
Musica Reservata, xiv, 186, 192, 422, 427, 472
Musica vulgalis, 271
Musical Union, 510, 512
Musicians of Swanne Alley, 197
Musiciens du Louvre, Les, 193
Musikverein
  Düsseldorf, 300
  Vienna, 648–9
Mute, 427
  brass, 428
  cello, 121
  horn, 428
  violin, 427, 670
Mute cornett, 151
Muziekkring Obrecht, 192
My Ladye Nevells Booke, 309

Nagy, Debra, 197
Napper, Susie, 197
Nardini, Pietro, 112–13, 570, 671
  Sonate énigmatique, 570
Nathan, Isaac, 154
National idioms/styles, 292, 335, 392, 420, 430, 517, 601, 625, 634
  vibrato production, 658

725

Naudot, Jacques-Christophe, 316
Nawrot, Piotr, 240
Nebenstimme, 72
Neefe, Christian Gottlob, 138
Neidhardt, Johann Georg, 432, 605
Nelson, Judith, 198
Nero, Emperor, 51
Neue Wiener Streichquartett, 352
Neuhold, Peter, 687
Neukomm, Edmond, 411
Neukomm, Sigismund
  Requiem, 687
Neumann, Anton, 60
Neumann, Frederick, 178, 432, 441–2, 627
Neumeyer, Fritz, 191
Neupert, J. C., of Bamberg, 348
Neusidler (Newsidler), Hans, 330, 375
New England Consort of Viols, 197
New Josquin Edition, 206
New London Consort, 192
New York Court Dance Company, 198
New York Ensemble for Early Music, 196
New York Pro Musica [Antiqua], 97, 196, 269, 433
Newberry Consort, 198
Newcomb, Anthony, 12, 425
Newman, Robert, 35, 423
Ney, Elly, 366
Nézet-Séguin, Yannick, 455
Ngoniba, 695
Nichols, Mary, 612
Nicholson, Charles, 243, 434, 502
Nicomachus, 79
Nicolai, J. C., 181
Nicolas, Prince, 60
Nicolet, Aurèle, 531
Niedt, Friedrich Erhard, 434, 509
Niehoff, Hendrik, 462
Niemann, Walter, 356
Nijinsky, Vaslav, 590
Nikisch, Arthur, 146, 384
Niquet, Hervé, 193
Nivers, Guillaume Gabriel, 229, 435, 441, 521, 560
Nolan, Rev. Frederick, 243
Nono, Luigi, 586
Noorman, Jantina, 427
Norblin, Louis-Pierre, 368
Nordstrom, Lyle, 197
Nordwestdeutscher Rundfunk (later WDR), 96
Norin, Lena Susanne, 572
Norrington, Sir Roger, xiii, xv, 24, 71, 146, 192–3, 213, 307–8, 359, 436, 455, 480, 556, 613
North, Roger, 437, 511
  on vibrato, 651
Northern Soul, 337
Nosky, Aisslinn, 613

Notation, 28, 124, 139, 207, 212, 284, 372, 388, 413, 437, 449, 466, 499
  alfabeto notation, 274
  Beauchamp Feuillet notation system, 163
  note buone, 5
  Notentexttreue, 689
  notes égales, 156
  notes inégales, 153, 156, 215, 420, 430, 439, 537, 540
Nottebohm, Gustav, 408, 443, 586
Nourrit, Adolphe, 260
Nucius, Johannes, 227, 617
  Musices poeticae, 16
Nurse, Ray, 196
Nussbaum, Jeffrey, 194
Nyastaranga, 257

Oberlin Baroque Performance Institute (BPI), 195
Oberlin, Russell, 269
Oboe, 77, 132, 148, 445
  muting, 454
Oboe da caccia, 446
Oboe d'amore, 446
Ockeghem, Johannes
  masses, 673
O'Dette, Paul, 197–8, 448
Odington, Walter, 331
Offenbach, Jacques
  Les brigands, 367
Ondes martenot, 211
Ondříček, František, 432
Ong, Walter, 449
Oni Wytars, 194
Online Chopin Variorum Edition, 200
Online editions, 200
Opera Atelier, Toronto, 197
Opera house claque, 24
Opera Lafayette, 197
Opera Restor'd, 309
Ophicleide, 411, 564, 573, 636
Opus 111, 216
Oral tradition, 52, 448
Orchestra of the Age of Enlightenment, xv, 99, 186, 192–3, 361, 365, 368, 380, 454–5, 524, 636
Orchestra of the Eighteenth Century, 99, 192, 197, 456
Orchestral placement, 74, 280, 367, 436, 451, 626
Orchestre de Paris, 471
Orchestre Révolutionnaire et Romantique, 215, 261, 368, 456
Orchestrion, 399
Orff, Carl
  Carmina Burana, 125, 591
Organ, 457
  England, 460
  France, 459
  Italy, 458
  North Germany and The Netherlands, 462

'Romantic', 464
Spain and Portugal, 459
Organ registrations, 64
Organistrum, 316
Orgue-mélodium, 74
Ornamentation, 17–19, 21, 29, 37, 41, 44, 46–7, 52–3, 57–9, 71–2, 83, 90, 94, 96, 99, 104, 107, 123, 130, 139, 147, 153, 155, 160, 165, 168–9, 173, 175, 208, 215, 223, 226, 250, 258, 263–4, 279, 284, 297, 301, 314–15, 322, 340–1, 353–4, 356–7, 359, 365, 368, 371, 381, 383, 390–1, 393, 396, 399, 402, 405, 412, 420, 430, 433, 443, 452, 486, 501, 509, 516, 531, 550, 552, 560, 594, 599, 602, 621, 625, 640, 663, 678–9, 684, 688, 692
Ornithoparchus, Andreas, 465–6
Orso, Francesco, 604
Ortiz, Diego, 107, 180, 466, 660, 662–3, 688
Österreich, Georg
  Actus funebris, 65
Otten, Kees, 192
Ottoboni, Cardinal Pietro, 150
Oxted and Limpsfield Players, 619
Ozi, Étienne, 31, 467, 626

Pacchierotti, Gaspari, 679
Pace, Charles, 312
Pachelbel, Johann, 684
Pachelbel, Wilhelm Hieronymus, 684
Pacher, Michael, 638
Paderewski, Ignacy, 100, 366–7
Padmore, Mark, 366
Paër, Ferdinando, 469
Paganini, Nicolò, 19, 29, 73, 234, 273, 282, 402, 468, 672
  performing style, 273
  24 Caprices, Op. 1, 469
  Caprice No. 24, 37
  Violin Concerto No. 1, Op. 6, 570
Page, Christopher, 469, 480
Page, Walter, 182
Paisible, James, 598
Paisiello, Giovanni
  La molinara, 273
Pajeot, Louis Simon, 87
Palau de la Música Catalana, 215
Palestrina, Giovanni, 128, 304, 619
  Missa Papae Marcelli, 91
  Pulcra es amica mea, 551
Palmer, Tony, 215
Palsa, Johann, 311
Palsgrave, John, 627
Panharmonicon, 399
Panofsky, Erwin, 317
Papini, Guido, 266
Paraphonistes de St Jean-des-Matines, 190
Parent, Michiel, 527
Paris Conservatoire, 31, 132, 174, 189, 236, 306, 328, 421, 447, 470, 477, 573, 625, 635

Parker, Charlie, 564
Parley of Instruments, The, 192, 309
Parlophone
  Two Thousand Years of Music, 191
  L'Anthologie Sonore, 191
Parlow, Kathleen, 37
Parrott, Andrew, 192, 427, 472, 480, 547
Parry, Milman, 449
Parsoneault, Catherine, 645
Partch, Harry, 333
Parthenia, 197
Partimento, 473
Pasquali, Niccolò, 230, 341
Pasquier, Jean, 568
Pasquini, Bernardo, 262, 419
Passaggio, 577
Paston, Edward, 330
Patti, Adelina, 503
Pauer, Ernst, 280, 292
Paulirinus, Paulus, 289, 674
Paumann, Conrad, 265, 374, 595, 673
Paxton, Stephen, 121
Pearlman, Martin, 197
Pears, Peter, 94
Peck, Ben, 194
Pedalling, 7, 29, 138, 315, 409, 493, 686
Pedersøn, Mogens, 253
Peile, John
  Bréval's New Instructions for the Violoncello, 94
Pelitti, Giuseppe, 638
Pellegrini, Domenico, 275
Penderecki, Krzysztof
  String Quartet No. 1, 655
Penna, Lorenzo, 62
Pepusch, Johann Christoph, 2, 476
Percussion, 26, 51, 453, 473
  in military music, 486
Perényi, Miklós, 518
Performance practice, 71, 494, 500, 587
  of repeats, 533
  scholarship, 476
Performance related journals, 483
Performing from memory, 140
  see also Memory
Pergolesi, Giovanni Battista
  Stabat Mater, 305
Peri, Jacopo, 63, 99
  Euridice, 62, 99
Périnet, François, 312
Periodicals, 482
Pérotin, 303
Perrine, 484
Petibon, Patricia, 366
Petits Violons, 668
Petrarch (Francesco Petrarca)
  'Vago augelletto che cantando vai', 382
Petrassi, Goffredo
  Suoni notturni, 276
Petri, Johann Samuel, 626, 671

Petrus de Cruce, 485, 514
Petrus Le Viser, 485
Pettiford, Oscar, 182
Petzold, Christian, 302
Pezze, Alexander, 517
Pfitzner, Hans
  Palestrina, 302
Phantasm, 183
Philadelphia Renaissance Wind Band, 197
Philharmonia Baroque, 197, 368
Philharmonic de Paris, 649
Philharmonic Hall, New York's Lincoln Center, 649
Philharmonic Society, 648
Philidor, André, 485
  Le mariage de la couture avec la grosse cathos, 486
Philidor, Anne-Danican, 486
  Sonata in D minor for recorder and bc, 527
Philidor, François-André, 486
Philidor, Jacques Danican, 69
Philidor, Jacques, *le cadet*, 486
Philidor, Pierre, 486
Philidor family, 445
Philip, Robert, 487, 609
Phillips, Peter, 187, 193
Philomathes, 414
Philomusica of London, 96, 167, 191
Philpot, Stephen, 341
Phonograph, 202, 205, 487
Piano roll, 202, 608
Pianoforte, 70, 489
Piatti, Alfredo, 115, 120–1, 155, 179, 517, 626
Piau, Sandrine, 366
Picasso, Pablo, 268
Picchianti, Luigi, 266
Piccinini, Alessandro, 275, 358, 376, 615, 629, 651
Pichl, Wenzel, 131
Pickett, Philip, 192
Pidoux, Raphael, 518
Pieranzovini, Pietro, 79
Pietrobono del Chitarino, 618
Piffaro (originally the Philadelphia Renaissance Wind Band), 197
Pincherle, Marc, 401
Pinel, Germain, 552
Pinnock, Trevor, xiii, xv, 307, 359, 495, 562
Pipe and tabor, 473, 495
Pirlinger, Joseph, 415
Pisendel, Johann Georg, 423
Pitch, 346, 411, 497
Pittsburgh's Renaissance and Baroque Society, 195
Pizzicato, 29
Plaidy, Louis, 101
Plainchant, 435, 458, 499
Plantade, Charles-Henri, 130
Plato, 240, 450, 627
  De Re Publica, 9
Platti, Giovanni Benedetto, 262

Play of Daniel, The, 269, 433
Play of Herod, The, 433
Player pianos, 399
Playford family, 501
Playford, Henry, 501
Playford, John, 501, 570, 661, 663, 672
  Select Musicall Ayres, 65
Pleeth, Anthony, 495
Pleeth, William, 122
Pleyel (et Cie), 175, 209, 246, 287, 292, 305, 343
  Salle Pleyel, 305
Pleyel harpsichord, 175, 360, 385
Pleyel piano, 471, 491
Pluche, Noël-Antoine, 520
Poel, William, 164
Poerschmann, Johann, 67
Pohl, Carl Ferdinand, 91
Polidori, 52
Poll, Hermann, 289
Pollani, 52
Pollet, Benôit
  Méthode, 286
Pollitzer, Adolf, 19, 213
Polyphon-Bogen, 42
Polyphony, 125
Ponte, Lorenzo da, 648
Pomerium, 198
Pompadour, Madame de, 72
Pompidou, President Georges, 83
Poppen, Christoph, 302
Popper, David, 120, 122, 237
Popular music, 182, 335–6, 502
Porphyry, 134
Porpora, Nicola, 154, 579
Porta, Carlo, 35, 175
Portamento, 30, 37, 52, 73–4, 112, 115, 121, 146, 165, 169, 179, 184, 203, 212, 219, 233, 235, 258–9, 272, 279, 339, 363, 385–6, 416, 502, 518, 531, 549, 552, 567, 583, 643, 672
Porthaux, Dominique Antony, 68
Potter, John, 302
Potter, Samuel, 410
Pottgieser, Dr H. W., 243
Potts, Mary, 308
Poulenc, Francis, 360
Poulin, Pamela, 585
Powell, Ardal, 196
Powell, Maud, 165
Praetorius, Michael, 17, 64, 67, 69, 120, 134, 163, 425, 473, 507, 617, 626, 630, 655, 669–70
  'Es ist ein Ros entsprungen' ('Lo, how a Rose e'er blooming'), 507
  gemeine Harfe, 284
  Syntagma Musicum, 571–2, 598, 627
  Terpsichore, 507
Pratten, Madame Sidney (Catharina Josepha Pratten, née Pelzer), 276
Prelleur, Peter, 341, 508
Prelude, 324
Preluding, 53, 314, 509
Presley, Elvis, 337

Preston, Stephen, 495
Primavera Singers, 433
Primrose, William, 666
Prinner, Johann, Jacob, 670, 672
Printz, Wolfgang Caspar, 15
Pro Arte Quartet, 352
Pro Cantione Antiqua, 192
Pro Musica Antiqua, 191, 196
Programmes, 510–11
Promenade Concerts, 35
Pronunciation, 48, 72, 75, 466, 514, 569, 621, 643
Proportions, system of, 514
Prospero, Bernadino, 180
Proto, Frank, 182
Prudenzani, Simone de, 515
Prume, François-Hubert, 279, 570
Prumier, Antoine, 286
Prunières, Henri, 81
Psalette de Notre Dame, 190
Psaltery, 284
Pseudo-Guido, 500
Ptolemy, Claudius, 79
Puccini, Giacomo
    Il tabarro, 624
    La bohème, 624
    Madama Butterfly, 665
Pugin, Laurent, 201
Pugnani, Gaetano, 453, 668, 692
Puliaschi, Giovanni Domenico, 449
Punto, Giovanni, 281, 311
Purcell, Henry, 172, 364, 501, 668
    trumpet writing, 634
    Catches, Rounds, Two-Part and Three-Part Songs, 251
    'Come ye Sons of Art', 171
    Dido and Aeneas, 190
    Fairy Queen, The, 81, 129, 369, 427
    Ode on St Cecilia's Day, 171, 251, 619
    Queen Mary's Funeral Music, 634
    Suite No. 3 in G major, 442
    Suite No. 4 in A minor, 540
    Twelve Sonatas of Three Parts, 251
Purcell Consort of Voices, 192
Purcell Quartet, 192
Purksteiner, Joseph, 60
Puyana, Rafael, 308
Puzzi, Giovanni, 311
Pynkosky, Marshall, 197
Pythagoras (of Samos), 136, 331
Pythagorean tuning, 136, 255, 331, 604

Quadro Amsterdam, 568
Quantz, Joseph Joachim, xvi, xviii, 31–2, 107, 119–20, 181, 217, 238, 243, 262, 310, 371, 383, 386, 395, 427, 430, 441–2, 446, 452–3, 516, 548, 626, 632, 666, 671
    on violin leadership, 144
    Versuch, 601, 625, 655
Quarenghi, Guglielmo, 517
    6 *Capricci* for solo cello, 517
    Capriccio for cello and piano, 518

Quarrington, Joel, 182
Quartetto Esterházy, 193, 568
Quatuor Baillot, 52
Quatuor Mosaïques, 142, 193, 518
Queen's Hall, Langham Place, London, 649
Quickelberg, Samuel, 426
Quicksilver, 197
Quintilian, 56, 534–5, 680
    Institutio Oratoria, 10
Quitschreiber, Georg, 657

Raatz-Brockman, Julius von, 299
Rabaud, Henri, 237
Rabelais, François
    Gargantua et Pantagruel, 242
Rachmaninov, Sergei
    piano playing of, 219
Radif, 695
Rafi family, 242
Raguenet, François, 520, 601, 625, 658
Raison, André, 32, 229, 521
Rambaux, Claude Victor, 620
Rameau, Jean-Philippe, 28, 32, 51, 80, 129, 131, 139, 160, 229, 242, 291, 304, 328, 345, 358–9, 393, 398, 412, 520–1, 530, 553
    inversion theory, 484
    Castor et Pollux, 190
    Hippolyte et Aricie, 129
    Les Boréades, 524
    Les Indes galantes, 589
    Pièces de clavecin en concerts, 355
    Platée, 398
    Zais, 361
Ramis de Pareia, Bartolomeus, 580
Ramm, Andrea von, 76, 196, 446, 522, 591
Ramos de Pareja [Ramis de Pareia], Bartolomé, 523
Rampal, Jean-Pierre, 174, 421, 562
Rampe, Siegbert, 542
Ramsier, Paul, 182
Ranke, Leopold von, 478
Raoux, Lucien-Joseph, 311
Raphael
    Allegory of St Cecilia, 660
Rapp, Regula, 567
Rasgueado, 274
Rasi, Francesco, 579
Rastell, John, 350
Rathbone, Joyce, 96
Rattle, Sir Simon, xiii, xv, 186, 455, 523
Ratzel, Friedrich, 558
Ravel, Maurice, 647
    Introduction and Allegro, 287
    La Valse, 245
    Sonatine, 533
Reber, Napoléon Henri, 620
Rebillé, Philbert, 242
Recitar cantando, 678
Reconstructed pronunciation, 524–5, 627
Recorder, 19, 30, 77, 99, 131, 152, 174, 177, 190, 239–40, 248, 257, 270, 295, 354–5, 386,

422, 446, 481, 501, 508, 526, 557, 567,
  596–7, 602, 619, 625, 628, 639, 655, 673
Rectigraph Company, 221
Redlich, Hans, 620
Rees, Abraham
  Cyclopaedia, 101
Reger, Max, 217, 401
Regis, Johannes, 424
Regondi, Giulio, 275
Rehearsal, 528
Reich, Steve, 40
Reicha, Antoine [Anton], 171, 258, 529
Reicha, Josef, 529
Reichardt, Johann Friedrich, 145, 371, 453,
  504, 530, 549, 609, 626, 671
Reiche, Gottfried, 634
Reidemeister, Peter, 531, 567
Reinagle, Hugh, 277
Reinecke, Carl, 110, 203–4, 272, 608–9
Reinecke, Hans Peter, 135
Renaissance Dancers, 163
Renz, Frederick, 196
Repeats, 326, 532, 640
Répertoire international de la presse
  musicale (RIPM), 483
Répertoire international de littérature
  musicale (RILM), 483
Répertoire International d'Iconographie
  Musicale (RIdIM), 317
Répertoire international des sources
  musicales (RISM), 200
Replicas, 28, 292, 384, 489, 620, 627, 662
  of Viennese pianos, 489
Respighi, Ottorino
  Pini di Roma, 571
Retrospect Ensemble, 614
Reusner, Esaias, 377
Reutter, Georg, II
  Il Parnasso, 635
Reynolds, Sir Joshua, 293
Rhau, Georg, 617
Rhetoric, 148, 185, 216, 225, 291, 297, 315, 534,
  585, 608, 617, 639
Rhythmic interpretation, 370, 441, 537, 590
Ribayaz, Lucas Ruiz de
  Luz y norte, 285
Riccio, Giovanni Battista, 527
Richards & Fowkes, 196
Richardson, Arthur, 665
Richman, James, 198
Richter, Franz Xavier, 78, 421, 635
Richter, Hans, 23, 384
Richter, Karl, 191, 359
Richter, Ludwig, 319
Rickenbacker International Corporation, 182
Riedsche songbook, 610
Riemann, Hugo, 4, 71, 190, 374, 478, 546
Riemenschneider, Albert, 194
Riemenschneider, J. A., 582
Riepel, Joseph, 635
Ries, Hubert, 218, 583

Rietz, Eduard, 549
Rifkin, Joshua, xiii, 215, 319, 472, 547
Rihm, Wolfgang, 584, 587
Rilling, Helmuth, 359, 368
Rimsky-Korsakov, Nikolai, 626
Rinforzando, 6
Rippe, Albert de, 376
Risler, Édouard, 471
Ritter, Hermann, 665
Robberechts, André, 73
Robertsbridge Codex, 140, 330
Robins, Brian, 393
Robinson, Thomas, 663
Roche, Elizabeth, 186
Rochlitz, Johann Friedrich, 453
Rockstro, Richard Shepherd, 548
Rockstro, William Smith, 251
Rode, Pierre, 52–3, 73, 169, 234, 273, 341, 353,
  394, 430, 471, 504, 548, 582, 626, 653,
  671–2, 692
  24 Caprices, 549
  Air varié, Op. 12, 549
  Violin Concerto No. 7, 505, 583
Rodenkirchen, Norbert, 572
Roentgen, David, 399
Roeser, Valentin, 131, 549
Rogers, Nigel, 76, 522, 591
Rogg, Lionel, 401
Rognoni, Francesco, 502, 550, 662, 697
  Selva de varii passaggi, 551
Rognoni, Riccardo, 550
Rolla, Alessandro, 267
Rolland, Paul, 655
Roman de Fauvel, The, 330
Romberg, Bernhard, 87, 120–1, 155, 178–9,
  183–4, 551, 626
  Cello Concerto No. 2, Op. 3, 552
Rooley, Anthony, 347, 612
Rosbaud, Hans, 82
Rose Ensemble, 198
Rose the younger, 661
Rose, Leonard, 182
Rose, Mademoiselle, 218
Rose, Michael, 454
Rosenthal, Moriz, 366
Rossbach, Franz, 635
Rosseter, Philip, 147
Rossi, Luigi, 80
Rossini, Gioachino, 128, 130, 259, 564
  cadenzas, 110
  Elisabetta regina d'Inghilterra, 259
  Guillaume Tell, 579
  Il barbiere di Siviglia, 259
  L'italiana in Algeri, 259
Rostal, Max, 371, 432
Rostropovich, Mstislav, 36, 43, 115, 122
Roth, Daniel, 367
Roth, François-Xavier, 97, 367, 590
Rothschild, Charlotte de, 209
Rousseau, Jean, 143, 231, 358, 371, 509, 552, 663,
  688

Méthode claire, 345
Rousseau, Jean-Jacques, 101, 179, 441, 520, 553
  Dictionnaire de musique, 208
  Le devin du village, 553
Rousset, Christophe, 193, 366
Rowland-Jones, Simon, 614
Roxburgh, Edwin, 556
Royal Academy of Music (London), 554
Royal Albert Hall, London, 649
Royal College of Music (London), 240, 554–5
Royal Conservatory of The Hague, 556
Royal Festival Hall, London, 649
Roze, Abbot Nicolas, 573
Rubato, 59, 95, 203, 220, 280, 286, 340, 360, 365, 367, 385, 438, 625, 639
  see also tempo rubato
Rubini, Giovanni Battista, 577
Rubinlicht, Janine, 355
Rubinstein, Anton, 102, 280, 366, 373, 513
Ruckers family of Antwerp, 289, 674
Rudall and Rose, 244
Ruffo, Vincenzo, 253
Rugeri, Francesco, 119
Ruhland, Konrad, 192
'Rule of the Octave', 63
Rust, Friedrich, 71, 302
Rutland Psalter, 457
Růžičková, Zuzana, 308
Rybar, Peter, 401
Rynar, Dyno, 655

Saariaho, Kaija
  Spins and spells, 571
Sabine, Wallace Clement, 649
Sacher, Paul, 191, 454, 480
Sachs, Curt, 134, 302, 384, 478, 558
Sächsische Landesbibliothek, Dresden, 200
Sackbut, 630
Sadie, Stanley, 99, 417, 456, 559
Saenger, Gustav, 37
Saint Lambert, Monsieur de, 32, 262, 440, 442, 559, 605–6
Sainte-Colombe, Jean de, 231, 390, 661
Sainte-Marie, 52
Sainton, Prosper, 279
Saint-Saëns, Camille, 114, 306, 328, 343, 447, 560
  Danse macabre, 570
  Symphony No. 3 in C minor ('Organ'), Op. 78, 367
  Piano Concerto No. 2, Op. 22, 560
Salieri, Antonio, 343, 414, 443, 474, 688
Salmon, Kathleen, 124
Salom, Tomas, 496
Salomon de Caus, 345
Salomon Quartet, 193
Salomon, Johann Peter, 65, 71, 144, 453
Salzedo, Carlos, 287
Sammartini, Giuseppe, 446
Sampson, Carolyn, 614

Sandrin, Pierre
  'Doulce mémoire', 467
Sankt Gallen manuscripts, 610
Santa María, Tomás de, 62, 104, 107, 137, 229, 537, 561
Santley, Charles, 261
Sanz, Gaspar, 274
Sarasate, Pablo de, 19, 268, 506, 654
Sarti, Federico, 266, 391
Sartorius, Georg Kaspar, 623
Sassoon, Siegfried, 268
Sattler, C. F., 312
Sauzay, Eugène, 52
Savall, Jordi, 193, 480, 562, 567, 689
Savart, Félix, 665
Savary, Jean Nicolas (*Savary jeune*), 68
Sax, Adolphe, 133, 344, 411, 431, 563, 637
Saxhorn, 563
Saxophone, 454
Saxotromba family, 564
Sbolci, Jefte, 266
Scarlatti, Alessandro, 520, 634
Scarlatti, Domenico, 139, 262, 268, 304, 348
  Sonatas, 348
Scelsi, Giacinto
  String Quartets Nos. 3 and 4, 570
  Triphon, 655
  Xnoybis, 570
Schachtner, Johann, 635
Schafhäutl, Carl Emil von, 244
Schaichet, Alexander, 401
Schatzberger, Lesley, 614
Scheibe, Johann Adolf, 16, 46, 76, 227, 535, 565
Scheinhardt, Christoph Stephan, 208
Schelble, Johann Nepomuk, 300
Schelle, Johann, 250
Scheller, Jakob, 282
Schenck, Johann, 662
Scherer, G. H., 67
Schering, Arnold, xiii, 42
Schetky, Johann, 93
Schiedermayr, Johann Baptist, 415
Schiever, Ernest, 250
Schiff, András, 518
Schildt, Melchior, 622
Schiller, Johann Christoph Friedrich von, 682
Schilling, Gustav, 395
Schillings, Max von
  Das Hexenlied, 584
Schindler, Anton, 407, 528
Schlick, Arnolt, 462, 565
  Ascendo ad Patrem meum, 566
  Salve regina, 566
Schmelzer, Johann Heinrich, 142, 427, 570
  Sonatae unarum fidium, 668
Schmidt, Wilhelm, 558
Schmitt, Alois, 299
Schmitt, Friedrich, 298–9
Schnabel, Artur, 273, 366
Schneider, Friedrich, 443

Schnitzer, Erasmus, of Nuremberg, 630
Schoenberg, Arnold, 5, 72, 82, 111, 115, 219, 352, 566
  on transcription, 623
  Chamber Symphony, 454
  Die glückliche Hand, Op. 18, 584
  Die Jakobsleiter, 12, 584
  Gurre-Lieder, 584
  Modern Psalm, Op. 50c, 584
  Moses und Aron, 584
  Ode to Napoleon Buonaparte, Op. 41, 584
  Pierrot Lunaire, Op. 21, 245, 584
  Survivor from Warsaw, A, Op. 46, 584
  'Vorgefühl', Op. 22 No. 4, 12
Schola Cantorum Basiliensis, xiv, 80, 190–1, 196, 198, 307, 328, 334, 347, 364, 448, 480, 522, 531, 567–8, 572, 591, 612, 636, 688–9
Schonbrun, Sheila, 269
Schop, Johann (elder), 223
Schrade, Leo, 478
Schradieck, Henry, 169, 672
Schröder, Jaap, 192, 365, 568, 698
Schröder-Devrient, Wilhelmine, 682
Schroeder, Carl, 94, 179, 618
Schroeder, Rolph, 42
Schubart, Christian Friedrich Daniel, 131, 346, 387
Schubert, Franz, 504
  accents, use of, 6
  'Auf dem Strom', D943, 312
  'Erlkönig', D328, 681
  on expression, 218
  Moment musical, Op. 94 No. 5, 6
  Octet, D803, 133, 141
  on pedalling, 492
  Piano Quintet ('Trout'), D667, 141
  Symphony No. 9 in C Major ('Great') D944, 35, 381, 455
  Vogl and, 681
  'Wasserflut' (*Winterreise* No. 6), 545
Schubert, Johann Friedrich, 569
  Die nächtliche Erscheinung, 569
  Neue Singe-Schule, 569
Schuberth, Karl, 179
Schuchart, Charles, 386
Schuh, Ernst von, 384
Schuller, Gunther, 182, 336
Schulz, Johann Adolph Peter, 5, 218, 592
Schumann, Clara, 170, 250, 272, 303, 510, 513
  cadenza for Mozart's Piano Concerto in D minor K466, 110
Schumann, Eugenie, 91
Schumann, Ferdinand, 92
Schumann, Robert, 91, 300, 339, 414, 443, 453
  on expression, 218
  on Paganini, 469
  Cello Concerto, Op. 29, 272
  Drei Romanzen, Op. 94, 447
  Fantasia in C, Op. 17, 90
  Fantasiestücke, Op. 73, 133
  Humoreske, Op. 20, 545
  Konzertstück, Op. 86, 312
  Märchenerzählungen, Op. 132, 615
  Piano Concerto in A minor, Op. 54, 5, 90, 170
  Piano Quartet, Op. 47, 120, 571
  Romance in B minor, Op. 28 No. 1, 545
  Symphony No. 4 in D minor, Op. 20, 35
  Träumerei (*Kinderszenen* No. 7), 272
  Violin Sonata No. 2 in D minor, Op. 121, 272
Schumann-Heink, Ernestine, 299
Schuppanzigh, Ignaz, 512
Schürmann, G. C., 131
Schütz Choir of London, 436
Schütz, Heinrich, 63–4, 148, 190, 222, 253, 507, 547, 662
  Cantiones sacrae, 216
  Geistliche Chormusik, 63
  Historia der Auferstehung, 64, 81
  'Saul, Saul, was verfolgst du mich' from the *Symphoniarum sacrarum*, 91
Schütze, Rainer, 292
Schweigl, Ignaz, 671
Schweitzer, Albert, 42, 360
Schwendler, Maximilian, 656
Scimone, Claudio, 191
Scordatura, 53, 114, 120, 232, 273, 469, 569, 662, 666
Scott, Anneke, 313
Scriabin, Alexander, 217
Sculthorpe, Peter
  Requiem, 571
Sechter, Simon, 443
Seebass, Tilman, 318
Segovia, Andrés, 268
Segovia Codex, 141
Seguin, Armand, 111
Sekles, Bernhard, 8
Seletsky, Robert, 84
Sellars, Peter, 129
Sellner, Joseph, 447, 626
Selma y Salaverde, Bartolomé de, 67
Senfl, Ludwig, 617
Senleches, Jacob de, 284
Sepulcro, 662
Sequentia, 193, 197, 572
Serpent, 74, 411, 572, 636
Servais, Adrien, 120
Serwaczyński, Stanislaus, 339
Ševčík, Otokar, 432
Shackleton, Sir Nicholas, xvi
Shakespeare, William, 101
  Hamlet, 527
Shankar, Lakshminarayana, 669
Shapey, Ralph
  Krosnick Soli, 571
Sharp, Cecil, 496
Shaw, Arnold, 337
Shaw, George Bernard, 177, 268, 649

INDEX

Shawm, 19, 51, 98, 163, 422, 445, 562, 573
Sheppard, Honor, 172
Shield, William, 40
Shinn, Frederick, 402
Shinohara, Makoto
   Fragmente, 528
Shore, John, 598, 638
Shortwave radios, 212
Shostakovich, Dmitri
   Piano Trio No. 2, Op. 67, 121
   Symphony No. 10, Op. 93, 36
   Violin Concerto No. 1, Op. 77, 110
Shudi, Burkat, 290
Shumsky, Oscar, 37
Silbermann, Andreas, 574
Silbermann, Gottfried, 137, 463, 493, 574, 690
Simandl, Franz, 181
Simandl bow, 181
Simandl system, 238
Simmons, Beverly, 195
Simpson, Christopher, 148, 231, 479, 575, 625, 661, 663, 688
Sinatra, Frank, 337
Singing, 18, 30, 154, 576
   alla bastarda, 577
   see also Vocal performance
'Singing recitation' (*recitar cantando*), 105
Singspiel, 301
Sitt, Hans, 666
Sitwells, The, 268
Sivori, Camillo, 469
Sixteen, The, 193
Sixtus Rauwolf of Augsburg, 377
Skálholt Quartet, 568
Skinner, David, 197
Skowroneck, Martin, 292
Sloper, Lindsay, 280
Slowik, Kenneth, 196–7
Smith, Bernard, 461
Smith, Father, 598
Smith, Hopkinson, 198
Smith, John Christopher, senior, 389
Smith, Thomas, 648
Smithers, Don, 636
Smithson String Quartet, 568
Smithsonian Chamber Players, 197
Smithsonian Jazz Masterworks Orchestra, 336
Smyth, Ethel, 268
Sneak's Noyse, 562
Snow, Valentine, 634
Società del Quartetto, 266
Société de Musique d'Autrefois, 97, 190
Société des Instruments Anciens, 175, 189, 190, 305
Société d'Instruments à Vent, 244
Société des Concerts du Conservatoire, 305
Society for Private Musical Performances, 72, 352, 566
Socrates, 217
Soldat(-Roger), Marie, 339

Soli Deo Gloria, 215
Solomon, Ashley, 556
Solway, Kenneth, 597
Somfai, László, 59
Somis, Giovanni Battista, 668
Sonatori de la Gioiosa Marca, 193
Sophocles
   Oedipus Tyrannus, 253
Sor, Fernando, 275
   Les Deux Amis, Op. 41, 276
Sorge, Georg Andreas
   Compendium harmonicum, 370
Sorrell, Jeannette, 197
Sostenuto pedal, 30
Sour Cream, 99
Sousa, John Philip, 513
Souster, Tim, 587
Soyer, David, 115
Spadina, Stefano, 113
Spangenberg, Johannes, 617
Spataro, Giovanni, 580
Speer, Daniel, 67, 630, 670
Spencer, Joseph, 195, 199
Spencer, Robert, 172, 555, 580
Sperger, Johann Matthias, 181, 666
Speth, Johann, 137, 581
   Ars magna, 137, 581
Spiegl, Fritz, 96
Spiess, Meinrad, 535
Spinacino, Francesco, 330
Spinet, 288, 581, 675
Spinetti, Giovanni, 582
Spitta, Philipp, 7, 158, 477
Spitzer, John, 585
Spivakovsky, Tossy, 42
Spohr, Louis, 48, 70, 86–7, 98, 132, 145, 168, 179, 219, 234, 282, 286, 321, 339, 504–5, 549, 570, 582, 626, 650, 653, 670, 672
   on vibrato, 169, 650, 653
   Violin Concerto No. 9, Op. 55, 583
   Violin Concerto No. 10, Op. 62, 505
   Violinschule, 29, 265, 672
Spontini, Gaspare, 145, 529
   Fernand Cortez, 428
   La vestale, 453
Sporck, Count Anton von, 310
Sprechgesang, 584
Sprechstimme, 72, 567, 584
Sprenger, Eugen, 665
Springfels, Mary, 197, 572
Squire, William Barclay, 252
Sramek, Jordan, 198
St Cecilia Players, 433
Stadlen, Peter, 686
Stadler, Anton, 21, 132, 584–6
Stadler, Johann, 585
Stadlmann, Johann Joseph, 60
Stainer & Bell, 201
Stamaty, Camille, 343
Stamitz, Anton, 113, 353, 668
Stamitz, Carl, 141, 302, 666, 668

733

Stamitz, Johann, 113, 383, 668
Stanesby, Thomas, junior, 67, 69
Stanfield, Milly Bernardine, 655
Stanford, Charles Villiers, 91, 190, 257
Stanley, John, 462
Starzer, Josef
  Musica da camera, 131
Steblin, Rita, 346
Steckler, Christian, 286
Steele-Perkins, Crispian, 636
Steffani, Agostino, 131
Steglich, Hermann, 312
Steibelt, Daniel, 409
Stein family, 246
Stein, Erwin, 6
Steinbach, Emil, 586
Steinbach, Fritz, 381, 401, 586
Steinert, Morris, 196
Steinmeyer, G. F., 465
Steinway piano, 491
'Steinway system', 29
Stepner, Daniel, 613
Stern, Julius, 395
Sterndale Bennett, William, 280, 554
Sterne, Colin, 195
Steuermann, Eduard, 8
Stevens, Denis, 3, 82, 191
Stewart, Rod, 337
Stiedry-Wagner, Erika, 584
Stile antico, 46
Stirling, Jane, 209
Stivori, Francesco, 253
Stockhausen, Julius, 90
Stockhausen, Karlheinz, 359, 547, 586
  Aus den sieben Tagen, 587
  Kreuzspiel, 587
  Mikrophonie I, 211
  use of Maihak W49 filter, 211
  use of shortwave radio, 212
Stokowski, Leopold, 698
Stölzel, Heinrich, 311, 635
Storch, Emanuel, 181
Storioni, Lorenzo, 665
Stour Festival, Kent, 172
Stowell, Robin, xviii, 85, 362, 588
Stradella, Alessandro, 225, 668
Stradivari, Antonio, 119, 350, 661, 664, 667, 669
Stradner, G., 638
Straeten, Edmond van der, 654
Straube, Karl, 96, 190
Strauss, Johann, I, 513
Strauss, Johann, II, 623
Strauss, Richard, 132, 219, 245, 384, 447, 586, 588, 626, 635, 683
  Ariadne auf Naxos, Op. 60, 589
  Capriccio, Op.85, 589
  Die Bürger als Edelman, Op. 60, 589
  Don Quixote, Op. 35, 250, 272, 570
  Ein Heldenleben, Op. 40, 570
  Enoch Arden, Op.38, 584
  Horn Concerto No. 1, Op. 11, 401
Stravinsky, Igor, 3, 359, 431, 438, 589, 600
  Agon, 590
  on dynamics, 6
  Firebird, 367, 590
  Les Noces, 590
  L'Histoire du soldat, 590
  Petrushka, 590
  Pulcinella, 590
  Sacre du printemps, Le (*Rite of Spring, The*), xviii, 35, 69, 83, 571, 590, 635–6
  Three Pieces for clarinet, 132
Striggio, Alessandro
  '*Ecce beatam lucem*', 62
Stroh, (John Matthias) Augustus, 669
Strungk, Nicholaus Adam, 570
Stubbs, Stephen, 197
Studio de Musique Ancienne de Montréal, 198
Studio der frühen Musik, 76, 192, 196, 522, 567, 591
Sturton, Edmundus
  Gaude virgo mater Christi, 424
Stutschewsky, Joachim, 121, 237, 655
Stuttgart Radio Symphony Orchestra, xv
Stuttgarter Kammerorchester, 191
Sudre, François, 170
Suetonius, *see* Gaius Suetonius Tranquillus
Suggia, Guilhermina, 655
Sullivan, Sir Arthur, 415, 554
Sulzer, Johann Georg, 218, 351, 591
Susato, Tielman, 163
Süssmayr, Franz Xaver, 681
Sutton, Julia, 433
Suzuki, Masaaki, 3, 592
Svetlanov, Yevgeny, 36
Švihlíková, Viktorie, 421
'swan bill' bow, 86
Sweelinck, Jan Pieterszoon, 462, 566
Swieten, Baron Gottfried van, 189, 417, 622
Symphonia, 316
Symphony Hall, Birmingham, 649
Symphony Hall, Boston, 649
Syntagma Musicum, 192
Synthesisers, 211
Szell, George, 49
Szymanowska, Maria, 218
Szymanowski, Karol
  written-out concerto cadenzas, 109

Tabel, Hermann, 290
Tablature, 8, 17, 22, 60–1, 104–5, 140, 153, 206, 231, 263, 266, 274, 329, 374, 379, 425, 484, 501, 559, 571, 594, 596, 623–4, 661, 673, 693, 697
Tabourot, Jehan, 163
Tactus, 143, 251, 254, 466, 596
Taddeo del Guasto, 253
Tafelmusik, 197, 597
Tafelmusik Chamber Choir, 597
Taffanel, Paul, 22, 244, 471
Taglietti, Giulio
  Sonata, Op. 1 No. 2, 570

Tagore, Rajah Sourindro Mohun, 257
Taillesfer, 283
Tainter, Charles Sumner, 488
Takács-Nagy, Gábor, 59
Talbot, James, 573, 598
Talbot Manuscript, 54, 598
Talich, Václav, 380, 421
Tallis, Thomas, 126
  'If ye Love Me', 608
  Spem in alium, 63, 620
Tallis Scholars, The, 187, 193
Tarade, Théodore-Jean, 114
Tarling, Judy, 309
Tarr, Edward H., 152, 636
Tárrega, Francisco, 276
  Fantasia sobre los Motivos de La Traviata, 276
Tartini, Giuseppe, 90, 108, 112, 151, 302, 415–16, 570, 599, 662, 668, 692
  on vibrato, 652
  L'arte del arco, 114
  'Devil's Trill' Sonata, 113, 599
  Traité des agrémens, 671
Taruskin, Richard, xviii, 33, 39–40, 187, 308, 436, 450, 600
Taskin, Pascal, 290
Tasnier, Jean, 426
Taste, 6, 10, 22, 28, 37, 70, 129, 146, 218, 248, 255, 263–4, 285, 291, 296, 354, 362–3, 388, 390, 414, 425, 442, 471, 510, 512, 517, 520, 524, 531, 549, 583, 600, 609, 623, 625, 629, 658–9
Taurins, Ivars, 597
Tausch, Julius, 300
Taverner Choir, 347, 472
Taverner Consort and Players, 192, 472
Taylor, Daniel, 198
Taylor, George, 196
Tchaikovsky, Piotr, 649
  use of valve horn, 312
  Eugene Onegin, 623
  Piano Concerto No. 1, Op. 23, 492
  Variations on a Rococo Theme, Op. 33, 250
  Violin Concerto in D major, Op. 35, 37
Teatro San Carlo, Naples, 647
Teatro San Cassiano, Venice, 647
Telemann, Georg Philipp, 131, 310, 430, 602, 662, 688
  Continuation des sonates méthodiques, 603
  Flute Quartets, 424
  Harmonischer Gottesdienst, 602
  III Trietti methodichi e III scherzi, 603
  Musicalisches Lob Gottes, 603
  Musique de table, 247
  Ouverture-Suite in D major, 689
  'Paris' Quartets, 247
  Singe- Spiel- und General-Bass-Übungen, 603
  Sonate metodiche, 603
  Wassermusik, 423
Telmányi, Emil, 42

Temperament, 1, 8, 160, 173, 248, 275, 289, 293, 295, 303, 315, 324, 332, 349, 393, 432, 446, 553, 603, 636, 640, 697, 700
Tempo, 605
Tempo rubato, 538
Terry, Richard, 190
Tertis, Lionel, 268, 655, 665
Tertullian (of Carthage), 216
Terzi, Giovanni Antonio, 376
Tessarini, Carlo, 233
Text underlay, 206, 610, 626, 641
Thalberg, Sigismond, 415
Théâtre des Champs-Elysées, 35
Theorbo, 65, 124, 284, 376, 397, 484, 615, 625
Theremin, 211
Thibaud, Jacques, 568
Thibault, Geneviève, 190
Thibaut de Champagne
  'Ausi com l'unicorne sui', 271
Thibaut, A. F. J., 189, 404, 471
Thieme, C. A., 435
Thiériot, Prudent, 68
Thierry, Alexandre, 459
Thoene, Helga, 302
Thomas, Ambroise
  Hamlet, 454
Thomas, Thomas, 4
Thomas, David, 612
Thomas, Jeffrey, 195
Thompson, John, 481
Thomsen, Magnus, 633
Thornton, Barbara, 197, 572
Thoroughbass, 93, 277, 296, 341, 349, 435, 585
Three Choirs Festival, 649
Thuringus, Joachim, 227, 617
Tiby, Jean-François, 73
Ticciati, Robin, xv, 455
Tickell, Kenneth, 465
Tieffenbrucker, Magno, 376
Tielke, Joachim, 350, 662
Tiersot, Julien, 279
Tillet, Titon du, 314
Tillière, Joseph Bonaventure, 618
Timpani, 21, 79–80, 101, 109, 210, 381, 386–7, 428, 454, 473, 645
Tinctoris, Johannes, 254, 374, 425, 465, 515, 523, 618
Tindemans, Margriet, 572
Tippett, Sir Michael, 171, 472, 619
  Divertimento on Sellinger's Round, 620
  Fantasia Concertante on a Theme of Corelli, 620
  Ice Break, The, 89
Tischler, Hans, 478
Tisdale, William
  Virginal Book, 622
Toet, Charles, 174
Toft, Robert, 425
Tolbecque, Auguste, 620, 662

Tomasini, Aloisio Luigi, 60, 687
Tomkins, Thomas, 461
Tomko, Linda, 198
Tomlinson, Grant, 196
Tonguing, 19, 77, 162, 167, 174, 256, 258, 281, 550, 632
Torelli, Giuseppe, 107, 570, 634
Toronto Consort, The, 197
Tortelier, Paul, 115, 120, 122
Toscanini, Arturo, 24, 74, 146
Tosi, Pier Francesco, 18, 32, 107, 154, 260, 301, 386, 502, 538, 569, 579, 602, 621, 625
   Opinioni, 30, 577
Touche, Firmin, 401
Tournemire, Charles, 471
Tours, Berthold, 666
Tourte, François, 87–8, 120
Tourte, Nicolas Pierre (*père*), 87–8
Tourte bow, 52–3, 84, 86–7, 120, 184, 430, 552, 668
Tovey, Sir Donald Francis, 115
Townley, Charles, 243
Trachtenberg, Alan, 318
Tractulus, 485
Tracy, Bradford, 198
Tragicomedia, 194
Transcriptions, 37, 51, 70, 102, 107, 200, 287, 291, 517, 622
   cello, 122
   guitar, 92
   harpsichord, 166
   jazz, 336
Transposition, 17, 19, 153, 173, 176, 251, 371, 498, 508, 602, 623
   choral, 125
Trasuntino, Alessandro, 604
Tre corde, 489
Treatises, 624
Treble violin, 349
Treichler, 688
Treitler, Leo, 449
Tremais, 570
Tremolo, 75, 77, 147–8, 162, 223, 291, 330, 628, 650
Trichet, Pierre, 485, 629, 661
Tricklir, Jean Balthasar
   Adagio and Rondo (cello/piano), 250
Triébert, Guillaume and family, 447
Trio Sonnerie, 192
Trombetta da Modon, Zorzi, 633
Trombone, 152, 451, 564, 630
   double-slide, evolution of, 633
   mutes, 685
   valve, 74
Tromlitz, Johann George, 31, 107, 243, 270, 502, 626, 632, 656
Trompe de chasse, 310
Trumpet, 633
   'Bach', 189, 635
   Baroque, xvii, 319
   French, 367
   muting, 428
   natural, 21, 74, 219
   piston valves, 431
   slide, 574
   tuning, 219
   Weidinger, 686
Tuba, 411, 636
Tubb, Evelyn, 612
Tudor, David, 111
Tulou, Jean-Louis, 22
Tuning fork, 638
Turetzky, Bertram, 182
Turina, Joaquin, 276
Türk, Daniel Gottlob, xvi, 47, 64, 217, 534, 625, 639
   Klavierschule, 33, 307, 449
   on cadenzas, 108–9
   use of baton, 145
Turner, John, 167
Turocy, Catherine, 198
Türrschmidt, Karl, 311
Tutmarc, Paul, Jr, 182
Twentieth-Century Ensemble, 556
Twenty-Four Violins, 364, 668
Tyard, Pontus de, 426
Tyler, James, 188, 199, 612

Uccellini, Marco, 568
Ugolini, Disma, 266
Ugolino of Orvieto, 424
Uilleann pipes, 51
Una corda, 7, 234, 273, 428, 469, 489, 492–4
Unger, Georg, 299
Urhan, Chrétien, 52
Urquhart (recorder maker), 526
Urtext editions, 11, 206, 641, 689
USSR State Symphony Orchestra, 36
Ut queant laxis, 26

Vaccai, Nicola, 643
   Metodo pratico, 643
Vaillant, Jehan, 644
Valckenborch [Falckenberg], Frederik van, 675
Valentini, Giuseppe
   Cello Sonata in D major, 115
Valle, Pietro della, 578
Van den Borren, Charles, 166
Van Immerseel, Jos, 193
Van Nevel, Paul, 193
Van, Guillaume de, 644
Vandenbroek, Othon-Joseph, 645
Vanderhagen, Amand, 239, 646
Vanhal, Johann Baptist, 181, 666
Varèse, Edgard
   Déserts, 35
Vaslin, Olive-Charlier, 368, 552, 620, 654
Vaucanson, Jacques de, 399
Vaughan Williams, Ralph, 268, 647

Fantasia on a Theme by Thomas Tallis, 647, 649
Vauxhall Gardens, 34
Vega Company, 182
Végh Quartet, 518
Vejvanovský, Pavel, 634
Veldhoven, Jos van, 547
Velluti, Giovanni, 30
Venegas de Henestrosa, Luis, 105, 229
Venere, Wendelio, 376
Venice Baroque Orchestra, 193
Venues and functions, 647
Veracini, Francesco Maria, 568, 599, 668
Verardi, Carlo, 266
Verdi, Giuseppe, 638, 679
  Aida, 81
  Alzira, 455
  cadenzas, 110
  Falstaff, 457
  Il Trovatore, 529
  Otello, 36
  Rigoletto, 623
Veroli Casket, 240
Verri, Pietro, 391
Verschuere Reynvaan, Joos, 67
Verstappen, José, 195
Verster, Sieuwert, 456
Vestergaard, Knud, 42
Viadana, Lodovico, 61
Viardot, Pauline, 30, 260, 549
Vibraphone, 475
Vibrato, 19, 37, 53, 73-4, 93, 113, 133, 138, 146, 169, 179, 241, 245, 254, 272, 277, 308, 332, 339, 348, 371, 381, 385, 390, 401, 447, 471, 531, 552, 583, 587, 607, 629, 632, 650, 663, 666, 670
  bow-vibrato, 179
  finger, 486
  string playing, 651
  vocal, 422, 657
  wind playing, 655
Vicentino, Nicola, 426, 604, 698
Victor Talking Machine, 205, 488
Vienna Capella Academica, 401
Vierdanck, Johann, 223
Vierne, Louis, 326
Vieuxtemps, Ernest, 250
Vieuxtemps, Henri, 73, 165, 469, 471, 570, 654
Viéville, Jean Laurent le Cerf de la, 520, 601, 658
Vihuela, 104, 595, 659-60
Vikárius, László, 60
Villazón, Rolando, 216
Vincentius (Livigimeno, Vincentius), 289
Vingt-quatre Violons du Roi, 452, 556, 664, 667-8
  Violons Ordinaires de la Chambre du Roy, 667
Viol, 660, 662
  viole d'Orphée, 153
Viola, 664
  bow, 85
  fingering, 230
  pitch, 119

Ritter, 101
  scordatura, 570
Viola alta, 665
Viola da braccio, 273, 664
Viola da gamba, 85, 124, 180, 664
Viola da Gamba Society of America, The, 194
Viola d'amore, 570, 665
Viola di fagotto, 665
Viola pomposa, 665
Violalin, 665
Violectra, 669
Violin, 667
  bow, 85, 392
  fingering, 232
  hold, 341, 396
  mute, 427
  scordatura, 570
Violon-alto, 665
Violoncello, 120
  see also, Cello
Violone, 180
Viotti, Giovanni, Battista, 19, 52-3, 73, 113, 183, 278, 354, 548, 653, 668, 671
Virdung, Sebastian, 19, 134, 598, 630, 674, 675
Virgiliano, Aurelio, 630
  Il dolcimelo, 152, 242
Virgin Classics, 216
Virginal, 32, 257, 288, 581-2, 674-5
  Paul Wismayer, 673
Vismes, Jacques de, 358
Visse, Dominique, 193, 366
Vitali, Giovanni Battista, 302, 668
Vitry, Philippe de, 675
Vivaldi, Antonio, 67, 131, 302, 310, 570, 668, 670
  Bajazet, 216
  on cadenzas, 107
  Ercole sul Termodonte, 216
  Le quattro stagioni, 142, 216, 247, 495, 568, 614
  L'oracolo in Messenia, 216
  on mutes, 427
  Nisi Dominus, 427
Vlijmen, Jan van, 557
Vocal performance, 73, 187, 359, 470, 472, 576-7, 676, 680
Vogl, Johann Michael, 681
Vogler, Georg Joseph, 346
Voice flute, 77
Voigt, 666
  Viola Concerto in C major, Op. 11, 468
Volans, Kevin, 587
Volbach, Fritz, 299
Voltaire, 520
Vuillaume, Jean-Baptiste, 665, 670
Vulpius, Melchior, 617

Wagner, Joachim, 575
Wagner, Richard, 74, 145-6, 278, 298, 311, 384, 453, 474, 665, 679, 682
  on conducting (*Über das Dirigieren*), 145, 626

Wagner, Richard (cont.)
　instituted production rehearsals, 529
　Das Rheingold, 524
　Der Ring des Nibelungen, 36, 683
　Die Meistersinger von Nürnberg, 101, 682
　Flying Dutchman (*Der fliegende Holländer*), 623
　Götterdämmerung, 36
　Lohengrin, 392
　Parsifal, 23, 83, 683
　Tannhäuser, 392, 529
　Tristan und Isolde, 101, 133, 320, 623
Wagner tuba, 683
Wailes, Marilyn, 54
Walcker's organs, 464
Waldbauer-Kerpely Quartet, 59
Walden, Valerie, xviii
Walpole, Horace, 293
Walraef, L'Abbé, 113
Walsh, John, 383
Walter, Bruno, 23, 94
Walther, Johann Gottfried, 319, 355, 535, 542, 565, 650, 662, 681, 684
　Hortulus chelicus, 668
　Scherzi da violino solo, 668
Walton, William, 268
　Cello Concerto, 110
Ward, Cornelius, 244
Ward, John, 612
Warlock, Peter, 268
Warrack, John, 249
Wasielewski, Wilhelm von, 168
Watkin, David, 151
Watrous, Hazel, 194
Waverly Consort, 196
Weaver, James, 197
Web Library of Seventeenth-Century Music, 201
Weber, Bedřich Diviš
　Variations in F major for trumpet and orchestra, 635
Weber, Carl Maria von, 68, 132, 407, 609
　on conducting, 145
　Clarinet Quintet, Op. 34, 615
　Der Freischütz, 453, 457
　Grand Duo Concertant, Op. 48, 615
　Oberon, 457
Weber, Gottfried, 68, 407-8, 684
Weber, Max, 14
　'value-relation', 14
Weber, William, 35, 512
Webern, Anton, 82, 220, 685
　Six Pieces Op. 6, 82
Weelkes, Thomas, 619
Weichenberger, Johann Georg, 377
Weidinger, Anton, 635, 686
Weigl, Joseph Franz, 687
Weil, Bruno, 455, 597
Weill, Kurt
　Mahagonny, 584
Weingartner, Felix, 626

Weisberg, Arthur, 656
Weissensee, Friedrich, 617
Weiss, Silvius Leopold, 377
Welcker von Gontershausen, Heinrich, 669
Weldre, Matthew de, 661
Wellesz, Egon
　Violin Concerto, Op. 84, 402
Welsh triple harp, 285-6
Welte-Mignon reproducing piano, 170
Wenzinger, August, xiii-xiv, 96, 191, 307, 480, 562, 567, 663, 688
Werckmeister, Andreas, 345, 432, 604, 625, 684
Werktreue, 39, 306, 439, 689
Werner, Josef, 272
Wesley, Samuel, 189
West Deutscher Rundfunk, 82, 481
West, Henry, 341
Westermann, Peter, 518
Westhoff, Johann Paul von, 668
Westrup, Sir Jack Allan, 369, 480, 689
Wettengel, Gustav Adolph, 181
White, John Reeves, 433
Whittall, Gertrude Clarke, 196
Wich, Sir John, 396
Widor, Charles-Marie, 326, 471
Wieck, Clara, 402
Wieck, Friedrich, 101
Wiemken, Robert, 197
Wiener Singakademie, 91
Wieniawski, Henryk, 37, 469, 654
Wieprecht, Wilhelm, 411, 431, 637
Wiesner, Samuel Gottfried, 270
Wigmore Hall, London, 649
Wijne, Robert, 526
Wilbye, John, 619
Wilderer, Johann Hugo von, 131
Wilhelmj, August, 168, 272, 305, 583
Willaert, Adrian, 126, 253, 604, 697
　'Quid non ebrietas?', 424, 580
Willent-Bordogni, Jean-Baptiste-Joseph, 502
Williams, Mary Lou, 336
Williams, Peter, 690
Willman, Thomas Lindsay, 691
Wilson, Nick, 39
Winkel, Dietrich, 406
Winschermann, Helmut, 531
Winterfeld, Carl, 91
Winternitz, Emanuel, 196, 317
Wistreich, Richard, 612
Wittgenstein, Ludwig, 220
Witthauer, Johann Georg, 370
Wobisch, Helmut, 635
Woldemar, Michel, 84, 415, 504, 653, 665-6, 671, 692
Wolff, Christian, 111
Wolff, Christoph, 182, 547
Wolff, Hermann, 511
Wolkenstein, Oswald von, 591
Wollheim, Richard, 11
Woltz, Johann, 595
Wood, Charles, 190

Wood, Melusine, 164
Wood, Richard, 186
Wood, Sir Henry, 35, 423, 555
World music: historical dimensions, 693
Wu Man, 695
Wulfstan of Winchester, 457
Wulstan, David, 192
Wunderlich, Jean-Georges, 31, 174, 626
Wynne, Shirley, 198

Xenakis, 359
  Nomos Alpha, 122
Xerox Corporation, 221
Xylophone, 475

Yamaha DX7, 211
York Early Music Week, 187
York, Deborah, 614
Yost, Michael, 363
Young, Anne, 277
Young, Crawford, 572
Young, Lester, 564
Young, Phillip, 270
Young, Thomas, 605
Ysaÿe, Eugène, 219, 471, 649, 654

Zabaleta, Nicanor, 287
Zabern, Conrad von, 500, 625, 696
Zacconi, Lodovico, 253, 626, 657, 696
  Prattica di Musica, 30
Zachow, Friedrich Wilhelm, 285
Zak, Albin, 337
Zanetti [Zannetti], Gasparo, 233, 670, 697
Zangius, Nikolaus, 617
Zarlino, Gioseffo, 33, 62, 127, 175, 256, 345, 626, 697
Zaslaw, Neal, 585, 698
Zeffirelli, Franco, 36
Zelenka, Jan Dismas, 310, 421, 516, 614
Zelter, Carl F., 395, 404–5
Zeno, Apostolo, 382
Zenobi, Luigi, 580, 677, 699
Zenti, Girolamo, 582
Zimbalist, Efrem, 37, 654
Zimmermann, Walter, 43
Zimmermann Coffee House, Leipzig, 648
Zingarelli, Niccolò Antonio
  Pirro, Re di Epiro, 391
Zingg, Jeannette, 197
Zwolle, Henri Arnaut de, 136, 289, 458, 604, 699

Lightning Source UK Ltd.
Milton Keynes UK
UKHW022248100321
380143UK00011B/74